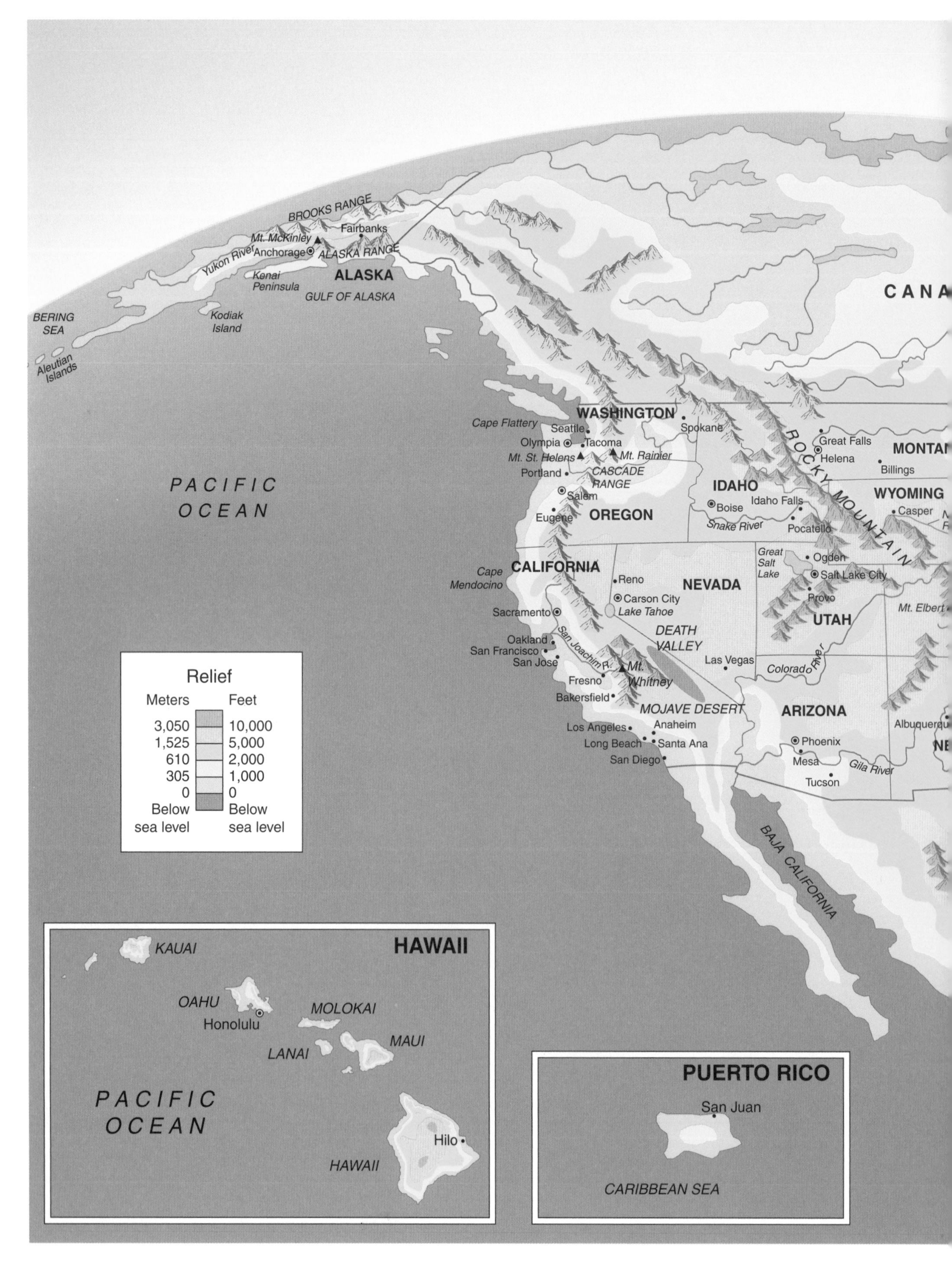
BROOKS RANGE
Fairbanks
Mt. McKinley
Yukon River
Anchorage
ALASKA RANGE
Kenai Peninsula
ALASKA
GULF OF ALASKA
BERING SEA
Kodiak Island
Aleutian Islands
CANA
PACIFIC OCEAN
WASHINGTON
Cape Flattery
Seattle
Olympia
Tacoma
Mt. St. Helens
Mt. Rainier
Portland
CASCADE RANGE
Salem
Eugene
OREGON
Spokane
ROCKY MOUNTAIN
Great Falls
Helena
MONTA
Billings
IDAHO
Boise
Idaho Falls
Snake River
Pocatello
WYOMING
Casper
Great Salt Lake
Ogden
Salt Lake City
Provo
UTAH
Mt. Elbert
Cape Mendocino
CALIFORNIA
Reno
Carson City
Lake Tahoe
NEVADA
Sacramento
Oakland
San Francisco
San Jose
San Joaquin R.
Mt. Whitney
DEATH VALLEY
Las Vegas
Colorado River
Fresno
Bakersfield
MOJAVE DESERT
ARIZONA
Los Angeles
Anaheim
Long Beach
Santa Ana
San Diego
Phoenix
Mesa
Gila River
Tucson
Albuquerqu
BAJA CALIFORNIA
Relief
Meters
Feet
3,050
10,000
1,525
5,000
610
2,000
305
1,000
0
0
Below sea level
Below sea level
HAWAII
KAUAI
OAHU
Honolulu
MOLOKAI
MAUI
LANAI
PACIFIC OCEAN
Hilo
HAWAII
PUERTO RICO
San Juan
CARIBBEAN SEA

HUDSON BAY
MINNESOTA
Grand Forks
Fargo
Bismarck
SOUTH DAKOTA
Pierre
Sioux Falls
Duluth
St. Paul
Minneapolis
Lake Superior
MICHIGAN
WISCONSIN
Green Bay
Madison
Milwaukee
Mississippi River
Lake Michigan
Lake Huron
Grand Rapids
Lansing
Detroit
IOWA
Cedar Rapids
Davenport
Des Moines
Omaha
Grand Island
Lincoln
NEBRASKA
Platte River
South Platte River
Rockford
Chicago
Gary
ILLINOIS
Peoria
Springfield
Toledo
Fort Wayne
Indianapolis
INDIANA
OHIO
Columbus
Cleveland
Akron
Lake Erie
Buffalo
Lake Ontario
Rochester
Syracuse
NEW YORK
Albany
Adirondack Mts.
St. Lawrence River
NEW HAMPSHIRE
VERMONT
Burlington
Montpelier
MAINE
Augusta
Lewiston
Portland
Concord
Manchester
Worcester
Boston
MASSACHUSETTS
Hartford
Providence
RHODE ISLAND
CONNECTICUT
New York
Newark
Trenton
NEW JERSEY
Wilmington
Dover
DELAWARE
Washington, D.C.
MARYLAND
PENNSYLVANIA
Pittsburgh
Harrisburg
Philadelphia
Baltimore
Annapolis
Wheeling
W. VIRGINIA
Charleston
Huntington
APPALACHIAN MTS.
BLUE RIDGE MTS.
VIRGINIA
Richmond
Newport News
Norfolk
Cincinnati
Frankfort
Ohio River
Louisville
Lexington
KENTUCKY
Kansas City
MISSOURI
Kansas City
St. Louis
Jefferson City
Springfield
KANSAS
Springs
Topeka
Arkansas River
Wichita
Oklahoma City
Tulsa
OKLAHOMA
Amarillo
Lawton
Red River
ARKANSAS
Fort Smith
Little Rock
Pine Bluff
Memphis
TENNESSEE
Nashville
Knoxville
Mt. Mitchell
Huntsville
Tennessee River
Winston Salem
Greensboro
NORTH CAROLINA
Charlotte
Raleigh
Cape Hatteras
Greenville
SOUTH CAROLINA
Columbia
Cape Fear
Charleston
Atlanta
Macon
Columbus
GEORGIA
Savannah
MISSISSIPPI
Birmingham
ALABAMA
Meridian
Jackson
Montgomery
Mobile
Biloxi
Lubbock
Fort Worth
Dallas
Brazos River
TEXAS
Shreveport
LOUISIANA
Baton Rouge
New Orleans
Mississippi Delta
Austin
San Antonio
Houston
Corpus Christi
Tallahassee
Jacksonville
FLORIDA
Cape Canaveral
Tampa
St. Petersburg
Fort Lauderdale
Miami
Florida Keys
ATLANTIC OCEAN
GULF OF MEXICO
MEXICO
BAHAMAS
CUBA
DOMINICAN REPUBLIC
HAITI
JAMAICA

Why Do You Need This New Edition?
6 good reasons why you should buy this new edition of The American Journey!
1 A greater emphasis on the personal and collective journeys that have shaped America's history, from the personal documents (now called One American Journey) that open each chapter to the narrative that defines the journey. New American Journey features introduce the journeys of the English clergyman Andrew Burnaby, poet Frances E. W. Harper, Franklin Delano Roosevelt, Dolores Huerta, and a Katrina survivor.
2 Chapter 5, Imperial Breakdown, has been substantially revised. A new American Journey features the English clergyman Andrew Burnaby, and shows how few people predicted the coming of the Revolution. The chapter has been rewritten for clarity, with greater emphasis on this theme of contingency with regard to the Revolutionary movement. There is also an expanded discussion of republican ideology.
3 There are 16 new topics in the book's main features, One American Journey, American Views, and Global Connections that highlight environmental and economic issues, black freedom struggles, civil war in Europe, and other engaging topics.
4 Chapter 31, Complacency, Crisis, and Global Reengagement, has been thoroughly updated. The chapter includes an updated discussion of the "Internet society," a new section on "Hurricane and Financial Storm" that provides coverage of the housing bubble, Crash of 2008, TARP, and the Great Recession.
5 A new section on "The Obama Phenomenon" covers the election of 2008. A new map highlights the 2008 election results.
6 There is a new discussion of the first fifteen months of the Obama administration through the passage of health insurance reform.
PEARSON

A History of the United States

Brief Sixth Edition

Combined Volume

David Goldfield
University of North Carolina, Charlotte

Carl Abbott
Portland State University

Virginia DeJohn Anderson
University of Colorado, Boulder

Jo Ann E. Argersinger
Southern Illinois University

Peter H. Argersinger
Southern Illinois University

William L. Barney
University of North Carolina, Chapel Hill

Robert M. Weir
University of South Carolina

PEARSON

Boston Columbus Indianapolis New York San Francisco Upper Saddle River
Amsterdam Cape Town Dubai London Madrid Milan Munich Paris Montréal Toronto
Delhi Mexico City São Paulo Sydney Hong Kong Seoul Singapore Taipei Tokyo

For our students, who helped us write this book.

Editor-in-Chief: Dickson Musslewhite
Publisher: Charlyce Jones Owen
Editorial Assistant: Maureen Diana
Supplements Editor: Emsal Hasan
Senior Manufacturing and Operations Manager for Arts & Sciences: Nick Sklitsis
Operations Specialist: Christina Amato
Director of Marketing: Brandy Dawson
Senior Marketing Manager: Maureen E. Prado Roberts
Senior Managing Editor: Ann Marie McCarthy
Senior Project Manager: Denise Forlow
Director of Media and Assessment: Brian Hyland
Media Project Manager: Tina Rudowski
Digital Media Editor: Andrea Messineo
Senior Art Director: Maria Lange
Cover Design: Red Kite Project
Cover Image: Winslow Homer (1836–1910), "Near Andersonville," 1865. Oil on canvas. Art Resource, N.Y.
AV Project Manager: Mirella Signoretto
Full-Service Production, Interior Design, and Composition: Ashley Schneider/ S4Carlisle Publishing Services
Manager,Visual Research: Beth Brenzel
Printer/Binder: Courier/Kendallville
Cover Printer: Lehigh-Phoenix Color/Hagerstown
Text Font: Adobe Jenson Regular

Credits and acknowledgments for illustrations from other sources reproduced, with permission, in this textbook appear on appropriate page within text (or on pages C-1–C-3).

Library of Congress Cataloging-in-Publication Data

The American journey : a history of the United States / David Goldfield . . . [et al.]. — Brief 6th ed.
p. cm.
ISBN-13: 978-0-205-24595-6 (combined volume)
ISBN-10: 0-205-24595-1 (combined volume)
ISBN-13: 978-0-205-24596-3 (volume 1)
ISBN-10: 0-205-24596-X (volume 1)
ISBN-13: 978-0-205-24597-0 (volume 2)
ISBN-10: 0-205-24597-8 (volume 2)
[etc.]
1. United States—History—Textbooks. I. Goldfield, David R., II. Title.

E178.1.A4925 2010
973—dc22

10 9 8 7 6 5 4 3 2 1

Combined Volume:
ISBN 10: 0-205-24595-1
ISBN 13: 978-0-205-24595-6

Examination Copy:
ISBN 10: 0-205-01184-5
ISBN 13: 978-0-205-01184-1

Volume 1:
ISBN 10: 0-205-24596-X
ISBN 13: 978-0-205-24596-3

Books à la carte Volume 1:
ISBN 10: 0-205-24604-4
ISBN 13: 978-0-205-24604-5

Volume 2:
ISBN 10: 0-205-24597-8
ISBN 13: 978-0-205-24597-0

Books à la carte Volume 2:
ISBN 10: 0-205-24606-0
ISBN 13: 978-0-205-24606-9

PEARSON

BRIEF CONTENTS

4 English Colonies in an Age of Empire, 1600s–1763 84

5 Imperial Breakdown, 1763–1774 116

6 

THE WAR FOR INDEPENDENCE, 1774–1783 140

7

THE FIRST REPUBLIC, 1776–1789 168

8 

A NEW REPUBLIC AND THE RISE OF PARTIES, 1789–1800 194

11

SLAVERY AND THE OLD SOUTH, 1800–1860 276

12

THE MARKET REVOLUTION AND SOCIAL REFORM, 1815–1850 302

13

THE WAY WEST, 1815–1850 336

21

23

24

25 

The Great Depression and the New Deal, 1929–1939 688

26 

World War II, 1939–1945 718

27 The Cold War at Home and Abroad, 1946–1952 750

28 The Confident Years, 1953–1964 778

29 

30 

31 

SPECIAL FEATURES

American Views

Global Connections

Maps

Figures and Tables

FIGURES

TABLES

Overview Tables

PREFACE

The path that led us to *The American Journey* began in the classroom with our students. Our primary goal is to make American history accessible to them. The key to that goal—the core of the book—is a strong, clear narrative. We chose our book's title because we believe the theme of *journey* offers an ideal way to give coherence to our narrative and yet fairly represent the complexities of our nation's past.

We employ this theme throughout the book, in its chapters, its pedagogical features, and its selection of primary source documents. The journeys we describe can be geographical, focusing on the movement of people, goods, ideas, or even germs from one place to another. They can also be ideological, political, or social—some eventually codified in our founding documents and institutions, others culminating in patterns of personal behavior and social relationships, still others reaching a dead end because of popular opposition, political or economic changes, or even war.

Not all journeys were straightforward in reaching their destinations. American history contains many examples of thwarted personal hopes and national promises that remained unfulfilled for generations. Americans debated the meaning of the liberty they hailed as their nation's founding principle and the extent of power they were willing to entrust to their government. Did the full measure of liberty apply to all its peoples irrespective of race, gender, or ethnicity? Were American freedoms defined only in the political terms set out in the Bill of Rights of 1791 or were they also to include freedom from economic insecurity and social injustice? Some of the journeys assumed a regional dimension as the environment and inherited cultural patterns imparted a distinctive approach to issues affecting the entire nation.

Most of all, the journeys have been those of individuals. We have tried to include as many of them as possible and to blend their stories into the larger national narrative of which they were and are a part. The voices of contemporaries open each chapter, describing their personal journeys—and detours—toward fulfilling their dreams, hopes, and ambitions as part of the broader American journey. These voices provide a personal window on our nation's history, and the themes they express resonate throughout the narrative. Embedding these individual stories within a broader narrative allows us to address questions of culture, identity, politics, and ideas as they shaped the lives of elites and common people alike.

By including stories from the perspectives of different individuals and groups in the text and Web-based features, we aim to provide students with a balanced overview of the American past. We do not shy away from controversial issues, such as the effects of early contacts between Native Americans and Europeans, why the political crisis of the 1850s ended in a bloody civil war, how Populists fit into the American political spectrum, or why the United States used nuclear weapons against Japan. If our treatment of these topics provokes debate between students and instructors, we encourage such discussions as an important catalyst to learning.

We invite students and teachers to think about how their own stories and those of their families relate to the theme of our book. Most of all, we hope that *The American Journey* can guide students along their own intellectual paths toward a better understanding of American history and their own place in it.

Approach

In telling our story, we had some definite ideas about what we might include and emphasize that other texts do not—information we felt that the current and next generations of students will need to know about our past to function best in a new society.

Chronological Organization A strong chronological backbone supports the book. We have found that jumping back and forth in time confuses students. They abhor dates but need to know the sequence of events in history. A chronological presentation is the best way to help students.

Geographical Literacy We also want students to be geographically literate. We expect them not only to know what happened in American history, but where it happened as well. Physical locations and spatial relationships were often important in shaping historical events. The abundant maps in *The American Journey*—all numbered and called out in the text—are an integral part of our story.

Regional Balance *The American Journey* presents balanced coverage of all regions of the country. In keeping with this balance, the South and the West receive more coverage in this text than in comparable books.

Religion This text stresses the importance of religion in American society as a cultural force and an influence on political action.

Pedagogical Support *The American Journey* includes many pedagogical tools to help students understand, analyze, and think critically about the events that unfold in each chapter. The **Student Tool Kit** (see pages xxxv–xlv) provides detailed highlights of these special features, including the MyHistoryLab (www.myhistorylab.com) website that accompanies the text. MyHistoryLab provides many additional resources that expand on the book's themes and content.

What's New in the Sixth Edition

In this edition, there is greater emphasis on the personal and collective journeys that have shaped America's history, from the personal documents that open each chapter to the narrative that defines the journey. In addition, every chapter has been thoroughly revised and improved with new special features as well as updated scholarship. Throughout the text, there is an increased emphasis on environmental history in both the chapter narrative and special features. A new **Key Topics** section provides critical thinking questions for each main section of the chapter for study and review. New MyHistoryLab icons are included within the chapters to indicate documents, audio and video clips, interactive maps, and activities available on the MyHistoryLab website that connect to content in the text. There is also a new section, **MyHistoryLab Connections**, listing these and other available resources at the end of each chapter.

Changes by Chapter:

Chapter 1

A new **Global Connections** feature, "Learning about Chocolate" describes Spanish colonists' fascination with chocolate, a New World food, and their efforts to learn how to make chocolate drinks back in Europe.

Chapter 2

A new **American Views** document, "A Colonist Marvels at New England's Abundant Wildlife," introduces environmental themes, describing the richness of New England nature at the time of colonization and the colonists' assumptions about exploiting natural resources.

Chapter 3

There are two new "Where to Learn More" sites that relate to the African American experience in colonial America.

Chapter 4

A new, expanded section provides discussion on Salem witchcraft.

Chapter 5

A new **American Journey** features the English clergyman, Andrew Burnaby, and shows how few people predicted the coming of the Revolution. The chapter has been rewritten for clarity, with greater emphasis on this theme of contingency with regard to the Revolutionary movement. There is also an expanded discussion of republican ideology.

Chapter 7

A new **American Views** focuses on black freedom struggles in the immediate aftermath of the Revolution.

Chapter 8

A new **American Views** highlights an environmental issue by examining contemporary thinking in the 1790s on water pollution in Philadelphia.

Chapter 11

A new **Global Connections**, "Cotton Is King," examines the international aspects of the cotton industry.

Chapter 14

The **American Journey** feature now connects Harriet Beecher Stowe's personal journey to America's journey. The chapter now emphasizes slavery as the primary cause of secession and war, both in the narrative and in the **American Views** feature, "The Cause of the Civil War." A new illustration connects the Revolutions of 1848 (the theme of the Global Connections feature in this chapter) to events in the United States in the 1850s. A second new illustration, the John Brown mural in the Kansas State House, enables students to discuss how art can mix memory and history.

Chapter 15

There is a new discussion, "The Southern Landscape," on the natural environment and geography of the South and how that affected battles and strategies. A new subhead, "The Real War," includes a quotation from Walt Whitman who lamented that the "real war" would never get into the history books. The narrative now emphasizes the blood, gore, and unnecessary carnage of the war. More information is included on the Native American involvement in the Civil War. The new **Global Connections**, "The Civil War in Europe," covers the reaction to the Civil War in Great Britain, France, and Russia, and their policies. A new **American Views,** "The Costs of War," is a collection of comments from soldiers and civilians from both sides on the carnage of the war.

Chapter 16

The major change in this chapter is the emphasis on the theme that Reconstruction did not fail, it was overthrown. The chapter stresses the violence against southern Republican governments, particularly blacks, as the key factor in ending Reconstruction. The new **American Journey** chapter opener is a poem by black poet Frances E. W. Harper, "An Appeal to the American People," that urged northerners not to abandon southern blacks to southern whites. The section "The Democrats' Violent Resurgence" gives more details on the extent and nature of the organized violence. "The Memory of Reconstruction" is expanded, especially on the openness with which future generations of white southerners commended the violence which overthrew Reconstruction.

Chapter 17
There is more emphasis on how "old" the New South was, particularly with respect to race relations. An expanded discussion is found in "Lynch Law." A new section on "History and Memory" discusses the excising of black history from the New South. There is a new **American Views** feature, "An Account of a Lynching."

Chapter 18
A more nuanced portrait is given of the great entrepreneurs, in line with recent scholarship that stresses their innovative business techniques. The chapter includes more discussion on the possibilities of employment for young working women, using Louisa May Alcott's novel *Little Women* as a harbinger.

Chapter 19
A new discussion of the role of the army in the West emphasizes military tactics.

Chapter 20
There is a new **Global Connections** feature on the money issue of the late 1800s.

Chapter 21
The new **American Journey** chapter opening features the nearly mythical labor agitator Mother Jones and her crusade against child labor. The chapter also expands its consideration of the importance of women in progressivism, particularly of feminist challenges to conventional ideas about women's domestic social role.

Chapter 22
A new section on U.S. relations with Europe in the early twentieth century before World War I helps to put into context America's ultimate involvement in that war. A new **American Views**, "A Southern Senator Opposes Annexation," is a speech from an Arkansas senator that gives appropriately more attention to the opponents of imperialism.

Chapter 24
There is new material on ethnicity and immigration, including a discussion of Sacco and Vanzetti.

Chapter 25
A new **American Journey** chapter opener is drawn from one of FDR's "fireside chats."

Chapter 26
Expanded coverage of the controversial Dresden bombing and expanded data on military and civilian deaths around the world emphasize the global nature of the conflict and the character of total war. Two new images highlight the experience of children on the home front.

Chapter 27
There is a new **American Journey** on the community of Lakewood, California. The treatment of the "second red scare" notes the bipartisan breadth of the anti-Communist efforts.

Chapter 28
A new **American Views** document, William Whyte on open space, shows the roots of the modern environmental movement as a reaction against suburban sprawl. The new **Global Connections** box discusses alliances and alignments in the 1950s, placing NATO in its global context and introducing the concept of first, second, and third worlds. There is new coverage of civil rights activism in the North and emphasis on the long time span of civil rights efforts.

Chapter 29
A new **American Journey** on Dolores Huerta opens the chapter. There is new emphasis on the breadth of Martin Luther King Jr.'s analysis of America's problems and concerns. The chapter reevaluates the Nixon-Kissinger diplomatic strategy.

Chapter 30
A new **American Journey** tells the story of Celia Noup's experience as a new immigrant from Cambodia. The new map on federal land holdings emphasizes the basis for different responses to environmental issues in the western states.

Chapter 31
There is a new **American Journey** from a Katrina survivor and a new Overview table on Core Support for Republicans and Democrats in 2008. There is updated discussion of the "Internet society" and a new section, "Hurricane and Financial Storm," that adds coverage of the housing bubble, Crash of 2008, TARP, and the Great Recession. The new section "The Obama Phenomenon" covers the election of 2008 (including a map) and the first fifteen months of the Obama administration through the passage of health insurance reform.

SUPPLEMENTARY INSTRUCTIONAL MATERIALS

For Instructors	For Students
myhistorylab www.myhistorylab.com **Save Time. Improve Results.** MyHistoryLab is a dynamic website that provides a wealth of resources geared to meet the diverse teaching and learning needs of today's instructors and students. MyHistoryLab's many accessible tools will encourage students to read their text and help them improve their grade in the course.	**myhistorylab** www.myhistorylab.com **Save Time. Improve Results.** MyHistoryLab is a dynamic website that provides a wealth of resources geared to meet the diverse teaching and learning needs of today's instructors and students. MyHistoryLab's many accessible tools will encourage you to read your text and help you improve your grade in your course.
Instructor's Resource Center www.pearsonhighered.com/irc This website provides instructors with additional text-specific resources that can be downloaded for classroom use. Resources include the Instructor's Resource Manual, PowerPoint presentations, and the test item file. Register online for access to the resources for *The American Journey*.	www.coursemart.com CourseSmart eTextbooks offer the same content as the printed text in a convenient online format—with highlighting, online search, and printing capabilities. You **save 60% over the list price** of the traditional book.
Instructor's Resource Manual Available for download at www.pearsonhighered.com/irc, the Instructor's Resource Manual contains chapter outlines, detailed chapter overviews, lecture outlines, topics for discussion, and information about audio-visual resources.	**Books à la Carte** These editions feature the exact same content as the traditional printed text in a convenient, three-hole-punched, loose-leaf version at a discounted price—allowing you to take only what you need to class. You'll **save 35% over the net price** of the traditional book.
Test Item File Available for download at www.pearsonhighered.com/irc, the Test Item File contains more than 1,500 multiple-choice, identification, matching, true-false, and essay test questions and 10–15 questions per chapter on the maps found in each chapter.	**Library of American Biography Series** www.pearsonhighered.com/educator/series/Library-of-American-Biography/10493.page Pearson's renowned series of biographies spotlighting figures who had a significant impact on American history. Included in the series are Edmund Morgan's *The Puritan Dilemma: The Story of John Winthrop*, B. Davis Edmund's *Tecumseh and the Quest for Indian Leadership*, J. William T. Youngs's *Eleanor Roosevelt: A Personal and Public Life*, and John R. M. Wilson's *Jackie Robinson and the American Dilemma*.
PowerPoint Presentations Available for download at www.pearsonhighered.com/irc, the PowerPoints contain chapter outlines and full-color images of maps, figures, and images.	***American Stories: Biographies in United States History*** This two-volume collection of sixty-two biographies provides insight into the lives and contributions of key figures as well as ordinary citizens to American history. Introductions, pre-reading questions, and suggested resources helps students connect the relevance of these individuals to historical events. Volume 1 **ISBN-10: 0131826549 ISBN-13: 9780131826540**; Volume 2 **ISBN-10: 0131826530 ISBN-13: 9780131826533**
MyTest www.pearsonmytest.com MyTest is a powerful assessment generation program that helps instructors easily create and print quizzes and exams. Questions and tests can be authored online, allowing instructors ultimate flexibility and the ability to efficiently manage assessments anytime, anywhere! Instructors can easily access existing questions and edit, create, and store using simple drag-and-drop and Word-like controls.	**Penguin Valuepacks** www.pearsonhighered.com/penguin A variety of Penguin-Putnam texts is available at discounted prices when bundled with *The American Journey, Brief 6/e*. Texts include Benjamin Franklin's *Autobiography and Other Writings*, Nathaniel Hawthorne's *The Scarlet Letter*, Thomas Jefferson's *Notes on the State of Virginia*, and George Orwell's *1984*.

(*continued*)

For Instructors	For Students
Retrieving the American Past (www.pearsoncustom.com, **keyword search | rtap**) Available through the Pearson Custom Library, the *Retrieving the American Past* (RTAP) program lets you create a textbook or reader that meets your needs and the needs of your course. RTAP gives you the freedom and flexibility to add chapters from several best-selling Pearson textbooks, in addition to *The American Journey, Brief 6/e,* and/or 100 topical reading units written by the History Department of Ohio State University, all under one cover. Choose the content you want to teach in depth, in the sequence you want, at the price you want your students to pay.	***A Short Guide to Writing About History, 7/e*** Written by Richard Marius, late of Harvard University, and Melvin E. Page, Eastern Tennessee State University, this engaging and practical text helps students get beyond merely compiling dates and facts. Covering brief essays and the documented resource paper, the text explores the writing and researching processes, identifies different modes of historical writing, including argument, and concludes with guidelines for improving style. **ISBN-10: 0205673708; ISBN-13: 9780205673704**
	Longman American History Atlas This full-color historical atlas designed especially for college students is a valuable reference tool and visual guide to American history. This atlas includes maps covering the scope of American history from the lives of the Native Americans to the 1990s. Produced by a renowned cartographic firm and a team of respected historians, the Longman American History Atlas will enhance any American history survey course. **ISBN: 0321004868; ISBN-13: 9780321004864**

PEARSON myhistorylab (www.myhistorylab.com)

FOR INSTRUCTORS AND STUDENTS

Save TIME. Improve Results.

MyHistoryLab is a dynamic website that provides a wealth of resources geared to meet the diverse teaching and learning needs of today's instructors and students. MyHistoryLab's many accessible tools will encourage students to read their text and help them improve their grade in their course.

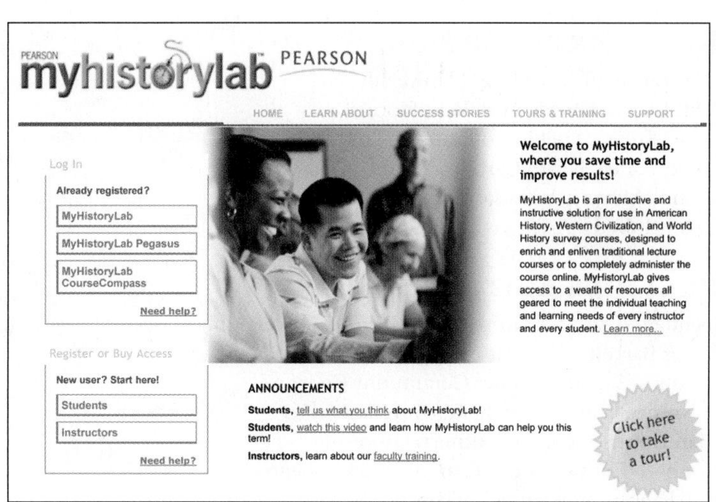

- **Pearson eText**—An e-book version of *The American Journey* is included in MyHistoryLab. Just as with the printed text, students can highlight and add their own notes as they read the book online.
- **Gradebook**—Students can follow their own progress and instructors can monitor the work of the entire class. Automated grading of quizzes and assignments helps both instructors and students save time and monitor their results throughout the course.
- **History Bookshelf**—Students may read, download, or print 100 of the most commonly assigned history works like Homer's *The Iliad* or Machiavelli's *The Prince.*
- **Audio Files**—Full audio of the entire text is included to suit the varied learning styles of today's students.
- **MySearchLab**—This website provides students access to a number of reliable sources for online research, as well as clear guidance on the research and writing process.

NEW IN-TEXT REFERENCES TO MYHISTORYLAB RESOURCES

Read/View/See/Watch/Hear/Study and Review Icons integrated in the text connect resources on MyHistoryLab to specific topics within the chapters. The icons are not exhaustive; many more resources are available than those highlighted in the book, but the icons draw attention to some of the most high-interest resources available on MyHistoryLab.

Read the **Document**

Primary and secondary source documents on compelling topics such as *Brown v. Board of Education of Topeka, Kansas* and Engel, Address by a Haymarket Anarchist enhance topics discussed in each chapter.

See the **Map**

Atlas and interactive maps present both a broad overview and a detailed examination of historical developments.

Watch the **Video**

Video lectures highlight topics ranging from Columbus to Lincoln to Obama, engaging students on both historical and contemporary topics. Also included are archival videos, such as footage of Ellis Island immigrants in 1903 and the Kennedy-Nixon debate.

Hear the **Audio**

For each chapter there are audio files of the text, speeches, readings, and other audio material, such as "Battle Hymn of the Republic" and "The Star Spangled Banner" that will enrich students' experience of social and cultural history.

Study and **Review**

MyHistoryLab provides a wealth of practice quizzes, tests, flashcards, and other study resources available to students online.

We would like to thank the reviewers whose thoughtful and often detailed comments helped shape the brief sixth edition and previous editions of *The American Journey*.

Brief Sixth Edition:

Troy Bickham, Texas A&M University
Matt Clavin, University of West Florida
Cathy Koken, Pueblo Community College
Susanna Lee, North Carolina State University
Brenda Murray, Arkansas Tech University
Carey Roberts, Arkansas Tech University

Previous Editions:

Jacqueline Akins, Community College of Philadelphia
James Barrett, University of Illinois–Urbana-Champaign
Caroline Barton, Holmes Community College
Lawrence Culver, Utah State University
Alan Downs, Georgia Southern University
Kimberly Earhart, Mount San Antonio College
E. J. Fabyan, Vincennes University
Jennifer Fry, Kings College
Michael Gabriel, Kutztown University
Mark Goldman, Tallahassee Community College
Kathleen Gorman, Minnesota State University–Mankato
Don Jacobson, Oakton Community College
Hasan Jeffries, Ohio State University
Thomas Jorsch, Ferris State University
John Klee, Maysville Community and Technical College
Jonathan Mercantini, Canisius College
Loyce Miles, Hinds Community College
James Owens, Oakton Community College
James Page, North Central Texas College
Joshua Schier, Western Michigan University
Larry Wilson, San Jacinto College Central

All of us are grateful to our families, friends, and colleagues for their support and encouragement. Jo Ann and Peter Argersinger would like in particular to thank Anna Champe, Linda Hatmaker, and John Willits; William Barney thanks Pamela Fesmire and Rosalie Radcliffe; Virginia Anderson thanks Fred Anderson, Kim Gruenwald, Ruth Helm, Eric Hinderaker, and Chidiebere Nwaubani; and David Goldfield thanks Frances Glenn and Jason Moscato.

Finally, we would like to acknowledge the members of our Prentice Hall family. They are not only highly competent professionals but also pleasant people. We regard them with affection and appreciation. None of us would hesitate to work with this fine group again. We would especially like to thank our editorial team: Charlyce Jones Owen, Publisher; our marketing team: Maureen Prado Roberts, Senior Marketing Manager, and Brandy Dawson, Director of Marketing; our production team: Ann Marie McCarthy, Denise Forlow, Ashley Schneider, S4Carlisle Publishing Services; Christina Amato, Manufacturing Manager, Craig Campanella, Editorial Director, and Yolanda deRooy, president of Prentice Hall's Humanities and Social Sciences division.

DG
CA
VDJA
JEA
PHA
WLB
RMW

David Goldfield received his Ph.D. in history from the University of Maryland. Since 1982 he has been Robert Lee Bailey Professor of History at the University of North Carolina in Charlotte. He is the author or editor of fifteen books on various aspects of southern and urban history. Two of his works—*Cotton Fields and Skyscrapers: Southern City and Region, 1607–1980* (1982) and *Black, White, and Southern: Race Relations and Southern Culture, 1940 to the Present* (1990)—received the Mayflower Award for nonfiction and was nominated for the Pulitzer Prize in history. His most recent book is *America Aflame: How the Civil War Created a Nation* (2011). When he is not writing history, Dr. Goldfield applies his historical craft to history museum exhibits, voting rights cases, and local planning and policy issues.

Carl Abbott is a professor of Urban Studies and planning at Portland State University. He taught previously in the history departments at the University of Denver and Old Dominion University, and held visiting appointments at Mesa College in Colorado and George Washington University. He holds degrees in history from Swarthmore College and the University of Chicago. He specializes in the history of cities and the American West and serves as coeditor of the Pacific Historical Review. His books include *The New Urban America: Growth and Politics in Sunbelt Cities* (1981, 1987), *The Metropolitan Frontier: Cities in the Modern American West* (1993), *Planning a New West: The Columbia River Gorge National Scenic Area* (1997), *Political Terrain: Washington, D.C. from Tidewater Town to Global Metropolis* (1999), and *How Cities Won the West: Four Centuries of Urban Change in Western North American* (2008).

Virginia DeJohn Anderson is Professor of History at the University of Colorado at Boulder. She received her B.A. from the University of Connecticut. As the recipient of a Marshall Scholarship, she earned an M.A. degree at the University of East Anglia in Norwich, England. Returning to the United States, she received her A.M. and Ph.D. degrees from Harvard University. She is the author of *New England's Generation: The Great Migration and the Formation of Society and Culture in the Seventeenth Century* (1991) and *Creatures of Empire: How Domestic Animals Transformed Early America* (2004). Her current research focuses on the American Revolution.

Jo Ann E. Argersinger received her Ph.D. from George Washington University and is Professor of History at Southern Illinois University. A recipient of fellowships from the Rockefeller Foundation and the National Endowment for the Humanities, she is a historian of social, labor, and business policy. Her publications include *Toward a New Deal in Baltimore: People and Government in the Great Depression* (1988), *Making the Amalgamated: Gender, Ethnicity, and Class in the Baltimore Clothing Industry* (1999), and *The Triangle Fire: A Brief History with Documents* (2009). She is currently writing a study of citizenship rights and public housing, placing the American experience in the international arena.

Peter H. Argersinger received his Ph.D. from the University of Wisconsin and is Professor of History at Southern Illinois University. He has won several fellowships as well as the Binkley-Stephenson Award from the Organization of American Historians, and he is currently president of the Society for Historians of the Gilded Age and Progressive Era. Among his books on political and rural history are *Populism and Politics* (1974), *Structure, Process, and Party* (1992), and *The Limits of Agrarian Radicalism* (1995). His most recent book, integrating legal and political history, is *Courting Chaos: The Politics of Apportionment in the Midwest, 1870–1910* (2011). His current research focuses on the political crisis of the 1890s.

William L. Barney is Professor of History at the University of North Carolina at Chapel Hill. A native of Pennsylvania, he received his B.A. from Cornell University and his M.A. and Ph.D. from Columbia University. He has published extensively on nineteenth-century U.S. history and has a particular interest in the Old South and the coming of the Civil War. Among his publications are *The Road to Secession* (1972), *The Secessionist Impulse* (1974), *Flawed Victory* (1975), *The Passage of the Republic* (1987), *Battleground for the Union* (1989), and *The Civil War and Reconstruction: A Student Companion* (2001). Most recently, he has finished *The Making of a Confederate: Walter Lenoir's Civil War* (2007).

Robert M. Weir is Distinguished Professor of History Emeritus at the University of South Carolina. He received his B.A. from Pennsylvania State University and his Ph.D. from Case Western Reserve University. He has taught at the University of Houston and, as a visiting professor, at the University of Southampton in the United Kingdom. His articles have won prizes from the Southeastern Society for the Study of the Eighteenth Century and the *William and Mary Quarterly*. Among his publications are *Colonial South Carolina: A History*, *"The Last of American Freemen": Studies in the Political Culture of the Colonial and Revolutionary South*, and, more recently, a chapter on the Carolinas in the new *Oxford History of the British Empire* (1998).

USING *THE AMERICAN JOURNEY*

When writing history, historians use maps, tables, graphs, and visuals to help their readers understand the past. What follows is an explanation of how to use the historian's tools that are contained in this book.

TEXT

Whether it is a biography of George Washington, an article on the Civil War, or a survey of American history such as this one, the text is the historian's basic tool for discussing the past. Historians write about the past using narration and analysis. Narration is the story line of history. It describes what happened in the past, who did it, and where and when it occurred. Narration is also used to describe how people in the past lived, how they spent their days and even, when the historical evidence makes it possible for us to know, what they thought, felt, feared, or desired. Using analysis, historians explain why they think events in the past happened the way they did and try to offer an explanation. In this book, narration and analysis are interwoven in each chapter.

VISUALS

Visual images embedded thoughout the text can provide as much insight into our nation's history as the written word. Within photographs and pieces of fine art lies emotional and historical meaning. Captions provide valuable information, such as in the example below. When studying the images, consider questions such as: "Who are the people?"; "How were they feeling?"; "What event motivated this photograph or painting?"; and "What can be learned from the backdrop surrounding the focal point?" Such analysis allows for a fuller understanding of the people who lived the American journey.

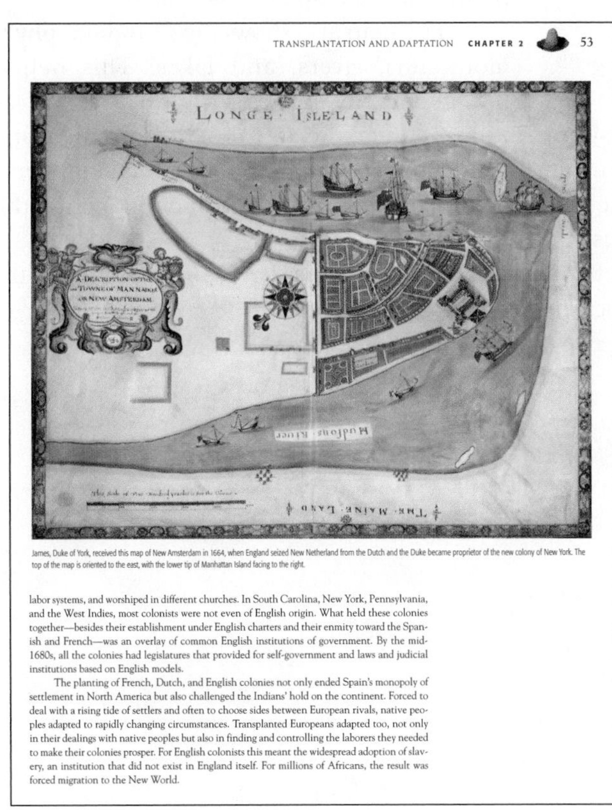
TRANSPLANTATION AND ADAPTATION **CHAPTER 2** 53

James, Duke of York, received this map of New Amsterdam in 1664, when England seized New Netherland from the Dutch and the Duke became proprietor of the new colony of New York. The top of the map is oriented to the east, with the lower tip of Manhattan Island facing to the right.

labor systems, and worshiped in different churches. In South Carolina, New York, Pennsylvania, and the West Indies, most colonists were not even of English origin. What held these colonies together—besides their establishment under English charters and their enmity toward the Spanish and French—was an overlay of common English institutions of government. By the mid-1680s, all the colonies had legislatures that provided for self-government and laws and judicial institutions based on English models.

The planting of French, Dutch, and English colonies not only ended Spain's monopoly of settlement in North America but also challenged the Indians' hold on the continent. Forced to deal with a rising tide of settlers and often to choose sides between European rivals, native peoples adapted to rapidly changing circumstances. Transplanted Europeans adapted too, not only in their dealings with native peoples but also in finding and controlling the laborers they needed to make their colonies prosper. For English colonists this meant the widespread adoption of slavery, an institution that did not exist in England itself. For millions of Africans, the result was forced migration to the New World.

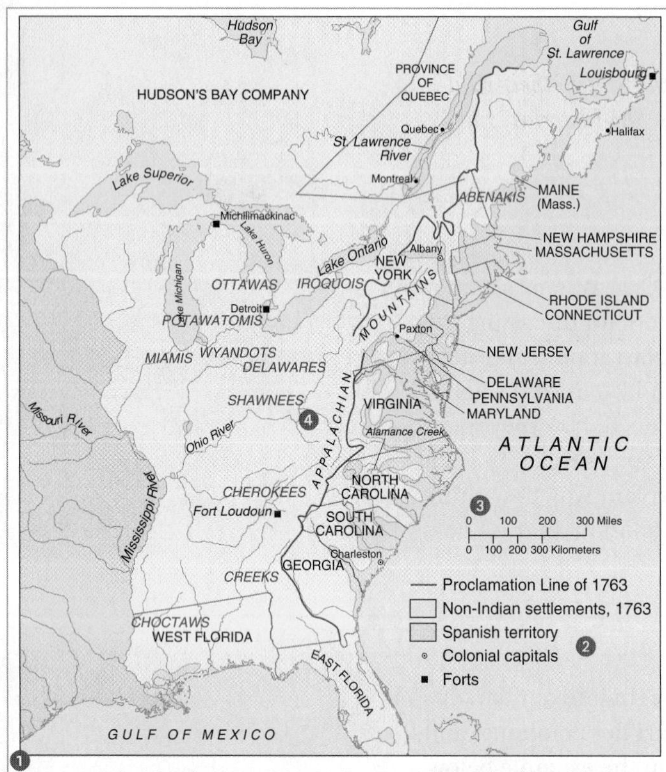

1 MAP 5–1 **Colonial Settlement and the Proclamation Line of 1763** This map depicts the regions claimed and settled by the major groups competing for territory in eastern North America. With the Proclamation Line of 1763, positioned along the crest of the Appalachian Mountains, the British government tried to stop the westward migration of settlers under its jurisdiction and thereby limit conflict with the Indians. The result, however, was frustration and anger on the part of land-hungry settlers.

5 **Why do** you think the Proclamation Line of 1763 was positioned along the crest of the Appalachian Mountains?

MAPS

Maps are important historical tools. They show how geography has affected history and concisely summarize complex relationships and events. Knowing how to read and interpret a map is important to understanding history. Map 5–1 from Chapter 5 shows the British colonies on the eastern seaboard of North America in 1763, about twelve years before the American Revolution. It has three features to help you read it: a caption, a legend, and a scale. The 1 **caption** explains the historical significance of the map. Here the caption tells us that in 1763 the British government sought to restrict colonial settlement west of the Appalachian Mountains to prevent conflict between colonists and Indians. Colonial frustration with this policy contributed to the outbreak of the American Revolution.

The legend and the scale appear in the lower right corner of the map. The 2 **legend** provides a key to what the symbols on the map mean. The solid line stretching along the Appalachian Mountains from Maine to Georgia represents the Proclamation Line of 1763. Cities are marked with a dot, capitals with a dot in a circle, and forts by a black square. Spanish territory west of the Mississippi River is represented in gold; territory settled by Europeans is represented in green. The 3 **scale** tells us that 7/8ths of an inch on the map represents 300 miles (about 480 kilometers) on the ground. With this information, estimates of the distance between points on the map are easily made.

The map also shows the 4 **topography** of the region—its mountains, rivers, and lakes. This helps us understand how geography influenced history in this case. For example, the Appalachian Mountains divide the eastern seaboard from the rest of the continent. The mountains obstructed colonial migration to the west for a long time. By running the Proclamation Line along the Appalachians, the British hoped to use this natural barrier to separate Indians and colonists.

A 5 **critical thinking question** asks for careful consideration of the spatial connections between geography and history.

STUDY AIDS

Each chapter begins with a collection of historically significant illustrations that provide visual context for the chapter. To help you look ahead at the chapter content, the second page shows the main chapter topics with a question for each to help you carefully consider important themes and developments.

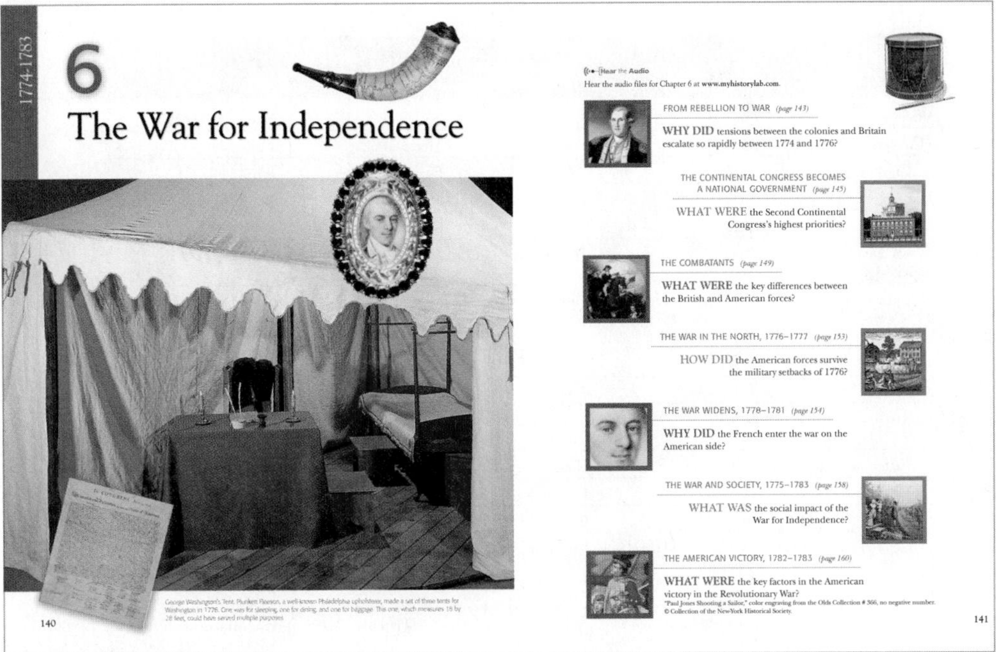

1774–1783

6

The War for Independence

Hear the Audio

Hear the audio files for Chapter 6 at www.myhistorylab.com.

FROM REBELLION TO WAR (page 143)

WHY DID tensions between the colonies and Britain escalate so rapidly between 1774 and 1776?

THE CONTINENTAL CONGRESS BECOMES A NATIONAL GOVERNMENT (page 145)

WHAT WERE the Second Continental Congress's highest priorities?

THE COMBATANTS (page 149)

WHAT WERE the key differences between the British and American forces?

THE WAR IN THE NORTH, 1776–1777 (page 153)

HOW DID the American forces survive the military setbacks of 1776?

THE WAR WIDENS, 1778–1781 (page 154)

WHY DID the French enter the war on the American side?

THE WAR AND SOCIETY, 1775–1783 (page 158)

WHAT WAS the social impact of the War for Independence?

THE AMERICAN VICTORY, 1782–1783 (page 160)

WHAT WERE the key factors in the American victory in the Revolutionary War?

140

141

MARGINAL QUESTIONS

The **Questions** that begin each chapter are repeated at the appropriate place in the margin of the text. You can use these questions to review your understanding of the chapter content.

WHO WERE the Regulators, and what were the Regulator movements?

MARGINAL KEY TERMS/GLOSSARY

Significant historical terms are called out in bold type throughout the text, defined in the margin, and listed at the end of each chapter with appropriate page numbers. All **key terms** in the text are listed alphabetically and defined in a glossary at the end of the book.

Pilgrims Settlers of Plymouth Colony, who viewed themselves as spiritual wanderers.

QUICK REVIEWS

The **Quick Reviews,** placed at key locations in the margins of each chapter, provide pinpoint summaries of important concepts, events, or topics in American history and serve as a mini-review resource.

QUICK REVIEW

Financial Strain on the Empire

- £146-million-pound national debt after French and Indian War.
- Many Britons believed Americans should bear more of the burden of empire.
- Economic recession increased pressure for new taxes.

OVERVIEW TABLES

The **Overview tables** in this text are a special feature designed to highlight and summarize important topics within a chapter. The Overview table shown here, for example, shows the predominant colonial labor systems in 1750 by geographic area.

52 CHAPTER 2 TRANSPLANTATION AND ADAPTATION

OVERVIEW English Colonies in the Seventeenth Century

Colony	Date of Founding	Established Religion	Economy	Government
Virginia	1607	Anglican	Tobacco	Royal (after 1625)
Plymouth	1620	Puritan	Mixed farming	Corporate
St. Christopher	1624	Anglican	Sugar	Royal
Barbados	1627	Anglican	Sugar	Royal
Nevis	1628	Anglican	Sugar	Royal
Massachusetts (including present-day Maine)	1630	Puritan	Mixed farming, fishing, shipbuilding	Corporate
New Hampshire	1630 (first settlement, annexed to Massachusetts 1643–1679)	Puritan	Mixed farming	Corporate (royal after 1679)
Antigua	1632	Anglican	Sugar	Royal
Montserrat	1632	Anglican	Sugar	Royal
Maryland	1634	None (Anglican after 1692)	Tobacco	Proprietary
Rhode Island	1636	None	Mixed farming	Corporate
Connecticut	1636	Puritan	Mixed farming	Corporate
New Haven	1638	Puritan	Mixed farming	Corporate
Jamaica	1655 (captured from Spanish)	Anglican	Sugar	Royal
Carolina	1663	Anglican	Rice	Proprietary
New York	1664 (captured from Dutch)	None	Mixed farming, furs	Proprietary (royal after 1685)
New Jersey	1664	None	Mixed farming	Proprietary
Pennsylvania	1681	None	Wheat, mixed farming	Proprietary

CONCLUSION

Even as England gained a permanent foothold in North America, it faced vigorous competition from France and the Netherlands. A new Atlantic world was beginning to emerge as the migration of people and goods across the ocean linked the Old and New Worlds as never before.

Commerce was the main focus of the short-lived New Netherland colony and a more durable New France. Profits from the fur trade encouraged the French to maintain friendly relations with their Indian allies and ensured that French kings would closely monitor the colony's affairs. English colonization was a more haphazard process. English kings granted charters for new colonies and let them develop more or less on their own. England had no equivalent in the seventeenth century of the imperial bureaucracies Spain and France created to manage their New World holdings.

The result was a highly diverse set of English colonies stretching from the Maine coast to the Caribbean. Settlers adjusted to different environments, developed different economies and

CHRONOLOGIES

Each chapter includes a **Chronology,** a list of the key events discussed in the chapter arranged in chronological order. Chronologies provide a review of important events and their relationship to one another.

CHRONOLOGY

c. 40,000–8000 B.C.E.	Ancestors of Native Americans cross Bering land bridge.	**1430s**	Beginnings of Portuguese slave trade in West Africa.
c. 10,000–9000 B.C.E.	Paleo-Indians expand through the Americas.	**1492**	End of *reconquista* in Spain.
c. 9000 B.C.E.	Extinction of large land mammals in North America.		Columbus's first voyage.
c. 8000 B.C.E.	Beginnings of agriculture in the Peruvian Andes and Mesoamerica.	**1494**	Treaty of Tordesillas.
c. 1500 B.C.E.	Earliest mound-building culture begins.	**1497**	John Cabot visits Nova Scotia and Newfoundland.
c. 500 B.C.E.–400 C.E.	Adena-Hopewell mound-building culture.	**1497–1499**	Vasco da Gama sails around Africa to reach India.
c. 700–1600 C.E.	Rise of West African empires.	**1517**	Protestant Reformation begins in Germany.
c. 900	First mounds built at Cahokia.	**1519–1521**	Hernán Cortés conquers the Aztec empire.
	Ancestral Puebloan expansion.	**1532–1533**	Francisco Pizarro conquers the Incan empire.
c. 1000	Spread of Islam in West Africa.	**1534–1542**	Jacques Cartier explores eastern Canada for France.
c. 1000–1015	First Viking voyages to North America.	**1540–1542**	Coronado explores southwestern North America.
c. 1000–1500	Last mound-building culture, the Mississippian.	**1542–1543**	Roberval's failed colony in Canada.
c. 1290s	Ancestral Puebloan dispersal into smaller villages.	**1558**	Elizabeth I becomes queen of England.
1400–1600	Renaissance in Europe.	**1565**	Spanish establish outpost at St. Augustine in Florida.
		1560s–1580s	English renew attempts to conquer Ireland.
		1587	Founding of "Lost Colony" of Roanoke.
		1598	Spanish found colony at New Mexico.

NATIVE AMERICAN SOCIETIES BEFORE 1492

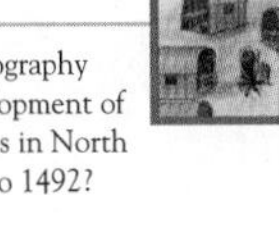

HOW DID geography shape the development of regional cultures in North America prior to 1492?

In 1492 perhaps 70 million people—nearly equal to the population of Europe at that time—lived on the continents of North and South America, most of them south of the present border between the United States and Mexico. They belonged to hundreds of groups, each with its own language or dialect, history, and way of life.

From the start, the original inhabitants of the Americas were peoples in motion. The first migrants may have arrived over forty thousand years ago, traveling from central Siberia and slowly making their way to southern South America. These people, and subsequent migrants from Eurasia, probably traveled across a land bridge that emerged across what is now the Bering Strait. During the last Ice Age, much of the earth's water was frozen in huge glaciers. This process lowered ocean levels, exposing a 600-mile-wide land bridge between Asia and America. Recent research examining genetic and linguistic similarities between Asian and Native American populations suggests that there may also have been later migrations.

See the **Map**
at **www.myhistorylab.com**
Pre-Columbian Societies of the Americas

HUNTERS, HARVESTERS, AND TRADERS

The earliest Americans adapted to an amazing range of environmental conditions, from the frozen Arctic to southwestern deserts to dense eastern woodlands. At first, they mainly subsisted by hunting the mammoths, bison, and other large game that roamed throughout North America.

NEW! MYHISTORYLAB ICONS

References to relevant primary source documents, audio files, visual sources, interactive maps, and activities available on the MyHistoryLab website have been added throughout each chapter. These references are identified by icons that connect the MyHistoryLab sources to the specific content within the text. Look for these icons as you read the chapter and explore the additional content online at www.myhistorylab.com.

Read the **Document**

Primary Source Documents, the History Bookshelf, and Activities.

See the **Map**

Interactive and Atlas Maps.

Hear the **Audio**

Audio files of *The American Journey* textbook and audio clips of readings, music, and speeches.

Watch the **Video**

Video Lectures and archival footage.

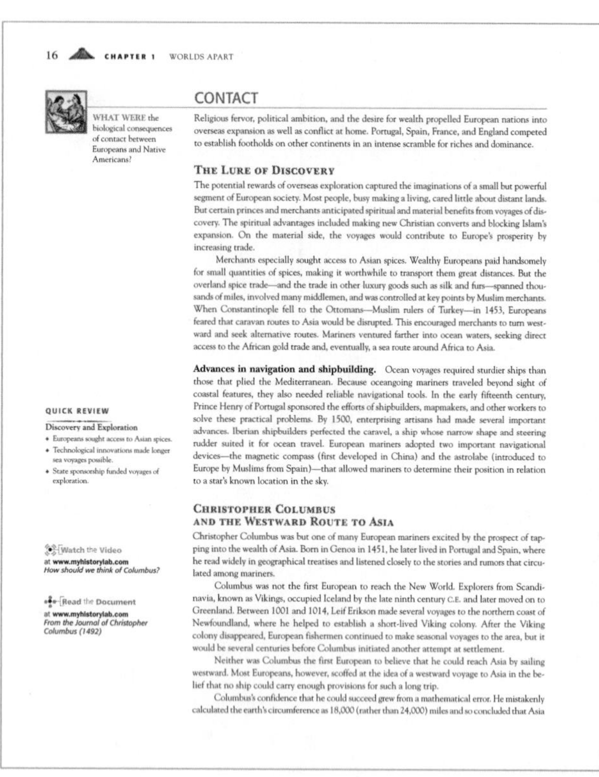

16 CHAPTER 1 WORLDS APART

WHAT WERE the biological consequences of contact between Europeans and Native Americans?

CONTACT

Religious fervor, political ambition, and the desire for wealth propelled European nations into overseas expansion as well as conflict at home. Portugal, Spain, France, and England competed to establish footholds on other continents in an intense scramble for riches and dominance.

THE LURE OF DISCOVERY

The potential rewards of overseas exploration captured the imaginations of a small but powerful segment of European society. Most people, busy making a living, cared little about distant lands. But certain princes and merchants anticipated spiritual and material benefits from voyages of discovery. The spiritual advantages included making new Christian converts and blocking Islam's expansion. On the material side, the voyages would contribute to Europe's prosperity by increasing trade.

Merchants especially sought access to Asian spices. Wealthy Europeans paid handsomely for small quantities of spices, making it worthwhile to transport them great distances. But the overland spice trade—and the trade in other luxury goods such as silk and furs—spanned thousands of miles, involved many middlemen, and was controlled at key points by Muslim merchants. When Constantinople fell to the Ottomans—Muslim rulers of Turkey—in 1453, Europeans feared that caravan routes to Asia would be disrupted. This encouraged merchants to turn westward and seek alternative routes. Mariners ventured farther into ocean waters, seeking direct access to the African gold trade and, eventually, a sea route around Africa to Asia.

QUICK REVIEW

Discovery and Exploration

- Europeans sought access to Asian spices.
- Technological innovations made longer sea voyages possible.
- State sponsorship funded voyages of exploration.

Advances in navigation and shipbuilding. Ocean voyages required sturdier ships than those that plied the Mediterranean. Because oceangoing mariners traveled beyond sight of coastal features, they also needed reliable navigational tools. In the early fifteenth century, Prince Henry of Portugal sponsored the efforts of shipbuilders, mapmakers, and other workers to solve these practical problems. By 1500, enterprising artisans had made several important advances. Iberian shipbuilders perfected the caravel, a ship whose narrow shape and steering rudder suited it for ocean travel. European mariners adopted two important navigational devices—the magnetic compass (first developed in China) and the astrolabe (introduced to Europe by Muslims from Spain)—that allowed mariners to determine their position in relation to a star's known location in the sky.

CHRISTOPHER COLUMBUS AND THE WESTWARD ROUTE TO ASIA

Watch the Video at www.myhistorylab.com *How should we think of Columbus?*

Read the Document at www.myhistorylab.com *From the Journal of Christopher Columbus (1492)*

Christopher Columbus was but one of many European mariners excited by the prospect of tapping into the wealth of Asia. Born in Genoa in 1451, he later lived in Portugal and Spain, where he read widely in geographical treatises and listened closely to the stories and rumors that circulated among mariners.

Columbus was not the first European to reach the New World. Explorers from Scandinavia, known as Vikings, occupied Iceland by the late ninth century C.E. and later moved on to Greenland. Between 1001 and 1014, Leif Erikson made several voyages to the northern coast of Newfoundland, where he helped to establish a short-lived Viking colony. After the Viking colony disappeared, European fishermen continued to make seasonal voyages to the area, but it would be several centuries before Columbus initiated another attempt at settlement.

Neither was Columbus the first European to believe that he could reach Asia by sailing westward. Most Europeans, however, scoffed at the idea of a westward voyage to Asia in the belief that no ship could carry enough provisions for such a long trip.

Columbus's confidence that he could succeed grew from a mathematical error. He mistakenly calculated the earth's circumference as 18,000 (rather than 24,000) miles and so concluded that Asia

NEW! myhistorylab CONNECTIONS

At the end of each chapter, the references in the chapter are listed again along with additional resources that relate directly to the content you will have read in the chapter.

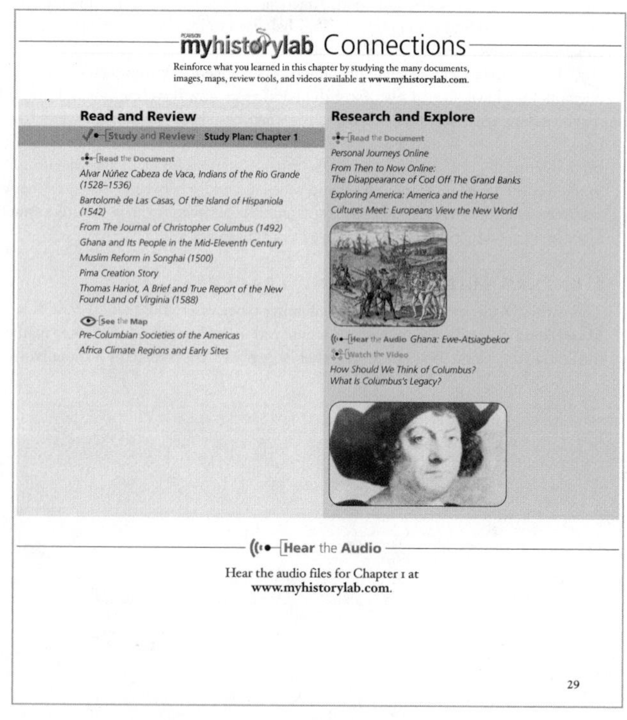

PEARSON myhistorylab Connections

Reinforce what you learned in this chapter by studying the many documents, images, maps, review tools, and videos available at www.myhistorylab.com.

Read and Review

Study and Review Study Plan: Chapter 1

Read the Document

Alvar Núñez Cabeza de Vaca, Indians of the Rio Grande (1528–1536)

Bartolomè de Las Casas, Of the Island of Hispaniola (1542)

From The Journal of Christopher Columbus (1492)

Ghana and Its People in the Mid-Eleventh Century

Muslim Reform in Songhai (1500)

Pima Creation Story

Thomas Hariot, A Brief and True Report of the New Found Land of Virginia (1588)

See the Map

Pre-Columbian Societies of the Americas

Africa Climate Regions and Early Sites

Research and Explore

Read the Document

Personal Journeys Online

From Then to Now Online: The Disappearance of Cod Off The Grand Banks

Exploring America: America and the Horse

Cultures Meet: Europeans View the New World

Hear the Audio *Ghana: Ewe-Atsiagbekor*

Watch the Video

How Should We Think of Columbus?

What Is Columbus's Legacy?

Hear the Audio

Hear the audio files for Chapter 1 at www.myhistorylab.com.

29

WHERE TO LEARN MORE, REVIEW QUESTIONS, AND KEY TERMS

At the end of each chapter there are a number of review and enrichment resources. The section called ❶ **Where to Learn More** lists important historical sites and museums around the country and related websites (many of which are also cited at appropriate places in the margins of the text) that provide exposure to historical artifacts and settings. ❷ **Review questions** reconsider the main topics of each chapter. ❸ **Key Terms** reference the page within the chapter where the term is defined.

WHERE TO LEARN MORE ❶

Jamestown Settlement, near Williamsburg, Virginia. Site includes replicas of first English passenger ships to Virginia, a reconstructed Powhatan Village, the re-created James Fort, and galleries with Indian and English artifacts. Visitors can also see archaeological excavations of site of the actual James Fort, as well as sample artifacts recovered from the area. The website http://www.virtualjamestown.org/ offers a wealth of fascinating information about English and Indian settlement in the Jamestown area.

St. Mary's City, Maryland. Visitors to this site of the first permanent settlement under the Calvert family may tour the area and view exhibits and living history programs that describe life in early Maryland. The website http://www.stmaryscity.org/ contains information about the historic site of St. Mary's City and has links to a virtual tour of the area.

Plimoth Plantation, Plymouth, Massachusetts. A living history museum, Plimoth Plantation re-creates colony life in the year 1627. There are reproductions of the English village and a Wampanoag settlement. Visitors may also see a replica of the *Mayflower*. The website http://www.plimoth.org/ provides information for visitors.

Pennsbury Manor, Morrisville, Pennsylvania. A reconstruction of William Penn's seventeenth-century plantation, this site includes furnished buildings and restored gardens. Visitor information about the site and William Penn's life can be found at http://www.pennsburymanor.org/.

REVIEW QUESTIONS 

1. To what extent was Richard Frethorne's experience typical of that of English colonists in the New World? What were the causes of his distress?
2. Comparing French, Dutch, and English colonies, which ones attracted the most settlers, and which the fewest? In what colonies were women scarce? What impact did these differences in emigration have on the various colonies' development?
3. Which English settlements were proprietary colonies? Did they share any common characteristics? What plans did the various proprietors have for their colonies, and to what extent were those plans put into effect?
4. When Virginia's settlers first arrived, they encountered a numerous and powerful confederation of Powhatan Indians. New England's colonists, in contrast, began their settlements after epidemics had drastically reduced the local native population. In what ways did the presence or absence of substantial Indian populations affect each region's early history?
5. In both Massachusetts and Pennsylvania, religion figured prominently as a motive for settlement. What were the religious beliefs of the settlers in each colony, and how did those beliefs help shape each colony's development?
6. Three colonial regions—the Chesapeake, the West Indies, and Carolina—developed economies dependent on staple crops. What were those crops? In what ways did staple-crop agriculture shape society in each region?
7. In what ways did events in Europe affect the founding of colonies in North America?

KEY TERMS 

Act for Religious Toleration (p. 41)
Anglican (p. 42)
Coureurs de bois (p. 34)
Covenant (p. 44)
Frame of Government (p. 51)
Fundamental Constitutions of Carolina (p. 49)
Headright system (p. 38)
House of Burgesses (p. 38)
Indentured servants (p. 34)
Joint-stock company (p. 37)
Pequot War (p. 44)
Pilgrims (p. 43)
Proprietary colony (p. 40)
Puritans (p. 40)
Quakers (p. 50)
Separatists (p. 43)
Slave codes (p. 48)

54

SPECIAL FEATURES

Historians find most of their information in written records and original documents that have survived from the past. These include government publications, letters, diaries, newspapers—whatever people wrote or printed, including many private documents never intended for publication. Several features in the text highlight the written record so important to understanding historical events.

ONE AMERICAN JOURNEY

Each chapter begins with **One American Journey,** a brief firsthand account of a time in history. Each of these personal journeys relates to the themes that follow in the chapter.

Personal Journeys Online

At the end of each document is a list of additional firsthand accounts that are included on the *MyHistoryLab* website.

4 **CHAPTER 1** WORLDS APART

ONE AMERICAN JOURNEY

After a difficult journey of over two hundred miles, the exhausted man arrived at the royal palace in the grand city of Tenochtitlán. He had hurried all the way from the Gulf Coast with important news for the Aztec leader, Moctezuma.

Our lord and king, forgive my boldness. I am from Mictlancuauhtla. When I went to the shores of the great sea, there was a mountain range or small mountain floating in the midst of the water, and moving here and there without touching the shore. My lord, we have never seen the like of this, although we guard the coast and are always on watch.

[When Moctezuma sent some officials to check on the messenger's story, they confirmed his report.]

Our lord and king, it is true that strange people have come to the shores of the great sea. They were fishing from a small boat, some with rods and others with a net. They fished until late and then they went back to their two great towers and climbed up into them.... They have very light skin, much lighter than ours. They all have long beards, and their hair comes only to their ears.

Miguel Leon–Portilla, *The Broken Spears: The Aztec Account of the Conquest of Mexico* (Boston, 1962).

Read the **Document** at **www.myhistorylab.com**

Personal Journeys Online

- **Christopher Columbus, *Journal of the First Voyage*, October 12, 1492. Account of his first meeting with Caribbean islanders.**
- **Martin Frobisher, *Account of First Voyage to the New World*, 1576. Description of his arrival in Canada and his encounter with native people.**

MOCTEZUMA was filled with foreboding when he received the messenger's initial report. Aztec religion placed great emphasis on omens and prophecies, which were thought to foreshadow coming events. Several unusual omens had recently occurred—blazing lights in the sky, one temple struck by lightning and another that spontaneously burst into flames. Now light-skinned strangers appeared offshore. Aztec spiritual leaders regarded these signs as unfavorable and warned that trouble lay ahead.

The messenger's journey to Tenochtitlán occurred in 1519. The "mountains" he saw were in fact the sails of European ships, and the strange men were Spanish soldiers under the command of Hernán Cortés. Before long, a variety of peoples—Native Americans, Africans, and Europeans—who had previously lived worlds apart would come together to create a world that was new to all of them.

This new world reflected the diverse experiences of the many peoples who built it. Improving economic conditions in the fifteenth and early sixteenth centuries propelled Europeans overseas to seek new opportunities for trade and settlement. Spain, Portugal, France, and England competed for political, economic, and religious domination within Europe, and their conflict carried over into the Americas. Native Americans drew upon their familiarity with the land and its resources, patterns of political and religious authority, and systems of trade and warfare to deal with the European newcomers. Africans did not come voluntarily to the Americas but were brought by the Europeans to work as slaves. They too would draw on their cultural heritage to cope with a new land and a new, harsh condition of life. ✦

AMERICAN VIEWS

Included in each chapter is a selection from a primary source document. The example shown here is the published account of Mary Rowlandson from Lancaster, Massachusetts, who in 1676 was taken captive with two of her children by Indian warriors. Each American Views feature begins with a brief introduction followed by several questions—for discussion or written response—on what the document reveals about key issues and events.

the Indians too far. Officials reduced demands for tribute and ended the *encomienda* system. The Franciscans eased their attacks on Pueblo religion. New Spanish governors, backed by military force, kept the peace as best they could in a place where Indians still outnumbered Europeans.

Resumption of the Beaver Wars. The Iroquois experience in the last phase of the Beaver Wars threatened to parallel that of the Indians of New England and Virginia. What began as a struggle between the Iroquois and western native peoples for control of the fur trade blossomed into a larger

AMERICAN VIEWS

Mary Rowlandson among the Indians

In February 1676, in the midst of King Philip's War, Indian warriors attacked the town of Lancaster, Massachusetts. They killed many inhabitants and took 23 colonists captive, including Mary Rowlandson and three of her children. Rowlandson spent the next three months traveling with various groups of Nipmucs, Narragansetts, and Wampanoags. She suffered physically and emotionally, watching her youngest daughter die in her arms and worrying about her other two children, from whom she was frequently separated. During her captivity, Rowlandson survived by accepting her fate and adapting to the Indians' way of life. Finally, with an English victory imminent, Rowlandson was ransomed and rejoined her husband (who had been away at the time of the attack) and family. In 1682, she published an account of her captivity in which she explored the meaning of her experience. Rowlandson's narrative proved so popular that three editions were printed in the first year.

- **How** did Rowlandson describe the Indians? How did she characterize her encounter with King Philip?
- **In** what ways did Rowlandson accommodate herself to the Indians' way of life? How did she employ her skills to fit in? Did her gender make a difference in her experience of captivity?
- **How** did Rowlandson's Puritan faith shape her narrative?

We travelled on till night; and in the morning, we must go over the River to Philip's crew. When I was in the Cannoo, I could not but be amazed at the numerous crew of Pagans that were on the Bank on the other side. When I came ashore, they gathered all about me, I sitting alone in the midst: I observed they asked one another questions, and laughed, and rejoyced over their Gains and Victories. Then my heart began to fail: and I fell a weeping which was the first time to my remembrance that I wept before them. Although I had met with so much Affliction, and my heart was many times ready to break, yet could I not shed one tear in their sight: but rather had been all this while in a maze, and like one astonished: but now I may say as, Psal. 137.1 By *the rivers of Babylon, there we sat down: yea, we wept when we remembered Zion*. There one of them asked me, why I wept, I could hardly tell what to say: yet I answered, they would kill me: No, said he, none will hurt you. Then came one of them and gave me two spoon-fulls of Meal to comfort me.... Then I went to see King Philip, he bade me come in and sit down, and asked me whether I would smoke (a usual Complement now adayes amongst Saints and Sinners) but this no way suited me. For though I had formerly used Tobacco, yet I had left it ever since I was first taken, *It seems to be a bait, the devil lays to make men loose their precious time*....

During my abode in this place, Philip spake to me to make a shirt for his boy, which I did, for which he gave me a shilling: I offered the money to my master, but he bade me keep it: and with it I bought a piece of Horse flesh. Afterwards he asked me to make a Cap for his boy, for which he invited me to Dinner. I went, and he gave me a Pancake, about as big as two fingers; it was made of parched wheat, beaten, and fryed in Bears grease, but I thought I never tasted pleasanter meat in my life. There was a Squaw who spake to me to make a shirt for her *Sannup* [husband], for which she gave me a piece of Bear. Another asked me to knit a pair of Stockins, for which she gave me a quart of Pease.... Hearing that my son was come to this place, I went to see him, and found him lying flat upon the ground: I asked him how he could sleep so? He answered me, *That he was not asleep, but at Prayer*; and lay so, that they might not observe what he was doing. I pray God he may remember these things now he is returned in safety.

Source: Neal Salisbury, ed., *The Sovereignty and Goodness of God, Together with the Faithfulness of His Promises Displayed*.... (Boston, 1997), pp. 82–83.

GLOBAL CONNECTIONS

This feature places the American journey within a broader, worldwide context. That journey not only influenced other countries and peoples, but we in turn have been shaped by global economic, migratory, technological, and political trends. Critical thinking questions encourage analysis of the global connections.

GLOBAL CONNECTIONS

NORTH AMERICA'S FIRST JEWISH COMMUNITY

In 1654, twenty-three Jews arrived in New Amsterdam after a long voyage from Brazil. The reasons why they ended up in the Dutch colonial town relate to a much larger story of repeated Jewish migrations, undertaken time and again to escape religious persecution. In New Amsterdam these settlers found a home, establishing the first permanent Jewish community in North America.

Many of them could trace their ancestry back to Spain, where there had been a flourishing Jewish community during the Middle Ages. By the fifteenth century, however, the same Christian militancy that inspired the *reconquista* against the Muslims brought trouble for Spain's Jewish population in the form of the Inquisition. Jews who refused to convert to Christianity risked execution as heretics. In 1492, the same year as Columbus's first voyage, Spanish authorities ordered all Jews to leave Spain. Refugee Spanish Jews relocated all over the Mediterranean world, with perhaps a hundred thousand settling in Portugal, Spain's neighbor on the Iberian Peninsula. Many who did so were forced to accept Christian baptism, but continued to follow their own faith in secret. When the authorities threatened to prevent such practices, many Jews chose to leave Portugal. Some sought refuge in the Netherlands, where they found religious toleration and commercial opportunities.

In the early seventeenth century, the same Dutch West India Company that founded New Netherland tried to dislodge the Portuguese from their prosperous sugar-producing colony of Brazil. The company succeeded in capturing the city of Recife in 1630, and for the next twenty-four years the Dutch ruled over northeastern Brazil. During that time, more than a thousand Jews moved to the colony from the Netherlands. But when the Portuguese regained control of Brazil in 1654, the Jews were forced to move yet again. Most returned to the Netherlands, but a few decided to take their chances in New Amsterdam. At last they found a place where they could stay. When New Netherland became New York in 1664, English authorities continued the Dutch practice of toleration. Even though Jewish colonists were only supposed to worship in private, there was a synagogue in New York City by 1700. Jews eventually settled in other colonies, such as Rhode Island, Pennsylvania, and South Carolina. Wherever they formed their communities, they contributed to the remarkable religious diversity of England's New World empire.

- How did religious persecution in early modern Europe affect the lives of its Jewish inhabitants?

Roanoke's dismal fate. But it endured, eventually developing into the prosperous colony of Virginia. The reason for Virginia's success was an American plant—tobacco—that commanded good prices from European consumers. Tobacco also underlay the economy of a neighboring colony, Maryland, and had a profound influence on the development of Chesapeake society.

THE ORDEAL OF EARLY VIRGINIA

In 1606, several English merchants petitioned King James I for a charter incorporating two companies to attempt New World settlement. One, the London, or Virginia, Company, included merchants from the city of London; the other, the Plymouth Company, included merchants from England's western ports. These **joint-stock companies** sold shares to investors (who expected a profit in return) to raise money for colonization.

joint-stock company Business enterprise in which a group of stockholders pooled their money to engage in trade or to fund colonizing expeditions.

The Jamestown colony. Three small ships carried 104 settlers, all men, to the mouth of Chesapeake Bay in May 1607 (see Map 2–2). On a peninsula about 50 miles up a river they named the James in honor of their king, the colonists built a fortified settlement they called Jamestown. Hoping to earn quick profits for Virginia Company investors, they immediately began hunting for gold and searching for the Northwest Passage to Asia. Spending all their time searching for riches, the settlers neglected to plant crops, and their food supplies dwindled. By January 1608, only thirty-eight colonists were still alive.

Read the Document at **www.myhistorylab.com** *Exploring America: Jamestown*

INTERPRETING THE PAST

These two-page features at the end of selected chapters analyze important topics in U.S. history through images and short document excerpts. A focus question and an introductory narrative give a careful examination of the historical implication of each topic in question. In this example, the accounts of an African and a slave trader on their voyages across the Atlantic from Africa are underscored by the stark images of the slave trade to provide an in-depth perspective on this topic.

INTERPRETING the PAST

The Voyage to Slavery

WHAT WERE the dehumanizing experiences faced by Africans as they were kidnapped and transported to the New World as slaves? Under what conditions were Africans taken for slavery, and what was their fate when they arrived in the New World?

Most Africans were captured by other Africans in interior wars between tribes or specifically for sale as slaves. The slaves were moved to the West Coast of Africa where European and American slavers awaited to purchase a human cargo. Slavers inspected their potential cargo for health and strength. Males were preferred because the work on New World plantations would be hard. Human cargo was packed into ships' holds in the most efficient manner and carried under horrible, inhumane conditions to the New World for sale to the highest bidder. It was not unusual for Africans to prefer death to such a fate and individuals would dive overboard or even throw their children into the sea because drowning was considered a better end than that of slavery. For this reason slaves would be kept below decks in leg irons with the exception of an hour or so of exercise each day. During the exercise period slaves would be forced to jump up and down or "dance" to keep their muscles limber and the sale price for each individual at its highest level. Each day dead slaves would be cast overboard and tales abound of schools of sharks trailing slave ships for hundreds of miles.

The shrieks of the women, ...

Olaudah Equiano, captured in Nigeria at a very early age, later gave this report of the experience crossing the Atlantic in a slave ship in 1789.

The closeness of the place [ship's hold], and the heat of the climate, added to the number in the ship, which was so crowded that each had scarcely room to turn himself, almost suffocated us. This produced copious perspirations, so that the air soon became unfit for respiration, from a variety of loathsome smells, and brought on a sickness amongst the slaves, of which many died, thus falling victims to the improvident avarice, as I may call it, of their purchasers. This wretched situation was again aggravated by the galling of the chains, now become insupportable; and the filth of the necessary tubs, into which the children often fell, and were almost suffocated. The shrieks of the women, and the groans of the dying, rendered the whole a scene of horror almost inconceivable. Happily perhaps for myself I was soon reduced so low here that it was thought necessary to keep me almost always on deck; and from my extreme youth I was not put in fetters. In this situation I expected every hour to share the fate of my companions, some of whom were almost daily brought upon deck at the point of death, which I began to hope would soon put an end to my miseries. . . . One day, when we had a smooth sea and moderate wind, two of my wearied countrymen who were chained together (I was near them at the time), preferring death to such a life of misery, somehow made through the nettings and jumped into the sea: immediately another quite dejected fellow, who on account of his illness, was suffered to be out of irons, also followed their example; and I believe many more would very soon have done the same if they had not been prevented by the ship's crew who were instantly alarmed. Those of us that were the most active were in a moment put down under the deck, and there was such a noise and confusion amongst the people of the ship as I never heard before, to stop her, and get the boat out to go after the slaves. However two of the wretches were drowned, but they got the other, and afterwards flogged him unmercifully for thus attempting to prefer death to slavery.

This eighteenth-century engraving of a slave ship shows how tightly Africans were packed below the decks of these vessels, evidence that the thirst for profit overrode concerns for their health or welfare.

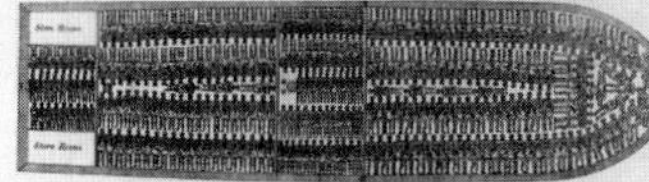

82

Alexander Falconbridge served as a ship's surgeon aboard a slaver in 1788. He was so horrified by what he witnessed during that time that he became involved in the British abolition movement.

When the Negroes, whom the black traders have to dispose of, are shown to the European purchasers, they first examine them relative to their age. They then minutely inspect their persons, and inquire into the state of their health; if they are afflicted with any infirmity, or are deformed; or have bad eyes or teeth; if they are lame, or weak in their joints, or distorted in the back, or of a slender make, or are narrow in the chest; in short, if they have been, or are afflicted in any manner, so as to render them incapable of much labour; if any of the foregoing defects are discovered in them, they are rejected. But if approved of, they are generally taken on board the ship the same evening. The purchaser has liberty to return on the following morning, but not afterwards, such as upon re-examination are found exceptionable.

The traders frequently beat those Negroes which are objected to by the captains and use them with great severity. It matters not whether they are refused on account of age, illness, deformity, or for any other reason. At New Calabar, in particular, the traders have frequently been known to put them to death. Instances have happened at that place that the traders, when any of their Negroes have been objected to, have dropped their canoes under the stern of the vessel, and instantly beheaded them, in sight of the captain.

African men, women, and children are tied together while walking in chains after being captured by slave traders.

Two men brand an African woman kneeling helplessly on the ground.

The purchaser has liberty to return...

83

The AMERICAN JOURNEY

1

Worlds Apart

Mexico: Hernán Cortés is greeted by Moctezuma's messenger in 1519. Mexican Indian painting, sixteenth century.

Hear the Audio
Hear the audio files for Chapter 1 at **www.myhistorylab.com**.

NATIVE AMERICAN SOCIETIES BEFORE 1492 *(page 5)*

HOW DID geography shape the development of regional cultures in North America prior to 1492?

WEST AFRICAN SOCIETIES *(page 10)*

WHAT WERE the key characteristics of West African society?

WESTERN EUROPE ON THE EVE OF EXPLORATION *(page 14)*

HOW DID events in Europe both shape and inspire exploration of the Americas?

CONTACT *(page 16)*

WHAT WERE the biological consequences of contact between Europeans and Native Americans?

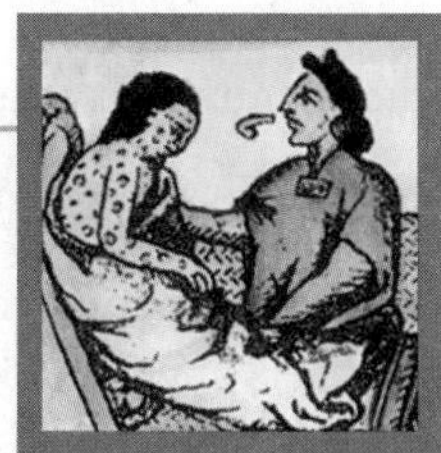

COMPETITION FOR A CONTINENT *(page 24)*

WHY DID early French and English efforts at colonization falter?

ONE AMERICAN JOURNEY

After a difficult journey of over two hundred miles, the exhausted man arrived at the royal palace in the grand city of Tenochtitlán. He had hurried all the way from the Gulf Coast with important news for the Aztec leader, Moctezuma.

Our lord and king, forgive my boldness. I am from Mictlancuauhtla. When I went to the shores of the great sea, there was a mountain range or small mountain floating in the midst of the water, and moving here and there without touching the shore. My lord, we have never seen the like of this, although we guard the coast and are always on watch.

[When Moctezuma sent some officials to check on the messenger's story, they confirmed his report.]

Our lord and king, it is true that strange people have come to the shores of the great sea. They were fishing from a small boat, some with rods and others with a net. They fished until late and then they went back to their two great towers and climbed up into them.... They have very light skin, much lighter than ours. They all have long beards, and their hair comes only to their ears.

Miguel Leon–Portilla, *The Broken Spears: The Aztec Account of the Conquest of Mexico* (Boston, 1962).

Read the **Document** at **www.myhistorylab.com**

Personal Journeys Online

- **Christopher Columbus, *Journal of the First Voyage,* October 12, 1492. Account of his first meeting with Caribbean islanders.**
- **Martin Frobisher, *Account of First Voyage to the New World,* 1576. Description of his arrival in Canada and his encounter with native people.**

MOCTEZUMA was filled with foreboding when he received the messenger's initial report. Aztec religion placed great emphasis on omens and prophecies, which were thought to foreshadow coming events. Several unusual omens had recently occurred—blazing lights in the sky, one temple struck by lightning and another that spontaneously burst into flames. Now light-skinned strangers appeared offshore. Aztec spiritual leaders regarded these signs as unfavorable and warned that trouble lay ahead.

The messenger's journey to Tenochtitlán occurred in 1519. The "mountains" he saw were in fact the sails of European ships, and the strange men were Spanish soldiers under the command of Hernán Cortés. Before long, a variety of peoples—Native Americans, Africans, and Europeans—who had previously lived worlds apart would come together to create a world that was new to all of them.

This new world reflected the diverse experiences of the many peoples who built it. Improving economic conditions in the fifteenth and early sixteenth centuries propelled Europeans overseas to seek new opportunities for trade and settlement. Spain, Portugal, France, and England competed for political, economic, and religious domination within Europe, and their conflict carried over into the Americas. Native Americans drew upon their familiarity with the land and its resources, patterns of political and religious authority, and systems of trade and warfare to deal with the European newcomers. Africans did not come voluntarily to the Americas but were brought by the Europeans to work as slaves. They too would draw on their cultural heritage to cope with a new land and a new, harsh condition of life. ✦

CHRONOLOGY

c. 40,000–8000 B.C.E.	Ancestors of Native Americans cross Bering land bridge.	**1430s**	Beginnings of Portuguese slave trade in West Africa.
c. 10,000–9000 B.C.E.	Paleo-Indians expand through the Americas.	**1492**	End of *reconquista* in Spain.
			Columbus's first voyage.
c. 9000 B.C.E.	Extinction of large land mammals in North America.	**1494**	Treaty of Tordesillas.
c. 8000 B.C.E.	Beginnings of agriculture in the Peruvian Andes and Mesoamerica.	**1497**	John Cabot visits Nova Scotia and Newfoundland.
		1497–1499	Vasco da Gama sails around Africa to reach India.
c. 1500 B.C.E.	Earliest mound-building culture begins.	**1517**	Protestant Reformation begins in Germany.
c. 500 B.C.E.–400 C.E.	Adena-Hopewell mound-building culture.	**1519–1521**	Hernán Cortés conquers the Aztec empire.
		1532–1533	Francisco Pizarro conquers the Incan empire.
c. 700–1600 C.E.	Rise of West African empires.	**1534–1542**	Jacques Cartier explores eastern Canada for France.
c. 900	First mounds built at Cahokia.	**1540–1542**	Coronado explores southwestern North America.
	Ancestral Puebloan expansion.	**1542–1543**	Roberval's failed colony in Canada.
c. 1000	Spread of Islam in West Africa.	**1558**	Elizabeth I becomes queen of England.
c. 1000–1015	First Viking voyages to North America.	**1565**	Spanish establish outpost at St. Augustine in Florida.
c. 1000–1500	Last mound-building culture, the Mississippian.	**1560s–1580s**	English renew attempts to conquer Ireland.
c. 1290s	Ancestral Puebloan dispersal into smaller villages.	**1587**	Founding of "Lost Colony" of Roanoke.
1400–1600	Renaissance in Europe.	**1598**	Spanish found colony at New Mexico.

NATIVE AMERICAN SOCIETIES BEFORE 1492

HOW DID geography shape the development of regional cultures in North America prior to 1492?

See the **Map** at **www.myhistorylab.com** *Pre-Columbian Societies of the Americas*

In 1492 perhaps 70 million people—nearly equal to the population of Europe at that time—lived on the continents of North and South America, most of them south of the present border between the United States and Mexico. They belonged to hundreds of groups, each with its own language or dialect, history, and way of life.

From the start, the original inhabitants of the Americas were peoples in motion. The first migrants may have arrived over forty thousand years ago, traveling from central Siberia and slowly making their way to southern South America. These people, and subsequent migrants from Eurasia, probably traveled across a land bridge that emerged across what is now the Bering Strait. During the last Ice Age, much of the earth's water was frozen in huge glaciers. This process lowered ocean levels, exposing a 600-mile-wide land bridge between Asia and America. Recent research examining genetic and linguistic similarities between Asian and Native American populations suggests that there may also have been later migrations.

HUNTERS, HARVESTERS, AND TRADERS

The earliest Americans adapted to an amazing range of environmental conditions, from the frozen Arctic to southwestern deserts to dense eastern woodlands. At first, they mainly subsisted by hunting the mammoths, bison, and other large game that roamed throughout North America.

Archaeologists working near present-day Clovis, New Mexico, have found carefully crafted spear points—some of which may be over thirteen thousand years old. Such efficient tools possibly contributed to overhunting, which, along with climate change, led to the extinction of many big-game species. By about 9000 B.C.E. the world's climate began to grow warmer, turning grasslands into deserts and reducing the animals' food supply. Humans too had to find other food sources.

Between roughly 8000 B.C.E. and 1500 B.C.E. the Native American societies changed in important ways. Native populations grew and men and women assumed more specialized roles in their villages. Men did most of the hunting and fishing, activities that required travel. Women remained closer to home, harvesting and preparing wild plant foods and caring for children.

QUICK REVIEW

The Earliest Americans

- The first North Americans were resourceful hunters.
- The earliest Americans adapted to a wide range of regional environments.
- Farming began in central Mexico nine to ten thousand years ago.

Across the continent, native communities also developed complex networks of trade. They not only exchanged material goods, but also marriage partners, laborers, ideas, and religious practices. Trade networks sometimes extended over great distances. Ideas about death and the afterlife also passed between groups. So too did certain burial practices, such as the placing of valued possessions in the grave along with the deceased person's body. In some areas, the increasing complexity of exchange networks, as well as competition for resources, encouraged concentrations of political power. Chiefs might manage trade relations and conduct diplomacy for groups of villages rather than for a single community.

The Development of Agriculture

No Native American adaptation was more momentous than the domestication of certain plants and the development of farming. Native Americans may have turned to farming when population growth threatened to outrun the wild food supply. Women, with their knowledge of wild plants, probably discovered how to save seeds and cultivate them, becoming the world's first farmers.

Wherever agriculture took hold, important social changes followed. Populations grew, because farming produced a more secure food supply than did hunting and gathering. Permanent villages appeared as farmers settled near their fields. In central Mexico, agriculture eventually sustained the populations of large cities. Trade in agricultural surpluses flowed through networks of exchange. In many Indian societies, women's status improved because of their role as the principal farmers. Even religious beliefs adapted to the increasing importance of farming.

culture areas Geographical regions inhabited by peoples who share similar basic patterns of subsistence and social organization.

The adoption of agriculture further enhanced the diversity of Native American societies that developed over centuries within broad regions, or **culture areas** (see Map 1–1). Within each area, inhabitants shared basic patterns of subsistence and social organization, largely reflecting the natural environment to which they had adapted. Most, but not all of them, eventually relied upon farming.

Nonfarming Societies

Agriculture was impossible in the challenging environment of the Arctic and Subarctic. There, nomadic bands of Inuits and Aleuts moved seasonally to fish or hunt whales, seals, and other sea animals, and, in the brief summers, gather wild berries.

Along the Northwest Coast and the Columbia River Plateau, one of the most densely populated areas of North America, abundant natural resources permitted native peoples to prosper without farming. Local rivers and forests supplied fish, game, and edible plants.

Farther south, in present-day California, hunter-gatherers once lived in smaller villages, which usually adjoined oak groves where Indians gathered acorns as an important food source. Nomadic hunting bands in the Great Basin, where the climate was warm and dry, learned to survive on the region's limited resources.

Women were the principal farmers in most Native American societies, growing corn, beans, and other crops in fields cleared by Indian men. Many of these New World foods would be transported across the Atlantic to become important to Old World diets.

Mesoamerican Civilizations

Mesoamerica, the birthplace of agriculture in North America, extends from central Mexico into Central America. A series of complex, literate, urban cultures emerged in this region beginning around 1200 B.C.E. The Olmecs, who flourished on Mexico's Gulf Coast from about 1200 to 400 B.C.E., and their successors in the region built cities featuring large pyramids, developed religious practices that included human sacrifice, and devised calendars and writing systems. Two of the most prominent Mesoamerican civilizations that followed the Olmecs were the Mayans in the Yucatán and Guatemala and the Aztecs of Teotihuacán in central Mexico.

The Mayans. Mayan civilization reached its greatest glory between about 150 and 900 C.E. in the southern Yucatán, creating Mesoamerica's most advanced writing and calendrical systems. The Mayans of the southern Yucatán suffered a decline after 900, but there were still many thriving Mayan centers in the northern Yucatán when Europeans arrived in the Americas. The great city of Teotihuacán dominated central Mexico from the first century to the eighth century C.E. and influenced much of Mesoamerica through trade and conquest.

The Aztecs. Some two hundred years after the fall of Teotihuacán, the Toltecs, a warrior people, rose to prominence, dominating central Mexico from about 900 to 1100. In the wake of the Toltec collapse, the **Aztecs** migrated from the north into the Valley of Mexico and built a great empire that soon controlled much of Mesoamerica. The magnificent Aztec capital, Tenochtitlán, was a city of great plazas, magnificent temples and palaces, and busy marketplaces. In 1492, Tenochtitlán was home to some 200,000 people, making it one of the largest cities in the world at the time.

Aztecs A warrior people who dominated the Valley of Mexico from 1100–1521.

The great pyramid in Tenochtitlán's principal temple complex was the center of Aztec religious life. Here Aztec priests sacrificed human victims. Human sacrifice had been part of Mesoamerican religion since the time of the Olmecs. People believed that such ceremonies pleased the gods and prevented them from destroying the earth. The Aztecs, however, practiced sacrifice on a much larger scale than ever before.

The Aztec empire expanded through military conquest, driven by a quest for sacrificial victims and tribute payments of gold, food, and handcrafted goods from hundreds of subject communities. But as the empire grew, it became increasingly vulnerable to internal division. Neighboring peoples submitted to the Aztecs out of fear rather than loyalty.

QUICK REVIEW

Mesoamerica

- Mesoamerica was the birthplace of agriculture in North America.
- Olmecs were the first literate urban culture in the region.
- Mayan civilization reached its height between 150 and 900 C.E.

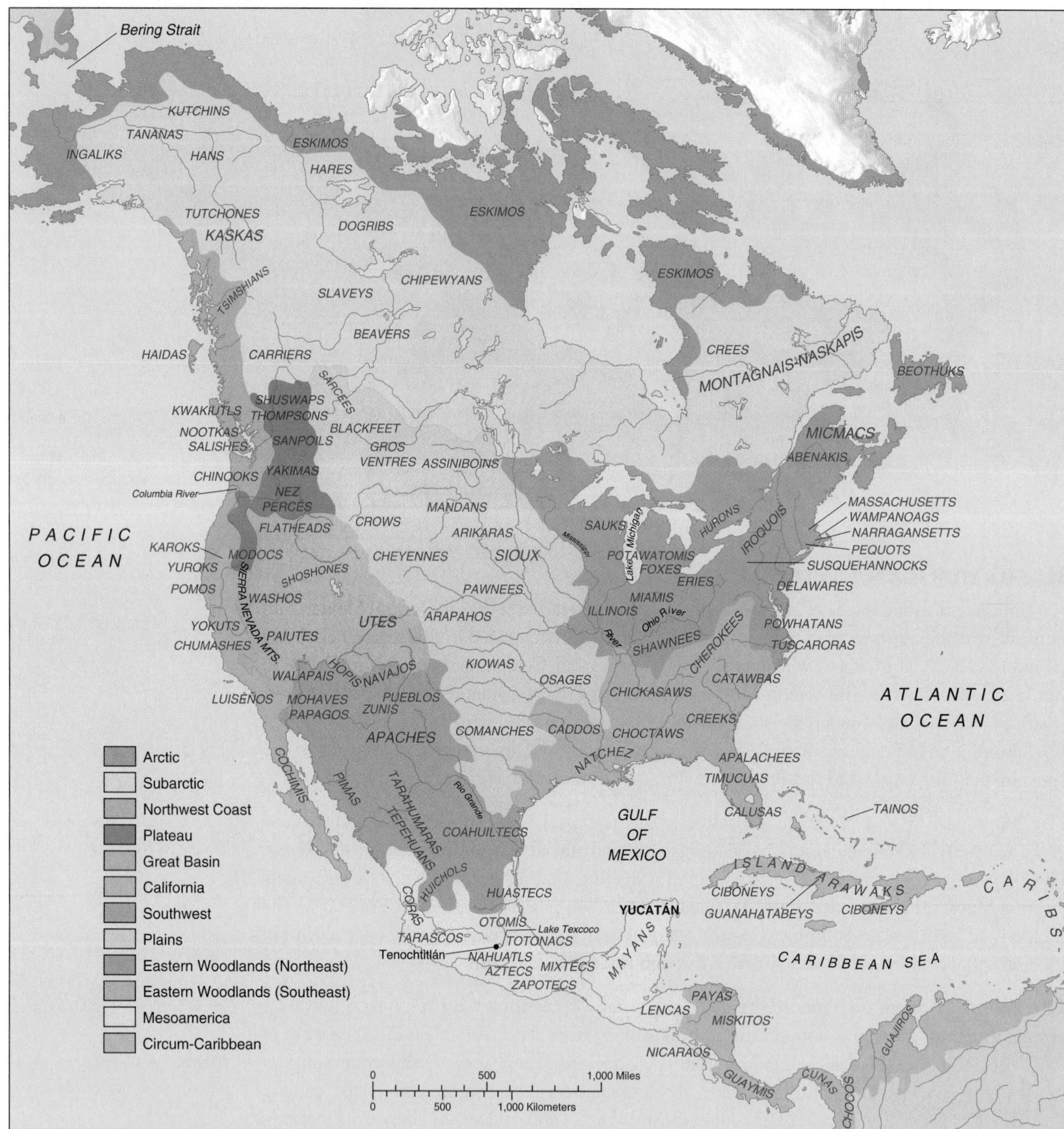

MAP 1–1 **North American Culture Areas, c. 1500** Over the course of centuries, Indian peoples in North America developed distinctive cultures suited to the environments in which they lived. Inhabitants of each culture area shared basic patterns of subsistence, craft work, and social organization. Most, but not all, Indian peoples combined farming with hunting and gathering.

How might major geographical features (mountains, rivers, deserts, etc.) have shaped the migration patterns and cultural development of the peoples of the Americas?

North America's Diverse Cultures

North of Mexico, the development of a drought-resistant type of maize around 400 B.C.E. enabled a series of cultures sharing certain characteristics with Mesoamerica to emerge. Beginning about 300 B.C.E., the Hohokams settled in villages in southern Arizona and devised elaborate irrigation systems that allowed them to harvest two crops of corn, beans, and squash each year. Trade networks linked the Hohokams to people living as far away as California and Mexico. Their culture endured for over a thousand years but mysteriously disappeared by 1450.

Ancestral Puebloans. Early in the first century C.E., Ancestral Puebloan peoples (sometimes called Anasazis) began to settle in farming communities where the borders of present-day Colorado, Utah, Arizona, and New Mexico meet. Scarce rainfall, routed through dams and hillside terraces, watered the crops. Ancestral Puebloans originally lived in villages, or pueblos (*pueblo* is the Spanish word for "village") built on mesas and canyon floors. In New Mexico's Chaco Canyon, perhaps as many as fifteen thousand people dwelled in a dozen large towns and hundreds of outlying villages. But after about 1200, villagers began carving multistoried stone houses into canyon walls, dwellings that could only be reached by difficult climbs up steep cliffs and along narrow ledges. Warfare and climate change may have worked together to force the Puebloans into these precarious homes.

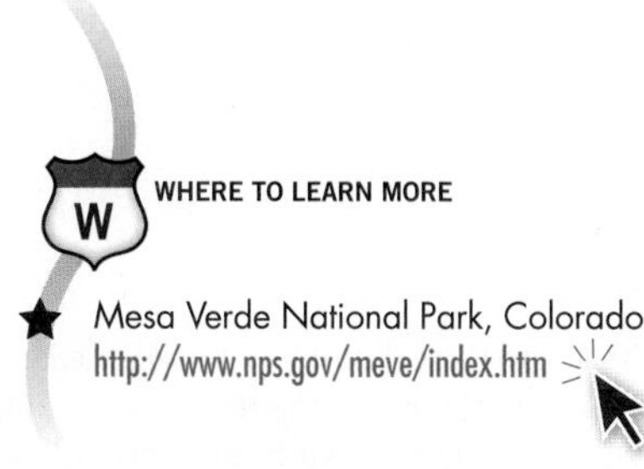

W
WHERE TO LEARN MORE
Mesa Verde National Park, Colorado
http://www.nps.gov/meve/index.htm

Around 1200, the climate of the Southwest grew colder, making it more difficult to grow enough to feed the large population. Food scarcity may have set village against village and encouraged attacks by outsiders. Villagers probably resorted to cliff dwellings for protection as violence spread in the region. By 1300, survivors abandoned the cliff dwellings and dispersed into smaller villages along the Rio Grande. Their descendants include the Hopis and Zunis, as well as other Puebloan peoples in the desert Southwest.

Read the **Document**
at **www.myhistorylab.com**
Alvar Núñez Cabeza de Vaca, Indians of the Rio Grande (1528–1536)

Plains Indians. The Great Plains of the continent's interior were much less densely settled than the desert Southwest. Mandans, Pawnees, and other groups settled along river valleys, where women farmed and men hunted bison. Plains Indians moved frequently, seeking more fertile land or better hunting. Wherever they went, they traded skins, food, and obsidian (a volcanic glass used for tools and weapons) with other native peoples.

W
WHERE TO LEARN MORE
Cahokia Mounds State Historic Site, Collinsville, Illinois
http://cahokiamounds.org/

Mound-building cultures. As agriculture spread to the Eastern Woodlands, a vast territory extending from the Mississippi Valley to the Atlantic seaboard, several "mound-building" societies—named for the large earthworks their members constructed—developed in the Ohio and Mississippi valleys. The oldest flourished in Louisiana between 1500 and 700 B.C.E. The members of the Adena-Hopewell culture, which appeared in the Ohio Valley between 500 B.C.E. and 400 C.E., built hundreds of mounds, often in the shapes of humans, birds, and serpents. Most were grave sites, where people were buried with valuable goods, including objects made from materials obtained through long-distance trade.

Cahokia One of the largest urban centers created by Mississippian peoples, containing 30,000 residents in 1250.

The last mound-building culture, the Mississippian, emerged between 1000 and 1500 in the Mississippi Valley. Mississippian farmers raised enough food to support sizable populations and major urban centers. The largest city by far was **Cahokia,** located near present-day St. Louis in a fertile floodplain with access to the major river systems of the continent's interior. Cahokia dominated the Mississippi Valley, linked by trade to dozens of villages in the midwestern region. Mississippian culture began to decline in the thirteenth century, perhaps due to an ecological crisis.

W
WHERE TO LEARN MORE
Mashantucket Pequot Museum, Mashantucket, Connecticut
http://pequotmuseum.org/

What followed in the Eastern Woodlands region was a century or more of warfare and political instability. In the vacuum left by Cahokia's decline, other groups sought to exert more power. In the Northeast, the Iroquois and Hurons moved from dispersed settlements into fortified villages. Both the Hurons and the Iroquois formed confederacies that were intended to diminish internal conflicts and increase their collective spiritual strength. Among the Iroquois, five separate nations—the Mohawks, Oneidas, Onondagas, Cayugas, and Senecas—joined to create the **Great League of Peace and Power** around the year 1450. Similar developments occurred in the Southeast, where chronic instability led to regional alliances and shifting centers of trade and political power.

Great League of Peace and Power Spiritual union of five Iroquois nations that aimed to maintain peace among them and unite them to fight against common enemies.

This artist's rendering, based on archaeological evidence, suggests the size and magnificence of the Mississippian city of Cahokia. By the thirteenth century, it was as populous as medieval London and served as a center of trade for the vast interior of North America.

Eastern Woodlands peoples were the first to encounter English explorers, and later, English settlers, at the start of the seventeenth century. By that point these native peoples relied on a mixture of agriculture and hunting, fishing, and gathering for their subsistence. They lived in villages with a few hundred residents, with greater densities of settlement in the South (where a warmer climate and longer growing season prevailed) than in the North.

The Caribbean Islanders

The Caribbean islands were peopled by mainland dwellers who began moving to the islands around 5000 B.C.E. Surviving at first by hunting and gathering, island peoples began farming perhaps in the first century C.E. Canoes carried trade goods throughout the Caribbean, as well as to Mesoamerica and coastal South America.

By 1492, as many as 4 million people may have inhabited the Caribbean islands. Powerful chiefs ruled over villages, conducted war and diplomacy, and controlled the distribution of food and other goods obtained as tribute from villagers.

Long before Europeans reached North America, the continent's inhabitants had witnessed centuries of dynamic change. Empires rose and fell, and new ones took their place. Large cities flourished and disappeared. Periods of warfare occasionally disrupted the lives of thousands of individuals. The Europeans' arrival, at the end of the fifteenth century, coincided with a period of particular instability, as various Native American groups competed for dominance in the wake of the collapse of the centralized societies at Cahokia and Chaco Canyon. Yet at the same time, Native American societies experienced important continuities. These included an ability to adapt to widely varying environmental conditions, the preservation of religious and ceremonial traditions, and an eagerness to forge relationships of exchange with neighboring peoples. Both continuities with past experience and more recent circumstances of political change would shape the ways native peoples responded to the European newcomers.

WEST AFRICAN SOCIETIES

WHAT WERE the key characteristics of West African society?

In the three centuries after 1492, six of every seven people who crossed the Atlantic to the Americas were not Europeans but Africans. Like the Americas, Africa had witnessed the rise of many ancient and diverse cultures (see Map 1–2). They ranged from the sophisticated Egyptian

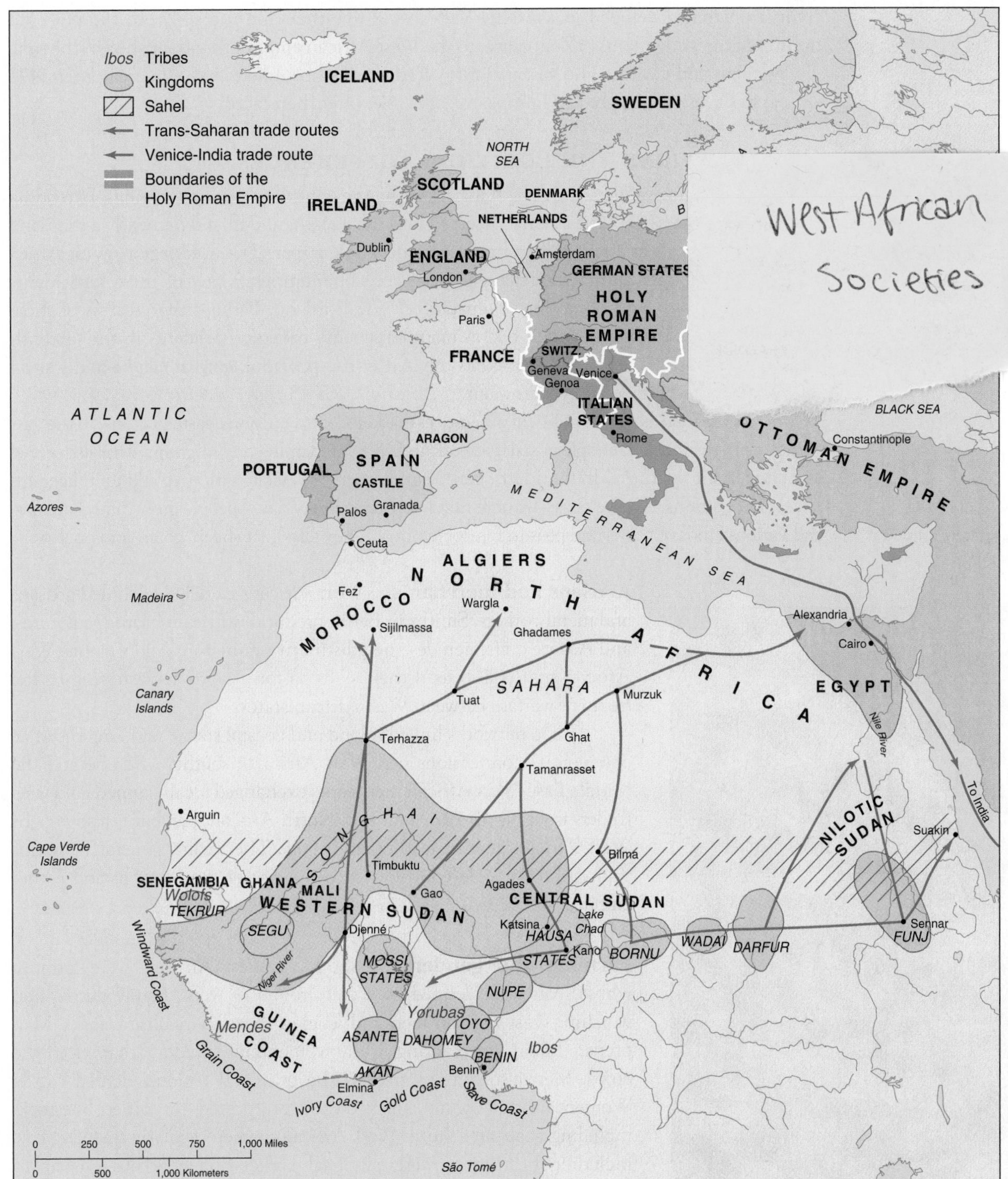

MAP 1–2 West Africa and Europe in 1492 Before Columbus's voyage, Europeans knew little about the world beyond the Mediterranean basin and the coast of West Africa. Muslim merchants from North Africa largely controlled European traders' access to African gold and other materials.

How does this map help explain the focus of Portuguese exploration in the fifteenth century?

civilization that developed in the Nile Valley over five-thousand years ago, to the powerful twelfth-century chiefdoms of Zimbabwe, to the West African empires that flourished in the time of Columbus and Cortés. The vast majority of Africans who came to the Americas after 1492 arrived as slaves, transported by Europeans eager to exploit their labor.

Geographical and Political Differences

Most African immigrants to the Americas came from the continent's western regions. Extending from the southern edge of the Sahara Desert toward the equator and inland for nearly a thousand miles, West Africa was an area of contrasts. On the whole a sparsely settled region, West Africa nevertheless contained numerous densely inhabited communities. Many of these settlements clung to the coast, but several important cities lay well inland. Perhaps the greatest of these metropolises was Timbuktu, which had as many as seventy-thousand residents in the fifteenth century. At that time, Timbuktu served as the seat of the powerful **Songhai Empire** and was an important center of trade and government.

Songhai Empire A powerful West African state that flourished between 1450 and 1591, when it fell to a Moroccan invasion.

QUICK REVIEW

West African Society

- West Africans were skilled artisans and metalworkers.
- Most West Africans were farmers.
- Most West African clans were patrilineal.

Geographical as well as political differences marked the inland and coastal regions. In the vast grasslands of the interior, people raised livestock and cultivated millet and sorghum. Rice also served as an important food crop. In the 1500s, Europeans brought an Asian variety to add to indigenous African rice strains. On the coast—where rain falls nearly every day—people grew yams, bananas, and various kinds of beans and peas in forest clearings. They also kept sheep, goats, and poultry.

Craftsmen from the West African kingdom of Benin were renowned for their remarkable bronze sculptures. This intricate bronze plaque depicts four African warriors in full military dress. The two tiny figures in the background may be Portuguese soldiers, who first arrived in Benin in the late fifteenth century.

Benin bronze plaque. National Museum of African Art, Smithsonian Institution, Washington, DC, U.S.A. Aldo Tutino/Art Resource, NY.

Artisans and merchants. West Africans excelled as skilled artisans and metalworkers. Smiths in Benin produced intricate bronze sculptures, and Asante craftsmen designed distinctive miniature gold weights. West African smiths also used their skills to forge weapons, attesting to the frequent warfare between West African states.

Trade networks linked inland and coastal states, and long-distance commercial connections tied West Africa to southern Europe and the Middle East. West African merchants exchanged locally mined gold with traders from North Africa for salt. North African merchants also bought West African pepper, leather, and ivory. The wealth generated by this trans-Saharan trade contributed to the rise of the Songhai and earlier empires.

Farming and gender roles. Most West Africans were farmers, whose lives were defined by a daily round of work, family duties, and worship. West African men and women shared agricultural tasks. Men prepared fields for planting, while women cultivated and harvested the crops. Men also hunted and, in the grassland regions, herded cattle. Women in the coastal areas owned and cared for other livestock, including goats and sheep. West African women regularly traded goods, including the crops they grew, in local markets and were thus essential to the vitality of local economies.

Family Structure and Religion

Family connections were exceedingly important to West Africans, helping to define each person's place in society. While ties between parents and children were of central importance, West Africans also emphasized their links with aunts, uncles, cousins, and grandparents. Groups of families formed clans that further extended an individual's kin ties within the village.

Elmina Castle, located on the coast of what is now Ghana, was founded by the Portuguese in 1482 as a trading post. In 1637, the Dutch West India Company seized the castle and converted it for use in the slave trade.

Religious beliefs magnified the powerful influence of family on African life. Ideas and practices focused on themes of fertility, prosperity, health, and social harmony. Because many West Africans believed that their ancestors acted as mediators between the worlds of the living and the dead, they held elaborate funerals for deceased members and performed public rituals at their grave sites.

West Africans believed that spiritual forces suffused the natural world, and they performed ceremonies to ensure the spirits' goodwill. West Africans preserved their faith through oral traditions, not written texts.

Islam began to take root in West Africa as early as the tenth century, introduced by Muslim traders and soldiers from North Africa. Urban dwellers, especially merchants, were more likely to convert to the new religion, as were some rulers. Farmers, however, accustomed to religious rituals that focused on agricultural fertility, tended to resist Islamic influence more strongly or adopt religious practices that mingled Islamic and traditional beliefs.

European Merchants in West Africa and the Slave Trade

Before the fifteenth century, Europeans knew little about Africa beyond its Mediterranean coast. But some Christian merchants had traded for centuries with Muslims in the North African ports. When stories of West African gold reached European traders, they tried to move deeper into the continent. But they encountered powerful Muslim merchants intent on monopolizing the gold trade.

The kingdom of Portugal sought to circumvent this Muslim monopoly. Portuguese forces conquered Ceuta in Morocco and gained a foothold on the continent in 1415. Because this outpost did not provide direct access to the sources of gold, Portuguese mariners began exploring the West African coast. They established trading posts along the way.

Read the **Document** at **www.myhistorylab.com** *Muslim Reform in Songhai (1500)*

By the 1430s, the Portuguese had discovered perhaps the greatest source of wealth they could extract from Africa—slaves. A vigorous market in African slaves had existed in southern Europe since the middle of the fourteenth century, and within West Africa itself for centuries. The expansion of this trade required not only eager buyers of slaves, but also willing suppliers. Most slaves within Africa lost their freedom because they were captured in war, but others had been kidnapped or were enslaved as punishment for a crime. First the Portuguese, and later other

Europeans, exploited rivalries among various West African states to encourage them to take war captives who could be sold into an expanding transatlantic slave trade. Virtually all of the African slaves who ended up in the New World had first been enslaved by fellow Africans.

European visitors who observed African slaves in their homeland often described them as "slaves in name only" because they were subject to so little coercion. African merchants who sold slaves to European purchasers had no reason to suspect that those slaves would be treated any differently by their new owners.

Africans caught in the web of the transatlantic slave trade, however, entered a much harsher world. Separated from the kinfolk who meant so much to them, isolated from a familiar landscape, and hard-pressed to sustain spiritual and cultural traditions in a new environment, Africans faced daunting challenges as they journeyed across the ocean and entered into the history of the New World.

WESTERN EUROPE ON THE EVE OF EXPLORATION

HOW DID events in Europe both shape and inspire exploration of the Americas?

When Columbus sailed from Spain in 1492, he left a continent recovering from the devastating warfare and disease of the fourteenth century and about to embark on the devastating religious conflicts of the sixteenth century. Between 1337 and 1453, England and France had exhausted each other in a series of conflicts known as the Hundred Years' War. And between 1347 and 1351, an epidemic known as the Black Death wreaked havoc on a European population already suffering from persistent malnutrition. Perhaps a third of all Europeans died, with results that were felt for more than a century.

The plague left Europe with far fewer workers, a result that contributed to southern Europeans' interest in the African slave trade. To help the economy recover, the survivors learned to be more efficient and rely on technological improvements. Innovations in banking, accounting, and insurance also fostered economic recovery. Although prosperity was distributed unevenly among social classes, on the whole, Europe had a stronger, more productive economy in 1500 than ever before.

In much of Western Europe, economic improvement encouraged an extraordinary cultural movement known as the Renaissance, a "rebirth" of interest in the classical civilizations of ancient Greece and Rome. The Renaissance originated in the city-states of Italy, where a prosperous and educated urban class promoted learning and artistic expression.

The daily lives of most Europeans, however, remained untouched by intellectual and artistic developments. Most Europeans resided in agricultural communities that often differed in important ways from Native American and West African societies. In European societies, men performed most of the heavy work of farming, while women focused on household production of such goods as butter, cheese, and cloth, as well as on caring for the family. Europeans lived in states organized into more rigid hierarchies than could be found in most parts of North America or West Africa, with the population divided into distinct classes. European society was also patriarchal, with men dominating political and economic life.

QUICK REVIEW

European Society

- European states were hierarchical.
- Most Europeans were peasant farmers.
- European society was patriarchal.

The Consolidation of Political and Military Authority

By the end of the fifteenth century, a measure of stability returned to the countries about to embark on overseas expansion. The monarchs of Spain, France, and England successfully asserted royal authority over their previously fragmented realms, creating strong state bureaucracies to control political rivals. They gave special trading privileges to merchants to gain their support, creating links that would later prove important in financing overseas expeditions.

The consolidation of military power went hand in hand with the strengthening of political authority. Before overseas expansion began, European monarchs exerted military force to extend their authority closer to home. Louis XI and his successors used warfare and intermarriage with the ruling families of nearby provinces to extend French influence. In the early sixteenth century, England's Henry VIII sent soldiers to conquer Ireland. And the Spain of 1492 was forged from the successful conclusion of the ***reconquista*** ("reconquest") of territory from Muslim control.

reconquista The long struggle (ending in 1492) during which Spanish Christians reconquered the Iberian peninsula from Muslim occupiers.

Muslim invaders from North Africa first entered Spain in 711 and ruled much of the Iberian Peninsula (which includes Spain and Portugal) for centuries. Beginning in the mid-eleventh century, Christian armies embarked on a long effort to reclaim the region. After the marriage of Ferdinand of Aragon and Isabella of Castile in 1469 united Spain's two principal kingdoms, their combined forces completed the *reconquista*. Granada, the last Muslim stronghold, fell in 1492, shortly before Columbus set out on his first voyage.

Religious Conflict and the Protestant Reformation

Even as these rulers sought to unify their realms, religious conflicts began to tear Europe apart. For more than a thousand years, Catholic Christianity had united Western Europeans in one faith. By the sixteenth century, the Catholic Church had accumulated enormous wealth and power. In reaction to this growing influence, many Christians, especially in Northern Europe, began to criticize the popes and the church itself for worldliness and abuse of power.

In 1517, a German monk, Martin Luther, invited open debate on a set of propositions critical of church practices and doctrines. Luther believed that the church had become too insistent on the performance of good works, such as charitable donations or other actions intended to please God. He called for a return to what he understood to be the purer beliefs of the early church, emphasizing that salvation came not by good deeds but only by faith in God. With the help of the newly invented printing press, his ideas spread widely, inspiring a challenge to the Catholic Church that came to be known as the **Reformation.**

Reformation Martin Luther's challenge to the Catholic Church, initiated in 1517, calling for a return to what he understood to be the purer practices and beliefs of the early church.

Luther urged people to take responsibility for their own spiritual growth by reading the Bible, which he translated for the first time into German. What started as a religious movement, however, quickly acquired an important political dimension.

Sixteenth-century Germany was a fragmented region of small kingdoms and principalities. They were officially part of a larger Catholic political entity known as the Holy Roman Empire, but many German princes were discontented with imperial authority. Many of these princes also supported Luther. When the Holy Roman Empire under Charles V (who was also king of Spain) tried to silence them, the reformist princes protested. From that point on, these princes—and all Europeans who supported religious reform—became known as **Protestants.**

Protestants All European supporters of religious reform under Charles V's Holy Roman Empire.

The Protestant movement took a more radical turn under the influence of the French reformer John Calvin, who emphasized the doctrine of **predestination.** Calvin maintained that an all-powerful and all-knowing God chose at the moment of Creation which humans would be saved and which would be damned. Nothing a person could do would alter that spiritual destiny. Once the ideas of Luther and Calvin began to spread in Europe, no one could contain the powerful Protestant impulse. In succeeding years, other groups formed, split, and split again, increasing Europe's religious fragmentation.

predestination The belief that God decided at the moment of Creation which humans would achieve salvation.

The Reformation fractured the religious unity of Western Europe and spawned a century of warfare unprecedented in its bloody destructiveness. Protestants fought Catholics in France and the German states. Popes initiated a "Counter-Reformation" to strengthen the Catholic Church—in part by internal reform and in part by persecuting its opponents and reimposing religious conformity. Europe thus fragmented into warring camps just at the moment when Europeans were coming to terms with their discovery of America. Some of the key participants in exploration, such as Spain and Portugal, rejected Protestantism, while others, including England and the Netherlands, embraced religious reform.

QUICK REVIEW

Religious Conflict in Europe

- 1517: Martin Luther sparks Reformation.
- John Calvin promotes a more radical vision of Protestantism.
- The Catholic Church launches a "Counter-Reformation."

WHAT WERE the biological consequences of contact between Europeans and Native Americans?

CONTACT

Religious fervor, political ambition, and the desire for wealth propelled European nations into overseas expansion as well as conflict at home. Portugal, Spain, France, and England competed to establish footholds on other continents in an intense scramble for riches and dominance.

The Lure of Discovery

The potential rewards of overseas exploration captured the imaginations of a small but powerful segment of European society. Most people, busy making a living, cared little about distant lands. But certain princes and merchants anticipated spiritual and material benefits from voyages of discovery. The spiritual advantages included making new Christian converts and blocking Islam's expansion. On the material side, the voyages would contribute to Europe's prosperity by increasing trade.

Merchants especially sought access to Asian spices. Wealthy Europeans paid handsomely for small quantities of spices, making it worthwhile to transport them great distances. But the overland spice trade—and the trade in other luxury goods such as silk and furs—spanned thousands of miles, involved many middlemen, and was controlled at key points by Muslim merchants. When Constantinople fell to the Ottomans—Muslim rulers of Turkey—in 1453, Europeans feared that caravan routes to Asia would be disrupted. This encouraged merchants to turn westward and seek alternative routes. Mariners ventured farther into ocean waters, seeking direct access to the African gold trade and, eventually, a sea route around Africa to Asia.

Advances in navigation and shipbuilding. Ocean voyages required sturdier ships than those that plied the Mediterranean. Because oceangoing mariners traveled beyond sight of coastal features, they also needed reliable navigational tools. In the early fifteenth century, Prince Henry of Portugal sponsored the efforts of shipbuilders, mapmakers, and other workers to solve these practical problems. By 1500, enterprising artisans had made several important advances. Iberian shipbuilders perfected the caravel, a ship whose narrow shape and steering rudder suited it for ocean travel. European mariners adopted two important navigational devices—the magnetic compass (first developed in China) and the astrolabe (introduced to Europe by Muslims from Spain)—that allowed mariners to determine their position in relation to a star's known location in the sky.

QUICK REVIEW

Discovery and Exploration

- Europeans sought access to Asian spices.
- Technological innovations made longer sea voyages possible.
- State sponsorship funded voyages of exploration.

Christopher Columbus and the Westward Route to Asia

Christopher Columbus was but one of many European mariners excited by the prospect of tapping into the wealth of Asia. Born in Genoa in 1451, he later lived in Portugal and Spain, where he read widely in geographical treatises and listened closely to the stories and rumors that circulated among mariners.

at **www.myhistorylab.com**
How should we think of Columbus?

at **www.myhistorylab.com**
From the Journal of Christopher Columbus (1492)

Columbus was not the first European to reach the New World. Explorers from Scandinavia, known as Vikings, occupied Iceland by the late ninth century C.E. and later moved on to Greenland. Between 1001 and 1014, Leif Erikson made several voyages to the northern coast of Newfoundland, where he helped to establish a short-lived Viking colony. After the Viking colony disappeared, European fishermen continued to make seasonal voyages to the area, but it would be several centuries before Columbus initiated another attempt at settlement.

Neither was Columbus the first European to believe that he could reach Asia by sailing westward. Most Europeans, however, scoffed at the idea of a westward voyage to Asia in the belief that no ship could carry enough provisions for such a long trip.

Columbus's confidence that he could succeed grew from a mathematical error. He mistakenly calculated the earth's circumference as 18,000 (rather than 24,000) miles and so concluded that Asia lay just 3,500 miles west of the Canary Islands. Columbus first sought financial support for a westward voyage from the king of Portugal, whose advisers disputed his calculations and warned him that he would starve at sea before reaching Asia. Undaunted, he turned to Portugal's rival, Spain.

Columbus tried to convince Ferdinand and Isabella that his plan suited Spain's national goals. If he succeeded, Spain could grow rich from Asian trade, send Christian missionaries to Asia (a goal in keeping with the religious ideals of the *reconquista*), and perhaps enlist the Great Khan of China as an ally in the long struggle with Islam. The Spanish monarchs nonetheless kept Columbus waiting nearly seven years—until 1492, when the last Muslim stronghold at Granada fell to Spanish forces—before they gave him their support.

A decidedly European view of Columbus's landing appears in this late sixteenth-century print. Columbus and his men, armed with guns and swords, are resplendent in European attire, while nearly naked Indians offer them gifts. To the left, Spaniards erect a cross to claim the land for Christianity. In the upper right, frightened natives flee into the woods.

After thirty-three days at sea, Columbus and his men reached the Bahamas. They spent four months exploring the Caribbean and visiting several islands. Although puzzled by his failure to find the fabled cities of China and Japan, Columbus believed that he had reached Asia. Three more voyages between 1493 and 1504, however, failed to yield clear evidence of an Asian landfall or Asian riches.

Frustrated in their search for wealth, Columbus and his men turned violent, sacking native villages and demanding tribute in gold. But Caribbean gold reserves, found mainly on Hispaniola, Puerto Rico, and Cuba, were not extensive. Dissatisfied with the meager results, Columbus sought to transform the Indians themselves into a source of wealth.

In 1494, Columbus suggested to the Spanish monarchs that the Indies could yield a profit if islanders were sold as slaves. In succeeding decades, the Spanish government periodically called for fair treatment of Indians and prohibited their enslavement, but such measures were ignored by colonists on the other side of the Atlantic.

Columbus died in Spain in 1506, still convinced he had found Asia. What he had done was to set in motion a process that would transform both sides of the Atlantic. It would eventually bring wealth to many Europeans and immense suffering to Native Americans and Africans.

QUICK REVIEW

Christopher Columbus

- Columbus believed he could sail westward to Asia and find wealth for Spain from Asian trade.
- Columbus convinced the Spanish monarchs to support his voyage.
- Columbus died in 1506 still believing he had found Asia.

The Spanish Conquest and Colonization

Of all European nations, Spain was best suited to take advantage of Columbus's discovery. Its experience with the *reconquista* gave it a religious justification for conquest (bringing Christianity to nonbelievers) and an army of seasoned soldiers—*conquistadores*—eager to seek their fortunes in America now that the last Muslims had been expelled from Spain. In addition, during the *reconquista*, Spain's rulers developed efficient techniques for controlling newly conquered lands that could be applied to New World colonies.

The Spanish first consolidated their control of the Caribbean, establishing outposts on Cuba, Puerto Rico, and Jamaica (see Map 1–3). The *conquistadores* were more interested in finding gold and slaves than in creating permanent settlements. Leaving a trail of destruction, they attacked native villages and killed or captured the inhabitants.

The end of the Aztec empire. In 1519, Hernán Cortés and six hundred soldiers landed on the coast of Mexico. Their subsequent actions more than fulfilled the Aztec king's belief that the Spaniards' arrival was an evil omen. By 1521, Cortés and his men had conquered the powerful Aztec empire, discovering riches beyond their wildest dreams.

The swift, decisive Spanish victory depended on several factors. In part, the Spanish enjoyed certain technological advantages. Their guns and horses often enabled them to overwhelm larger groups of Aztec foot soldiers armed with spears and wooden swords edged with

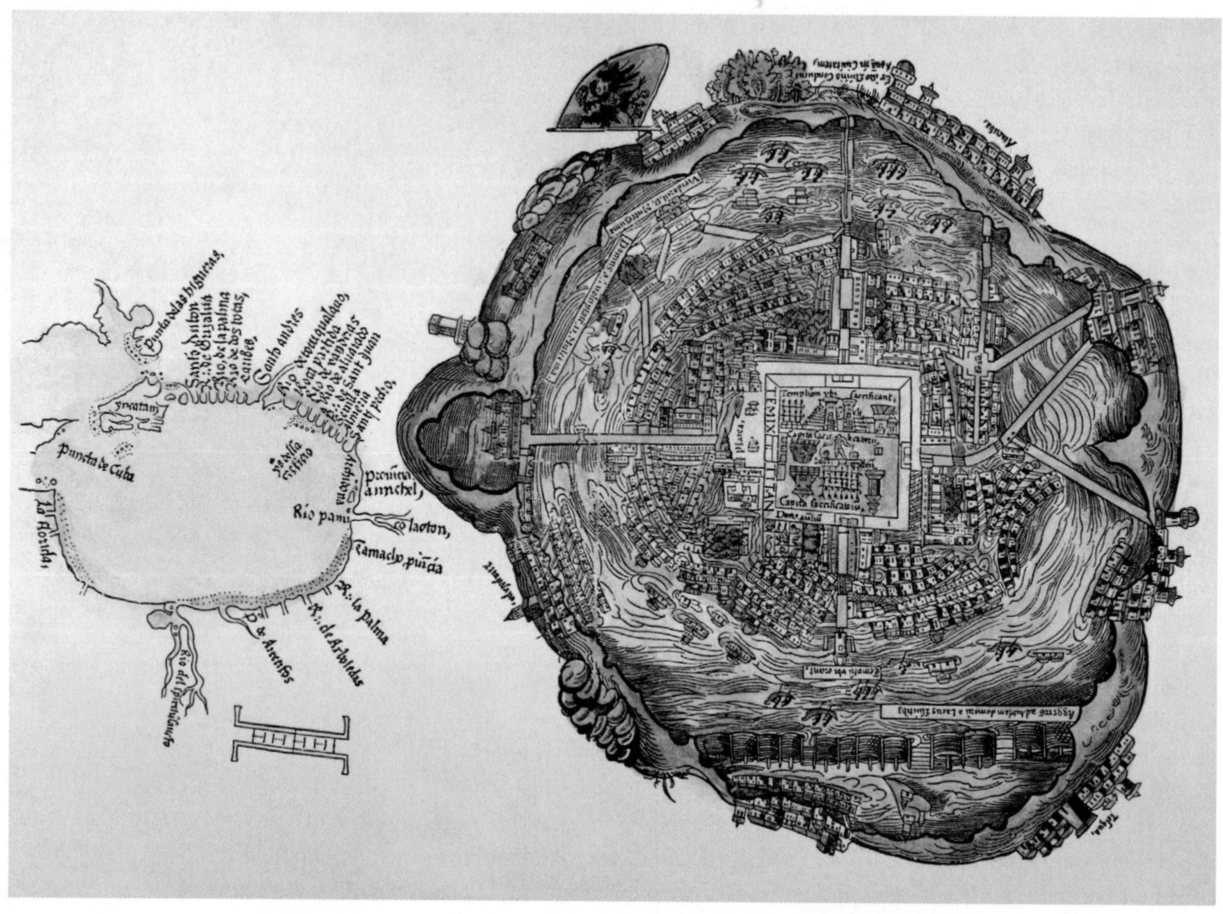

To conquer Tenochtitlán, Spanish soldiers had to gain control of the narrow causeways that led to the center of this distinctively designed city.

obsidian. But technology alone cannot account for the conquest of a vastly more numerous enemy, capable of absorbing far higher losses in combat.

Cortés benefited from two other factors. First, he exploited divisions within the Aztec empire. The Spanish acquired indispensable allies among subject Indians who resented Aztec domination, tribute demands, and seizure of captives for religious sacrifice.

A second and more important factor was disease. One of Cortés's men was infected with smallpox, which soon devastated the native population. European diseases had been unknown in the Americas before 1492, and Indians lacked resistance to them. Historians estimate that nearly 40 percent of the inhabitants of central Mexico died of smallpox within a year. Other diseases followed, including typhus, measles, and influenza. By 1600, the population of Mexico may have declined from over 15 million to less than 1 million people.

The fall of the Inca empire. In 1532, Francisco Pizarro and 180 men, following rumors of even greater riches than those of Mexico, discovered the Inca empire high in the Peruvian Andes. It was the largest empire in the Americas, stretching more than 2,000 miles from what is now Ecuador to Chile. An excellent network of roads and bridges linked this extensive territory to the imperial capital of Cuzco. The Spaniards arrived at a moment of weakness for the empire. A few years before, the Incan ruler had died, probably from smallpox, and civil war had broken out between two of his sons. The victor, Atahualpa, was on his way from the empire's northern provinces to claim his throne in Cuzco when Pizarro intercepted him. Pizarro took Atahualpa hostage and despite receiving a colossal ransom—a roomful of gold and silver—had him killed.

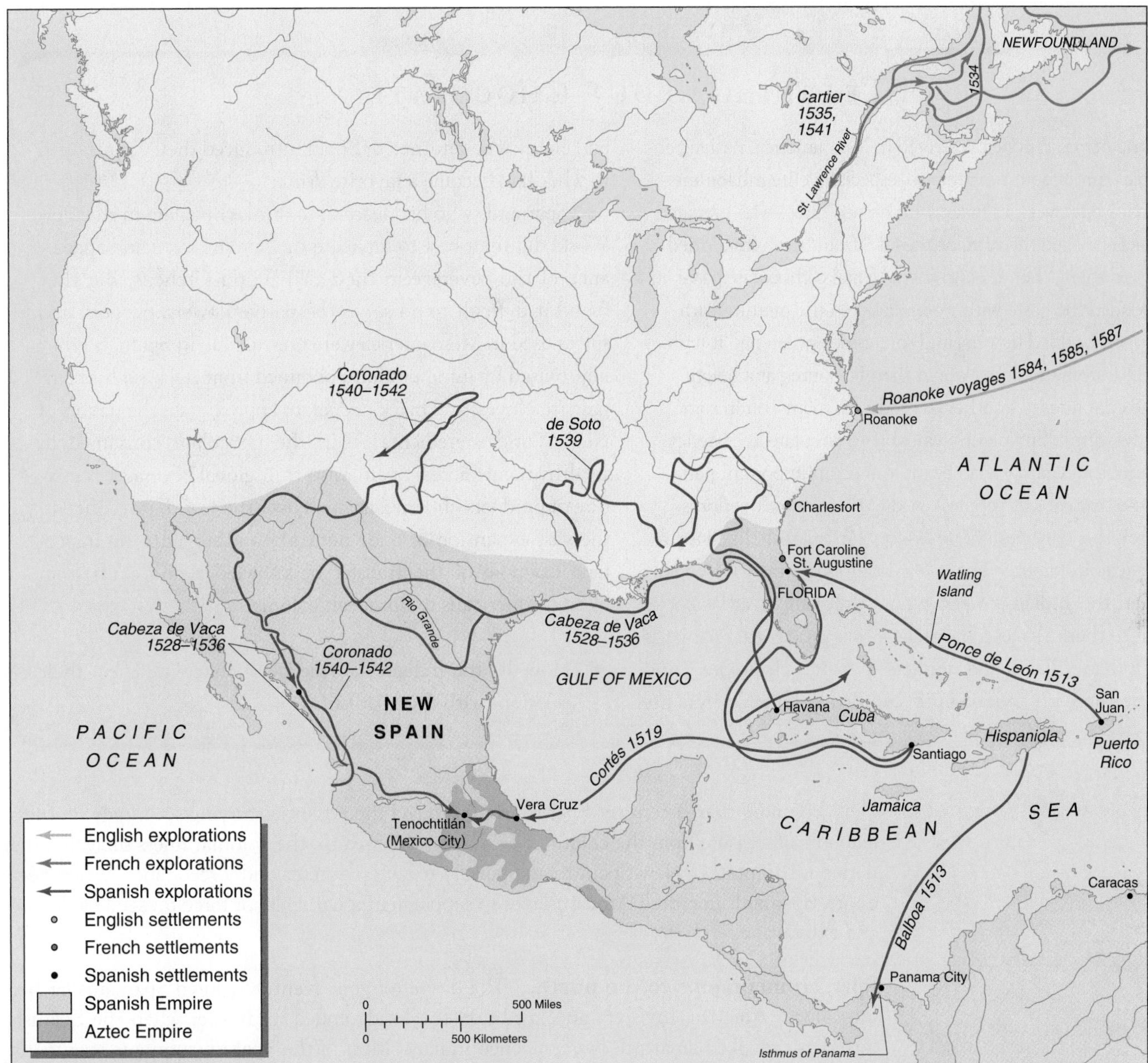

MAP 1–3 **Spanish, English, and French Settlements in North America in the Sixteenth Century** By the end of the sixteenth century, only Spain had established permanent settlements in North America. French outposts in Canada and at Fort Caroline, as well as the English settlement at Roanoke, failed to thrive. European rivalries for North America, however, would intensify after 1600.

Based on this map, what factors might help to explain why Spain was more successful in the establishment of permanent settlements before 1600 than either France or England? Do you think geographic location (climate, terrain, etc.) may have played a role?

The Spaniards then captured Cuzco, eventually extended control over the whole empire, and established a new capital at Lima.

By 1550, Spain's New World empire stretched from the Caribbean through Mexico to Peru. It was administered from Spain by the Council of the Indies, which enacted laws for the empire and supervised an elaborate bureaucracy charged with their enforcement. The council aimed to project royal authority into every village in New Spain in order to maintain political control and extract as much wealth as possible from the land and its people.

GLOBAL CONNECTIONS

 LEARNING ABOUT CHOCOLATE 

Long before Europeans arrived in Mesoamerica, native peoples throughout the region—especially elite inhabitants—enjoyed beverages made with cacao. Those who prepared the drinks removed the nibs, or "beans," from cacao fruit, dried and toasted them, then ground them to make chocolate paste. They blended the paste with water, flavored the mixture with chili peppers or dried flowers, and sometimes sweetened it with honey. The aromatic liquid would then be poured at a height from one container to another to produce a foamy, often somewhat bitter, drink. Sufficiently valuable to circulate as currency throughout the region, cacao beans formed an important part of the tribute that subject peoples owed to their Aztec overlords.

After the conquest of Mexico, the Spanish likewise received cacao as tribute. They also developed a taste for chocolate when the Indian women whom they employed as cooks served it to them. To learn how cacao was processed, Spaniards visited Indian villages and markets to watch chocolate being made. By the early seventeenth century, colonial merchants and clergy who returned to Spain introduced their countrymen to what had become a favorite drink.

Spaniards who had learned to drink chocolate in the New World did their best to replicate the familiar taste and appearance of the beverage in their Old World kitchens. But they found it difficult to do so, as the native flowers, peppers, and spices used in Mesoamerica were unavailable in Spain. So they improvised by using products obtained from Asia, such as cinnamon, cloves, and black pepper, to approximate the flavors of New World ingredients. Thus the chocolate consumed in wealthy homes across Spain was a truly global beverage. A mixture of products obtained from all over the world, it testified to the vast expansion of trade networks and served as an important example of the transfer of knowledge and skills from Native Americans to European colonists.

- How did the Indians' knowledge of chocolate affect their relations with the Spanish?

For more than a century, Spanish ships crossed the Atlantic carrying seemingly limitless amounts of treasure from the colonies. To extract this wealth, the colonial rulers subjected the native inhabitants of New Spain to compulsory tribute payments and forced labor. When necessary, Spaniards imported African slaves to supplement a native labor force ravaged by disease and exhaustion.

Spanish incursions to the north. The desire for gold eventually lured Spaniards farther into North America. In 1528, an expedition to Florida ended in disaster when the Spanish intruders provoked an attack by Apalachee Indians. Most of the Spanish survivors eventually perished, but Álvar Núñez Cabeza de Vaca and three other men (including an African slave) escaped from their captors and managed to reach Mexico after a grueling eight-year journey. In a published account of his ordeal, Cabeza de Vaca insisted that the interior of North America contained a fabulously wealthy empire (see "American Views: Cabeza de Vaca among the Indians").

This report inspired other Spaniards to seek such treasures that had eluded its author. In 1539, Hernán de Soto—who tried unsuccessfully to get Cabeza de Vaca to serve as a guide—led an expedition from Florida to the Mississippi River. Along the way, the Spaniards harassed the native peoples, demanding provisions, burning villages, and capturing women to be servants and concubines. In these same years, Francisco Vásquez de Coronado led three hundred troops on an equally destructive expedition through present-day Arizona, New Mexico, and Colorado on a futile search for the mythical Seven Cities of Cíbola, rumored to contain hoards of gold and precious stones.

The failure to find gold and silver halted Spain's attempt to extend its empire to the north. By the end of the sixteenth century, the Spanish maintained just two precarious footholds north of Mexico. One was at St. Augustine, on Florida's Atlantic coast. The other settlement was located far to the west in what is now New Mexico.

Almost from the start of the conquest, the bloody tactics used by the Spanish in the New World aroused protest back in Spain. The Indians' most eloquent advocate was Bartolomé de Las Casas, a Dominican priest shamed by his own role (as a layman) in the conquest of Hispaniola. In 1516, the Spanish king appointed him to the newly created office of Protector of the Indians, but his efforts had little effect.

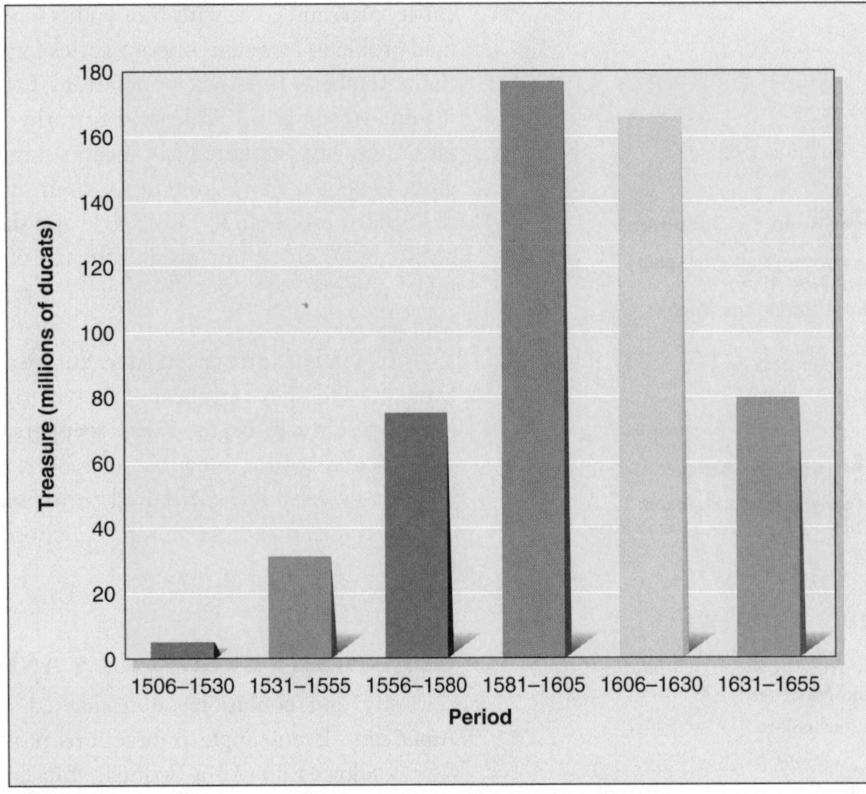

FIGURE 1–1 **Value of New World Treasure Imported into Spain, 1506–1655** During the sixteenth and early seventeenth centuries, Spain was the only European power to reap great wealth from North America. The influx of New World treasure, however, slowed the development of Spain's economy in the long run. [Note: A ducat was a gold coin.]
Data Source: J.H. Elliott, *Imperial Spain, 1469–1716* (1964), p. 175.

The seeds of economic decline. Meanwhile, the vast riches of Central and South America glutted Spain's treasury. Between 1500 and 1650, an estimated 181 tons of gold and 16,000 tons of silver were shipped from the New World to Spain, making it the richest and most powerful state in Europe (see Figure 1–1). But this influx of American treasure had unforeseen consequences that would soon undermine Spanish predominance.

In 1492, the Spanish crown, determined to impose religious conformity after the *reconquista*, expelled from Spain all Jews who refused to become Christians. The refugees included many leading merchants who had contributed significantly to Spain's economy. The remaining Christian merchants, now awash in American riches, saw little reason to invest in new trade or productive enterprises that might have sustained the economy once the flow of New World treasure diminished. As a result, Spain's economy eventually stagnated.

Read the **Document**
at **www.myhistorylab.com**
Bartolomé de Las Casas, Of the Island of Hispaniola (1542)

Compounding the problem, the flood of American gold and silver contributed to what historians have called a "price revolution" in Europe. Beginning in the late fifteenth century, as Europe's population recovered from the Black Death, demographic and economic factors led to a rise in prices. This inflationary cycle was made worse by the influx of New World gold and silver.

THE COLUMBIAN EXCHANGE

Spain's long-term economic decline was just one of many consequences of the conquest of the New World. In the long run, the biological consequences of contact—what one historian has called the **Columbian Exchange**—proved to be the most momentous (see the Overview table, The Columbian Exchange).

Columbian Exchange The transatlantic exchange of plants, animals, and diseases that occurred after the first European contact with the Americas.

The most catastrophic result of the exchange was the exposure of Native Americans to Old World diseases. Europeans and Africans, long exposed to these diseases, had developed some immunity to them. Native Americans, lacking such contact, had not. Epidemics of smallpox, measles, typhus, and influenza struck Native Americans with great force, killing half, and sometimes as many as 90 percent, of the people in communities exposed to them.

Another important aspect of the Columbian Exchange was the introduction of Old World livestock to the New World, which began when Columbus brought horses, sheep, cattle, pigs, and goats with him on his second voyage in 1493. The large European beasts created problems as well as opportunities for native peoples. With few natural predators to limit their numbers, livestock populations boomed in the New World, competing with native mammals for grazing. At least at first, the Indians' unfamiliarity with the use of horses in warfare often gave mounted European soldiers a decisive military advantage. But some native groups adopted these animals for their own purposes. Yaquis, Pueblos, and other peoples in the Southwest began to raise cattle and sheep. By the eighteenth century, Plains Indians had reoriented their culture around the use of horses, which had become essential for travel and hunting buffalo. Horses also became a primary object for trading and raiding among Plains peoples.

Read the Document at **www.myhistorylab.com** *Exploring America: America and the Horse*

Columbus introduced such European crops as wheat, chickpeas, melons, onions, and fruit trees to the Caribbean. Native Americans, in turn, introduced Europeans to corn, tomatoes, squash, beans, cacao, peppers, and potatoes, as well as nonfood plants such as tobacco and cotton. New World food crops enriched Old World diets and the nutritional benefits eventually contributed to a sharp rise in Europe's population. Over time, many of these more numerous Europeans chose to leave their overcrowded communities for the New World.

Read the Document at **www.myhistorylab.com** *Cultures Meet: Europeans View the New World*

QUICK REVIEW

Sources of Misunderstanding and Mistrust

- Technology.
- Religion.
- Gender.
- Social organization.

Cultural Perceptions and Misperceptions

Curiosity and confusion often marked early encounters between Europeans and Native Americans. Even simple transactions produced unexpected results. The first Indians whom Cortés allowed aboard a Spanish ship fainted at the sound of a large cannon being fired. French explorers were similarly taken by surprise when they choked while smoking Iroquois tobacco, which they thought tasted like "powdered pepper." These relatively minor mishaps were soon overshadowed by more substantial interactions that highlighted cultural differences between Indians and Europeans.

Cacao, from which chocolate is made, was one of many New World foods that entered Old World diets as part of the Columbian Exchange. This sixteenth-century illustration shows a native Mexican woman pouring chocolate from a great height to produce a frothy drink.

Most Indians believed that the universe contained friendly and hostile spiritual forces. People interacted with the spirit world through ceremonies that often involved exchanging gifts. North of Mexico, Indians (like West Africans) passed on religious beliefs through oral traditions, not in writing. To Europeans accustomed to worshiping one God in an organized church and preserving their beliefs in a written Bible, Indian spiritual traditions were incomprehensible. Many Europeans assumed that Indians worshiped the Devil. Indians, in turn, often found Christianity confusing and at first rejected European pressure to convert.

Different understandings of gender roles provided another source of confusion. Europeans regarded men as superior to women and thus the natural rulers of society. They disapproved of the less restrictive gender divisions among Native Americans. Europeans, accustomed to societies in which men did most agricultural work, objected to Indian women's dominant role in farming and assumed that men's hunting was more for recreation than subsistence. They concluded that Indian women lived "a most slavish life." Indians, in turn, thought that European men failed to make good use of their wives.

In order for Indians and Europeans to get along peaceably, each side would have to look past these and other cultural differences and adapt to the new circumstances under which both groups now lived. At first, such harmony seemed possible. But it soon became clear that Europeans intended to dominate the lands they discovered. Such claims to dominance sparked vigorous resistance from native peoples everywhere who strove to maintain their autonomy in a changed world.

AMERICAN VIEWS

Cabeza de Vaca among the Indians (1530)

Alvar Núñez Cabeza de Vaca came to the New World in 1527 in search of riches, not suffering. But the Spanish expedition of which he was a member met disaster shortly after it arrived in Florida on a mission to conquer the region north of the Gulf of Mexico. Of an original group of three hundred soldiers, only Cabeza de Vaca and three other men (including one African slave) survived. They did so by walking thousands of miles overland from the Gulf Coast to northern Mexico, an eight-year-long ordeal that tested the men's wits and physical endurance. Instead of entering Indian villages as proud conquistadors, Cabeza de Vaca and his companions encountered native peoples from a position of weakness. In order to survive, they had to adapt to the ways of the peoples across whose land they passed. After Cabeza de Vaca made it back to Mexico City, he described his experiences in an official report to the king of Spain. This remarkable document offers vivid descriptions of the territory extending from northern Florida to northern Mexico and the many peoples who inhabited it. It is equally interesting, as this extract suggests, for what it reveals about Cabeza de Vaca himself and the changes he made in the interest of survival.

- **While** living among the Capoques, what sort of work did Cabeza de Vaca have to do, and why?
- **Why** did Cabeza de Vaca decide to become a merchant? What advantages did this way of life offer him?
- **Why** did the Indians welcome Cabeza de Vaca into their communities even though he was a stranger?

[I remained with the Capoques] for more than a year, and because of the great labors they forced me to perform and the bad treatment they gave me, I resolved to flee from them and go to those who live in the forests and on the mainland, who are called those of Charruco, because I was unable to endure the life that I had with these others; because among many other tasks, I had to dig the roots to eat out from under the water and among the rushes where they grew in the ground. And because of this, my fingers were so worn that when a reed touched them it caused them to bleed, and the reeds cut me in many places. . . . And because of this, I set to the task of going over to the others, and with them things were somewhat better for me. And because I became a merchant, I tried to exercise the vocation as best I knew how. And because of this they gave me food to eat and treated me well, and they importuned me to go from one place to another to obtain the things they needed, because on account of the continual warfare in the land, there is little traffic or communication among them. And with my dealings and wares I entered inland as far as I desired, and I went along the coast for forty or fifty leagues. The mainstay of my trade was pieces of snail shell and the hearts of them; and conch shells with which they cut a fruit that is like frijoles [beans], with which they perform cures and do their dances and make celebrations. . . . And in exchange and as barter for it, I brought forth hides and red ocher with which they smear themselves and dye their faces and hair, flints to make the points of arrows, paste, and stiff canes to make them, and some tassels made from deer hair which they dye red. And this occupation served me well, because practicing it, I had the freedom to go wherever I wanted, and I was not constrained in any way nor enslaved, and wherever I went they treated me well and gave me food out of want for my wares, and most importantly because doing that, I was able to seek out the way by which I would go forward. And among them I was very well known; when they saw me and I brought them the things they needed, they were greatly pleased.

Source: Rolena Adorno and Patrick Charles Pautz, eds., *The Narrative of Cabeza de Vaca* (Lincoln: University of Nebraska Press, 2003), pp. 96–97.

OVERVIEW The Columbian Exchange

	From Old World to New World	From New World to Old World
Diseases	Smallpox, measles, plague, typhus, influenza, yellow fever, diphtheria, scarlet fever, whooping cough	Sexually transmitted strain of syphilis
Animals	Horses, cattle, pigs, sheep, goats, donkeys, mules, black rats, honeybees, cockroaches	Turkeys
Plants	Wheat, sugar, barley, apples, pears, peaches, plums, cherries, coffee, rice, dandelions, and other weeds	Maize, beans, peanuts, potatoes, sweet potatoes, manioc, squash, papayas, guavas, tomatoes, avocadoes, pineapple, chili pepper, cacao

WHY DID early French and English efforts at colonization falter?

Treaty of Tordesillas Treaty negotiated in 1494 to resolve the territorial claims of Spain and Portugal.

COMPETITION FOR A CONTINENT

Spain's New World bonanza attracted the attention of other European states eager to share in the wealth. Portugal soon acquired its own profitable piece of South America. In 1494, the conflicting claims of Portugal and Spain were resolved by the **Treaty of Tordesillas.** The treaty drew a north–south line approximately 1,100 miles west of the Cape Verde Islands. Spain received all lands west of the line, while Portugal held sway to the east. This limited Portugal's New World empire to Brazil, where settlers established sugar plantations worked by slave labor. But the treaty also protected Portugal's claims in Africa and Asia, which lay east of the line.

France and England, of course, rejected this division of the Western Hemisphere between Spain and Portugal. Their initial challenges to Spanish dominance in the New World, however, proved quite feeble. Domestic troubles—largely sparked by the Protestant Reformation—distracted the two countries from the pursuit of empire. By the close of the sixteenth century, both France and England insisted on their rights to New World lands, but neither had created a permanent settlement to support its claim.

EARLY FRENCH EFFORTS IN NORTH AMERICA

France was a relative latecomer to New World exploration. Preoccupied with European affairs, France's rulers paid little attention to America. But when news of Cortés's exploits in Mexico arrived in the 1520s, King Francis I wanted his own New World empire to enrich France and block further Spanish expansion. In 1524, Francis sponsored a voyage by Giovanni da Verrazano, an Italian navigator, who mapped the North American coast from present-day South Carolina to Maine. During the 1530s and 1540s, the French mariner Jacques Cartier made three voyages in search of rich mines to rival those of Mexico and Peru. He explored the St. Lawrence River up to what is now Montreal, hoping to discover a water route through the continent to Asia (the so-called Northwest Passage).

On his third voyage, in 1541, Cartier was to serve under the command of a nobleman, Jean-François de la Rocque, Sieur de Roberval, who was commissioned by the king to establish a permanent settlement in Canada. This first attempt to found a permanent French colony failed miserably. The Iroquois, suspicious of repeated French intrusions on their lands, saw no reason to help them. A year after they arrived in Canada, Roberval and the surviving colonists were back in France.

Disappointed with their Canadian expeditions, the French made a few forays to the south, establishing outposts in what is now South Carolina in 1562 and Florida in 1564. They soon abandoned the Carolina colony, and Spanish forces captured the Florida fort. Then, back in France, a prolonged civil war broke out between Catholics and Protestants. Renewed interest in colonization would have to await the return of peace at home.

English Attempts in the New World

The English were quicker than the French to stake a claim to the New World but no more successful at colonization. In 1497, King Henry VII sent John Cabot, an Italian mariner, to explore eastern Canada on England's behalf. But neither Henry nor any of his wealthy subjects would invest the funds necessary to follow up on Cabot's discoveries.

Read the **Document**
at **www.myhistorylab.com**
From Then to Now Online: The Disappearance of Cod Off The Grand Banks

The lapse in English activity in the New World stemmed from religious troubles at home. Between 1534 and 1558, England changed its official religion several times. King Henry VIII, who had once defended the Catholic Church against its critics, took up the Protestant cause when the pope refused to annul his marriage to Catherine of Aragon. In 1534, Henry declared himself the head of a separate Church of England and seized the Catholic Church's English property. Because many English people sympathized with the Protestant cause, there was relatively little opposition to Henry's actions. But in 1553, Mary—daughter of the spurned Catherine of Aragon—became queen and tried to bring England back to Catholicism. She had nearly three hundred Protestants burned at the stake for their beliefs (earning her the nickname "Bloody Mary"), and many others went into exile in Europe.

Mary's brief but destructive reign ended in 1558, and her half-sister Elizabeth, a committed Protestant, became queen. Elizabeth ruled for forty-five years (1558–1603), restoring Protestantism as the state religion, bringing stability to the nation, and renewing England's interest in the New World. She and her subjects saw colonization not only as a way to gain wealth and political advantage but also as a Protestant crusade against Catholic domination.

The colonization of Ireland. England's first target for colonization, however, was not America but Ireland. Henry VIII had tried, with limited success, to bring the island under English control in the 1530s and 1540s. Elizabeth renewed the attempt in the 1560s with a series of brutal expeditions that destroyed Irish villages and slaughtered the inhabitants. Several veterans of these campaigns later took part in New World colonization and drew on their Irish experience for guidance.

Two aspects of that experience were particularly important. First, the English transferred their assumptions about Irish "savages" to Native Americans. Englishmen in America frequently observed similarities between Indians and the Irish. Because the English held the "wild Irish" in contempt, these observations encouraged them to scorn the Indians. When Indians resisted their attempts at conquest, the English recalled the Irish example, claiming that native "savagery" required brutal suppression.

Second, the Irish experience influenced English ideas about colonial settlement. English conquerors set up "plantations" surrounded by palisades on seized Irish lands. These plantations were meant to be civilized outposts in a savage land. Their aristocratic owners imported Protestant tenants from England and Scotland to farm the land. Native Irish people, considered too wild to join proper Christian communities, were excluded. English colonists in America followed this precedent when they established plantations that separated English and native peoples.

Expeditions to the New World. Sir Humphrey Gilbert, a notoriously cruel veteran of the Irish campaigns, became fascinated with the idea of New World colonization. He composed a treatise to persuade Queen Elizabeth to support such an endeavor. The queen authorized several exploratory voyages, including Martin Frobisher's three trips in 1576–1578 in search of the Northwest Passage to Asia. Frobisher failed to find the elusive passage and sent back shiploads of glittering ore that proved to be fool's gold. Elizabeth had better luck in allowing privateers, such as John Hawkins and Francis Drake, to raid Spanish ships and New World ports for gold and silver. The plunder taken during these raids enriched both the sailors and their investors—one of whom was the queen herself.

John White's picture of the village of Pomeiooc offers a rare glimpse of a sixteenth-century Eastern Woodlands Indian community. The village is surrounded by a palisade with two entrances; evidence suggests that White exaggerated the spacing of the poles in order to depict the houses inside. Eighteen dwellings constructed of poles and mats are clustered around the village circumference; inside some of them raised sleeping platforms can be seen. Many of the villagers are clustered around a central fire, while others are working or conversing.

Algonquian Indian village of Pomeiooc (North Carolina) watercolor, c. 1585 by John White.

Meanwhile, Gilbert continued to promote New World settlement, arguing that it would increase England's trade and provide a place to send unemployed Englishmen. Gilbert suggested offering free land in America to English families willing to emigrate.

In 1578, Gilbert received permission to set up a colony along the North American coast. It took him five years to organize an expedition to Newfoundland, which he claimed for England. After sailing southward seeking a more favorable site for a colony, Gilbert headed home, only to be lost at sea during an Atlantic storm. The impetus for English colonization did not die with him, however, for his half-brother, Sir Walter Raleigh (another veteran of the Irish wars), took up the cause.

The Roanoke Colony. In 1584, Raleigh sent an expedition to find a suitable location for a colony. The Carolina coast seemed promising, so Raleigh sent men in 1585 to build a settlement on Roanoke Island. Most of the colonists were soldiers fresh from Ireland who refused to grow their own food, insisting that the Roanoke Indians should feed them. When the local chief, Wingina, organized native resistance, they killed him. Eventually, the colonists, disappointed not to have found any treasure and exhausted by a harsh winter, returned to England in 1586.

Two members of these early expeditions, however, left a more positive legacy. Thomas Hariot studied the Roanoke and Croatoan Indians and identified plants and animals in the area, hoping that some might prove to be profitable commodities. John White drew maps and painted a series of watercolors depicting the natives and the coastal landscape. When Raleigh tried once more, in 1587, to found a colony, he chose White to be its leader. This attempt also failed. The ship captain dumped the settlers—who, for the first time, included women and children—on Roanoke Island so that he could pursue Spanish treasure ships. White waited until his granddaughter, Virginia Dare (the first English child born in America), was born and then sailed to England for supplies. But the outbreak of war with Spain delayed his return for three years. When he finally returned in 1590, White found the colony deserted. The actual fate of the "Lost Colony" at Roanoke will probably never be known.

Read the Document

at **www.myhistorylab.com**
Thomas Hariot, A Brief and True Report of the New Found Land of Virginia (1588)

QUICK REVIEW

Roanoke

- 1578: Gilbert receives permission to set up a colony.
- 1585: Raleigh sends men to build a settlement on Roanoke Island.
- 1587: Raleigh sends a second expedition led by White.
- 1590: White returns to find Roanoke deserted.

At this point, Raleigh gave up on North America and turned his attention to his Irish plantations. But England's interest in colonization did not wane. In 1584, Richard Hakluyt had aroused enthusiasm for America by writing the *Discourse on the Western Planting* for the queen and her advisers. He argued that England would prosper from trade and the sale of New World commodities. Once the Indians were civilized, Hakluyt added, they would eagerly purchase English goods. Equally important, England could plant "sincere religion" (that is, Protestant Christianity) in the New World and block Spanish expansion. Hakluyt's arguments fired the imaginations of many people, and the defeat of the Spanish Armada emboldened England to challenge Spain's New World dominance. The experience of Roanoke should have tempered that enthusiasm, illustrating the difficulty of establishing colonies. But the English were slow to learn these lessons; when they resumed colonization efforts in 1607, they repeated Roanoke's mistakes, with disastrous results for the people involved. As it was, the sixteenth century ended with no permanent English settlement in the New World.

CONCLUSION

Dramatic changes occurred in North America during the century after Moctezuma's messenger spotted the Spanish ships off the Mexican coast. Europeans, eager for wealth and power, set out to claim a continent that just a hundred years earlier they had not dreamed existed. African slaves were brought to the Caribbean, Mexico, and Brazil, and forced to labor under extremely harsh conditions for white masters. The Aztec and Incan empires collapsed in the wake of the Spanish conquest. In the Caribbean and parts of Mexico and Peru, untold numbers of native peoples succumbed to European diseases they had never before encountered.

And yet conditions in 1600 bore clearer witness to the past than to the future. Despite all that had happened, North America was still Indian country. Only Spain had established North American colonies, and even its soldiers struggled to expand north of Mexico. Spain's outposts in Florida and New Mexico staked claims to territory that it did not really control. Except in Mexico and the Caribbean, Europeans had merely touched the continent's shores. In 1600, despite the virulent epidemics, native peoples (even in Mexico) still greatly outnumbered European and African immigrants. The next century, however, brought many powerful challenges both to native control and to the Spanish monopoly of settlement.

Where to Learn More

Cahokia Mounds State Historic Site, Collinsville, Illinois. This site, occupied from 600 to 1500 C.E., was the largest Mississippian community in eastern North America. It now includes numerous exhibits, and archaeological excavations continue in the vicinity. The website http://cahokiamounds.org/ contains a wealth of information and an interactive map.

Mashantucket Pequot Museum, Mashantucket, Connecticut. This tribally owned and operated complex offers a view of Eastern Woodlands Indian life, focusing on the Pequots of eastern Connecticut. Exhibits include dioramas, films, interactive programs, and a reconstructed sixteenth-century Pequot village. The homepage for the Mashantucket Pequot Museum and Research Center is http://pequotmuseum.org/.

Mesa Verde National Park, Colorado. Occupied by Ancestral Puebloan peoples as early as A.D. 550, the area contains a variety of sites, from early pithouses to spectacular cliff dwellings. The official National Park webpage for Mesa Verde is http://www.nps.gov/meve/index.htm.

St. Augustine, Florida. Founded in 1565, St. Augustine is the site of the first permanent Spanish settlement in North America. Today the restored community resembles a Spanish colonial town, with narrow, winding streets and seventeenth- and eighteenth-century buildings. The site also contains the restored Castillo de San Marcos, now a national park. There is an informational website at http://www.augustine.com/history/.

Review Questions

1. How did the Aztecs who first glimpsed Spanish ships off the coast of Mexico describe to Moctezuma what they had seen? What details most captured their attention?
2. Compare men's and women's roles in Native American, West African, and European societies. What were the similarities and differences? How did differences between European and Native American gender roles lead to misunderstandings?
3. Many of the first European colonizers in North America were military veterans. What impact did this have on their relations with Indian peoples?
4. Why did Spain so quickly become the dominant colonial power in North America? What advantages did it enjoy over France and England?
5. What role did religion play in early European efforts at overseas colonization? Did religious factors always encourage colonization, or did they occasionally interfere with European expansion?
6. In what ways were trade networks important in linking different groups of people in the Old and New Worlds?

Key Terms

Aztecs (p. 7)
Cahokia (p. 9)
Columbian Exchange (p. 21)
Culture areas (p. 6)
Great League of Peace and Power (p. 9)
Predestination (p. 15)
Protestants (p. 15)
Reconquista (p. 15)
Reformation (p. 15)
Songhai Empire (p. 12)
Treaty of Tordesillas (p. 24)

myhistorylab Connections

Reinforce what you learned in this chapter by studying the many documents, images, maps, review tools, and videos available at **www.myhistorylab.com.**

Read and Review

Study and Review **Study Plan: Chapter 1**

Read the Document

Alvar Núñez Cabeza de Vaca, Indians of the Rio Grande (1528–1536)

Bartolomè de Las Casas, Of the Island of Hispaniola (1542)

From The Journal of Christopher Columbus (1492)

Ghana and Its People in the Mid-Eleventh Century

Muslim Reform in Songhai (1500)

Pima Creation Story

Thomas Hariot, A Brief and True Report of the New Found Land of Virginia (1588)

See the Map

Pre-Columbian Societies of the Americas

Africa Climate Regions and Early Sites

Research and Explore

Read the Document

Personal Journeys Online

From Then to Now Online:
The Disappearance of Cod Off The Grand Banks

Exploring America: America and the Horse

Cultures Meet: Europeans View the New World

Hear the Audio *Ghana: Ewe-Atsiagbekor*

Watch the Video

How Should We Think of Columbus?
What Is Columbus's Legacy?

Hear the Audio

Hear the audio files for Chapter 1 at
www.myhistorylab.com.

1600-1685

2 Transplantation and Adaptation

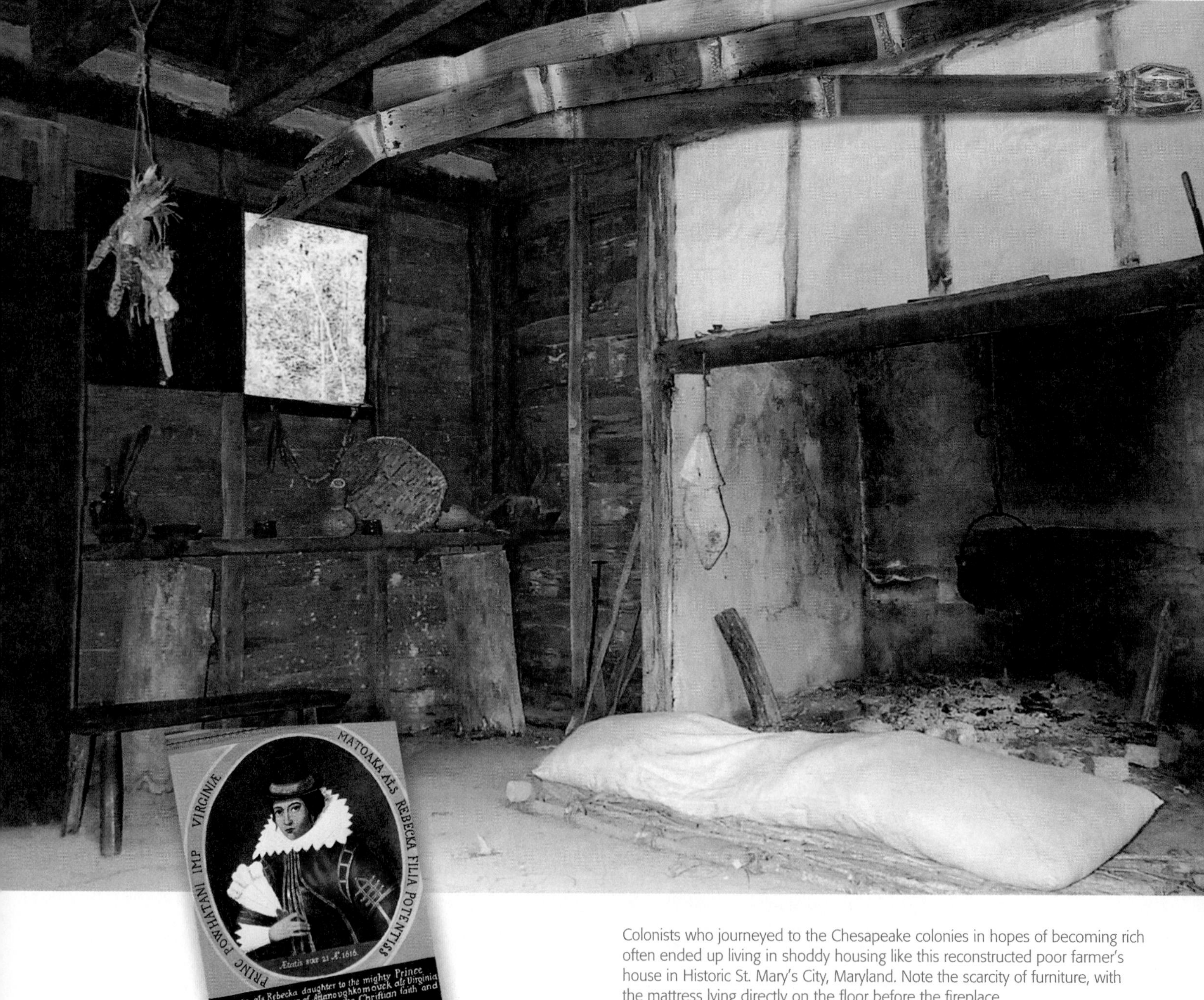

Colonists who journeyed to the Chesapeake colonies in hopes of becoming rich often ended up living in shoddy housing like this reconstructed poor farmer's house in Historic St. Mary's City, Maryland. Note the scarcity of furniture, with the mattress lying directly on the floor before the fireplace.

Hear the Audio

Hear the audio files for Chapter 2 at **www.myhistorylab.com**.

THE FRENCH IN NORTH AMERICA *(page 33)*

WHAT ROLE did the fur trade and fur traders play in the success of the French colonies?

THE DUTCH OVERSEAS EMPIRE *(page 35)*

HOW DID conflict between the English and the Dutch affect Dutch colonization in the Americas?

ENGLISH SETTLEMENT IN THE CHESAPEAKE *(page 36)*

HOW DID tobacco cultivation shape the development of Virginia society?

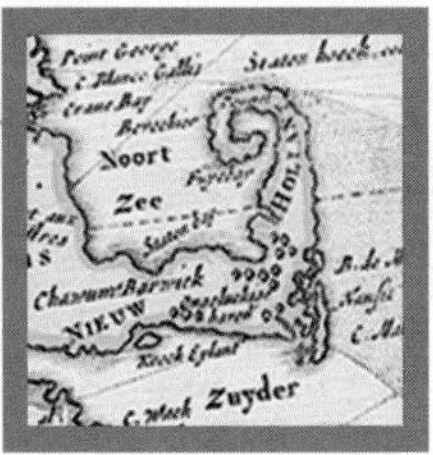

THE FOUNDING OF NEW ENGLAND *(page 42)*

WHY WERE the English colonies in New England so different from those in the Chesapeake?

COMPETITION IN THE CARIBBEAN *(page 47)*

WHAT WAS the connection between sugar cultivation and slavery in the Caribbean?

SLAVERY CODE

DISTRICT OF COLUMBIA,

THE RESTORATION COLONIES *(page 49)*

HOW DID the proprietors of the Restoration colonies shape their development?

ONE AMERICAN JOURNEY

Martin's Hundred in Virginia, 1623

Loving and kind father and mother:

My most humble duty remembered to you, . . . This is to let you understand that I your child am in a most heavy case by reason of the nature of the country, [which] is such that it causeth much sickness, as the scurvy and the bloody flux and diverse other diseases, which maketh the body very poor and weak. . . . [Since] I came out of the ship I never ate anything but peas, and loblollie (that is water gruel). . . . A mouthful of bread for a penny loaf must serve for four men which is most pitiful. . . . [We] live in fear of the enemy every hour . . . for our plantation is very weak by reason of the death and sickness of our company. . . .

But I am not half a quarter so strong as I was in England, and all is for want of victuals, for I do protest unto you that I have eaten more in [one] day at home than I have allowed me here for a week. . . .

[I] saith that if you love me you will redeem me suddenly, for which I do entreat and beg. . . . Good father, do not forget me, but have mercy and pity my miserable case. I know if you did but see me, you would weep to see me. . . .

Richard Frethorne

Susan M. Kingsbury, ed., *The Records of the Virginia Company of London,* 4 vols. (Washington, D.C., 1935), 4:58–62.

Read the **Document** at **www.myhistorylab.com**

Personal Journeys Online

- **Rev. Francis Higginson, July 1629. Letter from Massachusetts to his friends in Leicester, England.**
- **Father Isaac Jogues, *Novum Belgium*, 1646. Description of New Amsterdam.**
- **Hans Sloan, *A Voyage to the Islands*, 1707. Description of early eighteenth-century Jamaica.**

RICHARD FRETHORNE had journeyed across the Atlantic to seek his fortune in the new colony of Virginia. Like many emigrants, he surely hoped that one day he would become a prosperous landowner, a status beyond his reach in England. Instead of health and prosperity, Frethorne found sickness and starvation. Fears of an attack by enemy Indians compounded his misery. Yet the starving young Englishman could not simply board the next ship for England. He was under contract to work for the Virginia Company and could not leave until he had completed his term of service. Hence Frethorne's anguished plea to his father to "redeem" him, or buy out the remainder of his contract so that he could return home sooner.

Frethorne's experience reveals several important aspects of European colonization in the New World. Colonization offered opportunities for advancement, to be sure, but often at the price of sickness, suffering, and danger. Virginia turned out to be England's first permanent colony in the New World, but from Frethorne's perspective in 1623, it was a fragile settlement teetering on the brink of disaster.

Virginia's eventual success, and that of other English colonies, depended upon the willingness of thousands of individuals like Richard Frethorne to face the challenges posed by overseas settlement. Even as their emigration was inspired by hopes of improvement, their quest also reflected England's desire to claim a portion of the New World for itself. In this scramble for American colonies, England's greatest adversaries were France and the Netherlands. If ordinary colonists were often preoccupied with their own tribulations, their leaders could never forget the high stakes involved in the international race for overseas possessions. ✦

CHRONOLOGY

1581	Northern Provinces of Holland declare independence from Spain.
1589	King Henry IV of France signs Edict of Nantes, granting religious toleration to French Protestants and effectively ending civil war over religion.
1602	Founding of Dutch East India Company.
1603–1625	James I reigns as king of England.
1607	Founding of English colonies at Jamestown and Sagadahoc.
1608	Establishment of French colony at Quebec.
1619	First Africans arrive in Jamestown.
	Virginia's House of Burgesses meets for the first time.
1620	Founding of Plymouth Colony in New England.
	Mayflower Compact signed.
1620s	Tobacco boom in Virginia.
1624	Dutch found colony of New Netherland.
1625	Virginia becomes a royal colony.
	Fort Amsterdam founded.
1625–1649	Charles I reigns as king of England.
1627	English colony at Barbados founded.
1630	Massachusetts Bay Colony founded.
1630–1642	Great Migration to New England.
1634	Lord Baltimore (Cecilius Calvert) founds proprietary colony of Maryland.
1635–1636	Roger Williams banished from Massachusetts; founds Providence, Rhode Island.
1637	Anne Hutchinson banished from Massachusetts.
	Pequot War.
1638	New Haven colony founded.
1640s	Sugar cultivation and slavery established in West Indies.
1642–1660	English Civil War and Interregnum.
1649	Maryland's Act for Religious Toleration.
1654	Jewish emigrants from Brazil move to New Amsterdam, creating North America's first permanent Jewish community.
1660	Charles II restored to English throne; reigns until 1685.
1663	Founding of Carolina colony.
1664	New Netherland conquered by the English, becomes New York.
	New Jersey established.
1673	French explorers reach the Mississippi River.
1681	Founding of Pennsylvania.

THE FRENCH IN NORTH AMERICA

WHAT ROLE did the fur trade and fur traders play in the success of the French colonies?

In the mid-sixteenth century, religious warfare between Catholics and Protestants at home had interrupted France's efforts to establish a foothold in North America. The only French subjects who maintained regular contact with the New World were fishermen making seasonal voyages to the waters off the coast of Newfoundland. But in the early seventeenth century, after King Henry IV restored civil order in France, the situation changed. With the creation of permanent settlements first along the St. Lawrence River and later in the continent's interior, France staked its claim to a New World empire.

The Quest for Furs and Converts

French fishermen who dried their catch along the Newfoundland shore often encountered Indians interested in trading beaver pelts for European goods. There was a ready market for these furs in Europe, where beaver hats had become very fashionable. Thus furs joined fish as a source of wealth, and a reason for French explorers and entrepreneurs to establish the colony of New France.

In 1608, Samuel de Champlain led an expedition up the St. Lawrence River to found a permanent settlement at Quebec. This village was eventually joined by two others located farther up the river (see Map 2–1). For several decades, the colony was managed by the Company of New France, a private corporation working on its own behalf as well as in France's

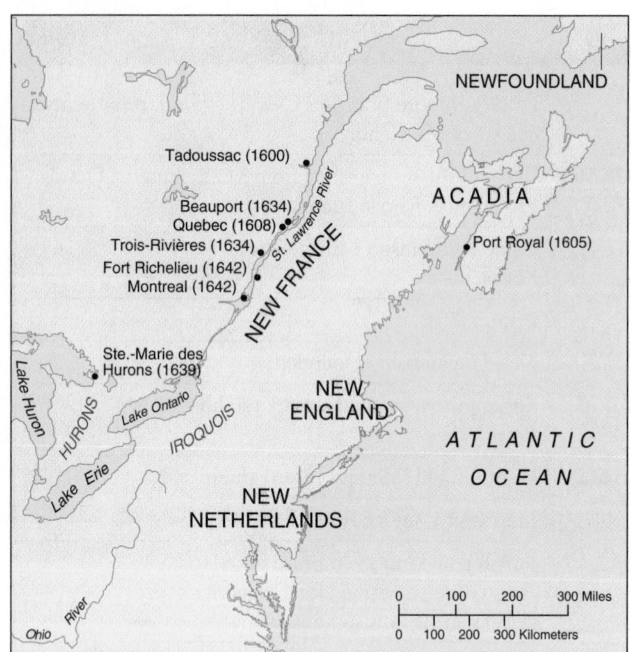

MAP 2–1 **New France, c. 1650** By 1650, New France contained a number of thinly populated settlements along the St. Lawrence River Valley and the eastern shore of Lake Huron. Most colonists lived in Quebec and Montreal; other sites served mainly as fur-trading posts and Jesuit missions to the Huron Indians.

Why were so many settlements in New France located along the banks of the St. Lawrence River? How did French settlement patterns reflect the economic goals of the French colonists?

coureurs de bois French for "woods runners," independent fur traders in New France.

QUICK REVIEW

The Fur Trade

- Fur traders were critical to New France's success.
- New France was ruled by royal appointees.
- *Coureurs de bois*: independent fur traders living among the Indians.

indentured servants Individuals who contracted to serve a master for a period of four to seven years in return for payment of the servant's passage to America.

QUICK REVIEW

New France under Royal Control

- 1663: King Louis XIV assumes direct control of the colony.
- French officials launch campaign to increase immigration.
- Campaign fails and population is only 15,000 in 1700.

imperial interests. New France grew slowly; by the 1660s, there were only 3,200 colonists clustered in and around the three main villages.

The fur trade supporting the colony's development functioned as a partnership between Indians and Europeans. At first, some colonists anticipated that economic ties between the two peoples would be supplemented by marital ones as French traders took Indian wives. Intermarriage, however, was never widespread, occurring mainly among ***coureurs de bois*** ("woods runners"), independent fur traders who ventured into the forests to live and trade among native peoples.

Indian peoples such as the Montagnais and Hurons welcomed the French not only as trading partners, but also as military allies, making sure that the newcomers understood that the two roles had to be linked. As a result, the fur trade entangled the French in rivalries among Indian groups that long predated European contact.

Some French colonists regarded saving Indian souls as even more important than profiting from furs. Beginning in the 1630s, Jesuit missionaries—members of a Catholic religious order founded during the Counter-Reformation—tried to convince Indians to come to the French settlements to hear Christian preaching and learn European ways. When that tactic failed, Jesuits traveled to native villages and learned native languages, bringing Christianity directly to Indian populations.

The Development of New France

After 1663, New France underwent several important changes. King Louis XIV disbanded the Company of New France and assumed direct control of the colony. The French government also vastly improved Canada's military defenses, investing money in the construction of forts and sending over professional soldiers.

French officials launched a massive campaign to increase migration to the colony. They sent more than 700 orphaned girls and widows—called *filles du roi*, or "king's daughters"—to provide wives in a colony where there were six men of marriageable age for every unmarried French woman. Many male immigrants were *engagés*, or **indentured servants,** who agreed to work for three years in return for food, lodging, a small salary, and a return passage to France.

Despite these efforts, only about 250 French immigrants arrived each year. Several factors discouraged prospective colonists, not least of which was Canada's reputation as a distant and inhospitable place. Rumors circulated about frigid Canadian winters and surprise Indian attacks. In addition, the government required settlers to be Catholic (although Protestants often resided in Canada temporarily), reducing the pool from which colonists could be recruited. In the end, nearly three out of four immigrants who went to Canada returned home.

By 1700, the population had grown to about 15,000 (less than 7 percent of the English population in the mainland colonies that year; see Figure 2–1). This growth was mostly due to a remarkable level of natural increase.

French officials sought to restrict settlement to the St. Lawrence Valley, fearing that further expansion would render the empire impossible to defend. The impetus to move inland, however, could not be restrained. By the 1670s, French traders and missionaries had reached the Mississippi River. In 1681–1682, Robert, Sieur de La Salle, followed the Mississippi to the Gulf of Mexico, claiming the entire valley (which he named Louisiana in honor of the king) for France. When officials tried to restrict the direct trade between Indians and the *coureurs de bois*, many of these Frenchmen drifted off to settle in what became known as the *pays des Illinois* along the Mississippi. This expansion of French influence alarmed the English, who had founded colonies along the Atlantic seaboard and feared a growing French presence in the west.

Because Indians expected their trading partners also to be military allies, Europeans were often drawn into native conflicts. This illustration, from Samuel de Champlain's 1613 description of the founding of New France, shows him joining his Huron allies in an attack on the Iroquois.

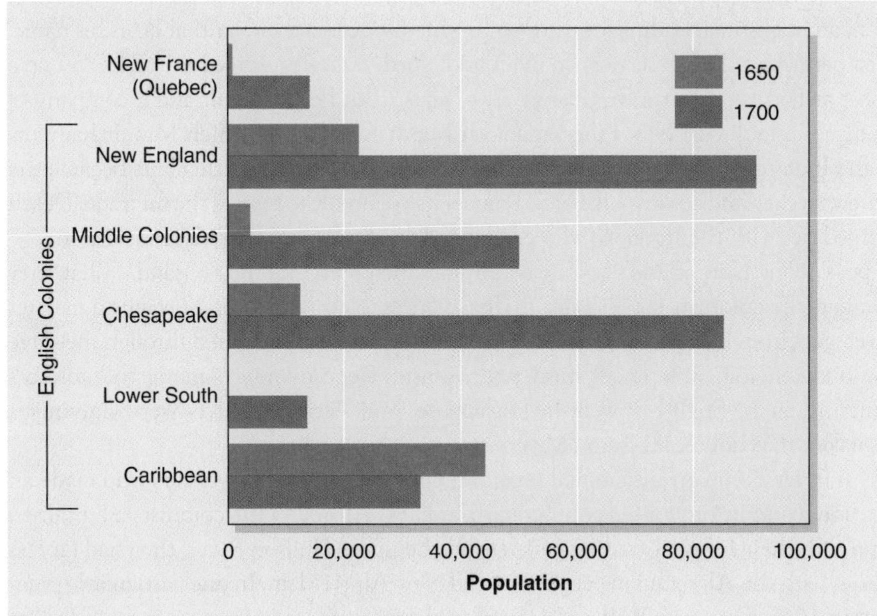

FIGURE 2–1 **European Populations of New France (Quebec) and English Colonies in 1650 and 1700**
Although New France's population grew rapidly between 1650 and 1700, it remained only a tiny fraction of the population of England's North American colonies. By 1700, English colonists on the mainland outnumbered New France's inhabitants by a factor of about 16 to 1.

Data Source: John J. McCusker and Russell R. Menard, *The Economy of British America, 1607–1789* (1985). University of North Carolina Press.

Prosperous and expansive, Canada provided France with a secure foothold on the North American mainland. Its successful establishment contributed to an escalating European competition for land and trade in the New World. Soon new rivals entered the scene.

THE DUTCH OVERSEAS EMPIRE

HOW DID conflict between the English and the Dutch affect Dutch colonization in the Americas?

The Dutch Republic joined the scramble for empire in the early seventeenth century. The Northern Provinces, sometimes known as Holland, had in 1581 declared their independence from Spain (whose kings ruled the region as part of the Holy Roman Empire), although sporadic fighting continued for another half-century. The new republic, dominated by Protestants, was intent on challenging Catholic Spain's power in the New World as well as the Old. More than any other factor, however, the desire for profit drove the Dutch quest for colonies.

Read the Document at **www.myhistorylab.com** *Exploring America: Exploitation of the Americas*

The Dutch East India Company

By 1600, the Dutch emerged as the leading economic power in Europe. The republic earned considerable wealth from manufacturing and Amsterdam soon became Europe's financial capital. The centerpiece of Dutch prosperity, however, was commerce, which expanded dramatically in the early seventeenth century. This commercial vitality provided the context for overseas expansion into both the Atlantic and Pacific.

The instrument of colonial dominance was the Dutch East India Company, founded in 1602 to challenge what had until then been a virtual Portuguese monopoly of Asian trade. Its first success was the capture of the Spice Islands (now Indonesia and East Timor), followed by the takeover of Batavia (Jakarta), Ceylon (Sri Lanka), and Sumatra. The company established slave-trading posts on the Gold Coast of West Africa, where it competed with the Portuguese, and at the Cape of Good Hope on Africa's southern tip. Its far-flung commercial net eventually encompassed parts of India and Formosa (Taiwan).

The West India Company and New Netherland

The Dutch next set their sights on the Americas, creating the West India Company in 1621. After taking control of West African slave-trading posts and temporarily occupying part of Brazil, the West India Company moved into the Caribbean (acquiring four islands by the 1640s) and North America. Its claim to the Connecticut, Hudson, and Delaware valleys stemmed from the 1609 voyage of Henry Hudson, an Englishman sailing for the Dutch, who discovered the river that bears his name.

The first permanent Dutch settlers on mainland North America arrived in 1624 to set up a fur-trading post at Fort Orange (now Albany). Two years later, Peter Minuit and a company of Protestant refugees established New Amsterdam on Manhattan Island, which Minuit had purchased from the Indians. The Hudson River corridor between these two settlements became the heart of the New Netherland colony. Like New France, its economic focus was the fur trade. Dutch merchants forged ties with the Iroquois, who exchanged furs for European tools and weapons.

At its peak, New Netherland's colonists only numbered about ten thousand. What they lacked in numbers the colonists made up for in divisiveness. New Netherland became a magnet for religious refugees from Europe, as well as a destination for Africans acquired through the slave trade. Ethnic and religious differences hindered a sense of community. Among the colony's Dutch, German, French, English, Swedish, Portuguese, and African settlers were Calvinists, Lutherans, Quakers, Catholics, Jews, and Muslims.

The West India Company dispatched several inept but aggressive governors who made an unstable situation worse by provoking conflict with Indians. Although the colonists maintained good relations with their Iroquois trading partners on the upper Hudson River, they had far less friendly dealings with the Algonquian peoples around New Amsterdam. In one particularly gruesome incident in 1645, Governor Willem Kieft ordered a massacre at an encampment of Indian refugees who had refused to pay him tribute. Ten years later, Governor Peter Stuyvesant antagonized Susquehannock Indians along the Delaware River by seizing a small Swedish colony where the Susquehannocks had traded.

Such actions provoked retaliatory raids by the Indians, further weakening the colony. Though profitable, the fur trade did not generate the riches to be found in other parts of the Dutch empire. By the 1650s, New Netherland increasingly looked like a poor investment to company officials back in Europe.

ENGLISH SETTLEMENT IN THE CHESAPEAKE

HOW DID tobacco cultivation shape the development of Virginia society?

Following the Roanoke Colony's disappearance after 1587 (see Chapter 1), twenty years passed before the English again attempted to settle in America. When they did, in 1607, it was in the lower Chesapeake Bay region. The new settlement, Jamestown, at first seemed likely to share

GLOBAL CONNECTIONS

 NORTH AMERICA'S FIRST JEWISH COMMUNITY 

In 1654, twenty-three Jews arrived in New Amsterdam after a long voyage from Brazil. The reasons why they ended up in the Dutch colonial town relate to a much larger story of repeated Jewish migrations, undertaken time and again to escape religious persecution. In New Amsterdam these settlers found a home, establishing the first permanent Jewish community in North America.

Many of them could trace their ancestry back to Spain, where there had been a flourishing Jewish community during the Middle Ages. By the fifteenth century, however, the same Christian militancy that inspired the *reconquista* against the Muslims brought trouble for Spain's Jewish population in the form of the Inquisition. Jews who refused to convert to Christianity risked execution as heretics. In 1492, the same year as Columbus's first voyage, Spanish authorities ordered all Jews to leave Spain. Refugee Spanish Jews relocated all over the Mediterranean world, with perhaps a hundred thousand settling in Portugal, Spain's neighbor on the Iberian Peninsula. Many who did so were forced to accept Christian baptism, but continued to follow their own faith in secret. When the authorities threatened to prevent such practices, many Jews chose to leave Portugal. Some sought refuge in the Netherlands, where they found religious toleration and commercial opportunities.

In the early seventeenth century, the same Dutch West India Company that founded New Netherland tried to dislodge the Portuguese from their prosperous sugar-producing colony of Brazil. The company succeeded in capturing the city of Recife in 1630, and for the next twenty-four years the Dutch ruled over northeastern Brazil. During that time, more than a thousand Jews moved to the colony from the Netherlands. But when the Portuguese regained control of Brazil in 1654, the Jews were forced to move yet again. Most returned to the Netherlands, but a few decided to take their chances in New Amsterdam. At last they found a place where they could stay. When New Netherland became New York in 1664, English authorities continued the Dutch practice of toleration. Even though Jewish colonists were only supposed to worship in private, there was a synagogue in New York City by 1700. Jews eventually settled in other colonies, such as Rhode Island, Pennsylvania, and South Carolina. Wherever they formed their communities, they contributed to the remarkable religious diversity of England's New World empire.

- How did religious persecution in early modern Europe affect the lives of its Jewish inhabitants?

Roanoke's dismal fate. But it endured, eventually developing into the prosperous colony of Virginia. The reason for Virginia's success was an American plant—tobacco—that commanded good prices from European consumers. Tobacco also underlaid the economy of a neighboring colony, Maryland, and had a profound influence on the development of Chesapeake society.

THE ORDEAL OF EARLY VIRGINIA

In 1606, several English merchants petitioned King James I for a charter incorporating two companies to attempt New World settlement. One, the London, or Virginia, Company, included merchants from the city of London; the other, the Plymouth Company, included merchants from England's western ports. These **joint-stock companies** sold shares to investors (who expected a profit in return) to raise money for colonization.

joint-stock company Business enterprise in which a group of stockholders pooled their money to engage in trade or to fund colonizing expeditions.

The Jamestown colony. Three small ships carried 104 settlers, all men, to the mouth of Chesapeake Bay in May 1607 (see Map 2–2). On a peninsula about 50 miles up a river they named the James in honor of their king, the colonists built a fortified settlement they called Jamestown. Hoping to earn quick profits for Virginia Company investors, they immediately began hunting for gold and searching for the Northwest Passage to Asia. Spending all their time searching for riches, the settlers neglected to plant crops, and their food supplies dwindled. By January 1608, only thirty-eight colonists were still alive.

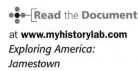

Read the **Document** at **www.myhistorylab.com** *Exploring America: Jamestown*

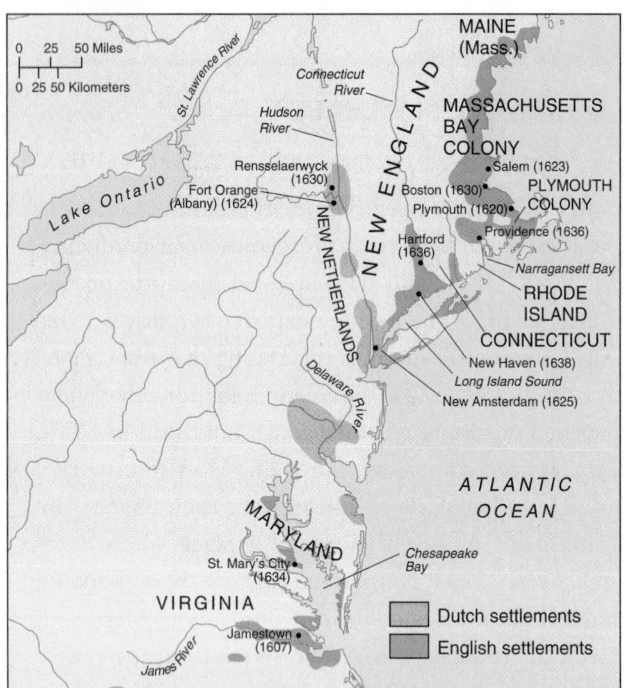

MAP 2–2 **English and Dutch Mainland Colonies in North America, c. 1655** Early English colonies clustered in two areas of the Atlantic seaboard—New England and the Chesapeake Bay. Between them lay Dutch New Netherland, with settlements stretching up the Hudson River. The Dutch also acquired territory at the mouth of the Delaware River in 1655 when they seized a short-lived Swedish colony located there.

> **Why might** the Dutch have sought to control the Hudson and Delaware Rivers? What does this map tell us about the differing goals of Dutch and English colonists?

headright system Instituted by the Virginia Company in 1616, this system gave fifty acres to anyone who paid his own way to Virginia and an additional fifty for each person (or "head") he brought with him.

House of Burgesses The legislature of colonial Virginia. First organized in 1619, it was the first institution of representative government in the English colonies.

After the disastrous first year, the colony's governing council turned to Captain John Smith for leadership. He imposed military discipline on Jamestown, organizing settlers into work gangs and decreeing that "he that will not worke shall not eate." When a gunpowder explosion wounded Smith in 1609 and forced him to return to England, his enemies had him replaced as leader.

Once again, the colony nearly disintegrated. More settlers arrived, only to starve or die of disease. Facing financial ruin, company officials back in England tried to conceal the state of the colony. They reorganized the company twice and sent more settlers, including glassmakers, winegrowers, and silkmakers, in a desperate effort to find a marketable colonial product. They experimented with harsh military discipline. When it became clear that such severity discouraged immigration, the company tried more positive inducements.

The first settlers had been expected to work in return for food and other necessities; only company stockholders were to share in the colony's profits. But settlers wanted land, so governors began assigning small plots to those who finished their terms of service to the company. In 1616, the company instituted the **headright system,** giving 50 acres to anyone who paid his own way to Virginia and an additional 50 for each person (or "head") he brought with him.

In 1619, three other important developments occurred. That year, the company began transporting women to become wives for planters and induce them to stay in the colony. It was also the year in which the first Africans arrived in Virginia. In addition, the company created the first legislative body in English America, the **House of Burgesses,** setting a precedent for the establishment of self-government in other English colonies. Landowners elected representatives to the House of Burgesses, which, subject to the approval of the company, made laws for Virginia.

Despite these changes, the settlers were still unable to earn the company a profit. To make matters worse, the headright system expanded English settlement beyond Jamestown. This strained the already tense relations between the English and the Indians onto whose lands they had intruded.

The Powhatan Confederacy and the colonists. When the English arrived in 1607, they planted their settlement in the heart of territory ruled by the powerful Indian leader Powhatan. Chief of a confederacy of about thirty tribes with some fourteen thousand people, including 3,200 warriors, Powhatan had little to fear at first from the struggling English outpost. After an initial skirmish with English soldiers, he sent gifts of food, assuming that by accepting the gifts, the colonists acknowledged their dependence on him. Further action against the settlers seemed unnecessary, because they seemed fully capable of destroying themselves.

This conclusion was premature. Armed colonists began seizing corn from Indian villages whenever native people refused to supply it voluntarily. In retaliation, Powhatan besieged Jamestown and tried to starve the colony to extinction. The colony was saved by the arrival of reinforcements from England, but war with the Indians continued until 1614.

The marriage of the colonist John Rolfe to Pocahontas, Powhatan's daughter, helped seal the peace in 1614. Pocahontas had briefly been held captive by the English during the war and had been instructed in English manners and religion by Rolfe. Sent to negotiate with Powhatan in the spring of 1614, Rolfe asked the chief for his daughter's hand. Powhatan gave his consent, and Pocahontas—baptized in the Church of England and renamed Rebecca—became Rolfe's wife.

WHERE TO LEARN MORE

Jamestown Settlement, near Williamsburg, Virginia
http://www.virtualjamestown.org/

Powhatan died in 1618, and his brother Opechancanough succeeded him as chief. Still harboring intense resentment against the English, the new chief made plans for retaliation. Early in the morning on March 22, 1622, hundreds of Indian men traveled to the English settlements, as if they meant to visit or trade. Instead, they attacked the unsuspecting colonists, killing 347 by the end of the day—more than one-fourth of the English population.

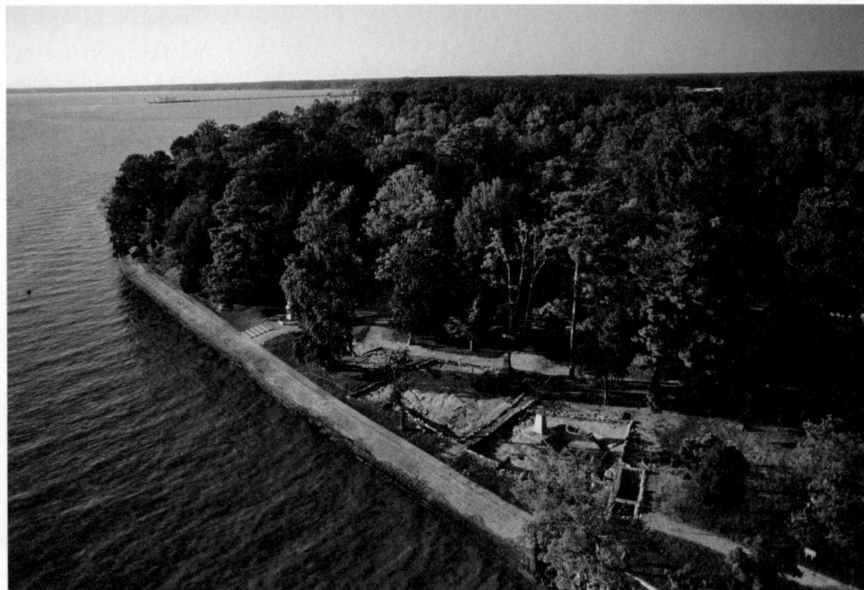

After years of work, archaeologists have excavated the original site of the English fort at Jamestown. This aerial view of the site shows its close proximity to the James River.

The surviving colonists almost immediately plotted revenge. English forces struck at native villages, killing the inhabitants and burning cornfields. During the ensuing nine years of war, the English treated the Indians with a ferocity that recalled their earlier subjugation of the Irish.

Although Opechancanough's attack failed to restrain the colonists, it destroyed the Virginia Company. Economic activity ceased as settlers retreated to fortified garrisons. The company went bankrupt, and a royal commission investigating the 1622 attack was shocked to discover that nearly ten times more colonists had died from starvation and disease than at the hands of Indians. King James had little choice but to dissolve the company in 1624, and Virginia became a royal colony the following year. The settlers continued to enjoy self-government through the House of Burgesses, but now the king chose the colony's governor and council, and royal advisers monitored its affairs.

QUICK REVIEW

Powhatan, Indian Leader

- Chief of a confederacy of about thirty tribes.
- Besieged Jamestown when colonists began stealing corn.
- Father of Pocahontas.

The Importance of Tobacco

Ironically, the demise of the Virginia Company helped the colony succeed. In their search for a marketable product, settlers had begun growing tobacco after 1610. Europeans acquired a taste for tobacco in the late sixteenth century when the Spanish brought samples from the West Indies and Florida. The first cargo of Virginia-grown tobacco arrived in England in 1617 and sold at a profitable 3 shillings per pound.

Between 1627 and 1669, annual tobacco exports climbed from 250,000 pounds to more than 15 million pounds. As the supply grew, the price per pound plunged from 13 pence in 1624 to a mere penny in the late 1660s, where it remained for the next half-century. What had once been a luxury product thus became affordable for Europeans of average means. Now thoroughly dependent on tobacco for their livelihood, the only way colonists could compensate for falling prices was to grow even more, pushing exports to England to more than 20 million pounds per year by the late 1670s (see Figure 2–2).

Tobacco shaped nearly every aspect of Virginia society, from patterns of settlement to the recruitment of colonists. Planters scrambled to claim lands near navigable rivers so that ships could reach their plantations and carry their crops to market. As a result, the colonists dispersed into plantations located along waterways instead of settling in compact communities. Settlers competed to produce the biggest and best crop and get it to market the fastest, hoping to enjoy even a small price advantage over everyone else.

Read the **Document**
at **www.myhistorylab.com**
From Then to Now Online: Tobacco and the American Economy

Tobacco kept workers busy nine months of the year. Planters sowed seeds in the early spring, transplanted seedlings a few weeks later, and spent the summer pinching off the tops of the plants (to produce larger leaves) and removing worms. After the harvest, the leaves were "cured"—dried in ventilated sheds—and packed in large barrels. During the winter, planters

This illustration shows John Smith seizing the scalplock of Opechancanough, Chief Powhatan's brother, during an English raid on an Indian village. Smith released his prisoner only after Indians ransomed him with corn. Thirteen years later, Opechancanough led a surprise attack against the colonists.

cleared and fenced more land and made barrels for next year's crop. Working on his own, one planter could tend two thousand plants, which yielded about 500 pounds of cured tobacco. When the price was high, this supplied a comfortable income. But as the price plummeted, planters could keep up only by producing more tobacco, and to do that they needed a large labor force.

The planters turned to England, importing thousands of indentured servants, or contract workers, who (like Richard Frethorne) agreed to a fixed term of labor, usually four to seven years, in exchange for free passage to Virginia. The master provided food, shelter, clothing, and, at the end of the term of service, "freedom dues" paid in corn and clothing. Between 1625 and 1640, one thousand or more indentured servants arrived each year. The vast majority, came from the ranks of England's unemployed, who emigrated in hopes of "bettering their condition in a Growing Country."

Most found such hopes quickly dashed. Servants died in alarming numbers from disease, and those who survived faced years of backbreaking labor. Masters squeezed as much work out of them as possible with long hours and harsh discipline. New obstacles faced servants who managed to survive their terms of indenture. For every ex-servant who became a landholder, dozens died in poverty. To prevent freed servants from becoming economic rivals, established planters avoided selling them good land, particularly after tobacco prices hit bottom in the 1660s. Many ex-servants found land only in places less suitable for tobacco cultivation and more vulnerable to Indian attack. As a result, they became a discontented group. In 1675, their discontent would flare into rebellion (discussed in Chapter 3).

Maryland: A Refuge for Catholics

The success of tobacco in Virginia encouraged further English colonization in the Chesapeake region. In 1632, King Charles I granted 10 million acres of land north of the bay to the nobleman George Calvert, Lord Baltimore. Unlike Virginia, which was founded by a joint-stock company, Maryland was a **proprietary colony**—the sole possession of Calvert and his heirs. They owned all the land, which they could divide up as they pleased, and had the right to set up the colony's government.

Calvert, who was Catholic, intended Maryland to be a refuge for others of his faith. When Queen Elizabeth's accession made England a Protestant nation, Catholics became a disadvantaged minority. In Maryland, Calvert wanted Catholic colonists to enjoy economic and political power. He intended to divide the land into manors—large private estates like those of medieval England—and distribute them to wealthy Catholic friends. These manorial lords would live on rents collected from tenant farmers.

Calvert died before settlement began, and it was the sad fate of his son, Cecilius, to see his father's plans unravel. The majority of colonists, who began arriving in 1634, were Protestants who despised Catholics. Refusing to live as tenants on Catholic estates, they claimed land of their own—a process that accelerated after 1640, when Maryland adopted a headright system like Virginia's as a way to recruit settlers.

Maryland's problems intensified when civil war broke out in England in 1642. For years, political and religious disputes had divided the nation. Charles I, who became king in 1625, clashed with the **Puritans,** who called for further reform of the Church of England. He also antagonized many government leaders by dissolving Parliament in 1629 and ruling on his own for

QUICK REVIEW

Tobacco

- 1617: Virginia-grown tobacco arrives in England.
- 1669: Tobacco exports reach 15 million pounds annually.
- Labor demand of tobacco farming stimulates immigration to the colonies.

proprietary colony A colony created when the English monarch granted a huge tract of land to an individual or group of individuals, who became "lords proprietor."

Puritans Individuals who believed that Queen Elizabeth's reforms of the Church of England had not gone far enough in improving the church. Puritans led the settlement of Massachusetts Bay Colony.

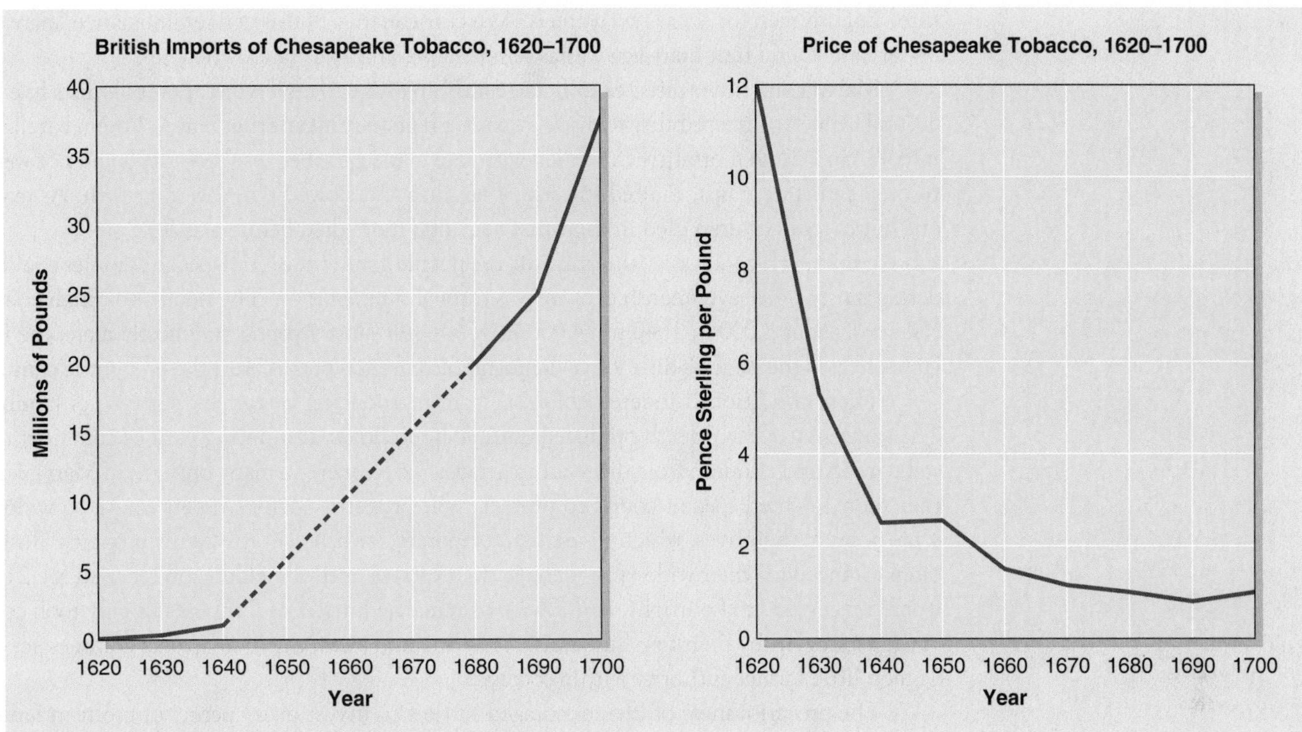

FIGURE 2–2 **The Supply and Price of Chesapeake Tobacco, 1620–1700** Tobacco cultivation dominated the economy of the Chesapeake region throughout the seventeenth century. As planters brought more and more land under cultivation, the amount of tobacco exported to Britain shot up and the price plummeted. (As the dashed line indicates, no data on tobacco imports are available for the years 1640–1680.)

Data Source: Russell R. Menard, "The Tobacco Industry in the Chesapeake Colonies, 1617–1730: An Interpretation," *Research in Economic History,* 5 (1980), app. Jai Press, Inc.

eleven years. Needing funds to suppress a rebellion in Scotland in 1640, however, Charles was forced to recall Parliament. Its leaders, sympathetic to the Puritan cause, quickly turned against him. Both king and Parliament recruited armies and went to war in 1642. Parliamentary forces triumphed, and in 1649, they executed Charles. For the next decade, England was governed as a protectorate, not a monarchy. Oliver Cromwell, a Puritan general, ruled until his death in 1658. His son, Richard, proved an inept successor, however, and in 1660 a group of army officers invited Charles's exiled son to accept the throne.

W
WHERE TO LEARN MORE
St. Mary's City, Maryland
http://www.stmaryscity.org/

During the 1640s and 1650s, Maryland Protestants took advantage of the upheaval in England to contest the Calverts' control of the colony. To pacify them, Cecilius Calvert established a legislature, assuming that Protestants would dominate the elective lower house while he could appoint Catholics to the upper house. In 1649, Calvert also approved the **Act for Religious Toleration,** the first law in America to call for freedom of worship for all Christians, but even this brought no peace. The Protestant majority continued to resist Catholic political influence.

Act for Religious Toleration The first law in America to call for freedom of worship for all Christians.

Instead of a peaceful Catholic refuge, Maryland soon resembled neighboring Virginia. Its settlers raised tobacco and imported as many indentured servants as possible. Throughout the seventeenth century, Protestants kept up their opposition to the proprietor's control and resisted Catholic efforts to govern the colony that was supposed to have been theirs.

Life in the Chesapeake Colonies

Few people could have predicted how much life in the Chesapeake colonies would differ from England. Many differences stemmed from the region's distinctive population. Because of their labor needs, masters preferred to recruit young men in their teens and twenties as indentured servants, importing three or four times as many of them as women. As a result, the populations of Virginia and Maryland were overwhelmingly young and male. Even as late as 1700, Virginia had three English men for every two women. As a consequence of this gender imbalance, many male ex-servants found that marriage was as remote a possibility as landownership.

Malaria and other diseases inflicted hardship on nearly everyone. Few colonists lived past 50, and women's susceptibility to disease during pregnancy meant that many of them barely made it to 40. Such high mortality, combined with late marriages (because servants could not wed until their terms were up), limited the size of families and slowed population growth. As many as one out of four children died in their first year, and more died before age 20.

Under such conditions, the only way the populations of the Chesapeake colonies could grow during most of the seventeenth century was through immigration. The number of English settlers rose from about 8,000 in 1640 to 24,000 in 1660. Still mostly young and mostly male, the immigrants helped the region's distinctive demographic patterns persist until the end of the century.

These conditions hindered colonists from reproducing customary patterns of family life. The frequency of early death produced unusual households, containing various combinations of stepparents and children from different marriages. There were so many orphans in Maryland that the colony created special courts to protect their property. Many women would be widows at some point in their lives, which gave them temporary control over the family property. Husbands often arranged for their widows to manage their estates until the eldest son reached age 21. Few women received land outright, and if widows remarried, their new spouses usually took control of the estates left by their first husbands. As in England itself, the Chesapeake colonies accorded women little formal authority within society.

The precariousness of life encouraged settlers to invest every penny of profit in land and labor, postponing investment in goods that would bring a more comfortable existence. Poor settlers slept on the floor on straw mattresses and had few other furnishings, often not even a chair or bench to sit on. Rich planters owned more goods, but often of poor quality. Nearly everyone subsisted on a rude diet of pork and corn.

Rough as these conditions were, they far surpassed the circumstances of most native peoples in the Chesapeake. The English population may have been growing slowly, but it still overwhelmed the Indian population, which suffered high mortality from European diseases. By 1685, there were more than ten colonists for every Indian living in eastern Virginia. By that point, many Native Americans in the Chesapeake had retreated to isolated towns, in hopes of preserving control over dwindling lands and maintaining some independence from English domination.

THE FOUNDING OF NEW ENGLAND

WHY WERE the English colonies in New England so different from those in the Chesapeake?

Even before permanent colonists arrived, New England's native population felt the effects of European contact. Between 1616 and 1618, a terrible epidemic swept through coastal New England, killing up to 90 percent of the Indians living there. The devastated survivors were struggling to cope with the consequences of this disaster just as the colonists began to arrive.

The Pilgrims and Plymouth Colony

Plymouth Colony, the first of the New England settlements, was founded in 1620. Its origins lay in religious disputes that had plagued England since the late sixteenth century. Most of Queen Elizabeth's subjects approved of her efforts to keep England a Protestant nation, but some reformers believed that she had not rid the Church of England of all Catholic practices. The enemies of these reformers, ridiculing them for wanting to purify the Church of England (or **Anglican** Church) of all corruption, called them Puritans.

Anglican Of or belonging to the Church of England, a Protestant denomination.

English Puritans believed in an all-powerful God who, at the moment of Creation, determined which humans would be saved and which would be damned. They held that salvation came through faith alone, not good works, and urged believers to seek a direct, personal relationship with God. The centerpiece of their spiritual life was conversion: the transforming experience that occurred when individuals felt the stirrings of grace in their souls and began to hope that they were among the saved. Those who experienced conversion were considered saints.

Puritans believed that certain Anglican practices interfered with conversion and the believer's relationship with God. But what they hated most about the Anglican Church was that anyone could be a member. Puritans believed that everyone should attend church services, but they wanted church membership, which conferred the right to partake in the Lord's Supper, or communion, to be limited to saints who had experienced conversion.

Elizabeth and the rulers who followed her—who as monarchs were the "supreme heads" of the Church of England—tried to silence the Puritans. Some Puritans, known as **separatists,** concluded that the Church of England would never change and left it to form their own congregations. One such group, mainly from the village of Scrooby, in Nottinghamshire, became the core of Plymouth Colony.

The Scrooby separatists left England in 1607–1608 for Holland, where they stayed for more than a decade. Although they could worship in peace there, many struggled to make a living and feared that their children were being tempted by the worldly pleasures of Dutch city life. Some Scrooby separatists contemplated moving to America and contacted the Plymouth Company. Called **Pilgrims** because they thought of themselves as spiritual wanderers, they were joined by other separatists and by nonseparatist "strangers" hired to help get the colony started. In all, 102 men, women, and children set sail on the *Mayflower* in September 1620.

After a long and miserable voyage, they landed near Massachusetts Bay. To prevent the colony from disintegrating into factions before their ship had even landed, the leaders drafted the Mayflower Compact, a document that bound all signers to abide by the decisions of the majority.

The Pilgrims settled at Plymouth, the site of a Wampanoag village recently depopulated by disease. Their first winter, the Pilgrims suffered through a terrible "starving time" that left nearly half of them dead.

When two English-speaking natives, Squanto and Samoset, emerged from the woods the next spring, the surviving Pilgrims marveled at them as "special instruments sent of God." Samoset had learned English from traders, and Squanto had learned it in England, where he lived for a time after being kidnapped by a sea captain. The two native men approached the Pilgrims on behalf of Massasoit, the Wampanoag leader. Although suspicious of the newcomers, the Wampanoags thought the Pilgrims might be useful allies against their enemies, the Narragansetts, who had escaped the recent epidemics.

In 1621, the Wampanoags and the Pilgrims signed a treaty of alliance, although each side understood its terms differently. The Pilgrims assumed that Massasoit had submitted to the superior authority of King James, whereas Massasoit assumed that he and the English king were equal partners.

Plymouth remained small, poor, and weak, never exceeding about seven thousand settlers. Although its families achieved a modest prosperity, the colony as a whole never produced more than small shipments of furs, fish, and timber to sell in England. After 1630, the first New England colony was overshadowed by a new and more powerful neighbor, Massachusetts Bay.

Massachusetts Bay Colony and Its Offshoots

The Puritans who founded Massachusetts shared many beliefs with the Pilgrims of Plymouth Colony—with one important exception. Unlike the Pilgrims, most Massachusetts settlers rejected separatism, insisting that the Anglican Church could be reformed. Their goal was to create godly churches to serve as models for the English church.

In 1629, a group of Puritan merchants and gentlemen received a royal charter for a joint-stock enterprise, the Massachusetts Bay Company, to set up a colony north of Plymouth. John Winthrop, a prosperous lawyer, was selected as the colony's governor. In the spring of 1630, a fleet of eleven ships carried Winthrop and about a thousand men, women, and children across the Atlantic.

QUICK REVIEW

The Pilgrims

- Pilgrims were separatists who believed the Church of England could not be reformed.
- First settled in the Netherlands before journeying to North America.
- Plymouth Colony founded in 1620.

separatists Members of an offshoot branch of Puritanism. Separatists believed that the Church of England was too corrupt to be reformed and hence were convinced they must "separate" from it to save their souls.

Pilgrims Settlers of Plymouth Colony, who viewed themselves as spiritual wanderers.

Read the Document at **www.myhistorylab.com**
***Agreement between the Settlers at New Plymouth (Mayflower Compact)* (1620)**

QUICK REVIEW

Mayflower Compact

- Mayflower Compact signed in 1620.
- Established self-government in the Plymouth Colony.
- Pilgrim leaders urged all adult males to sign the compact.

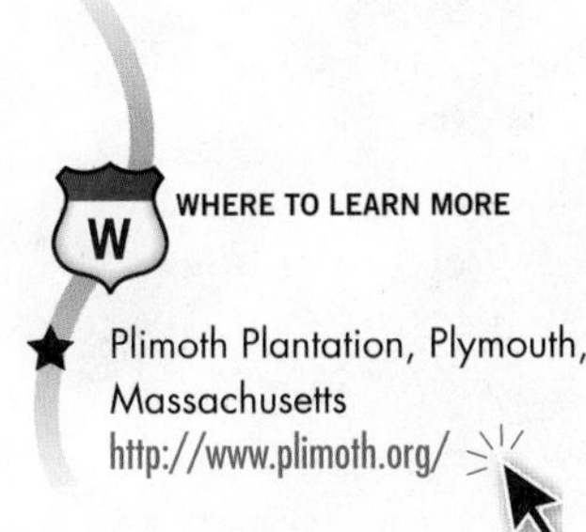

covenant A contract with God, binding settlers to meet their religious obligations in return for God's favor.

Read the Document at **www.myhistorylab.com** *John Winthrop, "A Model of Christian Charity"* (1630)

Stability, conformity, and intolerance. Winthrop described the settlers' mission in New England as a **covenant,** or contract, with God, binding them to meet their religious obligations in return for God's favor. The settlers also created covenants to define their duties to one another. When they founded towns, colonists signed covenants agreeing to live together in peace. Worshipers in each town's church likewise wrote covenants binding themselves to live in harmony.

The desire for peace and purity could breed intolerance. Settlers scrutinized their neighbors for signs of unacceptable behavior. Standards for church membership were strict; only those who could convincingly describe their conversion experiences were admitted. But the insistence on covenants and conformity also created a remarkably stable society.

That stability was enhanced by the development of representative government. By 1634, colony leaders had converted the charter of the Massachusetts Bay Company into a plan of government. The General Court, which initially included only the shareholders of the joint-stock company, was transformed into a two-house legislature. Freemen—adult males who held property and were church members—elected representatives to the lower house, as well as eighteen members (called "assistants") to the upper house. They also chose a governor and deputy governor.

Pequot War Conflict between English settlers and Pequot Indians over control of land and trade in eastern Connecticut.

The Connecticut Valley and the Pequot War. At least thirteen thousand settlers came to New England and established dozens of towns between 1630 and 1642, when the outbreak of the English Civil War halted emigration. The progress of settlement was generally untroubled in coastal Massachusetts, but when colonists moved into the Connecticut River Valley, tensions with Indians developed. These erupted in 1637 in the brief, tragic conflict called the **Pequot War.**

English settlers from Massachusetts first arrived in the Connecticut Valley in the mid-1630s. When English settlers poured into Connecticut and demanded Pequot submission to English authority, the Pequots turned against them. A struggle for control over the land and trade of eastern Connecticut began.

The colonists allied with the Pequots' enemies, the Narragansetts and Mohegans. Together they overwhelmed the Pequots. After the surviving Pequots had fled or been sold into slavery, more settlers moved to Connecticut, which soon declared itself a separate colony. In 1639, the settlers adopted the Fundamental Orders, creating a government similar to that of Massachusetts, and the English government granted them a charter in 1662.

John Winthrop (1588–1649) served as the Massachusetts Bay Colony's governor for most of its first two decades. Throughout his life, Winthrop—like many fellow Puritans—struggled to live a godly life in a corrupt world.

Roger Williams and the founding of Rhode Island. Massachusetts spun off other colonies as its population expanded in the 1630s and dissenters ran afoul of its intolerant government. Roger Williams, who founded Rhode Island, was one of these religious dissenters. Williams was a separatist minister who declared that because Massachusetts churches had not rejected the Church of England, they shared its corruption. He opposed government interference in religious affairs and argued for the separation of church and state. Williams even attacked the Massachusetts charter, insisting that the king had no right to grant Indian lands to English settlers.

When Williams refused to be silenced, the General Court banished him, intending to ship him back to England. But in the winter of 1635, Williams slipped away. He and a few followers found refuge among the Narragansett Indians, from whom he purchased land for the village of Providence, founded in 1636. More towns sprang up nearby when a new religious challenge sent additional refugees to Rhode Island from Massachusetts.

Anne Hutchinson's challenge to the Bay Colony. Anne Hutchinson arrived in Boston from England with her husband and seven children in 1634. Welcomed by the town's women for her talents as a midwife, she began to hold religious meetings in her house. During these meetings, she denounced several ministers, who had taught worshipers that there were spiritual exercises they could perform that might prepare them for sainthood.

Many people, including prominent Boston merchants, flocked to Hutchinson's meetings. But her critics believed her to be a dangerous antinomian (someone who claimed to be free from obedience to moral law), because she seemed to maintain that saints were accountable only to God and not to any worldly authority. Her opponents also objected to her teaching of mixed groups of men and women. Colony magistrates arrested her and tried her for sedition—that is, for advocating the overthrow of the government.

The court found her guilty and banished her. With many of her followers, she moved to Rhode Island, where Roger Williams had proclaimed a policy of religious toleration. Other followers returned to England or moved north to what became in 1679 the colony of New Hampshire.

Read the **Document**
at **www.myhistorylab.com**
The Trial of Anne Hutchinson (1638)

QUICK REVIEW

Anne Hutchinson

- Arrived in Boston with her family in 1634.
- Began to hold religious meetings in her house.
- Found guilty of sedition and banished from Massachusetts.

Families, Farms, and Communities in Early New England

"This plantation and that of Virginia went not forth upon the same reasons," declared one of Massachusetts's founders. Virginians came "for profit," whereas New Englanders emigrated to bear witness to their Puritan faith. Unlike the unmarried young men who moved in great numbers to Virginia, most New Englanders settled with their families. This had important implications for the development of New England society.

Even though emigration from England slowed to a trickle after 1642, New England's population continued to grow. By 1660, the number of colonists exceeded thirty-three thousand. This demographic expansion stemmed from the initial emigration of families. With a more balanced sex ratio (about three men to two women) than there was in the early Chesapeake, marriage and childbearing were more common.

Settling in a region with a healthier climate, New Englanders were largely spared early deaths from malaria and other diseases that ravaged the Chesapeake settlers. Most children survived to reach adulthood and form families of their own. Many New Englanders enjoyed unusually long lives for the seventeenth century, reaching their seventies and even eighties.

Women in early New England. In New England, as in other colonies and England itself, women were assumed to be legally and economically dependent on the men in their families. Since fewer New England marriages were shortened by the early death of a spouse, fewer New England women experienced widowhood, the one time in their lives when they might enjoy legal independence and exercise control over property.

Women's economic contributions were central to the family's success. In addition to caring for children, cooking, sewing, gardening, and cleaning, most women engaged in household production and traded the fruits of their labor with other families. They sold eggs, made butter and cheese, brewed beer, and wove cloth. Wives of shopkeepers and craftsmen occasionally managed their husbands' businesses when the men had to travel or became ill.

Community and economic life. New Englanders' lives were shaped not only by their families but also by their towns. Unlike Chesapeake colonists, who tended to disperse into separate plantations, New Englanders clustered into communities that might contain fifty or a hundred families. The Massachusetts government strongly encouraged town formation by granting land to groups of families who promised to settle together. Once they found a town they liked, families tended to stay in place. Grown children, inheriting parental estates and finding spouses nearby, often settled in the same community as their parents.

AMERICAN VIEWS

A Colonist Marvels at New England's Abundant Wildfowl (1634)

William Wood journeyed twice to Massachusetts, arriving first in 1629 for a four-year stay, and then returning from England in 1636 to remain in the colony for the rest of his life. In 1634, he published New England's Prospect, *an account of the natural resources of the region, its native inhabitants, and the new towns founded by the colonists. He described an abundance of animal life that would eventually diminish. The millions of pigeons mentioned below, for instance, were almost certainly passenger pigeons, which became extinct in 1914 due to overhunting and the disappearance of the large forests they needed to survive.*

- **What** do Wood's descriptions suggest about the colonists' approach to their environment?
- **Why** does Wood assign a monetary value to certain birds?
- **Why** does Wood repeatedly urge his readers to believe him when he describes such large numbers of wildfowl?

The pigeon of that country is something different from our dovehouse pigeons in England . . . They have long tails like a magpie. And they seem not so big, because they carry not so many feathers on their backs as our English doves, yet are they as big in body. These birds come into the country to go to the north parts in the beginning of our spring, at which time (if I may be counted worthy to believed in a thing that is not so strange as true) I have seen them fly as if the airy regiment had been pigeons, seeing neither beginning nor ending, length or breadth of these millions of millions. The shouting of people, the rattling of guns, and pelting of small shot could not drive them out of their course, but so they continued for four or five hours together. . . . Many of them build amongst the pine trees, . . . joining nest to nest and tree to tree by their nests, so that the sun never sees the ground in that place, from whence the Indians fetch whole loads of them. . . .

The turkey is a very large bird, of a black color yet white in flesh, much bigger than our English turkey. . . . Of these sometimes there will be forty, threescore, and an hundred of a flock, sometimes more and sometimes less. . . . Such as love turkey hunting must follow it in winter after a new fallen snow, when he may follow them by their tracks. Some have killed ten or a dozen in half a day. If they can be found towards an evening and watched where they perch, if one come about ten or eleven of the clock, he may shoot as often as he will; they will sit unless they be slenderly wounded. These turkey remain all the year long. The price of a good turkey cock is four shillings, and he is well worth it, for he may be in weight forty pound, a hen two shillings. . . .

The geese of the country be of three sorts: first a brant goose, which is a goose almost like the wild goose in England; the price of one of these is six pence. The second kind is a white goose, almost as big as an English tame goose. These come in great flocks about Michaelmas [September]. Sometimes there will be two or three thousand in a flock . . . The price of one of these is eight pence. The third kind of geese is a great gray goose with a black neck and a black and white head, strong of flight, and these be a great deal bigger than the ordinary geese of England . . . the price of a good gray goose is eighteen pence. . . .

The ducks of the country be very large ones and in great abundance, so is there of teal likewise. The price of a duck is six pence, of a teal three pence. If I should tell you how some have killed a hundred geese in a week, fifty ducks at a shot, forty teals at another, it may be counted impossible though nothing more certain.

Source: William Wood, *New England's Prospect,* ed. Alden T. Vaughan (Amherst, MA, 1977), pp. 50–52.

At the center of each town stood the meetinghouse, used as both a place of worship and a town hall. Massachusetts law required towns with at least fifty families to support a school (so children could learn to read the Bible), and men often wrangled at town meetings over the choice and salary of a schoolmaster. Townsmen tried, not always successfully, to reach decisions by consensus. To oversee day-to-day local affairs, they chose five to seven trusted neighbors to serve as selectmen. Each town could also elect two men to represent it in the colony legislature.

New England's stony soil and short growing season offered few ways to get rich, but most people achieved a modest prosperity. Their goal was to achieve a competency—enough property to ensure the family's economic independence. Without the income generated by a staple crop like tobacco, New England farmers could not hire large numbers of indentured servants and so relied on family labor.

New Englanders regularly traded goods and services with their neighbors. A carpenter might erect a house—usually larger and sturdier than the ramshackle Chesapeake dwellings—in return for barrels of salted beef. Men with several teenaged sons sent them to help neighbors whose children were still small. Midwives delivered babies in return for cheese or eggs. Women nursed sick neighbors, whom they might later call on for similar help. These transactions allowed most New Englanders to enjoy a comfortable life, one that many Virginians might have envied.

New England prospered by developing a diversified economy less vulnerable to depression than Virginia's. New Englanders became such skilled shipbuilders and seafaring merchants that by the 1670s, London merchants complained about competition from them. England itself had little use for the dried fish, livestock, salted meat, and wood products that New England vessels carried, but enterprising merchants found exactly the market they needed in the West Indies.

QUICK REVIEW

Childhood in New England

- Children went to work shortly after their fifth birthday.
- Around age 10 children began doing more complex work.
- Many early teens performed work similar to that of adults.

COMPETITION IN THE CARIBBEAN

WHAT WAS the connection between sugar cultivation and slavery in the Caribbean?

The Spanish claimed all Caribbean islands by right of Columbus's discovery, but during the seventeenth century, France, the Netherlands, and England acquired their own island colonies. Europeans competed for these islands at first in the hope that they would yield precious metals and provide bases for privateering expeditions. It eventually became clear that the islands would produce treasure of another sort—sugar, which was in great demand in Europe. In order to reap the enormous profits that sugar could bring, Caribbean planters of all nationalities imported enormous numbers of African people to work as slaves under the harshest conditions to be found in the New World.

SUGAR AND SLAVES

The Spanish and Portuguese first experimented with sugar production on the Canaries and other Atlantic islands in the fifteenth century. Europeans prized sugar as a sweetener, preservative, decoration—even a medicine—and paid high prices for it. Columbus accordingly brought sugar canes to the New World on his second voyage, in 1493. Soon after the Spanish began growing sugar on Santo Domingo, they began importing African slaves as workers, because Indian slaves were dying in great numbers. The Spanish brought sugar to the South American mainland, as did the Portuguese, who turned Brazil into one of the world's major producers.

At first, English colonists who came to the West Indies in the 1620s and 1630s raised tobacco and imported indentured servants to work their fields. By that time, however, tobacco prices were dropping. Moreover, the disease environment of the West Indies proved even harsher than in the Chesapeake, and settlers died in great numbers.

By the 1640s, a Barbados planter boasted of "a great change on this island of late from the worse to the better, praised be God." That change was a shift from tobacco to sugar cane. Dutch merchants helped finance this transition. Sugar rapidly transformed the West Indies. Planters deforested whole islands to raise sugar cane. They stopped planting food crops and raising livestock—thereby creating a demand for lumber and provisions that boosted New England's economy.

For some years after the transition to sugar, English planters continued to import white indentured servants, including kidnapped English and Irish youths, and supplemented the labor force with African slaves. Due to the islands' unhealthy environment and harsh working conditions, servants died in great numbers. England could barely meet the demand for workers, and English workers, if they survived, often proved rebellious. The English switched to African laborers, whom they considered better suited to agricultural work in a tropical climate. The planters' decision had an enormous impact on English colonial life, first in the islands and then on the mainland, where slavery would develop later in the seventeenth century (see Chapter 3).

African slaves working at a sugar mill in the West Indies, probably on a Dutch-owned island: line engraving, 17th century.

A Biracial Society

As happened on virtually all the Caribbean islands, the English West Indies developed a biracial plantation society—the first in the English colonial world. By 1700, more than 250,000 slaves had been brought to the English islands, and they soon constituted a majority of the population.

slave codes A series of laws passed mainly in the southern colonies in the late seventeenth and early eighteenth centuries to define the status of slaves and codify the denial of basic civil rights to them.

Laws, sometimes called **slave codes,** declared slavery to be a lifelong condition that passed from slave parents to their children. Slaves had no legal rights and were under the complete control of their masters. Only rarely would masters who killed slaves face prosecution, and those found guilty were subject only to fines. Slaves, in contrast, faced appalling punishments even for minor offenses. They could be whipped, branded, or maimed for stealing food or harboring a runaway compatriot. Serious crimes such as murder or arson brought execution without trial. Slaves who rebelled were burned to death.

QUICK REVIEW

Slave Codes

- Slavery was a lifelong condition that passed from parents to children.
- Slaves had no legal rights.
- Masters were all but exempt from prosecution for mistreatment of slaves.
- Slaves were subject to punishment at the discretion of masters.

Astonishingly, slaves maintained some elements of normal life even under these brutal conditions. When masters began to import African women as well as men—hoping to create a self-reproducing labor force—slaves formed families and preserved at least some African traditions. They gave their children African names. They celebrated and worked to the rhythms of African music. And slaves drew on their West African heritage to perform elaborate funeral rituals, often burying their dead with food and other goods to accompany them on the journey to the afterlife.

White planters, profiting handsomely from their slaves' toil, lived better than many English gentlemen. But sugar made relatively few white colonists wealthy. Its production required a heavy investment in land, slaves, mills, and equipment. As great planters took vast amounts of land for themselves, freed servants and small farmers struggled to survive. After 1650, many of these poor men, looking for other places to live, headed for the mainland. They were joined by planters looking for a place to expand their operations.

THE RESTORATION COLONIES

HOW DID the proprietors of the Restoration colonies shape their development?

The initial burst of English colonization ended in 1640 when England tottered on the brink of civil war. With the restoration of Charles II to the throne in 1660, however, interest in North America revived. During his reign (1660–1685), four new colonies—Carolina, Pennsylvania, New Jersey, and New York—were created (see Map 2–3). All were proprietary colonies, essentially the private property of the people to whom they had been given. (See the Overview table, English Colonies in the Seventeenth Century.)

EARLY CAROLINA: COLONIAL ARISTOCRACY AND SLAVE LABOR

In 1663, Charles II granted a group of supporters an enormous tract of land stretching from southern Virginia to northern Florida. The proprietors, who included several Barbados planters, called their colony Carolina, after *Carolus*, the Latin form of the king's name.

One of the proprietors, Anthony Ashley Cooper, worked closely with his secretary, John Locke, to devise the **Fundamental Constitutions of Carolina.** This plan to ensure the colony's stability linked property ownership and political rights to a hierarchical social order. It called for the creation of a colonial aristocracy, who would own two-fifths of the land and wield extensive political power. Below them, a large class of freeholders would own small farms and elect representatives to an assembly. At the bottom of the social order would be slaves. This plan never went into effect. People moved in from Virginia and the West Indies and settled where they pleased. They even voted in the assembly to reject the Fundamental Constitutions.

Fundamental Constitutions of Carolina A complex plan for organizing the colony of Carolina, drafted in 1669 by Anthony Ashley Cooper and John Locke.

The colonists at first raised livestock to be sold to the West Indies. But the introduction of rice in the 1690s transformed the settlers' economy, making it, as one planter noted, "as much their staple Commodity, as Sugar is to Barbados and Jamaica, or Tobacco to Virginia and Maryland." The English had never grown rice, but West Africans had. Rice cultivation in Carolina coincided with an increase in the number of African slaves there, who probably introduced the crop. Ironically, the profits earned from rice persuaded Carolina planters to invest even more heavily in slave labor.

Carolina society soon resembled the sugar islands from which many of its founders had come. By 1708, there were more black slaves than white settlers; two decades after that, black people outnumbered white people by two to one. Rice farming required a substantial investment in land, labor, and equipment, including dikes and dams for flooding fields. Those who could afford such an investment set themselves up as planters in Carolina's coastal rice district, acquiring large estates and forcing poorer settlers to move elsewhere.

Some of these dislocated settlers went to the northern part of Carolina, where the land and climate were unsuited to rice. There they raised tobacco and livestock, and produced pitch, tar, and timber products from the region's pine forests. So different were the two regions that the colony formally split into two provinces—North and South Carolina—in 1729.

South Carolina rice planters became some of the wealthiest colonists on the mainland. But their luxurious style of life came at a price. As Carolina's slave population grew, planters dreaded the prospect of slave rebellion. To avert this nightmare, they enacted slave codes as harsh as those of the sugar islands. Carolina evolved into a racially divided society founded on the oppression of a black majority and permeated by fear.

QUICK REVIEW

Rice and Slavery

- 1690s: Rice introduced in Carolina.
- 1708: Black slaves outnumber white settlers.
- 1730s: Blacks outnumber whites two to one.

PENNSYLVANIA: THE DREAM OF TOLERATION AND PEACE

Even as early Carolina diverged from the plans of its founders, another Englishman dreamed of creating a colonial utopia. William Penn put his plans into action in 1681, when Charles II

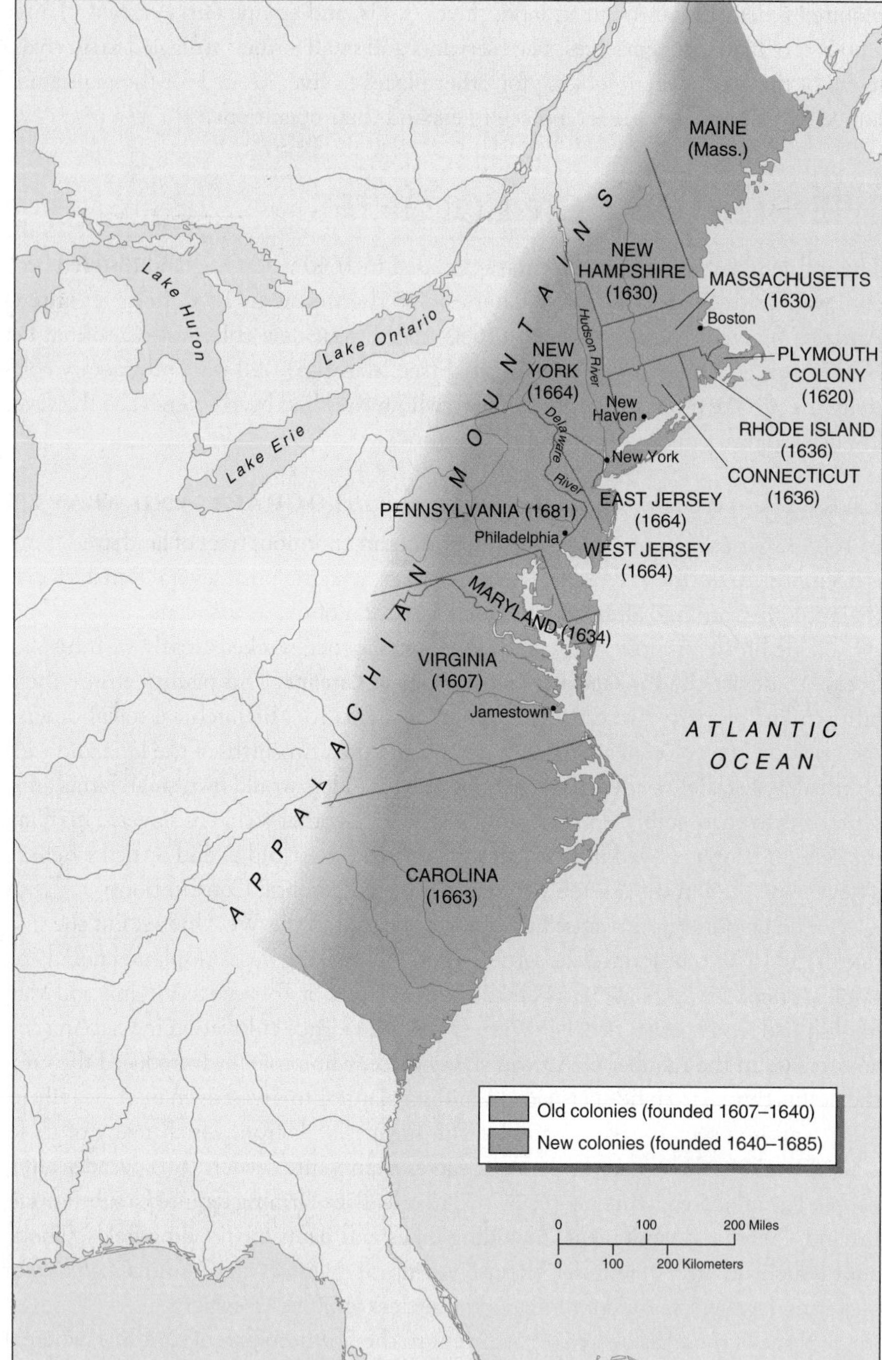

MAP 2–3 **English North American Colonies, c. 1685** After the restoration of Charles II in 1660, several large proprietary colonies joined earlier English settlements in New England and the Chesapeake. By 1685, a growing number of English settlers solidified England's claim to the Atlantic coast from Maine (then part of Massachusetts Bay Colony) to the southern edge of Carolina.

How might the establishment of the new colonies (founded 1640–1685) have shaped the development of the old colonies (founded 1607–1640)? What connections were beginning to emerge between the British colonies by the end of the seventeenth century?

Quakers Members of the Society of Friends, a radical religious group that arose in the mid-seventeenth century. Quakers rejected formal theology, focusing instead on the Holy Spirit that dwelt within them.

granted him a huge tract of land north of Maryland. Penn intended his colony to be a model of justice and peace, as well as a refuge for members of the Society of Friends, or **Quakers,** a persecuted religious sect to which Penn belonged.

The Society of Friends was one of many radical religious groups that emerged in England during the civil war. Rejecting predestination, they maintained that every soul had a spark of grace and that salvation was possible for all who heeded that "Inner Light." Instead of formal religious services, Quakers held meetings at which silence reigned until someone, inspired by the Inner Light, rose to speak.

Quaker beliefs had disturbing social and political implications. Although they did not advocate complete equality of the sexes, Quakers granted women spiritual equality with men, allowing them to preach, hold separate prayer meetings, and exercise authority over "women's matters." Arguing that social distinctions were not the work of God, Quakers refused to defer to their "betters." Because their faith required them to renounce the use of force, Quakers refused to perform military service, which their enemies considered tantamount to treason.

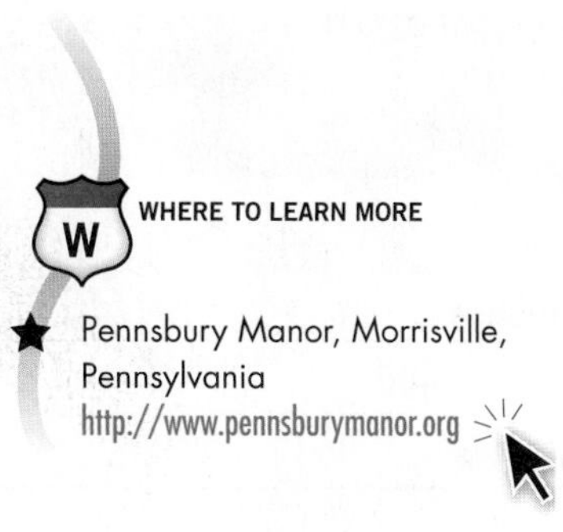

W
WHERE TO LEARN MORE
Pennsbury Manor, Morrisville, Pennsylvania
http://www.pennsburymanor.org

When English authorities began harassing Quakers, William Penn, who was himself jailed briefly, conceived his plan for a New World refuge. Using his father's connection with the king, he acquired the land that became Pennsylvania ("Penn's Woods") and recruited settlers from among Europe's oppressed peoples and persecuted religious sects. By 1700, about eighteen thousand emigrants had left England, Wales, Scotland, Ireland, and various German provinces for the new colony.

Many came in families and settled in an area occupied by the Delaware Indians, whose numbers, though still substantial, had recently been reduced by disease and warfare. The "holy experiment" required colonists to live "as Neighbours and friends" with the Indians as well as with one another. Penn aimed to accomplish this by paying Indians for land and regulating trade. As long as Penn controlled his colony, relations between the settlers and the Indians were generally peaceful. Relations between Penn and the settlers, however, were less cordial.

In the **Frame of Government** he devised for Pennsylvania, Penn remained true to his Quaker principles with a provision allowing for religious freedom. But true to his aristocratic origins, he designed a legislature with limited powers and reserved considerable authority for himself. When Penn returned to England after a brief stay in the colony (1682–1684), the settlers began squabbling among themselves. The governor and council, both appointed by Penn, fought with elected members of the assembly. Penn's opponents—many of whom were fellow Quakers—objected to his proprietary privileges, including his control of foreign trade and his collection of fees from landholders. Settlers on the lower Delaware River, which the crown had added to Penn's colony to give its port city, Philadelphia, access to the sea, gained autonomy for themselves with their own legislature, in effect creating an unofficial colony that later became Delaware.

Frame of Government William Penn's constitution for Pennsylvania, which included a provision allowing for religious freedom.

By 1720, Pennsylvania's ethnically and religiously diverse colonists numbered more than thirty thousand. The colony, with some of the richest farmland along the Atlantic coast, was widely known as the "best poor man's country in the world." Growing wheat and other crops, the settlers lived mostly on scattered farms rather than in towns. From the busy port of Philadelphia, ships carried much of the harvest to markets in the West Indies and southern Europe.

New Netherland Becomes New York

The proprietary colonies of New York and New Jersey were carved out of the Dutch colony of New Netherland. Competition between the English and the Dutch intensified in the mid-seventeenth century as the two peoples struggled for trade supremacy on the high seas. Their antagonism generated two Anglo-Dutch wars in 1652–1654 and 1665–1667. In the New World, tensions were heightened by the presence of English colonists on Long Island, which the Dutch claimed for themselves.

In 1664, Charles II brought matters to a head by claiming that since the site of New Netherland lay within the bounds of the original charter of Virginia, the land belonged to England. He granted the territory to his brother James, duke of York, who sent ships to back up England's claim. Their arrival provoked a rebellion by Long Island's English colonists, leading the Dutch governor, Peter Stuyvesant—who commanded just 150 soldiers—to surrender without firing a shot.

The duke of York became proprietor of this new English possession, which was renamed New York. James immediately created another colony, New Jersey, which he granted to his supporters.

New York, which James retained for himself, was the most valuable part of the former Dutch colony. It included the port of New York City (the former New Amsterdam) and the Hudson Valley with its fur trade. James encouraged Dutch colonists to remain and promoted immigration from England to strengthen the colony and gain income from land sales. By 1700, the settlers numbered twenty thousand.

OVERVIEW English Colonies in the Seventeenth Century

Colony	Date of Founding	Established Religion	Economy	Government
Virginia	1607	Anglican	Tobacco	Royal (after 1625)
Plymouth	1620	Puritan	Mixed farming	Corporate
St. Christopher	1624	Anglican	Sugar	Royal
Barbados	1627	Anglican	Sugar	Royal
Nevis	1628	Anglican	Sugar	Royal
Massachusetts (including present-day Maine)	1630	Puritan	Mixed farming, fishing, shipbuilding	Corporate
New Hampshire	1630 (first settlement, annexed to Massachusetts 1643–1679)	Puritan	Mixed farming	Corporate (royal after 1679)
Antigua	1632	Anglican	Sugar	Royal
Montserrat	1632	Anglican	Sugar	Royal
Maryland	1634	None (Anglican after 1692)	Tobacco	Proprietary
Rhode Island	1636	None	Mixed farming	Corporate
Connecticut	1636	Puritan	Mixed farming	Corporate
New Haven	1638	Puritan	Mixed farming	Corporate
Jamaica	1655 (captured from Spanish)	Anglican	Sugar	Royal
Carolina	1663	Anglican	Rice	Proprietary
New York	1664 (captured from Dutch)	None	Mixed farming, furs	Proprietary (royal after 1685)
New Jersey	1664	None	Mixed farming	Proprietary
Pennsylvania	1681	None	Wheat, mixed farming	Proprietary

CONCLUSION

Even as England gained a permanent foothold in North America, it faced vigorous competition from France and the Netherlands. A new Atlantic world was beginning to emerge as the migration of people and goods across the ocean linked the Old and New Worlds as never before.

Commerce was the main focus of the short-lived New Netherland colony and a more durable New France. Profits from the fur trade encouraged the French to maintain friendly relations with their Indian allies and ensured that French kings would closely monitor the colony's affairs. English colonization was a more haphazard process. English kings granted charters for new colonies and let them develop more or less on their own. England had no equivalent in the seventeenth century of the imperial bureaucracies Spain and France created to manage their New World holdings.

The result was a highly diverse set of English colonies stretching from the Maine coast to the Caribbean. Settlers adjusted to different environments, developed different economies and

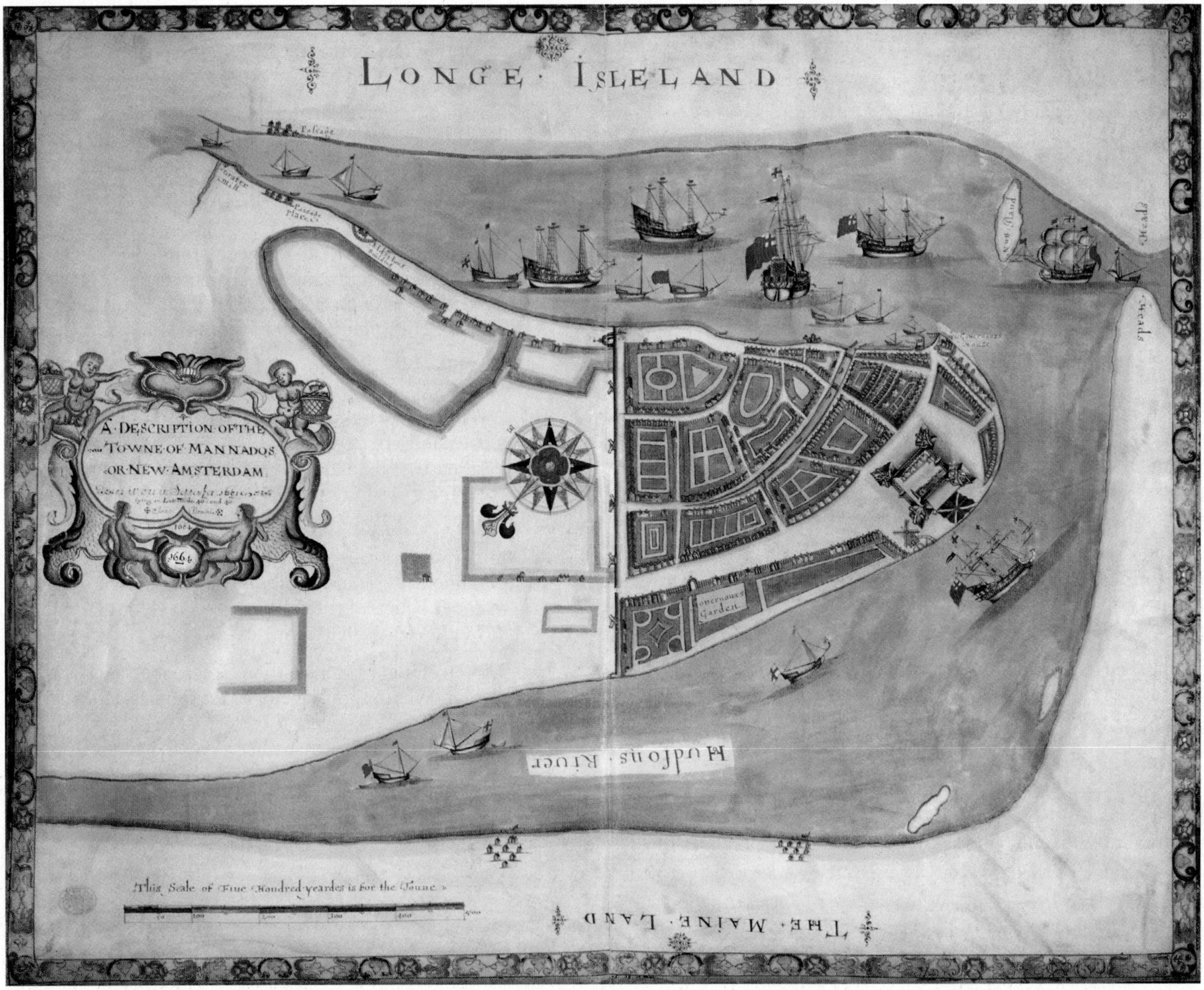

James, Duke of York, received this map of New Amsterdam in 1664, when England seized New Netherland from the Dutch and the Duke became proprietor of the new colony of New York. The top of the map is oriented to the east, with the lower tip of Manhattan Island facing to the right.

labor systems, and worshiped in different churches. In South Carolina, New York, Pennsylvania, and the West Indies, most colonists were not even of English origin. What held these colonies together—besides their establishment under English charters and their enmity toward the Spanish and French—was an overlay of common English institutions of government. By the mid-1680s, all the colonies had legislatures that provided for self-government and laws and judicial institutions based on English models.

The planting of French, Dutch, and English colonies not only ended Spain's monopoly of settlement in North America but also challenged the Indians' hold on the continent. Forced to deal with a rising tide of settlers and often to choose sides between European rivals, native peoples adapted to rapidly changing circumstances. Transplanted Europeans adapted too, not only in their dealings with native peoples but also in finding and controlling the laborers they needed to make their colonies prosper. For English colonists this meant the widespread adoption of slavery, an institution that did not exist in England itself. For millions of Africans, the result was forced migration to the New World.

WHERE TO LEARN MORE

Jamestown Settlement, near Williamsburg, Virginia. Site includes replicas of first English passenger ships to Virginia, a reconstructed Powhatan Village, the re-created James Fort, and galleries with Indian and English artifacts. Visitors can also see archaeological excavations of site of the actual James Fort, as well as sample artifacts recovered from the area. The website http://www.virtualjamestown.org/ offers a wealth of fascinating information about English and Indian settlement in the Jamestown area.

St. Mary's City, Maryland. Visitors to this site of the first permanent settlement under the Calvert family may tour the area and view exhibits and living history programs that describe life in early Maryland. The website http://www.stmaryscity.org/ contains information about the historic site of St. Mary's City and has links to a virtual tour of the area.

Plimoth Plantation, Plymouth, Massachusetts. A living history museum, Plimoth Plantation re-creates colony life in the year 1627. There are reproductions of the English village and a Wampanoag settlement. Visitors may also see a replica of the *Mayflower*. The website http://www.plimoth.org/ provides information for visitors.

Pennsbury Manor, Morrisville, Pennsylvania. A reconstruction of William Penn's seventeenth-century plantation, this site includes furnished buildings and restored gardens. Visitor information about the site and William Penn's life can be found at http://www.pennsburymanor.org/.

REVIEW QUESTIONS

1. To what extent was Richard Frethorne's experience typical of that of English colonists in the New World? What were the causes of his distress?
2. Comparing French, Dutch, and English colonies, which ones attracted the most settlers, and which the fewest? In what colonies were women scarce? What impact did these differences in emigration have on the various colonies' development?
3. Which English settlements were proprietary colonies? Did they share any common characteristics? What plans did the various proprietors have for their colonies, and to what extent were those plans put into effect?
4. When Virginia's settlers first arrived, they encountered a numerous and powerful confederation of Powhatan Indians. New England's colonists, in contrast, began their settlements after epidemics had drastically reduced the local native population. In what ways did the presence or absence of substantial Indian populations affect each region's early history?
5. In both Massachusetts and Pennsylvania, religion figured prominently as a motive for settlement. What were the religious beliefs of the settlers in each colony, and how did those beliefs help shape each colony's development?
6. Three colonial regions—the Chesapeake, the West Indies, and Carolina—developed economies dependent on staple crops. What were those crops? In what ways did staple-crop agriculture shape society in each region?
7. In what ways did events in Europe affect the founding of colonies in North America?

KEY TERMS

Act for Religious Toleration (p. 41)
Anglican (p. 42)
Coureurs de bois (p. 34)
Covenant (p. 44)
Frame of Government (p. 51)
Fundamental Constitutions of Carolina (p. 49)
Headright system (p. 38)
House of Burgesses (p. 38)
Indentured servants (p. 34)
Joint-stock company (p. 37)
Pequot War (p. 44)
Pilgrims (p. 43)
Proprietary colony (p. 40)
Puritans (p. 40)
Quakers (p. 50)
Separatists (p. 43)
Slave codes (p. 48)

PEARSON myhistorylab Connections

Reinforce what you learned in this chapter by studying the many documents, images, maps, review tools, and videos available at **www.myhistorylab.com**.

Read and Review

Study and **Review** **Study Plan: Chapter 2**

Read the **Document**

Richard Frethorne, Letter to His Parents (1623)

John Winthrop, "A Model of Christian Charity" (1630)

Agreement between the Settlers at New Plymouth (Mayflower Compact) (1620)

Captain John Smith to Queen Anne (1617)

Father Isaac Jogues, Description of New York (1646)

Laws of Virginia (1610–1611)

Prenuptial Agreement (1653)

The Trial of Anne Hutchinson (1638)

See the **Map** *The Colonies to 1740*

Research and Explore

Read the **Document**

Personal Journeys Online

From Then to Now Online: Tobacco and the American Economy

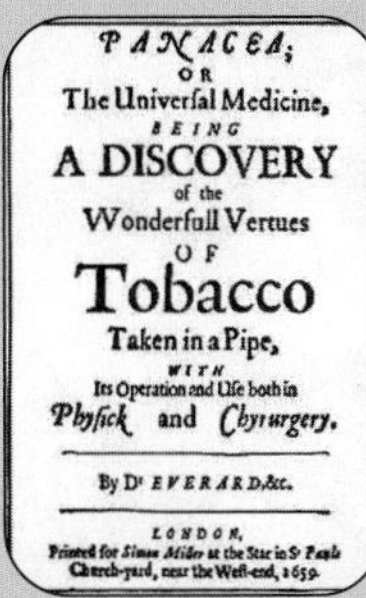
PANACEA; OR The Universal Medicine, BEING A DISCOVERY of the Wonderfull Vertues OF Tobacco Taken in a Pipe, WITH Its Operation and Use both in Physick and Chyrurgery. By Dr EVERARD, &c. LONDON, Printed for Simon Miller at the Star in St Pauls Church-yard, near the West-end, 1659.

Exploring America: Exploitation of the Americas

Estate Inventories of Early Virginians

Exploring America: Jamestown

Hear the **Audio**

Hear the audio files for Chapter 2 at **www.myhistorylab.com**.

3

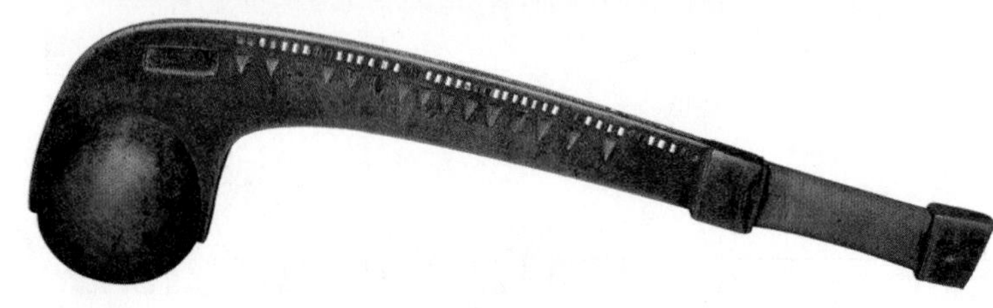

A Meeting of Cultures

NEGROES
FOR SALE.

I will sell by Public Auction, on Tuesday of next Court, being the 29th of November, *Eight Valuable Family Servants*, consisting of one Negro Man, a first-rate field hand, one No. 1 Boy, 17 years o: age, a trusty house servant, one excellent Cook, one House-Maid, and one Seamstress. The balance are under 12 years of age. They are sold for no fault, but in consequence of my going to reside North. Also a quantity of Household and Kitchen Furniture, Stable Lot, &c. Terms accommodating, and made known on day of sale.

Jacob August.
P. J. TURNBULL, *Auctioneer*.

Warrenton, *October* 28, 1859.

Printed at the *News* office, Warrenton, North Carolina.

This illustration of the African slave trade shows a group of Africans taken from a slave ship that was captured by HMS *Undine*.
Top photo: King Philip's War Club. Published courtesy of Fruitlands Museums, Harvard, Massachusetts.

Hear the Audio
Hear the audio files for Chapter 3 at **www.myhistorylab.com**.

INDIANS AND EUROPEANS *(page 59)*

WHAT WERE the consequences of trade between Indians and Europeans?

AFRICANS AND EUROPEANS *(page 67)*

HOW AND why did race-based slavery develop in British North America?

EUROPEAN LABORERS IN EARLY AMERICA *(page 76)*

WHAT METHODS did Europeans employ to acquire and manage labor in colonial America?

ONE AMERICAN JOURNEY

One day [in 1756], when all our people were gone out to their work as usual, and only I and my sister were left to mind the house, two men and a woman got over our walls, and in a moment seized us both; and without giving us time to cry out, or to make any resistance, they stopped our mouths and ran off with us into the nearest wood. Here they tied our hands, and continued to carry us as far as they could. . . . Thus I continued to travel, both by land and by water, through different countries and various nations, till at the end of six or seven months after I had been kidnapped, I arrived at the sea coast. . . .

The first object that saluted my eyes when I arrived on the coast was the sea, and a slave ship, which was then riding at anchor, and waiting for its cargo. These filled me with astonishment, that was soon converted into terror, which I am yet at a loss to describe. . . . I was immediately handled and tossed up to see if I was sound, by some of the crew; and I was now persuaded that I had got into a world of bad spirits, and that they were going to kill me. Their complexions too, differing so much from ours, their long hair, and the language they spoke, which was very different from any I had ever heard, united to confirm me in this belief. . . . I asked. . . . if we were not to be eaten by those white men with horrible looks, red faces, and long hair. . . .

In a little time after, amongst the poor chained men, I found some of my own nation. . . . They gave me to understand we were to be carried to these white people's country to work for them. . . . [Many weeks later] we were landed up a river a good way from the sea, about Virginia county, where we saw few of our native Africans, and not one soul who could talk to me.

Olaudah Equiano, *The Interesting Narrative of the Life of Olaudah Equiano, or Gustavus Vassa, The African.*

Read the **Document** at **www.myhistorylab.com**

Personal Journeys Online

- **Pedro Naranjol, *Indian Account of the Pueblo Revolt,* 1680.**
- **Job ben Solomon, *Some Memoirs of the Life of Job,* 1734. Description of Job's capture and sale into slavery.**
- **Gottlieb Mittelberger, *Journey to Pennsylvania,* 1756. Description of the arrival of German redemptioners to Pennsylvania.**

OLAUDAH EQUIANO, born in 1745 in the African kingdom of Benin, was only a boy when his terrifying journey to America began. The son of an Igbo chief, he was caught in the web of an expanding transatlantic slave trade that reached from the African interior to nearly every port town in the Americas and the Caribbean. From modest beginnings in the sixteenth century, the slave trade had expanded dramatically, transforming every society it touched. Equiano's Virginia scarcely resembled that of John Smith. Tobacco still reigned supreme, but by the mid-eighteenth century, more workers were black than white.

At the same time, in Virginia and elsewhere in North America, Indian peoples faced new challenges as they endeavored to maintain their independence despite a flood of immigrants from Europe and Africa. Indians employed different tactics—adaptation, coexistence, diplomacy, resistance—to assert their claims to land and their right to participate in the events and deliberations that affected their lives. The America to which Olaudah Equiano had been forcibly transported remained a place where Indian voices had to be heeded.

Equiano's journey did not end in Virginia. Over the next quarter-century, he traveled to other mainland colonies, the West Indies, England, Turkey, Portugal, and Spain. He worked as the servant of a naval officer, a barber, a laborer, an overseer, saving money to purchase his freedom. Such an extraordinary career testified to Equiano's resilience and determination. It also bore witness to the emergence of an international market for laborers, which—like slavery and Indian relations—shaped the development of North America. Thousands of people from England, Scotland, Ireland, and Germany attempted to take advantage of that market and seek their fortunes in America, increasing the white population and expanding onto new lands. The interactions of Indians, Africans, and Europeans created not one but many New Worlds. ✦

INDIANS AND EUROPEANS

WHAT WERE the consequences of trade between Indians and Europeans?

Although, by 1750, European colonists and African slaves together outnumbered Indians north of the Rio Grande, Native Americans still dominated much of the continent. Colonists remained clustered along the coasts, and some native peoples had scarcely seen any Europeans.

The character of the relationship between Indians and Europeans depended on more than relative population size and the length of time they had been in contact. It was also shaped by the intentions of the newcomers—whether they came to extract resources, to trade, to settle, or to gain converts—and by the responses of Native American groups intent on preserving their cultures. The result was a variety of regionally distinctive New World communities.

Indian Workers in the Spanish Borderlands

More than any other European colonists, the Spanish sought direct control over Indian laborers. Their success in doing so depended on two factors: the existence of sizable Indian communities and Spanish military force. Native villages provided workers and existing structures of government that the Spanish converted to their own uses. At the same time, Spanish soldiers ensured that the Indians obeyed orders even though they greatly outnumbered the colonists.

CHRONOLOGY

1440s	Portuguese enter slave trade in West Africa.
c. 1450	Iroquois form Great League of Peace and Power.
1610–1614	First war between English settlers and Powhatan Indians.
1619	First Africans arrive in Virginia.
1622–1632	Second war between English settlers and Powhatan Indians.
1637	Pequot War in New England.
1640s	Slave labor begins to dominate in the West Indies.
	First phase of the Beaver Wars.
1651	First "praying town" established at Natick, Massachusetts.
1661	Maryland law defines slavery as lifelong, inheritable status.
1670	Virginia law defines status of slaves.
1675–1676	King Philip's War in New England.
1676	Bacon's Rebellion in Virginia.
1680	Pueblo Revolt in New Mexico.
1680s	Second phase of Beaver Wars begins.
1688–1697	England and France fight the War of the League of Augsburg (known in America as King William's War).
1690s	Shift from white indentured servants to black slaves as principal labor force in the Chesapeake.
1701	Iroquois adopt policy of neutrality toward French and English.
1711–1713	Tuscarora War in Carolina.
1713	Beginnings of substantial Scottish, Scots-Irish, and German immigration to colonies.
1715–1716	Yamasee War in Carolina.
1720s	Black population begins to increase naturally in English mainland colonies.
1730	Major slave insurrection in Virginia.
1732	Georgia established.
1739	Stono Rebellion in South Carolina.
1741	Slave conspiracy discovered in New York City.
1750	Slavery legalized in Georgia.
1760–1775	Peak of European and African immigration to English colonies.

encomienda In the Spanish colonies, the grant to a Spanish settler of a certain number of Indian subjects, who would pay him tribute in goods and labor.

repartimiento In the Spanish colonies, the assignment of Indian workers to labor on public works projects.

One important method of labor control was the ***encomienda.*** *Encomiendas*, granted to influential Spaniards in New Mexico, gave these colonists the right to collect tribute from the native peoples living on a specific piece of land. The tribute usually took the form of corn, blankets, and animal hides. It was not supposed to include forced labor, but often it did.

The Spanish also relied on the ***repartimiento,*** a mandatory draft of Indian labor for public projects. Laws stated that native workers should be paid and limited the length of their service, but the Spanish often ignored these provisions and sometimes compelled Indians to work on private estates.

The native peoples strongly resented these Spanish strategies. Spanish demands for labor and tribute remained constant, even when Indian populations declined from disease or crops failed, and workers who resisted were severely punished. Resentments simmered beneath a surface of cooperation until late in the seventeenth century, when long-standing native anger burst forth in rebellion.

The Web of Trade

Not all economic exchanges between Indians and Europeans were directly coercive. Indians sometimes used trade relations to exert influence over Europeans. Native Americans thought of trade as one aspect of a broader alliance between peoples. Europeans who wished to trade with Indians had to prove their friendship by offering gifts and military aid as well as manufactured goods.

The French readily adapted to the Native American understanding of trade, realizing that good relations were essential to keeping New France's fur trade operating smoothly. The fur trade benefited Indians too. "The Beaver does everything perfectly well," noted one native leader, "it makes kettles, hatchets, swords, knives, bread; and, in short, it makes everything."

The benefits of trade were immediate and obvious; the problems were slower to appear. The one exception was the problem of disease, which followed almost immediately from Indians' contacts with European traders (see Figure 3–1). The Huron population declined by half in just six years between 1634 and 1640.

This detail from a map illustration depicts an encounter between a French trader and an Indian hunter in the Canadian wilderness. The exchange of European goods for furs was central to the economy of New France.

Although Indian hunters enjoyed considerable autonomy in their work, French merchants began to use economic pressure to control them. By supplying Indians with trade goods in advance, merchants obligated them to bring in furs as payment. Extending credit in this way allowed the French to control native workers without having to subjugate them.

The French could control the Indians through credit because native peoples had grown increasingly dependent on European manufactures. In many communities, Indians abandoned native crafts and instead relied on imported goods. As a result, they had no alternative but to increase their hunting in order to have furs to trade for what they needed. One consequence of this situation was overhunting; as early as the 1640s, beaver could no longer be found in much of New England, New York, and Pennsylvania.

Trade with Europeans eventually encouraged violence and warfare. Indians had fought one another before European colonization, but these wars were generally limited in scope and destructiveness. Warriors conducted raids mainly to seize captives rather than to kill large numbers of their enemies. After Europeans arrived, warriors raided their enemies to replace family members lost to disease and fought to avenge losses resulting from the fierce competition for a diminishing supply of fur-bearing animals. The proliferation of firearms made the conflicts deadlier, and more casualties led to further wars.

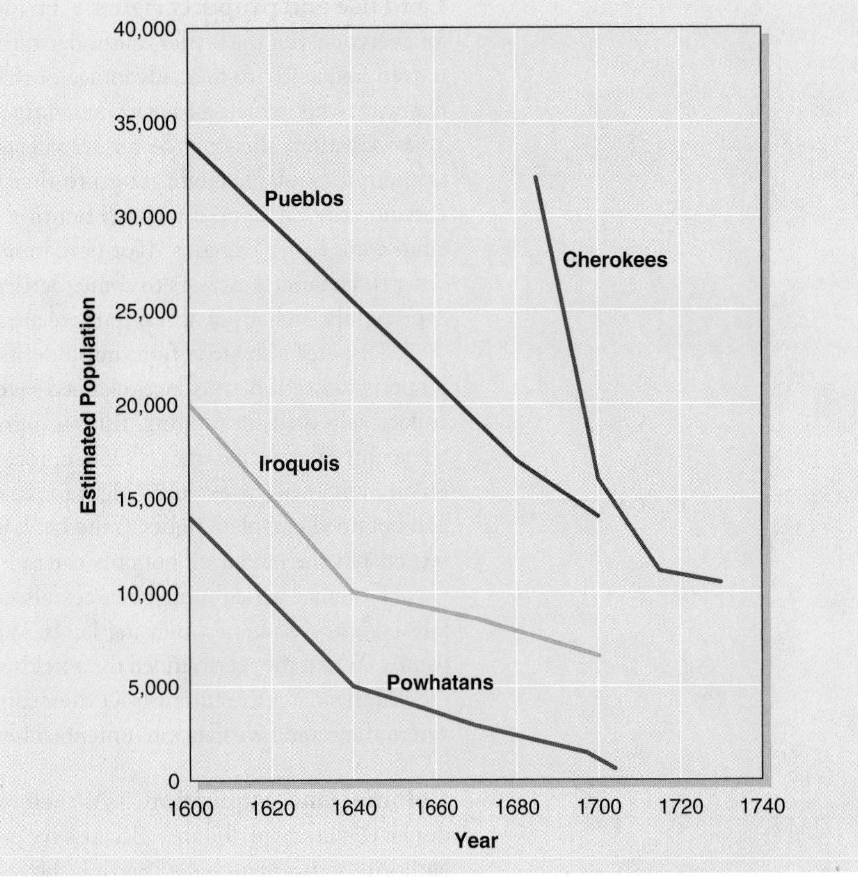

FIGURE 3–1 **Estimated Populations of Selected Indian Peoples, 1600–1730** Indian populations shrank dramatically due to diseases brought by Europeans from the Old World. By about 1750, native peoples had become a minority of the inhabitants of America north of the Rio Grande.

Data Sources: Daniel Richter, *The Ordeal of the Longhouse* (1992); Helen Rountree, *Pocahontas's People* (1990); David Weber, *The Spanish Frontier in North America* (1992); Peter Wood et al., eds., *Powhatan's Mantle* (1989).

The **Beaver Wars,** a long struggle between the Hurons and the Iroquois that began in the 1640s, illustrated the ferocity of such contests. The Hurons were trading partners and allies with the French, and the Iroquois had forged ties with Dutch merchants in the Hudson River Valley. To satisfy the European demand for furs, the Hurons and Iroquois both hunted beaver at an unsustainable rate. By the 1630s, they had killed nearly all the beavers on their own lands and began to look elsewhere. The Hurons raised more corn to trade for furs with Indians living north of the Great Lakes, where beavers were still abundant. The Iroquois, however, began to raid Huron trading parties and attack Huron villages.

Beaver Wars Series of bloody conflicts, occurring between 1640s and 1680s, during which the Iroquois fought the Hurons and French for control of the fur trade in the east and the Great Lakes region.

The Iroquois triumphed in this struggle largely because the Dutch supplied them with guns, whereas the French were reluctant to arm the Hurons. In the end, thousands of Hurons were killed or captured, and many others fled westward. The cycle of warfare did not end with the Hurons' destruction. The victorious Iroquois went on to challenge Indian nations near the Great Lakes and in the Ohio Valley.

QUICK REVIEW

French-Indian Trade: The Costs for Indians

- Disease.
- Dependence on European technology.
- Increased violence and warfare.

Displacing Native Americans in the English Colonies

In New France and New Netherland, where the fur trade took precedence over farming, Indians outnumbered Europeans. This numerical superiority and their key role as suppliers of furs allowed native peoples to negotiate with settlers from a position of strength. The situation was different in the English colonies, whose settlers came to farm and thus competed directly with Indians for land.

Land use and property rights. English settlers at first assumed that there was enough land for everyone. But the settlers misunderstood how Indians used land. Eastern Algonquian peoples moved frequently to take advantage of the land's diversity. They cleared areas for villages and planting fields, which native women farmed until the soil grew less fertile. Then they moved to a new location, allowing the former village site to return to forest. In ten to twenty years, they or their descendants might return to that site to clear and farm it again. In the winter, village communities broke up into small hunting bands. Thus what the colonists considered "vacant" lands were either being used for nonfarming activities such as hunting or regaining fertility in order to be farmed in years to come. Settlers who built towns on abandoned native village sites deprived the Indians of access to these areas.

Disputes also arose from misunderstandings about the definition of land ownership and property rights. Indian villages claimed sovereignty over a certain territory, which their members collectively used for farming, fishing, hunting, and gathering. No Indian claimed individual ownership of a specific tract of land. Europeans, of course, did, and for them ownership conferred on an individual the exclusive right to use or sell a piece of land. The settlers assumed that they had obtained complete rights to the land, whereas the Indians assumed that they had given the settlers not the land itself but only the right to use it.

Colonial agricultural practices also strained relations with the Indians. Cutting down forests destroyed Indian hunting lands. When colonists dammed rivers, they disturbed Indian fishing. When they surrounded their fields with fences, colonists made trespassers of natives who crossed them. Yet the colonists let their cattle and pigs loose to graze in the woods and meadows, where they could wander into unfenced Indian cornfields and damage the crops.

Colonial land acquisition. As their numbers grew, the colonists acquired Indian lands and displaced native inhabitants. Because Indians owned land collectively, only their leaders had the authority to negotiate sales. Settlers, however, sometimes bought land from individual Indians who had no right to sell it. Because land transfers were usually arranged through interpreters and recorded in English, Indians were not always fully informed of the terms of sale. Even Indians who willingly sold land grew resentful as colonists approached them for more. Finally, native peoples could be forced to sell land to settle debts to English creditors.

QUICK REVIEW

Native Americans and English Settlers

- Influx of settlers exposed native peoples to disease.
- Settlers' desire for land led to violence between settlers and Indians.
- By 1650 settlers outnumbered Indians in some areas.

Settlers occasionally obtained land by fraud. Some colonists simply settled on Indian lands and appealed to colonial governments for help when the Indians objected. Land speculators amplified this kind of unrest as they sought to acquire land as cheaply as possible and sell it for as much as they could.

Finally, colonists often seized Indian lands in the aftermath of war, as befell, among many others, the Pequots in 1637 in Connecticut and, in Carolina, the Tuscaroras in 1713 and the Yamasees in 1715. In each case, settlers moved onto land left vacant after colonial forces killed, captured, and dispersed native peoples. The colonists' hunger for land generated relentless pressure on native peoples. The pattern of mutual suspicion and territorial competition would be difficult to alter.

Bringing Christianity to Native Peoples

In addition to trade and settlement, religion played a powerful role in shaping relations between Native Americans and Europeans. The three major New World empires of Spain, France, and England competed for Indians' souls as well as their lands and riches.

Catholic missionaries in Spanish colonies. Franciscan priests were the driving force behind Spain's efforts to control New Mexico and Florida (see Map 3–1). Spain valued both regions for strategic reasons. Neither colony attracted many settlers, however, because neither offered much opportunity for wealth. When Franciscan missionaries proposed to move in, Spanish officials, eager to back up their claims with a more visible Spanish presence, provided financial support. Franciscans settled near native villages in New Mexico and Florida in order to

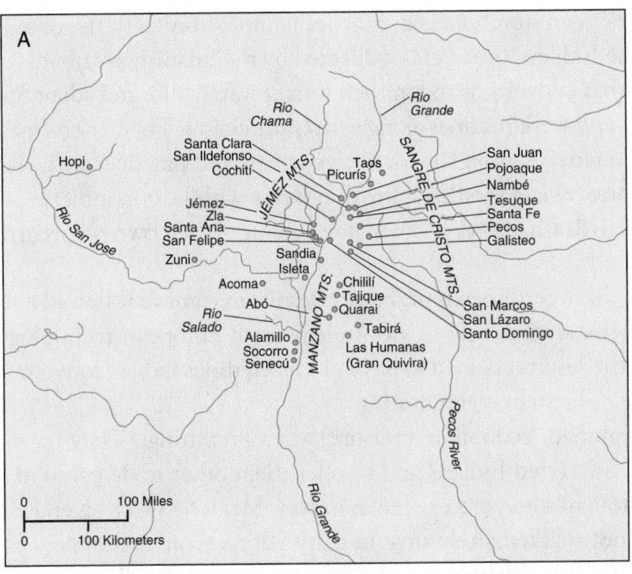

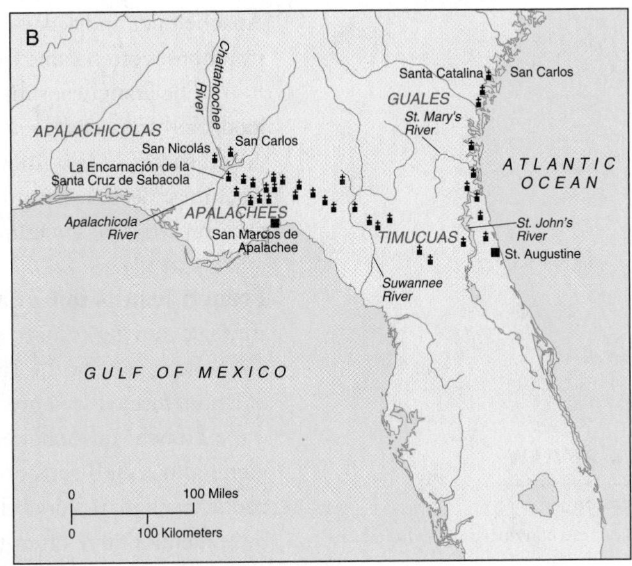

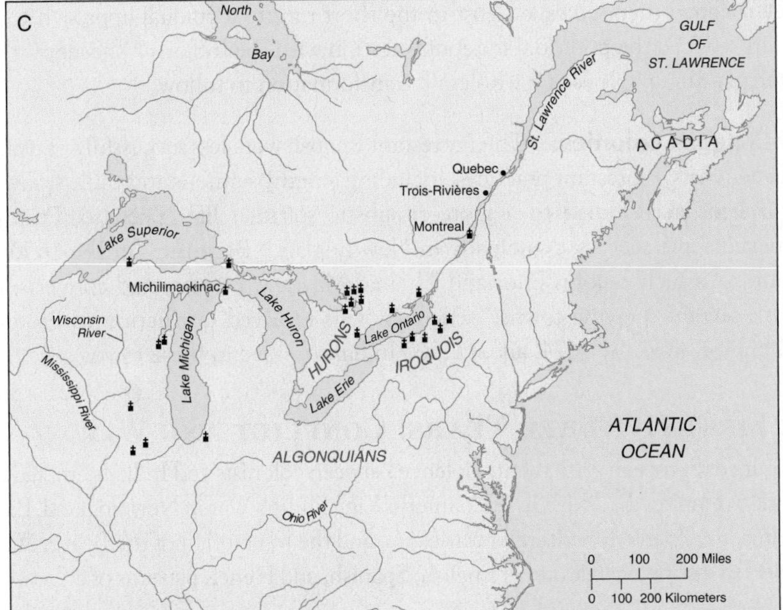

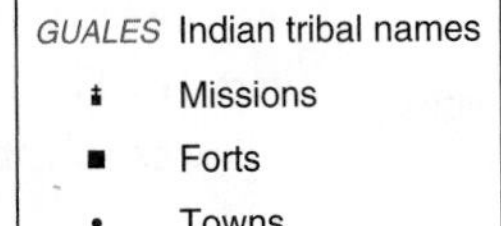

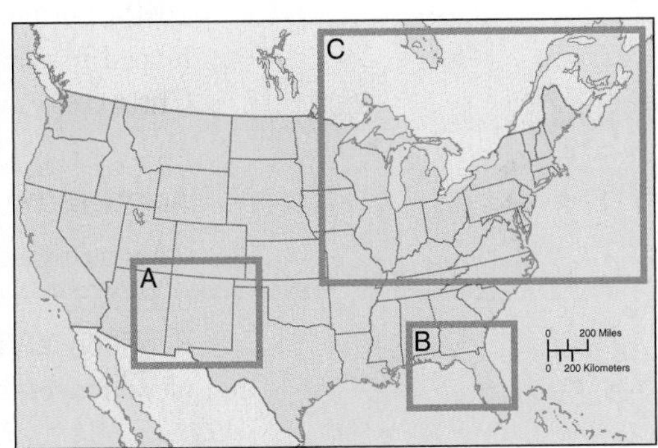

MAP 3–1 **Spanish and French Missions in Seventeenth-Century North America** Spanish Franciscans in New Mexico (A) and Florida (B) and French Jesuits in New France (C) devoted considerable effort to converting native peoples to Catholic Christianity.

What might explain the geographic distribution of Spanish and French missions? Why were French missions clustered around the Great Lakes? Why did the Spanish missions in Florida form lines of closely connected outposts?

convert their inhabitants to Catholicism. The priests wore their finest vestments and displayed religious paintings and statues, trying to impress the Indians. They gave away bells, knives, cloth, and food. The natives believed that accepting these gifts obliged them to listen to the priests' Christian message and help the Franciscans build houses and churches.

After brief religious instruction, the missionaries convinced many Indians to accept baptism into the Catholic Church. Many of these conversions were doubtless genuine, but they also had practical motivations. Conversions often followed epidemics that devastated native villages but spared the Spanish, leading Indians to wonder if the Christian God might be more powerful than their own gods. In New Mexico, the Spanish promised Pueblo converts protection against

Apache raids and access to Franciscan storehouses in times of famine. Ironically, the corn in the storehouses often came from the Indians' own fields, collected by the Spanish as tribute.

The Franciscans insisted that converts abandon their former ways of life and adopt Spanish food, clothing, gender relations, and work routines along with Catholicism. Their efforts met with mixed success. Many Indians preferred to supplement native beliefs and practices with the new teachings. Because the missionaries reacted to this spiritual mixture with horror, inflicting severe punishments that sometimes led to death, native peoples often practiced their own rituals in secret.

French Jesuits in Canada. To a certain extent, French Jesuits in Canada followed a similar strategy, moving to native villages and seeking to awe Indians with European technology and Catholic rituals. By the 1650s, the Jesuits claimed to have produced thousands of converts, some of whom formed separate native Christian communities.

French missionaries combined economic pressure with preaching. They persuaded merchants to sell guns only to converted Indians and to offer them other trade goods at a discount. Such tactics doubtless brought some success, but as in New Mexico, the crises engendered by epidemics more often than not sparked an upsurge in conversions. Converts in New France also preferred to meld Catholic teachings with native beliefs. Missionaries hardly condoned this response but they resigned themselves, at least in the short run, to a gradual approach to conversion. The Jesuits reduced the potential for confrontation with the Indians by accepting small changes in converts at first in hopes of a wholesale transformation to follow.

QUICK REVIEW

Conversion

- Missionaries convinced many Indians to accept baptism.
- Many Indians did not understand the implications of baptism.
- Converts blended Christianity and native religion.

Missionaries in English colonies. The Protestant English were less successful at attracting Native American converts. Protestant practices, including lengthy sermons and Bible study, held little allure for Indians accustomed to a more ritualistic spiritual life. Even so, Protestant missionaries achieved some success, principally in New England. Beginning in the 1650s and 1660s, Puritan ministers such as John Eliot and Thomas Mayhew, Jr., attracted converts. Eliot helped to establish several "praying towns," where Indians received instruction in Protestant Christianity and English ways. By 1674, about 2,300 Indians resided in these towns.

After the First Hundred Years: Conflict and War

After nearly a century of European settlement, violence between colonists and Indians erupted in all three North American empires. Each deadly encounter—King Philip's War in New England, Bacon's Rebellion in Virginia, the Pueblo Revolt in New Mexico, and the resumption of the Beaver Wars in New France—reflected distinctive features of English, Spanish, and French patterns of colonization.

King Philip's War. The growing frustration of the Wampanoags, who had befriended the Pilgrims more than a half-century earlier, with the land-hungry settlers whose towns now surrounded them, sparked **King Philip's War,** which broke out in 1675. Massasoit's younger son, Metacom—called King Philip by the English—led the Wampanoags in the struggle to preserve their independence. He had little reason to trust English settlers.

King Philip's War Conflict in New England (1675–1676) between Wampanoags, Narragansetts, and other Indian peoples against English settlers; sparked by English encroachments on native lands.

In the spring of 1675, a colonial court found three Wampanoags guilty of murdering a Christian Indian who had warned the English of Wampanoag preparations for war. Despite Philip's protest that the evidence against the men was tainted, the court sentenced them to be hanged. This act convinced the Wampanoags that they had to strike back against the English before it was too late. Only "a small part of the dominion of my ancestors remains," declared Philip. "I am determined not to live until I have no country."

Native warriors attacked outlying villages in Plymouth Colony, moved into the Connecticut River Valley, and then turned eastward to strike towns within 20 miles of Boston. As the Narragansetts and other groups joined the uprising, Philip successfully eluded the combined forces of Massachusetts, Connecticut, and Plymouth (see American Views: Mary Rowlandson among the Indians). By the summer of 1676, however, the Indians were exhausted, weakened by disease and food shortages. Philip moved into western New England, where his men clashed with the powerful Mohawks, long-standing enemies of the Wampanoags and allies of English fur traders in New York. Philip died in an ambush in August 1676, and the war ended soon after.

At least a thousand colonists and perhaps three thousand Indians died in King Philip's War. The Indians forced back the line of settlement but lost what remained of their independence in New England. The victorious English sold many native survivors, including Philip's wife and young son, into slavery in the West Indies. Philip's head, impaled on a stake, was left for decades just outside Plymouth as a grisly warning of the price to be paid for resisting colonial expansion.

Bacon's Rebellion. As King Philip's War raged in New England, **Bacon's Rebellion** erupted in Virginia and had a similarly devastating effect on that colony's native population. Frustrated by shrinking economic opportunities in eastern Virginia, where established planters controlled the good land, many settlers, including new arrivals and recently freed indentured servants, moved to Virginia's western frontier. There they came into conflict with the region's resident Indians. In the summer of 1675, a group of frontier settlers attacked the Susquehannocks to seize their lands. The Indians struck back, prompting Nathaniel Bacon, a wealthy young planter who had only recently arrived in Virginia, to lead a violent campaign against all Indians, even those at peace with the colonial government. Governor William Berkeley ordered Bacon and his men to stop their attacks. They defied him and marched on Jamestown, turning a war between settlers and Indians into a rebellion of settlers against the colonial authorities.

Bacon's Rebellion Violent conflict in Virginia (1675–1676), beginning with settler attacks on Indians but culminating in a rebellion led by Nathaniel Bacon against Virginia's government.

The rebels believed that Berkeley and the colonial government represented the interests of established tobacco planters who wanted to keep men like themselves from emerging as potential competitors. Desperate because of the low price of tobacco, the rebels demanded voting rights, lower taxes, and easier access to land—meaning, in effect, the right to take land from the Indians. They captured and burned the colonial capital at Jamestown, forcing Berkeley to flee. Directing their aggression against Indians once more, they burned Indian villages and massacred the inhabitants.

By the time troops arrived from England to put down the rebellion, Bacon had died of dysentery and most of his men had drifted home. Berkeley hanged twenty-three rebels, but the real victims of the rebellion were Virginia's Indians. The remnants of the once-powerful Powhatans lost their remaining lands and either moved west or lived in poverty on the edges of English settlement. Hatred of Indians became a permanent feature of frontier life in Virginia, and government officials appeared more eager to spend money "for extirpating all Indians" than for maintaining peaceful relations.

The Pueblo Revolt. In 1680, the **Pueblo Revolt** against the Spanish in New Mexico had a very different outcome than did the rebellion in Virginia or the war in New England. Nearly 20,000 Pueblo Indians had grown restless under the harsh rule of only 2,500 Spaniards. The spark that ignited the revolt was an act of religious persecution. Spanish officials unwisely chose this troubled time to stamp out the Pueblo religion. In 1675, the governor arrested forty-seven native religious leaders on charges of sorcery. The court ordered most of them to be publicly whipped and released but sentenced four to death.

Pueblo Revolt Rebellion in 1680 of Pueblo Indians in New Mexico against their Spanish overlords, sparked by religious conflict and excessive Spanish demands for tribute.

Led by Popé, one of the freed leaders, the outraged Pueblos organized for revenge. A growing network of rebels emerged as Spanish soldiers marched into Pueblo villages and destroyed *kivas*, the chambers that Indians used for religious ceremonies. Working from the village of Taos in northern New Mexico, by the summer of 1680, Popé commanded an enormous force of rebels drawn from twenty Pueblo villages. On August 10, they attacked the Spanish settlements. Popé urged them to destroy "everything pertaining to Christianity." By October, all the surviving Spaniards had fled New Mexico.

W
WHERE TO LEARN MORE
Taos Pueblo, Taos, New Mexico
http://www.nps.gov/history/worldheritage/taos.htm

They did not return for thirteen years. By then, internal rivalries had split the victorious Pueblo coalition, and Popé had been overthrown as leader. Few Pueblo villages offered much resistance to the new Spanish intrusion. Even so, the Spanish now understood the folly of pushing the Indians too far. Officials reduced demands for tribute and ended the *encomienda* system. The Franciscans eased their attacks on Pueblo religion. New Spanish governors, backed by military force, kept the peace as best they could in a place where Indians still outnumbered Europeans.

Resumption of the Beaver Wars. The Iroquois experience in the last phase of the Beaver Wars threatened to parallel that of the Indians of New England and Virginia. What began as a struggle between the Iroquois and western native peoples for control of the fur trade blossomed into a larger

AMERICAN VIEWS

Mary Rowlandson among the Indians

In February 1676, in the midst of King Philip's War, Indian warriors attacked the town of Lancaster, Massachusetts. They killed many inhabitants and took 23 colonists captive, including Mary Rowlandson and three of her children. Rowlandson spent the next three months traveling with various groups of Nipmucs, Narragansetts, and Wampanoags. She suffered physically and emotionally, watching her youngest daughter die in her arms and worrying about her other two children, from whom she was frequently separated. During her captivity, Rowlandson survived by accepting her fate and adapting to the Indians' way of life. Finally, with an English victory imminent, Rowlandson was ransomed and rejoined her husband (who had been away at the time of the attack) and family. In 1682, she published an account of her captivity in which she explored the meaning of her experience. Rowlandson's narrative proved so popular that three editions were printed in the first year.

- **How** did Rowlandson describe the Indians? How did she characterize her encounter with King Philip?
- **In** what ways did Rowlandson accommodate herself to the Indians' way of life? How did she employ her skills to fit in? Did her gender make a difference in her experience of captivity?
- **How** did Rowlandson's Puritan faith shape her narrative?

We travelled on till night; and in the morning, we must go over the River to Philip's crew. When I was in the Cannoo, I could not but be amazed at the numerous crew of Pagans that were on the Bank on the other side. When I came ashore, they gathered all about me, I sitting alone in the midst: I observed they asked one another questions, and laughed, and rejoyced over their Gains and Victories. Then my heart began to fail: and I fell a weeping which was the first time to my remembrance that I wept before them. Although I had met with so much Affliction, and my heart was many times ready to break, yet could I not shed one tear in their sight: but rather had been all this while in a maze, and like one astonished: but now I may say as, Psal. 137.1 *By the rivers of Babylon, there we sat down: yea, we wept when we remembered Zion.* There one of them asked me, why I wept, I could hardly tell what to say: yet I answered, they would kill me: No, said he, none will hurt you. Then came one of them and gave me two spoon-fulls of Meal to comfort me. . . . Then I went to see King Philip, he bade me come in and sit down, and asked me whether I would smoke (a usual Complement now adayes amongst Saints and Sinners) but this no way suited me. For though I had formerly used Tobacco, yet I had left it ever since I was first taken, *It seems to be a bait, the devil lays to make men loose their precious time. . . .*

During my abode in this place, Philip spake to me to make a shirt for his boy, which I did, for which he gave me a shilling: I offered the money to my master, but he bade me keep it: and with it I bought a piece of Horse flesh. Afterwards he asked me to make a Cap for his boy, for which he invited me to Dinner. I went, and he gave me a Pancake, about as big as two fingers; it was made of parched wheat, beaten, and fryed in Bears grease, but I thought I never tasted pleasanter meat in my life. There was a Squaw who spake to me to make a shirt for her *Sannup* [husband], for which she gave me a piece of Bear. Another asked me to knit a pair of Stockins, for which she gave me a quart of Pease. . . . Hearing that my son was come to this place, I went to see him, and found him lying flat upon the ground: I asked him how he could sleep so? He answered me, *That he was not asleep, but at Prayer;* and lay so, that they might not observe what he was doing. I pray God he may remember these things now he is returned in safety.

Source: Neal Salisbury, ed., *The Sovereignty and Goodness of God, Together with the Faithfulness of His Promises Displayed. . . .* (Boston, 1997), pp. 82–83.

conflict that was absorbed into the imperial rivalry between England and France. Although the Iroquois suffered devastating losses, they did not lose their independence. The key to Iroquois survival in the war's aftermath was the adoption of a position of neutrality between the European powe

Looking for new trading partners to replace the Hurons, the French turned in the to various Indian peoples living near the Great Lakes. But the Iroquois had begun to raic same peoples for furs and captives, much as they had attacked the Hurons in the first p the Beaver Wars in the 1640s. They exchanged the furs for European goods with English who had replaced the Dutch as their partners after the conquest of New Netherland.

The French attacked the Iroquois to prevent them and their English allies from extend influence in the west. In June 1687, a combined force of French and Christian Indian soldiers the lands of the Senecas, the westernmost of the five nations of the Iroquois League. The Iroquois retaliated by besieging a French garrison at Niagara, where nearly two hundred soldiers starved to death, and killing hundreds of colonists in attacks on French villages along the St. Lawrence River.

The French participated much more directly and suffered greater losses in this renewal of the Beaver Wars than they had in the earlier fighting. In 1688 France and England went to war in Europe, and the struggle between them and their Indian allies for control of the fur trade in North America became part of a larger imperial contest. The European powers made peace in 1697, but calm did not immediately return to the Great Lakes region.

The conflict was even more devastating for the Iroquois. Perhaps a quarter of their population died from disease and warfare by 1689. The devastation encouraged Iroquois diplomats to find a way to extricate themselves from future English–French conflicts. The result, in 1701, was a pair of treaties, negotiated separately with Albany and Montreal, that recognized Iroquois neutrality and, at least for several decades, prevented either the English or the French from dominating the western lands.

AFRICANS AND EUROPEANS

HOW AND why did race-based slavery develop in British North America?

The movement of Africans to the Americas was one of the largest forced migrations in world history. By the time New World slavery finally ended, with its abolition in Brazil in 1888, over twelve million Africans had arrived on American shores. From a relatively small stream in the sixteenth century, African migration accelerated to a great flood by the 1700s.

Virtually all Africans arrived as slaves, making the history of the African experience in the Americas inseparable from the history of slavery and the slave trade. As one eighteenth-century Englishman noted, Africans were "the strength and sinews of this western world," performing much of the labor of colonization. The vast majority of African slaves ended up in Brazil, the West Indies, or New Spain. Only 1 out of 20 Africans came to the British mainland colonies, but this still amounted to nearly 350,000 individuals (see Figure 3–2). Their presence transformed English colonial societies everywhere, but particularly in the South. At the same time, Africans were themselves transformed. Out of their diverse African ethnic backgrounds and the experience of slavery itself they forged new identities as African American peoples.

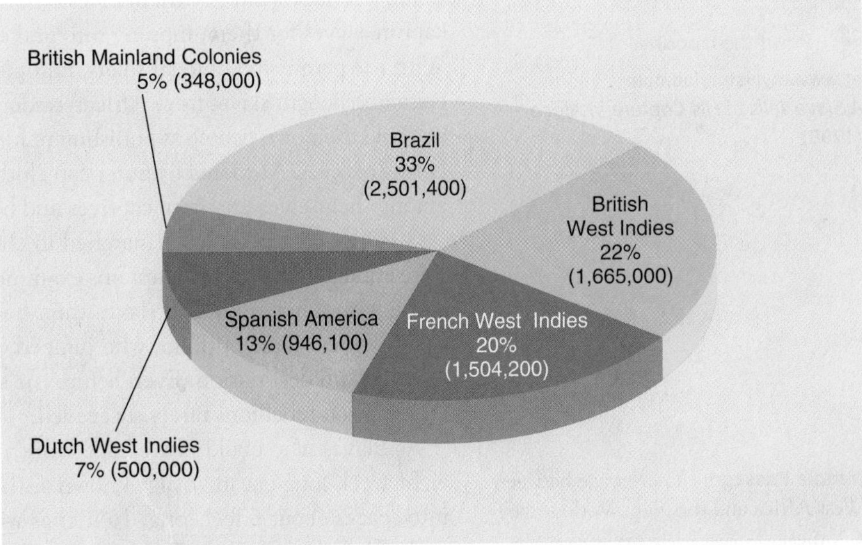

FIGURE 3–2 **Destination of Slaves Imported from Africa to the Americas between 1451 and 1810** Approximately 7.5 million Africans were brought as slaves to the Americas before 1810. The vast majority went to the Caribbean, Mexico, and South America, where they toiled in mines and on sugar plantations.

Data Source: Philip Curtin, *The Atlantic Slave Trade: A Census* (1969), p. 268.

See the Map at www.myhistorylab.com *African Slave Trade,* 1500–1870

QUICK REVIEW

The Demand for Labor

- Indians first forced into slavery in the Americas.
- By 1700 Indian slave trade replaced by slaves from Africa.
- Over time slaves replaced servants on tobacco plantations.

Labor Needs and the Turn to Slavery

Europeans in the New World were thrilled to find that land was abundant and quite cheap by European standards. They were perplexed, however, by the unexpectedly high cost of labor. In Europe, the reverse had been true. There land was expensive but labor cheap, because competition for jobs among large numbers of workers pushed wages down. Colonial workers commanded high wages because there were so few of them compared to the supply of land to be developed. In addition, few settlers wanted to work for others when they could get farms of their own. The scarcity and high cost of labor led some colonial employers to turn to enslaved Africans as a solution.

The development of slavery in the colonies was not inevitable. Europeans had owned slaves (both white and black) long before the beginning of American colonization, but slaves formed a small—and shrinking—minority of European laborers. By the fifteenth century, slavery had all but disappeared in northern Europe except as punishment for serious crimes.

Slavery persisted longer in southern Europe and the Middle East. In both regions, religion influenced the choice of who was enslaved. Because neither Christians nor Muslims would hold as slaves members of their own faiths, Arab traders turned to sub-Saharan Africa to find slaves. By the fifteenth century, a durable link between slave status and black skin had been forged in European minds.

Europeans in the New World, beginning with Columbus, first enslaved Indians as a way of addressing the labor shortage. Native American slaves, however, could not fill the colonists' labor needs. Everywhere disease and harsh working conditions reduced their numbers. English colonists also discovered problems with enslaving Indians. When traders incited Indian wars to gain slaves, bloodshed often spread to English settlements. Enslaved Indian men refused to perform agricultural labor, which they considered women's work. And because they knew the land so well, Indians could easily escape. As a result, although the Indian slave trade persisted in the English colonies through the eighteenth century (and into the nineteenth century), by 1700 it had given way to a much larger traffic in Africans.

Interpreting the Past
The Voyage to Slavery (pp. 82–83)

Read the Document at www.myhistorylab.com *A Slave Tells of His Capture in Africa* (1798)

The Shock of Enslavement

European traders did not themselves enslave Africans. Instead, they relied on other Africans to capture slaves for them, tapping into and expanding a preexisting internal African slave trade. With the permission of local rulers, Europeans built forts and trading posts on the West African coast and bought slaves from African traders (see Map 3–2). African rulers occasionally enslaved and sold their own people as punishment for crimes, but most slaves were seized in raids on neighboring peoples. Attracted by European cloth, liquor, guns, and other goods, West Africans fought among themselves to secure captives and began kidnapping individuals from the interior.

Once captured, slaves marched in chains to the coast, to be confined in cages until there were enough to fill a ship. Captains examined them to ensure their fitness and branded them like cattle with a hot iron. The slaves then boarded canoes to be ferried to the ships. Desperation overwhelmed some of them, who jumped overboard and drowned rather than be carried off to an unknown destination. Even before the ships left African shores, slaves sometimes mutinied, though such rebellions rarely succeeded.

Middle Passage The voyage between West Africa and the New World slave colonies.

Read the Document at www.myhistorylab.com *Olaudah Equiano, The Middle Passage* (1788)

Slaves who could not escape while still in Africa suffered through a horrendous six- to eight-week-long ocean voyage known as the **Middle Passage.** Captains wedged men below decks into spaces about 6 feet long, 16 inches wide, and 30 inches high. Women and children were packed even more tightly. Except for brief excursions on deck for forced exercise, slaves remained below decks, where the air grew foul from the vomit, blood, and excrement in which the terrified victims lay. Some slaves went insane; others refused to eat. On many voyages, between 5 and 20 percent of the slaves perished from disease and other causes, but captains had usually packed the ships tightly enough to make a profit from selling the rest.

Those who survived the dreadful voyage endured the fear and humiliation of sale. Ship captains sometimes sold slaves at public auctions, where purchasers poked them, looking for signs of disease. Many terrified Africans, like Equiano, thought they were going to be eaten.

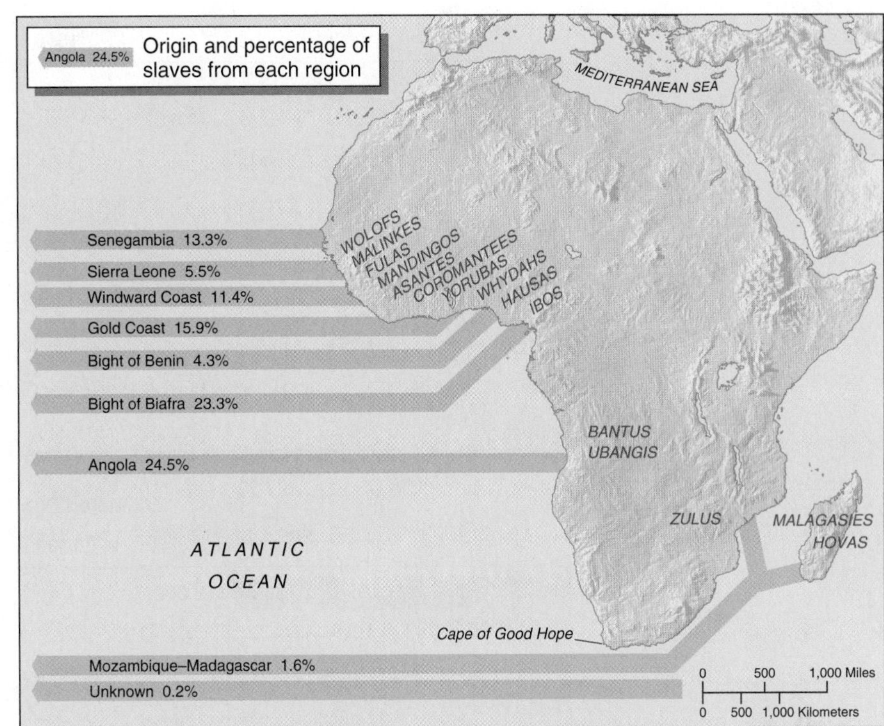

MAP 3–2 **African Origins of North American Slaves, 1690–1807** Nearly all slaves in English North America were West Africans. Most had been captured or purchased by African slave traders, who then sold them to European merchants.

Why might the Bight of Biafra and Angola together have made up nearly 50 percent of all slave trading out of West Africa?

African Slaves in the New World

The Spanish and Portuguese first brought Africans to the Americas to replace or supplement the dwindling numbers of Indian slaves toiling in silver mines and on sugar plantations. The Dutch, who scrambled for a share of the lucrative slave trade, quickly followed suit. English colonists, less familiar with slavery, adopted it more slowly. West Indian planters were the first English settlers to do so on a large scale in the 1640s. In most other English colonies, however, different economic conditions either postponed or prevented slavery's widespread adoption.

Slavery in the southern colonies. Slavery did not fully take hold in Virginia until the end of the seventeenth century, at which point Africans comprised a significant portion of the population (see Figure 3–3). For decades, tobacco planters saw no reason to stop using white indentured servants. Servants (because they worked for masters only for a period of years rather than for life) cost less than slaves, were readily available, and were familiar. By the 1680s, however, planters in Virginia and Maryland began to shift from servants to slaves.

Two related developments caused this change. First, white indentured servants became harder to find. Fewer English men and women chose to emigrate as servants after 1660 because an improving economy in England provided jobs at home. At the same time, Virginia's white population tripled between 1650 and 1700, increasing the number of planters competing for a shrinking supply of laborers. Planters also faced competition from newer colonies such as Pennsylvania and New Jersey, which had more generous land policies for immigrants.

Second, as white servants grew scarcer, changes in the slave trade made African slaves more available. Before the 1660s, the Dutch and Portuguese merchants who dominated the trade mainly supplied their own colonies and the profitable West Indian market. But beginning in 1674, England's Royal African Company began shipping slaves directly to English buyers. The supply of slaves surged after 1698, when the Royal African Company lost its special trading rights, and many English merchants and New Englanders entered the fiercely competitive trade.

Chesapeake planters eventually found reasons besides availability to prefer slaves to servants. Slaves were a better long-term investment. Because slave status passed from slave mothers to their children, buying both men and women gave planters a self-reproducing labor force. Runaway black slaves were more easily recaptured than escaped servants, who blended into the white population. And unlike indentured servants, slaves were slaves for life.

Chesapeake planters had already come to see white servants as possessions, people whose labor could be bought and sold like any other commodity. This attitude doubtless eased the

See the **Map**
at **www.myhistorylab.com**
The Atlantic and Islamic Slave Trades

Read the **Document**
at **www.myhistorylab.com**
Virginia Law on Indentured Servitude (1705)

Read the **Document**
at **www.myhistorylab.com**
Wessell Webling, His Indenture (1622)

Read the **Document**
at **www.myhistorylab.com**
A Virginian Describes the Difference between Servants and Slaves (1722)

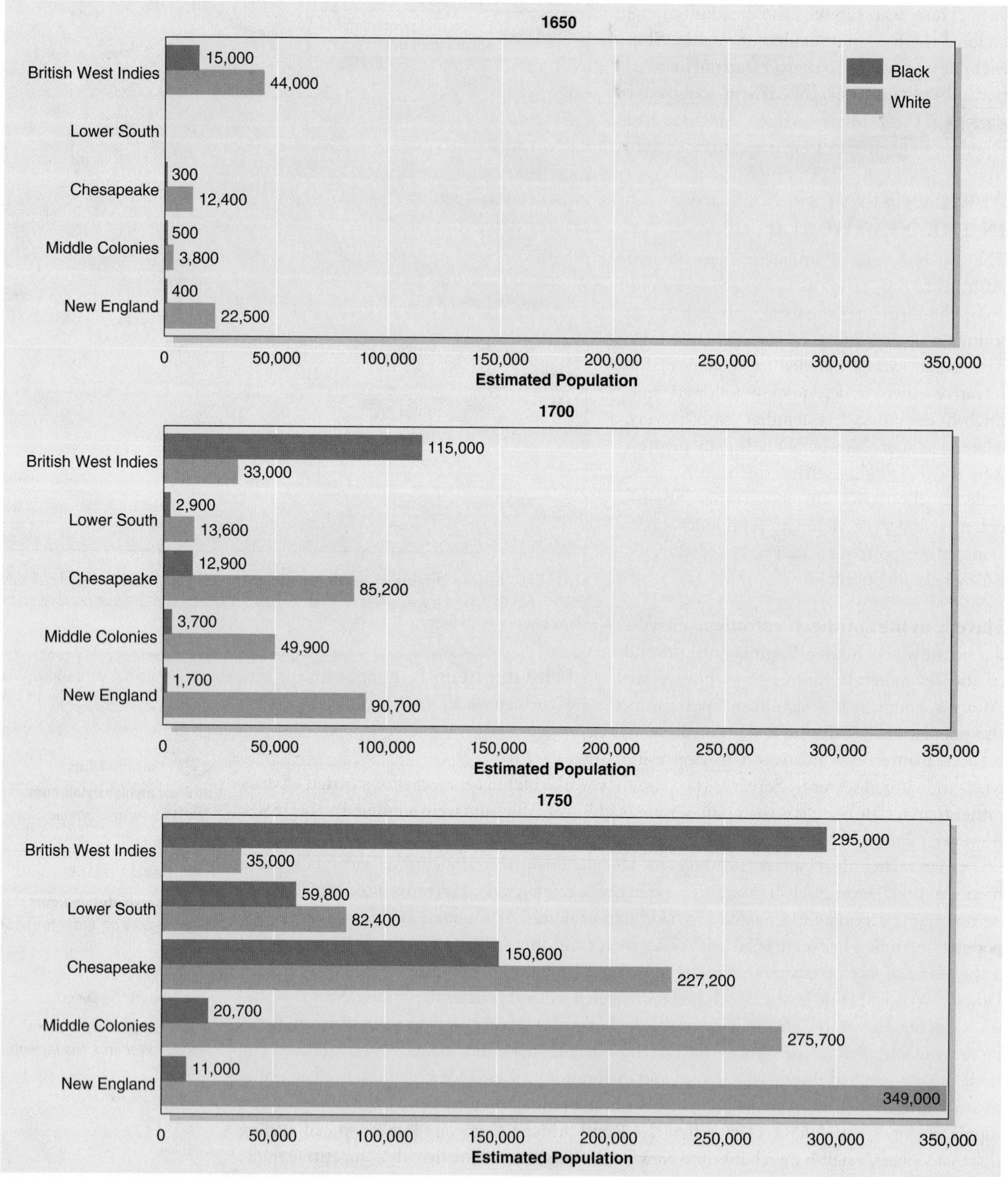

1650

British West Indies
15,000
44,000
Lower South
Chesapeake
300
12,400
Middle Colonies
500
3,800
New England
400
22,500

Black
White

0 50,000 100,000 150,000 200,000 250,000 300,000 350,000
Estimated Population

1700

British West Indies
115,000
33,000
Lower South
2,900
13,600
Chesapeake
12,900
85,200
Middle Colonies
3,700
49,900
New England
1,700
90,700

0 50,000 100,000 150,000 200,000 250,000 300,000 350,000
Estimated Population

1750

British West Indies
295,000
35,000
Lower South
59,800
82,400
Chesapeake
150,600
227,200
Middle Colonies
20,700
275,700
New England
11,000
349,000

0 50,000 100,000 150,000 200,000 250,000 300,000 350,000
Estimated Population

FIGURE 3–3 **Estimated Population of Black and White Settlers in British Colonial Regions, 1650–1750** Settler populations increased rapidly in all colonial regions, but the racial composition varied. By 1750, black people overwhelmingly predominated in the West Indies and were quite numerous in the southern colonies; north of Maryland, however, their numbers remained small.

Data Source: John J. McCusker and Russell Menard, *The Economy of British America, 1607–1789* (1985).

transition in the 1680s and 1690s to the much harsher system of slavery. In Carolina, of course, slaves were there from the start, brought in the 1670s by colony founders accustomed to slavery in Barbados. By 1720, slavery was firmly embedded in all the southern colonies except sparsely settled North Carolina. In that year, one-third of Virginia's settler population, and nearly three-quarters of South Carolina's, were black.

Slavery grew rapidly in the southern colonies because it answered the labor needs of planters engaged in the commercial production of tobacco and rice. The demand for slaves became so powerful that it destroyed James Oglethorpe's plan to keep them out of Georgia, the last of England's mainland colonies, founded in 1732. Oglethorpe intended Georgia to be a refuge for English debtors, who normally were jailed until they could repay their creditors. Slaves were initially prohibited not only to prevent them from competing with the debtors, but also to make it difficult for fugitive slaves from South Carolina to escape there. With slavery forbidden, any black person seen in Georgia would be immediately recognizable as a runaway. But when Georgia's colonists began to grow rice, they demanded the right to have slaves. In 1750, the colony's founders reluctantly legalized slavery; by 1770, slaves made up nearly half of the colony's population.

Slavery in the northern colonies. Far fewer slaves lived north of the Chesapeake, although they were present in every British colony. They were too expensive for most northern farmers—who mainly produced food for their families, not staple crops for an international market—to use profitably. This was not true, however, for farmers with larger properties in parts of Long Island, the Hudson Valley, Rhode Island, northern New Jersey, and southeastern Pennsylvania, where commercial wheat farming and livestock raising prevailed. In the eighteenth century, these landowners acquired significant numbers of slaves.

Northern slaves could often be found in cities, especially ports such as Newport, Rhode Island, where newly arrived Africans landed. At the start of the eighteenth century, one out of six Philadelphia residents was a slave; by 1740, slaves made up 15 percent of the city's workingmen. In mid-eighteenth-century New York City, slaves comprised between 12 and 14 percent of the population. Many urban slaves were domestic servants in the homes of rich merchants and professionals. Substantial numbers also labored as artisans.

The freed slave Olaudah Equiano appears in this 1780 portrait by an unknown artist. After purchasing his freedom, Equiano wrote a vivid account of his capture in Africa and his life in slavery. One of the first such accounts to be published (in 1789), this narrative testified to slavery's injustice and Equiano's own fortitude and talents.

Royal Albert Memorial Museum, Exeter, Devon, UK/Bridgeman Art Library.

Changing race relations in the colonies. Race relations in the mainland colonies were less rigid in the seventeenth century than they would later become. Before 1700, slaves did not form a majority of the population in any colony, a situation that may have made them seem less threatening to white people. In some areas, free black people—often slaves who had bought their own freedom—prospered in an atmosphere of racial tolerance that would be unthinkable by the eighteenth century.

The career of an ambitious black Virginian named Anthony Johnson, for example, resembled that of many white settlers. Johnson's master allowed him to marry and start a family while he was still a slave and may even have allowed Anthony to purchase his and his family's liberty. Once free, the Johnsons settled in eastern Virginia, where Anthony and his sons eventually acquired substantial plantations. He and his sons also owned slaves. Anthony Johnson belonged to the first or what one historian has called the "charter" generation of American slaves, and his experience reveals how much slavery changed over time. This generation of slaves mainly came from African port towns, where Europeans and Africans had mingled for generations, or by way of the West Indies or New Netherland. Familiar with European ways, often fluent in European

QUICK REVIEW

Growth of Slavery

- Slavery grew rapidly in the South.
- The use of slaves made economic sense on tobacco and rice plantations.
- Northern slaves worked as servants, craftsmen, and day laborers.

languages, they acquired skills and knowledge that enabled them to bargain with their masters in ways their descendants would not be able to replicate. They came in small groups, cultivated their masters as patrons, negotiated for their own property, and often gained their freedom. They enjoyed such advantages because they came to colonies where slavery had not yet become firmly embedded, where the meaning of bondage was still being worked out.

Repressive laws and slave codes. But Johnson's descendants, and the generations of slaves and free black people who came after them, encountered much harsher conditions. Once slavery became the dominant labor system in the Chesapeake, tobacco planters no longer welcomed free black people, fearing that they might encourage slaves to escape. In 1691, Virginia's legislature prohibited individual masters from freeing their slaves. Lawmakers passed another measure in 1699 requiring newly freed black people to leave the colony altogether. Black families like the Johnsons, who were already free, suffered under increasing discrimination.

Read the **Document** at **www.myhistorylab.com** *Exploring America: Racism in America*

Bad as the situation of free black people had grown, the condition of slaves was far worse. Slave codes, laws governing slavery, essentially reduced an entire class of human beings to property. In Virginia, from the middle of the seventeenth century on, new laws added to slaves' oppression. A 1662 measure defined slavery as a lifelong and inherited status that passed from slave mothers to their children—even children with white fathers. Masters who might have felt uneasy about holding fellow Christians as slaves were relieved in 1667 when another law stated that baptism would not release slaves from bondage. Two years later, the House of Burgesses gave masters the power of life and death over their slaves, decreeing that masters would not be charged with a felony if their slaves died during punishment. These and other measures were gathered into a comprehensive slave code in Virginia in 1705.

Read the **Document** at **www.myhistorylab.com** *From Then to Now Online: The Legacy of Slavery*

Slave codes appeared virtually everywhere, North and South, but were particularly harsh in the southern colonies. White colonists in the Tidewater Chesapeake and South Carolina feared the consequences of a growing black population. One South Carolina planter predicted in 1720 that slaves would soon rise up against their masters because black people were "too numerous in proportion to the White Men there."

AFRICAN AMERICAN FAMILIES AND COMMUNITIES

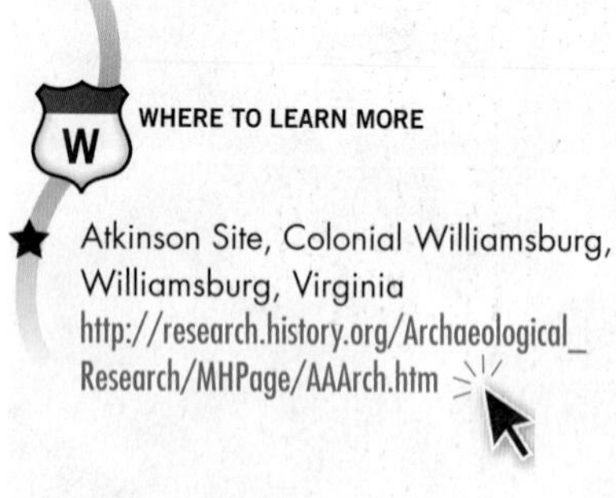

W
WHERE TO LEARN MORE
Atkinson Site, Colonial Williamsburg, Williamsburg, Virginia
http://research.history.org/Archaeological_Research/MHPage/AAArch.htm

The harshness of the slaves' condition could be relieved somewhat by the formation of close ties with others who shared their circumstances. For such ties to be created, however, several developments had to occur. Slaves had to become sufficiently numerous in specific localities so that black people could have regular contact with one another. Ethnic and language barriers carried over from Africa had to erode so that slaves could communicate. And for families to be formed, there had to be enough slave women as well as men. Because these conditions were slow to develop, occurring at different rates in different colonies, the formation of African American families and communities was delayed until well into the eighteenth century.

The rise of the creole slave population. Slaves were most numerous in the southern colonies, and it was there that African American families and communities emerged with greater success. This was especially true in South Carolina and parts of the Tidewater Chesapeake, where in certain localities slaves formed a majority of the population. Even more significant, these regions witnessed the rise of a creole, or American-born, slave population by about the 1750s. This development distinguished slavery in the mainland British colonies from that in the West Indies, where disease and overwork killed so many slaves that the black population grew only because of the constant importation of Africans.

QUICK REVIEW

Creole Slaves

- Slaves born in America, not Africa.
- Lived longer and had more children than African-born slaves.
- Played key role in the development of African American identity.

The rise of a creole slave population in the Chesapeake and in Carolina set off a chain of related events that fostered family and community life. Creoles lived longer than African immigrants, and creole women usually bore twice as many children as African-born mothers. This circumstance allowed the slave population to grow by natural increase and more closely resemble a normal population of men and women, children and elders. At the same time, creole slaves grew up without personal memories of Africa, and thus African ethnic differences receded in importance.

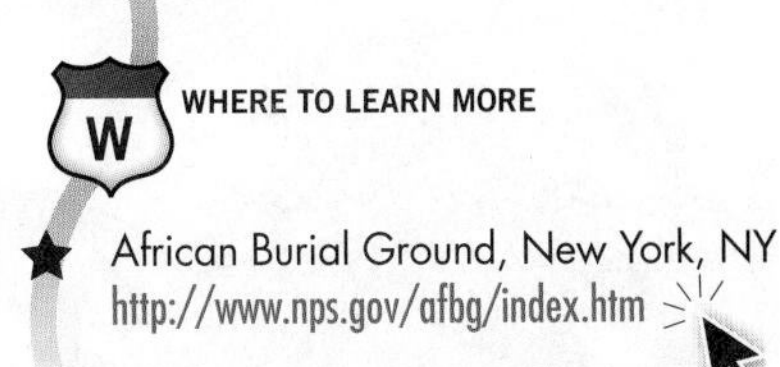

WHERE TO LEARN MORE

★ African Burial Ground, New York, NY
http://www.nps.gov/afbg/index.htm

Work and family life. Most of a slave's life was structured by work. The vast majority of southern slaves were field hands. On large plantations, masters selected some slave men to be trained as shoemakers, weavers, or tailors and chose others as drivers or leaders of work gangs.

Although this watercolor of a slave ship bound for Brazil dates from the nineteenth century, it depicts a scene common on slavers in the 1700s. The artist's attention to detail suggests both the misery of the slaves' surroundings and the dignity of the individuals forced to live under such conditions.

The Granger Collection, New York.

This English woodcut, dating from about 1700, served as a label on a tobacco package. In the foreground, planters smoke and take their ease, while in the background, slaves toil under the hot sun.

With the exception of nurses and cooks, few slave women avoided the drudgery of field labor. If they had families, the end of the day's work in the fields only marked the start of domestic duties back in the slave quarters. But no matter how onerous, work did not absorb every minute of the slaves' lives, and in the intervals around their assigned duties many slaves nurtured ties of family and community that combined African traditions with New World experience.

By the late eighteenth century, more than half of Chesapeake and Carolina slaves lived in family groups. These were fragile units, subject to the whims of masters who did not recognize slave marriages as legal, broke up families by sale, and could take slave women as sexual partners at will. Over time, dense kinship networks formed, reflecting West African influences. Slaves placed great emphasis on kin connections, even using familiar terms such as "aunt" and "uncle" to address friends. Some slave husbands, as was customary in West Africa, took more than one wife. In naming their children, slaves mingled old and new practices, sometimes giving them the African names of distant kin and sometimes using English names.

Community life and religion. Community life forged ties between slave families and single slaves on the plantations and offered further opportunities to preserve elements of African heritage. Traces of African religious practices endured in America. Magical charms and amulets have been found buried in slave quarters, indicating that spiritual ceremonies may have been conducted out of sight of white masters. Reflecting their West African background, slaves placed great emphasis on funerals, in the belief that relatives remained members of kin communities even after death. Christianity offered little competition to African religious practices during most of the colonial period. Few masters showed much interest in converting their slaves before the Revolution.

QUICK REVIEW

Slave Society

- Traces of African culture remained in slave society.
- Labor consumed most of slave's time.
- Growth of slave families and communities inhibited escape and rebellion.

African influences shaped aspects of slaves' recreational activity and material life. Slave musicians used African-style instruments, including drums and banjos, to accompany traditional songs and dances. Where slaves were allowed to build their own houses, they incorporated African elements into the designs—for instance, by using mud walls and roofs thatched with palmetto leaves. Their gardens frequently contained African foods, such as millet, yams, peppers, and sesame seeds, along with European and Native American crops.

Resistance and Rebellion

Even as family ties made a life in bondage more tolerable, they made it more difficult for slaves to attempt escape or contemplate rebellion. Slaves who resisted their oppression ran the risk of endangering families and friends as well as themselves. But the powerful desire for freedom was not easily suppressed, and slaves found ways to defy the dehumanization that slavery entailed.

Running away from a master was a desperate act, but thousands of slaves did just that. Deciding where to go posed a problem. Escape out of the South did not bring freedom, because slavery was legal in every colony. After 1733, some runaways went to Florida, where Spanish officials promised them freedom. Others tried to survive on their own in the woods or join the Indians—a choice that carried the risk of capture or death. Perilous as it was, escape proved irresistible to some slaves, especially young males. In a few isolated areas on the South Carolina frontier, runaways formed outlaw "maroon" settlements.

This eighteenth-century painting from South Carolina records the preservation of certain African traditions in American slave communities. The dance may be Yoruba in origin, while the stringed instrument and drum were probably modeled on African instruments.

Abby Aldrich Rockefeller Folk Art Museum, The Colonial Williamsburg Foundation Williamsburg, VA.

Many slaves chose less perilous ways to resist their bondage. Slaves worked slowly, broke tools, and pretended to be ill in order to exert some control over their working lives. When provoked, they also took more direct action, damaging crops, stealing goods, and setting fires. Slaves with knowledge of poisonous plants occasionally tried to kill their owners, although the penalty for being caught was to be burned to death.

The most serious, as well as the rarest, form of resistance was organized rebellion. South Carolinians and coastal Virginians, who lived in regions with slave majorities, had a particular dread of slave revolt. But because rebellions required complete secrecy, careful planning, and access to weapons, they were extremely hard to organize. No slave rebellion succeeded in the British colonies. Rumors usually leaked out before any action had been taken, prompting severe reprisals against the alleged conspirators.

Three major slave revolts did occur and instilled lasting fear in white colonists. In 1712 in New York City, where black people made up 20 percent of the population, about twenty slaves set a building on fire and killed nine white men who came to put it out. The revolt was quickly suppressed, with twenty-four rebels sentenced to death. Another slave insurrection occurred in Virginia in 1730, sparked by a false rumor that local officials had suppressed a royal edict calling for the emancipation of Christian slaves. More than three hundred rebels escaped into the Dismal Swamp along the border with North Carolina, attacking white settlers in the area. Using Indians to hunt down the fugitives, Virginia authorities captured and executed twenty-four of the rebellion's leaders. Another major revolt, the **Stono Rebellion,** struck South Carolina in 1739. About twenty slaves—including several recently arrived Angolans—broke into a store and armed themselves with stolen guns. Marching southward along the Stono River, their ranks grew

Stono Rebellion Uprising in 1739 of South Carolina slaves against whites; inspired in part by Spanish officials' promise of freedom for American slaves who escaped to Florida.

to perhaps a hundred. Heading for freedom in Spanish Florida, they attacked white settlements along the way. White troops (with Indian help) defeated the rebels within a week, but tensions remained high for months. The death toll, in the end, was about two dozen white people and perhaps twice as many black rebels.

In the wake of these rebellions, colonial assemblies passed laws requiring stricter supervision of slave activities. In South Carolina, other measures encouraged more white immigration to offset the colony's black majority. Planters in the southern colonies in particular considered slavery indispensable to their economic survival, even though this labor system generated so much fear and brutality. Their slaves, in turn, obeyed when necessary, resisted when possible, and kept alive the hope that freedom would one day be theirs.

Read the **Document** at **www.myhistorylab.com** *Slaves Revolt in South Carolina* (1739)

EUROPEAN LABORERS IN EARLY AMERICA

WHAT METHODS did Europeans employ to acquire and manage labor in colonial America?

Slavery was one of several responses to the scarcity of labor in the New World. It took hold mainly in areas where the profits from export crops such as sugar, rice, and tobacco offset the high purchase price of slaves and where a warm climate permitted year-round work. Elsewhere European masters and employers found various ways to acquire and manage European laborers.

A Spectrum of Control

Slavery was the most oppressive extreme in a spectrum of practices designed to exert control over workers and relieve the problems caused by the easy availability of land and the high cost of labor. Most colonial laborers were, in some measure, unfree (see the Overview table, Predominant Colonial Labor Systems, 1750). One-half to two-thirds of all white immigrants to the English colonies arrived as indentured servants, bound by contract to serve masters for a period of years. But indentured servants, though less costly than slaves, carried too high a price for farmers who raised crops mainly for subsistence. Servants could be found in every colony, but were most common in the Chesapeake and, to a lesser extent, in Pennsylvania, where they worked for farmers producing export crops.

Slaves replaced white indentured servants in Chesapeake tobacco fields during the eighteenth century. Masters continued to import servants for a while to fill skilled jobs but in time trained slaves to fill those positions. Thus, by the middle of the eighteenth century, white servitude, although it still flourished in some places, was in decline as a dominant labor system.

Eighteenth-century Chesapeake planters also availed themselves of another unfree labor source: transported English convicts. Lawmakers in England saw transportation as a way of getting rid of criminals who might otherwise be executed. Between 1718 and 1775, nearly fifty thousand convicts were sent to the colonies, 80 percent of whom ended up in the Chesapeake region. Most were young, lower-class males forced by economic hardship to turn to crime. A few convicts eventually prospered in America, but most faced lives as miserable as those they had known in England.

redemptioner Similar to an indentured servant, except that a redemptioner signed a labor contract in America rather than in Europe.

An arrangement similar to indentured servitude—the **redemptioner** system—brought many families, especially from German provinces, to the colonies in the eighteenth century. Instead of negotiating contracts for service before leaving Europe, as indentured servants did, redemptioners promised to redeem, or pay, the costs of passage on arrival in America. They often paid part of the fare before sailing. If they could not raise the rest soon after landing, the ship captain who brought them sold them into servitude. The length of their service depended on how much they still owed.

Purchasing slaves, servants, or convicts did not make sense for everyone. Colonists who owned undeveloped land faced many tasks—cutting trees, clearing fields, building fences and barns—that brought no immediate profit. Rather than buy expensive laborers to accomplish these ends, landowners rented undeveloped tracts to families without property. Both tenants and landlords benefited from this arrangement. Tenants enjoyed greater independence than servants

OVERVIEW Predominant Colonial Labor Systems, 1750

	Colony	Labor System
New England	Massachusetts	Family farms
	Connecticut	Family farms
	New Hampshire	Family farms
	Rhode Island	Family farms
Middle Colonies	New York	Family farms, tenancy
	Pennsylvania and Delaware	Indentured servitude, tenancy, family farms
	New Jersey	Family farms, tenancy
South	Maryland	Slavery
	Virginia	Slavery
	North Carolina	Family farms, slavery
	South Carolina	Slavery

and could save toward the purchase of their own farms. The landlord secured the labor necessary to transform his property into a working farm, thus increasing the land's value. He also received an annual rent payment and eventually profited from selling the land, often to the tenant family who had rented it.

Merchants eager to develop New England's fisheries devised other means to fill their labor needs. Because it was fairly easy to get a farm, few New Englanders took on the risky job of fishing. Moreover, few could afford the necessary equipment, including boats, provisions, and salt (used for preserving fish). Merchants recruited fishermen by advancing credit to coastal villagers so that they could outfit their own boats. Many fishermen ran up such large debts that they were obliged to continue supplying fish to their creditors, whether they wanted to or not.

In the northern colonies, the same conditions that made men reluctant to become fishermen deterred them from becoming farm laborers, except perhaps for high wages. Paying high wages, however, or the high cost of servants or slaves was difficult for New Englanders with farms that produced no export crops and could not be worked during cold winter months. So northern farmers turned to the cheapest and most dependable workers they could find—their children.

Children as young as 5 or 6 years old began with simple tasks and moved on to more complex work as they grew older. By the time they were in their late teens, girls knew how to run households, and boys knew how to farm. Fathers used their ownership of property to prolong the time their sons worked for them. Young men could not marry until they could set up their own households and relied on their fathers to provide them with land to do so. Fathers often waited until their sons were in their mid-twenties, compelling them until then to invest their labor in the paternal estate.

QUICK REVIEW

Child Labor in New England

- Children began work as young as 5 or 6.
- Teenagers took on adult tasks.
- Fathers used ownership of property to tie sons to the land.

New European Immigrants

European immigrants flooded into America in the seventeenth and eighteenth centuries (see Figure 3–4). Nearly 250,000 Scots-Irish people—descendants of Protestant Scots who had settled in northern Ireland in the sixteenth and seventeenth centuries—came to the colonies after

GLOBAL CONNECTIONS

Early Modern Europe's Biggest Mass Migration

The stream of German immigrants moving to America in the late seventeenth and eighteenth centuries formed only a small part of a much larger flow of emigrants from the Rhineland to many parts of the globe. The Rhineland was not a single political unit, but a region of small states and principalities located along one of Europe's major rivers. Political fragmentation brought religious diversity, with German Reformed or Lutheran churches dominant in some areas and Catholics in others.

Large-scale emigration of Rhineland inhabitants stemmed from many causes, especially warfare. During the Thirty Years' War (1618–1648), much of the Rhineland area was devastated by intense religious conflict and famine. In the 1680s and 1690s, Louis XIV of France invaded the region, sparking more turmoil. Almost continual warfare from the 1730s to the 1760s made the lives of Rhineland inhabitants even worse.

Economic hardship and political repression also spurred emigration. Harsh winters in 1708–1709 and 1709–1710, for instance, destroyed orchards and vineyards, threatening many farmers with impoverishment and even starvation. Harvests failed in many parts of the Rhineland in the 1740s. In addition, religious minorities suffered from persecution, and everyone bore the burden of increasing taxes and arbitrary rule by local princes. For all of these reasons, over the course of the eighteenth century, hundreds of thousands of Rhinelanders decided to flee their homeland.

Many promoters, land speculators, and even governments sought to direct the flow of emigrants to a favored region. Officials from Russia and Prussia offered cheap land and tax exemptions to lure migrants to their countries. As a result of this promotional campaign, by far the largest number of Rhineland refugees relocated to various parts of Eastern Europe, including Prussia, Russia, Hungary, and Poland. A smaller flow of emigrants, mostly Protestants, made their way to North America, settling principally in Pennsylvania, New York, and the Carolinas. Still others moved to Cayenne (French Guiana) in South America. The exodus of these German-speaking emigrants to destinations in the Old and New Worlds constituted the most significant mass migration in early modern Europe.

- Why might more Rhineland migrants have moved within Europe instead of going to the North American colonies?

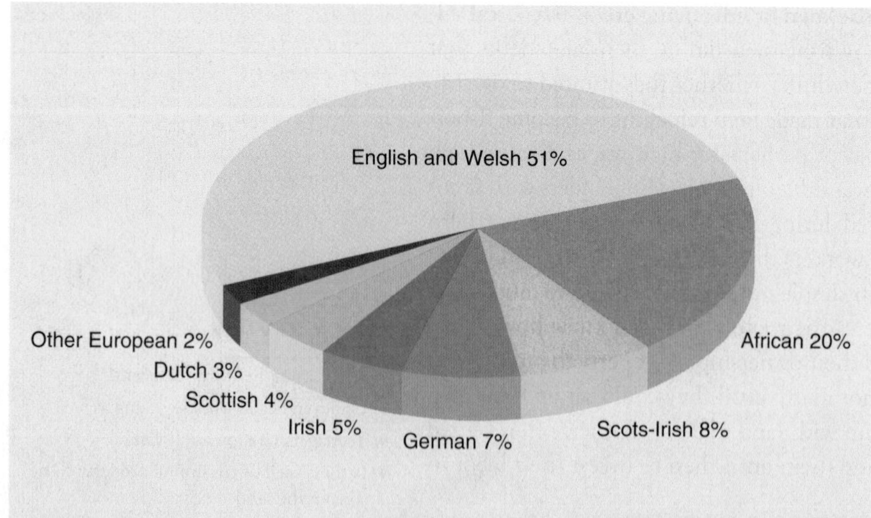

FIGURE 3–4 **Ethnic Distribution of Non-Indian Inhabitants of British Mainland Colonies, c. 1770** By the third quarter of the eighteenth century, the colonial population was astonishingly diverse. Only two out of three settlers claimed British ancestry (from England, Wales, Scotland, or northern Ireland), while one out of five was African in origin.

Data Source: Thomas L. Purvis, "The European Ancestry of the United States Population, 1790," *William and Mary Quarterly*, 3d series, 41 (1984), p. 98.

1718, when their landlords raised rents to intolerable levels. Tens of thousands of immigrants arrived from Scotland during the same period, some seeking economic improvement and some sent as punishment for rebellions against the king in 1715 and 1745. Thousands of Irish Catholics arrived as servants, redemptioners, and convicts.

Continental Europe contributed another stream of emigrants. Perhaps 100,000 German Protestants left the Rhine Valley, where war, economic hardship, and religious persecution had brought misery. French Protestants (known as Huguenots) began emigrating after 1685, when their faith was made illegal in France. Swiss Protestants likewise fled religious persecution. Even a few Poles, Greeks, Italians, and Jews reached the colonies in the eighteenth century.

Many emigrants responded to pamphlets and newspaper articles that exaggerated the bright prospects of life in America. Others studied more realistic accounts from friends and relatives who had already emigrated. Landowners sent agents to port towns to recruit new arrivals to become tenants, often on generous terms.

Streams of emigrants flowed to places where land was cheap and labor most in demand (see Map 3–3). Few went to New England, where descendants of the first settlers occupied the best land. They also avoided areas where slavery predominated—the Chesapeake Tidewater and lowland South Carolina—in favor of the foothills of the Appalachian Mountains, from western Pennsylvania to the Carolinas. There, one emigrant declared, a "poor man that will incline to work may have the value of his labour."

This observation, though partly true, did not tell the whole story. Any person who came as a servant, redemptioner, or tenant learned that his master or landlord received much of "the value of his labour." Not all emigrants realized their dreams of becoming independent landowners. The scarcity of labor in the colonies led as easily to the exploitation of white workers as of slaves and Indians. Even so, for many people facing bleak prospects in Europe, the chance that emigration might bring prosperity was too tempting to ignore.

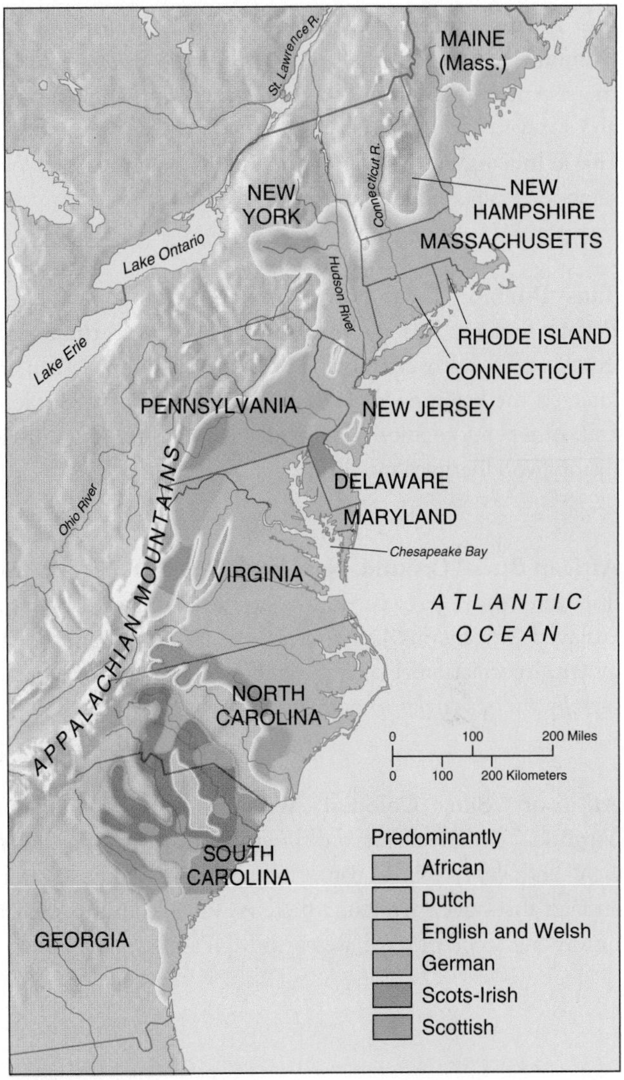

MAP 3–3 **Ethnic Distribution of Settler Population in British Mainland Colonies, c. 1755** Settlers of different ethnic backgrounds tended to concentrate in certain areas. Only New Englanders were predominantly English, while Africans dominated in the Chesapeake Tidewater and South Carolina. German, Scottish, and Scots-Irish immigrants often settled in the backcountry.

What factors explain the geographic concentration of colonists of particular ethnic backgrounds?

CONCLUSION

The ocean voyage that brought Olaudah Equiano across the Atlantic carried him to a land containing a strikingly diverse mosaic of peoples and communities. In communities across North America, peoples from three continents adapted to one another and to American conditions. For some of the people in these communities, emigration and settlement had brought opportunity; for others, including Equiano and his fellow Africans, it brought oppression. For many, though not all, European immigrants, the colonies offered the chance for economic improvement.

Yet at the same time, millions of African slaves suffered under the most repressive colonial labor regime, fighting its grip whenever possible. And even as Europeans and Africans adapted to different New World circumstances, Indians struggled with the consequences of disease, trade, religious conversion, settlement, and warfare resulting from European immigration. Some native peoples managed to preserve their autonomy, others did not.

As the eighteenth century wore on, the North American colonies attracted more attention from their home countries. Spain, France, and England recognized the colonies' growing economic power and strove to harness it to block the expansion of their rivals. Everywhere the effort to strengthen imperial ties created ambivalence among colonists. Because the English settlers were by far the most numerous, their responses were the most pronounced. As they saw more clearly the differences between themselves and England itself, some colonists began to defend their distinctive habits, while others tried more insistently than ever to imitate English ways. The tension between new and old had characterized colonial development from the start. What made the eighteenth century distinctive were the many ways in which the tensions worked themselves out.

Where to Learn More

Ste. Marie among the Hurons, near Midland, Ontario, Canada. This site contains a reconstructed Jesuit mission from the seventeenth century. There is a museum with information about seventeenth-century France as well as life among the Huron Indians. Further information may be found at http://www.saintemarieamongthehurons.on.ca.

Taos Pueblo, Taos, New Mexico. Still a residence for Pueblo Indians, this multistoried pueblo has portions dating from the fifteenth century. This is the site from which Popé directed the beginnings of the Pueblo Revolt in 1680. Pictures and other information are available at http://www.nps.gov/history/worldheritage/taos.htm.

African Burial Ground, New York City, NY. This recently discovered site of an eighteenth-century burial ground for free and enslaved Africans on Manhattan is now a national park and monument. Information about visits and exhibitions can be found at http://www.nps.gov/afbg/index.htm.

Atkinson Site, Colonial Williamsburg, Williamsburg, Virginia. Archaeologists are currently excavating this site of an eighteenth-century slave quarter. Information about the site and the artifacts that have been found there is available at http://research.history.org/Archaeological_Research/MHPage/AAArch.htm.

Review Questions

1. The first phase of Olaudah Equiano's journey into slavery took him from Africa's interior to the coast. What part of this journey most frightened him? Why? How did the development of a transatlantic labor market shape Equiano's experiences in the New World and the Old?
2. English colonists experienced more frequent, and more violent, conflicts with Indians than the settlers of New France did. Why was this so? What factors affected Indian-European relations in the two colonial regions?
3. Why were Catholic missionaries more successful than Protestants in converting Indians to Christianity in early America?
4. When did Chesapeake planters switch from servants to slaves? What factors contributed to their decision to make this change?
5. By about 1750, more slaves in the mainland British colonies were creoles (American-born) than African-born. What effects did this have on the formation of African American communities in America?
6. Different labor systems predominated in various regions of British America. How did the economy of each region help determine its labor system?
7. Tens of thousands of European immigrants came to America in the eighteenth century, but they tended to settle only in certain colonial regions. What destinations did they favor and why?

Key Terms

Bacon's Rebellion (p. 65)
Beaver Wars (p. 61)
Encomienda (p. 60)
King Philip's War (p. 64)
Middle Passage (p. 68)
Pueblo Revolt (p. 65)
Redemptioner (p. 76)
Repartimiento (p. 60)
Stono Rebellion (p. 75)

myhistorylab Connections

Reinforce what you learned in this chapter by studying the many documents, images, maps, review tools, and videos available at **www.myhistorylab.com**.

Read and Review

Study and Review **Study Plan: Chapter 3**

Read the Document

Olaudah Equiano, The Middle Passage (1788)

A Slave Tells of His Capture in Africa (1798)

A Virginian Describes the Difference between Servants and Slaves (1722)

Runaway Indentured Servants (1640)

Runaway Notices from The South Carolina Gazette *(1732, 1737)*

Slaves Revolt in South Carolina (1739)

Virginia Law on Indentured Servitude (1705)

Wessell Webling, His Indenture (1622)

See the Map

African Slave Trade, 1500–1870

The Atlantic and Islamic Slave Trades

Research and Explore

Read the Document

Personal Journeys Online

From Then to Now Online: The Legacy of Slavery

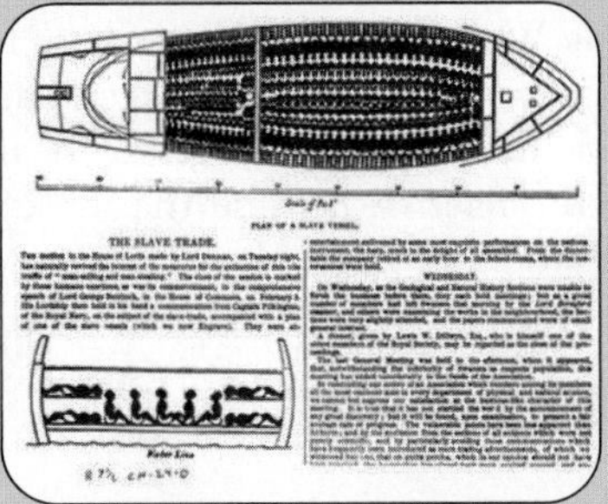

Exploring America: Racism in America

Watson and the Shark: Reading the Representation of Race

Hear the Audio *I Just Come from the Fountain*

Hear the Audio

Hear the audio files for Chapter 3 at **www.myhistorylab.com**.

INTERPRETING the PAST

The Voyage to Slavery

WHAT WERE the dehumanizing experiences faced by Africans as they were kidnapped and transported to the New World as slaves? Under what conditions were Africans taken for slavery, and what was their fate when they arrived in the New World?

Most Africans were captured by other Africans in interior wars between tribes or specifically for sale as slaves. The slaves were moved to the West Coast of Africa where European and American slavers awaited to purchase a human cargo. Slavers inspected their potential cargo for health and strength. Males were preferred because the work on New World plantations would be hard. Human cargo was packed into ships' holds in the most efficient manner and carried under horrible, inhumane conditions to the New World for sale to the highest bidder. It was not unusual for Africans to prefer death to such a fate and individuals would dive overboard or even throw their children into the sea because drowning was considered a better end than that of slavery. For this reason slaves would be kept below decks in leg irons with the exception of an hour or so of exercise each day. During the exercise period slaves would be forced to jump up and down or "dance" to keep their muscles limber and the sale price for each individual at its highest level. Each day dead slaves would be cast overboard and tales abound of schools of sharks trailing slave ships for hundreds of miles.

The shrieks of the women, ...

Olaudah Equiano, captured in Nigeria at a very early age, later gave this report of the experience crossing the Atlantic in a slave ship in 1789.

The closeness of the place [ship's hold], and the heat of the climate, added to the number in the ship, which was so crowded that each had scarcely room to turn himself, almost suffocated us. This produced copious perspirations, so that the air soon became unfit for respiration, from a variety of loathsome smells, and brought on a sickness amongst the slaves, of which many died, thus falling victims to the improvident avarice, as I may call it, of their purchasers. This wretched situation was again aggravated by the galling of the chains, now become insupportable; and the filth of the necessary tubs, into which the children often fell, and were almost suffocated. The shrieks of the women, and the groans of the dying, rendered the whole a scene of horror almost inconceivable. Happily perhaps for myself I was soon reduced so low here that it was thought necessary to keep me almost always on deck; and from my extreme youth I was not put in fetters. In this situation I expected every hour to share the fate of my companions, some of whom were almost daily brought upon deck at the point of death, which I began to hope would soon put an end to my miseries. . . . One day, when we had a smooth sea and moderate wind, two of my wearied countrymen who were chained together (I was near them at the time), preferring death to such a life of misery, somehow made through the nettings and jumped into the sea: immediately another quite dejected fellow, who on account of his illness, was suffered to be out of irons, also followed their example; and I believe many more would very soon have done the same if they had not been prevented by the ship's crew who were instantly alarmed. Those of us that were the most active were in a moment put down under the deck, and there was such a noise and confusion amongst the people of the ship as I never heard before, to stop her, and get

This eighteenth-century engraving of a slave ship shows how tightly Africans were packed below the decks of these vessels, evidence that the thirst for profit overrode concerns for their health or welfare.

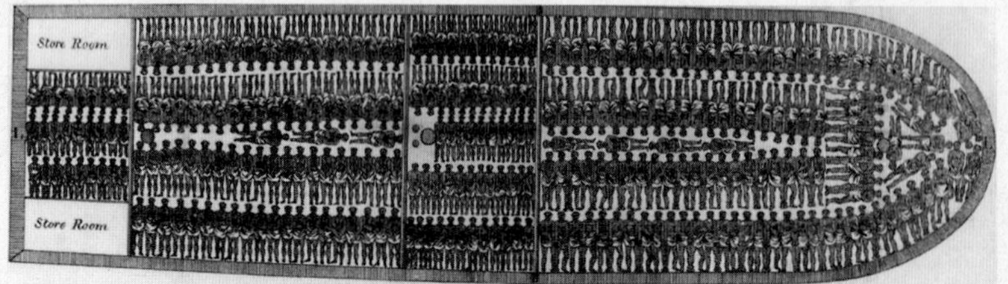

the boat out to go after the slaves. However two of the wretches were drowned, but they got the other, and afterwards flogged him unmercifully for thus attempting to prefer death to slavery.

Alexander Falconbridge served as a ship's surgeon aboard a slaver in 1788. He was so horrified by what he witnessed during that time that he became involved in the British abolition movement.

When the Negroes, whom the black traders have to dispose of, are shown to the European purchasers, they first examine them relative to their age. They then minutely inspect their persons, and inquire into the state of their health; if they are afflicted with any infirmity, or are deformed; or have bad eyes or teeth; if they are lame, or weak in their joints, or distorted in the back, or of a slender make, or are narrow in the chest; in short, if they have been, or are afflicted in any manner, so as to render them incapable of much labour; if any of the foregoing defects are discovered in them, they are rejected. But if approved of, they are generally taken on board the ship the same evening. The purchaser has liberty to return on the following morning, but not afterwards, such as upon re-examination are found exceptionable.

African men, women, and children are tied together while walking in chains after being captured by slave traders.

The traders frequently beat those Negroes which are objected to by the captains and use them with great severity. It matters not whether they are refused on account of age, illness, deformity, or for any other reason. At New Calabar, in particular, the traders have frequently been known to put them to death. Instances have happened at that place that the traders, when any of their Negroes have been objected to, have dropped their canoes under the stern of the vessel, and instantly beheaded them, in sight of the captain.

Two men brand an African woman kneeling helplessly on the ground.

The purchaser has liberty to return...

1600s-1763

4

English Colonies in an Age of Empire

New Amsterdam City Hall and Great Dock in the late seventeenth century.

Hear the Audio

Hear the audio files for Chapter 4 at **www.myhistorylab.com**.

ECONOMIC DEVELOPMENT AND IMPERIAL TRADE IN THE BRITISH COLONIES *(page 87)*

WHAT WERE the goals of British trade policy?

THE TRANSFORMATION OF CULTURE *(page 93)*

HOW DID new intellectual and religious trends reshape colonial culture?

THE COLONIAL POLITICAL WORLD *(page 98)*

HOW DID the "Glorious Revolution" affect colonial politics?

EXPANDING EMPIRES *(page 102)*

WHAT WAS the "backcountry"? Who settled there and why?

North Wind Picture Archives

A CENTURY OF WARFARE *(page 106)*

WHAT ROLE did the colonists play in the French and Indian War?

ONE AMERICAN JOURNEY

Virginia 26th April 1763

Mr. Lawrence

Be pleased to send me a genteel sute of Cloaths made of superfine broad Cloth handsomely chosen; I shou[l]d have Inclosed [for] you my measure but in a general way they are so badly taken here that I am convinced it wou[l]d be of very little service; I wou[l]d have you therefore take measure of a Gentleman who wears well made Cloaths of the following size—to wit—Six feet high & proportionably made; if any thing rather Slender than thick for a Person of that highth with pretty long arms & thighs—You will take care to make the Breeches longer than those you sent me last, & I wou[l]d have you keep the measure of the Cloaths you now make by you and if any alteration is required, in my next [letter] it shall be pointed out. Mr Cary will pay your Bill—& I am Sir Yr Very H[um]ble Serv[an]t . . .

George Washington

W. W. Abbot and Dorothy Twohig, eds., *The Papers of George Washington,* Colonial Series, vol. 7 (Charlottesville, 1990).

Read the Document at **www.myhistorylab.com**

Personal Journeys Online

- **Eliza Lucas Pinckney, *Letterbook,* 1742. Description of a South Carolina plantation mistress's day.**
- **Alexander Hamilton, *Itinerarium,* 1744. Description of sociability in eighteenth-century Philadelphia.**
- **Nathan Cole, "Spiritual Travels," October 23, 1740. A Connecticut farmer hears George Whitefield preach.**

GEORGE WASHINGTON, along with a few dozen other privileged Virginians, had traveled to Williamsburg for a visit that mixed politics, business, and pleasure. Like Washington, these men had come to the capital to represent their respective counties in the House of Burgesses. When not engaged in government business, they attended to private affairs. Washington was surely not the only one to take the opportunity to write to his London tailor and order the fashionable clothing that advertised his status as a gentleman.

April 1763 marked the fourth time Washington had gone to Williamsburg to take his seat in the legislature. Just 31 years old in that year, he had recently married Martha Custis, a wealthy widow, and inherited his older brother's plantation at Mount Vernon. Washington already owned more land than most English gentlemen. With land and wealth to support his ambitions, he wanted to live, look, and behave like an English country gentleman.

Throughout British America, colonists who had achieved wealth and power tried, like Washington, to imitate the habits and manners of the English gentry. Their aspirations testified to important developments in the eighteenth century. Prosperity and the demand of a growing population for English products tied the colonies ever more tightly into a trade network centered on the imperial metropolis, London. The flow of goods and information between Britain and America fueled the desires of Washington and other successful colonists for acceptance as transatlantic members of the British elite.

These developments in Great Britain's American colonies brought them to the attention of European statesmen, who increasingly factored North America into their calculations. Parliament devised legislation to channel colonial products into British ports and away from European competitors. Spain and France viewed the economic growth and geographic expansion of British North America as a threat to their own colonial possessions, and responded by augmenting their own territorial claims. With expansion came conflict, and with conflict, a series of four imperial wars, which themselves became powerful engines of change in the New World.

CHRONOLOGY

1651–1733	Parliament passes series of navigation acts to regulate imperial trade.
1660	Charles II becomes king of England.
1662	Halfway Covenant adopted by Massachusetts clergy.
1685	James II becomes king of England.
1686–1689	Dominion of New England.
1688	Glorious Revolution in England; James II loses the throne.
1689	William and Mary become English monarchs; Leisler's Rebellion begins in New York.
1689–1697	King William's War in America.
1691–1692	Witchcraft trials in Salem, Massachusetts.
1698	First French settlements near mouth of Mississippi River.
1701	Iroquois adopt policy of neutrality toward France and Britain.
1702–1713	Queen Anne's War in America.
1707	Act of Union joins England and Scotland to create Great Britain.
1718	San Antonio, Texas, and New Orleans founded.
1734–1735	Jonathan Edwards leads religious revival in Northampton, Massachusetts.
1739	Great Awakening begins in Middle Colonies with George Whitefield's arrival.
1744–1748	King George's War in America.
1754–1763	Seven Years' War in America.
1760s	Spanish begin establishing missions in California.

ECONOMIC DEVELOPMENT AND IMPERIAL TRADE IN THE BRITISH COLONIES

WHAT WERE the goals of British trade policy?

England's greatest assets in its competition with other European nations were a dynamic economy and a sophisticated financial system that put commerce at the service of the state. British leaders came to see colonies as indispensable to the nation's economic welfare. Colonies supplied raw materials unavailable in the mother country, and colonists and Indians provided a healthy market for British manufactured goods.

As the eighteenth century progressed, colonial economies grew in tandem with that of Great Britain. Parliament knitted the colonies into an empire with commercial legislation, while British merchants traded with and extended credit to growing numbers of colonial merchants and planters. Over time, these developments integrated the economies of the colonies with that of the mother country in a vast transatlantic system.

The Regulation of Trade

To improve its competitive position in transatlantic trade, England adopted a policy of **mercantilism.** The goal was to achieve a favorable balance of trade within the empire as a whole, with exports exceeding imports. Colonies played a crucial role, since they supplied commodities that British consumers would otherwise have to purchase from foreign competitors. Certain colonial products, such as tobacco or rice, could also be exported to foreign markets, further improving the balance of trade. Between 1651 and 1733, Parliament passed four types of mercantilist regulations to put this policy into action (see the Overview table, British Imperial Trade Regulations, 1651–1733).

mercantilism Economic system whereby the government intervenes in the economy for the purpose of increasing national wealth.

The first type of regulation aimed at ending Dutch dominance in overseas trade. Beginning with the Navigation Act of 1651, all trade in the empire had to be conducted in English or colonial ships, with crews of which at least half were Englishmen or colonists. The act stimulated rapid growth in England's merchant marine and New England's shipping industry, which soon became the most profitable sector of New England's economy.

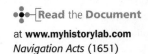

Read the **Document** at **www.myhistorylab.com** *Navigation Acts* (1651)

enumerated products Items produced in the colonies and enumerated in acts of Parliament that could be legally shipped from the colony of origin only to specified locations.

QUICK REVIEW

British Trade Policy

- All trade in empire to be conducted on English or colonial ships.
- Colonial trade to be channeled through England or another English colony.
- Subsidization of English goods offered for sale in the colonies.
- Colonists prohibited from large-scale manufacture of certain products.

The second type of legislation stipulated that certain colonial goods, called **enumerated products,** could be shipped only to England or to another English colony. These goods initially included tobacco, sugar, and indigo; other products, such as rice, were added later. These laws also required European goods to pass through England before they could be shipped to the colonies. When these goods entered English ports, they were taxed, making them more expensive and encouraging colonists to buy English-made items.

The third and fourth types of regulations further enhanced the advantage of English manufacturers who produced for the colonial market. Parliament subsidized certain goods, including linen and gunpowder, to allow manufacturers to undersell European competitors in the colonies. Other laws protected English manufacturers from colonial competition by prohibiting colonists from manufacturing wool, felt hats, and iron on a large scale.

England's commercial goals were largely achieved. The Dutch eventually lost their preeminence in the Atlantic trade. Colonial trade helped the English economy to grow and contributed to London's emergence as Western Europe's largest city. Colonists enjoyed protected markets for their staple crops and low prices on English imports. Colonial merchants took full advantage of commercial opportunities within the empire.

Occasionally, merchants evaded these laws by smuggling. Customs officials, sent over from England beginning in the 1670s, were hard-pressed to stop them. Smuggling tended to increase in wartime; the risks may have been higher, but so too were profits. Without the support of colonial authorities (some of whom might be involved in illicit trade themselves), customs officials struggled to enforce parliamentary regulations.

The Colonial Export Trade and the Spirit of Enterprise

By the mid-eighteenth century, the Atlantic had become a busy thoroughfare of international commerce (see Map 4–1). British and colonial vessels carried goods and people from Great Britain, continental Europe, and West Africa to the colonies and returned raw materials to the Old World. At the heart of Anglo-American trade lay the highly profitable commerce in staple crops, most of which were produced by slave labor.

West Indian sugar far surpassed all other colonial products in importance (see Figure 4–1). By the late 1760s, the value of sugar exports reached almost £4 million per year—nearly 50 percent more than the total value of all other exports from British American colonies.

Tobacco from the Chesapeake colonies was the second most valuable staple crop. Nearly 90 percent of the crop was reexported to continental Europe. Persistent low prices, however, led many tobacco planters to sow some of their land with wheat after about 1750. This change lessened their dependence on tobacco and allowed them to take advantage of the strong demand for flour in southern Europe and the West Indies.

Exports of rice and indigo (a plant that produced a blue dye used in textile manufacture) enriched many South Carolina planters. Parliament encouraged indigo production by granting subsidies to growers and placing stiff taxes on foreign indigo. It also subsidized colonial production of naval stores—such as tar, pitch, and turpentine—to reduce England's dependence on Swedish suppliers.

Wheat exports from the Middle Colonies boomed in the eighteenth century. Since farmers in Great Britain grew enough wheat to supply the domestic market, there was little demand there for colonial flour. But there was a strong market for it in the West Indies and Europe, particularly when a series of poor harvests and warfare disrupted European supplies.

New England had no staple crop and produced little for export. The region's merchants nevertheless prospered by carrying other colonies' goods to market. By 1770, New England's earnings from shipping fees, freight charges, and insurance exceeded the total value of its own exports.

QUICK REVIEW

Colonial Exports

- Chesapeake colonies: tobacco.
- South Carolina: rice and indigo.
- Middle Colonies: wheat.

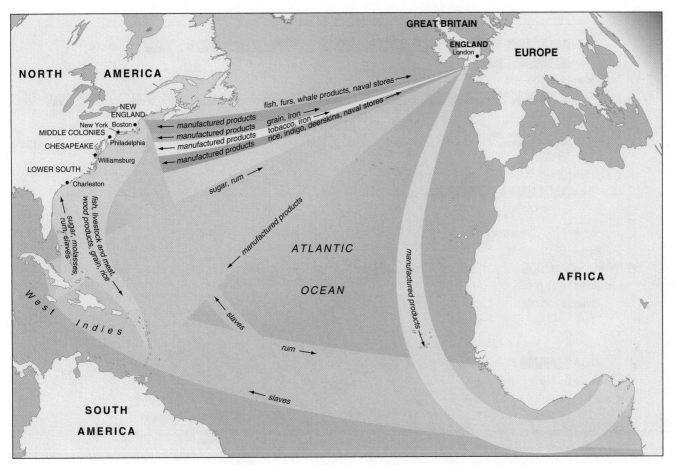

MAP 4–1 Anglo-American Transatlantic Commerce By the eighteenth century, Great Britain and its colonies were enmeshed in a complex web of trade. Britain exchanged manufactured goods for colonial raw materials, while Africa provided the enslaved laborers who produced the most valuable colonial crops.

The transatlantic commerce of this era is sometimes referred to as the "triangular trade." Does this map support or complicate this description?

New England merchants also strengthened trade links to the West Indies that had first been forged in the 1650s. By the mid-eighteenth century, more than half of all New England exports went to the islands. Merchants accepted molasses and other sugar by-products in payment, bringing them back to New England to be distilled into cheap rum. Traders then carried rum to Africa to exchange for slaves. Although British merchants dominated the African slave trade, New Englanders also profited. Less than 10 percent of New England's population were slaves, but because New Englanders trafficked in human cargo and provisioned the West Indies, their commercial economy nonetheless depended on slavery.

The Import Trade and Ties of Credit

By the late 1760s, over £4 million worth of British manufactured goods flowed into the colonies each year. This import trade satisfied a demand for items that could not be produced—at least not cheaply—in North America.

See the **Map** at **www.myhistorylab.com** *Colonial Products*

Imported weapons, woolen cloth, knives, and jewelry often made their way into Indian villages. Indians were discerning customers and rejected goods not made to their liking. Native leaders sometimes acquired imported goods for exchange with allies as well as for their own use.

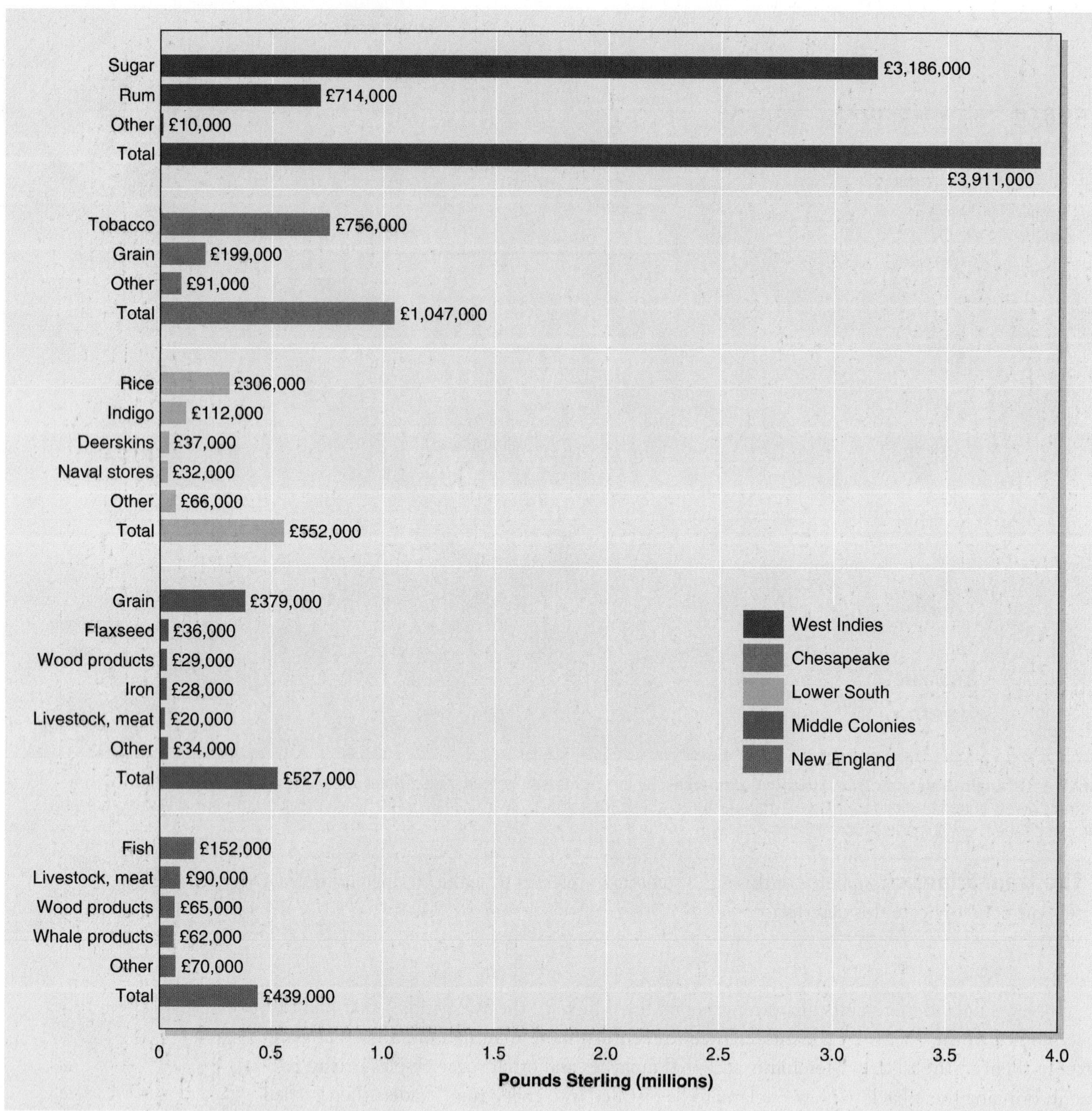

FIGURE 4–1 **Average Annual Value of Colonial Exports by Region, 1768–1772** Staple crops—especially sugar—produced by slave labor were the most valuable items exported from Britain's North American colonies.

Data Source: John J. McCusker and Russell R. Menard, *The Economy of British America, 1607–1789*, rev. ed. (1991). University of North Carolina Press.

The colonists' even heavier consumption of manufactured goods was vital to British overseas commerce. In terms of value, colonists imported more goods than they exported. This imbalance was remedied in good part by colonial earnings from shipping fees and payments from the British government for colonial military expenses.

British merchants extended credit to colonists on generous terms so they could buy British products. Major tobacco planters virtually lived on the easy credit that British merchants provided. These merchants marketed the planters' tobacco and supplied them with English goods, charging the costs of purchase and transportation against the profits they expected the next year's crop to bring.

Scenes like this were common in the dockyards at Deptford and other parts of eighteenth-century London. Boxes and barrels of English goods were loaded aboard sailing ships that returned months later with sugar, tobacco, rice, and other products from every part of England's worldwide empire.

Easy credit let planters indulge themselves with English goods, and many sank into debt. When trade was brisk and tobacco prices high, no one worried. But when tobacco prices dropped or an international crisis made overseas trading risky, creditors called in the debts owed to them. At such times, colonial debtors realized how much they (like the Indians involved in European trade) depended on goods and credit supplied by distant merchants.

Becoming More Like Britain: The Growth of Cities and Inequality

As colonial commerce grew, so did colonial cities—the connecting points in the economic network tying the colonies to London and other British ports. Boston, New York, Philadelphia, and Charleston were as large as many British provincial towns. Only about 5 percent of all mainland colonists lived in cities, but the influence of urban centers far outweighed their size.

OVERVIEW British Imperial Trade Regulations, 1651–1733

Name of Act	Key Features
Navigation Act of 1651	Aimed to eliminate Dutch competition in overseas trade Required most goods to be carried in English or colonial ships Required crews to be at least half English
Navigation Act of 1660	Required all colonial trade to be carried in English ships Required master and three-quarters of crew to be English Created list of enumerated goods, such as tobacco and sugar, that could be shipped only to England or another English colony
Staple Act of 1663	Required products from Europe, Asia, and Africa to be landed in England before being shipped to the colonies
Plantation Duty Act of 1673	Attempted to reduce smuggling Required captains of colonial ships to post bond that they would deliver enumerated goods to England or pay the "plantation duty" that would be owed in England
Navigation Act of 1696	Plugged loopholes in earlier laws Created vice-admiralty courts in colonies to enforce trade regulations
Woolens Act of 1699	Forbade export of woolen cloth made in the colonies, to prevent competition with English producers
Hat Act of 1732	Prohibited export of colonial-made hats
Molasses Act of 1733	Placed high tax on French West Indian and other foreign molasses imported into colonies to encourage importation of British West Indian molasses

All colonial cities (like Britain's major ones) were seaports. With their bustle and cosmopolitan atmosphere, colonial cities resembled British provincial cities more than they did the farming villages of the American countryside. Cities provided such amenities as inns, taverns, coffeehouses, theaters, and social clubs. Their populations were diverse in ethnic origin and religion. In addition, the African American population in the northern colonies tended to live in cities. By 1750, slaves made up 20 percent of New York City's population, about 10 percent of Philadelphia's, and nearly 9 percent of Boston's.

Hear the Audio at **www.myhistorylab.com** *The Connecticut Peddler*

Artisans in colonial cities. Colonial cities had higher proportions of artisans than did rural villages. Many of them labored at trades directly related to overseas commerce, such as shipbuilding or ropemaking. Others produced pottery, furniture, paper, glassware, and iron tools.

Colonial manufacturing took place in workshops often attached to artisans' houses. Artisans managed a workforce consisting of their wives and children, along with journeymen or apprentices. Usually teenage boys, apprentices contracted to work for a master for four to seven years. Like indentured servants, they received no wages but worked for food, clothing, shelter, and a small payment at the end of their service. Once an apprentice finished his training, he became a journeyman, working for a master but now earning wages and saving to set up his own shop.

Many artisans flourished in colonial cities, but prosperity was by no means guaranteed. In Philadelphia, skilled artisans typically earned enough for a modest subsistence. Yet workers at less skilled crafts often made only a bare living, and ordinary laborers faced seasonal unemployment.

This view of the Philadelphia waterfront dates from 1720. It shows how the city had developed into one of British America's principal ports just forty years after its founding.

Peter Cooper, "The Southeast Prospect of the City of Philadelphia," ca. 1720. The Library Company of Philadelphia.

Cities like Philadelphia, New York, and Charleston provided opportunities for some women to support themselves with craft work. Mary Wallace and Clementia Ferguson, for instance, stitched fashionable hats and dresses for New York customers. Nonetheless, even in cities, women's options were limited. Most employed women were widows striving to maintain a family business until sons grew old enough to take over.

The growing gap between rich and poor. Wherever colonists engaged heavily in commerce—in cities or on plantations—the gap between rich and poor widened during the eighteenth century. In 1687, the richest 10 percent of Boston's residents owned 46 percent of the taxable property in the town; by 1771, the top tenth held 63 percent of the taxable wealth. Similar changes occurred in Philadelphia. In South Carolina and the Chesapeake, many planters added to the already substantial holdings in land and slaves that they had inherited. It became increasingly difficult for newcomers to enter their ranks. At the same time, the colonies' growing reliance on slave labor—especially in the South—created a sizable class of impoverished people denied the chance to better their condition. By 1770, slaves, for whom America was anything but a land of opportunity, constituted one out of five residents of the British colonies.

QUICK REVIEW

Poverty in the Colonies

- Gap between rich and poor widened in the eighteenth century.
- Most cities had workhouses or shelters.
- Much smaller percentage of population depended on public assistance in the colonies than in England.

To address the growing problem of poverty among white colonists, cities built workhouses, and towns collected funds for poor relief in greater amounts than ever before. Many poor people were aged or ill, without families to help them. Able-bodied workers forced to accept public relief usually owed their misfortune to temporary downturns in the economy.

Even in the worst of times, no more than one out of ten white colonists (mainly city dwellers) depended on public assistance. For free black people who were unemployed and denied public relief, conditions were far worse. A Pennsylvania law went so far as to allow them to be enslaved. And, bad as it was, the problem of poverty among white colonists had not reached anything like the levels seen in Britain. As much as one-third of England's population regularly received relief, and the numbers swelled during hard times. Eighteenth-century white colonists, on average, enjoyed a higher standard of living than most British residents or other Europeans. So long as land was available—even if one had to move to the edges of settlement to get it—colonists could at least eke out a bare subsistence, and many did much better.

THE TRANSFORMATION OF CULTURE

HOW DID new intellectual and religious trends reshape colonial culture?

Despite the convergence of British and colonial society, many influential settlers worried that America remained culturally inferior to Great Britain. During the eighteenth century, some prosperous colonists strove to overcome this provincial sense of inferiority. They built grand houses and filled them with imported goods, cultivated what they took to be the manners of the British gentry, and followed British and European intellectual developments. Some colonial gentlemen

The Governor's Palace in Williamsburg, Virginia, completed in 1722, was one of the grandest and most expensive dwellings in the colony.

even reshaped their religious beliefs to reflect European notions that God played only an indirect role in human affairs.

These elite aspirations, however, were not shared by all settlers. Most colonists, although they might purchase a few imported goods, had little interest in copying the manners of the British elite, and few of them altered their spiritual beliefs to fit European patterns. Indeed, familiar religious practices flourished in eighteenth-century America, and when a tremendous revival swept through the colonies beginning in the 1730s, religion occupied center stage in American life.

Goods and Houses

Eighteenth-century Americans imported more manufactured products from England with every passing year. This practice did not simply reflect the growth of the colonial population, for the rate at which Americans bought British goods exceeded the rate of population increase. Colonists owned more goods, often of better quality, than their parents and grandparents had possessed.

Read the **Document**
at **www.myhistorylab.com**
Benjamin Wadsworth, from A Well-Ordered Family (1712)

In the less secure economic climate of the seventeenth century, colonists had limited their purchases of goods, investing instead in land to pass on to their children. But by the eighteenth century, prosperous colonists felt secure enough to buy goods to make their lives more comfortable. Colonists acquired such goods to advertise their more refined style of life.

Prosperous colonists built grand houses where they lived in greater comfort than ever before. By the 1730s, numerous southern planters had built "great houses" while others transformed older houses into more stylish residences. Washington extensively remodeled Mount Vernon, adding a second story and extra wings to create a home fit for a gentleman. In the northern colonies, merchants built the most impressive houses, often following architectural pattern books imported from England.

Berkeley and Westover Plantations, Charles City, Virginia
http://www.jamesriverplantations.org

These houses were not only larger but also different in design from the homes of less affluent colonists. Most settlers lived in one- or two-room dwellings and thus cooked, ate, and slept in the same chamber. But the owners of great houses could devote rooms to specialized uses, such as kitchens and private bedrooms.

Prosperous colonists did not build such homes merely to advertise their wealth. They wanted to create the proper setting for a refined way of life, emulating the English gentry in their country estates and London townhouses. But they knew that the true measure of their gentility lay not just in where they lived and what they owned but in how they behaved.

Mount Vernon, Virginia
http://www.mountvernon.org

Shaping Minds and Manners

Colonists knew that the manners of British gentlefolk set them apart from ordinary people. Many Americans therefore imported "courtesy books" containing the rules of polite behavior. These publications advised would-be gentlemen on how to show regard for social rank, practice personal cleanliness, and respect other people's feelings. Many colonists subscribed to English journals such as the *Tatler* and the *Spectator* that printed articles describing good manners.

Women, too, cultivated genteel manners. In Charleston, South Carolina, and other colonial cities, girls' boarding schools advertised instruction in "Polite Education." Female pupils received only the rudiments of intellectual training in reading, writing, and arithmetic, for it was assumed that women had little need of such accomplishments. The private schools' curricula instead focused on French, music, dancing, and fancy needlework. These were skills that advertised girls' genteel status and prepared them for married lives as elite ladies.

Some people expressed their gentility through more intellectual pursuits, taking advantage of the relatively high literacy rates among white colonists. In New England, where settlers placed great emphasis on Bible study, about 70 percent of men and 45 percent of women could read and write. Only a third of men in the southern colonies, and even fewer women, could read and write, but even these literacy rates were higher than among Britain's general population. Eighteenth-century colonists enjoyed greater access to printed material than ever before. In 1704, the *Boston News-Letter* became the first continuously published newspaper in British America. By the 1760s nearly every colony had a regularly published newspaper, and booksellers opened shops in several cities. Prominent colonists began to participate in a transatlantic world of ideas.

Educated colonists were especially interested in the new ideas that characterized what has been called the **Age of Enlightenment.** The European thinkers of the Enlightenment drew inspiration from recent advances in science that suggested that the universe operated according to natural laws that human reason could discover. The hallmark of Enlightenment thought was a belief in the power of human reason to improve the human condition.

Age of Enlightenment Major intellectual movement occurring in Western Europe in the late seventeenth and early eighteenth centuries.

This optimistic worldview marked a profound intellectual shift. Enlightenment thinkers rejected earlier ideas about God's unknowable will and continued intervention in human and natural events. They instead assigned God a less active role as the creator of the universe, who had set the world running according to predictable laws, and then let nature and humans shape events. Such ideas inspired a growing international community of scholars to try to discover the laws of nature and to work toward human progress.

Colonial intellectuals sought membership in this scholarly community. A few of them—the Reverend Cotton Mather of Massachusetts, William Byrd, Benjamin Franklin—gained election to the Royal Society, the most prestigious learned society in England. Most of their scholarly contributions were unimpressive, but Franklin achieved genuine intellectual prominence. His experiments with a kite proved that lightning was electricity (a natural force whose properties were poorly understood at the time) and gained him an international reputation.

QUICK REVIEW

Enlightenment Thought

- Inspired by scientific advances.
- Emphasis on the power of reason to improve human life.
- Assigned God a less active role in human affairs.

If Franklin's career embodied the Enlightenment ideal of the rational exploration of nature's laws, it also revealed the limited impact of Enlightenment thought in colonial America. Only a few prosperous and educated colonists could afford such intellectual pursuits. Franklin came from humble origins—his father was a maker of candles and soap—but his success as a printer allowed him to retire from business at the age of 42. Only then did he purchase the equipment for his electrical discoveries and have the leisure time to begin his scientific work. Franklin's equipment—and leisure—were as much badges of gentlemanly status as George Washington's London-made suit.

Most colonists remained ignorant of scientific advances and Enlightenment ideas, having little leisure to devote to literature and polite conversation. When they found time to read, they picked up not a courtesy book or the *Spectator* but the Bible, which was the best-selling book of the colonial era. Religion principally shaped the way in which they viewed the world and explained human and natural events.

Colonial Religion and the Great Awakening

Church steeples dominated the skylines of colonial cities. By the 1750s, Boston and New York each had eighteen churches, and Philadelphia boasted twenty. Churches and meetinghouses likewise dominated country towns. Often the largest and finest buildings in the community, they bore witness to the diverse and thriving condition of religion in America.

In every New England colony except Rhode Island, the Puritan (or Congregationalist) faith was the established religion. Congregational churches in the region, headed by ministers trained at Harvard College and Yale (founded in 1701), served the majority of colonists, who were required to pay taxes to support them. Though proud of the Puritan tradition that had inspired New England's origins, ministers and believers nonetheless had to adapt to changing social and religious conditions.

By the time he was in his forties, Benjamin Franklin had already achieved considerable fame as an author, scientist, and inventor.

Mason Chamberlain (1727–1787), "Portrait of Benjamin Franklin." 1762. Oil on canvas, 503/8 × 403/4 inches (128 × 103.5 cm). Gift of Mr. and Mrs. Wharton Sinkler, 1956. Location: Philadelphia Museum of Art, Philadelphia, Pennsylvania, U.S.A./Art Resource, NY.

The principal adaptation consisted of a move away from strict requirements for church membership. In order to keep their churches pure, New England's founders had required prospective members to give convincing evidence that they had experienced a spiritual conversion before they could receive communion and have their children baptized. By the 1660s, however, fewer colonists sought admission under such strict standards, which left them and their unbaptized children outside the church. To address this problem, the clergy in 1662 adopted the **Halfway Covenant.** This allowed adults who had been baptized (because their parents were church members), but who had not themselves experienced conversion, to have their own children baptized.

Congregational churches also had to accept a measure of religious toleration in New England. In 1691, Massachusetts received a royal charter granting "liberty of Conscience" to all Protestants, bringing the colony in line with England's religious policy. At the same time, some Congregationalist preachers began emphasizing personal piety and good works in their sermons, ideas usually associated with Anglicanism. These changes indicated a shift away from the Puritan exclusiveness of New England's early years.

In the South, the established Church of England consolidated its authority in the early eighteenth century but never exerted effective control over spiritual life. Many a parson in England could ride from one side of his parish to the other in an hour, but Anglican clergymen in the southern colonies served parishes that were vast and sparsely settled. One South Carolina parish contained 10,400 square miles and only seven hundred white residents. Ministers also found that influential planters, accustomed to running parishes when preachers were unavailable, resisted their efforts to take control of churches. Aware that the planters' taxes paid their salaries, many ministers found it easiest simply to preach and behave in ways that offered the least offense. Frontier regions often lacked Anglican churches and clergymen altogether. In such places, dissenting religious groups, such as Presbyterians, Quakers, and Baptists, gained followers among people neglected by the Anglican establishment.

Halfway Covenant Plan adopted in 1662 by New England clergy to deal with problem of declining church membership, allowing children of baptized parents to be baptized whether or not their parents had experienced conversion.

No established church dominated in the Middle Colonies of New York, New Jersey, and Pennsylvania. The region's ethnically diverse population and William Penn's policy of religious toleration guaranteed that a multitude of groups would compete for followers. Yet religion flourished in the Middle Colonies. By the middle of the eighteenth century, the region had more congregations per capita than even New England.

Groups such as the Quakers and the Mennonites, who did not have specially trained ministers, easily formed new congregations in response to local demand. Lutheran and German Reformed churches, however, required European-educated clergy, who were always scarce. Pious laymen held worship services in their homes even as they sent urgent letters overseas begging for ordained ministers. When more Lutheran and Reformed clergy arrived in the 1740s and 1750s, they sometimes discovered, as Anglican preachers did in the South, that laymen balked at relinquishing control of the churches.

Read the **Document** at **www.myhistorylab.com** *Exploring America: The Great Awakening*

Bewildering spiritual diversity, relentless religious competition, and a comparatively weak Anglican Church all distinguished the colonies from Britain. Yet in one important way, religious developments during the middle third of the eighteenth century drew the colonies closer to Britain. A great transatlantic religious revival, originating in Scotland and England, first touched the Middle Colonies in the 1730s. In 1740–1745, it struck the northern colonies with the force of a hurricane, and in the 1760s, the last phase of the revival spread through the South.

America had never seen anything like this immense revival, which came to be called the **Great Awakening.**

Great Awakening Tremendous religious revival in colonial America striking first in the Middle Colonies and New England in the 1740s and then spreading to the southern colonies.

By 1730, Presbyterians in Pennsylvania had split into factions over such issues as the disciplining of church members and the requirement that licensed ministers have university degrees. What began as a dispute among clergymen eventually blossomed into a broader challenge to religious authority. That challenge gained momentum in late 1739, when one of the most charismatic evangelists of the century, George Whitefield, arrived in the colonies from England.

Whitefield, an Anglican minister, had experienced an intense religious conversion while he was still a university student. Already famous in Britain as a preacher of great emotional fervor, he embarked on a tour of the colonies in the winter of 1739–1740. As soon as Whitefield landed in Delaware, his admirers whipped up local enthusiasm, ensuring that he would preach to huge crowds in Pennsylvania and New Jersey. Whitefield then moved on to New England, where some communities had already experienced local awakenings. In 1734–1735, for instance, the Congregationalist minister Jonathan Edwards had led a revival in Northampton, Massachusetts, urging his parishioners to recognize their sinfulness and describing hell in such a terrifying way that many despaired of salvation.

Read the **Document**
at **www.myhistorylab.com**
Jonathan Edwards, "Some Thoughts" **(1742)**

Whitefield's tour through the colonies knitted these scattered local revivals into the Great Awakening. Crowds gathered in city squares and open fields to listen to his sermons. Whitefield exhorted his audiences to examine their souls for evidence of the "indwelling of Christ" that would indicate that they were saved. He criticized other ministers for emphasizing good works and "head-knowledge" instead of the emotional side of religion.

Whitefield's open-air sermons scarcely resembled the colonists' accustomed form of worship. Settlers normally gathered with family and neighbors in church for formal, structured services. They sat in pews assigned on the basis of social status, reinforcing standards of order and community hierarchy. But Whitefield's sermons were highly dramatic performances. He preached for hours in a booming voice, gesturing wildly and sometimes even dissolving in tears. Thousands of strangers, jostling in crowds that often outnumbered the populations of several villages put together, wept along with him.

In the wake of Whitefield's visits, Benjamin Franklin noted, "it seem'd as if all the World were growing Religious." Revivals and mass conversions often followed his appearances, to the happy astonishment of local clergy. But their approval evaporated when more extreme revivalists appeared. Officials who valued civic order tried to silence such extremists by passing laws that prohibited them from preaching in a town without the local minister's permission.

Read the **Document**
at **www.myhistorylab.com**
Benjamin Franklin on George Whitefield **(1771)**

Disputes between individuals converted in the revivals—called **New Lights**—and those who were not (Old Lights) split churches. New Lights insisted, as the separatist founders of Plymouth once had, that they could not remain in churches with sinful members and unconverted ministers and so left to form new churches.

New Lights People who experienced conversion during the revivals of the Great Awakening.

The Awakening came late to the southern colonies, but it was there, in the 1760s, that it produced perhaps its greatest controversy. Many southern converts became Baptists, combining religious criticism of the Anglicans with condemnation of the wealthy planters' way of life. Plainly dressed Baptists criticized the rich clothes, drinking, gambling, and pride of Virginia's gentry. The planters, in turn, viewed the Baptists as dangerous people who could not "meet a man upon the road, but they must ram a text of Scripture down his throat." Most of all, they hated the Baptists for their willingness to preach to slaves.

Although the revivals themselves gradually waned, the Great Awakening had a lasting impact on colonial society. In addition to introducing colonists to a fervent evangelicalism, it forged new links between Great Britain and the colonies. Evangelical ministers on both sides of the Atlantic exchanged correspondence. Periodicals such as the *Christian History* informed British and American subscribers of advances in true religion throughout the empire.

The revivals also brought newcomers into Christian congregations. Chesapeake slaves responded to the evangelists' message and—often contrary to the intent of the white

During George Whitefield's tour of the American colonies in 1739–1741, the famous revivalist minister often preached to large crowds gathered outdoors to hear one of his powerful sermons.

preachers—drew lessons about the equality of humankind. A few black preachers circulated in the slave quarters, spreading the message of salvation and freedom. The impact of revivalism on Indians was less dramatic, but still significant. Evangelicals enjoyed their greatest success in small Native American communities, whose inhabitants were attracted to a less formal style of preaching, particularly in New England. Native converts often urged fellow Indians to heed the Christian message of self-discipline, not to emulate English colonists, but to revitalize villages beset by alcoholism and other problems linked to European domination.

The Awakening did not greatly increase women's church membership, since women already constituted majorities in many congregations. But by emphasizing the emotional power of Christianity, revivals accorded greater legitimacy to what was thought to be women's more sensitive temperament.

Everywhere, the New Light challenge to established ministers and churches undermined habits of deference to authority. Revivalists urged colonists to think for themselves in choosing which church to join, and not just to conform to what the rest of the community did. As their churches fractured, colonists faced more choices than ever before in their religious lives.

The exercise of religious choice also influenced political behavior. Voters noticed whether candidates for office were New or Old Lights and cast their ballots for men on their own side. Tactics first used to mobilize religious groups—such as organizing committees and writing petitions and letters—also proved useful for political activities. The Awakening thus fostered greater political awareness and participation among colonists.

THE COLONIAL POLITICAL WORLD

HOW DID the "Glorious Revolution" affect colonial politics?

The political legacy of the Great Awakening—particularly the emphasis on individual choice and resistance to authority—corresponded to developments in the colonial political world. For most of the seventeenth century, ties within the empire developed from trade rather than governance. But as America grew in wealth and population, king and Parliament sought to manage colonial affairs more directly.

The Dominion of New England and the Limits of British Control

Before 1650, England made little attempt to exert centralized control in North America. Each colony more or less governed itself, and most political activity occurred at the town or county level. Busy with the routines of daily life, most colonists devoted little time, and even less interest, to politics.

When Charles II became king in 1660, he initially showed little interest in the colonies except as sources of land and government offices with which he could reward his supporters. Charles's brother James, the duke of York, envisioned a more tightly controlled empire. He encouraged Charles to appoint military officers with strong ties of loyalty to him as royal governors. In 1675, James convinced Charles to create the Lords of Trade, a committee of the Privy Council (the group of nobles who served as royal advisers), to oversee colonial affairs.

When James II became king in 1685, the whole character of the empire abruptly changed. Seeking to transform it into something much more susceptible to England's control, James set out to reorganize it along the lines of Spain's empire, combining the colonies into three or four large provinces. He appointed powerful governors to carry out policies that he himself would formulate.

James began in the north, creating the **Dominion of New England** out of eight previously separate colonies stretching from Maine (then part of Massachusetts) to New Jersey. He chose Sir Edmund Andros, a former army officer, to govern the vast region with an appointive council but no elective assembly.

Dominion of New England James II's failed plan of 1686 to combine eight northern colonies into a single large province, to be governed by a royal appointee with no elective assembly.

Events in England ultimately sealed the fate of the Dominion. For years, English Protestants had worried about James's absolutist governing style and his conversion to Catholicism. Their fears increased in 1688, when the queen bore a son to carry on a Catholic line of succession. Parliament's leaders invited Mary, James's Protestant daughter from his first marriage, and her husband, William of Orange, the stadtholder of the Netherlands, to take over the throne. In November 1688, William landed in England and gained the support of most of the English army. In December, James fled to France, ending a bloodless coup known as the **Glorious Revolution.**

Glorious Revolution Bloodless revolt that occurred in England in 1688 when parliamentary leaders invited William of Orange, a Protestant, to assume the English throne.

Bostonians overthrew Andros the following April and shipped him back to England. Massachusetts colonists hoped that their original charter of 1629 would be reinstated, but a new one was issued in 1691. It made several important changes. Massachusetts now included the formerly separate Plymouth Colony as well as Maine. Its colonists no longer elected their governor, who would instead be appointed by the monarch. Voters no longer had to be church members, and religious toleration was extended to all Protestants. The new charter ended exclusive Puritan control in Massachusetts but also restored political stability.

The impact of the Glorious Revolution in other colonies likewise reflected local conditions. In Maryland, Protestants used the occasion of William and Mary's accession to the throne to lobby for the end of the Catholic proprietorship. They were partly successful. The Calvert family lost its governing powers but retained rights to vast quantities of land. The Anglican Church became the established faith, and Catholics were barred from public office.

Salem Witchcraft

In Massachusetts, during the three years between Andros's overthrow and the arrival of a royal governor in 1692, the colony lacked a legally established government. In this atmosphere of uncertainty, an outbreak of accusations of witchcraft in Salem grew to unprecedented proportions. Over the years, New Englanders had executed a dozen or so accused witches, usually older

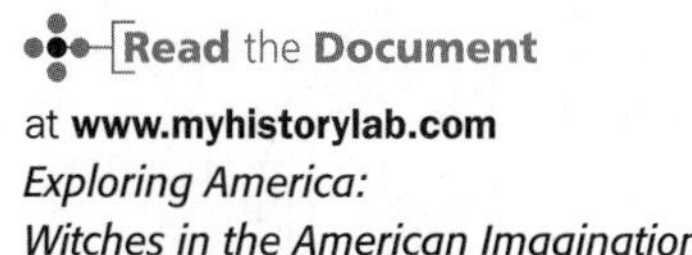
Read the **Document**
at **www.myhistorylab.com**
Exploring America: Witches in the American Imagination

women. But in the winter of 1691–1692, when several young girls of Salem experienced fits and other strange behavior, hundreds of settlers were accused of witchcraft and nineteen were hanged.

Salem's crisis occurred against a backdrop of local economic change, which created friction between agrarian and more commercial parts of the town. Recent conflicts with Indians on the nearby frontier also made many colonists worry that God was punishing them for their sins. Moreover, the town had recently experienced bitter controversy over the appointment of a minister. All of these tensions contributed to the frenzy of witchcraft accusations.

Read the **Document**
at **www.myhistorylab.com**
Ann Putnam's Confession (1706)

QUICK REVIEW

Glorious Revolution

- 1688: James II forced from throne in bloodless coup.
- Massachusetts receives new charter.
- Broad support for Glorious Revolution throughout colonies.

The Legacy of the Glorious Revolution

At the time of the Glorious Revolution, colonists rejected James II, not English authority in general. Their motives largely reflected powerful anti-Catholic sentiment. William's firm Protestantism reassured them, and most colonists assumed that life would return to normal. But the Glorious Revolution in England and the demise of the Dominion had long-lasting effects that shaped political life in England and America for years to come.

In England, the Glorious Revolution signaled a return to political stability after years of upheaval. English people celebrated the preservation of their rights from the threat of a tyrannical king. In 1689, Parliament passed the Bill of Rights, which justified James's ouster and bound future monarchs to abide by the rule of law. They could not suspend statutes, collect taxes, or engage in foreign wars without Parliament's consent, or maintain a standing army in peacetime. Parliamentary elections and meetings would follow a regular schedule, without royal interference. In sum, Parliament claimed to be the crown's equal partner in governing England.

Colonists, too, celebrated the vindication of their rights as Englishmen. They believed that their successful resistance to Andros confirmed that their membership in the empire was founded on voluntary allegiance, not forced submission to the mother country. Observing the similarity between Parliament and the colonial assemblies, they concluded that their own legislatures had a critical role in governance and in the protection of their rights and liberties. On both sides of the Atlantic, representative government had triumphed.

In fact, Parliament claimed full authority over the colonies and did not recognize their assemblies as its equal. For more than a half-century, however, it did not vigorously assert that authority. In addition, William and his immediate successors lacked James's compulsion to control the colonies. During the early eighteenth century, Parliament and royal ministers confined their attention to matters of trade and military defense and otherwise left the colonies on their own. This mild imperial rule, later called the era of "salutary neglect," allowed the colonies to grow in wealth, population, and self-government. It also encouraged colonists to assume equality with the English as members of the empire.

Diverging Politics in the Colonies and Great Britain

British people on both sides of the Atlantic believed that politics ought to reflect social organization. They often compared the state to a family. Just as fathers naturally headed families, adult men led societies. In particular, adult male property holders, who enjoyed economic independence, claimed the right to vote and hold office. Women (who generally could not own property), propertyless men, and slaves had no political role because they, like children, were subordinate to the authority of others. Their dependence on husbands, fathers, masters, or employers—who could influence their political decisions—rendered them incapable of exercising freedom of choice.

Eighteenth-century people also believed that government should reflect society's hierarchical organization. In Britain, this idea was embodied in the monarchy and Parliament. The crown, of course, represented the interests of the royal family. Parliament represented society's two main divisions: the aristocracy in the House of Lords and the common people in the House of Commons. Americans shared the view that government should mirror social hierarchies but found it much more difficult to put the idea into practice.

American society grew closer to the British model during the eighteenth century but was never identical to it. Thus, its political structure would never fully mirror that of Britain. One obvious difference was that America lacked an aristocracy. Elite colonists were often just two or three generations removed from humble beginnings. Hence the acute anxiety that inspired George Washington and other colonial gentlemen to seek refinement, to gain the automatic recognition that Britain's elites enjoyed.

In both Britain and America, land ownership was the prerequisite for political participation, because it freed people from dependence on others and gave them a stake in society. In Britain, this requirement sharply limited participation. Landholding in America, however, was much more widespread. A majority of white male farmers eventually owned the land they tilled, and in most colonies, 50 to 75 percent of white men were eligible to vote.

Distinctive social conditions in Britain and America also gave rise to different notions of political representation. Electoral districts for Parliament came in a confusing mixture of shapes, reflecting their status in past centuries. Once-important towns sent representatives on the basis of their former prominence. At the same time, rapidly growing cities, such as Manchester, lacked any representative at all. Most people in Britain, however, accepted the idea of **virtual representation,** which held that representatives served the interests of the nation as a whole, not just the locality from which they came. They maintained that since the colonists held interests in common with British people at home, they were virtually represented in Parliament, just like Manchester's residents.

virtual representation The notion that parliamentary members represented the interests of the nation as a whole, not those of the particular district that elected them.

Since the founding of their colonies, however, Americans had experienced **actual representation** and believed that elected representatives should be directly responsive to local interests. The Americans' experience with actual representation made them extremely skeptical of Parliament's claims to virtual representation. For the first half of the eighteenth century, however, Parliament did not press this claim, and the tensions between the two ideas remained latent.

actual representation The practice whereby elected representatives normally reside in their districts and are directly responsive to local interests.

The most direct political confrontations between Britain and the colonies instead focused on the role of colonial governors. In every colony except Connecticut and Rhode Island (where voters chose the executive), either the king or the proprietor appointed the governor. The governors' interests thus lay with their British patrons and not the colonies. More important, governors exercised great power over the colonial assemblies.

In practice, several conditions hampered governors' efforts to exercise their legal authority. Many arrived with detailed instructions on how to govern, which limited their ability to negotiate with colonists over sensitive issues. Governors controlled few offices or other prizes to use as patronage to buy the allegiance of their opponents. They struggled to dominate assemblies that grew in size as the colonial population expanded. And in several colonies, including Massachusetts and New York, governors relied on the assemblies to appropriate the money for their salaries—a financial dependence that restrained even the most autocratic executive.

Despite concerns about the power of governors, most colonists accepted the loose and sometimes contradictory political ties of empire. They saw their connections to Britain as voluntary, based on common identity and rights. So long as Parliament treated them as partners in empire and refrained from ruling by coercion, colonists could celebrate British government as "the most perfect combination of human powers in society . . . for the preservation of liberty and the production of happiness."

By the middle of the eighteenth century, the blessings of British government extended to more colonists than ever before. The population of British America grew rapidly and spread out over vast amounts of land. The expansion of British settlement, in turn, alarmed other European powers. Both Spain and France launched new settlements as the competition for the continent entered a new and volatile phase.

EXPANDING EMPIRES

WHAT WAS the "backcountry"? Who settled there and why?

During the first half of the eighteenth century, England, Spain, and France enlarged their North American holdings according to patterns established during the previous century. England's empire expanded in tandem with the unrelenting growth of its colonial population. Spain and France still relied on missionaries, soldiers, and traders to stake their claims to American territory. Over time, these empires came into closer contact with one another, intensifying the competition for land, trade, resources, and Indian allies (see Map 4–2).

British Colonists in the Backcountry

Population growth in eighteenth-century British North America was truly astonishing. The non-Indian population in the mainland colonies numbered about 260,000 in 1700; by 1760, it had increased to over 1.5 million (see Figure 4–2). Much of this growth stemmed from natural increase.

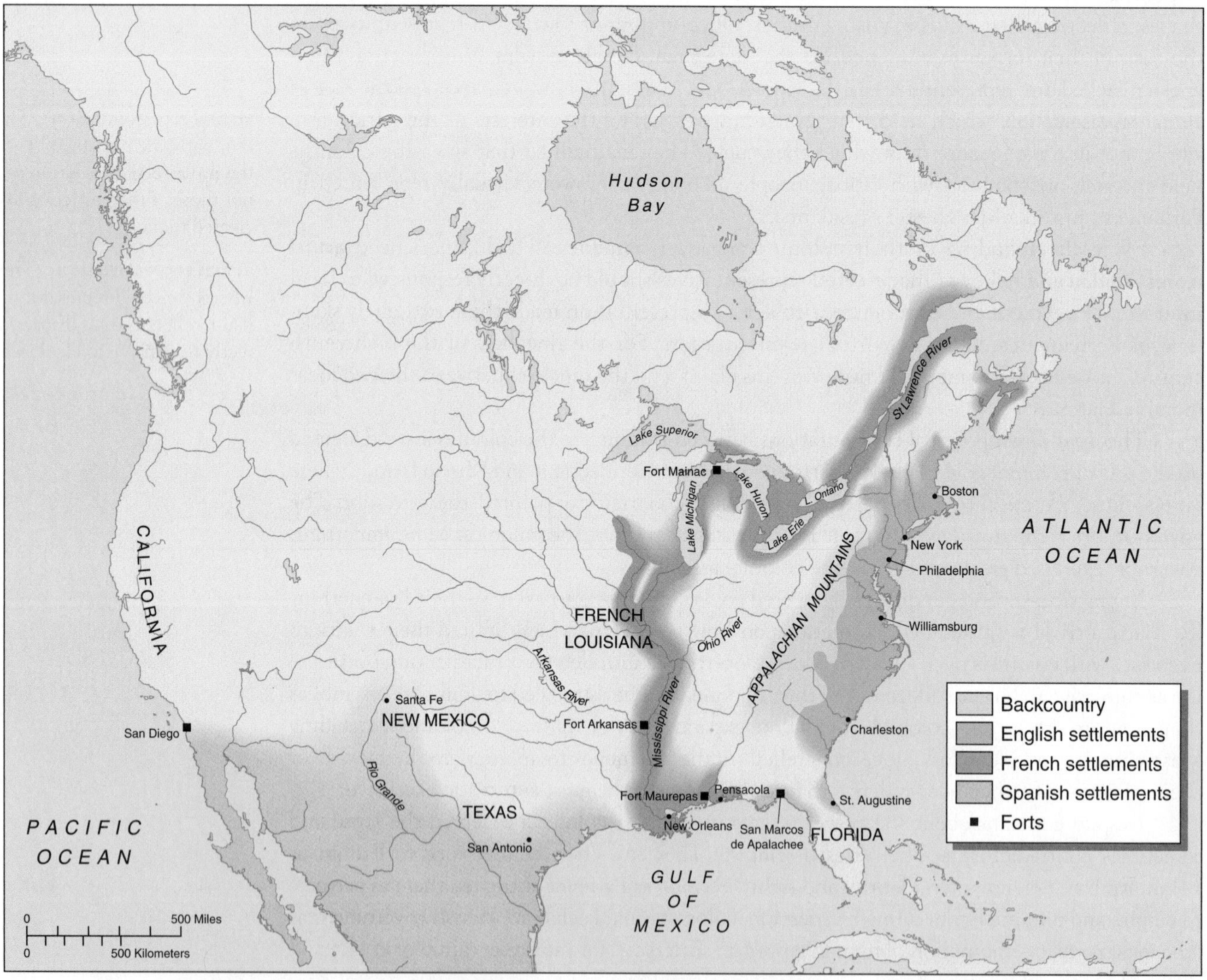

MAP 4–2 **Expanding Settlement, c. 1750** Imperial rivalries drove Spain, France, and England to expand their North American empires in the mid-eighteenth century. Once again, this sparked conflict with native peoples as well as with European competitors.

How does this map help pinpoint the role of English backcountry settlement in the escalation of imperial conflict in eighteenth-century North America?

Immigration also boosted the population. Thousands of Scots-Irish and German settlers, in addition to thousands of African slaves, helped the population of the Lower South increase at nearly twice the rate of New England, which attracted few immigrants (and therefore remained the most thoroughly English of all colonial regions). By 1770, Pennsylvania had 240,000 settlers, ten times the number it had in 1710.

Most of the coast from Maine to Georgia was settled by 1760, forcing new immigrants to move inland. The most dramatic expansion occurred in the foothills and valleys of the Appalachian Mountains from Pennsylvania to Georgia, a region known as the backcountry.

Between 1730 and 1770, nearly a quarter of a million German, Scots-Irish, and English colonists entered the backcountry. They mainly raised crops and livestock for subsistence on small, isolated farms. Community life developed slowly, because many backcountry settlers moved frequently and a surplus of men among the first settlers delayed the formation of families.

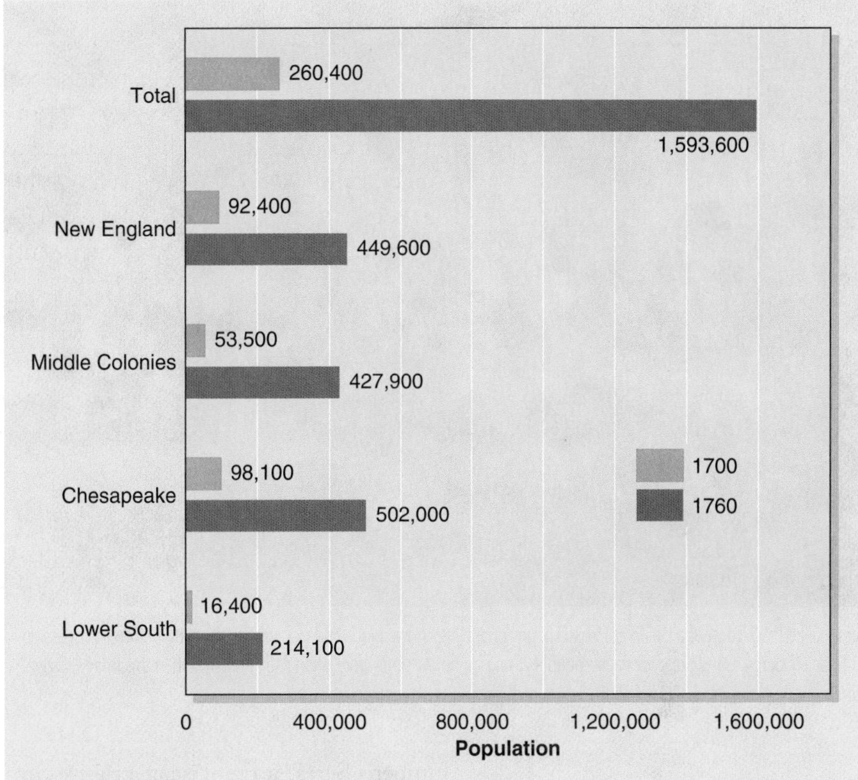

FIGURE 4–2 **Population Growth in British Mainland Colonies, 1700–1760** Both natural increase and immigration contributed to a staggering rate of population growth in British North America. Some colonists predicted that Americans would soon outnumber Britain's inhabitants—a possibility that greatly concerned British officials.

Data Source: John J. McCusker and Russell R. Menard, *The Economy of British America, 1607–1789*, rev. ed. (1991). University of North Carolina Press.

Contemporary observers, especially eastern elites, derided the crudeness of frontier life. Their disparaging comments reflected emerging tensions between backcountry settlements and older seacoast communities. Many eastern planters acquired vast tracts of western land with the intent of selling it to these "crude" settlers. Their interests collided with those of many backcountry settlers, including squatters who occupied the land without acquiring legal title in the hope that their labor in clearing farms would establish their property rights.

Backcountry settlers often complained that the rich eastern planters who dominated the colonial legislatures ignored western demands for adequate representation. They also argued that the crudeness of frontier life was only temporary. Perhaps the best measure of their desire to resemble eastern planters was the spread of slaveholding in the backcountry.

Tensions grew throughout the backcountry as colonists encroached on Indian lands. Indians moving to avoid friction with whites frequently encroached on lands claimed by other tribes—particularly those of the Iroquois Confederacy—leading to conflict among native peoples.

Even where British settlers had not yet appeared, English and Scottish traders could often be found, aggressively pursuing trade with the Indians. Spanish and French observers feared this commercial expansion even more than the movement of settlers. Knowing that the Indians viewed trade as a counterpart to military alliance, they worried that the British, with cheaper and better trade goods, would lure away their native allies. In response, the Spanish and French expanded their own territorial claims and tried to strengthen relations with Indian peoples.

QUICK REVIEW

Population Growth

- 1700: 265,000 black and white settlers in the mainland colonies.
- 1760: 1.5 million black and white settlers in the mainland colonies.
- Population growth due to natural increase and immigration.

The Spanish in Texas and California

To create a buffer zone around their existing colonies, the Spanish moved into Texas and California. Franciscan priests established several missions in east Texas between 1690 and 1720.

An idealized depiction of a California mission, this engraving shows pious Indian converts kneeling before a procession of Spanish clergy. Conditions for native peoples living in the missions were often much harsher than this image suggests.

San Antonio was founded in 1718 as a waystation between the Rio Grande and the east Texas missions; its fortified chapel, San Antonio de Valero, later became famous as the Alamo. The Spanish advance into Texas, however, met with resistance from the French (who also had outposts on the Gulf Coast) and from the Caddos and other Indians armed with French guns. Efforts to fill east Texas with settlers from Spain, Cuba, and the Canary Islands failed when Spanish officials could not guarantee their safety. With only 1,800 settlers there as late as 1742, Spain exerted a weak hold on Texas.

Sixteenth-century Spaniards had considered building outposts in California to supply ships traveling between Mexico and the Philippines but were deterred by the region's remoteness. Spanish interest revived in the 1760s, when it seemed that Russia, which had built fur-trading posts in Alaska, might occupy California. Largely through the efforts of two men—José de Gálvez, a royal official, and Junípero Serra, a Franciscan priest—the Spanish constructed a string of forts and missions from San Diego north to San Francisco between 1769 and 1776.

They initially encountered little opposition from California's Indians, who lived in small, scattered villages. With no European rivals nearby, the Spanish erected an extensive mission system designed to convert and educate Indians and set them to work. Thousands of native laborers farmed irrigated fields and tended livestock. They did so under extremely harsh conditions.

According to one observer, Christian Indians who settled at the missions endured a fate "worse than that of slaves." The Spanish worked them hard and maintained them in overcrowded, unsanitary dwellings. Native women suffered from sexual exploitation by Spanish soldiers. Epidemics of European diseases swept through the Indian population. Signs of native resistance met with quick and cruel punishment.

Spain's empire grew, even as it weakened, during the eighteenth century. Its scattered holdings north of the Rio Grande functioned as colonies of another colony—Mexico—shielding it from foreign incursions. From the beginning, Spain's vision of empire had rested not on extensive settlement but on subjugation of native peoples in order to control their labor. After 1700, the limitations of this coercive approach to empire became apparent.

The French along the Mississippi and in Louisiana

French expansion followed the major waterways of the St. Lawrence River, the Great Lakes, and the Mississippi into the heart of North America. Concerned about defending scattered settlements, French officials forbade colonists to move into the interior. But colonists went anyway, building six villages along the Mississippi in a place they called the *pays des Illinois*.

The first Illinois settlers were independent fur traders (*coureurs de bois*, or "woods runners") unwilling to return to Canada after the French government tried to prohibit their direct trade with Indians. Many found Christian Indian wives and farmed the rich lands along the river. The settlers, using the labor of their families and of black and Indian slaves, produced surpluses of wheat, corn, and livestock to feed the growing population of New Orleans and the lower Mississippi Valley.

See the **Map**
at **www.myhistorylab.com**
French America, 1608–1763

AMERICAN VIEWS

An English Minister Visits the Backcountry

In 1766, Charles Woodmason, a newly ordained Anglican minister, embarked on a six-year-long tour to bring religion to backcountry settlers. Born in England, he came to the colonies around 1752, settling first in Charleston, South Carolina. He lived in the area as a planter and merchant for more than a decade before deciding on a career in the ministry. Assigned to work in the backcountry, he was shocked to find crude living conditions and ethnically diverse settlers with little or no knowledge of religion. As the following excerpt shows, the journal Woodmason kept during these years contains a fascinating mix of his observations and prejudices.

- **How** does Woodmason characterize the behavior of backcountry settlers?
- **What** is Woodmason's opinion of the settlers' religious beliefs?
- **How** accurately do you think Woodmason's account reflects backcountry society? To what extent did his identity as an English-born gentleman shape his impressions of the region?

In this Circuit of a fortnight I've eaten Meat but thrice, and drank nought but Water—Subsisting on my Bisket and Rice Water and Musk Melons, Cucumbers, Green Apples and Peaches and such Trash. By which am reduc'd very thin. It is impossible that any Gentleman not season'd to the Clime, could sustain this. . . . Nor is this a Country, or place where I would wish any Gentleman to travel, or settle. . . . [The settlers'] Ignorance and Impudence is so very high, as to be past bearing—Very few can read—fewer write. . . . They are very Poor—owing to their extreme Indolence for they possess the finest Country in America, and could raise but ev'ry thing. They delight in their present low, lazy, sluttish, heathenish, hellish Life, and seem not desirous of changing it. Both Men and Women will do any thing to come at Liquor, Cloaths, furniture, &c. &c. rather than work for it. . . .

It is very few families whom I can bring to join in Prayer, because most of them are of various Opinions the Husband a Churchman, Wife, a Dissenter, Children nothing at all. . . . Few or no Books are to be found in all this vast Country. . . . Nor do they delight in Historical Books or in having them read to them, as do our Vulgar in England for these People despise Knowledge, and instead of honouring a Learned Person, or any one of Wit or Knowledge be it in the Arts, Sciences, or Languages, they despise and Ill treat them—And this Spirit prevails even among the Principals of this Province. . . . [At Flatt Creek] I found a vast Body of People assembled—Such a Medley! such a mixed Multitude of all Classes and Complexions I never saw. I baptized about 20 Children and Married 4 Couple—Most of these People had never before seen a Minister, or heard the Lords Prayer, Service, or Sermon in their Days. I was a Great Curiosity to them—And they were as great Oddities to me. After Service they went to Revelling Drinking Singing Dancing and Whoring—and most of the Company were drunk before I quitted the Spot—They were as rude in their Manners as the Common Savages, and hardly a degree removed from them.

Source: Richard J. Hooker, ed., *The Carolina Backcountry on the Eve of the Revolution: The Journal and Other Writings of Charles Woodmason, Anglican Itinerant* (Chapel Hill, 1953), pp. 52–56.

French Louisiana contained a remarkably diverse population of Indian peoples, French soldiers and settlers, and German immigrants, as well as African slaves, who by the 1730s outnumbered the European colonists. Discouraged by the lack of profits, French officials and merchants neglected Louisiana, and even Catholic missionaries failed to establish a strong presence. Significant European emigration to Louisiana essentially ceased after the 1720s.

But the French approach to empire in Louisiana as in Canada depended more on Indian alliances than on settlement. Louisiana's principal allies were the Choctaws, whom one military official called "the bulwark of the colony." The Choctaws and other native allies offered trade and military assistance in return for guns, trade goods, French help in fighting British raiders seeking Indian slaves, and occasional French mediation of Indian disputes.

French expansion along the Mississippi Valley drove a wedge between Florida and Spain's other mainland colonies; it also blocked the westward movement of English settlers. But France's enlarged empire was only as strong as the Indian alliances on which it rested. Preserving good relations was expensive, however, requiring the constant exchange of diplomatic gifts and trade goods. When France ordered Louisiana officials to limit expenses and reduce Indian gifts in 1745, the officials objected that the Choctaws "would ask for nothing better than to have such pretexts in order to resort to the English."

The fear of losing Indian favor preoccupied officials in 1745 because at that moment France's empire in America consisted of two disconnected pieces: New France, centered in the St. Lawrence Valley and the Great Lakes basin, and Louisiana, stretching from New Orleans to the *pays des Illinois*. Between them lay a thousand miles of wilderness, through which only one thoroughfare passed—the Ohio River. For decades, communication between the two parts of France's North American empire had posed no problem because Indians in the Ohio Valley allowed the French free passage through their lands. If that policy ended, however, France's New World empire would be dangerously divided.

A CENTURY OF WARFARE

WHAT ROLE did the colonists play in the French and Indian War?

The expansion of empires in North America reflected the policies of European states locked in a relentless competition for power and wealth. From the time of the Glorious Revolution, English foreign policy aimed at limiting the expansion of French influence. This, in turn, resulted in a series of four wars. As the eighteenth century wore on, the conflicts between the two countries increasingly involved their American colonies as well as Spain and its colonies. The outcome of each of the wars in America depended no less on the participation of colonists and Indians than on the policies and strategies of the European powers. The conclusion of the final conflict signaled a dramatic shift in North American history (see the Overview table, The Colonial Wars, 1689–1763).

Imperial Conflict and the Establishment of an American Balance of Power, 1689–1738

When he became king of England in 1688, the Dutch Protestant William of Orange was already fighting the War of the League of Augsburg against France's Catholic king, Louis XIV. Almost immediately, William brought England into the conflict. The war lasted until 1697 and ended, as most European wars of this period did, in a negotiated peace that reestablished the balance of power. Little territory changed hands, either in this war or in the War of the Spanish Succession (1702–1713), which followed it.

King William's War The first Anglo-French conflict in North America (1689–1697), the American phase of Europe's War of the League of Augsburg.

Queen Anne's War American phase (1702–1713) of Europe's War of the Spanish Succession.

In America, these two imperial wars—known to British colonists as **King William's War** and **Queen Anne's War,** after the monarchs on the throne at the time—ended with equal indecisiveness. Neither war caused more than marginal changes for the colonies in North America. Both had profound effects, however, on the English state and the Iroquois League.

All European states of the eighteenth century financed their wars by borrowing. But the English were the first to realize that wartime debts did not necessarily have to be repaid during the following peace. The government instead created a funded debt. Having borrowed heavily from large joint-stock corporations, the government used tax revenues to pay the interest on the loans but not to pay off the loans themselves.

Country (Real Whig) ideology Train of thought (focusing on the threat to personal liberty and the taxation of property holders) first appearing in England in the late seventeenth century in response to the growth of governmental power and a national debt.

As the debt grew larger, more taxes were necessary to pay interest on it. Taxes also rose to pay for a powerful navy and a standing army. When the treasury created a larger bureaucracy to collect taxes, many Englishmen grew nervous. Their anxiety emerged as a strain of thought known as **Country,** or **"Real Whig," ideology.** Country ideology stressed the threats that a standing army and a powerful state posed to personal liberty. It also emphasized the dangers of taxation to property rights and the need for property holders to retain their right to consent to taxation. Real Whig politicians publicized their fears but could not stop the growth of the state.

OVERVIEW The Colonial Wars, 1689–1763

Name in the Colonies	European Name and Dates	Dates in America	Results for Britain
King William's War	War of the League of Augsburg, 1688–1697	1689–1697	Reestablished balance of power between England and France
Queen Anne's War	War of the Spanish Succession, 1702–1714	1702–1713	Britain acquired Nova Scotia
King George's War	War of the Austrian Succession, 1739–1748	1744–1748	Britain returned Louisbourg to France British settlers began moving westward Weakening of Iroquois neutrality
French and Indian War	Seven Years' War, 1756–1763	1754–1763	Britain acquired Canada and all French territory east of Mississippi Britain gained Florida from Spain

In America, the first two imperial wars transformed the role of the Iroquois League. During King William's War, the Iroquois allied with the English, but received little help from them when the French and their Indian allies attacked Iroquois villages. By 1700, the Iroquois League had suffered such horrendous losses—perhaps a quarter of the population had died from causes related to the war—that its leaders sought an alternative to direct alliance with the English.

With the **Grand Settlement of 1701,** the Iroquois adopted a policy of neutrality with regard to the French and British empires. The Iroquois's strategic location between New France and the English colonies allowed them to serve as a geographical and diplomatic buffer. Neutral Iroquois diplomats could play the English against the French, gaining favors from one side in return for promises not to ally with the other. This neutralist policy ensured that for nearly fifty years neither Britain nor France could gain ascendancy in North America.

Grand Settlement of 1701 Separate peace treaties negotiated by Iroquois diplomats at Montreal and Albany that marked the beginning of Iroquois neutrality in conflicts between the French and the British in North America.

Iroquois neutrality offered benefits to the Europeans as well as the Indians. The British began to negotiate with them for land. The Iroquois claimed sovereignty over much of the country west of the Middle and Chesapeake colonies. To smooth relations with the British, the Iroquois sold them land formerly occupied by Delawares and Susquehannocks.

Meanwhile a neutral Iroquois League claiming control over the Ohio Valley and blocking British access across the Appalachian Mountains helped the French protect the strategic corridor that linked Canada and Louisiana. If the British ever established a permanent presence in the Ohio Valley, however, the Iroquois would cease to be of use to the French. The Iroquois remained reasonably effective at keeping the British out of the valley until the late 1740s. The next European war, however, altered these circumstances.

King George's War The third Anglo-French war in North America (1744–1748), part of the European conflict known as the War of the Austrian Succession.

King George's War Shifts the Balance, 1739–1754

The third confrontation between Britain and France in Europe, the War of the Austrian Succession—**King George's War** to the British colonists—began as a small war between Britain and Spain in 1739. But in 1744, France joined in the war against Britain and conflict once again erupted in North America.

New Englanders saw yet another chance to attack Canada. This time their target was the great fortress of Louisbourg on Cape Breton Island, a naval base that dominated the Gulf of St. Lawrence. An expedition from Massachusetts and Connecticut, supported by a squadron of Royal Navy warships, captured Louisbourg in 1745. This success cut Canada off from French reinforcement. English forces should now have been able to conquer New France.

W
WHERE TO LEARN MORE
Fortress of Louisbourg National Historic Site, Cape Breton Island, Canada
http://louisbourg.com/history.html

This contemporary map shows the British seizure of the French fortress at Louisbourg in 1758 during the French and Indian War. In 1745, during King George's War, New Englanders had helped capture the fort, which was returned to France at the war's end in 1748.

Instead, politically influential merchants in Albany, New York, chose to continue their profitable trade with the enemy across Lake Champlain, enabling Canada to hold out until the end of the war. When the peace treaty was signed in 1748, Britain, which had fared badly in the European fighting, returned Louisbourg to France. This diplomatic adjustment, routine by European standards, shocked New Englanders. At the same time, New York's illegal trade with the enemy appalled British administrators. They began thinking of ways to prevent such independent behavior in any future war.

King George's War furnished an equal share of shocks for New France, which had suffered more than in any previous conflict. Even before the war's end, traders from Pennsylvania began moving west to buy furs from Indians who had once traded with the French. The movements of these traders, along with the appearance of Virginians in the Ohio Valley after 1748, gravely concerned the French.

In 1749, the governor general of New France set out to assert direct control over the region by building a series of forts from Lake Erie to the Forks of the Ohio (where the Monongahela and Allegheny rivers meet to form the Ohio River). This decision signaled the end of France's commitment to Iroquois neutrality. The Iroquois now found themselves trapped between empires edging closer to confrontation in the Ohio Valley.

The Iroquois, in fact, had never exerted direct power in the Ohio Country. Their control instead depended on their ability to dominate the peoples who actually lived there. The appearance of English traders in the valley offering goods on better terms than the French or the Iroquois had ever provided undermined Iroquois dominance.

The Ohio Valley Indians increasingly pursued their own independent course. One spur to their disaffection from the Iroquois was the 1744 **Treaty of Lancaster,** by which Iroquois chiefs had sold the rights to trade at the Forks of the Ohio to Virginia land speculators. The Virginians assumed that these trading rights included the right to acquire land for eventual sale to settlers. The Ohio Valley Indians found this situation intolerable, as did the French. When, in 1754, the government of Virginia sent out a small body of soldiers under Lieutenant Colonel George Washington to protect Virginia's claim to the Forks of the Ohio, the French struck back.

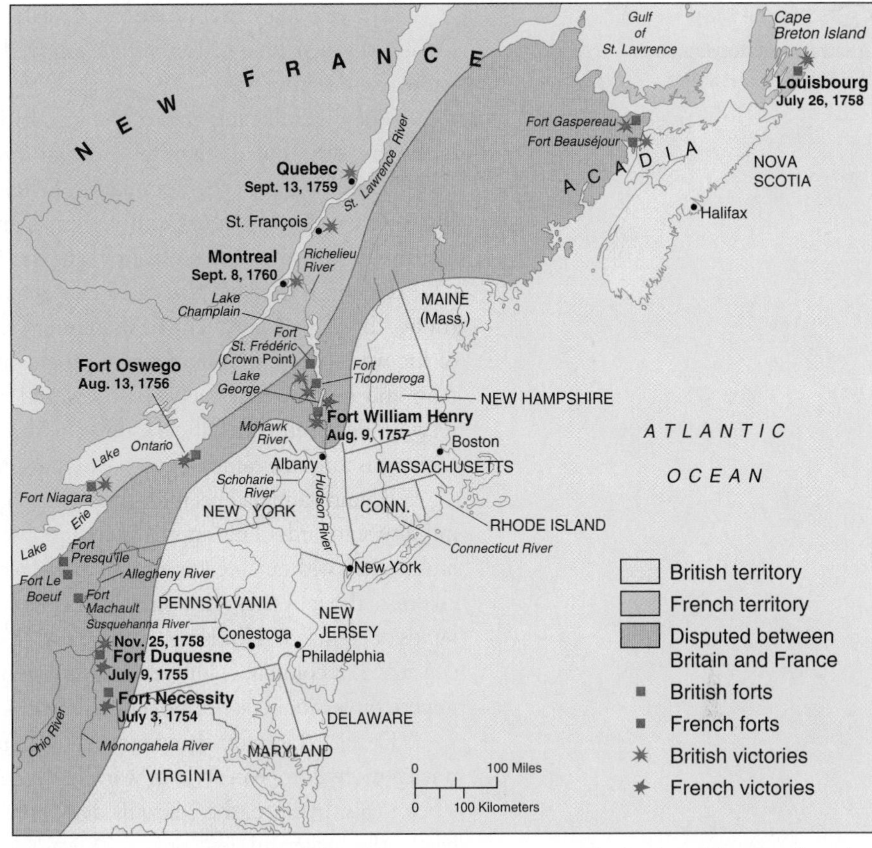

MAP 4–3 **The French and Indian War, 1754–1763** Most of the battles of the French and Indian War occurred in the frontier regions of northern and western New York and the Ohio Valley. The influx of settlers into these areas created tensions that eventually developed into war.

Why did most of the fighting in the French and Indian War take place in the backcountry? How does this map help explain the crucial importance of Louisbourg to the French?

THE FRENCH AND INDIAN WAR, 1754–1763: A DECISIVE VICTORY

In April 1754, French soldiers overwhelmed a group of Virginians who had been building a small fort at the Forks of the Ohio. They erected their own fort, Fort Duquesne, on the spot. The French intended to follow up by similarly ousting Washington's troops, who had encamped farther up the Monongahela River. However, at the end of May, Washington's men killed or captured all but one member of a small French reconnaissance party. The French decided to teach the Virginians a lesson. On July 3, they attacked Washington at Fort Necessity, forcing him to surrender.

Even before this news reached Britain, imperial officials worried that the Iroquois might ally with the French. Britain ordered New York's governor to convene an intercolonial meeting in Albany—known as the Albany Congress—to discuss matters with the Iroquois. Several prominent colonists, including Governor William Shirley of Massachusetts and Benjamin Franklin, took advantage of the occasion to put forward the **Albany Plan of Union,** which called for an intercolonial union to coordinate defense, levy taxes, and regulate Indian affairs. But the colonies, too suspicious of one another to see their common interests, rejected the Albany Plan, which British officials also disliked. Meanwhile, events in the west took a turn for the worse.

Treaty of Lancaster Negotiation in 1744 whereby Iroquois chiefs sold Virginia land speculators the right to trade at the Forks of the Ohio.

Albany Plan of Union Plan put forward in 1754 calling for an intercolonial union to manage defense and Indian affairs. The plan was rejected by participants at the Albany Congress.

The French expulsion of the Virginians left the Indians of the region, Delawares and Shawnees, with no choice but to ally with the French in what came to be called the French and Indian War (see Map 4–3). The Iroquois tried to remain neutral, but their neutrality no longer mattered. Europeans were at last contending directly for control of the Ohio Country.

The **French and Indian War** blazed in America for two years before it erupted as a fourth Anglo-French war in Europe in 1756. Known in Europe as the Seven Years' War (1756–1763), it involved fighting in the Caribbean, Africa, India, and the Philippine Islands as well as in Europe and North America. It was unlike any other eighteenth-century conflict, not only in its immense scope and expense but also in its decisive outcome.

French and Indian War The last of the Anglo-French colonial wars (1754–1763) and the first in which fighting began in North America. The war ended with France's defeat.

See the Map at www.myhistorylab.com The Seven Years' War

The war had two phases in North America—1754 to 1758 and 1758 through 1760. During the first phase, the French enjoyed a string of successes as they followed their proven strategy—guerrilla war.

The first full campaign of the war, in 1755, saw not only the British colonial frontiers collapsing in terror but also a notable defeat inflicted on the troops Britain had dispatched to attack Fort Duquesne under the command of Major General Edward Braddock. Braddock's defeat set the tone for virtually every military engagement of the next three years and opened a period of demoralization and internal conflict in the British colonies.

Britain responded to Braddock's defeat by sending a new commander in chief with more trained British soldiers. The new commander, Lord Loudoun, insisted on managing every aspect of the war effort, not only directing the campaigns but also dictating the amount of support, in men and money, that each colony would provide. Colonial soldiers, who had volunteered to serve under their own officers, objected to Loudoun's command. By the end of 1757, a year of disastrous military campaigns, colonial assemblies were also refusing to cooperate.

Britain's aim had been to "rationalize" the war by making it conform to European professional military standards. This approach required soldiers to advance in formation in the face of massed musket fire without breaking rank. Few colonial volunteers met professional standards, and few colonists thought them necessary, especially when British soldiers suffered defeat after defeat at the hands of French and Indian guerrillas. British officers assumed that colonial soldiers were simply lazy cowards. But colonial volunteers saw British officers as brutal taskmasters. They resisted all efforts to impose professional discipline on their own units, even to the point of desertion and mutiny.

Despite the astonishing success of their guerrilla tactics, the French, too, began moving toward a more European style of warfare. In the process, they destroyed their strategic and tactical advantages. In 1756, the Marquis de Montcalm assumed command of French forces. In his first battle, the successful siege of Fort Oswego, New York, Montcalm was horrified by the behavior of his Indian allies, who killed wounded prisoners, took personal captives, and collected scalps as trophies. He came to regard the Indians—so essential to the defense of New France—as mere savages.

Following his next victory, the capture of Fort William Henry, New York, Montcalm conformed to European practice by allowing the defeated garrison to go home in return for the promise not to fight again. Montcalm's Indian allies, a thousand or more strong, were not to take prisoners, trophies, or plunder. The tragic result came to be known as the Massacre of Fort William Henry. Feeling betrayed by their French allies, the Indians took captives and trophies anyway. This action not only outraged the New England colonies (most of the victims were New Englanders) but also alienated the Indians on whom the defense of Canada depended.

At the same time that the Europeanization of the war was weakening the French, the British moderated their policies and reached accommodation with the colonists. A remarkable politician came to power in London as England's chief war minister. William Pitt, who as secretary of state directed the British war effort from late 1757 through 1761, realized that friction arose from the colonists' sense that they were bearing all the financial burdens of the war without having any say in how the war was fought. Pitt's ingenious solution was to promise reimbursements to the colonies in proportion to their contribution to the war effort, reduce the power of the commander in chief, and replace the arrogant Loudoun with a less objectionable officer.

QUICK REVIEW

Pitt's Policies

- Reimbursements to the colonies in proportion to their contribution.
- Deemphasis of the power of the commander in chief.
- More British troops to fight alongside colonial troops.

Pitt's money and measures restored colonial morale and launched the second phase of the war. He sent thousands of British soldiers to America to fight alongside colonial troops. As the Anglo-American forces grew stronger, they operated more successfully, seizing Louisbourg again in 1758. Once more, Canada experienced crippling shortages of supplies. But this time, the Anglo-Americans were united and able to take advantage of the situation. British emissaries persuaded the Delawares and Shawnees to abandon their French alliance, and late in 1758, an Anglo-American force again marched on Fort Duquesne. In command of its lead battalion was Colonel George Washington. The French defenders, abandoned by their native allies and confronted by overwhelming force, blew up the fort and retreated to the Great Lakes.

GLOBAL CONNECTIONS

TEA AND EMPIRE

We went ashore [near Greenwich, New York] to fill water near a small log cottage on the west side of the river inhabited by one Stanespring and his family. . . . This cottage was very clean and neat but poorly furnished. Yet Mr. Milne observed severall superfluous things which showed an inclination to finery in these poor people, such as a looking glass with a painted frame, half a dozen pewter spoons and as many plates, . . . a set of stone tea dishes, and a tea pot. These, Mr. Milne said, were superfluous and too splendid for such a cottage. . . . As for the tea equipage it was quite unnecessary. . . .

Source: Wendy Martin, ed., *Colonial American Travel Narratives* (New York, 1994), p. 216.

Alexander Hamilton, a Scottish physician, made this observation while traveling from Maryland to New Hampshire in 1744. Few colonists would have agreed that the family's teapot and dishes were "quite unnecessary." By the eighteenth century, many colonists—even residents of Philadelphia's poorhouse—regarded tea as an essential part of their diet. How had a beverage from a native Chinese plant become commonplace in towns and villages located thousands of miles away? The answer lies in the expanding network of British commerce. By the start of the eighteenth century, Britain's East India Company had established a thriving trade in tea and silks with Chinese merchants in Canton. Large ships, specially designed to withstand the rigors of lengthy voyages around Africa's Cape of Good Hope, carried more tea every year. Imports rose from 50 tons in 1700 to 15,000 tons by 1800. Increased supplies meant that tea became affordable for all classes of British subjects and colonists. Poorer folk relied on the mild stimulant to help them endure hard days at work. For wealthier people, drinking tea became a marker of sociability. This was especially true for women, whose elegant tea parties offered opportunities to display fine porcelain tea pots and cups, silver or pewter spoons, sugar tongs, and other equipment. Until factories began producing porcelain in Britain itself, British and colonial consumers sipped their tea from cups that arrived as ballast aboard the East India Company ships. Only with the onset of the Revolutionary movement, when British taxes on tea discouraged colonial purchases, did American consumers reject the beverage that had previously linked them with Great Britain and, by extension, a commercial empire that virtually circled the globe.

- Why might Alexander Hamilton have thought it unsuitable for a poor family to drink tea?

From this point on, the Anglo-Americans suffered no setbacks, and the French won no victories. The war became a contest in which the larger, better-supplied army would triumph. Montcalm, forced back to Quebec, decided to risk everything in a European-style, open-field battle against a British force led by General James Wolfe. At the Battle of Quebec (September 13, 1759), Montcalm lost the gamble—and his life (as did the victorious General Wolfe).

The French had not yet lost the war. If they could revive their Indian alliances, they still had a chance. What finally decided the outcome of the war in America was two developments: the Battle of Quiberon Bay in France (November 20, 1759) and the Iroquois's decision to join the Anglo-American side in 1760. The sea battle cost the French navy its ability to operate in the Atlantic, preventing it from reinforcing Canada. Montcalm's successor could not rebuild the Indian alliances he so desperately needed. At the same time, the Iroquois decision to enter the war on the Anglo-American side tipped the balance irrevocably against the French. The last defenders of Canada surrendered on September 8, 1760.

THE TRIUMPH OF THE BRITISH EMPIRE, 1763

The war pitting Britain against France and Spain (which had entered the fighting as a French ally in 1762) concluded with an uninterrupted series of British victories. In the Caribbean, where every valuable sugar island the French owned came under British control, the culminating event was the

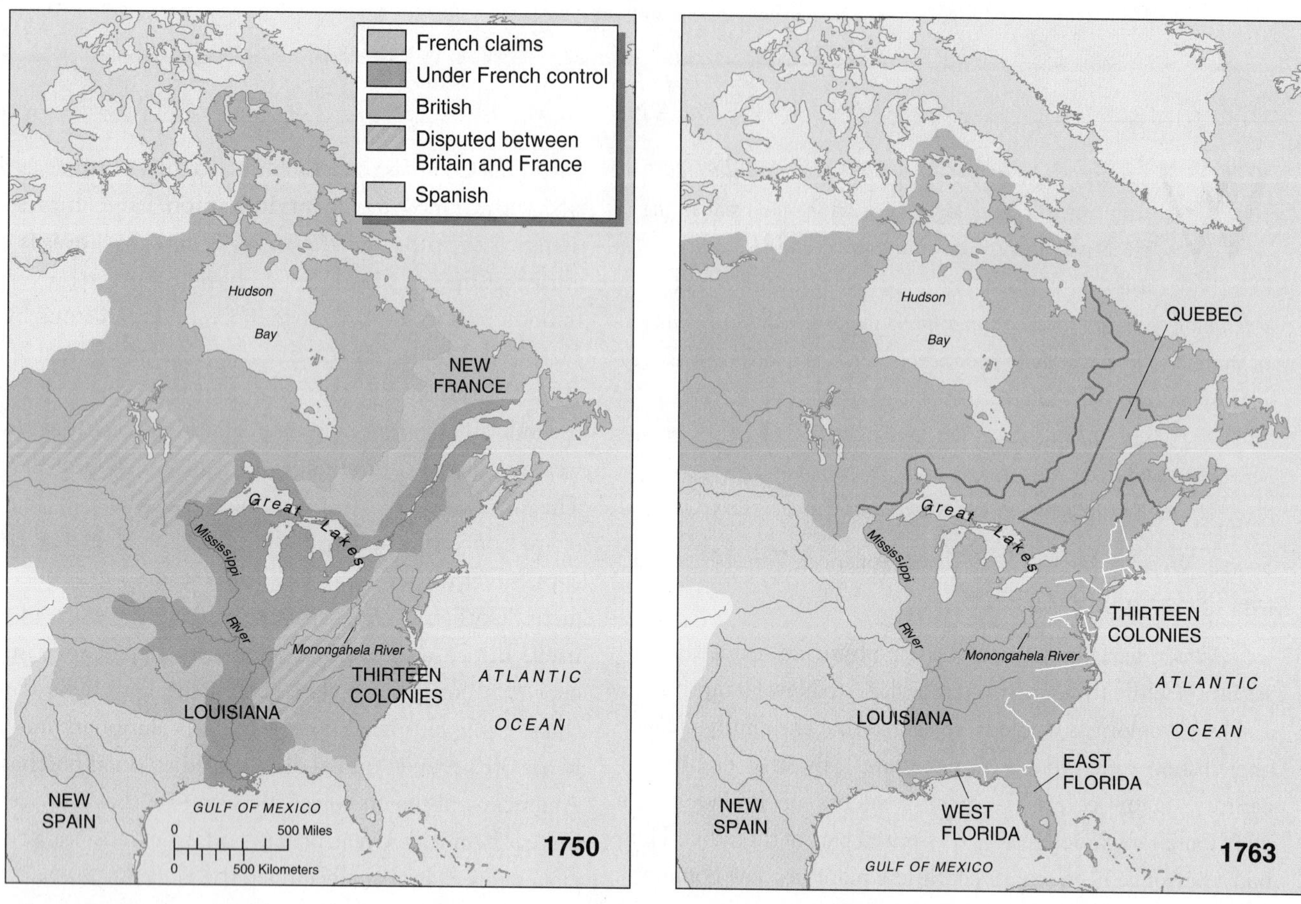

MAP 4–4 **European Empires in North America, 1750–1763** Great Britain's victory in the French and Indian War transformed the map of North America. France lost its mainland colonies, England claimed all lands east of the Mississippi, and Spain gained nominal control over the Trans-Mississippi West.

Using these two maps, explain why the position of Native Americans in colonial North America was much more precarious in 1763 than in 1750.

surrender of Havana on August 13, 1762. Even more spectacular was Britain's capture of the Philippine capital of Manila on October 5—a victory that literally carried British power around the world.

These conquests created the unshakable conviction that British arms were invincible. An immense surge of British patriotism spread throughout the American colonies. When news of the conquest of Havana reached Massachusetts, bells rang, cannons fired salutes, and bonfires blazed.

Treaty of Paris The formal end to British hostilities against France and Spain in February 1763.

Hostilities ended formally on February 10, 1763, with the conclusion of the **Treaty of Paris.** France regained its West Indian sugar islands—its most valuable colonial possessions—but lost the rest of its North American empire. France ceded to Britain all its claims to lands east of the Mississippi River (except the city of New Orleans) and compensated Spain for the losses it had sustained as an ally by handing over all claims to the Trans-Mississippi West and the port of New Orleans (see Map 4–4). Britain returned Cuba and the Philippines to Spain and in compensation received Florida. Now Great Britain owned everything east of the Mississippi, from the Gulf of Mexico to Hudson's Bay. With France and Spain both humbled and on the verge of financial collapse, Britain seemed preeminent in Europe and ready to dominate in the New World. Never before had Americans felt more pride in being British, members of the greatest empire on earth.

In his most famous painting, American artist Benjamin West depicted the death of the British general James Wolfe at the Battle of Quebec. He portrays Wolfe as a glorious martyr to the cause of British victory. In the left foreground, West added the figure of an Indian, a "noble savage" who contemplates the meaning of Wolfe's selfless sacrifice of his life.

Benjamin West (1738–1820), "The Death of General Wolfe," 1770, Oil on canvas, 152.6×214.5 cm. Transfer from the Canadian War Memorials, 1921 (Gift of the 2nd Duke of Westminster, Eaton Hall, Cheshire, 1918). National Gallery of Canada, Ottawa, Ontario.

CONCLUSION

The George Washington who ordered a suit from England in 1763 longed to be part of the elite of the great British Empire. If he feared any threat to his position in that elite, it was not Parliament and the king but the uncomfortably large debts he owed to his London agents or perhaps the unruly Baptists who challenged the superiority of the great planters. But such worries, though real, were merely small, nagging doubts, shared by most of his fellow planters.

What was more real to Washington was the great victory that the British had just gained over France, a victory that he had helped to achieve. For Washington, as for virtually all other colonial leaders and many ordinary colonists, 1763 was a moment of great promise and patriotic devotion to the British Empire. They hoped that the colonies had embarked on a new stage in a political and cultural journey, moving them closer to an equal partnership with England itself in the world's most powerful empire. It was a time for colonists to rejoice in the fundamental British identity and liberty and rights that seemed to ensure that their lives would be better and more prosperous than ever.

Where to Learn More

Colonial Williamsburg, Williamsburg, Virginia. A reconstruction of the capital of eighteenth-century Virginia, this site covers 173 acres and contains many restored and rebuilt structures, including houses, churches, the House of Burgesses, and the Governor's Palace. Many educational and cultural programs are available. Historical interpreters, dressed in period costume, provide information about eighteenth-century Chesapeake life. The website http://www.colonialwilliamsburg.com/history/index.cfm has a variety of links that include biographical information on eighteenth-century residents of Williamsburg, aspects of colonial life, and material culture.

Mount Vernon, Virginia. Site of George Washington's much-refurbished home. There is also a reconstructed gristmill and barn, as well as various outbuildings. Exhibits include information on Washington's agricultural experiments. The website http://www.mountvernon.org offers virtual tours of the house and grounds, as well as information on "George Washington, Pioneer Farmer."

Fortress of Louisbourg National Historic Site, Cape Breton Island, Canada. This site includes a reconstruction of the fortified French settlement that played a key role in the eighteenth-century wars between Britain and France. More information is available at the website http://louisbourg.com/history.html.

Berkeley and Westover Plantations, Charles City, Virginia. These two eighteenth-century James River plantations suggest the elegance of elite planters' lives. The house and grounds at Berkeley are open to the public, the grounds only at Westover, the home of William Byrd. Pictures, descriptions of the sites, and background on their owners can be found at http://www.jamesriverplantations.org/, which has links to each plantation.

Review Questions

1. Why did George Washington prefer to order a suit from London rather than trust a Virginia tailor to make him one? How does his decision reflect elite colonists' attitudes about American society and culture in the eighteenth century?
2. In what ways did economic ties between Britain and the colonies grow closer in the century after 1660?
3. What was the Great Awakening, and what impact did it have? How did it affect different groups in colonial society?
4. In what ways were colonial and British political ideas and practices similar? In what ways were they different?
5. Why did England, Spain, and France renew their competition for North America in the eighteenth century?
6. What role did warfare play in North America in the eighteenth century? What role did the Iroquois play?

Key Terms

Actual representation (p. 101)
Age of Enlightenment (p. 95)
Albany Plan of Union (p. 109)
Country (Real Whig) ideology (p. 106)
Dominion of New England (p. 99)
Enumerated products (p. 88)
French and Indian War (p. 109)
Glorious Revolution (p. 99)
Grand Settlement of 1701 (p. 107)
Great Awakening (p. 97)
Halfway Covenant (p. 96)
King George's War (p. 107)
King William's War (p. 106)
Mercantilism (p. 87)
New Lights (p. 97)
Queen Anne's War (p. 106)
Treaty of Lancaster (p. 109)
Treaty of Paris (p. 112)
Virtual representation (p. 101)

myhistorylab Connections

Reinforce what you learned in this chapter by studying the many documents, images, maps, review tools, and videos available at **www.myhistorylab.com.**

Read and Review

Study and Review **Study Plan: Chapter 4**

Read the Document

Benjamin Franklin, Observations Concerning the Increase of Mankind, Peopling of Countries (1751)

Ann Putnam's Deposition (1692)

Ann Putnam's Confession (1706)

Benjamin Franklin on George Whitefield (1771)

Benjamin Wadsworth, from A Well-Ordered Family (1712)

England Asserts Her Dominion through Legislation in 1660

Jonathan Edwards, "Some Thoughts" (1742)

Navigation Acts (1651)

See the Map

French America, 1608–1763

Colonial Products

The Seven Years' War

European Claims in North America, 1750 and 1763

Regions of Colonial North America, 1683–1763

Research and Explore

Read the Document

Personal Journeys Online

From Then to Now Online: The Diversity of American Religious Life

Exploring America: The Great Awakening

Exploring America: Witches in the American Imagination

Hear the Audio

Lookie There!

The Connecticut Peddler

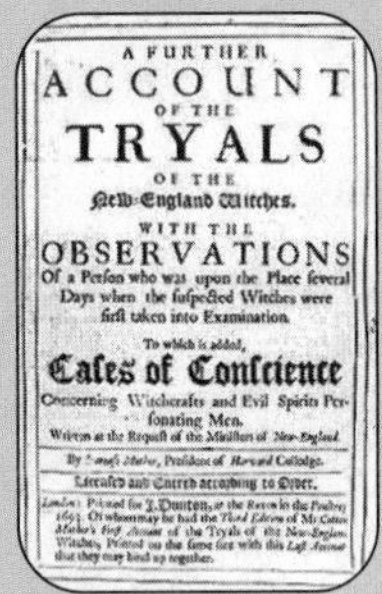

A FURTHER
ACCOUNT
OF THE
TRYALS
OF THE
New-England Witches.
WITH THE
OBSERVATIONS
Of a Person who was upon the Place several Days when the suspected Witches were first taken into Examination.
To which is added,
Cases of Conscience
Concerning Witchcrafts and Evil Spirits Personating Men.
Written at the Request of the Ministers of New-England.
Licensed and Entred according to Order.

Hear the Audio

Hear the audio files for Chapter 4 at **www.myhistorylab.com.**

1763-1774

5 Imperial Breakdown

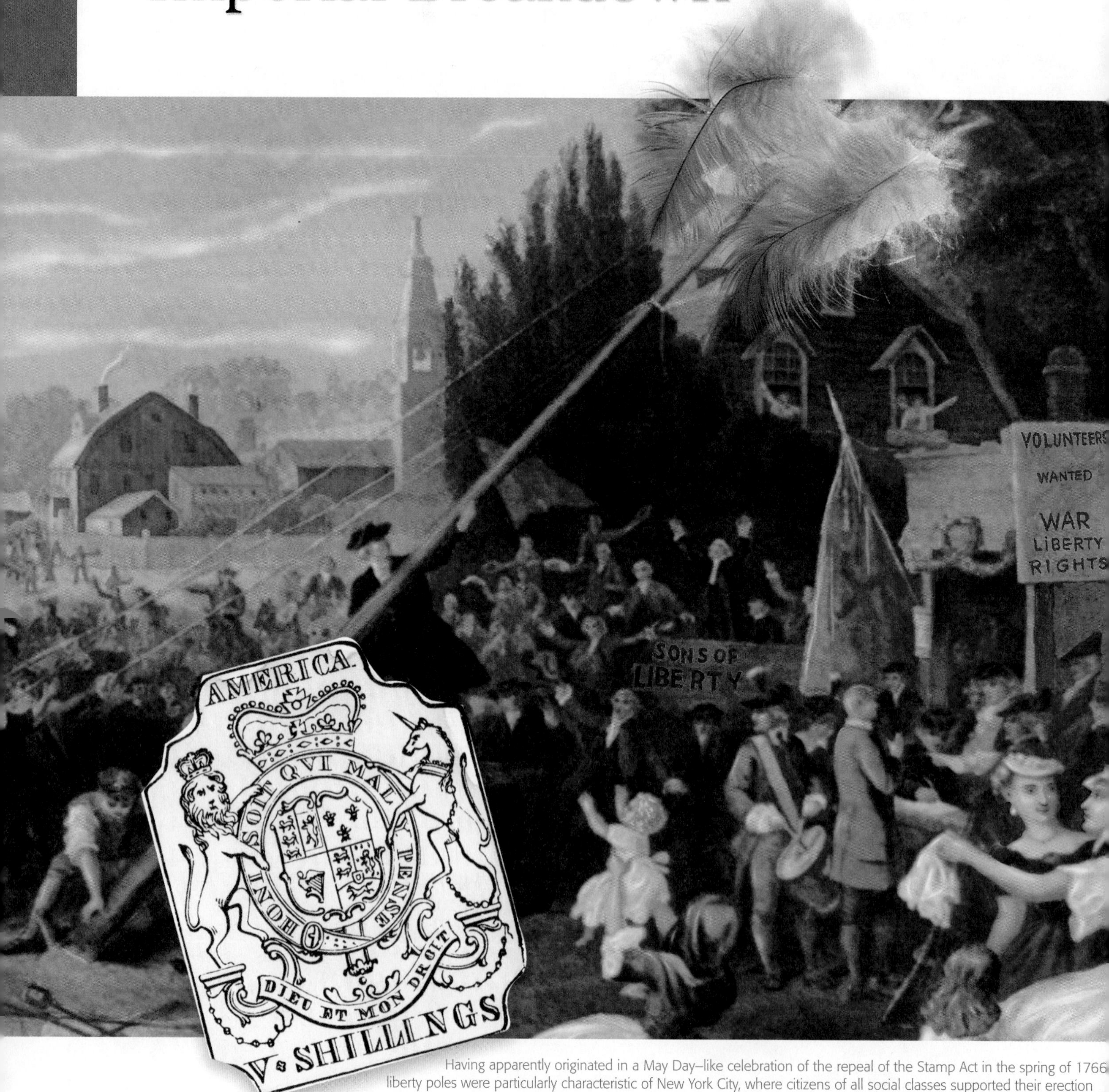

Having apparently originated in a May Day–like celebration of the repeal of the Stamp Act in the spring of 1766 liberty poles were particularly characteristic of New York City, where citizens of all social classes supported their erection (as in the picture). However, British soldiers repeatedly destroyed them, thereby prompting serious rioting. Elsewhere, liberty trees served similar symbolic functions. John C. McRae of New York published this print in 1875. © North Wind/North Wind Picture Archives

((•• Hear the Audio
Hear the audio files for Chapter 5 at **www.myhistorylab.com**.

THE CRISIS OF IMPERIAL AUTHORITY *(page 119)*

WHAT NEW challenges did the British government face in North America after 1763?

REPUBLICAN IDEOLOGY AND COLONIAL PROTEST *(page 123)*

HOW DID republican ideology inform the colonists' view of their relationship to Britain?

THE STAMP ACT CRISIS *(page 124)*

WHY DID the Stamp Act spark widespread unrest in the colonies?

THE TOWNSHEND CRISIS *(page 126)*

HOW DID the colonists respond to Townshend's colonial policies?

DOMESTIC DIVISIONS *(page 129)*

WHAT ISSUES and interests divided the colonists?

THE FINAL IMPERIAL CRISIS *(page 131)*

WHAT PUSHED the colonists from protest to rebellion?

One American Journey

Indeed, it appears to me a very doubtful point, even supposing all the colonies of America to be united under one head, whether it would be possible to keep in due order and government so wide and extended an empire, the difficulties of communication, of intercourse, of correspondence, and all other circumstances considered.

A voluntary association or coalition, at least a permanent one, is almost as difficult to be supposed: for fire and water are not more heterogeneous than the different colonies in North America. Nothing can exceed the jealousy and emulation which they possess in regard to each other. . . . Even the limits and boundaries of each colony are a constant source of litigation. In short, such is the difference of character, of manners, of religion, of interest, of the different colonies, that I think, if I am not wholly ignorant of the human mind, were they left to themselves, there would soon be a civil war from one end of the continent to the other; while the Indians and negroes would, with better reason, impatiently watch the opportunity of exterminating them all together.

Andrew Burnaby, *Travels Through the Middle Settlements in North America in the Years 1759 and 1760* [1775] (3rd edition, 1798; reprinted New York: Augustus M. Kelley, 1970), pp. 152–153.

Read the **Document** at **www.myhistorylab.com**

Personal Journeys Online

- **Mary Ambler, *Diary of M. Ambler,* 1770. This memoir records Ambler's trip to Baltimore to have her two young children inoculated for smallpox.**
- **Reverend John Ettwein, *Notes of Travel from the North Branch of the Susquehanna to the Beaver River, Pennsylvania,* 1772. This journal recorded the journey of about one hundred Christianized Indians through western Pennsylvania to their new homes at the village of Friedenstadt.**
- **Nicholas Cresswell, *The Journal of Nicholas Cresswell,* 1774–1777. A prospective immigrant sails, having decided to go to America, but the Revolution changes his mind.**

ANDREW BURNABY, an English clergyman, made these observations while on a tour of the colonies in 1759 and 1760. Few people on either side of the Atlantic would have disagreed with his assessment. The only union that he or anyone else at the time could imagine was the imperial connection that bound Great Britain to its American possessions. That connection seemed even stronger as Burnaby's journey came to a close in 1760, for by then Britain's victory in the French and Indian War was all but certain.

But the war had changed the British Empire in ways that few people immediately grasped. The first to understand the challenges of victory were British officials, who found themselves with a burdensome debt and vastly increased territory to administer—much of it occupied by erstwhile enemies. Their efforts to meet these challenges resulted in an unprecedented assertion of imperial control over the American colonies in order to secure the fruits of victory. From the vantage point of London, this new model of empire appeared both necessary and, to some officials, long overdue.

To many colonists, however, British reforms represented an unwarranted disruption of a well-functioning imperial relationship. Rather than seeing various reform measures as attempts to deal with practical problems, colonists regarded them as repeated assaults on their property and rights. For more than a decade, Great Britain and its American colonies engaged in an often acrimonious and occasionally violent debate over the proper structure of the postwar empire. Only at the end of that period did it become clear that the survival of the empire itself might be at stake. ✦

CHRONOLOGY

1759–1761	Cherokee War takes place.
1760	George III becomes king.
1761–1769	British, French, German, Russian, and American astronomers observe transit of Venus across the sun.
1763	Peace of Paris ends French and Indian War.
	Spanish accelerate imperial reforms.
	British troops remain in America.
	Proclamation Line of 1763 limits western expansion of colonial settlement.
	Pontiac's War begins.
	Paxton Boys murder peaceful Indians.
1764	Sugar Act passed.
	Currency Act passed.
1765	Quartering Act passed.
	Stamp Act passed.
	Stamp Act Congress meets in New York.
1766	Stamp Act repealed; Declaratory Act passed.
	New York Assembly refuses to comply with Quartering Act.
1767	Townshend duties imposed.
	Regulator movements begin in North and South Carolina.
1769	James Watt, a British inventor, patents a steam engine.
1769–1770	Famine kills one-third of the population in Bengal, India.
1770	Boston Massacre takes place.
	Tea duty retained, other Townshend duties repealed.
1771	North Carolina Regulator movement defeated.
1772	*Gaspée* burned.
	Committees of Correspondence formed.
1773	Boston Tea Party takes place.
1774	Coercive Acts passed.
	Quebec Act passed.
	First Continental Congress meets and agrees to boycott British imports.

THE CRISIS OF IMPERIAL AUTHORITY

WHAT NEW challenges did the British government face in North America after 1763?

As the French and Indian War drew to a close, political shifts at the heart of London did not make the task of imperial administration any easier. In 1760, a rather naïve new monarch, George III, ascended the throne at the age of 22. Disputes among his advisers soon led to the resignation of William Pitt, the popular war minister who had helped England achieve its great victory. Political infighting at the highest reaches of government persisted until April 1763, when George Grenville became first lord of the treasury and the man responsible for ushering Britain and her colonies into the postwar era.

Challenges of Control and Finance

Britain's empire in 1763 was immense, and the problems its rulers faced were correspondingly large. Moreover, it still faced threats, if diminished ones, from its traditional European enemies. French territory on the North American mainland had been reduced to two tiny islands in the Gulf of St. Lawrence. Yet France's spectacular defeat would only whet its appetite for revenge. Spain was a more significant presence on the North American mainland. At the end of the French and Indian War, it surrendered East and West Florida to Britain but got back its possessions in Cuba and the Philippines that the British had captured. Spain acquired Louisiana from its French ally as compensation for the loss of the Floridas.

Protecting Britain's enlarged empire from these familiar European rivals formed just part of the security problems facing British officials. With the Peace of Paris of 1763, Britain acquired

QUICK REVIEW

European Territories, 1763

- Britain: territories in North America from Hudson's Bay to the Caribbean, from the Atlantic to the Mississippi.
- France: territory on the mainland reduced to two small islands.
- Spain: Cuba, the Philippines, Louisiana, and California.

not only new lands but also new subjects—few of whom had any reason to feel loyal toward George III or the British nation. Thousands of French inhabitants remaining in Canada and the Mississippi Valley would likely side with France in the event of another war with Britain. Even greater numbers of Native Americans, most of whom sided with France during the war, populated these regions.

Concerns about imperial authority extended to the inhabitants of the existing colonies themselves. Worries about the colonists' wartime smuggling and their assemblies' frequent obstruction of military orders fed an ongoing debate in London about the need for a more centralized form of imperial control. The assertiveness of colonial legislatures, many British officials thought, contributed to an unacceptable level of American insubordination. Imperial reform would have to address this problem as well.

QUICK REVIEW

Financial Strain on the Empire

- British national debt rose to all-time high after French and Indian War.
- Many Britons believed Americans should bear more of the burden of empire.
- Economic recession increased pressure for new taxes.

But any plan for imperial restructuring, no matter how well designed, faced an enormous obstacle. Wartime expenses had caused England's national debt to balloon. Half of the money collected from hard-pressed British taxpayers went just to pay the interest on this massive debt, and no more revenue could be squeezed from them without risking domestic unrest. Moreover, it seemed unfair to do so. Since the comparatively lightly taxed Americans benefited the most from the war, officials believed they should shoulder more of the financial burden of victory.

Native Americans and Frontier Conflict

Cherokee War Conflict (1759–1761) on the southern frontier between the Cherokee Indians and colonists from Virginia southward.

As a first response to the new demands of empire, the British government decided to keep a substantial body of troops in America in peacetime—10,000 were initially planned. The soldiers would protect the new territories and existing colonies. More importantly, officials hoped that their presence would help to maintain peace with the Indians.

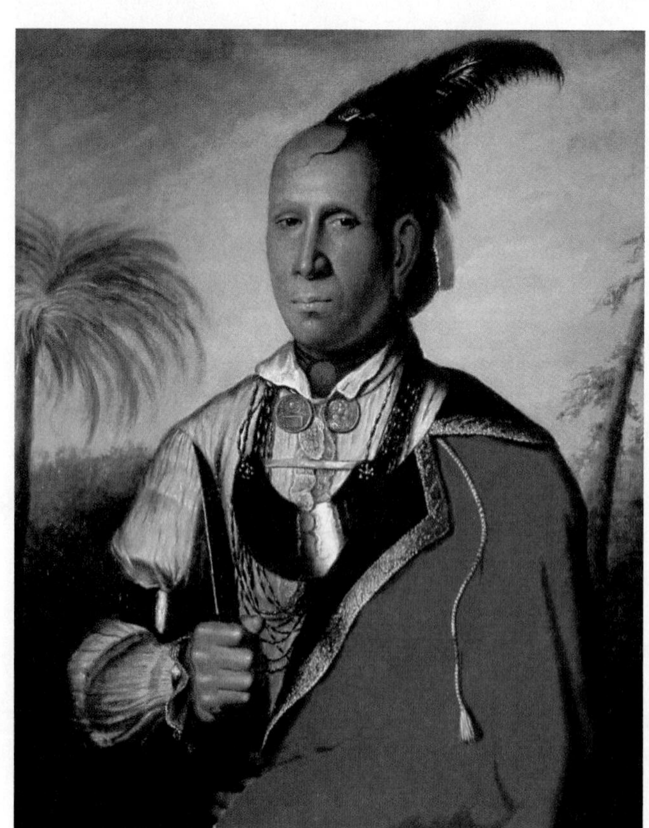

Cunne Shote, one of three Cherokee chiefs who visited London in 1762, had this portrait painted there by Francis Parsons.

Even as the war with France had been drawing to a close, conflict with Cherokee Indians on the southern frontier had flared into violence. Longtime allies and trading partners of South Carolina, the Cherokees resented repeated incidents of theft, encroachment on their lands, and violence perpetrated by frontier colonists. By early 1760, their frustration blossomed into the **Cherokee War** when they launched retaliatory attacks on western settlements in all the southern colonies. Three expeditions, manned by British as well as colonial troops, eventually forced the Cherokees to agree, in a 1761 treaty, to surrender land in the Carolinas and Virginia to the colonists.

The end of the Cherokee War did not necessarily ease frontier tensions. France's loss of its North American colonies deprived many Indians of a key ally, trading partner, and counterweight to British pressures for land. Britain's General Jeffrey Amherst confirmed their worst fears when he ordered a reduction in the gifts customarily supplied to the Iroquois and other Native American allies. He saw no reason to continue offering what he regarded as bribes to maintain ties to Indians who could no longer threaten to desert Britain and ally with France. Amherst further infuriated western Indians by reneging on a promise to construct trading posts in the interior and withdraw troops. The persistence of military garrisons and the establishment of farming settlements near them suggested nothing less than a British intent to occupy Indian lands permanently.

The Indian response stunned the British with its fierceness and geographical range. It was also remarkable as an unprecedented example of Indian unity in the face of European expansion. The sources of that unity were as much spiritual as political. In 1761, Neolin, sometimes known as the Delaware Prophet, experienced a vision in which God commanded the Indians to reject their dependence on European goods and ways and embrace their own ancestral practices.

By May 1763 the Indians were ready to strike. Led by an Ottawa chief named Pontiac, a loose coalition of at least eight major Native American peoples launched attacks on more than a dozen British forts in the west, beginning at Detroit. Within months, **Pontiac's War** raged along the frontier from the Great Lakes to Virginia. Horrified by the prospect of an Indian victory, General Amherst urged his troops to adopt desperate measures. British tactics included killing Indian prisoners and, most notoriously, distributing smallpox-infected blankets as diplomatic gifts to local chiefs who had come to Fort Pitt during a temporary truce.

It was not smallpox but starvation that ultimately ended Pontiac's War. British forces attacked Indian food supplies as they waited for their adversaries to run out of ammunition. By late summer 1764, the Indian coalition had begun to disintegrate and fighting ceased. Pontiac finally accepted a treaty in 1766. Chastened by the conflict, British officials agreed to follow the practices the French had once used in the Great Lakes area by supplying western Indians with diplomatic gifts, encouraging trade, and mediating disputes.

Yet frontier animosities whipped to a frenzy by the war did not easily dissipate. Few colonists in vulnerable western settlements cared any longer to distinguish between friendly and hostile Indians; as far as they were concerned, all Indians were enemies. This kind of thinking provoked a group of Scots-Irish settlers in Paxton Township, Pennsylvania, upset at the colonial assembly's lack of aggressiveness in dealing with Indians, to take matters into their own hands. Unable to catch the Indians who were attacking their settlements, they slaughtered a defenseless group of Christian Conestogas living nearby. The so-called Paxton Boys went on to murder another group of Christian Indians two weeks later.

Dealing with the New Territories

Even as Pontiac's War was going on, the king issued the **Proclamation of 1763.** The measure aimed to pacify Indians by prohibiting white settlement west of the ridgeline of the Appalachian Mountains. Colonists who had already moved to the western side of this Proclamation Line were required "forthwith to remove themselves" back to the east (see Map 5–1). The royal proclamation contained two other key features. First, it obligated Britain to establish a regulated Indian trade in the interior in an effort to supply desired

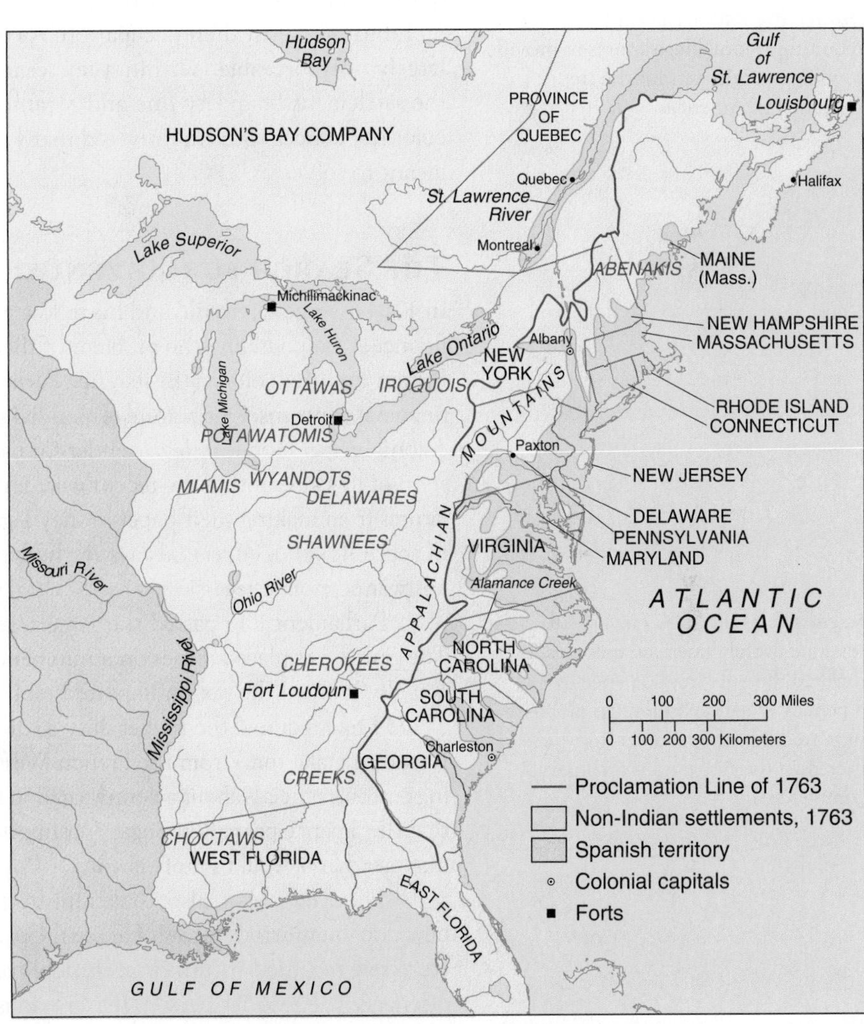

MAP 5–1 **Colonial Settlement and the Proclamation Line of 1763** This map depicts the regions claimed and settled by the major groups competing for territory in eastern North America. With the Proclamation Line of 1763, positioned along the crest of the Appalachian Mountains, the British government tried to stop the westward migration of settlers under its jurisdiction and thereby limit conflict with the Indians. The result, however, was frustration and anger on the part of land-hungry settlers.

Why do you think the Proclamation Line of 1763 was positioned along the crest of the Appalachian Mountains?

See the Map
at **www.myhistorylab.com**
Settlement in North America, c. 1763

Pontiac's War Indian uprising (1763–1766) led by Pontiac of the Ottawas and Neolin of the Delawares.

Proclamation of 1763 Royal proclamation setting the boundary known as the Proclamation Line that limited British settlements to the eastern side of the Appalachian Mountains.

Quartering Acts Acts of Parliament requiring colonial legislatures to provide supplies and quarters for the troops stationed in America.

goods and curb traders' cheating of their Native American customers. Second, it established civilian governments in East and West Florida. For the time being, Canada—inhabited by more than eighty thousand French Catholics—would remain under military rule.

The 10,000-man force that British officials planned to keep in America was not nearly large enough to ensure that the proclamation would be obeyed. Moreover, both the stationing of troops in peacetime and the establishment of the Proclamation Line aroused considerable resentment among colonists. Americans shared a traditional English distrust of standing armies, and worried that the soldiers could just as easily be used to coerce the colonists as to protect them. Their concerns were heightened when Parliament passed two **Quartering Acts** that required colonial assemblies to provide barracks and supplies for the soldiers.

News of the Proclamation Line was no more welcome. Colonial settlers and land speculators coveted the territories they had fought to win from France and resented the prohibition against their occupation. As it turned out, the prohibition against settlement was largely unenforceable. Within a few years, imperial authorities made several adjustments to the settlement boundary line and returned supervision of the Indian trade to the individual colonies, concessions that revived many of the problems that the Proclamation of 1763 had meant to solve.

The Search for Revenue: The Sugar Act

In 1764 George Grenville and his fellow ministers turned from territorial control to matters of finance. Compounding the problem of the soaring national debt, a postwar recession had both Britain and the colonies in its grip. Parliament passed two laws that year to address imperial financial concerns. One statute responded to London merchants' protest against Virginia's use of colonial paper money as legal tender for payment of debts, because the money had lost nearly a sixth of its value during the recent war. The Currency Act of 1764 prohibited all colonial legislatures from making their paper money legal tender. It allowed creditors to demand repayment in specie (gold or silver), always in short supply in the colonies, and even more so during the postwar economic recession.

Sugar Act Law passed in 1764 to raise revenue in the American colonies. It lowered the duty from 6 pence to 3 pence per gallon on foreign molasses imported into the colonies and increased the restrictions on colonial commerce.

Parliament also passed the American Revenue Act, commonly known as the **Sugar Act.** The Sugar Act placed duties on a number of colonial imports, but its most important provision actually lowered the tax on imported molasses from 6 to 3 pence per gallon. The Molasses Act of 1733 had required the higher duty to discourage colonists from importing molasses (much of it used to make rum) from the French West Indies. But merchants evaded the high tax by bribing customs officials about a penny a gallon to certify French molasses as British. Grenville hoped that the 3 pence per gallon Sugar Act tax was close enough to the going rate for bribes that colonial merchants would simply pay it.

The Sugar Act also took aim at smugglers by requiring that ships carry elaborate new documentation of their cargoes. Customs officials could seize ships for what their owners often regarded as minor technicalities. The act further ordered customs collectors to discharge their duties personally. Previously, these men had often lived in England, leaving the work of collection in the colonies to poorly paid deputies, who were susceptible to bribes. Finally, Parliament gave responsibility for trying violations of the laws to a new vice-admiralty court in Halifax, Nova Scotia. Vice-admiralty courts, with jurisdiction over maritime affairs, normally operated without a jury and were therefore more likely to enforce trade restrictions.

New Englanders predominated among those colonists actively opposed to the Sugar Act. They feared that enforcement of the tax on foreign molasses would damage the northern rum industry. Earnings from rum were crucial to the New England–West Indies trade and also helped to pay for imported British goods. The postwar recession was hardly the time to stir up colonial fears about their economies. The assemblies of eight colonies collaborated on a set of petitions sent to royal authorities to protest the Sugar Act. Officials in London, however, simply ignored the petitions even as they labored to devise new colonial taxes.

REPUBLICAN IDEOLOGY AND COLONIAL PROTEST

HOW DID republican ideology inform the colonists' view of their relationship to Britain?

Colonists stressed economic arguments in their petitions against the Sugar Act, but their unease about the measure also had political dimensions. Parliament had passed similar commercial regulations before, but its new assertiveness and its claim that additional taxes might be necessary stirred colonial fears that more than their pocketbooks were under threat. Colonists treasured their rights as Englishmen, but new imperial reforms threatened to encroach on their enjoyment of those rights as never before. Thus imperial reforms provoked colonists to reflect upon the character of the postwar empire and on the principles that governed their membership in it.

POWER VERSUS LIBERTY

Many colonists derived their understanding of politics from a set of ideas loosely grouped under the heading of **republicanism.** Influenced by writings from classical Rome, and linked to what was known in England as **Country,** or **"Real Whig," ideology** (see Chapter 4), republican political thinkers acknowledged that governments must exercise power, but simultaneously cautioned that power could easily overwhelm liberty. Too much power in the hands of a ruler meant tyranny. Too much liberty in the hands of the people, however, was no better; it meant anarchy.

republicanism The idea that governments must exercise power, but simultaneously cautioning that power could easily overwhelm liberty.

Country (Real Whig) ideology Train of thought (focusing on the threat to personal liberty and the taxation of property holders) first appearing in England in the late seventeenth century in response to the growth of governmental power and a national debt.

Republican ideology thus called upon the people to be ever vigilant against corruption and excessive power. Their main bulwark against tyranny was civil liberty, or maintaining the right of the people to participate in government. The people who did so, however, had to demonstrate virtue. To eighteenth-century republicans, virtuous citizens were those who focused not on their private interests but rather on what was good for the public as a whole. They were necessarily propertyholders, since only these individuals could exercise an independence of judgment impossible for those dependent on employers, landlords, masters, or (in the case of women and children) husbands and fathers.

QUICK REVIEW

Republican Ideology

- Sought to achieve a balance between power and liberty.
- Saw the British Constitution as the embodiment of political balance.
- Colonists saw in taxation the potential for tyranny.

THE BRITISH CONSTITUTION

The key to good government was preserving a balance between the exercise of power and the protection of liberty. Colonists agreed that no government performed this crucial task better than Great Britain's, based as it was on the **British Constitution.** Then, as now, the British Constitution was not a written document. It consisted instead of the governing institutions, laws, and political customs of the realm as they had evolved over the centuries. It was understood, in short, as the way in which British government and society together *were constituted*.

British Constitution The principles, procedures, and precedents that governed the operation of the British government.

The genius of Britain's government lay in the fact that its constitution was "mixed and balanced." Society was comprised of three elements—the monarchy, aristocracy, and common people—and they had their governmental counterparts in the Crown, the House of Lords, and the House of Commons. Liberty would be preserved so long as none of the elements acquired the ability to dominate or corrupt the others.

The British Constitution protected that balance in a number of ways. Both Houses of Parliament, for instance, had to consent to laws in order for them to go into effect. Because taxation was such a sensitive subject, the House of Commons—the governmental unit closest to the people—retained the right to initiate tax laws and no tax could pass without the consent of the representatives of both houses. This parliamentary control of taxation operated as a crucial check on the monarch's power.

Taxation and Sovereignty

Colonists who had absorbed republican ideas were especially concerned about taxation because anyone who paid taxes in effect surrendered some of his property to do so. As long as the taxpayer consented to those taxes, however, it was unlikely that they would become excessive enough to threaten his independence and liberty. Rumors from England that more taxes might follow passage of the Sugar Act encouraged some colonists to begin thinking about whether they really consented to taxes passed by a Parliament to which they elected no representatives.

The fiscal measures required by imperial reform thus drew attention to differences between British and colonial understandings of representation. British authorities contended that colonists, like all inhabitants of Britain, were virtually represented in Parliament because that body's members served the interests of the British nation and empire as a whole. Colonists, however, thought they could only be represented by men for whom they had actually voted—such as the members of their colonial legislatures (see Chapter 4). And they insisted that the right to be taxed only by their own elected representatives was one of the most basic rights of Englishmen.

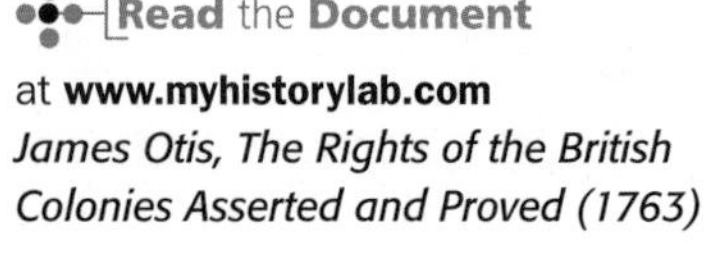

Read the Document at **www.myhistorylab.com** *James Otis, The Rights of the British Colonies Asserted and Proved (1763)*

Few colonists realized yet that their concerns about taxation connected to the more fundamental issue of political **sovereignty.** Sovereignty was the supreme authority of the state, and it included both the right to take life (as in the case of executions for capital crimes) and to tax. If the state were deprived of its authority, it ceased to be sovereign. Were colonists to reach the point where they denied Parliament's right to tax them, they would in effect be denying that the British government had sovereign power over the colonies.

sovereignty The supreme authority of the state, including both the right to take life (as in the case of executions for capital crimes) and to tax.

THE STAMP ACT CRISIS

WHY DID the Stamp Act spark widespread unrest in the colonies?

Because revenue from the Sugar Act was hardly enough to solve Britain's debt problems, George Grenville proposed another measure, the **Stamp Act.** This legislation required all valid legal documents, as well as newspapers, playing cards, and various other papers, to bear a government-issued stamp, for which there was a charge. Colonists who opposed the Sugar Act had difficulty justifying their opposition to a measure that appeared to fall within Britain's accepted authority to regulate commerce. The Stamp Act was different. It was the first internal tax (as opposed to an external trade duty) that Parliament had imposed on the colonies.

Read the Document at **www.myhistorylab.com** *Exploring America: The Stamp Act*

Colonial Assemblies React to the Stamp Tax

Colonial protests arose months before the Stamp Act was due to go into effect on November 1, 1765. Eight legislatures passed resolutions condemning the measure. In Virginia's House of Burgesses, 29-year-old Patrick Henry went so far as to propose a resolution asserting that Virginians could disobey any law to which their own legislature had not agreed. Neither this nor some of Henry's other inflammatory proposals passed, but they testified to colonial outrage at what many regarded as an unconstitutional tax.

Stamp Act Law passed by Parliament in 1765 to raise revenue in America by requiring taxed, stamped paper for legal documents, publications, and playing cards.

In October, nine colonies sent delegates to the **Stamp Act Congress** meeting in New York to coordinate the colonial response. The delegates affirmed their loyalty to the king and their "due subordination" to Parliament, but proceeded to adopt the **Declaration of Rights and Grievances.** This document denied Parliament's right to tax the colonies and petitioned king and Parliament to repeal both the Sugar and Stamp acts. Parliament, shocked at this challenge to its authority, refused to receive this declaration or any other colonial petitions.

Stamp Act Congress October 1765 meeting of delegates sent by nine colonies, which adopted the Declaration of Rights and Grievances and petitioned against the Stamp Act.

Read the Document at **www.myhistorylab.com** *Benjamin Franklin, Testimony against the Stamp Act (1766)*

While colonial assemblies and the Stamp Act Congress deliberated, a torrent of pamphlets and newspaper essays flowed from colonial presses. Some went beyond opposition to the Stamp

GLOBAL CONNECTIONS

A Frenchman Reports on the American Reaction to the Stamp Act

Britain emerged from the Great War for Empire as the victor, but France had no intention of quietly giving up the struggle. French officials therefore took a keen interest in what was happening in the British North American colonies. The Duc de Choiseul, who was in charge of foreign affairs in the 1760s, was in fact remarkably prescient in believing that the British acquisition of Canada would prompt the thirteen mainland colonies to revolt since they no longer needed protection from the French next door. Choiseul and his successor in office, the Comte de Vergennes, accordingly sent agents to take the temperature of affairs in America and report on items of interest such as fortifications, navigable rivers, and the like.

An anonymous traveler whose journal wound up in the French naval archives may have been such a spy, and his findings doubtless pleased French officials. After landing in North Carolina in early 1765, he went north through Williamsburg, Virginia; Annapolis, Maryland; Philadelphia, Pennsylvania; to New York City. On May 30 he was visiting the Virginia House of Burgesses when Patrick Henry gave an historic speech against the Stamp Act, and the traveler's account remains one of our best sources for what was actually said that day. But at all of his major stops, he found Americans condemning the Stamp Act and claiming that they "would fight to the last Drop of their blood before they would Consent to any such slavery." He was sure that this act "had made a great alteration in the Americans Disposition towards great britain" and turned them toward manufacturing goods for themselves. If the trend continued, he predicted that it would be a "fatal stroke to England, for their Chief Dependance is on their manufactures to which these colonys were a Considerable suport."

British officials, he believed, had encouraged religious and other differences among the colonists to keep them dependent on the mother country. But, he concluded, "great is their mistake in this, for the Inhabitants of north America Can lay aside their religion, when their Interest requires it as well as the English Can, and always have done."

- Do you think the Frenchman was right in his assessment of the American reaction to the Stamp Act and the value of the colonies to Great Britain?

Act itself to address broader issues. At the same time, merchants in several colonial cities resorted to economic pressure, pledging to cease importing British goods until the hated taxes were repealed. Important as these various measures were in solidifying colonial opposition, however, defeat of the Stamp Act came largely through actions, not words.

Declaration of Rights and Grievances Asserts that the Stamp Act and other taxes imposed on the colonists without their consent were unconstitutional.

Colonists Take to the Streets

In Boston, a group composed mainly of artisans and shopkeepers, with a few prominent citizens playing behind-the-scenes roles, organized themselves as the **Sons of Liberty.** As part of their general protest against the Stamp Act, they planned to intimidate Andrew Oliver, who had been appointed to the office of stamp distributor, into resigning. In August 1765, they took to the streets. Violent protests quickly spread to other locations. Up and down the coast, rioters forced nearly every stamp distributor to resign his office before the law went into effect on November 1. After that date, the law was essentially nullified, because there was no one to distribute the hated stamps.

Sons of Liberty Secret organizations in the colonies formed to oppose the Stamp Act.

Colonial elites sympathetic to the cause of the rioters were nonetheless appalled at their violent tactics. The Stamp Act Congress convened, in large part, so that elites could try to regain control of the situation. When news of the protests reached London, imperial authorities were astonished by the violence. British merchants, feeling the sting of colonial boycotts of British goods, petitioned Parliament to repeal the Stamp Act and resolve the crisis before matters got further out of hand.

QUICK REVIEW

The Stamp Act Crisis

- First internal tax imposed on colonists by Britain.
- Protest of the Stamp Act took many forms.
- Repeal of the Stamp Act accompanied by passage of the Declaratory Act.

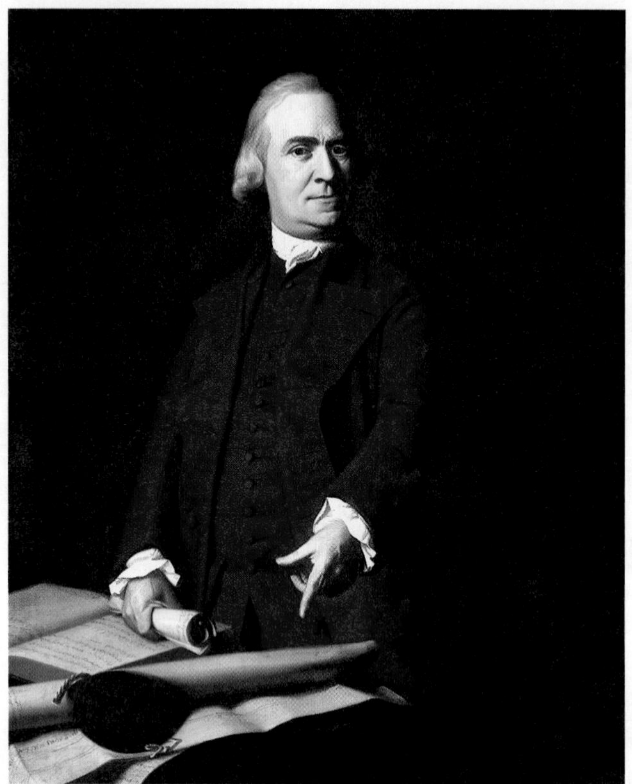

Samuel Adams, the leader of the Boston radicals, as he appeared to John Singleton Copley in the early 1770s. In this famous picture, thought to have been commissioned by another revolutionary leader, John Hancock, Adams points to legal documents guaranteeing American rights.

Source: John Singleton Copley (1738–1815), "Samuel Adams," ca. 1772. Oil on canvas 49 1/2 × 39 1/2 in. (125.7 cm × 100.3 cm). Deposited by the City of Boston, 30.76c Courtesy, Museum of Fine Arts, Boston. Reproduced with permission.

Repeal and the Declaratory Act

For reasons that had nothing to do with colonial unrest, George III decided to replace Grenville at the treasury with another man, the Marquis of Rockingham. Rockingham was convinced that repealing the Stamp Act was the only way to calm colonial tempers. He faced a delicate task, however, in getting Parliament and the king to agree to repeal.

Both Crown and Parliament thought it preposterous for the world's mightiest empire simply to give way to unruly American mobs. They did not wish to give the slightest impression that they agreed with the colonists' assertion that the Stamp Act was unconstitutional, for to do so would be to call into question Parliament's right to legislate for the colonies at all. In the end, Rockingham found a three-part solution that linked repeal to an unequivocal assertion of Parliament's sovereignty.

First, the Stamp Act would be repealed only because it had damaged British commercial interests, and not because it allegedly violated the colonists' rights. Second, Parliament passed the **Declaratory Act.** This measure affirmed Parliament's sovereignty, declaring that it had "full power and authority to make laws and statutes of sufficient force and validity to bind the colonies and people of America . . . in all cases whatsoever." Third, Parliament passed the Revenue Act of 1766, which reduced the tax on molasses from 3 pence per gallon to 1 penny, but imposed it on all molasses—British and foreign—that came to the mainland colonies.

In London, Parliament had saved face and calmed the merchant community. In the colonies, people rejoiced. They regarded repeal as a vindication of their claim that the Stamp Act had been unconstitutional, and they saw little threat in the Declaratory Act because it did not explicitly assert Parliament's right to tax the colonies, but only "make laws" for them. The Revenue Act attracted little notice, even though it in fact generated considerable income for the empire. Tacit acceptance of this measure suggested that colonists remained willing to pay "external" taxes that regulated trade.

Declaratory Act Law passed in 1766 to accompany repeal of the Stamp Act that stated that Parliament had the authority to legislate for the colonies "in all cases whatsoever."

THE TOWNSHEND CRISIS

HOW DID the colonists respond to Townshend's colonial policies?

Peace between Britain and the colonies did not last long. In 1766 there was another shake-up in the British ministry. The king replaced Rockingham with William Pitt, who had accepted a peerage and was now known as Lord Chatham. Leadership in the House of Commons passed from Pitt to Charles Townshend. Townshend was convinced that the colonists still needed to be taught a lesson in submission to Parliament's authority.

Townshend's Plan

One focus of Charles Townshend's concern was New York, where the legislature refused to comply with the Quartering Act of 1765 that required colonial assemblies to raise money for housing and supplying British troops. New Yorkers had concluded that this measure amounted to taxation without representation. Townshend's response was to get Parliament to pass an act in 1767 that suspended the New York legislature. Although the New York assembly gave in before the act went into effect, the measure revived concerns about imperial power and showed colonists that Townshend meant business.

A satirical British engraving from 1766 showing English politicians burying the Stamp Act, "born 1765 died 1766." The warehouses in the background symbolize the revival of trade with America.

Much of Britain's postwar debt remained unpaid. Nonetheless, Townshend's fiscal plan was not really designed to reduce that debt. Townshend proposed new duties for the colonies but at the same time lowered certain taxes in Britain itself. He and other British officials were primarily interested in asserting parliamentary sovereignty over the colonies. The result was the **Townshend Duty Act of 1767.** It imposed new duties on imports that colonists got from Britain, including tea, paper, lead, glass, and paint. Revenue from the act would pay the salaries of governors and judges in the colonies, freeing them from dependence on the colonial assemblies that normally paid them.

Townshend Duty Act of 1767 Act of Parliament, passed in 1767, imposing duties on colonial tea, lead, paint, paper, and glass.

Colonists suspected that Townshend's plan to pay governors and judges would ensure that these officials would support their parliamentary paymasters rather than the colonial assemblies. Their fears grew when news arrived that there would be a new American Board of Customs Commissioners to see that the Townshend duties were paid. The board would be located in Boston, the presumed home port of many smugglers and the site of the fiercest protests against the Stamp Act.

Renewed Resistance

Charles Townshend died suddenly in September 1767 and thus did not live to see the consequences of his actions. Colonial protests were swift, if unorganized. Once again, colonial radicals called for a boycott of British goods. But trade embargoes hurt merchants and consumers alike, making it difficult to guarantee compliance in all port towns. Yet unanimity was critical; a boycott in Boston was meaningless if British goods continued to flow into Philadelphia or New York. Support for nonimportation increased, however, after an incident in Boston in June 1768. When customs commissioners seized John Hancock's ship, *Liberty*, on charges of smuggling, their action sparked a riot. In response to the requests of the terrified commissioners, Britain sent two regiments of troops to Boston.

In the aftermath of the *Liberty* riot and with the impending arrival of British troops, merchants first in Boston and New York, and later Philadelphia, agreed to nonimportation. Enforcement of the trade boycotts energized the populace and drew more people, including artisans and laborers, into political action than ever before. Women, who normally had no

W
WHERE TO LEARN MORE
Charleston, South Carolina
http://www.nps.gov/nr/travel/charleston/

Read the **Document**
at **www.myhistorylab.com**
John Dickinson, from Letters from a Farmer in Pennsylvania (1768)

Hear the **Audio**
at **www.myhistorylab.com**
The Liberty Song

formal political role because of their dependent status, found that their responsibilities for household production and purchasing gained political meaning. They too could announce their solidarity with fellow colonists by spurning British imports and instead making and wearing homespun clothing. Colonists from all social groups forged a sense of common purpose in their resistance to the Townshend duties (see American Views: Social Status and the Enforcement of the Nonimportation Movement).

nonimportation movement A tactical means of putting economic pressure on Britain by refusing to buy its exports in the colonies.

Read the **Document** at **www.myhistorylab.com** *The Virginia Nonimportation Resolutions (1769)*

The **nonimportation movement** eventually produced a sharp drop in British imports. By early 1770, northern colonies had reduced imports by nearly two-thirds (see Figure 5–1). Once again, colonial economic pressure caught the attention of British merchants and members of Parliament. The troubles in America contributed to the king's decision to appoint a new prime minister, Frederick, Lord North, in January 1770. Lord North was prepared to concede that the Townshend duties had been counterproductive because they interfered with British trade. But even as he worked for their repeal, news arrived of another episode of violence in Boston—this time involving British troops.

The Boston Massacre

Ever since British troops had arrived in Boston in 1768, there had been friction between soldiers and civilians. By the summer of 1769, however, Boston seemed calm enough that British authorities thought it safe to remove half of the 1,000 troops stationed there. This action energized the Sons of Liberty, who saw an opportunity to confront the remaining soldiers more often. Crowds frequently gathered to taunt and throw stones at troops standing at guardposts. Townsmen also targeted off-duty soldiers who sought part-time employment at unskilled jobs. Many Bostonians, unemployed because of the weak economy, resented competition from soldiers who, because they derived some income from the army, could afford to accept lower wages from employers.

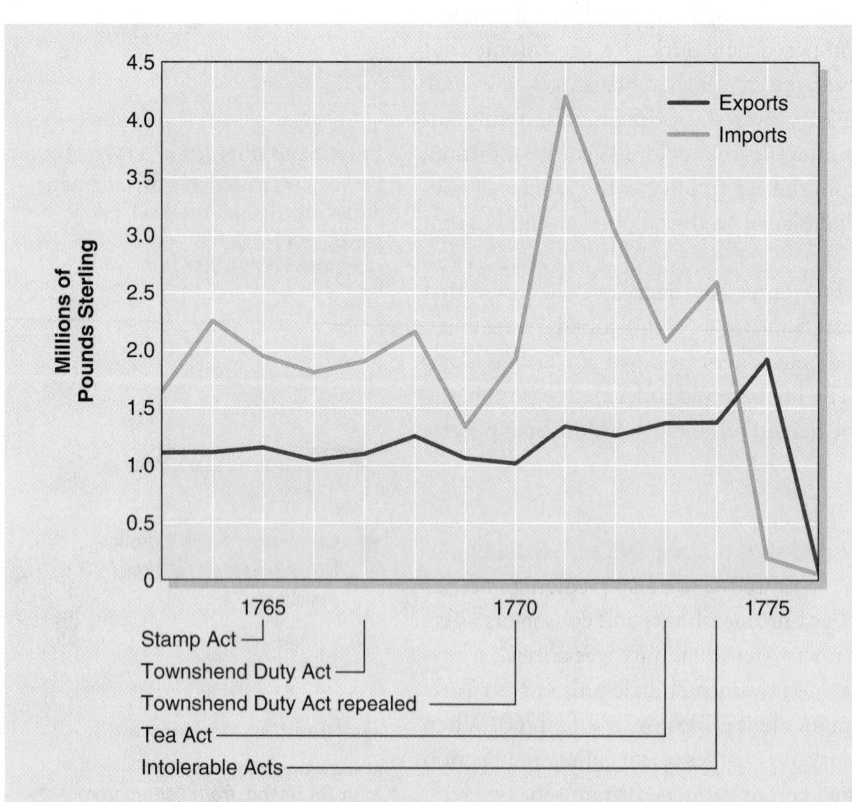

FIGURE 5–1 **Value of American Exports to and Imports from England, 1763–1776** This figure depicts the value of American exports to and imports from England. The decrease of imports in 1765–1766 and the even sharper drop in 1769 illustrate the effect of American boycotts in response to the Stamp Act and Townshend duties.

Data Source: U.S. Bureau of the Census, *Historical Statistics of the United States, Colonial Times to 1970,* Bicentennial Edition, Part 1 (1975).

In early March 1770, these sporadic incidents culminated in a fatal confrontation. On March 5, a crowd gathered outside the customs house and began pelting the guardsmen with snowballs and rocks. The British officer, Captain Thomas Preston, ordered his men to fix bayonets and push the crowd back. But then one soldier evidently slipped, and his musket discharged as he fell. The remaining soldiers, perhaps believing that in the tumult Preston had ordered them to fire, shot into the crowd, killing five Bostonians and wounding six. Four of the dead men were white artisans or laborers; the fifth was Crispus Attucks, a free black sailor.

Captain Preston and six soldiers were tried for murder. They were defended in court by two prominent Boston lawyers, John Adams and Josiah Quincy Jr. who—despite their radical political leanings—thought the soldiers deserved a proper legal defense.

Preston and four soldiers were acquitted; two others were convicted of the lesser charge of manslaughter.

The **Boston Massacre** seemed to fulfill dire republican prophecies about a tyrannical Britain using military coercion to take away American liberties. Boston's radicals worked to ensure that the memory of the Massacre remained fresh in colonists' minds. Each year, Bostonians commemorated March 5 as "Massacre Day," with public speeches and other events. Orators warned colonists in other cities to be vigilant, since their turn might be next.

Read the Document at **www.myhistorylab.com** *Boston Gazette, Description of the Boston Massacre (1770)*

Boston Massacre After months of increasing friction between townspeople and the British troops stationed in the city, on March 5, 1770, British troops fired on American civilians in Boston.

Partial Repeal and Its Consequences

Ironically, the Boston Massacre occurred on the same day that Lord North proposed that Parliament repeal all of the Townshend duties except the one on tea. As was the case after the Stamp Act, Parliament feared that complete repeal would make it seem that Britain had given in to the colonists. Retaining the tax on tea served as a statement of parliamentary authority; it also made fiscal sense in that most of the revenue raised by the Townshend duties came from the tax on tea.

The rejoicing that had followed the Stamp Act repeal was not repeated after partial repeal of the Townshend duties. For the colonists, this had been an incomplete victory, and recent events, especially the Boston Massacre, had seriously undermined their trust in British authority. On the surface, the years 1770–1773 looked like a time of relative calm. Underneath, however, colonial animosities against British policies continued to simmer.

Every now and then, some incident brought those animosities to a boil in a dramatic way. Such was the case in 1772, when a British customs vessel, the *Gaspée*, ran aground near Providence, Rhode Island. Because its crew had allegedly harassed local residents, Rhode Islanders got even. Led by John Brown, a local merchant, they boarded and burned the ship. The British government appointed a commission of inquiry with instructions to arrest the culprits and send them to England for trial. Despite its offer of a reward for information, the commission learned nothing.

Such incidents, and in particular the British threat to send Americans to England for trial, led colonial leaders to resolve to keep one another informed about British actions. Twelve colonies established **committees of correspondence** for this purpose. In 1773, Boston radicals established similar committees in towns throughout Massachusetts. The committees aimed not only to keep abreast of events in Britain and in other colonies, but also to try and anticipate what Parliament's next move might be. Radicals were especially concerned that colonists would let down their guard in the relative calm that followed the Townshend duty repeal.

committees of correspondence Committees formed in the colonies to keep Americans informed about British measures that would affect them.

DOMESTIC DIVISIONS

WHAT ISSUES and interests divided the colonists?

Even as growing mistrust of Britain encouraged many colonists to see themselves as having common interests, local animosities could still divide them. The same issues that sparked opposition to Britain—property rights and political representation—often pitted colonists against one another.

Regulator Movements

The end of the Cherokee War of 1760–1761 had not brought peace to backcountry South Carolina. Gangs of outlaws displaced by that conflict roamed the countryside, plundering the estates of prosperous farmers and challenging anyone to stop them. When the colonial government, based more than a hundred miles away in Charleston, failed to respond, the aggrieved farmers took matters into their own hands. In 1767, they organized what were in effect vigilante

Regulators Vigilante groups active in the 1760s and 1770s in the western parts of North and South Carolina. The South Carolina Regulators attempted to rid the area of outlaws; the North Carolina Regulators were more concerned with high taxes and court costs.

companies to fight against the marauders. Calling themselves **"Regulators,"** they aimed to bring law and order to the backcountry. By March 1768, the Regulators succeeding in killing or expelling most of the criminals.

The outlaws' threat to property and order, however, was symptomatic of a larger problem of political representation. By the 1760s, most South Carolina settlers lived in the backcountry, but because the creation of legislative districts in the region had not kept pace with settlement, they elected only 2 of 48 assembly representatives. Moreover, there was no court system in the region for the resolution of disputes. Once the outlaws had been eliminated, the Regulators—many of whom were relatively prosperous farmers and shopkeepers—took it upon themselves to "regulate" the poor settlers in their neighborhoods. The crisis diminished only when the governor agreed to create circuit courts in the backcountry and the assembly established new districts that increased the region's political representation.

At about the same time, a Regulator movement emerged in North Carolina. Once again, political representation was a major grievance, for the western counties elected only 17 of the assembly's 78 members. And while North Carolina's backcountry did have county courts, they were plagued by corruption. Once again, aggrieved westerners resorted to extralegal protests. They refused to pay taxes, closed county courts, and attacked the most detested of tax officials. Governor William Tryon matched force with force, sending a thousand militiamen from eastern counties to subdue the protestors. In May 1771, the militiamen defeated more than 2,000 poorly armed Regulators in a battle at Alamance Creek that left 29 men dead and 150 wounded.

QUICK REVIEW

Vigilante Justice

- 1766: Regulators form in response to corruption and lawlessness in North Carolina and South Carolina.
- Regulators conflict with local elites.
- Response to Regulators demonstrated inflexibility of British government.

The battle at Alamance Creek was the most serious episode of unrest, but the tensions that produced it simmered throughout the backcountry. Western settlers, often recent immigrants from Scotland, Northern Ireland, and Germany, paid little attention to the threats to liberty and property posed by parliamentary measures. As far as they were concerned, the sources of corruption lay much closer to home, in eastern capitals where officials ignored western demands for good government. Until legislative districts were created in the region, backcountry farmers could legitimately complain about taxation without representation—imposed by their own colonial assemblies.

This depiction of Governor William Tryon's confrontation with the North Carolina Regulators during May 1771 was produced at Philadelphia in 1876 by F.O.C. Darley (1822–1888).

The Beginnings of Antislavery

In a similar vein, African slaves could have argued that their experience of actual enslavement was far more real than any potential threat to white colonists' liberty posed by imperial reforms. Black colonists, both slave and free, watched white colonists march in parades and riot in the streets, and heard their orators make fervent speeches on behalf of liberty. Although slavery would far outlast these decades, some colonists began to question the legitimacy of the oppressive institution.

Some slaves, particularly in New England, employed the language of liberty when they sued their owners for freedom. In Massachusetts, groups of slaves petitioned both the legislature and the governor for release from bondage. While these legal maneuvers did bring freedom for some individual slaves, taking masters to court was expensive, and slavery as an institution was scarcely undermined.

The slave trade was temporarily interrupted in some colonies during the nonimportation movements. But the first significant attacks on the institution were generated by religious, not economic or political, concerns. Beginning in the 1750s, antislavery movements arose on both sides of the Atlantic. In England, Methodists led the way; in the colonies, Quakers were the first to create an antislavery society and, in 1774, to abolish slaveholding among their membership.

The majority of colonists were nowhere near ready to endorse the end of slavery, and slaveowners regarded calls for abolition as a threat to their property rights. Yet if the antislavery movement could claim few victories in these years, it in fact achieved a major accomplishment. For the first time, colonists who had grown accustomed to taking slavery for granted had to defend an institution that violated the very rights they claimed for themselves.

THE FINAL IMPERIAL CRISIS

WHAT PUSHED the colonists from protest to rebellion?

The relative calm that marked the years 1770 to 1773 might have lasted far longer had Parliament not passed another law that reignited colonial protests. Ironically, the despised measure had nothing to do with imperial reform.

The Boston Tea Party

The measure that outraged colonists was actually designed to help a failing British corporation. The East India Company was tottering on the brink of bankruptcy. Millions of pounds of unsold tea sat in its warehouses, and the imminent failure of Britain's largest corporation alarmed Lord North. If English and colonial consumers, who were purchasing cheaper smuggled Dutch tea, could be induced to buy East India Company tea, the corporation might be saved without needing a major government subsidy.

W
WHERE TO LEARN MORE
Boston, Massachusetts,
The Freedom Trail
http://www.cityofboston.gov/freedomtrail/

North's proposed solution was the **Tea Act of 1773.** The measure made East India Company tea cheaper by exempting it from the duty normally collected as the tea was transshipped through Britain. For colonial consumers, the only tax that remained on the tea was the old Townshend duty. North assumed that the lure of cheaper tea would allow the colonists to accept the Townshend duty, and their increased purchases would save the beleaguered East India Company.

Tea Act of 1773 Act of Parliament that permitted the East India Company to sell through agents in America without paying the duty customarily collected in Britain, thus reducing the retail price.

As it turned out, North spectacularly misjudged the colonial reaction. Merchants were outraged by a provision in the Tea Act that gave the company and its agents a monopoly on the sale of tea in the colonies. They were joined in protest by Americans in every colony, convinced that North meant to trick them into paying a tax to which they had not consented. Elite colonists and laborers, men and women, united in their opposition.

Colonial leaders realized that their most effective form of resistance was preventing the ships carrying tea from landing. In several ports, the Sons of Liberty threatened ship captains with violence, convincing them to return to England without unloading their cargo. But in Boston, the company agents responsible for the tea happened to be the sons of Governor Thomas Hutchinson. The governor was determined to have the tea unloaded in Boston and the tax paid.

Read the **Document** at **www.myhistorylab.com** *From Then to Now Online: The Tea Party Movement*

Boston's Sons of Liberty saw no alternative to taking decisive action. On December 16, 1773, a well-organized band of men disguised as Indians raced aboard the *Dartmouth* and two other tea ships, broke open 342 chests of tea, and heaved the contents into the harbor. In a similar action in 1774, residents of Annapolis, Maryland, forced some merchants to burn their own

Read the **Document** at **www.myhistorylab.com** *Hewes, "A Retrospect on the Boston Tea Party" (1834)*

Boston Tea Party Incident that occurred on December 16, 1773, in which Bostonians, disguised as Indians, destroyed £9,000 worth of tea belonging to the British East India Company in order to prevent payment of the duty on it.

Coercive Acts Legislation passed by Parliament in 1774; included the Boston Port Act, the Massachusetts Government Act, the Administration of Justice Act, and the Quartering Act of 1774.

ship when it arrived with dutied tea. But it was the **Boston Tea Party** that captured the attention of Parliament and inspired its angry reaction.

The Intolerable Acts

The destruction of property in the Boston Tea Party shocked many people in Britain and America. Parliament understood that such an affront to its sovereignty demanded a vigorous response. Thus in the spring of 1774, it passed a series of repressive measures known as the **Coercive Acts.**

The first of these, effective June 1, 1774, was the Boston Port Act, which closed the port of Boston until Bostonians paid for the tea and uncollected duties. The Administration of Justice Act allowed any British soldier or official who was charged with a crime while performing his duties to be tried in England (where he would almost certainly receive sympathetic treatment). A new Quartering Act permitted the army to lodge soldiers in any civilian building if necessary. The fourth and most detested measure, the Massachusetts Government Act, drastically modified that colony's charter of 1691. Henceforth, members of the governor's council and sheriffs would be appointed rather than elected. In addition, the act limited the number of town meetings that could be held without the governor's prior approval. As the Coercive Acts made their way through Parliament, the king chose General Thomas Gage, the commander of the British army in North America, as the new governor of Massachusetts.

On the same day that Parliament enacted these measures, it also passed an unrelated law, the **Quebec Act.** This statute extended Quebec's boundaries south to the Ohio River and stipulated that the colony was to be governed by an appointed governor and council but no elected assembly (see Map 5–2). Civil cases would be tried without a jury and the Catholic Church would enjoy the same privileges that it had under the French. The colonists linked the Quebec Act with the Coercive Acts and labeled them the **Intolerable Acts.**

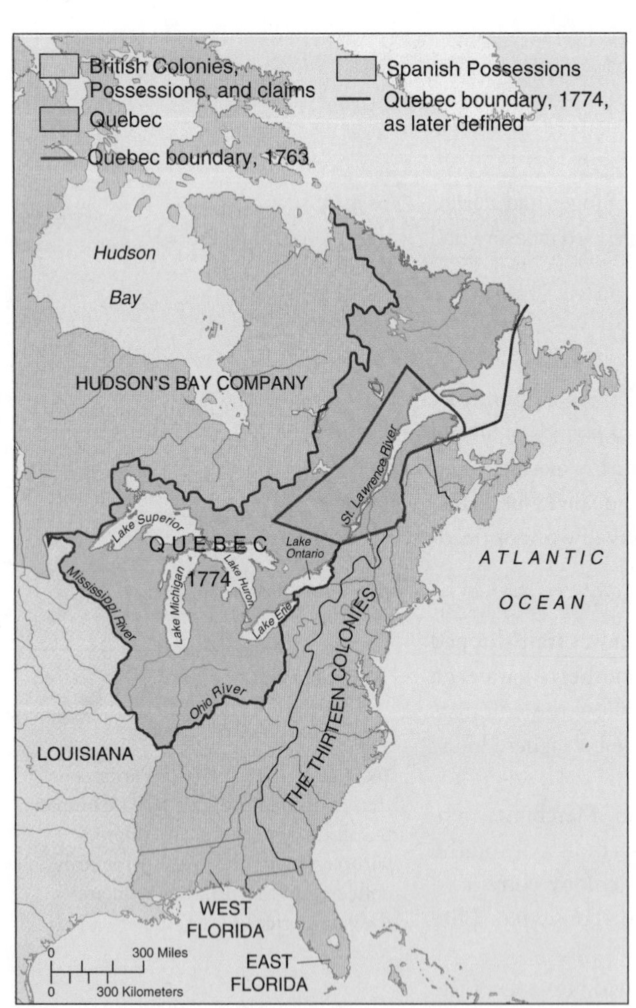

MAP 5–2 **The Quebec Act of 1774** The Quebec Act enlarged the boundaries of the Canadian province southward to the Ohio River and westward to the Mississippi, thereby depriving several colonies of claims to the area granted them by their original charters.

Which parts of Quebec were home to the most British colonists in 1774? Why did they object to the Quebec Act?

The Americans' Reaction

The Americans' response to all of these measures was swift, but also revealed divided opinions. The colonists came closest to unanimity in their opposition to the Quebec Act. As one colonist said, the establishment of the Catholic Church in Quebec "gave a General Alarm to all Protestants." Equally disturbing was the fact that the act gave Canada jurisdiction over lands north of the Ohio River claimed by Connecticut, Pennsylvania, and Virginia. Colonial settlers and land speculators in these colonies resented their exclusion from territory they had helped to win for Britain in the French and Indian War. Colonists also suspected that the autocratic government prescribed for Quebec loomed as a model of British plans for their own colonies.

There was little the colonists could do to stop Gage from closing the port of Boston. Many merchants argued that the town should just pay for the tea and thus avoid an economic crisis. They were outnumbered, however, by many more Bostonians who called for another intercolonial boycott of British goods. Yet in New York and Philadelphia, merchants balked at a form of protest that hurt their businesses, and instead wanted an intercolonial congress called to coordinate an American response.

Colonists everywhere expressed real concern about the other Coercive Acts. The Administration of Justice Act—which some with vivid imaginations dubbed the Murder Act—seemed to declare open season on colonists, allowing crown officials to kill them without fear of punishment. The Massachusetts Government Act suggested that no colonial charter was safe. Parliament might decide to abolish the lower houses of all the colonies (see the Overview table, New Restraints and Burdens on Americans, 1763–1774).

If Lord North thought that the Coercive Acts would drive a wedge between radical Boston and the rest of the colonies, he was utterly mistaken. Boston's committee of correspondence produced a steady stream of warnings about this latest and most serious threat to liberty that resonated throughout the colonies. As real economic hardship descended on the city, contributions of food and fuel flowed in from the countryside. The spirit of protest thus spread out from urban areas, where opposition to the Stamp Act and Townshend Acts had mainly occurred, into rural villages. More colonists were politicized than ever before.

When the assemblies in other colonies discussed joining the resistance movement, royal governors shut them down. This led colonists to organize "provincial congresses," or extralegal conventions that acted as proxies for the assemblies in mobilizing the public. Massachusetts's Provincial Congress, meeting in the town of Concord, became the colony's de facto government. It voted to accept the **Suffolk Resolves,** which had been passed at a convention in Suffolk County (where Boston was located). These resolutions called for the payment of taxes to the Provincial Congress, not to Gage in Boston, and demanded creation of an armed force of "minutemen" ready to respond to any emergency. The Provincial Congress also authorized the stockpiling of arms and ammunition in Concord.

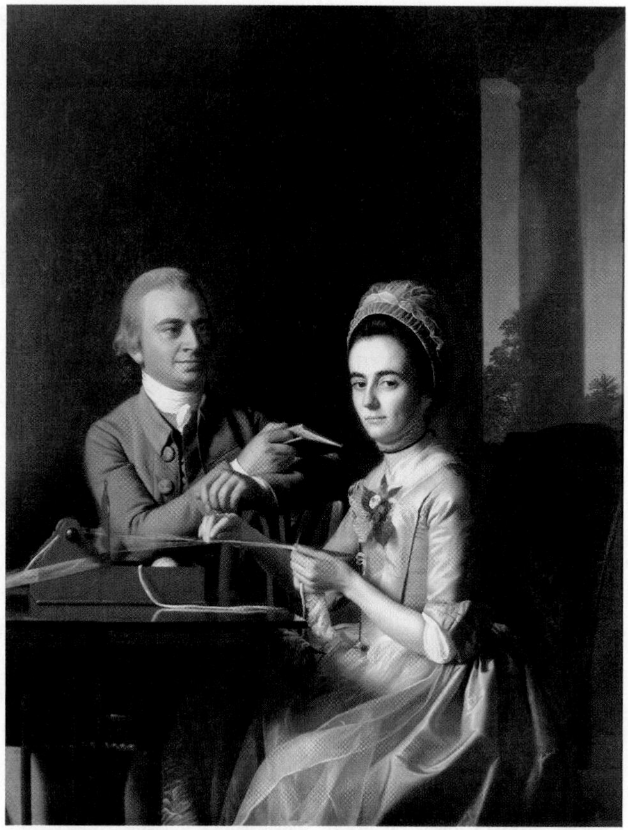

Mr. and Mrs. Thomas Mifflin of Philadelphia. Mifflin was a prominent merchant and radical opponent of British policy toward the colonies. He and his wife were visiting Boston in 1773, when John Singleton Copley painted them. Working at a small loom, Sarah Morris Mifflin weaves a decorative fringe. She no doubt did the same during the nonimportation movement against the Townshend duties, thereby helping to make importation of such goods from England unnecessary.

Quebec Act Law passed by Parliament in 1774 that provided an appointed government for Canada, enlarged the boundaries of Quebec, and confirmed the privileges of the Catholic Church.

Intolerable Acts American term for the Coercive Acts and the Quebec Act.

Suffolk Resolves Militant resolves adopted in 1774 in response to the Coercive Acts by representatives from the towns in Suffolk County, Massachusetts, including Boston.

First Continental Congress Meeting of delegates from most of the colonies held in 1774 in response to the Coercive Acts. The Congress endorsed the Suffolk Resolves, adopted the Declaration of Rights and Grievances, and agreed to establish the Continental Association.

The First Continental Congress

A consensus emerged in support of an intercolonial congress. In the end, twelve colonies (all except Georgia) sent representatives. The **First Continental Congress** met at Carpenter's Hall in Philadelphia from September 5 to October 26, 1774, with fifty-five delegates present at one time or another. The delegates quickly voted for nonimportation, remembering its utility in previous imperial confrontations. Virtually all of the delegates likewise agreed to a policy of nonexportation, to begin in August 1775 if Britain had not yet addressed colonial grievances. Radical delegates also succeeded in having the Congress endorse the Suffolk Resolves, declaring the Coercive Acts unconstitutional.

Delegates then engaged in an extended debate trying to define colonial rights, in effect specifying the terms by which the colonies would voluntarily retain their membership in the empire. The result was a declaration of rights and set of resolves that responded to a decade of imperial crises. The delegates went beyond declaring the Intolerable Acts unconstitutional to

AMERICAN VIEWS

Social Status and the Enforcement of the Nonimportation Movement

Many Americans enthusiastically supported the nonimportation movement called in response to the Townshend Duty Act crisis of the late 1760s. A few, however, openly opposed it. Among these was the aristocratic William Henry Drayton of South Carolina, who objected to the composition of the committee chosen to enforce the nonimportation agreement in his region. The committee included artisans and shopkeepers, men who, Drayton claimed, should have no role in public affairs. Their education prepared them only "to cut up a beast in the market to the best advantage, to cobble an old shoe in the neatest manner, or to build a necessary house [privy]," not to make public policy. As the following document makes clear, deference had its limits, and the committeemen emphatically disagreed with him. Drayton was later to reverse himself and actively support the Continental Association's ban on importing British goods in 1775. "The people" wanted it, he would later explain, and "it was our duty, to satisfy our constituents; as we were only servants of the public [at large]."

- **Who** makes policy in the United States today?
- **What** qualifications do you think they should have?
- **How** do your answers to these questions differ from Drayton's? From the "Mechanicks's"?
- **How** would you explain Drayton's later switch?

The Mechanicks of the General Committee to William Henry Drayton

The gracious Giver of all good things, has been pleased to bestow a certain principle on mankind, which properly may be called common sense: But, though every man hath a natural right to a determined portion of this ineffable ray of the Divinity, yet, to the misfortune of society, many persons fall short of this most necessary gift of God. . . .

The Mechanicks pretend to nothing more, than having a claim from nature, to their share in this inestimable favour, in common with Emperors and Kings, and, were it safe to carry the comparison still higher, they would say with William-Henry Drayton himself; who, in his great condescention, has been pleased to allow us a place amongst human beings: But whether it might have happened from an ill construction of his sensory, or his upper works being damaged by some rough treatment of the person who conducted his birth, we know not; however so it is, that, to us, he seems highly defective in this point, whatever exalted notions he may entertain of his own abilities.

By attending to the dictates of common sense, the Mechanicks have been able to distinguish between RIGHT and WRONG; in doing which indeed no great merit is claimed, because every man's own feelings will direct him thereto, unless he obstinately, or from a pertinacious opinion of his own superior knowledge, shuts his eyes, and stoickally submits to all the illegal encroachments that may be made on his property, by an ill-designing and badly-informed ministry.

Mr. Drayton may value himself as much as he pleases, on his having had a liberal education bestowed on him, tho' the good fruits thereof have not hitherto been conspicuous either in his public or private life: He ought however to know, that this is not so absolutely necessary to these, who move in the low sphere of mechanical employments. But still, though he pretends to view them with so contemptuous and oblique an eye, these men hope, that they are in some degree useful to society, without presuming to make any comparisons between themselves and him, except with regard to love for their country; for he has amply shewn, that an attachment of this sort is not one of his ruling passions. Nor does he appear in the least to have regarded the peace and good order of that community of which he is a member; otherwise he would not wilfully, and without any cause, have knocked his head against ninety-nine out of every hundred of the people, not only in this province, but of all North-America. . . .

Mr. Drayton may be assured, that so far from being ashamed of our trades, we are in the highest degree thankful to our friends, who put us in the way of being instructed in them; and that we bless God for giving us strength and judgment to pursue them, in order to maintain our families, with a decency suitable to their stations in life. Every man is not so lucky as to have a fortune ready provided to his hand, either by his own or his wife's parents, as has been his lot; nor ought it to be so with all men; and Providence accordingly hath wisely ordained otherwise, by appointing the greatest part of mankind, to provide for their support by manual labour; and we will be bold to say, that such are the most useful people in a community. . . .

We are, Yours, &c.

MECHANICKS of the COMMITTEE.

October 3d, 1769.

Source: South Carolina Gazette, October 5, 1769; reprinted in *The Letters of Freeman, etc.: Essays on the Nonimportation Movement in South Carolina* by William Henry Drayton, ed. Robert M. Weir (1977), University of South Carolina Press, pp. 111–114.

OVERVIEW New Restraints and Burdens on Americans, 1763–1774

	Limits on Legislative Action	Curbs on Territorial Expansion	Burdens on Colonial Trade	Imposition of New Taxes
1763		Proclamation Line keeps white settlement east of the Appalachians.	Peacetime use of navy and new customs officials to enforce Navigation Acts.	
1764	Currency Act limits the colonial legislatures' ability to issue paper money.		Vice-admiralty courts strengthened for Sugar Act.	Sugar Act imposes taxes for revenue (modified 1766).
1765				Quartering Act requires assemblies to provide facilities for royal troops. Stamp Act imposes internal taxes on various items (repealed 1766).
	Declaratory Act proclaims Parliament's right to legislate for colonies in all cases whatsoever.			
1767	Royal instructions limit size of colonial assemblies.		Vice-admiralty courts strengthened for Townshend duties. American Customs Service established in Boston.	Townshend duties imposed on some imported goods in order to pay colonial officials. (All but tax on tea repealed 1770.)
1773				Tea Act reduces duty and prompts Boston Tea Party.
1774 (Intolerable Acts)	Massachusetts Government Act limits town meetings, changes legislature, and violates Massachusetts charter.	Quebec Act enlarges Quebec at expense of colonies with claims in the Ohio River Valley.	Boston Port Act closes harbor until East India Company's tea is paid for.	Quartering Act of 1774 declares that troops could be lodged in virtually any uninhabited building in Boston.

criticize all revenue measures passed since the end of the French and Indian War. They denounced the dissolution of colonial assemblies and the keeping of troops in the colonies during peacetime. Congress defined the colonists' rights to include "life, liberty, and property," and stated that colonial legislatures had exclusive powers to make laws and pass taxes, subject only to the royal veto. About the only concession it made was to pledge that Americans would "cheerfully" consent to trade regulations for the good of the empire.

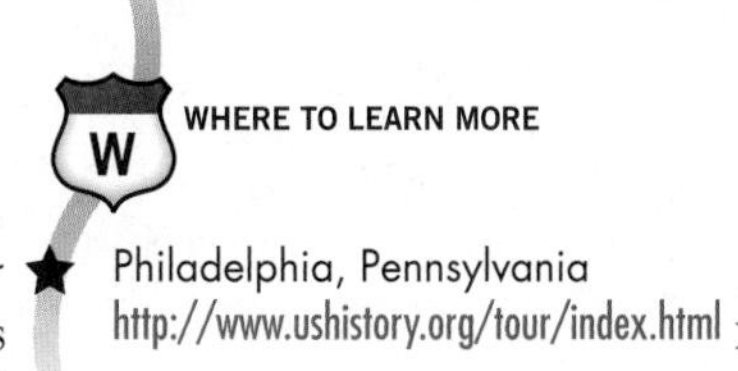

The Continental Association

As Congress's proceedings came to an end, some delegates began to tinker with its recommendations to protect their own colonies' interests. Members from the Chesapeake colonies wanted to ensure that, if the nonexportation policy had to go into effect in 1775, it would

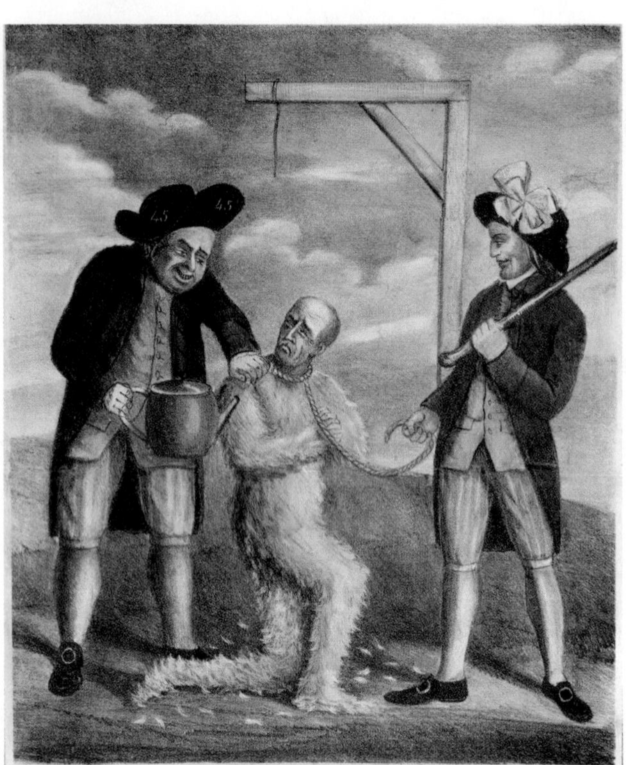
A NEW METHOD OF MACARONY MAKING AS PRACTISED AT BOSTON

This image shows John Malcolm, an unpopular customs commissioner, being tarred and feathered in Boston. By 1774, radicals threatened others who defended British measures with similar punishment.

not begin until that year's tobacco crop had been shipped. Carolina delegates went so far as to threaten to walk out of the meeting if rice was not exempted from the nonexportation agreement. Northern delegates agreed to the Carolinians' demand, but the incident demonstrated how fragile colonial unity was.

Two final tasks remained. First, Congress needed an enforcement mechanism to ensure that its agreed-upon measures were followed. It created the **Continental Association,** a mutual pledge by the delegates to see that their colonies ceased importing any British goods after December 1, 1774, and, if the dispute with Britain was not resolved by September 1775, make sure that their provinces ceased exporting goods to Britain and the West Indies. Voters in every town, city, and county throughout the colonies were to choose committees to enforce the terms of the Association. The approximately 7,000 men who served on these committees during the winter of 1774–1775 in effect formed grassroots radical governments.

Second, Congress concluded its proceedings with an address not to Parliament, but to the king and the British and American people. This gesture confirmed the fact that delegates no longer considered Parliament to be a legitimate legislature over the colonies. Delegates instead asked George III to use his "royal authority and interposition" to protect his loyal subjects in America. So long as the king protected colonial rights, he could count on the Americans' allegiance.

Political Polarization

Scarcely anyone called for independence at this point. Even so, many Americans had moved far from the positions they had taken at the start of the imperial crisis. Instead of urging a return to the pre-1763 status quo, they agreed with the Congress's rejection of Parliament's sovereignty and its assumption that only allegiance to the king tied Americans to Britain. But not all colonists accepted such a drastic reinterpretation of the imperial connection. Even if they regarded recent parliamentary measures as threats to American liberty, some colonists continued to recognize parliamentary authority over the colonies. Others had never quarreled with British policies at all. By late 1774, however, it became more dangerous to express such opinions. The local committees created under the Continental Association not only enforced the boycott against British goods but also intimidated their opponents into silence.

A new political order was emerging, requiring colonists to choose one side or the other in an atmosphere of increasing polarization. The advocates of colonial rights began to call themselves **Whigs** and condemned their opponents as **Tories.** These traditional English party labels dated from the late seventeenth century, when the Tories had supported the accession of the Catholic King James II, and the Whigs had opposed it. Colonial Whigs used this label to identify themselves as champions of liberty and called their opponents Tories to represent them as defenders of tyrannical royal government. As imperial ties proceeded to unravel, there appeared to be no third option.

QUICK REVIEW

Congressional Response to the Coercive Acts

- All agreed that acts were unconstitutional.
- A minority prepared to go to war with Britain.
- Most delegates thought of the interests of their own colony first.

Continental Association Agreement adopted by the First Continental Congress in 1774 in response to the Coercive Acts to cut off trade with Britain until the objectionable measures were repealed.

Whigs The name used by advocates of colonial resistance to British measures during the 1760s and 1770s.

CONCLUSION

Years of political turmoil inspired colonists to think more systematically about their rights than they had ever done before. As they did so, members of the elite and laborers, men and women, black colonists and white, were all drawn into the politics of resistance. They read (and sometimes wrote) letters and pamphlets, marched in the streets, boycotted tea, and wore homespun clothing. In so doing, they came to recognize their common interests as Americans and their differences from the British. They became aware, as Benjamin Franklin would later write, of the need to break "through the bounds, in which a dependent people had been accustomed to think, and act" so that they might "properly comprehend the character they had assumed."

In the winter of 1774–1775, however, the "character" of the Americans was not yet fully revealed. Although they had achieved an unprecedented level of unity in their opposition to Parliament, they did not all agree on where the path of resistance would lead. Americans had surely rebelled, but had not yet launched a revolution.

Tories A derisive term applied to loyalists in America who supported the king and Parliament just before and during the American Revolution.

Where to Learn More

Fort Michilimackinac National Historic Landmark, Mackinaw City, Michigan. Near the south end of the Mackinac Bridge, the present structure is a modern restoration of the fort as it was when Pontiac's War took a heavy toll on its garrison. The Mackinac State Historic Park's website, http://www.mackinacparks.com/ provides a brief description and photographs of the reconstructed colonial village and fort.

Charleston, South Carolina. Many buildings date from the eighteenth century. Officials stored tea in one of them, the Exchange, to prevent a local version of the Boston Tea Party. The website for Historic Charleston, http://www.nps.gov/nr/travel/charleston, provides a map, a list of buildings, and information about them.

Boston, Massachusetts, The Freedom Trail. Many important buildings and sites in this area date from the seventeenth and eighteenth centuries. They include Faneuil Hall (Dock Square), where many public meetings took place prior to the Revolution, and the Old State House (Washington and State streets), which overlooks the site of the Boston Massacre. The Freedom Trail, http://www.cityofboston.gov/freedomtrail/, provides a well-illustrated virtual tour of the historic sites.

Philadelphia, Pennsylvania. Numerous buildings and sites date from the eighteenth century. Independence National Historical Park contains Carpenter's Hall, where the First Continental Congress met, and the Pennsylvania State House (now known as Independence Hall), where the Declaration of Independence was adopted. Philadelphia's Historic Mile, http://www.ushistory.org/tour/index.html, provides a virtual tour of the great landmarks of the city, including Independence Hall.

Review Questions

1. What did Andrew Burnaby see as the main obstacles to colonial union? What did he foresee as the consequences of leaving the colonists "to themselves"?
2. How did the outcome of the French and Indian War affect the relations between Native Americans and white settlers? Between British authorities and Americans?
3. What was the relationship between the French and Indian War and changes in British policy toward America? How did the expectations of Americans and Britons differ in 1763? Why were the new policies offensive to Americans?
4. How was stationing British troops in America related to British taxation of the colonists? Why did the colonists consider taxation by Parliament an especially serious threat to their freedom as well as to their pocketbooks?
5. How did Americans oppose the new measures? Who participated in the various forms of resistance? How effective were the different kinds of resistance? What effect did resistance to British measures have on Americans' internal politics and sense of identity as Americans?
6. What led to the meeting of the First Continental Congress? What steps did the Congress take? What did it expect to achieve?

Key Terms

Boston Massacre (p. 129)
Boston Tea Party (p. 132)
British Constitution (p. 123)
Cherokee War (p. 120)
Coercive Acts (p. 132)
Committees of correspondence (p. 129)
Continental Association (p. 136)
Country (Real Whig) ideology (p. 123)
Declaration of Rights and Grievances (p. 125)
Declaratory Act (p. 126)
First Continental Congress (p. 133)
Intolerable Acts (p. 133)
Nonimportation movement (p. 128)
Pontiac's War (p. 122)
Proclamation of 1763 (p. 122)
Quartering Acts (p. 122)
Quebec Act (p. 133)
Regulators (p. 130)
Republicanism (p. 123)
Sons of Liberty (p. 125)
Sovereignty (p. 124)
Stamp Act (p. 124)
Stamp Act Congress (p. 124)
Suffolk Resolves (p. 133)
Sugar Act (p. 122)
Tea Act of 1773 (p. 131)
Tories (p. 137)
Townshend Duty Act of 1767 (p. 127)
Whigs (p. 136)

PEARSON myhistorylab Connections

Reinforce what you learned in this chapter by studying the many documents, images, maps, review tools, and videos available at **www.myhistorylab.com**.

Read and Review

Study and Review **Study Plan: Chapter 5**

Read the Document

Benjamin Franklin, Testimony against the Stamp Act (1766)

John Dickinson, from Letters from a Farmer in Pennsylvania (1768)

An Early Abolitionist Speaks Out against Slavery (1757)

Boston Gazette, Description of the Boston Massacre (1770)

Hewes, "A Retrospect on the Boston Tea Party" (1834)

John Andrews to William Barrell, Boston Tea Party (1773)

James Otis, The Rights of the British Colonies Asserted and Proved (1763)

Slave Petition to the Governor of Massachusetts (1774)

The Virginia Nonimportation Resolutions (1769)

See the Map *Settlement in North America, c. 1763*

Research and Explore

Read the Document

Personal Journeys Online

From Then to Now Online: The Tea Party Movement

Exploring America: The Stamp Act

Hear the Audio *The Liberty Song*

Hear the Audio

Hear the audio files for Chapter 5 at **www.myhistorylab.com.**

1774-1783

6

The War for Independence

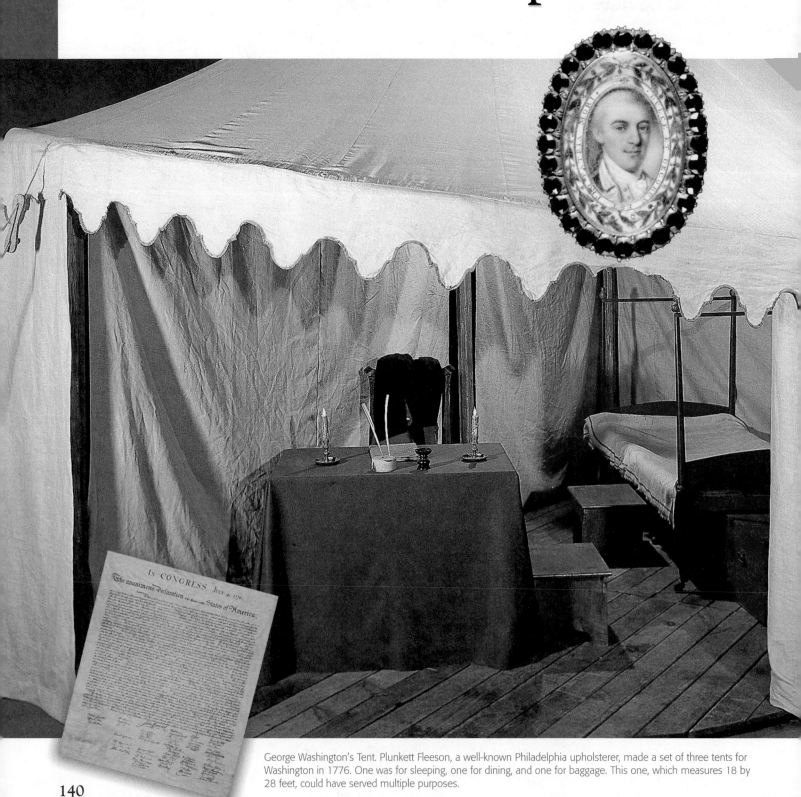

George Washington's Tent. Plunkett Fleeson, a well-known Philadelphia upholsterer, made a set of three tents for Washington in 1776. One was for sleeping, one for dining, and one for baggage. This one, which measures 18 by 28 feet, could have served multiple purposes.

Hear the Audio

Hear the audio files for Chapter 6 at **www.myhistorylab.com**.

FROM REBELLION TO WAR *(page 143)*

WHY DID tensions between the colonies and Britain escalate so rapidly between 1774 and 1776?

THE CONTINENTAL CONGRESS BECOMES A NATIONAL GOVERNMENT *(page 145)*

WHAT WERE the Second Continental Congress's highest priorities?

THE COMBATANTS *(page 149)*

WHAT WERE the key differences between the British and American forces?

THE WAR IN THE NORTH, 1776–1777 *(page 153)*

HOW DID the American forces survive the military setbacks of 1776?

THE WAR WIDENS, 1778–1781 *(page 154)*

WHY DID the French enter the war on the American side?

THE WAR AND SOCIETY, 1775–1783 *(page 158)*

WHAT WAS the social impact of the War for Independence?

THE AMERICAN VICTORY, 1782–1783 *(page 160)*

WHAT WERE the key factors in the American victory in the Revolutionary War?

"Paul Jones Shooting a Sailor," color engraving from the Olds Collection # 366, no negative number. © Collection of the New-York Historical Society.

ONE AMERICAN JOURNEY

Headquarters, Valley Forge

January 14, 1778

I barely hinted to you my dearest Father my desire to augment the Continental Forces from an untried Source. . . . I would solicit you to cede me a number of your able bodied men Slaves, instead of leaving me a fortune. I would bring about a twofold good, first I would advance those who are unjustly deprived of the Rights of Mankind to a State which would be a proper Gradation between abject Slavery and perfect Liberty and besides I would reinforce the Defenders of Liberty with a number of gallant Soldiers. . . .

Headquarters, Valley Forge

February 2, 1778

My dear Father,

The more I reflect upon the difficulties and delays which are likely to attend the completing our Continental Regiments, the more anxiously is my mind bent upon the Scheme which I lately communicated to you. . . .

You seem to think my dear Father, that men reconciled by long habit to the miseries of their Condition would prefer their ignominious bonds to the untasted Sweets of Liberty, especially when offer'd upon the terms which I propose. . . . I am tempted to believe that this trampled people have so much human left in them, as to be capable of aspiring to the rights of men by noble exertions, if some friend to mankind would point the Road, and give them prospect of Success.

I have long deplored the wretched State of these men and considered in their history, the bloody wars excited in Africa to furnish America with Slaves. The Groans of despairing multitudes toiling for the Luxuries of Merciless Tyrants. I have had the pleasure of conversing with you sometimes upon the means of restoring them to their rights. When can it be better done than when their enfranchisement may be made conducive to the Public Good.

John Laurens

Henry Laurens Papers, vol. 12, pp. 305, 390–392.

Read the **Document** at **www.myhistorylab.com**

Personal Journeys Online

- **Baikia Harvey, Letter to Thomas Baikie, Snowhill, South Carolina, December 30, 1775. A new immigrant describes conditions in Georgia in 1775.**
- **Joseph Martin, *The Revolutionary Adventures of Joseph Plumb Martin,* 1776–1783. A Continental soldier remembers the Revolution.**

JOHN LAURENS wrote these letters to his father, Henry, at one of the low points of the American Revolution, when victory seemed most remote. The letters reveal much, not only about the course of the war but also about the aspirations and limitations of the Revolutionary generation. Henry Laurens, a wealthy slaveholder from South Carolina, was president of the Continental Congress; his son John was an aide to General George Washington. The progress of the war had encouraged young John to take an intellectual journey that can only be understood in the context of that conflict.

John, 23 years old in 1778, had been born in South Carolina but educated for the most part in Geneva and London, where he

CHRONOLOGY

1775	April 19: Battles of Lexington and Concord.
	May 10: Second Continental Congress meets.
	June 17: Battle of Bunker Hill.
	December 31: American attack on Quebec.
1776	January 9: Thomas Paine's *Common Sense* published.
	July 4: Declaration of Independence.
	September 15: British take New York City.
	December 26: Battle of Trenton.
1777	January 3: Battle of Princeton.
	September 11: Battle of Brandywine Creek.
	October 17: American victory at Saratoga.
	Runaway inflation begins.
	Continental Army winters at Valley Forge.
1778	February 6: France and the United States sign an alliance.
	June 17: Congress refuses to negotiate with British peace commissioners.
	July 4: George Rogers Clark captures British post in the Mississippi Valley.
	December 29: British capture Savannah.
	Death of the great French Enlightenment writer, François-Marie Arouet Voltaire.
1779	June 21: Spain declares war on Britain.
	Americans devastate the Iroquois country.
	September 23: John Paul Jones captures the British ship *Serapis*.
1780	May 12: Fall of Charleston, South Carolina.
	October 7: Americans win Battle of Kings Mountain.
	December 3: Nathanael Greene takes command in the South.
1781	January 17: Americans defeat British at Battle of Cowpens.
	March 15: Battle of Guilford Court House.
	October 19: Cornwallis surrenders at Yorktown.
1783	March 15: Washington quells the Newburgh "Conspiracy."
	September 3: Peace of Paris signed.
	November 21: British begin evacuating New York.
	First manned balloon flight, in France.
	Quakers present first antislavery petition to the British parliament.
1784	United States vessel opens trade with Canton, China.
1788	Britain transports convicts to Australia.

had been exposed to some of the most progressive currents of the Enlightenment. Among these were compassion for the oppressed and the conviction that slavery should be abolished.

Laurens saw an opportunity to solve two problems at once when he returned to America in 1777. Enlisting slaves in the army would provide blacks with a stepping stone to freedom and American forces with desperately needed troops. Although his father detested slavery, however, he could never quite accept his son's radical proposition. John was further frustrated when he turned to state legislatures in the Deep South. Convincing them to allow black troops to enlist in return for their freedom proved impossible.

John's idealistic quest for social justice ended on the banks of the Combahee River in South Carolina, where he died in one of the last skirmishes of the war. "Where liberty is," he once wrote, "there is my country." Americans won their independence, but eight long years of warfare strained and in some ways profoundly altered the fabric of American society, though not as much as Laurens had wished. ✦

FROM REBELLION TO WAR

WHY DID tensions between the colonies and Britain escalate so rapidly between 1774 and 1776?

When the First Continental Congress adjourned in October 1774, no one quite knew what the future would hold. Matters indeed seemed to be approaching a crisis. Britain had adopted its harshest policies yet in response to the Boston Tea Party and appeared to be in no mood for reconciliation. At the same time, colonists in New England were stockpiling arms while committees of safety watched their neighbors in the cities and countryside, intimidating defenders of Britain into silence. Yet if tempers ran high, few people wished for bloodshed.

Contradictory British Policies

Britain held parliamentary elections in the fall of 1774, but if Americans hoped that the outcome would change the government's policy toward them, they were disappointed. Lord North's supporters won easily. Even so, a few members of Parliament urged their fellow legislators to adopt conciliatory measures before it was too late. However, such efforts failed to gain much support.

Lord North's next actions made matters worse. He ordered Thomas Gage, commander in chief of the British army in America and newly installed governor of Massachusetts, to destroy an arms stockpile in Concord and arrest the radical leaders John Hancock and Samuel Adams. North then introduced a measure that prohibited New Englanders from trading outside the British Empire or sending their ships to the North Atlantic fishing grounds. Both Houses of Parliament followed a similar hard line by declaring the colony of Massachusetts to be in rebellion.

Conciliatory Proposition Plan whereby Parliament would "forbear" taxation of Americans in colonies whose assemblies imposed taxes considered satisfactory by the British government.

Yet at the same time, Lord North introduced a **Conciliatory Proposition,** whereby Parliament pledged not to tax the colonies if their assemblies would voluntarily contribute to the defense of the empire and the costs of civil government and the judiciary in their own colonies. British officials, however, would decide what was a sufficient contribution—a provision that protected Parliament's claim to sovereignty—and could use force against colonies that did not pay their share. At one time, colonists might have found the Conciliatory Proposition acceptable. By the spring of 1775, it was too late.

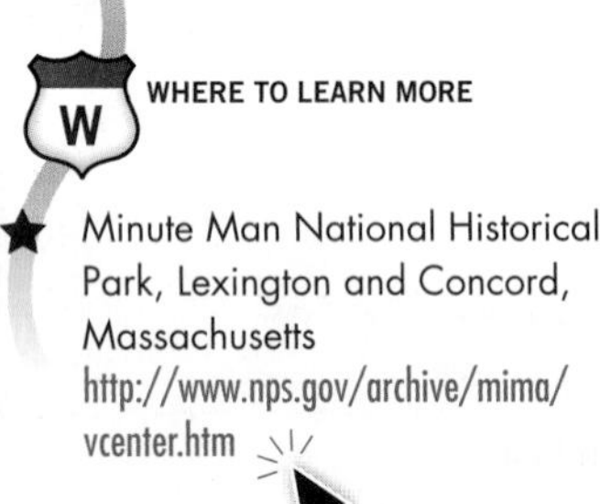

Minute Man National Historical Park, Lexington and Concord, Massachusetts http://www.nps.gov/archive/mima/vcenter.htm

Mounting Tensions in America

Colonists everywhere waited to hear what Britain's next move would be, but those in Massachusetts were most apprehensive. General Gage had begun fortifying Boston and had dissolved the Massachusetts legislature. The delegates assembled anyway, calling themselves the Provincial Congress. In October 1774, this body appointed an emergency executive body, the **Committee of Safety,** headed by John Hancock, to gather arms and ammunition and to organize militia volunteers. Some localities had already formed special companies of **Minute Men,** who were to be ready at "a minute's warning in Case of an alarm." Massachusetts had, in effect, created a revolutionary government.

Committee of Safety Any of the extralegal committees that directed the revolutionary movement and carried on the functions of government at the local level in the period between the breakdown of royal authority and the establishment of regular governments.

Minute Men Special companies of militia formed in Massachusetts and elsewhere beginning in late 1774.

As tensions grew, colonists everywhere found it increasingly dangerous to express opinions in favor of Britain, or even to avoid taking a position. Moderates who placed their hopes in George III were demoralized when the king declared the New England colonies to be in a state of rebellion. The king's threat that "blows must decide whether they are to be subject to this Country or independent" scarcely reassured those who hoped to avoid spilling blood. The initial clash between British and American forces was not long in coming.

Read the Document at **www.myhistorylab.com** *Royal Proclamation of Rebellion (1775)*

Read the Document at **www.myhistorylab.com** *Joseph Warren, "Account of the Battle of Lexington" (1775)*

The Battles of Lexington and Concord

Gage received his orders to seize the weapons at Concord and arrest Samuel Adams and John Hancock on April 14, 1775. On the night of April 18, hoping to surprise the colonists, he assembled 700 men on the Boston Common for a predawn march toward the towns of Lexington and Concord, some 20 miles away (see Map 6–1). But the army's maneuvers were hardly invisible to vigilant colonists. Adams and Hancock, who were staying in Lexington, escaped. Throughout the night, patriot riders—including the silversmith Paul Revere—spread the alarm through the countryside.

When the British soldiers reached Lexington at dawn, they found about seventy armed militiamen drawn up in formation on the village green. Outnumbered ten to one, the Americans probably did not plan to begin a fight. More likely, they were there in a show of defiance, to demonstrate that Americans would not run at the sight of the king's troops. A British major ordered the militia to disperse. They were starting to obey when a shot from an unknown source shattered the stillness. The British responded with a volley that killed or wounded 18 Americans.

The British troops pressed on to Concord and burned what few supplies the Americans had not been able to hide. But when their rear guard came under fire at Concord's North Bridge, the British panicked. As they retreated to Boston, patriot Minute Men and other militia harried them from both sides of the road. By the time the column reached safety, 273 British soldiers were dead, wounded, or missing.

News of the **Battles of Lexington and Concord** spread quickly. The speed with which distant colonies heard about the outbreak of fighting testifies to the extraordinary efforts patriots made to spread word of it.

The shots fired that April morning would, in the words of the nineteenth-century Concord philosopher and poet Ralph Waldo Emerson, be "heard round the world." They signaled the start of the American Revolution, which would help to inspire many revolutions elsewhere.

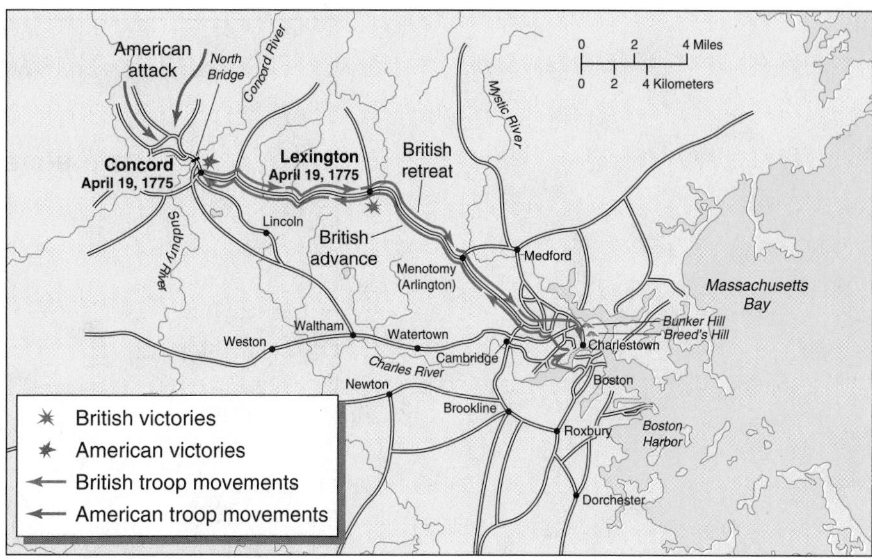

MAP 6–1 **The Battles of Lexington and Concord, April 19, 1775** This map shows the area around Boston, where in April 1775 British and American forces fought the first military engagements of the Revolution.

How did the fighting at Lexington and Concord differ from traditional European military engagements?

THE CONTINENTAL CONGRESS BECOMES A NATIONAL GOVERNMENT

WHAT WERE the Second Continental Congress's highest priorities?

The First Continental Congress had adjourned in October 1774 with virtually everyone hoping that the imperial crisis could be resolved without war. When the delegates reconvened in Philadelphia on May 10, 1775, however, war had begun. Gage's troops had limped from Concord back into Boston, besieged there by a gathering force of patriot militia from all over New England. With no other intercolonial body available to do the job, the Second Congress by default assumed management of the rebellion as its members also debated what the colonies' ultimate goal should be. Even before America had declared itself a nation, it had acquired a national government.

THE SECOND CONTINENTAL CONGRESS CONVENES

It would be difficult to overstate the enormity of the task facing the **Second Continental Congress.** On the very day that the Congress convened—May 10, 1775—American forces from Vermont and Massachusetts under, respectively, Ethan Allen and Benedict Arnold captured the British garrison at Fort Ticonderoga at the southern end of Lake Champlain. Just over a month later, General Gage attempted to fortify territory south of Boston, where his cannons could command the harbor. But the Americans seized the high ground first, entrenching themselves on Breed's Hill north of town. On June 17, 1775, Gage sent 2,200 well-trained soldiers to drive the 1,700 patriot forces from their new position. Misnamed for another hill nearby, this encounter has gone down in history as the Battle of Bunker Hill (see Map 6–2).

Taking leadership of the rebellion, the Congress in the succeeding months became, in effect, a national government. Such important tasks as making laws and imposing taxes remained with the colonial assemblies. Congress instead focused on the functions the Crown had formerly performed. It took command of the **Continental Army,** authorized the formation of a navy, established a post office, conducted diplomacy with Indian nations, and printed paper money to meet its expenses.

Battles of Lexington and Concord The first two battles of the American Revolution, which resulted in a total of 273 British soldiers dead, wounded, and missing and nearly one hundred Americans dead, wounded, and missing.

Second Continental Congress Convened in Philadelphia on May 10, 1775, the Second Continental Congress called for the patchwork of local forces to be organized into the Continental Army, authorized the formation of a navy, established a post office, and printed paper continental dollars to meet its expenses.

Continental Army The regular or professional army authorized by the Second Continental Congress and commanded by General George Washington during the Revolutionary War.

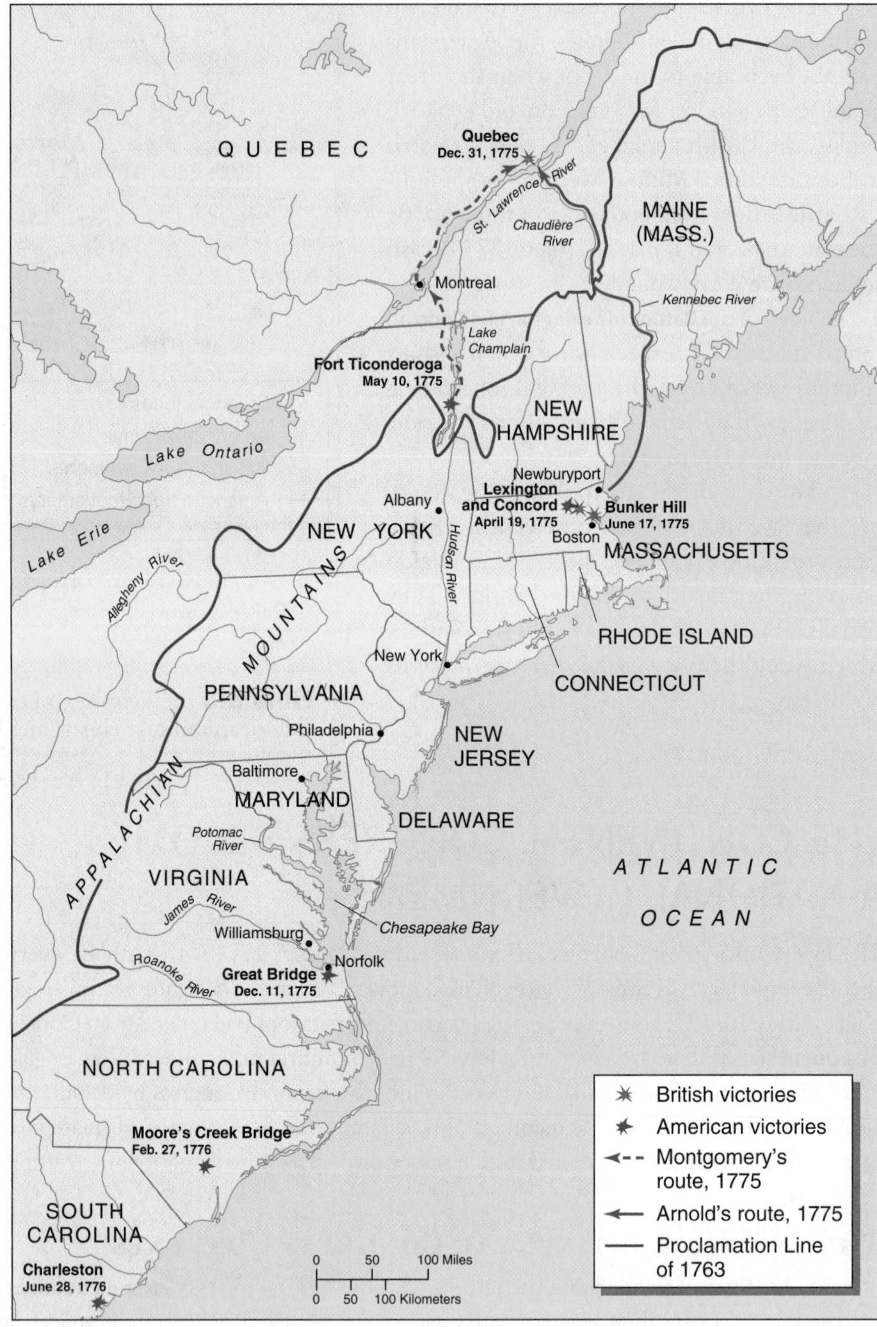

MAP 6–2 **Early Fighting, 1775–1776** As this map clearly reveals, even the earliest fighting occurred in widely scattered areas, thereby complicating Britain's efforts to subdue the Americans.

What were the key components of Britain's strategy in the early years of the war? Why did the British fail to suppress the rebellion?

Olive Branch Petition Petition adopted by the Second Continental Congress as a last effort of peace that avowed America's loyalty to George III and requested that he protect them from further aggressions.

Declaration of the Causes and Necessity of Taking Up Arms Declaration of the Second Continental Congress that Americans were ready to fight for freedom and liberty.

One of Congress's most momentous decisions was choosing a leader for the Continental Army. Although most of the patriot troops around Boston were New Englanders, delegates knew that they had to ensure military support from all colonies. Thus, at John Adams's suggestion, Congress asked a Virginian, George Washington, to take command.

Not yet ready to demand independence, Congress hoped that the fighting would compel Britain to accept a government that acknowledged the sovereignty of colonial assemblies and an imperial tie through allegiance to the Crown. Thus even as delegates managed the war, they approved the **Olive Branch Petition** on July 5, 1775, in which they asked George III to protect his American subjects from the military actions ordered by Parliament. The following day, Congress approved the **Declaration of the Causes and Necessity of Taking Up Arms,** which listed colonial grievances and asserted the resolve of American patriots "to die freemen, rather than to live slaves." And at the end of the month, it formally rejected North's Conciliatory Proposition.

This fine portrait of George Washington appears in multiple versions depicting the victorious general against different backgrounds, including the battles of Princeton and Yorktown. The painter, Charles Willson Peale, served under Washington at Princeton, and the French commander at Yorktown, the Count de Rochambeau, took an appropriate version home with him in 1783.

Early Fighting: Massachusetts, Virginia, the Carolinas, and Canada

Washington arrived in Boston in early July 1775 to take command of the American forces. Months of military standoff followed, with neither side able to dislodge the other. During the winter of 1775–1776, however, the Americans dragged some sixty cannons 300 miles through snow and over mountains from Fort Ticonderoga to Boston. In March 1776, Washington mounted the newly arrived guns to overlook Boston harbor, putting the British in an indefensible position. The British then evacuated the city and moved their troops to Halifax, Nova Scotia. New England was for the moment secure for the patriots.

Fighting in the South also went well for the Americans. Virginia's last royal governor, Lord Dunmore, fled the capital, Williamsburg, and set up a base in nearby Norfolk. Promising freedom to slaves who joined him, he succeeded in raising a small force of black and white loyalists and British marines. On December 9, 1775, most of these men died when they attacked a much larger force of 900 Virginia and North Carolina troops at Great Bridge, near Norfolk. On February 27, a force of loyalist Scots suffered a similar defeat at Moore's Creek Bridge in North Carolina. And in June 1776, colonial forces successfully repulsed a large British expedition sent to attack Charleston, South Carolina.

Independence

The American forces' stunning early successes bolstered their confidence. At the same time, Britain continued to lose whatever colonial support remained. In October 1775, the navy attacked and burned the town of Falmouth (now Portland) in Maine, an atrocity that outraged even those moderate colonists who held out hope for reconciliation. Slaveholders, particularly in Virginia, were equally appalled at Governor Dunmore's efforts to lure slaves away with a promise of freedom. When King George III rejected the Congress's Olive Branch Petition in August 1775 and proclaimed the colonies to be in rebellion, he unknowingly pushed more colonists toward independence.

It had taken more than a year of armed conflict to convince many Americans to accept the idea that independence from Britain, not reconciliation, should be the necessary outcome of their efforts. As it turned out, taking that final step required a push from an unexpected direction. It came from Thomas Paine, a ne'er-do-well Englishman, who had recently arrived on American soil. His pamphlet *Common Sense*, published in Philadelphia in January 1776, denounced King George and made a vigorously argued case for independence. *Common Sense*, which sold more than 100,000 copies throughout the colonies, helped propel many Americans toward independence.

Tactical considerations also influenced patriot leaders. Formal separation from Great Britain would make it easier for them to gain desperately needed aid from England's rival France and other foreign countries. France and Spain were already providing a small amount of secret aid, but would do much more for an independent nation. Declaring independence would also provide a better legal basis for American leaders' newly claimed authority. Accordingly, most of the states (as the rebellious colonies now called themselves) either instructed or permitted their delegates in the Congress to vote for independence.

QUICK REVIEW

The Continental Congress Takes Charge

- Commanded the Continental Army.
- Authorized the formation of a navy.
- Established a post office.
- Conducted diplomacy with Native American nations.
- Printed paper money.

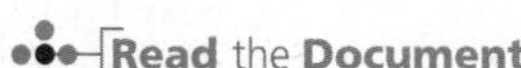

Read the **Document**

at **www.myhistorylab.com**
Exploring America: Exploring the Geography of the American Revolution

Thomas Jefferson, author of the Declaration of Independence and future president of the United States. Mather Brown, an American artist living in England, painted this picture of Jefferson for John Adams while the two men were in London on diplomatic missions in 1786. A companion portrait of Adams that Jefferson ordered for himself also survives. Brown's sensitive portrait of a thoughtful Jefferson is the earliest known likeness of him.

On June 7, 1776, Virginian Richard Henry Lee introduced in the Congress a resolution stating that the united colonies "are, and of right ought to be, free and independent States." Postponing a vote on the issue, the Congress appointed a committee to draw up a declaration of independence. On June 28, after making revisions in Thomas Jefferson's proposed text, the committee presented the document to Congress. In the debate that followed, a few delegates clung to the hope of remaining loyal to the crown. But when the Congress voted on the resolution for independence on July 2, 1776, all voting delegations approved it. After further tinkering with the wording, the Congress officially adopted the **Declaration of Independence** on July 4, 1776.

Congress intended the declaration to be a justification for America's secession from the British Empire and an invitation to potential allies. But Jefferson's prose transformed a version of the **contract theory of government** into one of history's great statements of human rights. Developed by the late-seventeenth-century English philosopher John Locke and others, the contract theory maintains that legitimate government rests on an agreement between the people and their rulers. The people are bound to obey their rulers only so long as the rulers offer them protection.

The Declaration of Independence consists of a magnificently stated opening assumption, two premises, and a powerful conclusion. The opening assumption is that all men are created equal, that they therefore have equal rights, and that they can neither give up these rights nor allow them to be taken away. The first premise—that people establish governments to protect their fundamental rights to life, liberty, and property—is a restatement of contract theory. The second premise is a long list of charges meant to prove that George III had failed to defend his American subjects' rights. This indictment, the heart of the declaration, justified the Americans' rejection of their hitherto legitimate ruler. Then followed the dramatic conclusion: that Americans could rightfully overthrow King George's rule and replace it with something more satisfactory to them.

Although Jefferson proclaimed "all men" as being equal, in fact many people were excluded from full participation in eighteenth-century American society. Women, Native Americans, slaves, and free black people fell outside the scope of that sweeping phrase. So too did men without property, who had restricted rights in colonial society. But if the words "all men are created equal" had limited practical meaning in 1776, they have ever since confronted Americans with a moral challenge to make good on them.

Declaration of Independence
The document by which the Second Continental Congress announced and justified its decision to renounce the colonies' allegiance to the British government.

contract theory of government
The belief that government is established by human beings to protect certain rights—such as life, liberty, and property—that are theirs by natural, divinely sanctioned law and that when government protects these rights, people are obligated to obey it.

The Loyalists

The Declaration of Independence may have clarified matters for American Whigs, but it made the position of Tories—those who professed loyalty to Britain—untenable. With the Declaration of Independence, these loyal subjects of Britain suddenly became enemies of the American people.

An estimated half a million colonists—20 percent of the free population—sided with Britain. Their numbers included rich merchants and farmers as well as poor settlers, and they could be found in every colony. Some were recent immigrants, especially Scots or Scots-Irish newcomers, who trusted the British government more than colonial elites to protect them. In New England, where they were a minority, Anglicans held fast to political as well as religious ties to Britain. Their experiences underscored the important point that the American Revolution

W WHERE TO LEARN MORE

★ Independence National Historical Park, Philadelphia, Pennsylvania
http://www.nps.gov/inde/index.htm

was a civil conflict as well as a war for independence. It set neighbor against neighbor and created permanent rifts within families.

These divisions were intensified by the actions of the legislatures of newly independent states. Refusing to swear allegiance to the state and nation brought criminal penalties; taking up arms on behalf of Britain became a capital crime. Even so, about 19,000 colonists fought with the British, often in special units made up solely of loyalists.

Up to 70,000 more loyalists became refugees, fleeing mainly to Nova Scotia and Upper Canada (later the province of Ontario). In addition, some 20,000 escaped slaves who sought freedom with British forces likewise dispersed to other parts of the British Empire. By propelling thousands of people northward, the American Revolution can be said to have created two nations—the United States and, eventually, Canada.

Read the **Document**
at **www.myhistorylab.com**
Thomas Jefferson, "Original Rough Draught" of the Declaration of Independence (1776)

Interpreting the Past
Democratic Roots in New England Soil (pp. 166–167)

Read the **Document**
at **www.myhistorylab.com**
The Declaration of Independence (1776)

THE COMBATANTS

WHAT WERE the key differences between the British and American forces?

Republican theory mistrusted professional armies as the instruments of tyrants. A free people, republicans insisted, relied for defense on their own patriotism. But militiamen, as one American general observed, had trouble coping with "the shocking scenes of war" because they were not "steeled by habit or fortified by military pride." In real battles, they often proved unreliable. Americans therefore faced a hard choice: Develop a professional army or lose the war. In the end, they did what they had to do.

Professional Soldiers

Drawing on their colonial experience and on republican theory, the new state governments first tried to meet their military needs by relying on the militia and by creating new units based on short-term enlistments. Officers, particularly in the North, were often elected, and their positions depended on personal popularity. Discipline became a major problem in both the militia and the new state units, and often volunteers had barely received basic training before their term of duty ended and they returned home.

Read the **Document**
at **www.myhistorylab.com**
Peter Oliver, Origin and Progress of the American Rebellion: A Tory View (1781)

Read the **Document**
at **www.myhistorylab.com**
From Then to Now Online: Anti-war Churches

Washington sought to avoid these problems by professionalizing the new Continental Army. He eventually prevailed on Congress to adopt stricter regulations and to require enlistments for three years or the duration of the war. Although he used militia effectively, his consistent aim was to turn the Continental Army into a disciplined force that could defeat the British in the large engagements of massed troops characteristic of eighteenth-century European warfare, for only such victories could impress the other European powers and establish the legitimacy of the United States.

The enemy British soldiers—and the nearly 30,000 German mercenaries (Americans called them "Hessians") whom the British government employed—offered Americans the clearest model of a professional army. British regulars were not (as Americans assumed) the "dregs of society." Although most of the enlisted men came from the lower classes and from economically depressed areas, many also had skills. British officers usually came from wealthy families and had simply purchased their commissions. Only rarely could a man rise from the enlisted ranks to commissioned-officer status.

The life of a British soldier was tough. They were frequently undernourished, and many more died of disease

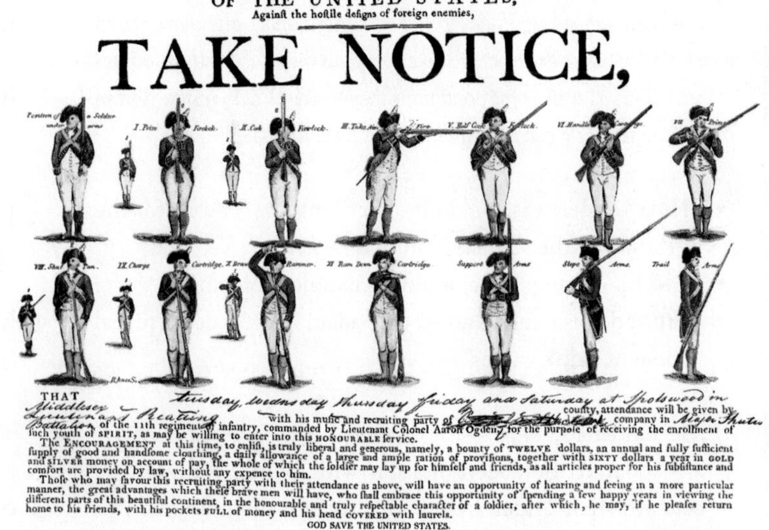

Posters like this one appeared in many cities and towns to recruit soldiers to join the Continental Army. Washington hoped to be able to turn inexperienced young men into a disciplined, professional fighting force.

Read the **Document**
at **www.myhistorylab.com**
Letter from a Revolutionary War Soldier (1776)

than of injury in battle. Medical care was, by modern standards, primitive. Severe discipline held soldiers in line. Striking an officer or deserting could bring death; lesser offenses usually incurred a beating.

After the winter of 1777–1778, conditions in the Continental Army more closely resembled those in the British army. Like British regulars, American recruits tended to be low on the social scale. They included young men without land, indentured servants, some criminals and vagrants—in short, men who lacked better prospects. The chances for talented enlisted men to win an officer's commission were greater than in the British army. But Continental soldiers frequently had little more than "their ragged shirt flaps to cover their nakedness," and their bare marching feet occasionally left bloody tracks in the snow.

The British and the Americans both had trouble supplying their troops. The British had plenty of sound money, which many American merchants and farmers were happy to take in payment for supplies. But they had to rely mostly on supplies shipped to them from the British Isles. The Continental Army, by contrast, had to pay for supplies in depreciating paper money. After 1780, the burden of provisioning the Continental Army fell on the states, which did little better than Congress had done. Unable to obtain sufficient supplies, the army sometimes threatened to seize them by force. Washington, however, did all he could to prevent his soldiers from foraging through the countryside, stealing much-needed provisions. He knew that such actions would erode public support for the army and the patriot cause and thus had to be stopped.

QUICK REVIEW

Military Life
- Soldiers suffered from disease and lack of food.
- Discipline was severe.
- Soldiers of the Continental Army developed a community of their own.

Often feeling ignored by an uncaring society, the professional soldiers of the Continental Army developed a community of their own. They groused, to be sure—sometimes alarmingly. In May 1780, Connecticut troops at Washington's camp in Morristown, New Jersey, staged a brief mutiny. On January 1, 1781, armed units from Pennsylvania stationed in New Jersey marched to Philadelphia demanding their back pay. The Pennsylvania Executive Council met part of the soldiers' demands, but some of the men left the service. Washington ordered subsequent mutinies by New Jersey and Pennsylvania troops suppressed by force.

AMERICAN VIEWS

An American Surgeon Reflects on the Winter at Valley Forge, 1777–1778

Dr. Albigence Waldo was a surgeon in the First Connecticut Infantry Regiment of the Continental Army while it was encamped at Valley Forge, Pennsylvania. His diary, from which the following excerpts are taken, reveals much about the attitudes of the soldiers as well as the conditions they faced. Waldo resigned from the service in 1779 because of illness but lived until 1794.

- **How** serious was Waldo in describing the reasons for the location of the soldiers' winter quarters?
- **Did** his griping reflect a serious morale problem?
- **What** do his remarks about the Indian soldier's death reveal about Waldo's values?

[December 13, 1777.—] It cannot be that our Superiors are about to hold consultation with Spirits infinitely beneath their Order, by bringing us into these [remote] regions. . . . No, it is, upon consideration for many good purposes since we are to Winter here—1st There is plenty of Wood & Water. 2dly There are but few families for the soldiery to Steal from—tho' far be it from a Soldier to Steal. 4ly [sic] There are warm sides of Hills to erect huts on. 5ly They will be heavenly Minded like Jonah when in the Belly of a Great Fish. 6ly They will not become home Sick as is sometimes the case when Men live in the Open World—since the reflections which will naturally arise from their present habitation, will lead them to the more noble thoughts of employing their leisure hours in filling their knapsacks with such materials as may be necessary on the Journey to another Home.

December 14.—Prisoners & Deserters are continually coming in. The Army which has been surprisingly healthy hitherto, now begins to grow sickly from the continued fatigues they have suffered this Campaign. Yet they still show a spirit of Alacrity & Contentment not to be expected from so young Troops. I am Sick—discontented—and out of humour. Poor food—hard lodging—Cold Weather—fatigue—Nasty Cloaths—nasty Cookery—Vomit half my time—smoak'd out of my senses—the Devil's in't—I can't Endure it—Why are we sent here to starve and Freeze—What sweet Felicities have I left at home; A charming Wife—pretty Children—Good Beds—good food—good Cookery—all agreeable—all harmonious. Here all Confusion—smoke & Cold—hunger & filthyness—A pox on my bad luck. There comes a bowl of beef soup—full of burnt leaves and dirt, sickish enough to make a Hector spue—away with it Boys—I'll live like the Chameleon upon Air. Poh! Poh! Crys Patience within me—you talk like a fool. Your being sick Covers your mind with a Melancholic Gloom, which makes everything about you appear gloomy. See the poor Soldier, when in health—with what cheerfulness he meets his foes and encounters every hardship—if barefoot, he labours thro' the Mud & Cold with a Song in his mouth extolling War & Washington—if his food be bad, he eats it notwithstanding with seeming content—blesses God for a good Stomach and Whistles it into digestion. But harkee Patience, a moment—There comes a Soldier, his bare feet are seen thro' his worn out Shoes, his legs nearly naked from the tatter'd remains of an only pair of stockings, his Breeches not sufficient to cover his nakedness, his Shirt hanging in Strings, his hair dishevell'd, his face meager; his whole appearance pictures a per-son forsaken & discouraged. He comes, and crys with an air of wretchedness & despair, I am Sick, my feet lame, my legs are sore, my body cover'd with this tormenting Itch—my Cloaths are worn out, my Constitution is broken, my former Activity is exhausted by fatigue, hunger & Cold, I fail fast. I shall soon be no more! And all the reward I shall get will be—"Poor Will is dead."

December 21.—[Valley Forge.] Heartily wish myself at home, my Skin & eyes are almost spoil'd with continual smoke. A general cry thro' the Camp this evening among the Soldiers, "No Meat! No Meat!"—the Distant vales Echo'd back the melancholy sound—"No Meat! No Meat!" Immitating the noise of Crows & Owls, also, made a part of the confused Musick.

What have you for your Dinners Boys? "Nothing but Fire Cake & Water, Sir." At night, "Gentlemen the Supper is ready." What is your Supper Lads? "Fire Cake & Water, Sir."

December 30.—Eleven Deserters came in to-day—some Hessians & some English—one of the Hesns took an Ax in his hand & cut away the Ice of the Schuylkill which was 1 1/2 inches thick & 40 Rod wide and waded through to our Camp—he was 1/2 hour in the Water. They had a promise when they engag'd that the war would be ended in one year—they were now tired of the Service.

[January 3, 1778.—] I was call'd to relieve a Soldier tho't to be dying—he expir'd before I Reach'd the Hutt. He was an Indian—an excellent Soldier—and an obedient good natur'd fellow. He engaged for money doubtless as others do;—but he has serv'd his country faithfully—he has fought for those very people who disinherited his forefathers—having finished his pilgrimage, he was discharged from the War of Life & Death. His memory ought to be respected, more than those rich ones who supply the world with nothing better than Money and Vice.

Source: "Valley Forge, 1777–1778. Diary of Surgeon Albigence Waldo, of the Connecticut Line," *Pennsylvania Magazine of History and Biography,* 21 (1897): 306–7, 309, 315–16, 319.

What was perhaps the most serious expression of army discontent—one that might have threatened the future of republican institutions and civilian government in the United States—occurred in March 1783, after the fighting was over. Washington's troops were then stationed near Newburgh, New York, waiting for their pay before disbanding. When the Congress failed to grant real assurances that any pay would be forthcoming, hotheaded young officers called a meeting that could have led to an armed coup. General Washington, who had scrupulously deferred to civilian authority throughout the war, asked permission to address the gathering and, in a dramatic speech, subtly warned the men of all that they might lose by insubordination. A military coup would "open the flood Gates of Civil discord" and "deluge" the nation in blood; loyalty now, he said, would be "one more distinguished proof" of their patriotism. With the fate of the Revolution apparently hanging in the balance, the movement collapsed. Washington's quick response set a precedent for the subordination of the military to civilian government.

Women in the Contending Armies

Women accompanied many units on both sides, as was common in eighteenth-century warfare. A few were prostitutes. Some were officers' wives or mistresses, but most were the married or common-law consorts of ordinary soldiers." These "camp followers" fulfilled many of the support functions necessary to sustain the army. They cooked and washed for the troops, occasionally helped load artillery, and provided most of the nursing care. A certain number in a company were subject to military orders and were authorized to draw rations and pay.

African American Participation in the War

Early in the war, as we have seen, some royal officials like Lord Dunmore recruited slaves with promises of freedom. But these efforts often proved counterproductive, frightening potentially loyalist slaveowners and driving them to the Whig side. Thus it was not until June 30, 1779, that the British commander in chief, Sir Henry Clinton, promised to allow slaves who fled from rebel owners to join the royal troops to "follow . . . any Occupation" they wished. Hedged as this promise of freedom was, news of it spread quickly among the slave communities, and late in the war, African Americans flocked to the British army in South Carolina and Georgia.

Sharing prevailing racial prejudices, the British were often reluctant to arm blacks. Instead, they put most of the ex-slaves to work as agricultural or construction workers (many of the free and enslaved blacks accompanying American troops were similarly employed). However, a few relatively well-equipped black British dragoons (mounted troops) did see combat in South Carolina.

On the other hand, approximately 5,000 African Americans fought against the British and for American independence, hundreds of them in the Continental Army. Many were freemen from Massachusetts and Rhode Island.

But farther south, as discussed above, John Laurens, a young Carolina patriot, repeatedly but vainly tried to convince the South Carolina assembly to raise and arm black troops. Instead, the legislature eventually voted to give slaves confiscated from loyalists to white volunteers as a reward for their service. It is therefore scarcely surprising that, as one Whig put it, many African Americans were "a little Toryfied," especially in the South.

QUICK REVIEW

African Americans and the Revolutionary War

- June 30, 1779: British promise freedom to slaves who will join the British army.
- Both sides reluctant to use African Americans in combat roles.
- Approximately 5,000 African Americans fought against the British.

Native Americans and the War

At first, most of the approximately 200,000 Native Americans east of the Mississippi River would probably have preferred to remain neutral, and both sides initially took them at their word. But Indians' skills and manpower were valuable, and by 1776 both the British and Americans sought their assistance. Forced to choose, many Native Americans favored the British, hoping thereby to safeguard their lands.

Prewar experience convinced Native Americans that British officials would be more apt to protect them against white settlers, and the British could provide more trade goods and arms. Many Indians, including the Cherokees, Creeks, Choctaws, and Chickasaws, therefore decided to back the British, and Cherokee warriors raided the southern frontier starting in 1776. Southern colonists countered with expeditions that repeatedly devastated Cherokee towns. But when older chiefs sought peace, Dragging Canoe (Tsi'yugunsi'ny) and the more militant younger men established new communities on the Chickamauga River in northern Georgia and continued to fight.

Caught between the British and the Americans, other Indian groups also split. Among these was the powerful Iroquois Confederation in upstate New York. Under the leadership of Thayendanegea—known to whites as Joseph Brant—the Mohawks and Senecas supported the British, while a minority of the Oneidas and Tuscaroras joined the Americans. The Revolution thus created an irreparable divide among the Iroquois, leading many to move to Canada during and after the war.

Frontier racism, which had scarcely dissipated since Pontiac's War (see Chapter 5), flared up again. Few Americans were willing to trust Indian claims of neutrality, and during the war conducted raids against native villages. In 1782, in an event that recalled the earlier Paxton Boys massacre in Pennsylvania (see Chapter 5), a group of Americans slaughtered 100 defenseless Moravian Christian Indians at Gnadenhutten in the Ohio country. Thus American behavior during the war did little to calm native fears for their lives and property in an independent United States.

THE WAR IN THE NORTH, 1776–1777

HOW DID the American forces survive the military setbacks of 1776?

The Revolutionary War can be divided into three phases. In the first, from the outbreak of fighting in 1775 through 1777, most of the important battles took place in New England, New York, New Jersey, and Pennsylvania, while the Americans faced the British alone. But in 1778, France entered the war on the American side, opening the second phase of the war in which fighting would rage from 1778 to 1781, mainly in the South, at sea, and on the western frontier. The third phase of the war, from late 1781 to 1783, saw little actual fighting. With American victory assured, attention shifted to the diplomatic maneuvering leading up to the Peace of Paris (1783).

Britain Hesitates: Crucial Battles in New York and New Jersey

During the first phase of the war, the British concentrated on subduing New England. Replacing General Gage, the government appointed Sir William Howe as commander in chief of British forces and his brother, Richard Howe, as admiral of the naval forces in North American waters. New York City had been the headquarters of the British army during the late colonial period, and the Howes made it their base of operations. To counter this move, Washington moved his forces to New York in the spring of 1776. In August 1776, the Howes landed troops on Long Island and, in the Battle of Brooklyn Heights, quickly drove the American forces deployed there back to Manhattan Island.

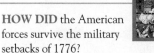

See the **Map**
at **www.myhistorylab.com**
The American Revolution

Following instructions to negotiate peace as well as wage war, Richard Howe then met with three envoys from Congress on Staten Island on September 11, 1776. The British commanders were prepared to offer fairly generous terms but could not grant independence. The Americans would accept nothing less. So the meeting produced no substantive negotiations.

In the ensuing weeks, British forces overwhelmed Washington's troops, driving them out of Manhattan and then, moving north, clearing them from the area around the city at the Battle of White Plains. But the Howes were hesitant to deal a crushing blow, and the Americans were able to retreat across New Jersey into Pennsylvania. The American cause seemed lost, however, and the Continental Army almost melted away. Realizing that without a success he would soon be without troops, Washington led his forces back across the icy Delaware and launched a successful surprise attack on a garrison of Hessian mercenaries at Trenton, New Jersey, on the morning of December 26. A week later, Washington overwhelmed a British force at Princeton, New Jersey. By raising morale, the victories at Trenton and Princeton probably saved the American cause.

QUICK REVIEW

Victories at Trenton and Princeton

- 1776: A series of defeats devastated the Continental Army.
- Christmas night 1776: Washington crosses the Delaware and launches a surprise attack.
- Victories at Trenton and Princeton revive the American cause.

The Year of the Hangman: Victory at Saratoga and Winter at Valley Forge

Contemporaries called 1777 the Year of the Hangman because the triple sevens suggested a row of gallows. It was in fact a critical year for the American cause. Mounting a major effort to end the rebellion, the British planned to send an army down the Hudson River from Canada. The goal was to have it link up with the Howes in New York City, isolate New England, and defeat the rebellion there. But there was little effort to coordinate strategy between the forces advancing from Canada and those in New York. Thus, the poorly planned and poorly executed campaign ended in disaster for the British.

Some 5,000 Redcoats and 3,000 German mercenaries assembled in Canada during the winter of 1776–1777. Under the command of the high-living and popular "Gentleman Johnny" Burgoyne, the army finally set off in June with 1,500 horses hauling its heavy artillery and ponderous supply

George Washington viewing troops at Valley Forge during the winter of 1777–78. This modern depiction is somewhat romanticized. While making a similar tour on foot, Washington once saw a soldier who was literally clothed in nothing but a blanket.

train. A second, smaller column, supported by an Indian force under Thayendanegea (Joseph Brant) moved to the west to capture an American fort near Oriskany, New York, and then join up with Burgoyne's main force. On July 5, Burgoyne's army recaptured Fort Ticonderoga, but success eluded him after that.

Trouble began as the troops started overland through the woods at the southern end of the lake. Huge trees felled by American axmen blocked their way, and the army crawled along at only two or three miles a day. Early in August, the column sent to capture the American fort near Oriskany turned back to Canada. Burgoyne's Indian allies under Joseph Brant likewise went home. Promised reinforcements never arrived. Ten days later, a Whig militia force wiped out a force of 800 men trying to gather supplies in Vermont.

By October 1777, Burgoyne's army was down to fewer than 6,000 men and faced disaster. Nearly 3,000 Continentals and 9,000 American militia, commanded by General Horatio Gates, exerted relentless pressure on the increasingly dispirited invaders. Unable to break through the American lines, Burgoyne surrendered his entire army to Gates following the Battle of Saratoga on October 17, 1777.

Meanwhile, General William Howe, rather than moving north to support Burgoyne, made plans to destroy Washington's army and capture Philadelphia. In July 1777, Howe's troops sailed from New York to Chesapeake Bay and from there marched on Philadelphia from the south. They met Washington's army on the banks of Brandywine Creek, near the Pennsylvania-Delaware border. The Americans put up a good fight before giving way with a loss of 1,200 killed or captured (twice as many as the British).

Valley Forge Area of Pennsylvania approximately 20 miles northwest of Philadelphia where General George Washington's Continental troops were quartered from December 1777 to June 1778 while British forces occupied Philadelphia during the Revolutionary War.

Howe occupied Philadelphia, and his men settled down in comfortable winter quarters. The Congress fled to York, Pennsylvania, and the Continental Army established its own winter camp outside Philadelphia at Valley Forge. The Continental Army's miserable winter at **Valley Forge** has become famous for its hardships. Suffering from cold, disease, and starvation, as many as 2,500 soldiers died. Yet despite the difficulties, the Continental Army completed its transformation into a disciplined professional force. By spring, pleased observers felt that Washington at last had an army capable of meeting the British on equal terms.

THE WAR WIDENS, 1778–1781

WHY DID the French enter the war on the American side?

Since late 1776, Benjamin Franklin and a team of American diplomats had been in Paris negotiating French support for the patriot cause. In the winter of 1777–1778, aware that a Franco-American alliance was close, Parliament belatedly tried to end the rebellion by giving the Americans everything they wanted except independence itself. But France and the United States concluded an alliance on February 6, 1778, and Congress refused to negotiate with the British.

Foreign intervention transformed the American Revolution into a virtual world war, engaging British forces in heavy fighting not only in North America but also in the West Indies and India. In the end, had it not been for French assistance, the American side probably would not have won the clear-cut victory it did.

The United States Gains an Ally

The American victory at Saratoga in October 1777 had persuaded the French that the United States had a viable future. Eager for revenge against their old British enemy, French officials decided to act quickly lest any military reverses force the Americans to agree to reconciliation with Britain. In a move that astonished the British, France accordingly signed a commercial treaty and a military alliance with the United States. Both sides promised to fight together until Britain recognized the independence of the United States, and France pledged not to seek the return of lands in North America.

French entry into the war was the first step in the consolidation of a formidable alliance of European powers eager to see Britain humbled and to gain trading rights in the former British colonies. France persuaded Spain to declare war on Britain in June 1779. Much of the salt used to preserve American soldiers' provisions came from Spanish territories, and New Orleans became a base for American privateers. More important, the Spanish fleet increased the naval power of the countries arrayed against Great Britain.

Meanwhile, Catherine the Great of Russia suggested that the European powers form a League of Armed Neutrality to protect their trade with the United States and other warring countries against British interference. Denmark and Sweden soon joined; Austria, Portugal, Prussia, and Sicily eventually followed. Britain, which wanted to cut off Dutch trade with the United States, used a pretext to declare war on the Netherlands before it could join. Great Britain thus found itself isolated and even, briefly, threatened with invasion. These threats did not frighten the British leaders into suing for peace, but they forced them to make important changes in strategy.

Accordingly, in the spring of 1778, the British replaced the Howes with a new commander, Sir Henry Clinton, and instructed him to send troops to attack the French West Indies. Knowing that he now faced a serious French threat, Clinton began consolidating his forces by evacuating Philadelphia and pulling his troops slowly back across New Jersey to New York.

On June 28, 1778, Washington caught up with the British at Monmouth Court House. This inconclusive battle proved to be the last major engagement in the North. Clinton withdrew to New York, and Continental troops occupied the hills along the Hudson Valley north of the city. The war shifted to other fronts.

QUICK REVIEW

Britain Isolated

- League of Armed Neutrality formed to protect trade with United States free from British interference.
- Members: Russia, Denmark, Sweden, Austria, the Netherlands, Portugal, Prussia, and Sicily.
- Britain declares war on the Dutch to cut off trade with United States.

Fighting on the Frontier and at Sea

Known as "a dark and bloody ground" to Native Americans, Kentucky became even bloodier after the British instructed their Indian allies to raid the area in 1777. Because the British post at Detroit coordinated these attacks, the Americans tried to take it in 1778. Three expeditions failed for various reasons, but the last, under a Virginian, George Rogers Clark, did capture three key British settlements in the Mississippi Valley: Kaskaskia, Cahokia, and Vincennes (see Map 6–3). These successes may have strengthened American claims to the West at the end of the war.

In 1778 bloody fighting also occurred on the eastern frontiers. During the summer, a British force of 100 loyalists and 500 Indians struck the Wyoming Valley of Pennsylvania. Four months later, a similar group of attackers burned farmsteads and slaughtered civilians at Cherry Valley, New York. Both raids stimulated equally savage reprisals against the Indians.

The Americans and British also clashed at sea throughout the war. Great Britain was the preeminent sea power of the age, and the United States never came close to matching it. But in 1775 Congress authorized the construction of 13 frigates—medium-sized, relatively fast ships, mounting 32 guns—as well as the purchase of several merchant vessels for conversion to warships. By contrast, the Royal Navy in 1779 had more than a hundred large, heavily armed "ships of the line." The Americans therefore engaged in what was essentially a guerrilla war at sea.

The Congress and the individual states also supplemented America's naval forces by commissioning privateers. In effect legalized pirates, privateers preyed on British shipping. Captured goods were divided among the crew according to rank; captured sailors became prisoners of war. Some 2,000 American privateers took more than 600 British ships and forced the British navy to spread itself thin doing convoy duty.

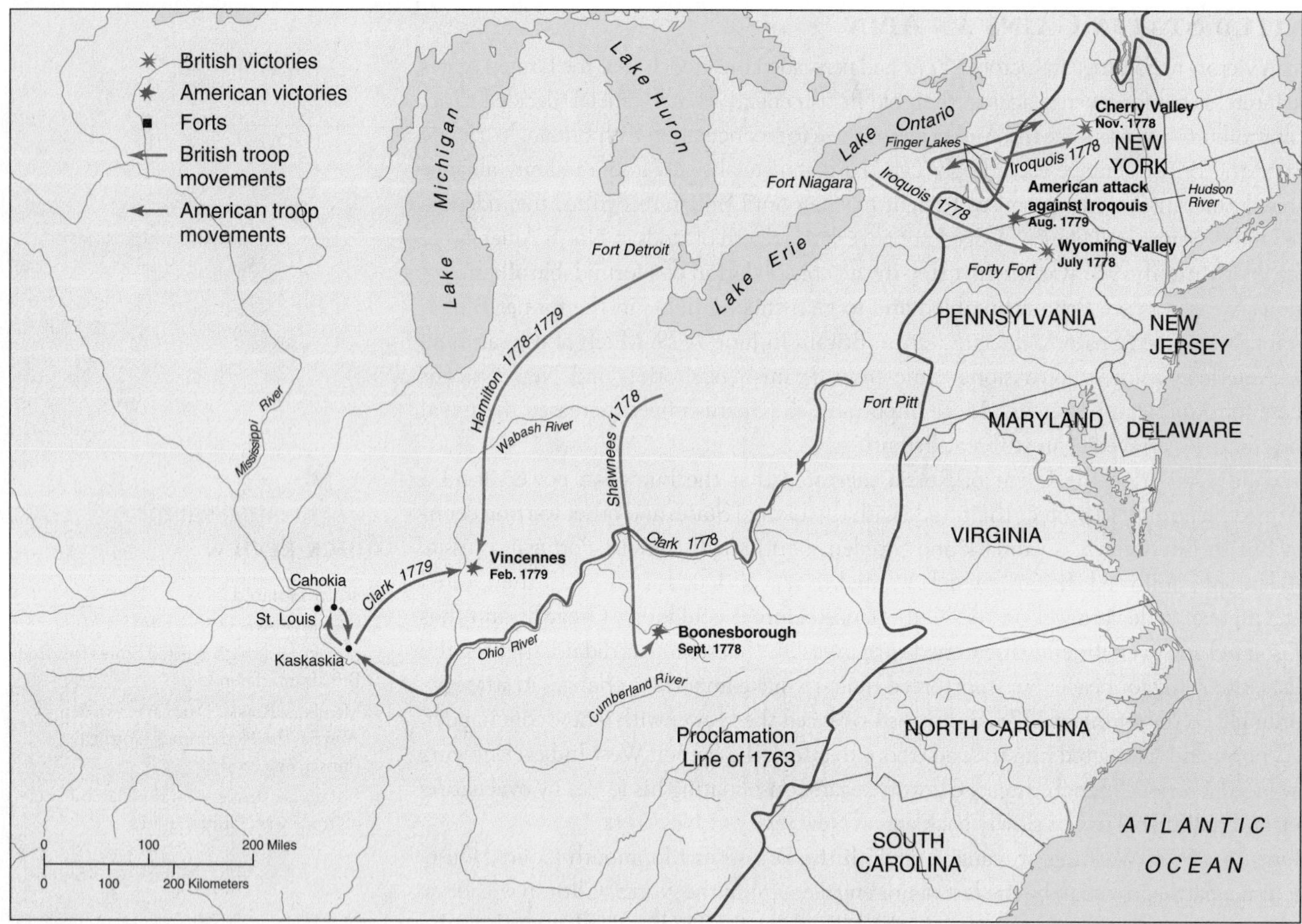

MAP 6–3 **The War on the Frontier, 1778–1779** Significant battles in the Mississippi Valley and the frontiers of the seaboard states added to the ferocity of the fighting and strengthened some American claims to western lands.

Why were the British at more of a disadvantage the farther from the coast they fought?

The Land War Moves South

During the first three years of the war, the British made little effort to mobilize what they believed to be considerable loyalist strength in the South. But in 1778, the enlarged threat from France prompted a change in strategy: Redcoats would sweep through a large area and then leave behind a Tory militia to reestablish loyalty to the crown and suppress local Whigs. The British hoped thereby to recapture everything from Georgia to Virginia; they would deal with New England later.

The British southern strategy unfolded in November 1778, when General Clinton dispatched 3,500 troops to take control of Georgia. Meeting only light resistance, they quickly seized Savannah and Augusta and restored the old colonial government under civilian control. After their initial success, however, the British suffered some serious setbacks. Spain entered the war and seized British outposts on the Mississippi and Mobile rivers while Whig militia decimated a loyalist militia at Kettle Creek, Georgia.

QUICK REVIEW

The Southern Strategy

- Little effort before 1778 by British to mobilize southern loyalists.
- Threat from France forced a new strategy.
- Early successes were followed by setbacks.
- American victory at Yorktown effectively ended the war.

But the Americans could not beat the British army. In late September and early October 1779, a combined force of 5,500 American and French troops, supported by French warships, laid siege to Savannah. The assault failed, and the French sailed off.

The way was now open for the British to attack Charleston, the military key to the Lower South. In December 1779, Clinton sailed through stormy seas from New York to the Carolina coast with about 9,000 troops. In the Battle of Charleston, he encircled the city, trapping the patriot forces inside. On May 12, 1780, more than 5,000 Continentals and militia laid down their arms in the worst American defeat of the war.

The British were now poised to sweep the entire South. Most local Whigs, thinking the Revolution over, at first offered little resistance to the Redcoats striking into the Carolina backcountry. The British success seemed so complete that Clinton tried to force American prisoners to resume their duties as British subjects and join the loyalist militia. Thinking that matters were now well in hand, Clinton sailed back to New York, leaving the southern troops under the command of Lord Cornwallis. Clinton's confidence that the South had returned to British allegiance was premature.

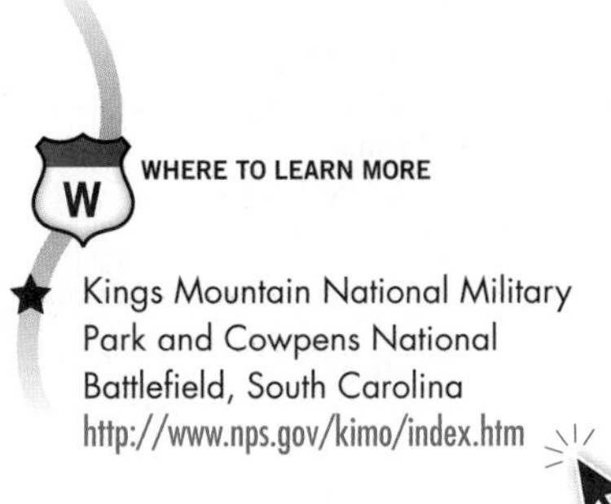

WHERE TO LEARN MORE

Kings Mountain National Military Park and Cowpens National Battlefield, South Carolina
http://www.nps.gov/kimo/index.htm

Watch the Video
at **www.myhistorylab.com**
The American Revolution as Different Americans Saw It

American Counterattacks

In the summer of 1780, Congress dispatched a substantial Continental force to the South under General Horatio Gates, the hero of Saratoga. Local patriots flocked to join him. But instead of achieving another great victory, Gates and his men blundered into Cornwallis's British army near Camden, South Carolina, on August 16, and suffered a complete rout. More than 1,000 Americans were killed or wounded and many captured. Gates—transformed from the hero of Saratoga into the goat of Camden—fled to Hillsborough, North Carolina.

American morale revived on October 7, 1780, when "overmountain men" (militia) from Virginia, western North Carolina, and South Carolina defeated the British at Kings Mountain, South Carolina. And in December 1780, Nathanael Greene replaced the discredited Gates, bringing competent leadership to the Continentals in the South.

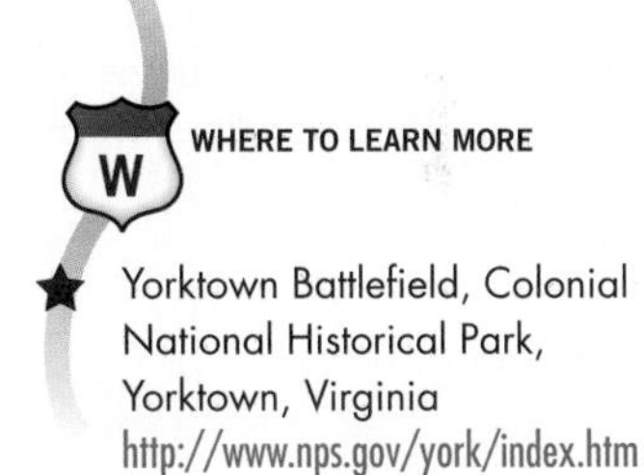

WHERE TO LEARN MORE

Yorktown Battlefield, Colonial National Historical Park, Yorktown, Virginia
http://www.nps.gov/york/index.htm

Ever resourceful, Greene divided his small forces, keeping roughly half with him in northeastern South Carolina and sending the other half westward under General Daniel Morgan. Cornwallis ordered Colonel Banastre Tarleton to pursue Morgan, who retreated northward until he reached Cowpens, South Carolina. There, on January 17, 1781, Morgan cleverly posted his least reliable troops, the militia, in the front line and ordered them to retreat after firing two volleys. When they did as told, the British thought the Americans were fleeing and charged after them—straight into devastating fire from Morgan's Continentals.

Cornwallis now badly needed a battlefield victory. Burning his army's excess baggage, he set off in hot pursuit of Greene and Morgan, whose rejoined forces retreated northward ahead of the British. On February 13, 1781, Greene's tired men crossed the Dan River into Virginia, and Cornwallis gave up the chase, marching his equally exhausted Redcoats southward. To his surprise, Cornwallis now found himself pursued—though cautiously—by Greene. On March 15, the opposing forces met at Guilford Court House, North Carolina, in one of the war's bloodiest battles. Although the British held the field at the end of the day, an Englishman accurately observed, "another such victory would destroy the British Army." Cornwallis retreated to the coastal town of Wilmington, North Carolina, to rest and regroup.

The surrender of Lord Cornwallis at Yorktown on October 19, 1781, led to the British decision to withdraw from the war. Cornwallis, who claimed to be ill, absented himself from the ceremony and is not in the picture. Washington, who is astride the horse under the American flag, designated General Benjamin Lincoln (on the white horse in the center) as the one to accept the submission of a subordinate British officer. John Trumbull, who painted *The Battle of Bunker Hill* and some 300 other scenes from the Revolutionary War, finished this painting while he was in London about 15 years after the events depicted. A large copy of the work now hangs in the rotunda of the United States Capitol in Washington, D.C.
John Trumbull (American 1756–1843), *Surrender of Lord Cornwallis at Yorktown, October 1781,* oil on canvas, 20 7/8 × 30 5/8 inches. Yale University Art Gallery, Trumbull Collection.

By the late summer of 1781, British fortunes were waning in the Lower South. The Redcoats held only the larger towns and the immediately surrounding countryside. With their superior staying power, they won most major engagements, but these victories brought

QUICK REVIEW

Victory at Yorktown

- Summer 1781: Cornwallis marches to Yorktown, Virginia.
- 6,000 British face 8,800 Americans and 7,800 French.
- October 19, 1781: British army surrenders.

them no lasting gain. When the enemy pressed him too hard, Greene retreated out of reach, advancing again as the British withdrew.

Disappointed and frustrated, Cornwallis decided to conquer Virginia to cut off Greene's supplies and destroy Whig resolve. British forces were already raiding the state. Cornwallis marched north to join them, reaching Yorktown, Virginia, during the summer of 1781.

The final military showdown of the war was at hand. By now, French soldiers were in America ready to fight alongside the Continentals, and a large French fleet in the West Indies had orders to support an attack on the British in North America. Faking preparations for an assault on British-occupied New York, the Continentals (commanded by Washington) and the French headed for the Chesapeake. Cornwallis and his 6,000 Redcoats soon found themselves besieged behind their fortifications at Yorktown by 8,800 Americans and 7,800 French. A French naval victory gave the allies temporary command of the waters around Yorktown. Cornwallis had nowhere to go, and Clinton—still in New York—could not reinforce him quickly enough. On October 19, 1781, the British army surrendered.

THE WAR AND SOCIETY, 1775–1783

WHAT WAS the social impact of the War for Independence?

Regular combatants were not the only ones to suffer during the struggle for independence. Eight years of warfare also produced profound dislocations throughout American society. Military service wrenched families apart, sporadic raids brought the war home to vast numbers of people, and everyone endured economic disruptions. As a forge of nationhood, the Revolution tested all Americans, whatever their standing as citizens.

THE WOMEN'S WAR

Women everywhere had to see their loved ones go off to fight and die. Such circumstances elevated women's domestic status. Couples began referring to "our"—not "my" or "your"—property. Wives frequently became more knowledgeable about the family's financial condition than their long-absent husbands. Women also assumed new public roles during the conflict. Some nursed the wounded. More wove cloth for uniforms. The Ladies' Association of Philadelphia was established in 1780 to demonstrate women's patriotism and raise money to buy shirts for the army. Similar associations formed in other states.

Read the **Document** at **www.myhistorylab.com** *John Adams to Abigail Adams (July 3, 1776)*

Despite their increasing private responsibilities and new public activities, it did not occur to most women to encroach on traditional male prerogatives. When John Adams's wife, Abigail, urged him and the Second Continental Congress to "Remember the Ladies," she was not expecting equal political rights. What she wanted, rather, was some legal protections for women and recognition of their value and need for autonomy in the domestic sphere. "Remember," she cautioned, "all Men would be Tyrants if they could."

The Revolution in fact did little to change women's political status. Perhaps the most immediate outcome of the Revolution for American women was the politicization of their maternal responsibilities. As good "republican mothers," they could be trusted to instill patriotism in their sons, helping them to mature into virtuous citizens. Although this idea led to calls for enhancing women's educational opportunities, it was at best a limited improvement in their political role.

QUICK REVIEW

Women's Roles

- Elevation of women's domestic status.
- New public roles as supporters of independence.
- Limited encroachment on traditional male prerogatives.
- The war politicized women's maternal roles.

EFFECT OF THE WAR ON AFRICAN AMERICANS

In the northern states, where slavery was already economically marginal and where black men were welcome as volunteers in the Continental Army, the Revolutionary War helped to bring an end to slavery, although it remained legal there for some time (see Chapter 7). In the South, however, slavery was integral to the economy, and white planters viewed it as crucial to their postwar recovery. Thus, although British efforts to recruit black soldiers brought freedom to thousands and temporarily undermined slavery in the South, the war ultimately strengthened the institution, especially in the Carolinas and Georgia. Of the African Americans who left with the British at the end of the war, many, both slave and free, went to the West Indies. Others settled in Canada, and some eventually reached Africa, where Britain established the colony of Sierra Leone for them.

Ki-On-Twog-Ky, also known as Corn Planter (1732/40–1836) was a Seneca Indian chief who raided American settlements for the British, while he observed that "war is war, death is death, a fight is hard business." He later presided over the surrender of much land to the United States.

The War's Impact on Native Americans

Survivors among the approximately 13,000 Native Americans who fought for the British did not have the option of leaving with them at the end of the war. How many died during the conflict is not known, but certainly many did. Not only the Iroquois but other groups lost much. The Americans repeatedly invaded the Cherokees' homeland in the southern Appalachian Mountains. Americans also attacked the Shawnees of Ohio.

In the peace treaty of 1783, Britain surrendered its territory east of the Mississippi, shocking and infuriating the Native Americans living there. They had not surrendered, and none of them had been at the negotiations in Paris. Because it enabled Americans to claim Indian territory by conquest, the Revolutionary War was a disaster for many Native Americans that opened the floodgates to a torrent of white settlers.

Economic Disruption

The British and American armies both needed enormous quantities of supplies. This heavy demand disrupted the normal distribution of goods and drove up real prices seven- or eightfold; in addition, widespread use of depreciating paper money by the American side amplified the rise in prices and triggered severe inflation.

When the British did not simply seize what they needed, they paid for it in hard currency—gold and silver. American commanders, by contrast, had to rely on paper money because the Congress and the states had almost no hard currency at their disposal. The Continental dollar, however, steadily declined in value, and by March 1780, the Congress was forced to admit officially that it was worthless.

Necessity, not folly, drove Congress and the states to rely on the printing press. Rather than alienate citizens by immediately raising taxes to pay for the war, the states printed paper money supposedly redeemable through future tax revenues. But because the quantity of this paper money rose faster than the supply of goods and services, prices skyrocketed, and the value of the money plunged. Those who had paper money tried to spend it before its value could drop further; whereas those who had salable commodities such as grain tended to hoard them in the hope that the price would go even higher. Prices also climbed faster than wages, leaving many working people impoverished.

The rampant inflation was demoralizing and divisive. Lucky speculators and unscrupulous profiteers could grow rich, while ordinary and patriotic people suffered. As usual, war and its deprivations brought out both the best and the worst in human nature.

Most Americans somehow managed to cope. But during the last years of the conflict, their economic and psychological reserves ran low. The total real wealth of private individuals declined by an average of 0.5 percent annually from 1774 to 1805, even with the returning prosperity of the 1790s. Such statistics suggest the true economic cost of the War for Independence. And the atrocities committed on both sides provide a comparable measure of the conflict's psychological cost.

THE AMERICAN VICTORY, 1782–1783

WHAT WERE the key factors in the American victory in the Revolutionary War?

The British surrender at Yorktown marked the end of major fighting in North America, though skirmishes continued for another year. In April 1782, the Royal Navy defeated the French fleet in the Caribbean, strengthening the British bargaining position. Although George III insisted on continuing the war because he feared that defeat would threaten British rule in Canada and the West Indies, the majority in Parliament now felt that enough men and money had been wasted trying to keep the Americans within the empire. In March 1782, the king accepted Lord North's resignation and appointed a new prime minister, with a mandate to make peace.

THE PEACE OF PARIS

The peace negotiations, which took place in Paris, were lengthy. The Americans demanded independence, handsome territorial concessions, and access to the rich British-controlled fishing grounds in the North Atlantic. The current British prime minister, Lord Shelburne, was inclined to be conciliatory to help British merchants recover their lost colonial trade. The French had achieved their objective of weakening the British and now wanted out of an increasingly costly worldwide war. Spain had not won its most important goal, the recovery of British-held Gibraltar, and thus gave the Americans no support at all.

QUICK REVIEW

Peace of Paris

- Signed September 3, 1783.
- United States got virtually everything it sought at peace talks.
- Treaty addressed important economic issues, but said nothing about slavery.

The American negotiators, Benjamin Franklin, John Adams, and John Jay, skillfully threaded their way among these conflicting interests. With good reason, they feared that the French and Spanish might strike a bargain with the British at the expense of the United States. As a result, the Americans disregarded Congress's instructions to avoid making peace unilaterally and secretly worked out their own arrangements with the British. On November 30, 1782, the negotiators signed a preliminary Anglo-American treaty of peace whose terms were embodied in the final **Peace of Paris,** signed by all the belligerents on September 3, 1783.

Peace of Paris Treaties signed in 1783 by Great Britain, the United States, France, Spain, and the Netherlands that ended the Revolutionary War.

The Peace of Paris gave the United States nearly everything it sought. Great Britain acknowledged that the United States was "free, sovereign and independent." The northern boundary of the new nation extended west from the St. Croix River (which separated Maine from Nova Scotia) past the Great Lakes to what were thought to be the headwaters of the Mississippi River (see Map 6–4). The Mississippi itself—down to just north of New Orleans—formed the western border. Spain acquired the provinces of East and West Florida from Britain. This territory included parts of present-day Louisiana, Mississippi, Alabama, and Georgia.

This British political cartoon from 1779 shows the horse "America" throwing its British master. The figure in the distance on the right is a French soldier; his depiction suggests that the cartoonist thought the French alliance would enable America to win the war.

Several provisions of the treaty addressed important economic issues. Adams, on behalf of New Englanders, insisted on a provision granting American fishermen access to the waters off eastern Canada. The treaty also required that British forces, on quitting American soil, were to leave behind all American-owned property, including slaves. Another provision declared existing debts between citizens of Britain and the United States still valid, giving British merchants hope of collecting on their American accounts. Congress was to "recommend" that the states restore rights and property taken from loyalists during the war. Nothing was said about the slave trade, which Jay had hoped to ban.

THE COMPONENTS OF SUCCESS

The War for Independence was over. In December 1783, the last British troops left New York. The Continental Army had already disbanded during the summer of 1783. On December 4, Washington said farewell to his officers

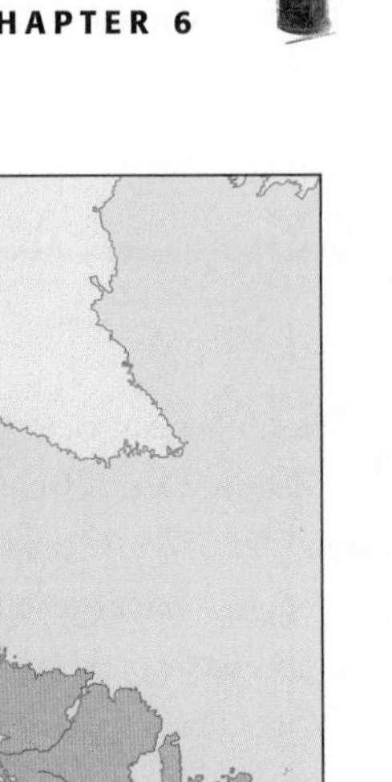

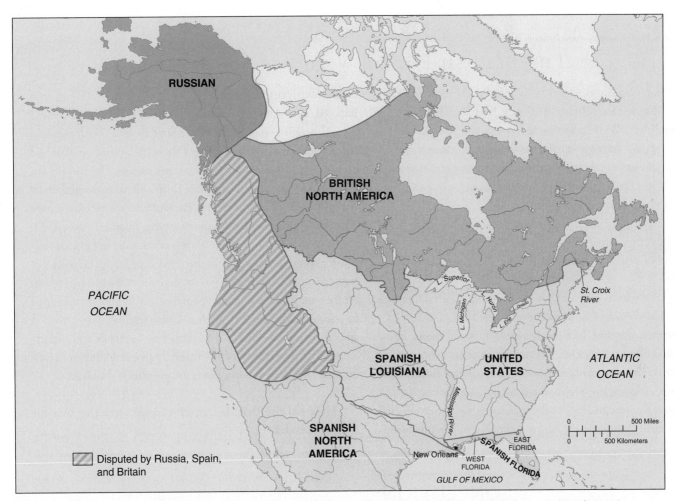

MAP 6–4 **North America after the Peace of Paris, 1783** The results of the American Revolution redrew the map of North America, confining Britain to Canada and giving the United States most of the area east of the Mississippi River, though Spain controlled its mouth for most of the next 20 years.

What factors helped determine the territorial settlement reached in the Peace of Paris?

at New York City's Fraunces Tavern and later that month resigned his commission to the Congress and went home to Mount Vernon. By now he had won the respect of friend and foe alike.

Washington's leadership was just one of the reasons why the Americans won the Revolutionary War. French assistance played a crucial role. Indeed, some historians contend that without the massive infusion of French men and money in 1781, the Revolution would have failed. The British also contributed heavily to their own downfall with mistakes that included bureaucratic inefficiency, hesitant command, and overconfidence. Finally, Great Britain had tried to solve a political problem by military means, but an occupying army is far more likely to alienate people than to secure their goodwill.

Yet it took 175,000 to 200,000 soldiers—Continentals and militia troops—to prevent Great Britain from recovering the colonies. Of these, some 7,000 died in battle. Perhaps 10,000 more succumbed to disease while on active duty, another 8,500 died while prisoners of war, and nearly 1,500 were reported missing in action. More than 8,000 were wounded and survived. Those who served in the Continental Army, probably more than half of all who fought, served the longest and saw the most action. Their casualty rate—30 to 40 percent—may have been the highest of any war in which the United States has been engaged. In proportion to the population, these losses would be the equivalent of more than 2 million people in the United States today.

GLOBAL CONNECTIONS

The British Empire without America

The American victory in the War for Independence did not deprive Great Britain of its entire New World empire. After 1783, Canada—which now counted thousands of loyalist refugees among its inhabitants—remained British, as did Jamaica, Barbados, and other lucrative sugar-growing Caribbean islands. Over the next few decades, however, the focus of the British Empire moved to the east.

Its centerpiece was India, where Britain expanded its territorial holdings, largely through conquest. Elsewhere, the first boatload of British convicts disembarked in Australia in 1788, and free settlers soon joined them to make good on Britain's claim to the island continent. By 1815, British imperial holdings also included parts of West and South Africa.

At the same time, Britain augmented its global empire by establishing commercial rather than territorial ties to other parts of the world. This was especially true for China, where British trade expanded dramatically, even as merchants' access was restricted to the port of Canton. In 1786, British merchants had also established a foothold at Penang on the Malay Peninsula. As the nineteenth century wore on, the mercantilist regulations that Britain had once imposed on its American colonies gave way to free trade policies.

Although Britain's so-called "second empire" encompassed the globe, it demonstrated some of the same weaknesses that had contributed to the loss of the American colonies. The Revolution had exposed crucial problems with British efforts to strengthen its imperial authority by asserting Parliamentary sovereignty over what had been essentially self-governing colonies. After 1783, imperial officials continued to allow a certain amount of local self-rule for white communities in the remaining British colonies but imposed more authoritarian governments on nonwhite majorities. At the same time, the imperial bureaucracy in London remained as uncoordinated as ever, with colonial responsibilities divided among numerous—and often competing—officials and departments. This new version of the British Empire would last until well into the twentieth century, but it too eventually dissolved.

- How did the British Empire change after the War for Independence?

CONCLUSION

Despite the devastation and divisiveness of the war, many people in Europe and the United States were convinced that it represented something momentous. The *Annual Register,* a popular and influential British magazine, commented accurately in 1783 that the American Revolution "has already overturned those favourite systems of policy and commerce, both in the old and in the new world, which the wisdom of the ages, and the power of the greatest nations, had in vain endeavored to render permanent; and it seems to have laid the seeds of still greater revolutions in the history and mutual relations of mankind."

Americans, indeed, had fired a shot heard round the world. Thanks in part to its heavy investment in the American Revolution, France suffered a financial crisis in the late 1780s. This, in turn, ushered in the political crisis that culminated in the French Revolution of 1789. The American Revolution helped to inspire among French people (including soldiers returning from service in America) an intense yearning for an end to arbitrary government and undeserved social inequalities. Liberty also proved infectious to thousands of German troops who had come to America as mercenaries but stayed as free citizens after the war was over. Once prosperous but distant provinces of a far-flung empire, the North American states had become an independent confederation, a grand experiment in republicanism whose fate mattered to enlightened men and women throughout the Western world. In his written farewell to the rank and file of his troops at the end of October 1783, Washington maintained that "the enlarged prospects of happiness, opened by the confirmation of our independence and sovereignty, almost exceed the power of description." He urged those who had fought with him to maintain their "strong attachments to the union" and "prove themselves not less virtuous and useful as citizens, than they have been persevering and victorious as soldiers." The work of securing the promise of the American Revolution, Washington knew, would now shift from the battlefield to the political arena.

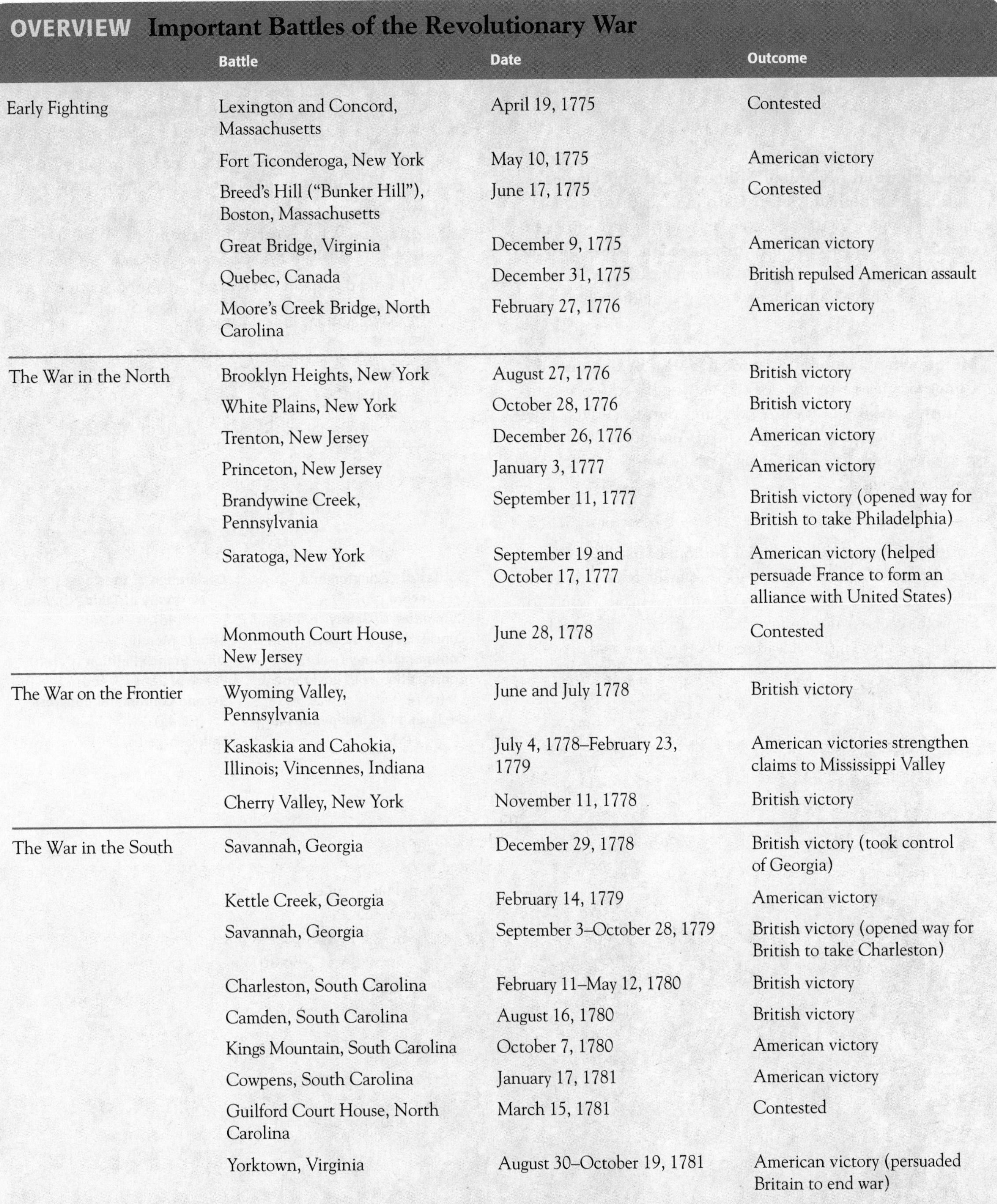

OVERVIEW Important Battles of the Revolutionary War

	Battle	Date	Outcome
Early Fighting	Lexington and Concord, Massachusetts	April 19, 1775	Contested
	Fort Ticonderoga, New York	May 10, 1775	American victory
	Breed's Hill ("Bunker Hill"), Boston, Massachusetts	June 17, 1775	Contested
	Great Bridge, Virginia	December 9, 1775	American victory
	Quebec, Canada	December 31, 1775	British repulsed American assault
	Moore's Creek Bridge, North Carolina	February 27, 1776	American victory
The War in the North	Brooklyn Heights, New York	August 27, 1776	British victory
	White Plains, New York	October 28, 1776	British victory
	Trenton, New Jersey	December 26, 1776	American victory
	Princeton, New Jersey	January 3, 1777	American victory
	Brandywine Creek, Pennsylvania	September 11, 1777	British victory (opened way for British to take Philadelphia)
	Saratoga, New York	September 19 and October 17, 1777	American victory (helped persuade France to form an alliance with United States)
	Monmouth Court House, New Jersey	June 28, 1778	Contested
The War on the Frontier	Wyoming Valley, Pennsylvania	June and July 1778	British victory
	Kaskaskia and Cahokia, Illinois; Vincennes, Indiana	July 4, 1778–February 23, 1779	American victories strengthen claims to Mississippi Valley
	Cherry Valley, New York	November 11, 1778	British victory
The War in the South	Savannah, Georgia	December 29, 1778	British victory (took control of Georgia)
	Kettle Creek, Georgia	February 14, 1779	American victory
	Savannah, Georgia	September 3–October 28, 1779	British victory (opened way for British to take Charleston)
	Charleston, South Carolina	February 11–May 12, 1780	British victory
	Camden, South Carolina	August 16, 1780	British victory
	Kings Mountain, South Carolina	October 7, 1780	American victory
	Cowpens, South Carolina	January 17, 1781	American victory
	Guilford Court House, North Carolina	March 15, 1781	Contested
	Yorktown, Virginia	August 30–October 19, 1781	American victory (persuaded Britain to end war)

Where to Learn More

Independence National Historical Park, Philadelphia, Pennsylvania. Independence Hall, where Congress adopted the Declaration of Independence, is the most historic building in Philadelphia. The informative website can be accessed through http://www.nps.gov/inde/index.htm.

Kings Mountain National Military Park and Cowpens National Battlefield, South Carolina. Situated approximately 20 miles apart, these were the sites of two battles in October 1780 and January 1781 that turned the tide of the war in the South. Both have museums and exhibits. The official site is accessible through http://www.nps.gov/kimo/index.htm.

Minute Man National Historical Park, Lexington and Concord, Massachusetts. There are visitors' centers at both Lexington and Concord with explanatory displays. Visitors may also follow the self-guided Battle Road Automobile Tour. The official website is accessible through http://www.nps.gov/archive/mima/vcenter.htm.

Yorktown Battlefield, Colonial National Historical Park, Yorktown, Virginia. The park commemorates the great American victory here. Innovative exhibits enable visitors to follow the course of the war from a multicultural perspective. The official website is accessible through http://www.nps.gov/york/index.htm.

Review Questions

1. Who were the loyalists, and how many of them were there? What attempts did the British and Americans make in 1775 to avert war? Why did these steps fail?
2. What actions did the Second Continental Congress take in 1775 and 1776? Why did it choose George Washington as the commander of its army? Why was he a good choice?
3. Why did Congress declare independence in July 1776? How did Americans justify their claim to independence?
4. Why were most of the early battles fought in the northern states? What effect did French entry into the war have on British strategy?
5. Why did the initial British victories in the South not win the war for them? Why did the United States ultimately win? What did it obtain by winning?
6. What were the effects of the war on Native Americans, African Americans, women, and American society in general?
7. What were some of the global effects of American independence?

Key Terms

Battles of Lexington and Concord (p. 145)
Committee of Safety (p. 144)
Conciliatory Proposition (p. 144)
Continental Army (p. 145)
Contract theory of government (p. 148)
Declaration of Independence (p. 148)
Declaration of the Causes and Necessity of Taking Up Arms (p. 146)
Minute Men (p. 144)
Olive Branch Petition (p. 146)
Peace of Paris (p. 160)
Second Continental Congress (p. 145)
Valley Forge (p. 154)

PEARSON myhistorylab™ Connections

Reinforce what you learned in this chapter by studying the many documents, images, maps, review tools, and videos available at **www.myhistorylab.com**.

Read and Review

Study and Review **Study Plan: Chapter 6**

Read the Document

Joseph Warren, "Account of the Battle of Lexington" (1775)

Thomas Jefferson, "Original Rough Draught" of the Declaration of Independence (1776)

Thomas Paine, A Freelance Writer Urges His Readers to Use Common Sense (1776)

John Adams to Abigail Adams (July 3, 1776)

Letter from a Revolutionary War Soldier (1776)

Peter Oliver, Origin and Progress of the American Rebellion: A Tory View (1781)

Royal Proclamation of Rebellion (1775)

The Declaration of Independence (1776)

See the Map

Revolutionary War: Northern Theater, 1775–1780

Territorial Claims in Eastern America after Treaty of Paris

The American Revolution

Research and Explore

Read the Document

Personal Journeys Online

From Then to Now Online: Anti-war Churches

Exploring America: Exploring the Geography of the American Revolution

Hear the Audio *The Liberty Song*

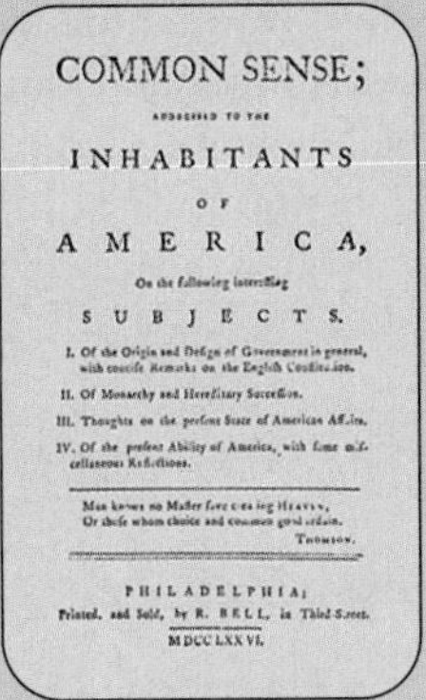
COMMON SENSE;
ADDRESSED TO THE
INHABITANTS
OF
AMERICA,
On the following interesting
SUBJECTS.

I. Of the Origin and Design of Government in general, with concise Remarks on the English Constitution.
II. Of Monarchy and Hereditary Succession.
III. Thoughts on the present State of American Affairs.
IV. Of the present Ability of America, with some miscellaneous Reflections.

Man knows no Master save creating Heaven,
Or those whom choice and common good ordain.
Thomson.

PHILADELPHIA;
Printed, and Sold, by R. BELL, in Third-Street.
MDCCLXXVI.

Watch the Video *The American Revolution as Different Americans Saw It*

Hear the Audio

Hear the audio files for Chapter 6 at **www.myhistorylab.com.**

Democratic Roots in New England Soil

WHY COULD New England society move from a firm condemnation of democracy to embracing the basic ideals that would lead to the Declaration of Independence and the Constitution of 1787?

The Puritans of New England were less than democratic in both beliefs and goals. Contrary to popular myth, Puritans did not migrate to the New World for the purpose of establishing religious freedom. They were seeking to establish a religious utopia to serve as what Governor John Winthrop called a "light upon a hill" for the world to copy. Once they created their utopia, Puritans wanted to keep it pristine, so they forbade the establishment of other religious doctrine, especially the Quaker and Roman Catholic faiths. In Puritan communities, nonconformist behavior was looked upon with deep suspicion, especially if it was religious in nature. The trials of Quaker evangelists and their public whippings and even execution provide evidence of Puritan intolerance.

However, the Puritans unknowingly planted the seeds for the very democracy that they hated as an abomination of the purity of God's social order. In the Mayflower Compact, Puritan separatists agreed to a governmental covenant that allowed for majority rule and later established the idea of the town meeting. In the charter of the Massachusetts Bay Colony, annual election of governors was provided for, as were the election of the colonial legislature and the General Court. Puritan customs forbade church ministers from serving in public office, an early version of separation of church and state although the Puritans would not see it in that way. Most important of all, the Puritans required that all church members be literate enough to read and interpret the Bible. Puritan laws directed all families to educate their children sufficiently to this purpose and towns were encouraged to establish free public schools. This emphasis upon the individual and his right to interpret the Bible, within certain doctrinal limits, without the intercession of a priest or minister would lead to political consequences.

A hundred years after the heyday of the Puritans, the political seeds that they planted would bear democratic fruit.

> We hold these truths to be self-evident, that all men are created equal, that they are endowed by their Creator with certain unalienable Rights, that among these are Life, Liberty and the pursuit of Happiness.—That to secure these rights, Governments are instituted among Men, deriving their just powers from the consent of the governed, . . .
>
> John Adams, *Coauthor of the Declaration of Independence*, 1776

Democracy I do not conceyve . . .

"The Signing of the Mayflower Compact," a painting by E. Percy Moran, shows the historic ceremonial signing on November 21, 1620, below the deck of the Mayflower.

Mayflower Compact (1620)

IN THE NAME OF GOD, AMEN. We, whose names are underwritten, the Loyal Subjects of our dread Sovereign Lord King James, by the Grace of God, of Great Britain, France, and Ireland, King, Defender of the Faith, &c. Having undertaken for the Glory of God, and Advancement of the Christian Faith, and the Honour of our King and Country, a Voyage to plant the first Colony in the northern Parts of Virginia; Do by these Presents, solemnly and mutually, in the Presence of God and one another, covenant and combine ourselves together into a civil Body Politick, for our better Ordering and Preservation, and Furtherance of the Ends aforesaid: And by Virtue hereof do enact, constitute, and frame, such just and equal Laws, Ordinances, Acts, Constitutions, and Officers, from time to time, as shall be thought most meet and convenient for the general Good of the Colony; unto which we promise all due Submission and Obedience. IN WITNESS whereof we have hereunto subscribed our names at Cape-Cod the eleventh of November, in the Reign of our Sovereign Lord King James, of England, France, and Ireland, the eighteenth, and of Scotland the fifty-fourth, Anno Domini; 1620.

The wooden Old Ship Meeting House in Hingham, Massachusetts, has served as church and community center for the Puritans of the town since 1681. The village meeting house hosted the annual town meeting where Puritans voted for their town selectmen (town council), voted on laws that would govern them for the next year, and openly debated town policy. All adult male members of the Church were usually allowed to vote.

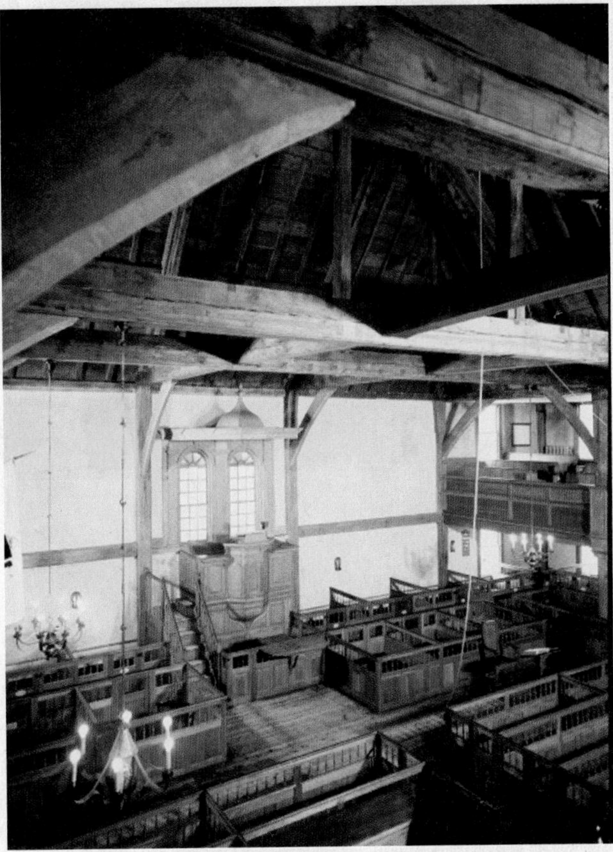

Fundamental Orders of Connecticut (1639)

It is Ordered, sentenced, and decreed, that there shall be yearly two General Assemblies or Courts, the one the second Thursday in April, the other the second Thursday in September following; the first shall be called the Court of Election, wherein shall be yearly chosen from time to time, so many Magistrates and other public Officers as shall be found requisite: Whereof one to be chosen Governor for the year ensuing and until another be chosen, and no other Magistrate to be chosen for more than one year: provided always there be six chosen besides the Governor, which being chosen and sworn according to an Oath recorded for that purpose, shall have the power to administer justice according to the Laws here established. . . .

It is Ordered, sentenced, and decreed, that the election of the aforesaid Magistrates shall be in this manner: every person present and qualified for choice shall bring in (to the person deputed to receive them) one single paper with the name of him written in it whom he desires to have Governor, and that he that hath the greatest number of papers shall be Governor for that year. And the rest of the Magistrates or public officers to be chosen in this manner: the Secretary for the time being shall first read the names of all that are to be put to choice and then shall severally nominate them distinctly, and every one that would have the person nominated to be chosen shall bring in one single paper written upon, and he that would not have him chosen shall bring in a blank; and every one that hath more written papers than blanks shall be a Magistrate for that year. . . .

It is Ordered, sentenced, and decreed, that the Secretary shall not nominate any person, nor shall any person be chosen newly into the Magistracy which was not propounded in some General Court before, to be nominated the next election; and to that end it shall be lawful for each of the Towns aforesaid by their deputies to nominate any two whom they conceive fit to be put to election. . . .

It is Ordered, sentenced, and decreed, that no person be chosen Governor above once in two years, and that the Governor be always a member of some approved Congregation, and formerly of the Magistracy within this Jurisdiction. . . .

Fundamental Agreement, or Original Constitution of the Colony of New Haven (June 4, 1639)

. . .

Query II. WHEREAS there was a covenant solemnly made by the whole assembly of free planters of this plantation, the first day of extraordinary humiliation, which we had after we came together, that as in matters that concern the gathering and ordering of a church, so likewise in all public officers which concern civil order, as choice of magistrates and officers, making and repealing laws, dividing allotments of inheritance, and all things of like nature, we would all of us be ordered by those rules which the scripture holds forth to US; this covenant was called a plantation covenant, to distinguish it from a church covenant. which could not at that time be made a church not being then gathered, but was deferred till a church might be gathered, according to GOD. It was demanded whether all the free planters do hold themselves bound by that covenant, in all businesses of that nature which are expressed in the covenant, to submit themselves to be ordered by the rules held forth in the scripture. . . .

Query III. THOSE who have desired to be received as free planters, and are settled in the plantation, with a purpose, resolution and desire, that they may be admitted into church fellowship, according to CHRIST, as soon as GOD shall fit them "hereunto, were desired to express it by holding up hands. According all did express this to be their desire and purpose by holding up their hands twice (viz.) at the proposal of it, and after when these written words were read unto them.

Query IV. All the free planters were called upon to express, whether they held themselves bound to establish such civil order as might best conduce to the securing of the purity and peace of the ordinance to themselves and their posterity according to GOD In answer hereunto they expressed by holding up their hands twice as before, that they held themselves bound to establish such civil order as might best conduce to the ends aforesaid.

7

The First Republic

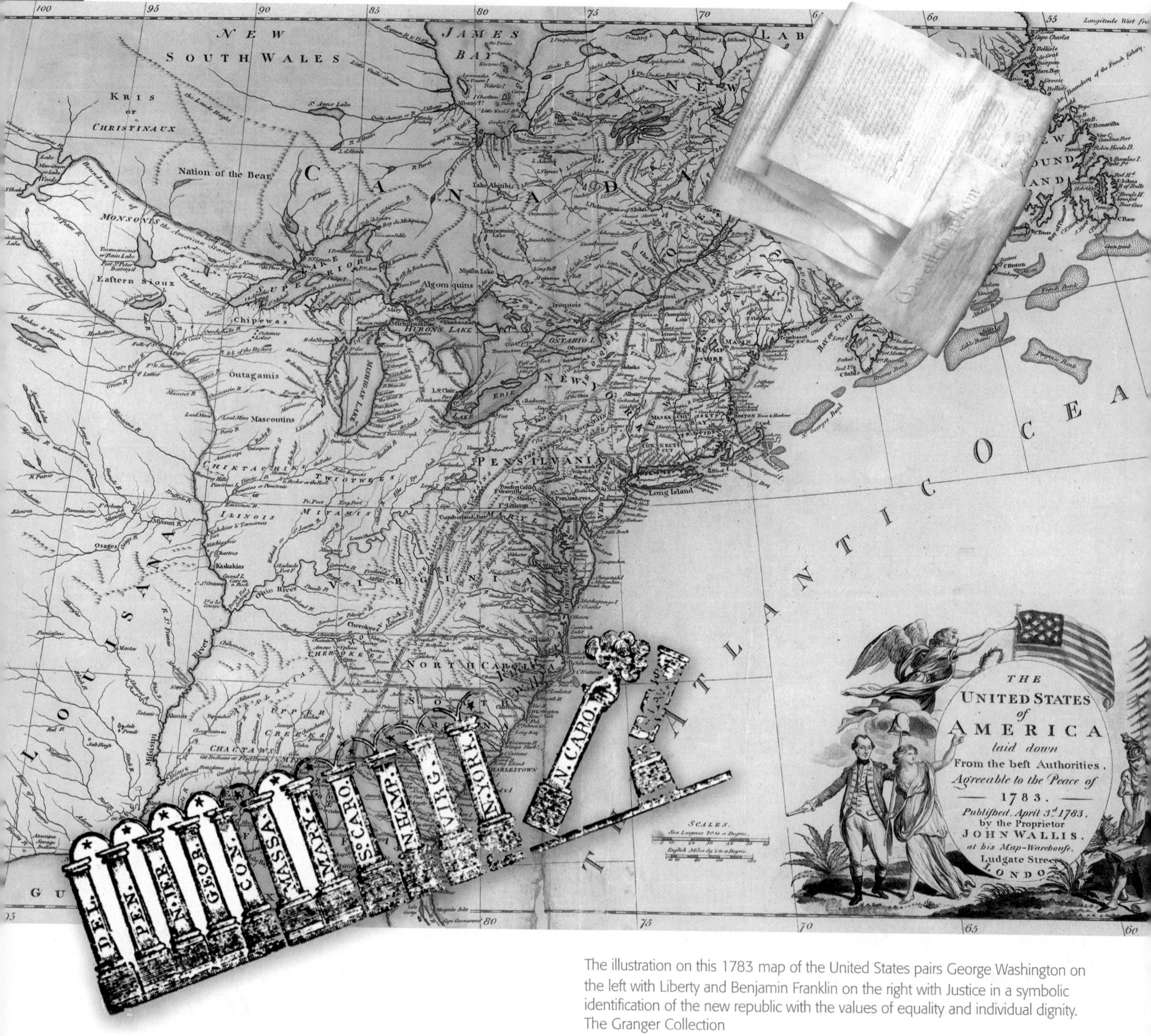

The illustration on this 1783 map of the United States pairs George Washington on the left with Liberty and Benjamin Franklin on the right with Justice in a symbolic identification of the new republic with the values of equality and individual dignity. The Granger Collection

Hear the Audio

Hear the audio files for Chapter 7 at **www.myhistorylab.com**.

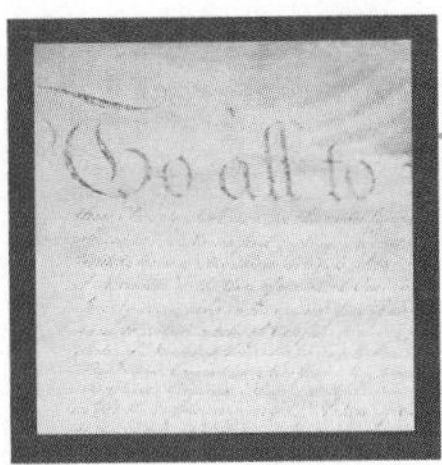

THE NEW ORDER OF REPUBLICANISM *(page 171)*

WHAT WERE the most significant weaknesses of the Articles of Confederation?

PROBLEMS AT HOME *(page 177)*

HOW DID economic problems lead to political conflict in the 1780s?

DIPLOMATIC WEAKNESSES *(page 182)*

WHAT STEPS did Britain and Spain take to block American expansion?

TOWARD A NEW UNION *(page 185)*

WHICH GROUPS in American society were most likely to support the Constitution? Why?

ONE AMERICAN JOURNEY

The jurors of the Commonwealth of Massachusetts upon their oath present that Moses Sash of Worthington . . . a negro man & Labourer being a disorderly, riotous & seditious person & minding & contriving as much as in him lay unlawfully by force of arms to stir up promote incite & maintain riots mobs tumults insurrections in this Commonwealth & to disturb impede & prevent the Government of the same & the due administration of justice in the same, & to prevent the Courts of justice from sitting as by Law appointed for that purpose & to promote disquiets, uneasiness, jealousies, animosities & seditions in the minds of the Citizens of this Commonwealth on the twentieth day of January in the year of our Lord Seventeen hundred & eighty seven & on divers other days & times as well before as since that time at Worthington . . . unlawfully & seditiously with force & arms did advise persuade invite incourage & procure divers persons . . . of this Commonwealth by force of arms to oppose this Commonwealth & the Government thereof & riotously to join themselves to a great number of riotous seditious persons with force & arms thus opposing this Commonwealth & the Government thereof . . . and in pursuance of his wicked seditious purposes . . . did procure guns, bayonets, pistols, swords, gunpowder, bullets, blankets & provisions & other warlike instruments offensive & defensive . . . & did cause & procure them to be carried & conveyed to the riotous & seditious persons as aforesaid in evil example to others to offend in like manner against the peace of the Commonwealth aforesaid & dignity of the same.

Source: Indictment of Moses Sash by the Supreme Judicial Court of Massachusetts for Suffolk County, April 9, 1787, cited in Sidney Kaplan and Emma Nogrady Kaplan, *The Black Presence in the Era of the American Revolution* (Amherst: University of Massachusetts Press, 1989), p. 259.

Read the **Document** at **www.myhistorylab.com**

Personal Journeys Online

- **William Shepard, Letter to Governor Bowdoin, Jan. 26, 1787. A militia captain describes the routing of the Shaysites at Springfield Arsenal.**
- **Henry Lee, Letter to George Washington, Oct. 1, 1786. One of Washington's former generals expresses his fears over the outbreak of agrarian insurgencies.**

THUS, in the dry, legalistic language of the highest court in Massachusetts was Moses Sash, a twenty-eight-year-old African American veteran of the Revolutionary War, indicted by a grand jury for his role in Shays's Rebellion. Named after its leader, Daniel Shays, another Revolutionary veteran, this armed insurgency pitted debt-ridden farmers in the western half of Massachusetts against conservative interests in the east. Farmers and laborers in western Massachusetts faced hard times in the 1780s. Faced with an unresponsive state legislature controlled by eastern merchants and creditors, angry farmers reacted much as they had during the revolutionary agitation against the British a decade earlier: They organized, protested, and shut down the county courts.

Routed in a battle at Springfield Arsenal in January 1787 by an army raised by Governor Bowdoin, the Shaysites fled into the hills. Nearly all of them, including Sash, were pardoned by the new administration of Governor John Hancock. Sash moved to Connecticut and died in poverty.

More than any other domestic disturbance in the 1780s, Shays's Rebellion dramatized the fragile nature and conflicting values of America's first republic under the Articles of Confederation. White Americans debated the meaning of liberty and whether greater powers should be granted to the very weak national government established by the Articles in 1781. Moses Sash and countless other African Americans—slave or free—insisted that the Revolution bequeathed a promise of greater human rights that extended to all Americans regardless of race. Americans favoring a stronger, more centralized government repeatedly cited Shays's Rebellion as an example of the impending chaos that would destroy the republic unless fundamental changes were made. Those changes came with the writing of the United States Constitution in 1787 and its ratification in 1788. ✦

CHRONOLOGY

1776	States begin writing the first constitutions.
1777	Articles of Confederation proposed.
1780s	English textile production begins to surge with new technological advances.
1781	Articles ratified.
1783	Americans celebrate independence and the peace treaty with Britain.
	British West Indies closed to U.S. traders.
1784	Onset of the postwar depression.
	Opening of China trade by the United States.
	Spain closes the Mississippi.
	Separatist plots in the West.
	Treaty of Fort Stanwix.
1785	Land Ordinance of 1785.
	States begin to issue more paper money.
	Treaty of Fort McIntosh.
1786	Shays's Rebellion breaks out.
	Jay-Gardoqui Treaty defeated.
	Annapolis Convention.
1787	Constitutional Convention at Philadelphia.
	Northwest Ordinance.
1788	Constitution ratified and goes into effect.
	Publication of *The Federalist*.

THE NEW ORDER OF REPUBLICANISM

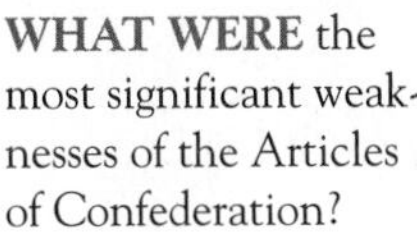

WHAT WERE the most significant weaknesses of the Articles of Confederation?

As royal authority collapsed during the Revolution, provincial congresses and committees assumed power in each of the former colonies. The Continental Congress, seeking to build support for the war effort, was concerned that these new institutions should have a firm legal and popular foundation. In May 1776, the Congress called on the colonies to form new state governments "under the authority of the people."

This call reflected the political philosophy of republicanism that animated the Revolution (see Chapter 6). To Americans, republicanism meant, first and foremost, that legitimate political authority derives from the people. Another key aspect of republicanism was the revolutionary idea that the people could define and limit governmental power through written constitutions. These core republican principles held that governmental authority should flow from the people, but it was not always clear just who was included in "the people."

Defining the People

Republicanism rested on the belief that the people were sovereign, but it also taught that political rights should be limited to those who owned private property. Only propertied people were thought to possess the independent will required for informed political judgment. This, in effect, restricted political participation to propertied white men. Virtually everyone else, property-less white men, servants legally bound to others, women, slaves, and most free black people, were denied political rights. As for Native Americans, they were outside the U.S. body politic and exercised political rights within their own nations.

Because the ownership of property was relatively widespread among white men, some 60 to 85 percent of adult white men could participate in politics, a far higher proportion than elsewhere in the world of the eighteenth century. The greatest concentration of the remaining 25 percent or so shut out of the political process were unskilled laborers and mariners living in port cities.

Women and the Revolution

The Revolution did little to change the traditional patriarchal assumption that politics and public life should be the exclusive domain of men. Women, according to republican beliefs, were part of the dependent class and belonged under the control of propertied men, their husbands and fathers.

With the exception of New Jersey, where women meeting the property qualifications were eligible to vote, the state constitutions of the Revolutionary era prohibited women from voting.

Under common law (the customary, largely unwritten, law that Americans had inherited from Britain), women surrendered their property rights at marriage unless they made special arrangements to the contrary. Legally and economically, husbands had complete control over their wives.

To be sure, some women saw in the political and social enthusiasm of the Revolution an opportunity to protest the most oppressive features of their subordination. Men, Eliza Wilkinson of South Carolina lamented, "won't even allow us liberty of thought and that is all I want." Such protests, however, had little enduring effect. Most women were socialized to accept that their proper place was in the home with their families.

Gender-specific language, including such terms as "men," "Freemen," "white male inhabitants," and "free white men," explicitly barred women from voting in almost all state constitutions of the 1770s. Only the New Jersey constitution of 1776 defined **suffrage,** the right to vote, in gender-free terms, extending it to all adults "worth fifty pounds." As a result, until 1807, when the state legislature changed the constitution, propertied women, including widows and single women, enjoyed the right to vote in New Jersey.

suffrage The right to vote in a political election.

Outside of the political realm, the Revolution did bring women a few limited gains. They benefited from slightly less restrictive divorce laws and gained somewhat greater access to educational and business opportunities, changes that reflected the relative autonomy of many women during the war when their men were off fighting. The perception of women's moral status also rose. As the Philadelphia physician Benjamin Rush argued in his *Thoughts upon Female Education* (1787), educated and morally informed women were needed to instruct "their sons in the principles of liberty and government." Often called republican motherhood, this more positive view of women's influence entrusted mothers with the responsibility of passing on republican virtues from one generation to the next.

QUICK REVIEW

Property, Race, Gender, and Citizenship

- Republicans limited political rights to white male property owners.
- 60 to 85 percent of adult white men owned property.
- The Revolution did not challenge exclusion of women from politics.

The Revolution and African Americans in the South. The Revolution had a more immediate impact on the lives of many African Americans, triggering the growth of free black communities and the development of an African American culture. Changes begun by the Revolution were the main factor in the tremendous increase of free blacks from a few thousand at mid-century to more than 100,000 by 1800 (see Figure 7–1). One key to this increase was a shift in the religious and intellectual climate. Revolutionary principles of liberty and equality and evangelical notions of human fellowship convinced many whites for the first time to challenge black slavery. As many whites grew more hostile to slavery, slaves in the North, drawing on republican political theory, submitted petitions for freedom to the new state legislatures and blacks everywhere began to seize opportunities for freedom.

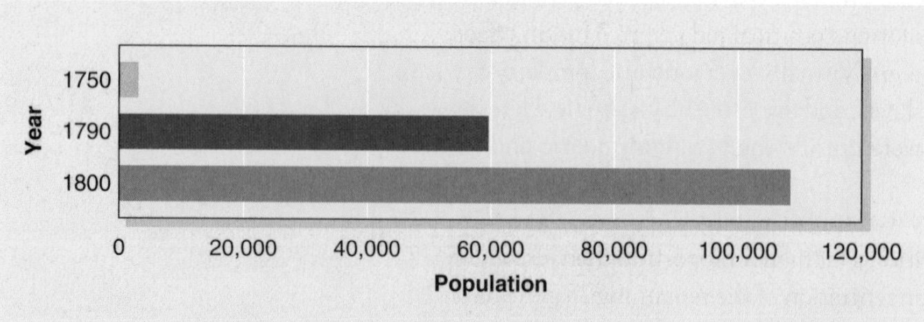

FIGURE 7–1 **Growth of the Free Black Population between 1750 and 1800** Gradual emancipation in the North, the freeing of many slaves by their owners in the South, and the opportunities for freedom offered by the Revolution, all contributed to an explosive growth in the free population of African Americans in the second half of the eighteenth century.

Data Source: A Century of Population Growth in the United States, 1790–1900 (1909). p. 80. Data for 1750 estimated.

Upwards of 50,000 slaves, or one in ten of those in bondage, gained their freedom as a result of the war. One route was through military service, which generally carried a promise of freedom. When the British began raising black troops, the Americans followed suit. All the states except Georgia and South Carolina recruited black regiments. Some 5,000 blacks served in the Continental Army along with Moses Sash, and they, like their counterparts in British units, were mostly slaves. Most of the slaves who gained freedom during the war, however, had fled their owners and made their way to the port cities of the North.

By making slave property generally less secure, the Revolution encouraged many masters to free their slaves. A manumission act passed by the Virginia assembly in 1782 (but tightened a decade later) allowed individual owners to free their slaves. As the number of free blacks increased, those still enslaved grew bolder in their efforts to gain freedom.

Read the **Document** at **www.myhistorylab.com** *A Free African American Petitions the Government for Emancipation of All Slaves (1777)*

Northern blacks and the Revolution. If the control mechanisms of slavery experienced some strain in the South during the Revolution, in the North, where slaves were only a small percentage of the population, they crumbled. Slaves pressured their owners for freedom by running away, damaging property, and committing arson. Most northern states ended slavery between 1777 and 1784. New York followed in 1799, and New Jersey in 1804. Nonetheless, although a majority of northern whites now agreed that slavery was incompatible a commitment to **natural rights** (the inherent human rights to life and liberty) and human freedom, they refused to sanction a sudden emancipation. The laws ending slavery in most of the northern states called for only the children of slaves to be freed, and only when they reached adulthood.

natural rights Political philosophy that maintains that individuals have an inherent right, found in nature and preceding any government or written law, to life and liberty.

Once free, northern blacks had to struggle to overcome white prejudice. Facing discrimination in jobs and housing, barred from juries, and denied a fair share of funds for schools, urban blacks had to rely on their own resources. With the help of the small class of property holders among them, they began establishing their own churches and self-help associations.

QUICK REVIEW

African Americans and the Revolution

- Revolutionary principles sparked some to challenge slavery.
- More than 50,000 slaves gained freedom as results of the war.
- By 1800 the free black population reached 100,000.

The Revolution's impact on Native Americans. Most Indian peoples had stayed neutral during the war or fought for the British (see Chapter 6). Just as the Americans sought to shake off British control, so the Indians, especially the western tribes and most of the Iroquois Confederation, sought to free themselves from American dominance. The British defeat was thus a double blow, depriving the Indians of a valuable ally and exposing them to the wrath of the victorious patriots.

The state governments, as well as the Confederation Congress, treated Indian lands as a prize of war to be distributed to white settlers. Territorial demands on the Indians escalated, and even the few tribes that had furnished troops for the American side struggled to maintain control over their homelands. As they did so, it was clear that white Americans did not consider Native Americans to be part of their republican society.

Most Native Americans did not want or expect equal rights within the new American republic. They viewed themselves as belonging to their own nations, composed of distinct villages and settlements, with a common culture and interests. They wanted political rights and control over the land within their nations. Above all, they wanted independence.

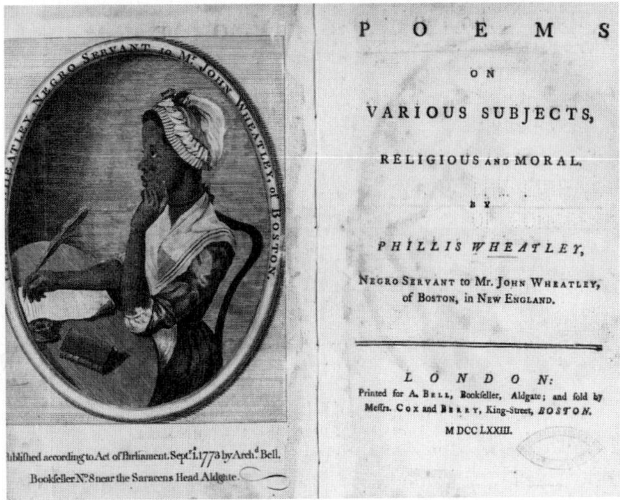

POEMS
ON
VARIOUS SUBJECTS,
RELIGIOUS AND MORAL.
BY
PHILLIS WHEATLEY,
NEGRO SERVANT to MR. JOHN WHEATLEY, of BOSTON, in NEW ENGLAND.

LONDON:
Printed for A. BELL, Bookseller, Aldgate; and sold by Messrs. COX and BERRY, King-Street, BOSTON.
M DCC LXXIII.

Phillis Wheatley was an acclaimed African American poet. Kidnapped into slavery as a child in Africa, she was a domestic slave to the Wheatley family of Boston when her first poems were published in 1773.

In seeking to defend their independence against the growing pressure of white Americans on their lands, Native Americans forged new confederacies in the 1780s that temporarily united them against a common enemy. They were encouraged in these efforts by the imperial powers of England and Spain, both of which sought to curb the westward expansion of the United States. Thus, the immediate impact of the

AMERICAN VIEWS

A Quaker Seeks Cooperative Action against Slavery

Quakers took the lead in pushing for the emancipation of slaves in the northern states. This letter, written in 1784 by James Pemberton, relates the efforts of a Pennsylvania Quaker to enlist the aid of British abolitionists in the cause of black freedom in the United States. It also outlines the struggles within the Society of Friends over admitting African Americans into membership.

- **What** plan of cooperation does Pemberton propose? What do you believe would be the keys to its success?
- **What** political bodies are cited for the delivery of antislavery petitions?
- **Why** were Quakers so reluctant to support the "unrestricted admission" of African Americans into their religious fellowship?
- **How** did some Quakers reason that racial intermarriage would upset a racial order ordained by Providence?

I am much obliged by the kindness in sending me the Essays on Slavery, the case of the oppressed blacks commands our attention to move in endeavors for their relief as opportunities are favorable; altho Congress has done as little in consequence of our address as your Parliament has in favor of your Petition, and I conclude on similar motives; An application is now about to be made by Friends to the Legislature of New Jersey on this Subject, and we have reprinted five hundred copies of the Petition of your yearly meeting and the Representation which followed it from your meeting . . . for general distribution among the people in these States, & the Rulers in particular, a fragment of a letter from T[homas] Day printed in London concise & serious has been reprinted by private procurement in newspapers & otherwise by which it has a general dispersion and will I hope prove useful.

The admission of members into our Religious Society is at all times a matter of weight, a base convincement of the rectitude of our principles and discipline, and a foundation sufficient without satisfactory proof of real conversion, the want of which has been productive of burdens & troubles to meetings in many instances, and in the case of Blacks, considerations of another nature occur which are of great importance, wherein friends here do not agree in sentiment tho religiously affected for the real welfare of those people, the concord of Society therefore requires a mature deliberate consideration of the Subject in a collective capacity, for which no occasion has yet offered and I know of no more than one instance of an application of this sort to any Monthly meeting; while some friends are advocates for an unrestricted admission, others plead if no limitation is proscribed they must become entitled to the privilege of intermarriage, and I believe there are few who would freely consent to such a union in their families which mixture some think would reverse the order of Divine Providence who in his wisdom inscrutable to us has been pleased to form distinction of Colour, for tho[ugh] of one blood he made all nations of men, yet it is also said he has fixed their habitation, which has been changed by avarice & ambition. However when the subject becomes necessary to be religiously discussed, I hope friends will be favored with the true spirit of judgment rightly determined &c.

Source: James Pemberton to James Phillips, in London, Nov. 18, 1784, Gilder Lehrman Collection of American History, 04237.

Revolution on Native Americans was a mixed one. On the one hand, the Revolution had created a new expansionist power in the United States that was intent on settling lands already occupied by Indians. On the other hand, American victory in the Revolution had broken the British monopoly of power in the region west of the Appalachian Mountains. Before the United States could consolidate its claim over the region, new imperial rivalries sprang up that allowed Native Americans to stake out a political middle ground between the competing powers. Throughout the 1780s, Native Americans continued to act as independent political agents in playing off outside powers against each other.

The State Constitutions

Ten new state constitutions were in place by the end of 1777. All these constitutions were written documents, a departure from the English practice of treating a constitution as a collection of customary rights and practices that had evolved over time. In the American view, a constitution was a formal expression of the people's sovereignty, a codification of the powers of government and the rights of citizenship that functioned as a fundamental law to which all public authority was held accountable.

Because Americans had come to associate tyranny with the privileges of royal governors, all the new state constitutions cut back sharply on executive power. Most important, for it struck at what patriots felt was the main source of executive domination and corruption, governors lost control over patronage, the power to appoint executive and judicial officials. As the new constitutions curbed the power of governors, they increased that of the legislatures, making them the focal point of government.

To make the legislatures more expressive of the popular will, the new constitutions included provisions that lowered property requirements for voting and officeholding, mandated annual elections, increased the number of seats in the legislatures, and made representation more proportional to the geographical distribution of population. Upper houses were made independent of the executive office and opened to popular election, as opposed to the colonial practice of having their members appointed by the governor.

In a final check on arbitrary power, each state constitution eventually included some form of a bill of rights that set explicit limits on the power of government to interfere in the lives of citizens. By 1784, the constitutions of all thirteen states had provisions guaranteeing religious liberty, freedom of the press, and a citizen's right to such fair legal practices as trial by jury.

QUICK REVIEW

New State Constitutions

- New constitutions guaranteed individual rights.
- Constitutions weakened tie between church and state.
- In general the legislature gained power at the expense of the executive.

Toward religious pluralism. The new constitutions weakened but did not always sever the traditional tie between church and state. Many states, notably in New England, levied taxes for the support of religion. The states of New England also continued to maintain Congregationalism as the established, or state-supported, religion, while allowing dissenting Baptists and Methodists to use funds from the compulsory religious taxes to support their ministers.

The mid-Atlantic states lacked the religious uniformity of New England. This pluralism checked legislative efforts to impose religious taxes or designate any denomination as the established church. In the South, where many Anglican (or Episcopalian) clergymen had been Tories, the Anglican Church lost its former established status.

Conflicting visions of republicanism. Although in general the executive lost power and the legislature gained power under the new state constitutions, the actual structure of each state government reflected the outcome of political struggles between radical and conservative visions of republicanism. The democratically inclined radicals wanted to open government to all male citizens. The conservatives wanted to limit government to an educated elite of substantial property holders. Although they agreed that government had to be derived from the people, most conservatives, like Jeremy Belknap of New Hampshire, thought that the people had to be "taught . . . that they are not able to govern themselves."

In South Carolina, where conservative planters gained the upper hand, the constitution mandated property qualifications that barred 90 percent of the state's white males from holding elective public office. By contrast, Pennsylvania had the most democratic and controversial constitution. Many of Pennsylvania's conservatives had discredited themselves during the Revolution by remaining neutral or loyal to the crown. The Scots-Irish farmers and Philadelphia artisans who stepped into the resulting political vacuum held an egalitarian view of republicanism. The constitution they pushed through in 1776 gave the vote to all free males who paid taxes, regardless of wealth, and eliminated property qualifications for officeholding. In addition, the constitution concentrated power in a unicameral (single-house) legislature, eliminating both the office of governor and the more elite upper legislative house. To prevent the formation of an entrenched class of officeholders, the constitution's framers also required legislators to stand for election annually and barred them from serving more than four years out of seven.

Unlike the colonial assemblies, the new state legislatures included substantially more artisans and small farmers and were not controlled by men of wealth. The proportion of legislators who came from a common background—those with property valued under £200—more than tripled to 62 percent in the North and more than doubled in the South from the 1770s to the 1780s.

Articles of Confederation Written document setting up the loose confederation of states that comprised the first national government of the United States.

The Articles of Confederation

Once the Continental Congress decided on independence in 1776, it needed to create a legal basis for a permanent union of the states. According to the key provision of the **Articles of Confederation** that the Congress finally submitted to the states in November 1777, "Each State retains its sovereignty, freedom and independence, and every power, jurisdiction and right, which is not by this confederation expressly delegated to the United States, in Congress assembled." The effect was to create a loose confederation of autonomous states.

The powers the Articles of Confederation delegated to the central government were extremely limited, in effect little more than those already exercised by the Continental Congress. There were no provisions for a national judiciary or a separate executive branch of government. The Articles made Congress the sole instrument of national authority but restricted it with a series of constitutional safeguards that kept it from threatening the interests of the states.

The Congress had authority primarily in the areas of foreign policy and national defense. It could declare war, make peace, conduct foreign affairs, negotiate with Native Americans, and settle disputes between the states. It had no authority, however, to raise troops or impose taxes; it could only ask the states to supply troops and money and hope that they would comply.

Most states quickly ratified the Articles of Confederation, but Maryland stubbornly held out until March 1781. Because they needed the approval of all thirteen states, only then did the Articles officially take effect. The issue in Maryland concerned the unsettled lands in the West between the Appalachian Mountains and the Mississippi River (see Map 7–1). Some states claimed these lands by virtue of their colonial charter rights, and led by Virginia and Massachusetts, they insisted on maintaining control over these territories. The so-called landless

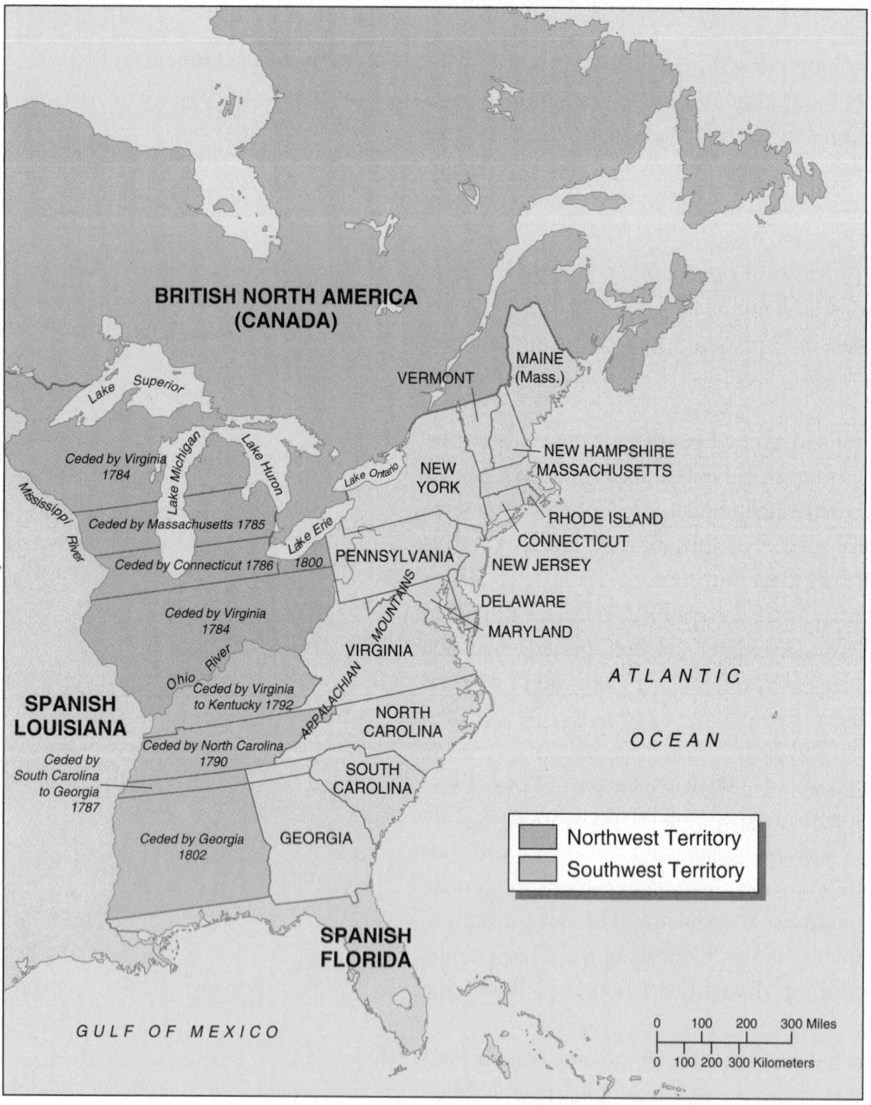

MAP 7–1 **Cession of Western Lands by the States** Eight states had claims to lands in the West after the Revolution, and their willingness to cede them to the national government was an essential step in the creation of a public domain administered by Congress.

Why did the question of control of western lands divide the states both during and after the Revolution? Which states were most in favor of federal control of western lands? Why?

states—those with no claim to the West—insisted that the territories should be set aside as a national domain, a reserve of public land controlled by Congress for the benefit of all the states.

Threatened by the British presence in the Chesapeake area in early 1781, Virginia finally broke the impasse over the Articles. Though it retained control of Kentucky, Virginia gave up its claim in the West to a vast area extending north of the Ohio River. In turn, Maryland, the last holdout among the landless states and now desperate for military aid from the Congress, agreed to ratify the Articles.

QUICK REVIEW

Powers of the Central Government under the Articles of Confederation

- No national judiciary.
- No separate executive branch.
- Congress sole national authority.
- No congressional authority to raise troops or impose taxes.

PROBLEMS AT HOME

HOW DID economic problems lead to political conflict in the 1780s?

Neither prosperity nor political stability accompanied the return of peace in 1783. The national government struggled to avoid bankruptcy, and in 1784, an economic depression struck. As fiscal problems deepened, creditor and debtor groups clashed angrily in state legislatures. When legislatures passed measures that provided relief to debtors at the expense of creditors, the creditors decried what they saw as the interference of ignorant majorities with the rights of private property. Raising the cry of "legislative despotism," the abuse of power by tyrannical lawmakers, the creditors joined their voices to those who early on had wanted the power of the states curbed by a stronger central government. The only solid accomplishment of the Confederation Congress during this troubled period was to formulate an orderly and democratic plan for the settlement of the West.

THE FISCAL CRISIS

The Continental Congress and the states had incurred heavy debts to finance the Revolutionary War. Unable to impose and collect sufficient taxes to cover the debts and without reserves of gold or silver, they had little choice but to borrow funds and issue certificates, or bonds, pledging repayment. By the end of the war in 1781, the national debt stood at $11 million. As Congress issued new securities to settle claims by soldiers and civilians, the debt rose to $28 million within just a few years.

The Congress never did put its tottering finances on a sound footing. Its fiscal problems ultimately discredited the Articles of Confederation in the eyes of the **nationalists,** a loose bloc of congressmen, army officers, and public creditors who wanted to strengthen the Confederation at the expense of the states. The nationalists first began to organize in the dark days of 1780 and 1781, when inflation was rampant, the army was going unpaid, the Congress had ceased paying interest on the public debt, and the war effort itself seemed in danger of collapsing. Galvanized by this crisis, the nationalists rallied behind Robert Morris, a Philadelphia merchant appointed as superintendent of finance for the Confederation government.

nationalists Group of leaders in the 1780s who spearheaded the drive to replace the Articles of Confederation with a stronger central government.

Morris sought to enhance national authority through a bold program of financial and political reform. He began by securing a charter from Congress in 1781 for the Bank of North America, the nation's first commercial bank. Morris temporarily brought order and economy to the nation's finances. Nonetheless, he was blocked in his efforts to gain the taxing power that was essential for restoring the shattered credit of the Confederation government.

In 1781, Morris proposed a national impost, or tariff, of 5 percent on imported goods. Because this was a national tax, it required an amendment to the Articles of Confederation and the consent of all thirteen states. Twelve of the states quickly ratified the impost amendment, but Rhode Island—critically dependent on its own import duties to finance its war debt—rejected it. When a revised impost plan was considered two years later, New York blocked its passage.

The failure of the impost tax was one of many setbacks that put the nationalists temporarily on the defensive. With the conclusion of peace in 1783, confidence in state government returned, taking the edge off calls to vest the central government with greater authority. The states continued to balk at supplying the money requisitioned by Congress and denied the Congress even limited authority to regulate foreign commerce. Most ominously for the nationalist cause, the states began to assume responsibility for part of the national debt. As Morris had warned in 1781, such a policy entailed "a principle of disunion . . . which must be ruinous." Without the power to tax, the Congress was a hostage to the sovereignty of the individual states with no real authority over the nation's economic affairs. When the economy plunged into a severe depression in 1784, Congress could only look on helplessly.

Economic Depression

During the Revolutionary War, Britain closed its markets to American goods. After the war, the British continued this policy, hoping to keep the United States weak and dependent. Meanwhile, British merchants were happy to satisfy America's pent-up demand for consumer goods after the war. Cheap British imports inundated the American market, and coastal merchants made them available to inland traders and shopkeepers by extending easy credit terms. In turn, these local businessmen sold the goods to farmers and artisans in the interior. Ultimately, however, the British merchants required payment in hard currency, gold and silver coins. Without access to its former export markets, America's only source of hard currency was foreign loans obtained by Congress and what money the French army had spent during the war. This was soon exhausted, and America's trade deficit with Britain—the excess of imports over exports—ballooned in the early 1780s (see Figure 7–2).

The result was an immense bubble of credit that finally burst in 1784, triggering a depression that would linger for most of the decade. As merchants began to press debtors for immediate payment, prices collapsed (they fell more than 25 percent between 1784 and 1786), and debtors were unable to pay. The best most could hope for was to avoid bankruptcy.

South Street Seaport Museum, New York City, New York
http://seany.org

In the cities, wages fell 25 percent between 1785 and 1789, and workers began to organize. They called for tariffs to protect them from cheap British imports and for legislative measures to promote American manufacturers. In the countryside, farmers faced lawsuits for the collection of debts and the dread possibility of losing their land.

With insufficient money in circulation to raise prices and reverse the downturn, the depression fed on itself. Congress was powerless to raise cash and was unable to pay off its old debts, including what it owed to the Revolutionary soldiers. Many state governments made things worse by imposing heavy taxes payable in the paper money they had issued during the Revolution. The result was to further reduce the amount of money in circulation, thus increasing deflationary pressures and forcing prices still lower.

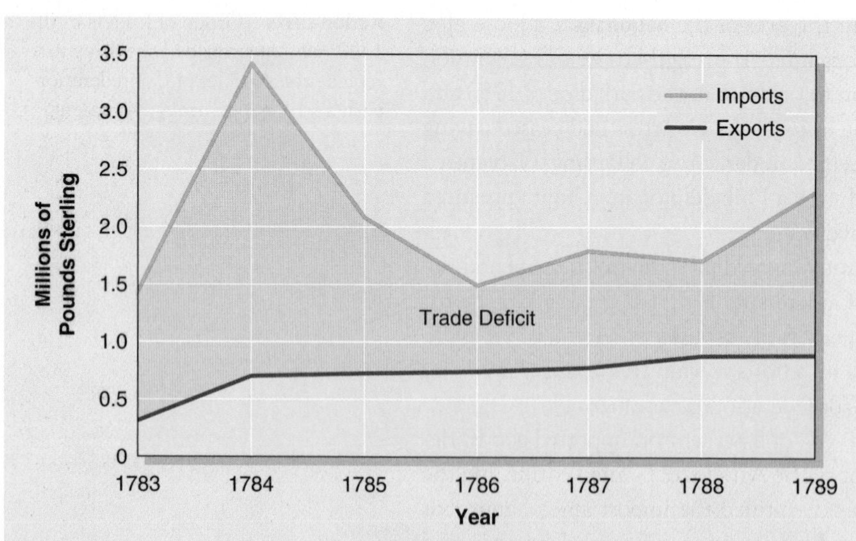

FIGURE 7–2 American Exports to and Imports from Britain between 1783 and 1789
During the 1780s, the United States imported far more from Britain than it exported there. The resulting huge trade deficit drained the country of gold and silver and was a major factor in the credit crisis that triggered an economic depression in the middle of the decade.

Data Source: U.S. Bureau of the Census, *Historical Statistics of the United States: Colonial Times to 1970*, pt. 2 (1975), p. 1176.

Britain's trade policies caused particular suffering among New England merchants. No longer protected under the old Navigation Acts as British vessels, American ships were now barred from most ports in the British trading empire. Incoming cargoes from the West Indies to New England fell off sharply, and the market for whale oil and fish, two of New England's major exports, dried up.

In the southern states, British policies compounded the problem of recovering from the physical damage and labor disruptions inflicted by the war. Some 10 percent of the region's slaves had fled during the war, and production levels on plantations fell in the 1780s. Chesapeake planters needed a full decade to restore the prewar output of tobacco, and a collapse in tobacco prices in 1785 left most of them in the same chronic state of indebtedness that had plagued them on the eve of the Revolution.

Farther south, in the Carolina low country, the plantation economy was crippled. War damage had been extensive, and planters piled up debts to purchase additional slaves and repair their plantations and dikes. Burdened by new British duties on American rice, planters saw their rice exports fall by 50 percent.

By the late 1780s, the worst of the depression was over and an upturn was under way in the mid-Atlantic states. Food exports to continental Europe were on the rise, and American merchants were developing new trading ties with India and China. Commercial treaties with the Dutch, Swedes, and Prussians also opened up markets that had been closed to the colonists. Nonetheless, a full recovery had to await the 1790s.

As the economy stagnated in the 1780s, the population was growing rapidly. There were 50 percent more Americans in 1787 than there had been in 1775. As a result, living standards fell and economic conflict dominated the politics of the states during the Confederation period.

QUICK REVIEW

Debt and the Balance of Trade

- Britain sought to keep America weak and dependent.
- Trade imbalance soared in the 1780s.
- Collapse of credit bubble in 1784 led to depression.

The Economic Policies of the States

The depression had political repercussions in all the states. Britain was an obvious target of popular anger, and merchants, artisans, and workers, especially in the North, pushed for tariff barriers against cheap British goods. Most northern states imposed anti-British measures, but these varied from state to state, limiting their impact and producing squabbles when goods imported in one state were shipped to another.

State legislatures in the North passed tariffs on foreign goods, but the lack of a uniform national policy doomed their efforts. Shippers evaded high tariffs by bringing their cargoes in through states with no tariffs or less restrictive ones. States without ports, such as New Jersey and North Carolina, complained of economic discrimination. When they purchased foreign goods from a neighboring shipping state, they were forced to pay part of the tariff cost, but all the revenue from the tariff accrued to the importing state.

Tariff policies also fed sectional tensions between northern and southern states that undermined efforts to confer on the Congress the power to regulate commerce. The agrarian states of the South, which had little in the way of mercantile or artisan interests to protect, generally favored free trade policies that encouraged British imports. Southern planters were also happy to take advantage of the low rates charged by British ships for transporting their crops to Europe; by doing so, they put pressure on northern shippers to reduce their rates.

The most bitter divisions exposed by the depression of the 1780s, however, were not between states but between debtors and creditors within states. As the value of debt securities the states had issued to raise money dropped during the Revolutionary War, speculators bought them up for a fraction of their face value from farmers and soldiers desperate for cash. The speculators then pressured the states to raise taxes and repay the debts in full in hard currency. Wealthy landowners and merchants likewise supported higher taxes and the rapid repayment of debts in hard currency.

Arrayed against these creditor groups by the mid-1780s was a broad coalition of debtors: middling farmers, small shopkeepers, artisans, laborers, and people who had overextended themselves speculating in western land. The debtors wanted the states to issue paper money that they could use instead of hard money—gold and silver—to pay their debts. The paper money would have an inflationary effect, raising wages and the prices of farm commodities and reducing the value of debts contracted in hard currency.

Shays's Rebellion. This was the economic context in which **Shays's Rebellion** exploded in the fall of 1786. Farm foreclosures and imprisonments for failure to pay debts had skyrocketed in western Massachusetts. When the creditor and seaboard interests in the legislature refused to pass any relief measures, some 2,000 farmers took up arms against the state government in Shays's Rebellion.

Shays's Rebellion An armed movement of debt-ridden farmers in western Massachusetts in the winter of 1786–1787. The rebellion created a crisis atmosphere.

Read the Document at **www.myhistorylab.com** *Military Reports on Shays's Rebellion (1787)*

Outside of western Massachusetts, discontented debtors generally stopped short of armed resistance because of their success in changing the monetary policy of their states. In 1785 and 1786, seven states enacted laws for new paper money issues. In most cases, the result was a qualified success. Controls on the supply of the new money kept it from depreciating rapidly, so that its inflationary effect was mild. Combined with laws that prevented or delayed creditors from seizing property from debtors to satisfy debts, the currency issues helped keep a lid on popular discontent.

The most notorious exception to this pattern of fiscal responsibility was in Rhode Island. A rural party that gained control of the Rhode Island legislature in 1786 pushed through a currency law that flooded the state with paper money that could be used to pay all debts. Creditors who balked at accepting the new money at face value were subject to heavy penalties. Shocked, they went into hiding or left the state entirely, and merchants denounced the law as outright fraud.

Debtors versus conservatives. The actions of the debtor party in Rhode Island alarmed conservatives everywhere, confirming their fears that legislative bodies dominated by common farmers and artisans rather than, as before the Revolution, by men of wealth and social distinction, were dangerous. Conservatives, creditors, and nationalists alike now spoke of a democratic tyranny that would have to be checked if the republic were to survive and protect its property holders.

Congress and the West

The Peace of Paris and the surrender of charter claims by the states gave the Congress control of a magnificent expanse of land between the Appalachian Mountains and the Mississippi River. This was the first American West. In what would prove the most enduring accomplishment of the Confederation government, the Congress set forth a series of effective provisions for its settlement, governance, and eventual absorption into the Union.

This clash between Shays's rebels and government troops at the Springfield arsenal marked the violent climax of the agrarian protests of the 1780s.

Asserting for the national government the right to formulate Indian policy, the Congress negotiated a series of treaties with the Indians beginning in 1784 for the abandonment of their land claims in the West. By threatening to use military force, congressional commissioners in 1784 coerced the Iroquois Confederation of New York to cede half of its territory to the United States in the Treaty of Fort Stanwix. Similar tactics in 1785 resulted in the Treaty of Fort McIntosh, in which the Wyandots, Chippewas, Delawares, and Ottawas ceded much of their land in Ohio. Against the opposition of states intent on grabbing Indian lands for themselves, Congress resolved in 1787 that its treaties were binding on all the states. And anxious for revenue, Congress insisted on payment from squatters who had filtered into the West before provisions had been made for land sales.

The most pressing political challenge was to secure the loyalty of the West to the new and fragile Union. To satisfy the demands of settlers for self-government, the Congress resolved as early as 1779 that new states would be carved out of the western domain with all the rights of the original states. An early plan for organizing the territories, the Ordinance of 1784, was largely the work of Thomas Jefferson. In it, he proposed to create ten districts, or territories, each of which could apply for admission as a state when its population equaled that of the free inhabitants in the least populous of the existing states. Jefferson also proposed that settlers be permitted to choose their own officials, and he called for the prohibition of slavery in the West after 1800. Shorn of its no-slavery features, the ordinance passed Congress but was never put into practice.

As settlers and speculators began pouring into the West in 1784, however, the Congress was forced to move quickly to formulate a policy for conveying its public land into private hands. If it could not regulate land sales and pass on clear titles, Congress would, in effect, have surrendered its claim to govern.

The Congress responded with the **Land Ordinance of 1785.** The crucial feature of this seminal legislation was its stipulation that public lands be surveyed in a rectangular grid pattern before being offered for sale (see Figure 7–3). By requiring that land first be platted into townships of 36 uniform sections of 640 acres each, the ordinance adopted the New England system of land settlement, an approach that promoted compact settlements and produced undisputed land titles.

Congress also attempted to attract a certain type of settler to the West by offering the plots of 640 acres at the then-hefty sum of no less than $640, or $1 per acre, payable in hard currency or its equivalent. The goal here was to keep out the shiftless poor and reserve the West for enterprising and presumably law-abiding farm families who could afford the entry cost. Concerned about westerners' reputation for lawlessness and afraid that the primitive living conditions might cause them to lapse into savagery, Congress also set aside the income from the sale of the sixteenth section in each township for the support of public schools.

Before any land sales occurred under the Ordinance of 1785, impatient settlers continued to push north of the Ohio River and claim homesteads as squatters. They clashed both with local Indian tribes and with the troops sent by the Congress to evict them. Impatient with the slow

QUICK REVIEW

Congressional Indian Policy

- Negotiated treaties for the abandonment of Indian land claims in the West.
- Made treaties binding on all states.
- Used the threat of military force to coerce Indians to cede their lands.

Land Ordinance of 1785 Act passed by Congress under the Articles of Confederation that created the grid system of surveys by which all subsequent public land was made available for sale.

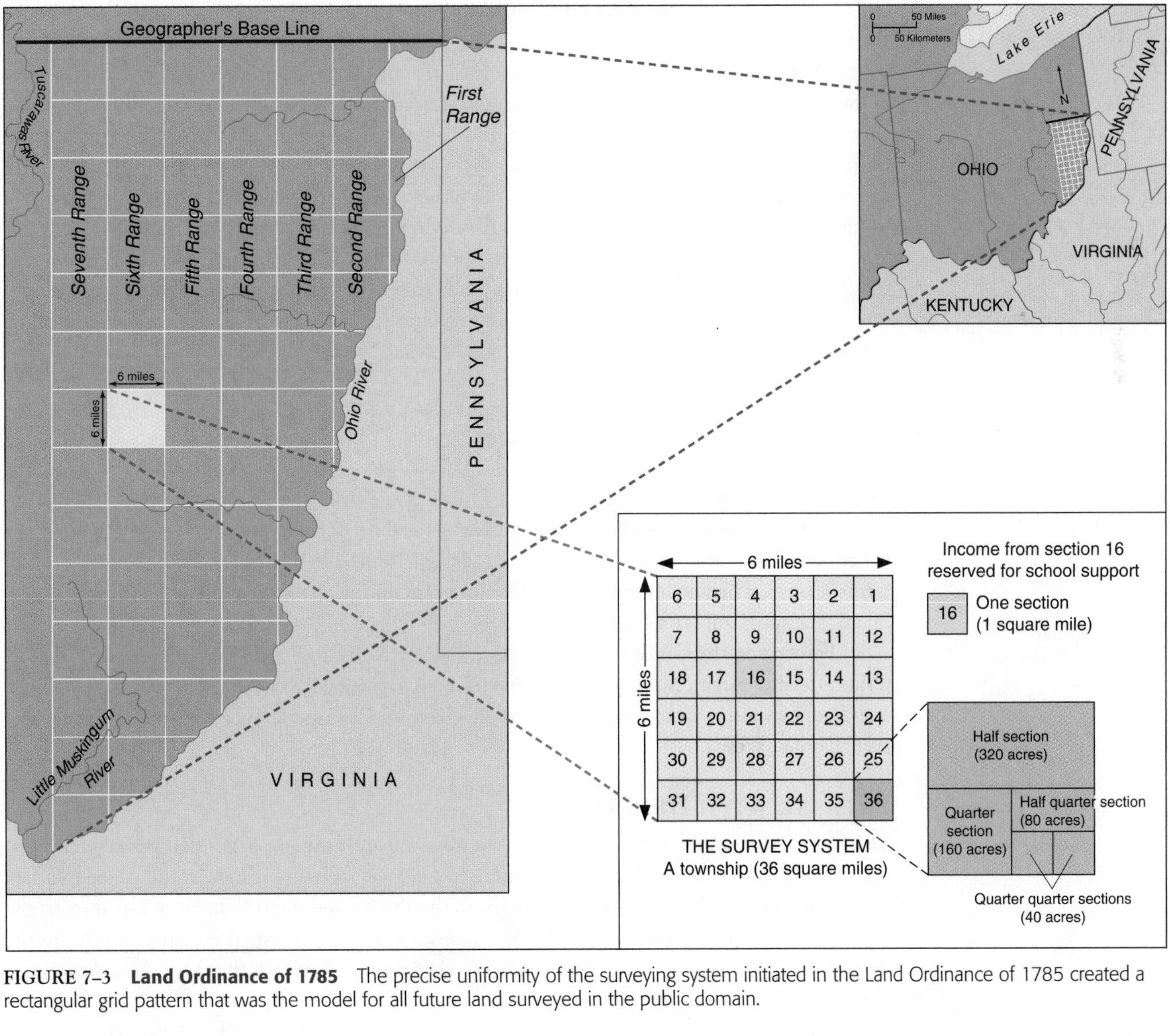

FIGURE 7–3 **Land Ordinance of 1785** The precise uniformity of the surveying system initiated in the Land Ordinance of 1785 created a rectangular grid pattern that was the model for all future land surveyed in the public domain.

process of surveying, the Congress sold off 1.5 million acres to a group of New England speculators organized as the Ohio Company. The speculators bought the land with greatly depreciated loan-office certificates that had been issued to Revolutionary War veterans, and their cost per acre averaged less than 10 cents in hard money. They now pressed their allies in Congress to establish a governmental structure for the West that would protect their investment by bringing the unruly elements in the West under control.

Both the Congress and speculators wanted political stability and economic development in the West and a degree of supervision for settlers. What was needed, wrote James Monroe of Virginia, were temporary controls—made acceptable by the promise of eventual statehood—that "in effect" would place the western territories under "a colonial government similar to that which prevail'd in these States previous to the revolution." The **Northwest Ordinance of 1787**, the most significant legislative act of the Confederation Congress, filled this need, creating a phased process for achieving statehood that neatly blended public and private interests.

Northwest Ordinance of 1787
Legislation that prohibited slavery in the Northwest Territories and provided the model for the incorporation of future territories into the union as coequal states.

Southwest Ordinance of 1790
Legislation passed by Congress that set up a government with no prohibition on slavery in U.S. territory south of the Ohio River.

According to the ordinance, controls on a new territory were to be strictest in the early stage of settlement, when Congress would appoint a territorial government consisting of a governor, a secretary, and three judges. When a territory reached a population of 5,000 adult males, those with 50 acres of land or more could elect a legislature. The actions of the legislature, however, were subject to an absolute veto by the governor. Once a territory had a population of 60,000, the settlers could draft a constitution and apply for statehood "on an equal footing with the original states in all respects whatsoever."

QUICK REVIEW

Slavery and New States

- Northwest Ordinance of 1787 establishes political structure for new territories.
- Northwest Ordinance prohibited slavery in the Northwest.
- Southwest Ordinance of 1790 allowed slavery in the region south of the Ohio River.

Most significant, it prohibited slavery. Southern congressmen agreed to the ban, in part because they saw little future for slavery in the region. More important, they expected slavery to be permitted in the region south of the Ohio River that was still under the administrative authority of Virginia, North Carolina, and Georgia in the 1780s. Indeed, slavery was allowed in this region when the **Southwest Ordinance of 1790** brought it under national control, a decision that would have grave consequences in the future sectionalization of the United States.

Although the Northwest Ordinance applied only to the national domain north of the Ohio River, it provided the organizational blueprint by which all future territory was brought into the Union. It went into effect immediately and set the original Union on a course of dynamic expansion through the addition of new states.

DIPLOMATIC WEAKNESSES

WHAT STEPS did Britain and Spain take to block American expansion?

In the international arena of the 1780s, the United States was a weak and often ridiculed nation. Under the Articles of Confederation, the Congress had the authority to negotiate foreign treaties but no economic or military power to enforce their terms. Unable to regulate commerce or set tariffs, Congress had no leverage with which to pry open the restricted trading empires of France, Spain, and most important, Britain.

France and the United States, allies during the Revolutionary War, remained on friendly terms after it. Britain, however, treated its former colonies with contempt, and Spain was also openly antagonistic. Both of these powers sought to block American expansion into the trans-Appalachian West.

Impasse with Britain

The Confederation Congress was unable to resolve any of the major issues that poisoned Anglo-American relations in the 1780s. Key among those issues were provisions in the peace treaty of 1783 that concerned prewar American debts to the British and the treatment of Loyalists by the patriots. Britain used what it claimed to be America's failure to satisfy these provisions to justify its own violations of the treaty. The result was a diplomatic deadlock that hurt American interests in the West and in foreign trade.

Article 4 of the peace treaty called for the payment of all prewar debts at their "full value in sterling money"—that is, in gold or silver coin. Among the most numerous of those with outstanding debts to British creditors were tobacco planters in the Chesapeake region of Virginia and Maryland. During the Revolution, the British army had carried off and freed many of the region's slaves without compensating the planters. Still angry, the planters were in no mood to repay their debts. Working out a scheme with their respective legislatures, they agreed only to pay the face value of their debts to their state treasuries in state or Continental paper money. Since this money was practically worthless, the planters in effect repudiated their debts.

During the Revolution, all the states had passed anti-Loyalist legislation, and many state governments had seized Loyalists' lands and goods, selling them to raise revenue for the war effort. Articles 5 and 6 of the peace treaty pledged the Congress to "recommend" to the states that they stop persecuting Loyalists and restore confiscated Loyalist property. But wartime animosities remained high, ebbing only gradually during the 1780s. Thus, the states were slow to rescind their punitive legislation or allow the recovery of confiscated property.

Combined with the matter of the unpaid debts, the continued failure of the states to make restitution to the Loyalists gave the British a convenient pretext to hold on to the forts in the West that they had promised to relinquish in the Treaty of Paris. Their refusal to abandon the forts, which extended from Lake Champlain in upstate New York westward along the Great Lakes, was part of an overall strategy to keep the United States weak, divided, and small. The continued British presence in the region effectively shut Americans out of the fur trade with the Indians. Moreover, it insulted the sovereignty of the United States and threatened the security of its northern frontier.

For all of the British provocations in the West, American officials viewed Britain's retaliatory trade policies as the gravest threat to American security and prosperity. John Adams, the American minister to London, concluded that the British would never lift their trading and shipping restrictions until forced to do so by a uniform American system of discriminatory duties on British goods. Retaliatory navigation acts by individual states did little good because they left the British free to play one state against another. Only with a strong, centralized government could Americans fashion a navigation system that would command Britain's respect.

QUICK REVIEW

British Foreign Policy

- Britain sought to keep the United States small, divided, and weak.
- Maintained forts in the West.
- Exploited divisions among Americans.
- Pursued retaliatory trade policies.

SPAIN AND THE MISSISSIPPI RIVER

At the close of the Revolutionary War, Spain reimposed barriers on American commerce within its empire. Spain also refused to recognize the southern and western boundaries of the United States as specified in the treaty with Britain in 1783, holding out instead for a more northerly border. And of greatest consequence, it denied the claim of the United States to free navigation of the entire length of the Mississippi River.

The Mississippi question was explosive because on its resolution hinged American settlement and control of the entire western region south of the Ohio River. Only with access to the Mississippi and the commercial right of deposit at New Orleans—that is, the right to transfer cargoes to oceangoing vessels—could the region's farmers, then mostly in what would become Tennessee and Kentucky, profitably reach national and international markets.

In the wake of the Revolution, the settlers of Kentucky, which was still part of Virginia, and Tennessee, which was still part of North Carolina, flirted with the idea of secession. Impatient to secure both political independence and the economic benefits that would come with access to the Mississippi, the separatists were not particular about whom they dealt with. They became entangled in a web of diplomatic intrigue that included the Spanish, the Indians, and American officials east of the mountains.

Spain sought to use the divided loyalties of American speculators and frontier settlers to its advantage, employing some of them as spies and informers. Spain likewise sought to exploit divisions among Indian groups. In a bewildering variety of treaties negotiated by the Congress, individual southern states, and land speculators, white Americans laid claim to much of the

GLOBAL CONNECTIONS

FOREIGN THREATS

"I think I have done all possible to make it possible for the Government of New Orleans to reap benefit from the present situation of the United States. . . . These people intend to live on friendly terms with Spain and we no longer hear the threats we formerly heard . . . we must not neglect them. I think time will bring them to the King."

In this letter of 1788 to the Spanish secretary of state, Don Diego de Gardoqui, the Spanish representative in Philadelphia, outlined Spain's efforts in the 1780s to detach the American settlements in Kentucky from the United States and draw them into an economic alliance with Spanish Louisiana. The goal was to protect Louisiana by both weakening the United States and expanding trading opportunities for the American goods and services desired by the Spanish subjects of Louisiana. Westward expansion by Americans was inevitable, but Spain hoped to control it and turn it to its advantage by offering trading rights on the Mississippi River that would lead to a partnership with the Spanish colony in New Orleans.

The efforts of Spain to draw Kentuckians into its empire, combined with the presence of the British in Canada and the willingness of both of these foreign powers to subsidize Native Americans as they fought to protect their tribal lands against encroachments by white settlers, threatened any effective American control of the trans-Appalachian territory. Meanwhile, British trading restrictions had largely succeeded in reducing the United States to a colonial dependency that furnished British factories with cheap raw materials and purchased British-made goods delivered in British ships. In struggling to establish its sovereign rights in a world of hostile imperial powers, the United States under the Articles of Confederation suffered the crippling disadvantage of lacking any means of formulating or implementing a uniform policy for its defense. More so than any of the other delegates at the Constitutional Convention, Alexander Hamilton drew the obvious conclusion. "You have to protect your rights against Canada in the north, Spain in the south, and your western frontier against the savages. . . . No Government could give us tranquility and happiness at home, which did not possess sufficient strength and stability to make us respectable abroad." Like any new nation confronted with threats to its security, the United States could not afford the luxury or indulge in the utopian hope of dispensing with power politics.

- How could Spain try to control the westward expansion of America and use that expansion to its advantage?

ancestral land of the major Indian nations in the Southeast. Fraud was rampant, and many Native Americans believed, with good reason, that they had never been consulted in the dispossession of their land. The Spanish responded by recruiting disaffected Indians into an alliance system of their own. Their staunchest allies came from a faction of the Creeks led by Alexander McGillivray, the son of a trader father and a half-French, half-Creek mother. Supplied with arms by the Spanish, these Creeks succeeded in forcing white settlers off their tribal land in Georgia.

Spain stepped up pressure on the West in the summer of 1784, when it closed the Mississippi River within Spanish territory to American trade. Hoping now to benefit from American weakness, Spain also opened negotiations for a long-term settlement with the United States. The Spanish negotiator, Don Diego de Gardoqui, offered a deal that cleverly played the interests of the North against those of the South and West. In exchange for an American agreement to surrender claims to navigate the Mississippi for the next thirty years, Gardoqui proposed to grant the United States significant trading concessions in the Spanish Empire that would open new markets and new sources of hard money to the financially pressed merchants of the northeastern states. John Jay, his American negotiating partner, reluctantly accepted the offer.

When Jay released the terms of the proposed treaty with Spain in 1786, southerners who had taken the lead in the settlement of the West, accused Jay of selling out their interests. The treaty threatened the agrarian alliance they hoped to forge with the West, increasing the odds that the West would break from the East and go its own way. Vowing that they would not surrender the West, southern congressmen united to defeat the treaty.

The regional antagonisms exposed by the Jay-Gardoqui talks heightened the alarm over the future of the republic provoked by Shays's Rebellion earlier in 1786. As the sense of crisis deepened in 1786, the nationalists grew in influence and numbers. Led by Alexander Hamilton of New York and James Madison of Virginia, they now argued that only a radical political change could preserve the republic and fulfill the promise of its greatness.

TOWARD A NEW UNION

WHICH GROUPS in American society were most likely to support the Constitution? Why?

In September 1786, delegates from several states met at the **Annapolis Convention,** in Annapolis, Maryland, seeking to devise a uniform system of commercial regulation for the country. While there, a group of nationalist leaders issued a call for a convention at Philadelphia "to devise such further provisions as shall appear to them necessary to render the constitution of the Federal Government adequate to the exigencies of the Union." The leaders who met at the **Constitutional Convention** in Philadelphia forged an entirely new framework of governance, the **Constitution of the United States,** which called for a federal republic with a powerful and effective national government. In 1788, after a close struggle in state ratifying conventions, the Constitution was adopted.

Annapolis Convention Conference of state delegates at Annapolis, Maryland, that issued a call in September 1786 for a convention to meet at Philadelphia to consider fundamental changes.

Constitutional Convention Convention that met in Philadelphia in 1787 and drafted the Constitution of the United States.

Constitution of the United States The written document providing for a new central government of the United States.

The Road to Philadelphia

Only nine states sent delegates to the Annapolis Convention, and only those from five states had actually arrived when the nationalists, at the prompting of James Madison and Alexander Hamilton, abruptly adjourned the meeting. They then called on the states and the Congress to approve a full-scale constitutional convention for Philadelphia in May 1787.

The timing of the call for the Philadelphia Convention could not have been better. During the fall and winter of 1786, the agrarian protests unleashed by Shays's Rebellion in Massachusetts spilled over into other states. Coupled with talk of a dismemberment of the Union in the wake of the Jay-Gardoqui negotiations, the agrarian unrest strengthened the case of the nationalists for more centralized authority.

All the states except Rhode Island, which wanted to retain exclusive control over its own trade, sent delegates to Philadelphia. The fifty-five men who attended the convention represented an extraordinary array of talent and experience. Chiefly lawyers by training or profession, most had served in the Confederation Congress, and more than one-third had fought in the Revolution. Extremely well educated by the standards of the day, the delegates were members of the intellectual as well as the political and economic elite. As a group, they were far wealthier than the average American. Most had investments in land and the public securities of the United States. At least nineteen owned slaves. Their greatest asset as a working body was their common commitment to a nationalist solution to the crisis of confidence they saw gripping the republic. Most of the strong supporters of the Articles of Confederation refused to attend.

W
WHERE TO LEARN MORE
Independence National Historical Park, Philadelphia, Pennsylvania
http://www.nps.gov/inde/index.htm

The Convention at Work

When it agreed to the Philadelphia Convention, the Congress authorized only a revision of the Articles of Confederation. Almost from the start, however, the delegates set about replacing the Articles altogether. The most ardent nationalists immediately seized the initiative by presenting the **Virginia Plan.** Drafted by James Madison, this plan replaced the Confederation Congress with a truly national government, organized like most of the state governments with a bicameral legislature, an executive, and a judiciary.

Virginia Plan Proposal calling for a national legislature in which the states would be represented according to population.

Two features of the Virginia Plan stood out. First, it granted the national Congress power to legislate "in all cases in which the separate states are incompetent" and to nullify any state laws that in its judgment were contrary to the "articles of Union." Second, it made representation in both houses of the Congress proportional to population. This meant that the most

This portrait, sketched in about 1790 by John Trumbull, is the only known likeness of Alexander McGillivray, a Creek leader who effectively played off Spanish and American interests in the Southeast to gain a measure of independence for the Creeks in the 1780s.

populous states would have more votes in Congress than the less populous states, giving them effective control of the government.

Delegates from the small states countered with the **New Jersey Plan,** introduced on June 15 by William Paterson. This plan kept intact the basic structure of the Confederation Congress—one state, one vote—but otherwise amended the Articles by giving the national government the explicit power to tax and to regulate domestic and foreign commerce. In addition, it gave acts of Congress precedence over state legislation, making them "the supreme law of the respective states."

The Great Compromise. The New Jersey Plan was quickly voted down, and the convention remained deadlocked for another month over how to apportion state representation in the national government. The issue was finally resolved on July 16 with the so-called **Great Compromise.** Small states were given equal footing with large states in the Senate, or upper house, where each would have two votes. In the lower house, the House of Representatives, the number of seats was made proportional to population, giving larger states the advantage. The Great Compromise also settled a sectional dispute over representation between the free (or about to be free) states and the slave states. The southern states wanted slaves counted for apportioning representation in the House but excluded from direct tax assessments. The northern states wanted slaves counted for tax assessments but excluded for apportioning representation. To settle the issue, the Great Compromise settled on an expedient, if morally troubling, formula: Free residents were to be counted precisely; to that count would be added, "excluding Indians not taxed, three-fifths of all other persons (meaning enslaved blacks)." Thus the slave states gained additional political representation, while the states in the North received assurance that the owners of nonvoting slaves would have to bear part of the cost of any direct taxes levied by the new government.

New Jersey Plan Proposal of the New Jersey delegation for a strengthened national government in which all states would have an equal representation in a unicameral legislature.

Read the **Document** at **www.myhistorylab.com** *The New Jersey Plan (1787)*

Read the **Document** at **www.myhistorylab.com** *The Virginia Plan (1787)*

Great Compromise Plan proposed at the 1787 Constitutional Convention for creating a national bicameral legislature in which all states would be equally represented in the Senate and proportionally represented in the House.

The Great Compromise ended the first phase of the convention, which had focused on the general framework of a stronger national government. In its next phase, the convention debated the specific powers to be delegated to the new government. It was at this point that the sectional cleavage between North and South over slavery and other issues came most prominently to the fore.

Regulation of commerce and the issue of slavery. The sectional clash first erupted over the power of Congress to regulate commerce. At issue was whether Congress could regulate trade and set tariffs by a simple majority vote. Southerners worried that a northern majority would pass navigation acts favoring northern shippers and drive up the cost of sending southern commodities to Europe. To counter this threat, delegates from the Lower South demanded that a two-thirds majority be required to enact trade legislation.

In the end, the delegates agreed that enacting trade legislation would require only a simple majority. In return, however, southerners exacted concessions on the slavery issue. When planters from South Carolina and Georgia made it clear that they would agree to join a new Union only if they could continue to import slaves, the convention abandoned a proposal to ban the foreign slave trade. Instead, Congress would be barred from acting against the slave trade for twenty years. In addition, bowing to the fears of planters that Congress could use its taxing power to undermine slavery, the convention denied Congress the right to tax exports from any state. And to alleviate southern concerns that slaves might escape to freedom in the North, the new

Constitution included an explicit provision calling on the states to return "persons held to Service or Labour" in any other state.

The office of the chief executive. After settling the slavery question, the convention had one last significant hurdle to clear: the question of the national executive. In large part because of their confidence in George Washington, whom nearly everyone expected to be the first president, the delegates fashioned a chief executive office with broad discretionary powers. The prerogatives of the president included the rank of commander in chief of the armed forces, the authority to conduct foreign affairs and negotiate treaties, the right to appoint diplomatic and judicial officers, and the power to veto congressional legislation. The president's term of office was set at four years, with no limits on how often an individual could be reelected.

QUICK REVIEW

Checks on Executive Power

- Senate given the authority to approve or reject presidential appointments.
- Congress, not the president, given the power to declare war.
- Congress given the power to override presidential vetoes.

Determining how to elect the president proved a thorny problem. The delegates envisioned a forceful, energetic, and independent executive, insulated from the whims of an uninformed public and the intrigues of the legislature. As a result, they rejected both popular election and election by Congress. The solution they hit upon was the convoluted system of an "electoral college." Each state was left free to determine how it would choose presidential electors equal to the number of its representatives and senators. These electors would then vote by ballot for two persons. The person receiving a majority of all the electoral votes would become president and the second highest vote-getter the vice president. If no candidate received a majority of the electoral votes, the election would be turned over to the House of Representatives, where each state would have one vote.

Overview of the Constitution

Although not as strong as the most committed nationalists would have liked, the central government outlined in the Constitution was to have far more powers than were entrusted to Congress under the Articles of Confederation (see the Overview table, The Articles of Confederation and the Constitution Compared). The Constitution's provision for a strong, single-person executive had no precedent in the Articles. Nor did the provision for a Supreme Court. The Constitution vested this court, as well as the lower courts that Congress was empowered to establish, with the judicial power of the United States. In addition, the Constitution specifically delegated to Congress the powers to tax, borrow and coin money, regulate commerce, and raise armed forces, all of which the Confederation government had lacked.

Read the Document at **www.myhistorylab.com** *The Constitution of the United States of America (1789), page A-5*

Read the Document at **www.myhistorylab.com** *From Then to Now Online: Reshaping the Constitution*

Most of the economic powers of Congress came at the expense of the states. Further curbing the sovereignty of the states was a clause stipulating that the Constitution and all national legislation and treaties were to be "the supreme law of the land." This clause has subsequently been interpreted as giving the central government the power to declare state laws unconstitutional.

A no-nonsense realism, as well as a nationalist outlook, infused the Constitution. Its underlying political philosophy was that, in Madison's wonderful phrase, "ambition must be made to counter ambition." Madison and the other members of the national elite who met at Philadelphia were convinced that self-interest, not disinterested virtue, motivated political behavior. Accepting interest-group politics as inevitable and seeking to prevent a tyrannical majority from forming at the national level, the architects of the Constitution designed a central government in which competing blocs of power counterbalanced one another.

The Constitution placed both internal and external restraints on the powers granted to the central government. The functional division of the government into executive, legislative, and judicial branches, each with ways to keep the others from exercising excessive power, created an internal system of checks and balances.

OVERVIEW The Articles of Confederation and the Constitution Compared

	Articles	Constitution
Sovereign power of central government	No power to tax or raise armies	Power granted on taxes and armed forces
Source of power	Individual states	Shared through federalism between states and national government
Representation in Congress	Equal representation of states in unicameral Congress	Bicameral legislature with equal representation of states in Senate and proportional representation in House
Amendment process	Unanimous consent of states	Consent of three-fourths of states
Executive	None provided for	Office of president
National judiciary	None provided for	Supreme Court

judicial review A power implied in the Constitution that gives federal courts the right to review and determine the constitutionality of acts passed by Congress and state legislature.

federalism The sharing of powers between the national government and the states.

Although the Constitution did not explicitly grant it, the Supreme Court soon claimed the right to invalidate acts of Congress and the president that it found to be unconstitutional. This power of **judicial review** provided another check against legislative and executive authority (see Chapter 9). To guard against an arbitrary federal judiciary, the Constitution empowered Congress to determine the size of the Supreme Court and to impeach and remove federal judges appointed by the president.

The external restraints on the central government were to be found in the nature of its relationship to the state governments. This relationship was based on **federalism,** the division of power between local and central authorities. By listing specific powers for Congress, the Constitution implied that all other powers were to be retained by the states. Thus, while strengthening the national government, the Constitution did not obliterate the sovereign rights of the states, leaving them free to curb the potential power of the national government in the ambiguous areas between national and state sovereignty.

Watch the **Video**
at **www.myhistorylab.com**
Slavery and the Constitution

This ambiguity in the federalism of the Constitution was both its greatest strength and its greatest weakness. It allowed both nationalists and advocates of states' rights to support the Constitution. But the issue of slavery, left unresolved in the gray area between state and national sovereignty, would continue to fester, sparking sectional conflict over the extent of national sovereignty that would plunge the republic into civil war three-quarters of a century later.

Read the **Document**
at **www.myhistorylab.com**
Exploring America: Ratification of the Constitution

Read the **Document**
at **www.myhistorylab.com**
Patrick Henry against Ratification of the Constitution (1788)

The Struggle over Ratification

The last article of the Constitution stipulated that it would go into effect when it had been ratified by at least nine of the states acting through specially elected popular conventions. Congress, influenced by the nationalist sentiments of many of its members, one-third of whom had attended the Philadelphia Convention, and perhaps weary of its own impotence, accepted this drastic and not clearly legal procedure, submitting the Constitution to the states in late September 1787.

Federalists A supporter of the Constitution who favored its ratification.

The delegates in Philadelphia had excluded the public from their proceedings. The publication of the Constitution lifted the veil of secrecy and touched off a great political debate. Although those who favored the Constitution could most accurately have been defined as nationalists, they referred to themselves as **Federalists,** a term that helped deflect charges that they favored an excessive centralization of political authority. By default, the opponents of the Constitution were known as **Antifederalists,** a negative-sounding label that obscured their support of the state-centered sovereignty that most Americans associated with federalism. Initially outmaneuvered in this way, the Antifederalists never did mount an effective campaign to counter the Federalists' pamphlets, speeches, and newspaper editorials (see the Overview table, Federalists Versus Antifederalists). The Antifederalists did attract some men of wealth and social standing. Most Antifederalists, however, were backcountry farmers, men with mud on their boots who lived far from centers of communication and market outlets for their produce. The Antifederalists clung to the belief that only a small republic, one composed of relatively homogeneous social interests, could secure the voluntary attachment of the people necessary for a free government. They argued that a large republic, such as the one framed by the Constitution, would inevitably become tyrannical because it was too distant and removed from the interests of common citizen-farmers.

Antifederalists Opponents of the Constitution in the debate over its ratification.

Read the Document at **www.myhistorylab.com** *James Madison, Defends the Constitution (1788)*

Read the Document at **www.myhistorylab.com** *The Federalist No. 51 (1788)*

However much the Antifederalists attacked the Constitution as a danger to the individual liberties and local independence that they believed the Revolution had been fought to safeguard, they were no political match for the Federalists. They lacked the wealth, social connections, access to newspapers, and self-confidence of the more cosmopolitan and better-educated Federalists. In addition, the Federalists could more easily mobilize their supporters, who were concentrated in the port cities and commercial farming areas along the coast. Conservatives shaken by Shays's Rebellion lined up behind the Constitution. So, too, did groups—creditors, merchants, manufacturers, urban artisans, commercial farmers—whose interests would be promoted by economic development.

In the early stages, the Federalists scored a string of easy victories. Delaware ratified the Constitution on December 7, 1787, and within a month, so, too, had Pennsylvania, New Jersey, Georgia, and Connecticut.

The Federalists faced their toughest challenge in the large states that had generally been more successful in going it alone during the 1780s. One of the most telling arguments of the Antifederalists in these and other states was the absence of a bill of rights in the Constitution. Realizing the importance of the issue, and citing Article 5 of the Constitution, which provided for an amendment process, the Federalists promised to recommend amending the Constitution with a bill of rights once it was ratified. By doing so, they split the ranks of the Antifederalists in Massachusetts. After the Federalists gained the support of two venerable heroes of the Revolution, John Hancock and Sam Adams, the Massachusetts convention approved the Constitution by a close vote in February 1788.

The major hurdles remaining for the Federalists were Virginia, the most populous state, and strategically located New York. To eke out victory in these crucial states, the Federalists drew on their pragmatism and persuasiveness. As in Massachusetts, they were helped by their promise of a bill of rights. And for the New York campaign, Madison, Jay, and Hamilton wrote an eloquent series of eighty-five essays known collectively as *The Federalist* to allay fears that the Constitution would so consolidate national power as to menace individual liberties. In the two most original and brilliant essays in *The Federalist*, essays 10 and 51, Madison turned traditional republican doctrine on its head. A large, diverse republic like the one envisaged by the Constitution, he reasoned,

This c. 1790 folk art depiction of Washington and his wife reveals how quickly Washington's fame became part of the public consciousness and made him the obvious choice to preside over the Constitutional Convention.

OVERVIEW Federalists versus Antifederalists

	Federalists	Antifederalists
Position on Constitution	Favored Constitution	Opposed Constitution
Position on Articles of Confederation	Felt Articles had to be abandoned	Felt Articles needed only to be amended
Position on power of the states	Sought to curb power of states with new central government	Felt power of states should be paramount
Position on need for bill of rights	Initially saw no need for bill of rights in Constitution	Saw absence of bill of rights in proposed Constitution as threat to individual liberties
Position on optimum size of republic	Believed large republic could best safeguard personal freedoms	Believed only a small republic formed on common interests could protect individual rights
Source of support	Commercial farmers, merchants, shippers, artisans, holders of national debt	State-centered politicians, most backcountry farmers

not a small and homogeneous one, offered the best hope for safeguarding the rights of all citizens. This was because a large republic would include a multitude of contending interest groups, making it difficult for any combination of them to coalesce into a tyrannical majority that could oppress minority rights. With this argument, Madison had developed a political rationale by which Americans could have both an empire and personal freedom.

North Carolina and Rhode Island did not ratify the Constitution until after the new government was functioning. North Carolina joined the Union in 1789 once Congress submitted the amendments that constituted the Bill of Rights. The obstinate Rhode Islanders stayed out until 1790, when Congress forced them in with a threat of commercial reprisal.

CONCLUSION

In freeing themselves from British rule, Americans embarked on an unprecedented wave of constitution-making that sought to put into practice abstract principles of republicanism that held that political power should derive from the people. Between 1776 and 1780, Americans developed a unique system of constitutionalism that went far beyond the British model of an unwritten constitution. They proclaimed the supremacy of constitutions over ordinary legislation, detailed the powers of government in a written document, provided protection for individual freedoms in bills of rights, and fashioned a process for framing governments through the election of delegates to a special constitutional convention and the popular ratification of the work of that convention. In all of these areas, Americans were pioneers in demonstrating to the rest of the world how common citizens could create their own governments.

In dealing with the legacy of slavery, however, white Americans were far more cautious, and most denied that their revolutionary experience included African Americans and should embrace black emancipation. Moses Sash and other African Americans, in keeping alive the dream of full black freedom, refused to passively accept the dictates of white authority. The revolution within a revolution they fought for was put off to the indefinite future by the delegates at the Constitutional

Convention in 1787. Instead, they focused on achieving a peaceful, political revolution in securing the ratification of the Constitution. Their victory in creating a new central government with real national powers was built on the foundation of constitutional concepts and mechanisms that Americans had laid down in their state constitutions. The new Constitution rested on the consent of the governed, and it endured because it could be amended to reflect shifts in popular will and to widen the circle of Americans granted the rights of political citizenship and the enjoyment of liberty.

Accepting as a given that self-interest drove political action, the framers of the Constitution designed the new national government to turn ambition against itself. They created rival centers of power that forced selfish factions to compete in a constant struggle to form a workable majority. The struggle occurred both within the national government and between that government and the states in the American system of federalism. The Constitution thus set the stage for an entirely new kind of national politics.

Where to Learn More

South Street Seaport Museum, New York City, New York. Maritime commerce was the lifeblood of the postrevolutionary economy. The artifacts and exhibits here offer a fine introduction to the seafaring world of the port city that became the nation's first capital in the new federal Union. See http://seany.org for more on the impact of trade on the development of New York and information on preservation projects underway in the city.

Independence National Historical Park, Philadelphia, Pennsylvania. Walks and guided tours through this historic district enable one to grasp much of the physical setting in which the delegates to the Constitutional Convention met. The website http://www.nps.gov/inde/index.htm includes a virtual tour of many of the collections at the park, a portrait gallery of leading figures in the Revolution, and a look at the archaeological projects underway in the park.

Northern Indiana Center for History, South Bend, Indiana. The permanent exhibition on the St. Joseph River valley of northern Indiana and southern Michigan explains the material world of this region and how it changed as first Europeans and then Americans mingled and clashed with the Native American population. At http://www.centerforhistory.org one can learn more about the center and the variety of programs it offers.

Review Questions

1. How did the Shaysites justify their taking up arms against the government of Massachusetts? Can you imagine any way in which the crisis could have been resolved short of violence?
2. Why do you think that the U.S. Constitution does not cite God or mention religion in any direct way?
3. What was so unprecedented about the new state constitutions, and what principles of government did they embody? What provisions do you think were made for the newly freed African Americans?
4. What were the problems of the economy in the 1780s, and why did clashes between debtors and creditors become so divisive? Do you think that an economic recovery could have been achieved under the Articles of Confederation?
5. Do you feel that the diplomatic weaknesses of the United States under the Articles were as serious as its internal problems? What were the sources of those weaknesses, and what threat did they pose for national unity?
6. What sorts of men drafted the Constitution in 1787, and how representative were they of all Americans? What explains the differences between the Federalists and the Antifederalists? Do you think they shared the same vision of what they wanted America to become? How widespread was the popular backing for the Constitution, and what accounts for its ratification?
7. Compare and contrast the options open to the United States in the 1780s in developing its economy with those of the new nations that have also emerged out of former colonial empires since World War II.

Key Terms

Annapolis Convention (p. 185)
Antifederalists (p. 189)
Articles of Confederation (p. 176)
Constitutional Convention (p. 185)
Constitution of the United States (p. 185)
Federalism (p. 188)
Federalists (p. 188)
Great Compromise (p. 186)
Judicial review (p. 188)
Land Ordinance of 1785 (p. 181)
Nationalists (p. 177)
Natural rights (p. 173)
New Jersey Plan (p. 186)
Northwest Ordinance of 1787 (p. 182)
Shays's Rebellion (p. 179)
Southwest Ordinance of 1790 (p. 182)
Suffrage (p. 172)
Virginia Plan (p. 185)

PEARSON myhistorylab Connections

Reinforce what you learned in this chapter by studying the many documents, images, maps, review tools, and videos available at **www.myhistorylab.com**.

Read and Review

Study and Review **Study Plan: Chapter 7**

Read the Document

Debates in the Federal Convention (1787)

James Madison Defends the Constitution (1788)

Patrick Henry against Ratification of the Constitution (1788)

A Free African American Petitions the Government for Emancipation of All Slaves (1777)

Alexander Hamilton, John Jay, and James Madison, The Federalist Papers (1787–1788)

The Federalist No. 51 (1788)

James Madison, The Virginia (or Randolph) Plan (1787)

Military Reports on Shays's Rebellion (1787)

The New Jersey Plan (1787)

Thomas Jefferson, Notes on the State of Virginia (1787)

Virginia Constitution (1776)

The New Jersey Plan (1787)

The Virginia Plan (1787)

Research and Explore

Read the Document

Personal Journeys Online

From Then to Now Online: Reshaping the Constitution

Are you an Anti-Federalist?

Exploring America: Ratification of the Constitution

Watch the Video *Slavery and the Constitution*

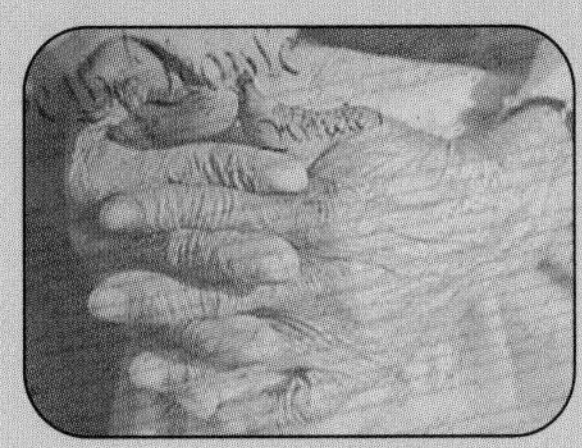

Hear the Audio

Hear the audio files for Chapter 7 at **www.myhistorylab.com**.

1789-1800

8 A New Republic and the Rise of Parties

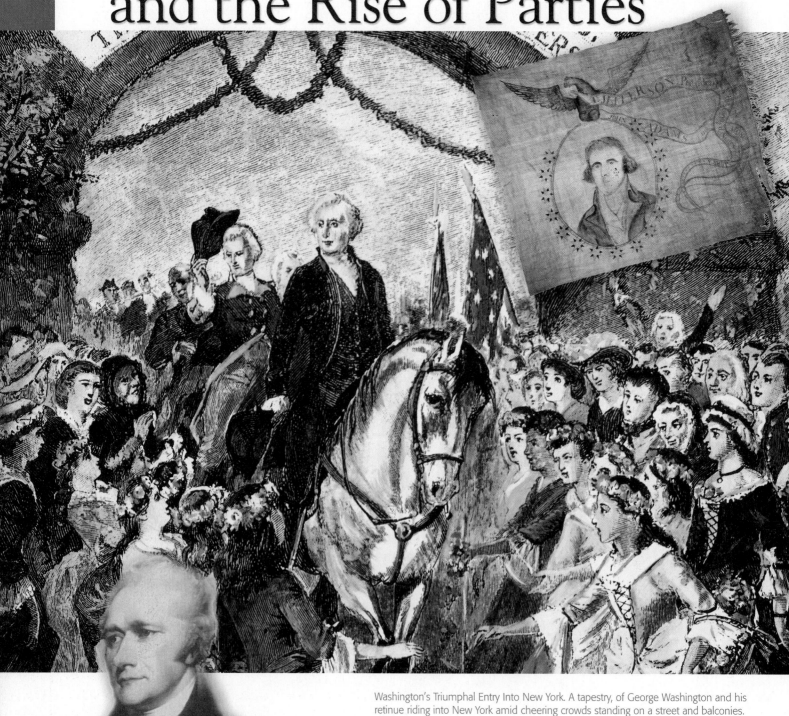

Washington's Triumphal Entry Into New York. A tapestry, of George Washington and his retinue riding into New York amid cheering crowds standing on a street and balconies.

Hear the Audio

Hear the audio files for Chapter 8 at **www.myhistorylab.com**.

WASHINGTON'S AMERICA *(page 197)*

WHAT EXPLAINS the differing role of slavery in the country's regional economies?

FORGING A NEW GOVERNMENT *(page 202)*

WHAT CHALLENGES faced the Congress that assembled in New York between 1789 and 1791?

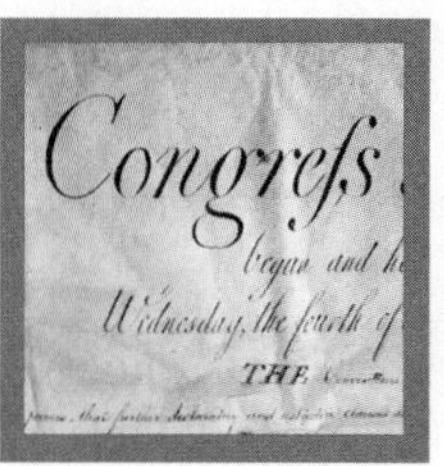

THE EMERGENCE OF PARTIES *(page 206)*

WHAT FORCES shaped the development of party politics in America?

THE LAST FEDERALIST ADMINISTRATION *(page 212)*

WHY WAS Adams defeated in the election of 1800?

ONE AMERICAN JOURNEY

April 30, 1789

New York City

This is the great important day. Goddess of Etiquette assist me while I describe it. . . . The President was conducted out of the middle window into the Gallery [of Federal Hall] and the Oath administered by the Chancellor [Robert R. Livingston, Chancellor of New York]. Notice that the Business was done, was communicated to the Croud by Proclamation . . . who gave three Cheers. . . . As the Company returned into the Senate Chamber, the president took the Chair, and the Senate and representatives their Seats. He rose & all arose also and [he] addressed them [in his inaugural address]. This great Man was agitated and embarrassed more than ever he was by the levelled Cannon or pointed Musket. He trembled and several times could scarce make out to read, tho it must be supposed he had often read it before. He put part of the fingers of his left hand, into the side, of what I think the Taylors call the fall, of his Breetches. Changing the paper into his left hand, after some time, he then did the same with some of the fingers of his right hand. When he came to the Words all the World, he made a flourish with his right hand, which left rather an ungainly impression. . . . He was dressed in deep brown, with Metal buttons, with an Eagle on them, White Stockings a Bag and Sword—from the Hall there was a grand Procession to St. Pauls Church where prayers were said by the Bishop. The Procession was well conducted and without accident, as far as I have heard. The Militias were all under Arms. [They] lined the Street near the Church, made a good figure and behaved well. The Senate returned to their Chamber after Service, formed & took up the Address. . . . In the Evening there were grand fire Works . . . and after this the People went to bed.

[William Maclay]

Kenneth R. Bowling and Helen E. Veit, eds., *The Diary of William Maclay and Other Notes on Senate Debates,* March 4, 1789–March 3, 1791 (Baltimore: Johns Hopkins University Press, 1988), pp. 11–13.

Read the **Document** at **www.myhistorylab.com**

Personal Journeys Online

- **New York *Daily Advertiser,* April 24, 1789. Newspaper description of Washington's arrival in New York.**
- **Tobias Lear, Diary, April 30, 1789. Account of presidential procession for Washington's inauguration.**
- **George Washington, Excerpts from the First Inaugural Address, April 30, 1789.**

SENATOR WILLIAM MACLAY of Pennsylvania wrote this account in his personal journal of the inauguration of George Washington as the first president of the United States at Federal Hall in New York City on April 30, 1789. A Presbyterian with a strong sense of rectitude that often made him overly critical of others, he was one of the first of the original Federalists to break with the Washington administration over its fiscal and diplomatic policies.

Washington's shakiness at his inaugural was understandable. He had every reason to dread taking on the burden of the presidency. As head of the new national government, he would put at risk the legendary status he had achieved during the Revolution. Most Americans intensely feared centralized authority, which is why the framers deliberately left the word *national* out of the Constitution. Washington somehow had to establish loyalty to a new government whose main virtue in the eyes of many was the very vagueness of its defined powers.

The Constitution had created the framework for a national government, but pressing problems demanded the fleshing out of that framework. The government urgently needed revenue to begin paying off the immense debt incurred during the Revolution. It also had to address the unstable conditions in the West, where the settlers wavered in their loyalties. Ultimately, the key to solving these and other problems was to inspire popular backing for the government's authority. ✦

WASHINGTON'S AMERICA

WHAT EXPLAINS the differing role of slavery in the country's regional economies?

The Americans whom Washington was called on to lead were hardly one unified people. They identified and grouped themselves according to many factors, including race, sex, class, ethnicity, religion, and degree of personal freedom. Geographical factors, including climate and access to markets, further divided them into regions and sections. The resulting hodgepodge sorely tested the assumption—and it was never more than an assumption in 1789—that a single national government could govern Americans as a whole (see Figure 8–1).

THE UNIFORMITY OF NEW ENGLAND

The national census of 1790 counted nearly 4 million Americans, one in four of whom lived in New England. Although often viewed as the most typically "American" part of the young nation, New England in fact was rather atypical. It alone of the nation's formative regions had largely shut itself off from outsiders. The Puritan notions of religious liberty that prevailed in the region extended only to those who subscribed to the Calvinist orthodoxy of the dominant Congregationalist Church. Geography conspired with this religious exclusiveness to limit

CHRONOLOGY

1789	Inauguration of Washington.
	Congress establishes the first federal departments.
	French Revolution begins.
1790	Hamilton submits the first of his financial reports to Congress.
1791	Bill of Rights ratified.
	Congress charters the Bank of the United States.
	Slave revolt breaks out in Saint-Domingue (Haiti).
1792	St. Clair's defeat along the Wabash.
	Reelection of Washington.
	Austria and Prussia invade France.
	Execution of King Louis XVI.
1793	France goes to war against Britain, Spain, and Holland.
	Genêt Mission.
	Washington issues Proclamation of Neutrality.
1794	Ohio is opened with the victory of General Anthony Wayne at the Battle of Fallen Timbers.
	Suppression of the Whiskey Rebellion in western Pennsylvania.
1795	Jay's Treaty with Britain ratified.
	Treaty of Greenville with Ohio Indians.
1796	Pinckney's Treaty with Spain ratified.
	Washington's Farewell Address.
	John Adams elected president.
1797	Beginning of the Quasi-War with France.
1798	XYZ Affair.
	Alien and Sedition Acts.
	Provisional army and direct tax.
	Virginia and Kentucky Resolutions.
1799	Fries's Rebellion in Pennsylvania.
	Napoleon assumes power in France.
1800	Franco-American Accord.
	Thomas Jefferson elected president.

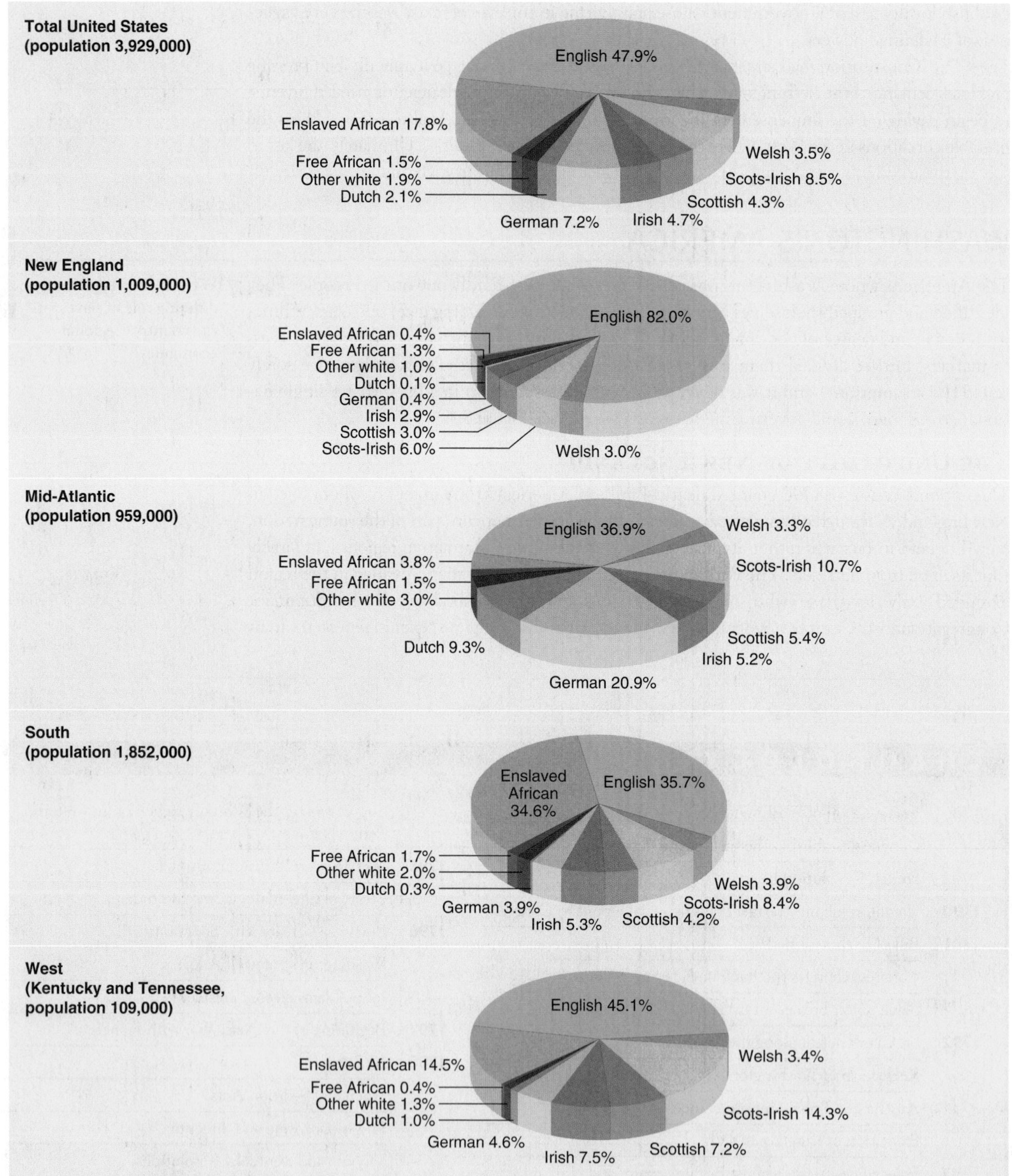

FIGURE 8–1 **Ethnic Breakdown of the United States in 1790, by Region** Unique racial and ethnic patterns shaped each of the nation's four major regions in 1790. New England was most atypical in its lack of racial or ethnic diversity.

Data Source: The Statistics of the Population of the United States, comp. Francis A. Walker (1872), pp. 3–7; Thomas L. Purvis, "The European Ancestry of the United States Population, 1790," *William and Mary Quarterly,* 41(1984), p. 98.

population diversity. New England's poor soils and long, cold winters made it an impractical place to cultivate cash crops like the tobacco and rice of the South. As a result, New England farmers had little need of imported white indentured servants or black slaves. Puritan values and a harsh environment thus combined to make New England the most religiously and ethnically uniform region in the United States. Most of the people living there were descended from English immigrants who had arrived in the seventeenth century.

New Englanders found slavery incompatible with the natural-rights philosophy that had emerged during the Revolution and gradually began to abolish it in the 1780s (though they remained profitably tied to slavery through shipping plantation crops). Slavery had, in any case, always been marginal in New England's economy. Owning slaves as domestic servants or artisans had been a status symbol for wealthy urban whites in Boston, Portsmouth, and Newport. As a result, about 20 percent of New England's small African American population lived in cities, where jobs were relatively easy to find, in contrast to the white population, only 10 percent of which lived in cities.

Women outnumbered men in parts of New England in 1789. This pattern—not found in other parts of the country—was the result of the pressure of an expanding population and the practice of dividing family farms among male heirs. As farms in the older, more densely settled parts of New England were divided into ever-smaller lots, many young men migrated west in search of cheap, arable land. Thus by 1789, women formed a slight majority in Connecticut, Massachusetts, and Rhode Island.

Despite their superior numbers, women in New England, as elsewhere, remained subordinate to men. Even so, the general testing of traditional authority that accompanied the Revolution led some New England women to question male power. The Massachusetts poet Judith Sargeant Murray, for example, published essays asserting that women were the intellectual equals of men. Republican ideology, emphasizing the need for women to be intellectually prepared to raise virtuous, public-spirited children, led reformers in New England to seek equal access for women to education. In 1789, Massachusetts became the first state to allocate funds specifically for girls' elementary education. Liberalized divorce laws in New England also allowed a woman to seek legal separation from an abusive or unfaithful spouse.

QUICK REVIEW

New Englanders

- Most of population were descendants of seventeenth-century English immigrants.
- Congregationalism deemed official religion in Connecticut and Massachusetts.
- Women outnumbered men in some parts of the region.
- Slavery abolished in 1780s.

In other respects, political and social life in New England remained rooted in the Puritan past. Age, property, and reputation determined one's standing in a culture that valued a clearly defined social order. The moral code that governed town life promoted curbs on individual behavior for the benefit of the community as a whole. With their notions of collective liberty, New Englanders subscribed to a version of republicanism that favored strong government, setting themselves apart from most other Americans, who embraced a more individualistic idea of liberty and a suspicion of government power. New Englanders perceived government as a divine institution with a moral responsibility to intervene in people's lives. Acting through town meetings, they taxed themselves for public services at rates two to four times higher than in the rest of the country. Their courts were also far more likely than those elsewhere to punish individuals for crimes against public order (like failing to observe the Sabbath properly) and sexual misconduct.

The Pluralism of the Mid-Atlantic Region

The states of the mid-Atlantic region—New York, New Jersey, and Pennsylvania—were the most ethnically and religiously diverse in the nation. People of English descent constituted somewhat less than 40 percent of the population. Other major ethnic groups included the Dutch and Scots-Irish in New York and Germans and Scots-Irish in New Jersey and Pennsylvania. With ethnic diversity came religious diversity. Transplanted New Englanders made up about 40 percent of New York's ethnic English population. Among others of English descent, Anglicans predominated in New York, and Quakers in New Jersey and Pennsylvania. The Dutch, concentrated in the lower Hudson Valley, had their own Dutch Reformed Church, and most Germans were either Lutherans or **pietists,** such as the Mennonites and the Moravians, who stressed personal piety over theological doctrine. The Presbyterian Scots-Irish settled heavily in the backcountry.

pietists Protestants who stress a religion of the heart and the spirit of Christian living.

Idealized classical images of women—white, chaste, and pure—were popular emblems in the early republic to portray national ideals of liberty and republican motherhood.

This mosaic-like pattern of ethnic and religious groupings was no accident. In contrast to Puritan New England, the Middle Colonies had offered freedom of worship to attract settlers. In addition, economic opportunities for newcomers were much greater than in New England. The soil was better, the climate was milder, and market outlets for agricultural products were more abundant. These conditions made the mid-Atlantic region the nation's first breadbasket. Commercial agriculture fed urban growth and created a greater demand for labor in both rural and urban areas than in New England. The influx of Germans and Scots-Irish into the region in the eighteenth century occurred in response to this demand.

The demand for labor had also been met by importing African slaves. Blacks, both free and enslaved, made up 5 percent of the mid-Atlantic population in 1790, and, as in New England, they were more likely than whites to live in the maritime cities. New York had more slaveholders in 1790 than any other American city except Charleston, South Carolina.

Despite its considerable strength in the port cities and adjacent rural areas, slavery was never an economically vital institution in most of the mid-Atlantic region. Commercial agriculture did not rest on a slave base, nor did it produce a politically powerful class of planters. As a result, slavery in the mid-Atlantic region gave way to the demands for emancipation inspired by the natural-rights philosophy of the Revolution.

Pennsylvania in 1780, New York in 1799, and New Jersey in 1804 all passed laws of gradual emancipation. These laws did not free adult slaves but provided that children born of a slave mother were to be freed at ages ranging between 18 and 28. Soon after the laws were passed, however, adult slaves began hastening their own freedom. They ran away, set fires, and pressured their owners to accept cash payments in return for a short, fixed term of labor service. But even as they gained their freedom, African Americans had to confront enduring white racism. The comments of one white New Yorker suggest what they were up against. "We may sincerely advocate the freedom of black men," he wrote, "and yet assert their moral and physical inferiority."

QUICK REVIEW

The Mid-Atlantic Region

- Most ethnically and religiously diverse area in the nation.
- Slavery concentrated in port cities and adjacent rural areas.
- Diversity created a complex political environment.

The diversity of the mid-Atlantic region created a complex political environment. Competing cultural and economic interests prevented the kind of broad consensus on the meaning of republicanism that had emerged in New England. Those who supported strong government included mercantile and financial leaders in the cities and commercial farmers in the countryside. These people tended to be Anglicans, Quakers, and Congregationalists of English descent. Those opposing them and favoring a more egalitarian republicanism tended to come from the middle and lower classes. They included subsistence farmers in the backcountry and artisans and day laborers in the cities. Fiercely independent and proud of their liberties, they resented the claims of the wealthy to political authority. They resisted government aid to business as a form of political corruption that unfairly enriched those who were already economically powerful.

The Slave South and Its Backcountry

In the South—the region from Maryland and Delaware to Georgia—climate and soil conditions favored the production of cash staples for world markets. Southern planters relied on the coerced labor of African slaves, whose numbers made the South the most populous region in the country.

Just under 40 percent of all southerners were slaves, but their concentration varied within the region. They were a majority in the Chesapeake Tidewater region, where slave ownership was widely distributed among white tobacco planters, including small and middling growers as well as the few great plantation owners. Farther south, in the tidal swamps of the South Carolina and Georgia lowcountry, where draining and clearing the land required huge inputs of labor, blacks outnumbered whites five to one. In the lowcountry, large planters, the richest men in the country, worked hundreds of slaves in the production of rice, indigo, and sea-island cotton.

Slaves were less numerous in the Piedmont, or foothills, region of the South that lies between the coastal plain and the Appalachian highlands. In the southern mountains, sloping to the southwest from the Blue Ridge in Virginia, the general absence of marketable crops diminished the demand for slave labor.

The free black population in the South had grown rapidly during the 1780s. Thousands of slaves fled behind British lines to win their freedom, and patriots freed others as a reward for enlisting in their forces. The Revolutionary values of liberty and equality also led many slave owners to question the morality of slavery. Legislatures in the Upper South passed laws making it financially easier than before for masters to manumit (free) their slaves. In Virginia alone, 10,000 slaves were manumitted in the 1780s. Slavery remained the foundation of the southern economy, however, and whites feared competition from freed blacks. As a result, no southern state embarked on a general program of emancipation, and slavery in the region survived the turbulence of the Revolutionary era.

Many German Lutherans settled in southeastern Pennsylvania. Hung above the gallery in this interior view of a Lutheran church in York are paintings of the 12 apostles and of figures drawn from the Old Testament.

Collection of the New-York Historical Society, Negative number 28824c.

Economic conditions in the South, where the raw poverty of the backcountry offset the great wealth of the low country, stamped the region's politics and culture. Tidewater planters were predominantly Anglican and of English descent. Piedmont farmers were more likely to be Scots-Irish Presbyterians and Baptists. More evangelical in their religion, and with simpler habits and tastes, the backcountry Baptists denounced the lowcountry planters for their luxury and arrogance. The planters retaliated by trying unsuccessfully to suppress the backcountry evangelicals.

The planters were indeed proud, domineering, and given to ostentatious displays of wealth. Planters understood liberty to mean the power of white males, unchecked by any outside authority, to rule over others. The only acknowledged check on this power was the planter's sense of duty, his obligation to adhere to an idealized code of conduct befitting a gentleman and a man of honor.

Backcountry farmers also jealously guarded their liberties. Backcountry farmers shared with the planters a disdain for government and restraints on the individual. But they opposed the planters' belief in a social hierarchy based on wealth and birth that left both poor whites and black slaves in a subordinate position.

W
WHERE TO LEARN MORE
Cincinnati Historical Society,
Cincinnati, Ohio
http://www.cincymuseum.org/

The Growing West

Between the Appalachian Mountains and the Mississippi River stretched the most rapidly growing region of the new nation, the West. Land-hungry settlers poured across the mountains once the British recognized the American claim to the region in the Treaty of Paris. During the 1780s, the white population of the West exploded from less than 10,000 to 200,000. The region's Native American population was about 150,000.

Indians strongly resisted white claims on their lands. A confederation of tribes in the Ohio Valley, led by the Miamis and supplied with firearms by the British in exchange for furs, kept whites out of the Old Northwest territory, the area north of the Ohio River. South of the Ohio, white settlements were largely limited to Kentucky and Tennessee. In what is today Alabama and Mississippi, the Creeks and their allies blocked American expansion.

Most white migrants in Kentucky and Tennessee were the young rural poor from the seaboard slave states. The West offered them the opportunity to claim their own farms and gain economic independence, free from the dominance of planters and the economic competition of slave labor. But planters also saw the West as a land of opportunity. The planters of Tidewater Virginia were especially likely to speculate in vast tracts of western land. And many planters' sons migrated to the West with a share of the family's slaves to become planters in their own right. This process laid the foundation for the extension of slavery into new regions.

Isolation and uncertainty haunted frontier life. The Appalachians posed a formidable barrier to social and economic intercourse with the East. Few settlers had the labor resources, which chiefly meant slaves, to produce an agricultural surplus for shipment to market down the Ohio and Mississippi rivers. Most farmers lived at a semisubsistence level. Many of them, mostly Scots-Irish, did not own the land they cultivated. These squatters, as they were called, occupied the land hoping someday to obtain clear title to it.

QUICK REVIEW

Westerners

- White population of West 200,000 by end of 1780s.
- Relationship between whites and Indians tense and sometimes violent.
- Most white migrants to Kentucky and Tennessee were young, rural poor from seaboard slave states.

In Kentucky, squatters, aligned with a small class of middling landowners, spearheaded the movement for political separation from Virginia that gained statehood for the territory in 1792. The settlers wanted to break the control that Tidewater planters had gained over most of the land and lucrative government offices in Kentucky. In their minds, planters, officeholders, land speculators, and gentlemen of leisure were all part of an aristocracy tied to the distant government in Richmond and intent on robbing them of their liberty.

Despite the movement in Kentucky for statehood, the ultimate political allegiance of the West was uncertain. Westerners wanted the freedom to control their own affairs and outlets for their crops. Apparently, they were willing to strike a deal with any outside power offering to meet these needs. Aware of the threat to the region posed by the British and Spanish, Washington had warned in 1784 that the political loyalties of the West wavered "on a pivot." The future of the region loomed as a major test for his administration.

FORGING A NEW GOVERNMENT

WHAT CHALLENGES faced the Congress that assembled in New York between 1789 and 1791?

The Congress that assembled in New York (the temporary capital) from 1789 to 1791 faced a challenge scarcely less daunting than that of the Constitutional Convention of 1787. It had to give form and substance to the framework of the new national government outlined in the Constitution. Executive departments had to be established, a federal judiciary organized, sources of revenue found, terms of international trade and foreign policy worked out, and the commitment to add a bill of rights to the Constitution honored.

"Mr. President" and the Bill of Rights

WHERE TO LEARN MORE

★ Federal Hall National Memorial, New York, New York
http://www.nps.gov/feha/index.htm

The first problem for Washington and Congress was to decide just how the chief executive of the new republic should be addressed. In a debate that tied up Congress for a month, agreement was finally reached on "Mr. President." Whatever his title, Washington was intent on surrounding the presidency with an aura of respectability.

Meanwhile, Congress got down to business. James Madison, now a representative from Virginia, early emerged as the most forceful leader in the House. He pushed for speedy action on the bill of rights, which the Federalists had promised to add to the Constitution during the ratification debate. To allay the fears of Antifederalists that the Constitution granted too much power to the national government, the Federalists had promised to consider amendments that protected both individual rights and liberties and the rights of states. But Madison astutely kept the focus of the amendments on personal liberties. He submitted nineteen amendments, and Congress soon settled on twelve. Ten of these, known collectively as the **Bill of Rights,** were ratified by the states and became part of the Constitution as of December 15, 1791.

Bill of Rights A written summary of inalienable rights and liberties.

The Bill of Rights is one of the most enduring legacies of the first Congress. Most of the first eight amendments are concerned with individual rights. They guarantee religious freedom, freedom of expression, and the safeguarding of individuals and their property against arbitrary legal proceedings. Only three amendments speak of state interests. Citing the necessity of a "well regulated Militia" for "the security of a free State," the Second Amendment guarantees "the right of the people to keep and bear Arms." This assured the states that they could rely on their militias for protection against federal tyranny. The Ninth and Tenth Amendments stipulate that the powers not granted to the national government in the Constitution are retained by the people and the states.

QUICK REVIEW

Amendments to the Constitution

- First eight amendments concerned with individual rights.
- Guarantees of religious freedom, freedom of expression, protection against arbitrary legal proceedings.
- Powers not granted to the national government retained by the people and the states.

The Bill of Rights broadened the government's base of popular support. Once Congress submitted the amendments to the states for ratification, North Carolina (1789) and Rhode Island (1790) overcame their lingering objections (see Chapter 7) and joined the Union. The Bill of Rights also assured Americans that the central government would not try to impose a uniform national culture.

Departments and Courts

In the summer of 1789, Congress authorized the first executive departments: the State Department for foreign affairs, the Treasury for finances, and the War Department for the nation's defense. These departments already existed under the Articles of Confederation, and the only debate about them concerned the extent of presidential control over the officials who would head them. The Constitution was silent on whether the president could dismiss an official without the Senate's consent. Congress decided that the president could do so, setting an important precedent that bolstered presidential power. Department heads would now be closely bound to the president. As a group, they would evolve into the cabinet, the president's chief advisory body.

Judiciary Act of 1789 Act of Congress that implemented the judiciary clause of the Constitution by establishing the Supreme Court and a system of lower federal courts.

Greater controversy attended the creation of the federal judiciary. The Constitution called for "one Supreme Court" but left it up to Congress to authorize lower federal courts. The framers were deliberately vague about the federal judiciary, because Antifederalists and proponents of states' rights did not want national courts enforcing a uniform judicial system.

The **Judiciary Act of 1789** represented an artful compromise that balanced the concerns of the Antifederalists and states' rights advocates with the concerns of nationalists who strongly opposed leaving matters of national law up to state courts. It created a hierarchical national judiciary based on thirteen federal district courts, one for each state. Appeals from these courts were to be heard in one of three circuit courts, and the Supreme Court was to have the final say in contested cases. In a major concession to the Antifederalists, however, the act limited jurisdiction in federal courts to legal issues stemming from the Constitution and the laws and treaties of the national government.

Waterborne commerce was the key in the early emergence of New York City as a trading center. Shown here is the Manhattan end of the Brooklyn Ferry in 1790.

Revenue and Trade

The government's most pressing need was for revenue. Aware that Congress under the Articles of Confederation had been crippled by its inability to secure a reliable source of income, Madison acted to put the finances of

Tariff Act of 1789 Apart from a few selected industries, this first tariff passed by Congress was intended to raise revenue and not protect American manufacturers from foreign competition.

WHERE TO LEARN MORE

Hamilton Grange National Memorial, New York, New York
http://www.nps/gov/hagr/index.htm

Read the **Document**
at **www.myhistorylab.com**
Alexander Hamilton, An Opinion on the Constitutionality of an Act to Establish a Bank (1791)

QUICK REVIEW

Hamilton's Reports

- Plan to address Revolutionary War debt.
- Call for an excise tax on distilled whiskey.
- Proposal to charter a national bank.
- Recommendation for government to promote industry.

the new federal government on a firm footing. Nearly everyone agreed that the government's chief source of income should be a tariff on imported goods and tonnage duties (fees based on cargo capacity) on ships entering American ports.

The **Tariff Act of 1789** was designed primarily to raise revenue, not to protect American manufacturers by keeping out foreign goods with high duties. It levied a duty of 5 percent on most imported goods but imposed tariffs as high as 50 percent on a limited number of items, such as steel, salt, cloth, and tobacco. The debate on the Tariff Act provoked some sectional sparring. Manufacturers, who were concentrated in the North, wanted high tariffs for protection against foreign competition. In contrast, farmers and southern planters wanted low tariffs to keep down the cost of the manufactured goods they purchased.

Hamilton and the Public Credit

The Treasury was the largest and most important new department. To its head, Alexander Hamilton of New York, fell the task of bringing order to the nation's ramshackle finances. The basic problem was the huge debt left over from the Revolution. With interest going unpaid, the debt was growing, and by 1789, it had reached $52 million. Until the government set up and honored a regular schedule for paying interest, the nation's public credit would be worthless. Unable to borrow, the government would collapse.

At the request of Congress, Hamilton prepared a series of reports on the nation's finances and economic condition. In the first, issued in January 1790, Hamilton proposed a bold plan to address the Revolutionary War debt. The federal government, he maintained, should fund the national debt at full face value. To do this, he proposed exchanging the old debt, including accrued interest, for new government bonds bearing interest at about 4 percent. In addition, Hamilton maintained that the federal government should assume the remaining war debt of the state governments. The intent of this plan was to give the nation's creditors an economic stake in the stability of the new nation and to subordinate state financial interests to those of the central government.

In his second report, issued in December 1790, Hamilton called for an excise tax (a tax on the production, sale, or consumption of a commodity) on distilled whiskey produced within the United States. The purpose of the tax was to raise additional revenue for interest payments on the national debt and establish the government's authority to levy internal taxes on its citizens.

The third report recommended the chartering of a national bank, the Bank of the United States. Hamilton patterned his proposed bank after the Bank of England and intended it to meet a variety of needs. Jointly owned by the federal government and private investors, it would serve as the fiscal (financial) and depository agent of the government and make loans to businesses. Through a provision that permitted up to three-fourths of the value of bank stock to be purchased with government bonds, the bank would create a market for public securities and hence raise their value. Most important, the bank would provide the nation with a stable currency. Hamilton proposed to allow the Bank of the United States to issue money in the form of paper banknotes that would be backed by a small reserve of specie and the security of government bonds. His goal was both to strengthen the economy and to consolidate the power of the national government.

Shown here in 1799, the neoclassical design of the First Bank of the United States in Philadelphia was a fitting expression of the grandeur of Hamilton's vision for a national bank.

Hamilton's final report, issued in December 1791, recommended government actions to promote industry. Looking, as always, to the British model of economic development, he argued that the United States would never become a great power until it diversified its largely agrarian economy. As long as the nation imported most of its manufactured goods,

Hamilton warned, it would be no more than a second-rate power. Hamilton advocated aid to American manufacturers in the form of protective tariffs (high tariffs meant to make imported goods more expensive than domestic goods) for such industries as iron, steel, and shoemaking—which had already begun to establish themselves—and direct subsidies to assist with start-up costs for other industries. Hamilton believed that such "patronage," as he called it, would ultimately foster interregional economic dependence. Thus, in Hamilton's vision, manufacturing, like a national currency, would be a great national unifier.

Reaction and Opposition

The breadth and boldness of Hamilton's program invited opposition. About half the members of Congress owned some of the nation's debt, and nearly all of them agreed with Hamilton that it should be paid off. Some opponents, however, were concerned that Hamilton's plan was unfair. Hard times had forced most of the original holders of the debt—by and large, ordinary citizens—to sell their certificates to speculators at a fraction of their face value. Should the government, asked Madison, reward speculators with a windfall profit when the debt was paid back in full and forget about the true patriots who had sustained the Revolution in its darkest hours?

Others objected, on republican grounds, that Hamilton had no intention of actually eliminating the government's debt. He envisioned instead a permanent debt, with the government making regular interest payments as they came due. The debt, in the form of government securities, would serve as a vital prop for the support of moneyed groups. One congressman saw this as a violation of "that great principle which alone was the cause of the war with Great Britain . . . that taxation and representation should go hand in hand." Future generations, he argued, would be unfairly taxed for a debt incurred by the present generation.

Opposition to Hamilton's proposal to have the federal government assume state debts reflected sectional differences. With the exception of South Carolina, the southern states had already paid back a good share of their war debts. Thus Hamilton's plan stood to benefit the northern states disproportionately. Because Hamilton had linked the funding of the national debt with the assumption of state debts, southern opposition threatened funding as well. Tensions mounted as the deadlock continued into the summer of 1790. Frustrated over southern intransigence, New Englanders muttered about seceding. Southerners responded in kind.

Tempers cooled when a compromise was reached in July. Southerners agreed to accept funding in its original form because, as Hamilton correctly noted, it would be impractical, if not impossible, to distinguish between the original and current holders of the national debt. Assumption passed after Hamilton cut a deal with Virginians James Madison and Thomas Jefferson. In exchange for southern support of assumption, Hamilton agreed to line up northern votes for locating the nation's permanent capital on the banks of the Potomac River, where it would be surrounded by the slave states of Maryland and Virginia. The package was sweetened by extra grants of federal money to states with small debts.

Hamilton's alliance with Madison and Jefferson proved short-lived, dissolving when Madison led the congressional opposition to Hamilton's proposed bank. Madison and most other southerners viewed the bank as evidence of a willingness to sacrifice the interests of the agrarian South in favor of the financial and industrial interests of the North. They feared that the bank, with its power to dispense economic favors, would re-create in the United States the kind of government corruption and privilege they associated with Great Britain. They argued that the Constitution did not explicitly authorize Congress to charter a bank or any other corporation.

The bank bill passed Congress on a vote that divided along sectional lines and Hamilton's bank was chartered for twenty years. Congress also passed a hefty 25 percent excise tax on distilled liquor. Little, however, of Hamilton's plan to promote manufacturing survived the scrutiny of the agrarian opposition. Tariff duties were raised moderately in 1792, but no funds were forthcoming to accelerate industrial development.

THE EMERGENCE OF PARTIES

WHAT FORCES shaped the development of party politics in America?

Federalists Supporters of Hamilton's program; they were American's most fully integrated into the market economy—and in control of it.

Republican Party headed by Thomas Jefferson that formed in opposition to the financial and diplomatic policies of the Federalist party; favored limiting the powers of the national government and placing the interests of farmers over those of financial and commercial groups.

By the end of Washington's first term, Americans were dividing into two camps. On one side stood those who still called themselves **Federalists.** These were the supporters of Hamilton's program—speculators, creditors, merchants, manufacturers, and commercial farmers. They were the Americans most fully integrated into the market economy and in control of it. Concentrated in the North, they included New England Congregationalists and mid-Atlantic Episcopalians (former Anglicans), members of the more socially prestigious churches. In both economic and cultural terms, the Federalists were drawn from the more privileged segments of society. Jefferson and Madison shrewdly gave the name **Republican** to the party that formed in opposition to the Federalists, thus identifying it with individual liberties and the heritage of the Revolution. The Republicans accused Hamilton and the Federalists of attempting to impose a British system of economic privilege and social exploitation. The initial core of the party consisted of southern planters and backcountry Scots-Irish farmers, Americans outside the market economy or skeptical of its benefits. They feared that the commercial groups favored by Hamilton would corrupt politics in their pursuit of power and foster commerce and manufacturing at the expense of agriculture. The Republicans were committed to an agrarian America in which power remained in the hands of farmers and planters.

In 1792, parties were still in a formative stage. The political divisions that had appeared first in Congress and then spread to Washington's cabinet did not yet extend very deeply into the electorate. Washington remained aloof from the political infighting and was still seen as a great unifier. Unopposed, he was reelected in 1792. However, a series of crises in his second term deepened and broadened the incipient party divisions. By 1796, rival parties were contesting the presidency and vying for the support of an increasingly politically organized electorate.

THE FRENCH REVOLUTION

The French Revolution began in 1789, and in its early phase, most Americans applauded it. France had been an ally of the United States during the Revolutionary War and now seemed to be following the example of its American friends in shaking off monarchical rule. By 1792, however, as threats against it mounted, the French Revolution turned violent and radical. Its supporters confiscated the property of aristocrats and the church, slaughtered suspected enemies, and executed the king, Louis XVI. In early 1793, republican France was at war against Britain and the European powers.

The excesses of the French Revolution and the European war that erupted in its wake touched off a bitter debate in America. Federalists drew back in horror from France's new regime. They insisted that the terror unleashed by the French was far removed from the reasoned republicanism of the American Revolution. For the Republicans, however, the French remained the standard-bearers of the cause of liberty for common people everywhere.

Franco-American relations. When the new French ambassador, Edmond Genêt, arrived in the United States in April 1793—just as the debate in America over the French Revolution was heating up—Franco-American relations reached a turning point. The two countries were still bound to one another by the Franco-American Alliance of 1778. The alliance required the United States to assist France in the defense of its West Indian colonies and to open U.S. ports to French privateers if France were attacked. Genêt, it soon became clear, hoped to embroil the United States in the French war against the British. He commissioned U.S. privateers to attack British shipping and tried to enlist an army of frontiersmen to attack Spanish possessions in Louisiana and Florida.

Genêt's actions, as well as the enthusiastic reception that greeted him as he traveled from Charleston to Philadelphia (chosen in 1790 as the temporary national capital), forced Washington

OVERVIEW Federalist Party versus Republican Party

Federalists	Republicans
Favored strong central government	Wanted to limit role of national government
Supported Hamilton's economic program	Opposed Hamilton's economic program
Opposed French Revolution	Generally supported French Revolution
Supported Jay's Treaty and closer ties to Britain	Opposed Jay's Treaty and favored closer ties to France
In response to threat of war with France, proposed and passed Direct Tax of 1798, Alien and Sedition Acts and legislation to enlarge army	Opposed Alien and Sedition Acts and enlarged army as threats to individual liberties
Drew strongest support from New England; lost support in mid-Atlantic region after 1798	Drew strongest support from South and West

to call a special cabinet meeting. The president feared that Genêt would stampede Americans into the European war, with disastrous results for the nation's finances. Over Jefferson's objections, Hamilton urged Washington to declare U.S. neutrality in the European war, maintaining that the president could commit the nation to neutrality on his own authority when Congress, as was then the case, was not in session. Washington accepted Hamilton's argument and issued a proclamation on April 22, 1793, stating that the United States would be "friendly and impartial toward the belligerent powers."

The growth of Democratic-Republican societies. Genêt quickly faded from public view, but U.S. politics became more open and aggressive in the wake of his visit. Pro-French enthusiasm lived on in a host of grassroots political organizations known as the Democratic-Republican societies. As their name suggests, these societies reflected a belief that democracy and republicanism were one and the same. This was a new concept in U.S. politics. Democracy had traditionally been equated with anarchy and mob rule. The members of the new societies argued, to the contrary, that only democracy—meaning popular participation in politics and direct appeals by politicians to the people—could maintain the revolutionary spirit of 1776, because the people were the only true guardians of that spirit.

The Democratic-Republican societies attacked the Washington administration for failing to assist France, and they expressed the popular feeling that Hamilton's program favored the rich over the poor. For the first time, Washington himself was personally assailed in the press.

The core members of the societies were urban artisans whose egalitarian views shocked the Federalists, who expected deference, not criticism and political activism, from the people. In their view, the Democratic-Republicans were rabble-rousers trying to dictate policy to the nation's natural leaders. The Federalists harshly condemned the emergence of organized political dissent from below, but in so doing they only enhanced the popular appeal of the growing Republican opposition.

Securing the Frontier

Control of the West remained an elusive goal throughout Washington's first term. Indian resistance in the Northwest Territory initially prevented whites from pushing north of the Ohio River. The powerful Miami Confederacy, led by Little Turtle, routed two ill-trained American armies in 1790 and 1791. The southern frontier was quieter, but the Spanish

GLOBAL CONNECTIONS

Neutrality in an Age of Revolution

Whereas it appears that a state of war exists between Austria, Prussia, Sardinia, Great Britain, and the United Netherlands on the one part and France on the other, and the duty and interest of the United States require that they should with sincerity and good faith adopt and pursue a conduct friendly and impartial toward the belligerent powers:

I have therefore thought fit . . . to exhort and warn the citizens of the United States carefully to avoid all acts and proceeding whatsoever which may in any manner tend to contravene such disposition.

In these words President Washington proclaimed the neutrality of the United States in the European war spawned by the French Revolution. He realized, as did most Americans, that the new and still weak nation had far more to lose than gain by embroiling itself in the European war. Still, before the French Revolution turned to regicide and the Reign of Terror in 1793–1794, Americans basked in pride for having first raised the revolutionary banner of liberty and equality that their former ally was now spreading over Europe. But by the mid-1790s exultation had turned into disillusionment and fears of social upheaval. By the time that Napoleon assumed what amounted to dictatorial powers in 1799, most Americans had reverted to their earlier belief in the uniqueness of the American Revolution. As Madison observed when reflecting on the French experience, America remained as "the only Theatre in which true liberty can have a fair trial."

Despite believing that the French had discredited the cause of liberty, Americans clung to the hope that the contagion of liberty they had first unleashed in their Revolution would topple autocratic regimes across the world. And spread it did in a wide arc of revolutionary movements that stretched across the Western world. The French colony of Saint-Domingue (Haiti) exploded in unrest in 1791 once the French Revolution had outlawed slavery. Touissant L'Ouverture, the slave grandson of an African king, led black armies in a ten-year war of liberation that resulted in the independence of Haiti in 1804. Napoleon's invasion of the Iberian Peninsula in 1809 created a power vacuum in Spain's American empire. A host of revolutions broke out to fill the vacuum, and Mexico, Argentina, Bolivia, Chile, Colombia, Ecuador, Peru, and Venezuela all gained their freedom from Spanish rule. None of these revolutions closely followed the American or French model. All, however, were united by a common political language of liberty, popular self-rule, and constitutionalism that the Americans and the French had bequeathed to global politics.

- In what ways did the American Revolution soon serve as a liberating example for revolutionary change elsewhere?

continued to use the Creeks and Cherokees as a buffer against American penetration south of the Tennessee River.

By 1793, many western settlers felt abandoned by the national government. They believed that the government had broken a promise to protect them against Indians and foreigners. Much of the popularity of the Democratic-Republican societies in the West fed off these frustrations. Westerners saw the French, who were at war with Britain and Spain, as allies against the foreign threat on the frontier, and they forwarded resolutions to Congress embracing the French cause. These resolutions also demanded free and open navigation on the Mississippi River. This, in the minds of Westerners, was their natural right. Without it, they would be forever impoverished. "If the interest of Eastern America requires that we should be kept in poverty," argued the Mingo Creek society of western Pennsylvania, "it is unreasonable from such poverty to exact contributions. The first, if we cannot emerge from, we must learn to bear, but the latter, we never can be taught to submit to."

Submission to national authority, however, was precisely what the Federalists wanted from both the Indians and the western settlers. By the summer of 1794, Washington's administration felt prepared to move against the Indians. This time, it sent into the Ohio region not the usual ragtag crew of militia and unemployed city dwellers but a force built around veterans from the professional army. The commander, General Anthony Wayne, was a savvy, battle-hardened war hero.

Wayne's victory on August 4, 1794, at the Battle of Fallen Timbers, near present-day Toledo, broke the back of Indian military resistance in Ohio. In the resulting **Treaty of Greenville,** signed in August 1795, twelve tribes ceded most of the present state of Ohio to the U.S. government in return for an annual payment of $9,500. The Ohio country was now open to white settlement.

Treaty of Greenville Treaty of 1795 in which Native Americans in the Old Northwest were forced to cede most of the present state of Ohio to the United States.

The Whiskey Rebellion

Within a few months of Wayne's victory at Fallen Timbers, another American army was on the move. Its target was the so-called whiskey rebels of western Pennsylvania, who were openly resisting Hamilton's excise tax on whiskey. Hamilton was determined to enforce the tax and assert the supremacy of national laws. Although resistance to the tax was widespread, he singled out the Pennsylvania rebels. It was easier to send an army into the Pittsburgh area than into the Carolina mountains. Washington, moreover, was convinced that the Democratic-Republican societies of western Pennsylvania were behind the defiance of federal authority there. He welcomed the opportunity to chastise these organizations, which he identified with the dangerous doctrines of the French Revolution.

Washington called on the governors of the mid-Atlantic states to supply militia forces to crush the **Whiskey Rebellion.** The army met no resistance and expended considerable effort rounding up 20 prisoners. Two men were found guilty of treason, but Washington pardoned both. Still, at Hamilton's insistence, the Federalists had made their point: When its authority was openly challenged, the national government would use military force to compel obedience.

Whiskey Rebellion Armed uprising in 1794 by farmers in western Pennsylvania who attempted to prevent the collection of the excise tax on whiskey.

The Whiskey Rebellion starkly revealed the conflicting visions of local liberty and national order that divided Americans of the early republic. The non-English majority on the Pennsylvania frontier, Irish, Scots-Irish, German, and Welsh, justified resistance to the whiskey tax with the same republican ideology that had fueled the American Revolution. Mostly poor farmers, artisans, and laborers, they appealed to notions of liberty, equality, and freedom from oppressive taxation that were deeply rooted in backcountry settlements from Maine to Georgia. In putting down the Pennsylvania rebels, Washington and Hamilton acted on behalf of more English and cosmopolitan groups in the East who valued central power as a check on any local resistance movement that might begin unraveling the still fragile republic.

Read the **Document**
at **www.myhistorylab.com**
George Washington, Proclamation Regarding the Whiskey Rebellion (1794)

Treaties with Britain and Spain

Much of the unrest in the West stemmed from the menacing presence of the British and Spanish on the nation's borders. Washington's government had the resources to suppress Indians and frontier dissidents but lacked sufficient armed might to push Spain and especially Britain out of the West.

The British, embroiled in what they saw as a life-or-death struggle against revolutionary France, clamped a naval blockade on France and its Caribbean colonies in the fall of 1793. They also supported a slave uprising on the French island of Saint-Domingue (present-day Haiti), enraging southern planters who feared that slave rebellions might spread to the United States. The French countered by opening their colonial trade, which had been closed to outsiders during peacetime, to neutral shippers. American merchants stepped in and reaped profits by supplying France. The British retaliated by seizing American ships involved in the French trade. They further claimed the right to search American ships and impress, or forcibly remove, sailors they suspected of having deserted from the British navy. News of these provocations reached America in early 1794 and touched off a major war scare. Desperate to avert a war, Washington sent John Jay, the chief justice of the United States, to London to negotiate an accord.

From the American point of view, the resulting agreement, known as **Jay's Treaty,** was flawed but acceptable. Jay had to abandon the American insistence on the right of neutrals to ship goods to nations at war without interference. He also had to grant Britain "most favored

Jay's Treaty Treaty with Britain negotiated in 1794 in which the United States made major concessions to avert a war over the British seizure of American ships.

AMERICAN VIEWS

An Architect on Water Pollution in Philadelphia

Benjamin Henry Latrobe, the first professional architect in the United States, was living in Philadelphia in 1798. Five years earlier, a major yellow fever epidemic had carried off two thousand of the city's inhabitants. Here, Latrobe offers his views on the sources of water pollution and what the city had to do to obtain a clean water supply and improve public health.

- **What** was the link between mosquitoes and yellow fever missed by Latrobe and his contemporaries?
- **How** then did doctors and others in the eighteenth century account for outbreaks of yellow fever and other diseases?
- **What** led Latrobe to conclude that foul air was not the source of the yellow fever?
- **How** did Philadelphia and other cities dispose of their human wastes and what does this tell us about the spread of waterborne diseases? How widespread in the world today do you suspect are the unsafe conditions that Latrobe described for Philadelphia in 1798?
- **What** solution did Latrobe offer for Philadelphia's water problems?

On inspecting the plan of the city of Philadelphia and observing the numerous wide and straight streets, it will not be easily believed that want of ventilation can be entirely the cause of the yellow fever which has made such dreadful and frequent devastations among the inhabitants. It is true that there are narrow and often very filthy alleys which intersect the interior of the squares bounded by the principal streets and in which the air may stagnate. The back yards of most of the houses are also depositories of filth. [Still,] there must be some cause more powerful and more specific. The cause, I believe, may be found in the following circumstance:

The soil between the Delaware and Schuylkill [rivers] is generally flat [and] consists of a bed of clay of different depth, from ten to thirty feet .... Below this bed of clay is universally a stratum of sand. In this sand runs a stratum of water, and as it is impossible to dig into it without finding clear and excellent water in an inexhaustible quantity, let the wells and pumps be ever so near to each other, it appears to me not at all extravagant to suppose that the waters of the two rivers unite through this sand stratum, which serves as a filtering bed . . . But this very circumstance, the inexhaustible supply of clean water to be found in every possible spot of ground . . . is the great cause, in my opinion, of the contagion which appears now to be an annual disease of Philadelphia, the yellow fever. The houses, being much crowded, and the situation flat, without subterraneous sewers to carry off the filth, every house has its privy and its drains which lodge their supplies in one boghole sunk into the ground at different depths. Many of them are pierced to the sand, and as those which are sunk thus low never fill up, there is a strong temptation to incur the expense of digging them deep at first to save the trouble and noisomeness of emptying them.

In every street, close to the footpath, is a range of pumps at the distance of about sixty or seventy feet from which all the water which is used for drinking or culinary purposes is drawn. The permeability of the stratum in which the water runs, and which the action of the pump draws to itself from all parts round it, must certainly contaminate the water of every pump in the neighborhood of a sink loaded with the filth of the family, and as the number of these sinks is very superior to that of the pumps, each of them is in a manner surrounded by noxious matter.

Thus . . . we have a proof that there does exist in the mode by which the city is supplied with water a very abundant source of disease, independent of the noxious exhalations of the narrow and filthy alleys and lanes [for] the evil lies in the constant fermentation of the stratum of water and production of mephitic [poisonous] air, to which the pumps are so many chimneys to convey it into the streets and open windows at all times, and from which it is regularly pumped up every time the handle is depressed.

The great scheme of bringing the water of the Schuylkill to Philadelphia to supply the city is now become an object of immense importance, though it is at present neglected from a failure of funds. The evil, however, which it is intended collaterally to correct is so serious . . . as to call loudly upon all who are inhabitants of Philadelphia for their utmost exertions to complete it.

Source: Benjamin Henry Latrobe, *The Journal of Latrobe: Being the Notes and Sketches of an Architect, Naturalist and Traveler in the United States from 1796 to* 1820 (New York: D. Appleton, 1905), pp. 92–98.

nation" status, giving up the American right to discriminate against British shipping and merchandise. And he had to reconfirm the American commitment to repay in full pre-Revolutionary debts owed to the British. In return for these major concessions, Britain pledged to compensate American merchants for the ships and cargoes it had seized in 1793 and 1794, to abandon the six forts it still held in the American Northwest, and to grant the United States limited trading rights in India and the British West Indies.

Signed in November 1794, Jay's Treaty caused an uproar in the United States when its terms became known in March 1795. Southerners saw in it another sellout of their interests. It required them to pay their prewar debts to British merchants but was silent about the slaves Britain had carried off during the Revolution. And the concessions Britain did make seemed to favor the North, especially New England merchants and shippers. Republicans, joined now by urban artisans, were infuriated that Jay had stripped them of their chief weapon, economic retaliation, for breaking free of British commercial dominance. The Senate ratified the treaty in June 1795, but only because Washington backed it.

Jay's Treaty, combined with a string of French victories in Europe in 1795, convinced Spain to adopt a more conciliatory attitude toward the United States. In the **Treaty of San Lorenzo** in 1795 (also known as Pinckney's Treaty), Spain accepted the American position on the 31st parallel as the northern boundary of Spanish Florida and granted American farmers free transit through the port of New Orleans with the right of renewal after three years.

Treaty of San Lorenzo Treaty with Spain in 1795 in which Spain recognized the 31st parallel as the boundary between the United States and Spanish Florida.

The First Partisan Election

Partisanship, open identification with one of the two parties, steadily rose in the 1790s, fueled in large measure by a new print culture. The first opposition newspaper, the *National Gazette*, appeared in 1791, and the number of newspapers more than doubled within the decade. Circulated and discussed in taverns and coffeehouses, newspapers helped draw ordinary Americans into the political process. Ongoing involvement in the raucous, celebratory political culture that Americans fashioned also politicized them. Through festivals, street parades and demonstrations favoring or opposing such events as the French Revolution or Jay's Treaty, and an endless stream of toasts, speeches, banquets, and broadsides, various groups publicly proclaimed and acted out their version of what it meant to be an American. No single version held sway. National self-identity varied by class, race, sex, and region, but as newspaper reports of local activities were copied and disseminated across the country, Americans could feel that they were joined in a collective effort to define what the nation meant to them. As a national identity was being forged and contested, lines of partisanship were marked and deepened.

Read the **Document** at **www.myhistorylab.com** *Exploring America: The Partisan Press*

Women also participated in this public arena of political activism. Although denied formal political rights, they wrote and attended plays with explicit political messages, joined in patriotic rituals, and organized their own demonstrations. By the late 1790s, both parties were seeking to broaden their popular appeal by including women in their partisan rallies.

As partisanship spread, no symbol of traditional authority, Washington included, was safe from challenge. He devoted most of his Farewell Address of September 1796 to a denunciation of partisanship. He also warned against any permanent foreign alliances and cautioned that the Union itself would be endangered if parties continued to be characterized "by geographical discriminations, *Northern* and *Southern*, *Atlantic* and *Western*."

Read the **Document** at **www.myhistorylab.com** *George Washington, Farewell Address (1796)*

Confirming Washington's fears, the election of 1796 was the first openly partisan election in American history. John Adams was the Federalist candidate, and Thomas Jefferson, the Republican candidate. Each was selected by a party caucus, a meeting of party leaders. As a result of disunity in the Federalist ranks, the election produced the anomaly of a Federalist president (Adams) and a Republican vice president (Jefferson). Written with no thought of organized partisan competition for the presidency, the Constitution simply stated that the presidential

Read the **Document** at **www.myhistorylab.com** *From Then to Now Online: Advice for an Empire*

QUICK REVIEW

The Election of 1796

- First openly partisan presidential election.
- Candidates: John Adams (Federalist); Thomas Jefferson (Republican).
- Adams won with support in New England and the mid-Atlantic states.

candidate with the second-highest number of electoral votes would become vice president. In this case, that candidate was Jefferson.

Despite the election's confused outcome, the sectional pattern in the voting was unmistakable. Only the solid support of regional elites in New England and the mid-Atlantic states enabled the Federalists to retain the presidency. Adams received all the northern electoral votes, with the exception of Pennsylvania's. Jefferson was the overwhelming favorite in the South.

THE LAST FEDERALIST ADMINISTRATION

WHY WAS Adams defeated in the election of 1800?

The Adams administration got off to a rocky start from which it never recovered. The vice president was the leader of the opposition party; key members of the cabinet, which Adams had inherited from Washington, owed their primary loyalty to Hamilton; and the French, who saw Adams as a dupe of the British, instigated a major crisis that left the threat of war hanging over the entire Adams presidency.

THE FRENCH CRISIS AND THE XYZ AFFAIR

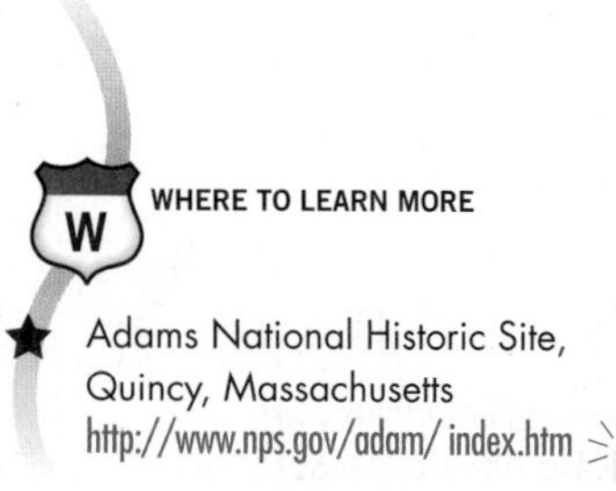

Adams National Historic Site, Quincy, Massachusetts
http://www.nps.gov/adam/ index.htm

An aggressive coalition known as the Directory gained control of revolutionary France in 1795 and denounced the Jay treaty as evidence of an Anglo-American alliance against France. When Jefferson and the pro-French Republicans lost the election of 1796, the Directory turned openly hostile. In short order, the French annulled the commercial treaty of 1778 with the United States, ordered the seizure of American ships carrying goods to the British, and declared that any American sailors found on British ships, including those forcibly pressed into service, would be summarily executed. By the time Adams had been in office three months, the French had confiscated more than 300 American ships.

In the fall of 1797, Adams sent three commissioners to Paris in an effort to avoid war. The French treated the three with contempt. Through three intermediaries, identified by Adams only as X, Y, and Z when he informed Congress of the negotiations, the French foreign minister demanded a large bribe to initiate talks and an American loan of $12 million.

XYZ Affair Diplomatic incident in 1798 in which Americans were outraged by the demand of the French for a bribe as a condition for negotiating with American diplomats.

Quasi-War Undeclared naval war of 1797 to 1800 between the United States and France.

In April 1798, the Senate published a full account of the insulting behavior of the French in what came to be called the **XYZ Affair.** The public was indignant, and war fever swept the country. The Federalists, who had always warned against the French, enjoyed greater popularity than they ever had or ever would again. Congress acted to upgrade the navy, and responsibility for naval affairs, formerly divided between the Treasury and War departments, was consolidated in a new Department of the Navy. By the fall of 1798, American ships were waging an undeclared war against the French in Caribbean waters, a conflict that came to be known as the **Quasi-War.**

The Federalists in Congress, dismissing Republican objections, also voted to create a vastly expanded army. They tripled the size of the regular army to 10,000 men and authorized a special provisional army of 50,000. Congress put the provisional army under Washington's command, but he declined to come out of retirement except for a national emergency. In the meantime, he insisted that Hamilton be appointed second in command and given charge of the provisional army's field operations. To pay for both the expanded army and the naval rearmament, the Federalists pushed through the Direct Tax of 1798, a levy on the value of land, slaves, and dwellings.

CRISIS AT HOME

The thought of Hamilton in charge of a huge army convinced many Republicans that their worst nightmares were about to materialize. One congressman shuddered that "the monarchy-loving Hamilton is now so fixed, as to be able, with one-step, to fill the place of our present commander in chief." Adams shared such fears. He was furious that Hamilton had been forced on him as commander of the provisional army. As Adams came to realize, Hamilton's supporters, known as the

High Federalists, saw the war scare with France as an opportunity to stamp out dissent, cement an alliance with the British, and strengthen and consolidate the powers of the national government.

The Federalists passed four laws in the summer of 1798, known collectively as the **Alien and Sedition Acts,** that confirmed the Republicans' fears. Three of these acts were aimed at immigrants, especially French and Irish refugees who voted for the Republicans. The president was empowered to deport foreigners who came from countries at war with the United States and to expel any alien resident he suspected of subversive activities. The Naturalization Act extended the residency requirement for U.S. citizenship (and hence the right to vote) from five to fourteen years. Worst of all in the minds of Republicans was the Sedition Act, a measure that made it a federal crime to engage in any conspiracy against the government or to utter or print anything "false, scandalous and malicious" against the government. Federalist judges were blatantly partisan in their enforcement of the Sedition Act. Twenty-five individuals, mostly Republican editors, were indicted under the act, and ten were convicted.

Alien and Sedition Acts Collective name given to four acts passed by Congress in 1798 that curtailed freedom of speech and the liberty of foreigners resident in the United States.

Read the Document at **www.myhistorylab.com** *The Alien and Sedition Acts (1798)*

Outraged at this threat to the freedom of speech, Jefferson and Madison turned to the safely Republican legislatures of Kentucky and Virginia for a forum from which to attack the constitutionality of the Alien and Sedition Acts. Taking care to keep their authorship secret, they each drafted a set of resolutions that challenged the entire centralizing program of the Federalists. In doing so, they produced the first significant articulation of the southern stand on **states' rights.**

states' rights Favoring the rights of individual states over rights claimed by the national government.

The resolutions—adopted in the fall of 1798—proposed a compact theory of the Constitution. They asserted that the states had delegated specific powers to the national government for their common benefit. It followed that the states reserved the right to decide whether the national government had unconstitutionally assumed a power not granted to it. If a state decided that the national government had exceeded its powers, it could "interpose" its authority to shield its citizens from a tyrannical law. In a second set of resolutions, the Kentucky legislature introduced the doctrine of **nullification,** the right of a state to render null and void a national law it deemed unconstitutional.

nullification A constitutional doctrine holding that a state has a legal right to declare a national law null and void within its borders.

Jefferson and Madison hoped that these resolutions would rally voters to the Republican Party as the defender of threatened U.S. liberties. Yet not a single additional state seconded them. In the end, what aroused popular rage against the Federalists was not legislation directed against aliens and subversives but the high cost of Federalist taxes.

The Direct Tax of 1798 fell on all owners of land, dwellings, or slaves and provoked widespread resentment. Enforcing it required an army of bureaucrats—more than 500 for the state of Pennsylvania alone. In February 1799, in the heavily German southeastern counties of Pennsylvania, a group of men led by an auctioneer named John Fries released tax evaders from prison in Bethlehem. President Adams responded to Fries's Rebellion with a show of force, but the fiercest resistance the soldiers he sent to Pennsylvania encountered was from irate farm wives, who doused them with hot water and the contents of chamber pots. Fries and two other men were arrested, convicted of treason, and sentenced to be executed. (Adams later pardoned them.) But the Federalists had now lost much of their support in Pennsylvania.

Interpreting the Past
Nullification as a Destructive Force in U.S. Politics (pp. 218–219).

The End of the Federalists

The events in Pennsylvania reflected the air of menace that gripped the country as the campaign of 1800 approached. The army was chasing private citizens whose only crime was resisting hateful taxes. Federal soldiers also roughed up Republican voters at polling places. Southern Republicans talked in private of the possible need to resist Federalist tyranny by force and, failing in that, to secede from the Union. Hamilton and the High Federalists saw in the Kentucky and Virginia resolutions "a regular conspiracy to overturn the government." Reports that Virginia intended to strengthen its militia heightened their anxieties, and they proposed to meet force with force.

No one did more to defuse the charged atmosphere than President Adams. The Federalists depended for their popular support on the expectation of a war with France, which as late as 1798 had swept them to victory in the congressional elections. Still, Adams refrained from asking for a

REPUBLICANS

Turn out, turn out and save your Country from ruin!

From an *Emperor*—from a *King*—from the iron grasp of a *British Tory Faction*—an unprincipled banditti of British speculators. The hireling tools and emissaries of his majesty king George the 3d have thronged our city and diffused the poison of principles among us.

DOWN WITH THE TORIES, DOWN WITH THE BRITISH FACTION,

Before they have it in their power to enslave you, and reduce your families to distress by heavy taxation. Republicans want no Tribute-liars—they want no ship Ocean-liars—they want no Rufus King's for Lords—they want no Varick to lord it over them—they want no Jones for senator, who fought with the British against the Americans in time of the war.—But they want in their places such men as

Jefferson & Clinton,

who fought their Country's Battles in the year '76

By associating their Federalist opponents with the hated Tories of the American Revolution, the Republicans appealed to the voters as the true defenders of American liberation.

Collection of the New-York Historical Society, Negative # 35609.

declaration of war. The United States had been successful in the Quasi-War and in Europe, the tide of war had turned against the French. As a result, Adams believed that the French would now be more open to conciliation. Of greater importance, Adams recognized that war with France could trigger a civil war at home. Hamilton and the High Federalists, he realized, would use war as an excuse to crush the Republican opposition in Virginia. Fearful of Hamilton's intentions and unwilling to run the risk of militarizing the government and saddling it with a huge war debt, Adams broke with his party and decided to reopen negotiations with France in February 1799.

The **Franco-American Accord of 1800** that resulted from Adams's initiative released the United States from its 1778 alliance with France. It also obligated the United States to surrender all claims against the French for damages done to U.S. shipping during the Quasi-War. Once peace with France seemed likely, the Hamiltonian Federalists lost their trump card in the election of 1800. The Republicans could no longer be branded as the traitorous friends of an enemy state. The enlarged army, with no foe to fight, became a political embarrassment, and the Federalists dismantled it. Although rumors of possible violence continued to circulate, the Republicans grew increasingly confident that they could peacefully gain control of the government.

The Federalists nonetheless ran a competitive race in 1800. Adams's peace policy bolstered his popularity. And because U.S. merchants had profited from supplying both sides in the European war, the country was enjoying a period of prosperity that benefited the president and his party. But the party wounds opened by Adams's decision to broker a peace with France continued to fester. Hamilton wrote a scathing attack on the president in a letter that fell into the hands of Aaron Burr, a crafty politician from New York whom the Republicans had teamed up with Jefferson for the presidential election. Burr published the letter, airing the Federalists' squabbling in public.

Franco-American Accord of 1800 Settlement reached with France that brought an end to the Quasi-War and released the United States from its 1778 alliance with France.

The Federalists, hampered by party disunity, could not counter the Republicans' aggressive organizational tactics. They found it distasteful to appeal to common people. Wherever they organized, the Republicans attacked the Federalists as monarchists plotting to undo the gains of the Revolution. The Federalists responded with emotional appeals that depicted Jefferson as a godless revolutionary whose election would usher in a reign of terror. "The effect," intoned the Reverend William Linn, "would be to destroy religion, introduce immorality, and loosen all bonds of society."

Attacks like Linn's reflected the fears of Calvinist preachers that a tide of disbelief was about to submerge Christianity in the United States. Church attendance had declined in the 1790s, particularly among men, and perhaps no more than one in twenty Americans was a member of any church. **Deism,** an Enlightenment religious philosophy popular among the leaders of the Revolutionary era, was now beginning to make inroads among ordinary citizens. Deists viewed God as a kind of master clockmaker who created the laws by which the universe runs but otherwise leaves it alone. They rejected revelation for reason, maintaining that the workings of nature alone reveal God's design.

Deism Religious orientation that rejects divine revelation and holds that the workings of nature alone reveal God's design for the universe.

QUICK REVIEW

Presidential Election of 1800

- Federalists could not overcome party disunity.
- Federalists depicted Republicans as godless revolutionaries.
- Strong party organization won election for Republicans Jefferson and Burr.

These developments convinced Calvinist ministers, nearly all of them Federalists, that the atheism of the French Revolution was infecting U.S. republicanism. They lashed out at the Republicans, the friends of the French Revolution, as perverters of religious and social order. Jefferson, a deist known for his freethinking in religion, bore the brunt of their attack in 1800.

The Republicans won the election by mobilizing voters through strong party organizations. Voter turnout in 1800 was twice what it had been in the early 1790s, and most of the new voters were Republicans. The Direct Tax of 1798 cost the Federalists the support of commercial farmers in the mid-Atlantic states. Artisans in port cities had already switched to the Republicans in protest over Jay's Treaty, which they feared left them exposed to a flood of cheap British imports. Adams carried New England and had a smattering of support elsewhere. With New York added to their solid base in the South and the backcountry, the Jeffersonians gained an electoral majority (see Map 8–1).

Party unity among Republican electors was so strong that Jefferson and Burr each received 73 electoral votes. Consequently, the election was thrown into the House of Representatives, which, until the newly elected Congress was seated, was still dominated by Federalists. Hoping to deny Jefferson the presidency, the Federalists in the House backed Burr. The result was a deadlock that persisted into the early months of 1801. On February 16, 1801, the Federalists yielded. Informed through intermediaries that Jefferson would not dismantle Hamilton's fiscal system, enough Federalists cast blank ballots to give Jefferson the majority he needed for election. The Twelfth Amendment to the Constitution, ratified in 1804, prevented a similar impasse from arising again by requiring electors to cast separate ballots for president and vice president.

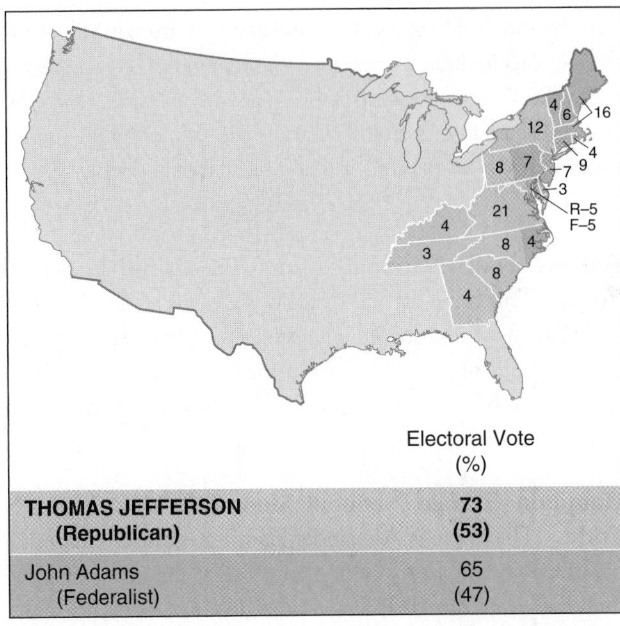

MAP 8–1 **The Election of 1800** The sharp erosion of Federalist strength in New York and Pennsylvania after 1798 swung the election of 1800 to the Republicans.

Where were the Federalists strongest? Where were the Republicans strongest? What explains the geographical distribution of political support for the two parties?

CONCLUSION

In 1789, the U.S. republic was little more than an experiment in self-government. The Federalists provided a firm foundation for that experiment. Hamilton's financial program, neutrality in the wars of the French Revolution, and the diplomatic settlement with Britain in Jay's Treaty bequeathed the young nation a decade of peace and prosperity.

Federalist policies, however, provoked strong opposition rooted in conflicting economic interests and contrasting regional views over the meaning of liberty and government in the new republic. As early as 1789 in the midst of debates in the Senate over a bill to establish a federal judiciary, William Maclay saw the outlines of a plan to subvert Republican liberties. As he put it, "The Constitution is meant to swallow up all the State Constitutions by degrees and this to Swallow by degrees all the State Judiciaries. This at least is the design some Gentlemen seem driving at."

Federalist leadership initially depended on a coalition of regional elites in New England, the mid-Atlantic region, and the slave districts of the South. Fully sharing Maclay's fears over a consolidated government, southern planters were the first of the elites to bolt the Federalist coalition when they joined urban artisans and backcountry Scots-Irish farmers in opposing Jay's Treaty and the commercially oriented program of the Federalists.

During John Adams's administration, Quaker and German farmers in the mid-Atlantic states defected from the Federalists over the tax legislation of 1798, and three of the four regions of the country lined up behind the Republicans. The new Republican majority was united by the belief that the actions of the New England Federalists threatened individual liberty and regional autonomy.

The openly partisan politics of the 1790s surprised the country's founders, who equated parties with the evils of factionalism. They had not foreseen that parties would forge a necessary link between the rulers and the ruled and create a mechanism by which group values and regional interests could be given a political voice. Party formation climaxed in the election of 1800, when the Republicans ended the Federalists' rule.

To the credit of the Federalists, they relinquished control of the national government peacefully. The importance of this precedent can scarcely be exaggerated. It marked the first time in modern political history that a party in power handed over the government to its opposition. It now remained to be seen what the Republicans would do with their newfound power.

Where to Learn More

Cincinnati Historical Society, Cincinnati, Ohio. Collections include written and visual materials on the history of the Old Northwest Territory. Visit its website, http://www.cincymuseum.org, for information on its programs and the accessibility of its printed and audiovisual collections.

Federal Hall National Memorial, New York, New York. This museum and historic site holds artifacts relating to President Washington's inauguration. Its website, http://www.nps.gov/feha/index.htm, includes a printable travel guide to various sites in Manhattan administered by the National Parks Service.

Hamilton Grange National Memorial, New York, New York. The home of Alexander Hamilton contains materials on his life. A brief history of the home and Hamilton's life can be found at its website, http://www.nps/gov/hagr/index.htm.

Adams National Historic Site, Quincy, Massachusetts. This site preserves buildings and manuscripts associated with four generations of the Adams family. See its website, http://www.nps.gov/adam/index.htm, for information on guided tours and the various homes that are part of the site.

Review Questions

1. What role did the "people" play in Washington's inauguration in 1789? What was the purpose of the grand procession, and why were the militia present?
2. What was distinctive about the four regions of the United States in 1790? What were the common values and goals that brought white Americans together?
3. What were the major problems confronting the Washington administration, and how effectively were they resolved? Why was Washington so cautious when confronted with the outbreak of war in Europe?
4. Who were the Federalists and the Republicans, and how did they differ over the meaning of liberty and the power of the national government? What were the major steps in the formation of two distinct parties in the early United States?
5. Why did regional differences tend to pit the North against the South by the late 1790s?
6. How did the XYZ Affair lead to a political crisis in the United States? Why did the Federalists believe that they would benefit from a war against France?
7. Jefferson called his election in 1800 the "revolution of 1800." What do you think he meant? Would you agree with him?

Key Terms

Alien and Sedition Acts (p. 213)
Bill of Rights (p. 203)
Deism (p. 214)
Federalists (p. 206)
Franco-American Accord of 1800 (p. 214)
Jay's Treaty (p. 209)
Judiciary Act of 1789 (p. 203)
Nullification (p. 213)
Pietists (p. 199)
Quasi-War (p. 212)
Republican (p. 206)
States' rights (p. 213)
Tariff Act of 1789 (p. 204)
Treaty of Greenville (p. 209)
Treaty of San Lorenzo (p. 211)
Whiskey Rebellion (p. 209)
XYZ Affair (p. 212)

PEARSON myhistorylab Connections

Reinforce what you learned in this chapter by studying the many documents, images, maps, review tools, and videos available at **www.myhistorylab.com**.

Read and Review

Study and Review **Study Plan: Chapter 8**

Read the Document

George Washington, Farewell Address (1796)

The Alien and Sedition Acts (1798)

The Jay Treaty (1794)

Alexander Hamilton, An Opinion on the Constitutionality of an Act to Establish a Bank (1791)

Proclamation of Neutrality (1793)

The Treaty of San Lorenzo (1796)

George Washington, Proclamation Regarding the Whiskey Rebellion (1794)

See the Map *Western Land Claims Ceded by the States*

Research and Explore

Read the Document
Personal Journeys Online

From Then to Now Online: Advice for an Empire

Exploring America: The Partisan Press

Hear the Audio

Hear the audio files for Chapter 8 at **www.myhistorylab.com**.

INTERPRETING the PAST

Nullification as a Destructive Force in U.S. Politics

TRACE the development of the concept of nullification from an attempt to protect civil liberties to a defense of slavery and a theory that led to secession and the attempt to destroy the Union.

The concept of nullification arose in the early years of the new republic. An undeclared naval war with France was under way and John Adams was president. French warships were seizing American merchant vessels in the Caribbean. Federalists controlled the presidency and the Congress. Hamilton and the High Federalists were clamoring for war with France. Thomas Jefferson and the Democratic Republicans were offering strong support for France and attacking the Adams administration for making war with the very nation that had helped secure American independence during the Revolution. Democratic Republican editors were torching Adams's name in their papers. In response, the Federalist Congress passed the Alien and Sedition Acts of 1798 that forbade "false, scandalous, and malicious writing" against the president and government officials.

Thomas Jefferson and James Madison were concerned about the violation of civil rights, and especially freedom of the press, contained within the Sedition Act of 1798. Jefferson and Madison secretly produced the Virginia and Kentucky Resolutions in opposition to the Alien and Sedition Acts. They argued the compact theory of government and suggested that states' rights were supreme over the authority of the federal government. Most important, they suggested that states had the authority to declare null and void any federal legislation that the state legislature considered to be unconstitutional. The power of the U.S. Supreme Court to declare federal laws to be unconstitutional had not yet been established; John Marshall was not yet Chief Justice of the U.S. Supreme Court. Jefferson and Madison, under the concept of states' rights, were attempting to assign that power to the states.

Protection is afforded to the minority ...

James Madison

Sedition Act of 1798

Section 1. Be it enacted by the Senate and House of Representatives of the United States of America, in Congress assembled, That if any persons shall unlawfully combine or conspire together, with intent to oppose any measure or measures of the government of the United States . . . he or they shall be deemed guilty of a high misdemeanor.

SEC. 2. And be it farther enacted, That if any person shall write, print, utter or publish, or shall cause or procure to be written, printed, uttered or published, or shall knowingly and willingly assist or aid in writing, printing, uttering or publishing any false, scandalous and malicious writing or writings against the government of the United States . . . (they) . . . shall be punished by a fine not exceeding two thousand dollars, and by imprisonment not exceeding two years.

James Madison, Virginia Resolution (1799)

That this Assembly doth explicitly and peremptorily declare, that it views the powers of the federal government, as resulting from the compact, to which the states are parties; as limited by the plain sense and intention of the instrument constituting the compact; as no further valid that they are authorized by the grants enumerated in that compact; and that in case of a deliberate, palpable, and dangerous exercise of other powers, not granted by the said compact, the states who are parties thereto, have the right, and are in duty bound, to interpose for arresting the progress of the evil, and for maintaining within their respective limits, the authorities, rights and liberties appertaining to them.

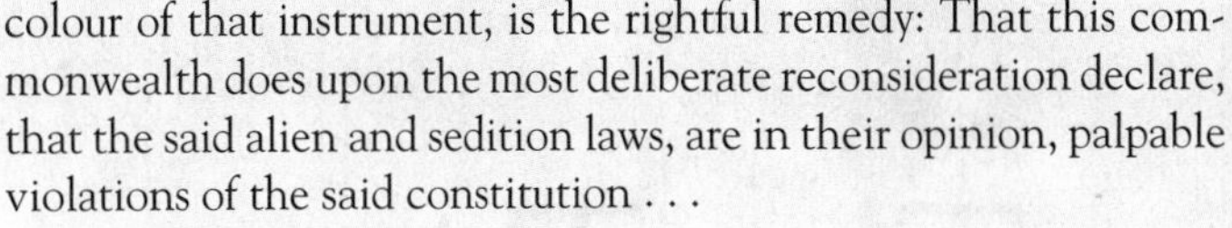

That the General Assembly doth particularly protest against the palpable and alarming infractions of the Constitution, in the two late cases of the "Alien and Sedition Acts" passed at the last session of Congress; the first of which exercises a power no where delegated to the federal government

. . . the General Assembly doth solemnly appeal to the like dispositions of the other states, in confidence that they will concur with this commonwealth in declaring, as it does hereby declare, that the acts aforesaid, are unconstitutional; and that the necessary and proper measures will be taken by each, for co-operating with this state, in maintaining the Authorities, Rights, and Liberties, referred to the States respectively, or to the people.

Kentucky Resolution (1799) (secretly authored by Thomas Jefferson)

RESOLVED, That this commonwealth considers the federal union, upon the terms and for the purposes specified in the late compact, as conducive to the liberty and happiness of the several states: That it does now unequivocally declare its attachment to the Union, and to that compact, agreeable to its obvious and real intention, and will be among the last to seek its dissolution: That if those who administer the general government be permitted to transgress the limits fixed by that compact, by a total disregard to the special delegations of power therein contained, annihilation of the state governments, and the erection upon their ruins, of a general consolidated government, will be the inevitable consequence: That the principle and construction contended for by sundry of the state legislatures, that the general government is the exclusive judge of the extent of the powers delegated to it, stop nothing short of despotism; since the discretion of those who administer the government, and not the constitution, would be the measure of their powers: That the several states who formed that instrument, being sovereign and independent, have the unquestionable right to judge of its infraction; and that a nullification, by those sovereignties, of all unauthorized acts done under colour of that instrument, is the rightful remedy: That this commonwealth does upon the most deliberate reconsideration declare, that the said alien and sedition laws, are in their opinion, palpable violations of the said constitution . . .

Thomas Jefferson

South Carolina's Exposition and Protest, 1828 (secretly authored by John C. Calhoun)

But the existence of the right of judging of their powers (the federal government), so clearly established from the sovereignty of States, as clearly implies a veto or control, within its limits, on the action of the General Government, on contested points of authority; and this very control is the remedy which the Constitution has provided to prevent the encroachments of the General Government on the reserved rights of the States; and by which the distribution of power, between the General and State Governments, may be preserved for ever inviolable, on the basis established by the Constitution. It is thus effectual protection is afforded to the minority, against the oppression of the majority. . . .

President Jackson's Proclamation Regarding Nullification, December 10, 1832

If this doctrine (nullification) had been established at an earlier day, the Union would have been dissolved in its infancy. . . . The discovery of this important feature in our Constitution was reserved to the present day. To the statesmen of South Carolina belongs the invention, and upon the citizens of that State will, unfortunately, fall the evils of reducing it to practice. . . .

I consider, then, the power to annul a law of the United States, assumed by one State, incompatible with the existence of the Union, contradicted expressly by the letter of the Constitution, unauthorized by its spirit, inconsistent with every principle on which It was founded, and destructive of the great object for which it was formed. . . .

South Carolina Ordinance of Secession, 1860

AN ORDINANCE to dissolve the union between the State of South Carolina and other States united with her under the compact entitled "The Constitution of the United States of America."

We, the people of the State of South Carolina, in convention assembled, do declare and ordain, and it is hereby declared and ordained, That the ordinance adopted by us in convention on the twenty-third day of May, in the year of our Lord one thousand seven hundred and eighty-eight, whereby the Constitution of the United States of America was ratified, and also all acts and parts of acts of the General Assembly of this State ratifying amendments of the said Constitution, are hereby repealed; and that the union now subsisting between South Carolina and other States, under the name of the "United States of America," is hereby dissolved.

The union . . . is hereby dissolved. . .

9 The Triumph and Collapse of Jeffersonian Republicanism

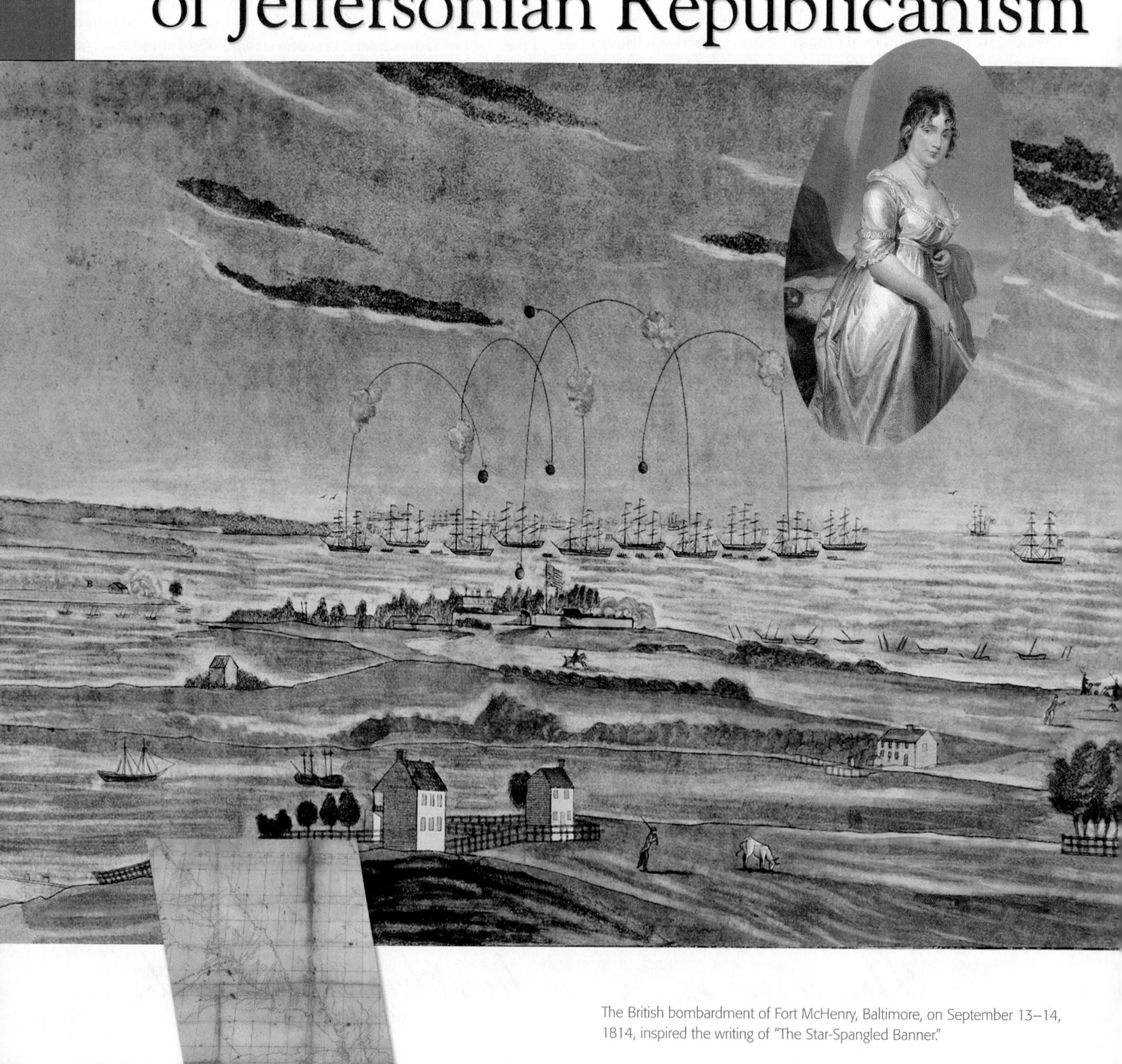

The British bombardment of Fort McHenry, Baltimore, on September 13–14, 1814, inspired the writing of "The Star-Spangled Banner."

Hear the Audio

Hear the audio files for Chapter 9 at **www.myhistorylab.com**.

JEFFERSON'S PRESIDENCY *(page 224)*

WHY WAS the expansion of the United States so important to Jefferson?

MADISON AND THE COMING OF WAR *(page 229)*

WHAT FACTORS pushed Madison into a war with Britain?

THE WAR OF 1812 *(page 232)*

WHAT WERE the consequences of the War of 1812?

THE ERA OF GOOD FEELINGS *(page 235)*

HOW DID rising nationalism contribute to the spirit of the Era of Good Feelings?

THE BREAKDOWN OF UNITY *(page 239)*

WHY DID slavery become such a divisive issue in the years preceding the Missouri Compromise?

One American Journey

Riversdale, 30 August 1814

My dear Sister,

Since I started this letter [on Aug. 9] we have been in a state of continual alarm, and now I have time to write only two or three lines to ask you to tell Papa that we are alive, in good health, and I hope safe from danger. I am sure that you have heard the news of the battle of Bladensburg where the English defeated the American troops with Madison 'not at their head, but at their rear.'

From there they went to Washington where they burned the Capitol, the President's House, all the public offices, etc. During the battle I saw several cannonballs with my own eyes, and I will write all the details to your husband. At the moment the English ships are at Alexandria which is also in their possession.

I don't know how all this will end, but I fear very badly for us. It is probable that it will also bring about a dissolution of the union of the states, and in that case, farewell to the public debt. You know I have predicted this outcome for a long time. Wouldn't it be wise to send your husband here without delay, in order to plan with me the best course to pursue for Papa's interests as well as yours?

This letter will go, I think, by a Dutch ship. If I have time with the confusion we are in, I will write again in a few days, perhaps by the same vessel. At present my house is full of people every day and at night my bedroom is full of rifles, pistols, sabers, etc. Many thanks to your husband for the information in his letter of 27 April, and tell him that I invested all his money in the May loan [of the U.S. Treasury]. Please give many greetings to my dear Father and to Charles [her brother]. Embrace your children for me and believe me,

Your affectionate sister,

Rosalie E. Calvert

Margaret Law Callcott, ed., *Mistress of Riversdale: The Plantation Letters of Rosalie Stier Calvert, 1795–1821* (Baltimore: Johns Hopkins University Press, 1991), pp. 271–272.

Read the Document at **www.myhistorylab.com**

Personal Journeys Online

- **George Robert Gleig, *Burning of Washington*, August 23, 1814. A British soldier describes the destruction in Washington.**
- **Dolley Madison, Letter to her sister, August 23, 1814. Dolley Madison describes the abandonment of the White House.**
- **Lt. Col. R. E. Parker, Letter to the governor, June 11, 1814. A Virginia soldier relates how the slaves plotted to escape behind British lines.**

Rosalie Calvert was the youngest of the three children of a wealthy Belgian family that had fled the advancing armies of revolutionary France in 1794. Her father, Henri J. Stier, had planned in advance for his family's departure and brought with him a sizable fortune in gold, U.S. currency, and paintings. The family, unsurprisingly, was strongly Federalist in its political leanings. In 1799, Rosalie married George Calvert, a descendant of the proprietors of the Maryland colony and a kinsman of the Washingtons.

The coming to power of the Jeffersonian Republicans in 1801 triggered bitter memories of the revolutionary turmoil Rosalie had experienced as a young woman in Belgium. In her eyes, Jefferson and his followers were demagogues who catered to the poor and threatened to infect the United States with the political radicalism of the French Revolution. She blamed the War of 1812 on ignorant, ill-conceived Republican policies and feared that the war would unleash massive unrest. Particularly

CHRONOLOGY

1801	Thomas Jefferson is inaugurated, the first Republican president.
	John Marshall becomes chief justice.
1802	Congress repeals the Judiciary Act of 1801.
1803	*Marbury v. Madison* sets the precedent of judicial review by the Supreme Court.
	Louisiana Purchase.
	Lewis and Clark expedition begins.
	Britain and France resume their war after a brief peace.
1804	Vice President Aaron Burr kills Alexander Hamilton in a duel.
	Judges John Pickering and Samuel Chase impeached by Republicans.
1806	Britain and France issue orders restricting neutral shipping.
	Betrayal of the Burr conspiracy.
1807	*Chesapeake* affair.
	Congress passes the Embargo Act.
	Congress prohibits the African slave trade.
1808	James Madison elected president.
1809	Repeal of the Embargo Act.
	Passage of the Nonintercourse Act.
1810–1825	Revolutions and independence movements in Latin America.
1810	Macon's Bill No. 2 reopens trade with Britain and France.
	United States annexes part of West Florida.
	Georgia state law invalidated by the Supreme Court in *Fletcher v. Peck*.
1811	Battle of Tippecanoe and defeat of the Indian confederation.
	Charter of the Bank of the United States expires.
1812	Congress declares war on Britain.
	American loss of Detroit.
	Napoleon invades Russia.
1813	Perry's victory at Battle of Put-in-Bay.
	Battle of the Thames and death of Tecumseh.
1814	Jackson crushes the Creeks at the Battle of Horseshoe Bend.
	British burn Washington, DC, and attack Baltimore.
	Macdonough's naval victory on Lake Champlain turns back a British invasion.
	Hartford Convention meets.
	Treaty of Ghent signed.
1815	Jackson routs British at the Battle of New Orleans.
	Congress of Vienna arranges a peace settlement for Europe after Napoleon's defeat at Waterloo.
1816	Congress charters the Second Bank of the United States and passes a protective tariff.
	James Monroe elected president.
1817	Rush-Bagot Treaty demilitarizes the Great Lakes.
1818	Anglo-American Accords on trade and boundaries.
	Jackson's border campaign in Spanish East Florida.
1819	Trans-Continental Treaty between United States and Spain.
	Beginning of the Missouri controversy.
	Financial panic sends economy into a depression.
	McCulloch v. Maryland upholds constitutionality of the Bank of the United States.
1820	Missouri Compromise on slavery in the Louisiana Purchase.
	Monroe reelected.
1821	Greek revolt against the Turks.
1822	The United States extends diplomatic recognition to the new nations of Latin America.
1823	Monroe Doctrine proclaims Western Hemisphere closed to further European colonization.
1825	John Quincy Adams elected president by the House of Representatives.

alarming was the news that a mob in Baltimore had brutally beaten twelve prominent Federalists for their antiwar stand. Thus the sense of "continual alarm" that runs through her letter in August 1814, at a time when the war had spilled over into her home.

Despite Rosalie's denunciations of the Republicans, Jefferson's party succeeded in promoting the growth and independence of the United States in the first quarter of the nineteenth century. Expansionist policies to the south and west more than doubled the size of the republic and fueled the westward spread of slavery. The war against Britain from 1812 to 1815, if less than a military triumph, nonetheless freed Americans to look inward for economic development.

At the height of Republican success just after the War of 1812, the Federalist Party collapsed, and with it the social and political elitism championed by Rosalie Calvert and her father. Without an organized opposition to enforce party discipline, the Republicans soon followed the Federalists into political oblivion. The nation's expansion produced two crises—a financial panic and a battle over slavery in Missouri—that shattered the facade of Republican unity. By the mid-1820s, a new party system was emerging.

JEFFERSON'S PRESIDENCY

WHY WAS the expansion of the United States so important to Jefferson?

Read the Document at **www.myhistorylab.com** *Margaret Bayard Smith, Reflections Upon Meeting Thomas Jefferson (1801)*

Read the Document at **www.myhistorylab.com** *Thomas Jefferson, First Inaugural Address (1801)*

WHERE TO LEARN MORE

Monticello, Charlottesville, Virginia http://www.monticello.org/

Thomas Jefferson believed that a true revolution had occurred in 1800, a peaceful overthrow of the Federalist Party and its hated principles of government consolidation and military force. In his eyes, the defeat of the monarchical Federalists reconfirmed the true political legacy of the Revolution by restoring the Republican majority to its rightful control of the government.

Unlike the Hamiltonian Federalists, whose commercial vision of the United States accepted social and economic inequalities as inevitable, the Jeffersonians wanted a predominantly agrarian republic based on widespread economic equality for white yeomen families to counter any threat posed by the privileged few to the people's liberties. Thus, they favored territorial expansion as a means of adding enough land to maintain self-reliant farmers as the guardians of republican freedoms. They also favored the spread of slavery. As long as racial slavery promoted a sense of unity among free white men, they were confident that a populist democracy could coexist with elite rule.

REFORM AT HOME

The cornerstone of Republican domestic policy was a return to the frugal, simple federal establishment the Jeffersonians believed to be the original intent of the Constitution. Determined to root out what they viewed as Federalist corruption and patronage, the Republicans began by reforming fiscal policy. Jefferson's secretary of the treasury was Albert Gallatin, a native of Switzerland who emerged in the 1790s as the best financial mind in the Republican Party. He convinced Jefferson that the Bank of the United States was essential for financial stability and blocked efforts to dismantle it. Unlike Hamilton, however, Gallatin thought that a large public debt was a curse, a drag on productive capital, and an unfair burden on future generations. He succeeded in reducing the national debt from $83 million in 1800 to $57 million by 1809.

Gallatin's conservative fiscal policies shrank both the spending and taxes of the national government. The Republicans eliminated all internal taxes, including the despised tax on whiskey. Slashes in the military budget kept government expenditures below the level of 1800. The cuts in military spending, combined with soaring revenues from customs collections, left Gallatin with a surplus in the budget that he could devote to debt repayment.

QUICK REVIEW

Republican Fiscal Reforms

- Reduced the size of federal government.
- Eliminated all internal taxes.
- Cut military spending.
- Created budget surplus.

Jeffersonian reform targeted the political character, as well as the size, of the national government. He moved to break the Federalist stranglehold on federal offices by appointing officials with sound Republican principles. Arch-Federalists, those Jefferson deemed guilty of misusing their offices for openly political reasons, were immediately replaced, and Republicans filled other posts opened up by attrition. By the time Jefferson left the presidency in 1809, Republicans held nearly all the appointive offices.

Jefferson moved most aggressively against the Federalists in the judiciary. Just days before they relinquished power, the Federalists passed the Judiciary Act of 1801, legislation that both enlarged the judiciary and packed it with more Federalists appointed by Adams, the outgoing president.

The Republicans fought back. Now dominant in Congress, they quickly repealed the Judiciary Act of 1801. Frustrated Federalists now turned to John Marshall, a staunch Federalist appointed chief justice of the United States by President Adams in 1801, hoping that he would

The classical design and bucolic setting of Monticello, Jefferson's home outside Charlottesville, Virginia, visually expressed both his aristocratic tastes and his vision of a harmonious agrarian republic.

Jane Braddick Petticolas (1791–1852), "View of the West Front of Monticello and Garden," 1825, watercolor on paper, 13 5/8 × 18 1/18 inches. Edward Owen/Monticello/Thomas Jefferson Foundation, Inc.

rule that Congress had acted unconstitutionally in removing the recently appointed federal judges. Marshall moved carefully to avoid an open confrontation. He was aware that the Republicans contended that Congress and the president had at least a coequal right with the Supreme Court to decide constitutional questions.

The issue came to a head in the case of ***Marbury v. Madison*** (1803), which centered on Secretary of State James Madison's refusal to deliver a commission to William Marbury, one of Adams's "midnight appointments" (so-called because Adams made them on his next-to-last day in office) as a justice of the peace for the District of Columbia. Marshall held that although Marbury had a legal right to his commission, the Court had no jurisdiction in the case. The Court ruled that the section of the Judiciary Act of 1789 granting it the power to order the delivery of Marbury's commission was unconstitutional because it conferred on the Court a power not specified in the Constitution. Stating that it was "emphatically the province and duty of the judicial department to say what the law is," Marshall created the precedent of judicial review, the power of the Supreme Court to rule on the constitutionality of federal law. This doctrine was of pivotal importance for the future of the Court.

Marbury v. Madison Supreme Court decision of 1803 that created the precedent of judicial review by ruling as unconstitutional part of the Judiciary Act of 1789.

Read the **Document**
at **www.myhistorylab.com**
Marbury v. Madison (1803)

QUICK REVIEW

Judiciary Act of 1801

- Enlarged the judiciary and packed it with Adams's appointees.
- Repealed by Republican Congress.
- Conflict came to head in case of *Marbury v. Madison* (1803).

The Louisiana Purchase

In foreign affairs, fortune smiled on Jefferson during his first term. The European war that had almost sucked in the United States in the 1790s subsided. Britain and France agreed on a truce in 1802. The Anglo-French peace allowed Spain and France to reclaim their colonial trade in the Western Hemisphere. The new ruler of France, Napoleon Bonaparte, was also now free to

See the **Map**
at **www.myhistorylab.com**
The Louisiana Purchase

Masterful hunters, the Plains Indians encountered by Lewis and Clark depended on the buffalo for their economic survival.

develop his plans for reviving the French empire in America. In a secret treaty with Spain in 1800, Napoleon reacquired for France the Louisiana Territory, a vast, vaguely defined area stretching between the Mississippi River and the Rocky Mountains.

Sketchy, unconfirmed reports of the treaty reached Jefferson in the spring of 1801, and he was immediately alarmed. French control of the Mississippi Valley, combined with the British presence in Canada, threatened to hem in the United States and deprive Jefferson's farmers of their empire of liberty.

Jefferson was prepared to reverse his party's traditional foreign policy to eliminate this threat. He opened exploratory talks with the British on an Anglo-American alliance to drive the French out of Louisiana. He also strengthened U.S. forces in the Mississippi Valley and secured congressional approval for the Lewis and Clark expedition through upper Louisiana. Although best known for its scientific discoveries, this expedition was designed initially as a military mission. Jefferson applied diplomatic and military pressure to induce Napoleon to sell New Orleans and a small slice of coastal territory to its east to the United States. This was his main objective: to possess New Orleans and control the mouth of the Mississippi River, outlet to world markets. To his surprise, Napoleon suddenly decided in early 1803 to sell all of the immense Louisiana Territory to the United States.

Watch the **Video**
at **www.myhistorylab.com**
Lewis and Clark: What were they trying to accomplish?

Napoleon's failure to reconquer Saint-Domingue (modern-day Haiti) was instrumental in his about-face on plans for a revived French empire in America. He had envisioned this rich sugar island as the jewel of his new empire and intended to use the Louisiana Territory as a granary to supply the island. During the upheavals of the French Revolution, the slaves on the island, led by Toussaint L'Ouverture, rebelled in a bloody and successful bid for independence. Napoleon sent a large army to reassert French control, but it succumbed to disease and the islanders' fierce resistance. Without firm French control of Saint-Domingue, Louisiana was of little use to Napoleon. For $15 million (including about $4 million in French debts owed to American citizens), he offered to part with the whole of Louisiana. The cost to the United States was about 3.5 cents per acre.

Read the **Document**
at **www.myhistorylab.com**
From Then to Now Online: The Lewis and Clark Expedition in Their World and Ours

Jefferson, the strict constructionist, now turned pragmatist. Despite the lack of any specific authorization in the Constitution for the acquisition of foreign territory or the incorporation as U.S. citizens of the 50,000 French and Spanish descendants then living in Louisiana, he accepted Napoleon's deal. The Louisiana Purchase doubled the size of the United States and offered seemingly endless space to be settled by yeoman farmers. It also opened up another frontier for slaveholders in the lower Mississippi Valley.

Read the **Document**
at **www.myhistorylab.com**
Constitutionality of the Louisiana Purchase (1803)

Florida and Western Schemes

The magnificent prize of Louisiana did not satisfy Republican territorial ambitions. Still to be gained were river outlets on the Gulf Coast essential for the development of plantation agriculture in Alabama and Mississippi. The boundaries of the Louisiana Purchase were so vague that Jefferson felt justified in claiming Spanish-held Texas and the Gulf Coast eastward from New Orleans to Mobile Bay, including the Spanish province of West Florida. Against stiff Spanish

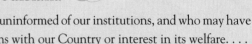

AMERICAN VIEWS

Protest of French Settlers in Louisiana

In the Louisiana Ordinance of 1804, Congress divided the Louisiana Purchase territory into northern and southern parts along a line that later separated the future state of Louisiana (originally designated the Territory of Orleans) from the territory to the north. No rights of self-government were extended to the settlers in Louisiana. Instead, a territorial government was established for which the president appointed both the governor and his advisory council. Congress also prohibited the inhabitants from engaging in the foreign slave trade and restricted the admission of future slaves to the bona-fide property of the actual settlers. A bill limiting the bondage of incoming slaves to one year passed the House but was rejected in the Senate. The following memorial to Congress registers the grievances of the French settlers over their treatment.

- **What** feature of congressional policy did the settlers single out as a major grievance?
- **Why** were the settlers so insistent that slavery was essential to their economic progress?
- **Why** do you think that Congress quickly abandoned its initial effort to restrict the growth of slavery in the Territory of Orleans?

We the subscribers, Planters, Merchants and other inhabitants of Louisiana respectfully approach the Legislature of the United States with a memorial of our rights, [and] a remonstrance against certain laws which contravene them. . . .

Without any agency in the events which have annexed our country to the United States, we yet considered them as fortunate, and thought our liberties secured even before we knew the terms of the cession. Persuaded that a free people would acquire territory only to extend the blessings of freedom, that an enlightened nation would never destroy those principles on which its government was founded, and that their Representatives would disdain to become the instruments of oppression, we calculated with certainty that their first act of sovereignty would be a communication of all the blessings they enjoyed. . . .

We pray leave to examine the law for erecting Louisiana. . . . This act does not "incorporate us into the Union," that it vests us with none of the "Rights," gives us no advances and deprives us of all the "immunities" of American citizens. . . .

A Governor is to be placed over us, whom we have not chosen, whom we do not even know, who may be ignorant of our language, uninformed of our institutions, and who may have no connections with our Country or interest in its welfare. . . .

We know not with what view the territory North of the 33d degree has been severed from us. . . . If this division should operate as to prolong our state of political tutelage, on account of any supposed deficiency of numbers, we cannot but consider it as injurious to our rights, and therefore enumerate it among those points of which we have reason to complain. . . .

There is one subject however extremely interesting to us, in which great care has been taken to prevent any interference even by the Governor and Council, selected by the President himself. The African trade is absolutely prohibited, and severe penalties imposed on a traffic free to all the Atlantic states, who choose to engage in it, and as far as it relates to procuring the subjects of it from other states [the domestic slave trade], permitted even in the territory of the Mississippi.

It is not our intention to enter into arguments that have become familiar to every reasoner on this question. We only ask the right of deciding it for ourselves, and of being placed in this aspect on an equal footing with other states. To the necessity of employing African labourers, which arises from climate, and the species of cultivation [sugar], pursued in warm latitudes, is added reason in this country peculiar to itself. The banks raised to restrain the waters of the Mississippi can only be kept in repair by those whose natural constitution and habits of labour enable them to resist the combined effects of a deleterious moisture, and a degree of heat intolerable to whites; this labour is great, it requires many hands and it is all important to the very existence of our country. . . .

Another subject . . . of great moment to us, is the sudden change of language in all the public offices and administration of justice. The great mass of the inhabitants speak nothing but the French: the late government was always very careful in their selection of officers, to find men who possessed our language and with whom we could personally communicate. . . .

We therefore respectfully pray that so much of the law mentioned above as provides for the temporary government of this country, as divides it into two territories, and prohibits the importation of slaves, be repealed.

Source: Pierre Derbigney, Memorial Presented by the Inhabitants of Louisiana to the Congress of the United States, Washington: Samuel H. Smith, 1804, Gilder Lehman Collection of American History, Pierpont Morgan Library, cited in *The Boisterous Sea of Liberty: A Documentary History of America from Discovery through the Civil War,* ed. by David Brion Davis and Steven Mintz (New York: Oxford University Press, 1998), pp. 290–293.

The PRAIRIE DOG sickened at the sting of the HORNET
or a Diplomatic Puppet exhibiting his Deceptions!

This Federalist cartoon satirizes Jefferson, in the form of a prairie dog, coughing up the $2 million bribe to Napoleon for the acquisition of West Florida, while a French diplomat stands by dancing and taunting Jefferson.

opposition, he pushed ahead with his plans to acquire West Florida. This provoked the first challenge to his leadership of the party.

Once it was clear that Spain did not want to sell West Florida to the United States, Jefferson accepted Napoleon's offer to act as a middleman in the acquisition. Napoleon's price was $2 million. He soon lost interest in the project, however, and Jefferson lost prestige in 1806, when he pushed an appropriations bill through Congress to pay for Napoleon's services. Former Republican stalwarts in Congress denounced the bill as bribe money and staged a party revolt against the president's devious tactics.

Jefferson's failed bid for West Florida emboldened westerners to demand that Americans seize the territory by force. In 1805 and 1806, Aaron Burr, Jefferson's first vice president, apparently became entangled in an attempt at just such a land grab.

Republicans had been suspicious of Burr since his dalliance with the Federalists in their bid to make him, rather than Jefferson, president in 1800. He further alienated the party when he involved himself with the efforts of a minority of die-hard Federalists known as the Essex Junto. The members of this group feared that incorporation of the vast Louisiana Purchase into the United States would leave New England powerless in national affairs. They concocted a plan for a northern confederacy in which New York would play a key role. Rebuffed by Hamilton, they turned to Burr and backed him in the New York gubernatorial race of 1804. Burr lost, largely because Hamilton denounced him. The enmity between the two men reached a tragic climax in July 1804, when Burr killed Hamilton in a duel at Weehawken, New Jersey. Burr, indicted for murder in the state of New Jersey, was nonetheless able to return to Washington where he both resumed his duties as vice president and hatched a separatist plot for the West.

QUICK REVIEW

Jefferson and Florida

- Jefferson failed in attempts to buy West Florida.
- Westerners demanded that the territory be taken by force.
- Aaron Burr involved in failed conspiracy to seize land in Florida.

The Burr conspiracy remains mysterious. Burr was undoubtedly eager to pry land loose from the Spanish and Indians, and he may have been thinking of carving out a separate western confederacy in the lower Mississippi Valley. Whatever he had in mind, he blundered in relying on General James Wilkinson as a co-conspirator. Wilkinson, the military governor of the Louisiana Territory and also a double agent for Spain, betrayed Burr. He was tried for treason in 1807, and Jefferson made extraordinary efforts to secure his conviction. He was saved by the insistence of Chief Justice Marshall that the Constitution defined treason only as the waging of war against the United States or the rendering of aid to its enemies. The law also required the direct testimony of two witnesses to an "overt act" of treason for conviction. Lacking such witnesses, the government failed to prove its case, and Burr was acquitted.

Embargo and a Crippled Presidency

Concern about a possible war against Britain in 1807 soon quieted the uproar over Burr's trial. After Britain and France had resumed their war in 1803, the United States became enmeshed in the same quarrels over neutral rights, blockades, ship seizures, and **impressment** of U.S. sailors that had almost dragged the country into war in the 1790s. Britain proclaimed a blockade of the European continent, which was controlled by Napoleon, and confiscated the cargoes of ships attempting to run the blockade. Napoleon retaliated with seizures of ships that submitted to

impressment The coercion of American sailors into the British navy.

British searches and accepted the British-imposed licensing system for trading with Europe. Caught in the middle, but eager to supply both sides, was the U.S. merchant marine, the world's largest carrier of neutral goods.

U.S. merchants and shippers had taken full advantage of the opportunities opened by the European war. Despite French and British restrictions, American merchants traded with anyone they pleased. They dominated commerce, not only between Britain and the United States, but also between the European continent and the French and Spanish colonies in the West Indies. Profits were so great that merchants made money even when only one-third of their ships evaded the blockades.

In June 1807, however, a confrontation known as the ***Chesapeake* Incident** nearly triggered an Anglo-American war. A British ship, the *Leopard*, ordered a U.S. frigate, the *Chesapeake*, to submit to a search in coastal waters off Norfolk, Virginia. When the commander of the *Chesapeake* refused, the *Leopard* opened fire. Jefferson resisted the popular outcry for revenge. Instead, he barred U.S. ports to British warships and called both for monetary compensation and an end to impressments, not only because the country was woefully unprepared for war but also because he passionately believed that international law should settle disputes between nations.

***Chesapeake* Incident** Attack in 1807 by the British ship *Leopard* on the American ship *Chesapeake* in American territorial waters.

In a last burst of the idealism that had animated the republicanism of the Revolution, Jefferson resorted to a trade embargo as a substitute for war. The **Embargo Act of 1807**, an expression of Jefferson's policy of "peaceable coercion," prohibited U.S. ships from leaving port to any nation until Britain and France repealed their trading restrictions on neutral shippers.

Embargo Act of 1807 Act passed by Congress in 1807 prohibiting American ships from leaving for any foreign port.

The premise of the embargo was that Europe was so dependent on American foods and raw materials that it would do America's bidding if faced with a cutoff. This premise was not so much wrong as unrealistic. The embargo did hurt Europe, but the people who first felt the pain were British textile workers and slaves in the colonies, hardly those who wielded the levers of power. Meanwhile, politically influential landlords and manufacturers benefited from short-term shortages by jacking up prices.

QUICK REVIEW

Growth of American Trade: 1793–1807

- Britain and France resumed war in 1803.
- American merchants wanted to supply both sides.
- Value of American exports increased fivefold between 1793 and 1807.

The U.S. export trade and its profits dried up with Jefferson's self-imposed blockade. Except for manufacturers, who now had the U.S. market to themselves, nearly all economic groups suffered under the embargo. Especially hard hit were New England shippers and merchants, and they accused the Republicans of near-criminal irresponsibility for forcing a depression on the country. Jefferson responded to these criticisms and to widespread violations of the embargo with a series of enforcement acts that consolidated executive powers far beyond what the Federalists themselves had been able to achieve while in power.

As the embargo tightened and the 1808 presidential election approached, the Federalist Party revived. The Federalist presidential candidate, Charles C. Pinckney, running against Secretary of State James Madison, Jefferson's handpicked successor, polled three times as many votes as he had in 1804. Madison won only because he carried the South and the West, the Republican heartland.

Before Madison took office, the Republicans abandoned Jefferson's embargo, replacing it with the Nonintercourse Act, a measure that prohibited U.S. trade only with Britain and France. At the president's discretion, trade could be reopened with either nation once it lifted its restrictions on U.S. shipping.

MADISON AND THE COMING OF WAR

WHAT FACTORS pushed Madison into a war with Britain?

Frail-looking and short, Madison struck most contemporaries as an indecisive and weaker version of Jefferson. Yet in intellectual toughness and resourcefulness he was at least Jefferson's equal. He failed because of an inherited foreign policy that was partly of his own making as Jefferson's secretary of state. The Republicans' idealistic stand on neutral rights was ultimately untenable unless backed up by military and political force. Madison concluded as much when he decided on war against Britain in the spring of 1812.

A war against America's old enemy also promised to restore unity to a Republican Party increasingly divided over Madison's peaceful diplomacy. Thus did Madison and his fellow Republicans push for a war they were eager but unprepared to fight.

The Failure of Economic Sanctions

As pressure mounted to reopen all trade routes, Congress responded in 1810 by replacing the Nonintercourse Act with Macon's Bill No. 2, named after Congressman Nathaniel Macon. This measure threw open American trade to everyone but stipulated that if either France or England lifted its restrictions, the president would resume trading sanctions against the other. Napoleon now duplicitously promised to withdraw his decrees against U.S. shipping on the condition that if Britain did not follow suit, Madison would force the British to respect U.S. rights. To Madison's chagrin, French seizures of U.S. ships continued. By the time Napoleon's duplicity became clear, he had already succeeded in worsening Anglo-American tensions. In November 1810, Madison reimposed nonintercourse against Britain, putting the two nations on a collision course.

The Frontier and Indian Resistance

Mounting frustrations in the South and West also pushed Madison toward a war against Britain. Nearly a million Americans lived west of the Appalachian Mountains in 1810, a tripling of the western population in just a decade. Farm prices, including those for the southern staples of cotton and tobacco, plunged when Jefferson's embargo shut off exports, and they stayed low after the embargo was lifted. Blame for the persistent agricultural depression focused on the British and their stranglehold on overseas trade after 1808. Western settlers also accused the British of inciting Indian resistance. However, it was the unceasing demand of Americans for ever more Indian land, not any British incitement, that triggered the **pan-Indian resistance movement** that so frightened western settlers on the eve of the War of 1812.

pan-Indian resistance movement Movement calling for the political and cultural unification of Indian tribes in the late eighteenth and early nineteenth centuries.

In the Treaty of Greenville (1795) (see Chapter 8), the U.S. government had promised that any future acquisitions of Indian land would be approved by all native peoples in the region. Nonetheless, government agents continued to play one group against another and divide groups from within by lavishing money and goods on the more accommodationist Christianized Indians. By such means, William Henry Harrison, the governor of the Indiana Territory, procured most of southern Indiana in the Treaty of Vincennes of 1804. Two extraordinary leaders, the Shawnee chief Tecumseh and his brother, the Prophet Tenkswatawa, channeled Indian outrage over this treaty into a movement to unify tribes throughout the West for a stand against the white invaders.

The message of pan-Indianism was unwavering: White encroachments had to be stopped and tribal and clan divisions submerged in a return to native rituals and belief systems. With the assistance of Tecumseh, Tenkswatawa established the Prophet's Town in 1808. At the confluence of the Wabash and Tippecanoe rivers in north-central Indiana, this encampment became headquarters of an intertribal confederation. As he tried to explain to the worried Governor Harrison, his goals were peaceful. He admonished his followers, "[Do] not take up the tomahawk, should it be offered by the British, or by the long knives [Virginians]: do not meddle with any thing that does not belong to you, but mind your own business, and cultivate the ground, that your women and your children have enough to live on."

That ground, of course, was the very reason the Indians could not live in peace and dignity. White settlers wanted it and would do anything to get it. In November 1811, Harrison marched an army to Prophet's Town and provoked the Battle of Tippecanoe. Losses were heavy on both sides, but Harrison regrouped his forces, drove the surviving Indians away, and burned the abandoned town. Harrison's victory came at a high cost: Tecumseh now joined forces with the British, leaving the frontier more unsettled than ever.

While Harrison's aggressiveness was converting fears of a British-Indian alliance into a self-fulfilling prophecy, expansionist-minded southerners struck at Britain through Spain, now its ally against Napoleon. With the covert support of President Madison, U.S. adventurers staged a bloodless revolt in Spanish West Florida between Louisiana and the Pearl River. This "republic" was quickly recognized by the U.S. government and annexed as part of Louisiana in 1811.

Hatred of Native Americans, expansionist pressures, the lingering agricultural depression, and impatience with the administration's policy of economic coercion all pointed in the same direction: a war against Britain coupled with a U.S. takeover of British Canada and what remained of Spanish Florida. This was the rallying cry of the **War Hawks,** the forty or so prowar congressmen swept into office in 1810. Generally younger men from the South and West, the War Hawks were led by Henry Clay of Kentucky. Along with other outspoken nationalists, such as John C. Calhoun of South Carolina, Clay played a key role in building congressional support for Madison's growing aggressiveness on the British issue.

The Prophet Tenkswatawa was the spiritual leader of the pan-Indian movement that sought to revitalize native culture and block the spread of white settlement in the Old Northwest.

Decision for War

In July 1811, Madison issued a Proclamation calling Congress into an early session on November 4. When Congress met, Madison tried to lay the groundwork for war. But the Republican-controlled Congress balked at strengthening the military or raising taxes to pay for war. On June 1, he sent a war message to Congress in which he laid out the stark alternative of submission or resistance to British control of U.S. commerce. Madison was now convinced that British commercial restrictions were not just a defensive measure aimed at France but an aggressive attempt to reduce the United States to the permanent status of colonial dependent.

For Madison and most other Republicans, the impending conflict was a second war for independence. Free and open access to world markets was certainly at stake, but so was national pride. The arrogant British policy of impressment was a humiliating affront to U.S. honor and headed the list of grievances in Madison's war message.

A divided Congress declared war on Britain. Support for the war was strongest in regions whose economies had been damaged the most by the British blockade and control of Atlantic commerce. Thus, the South and the West, trapped in an agricultural depression and anxious to eliminate foreign threats at their frontiers, favored war. Conversely, mercantile New England, a region that had, ironically, prospered as a result of British interference with ocean commerce, opposed the war.

The votes that carried the war declaration came from northern Republicans, who saw the impending struggle as a defense of America's experiment in self-government. Nine-tenths of the congressional Republicans voted for war, but not a single Federalist did so. For the Federalists, the real enemy was France, which had actually seized more U.S. ships than had the British. From their strongholds in coastal New England, the Federalists condemned the war as a French-inspired plot and predicted that it would end in financial ruin.

The Federalists' anger increased when they learned that the British had been prepared to yield on one of the most prominent issues. On June 23, the British government revoked for one year its Orders in Council against the United States. This concession, however, did not address impressment or monetary compensation, and news of it reached America too late to avert a war.

W
WHERE TO LEARN MORE
Tippecanoe Battlefield Museum, Battle Ground, Indiana http://www.tcha.mus.in.us/battlefield.htm

QUICK REVIEW

Treaties and Resistance

- Treaty of Greenville (1795) promised all further acquisitions of Indian land would be approved by all native peoples in the region.
- Treaty of Vincennes (1804) procured most of southern Indiana in violation of Treaty of Greenville.
- Indian tribes throughout West unified for stand against settlers.

War Hawks Members of Congress, predominantly from the South and West, who aggressively pushed for a war against Britain after their election in 1810.

THE WAR OF 1812

WHAT WERE the consequences of the War of 1812?

The Republicans led the nation into a war it was unprepared to fight. (See Map 9–1.) Still, the apparent vulnerability of Canada to invasion and the British preoccupation with Napoleon in Europe made it possible to envision a U.S. victory.

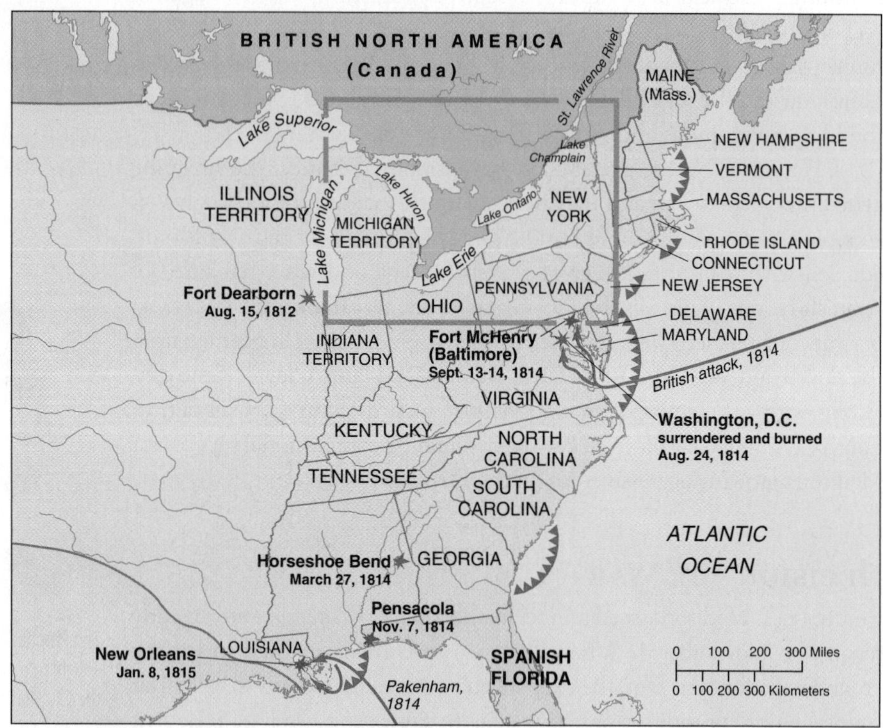

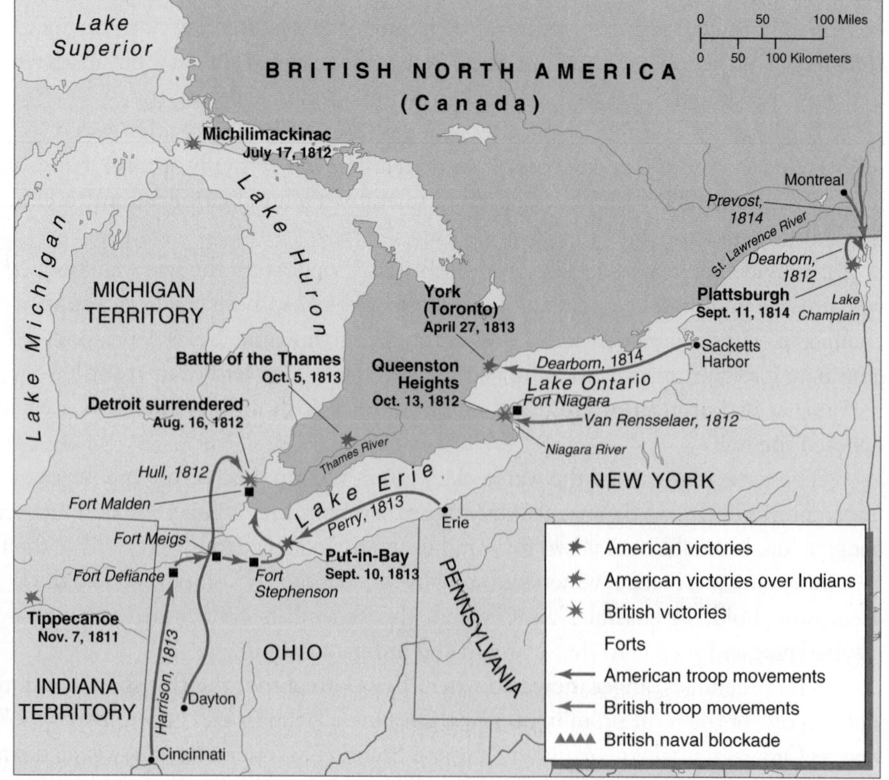

See the **Map**

at **www.myhistorylab.com**
The War of 1812

MAP 9–1 **The War of 1812** Most of the battles of the War of 1812 were fought along the Canadian-American border, where American armies repeatedly tried to invade Canada. Despite the effectiveness of the British naval blockade, the American navy was successful in denying the British strategic control of the Great Lakes. Andrew Jackson's smashing victory at the Battle of New Orleans convinced Americans that they had won the war.

Why was control of the Great Lakes so important to both sides? Why was the Battle of New Orleans so important in shaping the final terms of the peace treaty that ended the war?

Setbacks in Canada

The **War of 1812** unleashed deep emotions that often divided along religious lines. From their strongholds in the Congregationalist churches in New England, the Federalists preached that all true Christians opposed a war "against the nation from which we are descended, and which for many generations has been the bulwark of the religion we profess." Such antiwar sentiments, however, outraged the Baptists and Methodists, the largest and most popularly rooted denominations. They believed, as resolved by the Georgia Baptist Association in 1813, that the British government was "corrupt, arbitrary, and despotic" and that the war was "just, necessary, and indispensable."

War of 1812 War fought between the United States and Britain from June 1812 to January 1815 largely over British restrictions on American shipping.

Fiercely loyal to Madison, who had championed religious freedom in Virginia, these Methodists and Baptists harbored old grudges against the established churches of both Britain and New England for suppressing their religious rights. Especially for the Baptists, the war became something of a crusade to secure civil and religious liberties against their traditional enemies.

Fort Meigs Historic Site, Perrysburg, Ohio http://www.fortmeigs.org

Madison hoped to channel this Christian anti-British patriotism into the conquest of Canada. Two out of three Canadians were native-born Americans who, it was assumed, would welcome the United States Army with open arms. Only 5,000 British troops were initially stationed in Canada, and Canadian militia were outnumbered nine to one by their U.S. counterparts.

Canada was also the only area where the United States could strike directly against British forces. Although officially a war to defend America's neutrality on the high seas, the War of 1812 was largely a land war. The United States simply did not have enough ships to do more than harass the powerful British navy.

By seizing Canada, Madison also hoped to weaken Britain's navy and undercut its maritime system. Madison had been convinced that withholding U.S. foodstuffs and provisions from the British West Indies would quickly force the British to yield to U.S. economic pressure. But the British had turned to Canada as an alternative source of supplies. Madison hoped to close off that source. And if, as Madison expected, Napoleon denied the British access to the naval stores of the Baltic region in Europe, a U.S. monopoly on Canadian lumber would cripple British naval power. Facing such a threat, the British would have to end the war on U.S. terms.

Madison's strategic vision was clear, but its execution was pathetic. Three offensives against Canada in 1812 were embarrassing failures (see Map 9–1). Republican expectations of victory in Canada had been wishful thinking. Most Canadians fought against, not with, the Americans. Reliance on state militias proved disastrous. Poorly trained and equipped, the militias, when they did show up for battle, could not match the discipline of British soldiers or the fighting skills of their Native American allies. Nor was U.S. generalship on a par with that of the British. Primitive land communications made the movement and coordination of troops a nightmare. New England, the obvious base for operations against the strategically critical St. Lawrence River Valley—the entry point for all British supplies and reinforcements—withheld many of its state forces from national service. Consequently, the invasions were piecemeal, ineffective forays launched from western areas where anti-British and anti-Indian sentiment ran high. All the Republicans had to show for the first year of the war were morale-boosting but otherwise insignificant naval victories. In individual combat between ships, the small U.S. navy acquitted itself superbly. Early in the war, U.S. privateers harassed British merchant vessels, but the easy pickings were soon gone. British naval squadrons were redeployed to protect shipping, and other warships kept up a blockade that stifled U.S. commerce.

QUICK REVIEW

Invasion of Canada

- Madison hoped to conquer Canada.
- Three offensives against Canada in 1812 were failures.
- By the end of 1812 British controlled half of Old Northwest.

Military setbacks and antiwar feeling in much of the Northeast hurt the Republicans in the election of 1812. Madison won only narrowly over DeWitt Clinton, an antiadministration Republican from New York. The now familiar regional pattern in voting repeated itself. Madison swept the electoral vote of the South and West. He ran poorly in the Northeast and won only because his party held on to Pennsylvania.

Western Victories and British Offensives

U.S. forces fared better in 1813. In September, the navy won a major engagement on Lake Erie that opened up a supply line in the western theater. Commodore Oliver Hazard Perry attacked the British fleet in the **Battle of Put-in-Bay,** on the southwestern shore of the lake, and forced the surrender of all six British ships. The victory signaled General William Henry Harrison to launch an offensive in the West.

Battle of Put-in-Bay American naval victory on Lake Erie in September 1813 in the War of 1812 that denied the British strategic control over the Great Lakes.

With the loss of Lake Erie, the British were forced to abandon Detroit, a place they had captured in the first year of the war. Harrison caught up with the British garrison and their Indian allies on the banks of the Thames River in southern Ontario. Demonstrating bold leadership and relying on battle-tested western militias, Harrison won a decisive victory. Tecumseh, the most visionary of the Indian warriors, was killed, and the backbone of the Indian resistance was broken. The Old Northwest was again safe for U.S. settlement.

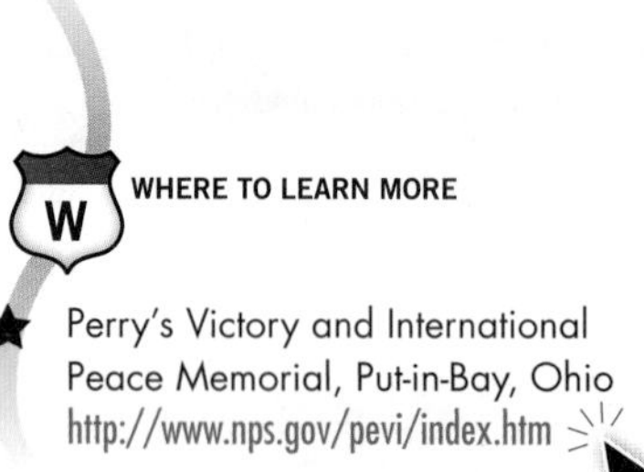

Perry's Victory and International Peace Memorial, Put-in-Bay, Ohio
http://www.nps.gov/pevi/index.htm

The Battle of the Thames ended British plans for an Indian buffer state. But by 1814, Britain had bigger goals in mind. A coalition of European powers forced Napoleon to abdicate in April 1814, thus freeing Britain to focus on the U.S. war. It now seemed poised to win the war with a clear-cut victory. British strategy in 1814 called for two major offensives—an invasion south from Montreal down Lake Champlain in upstate New York, and an attack on Louisiana aimed at seizing New Orleans with a task force out of Jamaica. The overall objective was nothing less than a reversal of America's post-1783 expansion.

The British attacks could hardly have come at a worse time for the Madison administration. The Treasury was nearly bankrupt. Lacking both a centralized means of directing wartime finances and any significant increase in taxes, the Treasury was forced to rely on makeshift loans. These loans were poorly subscribed, largely because the cash-rich New England banks refused to buy them. Inflation also became a problem when state banks, no longer restrained by the control of a national bank, overissued paper money in the form of bank notes.

As the country's finances tottered toward collapse, political dissent in New England was reaching a climax. In 1814, the British extended their blockade of U.S. commerce northward to include New England. Federalist merchants and shippers, who had earlier profited from their illegal trade with the British, now felt the economic pinch of the war. Cries for resistance against "Mr. Madison's war" culminated in a call issued by the Massachusetts legislature for a convention to consider "a radical reform of the national compact." The convention was scheduled for December in Hartford, Connecticut.

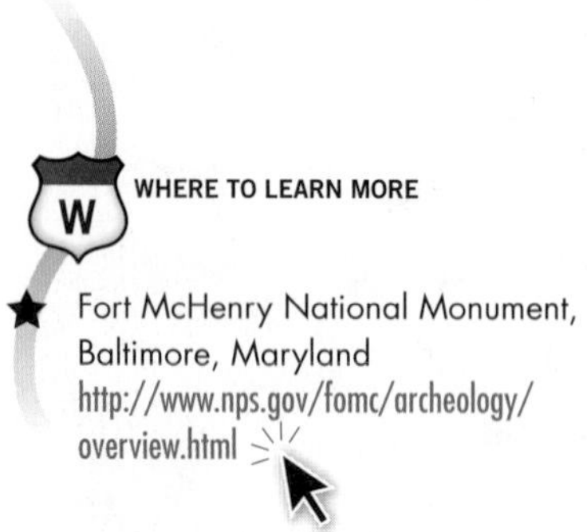

Fort McHenry National Monument, Baltimore, Maryland
http://www.nps.gov/fomc/archeology/overview.html

The darkest hour came in August 1814. A British amphibious force occupied and torched Washington, DC, in retaliation for a U.S. raid on York (now Toronto), the capital of Upper Canada. Still, the British actions stiffened U.S. resistance, and the failure of a follow-up attack on Baltimore deprived the British of any strategic gain.

The Chesapeake raids were designed to divert U.S. attention from the major offensive General George Prevost was leading down the shores of Lake Champlain. Prevost commanded the largest and best-equipped army the British had yet assembled, but he was forced to turn back when Commodore Thomas McDonough defeated a British fleet on September 11 at the **Battle of Plattsburgh.**

Battle of Plattsburgh Victory of Commodore Thomas McDonough over a British fleet in Lake Champlain, September 11, 1814.

The tide had turned. When news of the setbacks at Baltimore and Plattsburgh reached England, the Foreign Office scaled back the demands it had been making on U.S. negotiators at peace talks in the city of Ghent, in present-day Belgium. The British were ready for peace, but one of their trump cards had yet to be played—the southern offensive against New Orleans. The outcome of that campaign could still upset whatever was decided at Ghent.

The Treaty of Ghent and the Battle of New Orleans

By the fall of 1814, the British were eager to redraw the map of post-Napoleonic Europe, restore profitable relations with America, and reduce their huge war debt. The British negotiators at Ghent agreed to a peace treaty on terms the Americans were delighted to accept. The **Treaty of Ghent,** signed on Christmas Eve, 1814, simply restored relations to their status at the start of the war. No territory changed hands, and nothing was said about impressment or the rights of neutrals. The ink had barely dried on the Treaty of Ghent when the British government sent reinforcements to General Edward Pakenham, the commander of the Louisiana invasion force. By this action, the British indicated that they were not irrevocably committed to the peace settlement, which, though signed, could not be formally ratified until weeks later, when it was sent across the Atlantic. Far from being an anticlimax to a war that was already over, the showdown between British and U.S. forces at the **Battle of New Orleans** in January 1815 had immense strategic significance for the United States.

Among the troops that Jackson led to victory at the Battle of New Orleans were a contingent of African Americans, the free men of color from New Orleans.

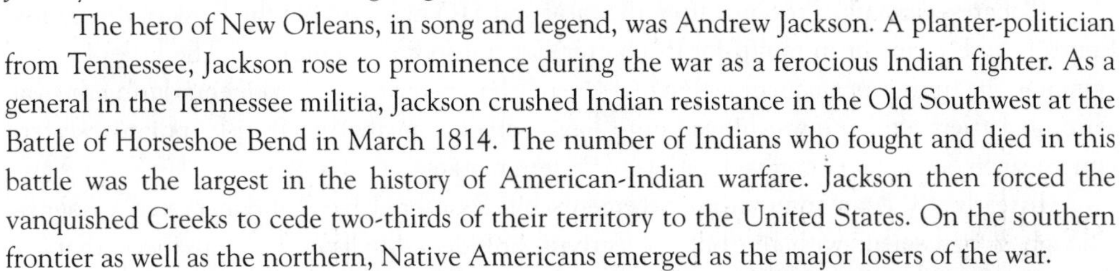

The hero of New Orleans, in song and legend, was Andrew Jackson. A planter-politician from Tennessee, Jackson rose to prominence during the war as a ferocious Indian fighter. As a general in the Tennessee militia, Jackson crushed Indian resistance in the Old Southwest at the Battle of Horseshoe Bend in March 1814. The number of Indians who fought and died in this battle was the largest in the history of American-Indian warfare. Jackson then forced the vanquished Creeks to cede two-thirds of their territory to the United States. On the southern frontier as well as the northern, Native Americans emerged as the major losers of the war.

After his Indian conquests, Jackson was promoted to general in the regular army and given command of the defense of the Gulf Coast. In November 1814, he seized Pensacola in Spanish Florida to deny the British its use as a supply depot and then hurried to defend New Orleans. The overconfident British frontally attacked Jackson's lines on January 8, 1815. The result was a massacre. More than 2,000 British soldiers were killed or wounded. U.S. casualties totaled 21.

Strategically, Jackson's smashing victory at New Orleans ended any possibility of a British sphere of influence in Louisiana. Politically, it was a deathblow to Federalism. At the Hartford Convention in December 1814, party moderates had forestalled talk of secession with a series of proposed constitutional amendments designed to limit southern power in national affairs. Set against the revived nationalism that marked the end of the war, the Federalists now seemed to be parochial sulkers who put regional interests above the national good. Worse yet, they struck many Americans as quasi-traitors who had been prepared to desert the country in the face of the enemy. As a significant political force, Federalism was dead.

Treaty of Ghent Treaty signed in December 1814 between the United States and Britain that ended the War of 1812.

Read the Document
at **www.myhistorylab.com**
The Treaty of Ghent (1814)

Battle of New Orleans Decisive American War of 1812 victory over British troops in January 1815 that ended any British hopes of gaining control of the lower Mississippi River Valley.

Read the Document
at **www.myhistorylab.com**
Report and Resolutions of the Hartford Convention (1814)

THE ERA OF GOOD FEELINGS

In 1817, on the occasion of a presidential visit by James Monroe, a Boston newspaper proclaimed the **Era of Good Feelings,** an expression that nicely captured the spirit of political harmony and sectional unity that washed over the republic in the immediate postwar years. National pride surged with the humbling of the British at New Orleans, the demise of the Federalists lessened political tensions, and the economy was booming. The Republicans had been vindicated, and for a short time they enjoyed de facto status as the only governing party.

HOW DID rising nationalism contribute to the spirit of the Era of Good Feelings?

Economic Nationalism

The War of 1812 had taught the Republicans to appreciate the old Federalist doctrines on centralized national power. In his annual message of December 1815, Madison outlined a program of economic nationalism that was pushed through Congress by Henry Clay and

Era of Good Feelings The period from 1817 to 1823 in which the disappearance of the Federalists enabled the Republicans to govern in a spirit of seemingly nonpartisan harmony.

John C. Calhoun, the most prominent of the new generation of young, nationalist-minded Republicans.

The first order of business was to create a new national bank. Reliance on state banks for wartime financing had proved a major mistake. Fiscal stability required the monetary coordination and restraint that only a new Bank of the United States could provide. Introduced by Calhoun, the bank bill passed Congress in 1816. Modeled after Hamilton's original bank and also headquartered in Philadelphia, the **Second Bank of the United States** was capitalized at $35 million, making it by far the nation's largest bank. Its size and official status as the depository and dispenser of the government's funds gave the bank tremendous economic power.

Second Bank of the United States A national bank chartered by Congress in 1816 with extensive regulatory powers over currency and credit.

After moving to repair the fiscal damage of the war, the Republicans then acted to protect what the war had fostered. Embargoes followed by three years of war had forced U.S. businessmen to manufacture goods they previously had imported. This was especially the case with iron and textile goods long supplied by the British. In 1815 and again in 1816, the British inundated the U.S. market with cheap imports to strangle U.S. industry in its infancy. Responding to this challenge to the nation's economic independence, the Republicans passed the Tariff of 1816, the first protective tariff in U.S. history.

Congress earmarked revenue from the tariff and $1.5 million from the Bank of the United States (a cash payment in return for its charter) for transportation projects. The lack of a road system in the trans-Appalachian region had severely hampered troop movements during the war. Also, as settlers after the war moved onto lands seized from the pro-British Indians, western congressmen demanded improved outlets to eastern markets.

QUICK REVIEW

Economic Nationalism

- Second Bank of the United States established.
- Tariff of 1816 protected American manufacturers.
- Revenue from the tariff earmarked for transportation projects.

In early 1817, an internal-improvements bill sponsored by Calhoun passed Congress. Though in agreement with the bill's objectives, President Madison was convinced that the Constitution did not permit federal financing of primarily local projects. He vetoed the bill just before he left office.

Congressional passage of Calhoun's internal-improvements bill marked the pinnacle of the Republicans' economic nationalism. Frightened by the sectional disunity of the war years, a new generation of Republicans jettisoned many of the ideological trappings of Jefferson's original agrarian party. Their program was a call for economic, and therefore political, unity. Support for this program was strongest in the mid-Atlantic and western states, the regions that stood to gain the most economically. Opposition centered in the Southeast, notably among die-hard proponents of states' rights in the old tobacco belt of Virginia and North Carolina and in New England, a region not only well served already by banks and a road network but also anxious not to be politically overshadowed by the rising West. This opposition took on an increasingly hard edge in the South as the Supreme Court outlined an ever more nationalist interpretation of the Constitution.

Judicial Nationalism

Under Chief Justice John Marshall, the Supreme Court had long supported the nationalist perspective Republicans began to champion after the war. Two principles defined Marshall's jurisprudence: the primacy of the Supreme Court in all matters of constitutional interpretation and the sanctity of contractual property rights. In ***Fletcher v. Peck*** (1810), for example, the Court ruled that a Georgia law voiding a land grant made by an earlier legislature—on the grounds that it had involved massive fraud—violated the constitutional provision barring any state from "impairing the obligation of contracts." Marshall held that despite the fraud, the original land grant constituted an unbreakable legal contract.

Fletcher v. Peck Supreme Court decision of 1810 that overturned a state law by ruling that it violated a legal contract.

Out of the political limelight since the Burr trial in 1807, the Court was thrust back into it by two controversial decisions in 1819. The first involved Dartmouth College and the attempt by the New Hampshire legislature to amend its charter in the direction of greater public control over this private institution. In ***Dartmouth College v. Woodward,*** the Court ruled

Dartmouth College v. Woodward Supreme Court decision of 1819 that prohibited states from interfering with the privileges granted to a private corporation.

that Dartmouth's original royal charter of 1769 was a contract protected by the Constitution. Therefore, the state of New Hampshire could not alter the charter without the prior consent of the college. By sanctifying charters, or acts of incorporation, as contracts, the Court prohibited states from interfering with the rights and privileges they had bestowed on private corporations.

The second important decision in 1819, ***McCulloch v. Maryland,*** rested on a positive assertion of national power over the states. The case involved the Bank of the United States. In 1818, the Maryland legislature placed a heavy tax on the branch of the Bank of the United States established in Baltimore (and on all other banks in the state established without state legislative authority). James McCulloch, the cashier of the Baltimore branch, refused to pay the tax. This set up a test case that involved two fundamental legal issues: Was the bank itself constitutional? And could a state tax federal property within its borders?

A unanimous Court, in language similar to but even more sweeping than that used by Alexander Hamilton in the 1790s, upheld the constitutional authority of Congress to charter a national bank and thereby regulate the nation's currency and finances. As long as the end was legitimate "within the scope of the Constitution," Congress had full power to use any means not expressly forbidden by the Constitution to achieve that end. As for Maryland's claim of a constitutional right to tax a federal agency, Marshall stressed that "the power to tax involves the power to destroy." Surely, he reasoned, when the people of the United States ratified the Constitution, they did not intend the federal government to be controlled by the states or rendered powerless by state action. Here was the boldest statement to date of the loose, or "implied powers," interpretation of the Constitution.

McCulloch v. Maryland Supreme Court decision of 1819 that upheld the constitutional authority of Congress to charter a national bank, and thereby to regulate the nation's currency and finances.

Rush-Bagot Agreement Treaty of 1817 between the United States and Britain that effectively demilitarized the Great Lakes by sharply limiting the number of ships each power could station on them.

Anglo-American Accords Series of agreements reached in the British-American Conventions of 1818 that fixed the western boundary between the United States and Canada, allowed for joint occupation of Oregon, and restored American fishing rights.

Toward a Continental Empire

Marshall's legal nationalism paralleled the diplomatic nationalism of John Quincy Adams, secretary of state from 1817 to 1825. A former Federalist and the son of the second president, Adams broke with the party over its refusal to support an expansionist policy and held several diplomatic posts under the Madison administration. Adams shrewdly exploited Britain's desire for friendly and profitable relations after the War of 1812. The British wanted access to U.S. cotton and foodstuffs in exchange for manufactured goods and investment capital. The United States wanted more trading opportunities in the British Empire and a free hand to deal with Spain's disintegrating empire in the Americas.

The **Rush-Bagot Agreement** of 1817 signaled the new pattern of Anglo-American cooperation. The agreement strictly limited naval armaments on the Great Lakes, thus effectively demilitarizing the border with Canada. The **Anglo-American Accords** of the following year resolved several issues left hanging after the war. The British once again recognized U.S. fishing rights off Labrador and Newfoundland, a concession that was of great importance to New England. The boundary of the Louisiana Territory abutting Canada was set at the 49th parallel, and both nations agreed to the joint occupation of Oregon, the territory in the Pacific Northwest that lay west of the Rocky Mountains.

Having secured the northern flank of the United States, Adams was now free to deal with the South and West. Adams wanted all of Florida and an undisputed American window on the Pacific. The adversary here was Spain. Spain resorted to delaying tactics in trying to hold off the tenacious Adams. Negotiations remained deadlocked until Andrew Jackson gave Adams the leverage he needed.

As secretary of state, John Quincy Adams was unrelenting in his pursuit of a continental empire for the United States.

Dagli Orti/Picture Desk, Inc./Kobal Collection

Trans-Continental Treaty of 1819 Treaty between the United States and Spain in which Spain ceded Florida to the United States, surrendered all claims to the Pacific Northwest, and agreed to a boundary between the Louisiana Purchase territory and the Spanish Southwest.

Read the **Document** at **www.myhistorylab.com** *Exploring America: Continentalism*

In March 1818, Jackson led his troops across the border into Spanish Florida. He destroyed encampments of the Seminole Indians, seized two Spanish forts, and executed two British subjects on the grounds that they were selling arms to the Seminoles for raids on the Alabama-Georgia frontier. Despite later protestations to the contrary, Jackson had probably exceeded his orders. He might well have been censured by the Monroe administration had not Adams supported him, telling Spain that Jackson was defending U.S. interests and warning that he might be unleashed again.

Spain yielded to the U.S. threat in the **Trans-Continental Treaty of 1819.** The United States annexed East Florida, and Spain recognized the prior U.S. seizures of West Florida in 1810 and 1813. Adams secured a U.S. hold on the Pacific Coast by drawing a boundary between the Louisiana Purchase and the Spanish Southwest that ran stepwise up the Sabine, Red, and Arkansas rivers to the Continental Divide and then due west along the 42nd parallel to the Pacific (see Map 9–2). Spain renounced any claim to the Pacific Northwest; the United States

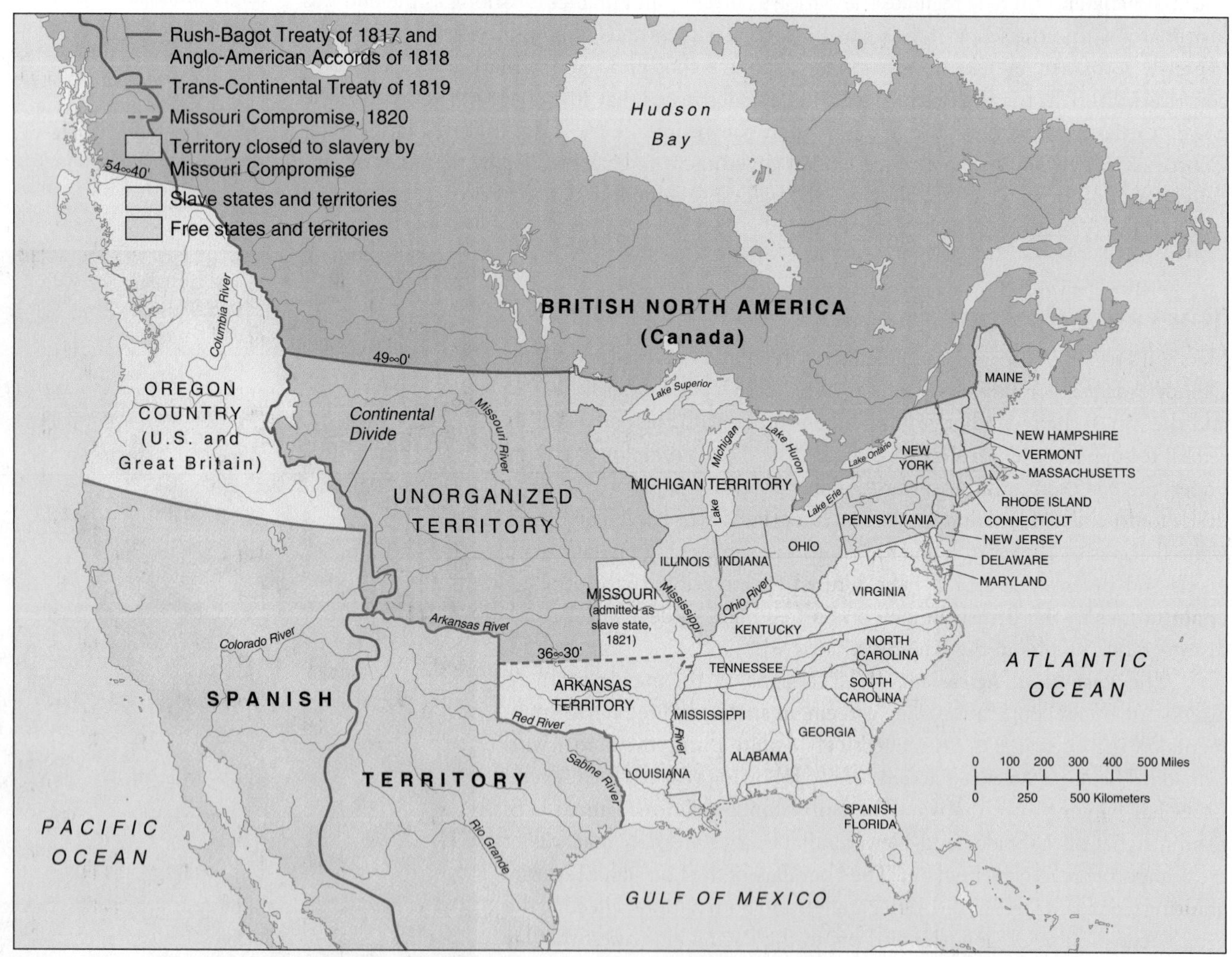

MAP 9–2 **The Missouri Compromise of 1820 and Territorial Treaties with Britain and Spain, 1818–1819** Treaties with Britain and Spain in 1818 and 1819 clarified and expanded the nation's boundaries. Britain accepted the 49th parallel as the boundary between Canada and the United States and agreed to joint occupation from the Trans-Mississippi West to the Oregon Country. Spain ceded Florida to the United States and agreed to a boundary stretching to the Pacific between the Louisiana Purchase territory and Spanish possessions in the Southwest. Sectional disputes over slavery led to the drawing of the Missouri Compromise line of 1820 that prohibited slavery in the Louisiana Territory north of 36° 30′.

Considering this map, where would you predict future conflicts over slavery might occur?

Fittingly placing Monroe next to a globe, this painting depicts one of the cabinet meetings that led to the formulation of the Monroe Doctrine.

in turn renounced its shaky claim to Texas under the Louisiana Purchase and assumed $5 million in Spanish debts to American citizens.

See the **Map** at **www.myhistorylab.com** *The Missouri Compromise of 1820–1821*

Adams's success in the Spanish negotiations turned on the British refusal to threaten war or assist Spain in the wake of Jackson's high-handed actions in Florida. Spanish possessions were worth little when weighed against the economic advantages of retaining close trading ties with the United States. Moreover, Britain, like the United States, had a vested interest in developing trade with the newly independent Latin American countries. Recognizing this common interest, George Canning, the British foreign minister, proposed in August 1823 that the United States and Britain issue a joint declaration opposing any European attempt to recolonize South America or to assist Spain in regaining its colonies.

President Monroe rejected the British overture, but only at the insistence of Adams. Adams wanted to maintain the maximum freedom of action for future U.S. policy and avoid any impression that America was beholden to Britain. He also wanted to cement relations with the new nations of Latin America that he had refused to recognize formally until 1822. Thus originated the most famous diplomatic statement in early American history, the **Monroe Doctrine.**

Monroe Doctrine In December 1823, Monroe declared to Congress that the Americas "are henceforth not to be considered as subjects for future colonization by any European power."

In his annual message to Congress in December 1823, Monroe declared that the Americas "are henceforth not to be considered as subjects for future colonization by any European power." In turn, Monroe pledged that the United States would not interfere in the internal affairs of European states. With its continental empire rapidly taking shape and new Latin American republics to be courted, the United States was more than willing to proclaim a special position for itself as the guardian of New World liberties.

THE BREAKDOWN OF UNITY

WHY DID slavery become such a divisive issue in the years preceding the Missouri Compromise?

For all the intensity with which he pursued his continental vision, John Quincy Adams worried in early 1819 that "the greatest danger of this union was in the overgrown extent of its territory, combining with the slavery question." His words were prophetic. A sectional crisis flared in 1819 over slavery and its expansion when the territory of Missouri sought admission to the Union as a slave state. Simultaneously, a financial panic ended postwar prosperity and crystallized regional discontent over banking and tariff policies. Party unity cracked under these pressures, and each region backed its own presidential candidate in the wide-open election of 1824.

The Panic of 1819

From 1815 to 1818, Americans enjoyed a wave of postwar prosperity. European markets were starved for U.S. goods after a generation of war and trade restrictions, so farmers and planters expanded production and brought new land into cultivation. The availability of public land in the West on easy terms of credit sparked a speculative frenzy, and land sales soared. State banks and, worse yet, the Bank of the United States fed the speculation by making loans in the form of bank notes far in excess of their hard-currency reserves.

European markets for U.S. cotton and food supplies returned to normal by late 1818. In January 1819, cotton prices sank in England, and the Panic of 1819 was on. Cotton was the most valuable U.S. export, and expected returns from the staple were the basis for an intricate credit network anchored in Britain. The fall in cotton prices triggered a credit contraction that soon engulfed the overextended U.S. economy. Commodity prices fell across the board, and real-estate values collapsed, especially in and around western cities.

A sudden shift in policy by the Bank of the United States virtually guaranteed that the economic downturn would settle into a depression. The Bank stopped all loans, called in all debts, and refused to honor drafts drawn on its branches in the South and West. Hardest hit by these policies were farmers and businessmen in the West, who had mortgaged their economic futures. Bankruptcies mushroomed as creditors forced the liquidation of farms and real estate. For westerners, the Bank of the United States now became "the Monster," a ruthless institution controlled by eastern aristocrats who callously destroyed the hopes of farmers.

Southern resentment over the hard times brought on by low cotton prices focused on the tariff. Planters charged that the Tariff of 1816 unfairly raised their costs and amounted to an unconstitutional tax levied for the sole benefit of northern manufacturers. Unreconstructed Jeffersonians, now known as the Old Republicans, spearheaded a sharp reaction against the South's flirtation with nationalist policies in the postwar period by demanding a return to strict doctrines of states' rights.

The Missouri Compromise

Until 1819, slavery was not a major divisive issue in U.S. politics. The Northwest Ordinance of 1787, which banned slavery in federal territories north of the Ohio River, and the Southwest Ordinance of 1790, which permitted slavery south of the Ohio, represented a compromise that had allowed slavery in areas where climate and soil conditions favored slave-based agriculture. What was unforeseen in the 1780s, however, was the explosive demand for slave-produced cotton generated by the English textile industry in the early nineteenth century (see Chapter 11). A thriving cotton market was underwriting slavery's expansion across the South, and even Missouri, a portion of the Louisiana Purchase that northerners initially assumed would be inhospitable to slavery, fell under the political control of slaveholders.

The Missouri issue increased long-simmering northern resentment over the spread of slavery and the southern dominance of national affairs under the Virginia presidents. In February 1819, James Tallmadge, a Republican congressman from New York, introduced an amendment in the House mandating a ban on future slave imports and a program of gradual emancipation as preconditions for the admission of Missouri as a state.

Without a two-party system in which each party had to compromise to protect its interests, voting followed sectional lines. The amendment passed in the northern-controlled House, but it was repeatedly blocked in the Senate, which was evenly divided between free and slave states. The debates were heated, and southerners spoke openly of secession if Missouri were denied admission as a slave state.

QUICK REVIEW

Tallmadge Amendment

- Proposed 1819 amendment banning future slave importations and imposing a program of gradual emancipation as condition of Missouri statehood.
- Passed by the House but rejected by the Senate.
- Voting broke down on regional lines.

The stalemate over Missouri persisted into the next session of Congress. Finally, Speaker of the House Henry Clay engineered a compromise in March 1820. Congress put no restrictions on slavery in Missouri, and the admission of Missouri as a slave state was balanced by the admission of Maine (formerly part of Massachusetts) as a free state. In return for their concession on Missouri, northern congressmen demanded a prohibition on slavery in the remainder of the Louisiana Purchase north of the 36°30' parallel, the southern boundary of Missouri (see Map 9–2). With the **Missouri Compromise,** the Louisiana Purchase was closed to slavery in the future, except for the Arkansas Territory and what would become the Indian Territory of Oklahoma. The compromise almost unraveled when Missouri submitted a constitution the following November that required the state legislature to bar the entry of free black people. Missouri's restrictionist policy obviously denied African American citizens the constitutional right to move from one state to any other state.

Missouri Compromise Sectional compromise in Congress in 1820 that admitted Missouri to the Union as a slave state and Maine as a free state and prohibited slavery in the northern Louisiana Purchase territory.

The nearly universal acceptance by white Americans of second-class citizenship for free black Americans permitted Clay to dodge the issue. Missouri's constitution was accepted with the proviso that it "shall never be construed" to discriminate against citizens in other states. With these meaningless words, the Missouri Compromise was salvaged. By sacrificing the claims of free black citizens for equal treatment, the Union survived its first great sectional crisis over slavery.

American System The program of government subsidies favored by Henry Clay and his followers to promote American economic growth and protect domestic manufacturers from foreign competition.

The Missouri crisis made white southerners aware that they were now a political minority within the Union. More rapid population growth in the North had reduced southern representation in the House to just over 40 percent. Of greater concern was the crystallization in Congress of a northern majority array against the expansion of slavery. Southern threats of secession died out in the aftermath of the Missouri Compromise, but it was an open question whether the sectional settlement really solved the intertwined issues of slavery and expansion or merely sidestepped them for a day of final reckoning.

The Election of 1824

The election of 1820 made Monroe, like both his Republican predecessors, a two-term president. The Federalists were too weak to run a candidate, and although Monroe won all but one of the electoral votes, Republican unity was more apparent than real. After Monroe's victory, Republicans split into factions as they began jockeying almost immediately for the election of 1824 (see Map 9–3).

Monroe had no obvious successor, and five candidates competed to replace him. All of them were nominal Republicans, and three were members of his cabinet. Secretary of War John C. Calhoun soon dropped out. He preferred to accept a nomination as vice president, confident that his turn would come in 1828. The other candidates, Secretary of the Treasury William Crawford from Georgia, Secretary of State John Quincy Adams from Massachusetts, Henry Clay from Kentucky, and Andrew Jackson from Tennessee, each had a strong regional following. As the Republican Party fragmented, sectional loyalties were replacing partisan allegiances.

None of the candidates ran on a platform, but Crawford was identified with states' rights, and Clay and Adams with centralized government. Clay in particular was associated with the national bank, protective tariffs, and federally funded internal improvements, a package of federal subsidies he called the **American System.** Jackson took no stand on any of the issues.

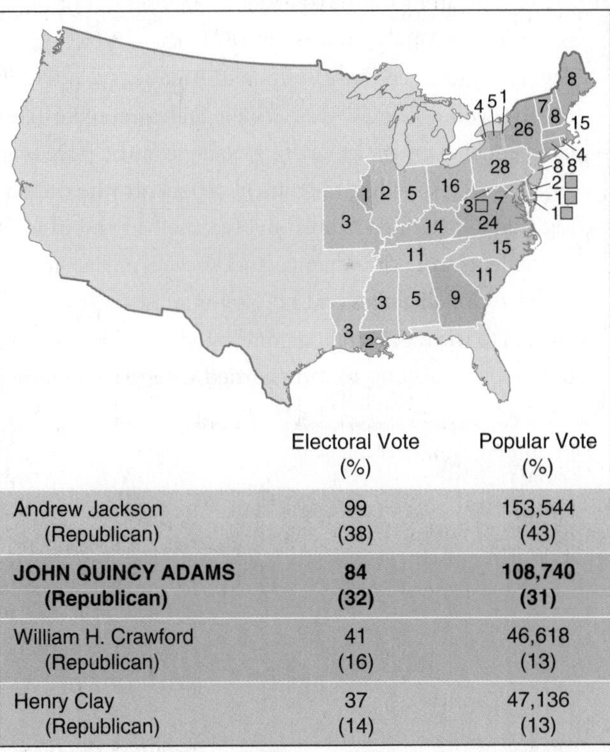

	Electoral Vote (%)	Popular Vote (%)
Andrew Jackson (Republican)	99 (38)	153,544 (43)
JOHN QUINCY ADAMS (Republican)	**84 (32)**	**108,740 (31)**
William H. Crawford (Republican)	41 (16)	46,618 (13)
Henry Clay (Republican)	37 (14)	47,136 (13)

MAP 9–3 **The Election of 1824** The regional appeal of each of the four presidential candidates in the election of 1824 prevented any candidate from receiving a majority of the electoral vote. Consequently, and as set forth in the Constitution, the House of Representatives now had to choose the president from the three leading candidates. Its choice was John Quincy Adams.

What does this map tell you about the state of the Republican Party in 1824?

GLOBAL CONNECTIONS

The U.S. Response to Independence Movements

"America . . . proclaimed to mankind the inextinguishable rights of human nature, and the only lawful foundations of government. . . . Wherever the standard of freedom and Independence has been or shall be unfurled, there will her heart, her benedictions and her prayers be. But she goes not abroad, in search of monsters to destroy. . . . She well knows that by once enlisting under other banners than her own, were they even the banners of foreign independence, she would involve herself beyond the power of extrication, in all the wars of interest and intrigue, of individual avarice, envy, and ambition, which assume the colors and usurp the standards of freedom. The fundamental maxims of her policy would insensibly change from liberty to force*. . . . She might become the dictatress of the world. She would no longer be the ruler of her spirit. . . . [America's] glory is not dominion, but liberty. Her march is the march of the mind."*

Drawn from the Independence Day speech of Secretary of State John Quincy Adams in 1821, these words gave classic expression to an enduring tension in America's relations with the outside world: Should the United States promote liberty and independence by the force of its example or the force of its arms? Adams was responding to political opponents who were demanding that the United States involve itself in the independence movements in Latin America and Greece. Adams refused to do so. The United States had no vital interests at stake in Greece, and aid to the rebels or premature recognition of the government they were struggling to form carried the risk of embroiling the United States in a conflict with their enemies, the Turks and Russians. Moreover, direct involvement in a European affair would set a dangerous precedent that Europeans could cite to intervene in the Western Hemisphere, where Adams wanted the United States to have a free hand.

As for the Latin American revolutionaries, Adams noted their disregard of the civil rights for which Americans had contended during the Revolution. He had no doubt that the independence movements to the south would eventually succeed, but he believed that the United States could best support them and the cause of liberty by championing and vindicating its own freedom and independence. To intervene abroad in an effort to transform foreign societies was to endanger liberty at home.

At the insistence of President Monroe, Adams extended diplomatic recognition to the new Latin American nations in 1822. In so doing, he insisted that the United States would recognize only governments that promised to adhere to all of their international obligations. Recognition, he stressed, carried no moral approval. This was the recognition policy followed by the U.S. government for ninty years, until President Woodrow Wilson committed it to a policy of liberal interventionism abroad.

- What is your position on the stand taken by Adams against the involvement of the United States in wars of liberty and independence?

Jackson's noncommittal stance turned out to be a great asset. It helped him to project the image of a military hero, fresh from the people, who was unsullied by any connection with Washington politicians, whom the public associated with hard times and sectional controversies. He was the highest vote-getter (43 percent of the popular vote), but none of the four candidates had a majority in the electoral college.

As in 1800, the election was thrown into the House of Representatives. Clay, who had received the fewest electoral votes, was eliminated. Crawford had suffered a debilitating stroke and was no longer a viable candidate. Thus it came down to Adams or Jackson. Anxious to undercut Jackson, his chief rival in the West, Clay used his influence as speaker of the House to line up support for Adams, a fellow advocate of a strong centralized government. Adams won the election, and he immediately named Clay as his secretary of state, the office traditionally viewed as a stepping-stone to the presidency. Jackson and his followers were outraged. They smelled a "corrupt bargain" in which Clay had bargained away the presidency to the highest bidder. Vowing revenge, they began building a new party that would usher in a more democratic era of mass-based politics.

CONCLUSION

In 1800, the Republicans were an untested party whose rise to power frightened many Federalists into predicting the end of the Union and constitutional government. The Federalists were correct in sensing that their days of power had passed, but they underestimated the ideological flexibility the Republicans would reveal once in office and the imaginative ways in which Jefferson and his successors would wield executive power to expand the size of the original Union. Far from being anarchists and demagogues, the Republicans were shrewd empire builders astute enough to add to their base of political support in the South and West. They also paved the way for the nation to evolve as a democratic republic rather than the more aristocratic republic preferred by the Federalists and Rosalie Calvert and her family.

With no Federalist threat to enforce party discipline, the Republicans lost their organizational strength. Embracing economic nationalism after the war made the party's original focus on states' rights all but meaningless. Ideologically and organizationally adrift, the party split into regional coalitions in the wake of the Missouri controversy and the panic of 1819. But before it dissolved, the party left as its most enduring legacy the foundations of a continental empire.

Where to Learn More

Fort McHenry National Monument, Baltimore, Maryland. This historic site preserves the fort that was the focal point of the British attack on Baltimore and contains a museum with materials on the battle and the writing of "The Star-Spangled Banner." For the military history of the fort and the archaeological work at the site, see http://www.nps.gov/fomc/archeology/overview.html.

Fort Meigs Historic Site, Perrysburg, Ohio. Part of the War of 1812 Heritage Trail, this site features a reconstructed War of 1812 fort and museum. Information on visits and activities can be found at http://www.fortmeigs.org.

Tippecanoe Battlefield Museum, Battle Ground, Indiana. This museum includes artifacts from the Indian and white settlement of Indiana and visual materials on the Battle of Tippecanoe of 1811. The museum's website at http://www.tcha.mus.in.us/battlefield.htm includes an account of the battle and its aftermath.

Monticello, Charlottesville, Virginia. The architecturally unique home of Thomas Jefferson and the headquarters for his plantation serves as a museum that provides insights into Jefferson's varied interests. Information on educational programs and upcoming events at Monticello, as well as the new Jefferson Library in Charlottesville, can be found at http://www.monticello.org/.

Perry's Victory and International Peace Memorial, Put-in-Bay, Ohio. At the site of Perry's decisive victory on Lake Erie in 1813 now stands a museum that depicts the role of the Old Northwest in the War of 1812. For a printable travel guide and information on the new visitor center, see http://www.nps.gov/pevi/index.htm.

Review Questions

1. What changes did the Republicans bring to the federal government? How did their policies differ from those of their Federalist predecessors?
2. Why were the Republicans so intent on expanding the boundaries of the United States, and why did the Federalists oppose an expansionist program?
3. What factors accounted for the Federalists' inability to regain national power after they lost the election of 1800?
4. What external and internal factors drew the United States into war against Britain? Could the war have been avoided?
5. What accounted for the difficulties of the United States in waging the War of 1812, and why was the war widely viewed as a great U.S. victory? How did the war lead to an increasing pattern of diplomatic cooperation between the United States and Britain?
6. Why was Rosalie Calvert so critical of the Republican Party and U.S. entry into the War of 1812? To what extent would New England Federalists have shared her views?
7. What explains the upsurge of nationalism that underlay the Era of Good Feelings? Why were the Republicans unable to maintain their party unity after 1819?
8. What accounted for the noninvolvement of the United States in the revolutionary movements in Latin America and the long delay in extending formal recognition to the new governments established there?

Key Terms

American System (p. 241)
Anglo-American Accords (p. 237)
Battle of New Orleans (p. 235)
Battle of Plattsburgh (p. 234)
Battle of Put-in-Bay (p. 234)
***Chesapeake* Incident** (p. 229)
Dartmouth College v. Woodward (p. 236)
Embargo Act of 1807 (p. 229)
Era of Good Feelings (p. 235)
Fletcher v. Peck (p. 236)
Impressment (p. 228)
Marbury v. Madison (p. 225)
McCulloch v. Maryland (p. 237)
Missouri Compromise (p. 241)
Monroe Doctrine (p. 239)
Pan-Indian resistance movement (p. 230)
Rush-Bagot Agreement (p. 237)
Second Bank of the United States (p. 236)
Trans-Continental Treaty of 1819 (p. 238)
Treaty of Ghent (p. 235)
War Hawks (p. 231)
War of 1812 (p. 233)

myhistorylab Connections

Reinforce what you learned in this chapter by studying the many documents, images, maps, review tools, and videos available at **www.myhistorylab.com**.

Read and Review

Study and Review **Study Plan: Chapter 9**

Read the Document

Constitutionality of the Louisiana Purchase (1803)

Marbury v. Madison *(1803)*

Thomas Jefferson, First Inaugural Address (1801)

James Madison, First Inaugural Address (1809)

Margaret Bayard Smith, Reflections Upon Meeting Jefferson (1801)

Pennsylvania Gazette, "Indian hostilities" (1812)

The Treaty of Ghent (1814)

Dolley Payne Madison to Lucy Payne Todd (1814)

Opinion of the Supreme Court for McCulloch v. Maryland *(1819)*

Monroe Doctrine (1823)

Report and Resolutions of the Hartford Convention (1814)

The Star-Spangled Banner (1814)

See the Map

The Louisiana Purchase

Missouri Compromise of 1820–1821

The War of 1812

Research and Explore

Read the Document

Personal Journeys Online

From Then to Now Online: The Lewis and Clark Expedition in Their World and Ours

Exploring America: Continentalism

Hear the Audio

Jefferson and Liberty.

Star Spangled Banner

Watch the Video *Lewis and Clark: What Were They Trying to Accomplish?*

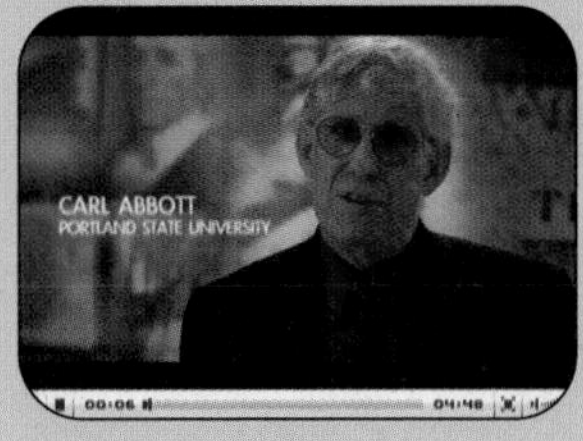

Hear the Audio

Hear the audio files for Chapter 9 at **www.myhistorylab.com.**

1824-1845

10 The Jacksonian Era

CHEROKEE PHŒNIX,
NEW ECHOTA, THURSDAY FEBRUARY 21, 1828.
VOL. I.
NO. 1.

President-elect Andrew Jackson addresses a crowd from a stage coach on his way to Washington in 1829.

Hear the Audio

Hear the audio files for Chapter 10 at **www.myhistorylab.com**.

THE EGALITARIAN IMPULSE *(page 249)*

WHAT FACTORS contributed to the democratization of American politics and religion in the early nineteenth century?

JACKSON'S PRESIDENCY *(page 254)*

HOW DID the Jacksonian Democrats capitalize on the new mass politics?

VAN BUREN AND HARD TIMES *(page 262)*

WHAT CHALLENGES did Van Buren face during his presidency?

THE RISE OF THE WHIG PARTY *(page 265)*

WHAT WAS the basis of Whig popularity? What did they claim to stand for?

THE WHIGS IN POWER *(page 268)*

WHY WAS William Henry Harrison's death such a blow to the Whig agenda?

ONE AMERICAN JOURNEY

Newport, New Hampshire

September 1828

Wherever a person may chance to be in company, he will hear nothing but politicks discussed. In the ballroom, or at the dinner table, in the Stagecoach & in the tavern; even the social chitchat of the tea table must yield up to the everlasting subject.

How many friendships are broken up! With what rancor the political war is carried on between the editorial corps! To what meanness[,] vulgarity & abuse is that champion of liberty, in proper hands, the press prostituted! With what lies and scandal does the columns of almost every political paper abound! I blush for my country when I see such things, & I often tremble with apprehension that our Constitution will not long withstand the current which threatens to overwhelm it. Our government is so based that an honest difference between American citizens must always exist. But the rancorous excitement which now threatens our civil liberties and a dissolution of this Union does not emanate from an honest difference of opinion, but from a determination of an unholy league to trample down an Administration, be it ever so pure, & be its acts ever so just. It must not be. There is a kind Providence that overlooks the destinies of this Nation and will not suffer it to be overthrown by a party of aspiring office seekers & political demagogues.

Benjamin B. French

Donald B. Cole and John J. McDonough, eds., *Witness to the Young Republic: A Yankee's Journal, 1828–1870* (Hanover, NH: University Press of New England, 1989), pp. 15–16.

Read the **Document** at **www.myhistorylab.com**

Personal Journeys Online

- **Alexis de Tocqueville, *Travel account*, 1835. A Frenchman gives his impressions of American democracy.**
- **Michael Chevalier, *Travel*, 1831. A Frenchman describes the spectacle of spectacle politics.**

BENJAMIN BROWN FRENCH, a young editor and county clerk in Newport, New Hampshire, penned these words in his journal in September 1828. Like most other Americans, he was amazed, indeed, shocked, by the intense, seemingly all-pervasive partisanship stirred up in the presidential election of 1828 between Andrew Jackson and John Quincy Adams. Whether measured by the vulgar personal attacks launched by a partisan press, the amount of whiskey and beef consumed at political barbecues, or the huge increase in voter turnout, this election marked the entrance of ordinary Americans onto the political stage.

The sense of shock soon wore off for French. The son of a wealthy Federalist lawyer with whom he was always at odds, French broke with his father at the age of 25, when he married without his permission. With no income, job, or family support, he now began to make a business out of law, politics, and journalism. In so doing he was part of the first generation of professional politicians, young men who compensated for their lack of social connections and family wealth by turning to politics. The partisanship that French found so disturbing in 1828 quickly became the basis of his livelihood. After rejecting his father's politics by joining the Democrats in 1831, he spent most of his subsequent years as a political officeholder in Washington, holding a variety of appointive jobs until his death in 1870.

What made French's career possible was the ongoing democratization of U.S. politics in the early decades of the nineteenth century. The number and potential power of the voters expanded, and professional politicians realized that party success now depended on reaching and organizing this enlarged electorate. Men like French, working for the party, could help them do this. ✦

CHRONOLOGY

1826	Disappearance of William Morgan.
1827	Emergence of the Anti-Masons, the first third party.
1828	Andrew Jackson elected president.
	John C. Calhoun writes *The South Carolina Exposition and Protest*.
1830	Congress passes the Indian Removal Act.
	Greek independence established.
	July Revolution in France.
	Revolutions break out in Belgium, Poland, and Italian states.
1831	William Lloyd Garrison starts publication of the *Liberator*.
	Nat Turner leads a slave uprising in Virginia.
1832	Jackson vetoes bill for rechartering the Second Bank of the United States; Bank War begins.
	South Carolina nullifies the Tariffs of 1828 and 1832.
	Jackson reelected.
	Election reform bill passes in Britain.
1833	Congress passes the Force Act and the Compromise Tariff.
	American Anti-Slavery Society established.
1834	Whig Party begins to organize.
1836	Texas War of Independence and establishment of the Republic of Texas.
	Congress passes first gag rule on abolitionist petitions.
	Van Buren elected president.
1837	Panic of 1837 sets off a depression.
1840	Independent Treasury Act passes.
	William Henry Harrison elected first Whig president.
1841	John Tyler succeeds to presidency on death of Harrison.
1842	United States and Britain sign the Webster-Ashburton Treaty.
1844	James K. Polk elected president.
	Gag rule repealed.
1845	Texas admitted to the Union.

THE EGALITARIAN IMPULSE

WHAT FACTORS contributed to the democratization of American politics and religion in the early nineteenth century?

Political democracy, defined as the majority rule of white males, was far from complete in early nineteenth-century America. Barriers to political participation, however, came under increasing attack after 1800 and were all but eliminated by the 1820s. As politics opened to mass participation, popular styles of religious leadership and worship emerged in a broad reaction to the formalism and elitism of the dominant Protestant churches. The same egalitarian impulse drove these twin democratic revolutions, and both represented an empowerment of the common man. Popular movements now spoke his language and appealed to his quest for republican equality. (Women would have to wait longer.)

The Extension of White Male Democracy

In 1789, Congress set the pay of representatives and senators at $6 a day plus travel expenses. By 1816, inflation had so eroded this salary that many government clerks earned more than members of Congress. Thus Congress thought itself prudent and justified when it voted itself a hefty raise to $1,500 a year. The public thought otherwise. So sharp was the reaction against the Salary Act of 1816 that 70 percent of the members of Congress were turned out of office at the next election. Chastised congressmen quickly repealed the salary increase.

QUICK REVIEW

Salary Act of 1816

- 1816: Congress votes itself a pay raise.
- Outraged public rejects 70 percent of incumbents at next election.
- Conflict represents turn toward the politics of Jacksonian era.

The uproar over the Salary Act marked a turning point in the transition from the deferential politics of the Federalist-Republican period to the egalitarianism of the coming Jacksonian era. The public would no longer passively accept decisions handed down by local elites or established national figures. Individual states, not the federal government, defined who could vote. Six states, Indiana, Mississippi, Illinois, Alabama, Missouri, and Maine, entered the Union between 1816 and 1821, and none of them required voters to own property. Meanwhile, proponents of suffrage liberalization won major victories in the older states. Constitutional conventions in Connecticut in 1818 and Massachusetts and New York in 1821 eliminated property requirements for voting. By the end of the 1820s, near universal white male suffrage was the norm everywhere except Rhode Island, Virginia, and Louisiana.

Extending the suffrage and democratic reform. Broadening the suffrage was part of a general democratization of political structures and procedures in the state governments. Most significant for national politics, voters acquired the power to choose presidential electors. In 1800, only two states had provided for a statewide popular vote in presidential elections. By 1824, most did so, and by 1832 only South Carolina still clung to the practice of having the state legislature choose the electors.

QUICK REVIEW

Expansion of the Franchise

- Opposition to land ownership as qualification for voting.
- Demands that all white men be treated equally.
- As political rights for white men expanded, political opportunities shrank for women and free black people.

Several currents swelled the movement for democratic reform. Limiting voting rights to those who owned land property seemed increasingly elitist when economic changes were producing new classes—workers, clerks, and small tradesmen—whose livelihoods were not tied directly to the land. Renters, more than 77 percent of the voters in New York City by 1814, joined homeowners in an expanded electorate. The middling and lower ranks of society demanded the ballot and access to offices to protect themselves from the commercial and manufacturing interests that benefited most from economic change.

Of greatest importance, however, was the incessant demand that all white men be treated equally. The logical extension of the ideology of the American Revolution, with its leveling attacks against kings and aristocrats, this demand for equality made republicanism by the 1820s synonymous with simple majority rule. If any white male was the equal of any other, regardless of wealth or property holdings, then only the will of the majority could be the measure of a republican government.

The disfranchisement of free blacks and women. As political opportunities expanded for white males, they shrank for women and free black people. In the state constitutions of the Revolutionary era, free black males who met the minimum property requirements usually had the same voting rights as white males. By the early 1800s, race and gender began to replace wealth and status as the basis for defining the limits of political participation. In state after state, the same constitutional conventions that embraced universal suffrage for white men deprived black men of the vote or burdened them with special property qualifications. Moreover, none of the ten states that entered the Union from 1821 to 1861 allowed black suffrage.

Advocates of greater democratization explicitly argued that only white males had the intelligence and love of liberty to be entrusted with political rights. Women, they said, were too weak and emotional, black people too lazy and lascivious. In denouncing distinctions drawn on property as artificial and demeaning, the white egalitarians simultaneously erected new distinctions based on race and sex that were supposedly natural and hence immutable. Thus personal liberties were now to be guarded not by propertied gentlemen but by all white men, whose equality ultimately rested on assumptions of their shared natural superiority over women and nonwhite people.

THE POPULAR RELIGIOUS REVOLT

In religion as well as politics, ordinary Americans demanded a greater voice in the early nineteenth century. Insurgent religious movements rejected the formalism and traditional Calvinism of the Congregational and Presbyterian churches, the dominant Protestant denominations in Washington's America. In a blaze of fervor known as the **Second Great Awakening** (recalling the Great Awakening of colonial America), evangelical sects led by the Methodists and Baptists radically transformed the religious landscape between 1800 and 1840. A more popularly rooted

Second Great Awakening Series of religious revivals in the first of the nineteenth century characterized by great emotionalism in large public meetings.

GLOBAL CONNECTIONS

An Age of Reform

"Turn where we may—within, around—the voice of great events is proclaiming to us, 'Reform, that you may preserve.' Now, therefore . . . take counsel . . . of the signs of this most portentous time. . . . The danger is terrible. The time is short. If this Bill should be rejected, I pray to God that none of those who concur in rejecting it may ever remember their votes with unavailing regret, amidst the wreck of laws, the confusion of ranks, the spoliation of property, and the dissolution of social order."

Thomas Babington Macaulay used this argument in the British Parliament to support the Reform Bill of 1832, legislation that extended the vote to Britain's industrial middle classes. Social changes produced by the Industrial Revolution had resulted in massive inequities and corruption in an electoral system that traditionally had consolidated power in the hands of wealthy conservative landowners. Events on the European continent gave greater weight to Macaulay's warning that England must reform or face revolution at home. The July Revolution of 1830 in France had deposed a conservative king and replaced him with one acceptable to the upper middle class. In the same year the Belgians succeeded in establishing their independence, but Austrian troops crushed a nationalist revolution in Italy, and Russian troops did likewise in Poland.

The revolutions of 1830 made it clear that the conservative order imposed on Europe at the Congress of Vienna in 1815 could not withstand the demands for political change unleashed by the American and French Revolutions or the economic change associated with the Industrial Revolution. Revolutionary ideals of legal equality and the right of cultural communities to determine their own fate as independent nations intersected with demands by the new middle and working classes for access to political power. The result was a continuing challenge to the status quo that periodically erupted into uprisings and revolutions. The next great wave of unrest that spilled over Europe after 1830 was the revolutions of 1848.

With the glaring exception of slavery, the United States by the 1830s was already a reformed society by the standards of Europe and the rest of the world. Liberal notions of individualism and self-improvement were wedded to mass democratic politics and a vibrant nationalism. But as long as slavery remained, America's national purpose would be tainted and tragically flawed.

- What lessons in establishing a republican government did the United States offer Europe in the nineteenth century?

Christianity moved outward and downward as it spread across frontier areas and converted marginalized and common folk. By 1850, one in three Americans was a regular churchgoer, a dramatic increase since 1800.

Read the **Document** at **www.myhistorylab.com** *Charles Finney, What a Revival of Religion Is (1835)*

Interpreting the Past *The Second Great Awakening and Religious Diversity in America* (pp. 334–335)

The Baptists and Methodists, both spinning off numerous splinter groups, grew spectacularly and were the largest religious denominations by the 1820s. The key to their success was their ability to give religious expression to the popular impulse behind democratic reform. Especially in the backcountry of the South and West, where the first revivals occurred, itinerant preachers reshaped religion to fit the needs and values of ordinary Americans.

The evangelical religion of the traveling preachers was democratic in its populist rejection of traditional religious canons and its encouragement of organizational forms that gave a voice to popular culture. Salvation was no longer simply bestowed by an implacable God, as taught by the Calvinist doctrine of individual predestination (see Chapter 1). Ordinary people could now actively choose salvation, and this possibility was exhilarating.

Evangelicalism and minority rights. Evangelicalism was a religion of the common people, and it appealed especially to women and African Americans. The revivals converted about twice as many women as men. Excluded from most areas of public life, women found strength and comfort in the evangelical message of Christian love and equality. As the wife of a Connecticut minister explained, church membership offered women a welcome release from "being treated like beasts of burden [and] drudges of domineering masters." In the first flush of

The Second Great Awakening originated on the frontier. Preachers were adept at arousing emotional fervor, and women in particular responded to the evangelical message of spiritual equality open to all who would accept Christ into their lives.

Collection of the New-York Historical Society, Negative #26275.

evangelical excitement, female itinerant preachers spread the gospel up and down the East Coast. By thus defying social convention, these women offered a model of independent action. Other women organized their own institutions within denominations still formally controlled by men. Women activists founded and largely directed hundreds of church-affiliated charitable societies and missionary associations.

QUICK REVIEW

Evangelical Christianity

- Second Great Awakening (1800–1840) transformed religious landscape.
- Evangelicals emphasized personal experience that would result in spiritual rebirth.
- Revivals converted about twice as many women as men.

Evangelicalism also empowered black Americans. African American Christianity experienced its first sustained growth in the generation after the Revolutionary War. As a result of their uncompromising commitment to convert slaves, the Baptists and Methodists led the way. Many of the early Baptist and Methodist preachers directly challenged slavery. In converting to Methodism, one slave stated that "from the sermon I heard, I felt that God had made all men free and equal, and that I ought not be a slave." Perceiving in it the promise of liberty and deliverance, the slaves received the evangelical gospel in loud, joyous, and highly emotional revivals. They made it part of their own culture, fusing Christianity with folk beliefs from their African heritage.

The limits of equality. But for all its liberating appeal to women and African Americans, evangelicalism was eventually limited by race and gender in much the same way as the democratic reform movement. Denied positions of authority in white-dominated churches and resentful of white opposition to integrated worship, free black northerners founded their own independent churches.

As increasing numbers of planters embraced evangelicalism after the 1820s, southern evangelicals first muted their attacks on slavery and then developed a full-blown religious defense of it based on the biblical sanctioning of human bondage. They similarly cited the Old Testament patriarchs to defend the unquestioned authority of fathers over their households, the masters of slaves, women, and children.

Whether in religion or politics, white men retained the power in Jacksonian America. Still, the Second Great Awakening removed a major intellectual barrier to political democracy. Traditional Protestant theology, whether Calvinist, Anglican, or Lutheran, viewed the mass of humanity as sinners predestined to damnation and hence was loath to accept the idea that those same sinners, by majority vote, should make crucial political decisions. In rejecting this theology, ordinary Americans made a fundamental intellectual breakthrough. "Salvation open to all" powerfully reinforced the legitimacy of "one man, one vote."

The Rise of the Jacksonians

The Jacksonian Democrats were the first party to mold and organize the democratizing impulse in popular culture. At the core of the Jacksonian appeal was the same rejection of established authority that marked the secular and religious populists. Much like the revivalists and the democratic reformers, the Jacksonians fashioned communications techniques that tapped into the hopes and fears of ordinary Americans. In so doing, they built the first mass-based party in U.S. history.

In Andrew Jackson the new **Democratic Party** that formed between 1824 and 1828 had the perfect candidate for the increasingly democratic temperament of the 1820s. Lacking any formal education, family connections, or inherited wealth to ease his way, Jackson relied on his own wits and raw courage to carve out a career as a frontier lawyer and planter in Tennessee. He won fame as the military savior of the republic with his victory at the Battle of New Orleans. Conqueror of the British, the Spanish, and the Indians, all of whom had blocked frontier expansion, he achieved incredible popularity in his native South.

Democratic Party Political Party formed in the 1820s under the leadership of Andrew Jackson; favored states' rights and a limited role for the federal government.

QUICK REVIEW

Andrew Jackson

- Self-made man from the southern backcountry.
- Frontier lawyer and planter in Tennessee.
- Hero of the Battle of New Orleans.

Jackson lost the election of 1824, but his defeat turned out to be a blessing in disguise. The wheeling and dealing in Congress that gave the presidency to John Quincy Adams enveloped his administration in a cloud of suspicion from the start. It also enhanced Jackson's appeal as the honest tribune of the people whose rightful claim to the presidency had been spurned by intriguing politicians in Washington by the "corrupt bargain" between Adams and Clay (see page 242).

When Adams delivered his first annual message to Congress in 1825, he presented a bold vision of an activist federal government promoting economic growth, social advancement, and scientific progress. Such a vision might have received a fair hearing in 1815, when postwar nationalism was in full stride. By 1825, postwar nationalism had dissolved into sectional bickering and burning resentments against banks, tariffs, and the political establishment, which were blamed for the hard times after the Panic of 1819.

To the opponents of the Jacksonians, elections had become a degrading spectacle in which conniving Democratic politicians, such as the one shown below handing a voting ticket to the stereotypical Irishman in the light coat, were corrupting the republic's political culture.

First State Election in Detroit, Michigan, 1837, c. 1837. Thomas Mickell Burnham. Gift of Mrs. Samuel T. Carson. Photograph ©1991 The Detroit Institute of Arts/ The Bridgeman Art Library, NY.

This bust portrait of Jackson in uniform, issued as print during the 1832 presidential race, invokes his military image and especially his victory at New Orleans in 1815.

Little of Adams's program passed Congress, and his nationalist vision drove his opponents into the Jackson camp. Southern planters jumped onto the Jackson bandwagon out of fear that Adams might use federal power against slavery; westerners joined because Adams revived their suspicions of the East. The most important addition came from New York, where Martin Van Buren had built the **Albany Regency,** a tightly disciplined state political machine.

Van Buren belonged to a new breed of professional politicians. In battling against the system of family-centered wealth and prestige on which politics had previously been based, Van Buren redefined parties as something good in and of themselves. Indeed, he and his followers argued that parties were indispensable instruments for the successful expression of the popular will against the dominance of elites.

State leaders such as Van Buren organized the first national campaign that relied extensively on new techniques of mass mobilization. In rallying support for Jackson against Adams in 1828, these state leaders put together chains of party-subsidized newspapers and coordinated a frantic schedule of meetings and rallies. Grassroots Jackson committees reached out to voters by knocking on their doors, pressing party literature into their hands, dispensing mass-produced medals and buttons with a likeness of Jackson, and lavishly entertaining all who would give them a hearing. Politics became a folk spectacle as torchlight parades awakened sleepy towns and political barbecues doled out whiskey and food to farmers from the surrounding countryside.

The election of 1828 centered on personalities, not issues. This in itself was a victory for Jackson's campaign managers, who proved far more skillful in the new presidential game of image making than did their Adams counterparts, now known as the National Republicans. Jackson carried every state south and west of Pennsylvania in 1828 and polled 56 percent of the popular vote. Voter turnout shot up to 55 percent from the apathetic 25 percent of 1824. Adams ran well only in New England and in commercialized areas producing goods for outside markets. Aside from the South, where he was virtually untouchable, Jackson's appeal was strongest among ordinary Americans who valued their local independence and felt threatened by outside centers of power beyond their control. He rolled up heavy majorities from Scots-Irish farmers in the Baptist–Methodist evangelical belt of the backcountry and from unskilled workers with an Irish Catholic background. To these voters, Jackson was a double hero, for he had defeated their hated British enemy and promised to do the same to the Yankee capitalists of the Northeast and all the elitist politicians.

Hear the Audio at **www.myhistorylab.com**
Van Buren

Albany Regency The tightly disciplined state political machine built by Martin Van Buren in New York.

JACKSON'S PRESIDENCY

HOW DID the Jacksonian Democrats capitalize on the new mass politics?

Read the Document at **www.myhistorylab.com**
Andrew Jackson, First Annual Message to Congress (1829)

Once in office, Jackson proved to be the most forceful and energetic president since Jefferson. Like a military chieftain tolerating no interference from his subordinates, Jackson dominated his presidency with the sheer force of his personality.

The Jacksonians had no particular program in 1828. Apart from removing Indians to areas west of the Mississippi River, Jackson's first term was notable primarily for its political infighting. Two political struggles that came to a head in 1832–1833, the Bank War and the nullification crisis, stamped the Jacksonians with a lasting party identity.

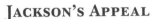

Jackson's Appeal

Although they were led by wealthy planters and entrepreneurs—hardly average Americans—the Jacksonians skillfully depicted themselves as the champions of the common man against aristocratic interests that had enriched themselves through special privileges granted by the government. Jackson proclaimed his task as one of restoring the federal government to the ideal of Jeffersonian republicanism, in which farmers and artisans could pursue their individual liberty free of any government intervention that favored the rich and powerful.

Jackson began his assault on special privilege by proclaiming a reform of the appointment process for federal officeholders. Accusing his predecessors, especially Adams, of having created a social elite of self-serving bureaucrats, he vowed to make government service more responsive to the popular will. He insisted that federal jobs required no special expertise or training and proposed to rotate honest, hard-working citizens in and out of the civil service.

Jackson's reform of the federal bureaucracy had more style than substance. He removed only about one-fifth of the officeholders he inherited, and most of his appointees came from the same relatively high-status groups as the Adams people. But by providing a democratic rationale for government service, he opened the way for future presidents to move more aggressively against incumbents. Thus emerged the **spoils system,** in which the victorious party gave government jobs to its supporters and removed the appointees of the defeated party.

Even at a Washington ball in his home in 1824, Adams, shown on the left, had to share the spotlight with his arch rival Jackson, the striking figure in the middle of the painting.

When Jackson railed against economic privilege, he most often had in mind Henry Clay's American System (see Chapter 9). Clay's program called for a protective tariff, a national bank, and federal subsidies for internal improvements; his goal was to bind Americans together in an integrated national market. To the Democrats, Clay's system represented government favoritism at its worst, a set of costly benefits at the public's expense for special-interest groups that corrupted politicians in their quest for economic power. In 1830, Jackson struck a blow for the Democratic conception of the limited federal role in economic development. He vetoed the Maysville Road Bill, which would have provided federal money for a road to be built entirely within Kentucky, Clay's home state. The bill was unconstitutional, he claimed, because it benefited only the citizens of Kentucky and not the U.S. people as a whole.

W
WHERE TO LEARN MORE
The Hermitage, Hermitage, Tennessee
http://www.thehermitage.com/

On the issue of internal improvements, as with bureaucratic reform, the Democrats placed party needs ahead of ideology. Jackson's Maysville veto did not rule out congressional appropriations for projects deemed beneficial to the general public. This pragmatic loophole gave Democrats all the room they needed to pass more internal-improvement projects during Jackson's presidency than during all of the previous administrations together. Having built a mass party, the Democrats soon discovered that they had to funnel federal funds to their constituents back home.

spoils system The awarding of government jobs to party loyalists.

The Democrats also responded to the demand for Indian removal that came out of their strongholds in the South and West. By driving Native Americans from these regions, Jackson more than lived up to his billing as the friend of the common (white) man.

Indian Removal

Some 125,000 Indians lived east of the Mississippi when Jackson became president. The largest concentration was in the South, where five Indian nations, the Cherokees, Creeks, Choctaws, Chickasaws, and Seminoles, controlled millions of acres of land in what soon would become the great cotton frontiers of southwestern Georgia and central Alabama and Mississippi. That, of

Interpreting the Past
Jacksonian Democracy and American Politics (pp. 274–275)

Sequoyah, a Cherokee scholar, developed a written table of syllables for the Cherokee language that enabled his people to publish a tribal newspaper in both Cherokee and English.

course, was the problem: Native Americans held land that white farmers coveted for their own economic gain.

Pressure from the states to remove the Indians had been building since the end of the War of 1812. It was most intense in Georgia. In early 1825, Georgia authorities finalized a fraudulent treaty that ceded most of the Creek Indians' land to the state. In 1828, Georgia moved against the Cherokees, the best-organized and most advanced (by white standards) of the Indian nations. By now a prosperous society of small farmers with their own newspaper and schools for their children, the Cherokees wanted to avoid the fate of their Creek neighbors. In 1827, they adopted a constitution declaring themselves an independent nation with complete sovereignty over their land. The Georgia legislature reacted by placing the Cherokees directly under state law, annulling Cherokee laws and even the right of the Cherokees to make laws, and legally defining the Cherokees as tenants on land belonging to the state of Georgia. By also prohibiting Indian testimony in cases against white people, the legislature stripped the Cherokees of any legal rights. Alabama and Mississippi followed Georgia's lead in denying Indians legal rights.

Thus the stage was set for what Jackson always considered the most important measure of the early days of his administration, the **Indian Removal Act.** Jackson had long considered the federal policy of negotiating with the Indians as sovereign entities a farce. But it was awkward politically for the president to declare that he had no intention of enforcing treaty obligations of the U.S. government. The way out of this dilemma was to remove Native Americans from the center of the dispute. In his first annual message, Jackson sided with state officials in the South and advised the Indians "to emigrate beyond the Mississippi or submit to the laws of those States."

Congress acted on Jackson's recommendation in the Indian Removal Act of 1830. The act appropriated $500,000 for the negotiation of new treaties under which the southern Indians would surrender their territory and be removed to land in the trans-Mississippi area (primarily present-day Oklahoma). Although force was not authorized and Jackson stressed that removal should be voluntary, no federal protection was provided for Indians harassed into leaving by land-hungry settlers.Ultimately, Jackson did deploy the U.S. Army, but only to round up and push out Indians who refused to comply with the new removal treaties.

And so most of the Indians left the eastern United States, the Choctaws in 1830, the Creeks and Chickasaws in 1832, and the Cherokees in 1838 (see Map 10–1). The government was ill prepared to supervise the removal. The private groups that won the federal contracts for transporting and provisioning the Indians were the ones that had entered the lowest bids; they were a shady lot, interested only in a quick profit. Thousands of Indians, perhaps as many as one-fourth of those who started the trek, died on the way to Oklahoma, the victims of cold, hunger, disease, and the general callousness of the white people they met along the way. It was indeed, as recalled in the collective memory of the Cherokees, a **Trail of Tears.**

Tribes that resisted removal were attacked by white armies. Federal troops joined local militias in 1832 in suppressing the Sauk and Fox Indians of Illinois and Wisconsin in what was called **Black Hawk's War.** More a frantic attempt by the Indians to reach safety on the west bank of the Mississippi than an actual war, this affair ended in the slaughter of 500 Indian men, women, and children by white troops and their Sioux allies. The Seminoles, many of whose leaders were runaway slaves adopted into the tribe, fought the army to a standstill in the swamps of Florida in what became the longest Indian war in U.S. history.

QUICK REVIEW

Georgia and the Cherokees

- Georgia stole land of Creek Indians in 1825.
- Georgia moved against Cherokees in 1828, stripping them of all legal rights.
- Stage was set for Indian Removal Act.

Indian Removal Act President Andrew Jackson's measure that allowed state officials to override federal protection of Native Americans.

Trail of Tears The forced march in 1838 of the Cherokee Indians from their homelands in Georgia to the Indian Territory in the West.

Black Hawk's War Short 1832 war in which federal troops and Illinois militia units defeated the Sauk and Fox Indians led by Black Hawk.

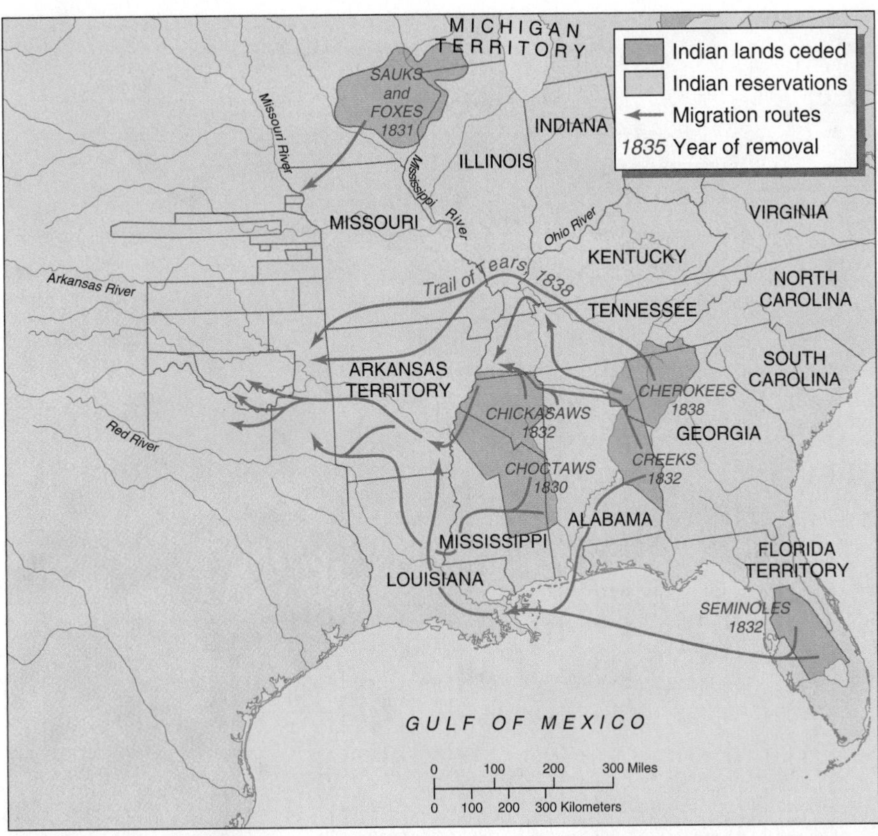

MAP 10–1 **Indian Removals** The fixed policy of the Jackson administration and pressure from the states forced Native Americans in the 1830s to migrate from their eastern homelands to a special Indian reserve west of the Mississippi River.

Which states were at the center of Indian Removal? What explains the intense pressure for removal in those states?

Jackson forged ahead with his removal policy despite the opposition of eastern reformers and Protestant missionaries. Aligned with conservatives concerned by Jackson's cavalier disregard of federal treaty obligations, they came within three votes of defeating the removal bill in the House of Representatives. Jackson ignored their protests (see American Views: Native Americans Speak Out) as well as the legal rulings of the Supreme Court. In *Cherokee Nation v. Georgia* (1831) and *Worcester v. Georgia* (1832), the Court ruled that Georgia had violated the U.S. Constitution in extending its jurisdiction over the Cherokees. Aware that southerners and westerners were on his side, Jackson ignored the Supreme Court rulings and pushed Indian removal to its tragic conclusion.

See the **Map** at **www.myhistorylab.com** *Native American Removal*

Read the **Document** at **www.myhistorylab.com** *Black Hawk, Autobiography of Ma-ka-tai-me-she-kia-kiak, or Black Hawk (1833)*

The Nullification Crisis

Jackson's stand on Indian removal confirmed the impression of many of his followers that when state and national power conflicted, he could be trusted to side with the states. But when states' rights forces in South Carolina precipitated the **nullification crisis** by directly challenging Jackson in the early 1830s over tariff policy, Jackson revealed himself to be an ardent nationalist on the issue of majority rule in the Union.

nullification crisis Sectional crisis in the early 1830s in which a states' rights party in South Carolina attempted to nullify federal law.

After the first protective tariff in 1816, rates increased further in 1824 and then jumped to 50 percent in 1828 in what was denounced as the "Tariff of Abominations," a measure contrived by northern Democrats to win additional northern support for Jackson in the upcoming presidential campaign. The outcry was loudest in South Carolina, an old cotton state losing population to the West in the 1820s as cotton prices remained low after the Panic of 1819. For all of

Read the **Document** at **www.myhistorylab.com** *Proclamation Regarding Nullification (1832)*

For the Cherokees, the Trail of Tears stretched 1,200 miles from the homeland in the East to what became the Indian Territory in Oklahoma.

the economic arguments against high tariffs, the tariff issue was a stalking-horse for the more fundamental issue of setting limits on national power so that the federal government could never move against slavery.

W
WHERE TO LEARN MORE
Rice Museum, Georgetown, South Carolina
http://www.ricemuseum.org

South Carolina was the only state where African Americans made up the majority of the population. Slaves were heavily concentrated in the marshes and tidal flats south of Charleston, the low-country district of huge rice plantations. Ever fearful that growing antislavery agitation in the North and in England was feeding slave unrest, state leaders such as James Hamilton, Jr. warned that the time had come to "stand manfully at the Safety Valve of Nullification."

With the low-country planters in charge, the antitariff forces in South Carolina controlled state politics by 1832. They called themselves the nullifiers, a name derived from the constitutional theory developed by John C. Calhoun. Calhoun argued that a state, acting through a popularly elected convention, had the sovereign power to declare an act of the national government null and inoperative. On the basis of this theory, a South Carolina convention in November 1832 nullified the tariffs of 1828 and 1832 (a compromise tariff that did not reduce rates to a low enough level to satisfy the nullifiers). The convention decreed that customs duties were not to be collected in South Carolina after February 1, 1833.

QUICK REVIEW

Fear of Rebellion and Northern Intentions

- African Americans were majority of South Carolina's population.
- Rebellions convinced planters that antislavery movement was feeding slave unrest.
- Southerners feared that protective tariffs were a prelude to emancipation.

Interpreting the Past
Nullification as a Destructive Force in U.S. Politics (pp. 218–219)

Jackson considered nullification a dangerous and nonsensical perversion of the Constitution, and he vowed to crush any attempt to block the enforcement of federal laws. In January 1833, Jackson, asked for and received from Congress the Force Bill giving him full authorization to put down nullification by military force. Meanwhile, a compromise tariff in 1833 provided for the lowering of tariff duties to 20 percent over a 10-year period. Up against this combination of the carrot and the stick, the nullifiers backed down, but not before they scornfully nullified the Force Bill.

Jackson's stand established the principle of national supremacy grounded in the will of the majority. Despite his victory, however, states' rights doctrines remained popular both in the South and among many northern Democrats. South Carolina had been isolated in its stand on nullification, but many southerners, and especially slaveholders, agreed that the powers of the national government had to be strictly limited. By dramatically affirming his right to use force against a state in defense of the Union, Jackson drove many planters out of the Democratic Party. In the shock waves set off by the nullification crisis, a new anti-Jackson coalition began to form in the South.

Read the **Document** at **www.myhistorylab.com** *The Force Bill (1833)*

The Bank War

What amounted to a war against the Bank of the United States became the centerpiece of Jackson's presidency and a defining event for the Democratic Party. The **Bank War** erupted in 1832, when Jackson vetoed draft legislation for the early rechartering of the national bank.

Bank War Successful effort by President Andrew Jackson to block the rechartering of the Second Bank of the United States.

Like most westerners, Jackson distrusted banks. Because gold and silver coins were scarce and the national government did not issue or regulate paper currency, money consisted primarily of notes issued as loans by private and state banks. These bank notes fluctuated in value according to the reputation and creditworthiness of the issuing banks. In the credit-starved West, banks were particularly unreliable. All of this struck many Americans, and especially farmers and workers, as inherently dishonest. They wanted to be paid in "real" money, gold or silver coin, and they viewed bankers as parasites who did nothing but fatten their own pockets by manipulating paper money. The largest and most powerful bank was the Bank of the United States, and citizens who were wiped out or forced to retrench drastically by the Panic of 1819 never forgave the Bank for saving itself at the expense of its debtors. Still, under the astute leadership of a new president, Nicholas Biddle of Philadelphia, the Bank performed well in the 1820s. Prosperous times had returned, and the Bank underwrote the economic expansion with its healthy credit reserves, stable bank notes, and policing of the state banks through its policy of returning their notes for redemption in specie. By 1832, the Bank was as popular as it ever would be.

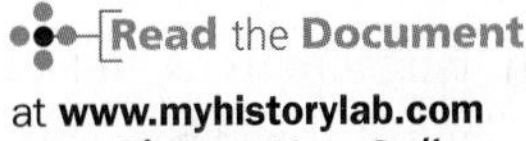

Read the **Document** at **www.myhistorylab.com** *From Then to Now Online: Banks and the Government*

Searching for an issue to use against Jackson in the presidential campaign of 1832, Clay forced Jackson's hand on the Bank. Clay convinced Biddle to apply to Congress for a new charter, even though the current charter would not expire until 1836. Confident of congressional approval, Clay reasoned that he had Jackson trapped. If Jackson went along with the new charter, Clay could take credit for the measure. If he vetoed it, Clay could attack Jackson as the enemy of a sound banking system.

Clay's clever strategy backfired. Jackson turned on him and the Bank with a vengeance. Jackson and his advisers realized that the Bank was vulnerable as a symbol of privileged monopoly, a monstrous institution that deprived common Americans of their right to compete equally for economic advantage. Moreover, many of these advisers were also state bankers and local developers, who backed Jackson precisely because they wanted to be free of federal restraints on their business activities. On July 10, 1832, Jackson vetoed the rechartering bill for the Bank in a message that appealed both to state bankers and to foes of all banks. He took a ringing "stand against all new grants of monopolies and exclusive privileges, against any prostitution of our Government to the advancement of the few at the expense of the many."

Read the **Document** at **www.myhistorylab.com** *Andrew Jackson, Veto of the Bank Bill (1832)*

The business community and eastern elites lashed out at Jackson's veto as the demagogic ravings of an economic fool. In rejecting Jackson's claims that the Bank had fostered speculative and corrupt financial practices, the pro-Bank forces had the better of the economic argument. But Jackson won the political battle, and he went to the people in the election of 1832 as their champion against the banking aristocracy. Although his support was no stronger than it had been in 1828, he easily defeated Clay, the candidate of the short-lived National Republican Party.

AMERICAN VIEWS

Native Americans Speak Out

Memorial and Protests of the Cherokee Nation, 1836

Of the major tribes in the Southeast, the Cherokees fought longest and hardest against the Jacksonian policy of Indian removal. Led by their principal chief, John Ross, the son of a Scot and a mixed-blood Cherokee woman, they submitted the following protest to Congress against the fraudulent 1835 Treaty of New Echota forced on them by the state of Georgia. Although clearly opposed by an overwhelming majority of the Cherokees, this treaty provided the legal basis for the forced removal of the Cherokee people from Georgia to the Indian Territory.

- **On what** legal grounds did the Cherokees base their protest? What pledges had been made to them by the U.S. government?
- **What** did the Cherokees mean when they said they had been "taught to think and feel as the American citizen"? If the Cherokees had become "civilized" by white standards, why did most whites still insist on their removal?
- **Why** would President Jackson have allowed white intruders to remain on land reserved by treaties for the Cherokees?
- **Do** you feel that the Cherokees were justified in believing that they had been betrayed by the U.S. government?

The undersigned representatives of the Cherokee nation, east of the river Mississippi, impelled by duty, would respectfully submit . . . the following statement of facts: It will be seen, from the numerous treaties between the Cherokee nation and the United States, that from the earliest existence of this government, the United States, in Congress assembled, received the Cherokees and their nation into favor and protection; and that the chiefs and warriors, for themselves and all parts of the Cherokee nation, acknowledged themselves and the said Cherokee nation to be under the protection of the United States of America, and of no other sovereign whatsoever: they also stipulated, that the said Cherokee nation will not hold any treaty with any foreign power, individual State, or with individuals of any State: that for, and in consideration of, valuable concessions made by the Cherokee nation, the United States solemnly guaranteed to said nation all their lands not ceded, and pledged the faith of the government, that "all white people who have intruded, or may hereafter intrude, on the lands reserved for the Cherokees, shall be removed by the United States, and proceeded against, according to the provisions of the act, passed 30th March, 1802," entitled "An act to regulate trade and intercourse with the Indian tribes, and to preserve peace on the frontiers." It would be useless to recapitulate the numerous provisions for the security and protection of the rights of the Cherokees, to be found in the various treaties between their nation and the United States. The Cherokees were happy and prosperous under a scrupulous observance of treaty stipulations by the government of the United States, and from the fostering hand extended over them, they made rapid advances in civilization, morals, and in the arts and sciences. Little did they anticipate, that when taught to think and feel as the American citizen, and to have with him a common interest, they were to be despoiled by their guardian, to become strangers and wanderers in the land of their fathers, forced to return to the savage life, and to seek a new home in the wilds of the far west, and that without their consent. An instrument purporting to be a treaty with the Cherokee people, has recently been made public by the President of the United States, that will have such an operation, if carried into effect. This instrument, the delegation aver before the civilized world, and in the presence of Almighty God, is fraudulent, false upon its face, made by unauthorized individuals, without the sanction, and against the wishes, of the great body of the Cherokee people. Upwards of fifteen thousand of those people have protested against it, solemnly declaring they will never acquiesce.

Source: U.S. Congress, *Executive Documents* (1836).

The Militant Consciousness of William Apess

Although virtually erased in the historical record, the Native Americans of New England had not vanished by the nineteenth century. They persisted, both as individuals and as a culture. Numbering no more than a few thousand, most lived impoverished on reservations where they were denied the local self-governance extended to whites. The young left early, searching for whatever paying jobs they could find. One of these marginalized, transient Indians, the Pequot William Apess, produced a remarkable collection of autobiographical and protest writings that he began publishing in pamphlet form in 1829. The following excerpts reveal the anger, passion, and eloquence he brought to his indictment of white injustices to his people in Massachusetts.

- **Why** does Apess link the plight of Indians in Massachusetts with that of Indians in Georgia?
- **How** does he use the military contributions of Indians on the patriot side in the American Revolution to stake a claim for himself and his people to the liberties of republicanism?
- **In what** way does his condemnation of the dispossession of Indian lands by whites change or complicate the traditional approach to American history as an unfolding story of freedom and opportunity?

Perhaps you have heard of the oppression of the Cherokees and lamented over them much, and thought the Georgians were hard and cruel creatures; but did you ever hear of the poor, oppressed and degraded Marshpee Indians in Massachusetts and lament over them?... And we do not know why the people of this Commonwealth want to cruelize us any longer, for we are sure that our fathers *fought, bled, and died for the liberties* of their now weeping and suffering children. . . . *Oh, white man! white man!* The blood of our fathers, spilt in the Revolutionary War, cries from the ground of our native soil, to break the chains of oppression, and let our children *go free!*" . . .

No doubt there are many good people in the United States who would not trample upon the rights of the poor, but there are many others who are willing to roll in their coaches upon the tears and blood of the poor and unoffending natives—those who are ready at all times to speculate on the Indians and defraud them out of their rightful possessions. Let the poor Indian attempt to resist the encroachments of his white neighbors, what a hue and cry is instantly raised against him. It has been considered as a trifling thing for the whites to make war on the Indians for the purpose of driving them from their country and taking possession thereof. This was, in their estimation, all right, as it helped to extend the territory and enriched some individuals. But let the thing be changed. Suppose an overwhelming army should march into the United States for the purpose of subduing it and enslaving the citizens; how quick would they fly to arms, gather in multitudes around the tree of liberty, and contend for their rights with the last drop of their blood. And should the enemy succeed, would they not eventually rise and endeavor to regain their liberty? And who would blame them for it?

Source: Barry O'Connell, ed., *On Our Own Ground: The Complete Writings of William Apess, a Pequot* (University of Massachusetts Press, 1992).

QUICK REVIEW

Jackson and the Bank of the United States

- Jackson and most westerners distrusted banks.
- Jackson vetoed rechartering the Bank of the United States.
- Struggle over future of Bank ended with victory for Jackson at expense of Democrat's image.

After Congress failed to override his veto, Jackson then set out to destroy the Bank. He claimed that the people had given him a mandate to do so by reelecting him in 1832. In Roger B. Taney he finally found a secretary of the treasury (his first two choices refused) who agreed to sign the order removing federal deposits from the Bank in 1833. Drained of its lifeblood, the deposits, the Bank was reduced by 1836 to seeking a charter as a private corporation in the state of Pennsylvania. In the meantime, the government's moneys were deposited in "pet banks," state banks controlled by loyal Democrats.

Jackson won the Bank War, but he left the impression that the Democrats had played fast and loose with the nation's credit system. The economy overheated in his second term. High commodity prices and abundant credit, both at home and abroad, propelled a buying frenzy of western lands. Prices soared, and inevitably the speculative bubble had to burst. When it did, the Democrats would be open to the charge of squandering the people's money by shifting deposits to reckless state bankers who were part of a corrupt new alliance between the government and private economic interests. Jackson was out of office when the Panic of 1837 hit; Van Buren, his successor, paid the political price for Jackson's economic policies.

VAN BUREN AND HARD TIMES

WHAT CHALLENGES did Van Buren face during his presidency?

Like John Adams and James Madison, Martin Van Buren followed a forceful president who commanded a strong popular following. Fairly or not, he would come out, as they did, second-best compared to his predecessor.

Facing a sharp economic downturn, Van Buren appeared indecisive and unwilling to advance a bold program. When the rise of a radical **abolitionist movement** in the North revived

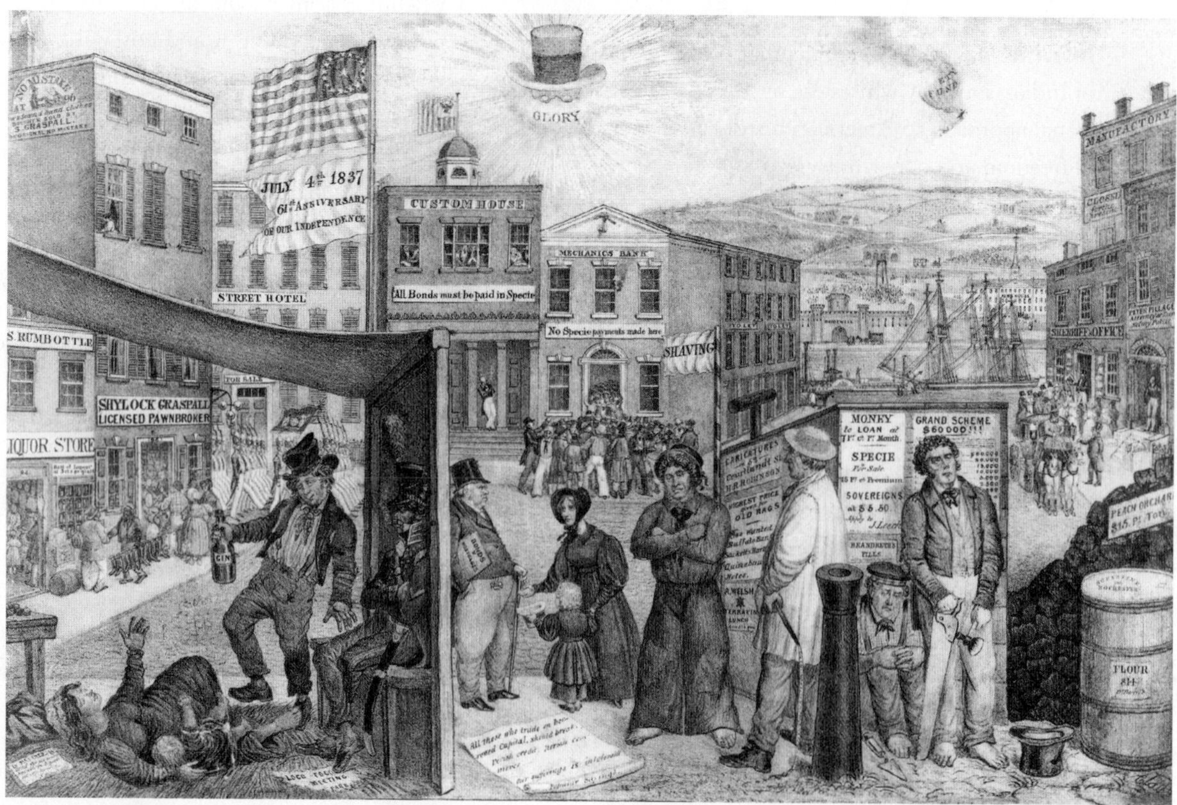

Broken families and demoralized workers were among the litany of evils blamed on the Panic of 1837.

sectional tensions over slavery, he awkwardly straddled the divisive issue. In the end, he undermined himself by failing to offer a compelling vision of his presidency.

abolitionist movement A radical antislavery crusade committed to the immediate end of slavery that emerged in the three decades before the Civil War.

The Panic of 1837

Van Buren was barely settled into the White House when the nation was rocked by a financial panic. For over a decade, the economy had benefited from a favorable business cycle. A banking crisis in 1837 painfully reintroduced economic reality.

Even as it expanded, the U.S. economy had remained vulnerable to disruptions in the supply of foreign capital and the sale of agricultural exports that underpinned prosperity. The key foreign nation was Britain, a major source of credit and demand for exports. In late 1836, the Bank of England tightened its credit policies. Concerned about the large outflow of specie to the United States, it raised interest rates and reduced the credit lines of British merchants heavily involved in U.S. trade. Consequently, the British demand for cotton fell and with it the price of cotton (see Figure 10–1). Because cotton, as the leading export, was the main security for most loans issued by U.S. banks and mercantile firms, its drop in value set off a chain reaction of contracting credit and falling prices. When panic-stricken investors rushed to the banks to redeem their notes in specie, the hard-pressed banks suspended specie payments.

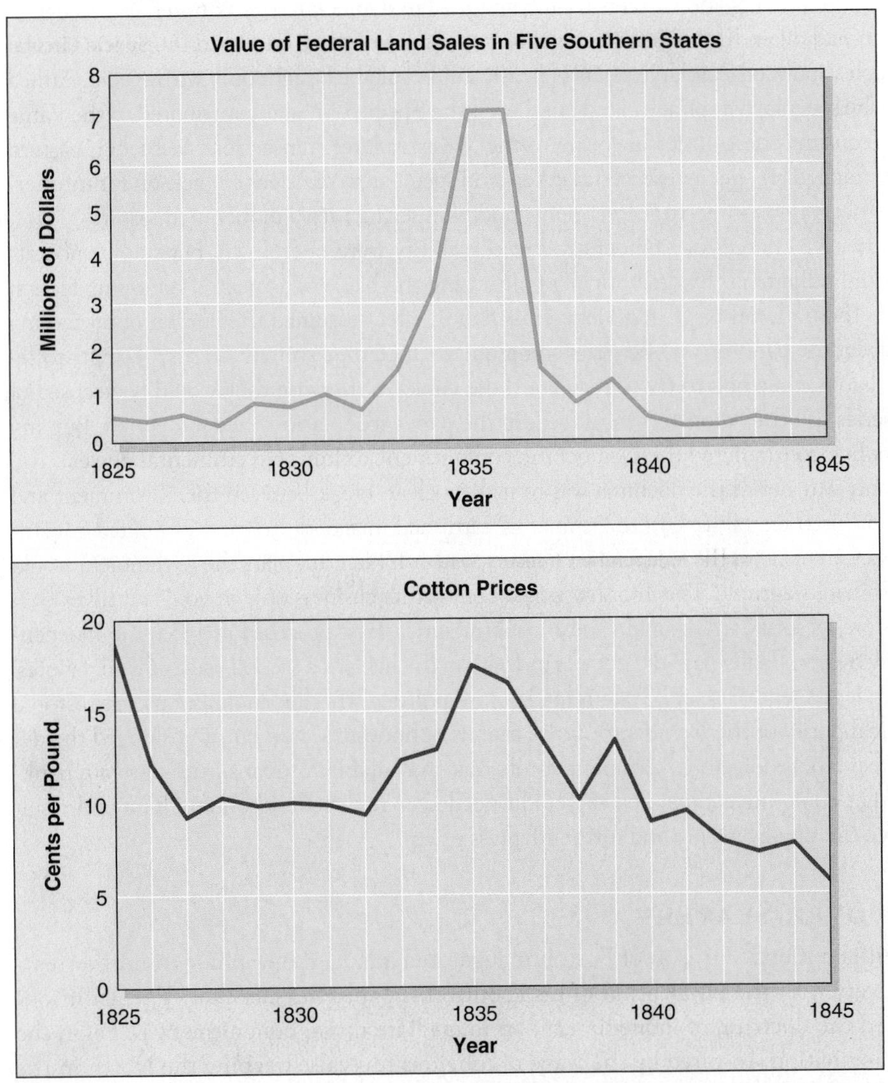

FIGURE 10–1 **Cotton Prices and the Value of Federal Land Sales in Five Southern States, 1825–1845.**

WHERE TO LEARN MORE

★ Martin Van Buren National Historic Site, Kinderhook, New York
http://www.nps.gov/mava/index.htm

What began as a bank panic soon dragged down the entire economy. As unemployment mounted and workers mobilized mass protest meetings in eastern cities, conservatives feared the worst. "Workmen thrown out of employ by the hundred daily," nervously noted a wealthy merchant in New York City in May 1837. He half expected that "we shall have a revolution here."

After a brief recovery in 1838, another round of credit contraction drove the economy into a depression that did not bottom out until 1843. In the manufacturing and commercial centers of the Northeast, unemployment reached an unheard-of 20 percent. The persistence of depressed agricultural prices meant that farmers and planters who had incurred debts in the 1830s faced the constant threat of losing their land or their slaves. Many fled west to avoid their creditors.

The Independent Treasury

Whig Party Political party, formed in the mid-1830s in opposition to the Jacksonian Democrats, that favored a strong role for the national government for promoting economic growth.

Specie Circular Proclamation issued by President Andrew Jackson in 1836 stipulating that only gold or silver could be used as payment for public land.

Independent Treasury System Fiscal arrangement first instituted by President Martin Van Buren in which the federal government kept its money in regional vaults and transacted its business in hard money.

Although the Democrats bore no direct responsibility for the economic downturn, they could not avoid being blamed for it. Their political opponents, now coalescing as the **Whig Party,** claimed that Jackson's destruction of the Bank of the United States had undermined business confidence. In their view, Jackson had then compounded his error by trying to force a hard-money policy on the state banks that had received federal deposits. The "pet banks" were required to replace small-denomination bank notes with coins or hard money. This measure, it was hoped, would protect the farmers and workers from being paid in depreciated bank notes.

Jackson had taken his boldest step against paper money when he issued the **Specie Circular** of 1836, which stipulated that large tracts of public land could be bought only with specie. Aimed at breaking the speculative spiral in land purchases, the Specie Circular contributed to the Panic of 1837 by requiring the transfer of specie to the West for land transactions just when eastern banks were strapped for specie reserves. Bankers and speculators denounced Jackson for interfering with the natural workings of the economy and blundering into a monetary disaster.

Conservative charges of Democratic irresponsibility were overblown, but the Democrats were caught in a dilemma. By dramatically politicizing the banking issue and removing federal moneys from the national bank, the Democrats had in effect assumed the burden of protecting the people from the banking and business community. Once they shifted treasury receipts to selected state banks, they had to try to regulate these banks. Otherwise they would be accused of creating a series of little "monsters" and feeding the paper speculation they so decried. But any regulatory policy contradicted the Democratic commitment to limit governmental power.

The only way out of the dilemma was to make a clean break between the government and banking. Van Buren reestablished the Democrats' tarnished image as the party of limited government when he came out for the **Independent Treasury System.** Under this plan, the government would dispense with banks entirely. The Treasury would conduct its business only in gold and silver coin and would store its specie in regional vaults or subtreasuries. First proposed in 1837, the Independent Treasury System finally passed Congress in 1840 on the heels of a second wave of bank failures.

The Independent Treasury System made more political than economic sense. It restored the ideological purity of the Democrats as the friends of honest money, but it prolonged the depression. Specie locked up in government vaults was unavailable for loans in the private banking system that could have expanded the credit needed to revive the economy. The end result was to reduce the money supply and further depress prices.

Uproar over Slavery

In 1831, William Lloyd Garrison of Boston inaugurated a radical new phase in northern attacks on slavery with the publication of his abolitionist paper the *Liberator*. The abolitionists embraced the doctrine of immediatism, an immediate moral commitment to begin the work of emancipation. Inspired by the wave of religious revivals sweeping the North in the late 1820s, they seized on slavery as the greatest sin of all. (For more on the abolitionists, see Chapter 12.)

The abolitionists touched off a political uproar when they launched a propaganda offensive in 1835. Taking advantage of technological improvements in the printing industry, they produced over a million pieces of antislavery literature, much of which was sent to the South through the U.S. mail. Alarmed white southerners vilified the abolitionists as fanatics intent on enticing the slaves to revolt. Abolitionist tracts were burned, and, with the open approval of Jackson, southern postmasters violated federal law by censoring the mail to keep out antislavery materials.

Unable to receive an open hearing in the South, the abolitionists now focused on Congress. Beginning in 1836 and continuing through Van Buren's presidency, hundreds of thousands of antislavery petitions, some with thousands of signatures, flooded into Congress. Most called for the abolition of slavery in the District of Columbia. Southern congressmen responded by demanding that free speech be repressed in the name of southern white security. Repression took the form of the **gag rule,** a procedural device whereby antislavery petitions were automatically tabled with no discussion.

gag rule A procedural device whereby antislavery petitions were automatically tabled in Congress with no discussion.

The gag rule first passed in 1836 and was renewed in a series of raucous debates through 1844. Only the votes of some three-fourths of the northern Democrats enabled the southern minority to have its way. With Van Buren's reluctant support, the gag rule became a Democratic Party measure, and it identified the Democrats as a prosouthern party in the minds of many northerners. Ironically, while Van Buren was attacked in the North as a lackey of the slave interests, he was damned in the South, if only because he was a nonslaveholder from the North, as being unsafe on the slavery issue. In short, tensions over slavery and the economy doomed Van Buren to be cast as a vacillating president fully trusted by neither section.

THE RISE OF THE WHIG PARTY

WHAT WAS the basis of Whig popularity? What did they claim to stand for?

The early opponents of the Democrats were known as the National Republicans, a label that captured the nationalist vision of former Jeffersonian Republicans who adhered to the economic program of Henry Clay and John Quincy Adams. The Bank War and Jackson's reaction to nullification shook loose pro-Bank Democrats and many southern states' righters from the original Jacksonian coalition, and these groups joined the opposition to Jackson. By 1834, the anti-Jacksonians started to call themselves Whigs, a name associated with eighteenth-century American and British opponents of monarchical tyranny. The name stuck because of the party's constant depiction of Jackson as King Andrew, a tyrant who ran roughshod over congressional prerogatives and constitutional liberties.

By 1840, the Whigs had mastered the techniques of political organization and mobilization pioneered by the Democrats in the late 1820s. They ran William Henry Harrison, their own version of a military hero, and swept to victory. The **second party system** of intense national competition between Whigs and Democrats was now in place (see the Overview table, The Second Party System). It would dominate politics until the rise of the antislavery Republican Party in the 1850s.

QUICK REVIEW

William Henry Harrison of Ohio

- Untainted by association with Bank of the United States, Masonic Order, or slaveholding.
- Hero of War of 1812.
- Selected John Tyler of Virginia as his running mate.

second party system The national two-party competition between Democrats and Whigs from the 1830s through the early 1850s.

THE PARTY TAKING SHAPE

The Whig Party was born in the congressional reaction to Jackson's Bank veto and his subsequent attacks on the national bank. What upset the congressional opposition, apart from the specific content of Jackson's policies, was how he enforced his will. Jackson wielded his executive power like a bludgeon. Whereas all earlier presidents together had used the veto only ten times, Jackson did so a dozen times. He openly defied the Supreme Court and Congress, and unlike his predecessors, he took each case directly to the people.

Local and state Whig coalitions sent an anti-Jackson majority to the House of Representatives in 1835. The most powerful of these coalitions was in New York, where a third party, the **Anti-Masons**, joined the Whigs. The party had originated in western New York in the late 1820s as a grassroots response to the sudden disappearance and presumed murder of William

Anti-Masons Third party formed in 1827 in opposition to the presumed power and influence of the Masonic order.

Whig political rally in 1840.

Morgan, an itinerant artisan who threatened to expose the secrets of the Order of Freemasons. An all-male order steeped in ritual and ceremony, the Masons united urban and small-town elites into a tightly knit brotherhood through personal contacts and mutual aid. When efforts to investigate Morgan's disappearance ran into a legal dead end, rumors spread that the exclusivist Masons constituted a vast conspiracy that conferred special privileges and legal protection on its members.

Western New York, an area of religious fervor and rapid economic change after the opening of the Erie Canal in 1825, provided fertile ground for the growth of the new party. With close ties to rural landlords and town creditors, the Masons were vulnerable to the charge of economic favoritism. In addition, evangelicals accused the Masons of desecrating the Christian faith with their secret rituals. The Anti-Masons were thus the first party to combine demands for equal opportunity with calls for the moral reform of a sinful society. They were also the first party to select their presidential ticket in a national nominating convention, a precedent immediately followed by the Whigs and Democrats.

Although it spread into New England and the neighboring mid-Atlantic states, the Anti-Mason Party was unable to sustain itself. Recognizing that the opponents of the Anti-Masons were usually the entrenched local interests of the Democratic Party, shrewd politicians, led by Thurlow Weed and William Seward of New York, took up the movement and absorbed most of it into the anti-Jackson coalition. They did so by calling for equal opportunity and for such evangelical reforms as a ban on the sale of alcohol. The Whigs thus broadened their popular base and added an egalitarian message to their appeal.

By 1836, the Whigs were strong enough to mount a serious challenge for the presidency. However, they still lacked an effective national organization that could unite their regional coalitions behind one candidate. Instead, they ran four sectional candidates. Van Buren won an electoral majority by holding on to the populous mid-Atlantic states and improving on Jackson's showing in New England. Still, the Whigs were encouraged by the results. Compared to Jackson, Van Buren did poorly in what had been the overwhelmingly Democratic South, which was now open to further Whig inroads.

OVERVIEW The Second Party System

	Democrats	Whigs
Ideology	Favor limited role of federal government in economic affairs and matters of individual conscience; support territorial expansion	Favor government support for economic development and controls over individual morality; opposed to expansion
Voter support	Mainly subsistence farmers, unskilled workers, and Catholic immigrants	Mainly manufacturers, commercial farmers, skilled workers, and northern evangelicals
Regional strength	South and West	New England and Upper Midwest

Whig Persuasion

Whereas the Democrats attributed the threat to those liberties to privileged monopolies of government-granted power, the Whigs found it in the expansive powers of the presidency as wielded by Jackson and in the party organization that put Jackson and Van Buren into office. In 1836, the Whigs called for the election of "a president of the nation, not a president of party." Underlying this call was the persistent Whig belief that parties undermined individual liberties and the public good by fostering and rewarding the selfish interests of the party faithful. Although the Whigs dropped much of this ideology when they matured as a party, they never lost their fear of the presidency as an office of unchecked, demagogic power.

Most Whigs viewed governmental power as a positive force to promote economic development. They favored the spread of banking and paper money, chartering corporations, passing protective tariffs to support U.S. manufacturers, and opening up new markets for farmers through government-subsidized transportation projects. Such policies, they held, would widen economic opportunities for Americans and provide incentives for material self-improvement.

Whether as economic promoters or evangelical reformers, Whigs believed in promoting social progress and harmony through an interventionist government. Whig ideology blended economic, social, and spiritual reform into a unified message of uplift. An activist government would provide economic opportunities and moral guidance for a harmonious, progressive society of freely competing individuals whose behavior would be shaped by the evangelical norms of thrift, sobriety, and self-discipline. Much of the Whigs' reform impulse was directed against non-English and Catholic immigrants, those Americans who the Whigs believed most needed to be taught the virtues of self-control and disciplined work habits. Not coincidentally, these groups, the Scots-Irish in the backcountry, the Reformed Dutch, and Irish and German Catholics, were the most loyal Democrats. They resented the Whigs' aggressive moralism and legislative attempts to interfere with their drinking habits and Sunday amusements. These Democrats were typically subsistence farmers on the periphery of market change and unskilled workers forced by industrial change to abandon their hopes of ever opening their own shops. They equated an activist government with special privileges for the economically and culturally powerful and identified with the Democrats' desire to keep the government out of the economy and individual religious practices.

The Election of 1840

One of the signs of the Whigs' maturing as a party was their decision in 1840 to place victory above principle. Because of the lingering economic depression, Democratic rule had been discredited for many voters. Henry Clay, who promised that his American System would revive

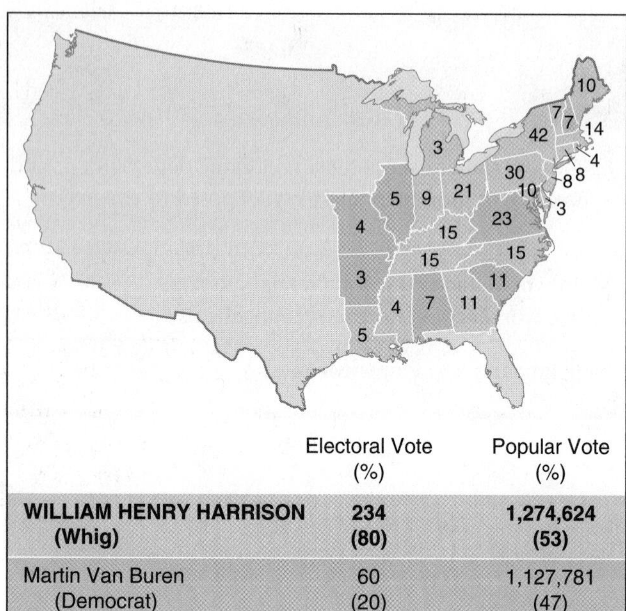

	Electoral Vote (%)	Popular Vote (%)
WILLIAM HENRY HARRISON (Whig)	**234 (80)**	**1,274,624 (53)**
Martin Van Buren (Democrat)	60 (20)	1,127,781 (47)

MAP 10–2 **The Election of 1840** Building upon their strength in the commercializing North, the Whigs attracted enough rural voters in the South and West to win the election of 1840.

Which Democratic strongholds proved vulnerable to the Whigs in 1840? Why?

the economy with government aid, appeared the most likely Whig candidate for president against Van Buren in 1840. Yet Whig power brokers dumped Clay, who represented the party's ideological heart, for a popular military hero, William Henry Harrison of Ohio.

Unlike Clay, Harrison was untainted by any association with the Bank of the United States, the Masonic Order, or slaveholding. As the victor at the Battle of Tippecanoe and a military hero in the War of 1812, he enabled Whig image-makers to cast him, like Jackson, as the honest, patriotic soldier worthy of the people's trust. In a decision that came back to haunt them, the Whigs geographically balanced their ticket by selecting John Tyler, a planter from Virginia, as Harrison's running mate. Tyler was an advocate of states' rights and a former Democrat who had broken with Jackson over the Force Bill.

Much to the disgust of Benjamin French, who accused the Whigs of running a campaign based on "fraud & humbug," the Whigs beat the Democrats at their own game of mass politics in 1840. They reversed the roles and symbolism of the Jackson-Adams election of 1828 and seized the high ground as the party of the people. In a further adaptation of earlier Democratic initiatives, the Whigs put together a frolicking campaign of slogans, parades, and pageantry.

The Whigs gained control of both Congress and the presidency in 1840. Harrison won 53 percent of the popular vote, and for the first time the Whigs carried the South (see Map 10–2). With the arrival of politics as mass spectacle, the turnout surged to an unprecedented 78 percent of eligible voters, a whopping increase over the average of 55 percent in the three preceding presidential elections (see Figure 10–2). The Whigs claimed most of the new voters and were now fully competitive with the Democrats in all parts of the nation. As the new majority party, they finally had the opportunity, or so they thought, to implement their economic program.

THE WHIGS IN POWER

WHY WAS William Henry Harrison's death such a blow to the Whig agenda?

Although the Whigs had been noncommittal on their plans during the campaign of 1840, it was common knowledge that Clay would move quickly on Whig economic policies by marshaling his forces in Congress and trying to dominate a pliant Harrison. But Harrison died from pneumonia in April 1841, barely a month after his inauguration, ruining Clay's plans.

Harrison and Tyler

QUICK REVIEW

The Election of 1844

- Henry Clay (Whig) versus James K. Polk (Democrat).
- Annexation of Texas and Oregon key issues.
- Polk's expansionist program united Democrats.
- Tyler used Polk's victory as mandate for annexation of Texas.

Harrison had pledged to follow the dictates of party leaders in Congress and defer to the judgment of his cabinet. Bowing to Clay's demands, he agreed to call Congress into special session to act on Whig Party measures. Precisely because he was the type of president the Whigs needed and wanted, his death was a real blow to Whig hopes of establishing the credibility of their party as an effective agent for positive change.

Just how serious that blow was soon became apparent when Tyler became president, the first vice president to succeed on the death of a president. Tyler subscribed to a states' rights agrarian philosophy that put him at odds with the urban and commercial elements of the Whig Party even in his home state of Virginia. Clay's economic nationalism struck him as a program of rank corruption that surrendered the constitutional rights of the South to power-hungry politicians and manufacturers in the North. Clay forged ahead with the party agenda, the repeal of the Independent Treasury System and its replacement by a new national bank, a protective tariff, and the distribution of the proceeds of the government's public land sales to the states as funds for internal improvements.

Tyler used the negative power of presidential vetoes to stymie the Whig program. He twice vetoed bills to reestablish a national bank. The second veto led to the resignation of the cabinet he had inherited from Harrison, save for Secretary of State Daniel Webster, who was in the midst of negotiations with the British. Enraged congressional Whigs then expelled Tyler from the party. Clay's legislative wizardry got him nowhere. In the end, Clay had no national bank, no funds for internal improvements, and only a slightly higher tariff. Although Clay's leadership of the Whigs was strengthened, Tyler had deprived that leadership of meaning by denying the Whigs the legislative fruits of their victory in 1840.

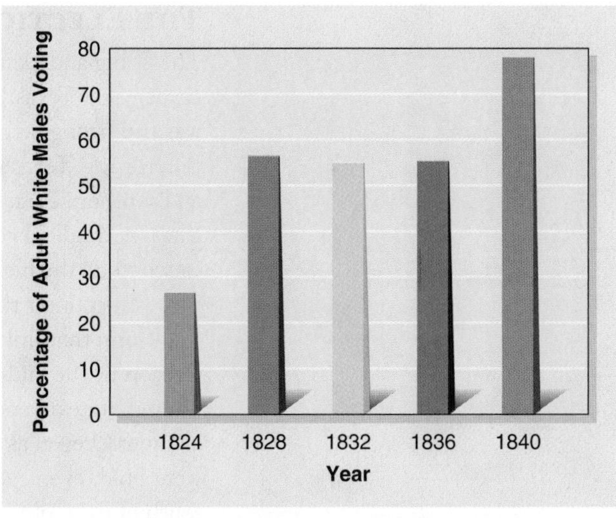

FIGURE 10–2 **Voter Turnout in Presidential Elections, 1824–1840** The creation of mass-based political parties dramatically increased voter turnout in presidential elections. Voting surged in 1828 with the emergence of the Jacksonian Democratic Party and again in 1840 when the Whig party learned to appeal to the mass electorate.

Data Source: Richard P. McCormick, "New Perspectives on Jacksonian Politics," in *The Nature of Jacksonian America*, ed. Douglas T. Miller (1972), p. 103.

The Texas Issue

Constrained by his states' rights view to a largely negative role in domestic policy, Tyler was a much more forceful president in foreign policy, an area in which the Constitution gives the chief executive considerable latitude. In 1842, Tyler's secretary of state, Daniel Webster, wrapped up his negotiations with the British over a long-standing boundary dispute. Webster now resigned from the cabinet to join his fellow Whigs, allowing Tyler to follow a pro-southern policy of expansion that he hoped would gain him the Democratic nomination for the presidency in 1844. His goal was the annexation of Texas.

Texas had been a slaveholding republic since 1836, when rebellious Americans, joined by some *tejanos* (Texans of Mexican descent), declared their independence from Mexico. Jackson extended diplomatic recognition before leaving office, but he refused the new nation's request to be annexed to the United States out of fear of provoking a war with Mexico, which did not recognize Texan independence, and damaging Van Buren's chances in the election of 1836.

For the sake of sectional harmony, party leaders sidestepped the Texas issue after 1836. Tyler renewed the issue in 1843 to curry favor among southern and western Democrats. He replaced Webster as secretary of state with a proannexationist Virginian, Abel P. Upshur, and secretly opened negotiations with the Texans. After Upshur's death in an accidental explosion on the battleship *Princeton*, John C. Calhoun, his successor, completed the negotiations and dramatically politicized the slavery issue. In the spring of 1844, Calhoun and Tyler submitted to the Senate a secretly drawn up treaty annexing Texas to the United States. Calhoun also made public his correspondence with Richard Pakenham, the British minister in Washington. In his letter, Calhoun accused the British of seeking to force emancipation on Texas in return for economic aid and a British-brokered Mexican recognition of Texan independence. These British efforts, warned Calhoun, were just the opening wedge in a master plan to block U.S. expansion and destroy slavery in the South. After pointedly defending slavery as a benign institution, Calhoun concluded that the security and preservation of the Union demanded the annexation of Texas. The Pakenham letter hit the Senate like a bombshell, convincing antislavery Northerners that the annexation of Texas was a slaveholders' conspiracy to extend slavery and swell the political power of the South. In June 1844, the Senate rejected Calhoun's treaty of annexation by a two-to-one margin. Still, the issue was hardly dead. Thanks to Tyler and Calhoun, Texas dominated the election of 1844.

The Election of 1844

The Whig and Democratic National Conventions met in the spring of 1844 in the midst of the uproar over Texas. Both Clay, who had the Whig nomination locked up, and Van Buren, who was the strong favorite for the Democratic one, came out against immediate annexation. Van Buren's anti-Texas stand cost him his party's nomination. In a carefully devised strategy, western and southern Democrats united to deny him the necessary two-thirds vote of convention delegates. A deadlocked convention turned to James K. Polk of Tennessee, a confirmed expansionist who had the blessing of Jackson, the party's patriarch.

To counter the charge that they were a prosouthern party, the Democrats ran in 1844 on a platform that linked Oregon to Texas as a territorial objective. Some 6,000 Americans were in Oregon by the mid-1840s, and demands mounted, especially from northern Democrats, that the United States abandon its 1818 agreement of joint occupation with the British and lay exclusive claim to Oregon as far north as the 54°4' parallel, the border with Russian-owned Alaska. These were bold, even reckless, demands, because the actual area of U.S. settlement in Oregon was south of the Columbia River, itself well south of even the 49th parallel.

The Democratic ticket in 1844 highlighted the Texas issue and linked Jackson's name to it.

Polk's expansionist program united the Democrats and enabled them to campaign with much more enthusiasm than in 1840. Acquiring Texas and Oregon not only held out the hope of cheap, abundant land to debt-burdened farmers in the North and planters in the South but also played on the anti-British sentiments of many voters. In contrast, the Whig campaign was out of focus. Clay sensed that his opposition to the immediate annexation of Texas was hurting him in the South, and he started to hedge by saying that he would accept Texas if the conditions were right. This wavering, however, failed to stem the defection of proslavery southern Whigs to the Democrats and cut into his support among antislavery Whigs in the North. Clay lost to Polk by less than 2 percent of the popular vote.

Tyler claimed Polk's victory as a mandate for the immediate annexation of Texas. He knew that it would still be impossible to gain the two-thirds majority in the Senate necessary for the approval of a treaty. Thus, he resorted to the constitutionally unprecedented expedient of a joint resolution in Congress inviting Texas to join the Union. By the narrow margin of 27 to 25, the Senate concurred with the House in favor of annexation. Tyler signed the joint resolution on March 1, 1845.

CONCLUSION

The Jacksonian era ushered in a revolution in U.S. political life. Responding to a surge of democratization that was in full swing by the 1820s, politicians learned how to appeal to a mass electorate and to build disciplined parties that channeled popular desires into distinctive party positions. In the two decades after 1824, voter participation in national elections tripled, and Democrats and Whigs competed on nearly equal terms in every region.

Although the origins of a national political culture can be traced back to the Federalists and the Jeffersonian Republicans, politics did not fully enter the mainstream of U.S. life until the rise of the second party system of Democrats and Whigs. The election of 1824 revived interest in presidential politics, and Jackson's forceful style of leadership highlighted the presidency as the focal point of U.S. politics. Professional politicians soon mastered the art of tailoring issues and images to reach the widest popular audience. Voters in favor of government aid for economic development and a social order based on Protestant moral controls turned to the Whigs. Conversely, those who saw an activist government as a threat to their economic and cultural equality turned to the Democrats.

The national issues around which the Democrats and Whigs organized and battled down to 1844 were primarily economic. As long as this was the case, party competition tended to diffuse sectional tensions and strengthen a national political culture. Slavery, in the form of the Texas question, replaced the economy as the decisive issue in the election of 1844. With this shift, party appeals began to focus on the place of slavery in U.S. society, creating an escalating politics of sectionalism that saw such loyal party workers as Benjamin French switch their allegiance to a new sectional party. Within a decade, the slavery issue would rip apart the second party system.

WHERE TO LEARN MORE

Rice Museum, Georgetown, South Carolina. Rice planters were the leaders of the nullification movement, and the interpretive materials here on the history of rice cultivation help one understand how slave labor was employed to produce their great wealth. Maps to the museum and news of special events can be found at http://www.ricemuseum.org.

The Hermitage, Hermitage, Tennessee. This site, the plantation home of Andrew Jackson, includes a museum with artifacts of Jackson's life. Its website, http://www.thehermitage.com, lists events and programs and examines the archaeological projects undertaken at the Hermitage.

Martin Van Buren National Historic Site, Kinderhook, New York. The site preserves Lindenwald, Van Buren's home after he left the presidency, and includes a library with materials on Van Buren and his political era. Its recently expanded website, http://www.nps.gov/mava/index.htm, discusses the history of Lindenwald and includes a virtual tour of its art collection.

Cherokee Trail of Tears Commemorative Park, Hopkinsville, Kentucky. Used as an encampment by the Cherokees in 1838 and 1839, this historic park is a documented site of part of the actual trail followed by the Cherokees during their forced removal. http://www.trailoftears.org.

Trail of Tears National Historic Trail. For access and information on the land and water routes followed by the Cherokees as they were forced out of the East, see http://www.nps.gov/trte/index.htm.

REVIEW QUESTIONS

1. Explain the democratic movements of the early nineteenth century. What role did race and gender play in these movements? What evidence is there for the existence of similar democratic sentiments in Europe?
2. What distinguished Jackson's presidency from those of his predecessors? How did he redefine the role of the president?
3. How was the Bank War central to the development of the Democratic and Whig parties? Why did the political debates of the 1830s focus on financial issues?
4. In terms of ideology and voter appeal, how did the Democrats and Whigs differ? How did each party represent a distinctive response to economic and social change?
5. How would you describe the changes in U.S. politics between 1824 and 1840? What accounted for these changes?
6. How did the annexation of Texas emerge as a political issue in the early 1840s? Why were the Democrats more in favor of territorial expansion than the Whigs?
7. What do you think accounted for the sense of shock, even outrage, with which Benjamin Brown French reacted to the partisanship of the election of 1828?

KEY TERMS

Abolitionist movement (p. 263)
Albany Regency (p. 254)
Anti-Masons (p. 265)
Bank War (p. 259)
Black Hawk's War (p. 256)
Democratic Party (p. 253)
Gag rule (p. 265)
Independent Treasury System (p. 264)
Indian Removal Act (p. 256)
Nullification crisis (p. 257)
Second Great Awakening (p. 250)
Second party system (p. 265)
Specie Circular (p. 264)
Spoils system (p. 255)
Trail of Tears (p. 256)
Whig Party (p. 264)

myhistorylab Connections

Reinforce what you learned in this chapter by studying the many documents, images, maps, review tools, and videos available at **www.myhistorylab.com**.

Read and Review

Study and Review **Study Plan: Chapter 10**

Read the Document

Andrew Jackson, First Annual Message to Congress (1829)

Andrew Jackson, Veto of the Bank Bill (1832)

Charles Finney, "What a Revival of Religion Is" (1835)

Memorial of the Cherokee Nation (1830)

Proclamation Regarding Nullification (1832)

The Force Bill (1833)

Black Hawk, Autobiography of Ma-ka-tai-me-she-kia-kiak, or Black Hawk (1833)

South Carolina's Ordinance of Nullification (1832)

See the Map

Native American Land Cessions to 1829

Native American Removal

The Slave, Free Black, and White Population of the United States in 1830

Research and Explore

Read the Document

Personal Journeys Online

From Then to Now Online: Banks and the Government

Hear the Audio *Van Buren*

Hear the Audio

Hear the audio files for Chapter 10 at **www.myhistorylab.com.**

Jacksonian Democracy and American Politics

TO WHAT degree was the election of 1824 a turning point in American political history? Considering the role of the common man, changes in party operations and campaign tactics, and the growing influence of political patronage, how did the events initiated in that election change American politics between 1824 and 1840?

Historians have referred to the years of Jackson's presidency as the Age of the Common Man and the Rise of Democracy. Perhaps this does carry a little too much elaboration with it, but the time of Andrew Jackson was a period of great ferment and change. The Second Great Awakening was stirring the religious and reform values of American citizens. The rise of the second two-party system was creating both conflict and confrontation in the American politics. The issues of national tariffs and slavery were beginning to divide the states, and the slow movement toward civil war was becoming clearly apparent. John Adams, Andrew Jackson, and Henry Clay and the election of 1824 comprise a turning point in U.S. politics. With a field of four candidates, the election for president was thrown to the U.S. House of Representatives, where Henry Clay was the Speaker of the House and had heavy influence upon the vote of the members of that chamber. After Adams was elected over Jackson, who had the largest share of popular votes, Adams appointed Clay as secretary of state then seen as a stepping stone to the presidency. Jackson's supporters immediately screamed "corrupt bargain" and the campaign of 1828 was under way before Adams was even inaugurated. Jackson's people coalesced into the Democratic Party. Adams's followers became the National Republicans, later evolving into the Whigs.

Mr. Clay came at six ...

9TH. . . . Mr. Clay came at six, and spent the evening with me in a long conversation explanatory of the past and prospective of the future. He said that the time was drawing near when the choice must be made in the House of Representatives of a President from the three candidates presented by the electoral colleges; that he had been much urged and solicited with regard to the part in that transaction that he should take, and had not been five minutes landed at his lodgings before he had been applied to by a friend of Mr. Crawford's, in a manner so gross that it had disgusted him; that some of my friends also, disclaiming, indeed, to have any authority from me, had repeatedly applied to him, directly or indirectly, urging considerations personal to himself as motives to his cause. He had thought it best to reserve for sometime his determination to himself: first, to give a decent time for his own funeral solemnities as a candidate; and, secondly, to prepare and predispose all his friends to a state of neutrality between the three candidates who would be before the House, so that they might be free ultimately to take that course which might be most conducive to the public interest. The time had now come at which he might be explicit in his communication with me, and he had for that purpose asked this confidential interview. He wished me, as far as I might think proper, to satisfy him with regard to some principles of great public importance, but without any personal considerations for himself. In the question to come before the House between General Jackson, Mr. Crawford, and myself, he had no hesitation in saying that his preference would be for me.

Henry Clay

Source: Charles Francis Adams, ed. Memoirs of John Quincy Adams, 12 Volumes (Philadelphia: J. B. Lippincott & Co., 1875).

Presidential Candidates and Political Parties, 1788–1840

IN THE slightly more than fifty years covered in this list, some parties flourished and some died. Some parties rose up to replace earlier parties and some changed into a new political alliance with a different name and evolved political goals.

1788	George Washington – No Party Designation
	John Adams – No Party Designation
1792	George Washington – No Party Designation
	John Adams – No Party Designation
	George Clinton – No Party Designation
1796	John Adams – Federalist
	Thomas Jefferson – Democratic-Republican
	Thomas Pinckney – Federalist
	Aaron Burr – Democratic-Republican
1800	Thomas Jefferson – Democratic-Republican
	Aaron Burr – Democratic-Republican
	John Adams – Federalist
	Charles C. Pinckney – Federalist
1804	Thomas Jefferson – Democratic-Republican
	Charles C. Pinckney – Federalist
1808	James Madison – Democratic-Republican
	Charles C. Pinckney – Federalist
	George Clinton – Democratic-Republican
1812	James Madison – Democratic-Republican
	De Witt Clinton – Federalist
1816	James Monroe – Democratic-Republican
	Rufus King – Federalist
1820	James Monroe – Democratic-Republican
	John Q. Adams – Independent Republican
1824	John Q. Adams – Democratic-Republican
	Andrew Jackson – Democratic-Republican
	William H. Crawford – Democratic-Republican
	Henry Clay – Democratic-Republican
1828	Andrew Jackson – Democratic
	John Q. Adams – National Republican
1832	Andrew Jackson – Democratic
	Henry Clay – National Republican
	William Wirt – Anti-Masonic
	John Floyd – National Republican
1836	Martin Van Buren – Democratic
	William H. Harrison – Whig
	Hugh L. White – Whig
	Daniel Webster – Whig
	W. P. Mangum – Whig
1840	William H. Harrison – Whig
	Martin Van Buren – Democratic

. . . to the victors belong the spoils

SENATOR WILLIAM Marcy gave the name "spoils system" to the practice of awarding political office to the supporters of your own party once you had won control of either state or federal government. His famous statement on the floor of the U.S. Senate: "When they are contending for victory, they avow the intention of enjoying it. If they are defeated, they expect to retire from office. If they are successful, they claim as matter of right the advantages of success. They see nothing wrong in the rule that to the victors belong the spoils of the enemy." This principle had been used heavily in the states of New York and Pennsylvania where Marcy engaged brutally in applying the practice. It was not until Jackson's election in 1828 that the spoils system was introduced at the federal level. Previous presidents had been circumspect in removing federal office servers from their jobs. Washington had removed only 9 in two terms, Adams had removed 9 in one term. After the Federalists were defeated in 1800 and the Democratic-Republicans took office, Jefferson refused to utilize the spoils system and removed only 39 federal office holders in two terms. Madison then dropped only 5 in two terms, Monroe removed only 9 in two terms and John Q. Adams fired only 2 in one administration. This changed in 1829 when Jackson removed a total of 734 federal office holders in a single year of his first administration. The age of the spoils system had arrived. The Democrats clearly used the spoils system to their advantage. How did the other political parties respond to this concept?

William Learned Marcy (1786–1857), American political leader.

11 Slavery and the Old South

NEGROES
FOR SALE.
Will be sold at public auction, at Spring Hill, in the County of Hempstead, on a credit of twelve months, on Friday the 28th day of this present month, 15 young and valuable Slaves, consisting of 9 superior Men & Boys, between 12 and 27 years of age, one woman about 43 years who is a good washer and cook, one woman about twenty-seven, and one very likely young woman with three children.
Also at the same time, and on the same terms, three Mules, about forty head of Cattle, plantation tools, one waggon, and a first rate Gin stand, manufactured by Pratt &Co.
Bond with two or more approved securities will be required.
Sale to commence at 10 o'clock.
E. E. Hundley,
W. Robinson,
H. M. Robinson.
Spring Hill, Jan. 6th, 1842.
NOTICE
NEGROES
FOR SALE
AT AUCTION
THIS DAY
AT 1 O'CLOCK
THE NEW YORK HERA
These shackles were found at a Plantation Slave Quarter site on Wadamalaw Island, S.C. approximately 25 miles from Charleston. They are blacksmith made.

"Slavery and the Old South, 1800–1860." A slave auction in Virginia, 1861. English engraving.

((•—[**Hear** the **Audio**

Hear the audio files for Chapter 11 at **www.myhistorylab.com**.

THE LOWER SOUTH *(page 279)*

HOW DID the increasing demand for cotton shape the development of slavery in the Lower South?

THE UPPER SOUTH *(page 282)*

WHAT CAUSED the decline of slavery after 1800 in the Upper South?

SLAVE LIFE AND CULTURE *(page 285)*

WHAT WAS life like for African American slaves in the first half of the nineteenth century?

FREE SOCIETY *(page 292)*

HOW WAS free society in the South structured?

THE PROSLAVERY ARGUMENT *(page 297)*

HOW DID the southern defense of slavery change between the early nineteenth century and the 1850s?

ONE AMERICAN JOURNEY

Had Mrs Wheeler condemned me to the severest corporal punish, or exposed me to be sold in the public slave market in Wilmington [New Carolina] I should probably have resigned myself with apparent composure to her cruel behests. But when she sought to force me into a compulsory union with a man whom I could only hate and despise it seemed that rebellion would be a virtue, that duty to myself and my God actually required it, and that whatever accidents or misfortunes might attend my flight nothing could be worse than what threatened my stay.

Marriage like many other blessings I considered to be especially designed for the free, and something that all the victims of slavery should avoid as tending essentially to perpetuate that system. Hence to all overtures of that kind from whatever quarter they might come I had invariably turned a deaf ear. I had spurned domestic ties not because my heart was hard, but because it was my unalterable resolution never to entail slavery on any human being. And now when I had voluntarily renounced the society of those I might have learned to love should I be compelled to accept one, whose person, and speech, and manner could not fail to be ever regarded by me with loathing and disgust. Then to be driven in to the fields beneath the eye and lash of the brutal overseer, and those miserable huts, with their promiscuous crowds of dirty, obscene and degraded objects, for my home I could not, I would not bear it.

Hannah Crafts

Henry Louis Gates, Jr., ed., *The Bondwoman's Narrative* (New York: Warner Books, 2002), pp. 206–207.

Read the **Document** at **www.myhistorylab.com**

Personal Journeys Online

- **Marie Perkins, Letter, 1852. A slave writes her husband informing him of the sale of their son.**
- **Lucy Skipwith, Letter, 1855. A slave writes her master in Virginia from his plantation in Alabama.**
- **Stephen Pembroke, Speech by a slave, 1854. A former slave describes his life under slavery.**

HANNAH CRAFTS was the name an African American woman adopted after she escaped from slavery in the late 1850s. This passage is from *The Bondwoman's Narrative*, a recently discovered manuscript that stands as the only known novel written by a female black slave. Although the precise identity of Crafts remains uncertain, the evidence strongly suggests that she was a house slave of John Hill Wheeler of North Carolina who fled north in the spring of 1857, married a Methodist clergyman, and merged into the black middle class of southern New Jersey. The novel contains searingly candid observations on the brutalized living conditions that field slaves were forced to endure.

Only the system of slavery that Crafts described with revulsion makes it possible to speak of the antebellum South as a single region despite its geographical and cultural diversity. It was black slavery that created a bond among white southerners and cast them in a common mold.

Not only did slavery make the South distinctive, it was also the source of the region's immense agricultural wealth, the foundation on which planters built their fortunes, the basis for white upward mobility, and the means by which white people controlled a large black minority. Precisely because slavery was so deeply embedded in southern life and customs, white leadership reacted to the mounting attacks on slavery after 1830 with an ever more defiant defense of the institution. That defense, in turn, reinforced a growing sense of sectionalism among white southerners, the belief that their values divided them from their fellow citizens in the Union.

Economically and intellectually, the Old South developed in stages. The South of 1860 was geographically much larger and

CHRONOLOGY

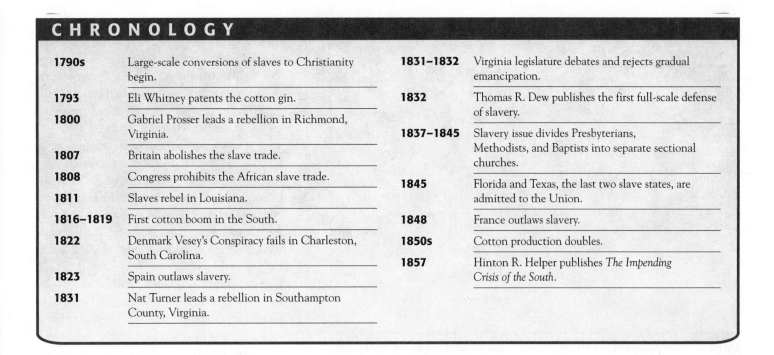

1790s	Large-scale conversions of slaves to Christianity begin.
1793	Eli Whitney patents the cotton gin.
1800	Gabriel Prosser leads a rebellion in Richmond, Virginia.
1807	Britain abolishes the slave trade.
1808	Congress prohibits the African slave trade.
1811	Slaves rebel in Louisiana.
1816–1819	First cotton boom in the South.
1822	Denmark Vesey's Conspiracy fails in Charleston, South Carolina.
1823	Spain outlaws slavery.
1831	Nat Turner leads a rebellion in Southampton County, Virginia.
1831–1832	Virginia legislature debates and rejects gradual emancipation.
1832	Thomas R. Dew publishes the first full-scale defense of slavery.
1837–1845	Slavery issue divides Presbyterians, Methodists, and Baptists into separate sectional churches.
1845	Florida and Texas, the last two slave states, are admitted to the Union.
1848	France outlaws slavery.
1850s	Cotton production doubles.
1857	Hinton R. Helper publishes *The Impending Crisis of the South*.

more diverse than it had been in 1800. It was also more uniformly committed to a single cash crop, cotton. Cotton became king, as contemporaries put it, and it provided the economic basis for southern sectionalism. During the reign of King Cotton, however, regional differences emerged between the Lower South, where the linkage between cotton and slavery was strong, and the Upper South, where slavery was relatively less important and the economy was more diversified. In both regions the control mechanisms of slavery were very tight, and Hannah Crafts was exceptional in her successful flight to freedom. ✦

THE LOWER SOUTH

HOW DID the increasing demand for cotton shape the development of slavery in the Lower South?

South and west of South Carolina stretched some of the best cotton land in the world. A long growing season, adequate rainfall, navigable rivers, and untapped fertility gave the Lower South incomparable natural advantages for growing cotton. Ambitious white southerners exploited these advantages by extending slavery to the newer cotton lands that opened up in the Lower South after 1800 (see Map 11–1). Cotton production and slavery thus went hand in hand.

Cotton and Slaves

Before 1800, slavery was associated with the cash crops of tobacco, rice, and sea island (or long-staple) cotton. Tobacco, the mainstay of the colonial Chesapeake economy, severely depleted the soil. Its production stagnated after the Revolutionary War, when it lost its formerly protected markets in Britain. Rice and long-staple cotton, named for its long, silky fibers, were profitable but geographically limited to the humid sea islands and tidal flats off the coast of South Carolina and Georgia. Like sugar cane, introduced into Louisiana in the 1790s, they required a huge capital investment in special machinery, dikes, and labor. Upland, or short-staple, cotton faced none of these constraints, once the cotton gin removed the technical barrier to its commercial production (see Chapter 12). It could be planted far inland, and small farmers could grow it profitably because it required no additional costs for machinery or drainage systems.

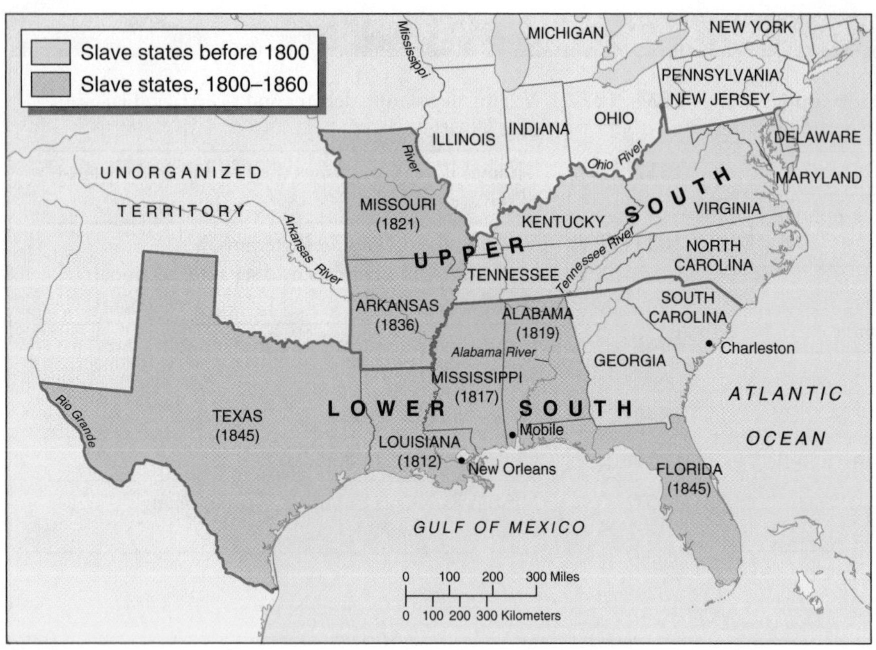

MAP 11–1 **The Spread of Slavery: New Slave States Entering the Union, 1800–1850**
Seven slave states entered the Union after 1800 as cotton production shifted westward.

Why was cotton production especially suited to slave labor?

As a result, after the 1790s, the production of short-staple cotton boomed. Moreover, like the South's other cash crops, upland cotton was well suited for slave labor because it required fairly continuous tending throughout the year. The long work year maximized the return on capital invested in slave labor.

The linkage of cotton and slaves was at the heart of the plantation system that spread westward after the War of 1812. From its original base in South Carolina and Georgia, the cotton kingdom moved into the Old Southwest and then into Texas and Arkansas. As wasteful agricultural practices exhausted new lands, planters moved to the next cotton frontier farther west. Cotton output exploded from 73,000 bales (a bale weighed close to 500 pounds) in 1800 to more than 2 million bales by midcentury, thanks to the fertility of virgin land and to technological changes, such as improved seed varieties and steam-powered cotton gins (see Figure 11–1). Slave labor accounted for more than 90 percent of cotton production.

Plantations, large productive units specializing in a cash crop and employing at least 20 slaves, were the leading economic institution in the Lower South. Planters were the most prestigious social group, and, although less than 5 percent of white families were in the planter class, they controlled more than 40 percent of the slaves, cotton output, and total agricultural wealth. Most had inherited or married into their wealth, but they could stay at the top of the South's class structure only by continuing to profit from slave labor.

W WHERE TO LEARN MORE

★ Cottonlandia Museum, Greenwood, Mississippi
http://www.cottonlandia.org/

Plantations were generally more efficient producers of cotton than small farms. A variety of factors contributed to this efficiency. Most important, the ownership of 20 or more slaves enabled planters to use gangs to do both routine and specialized agricultural work. This **gang system,** a crude version of the division of labor that was being introduced in northern factories, permitted a regimented work pace. Teams of field hands, made up of women as well as men, had to work at a steady pace or else feel the lash.

gang system The organization and supervision of slave field hands into working teams on southern plantations.

The plantation districts of the Lower South stifled the growth of towns and economic enterprise. Planters, as well as ordinary farmers, strove to be self-sufficient. The most significant economic exchange, exporting cotton, took place in international markets and was handled by specialized commission merchants in Charleston, Mobile, and New Orleans. The Lower South had amassed great wealth, but most outsiders saw no signs of progress there.

The Profits of Slavery

Slavery was profitable on an individual basis. Most modern studies indicate that the average rate of return on capital invested in a slave was about 10 percent a year, a rate that at least equaled that of alternative investments in the South or the North. Not surprisingly, the newer regions of the cotton kingdom in the Lower South, with the most productive land and the greatest commitment to plantation agriculture, consistently led the nation in per capita income.

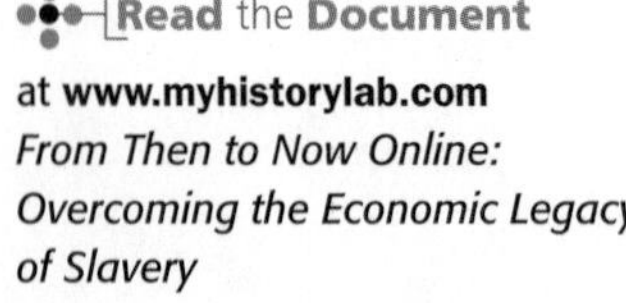
Read the **Document**
at **www.myhistorylab.com**
From Then to Now Online: Overcoming the Economic Legacy of Slavery

The profitability of slavery ultimately rested on the enormous demand for cotton outside the South. Demand was so strong that prices held steady at around 10 cents a pound in the 1850s, even as southern production of cotton doubled. Textile mills in Britain were always the largest market, but demand in continental Europe and the United States grew even faster after 1840.

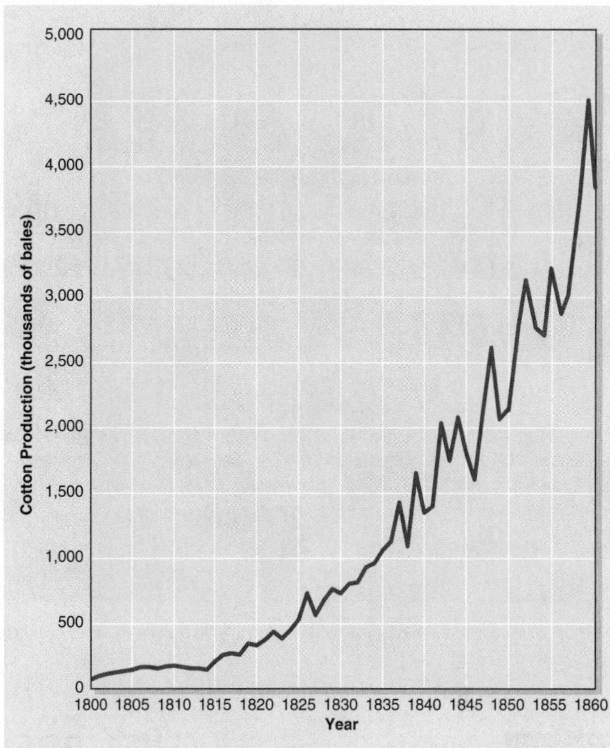

FIGURE 11–1 **U.S. Cotton Production, 1800–1860** Cotton production spiraled upward after 1800, and the South became the world's leading supplier.

Data Source: U.S. Bureau of the Census, *Historical Statistics of the United States* (1960).

The slave trade. Southern law defined slaves as chattel, the personal property of their owners, and their market value increased along with the profitability of slavery. Prices for a male field hand rose from $250 in 1815 to $900 by 1860. Prices at any given time varied according to the age, sex, and skills of the slave, as well as overall market conditions, but the steady rise in prices meant that slave owners could sell their human chattel and realize a profit over and above what they had already earned from the slaves' labor. This was especially the case with slave mothers; the children they bore increased the capital assets of their owners. Slave women of childbearing age were therefore valued nearly as much as male field hands.

The domestic slave trade brought buyers and sellers of slaves together. Slaves flowed from the older areas of the Upper South to the newer plantation districts in the Lower South. This trade was extensive: More than 800,000 slaves were moved between regions in the South from 1790 to 1860. The sheer size of the internal slave trade indicates just how profit-driven slave owners were. Few of them hesitated to break up slave families for sale when market conditions were right. About half of all slave sales separated family members. Slave children born in the Upper South after 1820 stood a one-in-three chance of being sold during their lifetime. Most of the profits from slave labor and sales went into buying more land and slaves. As long as slaves employed in growing cash staples returned 10 percent a year, slave owners had little economic incentive to shift their capital resources into manufacturing or urban development. The predictable result was that industrialization and urbanization fell far behind the levels in the free states.

Nowhere was the indifference of planters to economic diversification more evident than in the Lower South, which had the smallest urban population and the fewest factories. Planters here were not opposed to economic innovations that promised greater profits, but they feared social changes that might undermine the stability of slavery. Urbanization and industrialization both entailed such risks. Most planters suspected that the urban environment weakened slavery.

QUICK REVIEW

Economy of Slavery

- Prices for average male field hand: $250 in 1815, $900 in 1860.
- Female slaves of childbearing age valued almost as highly as male field hands.
- Large and profitable regional market in slaves.

Urban slavery. Urban slaves were artisans, semiskilled laborers, and domestics, and, unlike their rural counterparts, they usually lived apart from their owners. They had much more freedom than field hands to move around, interact with white people and other black people, and experiment with various social roles. Many of them, especially if they had a marketable skill, such as carpentry or tailoring, could hire out their labor and retain some of their wages for themselves after reimbursing their owners. In short, the direct authority of the slave owner was less clear-cut in the town than in the country.

Urban slavery declined from 1820 to 1860 as slaves decreased from 22 percent to 10 percent of the urban population. This decline reflected both doubts about the stability of slavery in an urban setting and the large profits that slave labor earned for slave owners in the rural cotton economy.

QUICK REVIEW

Urban Slavery

- 1820–1860: slaves decreased from 22 percent to 10 percent of urban population.
- Planters had a general ambivalence toward industrialization.
- Many planters saw factory work as a threat to slave discipline.

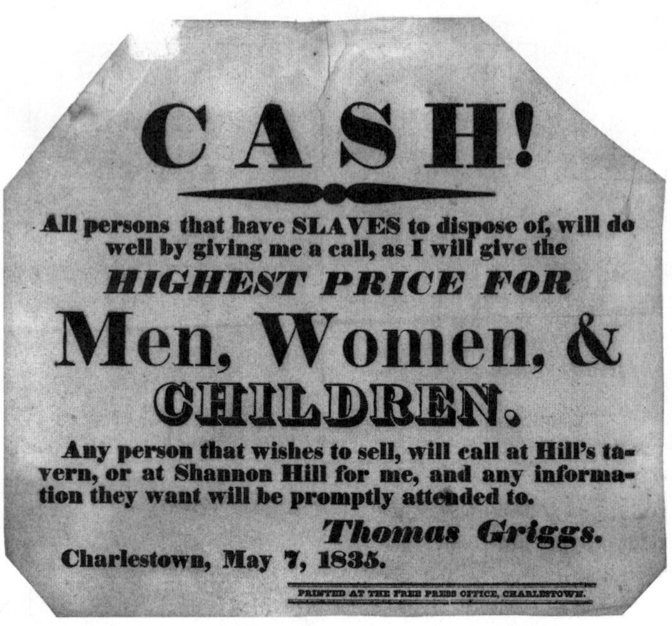

Like most slave traders, Thomas Griggs of Charleston offered cash for all slaves he purchased.

Industrial slavery. The ambivalence of planters toward urban slavery also characterized their attitudes toward industrial slavery and, indeed, to industrialization itself. If based on free labor, industrialization risked promoting an antislavery class consciousness among manufacturing laborers that would challenge the property rights of slave owners. But the use of slaves as factory operatives threatened slave discipline because an efficient level of production required special incentives. A Virginian noted of slaves that he had hired out for industrial work, "They were worked hard, and had too much liberty, and were acquiring bad habits. They earned money by overwork, and spent it for whisky, and got a habit of roaming about and *taking care of themselves;* because, when they were not at work in the furnace, nobody looked out for them."

No more than 5 percent of the slaves in the Lower South ever worked in manufacturing, and most of these were in rural enterprises serving local markets too small to interest northern manufacturers. Ever concerned to preserve slavery, planters would not risk slave discipline or the profits of cotton agriculture by embracing the unpredictable changes that industrialization was sure to bring.

THE UPPER SOUTH

WHAT CAUSED the decline of slavery after 1800 in the Upper South?

Climate and geography distinguished the Upper South from the Lower South. The eight slave states of the Upper South lay north of the best growing zones for cotton. The northernmost of these states—Delaware, Maryland, Kentucky, and Missouri—bordered on free states and were known as the Border South. The four states south of them—Virginia, North Carolina, Tennessee, and Arkansas—constituted a middle zone. Slavery was entrenched in all these states, but it was less dominant than in the cotton South.

The key difference between the Upper and Lower South was the suitability of the Lower South for growing cotton with gangs of slave laborers. Except for prime cotton districts in middle Tennessee, eastern Arkansas, and parts of North Carolina, the Upper South lacked the fertile soil and long growing season necessary for the commercial production of cotton, rice, or sugar (see Map 11–2). Consequently, the demand for slaves was weaker than in the Lower South. Percentages of slave ownership and of slaves in the overall population were roughly half those in the cotton South. While the Lower South was undergoing a cotton boom after the War of 1812, the Upper South was mired in a long economic slump, from which it did not emerge until the 1850s. The improved economy of the Upper South in the late antebellum period increasingly relied on free labor, a development that many cotton planters feared would diminish southern unity in defense of slavery.

A Period of Economic Adjustment

To inhabitants and visitors alike, vast stretches of the Upper South presented a dreary spectacle of exhausted fields and depopulation in the 1820s and 1830s. The soil was most depleted where tobacco had been cultivated extensively. Even where the land was still fertile, farmers could not compete against the fresher lands of the Old Southwest. Land values fell as farmers dumped their property and headed west.

Agricultural reform emerged in the 1830s as one proposed solution to this economic crisis. Its leading advocate was Edmund Ruffin, a Virginia planter who tirelessly promoted the use of marl (calcium-rich seashell deposits) to neutralize the overly acidic and worn-out soils of the Upper South. He also called for deeper plowing, systematic rotation of crops, and upgrading the breeding stock for animal husbandry.

Ruffin's efforts, and those of the agricultural societies and fairs spawned by the reform movement, met with some success, especially in the 1840s, when the prices of all cash staples fell. Still, only a minority of farmers ever embraced reform. These were generally the well-educated planters who read the agricultural press and could afford to change their farming practices.

Although soil exhaustion and wasteful farming persisted, agriculture in the Upper South had revived by the 1850s. A rebound in the tobacco market accounted for part of this revival, but the growing profitability of general farming was responsible for most of it.

Particularly in the Border South, the trend was toward agricultural diversification. Farmers and planters lessened their dependence on slave labor or on a single cash crop and practiced a thrifty, efficient agriculture geared to producing grain and livestock for urban markets. Western Maryland and the Shenandoah Valley and northern sections of Virginia grew wheat, and in the former tobacco districts of the Virginia and North Carolina Tidewater, wheat, corn, and garden vegetables became major cash crops.

Expanding urban markets and a network of internal improvements facilitated the transition to general farming. Both these developments were outgrowths of the movement for industrial diversification launched in the 1820s in response to the heavy outflow of population from the Upper South.

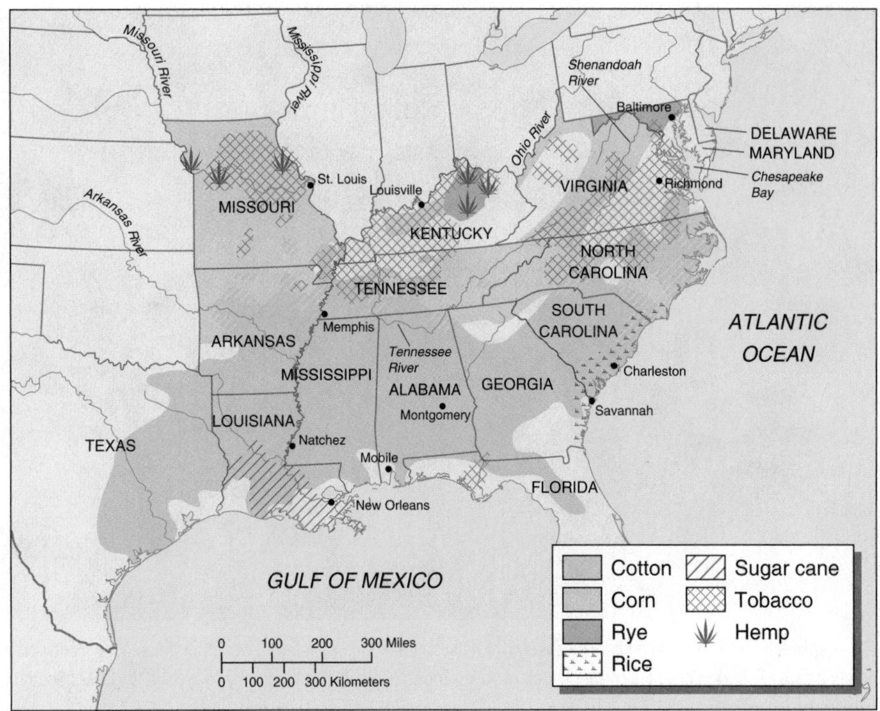

MAP 11–2 Cotton and Other Crops in the South, 1860 Most of the Upper South was outside the Cotton Belt, where the demand for slave labor was greatest.

Why was the increasing dominance of cotton cultivation in the Lower South accompanied by a growing concentration of slaves in that region? What agricultural trends help explain the relative decline of slavery in the Upper South?

QUICK REVIEW

Economic Trends in the Upper South

- Increased agricultural diversity.
- Expanding urban markets.
- Growing urbanization.
- Decreased reliance on plantation agriculture and slave labor.

Growing urbanization. Although not far advanced by northern standards, urbanization and industrialization in the Upper South were considerably greater than in the Lower South. The region had twice the percentage of urban residents of the cotton South, and it contained the leading manufacturing cities in the slave states, St. Louis, Baltimore, and Louisville. Canals and railroads linked cities and countryside in a denser transportation grid than in the Lower South.

With an economy more balanced among agriculture, manufacturing, and trade than a generation earlier, the Upper South at midcentury was gradually becoming less tied to plantation agriculture and slave labor. The rural majority increasingly prospered by growing foodstuffs for city-dwellers and factory workers. The labor market for railroad construction and manufacturing work attracted northern immigrants, helping to compensate for the loss of the native-born population through migration to other states.

The economic adjustment in the Upper South converted the labor surplus of the 1820s into a labor scarcity by the 1850s. "It is a fact," noted Edmund Ruffin in 1859, "that labor is greatly deficient in all Virginia, and especially in the rich western counties, which, for want of labor, scarcely yet yield in the proportion of one tenth of their capacity." Ruffin's commitment to agricultural reform was exceeded only by his devotion to slavery. He now feared that free labor was about to replace scarce and expensive slave labor in Virginia and much of the Upper South.

The Decline of Slavery

Slave owners tended to exaggerate all threats to slavery, and Ruffin was no exception. But slavery was clearly growing weaker in the Upper South by the 1850s (see Figure 11–2). The decline

The internal slave trade was the primary means by which the slaves of the Upper South were brought into the plantation markets of the Old Southwest. This illustration shows professional slave traders driving a chained group of slaves, known as a coffle, to prospective buyers in the Lower South.

Collection of The New-York Historical Society.

Read the **Document**
at www.myhistorylab.com
A Slave Tells of His Sale at Auction (1848)

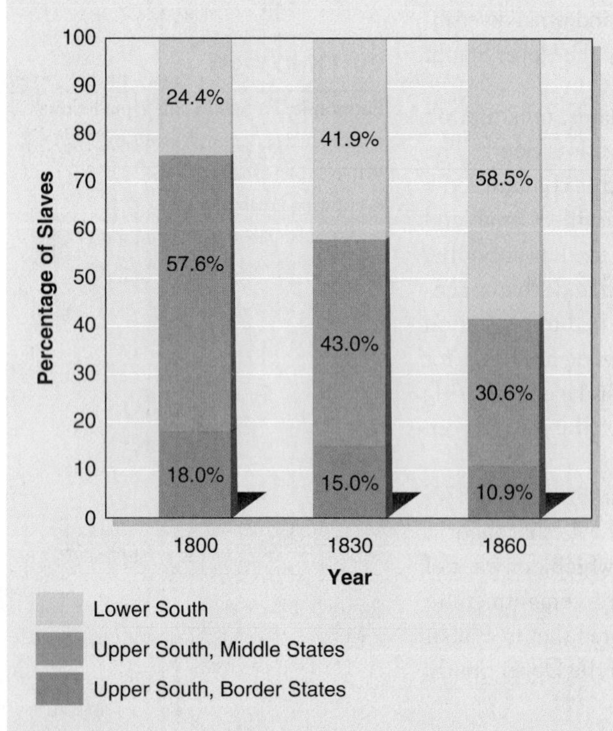

FIGURE 11–2 **The Changing Regional Pattern of Slavery in the South, 1800–1860** As the nineteenth century progressed, slavery increasingly became identified with the cotton-growing Lower South.

was most evident along the northern tier of the Upper South, where the proportion of slaves to the overall population fell steadily after 1830.

Elsewhere in the Upper South, slavery was holding its own by the 1850s. Tobacco and cotton planters in North Carolina and Tennessee continued to rely heavily on slave labor, but most small farmers were indifferent, if not opposed, to the institution. Only in Arkansas, whose alluvial lands along the Mississippi River offered a new frontier for plantation agriculture, was slavery growing rapidly.

The region's role as a slave exporter to the Lower South hastened the decline of slavery in the Upper South. In every decade after 1820, the internal slave trade drained off about 10 percent of the slaves in the Upper South, virtually the entire natural increase. Selling slaves to the Lower South reinforced the Upper South's economic stake in slavery at a time when the institution was otherwise barely profitable there. The sale of surplus slaves was a windfall for planters whose slaves had become an economic burden. This same windfall gave planters the capital to embark on agricultural reform and shift out of tobacco production. Investment capital in the Upper South was not flowing into slave property but into economic diversification that expanded urban manufacturing. Both of these structural changes increasingly put slavery at a competitive disadvantage against free labor.

The wheat, corn, oats, and fodder crops that replaced tobacco in much of the Upper South did not require continuous attention. Unlike tobacco, wheat needed intensive labor only at planting and harvest. Thus, as planters abandoned tobacco, they kept fewer slaves and relied on cheap seasonal workers to meet peak labor demand.

The cheapness and flexibility of free labor made it better suited than slave labor for general farming. Urban manufacturers likewise wanted workers who could be hired and fired at a moment's notice. Despite the successful use of slaves in tobacco manufacturing and at the

On June 8, 1857, the slaves on the Stirrup Branch plantation in Bishopville, South Carolina, had their picture taken in the rear of their owner's house. The occasion was the seventy-fifth birthday of Captain James Rembert.

large Tredegar Iron Works in Richmond, immigrant workers displaced slaves in most of the factories in the Border South. By 1860, slaves made up just 1 percent of the population in St. Louis and Baltimore, the South's major industrial cities.

Slavery was in economic retreat across the Upper South after 1830. There were still plantation districts with large concentrations of slaves, and slave owners retained enough political power to defeat all challenges to their property interests. Nevertheless, the gradual turn to free labor was unmistakable.

SLAVE LIFE AND CULTURE

WHAT WAS life like for African American slaves in the first half of the nineteenth century?

Nearly 4 million slaves lived in the South by 1860, a more than fivefold increase since the ratification of the Constitution. This population gain was overwhelmingly due to an excess of births over deaths. The British-led effort to suppress the foreign slave trade was successful in closing off fresh supplies from Africa after 1807.

Almost all southern slaves were thus native-born by the mid-nineteenth century. They were not Africans but African Americans, and they shared the common fate of bondage. By resisting an enslavement they could not prevent, they shaped a culture of their own that eased their pain and raised their hopes of someday being free. They retained their dignity in the face of continual humiliation and relied on their family life and religious beliefs as sources of strength under nearly intolerable circumstances.

Work Routines and Living Conditions

Being treated as a piece of property to be worked for profit and bought and sold when financially advantageous to one's owners, this was the legal and economic reality that all slaves confronted. Each southern state had its own **slave codes,** laws defining the status of slaves and the rights of masters; the codes gave slave owners near-absolute power over their human property.

slave codes A series of laws passed mainly in the southern colonies in the late seventeenth and early eighteenth centuries to defend the status of slaves and codify the denial of basic civil rights to them.

Read the **Document** at **www.myhistorylab.com** *Georgia Slave Codes (1848)*

Slaves could not own property, make contracts, possess guns or alcohol, legally marry (except in Louisiana), leave plantations without the owner's written permission, or testify against their masters or any other white person in a court of law. Many states also prohibited

GLOBAL CONNECTIONS

Cotton Is King

"But if there were no other reason why we should never have war, would any sane nation make war on cotton? Without firing a gun, without drawing a sword, should they make war on us we could bring the whole world to our feet. . . . What would happen if no cotton was furnished for three years? . . . England would topple headlong and carry the whole civilized world with her, save the South. No, you dare not make war on cotton. No power on earth dares to make war upon it. Cotton is king."

With these words delivered in a debate in the U.S. Senate on March 4, 1858, Senator James Henry Hammond of South Carolina popularized the phrase "Cotton is King," one that had first appeared in 1855 as the title of a work by the Cincinnati merchant David Christy decrying the world's dependence on southern-supplied cotton. Hammond would be proved wrong in his proclamation of the South's cotton-based invincibility, as Confederate diplomats discovered to their dismay during the Civil War, but by the 1850s the South's chief staple did indeed appear to be omnipotent.

As Hammond was speaking, the production, marketing, and consumption of cotton had spun a global web that constituted a veritable cotton empire of staggering proportions. Worldwide, perhaps as many 20 million workers were employed in the manufacturing of cotton and cotton cloth. No other manufacturing activity then rivaled cotton. Entire towns and regions stretching from the textile centers of New England to the mill districts of England, France, and Germany on to the suburbs of Moscow in Russia were critically dependent on a reliable and abundant source of cheap cotton. That source was overwhelmingly the American slave South. By the late 1850s cotton planters and their slaves provided England with 77 percent of its raw cotton, France 90 percent, Germany 60 percent, and Russia up to 92 percent. England's economy in particular, whether measured by its manufacturing, financial, or export sectors, seemed hostage to the South's continuing ability and willingness to keep it supplied with the product essential for its prosperity. No wonder Hammond was confident to the point of cockiness.

Hammond's speech politicized the growing faith of planters in the indispensability of their cotton to the global economy and pushed many of them to view secession from the Union as not only desirable but feasible. What Hammond and these planters overlooked was that cotton had become so important to the global economy that any major disruption in southern cotton would quickly compel foreign purchasers to develop alternative sources of cotton that were more directly under their political control. The cutting off of southern cotton during the Civil War resulted in a new global configuration of cotton production that permanently displaced King Cotton from its throne.

- What do you think were the main contours of the new global web of cotton production that emerged during and after the American Civil War, and what do you suspect was the likely impact on the rural populations of India, Egypt, and parts of Brazil?

teaching a slave to read or write. The murder of a slave by a master was illegal, but in practice, the law and community standards looked the other way if a disobedient slave was killed while being disciplined.

The slave codes penalized any challenge to a master's authority or any infraction of plantation rules. Whippings were the most commonly authorized punishment. Striking a master, committing arson, or conspiring to rebel were punishable by death. Most masters recognized that it made good business sense to feed, clothe, and house their slaves well enough to ensure productive labor and to encourage a family life that would enable the slave population to reproduce itself. Thus planters' self-interest probably improved the living standards for slaves in the first half of the nineteenth century, and the slave population grew at a rate only slightly below that of white southerners.

QUICK REVIEW

Health and Welfare

- Planters provided the bare necessities.
- Slave diets were insufficient in vitamins and nutrients.
- Clothing and shelter were rudimentary.
- Life expectancy at birth for slaves was roughly half that of whites.

Diet and housing. Planters rarely provided their slaves with more than the bare necessities. The slaves lived mainly on rations of cornmeal and salt pork, supplemented with vegetables they grew on the small garden plots that many planters permitted and with occasional catches of game and fish. This diet provided ample calories but was often insufficient in vitamins and nutrients. Infant mortality was twice as high among slaves as among white southerners in 1850; so was mortality among slave children up to age 14. According to one study, the life expectancy for slaves at birth was 21 to 22 years, roughly half the white life expectancy.

Planters furnished slaves with two sets of coarse clothing, one for summer and one for winter. Their housing, typically a 15-by-15-foot one-room cabin for five or six occupants, provided little more than basic shelter against the elements. Large planters placed these cabins in a row, an arrangement that projected precision and undifferentiated order. Slaves expressed their individuality by furnishing their cabins with handmade beds and benches and by pushing for the right to put in gardens.

Especially on large plantations, slave nursemaids cared for the young children in the white planter's family.

From the Collection of the Louisiana State Museum.

Working conditions. The diet and housing of most slaves may have been no worse than that of the poorest whites in both the North and the South, but their workload was undoubtedly heavier. Just over half of the slave population at midcentury was concentrated on plantation units with 20 or more slaves, and most of these slaves worked as field hands in gang labor. Overseers freely admitted that they relied on whippings to make slaves in the gangs keep at their work.

Most plantation slaves toiled at hard physical labor from sunup to sundown. The work was more intense and sustained than that of white farmers or white factory hands. The fear of the whip on a bare back set the pace.

Some 15 to 20 percent of plantation slaves were house servants or skilled artisans who had lighter and less regimented workloads than field hands. Some planters used the prospect of transfer to these relatively privileged positions as an incentive to field hands to work harder. Extra rations, time off on weekends, passes to visit a spouse on a nearby plantation, and the right to have a garden plot were among the other incentives planters used to keep labor productivity high. However, what a planter viewed as privileges, benevolently bestowed, slaves quickly came to see as customary rights. Despite the power of the whip, if planters failed to respect these "rights," slave morale would decline, and the work routine would be interrupted.

Nearly three-fourths of the slaves worked on plantations and medium-sized farms. Most of the remainder, those in units with fewer than 10 slaves, worked on small farms in close contact with the master's family. Their workloads were more varied and sometimes less taxing than those of plantation hands, but these slaves were also more directly exposed to the whims of their owners and less likely to live in complete family units. Slave couples on small holdings were more likely to live on separate farms. Owners with only a few slaves were also more vulnerable than planters to market downturns that could force them to sell slaves and further divide families.

Read the **Document**
at www.myhistorylab.com
Memoirs of a Monticello Slave (1847)

Of all slaves, 10 percent were not attached to the land, laboring instead at jobs that most white workers shunned. Every southern industry, but most particularly extractive industries such as mining and lumbering, relied heavily on slaves. Racial tensions often flared in southern industry, and when the races worked together, skilled white laborers typically insisted on being placed in supervisory positions.

Digging coal as miners or shoveling it as stokers for boilers on steamboats, laying down iron for the railroads or shaping hot slabs of it in a foundry, industrial slaves worked at least as hard as field hands. Compared to plantation slaves, however, they had more independence off the job and greater opportunities to earn money of their own. Because many of them had to house and feed themselves, they could also enjoy more time free from direct white scrutiny. By undertaking extra factory work, known as "overwork," industrial slaves could earn $50 or more a month, money they could use to buy goods for their families or, in rare cases, to purchase their freedom.

Families and Religion

The core institution of slave life was the family. Except in Louisiana, southern law did not recognize slave marriages, but masters permitted, even encouraged, marital unions in order to raise the morale of their labor force and increase its value by having it produce marketable children. Slaves embraced their families as a source of loving warmth and strength in a system that treated them as commodities.

Despite all the obstacles arrayed against them, many slave marriages produced enduring commitments and a supportive moral code for family members. Most slave unions remained intact until the death or, frequently, the sale of one spouse. Close to one-third of slave marriages were broken up by sales or forced removals.

Both parents were present in about two-thirds of slave families, the same ratio as in contemporary peasant families in Western Europe. Although the father's role as protector of and provider for his wife and children had no standing under slavery, most slave fathers struggled to help feed their families by hunting and fishing, and they risked beating and death to defend their wives against sexual abuse by the overseer or master. Besides their field labors, slave mothers had all the burdens of pregnancy, child care, laundry, and cooking.

No anguish under slavery was more heartrending than that of a mother whose child was sold away from her. "Oh, my heart was too full!" recalled Charity Bowery on being told that her boy Richard had been sold. "[My mistress] had sent me away on an errand, because she didn't want to be troubled with our cries. I hadn't any chance to see my poor boy. I shall never see my poor boy. I shall never see him again in this world. My heart felt as if it was under a great load."

QUICK REVIEW

Slave Families

- Both parents present in two-thirds of slave families.
- Most slave fathers did extra work and risked punishment to support and defend their families.
- Parents concentrated on teaching children survival skills.

Charity Bowery's experience was hardly unique. Slave parents had to suppress the rage they felt at their powerlessness to protect their children from the cruelties of slavery. Most parents could only teach their children the skills of survival in a world in which white people had a legal monopoly on violence. The most valuable of these skills was the art of hiding one's true feelings from white people and telling them what they wanted to hear.

Extensive kinship ties provided a support network for the vulnerable slave family. Thickest on the older and larger plantations, these networks included both blood relatives and other significant people. Children were taught to address elders as "Aunt" and "Uncle" and fellow slaves as "sister" and "brother." If separated from a parent, a child could turn to relatives or the larger slave community for care and assistance.

Slaves followed West African customs by prohibiting marriage between cousins and by often naming their children after departed grandparents. They also drew on an African heritage kept alive through folklore and oral histories to create a religion that fit their needs. The ancestors of nineteenth-century slaves brought no common religion with them when they were taken to the New World. However, beliefs common to a variety of African religions survived. Once slaves began to embrace Christianity in the late eighteenth century, they blended these beliefs into an African Christianity. In keeping with African traditions, the religion of the slaves fused the natural and spiritual worlds, accepted the power of ghosts over the living, and relied on an expressive form of worship in which the participants shouted and swayed in rhythm with the beat of drums and other instruments.

Read the **Document** at **www.myhistorylab.com**
Charles C. Jones, The Religious Instruction of the Negroes in the United States (1842)

By most estimates, no more than 30 percent of slaves ever converted to Christianity. Those who did found in Christianity a message of deliverance rooted in the liberation of Moses's people from bondage in Egypt. The Jesus of the New Testament spoke to them as a compassionate God who had shared their burden of suffering, so that all peoples could hope to find the Promised Land of love and justice. By blending biblical imagery into their spirituals, the slaves expressed their yearning for freedom: "Didn't my Lord deliver Daniel/Then why not every man?"

The initial exposure of slaves to Christianity usually came from evangelical revivalists, and slaves always favored the Baptists and Methodists over other denominations. The evangelical message of universal spiritual equality confirmed the slaves' sense of personal worth. Less formal in both their doctrines and organization than the Presbyterians and Episcopalians, the evangelical sects allowed the slaves more leeway to choose their own preachers and engage in their physical call-and-response pattern of worship.

Most planters were pragmatic about encouraging Christianity among their slaves. They wished to control religion, as they did other aspects of slaves' lives. Thus, while many planters allowed black preachers at religious services on their plantations, they usually insisted that white observers be present. Worried that abolitionist propaganda might attract the slaves to Christianity as a religion of secular liberation, some planters in the late antebellum period tried to convert their slaves to their own version of Christianity. They invited white ministers to their plantations to preach a gospel of passivity and obedience, centered on Paul's call for servants to "obey in all things your Masters."

Although most slaves viewed the religion of their owners as hypocritical and the sermons of white ministers as propaganda, they feigned acceptance of the religious wishes of their masters. As much as they could, the slaves hid their genuine religious life from white people. Many slaves experienced religion as a spiritual rebirth that gave them the inner strength to endure their bondage. As one recalled, "I was born a slave and lived through some hard times. If it had not been for my God, I don't know what I would have done."

QUICK REVIEW

Fear of Rebellion and Northern Intentions

- African Americans were the majority of South Carolina's population.
- Rebellions convinced planters that the antislavery movement was feeding slave unrest.
- Southerners feared that protective tariffs were a prelude to emancipation.

See the **Map** at **www.myhistorylab.com** *Slave Conspiracies and Uprisings, 1800–1831*

RESISTANCE

Open resistance to slavery was futile. The persistently disobedient slave would be sold "down river" to a harsher master or, in extreme cases, killed. Although the odds of succeeding were infinitesimal, desperate slaves did plot rebellion in the nineteenth century. The first major uprising, **Gabriel Prosser's Rebellion** in 1800, involved about 50 armed slaves around Richmond, though perhaps as many as 1,000 slaves knew about Prosser's plans. The rebels' failure to seize a key road to Richmond and a slave informer's warning to white authorities doomed the rebellion before it got under way. State authorities executed Prosser and 25 of his followers.

Gabriel Prosser's Rebellion Slave revolt that failed when Gabriel Prosser, a slave preacher and blacksmith, organized a thousand slaves for an attack on Richmond, Virginia, in 1800.

A decade later, in what seems to have been a spontaneous bid for freedom, several hundred slaves in the river parishes (counties) above New Orleans marched on the city. Poorly armed, they were no match for the U.S. Army troops and militiamen who stopped them. More than 60 slaves died, and the heads of the leading rebels were posted on poles along the Mississippi River to warn others of the fate that awaited rebellious slaves.

The most carefully planned slave revolt (at least in the minds of whites who resorted to torture to gain "confessions"), **Denmark Vesey's Conspiracy,** like Prosser's, failed before it got started. Vesey, a literate carpenter and lay preacher in Charleston who had purchased his freedom, allegedly planned the revolt in the summer of 1822. The plot collapsed when two domestic servants betrayed it. White authorities responded swiftly and savagely. They hanged 35 conspirators, including Vesey, and banished 37 others from the state. After destroying the African Methodist Episcopal church where Vesey had preached and the purported conspirators had met, they tried to seal off the city from subversive outsiders by passing the Negro Seamen's Act, which mandated the imprisonment of black sailors while their ships were berthed in Charleston.

Denmark Vesey's Conspiracy The most carefully devised slave revolt in which rebels planned to seize control of Charleston in 1822 and escape to freedom in Haiti, a free black republic, but they were betrayed by other slaves, and seventy-five conspirators were executed.

One slave revolt, **Nat Turner's Rebellion,** in Southampton County, Virginia, did erupt before it could be suppressed. Turner was a literate field hand driven by prophetic visions of black vengeance against white oppressors. Convinced by what he called "signs in heaven" that he should "arise and prepare myself and slay my enemies with their own weapons," he led a small band of followers on a murderous rampage in late August 1831. The first white man to be killed was Joseph Travis, Turner's owner. In the next two days, the rebels killed 60 other white people. An enraged posse, aided by slaves, captured or killed most of Turner's party. Turner hid for two months before being apprehended. He and more than 30 other slaves were executed, and panicky white people killed more than 100 others.

Nat Turner's Rebellion Uprising of slaves led by Nat Turner in Southampton County, Virginia, in the summer of 1831 that resulted in the death of 55 white people.

Read the **Document** at **www.myhistorylab.com** *Nat Turner, Confession (1831)*

Slaves well understood that the odds against a successful rebellion were insurmountable. They could see who had all the guns. White people were also more numerous. Surveillance by

This contemporary woodcut of Nat Turner's Rebellion depicts the fervency of both the actions of the slaves and the response of the whites.

Watch the Video
at **www.myhistorylab.com**
Underground Railroad

Underground Railroad Support system set up by antislavery groups in the Upper South and the North to assist fugitive slaves in escaping the South.

mounted white patrols, part of the police apparatus of slavery, limited organized rebellion by slaves to small, local affairs that were quickly suppressed.

Nor could many slaves escape to freedom. Few runaways made it to Canada or to a free state. White people could stop black people and demand to see papers documenting their freedom or right to travel without a master. The **Underground Railroad,** a secret network of stations and safe houses organized by Quakers and other black and white antislavery activists, provided some assistance. However, fellow slaves or free black people, especially in the cities of the Border South, provided the only help most runaways could count on. Out of more than 3 million slaves in the 1850s, only about 1,000 a year permanently escaped. (See American Views: A Letter from an Escaped Slave to His Former Master.)

After fleeing from slavery in Maryland in 1849, Harriet "Moses" Tubman, standing on the left, risked reenslavement by returning to the South on several occasions to assist in the escapes of other slaves. She is photographed here with some of those she helped free.

AMERICAN VIEWS

A Letter from an Escaped Slave to His Former Master

In 1859, Jackson Whitney was one of 6,000 fugitive slaves living in Canada, a sanctuary of freedom beyond the reach of the Fugitive Slave Act of 1850. Like most fugitives, he was male, and he had been forced to leave his family behind in Kentucky. His letter, as well as other direct testimony by African Americans about their experiences and feelings while enslaved, gives us information about slavery that only the slaves could provide.

- **How** would you characterize the tone of Whitney's letter? How did he express his joy at being a free man?
- **How** did Whitney feel that Riley, his former owner, had betrayed him?
- **What** did Whitney mean by the phrase "a slave talking to 'massa' "? How did he indicate that he had been hiding his true feelings as a slave?
- **How** did Whitney contrast his religious beliefs and those of Riley? How did he expect Riley to be punished?
- **What** pained Whitney about his freedom in Canada, and what did he ask of Riley?

March 18, 1859

Mr. Wm. Riley, Springfield, Ky.,
Sir:
I take this opportunity to dictate a few lines to you, supposing you might be curious to know my whereabouts. I am happy to inform you that I am in Canada, in good health, and have been here several days. Perhaps, by this time, you have concluded that robbing a woman of her husband, and children of their father does not pay, at least in your case; and I thought, while lying in jail by your direction, that if you had no remorse or conscience that would make you feel for a poor, broken-hearted man, and his worse-than-murdered wife and child, . . . and could not by any entreaty or permission be induced to do as you promised you would, which was to let me go with my family for $800, but contended for $1,000, when you had promised to take the same you gave for me (which was $660.) at the time you bought me, and let me go with my dear wife and children! but instead would render me miserable, and lie to me, and to your neighbors . . . and when you was at Louisville trying to sell me! then I thought it was time for me to make my feet feel for Canada, and let your conscience feel in your pocket. Now you cannot say but that I did all that was honorable and right while I was with you, although I was a slave. I pretended all the time that I thought you, or some one else had a better right to me than I had to myself, which you know is rather hard thinking.

You know, too, that you proved a traitor to me in the time of need, and when in the most bitter distress that the human soul is capable of experiencing; and could you have carried out your purposes there would have been no relief. But I rejoice to say that an unseen, kind spirit appeared for the oppressed, and bade me take up my bed and walk, the result of which is that I am victorious and you are defeated. I am comfortably situated in Canada, working for George Harris [another fugitive slave from Kentucky who had bought a farm in Canada] . . .

There is only one thing to prevent me being entirely happy here, and that is the want of my dear wife and children, and you to see us enjoying ourselves together here. I wish you could realize the contrast between Freedom and slavery; but it is not likely that we shall ever meet again on this earth.

But if you want to go to the next world and meet a God of love, mercy, and justice, in peace; who says, "Inasmuch as you did it to the least of them my little ones, you did it unto me," making the professions that you do, pretending to be a follower of Christ, and tormenting me and my little ones as you have done, [you] had better repair the breaches you have made among us in this world, by sending my wife and children to me; thus preparing to meet your God in peace; for, if God don't punish you for inflicting such distress on the poorest of His poor, then there is no use of having any God, or talking about one . . .

I hope you will consider candidly, and see if the case does not justify every word I have said, and ten times as much. You must not consider that it is a slave talking to 'massa' now, but one as free as yourself.

I subscribe myself one of the abused of America, but one of the justified and honored of Canada.

Jackson Whitney

Source: John W. Blassingame, ed., *Slave Testimony: Two Centuries of Letters, Speeches, Interviews, and Autobiographies* (Louisiana State University Press, 1977).

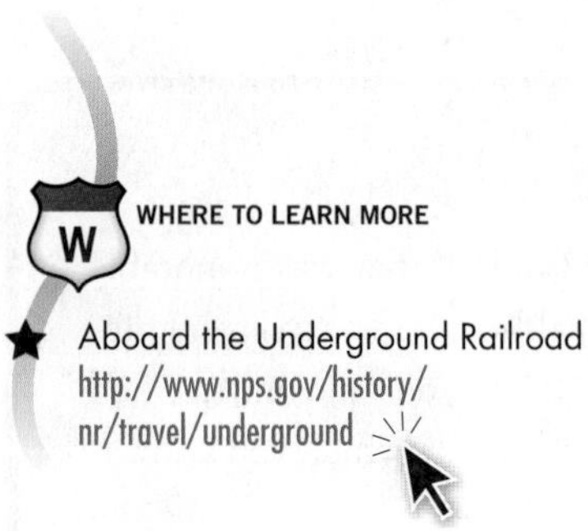

WHERE TO LEARN MORE

Aboard the Underground Railroad
http://www.nps.gov/history/nr/travel/underground

Running away was common, but most runaways fled no farther than to nearby swamps and woods. Most voluntarily returned or were tracked down by bloodhounds within a week. Aside from those who were protesting a special grievance or trying to avoid punishment, slaves who ran away usually did so to visit a spouse or loved one. Occasionally, runaways could bargain for lenient treatment in return for faithful service in the future. Most were severely punished. Such temporary flights from the master's control siphoned off some of the anger that might otherwise have erupted in violent, self-destructive attacks on slave owners. All planters had heard about the field hand who took an ax to an overseer, the cook who poisoned her master's family, or the house servant who killed a sleeping master or mistress.

Slaves resisted complete domination by their masters in less overt ways. They mocked white people in folktales like those about Br'er Rabbit, for example, in which weak but wily animals cunningly outsmart their stronger enemies. Slave owners routinely complained of slaves malingering at work, abusing farm animals, losing tools, stealing food, and committing arson. These subversive acts of protest never challenged the system of slavery itself, but they did help slaves to maintain a sense of dignity and self-respect.

FREE SOCIETY

HOW WAS free society in the South structured?

The abolitionists and the antislavery Republican party of the 1850s portrayed the social order of the slave South as little more than haughty planters lording it over shiftless poor white people. The reality was considerably more complex. Planters, who set the social tone for the South as a whole, did act superior, but they were a tiny minority and had to contend with an ambitious middle class of small slaveholders and a majority of nonslaveholding farmers. Some landless white people on the margins of rural society fit the stereotype of "poor whites," but they were easily outnumbered by self-reliant farmers who worked their own land. Southern cities, though small by northern standards, provided jobs for a growing class of free workers who increasingly clashed with planters over the use of slave labor. These same cities, notably in the Upper South, were also home to the nation's largest concentration of free black people.

Hear the Audio
at **www.myhistorylab.com**
Remembering Slavery

The Slaveholding Minority

Large planters. Only in the rice districts of the South Carolina low country and in the rich sugar- and cotton-growing areas of the Mississippi Delta were large planters more than a small minority of the slaveholding class, let alone the general white population. Families of the planter class, those who held a minimum of 20 slaves, constituted only around 3 percent of all southern families in 1860. Fewer than one out of five planter families, less than 1 percent of all families, owned more than 50 slaves. Far from conspicuously exhibiting their wealth, most planters lived in drab log cabins, not grand, white-columned houses. Most planters wanted to acquire wealth, not display it. They were restlessly eager to move on and abandon their homes when the allure of profits from a new cotton frontier promised to relieve them of the debts they had incurred to purchase their slaves.

Planters' wives. Most planters expected their wives to help supervise the slaves and run the plantation. Besides raising her children, the plantation mistress managed the household staff, oversaw the cooking and cleaning, gardened, dispensed medicine and clothing to the slaves, and often assisted in their religious instruction. When guests or relatives came for an extended visit, the wife had to make all the special arrangements that such occasions entailed. When the master was called off on a business or political trip, she kept the plantation accounts. In many respects, she worked harder than her husband.

QUICK REVIEW

Plantation Mistresses

- Mistresses ran the household staff.
- Mistresses were responsible for arrangements for visitors.
- Planter's wives found the management of slaves a burden.

OVERVIEW Structure of Free Society in the South, c. 1860

Group	Size	Characteristics
Large planters	Less than 1 percent of white families	Owned 50 or more slaves and plantations in excess of 1,000 acres; the wealthiest class in United States
Planters	About 3 percent of white families	Owned 20 to 49 slaves and plantations in excess of 100 acres; controlled bulk of southern wealth and provided most of the political leaders
Small slaveholders	About 20 percent of white families	Owned fewer than 20 slaves and most often fewer than five; primarily farmers, though some were part of a small middle class in towns and cities
Nonslaveholding whites	About 75 percent of white families	Mostly yeomen farmers who owned their own land and stressed production for family use; one in five owned neither slaves nor land and squatted on the least desirable land where they planted some corn and grazed some livestock; in cities they worked as artisans or, more typically, day laborers
Free blacks	About 3 percent of all free families	Concentrated in the Upper South; hemmed in by legal and social restrictions; mostly tenants or farm laborers; about one-third lived in cities and generally were limited to lowest paying jobs

Planters' wives often complained in their journals and letters of their isolation from other white women and the physical and mental toil of managing slaves. The women with whom they had the closest daily contact were often their female domestic slaves. As Hannah Crafts noted, they treated some of these slaves with an intimacy that abolitionist propaganda refused to acknowledge. Whatever their misgivings about slavery, plantation mistresses enjoyed a wealth and status unknown to most southern women and only rarely questioned the institution of slavery. Their deepest anger stemmed from their humiliation by husbands who kept slave mistresses or sexually abused slave women. Bound by their duties as wives not to express this anger publicly, and unwilling to renounce the institution that both victimized and benefited them, white women tended to vent their frustrations on black women whose alleged promiscuity they blamed for the sexual transgressions of white males.

Small slaveholders. Despite the tensions and sexual jealousies it aroused, owning slaves was the surest means of social and economic advancement for most white families. Most slave owners, however, never attained planter status. Nine out of 10 slave owners in 1860 owned fewer than 20 slaves, and fully half of them had fewer than five. Many white people also rented a few slaves on a seasonal basis.

Generally younger than the planters, small slaveholders were a diverse lot. About 10 percent were women, and another 20 percent or so were merchants, businessmen, artisans, and urban professionals. Most were farmers trying to acquire enough land and slaves to become planters. To keep costs down, they often began by purchasing children, the cheapest slaves available, or a young slave family, so that they could add to their slaveholdings as the slave mother bore more children.

Small slaveholders had scant economic security. A deadly outbreak of disease among their slaves or a single bad crop could destroy their credit and force them to sell their slaves to clear their debts. Owners of fewer than ten slaves stood a fifty-fifty chance within a decade of dropping out of the slaveholding class. Nor could small holders hope to compete directly with the planters. In any given area suitable for plantations, they were gradually pushed out as planters bought up land to raise livestock or more crops. In general, only slave owners who had established themselves in business or the professions had the capital reserves to rise into the planter elite.

The White Majority

Three-fourths of southern white families owned no slaves in 1860. Although most numerous in the Upper South, nonslaveholders predominated wherever the soil and climate were not suitable for plantation agriculture. Most were yeoman farmers who worked their own land with family labor.

These farmers were quick to move when times were bad and their land was used up, but once settled in an area, they formed intensely localized societies in which fathers and husbands held sway over their families. The community extended 5 to 10 miles around the nearest country store or county courthouse. Networks of kin and friends provided labor services when needed, fellowship in evangelical churches, and staple goods that an individual farm could not produce. Social travel and international markets, so central to the lives of planters, had little relevance in the farmers' community-centered existence. The yeomanry aimed to be self-sufficient and limited their market involvement to the sale of livestock and an occasional cotton crop that could bring in needed cash.

Yeoman farmers jealously guarded their independence, and in their tight little worlds of face-to-face relationships, they demanded that planters treat them as social equals. Ever fearful of being reduced to dependence, they avoided debt and sought to limit government authority. Rather than risk financial ruin by buying slaves on credit to grow cotton, they grew food crops and depended on their sons and, when needed, their wives and daughters to work the fields.

Nonslaveholding farmers from the mountains and planters on the bottomlands rarely mixed, and their societies developed in isolation from each other. In areas where there were both small farms and scattered plantations, the interests of the yeomen and the planters were often complementary. Planters provided local markets for the surplus grain and livestock of nonslaveholders and, for a small fee, access to gristmills and gins for grinding corn and cleaning cotton. They lent small sums to poorer neighbors in emergencies or to pay taxes. The yeomen staffed the slave patrols and became overseers on the plantations. Both groups sought to protect property rights from outside interference and to maintain a system of racial control in which white liberties rested on black degradation.

When yeomen and planters clashed, it was usually over economic issues. Large slaveholders needing better credit and marketing facilities gravitated toward the Whig Party, which called for banks and internal improvements. Nonslaveholding farmers, especially in the Lower South, tended to be Democrats who opposed banks and state-funded economic projects. They viewed bankers as grasping outsiders who wanted to rob them of their economic independence, and they suspected that state involvement in the economy led only to higher taxes and increased public debt. These partisan battles, however, rarely involved a debate about the merits of slavery. As long as planters deferred to the egalitarian sensibilities of the yeomen by courting them at election time and promising to safeguard their liberties, the planters were able to maintain broad support for slavery across class lines.

Around 15 percent of rural white families owned neither land nor slaves. These were the so-called poor whites, stigmatized by both abolitionists and planters as lazy and shiftless. The abolitionists considered them a kind of underclass who proved that slavery so degraded the dignity of labor that it led people to shun work and lapse into wretched poverty. To the planters, they were a constant nuisance and a threat to slave discipline. Planters habitually complained that poor whites demoralized their slaves by showing that a person could survive without steady labor.

Some landless white people did live down to their negative stereotype. Still, the "poor white trash" label with which they were stigmatized is misleading. Most were resourceful and enterprising enough to supply themselves with all the material comforts they wanted. Not having to do steady work for survival, they hunted, fished, and took orders from no one. Although poor by most standards, they were also defiantly self-reliant.

Nonslaveholders were a growing majority in southern cities, especially among the working classes. These urban workers shared no agricultural interests or ties with the planters. Nor were most of them, especially in the unskilled ranks, southern-born. Northerners and immigrants dominated the urban work force. Free workers, especially Irish and German immigrants, increasingly replaced slaves in urban labor markets. These white workers bitterly resented competition from black slaves, and their demands to exclude slaves from the urban workplace reinforced planters' belief that cities bred abolitionism.

Free Black People

A small minority of southern black people, 6 percent of the total in 1860, were "free persons of color." They constituted 3 percent of the free population in the South (see Figure 11–3). These free black people occupied a precarious and vulnerable position between degraded

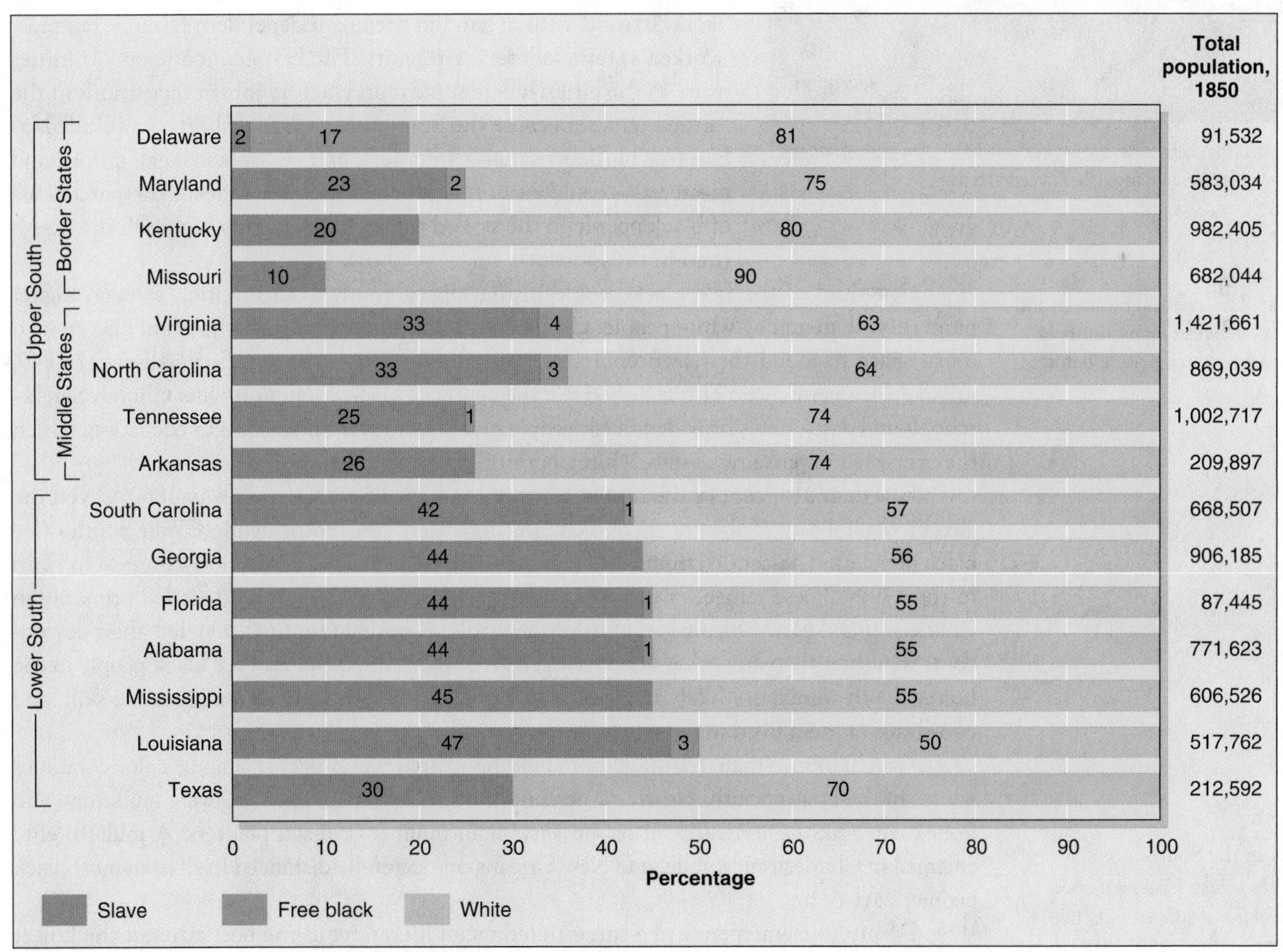

FIGURE 11–3 **Slave, Free Black, and White Population in Southern States, 1850** Except for Texas, slaves by 1850 comprised over 40 percent of the population in every state of the Lower South. The small population of free black people was concentrated in the Upper South.

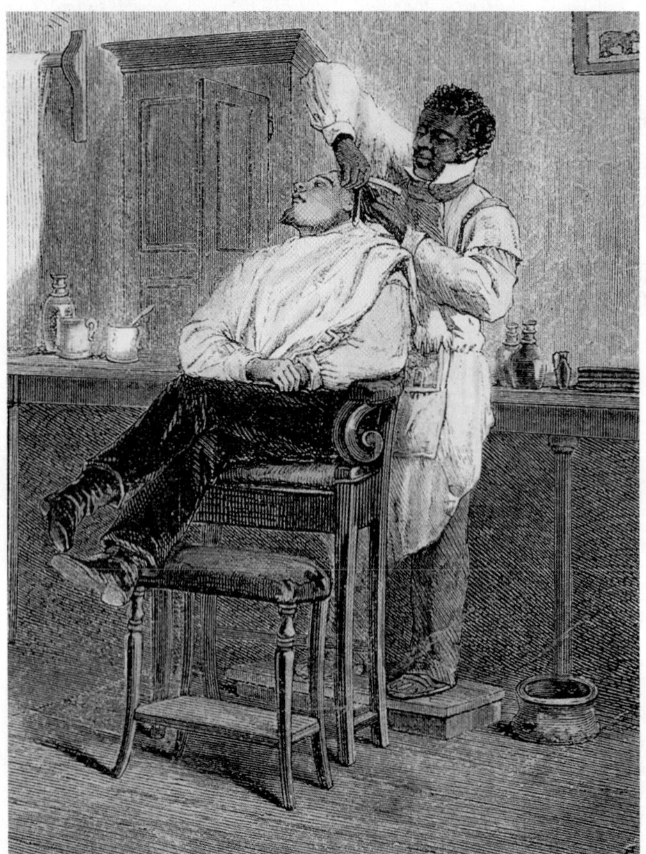

Barbering was one of the skilled trades open to black men during the antebellum years. Several wealthy African Americans began their careers as barbers.

The Granger Collection, New York.

enslavement and meaningful freedom. White intimidation and special legal provisions known as **black codes** (found throughout the North as well) denied them nearly all the rights of citizenship. Because of the legal presumption in the South that all black people were slaves, they had to carry freedom papers, official certificates of their freedom. They were shut out of the political process and could not testify against white people in court. Many occupations, especially those involved in the communication of ideas, such as the printing trades, were closed to them.

Every slave state forbade the entry of free black people, and every municipality had rules and regulations that forced them to live as an inferior caste. Any sign of upward mobility or intimation of equal standing was ruthlessly suppressed. More than four-fifths of the southern free black population lived in the Upper South. Most were the offspring of slaves freed by private manumissions between 1780 and 1800, when slavery temporarily loosened in the Chesapeake region in the wake of the Revolutionary War. Manumissions dropped sharply after 1810, the result of heightened white anxieties after Prosser's Rebellion and the rising demand for slaves in the Lower South.

As in the North, legal barriers and white prejudice generally confined free black people to the poorest paying and most menial work. In rural areas, a handful became independent farmers, but most worked as farm laborers or tenants. The best economic opportunities were in the cities, where some found factory jobs and positions in the skilled trades. Because the South had a general shortage of skilled labor, free black artisans—carpenters, barbers, shoemakers, tailors, and plasterers—could earn a respectable income. Indeed, the percentage of black people in the skilled trades was generally higher in the South than in the North.

black codes Laws passed by states and municipalities denying many rights of citizenship to free black people before the Civil War.

One-third of the free black people in the Upper South lived in cities, a much higher proportion than among white people. Cities offered black people not only jobs but also enough social space to found their own churches and mutual-aid associations. Especially after 1840, urban African American churches became the center of black community life. Church Sunday schools and day schools provided black people practically their only access to education, which they persisted in pursuing despite white opposition.

Less than 2 percent of the black people in the Lower South were free in 1860. Given the greater profitability of slavery there, manumissions were rare. Most of the Lower South's free black population descended from black emigrants who had fled the revolutionary unrest in Haiti in the 1790s. These refugees were artisans, shopkeepers, and farmers who settled primarily in Charleston and New Orleans. Able to secure a solid economic footing, they left their descendants wealthier than any other free black people in the United States. Free black people in the Lower South were more likely than those in the Upper South to have a marketable skill, and two-thirds of them lived in cities.

A light skin enhanced the social standing of free black people among color-conscious whites in the Lower South. Nearly 70 percent of free black people in 1860 were mulattoes, and from their ranks came nearly all of the very small number of black planters. A mulatto elite emerged in Charleston, Mobile, and New Orleans that carefully distanced itself from most black people, slave or free.

QUICK REVIEW

Free Blacks in the South

- 6 percent of southern blacks were free.
- 80 percent of free southern blacks lived in the Upper South.
- Free black southerners faced a host of legal and social disabilities.

Despite the emergence of a three-tiered racial hierarchy in the port cities of the Lower South, white officialdom insisted on maintaining a white and black racial dichotomy. As the racial defense of slavery intensified in the 1850s, more calls were made for laws to banish or enslave free black people. Arkansas passed such a law in 1859, and similar bills were proposed in Florida, Tennessee, Mississippi, and Missouri. Even Maryland held a referendum in 1859 on whether to reenslave its free black population, among the largest in the South. Only the opposition of nonslaveholders heavily dependent on cheap free black labor defeated the referendum.

THE PROSLAVERY ARGUMENT

HOW DID the southern defense of slavery change between the early nineteenth century and the 1850s?

In the early nineteenth century, white southerners made no particular effort to defend slavery, because the institution was not under heavy outside attack. If pressed, most white people would have called slavery a necessary evil, an unfortunate legacy from earlier generations that was needed to maintain racial peace.

The 1830s marked a turning point. After the twin shocks of Nat Turner's Rebellion and the onset of the abolitionist crusade (for more on this crusade, see Chapter 12), white mobs emerged to stifle any open criticism of slavery in the Lower South. White southerners also began to develop a defense of slavery. By the 1850s, politicians, intellectuals, and evangelical ministers were arguing that slavery was a positive good.

Read the **Document** at **www.myhistorylab.com** *Thomas R. Dew's Defense of Slavery (1832)*

Religious Arguments

Evangelical Protestantism dominated southern religious expression by the 1830s, and its ministers took the lead in combating abolitionist charges that slavery was a moral and religious abomination. Except for a radical minority of antislavery evangelicals in the Upper South, southern churches had always supported slavery. This support grew more pronounced and articulate once the abolitionists stepped up their attacks on slavery in the mid-1830s.

Southern evangelicals accepted the Bible as God's literal word, and through selective reading they found abundant evidence to proclaim slavery fully in accord with His moral dictates. Southern evangelicals also turned to the Bible to support their argument that patriarchal authority, the unquestioned power of the father, was the basis of all Christian communities. Part of that authority extended over slaves, and slavery thus became a matter of family governance, a domestic institution in which Christian masters of slaves, unlike capitalist masters of free "wage slaves" in the North, accepted responsibility for caring for their workers in sickness and old age. Far from being a moral curse, therefore, slavery was part of God's plan to Christianize an inferior race and teach its people how to produce raw materials that benefited the world's masses.

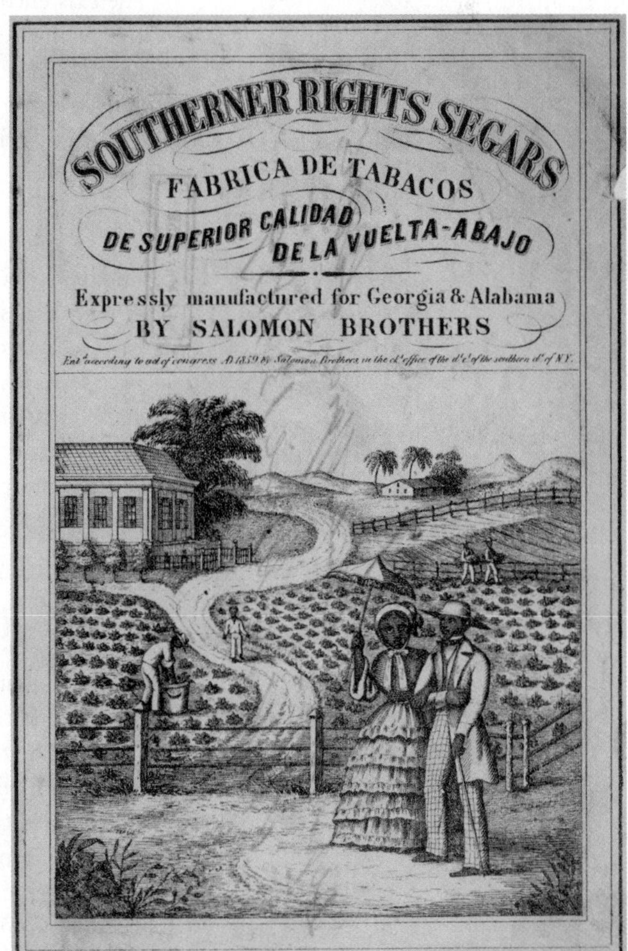

As this printed label from the 1850s for a box of cigars reveals, antebellum manufacturers of consumer goods produced by slave labor had every incentive to present an idealized picture of slave life in the South.

The growing commitment of southern evangelicals to slavery as a positive good clashed with the antislavery position and the generally more liberal theology of northern evangelicals. In 1837, the Presbyterians split along sectional lines in part because of differences over slavery. In 1844, as a direct result of the slavery issue, the Methodist Episcopal Church, the nation's largest, divided into northern and southern churches. The Baptists did the same a year later. These religious schisms foreshadowed the sectionalized political divisions of the 1850s; they also severed one of the main emotional bonds between whites in the North and the South. The religious defense of slavery was central to the slaveholding ethic of paternalism that developed after 1830. By the 1850s, planters commonly described slaves as members of an extended family who were treated better than free workers in the North.

The crusade to sanctify slavery won few converts outside the South. Most northern churches did not endorse abolitionism but did have moral qualms about slavery. In a particularly stinging rebuke to southern church leaders in the 1850s, black abolitionists succeeded in having slaveholders barred from international religious conventions.

Racial Arguments

More common than the biblical defense of slavery was the racial argument that black people were unfit for freedom. Drawing in part on the scientific wisdom of the day, the racial defense alleged that black people were naturally lazy and inherently inferior to white people. If freed, so went the argument, they would turn to crime and sexually assault white women. Only the controls of slavery enabled the races to coexist in the South.

The racial argument resonated powerfully among white people because nearly all of them, including those otherwise opposed to slavery, dreaded emancipation. The attitude of a Tennessee farmer, as recorded by a northern traveler in the 1850s, was typical: "He said he'd always wished there hadn't been any niggers here . . . , but he wouldn't like to have them free." Unable to conceive of living in a society with many free black people, most white people could see no middle ground between slavery and the presumed social chaos of emancipation.

The existence of *black* slavery also had egalitarian implications for the nonslaveholding majority of whites. Slavery supposedly spared white southerners from the menial, degrading labor that white northerners had to perform. Moreover, because slaves lacked political rights, champions of slavery argued that black bondage buttressed the political liberties of all white males by removing from politics the leveling demands of the poor and propertyless for a redistribution of wealth.

Despite its apparent success in forging white solidarity, the racial argument could be turned on its head and used to weaken slavery. Most white northerners were about as racist as their southern counterparts, but they were increasingly willing to end slavery on the grounds that the stronger white race should help black people improve themselves as free persons. In short, nothing in the internal logic of racist doctrines required enslaving black people. The same logic also encouraged some white southerners to challenge the economic prerogatives of slaveholders. Why, for example, should any white people, as members of the master race, be forced into economic competition against skilled slave artisans? Why should not all non-agricultural jobs be legally reserved for white people? Doctrines of black inferiority could not prevent white unity from cracking when the economic interests of nonslaveholders clashed with those of planters.

CONCLUSION

The proslavery argument depicted a nearly ideal society blessed by class and racial harmony. In reality, social conditions in the slave South were contradictory and conflict-ridden. Slaves were not content in their bondage. Hannah Crafts spoke for nearly all of them when she described slavery as a coarse, brutalizing institution that demeaned all it touched. They dreamed of freedom and sustained that dream through their own forms of Christianity and the support of family and kin. Relations between masters and their slaves were antagonistic, not affectionate, and wherever the system of control slackened, slaves resisted their owners. Nor did all white southerners, who confronted increasing economic inequality after 1830, accept racial slavery as in their best interests. It divided as well as united them.

During the 1850s, the size of the slaveholding class fell from 31 percent of southern white families to 25 percent. Slave owners were a shrinking minority, and slavery was in decline throughout the Upper South. In the Border South, free labor was replacing slavery as the dominant means of organizing economic production. In these states, slavery was a vulnerable institution. Planters were not fooled by the public rhetoric of white unity. They knew that slavery was increasingly confined to the Lower South, and that elsewhere in the South white support for it was gradually eroding. Planters feared the double-edged challenge to their privileged position posed by outside interference with slavery and internal white disloyalty. By the 1850s, many of them were concluding that the only way to resolve their dilemma was to make the South a separate nation.

Where to Learn More

Aboard the Underground Railroad. For a National Register of Historic Places Travel Itinerary that provides maps and descriptions and photographs of sixty historic places associated with the Underground Railroad, go to http://www.nps.gov/history/nr/travel/underground/.

The Anacostia Museum Center for African American History. This museum of the Smithsonian Institution explores American history and cultures from an African American perspective. Go to http://anacostia.si.edu for information on its exhibits and a calendar of events.

Appalachian Museum of Berea College, Berea, Kentucky. This museum is an excellent source for understanding the lifestyle and material culture of the nonslaveholding farmers in the Appalachian highlands. For an overview of its exhibits, see http://www.berea.edu/appalachiancenter/artifactsexhibits.asp.

Cottonlandia Museum, Greenwood, Mississippi. The library and museum depict the history of cotton in the Mississippi Delta. Special collections include some Native American artifacts. Information on its displays can be found at http://www.cottonlandia.org/.

Review Questions

1. What factors accounted for the tremendous expansion of cotton production in the South? How was this expansion linked to slavery and westward movement?
2. What differentiated the Upper South from the Lower South? What role did slavery play in each region after 1815?
3. How would you characterize the life of a plantation slave? What insights does Hannah Crafts's opening account provide into the special vulnerability of slave women? Why were religion and family such key features of the world that slaves built for themselves? What evidence is there of resistance and rebellion among the slaves?
4. How did most nonslaveholding white southerners live? What values did they prize most highly? Why did most nonslaveholders accept slavery or at least not attack it directly?
5. What was the position of free black southerners in southern society? How were their freedoms restricted?
6. How did white southerners attempt to defend slavery and reconcile it with Christianity?
7. How was the development of the Old South linked to the international cotton market?

Key Terms

Black codes (p. 296)
Denmark Vesey's Conspiracy (p. 289)
Gabriel Prosser's Rebellion (p. 289)
Gang system (p. 280)
Nat Turner's Rebellion (p. 289)
Slave codes (p. 285)
Underground Railroad (p. 290)

PEARSON **myhistorylab** Connections

Reinforce what you learned in this chapter by studying the many documents, images, maps, review tools, and videos available at **www.myhistorylab.com.**

Read and Review

Study and Review **Study Plan: Chapter 11**

Read the Document

Memoirs of a Monticello Slave (1847)

Nat Turner, Confession (1831)

A Slave Tells of His Sale at Auction (1848)

Georgia Slave Codes (1848)

Charles C. Jones, The Religious Instruction of the Negroes in the United States (1842)

Senator Sees Slavery as a "Positive Good" (1837)

Thomas R. Dew's Defense of Slavery (1832)

See the Map

Slavery in the South

Agriculture, Industry, and Slavery in the Old South, 1850

Slave Conspiracies and Uprisings, 1800–1831

The Underground Railroad

Research and Explore

Read the Document

Personal Journeys Online

From Then to Now Online: Overcoming the Economic Legacy of Slavery

Hear the Audio

Go Down Moses; sung by Bill McAdoo

Pick a Bale of Cotton

Remembering Slavery

Watch the Video *Underground Railroad*

Hear the Audio

Hear the audio files for Chapter 11 at **www.myhistorylab.com.**

1815-1850

12

The Market Revolution and Social Reform

An abolitionist freeing a slave from his shackles: colored woodcut, c. 1840, from an American antislavery almanac.
Top image: Map of proposed route of Erie Canal, 1811 Negative Number 420757, © Collection of the New-York Historical Society, New York City.

((•—Hear the **Audio**

Hear the audio files for Chapter 12 at **www.myhistorylab.com**.

INDUSTRIAL CHANGE AND URBANIZATION *(page 305)*

HOW DID industrialization contribute to growing inequality and the creation of new social classes?

REFORM AND MORAL ORDER *(page 317)*

WHAT ROLE did women play in the reform movements that followed the War of 1812?

INSTITUTIONS AND SOCIAL IMPROVEMENT *(page 321)*

HOW DID Enlightenment ideas shape the reform of institutions for the poor, criminals, and the mentally ill?

ABOLITIONISM AND WOMEN'S RIGHTS *(page 325)*

WHAT WAS the relationship between abolitionism and the women's rights movement?

ONE AMERICAN JOURNEY

East Boylston, Mass. 10th mo. 2d, 1837

Dear Friend: . . .

The investigation of the rights of the slave has led me to a better understanding of my own. I have found the Anti-Slavery cause to be the high school of morals in our land—the school in which human rights *are more fully investigated, and better understood and taught, than in any other. Here a great fundamental principle is uplifted and illuminated, and from this central light, rays innumerable stream all around. Human beings have* rights, *because they are* moral *beings: the rights of* all *men grow out of their moral nature; and as all men have the same moral nature, they have essentially the same rights. These rights may be wrested from the slave, but they cannot be alienated: his title to himself is as perfect* now, *as is that of Lyman Beecher [a prominent minister]: it is stamped on his moral being, and is, like it, imperishable. Now if rights are founded on the nature of our moral being, then the* mere circumstance of sex *does not give to man higher rights and responsibilities, than to woman. . . . My doctrine then is, that whatever it is morally right for man to do, it is morally right for woman to do. Our duties originate, not from difference of sex, but from the diversity of our relations in life, the various gifts and talents committed to our care, and the different eras in which we live.*

Angelina Emily Grimké

Angelina E. Grimke, *Letters to Catherine Beecher, in reply to an Essay of Slavery and Abolition,* Addressed to A. E. Grimke, rev. ed., Boston: Isaac Knapp, 1838, pp. 114–21.

Read the **Document** at **www.myhistorylab.com**

Personal Journeys Online

- **Margaret Fuller, Excerpt from *Women in the Nineteenth Century,* 1845. Arguments for women's rights.**
- **Lydia Maria Child, Letter, 1839. Issue of women's rights in the antislavery movement.**

BORN IN 1805 to a wealthy slaveholding family in Charleston, Angelina was the daughter of a prominent jurist. Despite all the social and economic benefits that membership in the planter class conferred upon her, she passionately rejected slavery when she became a young adult. As was also true for her sister Sarah, this rejection was part of a religious conversion to Quakerism. Angelina left her home in Charleston in 1829 and joined her sister in Philadelphia. The sisters joined the abolitionist movement in 1835, and within two years had become the crusade's most celebrated (and notorious) platform lecturers.

Although Angelina, in her commitment to radical reform, was hardly typical of antebellum U.S. women, let alone women of the planter class, her journey from a privileged life in Charleston to one of social activism in the North speaks to the radicalizing potential of the reform impulse that swept over the nation after the War of 1812. This reform impulse was strongest in the North, where traditional social and economic relations were undergoing wrenching changes as a market revolution accelerated the spread of cities, factories, and commercialized farms. New middle and working classes evolved in response to such changes, which were the most pronounced in the Northeast. The North was also the area where the emotional fires of evangelical revivals burned the hottest.

The religious message of the Second Great Awakening, which began in the early 1800s, provided a framework for responding to the changes that accompanied the market revolution. Evangelicalism taught that in both the spiritual and secular realms, individuals were accountable for their own actions. Through Christian activism, individuals could strive toward moral perfectibility and cleanse society of its evils.

The first wave of reform after the War of 1812 focused on individual behavior, targeting drinking, gambling, sexual misconduct, and Sabbath-breaking. By the 1830s, a second phase

CHRONOLOGY

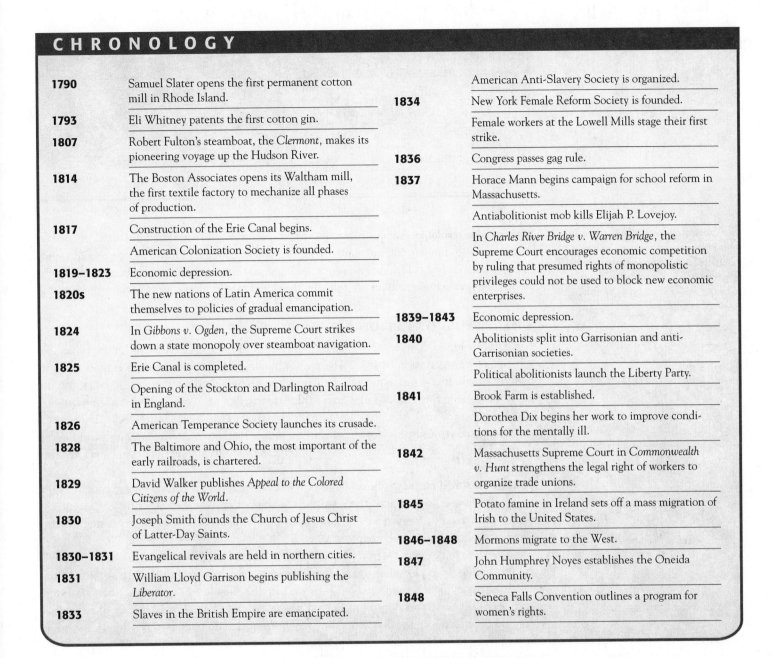

1790	Samuel Slater opens the first permanent cotton mill in Rhode Island.
1793	Eli Whitney patents the first cotton gin.
1807	Robert Fulton's steamboat, the *Clermont*, makes its pioneering voyage up the Hudson River.
1814	The Boston Associates opens its Waltham mill, the first textile factory to mechanize all phases of production.
1817	Construction of the Erie Canal begins.
	American Colonization Society is founded.
1819–1823	Economic depression.
1820s	The new nations of Latin America commit themselves to policies of gradual emancipation.
1824	In *Gibbons v. Ogden*, the Supreme Court strikes down a state monopoly over steamboat navigation.
1825	Erie Canal is completed.
	Opening of the Stockton and Darlington Railroad in England.
1826	American Temperance Society launches its crusade.
1828	The Baltimore and Ohio, the most important of the early railroads, is chartered.
1829	David Walker publishes *Appeal to the Colored Citizens of the World*.
1830	Joseph Smith founds the Church of Jesus Christ of Latter-Day Saints.
1830–1831	Evangelical revivals are held in northern cities.
1831	William Lloyd Garrison begins publishing the *Liberator*.
1833	Slaves in the British Empire are emancipated.
	American Anti-Slavery Society is organized.
1834	New York Female Reform Society is founded.
	Female workers at the Lowell Mills stage their first strike.
1836	Congress passes gag rule.
1837	Horace Mann begins campaign for school reform in Massachusetts.
	Antiabolitionist mob kills Elijah P. Lovejoy.
	In *Charles River Bridge v. Warren Bridge*, the Supreme Court encourages economic competition by ruling that presumed rights of monopolistic privileges could not be used to block new economic enterprises.
1839–1843	Economic depression.
1840	Abolitionists split into Garrisonian and anti-Garrisonian societies.
	Political abolitionists launch the Liberty Party.
1841	Brook Farm is established.
	Dorothea Dix begins her work to improve conditions for the mentally ill.
1842	Massachusetts Supreme Court in *Commonwealth v. Hunt* strengthens the legal right of workers to organize trade unions.
1845	Potato famine in Ireland sets off a mass migration of Irish to the United States.
1846–1848	Mormons migrate to the West.
1847	John Humphrey Noyes establishes the Oneida Community.
1848	Seneca Falls Convention outlines a program for women's rights.

of reform turned to institutional solutions for crime, poverty, and social delinquency, largely untouched by voluntary moral suasion. The third phase of the reform cycle rejected the social beliefs and practices that prescribed fixed and subordinate positions to certain Americans based on race and also on sex. This radical phase culminated in abolitionism and the campaign for women's rights, movements that came together in Angelina Grimké's journey out of her native South. ✦

INDUSTRIAL CHANGE AND URBANIZATION

HOW DID industrialization contribute to growing inequality and the creation of new social classes?

In 1820, 80 percent of the free labor force worked in agriculture, and manufacturing played a minor role in overall economic activity. Over the next three decades, however, the United States joined England as a world leader in industrialization.

The most direct cause of this rapid and sustained surge in manufacturing was increased consumption within the United States of the goods the country was producing. The

Table 12–1

Impact of the Transportation Revolution on Traveling Time

Route	1800	1830	1860
New York to Philadelphia	2 days	1 day	Less than 1 day
New York to Charleston	More than 1 week	5 days	2 days
New York to Chicago	6 weeks	3 weeks	2 days
New York to New Orleans	4 weeks	2 weeks	6 days

transportation revolution Dramatic improvements in transportation that stimulated economic growth after 1815 by expanding the range of travel and reducing the time and cost of moving goods and people.

transportation revolution dramatically reduced transportation costs and shipping times, opened up new markets for farmers and manufacturers alike, and provided an incentive for expanding production (see Table 12–1). As agricultural and manufactured goods were exchanged more efficiently, a growing home market continually stimulated the development of U.S. manufacturing.

The Transportation Revolution

Aside from some 4,000 miles of toll roads in the Northeast, the nation had nothing approaching a system of transportation in 1815. The cost of moving goods by land transportation was prohibitively high. It cost just as much to haul heavy goods by horsedrawn wagons 30 miles into the interior as to ship them 3,000 miles across the Atlantic Ocean. Water transportation was much cheaper, but it was limited to the coast or navigable rivers.Thus, only farmers located near a city or a river could grow surplus crops for sale in an outside market. Western farm surpluses followed the southerly flow of the Ohio and Mississippi river systems to market outlets in New Orleans.

W
WHERE TO LEARN MORE
Erie Canal Museum,
Syracuse, New York
http://www.eriecanalmuseum.org

Steamboats and canals. Steamboats provided the first transportation breakthrough. By the 1820s, steamboats had reduced the cost and the time of upriver shipments by 90 percent. As steamboats spread to western waters, more and more farmers could reap the economic benefits of exporting corn, pork, and other foodstuffs.

Western trade did not start to flow eastward until the completion of the Erie Canal in 1825, the first and most successful of the artificial waterways designed to link eastern seaboard cities with western markets (see Map 12–1). Funded by the New York legislature, the Erie Canal stretched 364 miles from Albany to Buffalo, a small port on Lake Erie. An immediate success, the Erie Canal reduced the cost of sending freight from Buffalo to New York City by more than 90 percent, and by the 1840s, it was pulling in more western trade than was being sent to New Orleans on the Mississippi River.

Anxious to match the Erie's success, other states launched plans for competing canals to the West. More than 3,000 miles of canal were in place by 1840, but no other canal could overcome the tremendous advantage of the Erie's head start in fixing trading patterns along its route.

Hear the **Audio** at **www.myhistorylab.com** *The Erie Canal*

Railroads. Railroads were the last and ultimately the most important of the transportation improvements that spurred economic development in Jacksonian America. Moving at 15 to 20 miles per hour, four times as fast as a canal boat and twice the speed of a stagecoach, the railroads of the 1830s were a radically new technology that overturned traditional notions of time and space.

In 1825, the same year the Erie Canal was completed, the world's first general-purpose railroad opened in England. The construction of the first American railroads began in the late 1820s, and they all pushed outward from seaboard cities eager to connect to the western market. By 1840, the railroads had become the most dynamic booster of interregional trade. Whereas the canal network stopped expanding after 1840, the railroads tripled their mileage in the 1840s. By

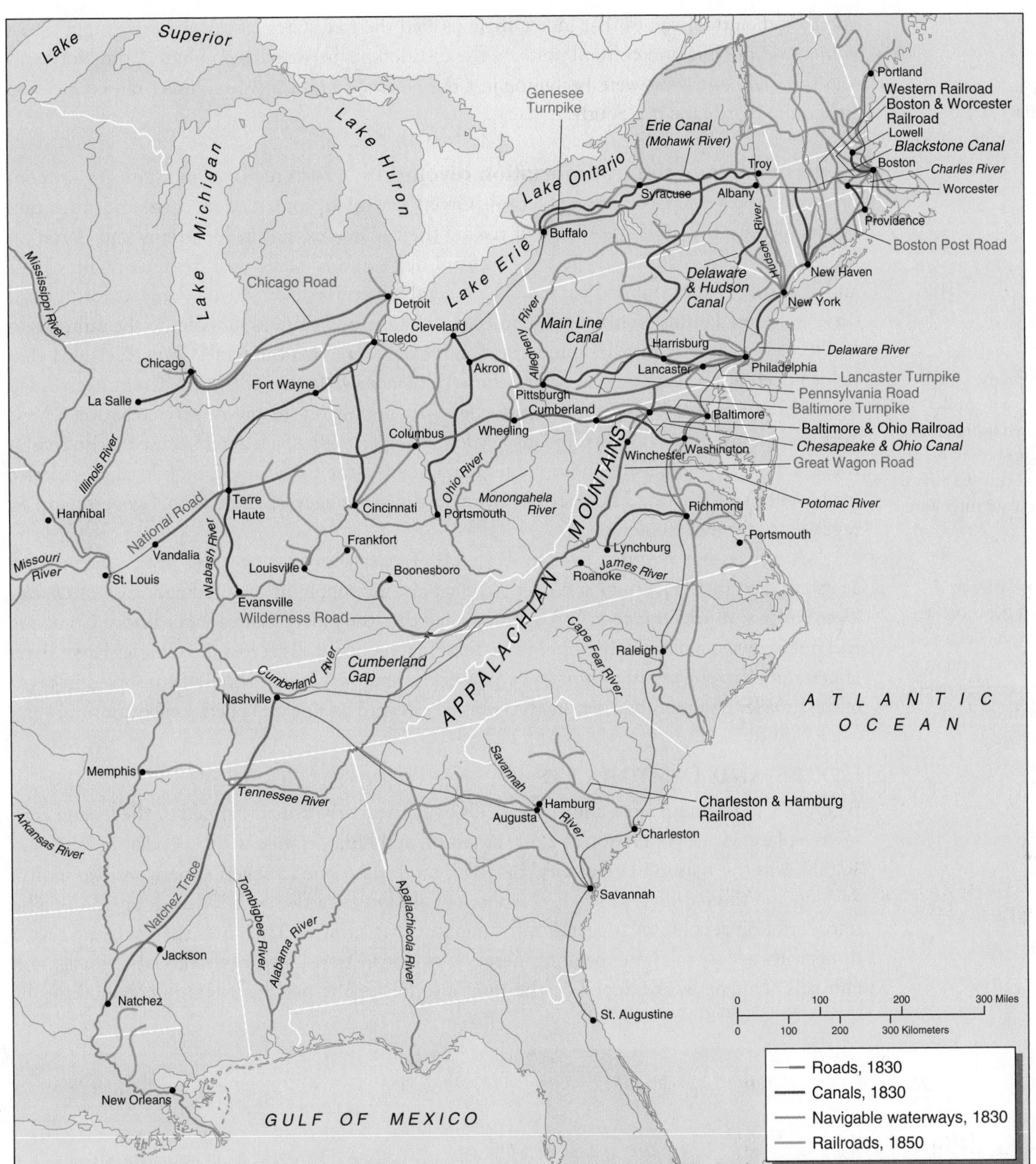

MAP 12–1 The Transportation Revolution By 1830, a network of roads, canals, and navigable rivers was spurring economic growth in the first phase of the transportation revolution. By 1850, railroads, the key development in the second phase of the transportation revolution, were opening up additional areas to commercial activity.

Which cities probably benefited the most from the new transportation infrastructure and why?

1849, trunk lines built westward from Atlantic Coast cities had reached the Great Lakes and the Ohio Valley and were about to enter the Mississippi Valley.

The rail network in place by midcentury was already altering the North-South sectional balance. The bulk of western trade no longer went downriver to New Orleans but was shipped east by rail. Moving in the opposite direction, to the West, were northern-born settlers, manufactured

QUICK REVIEW

Railroads

- Most important link in Jacksonian transportation revolution.
- 1825: first general-purpose railroad opened in England.
- By midcentury, railroads were a vital part of American economy.

goods, and cultural values that increasingly unified the free states east of the Mississippi into a common economic and cultural unit. As the distinctions between them blurred, the Northeast and the Old Northwest were becoming just the North. Significantly, no direct rail connection linked the North and the South.

Government and the transportation revolution. Both national and state government promoted the transportation revolution. Given the high construction costs and uncertain profits, private investors were leery of risking their scarce capital in long-term transportation projects. State legislatures stepped in and furnished some 70 percent of the funding for canals and about half of all railroad capital. The federal government provided engineers for railroad surveys, lowered tariffs on iron used in rail construction, and granted subsidies to the railroads in the form of public land. Most important, however, were two Supreme Court decisions that helped open up the economy to competition. In ***Gibbons v. Ogden*** (1824), the Court overturned a New York law that had given Aaron Ogden a monopoly on steamboat service between New York and New Jersey. Thomas Gibbons, Ogden's competitor, had a federal license for the coastal trade. The right to compete under the national license, the Court ruled, took legal precedence over Ogden's monopoly. The decision affirmed the supremacy of the national government to regulate interstate commerce.

Gibbons v. Ogden Supreme Court decision of 1824 involving coastal commerce that overturned a steamboat monopoly granted by the state of New York on the grounds that only Congress had the authority to regulate interstate commerce.

A new Court presided over by Roger B. Taney, who became chief justice when John Marshall died in 1835, struck a bolder blow against monopoly in the landmark case of ***Charles River Bridge v. Warren Bridge*** in 1837. Taney ruled that the older Charles River Bridge Company had not received a monopoly from Massachusetts to collect tolls across the Charles River. Any uncertainties in the charter rights of corporations, reasoned Taney, should be resolved in favor of the broader community interests that would be served by free and open competition.

Charles River Bridge v. Warren Bridge Supreme Court decision of 1837 that promised economic competition by ruling that the broader rights of the community took precedence over any presumed right of monopoly granted in a corporate charter.

CITIES AND IMMIGRANTS

Barely one in twenty Americans in the 1790s lived in an urban area (defined by the federal census as a place with a population of 2,500 or more), and Philadelphia, with a population just over 40,000, was the nation's largest city. By 1850, more than one in seven Americans was a city-dweller, and the nation had 10 cities whose population exceeded 50,000 (see Map 12–2). The transportation revolution triggered this surge in urban growth. The cities that prospered were those with access to the expanding network of cheap transport on steamboats, canals, and railroads. This network opened up the rural interior for the purchase of farm commodities by

Canal boats below a lock at the Junction of the Erie with the Northern (Champlain) Canal. Aquatint by John Hill.

Collection of the New-York Historical Society, Negative #34684.

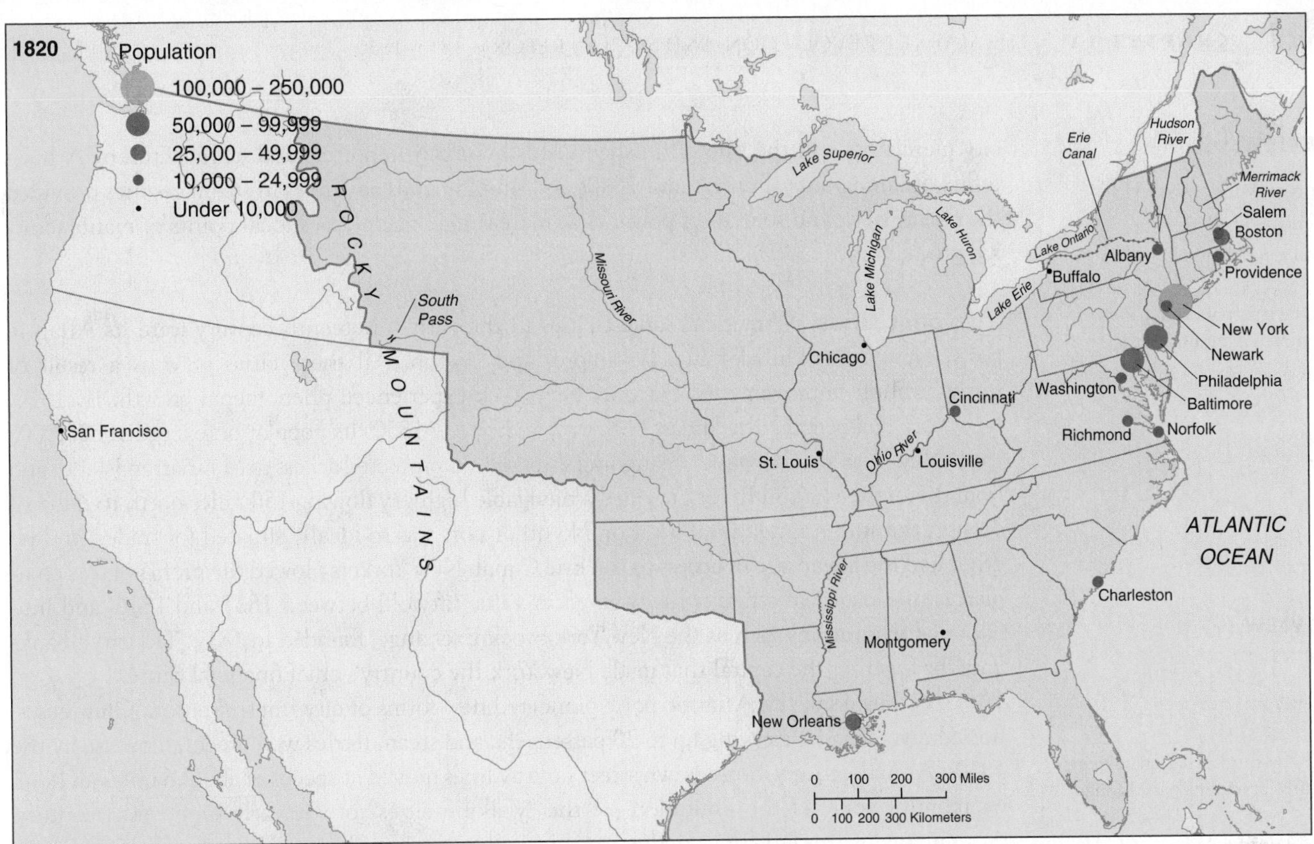

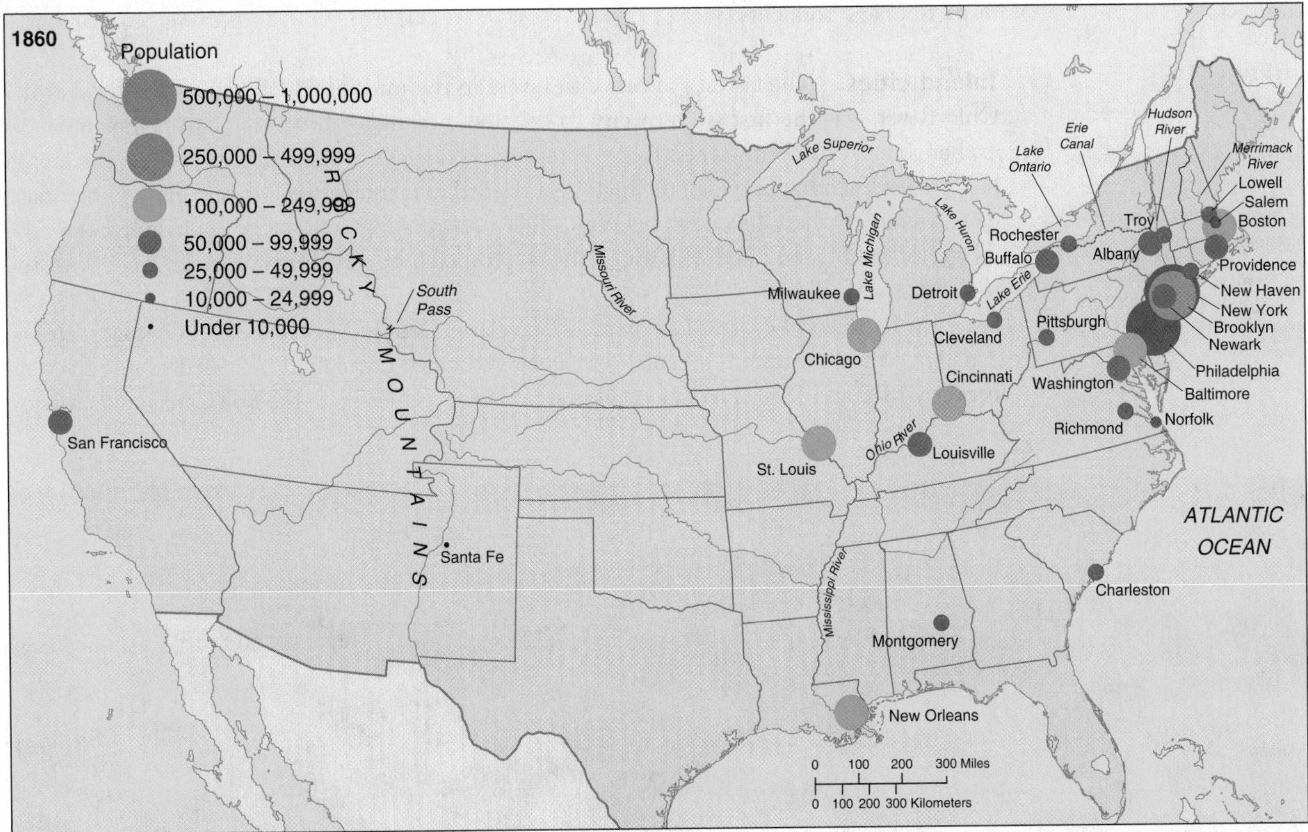

MAP 12–2 **The Growth of Cities, 1820–1860** In 1820, most cities were clustered along the Atlantic seaboard. By 1860, new transportation outlets—canals and railroads—had fostered the rapid growth of cities in the interior, especially at trading locations with access to navigable rivers or to the Great Lakes. Much of this growth occurred in the 1850s.

Data Source: Statistical Abstract of the United States.

Which region saw the least urban growth? Why?

QUICK REVIEW

Urbanization at Midcentury

- 1 in 7 Americans lived in a city.
- 10 cities had a population in excess of 50,000.
- An expanding transportation network fueled the growth of cities.

city merchants and the sale of finished goods by urban importers and manufacturers. A huge influx of immigrants after the mid-1840s and simultaneous advances in steam engines provided the cheap labor and sources of power that increasingly made cities focal points of manufacturing production.

The port cities. America's largest cities in the early nineteenth century were its Atlantic ports: New York, Philadelphia, Baltimore, and Boston. All these cities grew as a result of transportation improvements, but only New York experienced phenomenal growth. By 1810, New York had become the largest U.S. city, and by the 1850s its population exceeded 800,000.

New York's harbor gave oceangoing ships direct, protected access to Manhattan Island, and from there, the Hudson River provided a navigable highway flowing 150 miles north to Albany, deep in the state's agricultural interior. No other port was so ideally situated for trade. And no other had the advantage of access to the Erie Canal. New Yorkers plowed the profits of this commerce into local real estate, which soared in value fiftyfold between 1823 and 1836, and into financial institutions such as the New York Stock Exchange, founded in 1817. The city's banks brought together the capital that made New York the country's chief financial center.

QUICK REVIEW

New York

- By 1810 New York was America's largest city.
- 1820–1860: one-third of nation's exports and three-fifths of imports pass through New York.
- New York benefited from rich and extensive hinterland.

As they grew, the Atlantic ports pioneered new forms of city transportation. Omnibuses, horsedrawn coaches carrying up to 20 passengers, and steam ferries were in common use by the 1820s. At mid-century, horsedrawn street railway lines moved at speeds of about 6 miles an hour, overcoming some of the limitations of the "walking cities" of the early nineteenth century. Accompanying this growth were the first slums, the most notorious of which was the Five Points district of New York City.

QUICK REVIEW

Midwestern Cities

- America's fastest growing cities were in the interior.
- Pittsburgh became a center of iron and glass manufacturing.
- St. Louis, Buffalo, Cleveland, Detroit, Milwaukee, and Chicago were centers of western urbanization.

Inland cities. The fastest growing cities were in the interior. Pittsburgh, at the head of the Ohio River, was the first western city to develop a manufacturing sector to complement its exchange function. With access to the extensive coalfields of western Pennsylvania, Pittsburgh had a cheap fuel that provided the high heat needed to manufacture iron and glass. Cincinnati, downstream on the Ohio, was the West's first meatpacking center. St. Louis, just below the merger of the Missouri and Mississippi rivers, prospered by servicing American trade with the trans-Mississippi West.

By the 1840s, the Great Lake ports of Cleveland, Detroit, Milwaukee, and Chicago were the dynamic centers of western urbanization. Their combined population increased twenty-five-fold between 1830 and 1850. The Great Lakes served as an extension of the Erie Canal, and cities on

New York City's busy harbor was the entry to the largest metropolitan center that emerged in the nineteenth-century United States.

the lakes where incoming and outgoing goods had to be unloaded for transshipment benefited enormously. They attracted settlers and soon evolved into regional economic centers. They also aggressively promoted themselves into major rail hubs and thus reaped the economic advantages of being at the junctions of both water and rail transport.

W
WHERE TO LEARN MORE
Lowell National Historical Park
http://www.nps.gov/lowe/index.htm

New industrial cities. The only other cities growing as fast as the Great Lakes ports were the new industrial towns. The densest cluster of these was in rural New England along the fall line of rivers, where the rapidly falling water provided cheap power to drive the industrial machinery of factories and machine shops. Each town was tied to a transportation network that brought in raw cotton for the textile mills from the mercantile centers of Boston and Providence and shipped out the finished goods.

Read the **Document** at **www.myhistorylab.com** *The Harbinger, Female Workers of Lowell (1836)*

Lowell, Massachusetts, was America's first large-scale planned manufacturing city. Founded in 1822 by Boston businessmen, Lowell was built around the falls of the Merrimack River. Within a decade, rural fields had been transformed into a city of 18,000 people. Lowell's success became a model for others to follow, and by 1840, New England led the North in both urbanization and industrialization.

Immigration. Swelling the size of nearly all the cities was a surge of immigrants after the 1830s. The number of immigrants from 1840 to 1860, 4.2 million, represented a tenfold increase over the number that had come in the two preceding decades. Most of these immigrants were Irish and German (see Figure 12–1).

Read the **Document** at **www.myhistorylab.com** *From Then to Now Online: Immigration: An Ambivalent Welcome*

In the 1840s, economic and political upheavals in Europe spurred mass migration, mostly to the United States. Catholic peasants in Ireland, dominated by their Protestant English landlords, eked out a subsistence as tenants on tiny plots of land. A potato blight wiped out the crop in 1845 and 1846, and in the next five years about 1 million Irish died of malnutrition and disease. Another 1.5 million fled, many to the United States.

The Irish had no money to buy land or move west unless they joined construction gangs for canals and railroads. Without marketable skills, they had to take the worst and lowest paying jobs. Packed into dark cellars, unventilated attics, and rank tenements, the Irish suffered from very high mortality rates. Still, cash wages and access to food made the U.S. city preferable to the prospect of starvation in Ireland.

Lowell was the nation's leading textile center and the second-largest city in Massachusetts by 1850. The building with the cupola and the structure with dormers and chimneys were part of the mill complex. The two detached buildings were boardinghouses for the young women who worked in the mills.

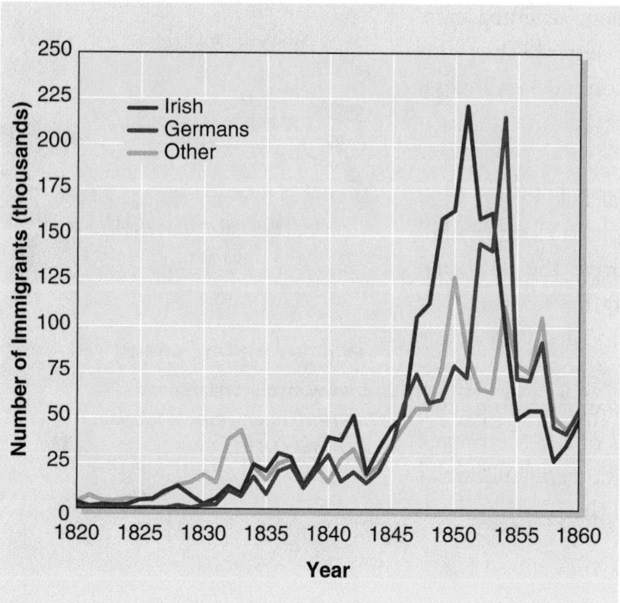

FIGURE 12–1 **Immigration to the United States, 1820–1860**
The potato famine in Ireland and economic and political unrest on the continent led to a surge in immigration in the 1840s. The pace slackened in the mid-1850s, when economic conditions in Europe improved.

Data Source: U.S. Bureau of the Census, *Historical Statistics of the United States, Colonial Times to 1957* (1960), p. 57.

German immigrants were second in number only to the Irish by the 1850s. They came to America to escape poor harvests and political turmoil. Far more Germans than Irish had owned property as farmers, artisans, and shopkeepers and had the capital to purchase land in the West and the skills to join the ranks of small businessmen in the cities. They were also more likely than the Irish to have entered the country through Baltimore or New Orleans, southern ports engaged in the tobacco and cotton trade with continental Europe. From there they fanned out into the Mississippi and Ohio valleys. With their diversified skills, they found ample economic opportunities in the fast-growing cities of the West and a setting in which to build tightly knit communities with German-speaking shops, churches, schools, and benevolent societies. About four in five of all the immigrants arriving after 1840 settled in the New England and mid-Atlantic states. Their sheer numbers transformed the size and ethnic composition of the working class, especially in the cities of the Northeast. And their cheap labor provided the final ingredient in the expansion of industrialization that began after the War of 1812.

QUICK REVIEW

Immigration at Midcentury

- Surge of immigrants fueled growth of cities after the 1830s.
- Economic and political upheaval spurred mass migration from Europe.
- Famine drove 1.5 million Irish to America.

putting-out system System of manufacturing in which merchants furnished households with raw materials for processing by family members.

The Industrial Revolution

The Northeast led America's industrial revolution. In 1815, this region had the largest cities, the most developed capital markets, the readiest access to the technological skills of artisans, and the greatest supply of available labor. The first large-scale factories, the textile mills, were erected in New England in the 1820s. For the next 30 years, the United States had the most rapidly developing industrial economy in the world.

The household and the small workshop were the sites of manufacturing in Jefferson's America. Wider markets for household manufactures began to develop in the late eighteenth century with the coming of the **putting-out system.** Local merchants furnished ("put out") raw materials to rural households and paid at a piece rate for the labor that converted the raw materials into manufactured products. The supplying merchant then marketed and sold these goods.

In the cities and larger towns, most manufacturing was done by artisans, skilled craftsmen known as mechanics. Working in their own shops and with their own tools, they produced small batches of finished goods. Each artisan had a specific skill that set him above common laborers—shoemaking, furniture making, silver smithing. These skills came from hands-on experience and craft traditions that were handed down from one generation to the next.

Master craftsmen taught the "mysteries of the craft" to the journeymen and apprentices who lived with them and worked in their shops. Journeymen had learned the skills of their craft but lacked the capital to open their own shops. Apprentices were adolescent boys legally sent by their fathers to live with and obey a master craftsman in return for being taught a trade.

The factory system of production that would undercut both household and artisanal manufacturing after 1815 could produce goods far more quickly and cheaply per worker than could artisans or rural households. Factories subdivided the specialized skills of the artisan into a series of semiskilled tasks, a process foreshadowed by the putting-out system. Factories also put workers under systematic controls. And in the final stage of industrialization, they boosted workers' productivity through the use of power-driven machinery.

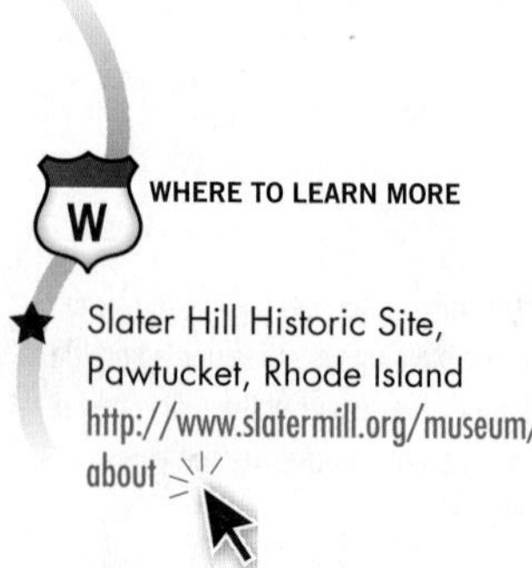

Slater Hill Historic Site, Pawtucket, Rhode Island
http://www.slatermill.org/museum/about

Britain pioneered the technological advances that drove early industrialization. The secrets of this technology, especially the designs for the machines that mechanized textile production, were closely guarded by the British government. Despite attempts to prohibit the emigration of artisans who knew how the machinery worked, some British mechanics made it to the United States. Samuel Slater was one of them, and he took over the operation of a fledgling mill in Providence,

Rhode Island. With his knowledge of how to build the water-powered spinning machinery, he converted the mill into the nation's first permanent cotton factory in 1790.

The first real spurt of factory building came with the closing off of British imports during the embargo and the War of 1812. Hundreds of new cotton and woolen mills were established from 1808 to 1815. But the great test of U.S. manufacturing came after 1815, when peace with Britain brought a flood of cheap British manufactured goods. If factories were to continue to grow, U.S. manufacturers had to reach more consumers in their home market and overcome the British advantage of lower labor costs.

Sources of labor. Industrial labor was more expensive in America than in England, where the high cost of land forced the rural poor into the cities to find work. In contrast, land was cheap and plentiful in the United States, and Americans preferred the independence of farm work to the dependence of factory labor. Consequently, the first mill workers were predominantly children. The owners set up the father on a plot of company-owned land, provided piecework for the mother, and put the children to work in the mills.

Although this so-called **Rhode Island system** of family employment sufficed for small mills, it was inadequate for the larger, more mechanized factories that were built in New England after the War of 1812. The owners of these mills recruited unmarried adolescent daughters of farmers from across New England as their laborers in the **Waltham system.** Although factory wages were low, they were more than these young women could earn doing piecework in the home or as domestics. The wages also brought a liberating degree of financial independence. "When they felt the jingle of silver in their pockets," recalled Harriet Hanson Robinson of her fellow workers at Lowell in the 1830s, "there for the first time, their heads became erect and they walked as if on air."

Rhode Island system During the industrialization of the early nineteenth century, the recruitment of entire families for employment in a factory.

Waltham system During the industrialization of the early nineteenth century, the recruitment of unmarried young women for employment in factories.

To overcome parental fears that their daughters might be exposed to morally corrupting conditions in the mills and mill towns, New England manufacturers set up paternalistic moral controls. Single female workers had to live in company-owned boardinghouses that imposed curfews, screened visitors, and mandated church attendance. The mill women worked six days a week from dawn to dusk for low wages. There were limits to what the women would endure, and in 1834 and 1836 the female hands at Lowell "turned out" to protest wage reductions in demonstrations that were the largest strikes in American history up to that time.

After the economic downturn of the late 1830s, conditions in the mills grew worse. By the mid-1840s, however, the Irish, desperate for work, sent their children into the mills at an earlier age than Yankee families. These workers did not leave after two or three years of building up a small dowry for marriage, as many New Englanders did. By the early 1850s, more than half the textile operatives were Irish women.

In the mid-Atlantic region, where the farm population was more prosperous than in New England and fewer young women were available for factory work, immigrants were an important source of manufacturing workers as early as the 1820s. They played an especially crucial role in urban manufacturing. The port cities lacked usable waterpower, but by drawing on a growing pool of cheap, immigrant labor, manufacturers could expand production while driving down the cost.

At midcentury most industrial work was still done by hand. Shown here are two foundry workers holding floor rammers used for packing sand against molds.

Except in New England textile factories and the smaller factories and shops in the seaboard cities, native-born males were the

QUICK REVIEW

Mill Work

- In the 1820s and 1830s most New England mill hands were young farm daughters.
- Young female workers were subject to paternalistic moral controls.
- Mill workers worked six-day weeks for low wages.

largest group of early manufacturing workers. They came from poor rural families that lacked enough land to pass on to male heirs. As late as 1840, women, including those working at home, made up about half of the manufacturing work force and one-quarter of the factory hands. Few of these workers brought any specific skills to their jobs, and thus they had little bargaining power. Economic necessity forced them to accept low wages and harsh working conditions. The sheer increase in their numbers, as opposed to any productivity gains from technological innovations, accounted by 1850 for two-thirds of the gains in manufacturing output.

Technological gains. After 1815, U.S. manufacturers began to close the technological gap with Britain by drawing on the versatile skills of U.S. mechanics. Mechanics experimented with new designs, improved old ones, and patented inventions that found industrial applications outside their own crafts.

The most famous early American invention was the cotton gin. Eli Whitney, a Massachusetts Yankee, built the prototype of the gin in 1793 while working as a tutor on a Georgia plantation. By cheaply and quickly removing the seeds from cotton fibers, the cotton gin spurred the cultivation of cotton across the South.

Whitney also pushed the idea of basing production on interchangeable parts. After receiving a federal contract to manufacture muskets, he designed new milling machines and turret lathes that transformed the technology of machine tool production. The new techniques were first applied in 1815 to the manufacture of wooden clocks and by the 1840s to sewing machines, farm machinery, and watch parts. The **American system of manufacturing,** low-cost, standardized mass production, built around interchangeable parts stamped out by machines, was America's unique contribution to the industrial revolution.

American system of manufacturing A technique of production pioneered in the United States in the first half of the nineteenth century that relied on precision manufacturing with the use of interchangeable parts.

As the pace of technological innovation accelerated after 1840, so did the growth of manufacturing. Indeed, the 1840s registered the highest rate of expansion in the manufacturing sector of the economy in the nineteenth century. The adoption of the stationary steam engine in urban manufacturing fueled much of this expansion. High-pressure steam engines enabled power-driven industry to locate in the port cities of the Northeast and the booming cities on the Great Lakes. With limited access to waterpower, early manufacturing in the West was confined to the processing of farm goods. By turning to steam power and new machine tools, western manufacturers after 1840 enlarged their region's industrial base and created a new industry, the mass production of agricultural implements. The West was the center of the farm-machinery industry, and the region produced 20 percent of the nation's manufacturing output by the 1850s.

A greater control over natural resources, as well as new technologies, drove industrial growth. To provide their mills with a steady, reliable source of water, one that would not be affected by the whims of nature, the Boston Associates constructed a series of dams and canals that

Shown here working at power looms under the supervision of a male overseer, young single women constituted the bulk of the labor force in the first textile factories of New England.

extended to the headwaters of the Merrimack River in northern New Hampshire. Inevitably, the ecology of the region changed. The level of the lakes was altered, the flow of rivers interrupted, the upward migration of spawning fish blocked, and the foraging terrain of wild game flooded. Farmers protested when their fields and pastures were submerged, but lawyers for the Boston Associates successfully argued that water, like other natural resources, should be treated as a commodity that could contribute to economic progress. Increasingly, the law treated nature as an economic resource to be engineered and bought and sold.

Growing Inequality and New Classes

In the first half of the nineteenth century, the economy grew three times faster than in the eighteenth century, and per capita income doubled. Living standards for most Americans improved. There was a price to be paid, however, for the benefits of economic growth. Half of the adult white males were propertyless at midcentury. Wealth had become more concentrated, and extremes of wealth and poverty eroded the Jeffersonian ideal of a republic of independent proprietors who valued liberty because they were economically free.

The gap between the rich and the poor widened considerably in the early phases of industrialization (see Figure 12–2). In 1800, the richest 10 percent of Americans owned 40 to 50 percent of the national wealth. By the 1850s, their share was about 70 percent. The most glaring discrepancies in wealth appeared in the large cities. In all cities by the 1840s, the top 10 percent of the population owned 80 percent of urban wealth.

QUICK REVIEW

A Growing Gap between Rich and Poor

- 1800: Richest 10 percent of Americans owned 40–50 percent of national wealth.
- 1850s: Richest 10 percent of Americans owned 70 percent of national wealth.

The new middle class. The faster pace of economic growth that enabled the urban rich to increase their wealth also created opportunities for a rapidly expanding new middle class. This class grew as the number of nonmanual jobs increased. Most of these jobs were in northern cities and bustling market towns, where the need was greatest for office and store clerks, managerial personnel, sales agents, and independent retailers. The result by midcentury was a new middle class superimposed on the older one of independent farmers, artisans, shopkeepers, and professionals. The separation of work and home constituted the first step in an evolving sense of class consciousness. As the market revolution advanced, the workplace increasingly became a specialized location of production or selling. Middle-class fathers now left for work in the morning, while mothers governed households that were primarily residential units and places of material comfort, where growing quantities of consumer goods were on display. Having servants became a status symbol. Shunned as degrading by most native-born white women, these low-paying jobs were filled by African American and young immigrant (especially Irish) women. Work had not left the middle-class home; instead, it was disguised as the "domestic duties" of middle-class wives who supervised the servants.

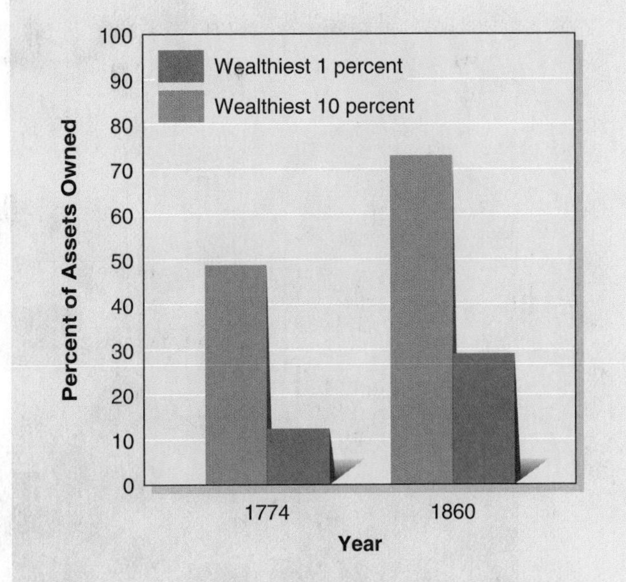

FIGURE 12–2 **Growth in Wealth Inequality, 1774–1860** The two benchmark years for the gathering of data on the nationwide distribution of wealth are 1774 and 1860. Specialized studies on regions and subregions indicate that wealth inequality increased most sharply from the 1820s to 1850, the period that coincides with early industrialization.

Data Source: Jeffrey G. Williamson and Peter H. Lindert, *American Inequality: A Macroeconomic History* (1980), p. 38.

Besides turning to etiquette books for advice on proper manners in public and in the home, the middle class also tried to shape its behavior by the tenets of evangelical religion. Revivals swept northern cities in the late 1820s. Preachers like Charles G. Finney stressed that both economic and moral success depended on the virtues of sobriety, self-restraint, and hard work. Aggressiveness and ambition at work were not necessarily sinful so long as businessmen reformed their own moral lives and helped others do the same. This message was immensely reassuring to employers and entrepreneurs, for it confirmed and sanctified their own pursuit of economic self-interest. It also provided them with a religious inspiration for

temperance Reform movement originating in the 1820s that sought to eliminate the consumption of alcohol.

attempting to exert moral control over their communities and employees. **Temperance,** the prohibition of alcoholic beverages, was the greatest of the evangelically inspired reforms, and abstinence from alcohol became the most telling evidence of middle-class respectability.

QUICK REVIEW

Class Consciousness

- Separation of home and work first step in evolving class consciousness.
- Home a place of material comfort for rising middle class.
- Having servants a sign of status.
- Middle class shaped by evangelical religion.

Read the **Document** at **www.myhistorylab.com**
Catharine Esther Beecher, American Woman's Home (1869)

cult of domesticity The belief that women, by virtue of their sex, should stay home as the moral guardians of family life.

Women and the cult of domesticity. In a reversal of traditional Calvinist doctrine, the evangelical ministers of the northern middle class enshrined women as the moral superiors of men. Though considered weak and passive, women were also held to be uniquely pure and pious. Women, who easily outnumbered men at Sunday services and weeknight prayer meetings, were now responsible for converting their homes into loving, prayerful centers of domesticity, and the primary task of motherhood became the Christian nurturing of souls entrusted to a mother's care.

This sanctified notion of motherhood reflected and reinforced shifting patterns of family life. Families became smaller as the birthrate fell by 25 percent in the first half of the nineteenth century. The decline was greatest in the urban middle class after 1820. Middle-class couples consciously limited the size of their families, and women stopped having children at an earlier age. As a result, parents devoted more care and financial resources to child rearing.

Beginning in the 1820s, ministers and female writers elevated the family role of middle-class women into a **cult of domesticity.** This idealized conception of womanhood insisted that the biological differences of God's natural order determined separate social roles for men and women. Characterized as strong, aggressive, and ambitious, men naturally belonged in the competitive world of business and politics. Women's providential task was to preserve religion and morality in the home and family.

The working classes. The economic changes that produced a new middle class also fundamentally transformed the working class. In the preindustrial United States, the working

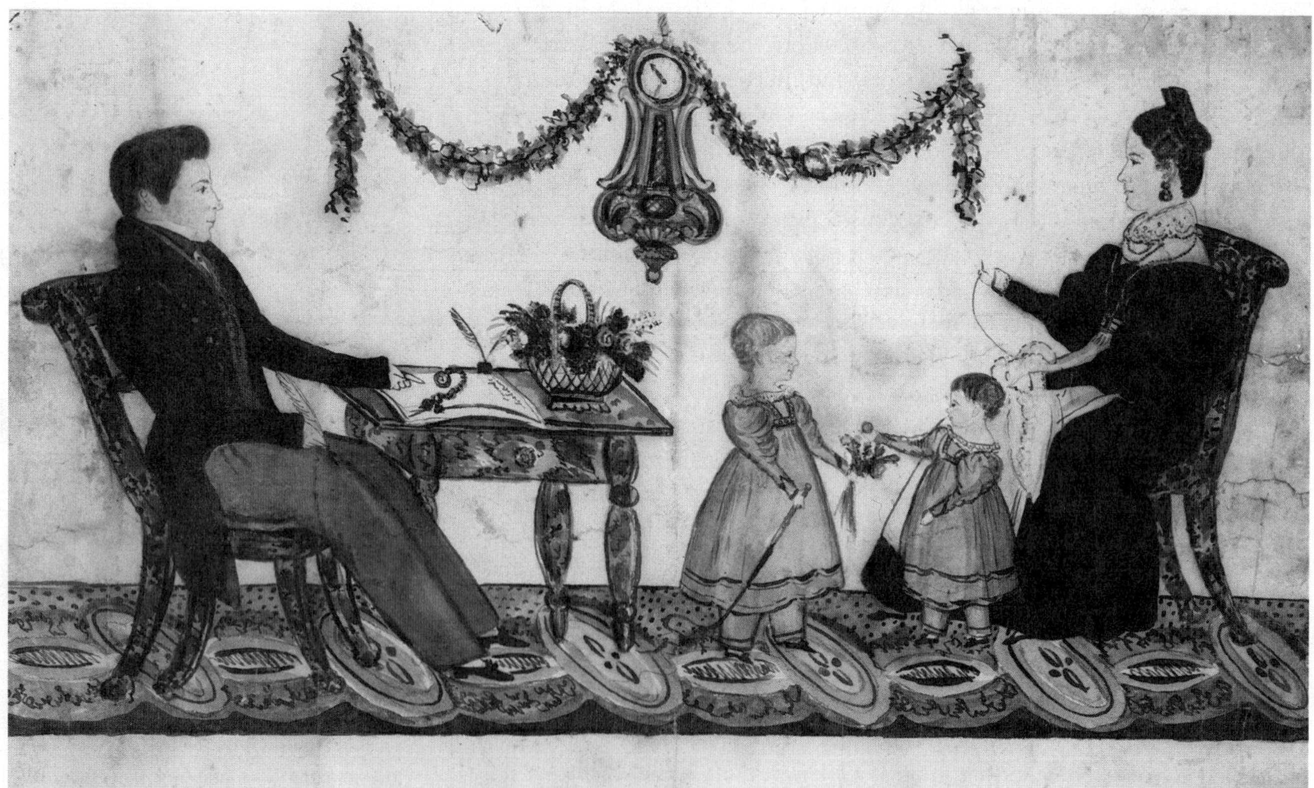

This pen-and-watercolor drawing of a middle-class family in 1832 illustrates how the home, as it lost its productive functions, became idealized as a center of domestic refinement and material comfort.

"Family Group," Joseph H. Davis, American, 1811–1865, Graphite pencil and watercolor on paper, Sheet: 24.8 × 41 cm (9 3/4 × 16 1/8 in.), Museum of Fine Arts, Boston, Gift of Maxim Karolik for the proposed M. and M. Karolik Collection of American Watercolors, class was predominantly native-born and of artisan origins. By midcentury, most urban workers were immigrants or the children of immigrants and had never been artisans in a skilled craft.

Job skills, sex, race, and ethnicity all divided workers after 1840. Master craftsmen were the most highly skilled and best-paid workers. As industrialization proceeded, the unity of the old artisan class splintered. Ambitious master craftsmen with access to capital rose into the ranks of small businessmen and manufacturers. They expanded output and drove down the cost of production by contracting out work at piece wages and hiring the cheapest workers they could find. The result was to transform the apprentice system into a system of exploited child labor.

By the 1830s, journeymen were becoming permanent wage earners with little prospect of opening their own shops. To protect their liberties from what they considered a new aristocracy of manufacturers, they organized workingmen's parties in the 1830s, centered in the eastern cities. At the top of these parties' lists of reforms were free public education, the abolition of imprisonment for debt, and a 10-hour workday.

Early trade unions. Journeymen also turned to trade union activity in the 1820s and 1830s to gain better wages, shorter hours, and enhanced job security. Benefiting from a strong demand for their skills, workers in the building trades organized the first unions. They were soon followed by shoemakers, printers, and weavers, workers in trades where pressure on urban journeymen was the most intense. Locals from various trades formed the National Trades Union, the first national union, in 1834. The new labor movement launched more than 150 strikes in the mid-1830s.

Although the Panic of 1837 decimated union membership, the early labor movement did achieve two notable victories. First, by the late 1830s, it had forced employers to accept the 10-hour day as the standard for most skilled workers. Second, in a landmark decision handed down in 1842, the Massachusetts Supreme Court ruled in *Commonwealth v. Hunt* that a trade union was not necessarily subject to laws against criminal conspiracies and that a strike could be used to force employers to hire only union members.

The unions defended artisanal rights and virtues, and they ignored workers whose jobs had never had craft status. As massive immigration merged with industrialization after 1840, this basic division between workers widened. On one side was the male, Protestant, and native-born class of skilled artisans. On the other side was the working-class majority of factory laborers and unskilled workers, predominantly immigrants and women who worked for a wage as domestics or factory hands.

Increasingly fearing these workers as a threat to their job security and Protestant values, in the 1840s U.S.-born artisans joined **nativist** organizations that sought to curb mass immigration from Europe and limit the political rights of Catholic immigrants. Whereas immigrants viewed temperance as business-class meddling in their lives, nativist workers tended to embrace the evangelical, middle-class ideology of temperance and self-help. One of the few issues that brought immigrants and nativists together was the nearly universal demand of white workers that black workers be confined to the most menial jobs.

Gender also divided workers. Working-class men shared the dominant ideology of female dependence. They measured their own status as husbands by their ability to support their wives and daughters. Beginning in the 1830s, male workers argued that their wages would be higher if women were barred from the labor force. With these views, male workers helped lock wage-earning women into the lowest paying and most exploited jobs.

nativist Favoring the interests and culture of native-born inhabitants over those of immigrants.

QUICK REVIEW

Unions

- In the late 1830s and early 1840s unions won important victories.
- Unions concentrated on artisanal rights and virtues.
- American-born artisans increasingly saw immigrants as a threat to job security.

REFORM AND MORAL ORDER

WHAT ROLE did women play in the reform movements that followed the War of 1812?

The rapidity and extent of the social and economic changes that accompanied the market revolution were disorienting, even frightening, to many Americans, particularly religious leaders and wealthy businessmen in the East. They saw signs of moral wickedness and disorder all around them in the more fluid, materialistic society that was emerging. Alarmed by what they perceived as a breakdown in moral authority, they sought to impose moral discipline on Americans.

These eastern elites, with the indispensable support of their wives and daughters, created a network of voluntary church-affiliated reform organizations known collectively as the **benevolent empire.** Revivals in the 1820s and 1830s broadened the base of reform to include the newly evangelicalized middle class in northern cities and towns.

benevolent empire Network of reform associations affiliated with Protestant churches in the early nineteenth century dedicated to the restoration of moral order.

The Benevolent Empire

Evangelical businessmen in the seaboard cities backed the call to restore moral order. Worried by the increasing number of urban poor, wealthy merchants contributed vital financial support for a network of reform associations. The reform societies built on the Second Great Awakening's techniques of organization and communication. The Protestant reformers sent out speakers on regular schedules along prescribed routes. They developed organizations that maintained a constant pressure for reform. National and local boards of directors supervised the work of salaried managers, who inspired volunteers to combat sin among the unconverted. When steam presses and stereotype plates halved the cost of printing and dramatically increased its speed, the American Bible Society was the first organization to exploit this revolution in the print media. Between 1790 and 1830, the number of religious newspapers grew from 14 to more than 600. By then, religious presses were churning out more than 1 million Bibles and 6 million tracts a year.

A host of local societies targeted individual vices. Their purpose, as summed up by a Massachusetts group, the Andover South Parish Society for the Reformation of Morals, was "to discountenance [discourage] immorality, particularly Sabbath-breaking, intemperance, and profanity, and to promote industry, order, piety, and good morals." These goals linked social and moral discipline, appealing both to churchgoers concerned about godlessness and profit-oriented businessmen eager to curb their workers' unruly behavior.

The boldest expression of the drive to enhance Protestant Christian power was the **Sabbatarian movement.** In 1828, evangelicals led by Lyman Beecher formed the General Union for Promoting the Observance of the Christian Sabbath. Their immediate goal was the repeal of a law passed by Congress in 1810 directing post offices to deliver mail on Sunday. Their broader mission was to enforce local statutes that shut down business and leisure activities on Sundays.

Sabbatarian movement Reform organization founded in 1828 by Congregationalist and Presbyterian ministers that lobbied for an end to the delivery of mail on Sundays and other Sabbath violations.

In 1829, insisting on the separation of church and state, the Democratic Congress upheld the postal law of 1810. The Sabbatarians had outraged canal operators, hotelkeepers, tavern owners, and other businesses threatened with the loss of their Sunday trade. Businessmen, workingmen, southern evangelicals, and religious conservatives all felt that the Sabbath purists had gone too far in a movement now seen as a threat to civil liberties and the rights of private property.

The General Union disbanded in 1832, but it left an important legacy for future reform movements. On the one hand, it developed techniques that converted the reform impulse into direct political action. In raising funds, training speakers, holding rallies, disseminating literature, lobbying for local Sunday regulations, and coordinating a petition to Congress, the Sabbatarians created an organizational model for other reformers to follow in mobilizing public opinion and influencing politicians. On the other hand, the failure of the Sabbatarians revealed that a new approach was needed that encouraged individuals to reform themselves without coercive controls. It soon emerged in the temperance movement.

QUICK REVIEW

The Birth of Reform

- Anxieties over social and economic change fueled reform efforts.
- Reform societies built on techniques and ideas of the Second Great Awakening.
- Local societies targeted individual vices.
- Reformers linked social and moral discipline to reform.

The Temperance Movement

Temperance, the drive against the consumption of alcohol, had the greatest impact on the most people of any reform movement. Its success rested on what Lyman Beecher called "a new moral power." Dismayed by popular resistance to the coercive moralism of the first wave of Protestant reform, evangelicals concluded that reform had to rest on persuasion, and it had to begin with the voluntary decision of individuals to free themselves from sin.

at **www.myhistorylab.com**
Drinking and the Temperance Movement in Nineteenth-Century America

OVERVIEW Changes Promoting Growth in the Transformed Economy

Sector	1815	1850
Travel and transportation	By foot and horsedrawn wagon	Cheaper and faster with canals, steamboats, and railroads opening up new markets
Population	Overwhelmingly native-born, rural, and concentrated east of Appalachian Mountains	Four times larger as a result of natural increase and surge of immigration after 1840; settlement of West and growth of cities
Wage labor	Native-born, primarily women and children in manufacturing	Expanding as rural poor and immigrants enter manufacturing workforce
Power	Water-driven mills	Steam-driven engines
Farming	Subsistence-oriented; surplus sold in localized markets	Commercialized agriculture spreading in response to improvements in transportation
Manufacturing	Small-scale production in household units and artisan shops	Large-scale production in eastern cities and factories

In 1826, evangelicals founded the **American Temperance Society.** Their goal was to bring about a radical change in U.S. attitudes toward alcohol and its role in social life. Taverns easily outnumbered churches as gathering places. Alcohol was used to pay common laborers and itinerant preachers on the early Methodist circuit. Masters and journeymen shared a drink as a customary way of taking a break from work, and no wedding, funeral, or meeting of friends was complete without alcohol.

American Temperance Society National organization established in 1826 by evangelical Protestants that campaigned for total abstinence from alcohol and was successful in sharply lowering per capita consumption of alcohol.

For the temperance crusade to succeed, the reformers had to finance a massive propaganda campaign and link it to an organization that could mobilize and energize thousands of people. They built such a mass movement by merging temperance into the network of churches and lay volunteers that the benevolent empire had developed and by adopting the techniques of revivals to win converts.

Evangelical reformers denounced intemperance as the greatest sin of the land. Alcohol represented all that was wrong in America, crime, poverty, insanity, broken families, boisterous politicking, Sabbath-breaking. This message thundered from the pulpit and the public lectern. Thanks to the generous financial subsidies of wealthy benefactors, it was also broadcast in millions of tracts printed on the latest high-speed presses. Like revivals, temperance rallies combined emotionally charged sermons with large, tearful prayer meetings to evoke guilt among sinners, who would then seek release by taking the pledge of abstinence.

Within a decade, the American Temperance Society had more than 5,000 local chapters and statewide affiliates, most in the Northeast.

Temperance cartoon.

A million members had pledged abstinence by 1833. Women constituted one-third to more than one-half of the members in local temperance societies. Lacking legal protections against abusive husbands who drank away the family resources, women had a compelling reason to join the crusade. As the moral protectors of the family, they pressured their husbands to take the teetotaler's pledge and stick by it, raised sons to shun alcohol, and banished liquor from their homes. By the 1840s, temperance and middle-class domesticity had become synonymous.

The first wave of temperance converts came from the upper and middle classes. Businessmen welcomed temperance as a model of self-discipline in their efforts to regiment factory work. Young, upwardly mobile professionals and petty entrepreneurs learned in temperance how to be thrifty, self-controlled, respectable, and creditworthy. Temperance made its first significant inroads among the working classes during the economic depression of 1839–1843. Joining together in what they called Washington Temperance Societies, small businessmen and artisans, many of them reformed drunkards, carried temperance into working-class districts. The Washingtonians insisted that workers could survive the depression only if they stopped drinking and adopted the temperance ethic of frugality and self-help. Their wives organized auxiliary societies and pledged to enforce sobriety and economic restraint at home. In a telling measure of the temperance movement's success, per capita alcohol consumption fell from an all-time high of 7.1 gallons per year in 1830 to less than 2 gallons per year by 1845.

Read the Document at **www.myhistorylab.com** *Lyman Beecher, "Six Sermons on Intemperance" (1828)*

Women's Role in Reform

The first phase of women's reform activities represented an extension of the domestic ideal promoted in the cult of domesticity. Assumptions about women's unique moral qualities permitted, and even encouraged, them to assume the role of "social mother" by organizing on behalf of the orphaned and the widowed. Founded in 1797, the Society for the Relief of Poor Widows with Small Children in New York typified these early approaches to reform. The women in the society came from socially prominent families. Motivated by religious charity and social duty, they visited poor women and children, dispensed funds, and set up work programs. However, they limited their benevolence to the "deserving poor," socially weak but morally strong people who had suffered personal misfortune, and screened out all who were thought to be unworthy.

A second phase in the reform efforts by women developed in the 1830s. Unlike their benevolent counterparts, the reformers now began to challenge male prerogatives and move beyond moral suasion. The crusade against prostitution exemplified the new militancy. Women seized leadership of the movement in 1834 with the founding of the New York Female Moral Reform Society. In the pages of their journal, *Advocate for Moral Reform*, members identified male greed and licentiousness as the causes for the fallen state of women. Identified, too, were the male patrons of the city's brothels. The society blamed businessmen for the low wages that forced some women to resort to prostitution and denounced lustful men for engaging in "a regular crusade against [our] sex."

In 1839, this attack on the sexual double standard became a national movement with the establishment of the **American Female Moral Reform Society.** With 555 affiliates throughout the evangelical heartland of the North, female activists mounted a lobbying campaign that, unlike earlier efforts, bypassed prominent men and reached out to a mass audience. By the 1840s, such unprecedented political involvement enabled women to secure the first state laws criminalizing seduction and adultery.

American Female Moral Reform Society Organization founded in 1839 by female reformers that established homes of refuge for prostitutes and petitioned for state laws that would criminalize adultery and the seduction of women.

Other women's groups developed a more radical critique of U.S. society and its male leadership. The Boston Seamen's Aid Society, founded in 1833 by Sarah Josepha Hale, a widow with five children, soon rejected the benevolent tradition of distinguishing between "respectable" and "unworthy" poor. Hale discovered that her efforts to guide poor women toward self-sufficiency flew in the face of the low wages and substandard housing that trapped her clients in poverty.

Hale attacked male employers for exploiting the poor. "Combinations of selfish men are formed to beat down the price of female labor," she wrote in her 1836 annual report, "and then they call the diminished rate the market price."

BACKLASH AGAINST BENEVOLENCE

Some of the benevolent empire's harshest critics came out of the populist revivals of the early 1800s. They considered the Protestant reformers' program a conspiracy of orthodox Calvinists from old-line denominations to impose social and moral control on behalf of a religious and economic elite.

These criticisms revealed a profound mistrust of the emerging market society. In contrast to the evangelical reformers, drawn from the well-educated business and middle classes who were benefiting from economic change, most evangelical members of the grassroots sects and followers of the itinerant preachers were unschooled, poor, and hurt by market fluctuations that they could not control. Socially uprooted and economically stranded, they found a sense of community in their local churches and resisted control by wealthier, better-educated outsiders. Above all, they clung to beliefs that shored up the threatened authority of the father over his household.

With the elevation of women to the status of moral guardians of the family and agents of benevolent reform outside the household, middle-class evangelicalism in the Northeast was becoming feminized. This new social role for women was especially threatening, indeed, galling, for men who were the casualties of the more competitive economy. Raised on farms where the father had been the unquestioned lawgiver and provider, these men attacked feminized evangelicalism for undermining their paternal authority. They found in Scripture an affirmation of patriarchal power for any man, no matter how poor or economically dependent.

The **Church of Jesus Christ of Latter-day Saints** (also known as the **Mormon Church**) represented the most enduring religious backlash of economically struggling men against the aggressive efforts of reforming middle-class evangelicals. Joseph Smith, who established the church in upstate New York in 1830, came from a New England farm family uprooted and impoverished by market speculations gone sour. He and his followers were alienated not only from the new market economy but also from what they saw as the religious and social anarchy around them. Based on Smith's divine revelations as set forth in the Book of Mormon (1830), their new faith offered converts both a sanctuary as a biblical people and a release from social and religious uncertainties.

Church of Jesus Christ of Latter-day Saints (Mormon Church) Church founded in 1830 by Joseph Smith and based on the revelations in a sacred book he called the Book of Mormon.

Mormonism provided a defense of communal beliefs centered on male authority. It assigned complete spiritual and secular authority to men. Only through subordination and obedience to their husbands could women hope to gain salvation. To be a Mormon was to join a large extended family that was part of a shared enterprise. Men bonded their labor in a communal economy to benefit all the faithful. Driven by a strong sense of social obligation, the Mormons forged the most successful alternative vision in antebellum America to the individualistic Protestant republic of the benevolent reformers. (For the Mormons' role in the westward movement, see Chapter 13.)

Interpreting the Past
The Second Great Awakening and Religious Diversity in America
(pp. 334–335)

INSTITUTIONS AND SOCIAL IMPROVEMENT

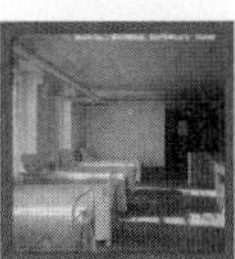

HOW DID Enlightenment ideas shape the reform of institutions for the poor, criminals, and the mentally ill?

Although evangelical Protestantism was its mainspring, antebellum reform also had its roots in the European Enlightenment. Like the evangelicals inspired by religious optimism, reformers drawing on Enlightenment doctrines of progress had unbounded faith in social improvement. They saw in the United States an unlimited potential to fashion a model republic of virtuous, intelligent citizens.

School Reform

Before the 1820s, schooling in America was an informal, haphazard affair that nonetheless met the basic needs for reading, writing, and arithmetic skills of an overwhelmingly rural population. Private tutors and academies for the wealthy, a few charitable schools for the urban poor, and rural one-room schoolhouses open for a few months each year constituted formal education at the primary level.

Workingmen's Movement Associations of urban workers who began campaigning in the 1820s for free public education and a ten-hour workday.

The first political demands for free tax-supported schools originated with the **Workingmen's Movement** in eastern cities in the 1820s. In pushing for "equal republican education," workers sought to guarantee that all citizens, no matter how poor, could achieve meaningful liberty and equality. Their proposals, however, met stiff resistance from wealthier property holders, who refused to pay taxes to support the education of working-class children.

The breakthrough in public education came in New England, where the disruptive forces of industrialization and urbanization were felt the earliest. Increased economic inequality, growing numbers of impoverished Irish Catholic immigrants, and the emergence of a mass democracy based on nearly universal white male suffrage convinced reformers of the need for state-supported schools.

Watch the **Video** at **www.myhistorylab.com** *Who was Horace Mann and why are so many schools named after him?*

In 1837, the Massachusetts legislature established the nation's first state board of education. The head of the board for the next twelve years was Horace Mann, a former Whig politician and temperance advocate who now tirelessly championed educational reform. Mann demanded that the state government assume centralized control over Massachusetts schools.

Democrats in the Massachusetts legislature denounced Mann's program as "a system of centralization and of monopoly of power in a few hands, contrary in every respect, to the true spirit of our democratical institutions." The laboring poor, who depended for economic survival on the wages their children could earn, resisted compulsory-attendance laws and a longer school year. Farmers fought to maintain local control over schooling and to block the higher taxes needed for a more comprehensive and professionalized system. The Catholic Church protested the thinly veiled attempts of the reformers to indoctrinate all students in the moral strictures of middle-class Protestantism. Catholics began, at great expense, to build their own parochial schools.

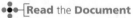

Read the **Document** at **www.myhistorylab.com** *Horace Mann on Education and National Welfare*

Mann and his allies nonetheless prevailed in most of the industrializing states, with strong support from the professional and business constituencies of the Whig Party. Manufacturers hoped that the schools would turn out a more obedient and punctual labor force, and the more skilled and prosperous workers saw in public education a key to upward mobility for their children. Most important for its political success, school reform appealed to the growing northern middle class. Schools would instill the moral and economic discipline that the middle class deemed essential for a progressive and ordered society.

Out of the northern middle class also came the young female teachers who increasingly staffed elementary schools. Presumed by their nature to be more nurturing than men, women now had an entry into teaching, the first profession open to them. Besides, women could also be paid far less than men; school boards assumed that they would accept low wages while waiting to be married.

Just over 50 percent of the white children between 5 and 19 years of age in the United States were enrolled in school in 1850, the highest percentage in the world at the time. Working-class parents pulled their children out of school at an earlier age than higher-income middle-class parents. Planters continued to rely on private tutors or academies, and southern farmers saw little need for public education. The slave states, especially in the Lower South, lagged behind the rest of the nation in public education.

Prisons, Workhouses, and Asylums

Up to this time, Americans had depended on voluntary efforts to cope with crime, poverty, and social deviance. Convinced that these efforts were inadequate, reformers turned to public authorities to establish a host of new institutions to deal with social problems.

The reformers held that people's environments shaped their character for good or evil. The Boston Children's Friend Society was devoted to the young, "whose plastic natures may be molded into images of perfect beauty, or . . . perfect repulsiveness." Samuel Gridley Howe, a prison reformer, proclaimed: "Thousands of convicts are made so in consequence of a faulty organization of society. . . ." In the properly ordered environment of new institutions, discipline and moral character would be instilled in criminals and other deviants who lacked the self-control to resist the society's corrupting vices and temptations.

Reformers had particularly high expectations for the penitentiary systems pioneered in Pennsylvania and New York in the 1820s. Unlike earlier prisons, the penitentiaries were huge, imposing structures that isolated the prisoners from each other and the outside world. No longer were criminals to be brutally punished or thrown together under inhumane conditions that perpetuated a cycle of moral depravity. Cut off from all corrupting influences, forced to learn that hard work teaches moral discipline, and uplifted by religious literature, criminals would be guided toward becoming law-abiding, productive citizens.

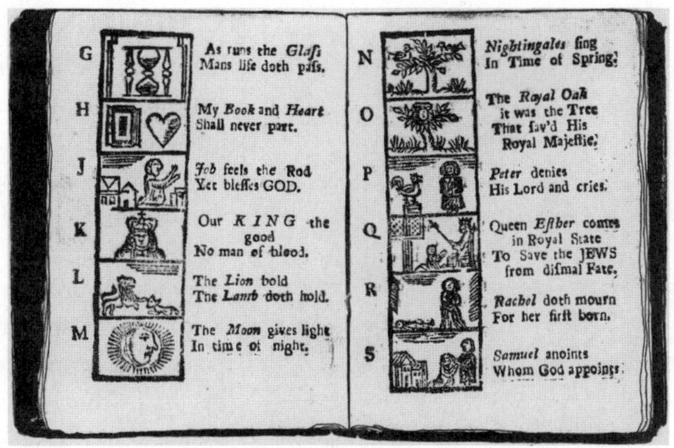
G As runs the *Glaſs* Mans life doth paſs.
H My *Book* and *Heart* Shall never part.
J *Job* feels the Rod Yet bleſſes GOD.
K Our *KING* the good No man of blood.
L The *Lion* bold The *Lamb* doth hold.
M The *Moon* gives light In time of night.
N *Nightingales* ſing In Time of Spring.
O The *Royal Oak* it was the Tree That ſav'd His Royal Majeſtie.
P *Peter* denies His Lord and cries.
Q Queen *Eſther* comes in Royal State To Save the JEWS from diſmal Fate.
R *Rachel* doth mourn For her firſt born.
S *Samuel* anoints Whom God appoints.

Moral lessons, such as this one for boys at play, filled the pages of the McGuffey's readers.

Library of Congress

Workhouses. The same philosophy of reform provided the rationale for asylums to house the poor and the insane. The number of transient poor and the size of urban slums increased as commercial capitalism uprooted farmers from the land and undercut the security of craft trades. Believing that the poor, much like criminals, had only themselves to blame, public officials and their evangelical allies prescribed a therapeutic regimen of discipline and physical labor to cure the poor of their moral defects. The structured setting for the regimen was the workhouse.

The custodians of the workhouses banished drinking, gambling, and idleness. Their prime responsibility was to supervise the inmates in a tightly scheduled daily routine built around manual labor. Once purged of their laziness and filled with self-esteem as the result of work discipline, the poor would be released to become useful members of society.

Asylums for the mentally ill. Public insane asylums offered a similar order for the mentally ill. Reformers believed that too many choices in a highly mobile, materialistic, and competitive society drove some people insane. Following the lead of New York and Massachusetts in the 1830s, 28 states had established mental hospitals by 1860. These facilities set rigid rules and work assignments to teach patients how to order their lives.

In the early 1840s Dorothea Dix, a Massachusetts schoolteacher, discovered that the insane in her home state were dumped into jails and almshouses, where they suffered filthy, inhumane treatment. Horrified, Dix lobbied state legislatures across the nation for the next twenty years to improve treatment for the mentally ill.

While the reformers did provide social deviants with cleaner, safer living conditions, their penitentiaries and asylums succeeded more in classifying and segregating inmates than in reforming them. Submission to routine turned out not to be the best builder of character. Penitentiaries, reformatories, and workhouses failed to eliminate or noticeably check poverty, crime, and vice. Refusing to question their basic premise that repressive institutions could promote individual responsibility, reformers abandoned their environmental explanations for deviance. By midcentury, they were defining deviants and dependents as permanent misfits with ingrained character defects. The asylums remained; but, stripped of their earlier optimism, they became little more than holding pens for the outcasts of society.

In the concern etched in her face, this photograph captures the compassion that Dorothea Dix brought to her crusade for mental health reform.

Utopian Alternatives

Unlike the reformers, who aimed to improve the existing order by guiding individuals to greater self-discipline, the utopians sought perfection by withdrawing from society and its confining institutions. A radically new social order, not an improved old one, was their goal.

Though following different religious and secular philosophies of communitarian living, all the utopians wanted to fashion a more rational and personally satisfying alternative to the competitive materialism of antebellum America. Nearly all the communities sought to transform the organization and rewards of work, thus challenging the prevailing dogmas about private property.

The most successful utopian communities were religious sects whose reordering of both sexual and economic relations departed sharply from middle-class norms. The **Shakers,** at their height in the 1830s, attracted some 6,000 followers. Organized around doctrines of celibate **communism,** Shaker communities held all property in common. The sexes worked and lived apart from each other. Dancing during religious worship brought men and women together and provided an emotional release from enforced sexual denial. In worldly as well as spiritual terms, women enjoyed an equality in Shaker life that the outside world denied them. For this reason, twice as many women as men joined the Shakers.

Shakers The followers of Mother Ann Lee, who preached a religion of strict celibacy and communal living.

communism A social structure based on the common ownership of property.

John Humphrey Noyes, a graduate of Dartmouth who studied for the ministry at Yale, established the **Oneida Community** in upstate New York in 1847. He attracted over 200 followers with his perfectionist vision of plural marriage, community nurseries, group discipline, and common ownership of property. Charged with adultery, Noyes fled to Canada in 1879, but the Oneida Community, reorganized in 1881 as a joint-stock company in the United States and committed thereafter to conventional sexual mores, survived into the twentieth century.

Oneida Community Utopian community established in upstate New York in 1848 by John Humphrey Noyes and his followers.

Secular utopians aspired to perfect social relations through rationally designed planned communities. Bitter critics of the social evils of industrialization, they tried to construct models for a social order free from poverty, unemployment, and inequality. They envisioned cooperative communities that balanced agricultural and industrial pursuits in a mixed economy that recycled earnings to the laborers who actually produced the wealth.

New Harmony Short-lived utopian community established in Indiana in 1825, based on the socialist ideas of Robert Owen, a wealthy Scottish manufacturer.

socialism A social order based on government ownership of industry and worker control over corporations as a way to prevent worker exploitation.

Despite their high expectations, nearly all the planned communities ran into financial difficulties and soon collapsed. The pattern was set by the first of the controversial socialist experiments, **New Harmony** in Indiana, the brainchild of the wealthy Scottish industrialist and philanthropist Robert Owen. A proponent of utopian **socialism,** Owen promised to create a new order where "the degrading and pernicious practices in which we are now well trained, of buying cheap and selling dear, will be rendered unnecessary" and "union and co-operation will supersede individual interest." But within two years of its founding in 1825, New Harmony fell victim to inadequate financing and internal bickering.

Brook Farm A utopian community and experimental farm established in 1841 near Boston.

transcendentalism A philosophical and literary movement centered on an idealistic belief in the divinity of individuals and nature.

About the only secular cooperative that gained lasting fame was **Brook Farm** in West Roxbury, Massachusetts (today part of Boston). Established in 1841, Brook Farm was a showcase for the transcendentalist philosophy of Ralph Waldo Emerson. A former Unitarian minister in Boston, Emerson taught that intuition and emotion could grasp a truer ("transcendent") reality than could the senses alone. Although disbanded after six years as an economic failure, Brook Farm inspired intellectuals such as Nathaniel Hawthorne, who briefly lived there. In turn, his writings and those of other writers influenced by **transcendentalism** flowed into the great renaissance of American literature in the mid-nineteenth century, an outpouring of work that grappled with Emersonian themes of individualism and the reshaping of the American character.

W
WHERE TO LEARN MORE
Historic New Harmony,
New Harmony, Indiana
http://www.usi.edu/hnh/index2.asp

Read the Document
at **www.myhistorylab.com**
Nathaniel Hawthorne, A Letter from Brook Farm (1841)

A distinctly national literature. In an 1837 address at Harvard titled "The American Scholar," Emerson called for a distinctly national literature devoted to the democratic possibilities of American life. Writers soon responded to Emerson's call.

Walt Whitman, whose *Leaves of Grass* (1855) foreshadowed modern poetry in its use of free verse, shared Emerson's faith in the possibilities of individual fulfillment, and his poems celebrated the democratic variety of the American people. Henry David Thoreau, Emerson's friend and neighbor, embodied the transcendentalist fascination with nature and self-discovery by living in relative isolation for 16 months at Walden Pond, near Concord, Massachusetts. His *Walden; or, Life in the Woods* (1854) became an American classic. Nathaniel Hawthorne and Herman Melville, the greatest novelists of the American renaissance, focused on the existence of evil and the human need for community.

Much of the appeal of the utopian communities flowed from the same concern about the splintering and selfishness of antebellum society that animated Hawthorne and Melville. The works of these novelists have endured, but the utopian experiments quickly collapsed. Promising economic security and social harmony to buttress a threatened sense of community, the utopians failed to lure all but a few Americans from the acquisitiveness and competitive demands of the larger society.

ABOLITIONISM AND WOMEN'S RIGHTS

WHAT WAS the relationship between abolitionism and the women's rights movement?

Abolitionism emerged from the same religious impulse that energized reform throughout the North. Like other reformers, the abolitionists came predominantly from evangelical, middle-class families, particularly those of New England stock. What distinguished the abolitionists was their insistence that slavery was *the* great national sin, an evil that mocked American ideals of liberty and Christian morality.

Read the **Document** at **www.myhistorylab.com** *National Convention of Colored People, Report on Abolition (1847)*

Rejecting Colonization

In the early nineteenth century, when slavery was expanding westward, almost all white Americans regardless of class or region were convinced that emancipation would lead either to a race war or the debasement of their superior status through racial interbreeding. This paralyzing fear of general emancipation, rooted in pervasive racism, long shielded slavery from sustained attack.

In 1817, antislavery reformers from the North and the South founded the **American Colonization Society.** Slaveholding politicians from the Upper South, notably Henry Clay, James Madison, and President James Monroe, were the leading organizers of the society. Gradual emancipation accompanied by the removal of black people from America to Africa was the only solution these white reformers could imagine for ridding the nation of slavery and avoiding a racial bloodbath. Their goal was to make America all free *and* all white.

American Colonization Society Organization, founded in 1817 by antislavery reformers, that called for gradual emancipation and the removal of freed blacks to Africa.

The American Colonization Society had no real chance of success. No form of emancipation, no matter how gradual, could appeal to slaveowners who could profit from the labor of their slaves. Moreover, the society could never afford to purchase the freedom of any significant number of slaves.

Free African Americans bitterly attacked the colonizers' central assumption that free black people were unfit to live as citizens in America. They were native-born and considered themselves Americans with every right to enjoy the blessings of republican liberty. Organizing through their own churches in northern cities, free African Americans founded some fifty abolitionist societies, offered refuge to fugitive slaves, and launched the first African American newspaper in 1827, *Freedom's Journal.* David Walker, a free black man who had moved from North Carolina to Massachusetts, published his *Appeal to the Colored Citizens of the World* in 1829. In a searing indictment of white greed and hypocrisy, he rejected colonization and insisted that "America is more our country, than it is the whites', we have enriched it with our *blood and tears*." He warned white America that "wo, wo, will be to you if we have to obtain our freedom by fighting."

As if in response to this call for revolutionary resistance by the enslaved, Nat Turner's Rebellion exploded in the summer of 1831 (see Chapter 11). Both alarmed and inspired by the increased tempo of black militancy, a small group of antislavery white people abandoned all illusions about colonization and embarked on a radically new approach for eradicating slavery.

OVERVIEW Types of Antislavery Reform

Type	Definition	Example
Gradualist	Accepts notions of black inferiority and attempts to end slavery gradually by purchasing the freedom of slaves and colonizing them in Africa	American Colonization Society
Immediatist	Calls for immediate steps to end slavery and denounces slavery and racial prejudice as moral sins	Abolitionists
Political antislavery	Recognizes slavery in states where it exists but insists on keeping slavery out of the territories	Free-Soilers

ABOLITIONISM

William Lloyd Garrison, a Massachusetts printer and the leading figure in early abolitionism, became coeditor of an antislavery newspaper in Baltimore in 1829. Before the year was out, Garrison was arrested and convicted of criminal libel for his editorials against a Massachusetts merchant engaged in the domestic slave trade, and he spent seven weeks in jail before a New York City philanthropist paid his $100 fine. Recognizing that his lack of freedom in jail paled against that of the slave, Garrison emerged with an unquenchable hatred of slavery. Returning to Boston, he launched his antislavery newspaper, the *Liberator,* in 1831. A year later, he was instrumental in founding the New England Anti-Slavery Society.

Hear the **Audio** at **www.myhistorylab.com** *The Liberator*

As militant as the free African Americans who comprised the bulk of the early subscribers to the *Liberator,* Garrison thundered, "If we would not see our land deluged in blood, we must instantly burst asunder the shackles of the slaves." He committed abolitionism to the twin goals of immediatism, an immediate moral commitment to end slavery, and racial equality. Only by striving toward these goals, he insisted, could white America ever hope to end slavery without massive violence.

The abolitionists' demand for the legal equality of black people was as unsettling to public opinion as their call for immediate, uncompensated emancipation. Denied the vote outside New England, segregated in all public facilities, prohibited from moving into several western states, and excluded from most jobs save menial labor, free black people everywhere were walled off as an inferior caste.

Garrison, harsh and uncompromising in denouncing slavery and advocating black rights, instilled the antislavery movement with moral urgency. But without the organizational and financial resources of a national society, the message of the early Garrisonians rarely extended beyond free black communities in the North. The success of British abolitionists in 1833, when gradual, compensated emancipation was enacted for Britain's West Indian colonies, inspired white and black abolitionists to gather at Philadelphia in December 1833 and form the **American Anti-Slavery Society.**

American Anti-Slavery Society The first national organization of abolitionists, founded in 1833.

The abolitionists spread their message through revivals, rallies, paid lecturers, children's games and toys, and the printed word. Drawing on the experience of reformers in Bible and tract societies, the abolitionists harnessed steam power to the cause of moral suasion. They distributed millions of antislavery tracts, and by the late 1830s, abolitionist sayings appeared on posters, emblems, song sheets, and even candy wrappers.

Women were essential in all of these activities. From the very beginning of the movement, they established their own antislavery societies as auxiliaries to the national organizations run and dominated by men. Initially, their role was limited to raising funds, circulating petitions, and visiting homes to gain converts. Often operating out of local churches, women were grass-roots organizers of a massive petition campaign launched in the mid-1830s. Women signed more than half of the antislavery memorials sent to Congress.

The abolitionists focused their energies on mass propaganda because they saw their role as social agitators who had to break through white apathy and change public opinion. By 1840 they had succeeded in enlisting nearly 200,000 northerners in 2,000 local affiliates of the American Anti-Slavery Society. Most whites, however, remained unmoved, and some violently opposed the abolitionists.

Antiabolitionist mobs in the North went on a rampage in the mid-1830s (see Figure 12–3). They disrupted antislavery meetings, beat and stoned speakers, destroyed printing presses, burned the homes of the wealthy benefactors of the movement, and vandalized free black neighborhoods in a wave of terror that drove many black people from several northern cities. Local elites, especially those with profitable ties to the slave economy of the South, often incited the mobs, whose fury expressed the anxiety of semiskilled and common laborers that they might lose their jobs if freed slaves moved north.

FIGURE 12–3 **Mob Violence and the Abolitionists** Civil disturbances resulting in attacks on individuals or property increased sharply in the 1830s. The abolitionist campaign to flood the country with antislavery literature triggered much of this surge. Nearly half of the mob activity in the 1830s was directed against abolitionists.

Data Source: Leonard L. Richards, *"Gentlemen of Property and Standing." Anti-Abolitionist Mobs in Jacksonian America* (1970).

In the South, the hostility to abolitionism took the form of burning and censoring antislavery literature, offering rewards for the capture of leading abolitionists to stand trial for allegedly inciting slave revolts, and tightening up slave codes and the surveillance of free black people. Meanwhile, Democrats in Congress yielded to slaveholding interests in 1836 by passing a gag rule that automatically tabled antislavery petitions with no debate.

The hostility and violence abolitionism provoked convinced Garrison and some of his followers that U.S. institutions and values were fundamentally flawed. In 1838, Garrison helped found the New England Non-Resistant Society, dedicated to the belief that a complete moral regeneration, based on renouncing force in all human relationships, was necessary if the United States were ever to live up to its Christian and republican ideals. The Garrisonian nonresistants rejected all coercive authority, whether expressed in capital punishment, human bondage, clerical support of slavery, male dominance in the patriarchal family, the racial oppression of back people, or the police power of government. The logic of their stand as Christian **anarchists** drove them to denounce all formal political activities and even the legitimacy of the Union, based as it was on a pact with slaveholders.

anarchists A person who believes that all government interferes with individual liberty and should be abolished by whatever means.

Garrison's opponents within the abolitionist movement accused him of alienating the public by identifying the antislavery cause with radical attacks on traditional authority. His support for the growing demand of antislavery women to be treated as equals in the movement brought the factional bickering to a head and split the American Anti-Slavery Society. In turn, the opposition of most male abolitionists to the public activities of their female counterparts provoked a militant faction of these women into founding their own movement to achieve equality in U.S. society.

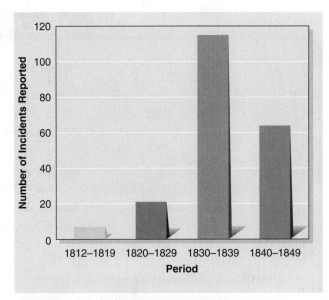

THE WOMEN'S RIGHTS MOVEMENT

Feminism grew out of abolitionism because of the parallels many women drew between the exploited lives of the slaves and their own subordinate status in northern society. "In striving to cut [the slave's] irons off, we found most surely that we were manacled *ourselves*," argued Abby Kelley, a Quaker abolitionist.

Read the **Document** at **www.myhistorylab.com** *Exploring America: Angelina Grimké*

In 1837, Angelina and Sarah Grimké, the South Carolina–born abolitionists, attracted large crowds of men and women to their antislavery lectures in New England. By publicly lecturing to a "promiscuous" (mixed) audience of men and women, they defied restrictions on women's proper role and enraged the Congregational clergy of Massachusetts. Harshly criticized

AMERICAN VIEWS

Appeal of a Female Abolitionist

Lydia Maria Child's Appeal, published in Boston in 1833, was a landmark in abolitionist literature for both the thoroughness of its attack on slavery and its refutation of racist ideology and discrimination. This condemnation of racial prejudice was the most radical feature of abolitionist ideology. It directly challenged the deeply held beliefs and assumptions of nearly all white Americans, in the North as well as the South. Racism and slavery, as Child shows in this excerpt from her Appeal, fed off one another in the national curse of slavery.

- **How** does Child argue that northern white people must bear some of the responsibility for perpetuating slavery?
- **What** arguments does Child make against racial discrimination in northern society?
- **What** did Child mean when she wrote that "the Americans are peculiarly responsible for the example they give"? Do you agree with her?
- **How** does Child deal with the charge that the abolitionists threatened the preservation of the Union?

While we bestow our earnest disapprobation on the system of slavery, let us not flatter ourselves that we are in reality any better than our brethren of the South. Thanks to our soil and climate, and the early exhortions of the Quakers, the form of slavery does not exist among us; but the very spirit of the hateful and mischievous thing is here in all its strength. . . . Our prejudice against colored people is even more inveterate than it is at the South. The planter is often attached to his negroes, and lavishes caresses and kind words upon them, as he would on a favorite hound: but our cold-hearted, ignoble prejudice admits of no exception, no intermission.

The Southerners have long continued habit, apparent interest and dreaded danger, to palliate the wrong they do; but we stand without excuse. . . . If the free States wished to cherish the system of slavery forever, they could not take a more direct course than they now do. Those who are kind and liberal on all other subjects, unite with the selfish and the proud in their unrelenting efforts to keep the colored population in the lowest state of degradation; and the influence they unconsciously exert over children early infuses into their innocent minds the same strong feelings of contempt. . . .

The state of public feeling not only makes it difficult for the Africans to obtain information, but it prevents them from making profitable use of what knowledge they have. A colored man, however intelligent, is not allowed to pursue any business more lucrative than that of a barber, a shoeblack, or waiter. These, and all other employments, are truly respectable, whenever the duties connected with them are faithfully performed; but it is unjust that a man should, on account of his complexion, be prevented from performing more elevated uses in society. Every citizen ought to have a fair chance to try his fortune in any line of business, which he thinks he has ability to transact. Why should not colored men be employed in the manufactories of various kinds? If their ignorance is an objection, let them be enlightened, as speedily as possible. If their moral character is not sufficiently pure, remove the pressure of public scorn, and thus supply them with motives for being respectable. All this can be done. It merely requires an earnest wish to overcome a prejudice, which . . . is in fact opposed to the spirit of our religion, and contrary to the instinctive good feelings of our nature. . . . When the majority heartily desire a change, it is effected, be the difficulties what they may. The Americans are peculiarly responsible for the example they give; for in no other country does the unchecked voice of the people constitute the whole of government. . . .

The strongest and best reason that can be given for our supineness on the subject of slavery, is the fear of dissolving the Union. The Constitution of the United States demands our highest reverence. . . . But we must not forget that the Constitution provides for any change that may be required for the general good. The great machine is constructed with a safety valve, by which any rapidly increasing evil may be expelled whenever the people desire it.

If the Southern politicians are determined to make a Siamese question of this also, if they insist that the Union shall not exist without slavery, it can only be said that they join two things, which have no affinity with each other, and which cannot permanently exist together. They chain the living and vigorous to the diseased and dying; and the former will assuredly perish in the infected neighborhood.

The universal introduction of free labor is the surest way to consolidate the Union, and enable us to live together in harmony and peace. If a history is ever written entitled "The Decay and Dissolution of the North American Republic," its author will distinctly trace our downfall to the existence of slavery among us.

Source: Lydia Maria Child, *An Appeal in Favor of That Class of Americans Called Africans* (originally published 1833), ed. Carolyn L. Karcher (University of Massachusetts Press, 1996).

for their unwomanly behavior, the Grimkés publicly responded with an indictment of the male patriarchy and the shocking assertion that "men and women are *created equal!* They are both moral and accountable beings and whatever is right for man to do is right for woman."

Now more sensitive than ever to the injustice of their assigned role as men's submissive followers, antislavery women demanded an equal voice in the abolitionist movement. Despite strong opposition from many of his fellow male abolitionists, Garrison helped Abby Kelley win a seat on the business committee of the American Anti-Slavery Society at its convention in 1840. The anti-Garrisonians walked out of the convention and formed a separate organization, the American and Foreign Anti-Slavery Society.

Hear the Audio at **www.myhistorylab.com** *What If I Am a Woman; speech by Maria W. Stewart; read by Ruby Dee*

WHERE TO LEARN MORE
W
Women's Rights Historical Park,
Seneca Falls, New York
http://www.nps.gov/wori/index.htm

What was rapidly becoming known as the "woman question" also disrupted the 1840 World Anti-Slavery Convention in London. The refusal of the convention to seat the U.S. female delegates was the final indignity that transformed the discontent of women into a self-conscious movement for women's equality. Two of the excluded delegates, Lucretia Mott and Elizabeth Cady Stanton, vowed to build an organization to "speak out for *oppressed* women."

Their work went slowly. Early feminists were dependent on the abolitionists for most of their followers, and they were unable to do more than hold local meetings and sponsor occasional speaking tours. In 1848, Stanton and Mott were finally able to call the first national convention ever devoted to women's rights at Seneca Falls, in upstate New York. The **Seneca Falls Convention** issued the **Declaration of Sentiments,** a call for full female equality. Modeled directly on the Declaration of Independence, it identified male patriarchy as the source of women's oppression and demanded the vote for women as a sacred and inalienable right of republican citizenship. This call for suffrage raised the prospect of women's self-determination as independent citizens. The Seneca Falls agenda defined the goals of the women's movement for the rest of the century. The feminists' few successes before the Civil War came in economic rights. By 1860, 14 states had granted women greater control over their property and wages.

Seneca Falls Convention The first convention for women's equality in legal rights, held in upstate New York in 1848.

Declaration of Sentiments The resolutions passed at the Seneca Falls Convention of 1848 calling for full female equality, including the right to vote.

Despite such successes, the feminist movement did not attract broad support. Most women found in the doctrine of separate spheres a reassuring feminine identity that they could express either at home or in benevolent and reform societies. Within the reform movement as a whole, women's rights were always a minor concern. Abolitionists focused on emancipation.

Watch the Video at **www.myhistorylab.com** *The Women's Rights Movement in Nineteenth-Century America*

POLITICAL ANTISLAVERY

Most of the abolitionists who had broken with Garrison in 1840 believed that emancipation could best be achieved by moving abolitionism into the mainstream of U.S. politics. Political abolitionism had its roots in the petition campaign of the late 1830s. Congressional efforts to suppress the discussion of slavery backfired when John Quincy Adams, the former president who had become a Massachusetts congressman, resorted to an unending series of parliamentary ploys to get around the gag rule (see Chapter 10). Adams became a champion of the constitutional right to petition Congress for redress of grievances. White northerners who had shown no interest in abolitionism as a moral crusade for black people now began to take a stand against slavery when the issue involved the civil liberties of whites and the dominant political power of the South. The hundreds of thousands, they signed abolitionist petitions in 1837 and 1838 to protest the gag rule and the admission of Texas as a slave state.

In 1840, anti-Garrisonian abolitionists tried to turn this new antislavery constituency into an independent political party, the **Liberty Party.** The Liberty Party opposed any expansion of slavery in the territories, condemned racial discrimination in the North as well as slavery in the South, and won the support of most black abolitionists. "To it," recalled Samuel Ward of New York, "I devoted my political activities; with it I lived my political life." In 1843, a national African American convention in Buffalo endorsed the Liberty Party.

Liberty Party The first antislavery political party, formed in 1840.

This political activism was part of a concerted effort by African Americans to assert leadership in an antislavery movement that rarely treated them as equals. Frederick Douglass was

GLOBAL CONNECTIONS

THE INTERNATIONAL DIMENSIONS OF ABOLITION

"The trumpet has sounded through all the colonial dependencies of our country, which proclaims 'liberty to the captives.' O! what heart is there so cold, so seared, so dead, as to feel no thrill of exulting emotion at the thought, that on the morning of this day, eight hundred thousand fellow-men and fellow-subjects, who, during the past night, slept bondmen, awoke freemen! [British emancipation will be] but the first day of a Jubilee year,—of a period of successive triumphs . . . of continuous and rapidly progressive prosperity, to the cause of freedom. [Once America joins Britain in the work of emancipation] the world will be shamed into imitation:—and in no long period, there will not be found on earth a remnant of it."

On August 1, 1834, the day that the British Emancipation Act of 1833 took effect, the Reverend Ralph Wardlaw of Glasgow, Scotland, spoke these words of millennial joy and hope for the future. It was a day of exultation for reformers on both sides of the Atlantic. The spark of freedom was first struck in Britain by the creation in 1787 of the Quaker-inspired Society for the Abolition of the Slave Trade. It exploded into a revolutionary conflagration when the slaves in Saint-Domingue rose up in rebellion in 1791 and unleashed the greatest slave revolt in the Western Hemisphere. By 1808, reformers in Britain and the United States had prohibited the African slave trade. When the Spanish Empire in Latin America began to break up after 1810, the independence movements in Spain's former colonies committed themselves to emancipation. In a startling reversal from the situation in 1800, only Brazil and Cuba remained as major slave areas in Latin America by the 1820s. Then, as the result of a massive grassroots campaign that inundated Parliament with 5,000 petitions and half a million signers, Britain passed the Emancipation Act of 1833, which emancipated the slaves in its colonies as of August 1, 1834.

British emancipation buoyed the abolitionist cause in the United States and was a major factor in emboldening the abolitionists to organize a national society in 1833. It also convinced them, as the Reverend Wardlaw had argued, that Protestant Christianity was poised to take the lead in an epic struggle for human betterment. That was the vision that inspired the abolitionists as they set out to redeem America's revolutionary heritage by cleansing the nation of slavery.

- How does placing the American antislavery movement in a transatlantic context broaden our understanding of the antislavery cause and its place in the intellectual history of the nineteenth century?

their most dynamic spokesman. Increasingly dissatisfied with Garrison's Christian pacifism and his stand against political action, Douglass broke with Garrison in 1847 and founded a black abolitionist newspaper, the *North Star*. The break became irreparable in 1851 when Douglass publicly denied the Garrisonian position that the Constitution was a proslavery document. If properly interpreted, Douglass insisted, "the Constitution is a *glorious liberty document*," and he called for a political war against slavery.

Hear the **Audio** at **www.myhistorylab.com**
If There is No Struggle, There is No Progress; excerpt from speech by Frederick Douglass; read by Ossie Davis

Led by Joshua R. Giddings, a small but vocal bloc of antislavery politicians began to popularize the frightening concept of "the Slave Power," a vast conspiracy of planters and their northern lackeys that controlled the federal government and was plotting to spread slavery and subvert any free institutions that opposed it. As proof, they cited the gag rule, which had shut off debate on slavery, and the campaign of the Tyler administration to annex slaveholding Texas.

The specter of the Slave Power made white liberties, and not black bondage, central to northern concerns about slavery. This shift redefined the evil of slavery to appeal to the self-interest of white northerners who had rejected the moral appeals of the Garrisonians. White people who had earlier been apathetic now began to view slavery as a threat to their rights of free speech and self-improvement.

The image of the Slave Power predisposed many northerners to see the expansionist program of the incoming Polk administration as part of a southern plot to secure more territory for slaveholders at the expense of northern farmers. Northern fears that free labor would be shut out of the new territories won in the Mexican War provided the rallying cry for the Free-Soil Party of 1848, which foreshadowed the more powerful Republican Party of the late 1850s.

Shown here are seven leaders of the founding generation of American feminists. Clockwise from the top: Lucretia Mott, Elizabeth Cady Stanton, Mary A. Livermore, Lydia Maria Child, Susan B. Anthony, and Grace Greenwood. In the center is Anna E. Dickinson.

CONCLUSION

With surprising speed after 1815, transportation improvements, technological innovations, and expanding markets drove the economy toward industrialization. Wealth inequality increased, old classes were reshaped, and new ones formed. These changes were most evident in the Northeast, where capital, labor, and growing urban markets spurred the acceleration of manufacturing. The reform impulse that both reflected and shaped these changes was also strongest in the Northeast. The new evangelical Protestantism promised that human perfectibility was possible if individuals strove to free themselves from sin. Influenced by this promise, the northern middle class embraced reform causes that sought to improve human character. Temperance changed U.S. drinking habits and established sobriety as the cultural standard for respectable male behavior. Middle-class reform also emphasized institutional solutions for what were now defined as the social problems of ignorance, crime, and poverty.

The most radical of the reform movements focused on women's equality and the elimination of slavery. The women's rights movement emerged out of women's involvement in reform, especially in abolitionism. Feminism and abolitionism triggered a backlash from the more conservative majority, a response that strengthened the resolve of reformers such as Angelina Grimké. This backlash prevented women from gaining legal and political equality, the major demand of the feminists, and convinced most abolitionists that they had to switch from moral agitation to political persuasion. The political abolitionists soon found that the most effective approach in widening the antislavery appeal was their charge that a Slave Power conspiracy threatened the freedoms of white northerners.

Where to Learn More

Lowell National Historical Park. The park is a wonderful resource for visualizing the early stages of America's industrial revolution. *For hours and a schedule of events, see http://www.nps*.gov/lowe/index.htm.

Slater Hill Historic Site, Pawtucket, Rhode Island. The Sylvanus Brown House of 1758, the Slaren Mill of 1793, and the Wilkinson Mill of 1810 are on the site. An extensive library and holdings provide insight into the social and economic world of the early industrial revolution. Information on hours, collections, and exhibits can be found at http://www.slatermill.org/museum/about.

Erie Canal Museum, Syracuse, New York. The museum houses extensive collections on the building and maintenance of the Erie Canal, and its photo holdings visually record much of the history of the canal. In addition to information on exhibits, tours, *and school programs, its website, http://www.eriecanalmuseum*. org, includes pictures of a replica of an Erie Canal line boat.

Historic New Harmony, New Harmony, Indiana. The tours and museum holdings at this preserved site offer a glimpse into the communal living that Robert Owen tried to promote in his utopian plan. For a brief history of New Harmony and links to special events and programs at the site, go to http://www.usi.edu/hnh/index2.asp.

Women's Rights Historical Park, Seneca Falls, New York. The park provides an interpretive overview of the first women's rights convention and includes among its historical sites the restored home of Elizabeth Cady Stanton. Go to http://www.nps.gov/wori/index.htm for links to the museum's summer calendar of events and information on programs.

Review Questions

1. Why were improvements in transportation so essential to the growth of the economy after 1815? What were the nature and scope of these improvements?
2. What is an industrial revolution? How can we explain the surge in manufacturing in the United States from 1815 to 1850?
3. What was the religious impulse behind the first wave of reform? What innovations in reaching a mass audience did the benevolent reformers pioneer?
4. What drew women into reform? Why did many of them feel a special affinity for abolitionism?
5. Why was abolitionism the most radical reform of all? How was it linked to an international movement calling for the end of slavery?
6. Why do you think so few southern women of the plantation class followed Angelina Grimké on her journey from social privilege to social activism?

Key Terms

American Anti-Slavery Society (p. 326)
American Colonization Society (p. 325)
American Female Moral Reform Society (p. 320)
American system of manufacturing (p. 314)
American Temperance Society (p. 319)
Anarchists (p. 327)
Benevolent empire (p. 318)
Brook Farm (p. 324)
Charles River Bridge v. Warren Bridge (p. 308)
Church of Jesus Christ of Latter-Day Saints (Mormon Church) (p. 321)
Communism (p. 324)
Cult of domesticity (p. 316)
Declaration of Sentiments (p. 329)
Gibbons v. Ogden (p. 308)
Liberty Party (p. 329)
Nativist (p. 317)
New Harmony (p. 324)
Oneida Community (p. 324)
Putting-out system (p. 312)
Rhode Island system (p. 313)
Sabbatarian movement (p. 318)
Seneca Falls Convention (p. 329)
Shakers (p. 324)
Socialism (p. 324)
Temperance (p. 316)
Transcendentalism (p. 324)
Transportation revolution (p. 306)
Waltham system (p. 313)
Workingmen's Movement (p. 322)

myhistorylab Connections

Reinforce what you learned in this chapter by studying the many documents, images, maps, review tools, and videos available at **www.myhistorylab.com**.

Read and Review

Study and Review **Study Plan: Chapter 12**

Read the Document

Horace Mann on Education and National Welfare

National Convention of Colored People, Report on Abolition (1847)

The Harbinger, Female Workers of Lowell (1836)

Catharine Esther Beecher, American Woman's Home (1869)

Nathaniel Hawthorne, A Letter from Brook Farm (1841)

John Humphrey Noyes and Bible Communism (1845 and 1849)

Lyman Beecher, "Six Sermons on Intemperance" (1828)

See the Map

Expanding America and Internal Improvements

Utopian Communities before the Civil War

Research and Explore

Read the Document

Personal Journeys Online

From Then to Now Online: Immigration: An Ambivalent Welcome

Exploring America: Angelina Grimké

Hear the Audio

If There is No Struggle, There is No Progress; excerpt from speech by Frederick Douglass; read by Ossie Davis

The Erie Canal

The Liberator

What if I am a Woman; speech by Maria W. Stewart; read by Ruby Dee

Watch the Video

Drinking and the Temperance Movement in Nineteenth-Century America

The Women's Rights Movement in Nineteenth-Century America

Who Was Horace Mann and Why Are So Many Schools Named after Him?

Hear the Audio

Hear the audio files for Chapter 12 at **www.myhistorylab.com**.

INTERPRETING the PAST

The Second Great Awakening and Religious Diversity in America

The Second Great Awakening (1800–1830s) led to the creation of many new religious affiliations within the American religious community and an increased diversity within American religious life. What were the similarities and differences among some of these new denominations? How did this growing diversity impact American society?

One of the reasons that separation of church and state has worked so well in the United States is the wide diversity of religious affiliations within the American population. From the beginning of English colonial efforts to the time of the American Revolution this happy scenario was not necessarily present. In the northern colonies the Congregationalist Church was the established state religion among Puritan settlers. In the middle and southern colonies the Anglican Church or Church of England was the established church.

Religious diversity was slow in growing in the early years of the American colonies and nation. The First Great Awakening of the 1730s and 1740s strengthened the Presbyterian, Baptist, and Methodist churches in their quest to win over the followers of the Congregationalist and Anglican churches and create diversity in the camp of American religions. The Second Great Awakening of the 1800s through the 1830s created even greater diversity.

They are ancient men, men of another age . . .

Charles Grandison Finney was the quintessential revival preacher of the Second Great Awakening. Finney emphasized revivals and evangelism; he empowered women in the church, preached against slavery, and believed in salvation by faith rather than good works. He is credited with bringing hundreds of thousands of individuals to the Christian faith.

Charles Grandison Finney, Lectures on the Revival of Religion, 1835

I would say nothing to undervalue, or lead you to undervalue a thorough education for ministers. But I do not call that a thorough education, which they get in our colleges and seminaries. It does not fit them for their work. . . . Those fathers who have the training of our young ministers are good men, but they are ancient men, men of another age and different stamp from what is needed in these days of excitement, when the church and world are rising to new thought and action. Those dear fathers will not, I suppose, see this; and will perhaps think hard of me for saying it; but it is the cause of Christ.

From Autobiography of Peter Cartwright, The Backwoods Preacher

The revival or "camp meeting" was the signal event of the Second Great Awakening. The Cane Ridge experience became an annual event in Kentucky and was copied all over the nation in large and small camp meetings to revive the faith of Christians or to convert new believers.

Somewhere between 1800 and 1801, in the upper part of Kentucky, at a memorable place called "Cane Ridge," there was appointed a sacramental meeting by some of the Presbyterian ministers, at which meeting, seemingly unexpected by ministers or people, the mighty power of God was displayed in a very extraordinary manner; many were moved to tears, and bitter and loud crying for mercy. The meeting was protracted for weeks. Ministers of almost all denominations flocked in from far and near. The meeting was kept up by night and day. Thousands heard of the mighty work, and came on foot, on horseback, in carriages and wagons. It was supposed that there were in attendance at times during the meeting from twelve to twenty-five thousand people. Hundreds fell prostrate under the mighty power of

Shaker Dance, Joseph Becker, Frank Leslie's Illustrated Newspaper, 1873

God, as men slain in battle. Stands were erected in the woods from which preachers of different Churches proclaimed repentance toward God and faith in our Lord Jesus Christ, and it was supposed, by eye and ear witnesses, that between one and two thousand souls were happily and powerfully converted to God during the meeting.

Simple Gifts

"Simple Gifts" is a Shaker quick dance or dancing song used in worship services such as the one illustrated above. The hymn was written by Elder Joseph Brackett, Jr. in 1848.

'Tis the gift to be simple, 'tis the gift to be free,
'Tis the gift to come down where we ought to be,
And when we find ourselves in the place just right,
'Twill be in the valley of love and delight.
When true simplicity is gain'd,
To bow and to bend we shan't be asham'd,
To turn, turn will be our delight,
Till by turning, turning we come round right.

Joseph Smith, The Beginnings of Mormonism (1823)

While I was thus in the act of calling upon God, I discovered a light appearing in my room, which continued to increase until the room was lighter than at noonday, when immediately a personage appeared at my bedside, standing in the air, for his feet did not touch the floor. . . .

He called me by name, and said unto me that he was a messenger sent from the presence of God to me, and that his name was Moroni; that God had a work for me to do; and that my name should be had for good and evil among all nations, kindreds, and tongues, or that it should be both good and evil spoken of among all people. . . .

. . . I returned to my father in the field, and rehearsed the whole matter to him. He replied to me that it was of God, and told me to go and do as commanded by the messenger. I left the field, and went to the place where the messenger had told me the plates were deposited; and owing to the distinctness of the vision which I had had concerning it, I knew the place the instant that I arrived there. . . .

At length the time arrived for obtaining the plates, the Urim and Thummim, and the breastplate. . . . the same heavenly messenger delivered them up to me with this charge: that I should be responsible for them; that if I should let them go carelessly, or through any neglect of mine, I should be cut off; but that if I would use all my endeavors to preserve them, until he, the messenger, should call for them, they should be protected.

. . . For no sooner was it known that I had them, than the most strenuous exertions were used to get them from me. . . . The persecution became more bitter and severe than before, and multitudes were on the alert continually to get them from me if possible. But by the wisdom of God, they remained safe in my hands. When, according to arrangements, the messenger called for them, I delivered them up to him; and he has them in his charge until this day. . . .

On the 5th day of April, 1829, Oliver Cowdery came to my house, until which time I had never seen him. He stated to me that . . . the family related to him the circumstances of my having received the plates, and accordingly he had come to make inquiries of me.

Two days after the arrival of Mr. Cowdery (being the 7th of April) I commenced to translate the Book of Mormon, and he began to write for me.

Thousands heard of the mighty work . . .

13 The Way West

In his painting. *The Oregon Trail,* 1869, Albert Bierstadt (1830–1902) captures a wagon train progressing through the dramatic landscape of mountain cliffs and an expansive sky. Oil on canvas, 31 × 49" (78.74 × 124.46 cm).
Butler Institute of American Art, Youngstown, OH, USA/Gift of Joseph G. Butler III 1946/Bridgeman Art Library.

Hear the Audio

Hear the audio files for Chapter 13 at **www.myhistorylab.com**.

THE AGRICULTURAL FRONTIER *(page 339)*

HOW DID economic and demographic pressures in the East spur western migration?

THE FRONTIER OF THE PLAINS INDIANS *(page 344)*

WHAT STRATEGIES did the Sioux use to maintain their power on the Great Plains?

THE MEXICAN BORDERLANDS *(page 348)*

WHAT FORCES contributed to the Americanization of Texas?

POLITICS, EXPANSION, AND WAR *(page 355)*

WHY WAS James K. Polk so eager to provoke a war with Mexico?

ONE AMERICAN JOURNEY

On an occasion when I had interrogated a Sioux chief, on the upper Missouri, about their Government, their punishments and tortures of prisoners, for which I had freely condemned them for the cruelty of the practice, he took occasion, when I had got through, to ask me some questions relative to modes in the civilized world, which, with his comments upon them, were nearly as follows: and struck me, as I think they must every one, with great force.

He . . . told me he had often heard that white people hung their criminals by the neck, and choked them to death like dogs, and those their own people; to which I answered, "yes." He then told me he had learned that they shut each other up in prisons, where they keep them a great part of their lives because they can't pay money! I replied in the affirmative to this, which occasioned great surprise and excessive laughter, even among the women. . . . He said . . . that he had been along the Frontier, and a good deal amongst the white people, and he had seen them whip their little children, a thing that is very cruel, he had heard also, from several white medicine-men, that the Great Spirit of the white people was the child of a white woman, and that he was at the last put to death by the white people! This seemed to be a thing that he had not been able to comprehend, and he concluded by saying, "the Indians' Great Spirit got no mother—the Indians no kill him, he never die." He put me a chapter of other questions as to the trespasses of the white people on their lands, their continual corruption of the morals of their women, and digging open the Indians' graves to get their bones, &c. To all of which I was compelled to reply in the affirmative, and quite glad to close my note-book, and quietly to escape from the throng that had collected around me, and saying (though to myself and silently), that these and an hundred other vices belong to the civilized world, and are practiced upon (but certainly, in no instance, reciprocated by) the "cruel and relentless savage."

George Catlin

George Catlin, *Letters and Notes on the Manners, Customs, and Condition of the North American Indians,* Vol. II, pp. 756–57, 1841.

Read the **Document** at **www.myhistorylab.com**

Personal Journeys Online

- **Edward Harris, Journal excerpt, 1843. Account by a naturalist of the smallpox epidemic of 1837 on the Upper Missouri.**
- **Pierre Jean de Smet, S. J., Letter from a Catholic priest, 1841. Impressions of the character and intelligence of Indians in the Rocky Mountains.**

GEORGE CATLIN, one of the great illustrators of the American Indians, recorded these words in the 1830s when he traveled over the trans-Mississippi West painting and sketching, in his words, "the looks and customs of the vanishing races of native man in America." Unlike most whites of his generation, he approached Indian cultures with respect, and he realized that native peoples had a valid critique of the culture and values of white America.

From his first contact with the tribes along the upper Missouri River in the early 1830s, Catlin sensed that he was witness to a way of life that was about to vanish. He worked at a feverish pace to create a pictorial record of what he saw in a collection of art he called "Catlin's Indian Gallery." The proceeds from exhibiting his work in Europe enabled him to live quite comfortably in the 1840s, but he suffered a severe setback in 1852 when a financial speculation went sour. A failure as an entrepreneur, he nonetheless succeeded brilliantly as an artist in depicting the Native American peoples of the trans-Mississippi West just as they were about to be engulfed by a surging tide of white settlement.

CHRONOLOGY

1803–1806	Lewis and Clark travel up the Missouri River in search of a water route to the Pacific.	**1842**	First large parties of migrants set out on the Oregon Trail.
1816	Settlers surge into the trans-Appalachian region.	**1845**	United States annexes Texas.
1821	Mexico gains its independence from Spain.		Democrats embrace Manifest Destiny.
	Santa Fe Trail opens.		The Great Irish Famine begins.
	Stephen F. Austin establishes the first American colony in Texas.	**1846**	Mexican War breaks out.
1824	Rocky Mountain Fur Company begins the rendezvous system.		United States and Britain reach an agreement in Oregon.
1830	Congress creates the Indian Territory.	**1847**	Mormons begin settlement of Utah.
1834	Protestant missions are established in Oregon.	**1848**	Oregon Territory is organized.
	Santa Anna seizes power in Mexico.		Treaty of Guadalupe Hidalgo ends the Mexican War.
1836	Texas wins its independence from Mexico.		Revolutions sweep across Europe.
1837	Smallpox epidemic hits the Plains Indians.	**1851**	Fort Laramie Treaty with the Plains Indians is signed.

Some 300,000 Americans traveled the Oregon Trail in the 1840s and 1850s in a trek that eventually made the United States a nation that spanned the continent. These overlanders, as they came to be known, were part of a restless tide of white migration that eventually saw more than 50,000 Americans a year migrate west of the Appalachians after the War of 1812.

The West became a meeting ground of people from diverse cultures as Anglo-Americans came into contact and conflict with the Indians of the Plains and the Mexicans of the Southwest. Convinced of the superiority of their political and cultural values, Anglo-Americans asserted a God-given right to spread across the continent and impose their notions of liberty and democracy on peoples whose land they coveted. In the process, they forever changed much in the Native American culture that Catlin had so respectfully painted. ✦

THE AGRICULTURAL FRONTIER

HOW DID economic and demographic pressures in the East spur western migration?

The U.S. population ballooned from 5.3 million in 1800 to more than 23 million by 1850. As the population expanded, it shifted westward. Fewer than one in ten Americans lived west of the Appalachians in 1800; by 1850, about half did (see Map 13–1).

The tremendous amount of land available for settlement accounted for both phenomena. Through purchase and conquest, the land area of the United States more than tripled in the first half of the nineteenth century. Here was space where Americans could raise the large families of a rural society in which, on average, six to eight children survived to adolescence.

Declining soil fertility and rising population pressure in the rural East propelled these migrations. A common desire for greater economic opportunity, however, resulted in two distinct western societies by the 1840s. North of the Ohio River, in the Old Northwest, free labor and family farms defined the social order. South of the Ohio was the Old Southwest, a society dominated by slave labor and the plantation.

The Crowded East

By the early nineteenth century, land was scarce in the East, especially in New England. After generations of population growth and subdivisions of landholdings to male heirs, most New England communities no longer had enough arable land to satisfy all the young men who

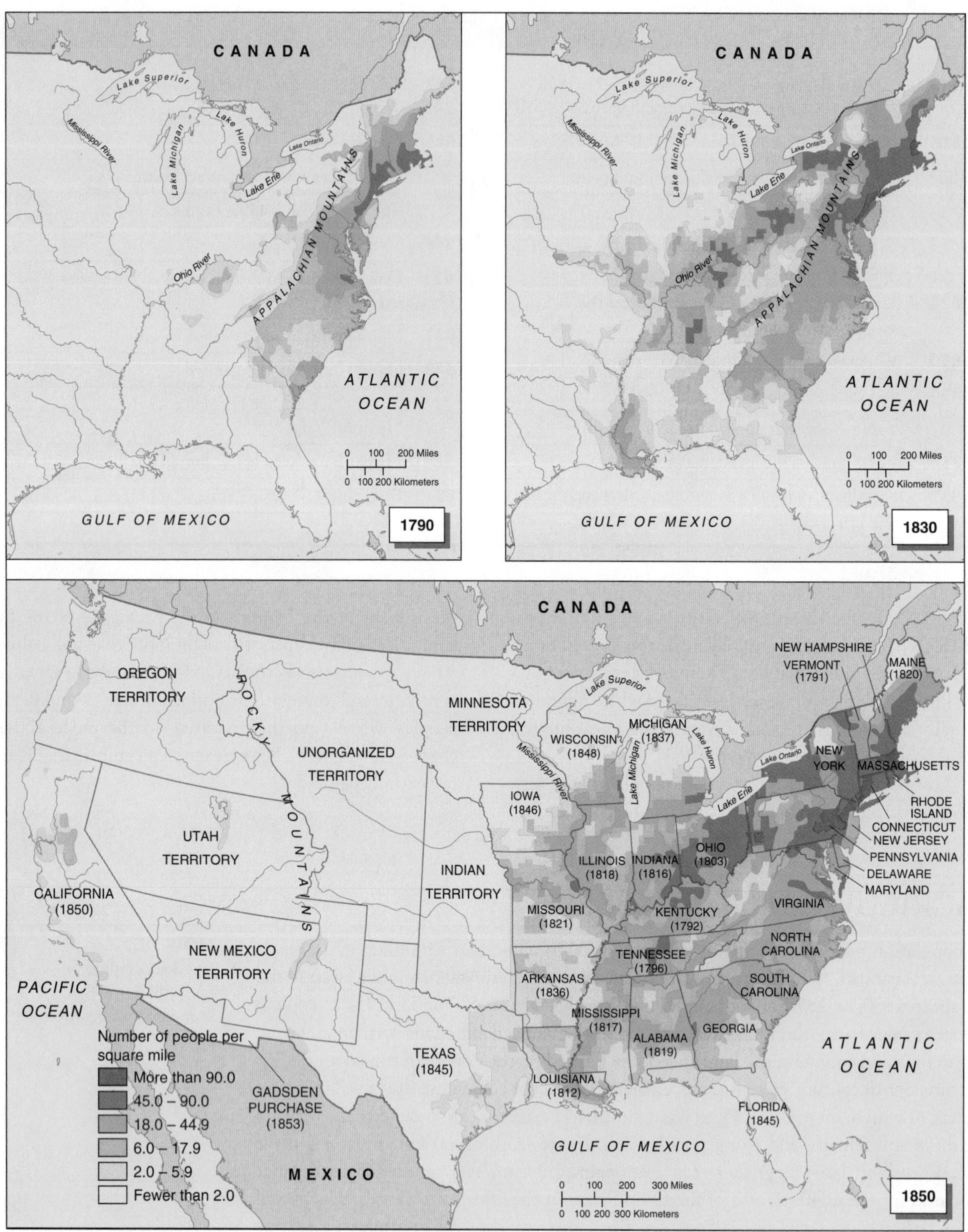

MAP 13–1 **The Westward Shift of the United States Population, 1790–1850** With a speed that was unimaginable in 1790, the United States quickly became a continental nation that stretched from the Atlantic to the Pacific by 1850. Particularly dramatic was the population growth in what became the Midwest.

What regions west of the Appalachian Mountains were most densely populated in 1850? What explains the demographic pattern shown in the 1850 map?

wanted their own farms. Even such recently opened areas as Vermont felt the pressure of rural overpopulation.

Land was more productive and expensive farther south, in the mid-Atlantic states. Keyed to the major export crop of wheat, agriculture was more commercialized than in New England, and economic inequality was thus higher. Successful farmers became wealthy by specializing in wheat and hiring the rural poor to work their fields. One-third to one-half of the young men in the commercialized agricultural districts of New Jersey and Pennsylvania were landless by the end of the eighteenth century. These men and their families, many of whom were recently arrived Scots-Irish and German immigrants, led the western migration from Pennsylvania. The pressure to move west was greatest in the slave states along the eastern seaboard. Although population density here was just two-thirds of that in New England, landholdings were more concentrated and the soil more exhausted than in the Northeast. Tenants who wanted their own land and small farmers tired of competing against slave labor were forced west across the mountains. They were joined by the sons of planters. Despite marriages arranged to keep land within the wealthy families, there was no longer enough good land left to carve out plantations for all the younger sons.

By the early 1800s, the young and the poor in the rural East had every incentive to head west, where fertile land was abundant, accessible, and, at $2 to $3 per acre, far cheaper than in the East. Land was the basis of wealth and social standing, and its ownership separated the independent from the dependent, the rooted from the rootless.

QUICK REVIEW

Why Go West?

- Scarcity of land in the East.
- Exhausted soil.
- Competition with slave labor.
- Cheap and abundant land in the West.

The western settler, observed a traveler on the Missouri frontier in the 1820s, wanted "to be a freeholder, to have plenty of rich land, and to be able to settle his children around him." Government policy under the Jeffersonian Republicans and Jacksonian Democrats attempted to promote these goals. Central to the land policy of the federal government after 1800 was the conviction that political liberties rested on the broadest possible base of land ownership. Thus, public policy and private aspirations merged in the belief that access to land was the key to preserving U.S. freedom.

When Jefferson took office in 1801, the minimum price for public land was $2 per acre, and a block of 320 acres had to be purchased at one time. By the 1830s, the price was down to $1.25 per acre, and the minimum purchase was only 80 acres. Congress also protected squatters, who had settled on public land before it was surveyed, from being outbid by speculators at land sales. The Preemption Act of 1841 guaranteed the right to purchase up to 160 acres at the minimum price of $1.25 when the public auction was held.

THE OLD NORTHWEST

The number of Americans who settled in the heartland of the Old Northwest, Ohio, Indiana, and Illinois, rose tenfold from 1810 to 1840. The end of the War of 1812 and the abandonment by the British of their former Indian allies opened the region to a flood of migrants.

Travelers passing through the Ohio Valley just after the war were astonished by the number of Americans trekking west. Wagonloads of migrants bounced along turnpikes to disembark on the Ohio River at Pittsburgh and Wheeling, where they bought flatboats to carry them down to the interior river valleys. Moving north across the Ohio were families from the hill country of Virginia and Kentucky. These two streams of migrants, one predominantly northern and the other southern, met in the lower Midwest and viewed each other as strangers.

A mosaic of settlements. The Old Northwest was less a melting pot in which regional cultures merged than a mosaic of settlements in which the different values and folkways of regional cultures from throughout the East took root and expanded. Belts of migration generally ran along a line from east to west as settlers sought out soil types and ecological conditions similar to those they had left behind. Thus, the same North-South cultural differences that existed along the Atlantic seaboard in 1800 were to be found half a century later in the Mississippi Valley.

A transplanted Yankee culture from New England and upstate New York spread over the upper Midwest, northern Ohio, Indiana, and Illinois, as well as Michigan and Wisconsin. These westerners were Whiggish in their politics, tended to be antislavery, and valued a communal sense of responsibility that regulated moral behavior and promoted self-improvement. The highland southerners who settled the lower Midwest, southern Ohio, Indiana, and Illinois, as well as Kentucky, were Democrats: They fiercely distrusted any centralized authority, political or moral, and considered Yankees intolerant do-gooders. Holding the balance of cultural and political power were the migrants from Pennsylvania and New Jersey, who were accustomed to ethnic diversity and the politics of competing economic groups. They settled principally in central Ohio, Indiana, and Illinois. By emphasizing economic growth and downplaying the cultural politics that pitted Yankees against southerners, they built a consensus around community development.

It took about ten years of backbreaking labor to create an 80-acre farm in heavily wooded sections. The work of women was essential for the success of the farm and the production of any salable surplus. Wives and daughters helped to tend the field crops, milked cows, and churned butter, and they produced the homespun cloth that, along with their dairy goods, found a market in the first country stores on the frontier.

claims clubs Groups of local settlers on the nineteenth-century frontier who banded together to prevent the price of their land claims from being bid up by outsiders at public land auctions.

Because outside labor was scarce and expensive, communities pooled their efforts for such tasks as raising a cabin. Groups of settlers also acted as cooperative units at public land auctions. Local associations known as **claims clubs** enforced the extralegal right of squatters to enter noncompetitive bids on land they had settled and improved. Members of the clubs physically intimidated speculators and refused to step aside until local settlers had acquired the land they wanted. The high cost of hauling goods to outside markets kept the early frontier economy barely above self-sufficiency. This initial economy, however, soon gave way to a more commercially oriented agriculture when steamboats, canals, and railroads opened up vast new markets (see Chapter 12).

The first large market was in the South, down the corridor of the Ohio and Mississippi rivers, and its major staples were corn and hogs. By the 1830s, the Erie Canal and its feeder waterways in the upper Midwest began to reorient much of the western farm trade to the Northeast. Wheat, because of its ready marketability for milling into flour, became the major cash crop for the northern market.

Cyrus McCormick pioneered the development of horse-drawn mechanical reapers. Shown here demonstrating his reaper to potential customers, McCormick helped revolutionize American agriculture with labor-saving machinery that made possible far larger harvests of grain crops.

Although southern cotton was the raw material that fueled New England textile factories in the first stages of industrialization, the commercialization of agriculture in the West also contributed to the growth of eastern manufacturing. Western farms supplied eastern manufacturers with inexpensive raw materials for processing into finished goods. By flooding national markets with corn and wheat, western produce not only supplied eastern workers with cheap food but also forced noncompetitive eastern farmers either to move west or to work in factories in eastern cities. In turn, the West itself became an ever-growing market for eastern factory goods. For example, nearly half of the nation's iron production in the 1830s was fashioned into farm implements.

In the 1820s, the Old Northwest was just emerging from semisubsistence and depended on the southern trade. Thirty years later it had become part of a larger Midwest whose economy was increasingly integrated with that of the Northeast. Settlers continued to pour into the region, and three additional states, Michigan (1837), Iowa (1846), and Wisconsin (1848), joined the Union.

The combination of favorable farm prices and steadily decreasing transportation costs generated a rise in disposable income that was spent on outside goods or invested in internal economic development. A network of canals and railroads was laid down, and manufacturing cities grew from towns favorably situated by water or rail transport. There was still room for subsistence farming, but the West north of the Ohio was now economically specialized and socially diverse.

QUICK REVIEW

Commercialization of Agriculture

- New technology spurred production.
- Commercialization of agriculture contributed to growth of eastern manufacturing.
- West became a market for eastern factory goods.

The Old Southwest

"The *Alabama Feaver* rages here with great violence and has carried off vast numbers of our Citizens," wrote a North Carolina planter in 1817 about the westward migration from his state. About as many people migrated from the old slave states in the East to the Old Southwest as those states gained by natural increase in the 1820s and 1830s. By 1850, more than 600,000 white settlers from Maryland, Virginia, and the Carolinas lived in slave states to the south and west, and many of them had brought their slaves with them. Indeed, from 1790 to 1860, more than 800,000 slaves were moved or sold from the South Atlantic region into the Old Southwest.

Soaring cotton prices after the War of 1812 and the smashing of Indian confederations during the war, which opened new lands to white settlement, propelled the first surge of migration into the Old Southwest (see Map 13–1). Before cotton prices plunged in the Panic of 1819, planters flooded into western Tennessee and the Black Belt, a crescent-shaped band of rich, black loamy soil arcing westward from Georgia through central Alabama and Mississippi. Migration surged anew in the 1830s when cotton prices were again high and the Chickasaws and Choctaws had been forced out of the incredibly fertile Delta country between the Yazoo and Mississippi rivers (see Chapter 10). The 1840s brought Texas fever to replace the Alabama fever of the 1810s, and a steady movement to the Southwest rounded out the contours of the cotton South. In less than thirty years, six new slave states—Mississippi (1817), Alabama (1819), Missouri (1821), Arkansas (1836), Florida (1845), and Texas (1845)—joined the Union (see the Overview table, Westward Expansion and the Growth of the Union, 1815–1850).

The southwestern frontier attracted both slaveholding planters and small independent farmers. The planters, though a minority, had the capital or the credit to acquire the best lands and the slave labor to make those lands productive. The slaveholders were responding both to the need for fresh land and to the extraordinary demand for short-staple cotton.

The most typical settlers on the southern frontier were the small independent yeomen farmers who generally owned no slaves. Usually settling in the valleys, on the ridges, and in the hill country, they often soon sold out to neighboring planters and headed west again.

The yeomanry moved onto the frontier in two waves. The first consisted of stockmen-hunters, a restless, transient group that spread from the pine barrens in the Carolina backcountry to the coastal plain of eastern Texas. These pioneers prized unfettered independence and measured their wealth in the livestock left to roam and fatten on the sweet grasses of uncleared forests. They were quick to move on when farmers, the second wave, started to clear the land for crops.

The yeoman farmers practiced a diversified agriculture aimed at feeding their families. Corn and pork were the mainstays of their diet, and both could readily be produced as long as there was room for the open-range herding of swine and for patches of corn. The more ambitious farmers, usually those who owned one or two slaves, grew some cotton, but most preferred to avoid the economic risks of cotton production. The yeoman's chief source of labor was his immediate family, and to expand that labor force to produce cotton meant going into debt to purchase slaves. The debt could easily cost the yeoman his farm if the price of cotton fell.

Measured by per capita income, and as a direct result of the profits from slave-produced cotton on virgin soils, the Old Southwest was a wealthier society than the Old Northwest in

OVERVIEW Westward Expansion and the Growth of the Union, 1815–1850

New Free States	New Slave States	Territories (1850)
Indiana, 1816	Mississippi, 1817	Minnesota
Illinois, 1818	Alabama, 1819	Oregon
Maine, 1820	Missouri, 1821	New Mexico
Michigan, 1837	Arkansas, 1836	Utah
Iowa, 1846	Florida, 1845	
Wisconsin, 1848	Texas, 1845	

1850. In the short term, the settlement of the Old Southwest was also more significant for national economic development. Cotton accounted for more than half the value of all U.S. exports after the mid-1830s. More than any other commodity, cotton paid for U.S. imports and underpinned national credit. But southern prosperity was not accompanied by the same economic development and social change as in the Old Northwest. Compared to the slave West in 1860, the free-labor West was twice as urbanized, and far more of its workforce was engaged in nonagricultural pursuits.

The Southwest Ordinance, enacted by Congress in 1790, opened all territories south of the Ohio River to slavery. Slaves, land, and cotton were the keys to wealth on the southern frontier, and agricultural profits were continually plowed back into more land and slaves to produce more cotton. In contrast, prosperous farmers in the Old Northwest had no slaves to work additional acres. Hence, they were much more likely to invest their earnings in promotional schemes designed to attract settlers whose presence would raise land values and increase business for local merchants and entrepreneurs. As early as the 1840s, rural communities in the Old Northwest were supporting bustling towns that offered jobs in trade and manufacturing on a scale far surpassing anything in the slave West. By the 1850s, the Midwest was almost as urbanized as the Northeast had been in 1830, and nearly half its labor force no longer worked on farms.

The Old Southwest remained overwhelmingly agricultural. Once the land was settled, the children of the first generation of slaveholders and yeomen moved west to the next frontier rather than compete for the good land that was left. Relatively few newcomers took their place. By the 1850s, Kentucky, Tennessee, Alabama, and Mississippi, the core states of the Old Southwest, were all losing more migrants than they were gaining.

THE FRONTIER OF THE PLAINS INDIANS

WHAT STRATEGIES did the Sioux use to maintain their power on the Great Plains?

Few white Americans had ventured west of the Mississippi by 1840. Moreover, Americans had no legal claim to much of the trans-Mississippi West, or merely the paper title of the Louisiana Purchase, to which none of the native inhabitants had acquiesced. Beyond Texas and the boundary line drawn by the Trans-Continental Treaty of 1819 lay the northern possessions of Mexico. Horse-mounted Indian tribes dominated by the Sioux were a formidable power throughout the central Plains.

Before the 1840s, only fur trappers and traders, who worked with and not against the powerful Sioux, had pushed across the Great Plains and into the Rockies. The 1840s brought a sudden change, a large migration westward that radically altered the ecology of the Great Plains. Farm families trapped in an agricultural depression and enticed by Oregon's bounty turned the trails blazed by the fur traders into ruts on the **Oregon Trail,** the route that led to the first large settlement of Americans on the Pacific Coast.

Oregon Trail Overland trail of more than two thousand miles that carried American settlers from the Midwest to new settlements in Oregon, California, and Utah.

Tribal Lands

At least 350,000 Native Americans lived in the plains and mountains of the trans-Mississippi West in 1840. They were loosely organized into tribal groups, each with its own territory and way of life. Most inhabited the Great Plains region, which lay north and west of the Indian Territory reserved for eastern tribes in the present state of Oklahoma. The point where the prairies of the Midwest gave way to the higher, drier plains marked a rough division between predominantly agricultural tribes to the east and nomadic, hunting tribes to the west.

In the 1830s, the U.S. government set aside a broad stretch of country between the Platte River to the north and the Red River to the south (most of what is now Oklahoma and eastern Kansas) exclusively for tribes resettled from the East under the Indian Removal Act of 1830 and for village-living groups native to the area. Many government officials envisioned this territory as a permanent sanctuary that would separate Indians from white people and allow them to live in peace on allotments of land granted as compensation for the territory they had ceded to the federal government. However, even as Congress was debating the idea of a permanent Indian reserve, the pressure on native peoples in the Mississippi Valley both from raiding parties of Plains Indians and the incessant demands of white farmers and speculators for land was rendering a stable Indian-white boundary meaningless.

On the eve of Indian removal in the East, the Sauks, Foxes, Potawatomis, and other Indian peoples inhabited Iowa. The defeat of the Sauks and Foxes in what white Americans called Black Hawk's War in 1832 opened Iowa to white settlement and forced tribes to cede land (see Chapter 10). In 1838, Congress created the Territory of Iowa, which encompassed all the land between the Mississippi and Missouri rivers north of the state of Missouri. The remaining Indians were now on the verge of being pushed completely out of the region. Throughout the upper Mississippi Valley in the 1830s, other groups suffered a similar fate, and the number of displaced Indians swelled.

The first to be displaced were farming peoples whose villages straddled the woodlands to the east and the open plains to the west. These border tribes were caught in a vise between the loss of their land to advancing white people and the seizure of their horses and agricultural provisions by Indian raiders such as the Sioux from the plains. The Pawnees were among the hardest hit.

By the 1830s, the Pawnees were primarily an agricultural people who embarked on seasonal hunts for game in the Platte River Valley. In 1833, they signed a treaty with the U.S. government in which they agreed to withdraw north of the Platte in return for subsidies and military protection from the hostile Indians on the plains. Once the Pawnees moved north of the Platte, Sioux attacked them and seized control of the prime hunting grounds. When the Pawnees in desperation filtered back south of the Platte, in violation of the treaty of 1833, they encountered constant harassment from white settlers. In vain the Pawnee leaders cited the provisions of the treaty that promised them protection from the Sioux. Forced back north of the Platte by the U.S. government, the Pawnees were eventually driven out of their homeland by the Sioux.

Shown here is a Lakota shirt, c. 1850, that was specially woven for Sioux warriors who had distinguished themselves in battle. The blue and yellow dyes symbolize sky and earth, and the strands of human hair represent acts of bravery performed in defense of the Lakota people.

Shirt, about 1860s, unknown Sioux artist. Deer skin, hair, quills, feathers, paint, Denver Art Museum Collection, Native Arts Acquisitions Funds, 1947. 235

QUICK REVIEW

The Pawnees

- By 1830s, the Pawnees were primarily an agricultural people.
- Agreed in 1833 treaty to move north.
- Attacked by Sioux in the north and white settlers in the south.

The Sioux were the dominant power on the northern and central Great Plains, more than able to hold their own against white Americans in the first half of the nineteenth century. In the eighteenth century, the western Sioux had separated from their woodland kin (known as the Santee Sioux), left their homeland along the headwaters of the Mississippi River, and pushed onto the Minnesota prairies. Armed with guns they had acquired from the French, the western Sioux dominated the prairies east of the Missouri River by 1800.

The Sioux learned to use the horse from the Plains Indians. Introduced to the New World by the Spanish, horses had revolutionized the lives of native peoples on the Great Plains. As they acquired more horses through trading and raids, the Plains Indians evolved a distinctly new nomadic culture. The Sioux were the most successful of all the tribes in melding two facets of white culture, the gun and the horse, into an Indian culture of warrior-hunters.

WHERE TO LEARN MORE

Indian Museum of North America, Crazy Horse, South Dakota
http://www.crazyhorsememorial.org/monument/

As the demand for buffalo hides from American and European traders increased in the early 1800s, the Sioux extended their buffalo hunts. In a loose alliance with the Cheyennes and Arapahos, Sioux war parties pushed aside or subjugated weaker tribes to the south and west of the Missouri River basin. Reduced to a dependent status, these tribes were forced to rely on the Sioux for meat and trading goods.

Epidemic diseases brought to the plains by white traders helped Sioux expansion. Because they lived in small wandering bands, the Sioux were less susceptible to these epidemics than the more sedentary village peoples. The Sioux were also one of the first tribes to be vaccinated against smallpox by doctors sent up the Missouri River by the Bureau of Indian Affairs in the early 1830s. Smallpox reached the plains in the 1780s, and a major epidemic in 1837 probably halved the region's Indian population. Particularly hard hit were tribes attempting to resist the Sioux advance. Sioux losses were relatively light and, unlike the other tribes, their population grew.

Read the **Document** at **www.myhistorylab.com** *Exploring America: America and the Horse*

By 1850, the Sioux had increased in power and numbers since they first encountered American officials during the Lewis and Clark Expedition in 1804 and 1805. Americans could vilify the Sioux, but they could not force them into dependence in the first half of the nineteenth century. The Sioux continued to extend their influence, and they were shrewd enough to align themselves with the Americans whenever their interests dictated conciliation.

QUICK REVIEW

Sources of Sioux Power

- Horses.
- Guns.
- Political skill.
- Relative insusceptibility to European diseases.

The Fur Traders

The western fur trade originated in the rivalry between British and U.S. companies for profitable furs, especially beaver pelts. Until the early 1820s, the Hudson's Bay Company, a well-capitalized

The annual rendezvous in Wyoming of fur trappers and traders was a multinational affair in which Anglo Americans, French Canadians, Mexican Americans, and Native Americans gathered to trade, drink, and swap stories.

The Denver Public Library, Western History Department.

British concern, dominated the trans-Mississippi fur trade. A breakthrough for U.S. interests came in 1824 when two St. Louis businessmen, William Henry Ashley and Andrew Henry of the Rocky Mountain Fur Company, developed the rendezvous system, which eliminated the need for permanent and costly posts deep in Indian territory. In keeping with Indian traditions of periodic intertribal meetings, the rendezvous system brought together trappers, Indians, and traders in a grand annual fair at a designated site in the high mountain country of Wyoming. White trappers and Indians exchanged the animal skins they had gathered in the seasonal hunt for guns, traps, tobacco, whiskey, textiles, and other trading goods with agents of the fur companies in St. Louis.

Read the **Document** at **www.myhistorylab.com** *Elizabeth Dixon Smith Geer, Oregon Trail Journal (1847, 1848)*

Living conditions in the wilderness were primitive, even brutal. Mortality rates among trappers ran as high as 80 percent a year. Death could result from an accidental gunshot wound, an encounter with a grizzly, or an arrow from an Indian whose hunting grounds a trapper had transgressed.

For all its dangers, the life of a trapper appealed to unattached young men. They were fleeing the confinements, as well as the comforts, of white civilization and were as free as they could be. When on a hunt with the Indians, they were part of a spectacle unknown to other white Americans, one that was already passing into history.

WHERE TO LEARN MORE

★ Scotts Bluff National Monument, Gering, Nebraska http://www.nps.gov/scbl/index.htm

Such spectacles were increasingly rare after 1840, the year of the last mountain men's rendezvous on the Green River in Wyoming. The most exploitative phase of the fur trade in the 1830s had ravaged the fur-bearing animals and accelerated the spread of smallpox among the tribes. Whiskey, the most profitable item among the white man's trading goods, had corrupted countless Indians and undermined the vitality of tribal cultures.

The mountain men were about to pass into legend, but before they did, they explored every trail and path from the front (or eastern) range of the Rockies to the Pacific. The main trading corridor of the fur trade, up the lower Missouri to the North Platte and across the plains to the South Pass, a wide plateau crossing the Continental Divide, and into the Wyoming basin, became the main overland route to the West in the 1840s. The mountain men had removed the mystery of western geography, and in so doing they hastened the end of the frontier conditions that had made their unique way of life possible.

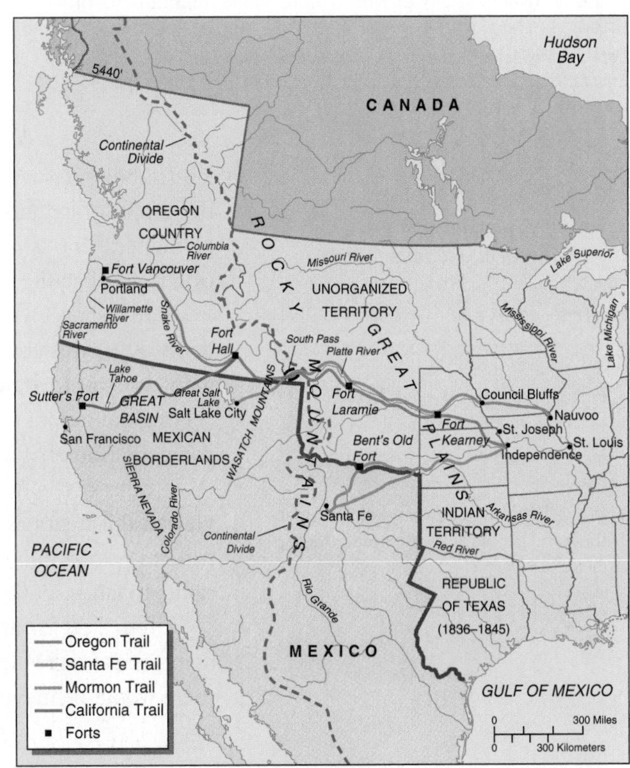

MAP 13–2 **Western Overland Trails** The great overland trails to the West began at the Missouri River. The Oregon Trail crossed South Pass in Wyoming and then branched off to Oregon, California, or Utah. The Santa Fe Trail carried American goods and traders to the Mexican Southwest.

What role did geography play in determining overland trails?

THE OREGON TRAIL

Before the 1830s, few Americans had heard of Oregon, and practically none lived there. Under an agreement reached in 1818, the Oregon Country was still jointly administered by the United States and Great Britain. Furs, whether beaver pelts or the skins of the Pacific sea otter, had attracted a few U.S. trappers and merchants, but the British-controlled Hudson's Bay Company dominated the region. Protestant missionaries established the first permanent white settlements in the 1830s. Reports of Oregon's fertility that the missionaries sent east sparked the first popular interest in the region, especially among midwestern farmers stuck in the agricultural depression that followed the Panic of 1837.

The first large party of overlanders on the Oregon Trail left Independence, Missouri, for the Willamette Valley in 1842. Independence and St. Joseph in Missouri and, by the 1850s, Council Bluffs in Iowa were the jumping-off points for the Oregon Trail. (See Map 13–2.) Most overlanders were young farm families from the Midwest, who had moved

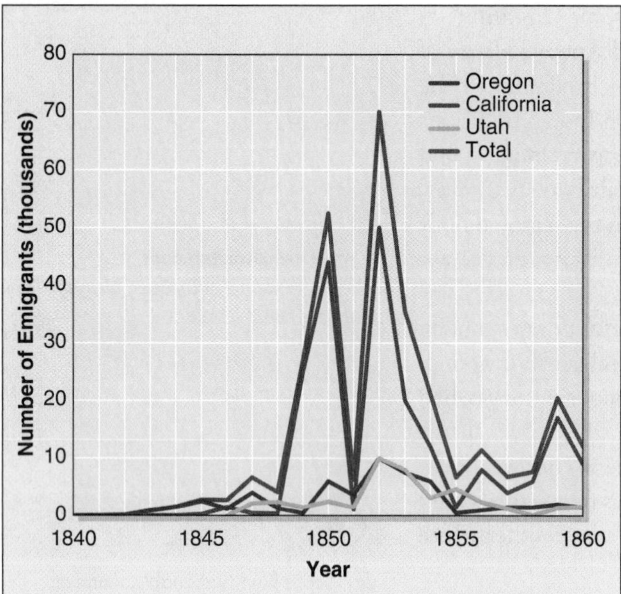

FIGURE 13–1 **Overland Emigration to the West, 1840–1860** Immigration to the trans-Mississippi West steadily increased in the 1840s as farm families moved to Oregon or Utah. After the discovery of gold in California in 1849, California attracted the bulk of the emigrants, many of whom were single men hopeful of striking it rich.

Data Source: John D. Unruh, Jr., *The Plains Across: The Overland Emigrants and the Trans-Mississippi West, 1840–60* (1982), pp. 84–85.

at least once before in their restless search for the perfect farm that would keep them out of debt. (See Figure 13–1.)

The journey was long and dangerous. In the 1840s, some 5,000 of the 90,000 men, women, and children who set out on the Oregon Trail died along the way. But although the overlanders were terrified of encountering Indians, who they assumed would be hostile, few died from Indian attacks. As long as the wagon trains were just passing through, the Plains Indians left the white people alone. At first they watched with bemused curiosity, and then, as the white migrants kept coming, they traded game for clothing and ammunition. Indians killed only 115 migrants in the 1840s, and trigger-happy white migrants provoked most of the clashes. Disease, especially cholera, was the great killer. Second to disease were accidents, especially drownings that resulted when drivers tried to force overloaded wagons across swollen rivers.

Cooperation between families was the key to a successful overland crossing. The men in a party often drew up a formal, written constitution at the start of a trip spelling out the assignments and work responsibilities of each wagon. Before the trail was well marked, former mountain men hired on as captains to lead wagon trains. Timing was crucial. A wagon train had to leave late enough in the spring to get good grass in Nebraska for the oxen and mules. Too early a departure, and the wagon train risked getting bogged down in spring mud; too late, and it risked being trapped in the snows of the Pacific coastal ranges.

Before "Oregon fever" had run its course, the flow of white settlers across the continent radically changed the economy and ecology of the Great Plains. Pressure mounted on plants and animals, reducing the land's ability to support all the tribes accustomed to living off it. Intertribal warfare intensified as the supply of buffalo and other game dwindled. Far from being separated from white people by a permanent line of division, the Plains Indians now stood astride the main path of white migration to the Pacific.

Read the **Document** at **www.myhistorylab.com** *The Treaty of Fort Laramie (1851)*

QUICK REVIEW

The Oregon Trail

- First large party of overlanders left Missouri in 1842.
- Most overlanders were young farm families.
- In the 1840s, five thousand of the ninety thousand people who attempted the trip died.

In response, officials in the Bureau of Indian Affairs organized a great gathering of the tribes in 1851. At this conference they pushed through the Fort Laramie Treaty, the first U.S. government attempt to draw boundaries within which to contain the Plains Indians. In exchange for accepting limitations on their movements and for the loss of game, the tribes were to receive annual compensation of $50,000 a year for fifty years (later reduced by the U.S. Senate to ten years).

Most of the Indians at the Fort Laramie conference were Sioux and their allies. The Sioux viewed the treaty as confirming their dominance on the Great Plains. When U.S. negotiators tried to restrict Sioux hunting to north of the Platte, the Sioux demanded and received treaty rights to lands south of the Platte as well.

The Fort Laramie Treaty represented a standoff between the Sioux and the U.S. government, the two great powers on the Plains. If neither yielded its claim to the region, war between them would be inevitable.

THE MEXICAN BORDERLANDS

WHAT FORCES contributed to the Americanization of Texas?

By the mid-1840s, parties of emigrant Americans were beginning to branch off the main Oregon Trail on their way to Utah and California, which were then part of Mexico's northern borderlands (see Map 13–2). Mostly a semiarid and thinly populated land of high plateaus, dry basins, and desert bisected north to south by mountain ranges, the borderlands had been part of the Spanish Empire in North America. Mexico inherited this territory when it won independence from Spain in 1821. Mexico's hold on the region was always weak. It lost Texas in 1837, and, in the next decade, the U.S. penetration of Utah and California set the stage for the U.S. seizure of most of the rest in the Mexican War.

The Peoples of the Southwest

Diverse peoples lived in the Southwest. Imperial Spain had divided them into four main groupings: Indians, full-blooded Native Americans who retained their own languages and customs; *mestizos*, people of racially mixed ancestry, usually Spanish and Indian; *criollos*, U.S.-born whites of Spanish ancestry; and Spaniards. By far the smallest group was the Spaniards. Compared to the English, few Spaniards emigrated to the New World, and most who did were men. Consequently, Spanish males married or lived with native women, creating a large class of *mestizos*. Despite their small numbers, the Spanish, along with the *criollos*, monopolized economic and political power. This wealthy elite controlled the labor of the *mestizos* in the predominantly ranching economy of the borderlands.

The largest single group in the borderlands were the Indians, about half the population in the 1820s. Most had not come under direct Spanish or Mexican control. Those who had were part of the mission system. This instrument of Spanish imperial policy forced Indians to live in a fixed area, convert to Catholicism, and work as agricultural laborers.

Spanish missions, most of them established by the Franciscan order, aimed both to Christianize and "civilize" the Indians, making them loyal imperial subjects. Mission Indians were forced to abandon their native economies and culture and settle in agricultural communities under the tight supervision of the friars (see Chapter 1). Spanish soldiers and royal officials, who lived in military garrisons known as *presidios*, accompanied the friars.

The largest concentration of Indians, some 300,000 when the Spanish friars arrived in the 1760s, was in California. Most of these, the Paiutes, Chumashes, Pomos, Shastas, and a host of smaller tribes, occupied their own distinct ecological zones where they gathered and processed what the rivers, forests, and grasslands provided. Fish and game were abundant, and wild plants and nuts, especially acorns, provided grain and flour.

The major farming Indians east of California were the Pueblo peoples of Arizona and New Mexico. Named after the adobe or stone communal dwellings in which they lived atop mesas or on terraces carved into cliffs, the Pueblo Indians were a peaceful people closely bound to small, tightly knit communities. (*Pueblo* is Spanish for "village.") Indeed, some of their dwellings, such as those of the Hopis in Arizona or the Acomas in New Mexico, have been continuously occupied for more than 500 years. Corn and beans were the staples of their irrigation-based agriculture. Formally a part of the Spanish mission system, they had incorporated the Catholic God and Catholic rituals into their own polytheistic religion, which stressed the harmony of all living things with the forces of nature. They continued to worship in their underground sanctuaries known as *kivas*.

Once the Pueblos made their peace with the Spaniards after their great revolt in 1680 (see Chapter 3), their major enemies were the nomadic tribes that lived by hunting and raiding. These tribes outnumbered the Pueblos four to one and controlled most of the Southwest until the 1850s. The horse, which many of the tribes acquired during Spain's temporary retreat from the region during the late seventeenth century in the wake of the Pueblo Revolt, was the basis of their way of life. As the horse frontier spread, the peoples of the southern Plains gained enormous mobility and the means of ranging far and wide for the economic resources that sustained their transformation into societies of mounted warriors.

This painting by Alfred James Miller depicts the busy interior of Fort Laramie in 1837.

Alfred Jacob Miller, "The Interior of Fort Laramie," 1858–60. The Walters Art Museum, Baltimore.

West of the pueblos around Taos was the land of the Navajos, who herded sheep, raised some crops, and raided other tribes from their

The paintings by George Catlin are among the best visual sources for understanding the material culture of the Plains Indians. Shown here in a c. 1837 painting are the circular lodges of a Mandan village.

Smithsonian American Art Museum, Washington, DC/Art Resource, NY

mountain fastnesses. Spilling over onto Navajo lands, the Southern Utes ranged up and down the canyon lands of Utah. The Gila Apaches were the dominant tribe south of Albuquerque and westward into Arizona. To the east in the Pecos River Valley roamed bands of Mescalero and Jicarillo Apaches. On the broad plains rolling northward from the Texas panhandle and southward into northern Mexico were war parties of Comanches and Kiowas.

The Comanches, a branch of the mountain Shoshonis who moved to the plains when horses became available, were the most feared of the nomadic peoples. Utterly fearless, confident, and masterful horsemen, they gained a reputation of mythic proportions for their prowess as mounted warriors. For food and clothing, they relied on the immense buffalo herds of the southern plains. For guns, horses, and other trading goods, they lived off their predatory raids. When the Santa Fe Trail opened in the early 1820s, their shrewdness as traders gave them a new source of firearms that strengthened their raiding prowess.

The three focal points of white settlement in the northern borderlands of Mexico, Texas, New Mexico, and Alta California (as distinguished from Lower, or Baja, California), were never linked by an effective network of communications or transportation. Each of these settlements was an isolated offshoot of Hispanic culture with a semiautonomous economy based on ranching and a mostly illegal trade with French, British, and U.S. merchants that brought in a trickle of needed goods.

WHERE TO LEARN MORE

Indian Pueblo Cultural Center, Albuquerque, New Mexico
http://www.indianpueblo.org/

Neither Spain, which tried to seal off its northern outposts from economic contact with foreigners, nor Mexico, which opened up the borderlands to outsiders, had integrated this vast region into a unified economic or political whole. Indeed, Mexico's most pressing problem in the 1820s was protecting its northern states from the Comanches. To serve as a buffer against the Comanches, the Mexican government in 1821 invited Americans into Texas, opening the way to the eventual U.S. takeover of the territory.

QUICK REVIEW

Peoples of the Southwest

- Indians.
- Spanish.
- Mestizos: those of racially mixed ancestry.
- Criollos: American-born whites of Spanish ancestry.

Tejano A person of Spanish or Mexican descent born in Texas.

THE AMERICANIZATION OF TEXAS

The Mexicans faced the same problems governing Texas that the Spanish had. Mexico City was about a thousand miles from San Antonio, the center of Hispanic settlement in Texas, and communications were slow and cumbersome. The ranching elite of ***Tejanos*** (Spanish-speaking Mexicans born in Texas) had closer economic ties to American Louisiana than they did to Coahuila, the Mexican state to which Texas was formally attached. The low agricultural productivity, combined with the low birthrate among mission Indians, outbreaks of disease, and the generally hostile frontier environment, sharply restricted population growth. Only some 5,000 Mexicans lived in Texas in the 1820s.

Sparsely populated and economically struggling, Mexican Texas shared a border with the United States along the Sabine River in Louisiana and the Red River in the Arkansas Territory (see Map 13–2). The threat that the nearby Americans posed to Mexico's security was obvious to Mexican officials. However, attempts to promote Mexican immigration into Texas failed. Reasoning that the Americans were going to come in any event and anxious to build up the population of Texas against Indian attacks, the Mexican government encouraged Americans to settle in Texas by offering huge grants of land in return for promises to accept Mexican citizenship, convert to Catholicism, and obey the authorities in Mexico City.

empresarios Agents who received a land grant from the Spanish or Mexican government in return for organizing settlements.

The first American ***empresario,*** the recipient of a large grant in return for a promise to bring in settlers, was Stephen F. Austin. After having the grant confirmed by the new Mexican government in 1821, Stephen Austin founded the first American colony in Texas. The Austin grant encompassed 18,000 square miles. Other grants were smaller but still lavish. The *empresarios* stood to grow wealthy by leasing out land, selling parcels to settlers, and organizing the rest into large-scale farms that produced cotton with slave labor in the bottomlands of the Sabine, Colorado, and Brazos rivers. As early as 1830, eastern and south-central Texas was becoming an extension of the plantation economy of the Gulf coastal plain. More than 25,000 white settlers, with around 1,000 slaves, had poured into the region (see American Views, A Mexican View of the Texans in 1828).

More Americans moved into Texas with slaves than the Mexicans had anticipated. Many settlers simply ignored Mexican laws, especially the Emancipation Proclamation of 1829, which forbade slavery in the Republic of Mexico. In 1830, the Mexican government attempted to assert its authority. It levied the first taxes on the Americans, prohibited the further importation of slaves, and closed the international border to additional immigration. Still, another 10,000 Americans spilled across the border in the early 1830s, and they continued to bring in slaves.

Unlike the *empresarios*, many of whom became Catholic and married into elite *Tejano* families, these newcomers lived apart from Mexicans and rejected Mexican citizenship. Cultural tensions escalated. Believing that they belonged to a superior race of liberty-loving white Anglo-Saxons, most of these new arrivals sneered at the Mexicans as a mongrelized race of black people, Indians, and Spaniards and resented having to submit to their rule. A clash became inevitable in 1835 when General Santa Anna, elected president of Mexico in 1833, overturned the liberal Mexican constitution of 1824. He established himself as a dictator in 1834, and his centralist rule ended any hope of the Americans *empresarios* and their *Tejano* allies that Texas might become an autonomous state within a federated Mexico. Skirmishing between Mexican troops and rebellious Texans began in the fall of 1835.

Alamo Franciscan mission at San Antonio, Texas, that was the site in 1836 of a siege and massacre of Texans by Mexican troops.

At first, the Anglo-*Tejano* leadership sought to overthrow Santa Anna, restore the constitution of 1824, and win separate statehood for Texas within a liberal Mexican republic. Santa Anna, however, refused to compromise. When he raised a large army to crush the uprising, he radicalized the rebellion and pushed its leaders to declare complete independence on March 2, 1836. Four days later, a Mexican army of 4,000 annihilated the 187 defenders of the **Alamo,** an abandoned mission in San Antonio. A few weeks later at Goliad, another 300 Texans were killed after they had agreed to surrender (see Map 13–3).

"Remember the Alamo!" and "Remember Goliad!" were powerful rallying cries for the beleaguered Texans. Volunteers from the U.S. South rushed to the aid of the main Texan army, commanded by Sam Houston. Houston's victory in April 1836 at the Battle of San Jacinto established the independence of Texas. Captured while trying to flee, Santa Anna signed a treaty in May 1836, recognizing Texas as an independent republic with a boundary on the south and west at the Rio Grande. However, the Nueces River to the north of the Rio Grande had been the administrative border of Texas under Mexican rule. The Mexican Congress rejected the treaty, and the boundary remained in dispute.

Soon forgotten during the ensuing eight years of Texas independence was the support that many *Tejanos* had given to the successful revolt against Mexican rule. In part because Mexico refused to recognize the Texas Republic, Anglos feared *Tejanos* as a subversive element. Pressure mounted on them to leave, especially after Santa Anna launched a major counterattack in 1842, capturing San Antonio. Those who stayed lost much of their land and economic power as Anglos used their knowledge of U.S. law or just plain chicanery to reduce the *Tejanos* to second-class citizens.

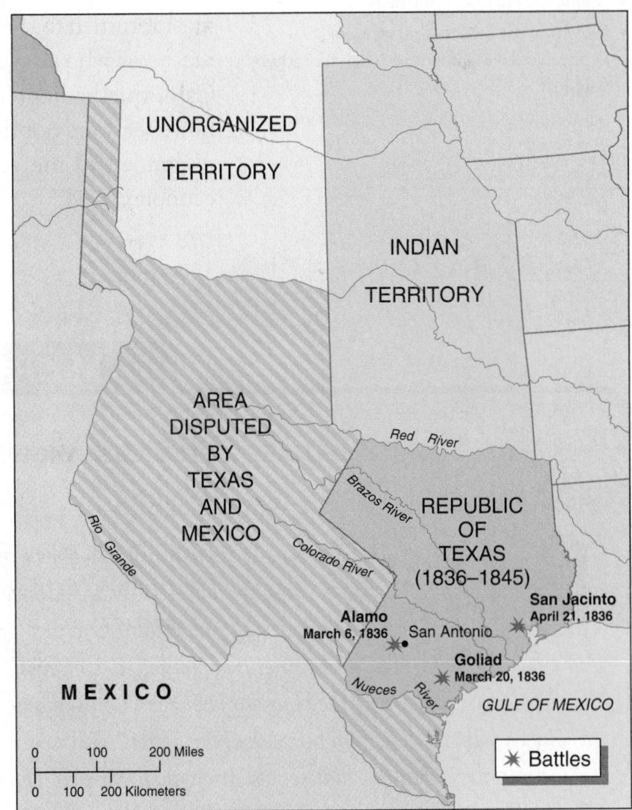

MAP 13–3 **Texas and Mexico after the Texas Revolt** The Battle of San Jacinto was the decisive American victory that gained the independence of Texas, but the border dispute between Texas and Mexico would not be resolved until the Mexican War a decade later.

Why might the Mexican government have thought it so important to establish the border of Texas at the Nueces River? What potential dangers might the government have seen in an expanded Texas?

More difficult to subordinate were the Comanches. While president of Texas, Houston tried to fix a permanent boundary between the Comanches and white settlers, but Texas pride and ongoing white encroachments on Indian land undercut his efforts. By the early 1840s, Texans and Comanches were in a state of nearly permanent war. Only the force of the federal army after the Civil War ended the Comanches' long reign over the high, dry plains of northern and western Texas.

The Push into California and the Southwest

California. Mexican rule in California was always weak. The Sonoran Desert and the resistance of the Yuman Indians in southeastern California cut off Mexico from any direct land contact with Alta California. Only irregular communications were maintained over a long sea route. For ***Californios,*** Californians of Spanish descent, Mexico was literally *la otra banda,* "the other shore." In trying to strengthen its hold on this remote and thinly populated region, the Mexican government relied on a program of economic development. As in Texas, however, Mexican policy had unintended consequences.

Californios Persons of Spanish descent living in California.

The centerpiece of the Mexican program was the secularization of the missions, opening up the landholdings of the Catholic Church to private ownership and releasing the mission Indians from paternalistic bondage. Small allotments of land were set aside for the Indians, but most returned to their homelands. Those who remained became a source of cheap labor for the *rancheros* who carved up the mission lands into huge cattle ranches. Thus, by the 1830s, California had entered what is called the *rancho* era. The main beneficiaries of this process, however, were not the Mexican authorities who had initiated it but the American traders who responded to the economic opportunities presented by the privatization of the California economy.

QUICK REVIEW

Mexican Rule in California

- Mexican rule in California weak.
- Government initiated program of economic development to help strengthen its control over region.
- Centerpiece of program: secularization of missions.

AMERICAN VIEWS

Mexican Views of the U.S. Expansion

A Mexican View of the Texans, 1828

By the late 1820s, Mexico was reassessing its policy of encouraging American immigration to Texas. Concerned over the large numbers and uncertain loyalties of the American settlers, the government appointed a commission in 1827 ostensibly to survey the boundary between Louisiana and the province of Texas. The real purpose of the commission was to recommend policy changes that would strengthen Mexico's hold on Texas. The following excerpt is from a journal kept by José María Sánchez, the draftsman of the boundary commission.

- **Why** was the Mexican government so ineffective in maintaining control over Texas?
- **What** was the appeal of Texas for Americans? How did most of them enter Texas and take up land?
- **Why** did Sánchez have such a low opinion of the Americans in the Austin colony? What did he think of Stephen Austin?
- **Why** did the Mexicans fear that they would lose Texas?

The Americans from the north have taken possession of practically all the eastern part of Texas, in most cases without the permission of the authorities. They immigrate constantly, finding no one to prevent them, and take possession of the *sitio* [location] that best suits them without either asking leave or going through any formality other than that of building their homes. Thus the majority of inhabitants in the Department are North Americans, the Mexican population being reduced to only Bejar, Nacogdoches, and La Bahía del Espíritu Santo, wretched settlements that between them do not number three thousand inhabitants, and the new village of Guadalupe Victoria that has scarcely more than seventy settlers. The government of the state, with its seat at Saltillo, that should watch over the preservation of its most precious and interesting department, taking measures to prevent its being stolen by foreign hands, is the one that knows the least not only about actual conditions, but even about its territory. . . . Repeated and urgent appeals have been made to the Supreme Government of the Federation regarding the imminent danger in which this interesting Department is of becoming the prize of the ambitious North Americans, but never has it taken any measures that may be called conclusive. . . .

[Sánchez goes on to describe the village of Austin and the American colony founded by Stephen Austin.]

Its population is nearly two hundred persons, of which only ten are Mexicans, for the balance are all Americans from the North with an occasional European. Two wretched little stores supply the inhabitants of the colony: one sells only whiskey, rum, sugar, and coffee; the other, rice, flour, lard, and cheap cloth. . . . The Americans from the North, at least the great part of those I have seen, eat only salted meat, bread made by themselves out of corn meal, coffee, and home-made cheese. To these the greater part of those who live in the village add strong liquor, for they are in general, in my opinion, lazy people of vicious character. Some of them cultivate their small farms by planting corn; but this task they usually entrust to their negro slaves, whom they treat with considerable harshness. Beyond the village in an immense stretch of land formed by rolling hills are scattered the families brought by Stephen Austin, which today number more than two thousand persons. The diplomatic policy of this empresario, evident in all his actions, has, as one may say, lulled the authorities into a sense of security, while he works diligently for his own ends. In my judgment, the spark that will start the conflagration that will deprive us of Texas, will start from this colony. All because the government does not take vigorous measures to prevent it. Perhaps it does not realize the value of what it is about to lose.

Source: José María Sánchez, excerpted from "A Trip to Texas in 1828," trans. Carlos E. Castaneda from *Southwestern Historical Quarterly*, vol. 29

A Mexican Rebel in 1859

The U.S. victory in the Mexican War intensified cultural conflict along the now expanded Hispanic frontier. The Anglos (as Mexicans called white Americans) quickly assumed positions of political and economic dominance. They broke treaties designed to protect the property rights and land titles of Mexican Americans and under the cover of legality bullied peoples of Mexican descent. The resulting anger and resentment flared up in a brief revolt in 1859 in the lower Rio Grande valley led by Juan Cortina, a ranch owner who had fought for Mexico in the Mexican War. The following is from one of the proclamations issued by Cortina.

- **What** was Cortina's opinion of the Anglos?
- **What** reasons did he cite for the uprising?
- **How** did he attempt to rally support for his cause?

Mexicans! When the State of Texas [became] an integrant part of the Union, flocks of vampires, in the guise of men, came and scattered themselves in the settlements, without any capital except the corrupt heart and the most perverse intentions. Some, brimful of laws, pledged to us their protection against the attacks of the rest; others assembled in shadowy councils, attempted and excited the robbery and burning of our relatives on the other side of the river Bravo; while others, to the abusing of our unlimited confidence, when we entrusted them with our titles [to land], which secured the future of our families, refused to return them under false and frivolous pretexts. . . . Many of you have been robbed of your property, incarcerated, chased, murdered, and hunted like wild beasts, because your labor was fruitful, and because your industry excited the vile avarice which led them.

Mexicans! Is there no remedy for you? . . . Mexicans! My part is taken; the voice of revelation whispers to me that to me is entrusted the work of breaking the chains of your slavery, and that the Lord will enable me, with powerful arm, to fight against our enemies, in compliance with the requirements of that Sovereign Majesty [God], who, from this day forward, will hold us under His protection. On my part, I am ready to offer myself as a sacrifice for your happiness; and counting upon the means necessary for the discharge of my ministry, you may count upon my cooperation, should no cowardly attempt put an end to my days.

Source: House Executive Documents, No. 52, 36th Congress, 1st session, 1860, pp. 80–82.

New England merchants had been trading in California since the 1780s. What first attracted them were the seal fisheries off the California coast, a source of otter pelts highly prized in the China trade. After the seals had been all but exterminated by the 1820s, Yankee merchants shipped out hides and tallow to New England for processing into shoes and candles. Ships from New England and New York sailed around Cape Horn to California ports, where they unloaded trading goods. Servicing this trade in California was a resident colony of American agents, some 300 strong by the mid-1840s.

Whereas Yankees dominated the American colonies in coastal California, it was mostly midwestern farm families who filtered into the inner valleys of California from the Oregon Trail in the 1830s and 1840s (see Map 13–2). Nearly a thousand Americans lived in the Sacramento River Valley by 1846.

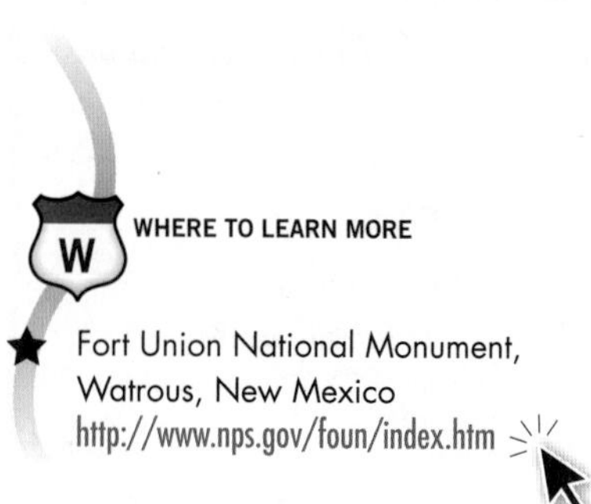

W
WHERE TO LEARN MORE
Fort Union National Monument,
Watrous, New Mexico
http://www.nps.gov/foun/index.htm

California belonged to Mexico in name only by the early 1840s. The program of economic development had strengthened California's ties to the outside world at the expense of Mexico. American merchants and California *rancheros* ran the economy, and both groups had joined separatist movements against Mexican rule. Unlike the *Californios*, who were ambivalent about their future political allegiance, the Americans wanted to be part of the United States and assumed that California would shortly be annexed. With the outbreak of the Mexican War in 1846, their wish became reality.

New Mexico. Except for Utah, the American push into the interior of the Mexican Southwest followed the California pattern of trade preceding settlement. When Mexico liberalized the formerly restrictive trading policies of Spain, American merchants opened up the 900-mile-long **Santa Fe Trail** from Independence, Missouri, to Santa Fe, New Mexico. Starved for mercantile goods, the New Mexicans were a small but highly profitable market. They paid for their American imports with gold, silver, and furs.

Santa Fe Trail The 900-mile trail opened by American merchants for trading purposes following Mexico's liberalization of the formerly restrictive trading policies of Spain.

Bent's Old Fort, an impregnable adobe structure built on the Arkansas River at the point where the Santa Fe Trail turned to the southwest, was the fulcrum for the growing economic influence of Americans over New Mexican affairs. Completed in 1832, the fort enabled the Bent brothers from Missouri to control a flourishing and almost monopolistic trade with Indians, trappers, caravans on the Santa Fe Trail, and the large landowners and merchants of New Mexico. This trade pulled New Mexico into the cultural and economic orbit of the United States and undermined what little sovereign power Mexico held in the region.

Although only a few hundred Americans were permanent residents of New Mexico in the 1840s, they had married into the Spanish-speaking landholding elite and were themselves beginning to receive large grants of land. Ties of blood and common economic interests linked this small group of American businessmen with the local elite. American merchants and New Mexican landlords were further united by their growing disdain for the instability of Mexican rule, Santa Anna's dictatorship, and sporadic attempts by Mexico to levy heavy taxes on the Santa Fe trade. Another bond was their concern over the aggressive efforts of the Texans to seize eastern New Mexico. After thwarting an 1841 Texan attempt to occupy Santa Fe, the leaders of New Mexico increasingly looked to the United States to protect their local autonomy. They quickly decided to cooperate with the U.S. army of invasion when the Mexican War got under way.

Utah. At the extreme northern and inner reaches of the Mexican borderlands lay Utah. Aside from trade with the Utes, Spain and Mexico had largely ignored this remote region. Its isolation and lack of white settlers, however, were precisely what made Utah so appealing to the Mormons, the Church of Jesus Christ of Latter-day Saints. For the Mormons in the 1840s, Utah became the promised land in which to build a new Zion.

Founded by Joseph Smith in upstate New York in the 1820s, Mormonism grew rapidly within a communitarian framework that stressed hard work and economic cooperation under the leadership of patriarchal leaders (see Chapter 12). The economic success of close-knit Mormon communities, combined with the righteous zeal of their members, aroused the fears and hostility of non-Mormons. Harassed out of New York, Ohio, and Missouri, the Mormons thought they had found a permanent home by the late 1830s in Nauvoo, Illinois. But the murder of Joseph Smith and his brother by a mob in 1844 convinced the beleaguered Mormons that they had to leave the settled East for a refuge in the West. In 1846 a group of Mormons migrated to the Great Basin in Utah. Under the leadership of Brigham Young, they established a new community in 1847 at the Great Salt Lake on the western slopes of the Wasatch Mountains. An annual influx of about 2,000 converts enabled the initial settlement to grow rapidly.

The Mormons succeeded by concentrating their farms along the fertile and relatively well-watered Wasatch Front. They dispensed land and organized an irrigation system that coordinated water rights with the amount of land under production. To their dismay, however, they learned in 1848 that they had not left the United States after all. The Union acquired Utah, along with the rest of the northern borderlands of Mexico, as a result of the Mexican War.

POLITICS, EXPANSION, AND WAR

WHY WAS James K. Polk so eager to provoke a war with Mexico?

The Democrats viewed their victory in the election of 1844 (see Chapter 10) as a popular mandate for expansion. James K. Polk, the new Democratic president, fully shared this expansionist vision. The greatest prize in his eyes was California. When he was stymied in his efforts to purchase California and New Mexico, he tried to force concessions from the Mexican government by ordering American troops to the mouth of the Rio Grande, far within the territory claimed by Mexico. When the virtually inevitable clash of arms occurred in late April 1846, war broke out between the United States and Mexico.

Victory resulted in the **Mexican Cession of 1848,** which added a half-million square miles to the United States. Polk's administration also finalized the acquisition of Texas and reached a compromise with the British on the Oregon Territory that recognized U.S. sovereignty in the Pacific Northwest up to the 49th parallel. The United States was now a nation that spanned a continent.

Mexican Cession of 1848 The addition of half a million square miles to the United States as a result of victory in the 1846 war between the United States and Mexico.

MANIFEST DESTINY

With a phrase that soon entered the nation's vocabulary, John L. O'Sullivan, editor and Democratic politician, proclaimed in 1845 America's "manifest destiny to overspread and to possess the whole of the continent which Providence has given us for the development of the great experiment of Liberty and federated self-government entrusted to us." Central to **Manifest Destiny** was the assumption that white Americans were a special people, a view that dated back to the Puritans' belief that God had appointed them to establish a New Israel cleansed of the corruption of the Old World.

Manifest Destiny Doctrine, first expressed in 1845, that the expansion of white Americans across the continent was inevitable and ordained by God.

What distinguished the special U.S. mission as enunciated by Manifest Destiny was its explicitly racial component. Between 1815 and 1850, the term Anglo-Saxon, originally loosely applied to English-speaking peoples, acquired racial overtones. Caucasian Anglo-Saxon Americans, as the descendants of ancient Germanic tribes that had purportedly brought the seeds of free institutions to England, were now said to be the foremost race in the world. The superior racial pedigree they claimed for themselves gave white Americans the natural right to expand westward, a chosen people carrying the blessings of democracy and progress. Only they, it was argued, had the energy, industriousness, and innate love of liberty to establish a successful free government.

Read the **Document** at **www.myhistorylab.com** *From Then to Now Online: Manifest Destiny and American Foreign Policy*

Manifest Destiny was closely associated with the Democratic Party. For Democrats, expansionism would counterbalance the debilitating effects of industrialization and urbanization. As good Jeffersonians, they stressed the need for more land to realize the ideal of a democratic republic rooted in the virtues and rough equality of independent farmers. For their working-class

GLOBAL CONNECTIONS

THE NINETEENTH-CENTURY FRONTIER

"If I was to till you of our own township how it is growing as if it were by m[a]gic and also our market town Castlemaine you would not feel much interest in them. But realy they astonish me. As to our digging there is little new but likely I will send you a newspaper which will give you all the information of these Things. . . . Our great railroad is now all the talk but is not begun yet. . . . There is a great many goldmining compenys starting up about this place I believe five or six some of them so large as 2000 shares. It is causing work to get more plenty for those who is willing to work for wages and if our great railway was started I think there need not be many idle. But I think that wages will never be high again as there is still a goodly number waiting in hops of the same perhaps more Than will work when they get the chance."

In this letter, with words and details that we might expect from an American prospecting for gold in California, John McCance, an Irish emigrant to Australia, wrote back home describing the conditions he faced in the goldfields in the province of Victoria. Settling a frontier, and displacing and subjugating native peoples in the process, was not a unique American experience in the nineteenth century. It was part of a worldwide process replicated by migrants, especially of European origin, in such areas as Latin America, Canada, South Africa, Australia, and New Zealand. Population growth on a global scale, combined with improved and cheap forms of international travel, fed a stream of migrants into the frontier regions of the Southern Hemisphere and the North American West. In a radical environmental adaptation that made possible a tremendous increase in global supplies of food, vast, open expanses of grasslands, increasingly accessible by railroads, were transformed for the commercial production of grain and livestock. As newcomers poured in, indigenous foraging and pastoral peoples were wiped out, displaced, herded onto reservations, or forced to fundamentally change their ways of living, the victims of disease and superior military force and technology. The advance of global frontiers and the growing dominance of European-based societies went hand-in-hand in the nineteenth century.

- How would you define a frontier?
- To what extent would you argue that the U.S. frontier experience has been unique?

Irish constituency, the Democrats touted the broad expanses of the West as the surest means to escape the misery of wage slavery.

Manifest Destiny captured the popular imagination when the country was still mired in depression after the Panic of 1837. The way out of the depression, according to many Democrats, was to revive the export trade to soak up the agricultural surplus.

In this late-1872 evocation of the spirit of Manifest Destiny, Indians retreat westward as white settlers, guided by a diaphanously clad America, spread the benefits of American civilization.

THE MEXICAN WAR

Once in office, Polk proved far more conciliatory with the British than with the Mexicans. Polk was willing to compromise on Oregon because he dreaded the possibility of a two-front war against both the Mexicans and the British. Mexico had severed diplomatic ties with the United States over the annexation of Texas (see Chapter 10), and a war could break out at any time.

In the spring of 1846, after Polk had abrogated the agreement on the joint occupation of Oregon, the British offered a compromise that they had earlier rejected. They agreed to a boundary at the 49th parallel if they were allowed to retain Vancouver Island in Puget Sound. Polk sent the offer to the Senate, which quickly approved it in June 1846.

Unlike Oregon, where he backed off from extravagant territorial claims, Polk refused to budge on the U.S. claim (inherited from the Texans when the

United States annexed Texas in 1845) that the Rio Grande was the border between Texas and Mexico. The Mexicans insisted that the Nueces River, 100 miles north of the Rio Grande, was the border, as it had been when Texas was part of Mexico.

Citing rumors of a Mexican invasion, Polk sent 3,500 troops under General Zachary Taylor to the Nueces River in the summer of 1845. Polk also stepped up his efforts to acquire California. He instructed Thomas Larkin, the U.S. consul in Monterey, California, to inform the *Californios* and Americans that the United States would support them if they revolted against Mexican rule. Polk also secretly ordered the U.S. Pacific naval squadron to seize California ports if war broke out with Mexico. Polk's final effort at peaceful expansion was the Slidell mission in November 1845. He sent John L. Slidell to Mexico City to offer $30 million to purchase California and New Mexico and to secure the Rio Grande boundary.

When Polk learned that the Mexican government had refused to receive Slidell, he set out to draw Mexico into a war that would result in the U.S. acquisition of California. In early 1846, he ordered General Taylor to advance to the Rio Grande, deep in the disputed border region. Taylor blockaded the mouth of the Rio Grande and built a fort on the northern bank across from the Mexican town of Matamoros. The Mexicans attacked and were repulsed on April 24.

Even before the news reached Washington, Polk had decided on war. Informed of the clash between Mexican and American troops in early May (it took ten days for the news to reach Washington), he sent a redrafted war message to Congress on May 9 asserting that Mexico "has invaded our territory, and shed American blood on American soil." Congress declared war on May 13, 1846.

The war was a stunning military success for the United States (see Map 13–4), in large measure because a decade of Comanche raids had so pillaged and demoralized settlements across northern Mexico that the local inhabitants were in no condition to resist any invader. The Mexicans fought bravely, but they lacked the leadership, modern artillery, and naval capacity to check the U.S. advances. By the end of 1846, Polk had gained his objectives in the Mexican borderlands. An army sent west under Colonel Stephen W. Kearny occupied New Mexico. The

QUICK REVIEW

Manifest Destiny

- Manifest Destiny distinguished by its explicitly racial component.
- Doctrine operated as a self-serving justification for territorial aggrandizement.
- Manifest Destiny associated with Democratic Party.

Read the **Document**

at **www.myhistorylab.com**
John O'Sullivan, Annexation (1845)

Read the **Document**

at **www.myhistorylab.com**
Thomas Corwin, Against the Mexican War (1847)

THE MEXICAN RULERS,
migrating from Matamoras, with their Treasures
T. B. Peterson Agent 98 Chesnut St. Philadelphia

This anti-Catholic lithograph sarcastically depicts the "rulers" of Mexico as lecherous Catholic clerics who were quick to desert the Mexican town of Matamor as when U.S. troops arrived in May 1846. The priest and monk ride out of Matamoras accompanied by young women, bottles of wine, and other booty.

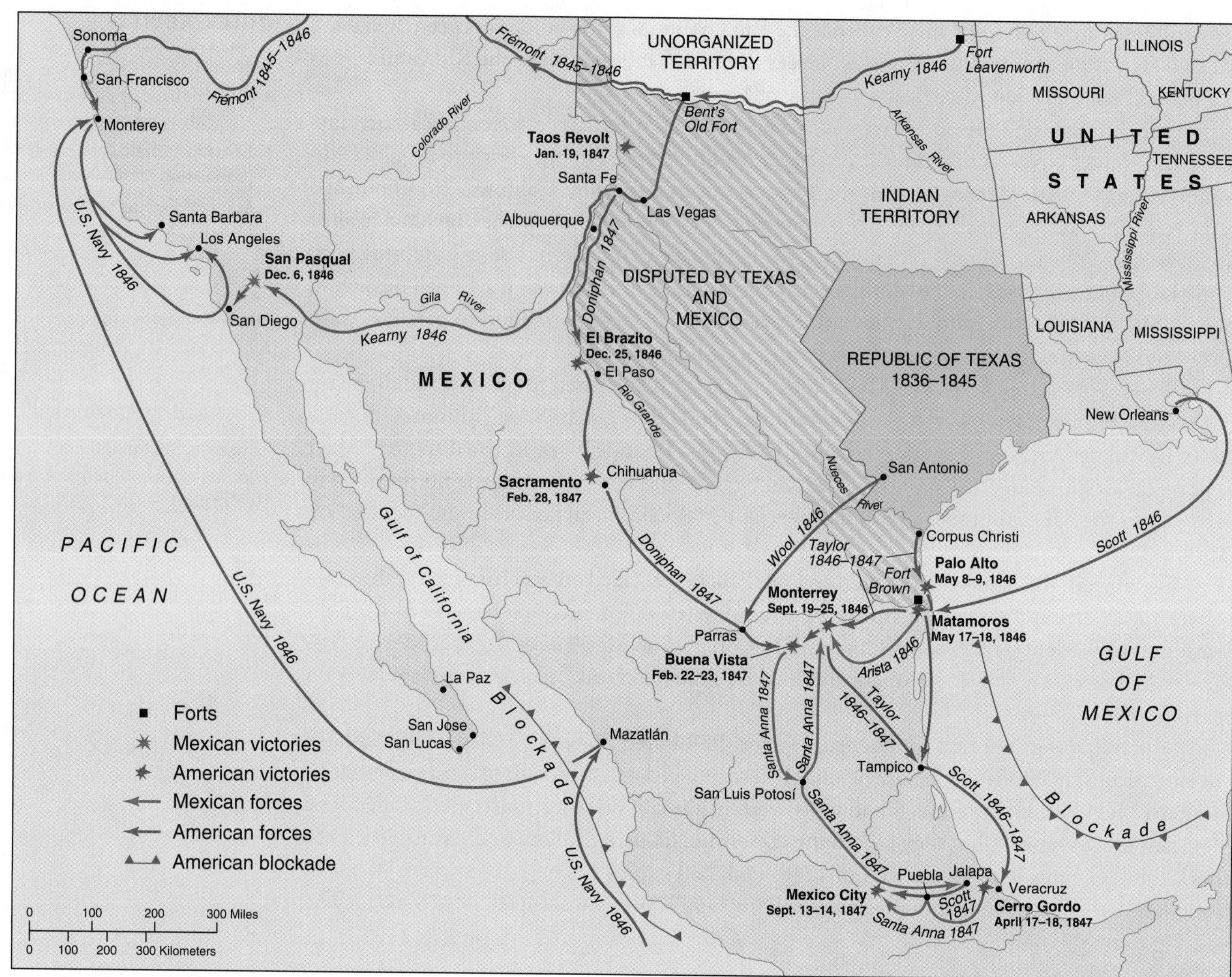

MAP 13–4 The Mexican War Victories by General Zachary Taylor in northern Mexico secured the Rio Grande as the boundary between Texas and Mexico. Colonel Stephen Kearny's expedition won control of New Mexico, and reinforcements from Kearny ensured the success of American troops landed by the Pacific Squadron in gaining Alta California for the United States. The success of General Winfield Scott's amphibious invasion at Vera Cruz and his occupation of Mexico City brought the war to an end.

Why did the United States feel the need to employ naval blockades to the east and west of Mexico?

See the Map at **www.myhistorylab.com** *Mexican-American War, 1846–1848*

Watch the Video at **www.myhistorylab.com** *The Annexation of Texas*

conquest was relatively bloodless, because most of the local elite cooperated with the U.S. forces. Sporadic resistance was largely confined to poorer Mexicans and the Pueblo Indians, who feared that their land would be confiscated.

Kearny's army then moved to Tucson and eventually linked up in southern California with pro-American rebels and U.S. forces sent ashore by the Pacific squadron. As in New Mexico, the stiffest resistance came from ordinary Mexicans and the Spanish-speaking Indians.

Despite the loss of its northern provinces, Mexico refused to concede defeat. After Taylor had established a secure defensive line in northeastern Mexico with a victory at Monterrey in September 1846 and repulsed a Mexican counterattack at Buena Vista in February 1847, Polk directed General Winfield Scott to invade central Mexico. Following an amphibious assault on Vera Cruz in March 1847, Scott captured Mexico City in September.

After a frustrating delay while Mexico reorganized its government, peace talks finally got under way and concluded in the Treaty of Guadalupe Hidalgo, signed on February 2, 1848. Mexico surrendered its claim to Texas north of the Rio Grande and ceded Alta California and

New Mexico (including present-day Arizona, Utah, and Nevada). The United States paid $15 million, assumed over $3 million in claims of American citizens against Mexico, and agreed to grant U.S. citizenship to Mexican residents in its new territories.

Polk had gained his strategic goals, but the cost was 13,000 American lives (most from diseases such as measles and dysentery), 50,000 Mexican lives, and the poisoning of Mexican-American relations for generations. The war also, as will be seen in Chapter 14, heightened sectional tensions over slavery and weakened the political structure that was vital to preserving the Union.

QUICK REVIEW

War with Mexico

- Polk sought a war that would give the United States control of California.
- Mexico fought bravely but could not match American military.
- Treaty of Guadalupe Hidalgo (1848): Mexico gave up claim to Texas north of Rio Grande, Alta California, and New Mexico.

CONCLUSION

Americans were an expansionist people. Their surge across the continent between 1815 and 1850 was fully in keeping with their restless desire for personal independence on a plot of land. Population pressure on overworked farms in the East impelled much of this westward migration, but by the 1840s, expansion had seemingly acquired a momentum all its own, one that increasingly rejected the claims of other peoples to the land. Far from being a process of peaceful, evolutionary, and democratic change, expansion involved the spread of slavery, violent confrontations, and the uprooting and displacement of native peoples. As Catlin sensed in the 1830s, the coming of white settlement quickly had a devastating impact on the native peoples he visited and befriended. By 1850, the earlier notion of reserving the trans-Mississippi West as a permanent Indian country had been abandoned. The Sioux and Comanches were still feared by white settlers, but their final subjugation was not far off. The derogatory stereotypes of Mexican Americans that were a staple of both popular thought and expansionist ideology showed clearly that U.S. control after the Mexican War would relegate Spanish-speaking people to second-class status. However misleading and false much of it was, the rhetoric of Manifest Destiny did highlight a central truth. Broad, popular support existed for expanding across the continent. As the Mexican War made clear, the United States was now unquestionably the dominant power in North America. The only serious threat to its dominance in the near future would come from inside, not outside, its domain.

Where to Learn More

Indian Pueblo Cultural Center, Albuquerque, New Mexico. This center provides an excellent orientation to the culture, crafts, and community life of the Pueblo and southwestern Indians. It also includes much material on archaeological findings. Visit http://www.indianpueblo.org for a calendar of events and an introduction to the history of the nineteen pueblos.

Indian Museum of North America, Crazy Horse, South Dakota. This is one of the best sources for learning about the culture of the Teton Sioux and other American and Canadian tribes on the Great Plains. Holdings include outstanding examples of Indian art and artifacts. For information on exhibits, educational and cultural programs, and special collections of Native American art, go to http://www.crazyhorsememorial.org/monument/.

Scotts Bluff National Monument, Gering, Nebraska. Scotts Bluff was a prominent landmark on the Oregon Trail, and the museum exhibits here have interpretive material on the trail and the western phase of expansion. Go to http://www.nps.gov/scbl/index.htm to print a park travel guide and to access a website devoted to the frontier photographer and artist William Henry Jackson.

Conner Prairie, Noblesville, Indiana. The museum and historic area re-create a sense of life on the Indiana frontier during the period of the Old Northwest. See http://www.connerprairie.org.

Fort Union National Monument, Watrous, New Mexico. Fort Union was a nineteenth-century military post, and the holdings and exhibits in the museum relate to frontier military life and the Santa Fe Trail. For a printable travel guide and a history of the park that includes bibliographical aids, go to http://www.nps.gov/foun/index.htm.

Review Questions

1. What accounted for the westward movement of Americans? How did the presence or absence of slavery affect developmental patterns in the new settlements?
2. How was the West of the Plains Indians transformed after 1830 as peoples migrated both within the region and into it from various directions? Why were the Sioux so powerful? How did they interact with other Native Americans and the U.S. government?
3. Who lived in the Mexican borderlands of the Southwest? Why was it so difficult for the Mexican government to maintain effective control of the region? What role did trade play in the American penetration of the Southwest?
4. What did Americans mean by Manifest Destiny? Why was territorial expansion so identified with the Democratic Party?
5. Who was responsible for the outbreak of the Mexican War? Were Mexicans the victims of American aggression? Why did the British make no effort to intervene?
6. How valid was the Sioux chief's indictment of the pretensions of white civilization as related to George Catlin?

Key Terms

Alamo (p. 351)
Californios (p. 352)
Claims clubs (p. 342)
Empresarios (p. 350)
Manifest Destiny (p. 355)
Mexican Cession of 1848 (p. 355)
Oregon Trail (p. 345)
Santa Fe Trail (p. 354)
Tejano (p. 350)

PEARSON myhistorylab Connections

Reinforce what you learned in this chapter by studying the many documents, images, maps, review tools, and videos available at **www.myhistorylab.com**.

Read and Review

Study and Review **Study Plan: Chapter 13**

Read the Document

Chief Seattle, Oration (1854)

Polk's 1st Inaugural Address (1845)

Elizabeth Dixon Smith Geer, Oregon Trail Journal (1847, 1848)

John O'Sullivan, Annexation (1845)

Lydia Allen Rudd, Diary of Westward Journey (1852)

The Treaty of Fort Laramie (1851)

Thomas Corwin, Against the Mexican War (1847)

William Barret Travis, Letter from the Alamo (1836)

History Bookshelf

James Fenimore Cooper, The Pioneers (1823)

Francis Parkman, The Oregon Trail: Sketches of Prairie and Rocky-Mountain Life (1847)

See the Map

Mexican-American War, 1846–1848

Native American Land Cessions, 1840

Research and Explore

Read the Document

Personal Journeys Online

From Then to Now Online: Manifest Destiny and American Foreign Policy

Exploring America: America and the Horse

Watch the Video *The Annexation of Texas*

Hear the Audio

Hear the audio files for Chapter 13 at **www.myhistorylab.com.**

1846-1861

14 The Politics of Sectionalism

The slave Eliza is attacked by vicious dogs while crossing a frozen river with her baby in this 1881 poster advertising a production of *Uncle Tom's Cabin*.

Hear the Audio

Hear the audio files for Chapter 14 at **www.myhistorylab.com**.

SLAVERY IN THE TERRITORIES *(page 366)*

WHY WAS the issue of slavery in the territories so contentious?

POLITICAL REALIGNMENT *(page 372)*

WHAT FACTORS contributed to the Republicans' rise to political prominence?

THE ROAD TO DISUNION *(page 381)*

WHY WERE southerners so alarmed by the election of Abraham Lincoln in 1860?

ONE AMERICAN JOURNEY

December 16, 1852

My Dear Madam,

So you want to know what sort of woman I am! Well, if this is any object, you shall have statistics free of charge. To begin, then, I am a little bit of a woman, somewhat more than forty, about as thin and dry as a pinch of snuff, never very much to look at in my best days and looking like a used up article now.

I was married when I was twenty-five years old to a man rich in Greek and Hebrew and Latin and Arabic, and alas, rich in nothing else. . . . But then I was abundantly furnished with wealth of another sort. I had two little curly headed twin daughters to begin with and my stock in this line has gradually increased, till I have been the mother of seven children, the most beautiful and the most loved of whom lies buried near my Cincinnati residence. It was at his dying bed and at his grave that I learned what a poor slave mother may feel when her child is torn away from her. In those depths of sorrow which seemed to me immeasurable, it was my only prayer to God that such anguish might not be suffered in vain. There were circumstances about his death of such peculiar bitterness, of what seemed almost cruel suffering that I felt that I could never be consoled for it unless this crushing of my own heart might enable me to work out some great good to others.

I allude to this here because I have often felt that much that is in that book had its root in the awful scenes and bitter sorrow of that summer. It has left now, I trust, no trace on my mind except a deep compassion for the sorrowful, especially for mothers who are separated from their children. . . .

This horror, this nightmare abomination! Can it be in my country! It lies like lead on my heart, it shadows my life with sorrow; the more so that I feel, as for my own brothers, for the South, and am pained by every horror I am obliged to write, as one who is forced by some awful oath to disclose in court some family disgrace. . . .

Yours affectionately,

H. B. Stowe

Harriet Beecher Stowe to Eliza Cabot Follen, December 16, 1852; from Jeanne Boydston, Mary Kelley, and Anne Margolis, *The Limits of Sisterhood* (Chapel Hill: University of North Carolina Press, 1988), pp. 178–180.

Read the **Document** at **www.myhistorylab.com**

Personal Journeys Online

- **Carl Schurz, *Reminiscences*, 1908. Account of his participation in Germany's failed Revolution of 1848 and his subsequent journey to freedom in the United States.**
- **Frederick Douglass, three excerpts: "What of the Night?" May 5, 1848; "A Letter to American Slaves," September 5, 1850; "Letter to James Redpath, June 29, 1860." These excerpts chart the famous black abolitionist's journey from a belief in moral suasion and political action as the best strategy to liberate the nation's slaves to an embrace of direct action and violence as the only remedy for emancipation.**

HARRIET BEECHER STOWE, in her letter to the poet and fellow abolitionist Eliza Cabot Follen in the year that *Uncle Tom's Cabin* became an international best seller, revealed how being a wife and a mother had influenced her perception of slavery and inspired her writing. When she was barely out of her teens, her family left their New England home for the raw frontier town of Cincinnati in 1832. Stowe's father, Lyman Beecher, already a famous Protestant evangelical preacher, moved there to save the West from Roman Catholicism. Stowe wrote a geography textbook, married a young scholar from her father's seminary,

CHRONOLOGY

1846	Wilmot Proviso is submitted to Congress but is defeated.
1848	Gold is discovered in California.
	Whig Party candidate Zachary Taylor defeats Democrat Lewis Cass and Free-Soiler Martin Van Buren for the presidency.
	Revolutions in Europe; publication of Karl Marx and Friedrich Engels's *Communist Manifesto*.
1850	California applies for statehood.
	President Taylor dies; Vice President Millard Fillmore succeeds him.
	Compromise of 1850 is passed.
1851	Harriet Beecher Stowe publishes *Uncle Tom's Cabin*.
1852	Democrat Franklin Pierce is elected president in a landslide over Whig candidate Winfield Scott.
	Whig Party disintegrates.
1853	National Black Convention convened in Rochester, New York, to demand repeal of the Fugitive Slave Act.
	Crimean War erupts between Russia and Turkey over Russian demand to protect Christian shrines in Palestine; soon engulfs Britain and France; eventually leads to the unification of Germany and Italy.
1854	Ostend Manifesto is issued.
	Kansas-Nebraska Act repeals the Missouri Compromise.
	Know-Nothing and Republican parties are formed.
1855	Civil war erupts in "Bleeding Kansas."
	William Walker attempts a takeover of Nicaragua.
1856	"Sack of Lawrence" occurs in Kansas; John Brown makes a retaliatory raid at Pottawatomie Creek.
	Democratic congressman Preston Brooks of South Carolina canes Massachusetts senator Charles Sumner in the U.S. Senate.
	Democrat James Buchanan is elected president over Republican John C. Frémont and American (Know-Nothing) candidate Millard Fillmore.
1857	Supreme Court issues *Dred Scott* decision.
	Kansas territorial legislature passes the proslavery Lecompton Constitution.
	Panic of 1857 begins.
1858	Senatorial candidates Abraham Lincoln and Stephen A. Douglas hold series of debates in Illinois.
1859	John Brown's Raid fails at Harpers Ferry, Virginia.
1860	Constitutional Union Party forms.
	Democratic Party divides into northern and southern factions.
	Republican candidate Abraham Lincoln is elected president over southern Democratic candidate John C. Breckinridge, northern Democratic candidate Stephen A. Douglas, and Constitutional Unionist candidate John Bell.
	South Carolina secedes from the Union.
1861	The rest of the Lower South secedes from the Union.
	Crittenden Plan and Tyler's Washington peace conference fail.
	Jefferson Davis assumes presidency of the Confederate States of America.
	Lincoln is inaugurated.
	Fort Sumter is bombarded; Civil War begins.
	Several Upper South states secede.
	Tsar Alexander II of Russia frees the serfs.

and settled into motherhood. The growing antislavery crusade prompted her to write a few articles on the subject. Not until the death of her beloved son, Charley, in a cholera epidemic in 1849, however, did she make the connection between her own tragedy and the national tragedy of human bondage.

Slavery was an abstract concept to most white northerners at the time. Stowe personalized it in a way that made them see it as an institution that did not just oppress black people but also destroyed families and debased well-meaning Christian masters. The deep piety expressed in the letter permeated the book and changed people's moral perceptions about slavery.

As slavery took on a personal and tragic meaning for Stowe, so it would move from being just another political issue to a moral crusade. Stowe's personal journey transformed it into a political passion; for the millions who read her book, the political became personal. Yet the anguish she expressed in her writing and the outrage it generated among her readers was hardly prefigured when a relatively obscure congressman from Pennsylvania stepped forward in 1846 with a modest proposal that not only placed slavery front and center as a national political issue, a position that only strengthened over the next fifteen years, but would shake the Union to its very core. ✦

Slavery was not, of course, a new political issue. But after 1846, the clashes between northern and southern congressmen over issues relating to slavery became more frequent and more difficult to resolve. In the coming years, several developments, including white southerners' growing consciousness of themselves as a minority, the mixture of political issues with religious questions, and the rise of the Republican Party, would aggravate sectional antagonism. The flash point was the issue of slavery in the territories acquired from Mexico.

SLAVERY IN THE TERRITORIES

WHY WAS the issue of slavery in the territories so contentious?

Whatever its boundaries over the years, the West symbolized the hopes and dreams of white Americans. It was the region of fresh starts, of possibilities. To exclude slavery from the western territories was to exclude white southerners from pursuing their vision of the American dream. Northern politicians disagreed. They argued that exclusion preserved equality, the equality of all white men and women to live and work without competition from slave labor or rule by despotic slaveholders. The issue of slavery in the territories became an issue of freedom for both sides. From the late 1840s until 1861, northern and southern leaders attempted to fashion a solution to the problem of slavery in the territories. Four proposals dominated the debate:

- Outright exclusion
- Extension of the Missouri Compromise line to the Pacific
- Popular sovereignty, allowing the residents of a territory to decide the issue
- Protection of the property of slaveholders (meaning their right to own slaves) even if few lived in the territory

The first major debate on these proposals occurred during the early days of the Mexican War and culminated in the Compromise of 1850.

THE WILMOT PROVISO

Wilmot Proviso The amendment offered by Pennsylvania Democrat David Wilmot in 1846 which stipulated that "as an express and fundamental condition to the acquisition of any territory from the Republic of Mexico . . . neither slavery nor involuntary servitude shall ever exist in any part of said territory."

In August 1846, David Wilmot, a Pennsylvania Democrat, offered an amendment to an appropriations bill for the Mexican War. The language of the **Wilmot Proviso** stipulated that "as an express and fundamental condition to the acquisition of any territory from the Republic of Mexico . . . neither slavery nor involuntary servitude shall ever exist in any part of said territory."

Wilmot explained that he wanted only to preserve the territories for "the sons of toil, of my own race and own color." By thus linking the exclusion of slavery in the territories to freedom for white people, he hoped to generate support across the North, regardless of party, and even in some areas of the Upper South. Linking freedom for white people to the exclusion of slaves infuriated southerners. It implied that the mere proximity of slavery was degrading and that white southerners were therefore a degraded people, unfit to join other Americans in the territories.

Northern lawmakers, a majority in the House of Representatives (because the northern states had a larger population than the southern states), passed more than 50 versions of the proviso between 1846 and 1850. In the Senate, however, where each state had equal representation, the proviso was consistently rejected and never became law.

The proviso debate sowed distrust and suspicion between northerners and southerners. Congress had divided along sectional lines before, but seldom had the divisions become so personal.

Religious differences also sharpened the sectional conflict over the proviso. The leading evangelical Protestant denominations—Methodists, Baptists, and Presbyterians—split along sectional lines by the mid-1840s. Growing numbers of northern evangelicals advocated political action. Southern evangelicals recoiled from such mixing of church and state, charging northerners with abandoning the basic tenets of evangelical Christianity: the importance of individual salvation above all, and the Bible as the unerring word of God. The leaders of the Democratic and Whig parties, disturbed that the issue of slavery in the territories could so

GLOBAL CONNECTIONS

The Revolutions of 1848

New Yorkers greeted the "Magnificent Magyar," Hungarian patriot Louis Kossuth, as a conquering hero in December 1851. Supporters rushed the stage from which he was to deliver a speech, and one female admirer tore off a section of his coat as a prized souvenir. To New Yorkers, Kossuth embodied the democratic ideals of their nation founded on the principles of liberty and equality.

Fueled by rapid industrial and urban transformation, democratic sentiment spread over the European continent among the new working and middle classes in the 1840s. France showed the way. When the government of King Louis-Philippe failed to respond to demands for economic and political reforms, these groups banded together to overthrow the monarchy in February 1848. But the resulting government and new constitution under Charles Louis Napoleon Bonaparte, the nephew of the famous ruler, offered only superficial change, as reformers squandered their advantage with internal bickering between radicals and moderates.

When students at the University of Bonn heard the news of Louis-Philippe's downfall, they rushed into the town square to demand civil and religious liberties and the formation of a German national state. "We were dominated by a vague feeling," one student recalled, "as if a great outbreak of elemental forces had begun, as if an earthquake was impending of which we had felt the first shock." But the authoritarian rulers of the nine German states, while they allowed the formation of an all-German parliament and the drafting of a republican constitution, ignored both and the revolution failed.

A similar scenario played out in the Austrian Empire, a conglomeration of eleven different ethnic peoples, including Kossuth's Hungary. The ruling Hapsburg monarchy initially accepted some of the reformers' demands but then ruthlessly suppressed uprisings in Prague, Vienna, and Buda (Hungary). The Austrians also reestablished their control over portions of Italy, successfully overcoming a movement for Italian unity and reform.

These setbacks troubled Americans. Their initial enthusiasm for the revolutionary movements of 1848 was rooted in the belief that mankind naturally prefers liberty and equality and that the American experiment was exportable to other peoples. President James K. Polk hailed developments in Europe in 1848: "The great principles of popular sovereignty which were proclaimed in 1776 by the immortal author of our Declaration of Independence, seem now to be in the course of rapid development throughout the world."

The failure of these revolutionary movements made the American experiment that much more precious, and it also highlighted some contradictions in American democratic life. Frederick Douglass wondered how Americans could lionize a Hungarian freedom fighter, but hunt down Americans with the same aspirations. Events of the 1850s would sorely test that experiment.

- How did Americans come to view their own ideals in the aftermath of the revolutions of 1848 in Europe?

monopolize Congress and poison sectional relations, sought to defuse the issue as the presidential election of 1848 approached.

The Election of 1848

Both Democrats and Whigs wanted to avoid identification with either side of the Wilmot Proviso controversy, and they selected their 1848 presidential candidates accordingly. The Democrats nominated Michigan senator Lewis Cass, a party stalwart, whose public career stretched back to the War of 1812. Cass understood the destructive potential of the slavery issue. In 1847, he suggested that territorial residents, not Congress, should decide slavery's fate. This solution, **popular sovereignty,** had a do-it-yourself charm: Keep the politicians out of it, and let the people decide. Cass was deliberately ambiguous, however, on when the people should decide. The timing was important. If residents could decide only when applying for statehood, slavery would be legal up to that point. The ambiguity aroused more fears than it allayed.

popular sovereignty A solution to the slavery crisis suggested by Michigan senator Lewis Cass by which territorial residents, not Congress, would decide slavery's fate.

The Whigs were silent on the slavery issue. Reverting to their winning 1840 formula of nominating a war hero, they selected General Zachary Taylor of Mexican War fame. Taylor belonged to no party and had never voted. If one had to guess his views, his background provided some clues. He owned a hundred-slave plantation in Louisiana, and his now-deceased daughter had been married to Jefferson Davis, Mississippi's staunch proslavery senator.

Taylor's background disturbed many antislavery northern Whigs. These Conscience Whigs, along with remnants of the old Liberty Party and a scattering of northern Democrats, bolted their parties and formed the Free-Soil Party. The name reflected the party's vow to keep the territories free. Its slogan, "Free soil, free speech, free labor, free men," was a catalog of white liberties that the South had allegedly threatened over the previous decade. The Free-Soilers' appeal centered on their opposition to slave labor in the territories. Free labor, they believed, could not compete with bonded labor. The party nominated former president Martin Van Buren.

Chalking up one out of seven northern votes, Van Buren ran strongly enough in 11 of the 15 northern states to deny the winning candidate in those states a majority of the votes cast. But he could not overcome Taylor's strength in the South. Taylor was elected, giving the nation its first president from the Lower South.

QUICK REVIEW

Slavery and the Election of 1848

- Democratic candidate Lewis Cass argued that territorial residents should decide the issue of slavery.
- Whig nominee Zachary Taylor remained silent on slavery issue.
- Taylor's election gave the country its first president from the Lower South.

The Gold Rush

Events in distant California, recently acquired from Mexico, would leave Taylor little time to savor his victory. By the time he took office in March 1849, a gold rush was under way there.

Through 1849 and 1850, more than 100,000 hopefuls flooded into California. Though the trek to California took months, whether overland or by the sea route, and travelers battled disease, weather, and each other, the lure of gold, easy to get at with just simple tools, was a powerful motivator.

Huge fortunes accrued, not only from the gold, but from supplying the miners. Young Levi Strauss experimented with trousers made out of canvas that miners particularly favored; two brothers, Henry Wells and William Fargo, offered banking, transportation, and mail services for the newcomers. The rush also attracted migrants from around the world. California soon became a polyglot empire of Chinese, Chileans, Mexicans, Irish, Germans, and Turks. Blacks, mostly slaves brought by southern masters, also roamed the gold fields.

By 1853 gold-mining operations had undergone structural and technological changes that made many miners superfluous. The new hydraulic extraction techniques severely damaged the pristine rivers of central California. Almost overnight, San Francisco was transformed from a modest port to a cosmopolitan metropolis. The image of California, and of the West in general, as wild or golden, dates from this era. But the romance of California and the wealth it generated loomed more troubling back east as the territory filled up with people in 1849. For the western dream would soon become ensnared in the conflict over slavery.

QUICK REVIEW

The Gold Rush

- 1849–1850: 100,000 would-be miners arrive in California.
- Rush attracted migrants from around the world.
- By 1853 large mining companies had taken over.
- California's population growth intensified conflict over slavery.

The California Gold Rush attracted a multinational population. Here, Chinese miners relax at their camp. The placid scene masks the occasionally violent confrontations between different racial and ethnic groups drawn to the gold fields.

The Compromise of 1850

When the California territory's new residents began asking for statehood and drafted a state constitution, the document contained no provision for slavery. The constitution reflected antiblack rather than antislavery sentiment. Keeping California white would shield residents against social and economic interaction with black people. If Congress accepted the residents' request for statehood, California would enter the Union as a free state. The Union at the time consisted of 15 free states and 15 slave states. The admission of California would tip the balance. New Mexico appeared poised to follow suit and enter the Union as the seventeenth free state. Southerners saw their political power slipping away. Northern leaders saw an opportunity to stop the extension of slavery and reduce southern influence in the federal government.

When Congress confronted the issue of California statehood in December 1849, partisans on both sides began marshaling forces for what promised to be a long and bitter struggle. Because nine Free-Soil candidates had won seats in the House of Representatives, neither Whigs nor Democrats held a majority there.

Read the **Document** at **www.myhistorylab.com** *The Compromise of 1850*

No one, at first, knew where Taylor stood. He supported, it turned out, a version of popular sovereignty and favored allowing California and the other territories acquired from Mexico to decide the slavery issue for themselves. Under normal circumstances, the residents of a new territory organized a territorial government under the direction of Congress. When the territory's population approached 30,000 or so, residents could draft a constitution and petition Congress for statehood. California already easily exceeded the population threshold. Taylor proposed bypassing the territorial stage, and congressional involvement in it, and having California and New Mexico admitted as states directly. The result would be to bring both into the Union as free states.

Southerners resisted Taylor's plan, and Congress deadlocked on the territorial issue. Henry Clay then stepped forward with his last great compromise. To break the impasse, Clay urged that Congress should take five steps:

- Admit California as a free state, as its residents clearly preferred.
- Allow the residents of the New Mexico and Utah territories to decide the slavery issue for themselves.
- End the slave trade in the District of Columbia.
- Pass a new fugitive slave law to enforce the constitutional provision stating that a person "held to Service or Labor in one state . . . escaping into another . . . shall be delivered upon Claim of the party to whom such Service or Labor may be due."
- Set the boundary between Texas and New Mexico and pay Texas $10 million for the territory given up to New Mexico. (Texas, incidentally, would use this payment to retire its state debt and fund a public school system.)

Clay's proposal provoked a historic Senate debate that began in February 1850, featuring America's three most prominent statesmen, Clay, John C. Calhoun, and Daniel Webster, together for the last time. Calhoun argued that the compromise did not resolve the slavery issue to the South's satisfaction, and he proposed to give southerners in Congress the right to veto legislation as a way to safeguard their minority rights. Webster stood up to support the compromise, at deep political peril to himself. His Massachusetts constituents detested the fugitive slave provision, which gave southern slaveholders the right to "invade" northern states to reclaim escaped slaves. After tumultuous deliberation that lasted into the summer of 1850, the Senate rejected the compromise.

QUICK REVIEW

The Compromise of 1850: Key Figures

- Senator Henry Clay: Kentucky (Whig).
- Senator John C. Calhoun: South Carolina (Democrat).
- Senator Daniel Webster: Massachusetts (Whig).

President Taylor, who had vowed to veto any compromise, died unexpectedly of a stomach ailment after overindulging in cherries and milk in the hot sun at a July 4 celebration in Washington. Vice President Millard Fillmore, a pro-Clay New Yorker, assumed the presidency after Taylor's death. Fillmore let it be known that he favored Clay's package and would sign it if passed.

Although the Senate had rejected the compromise, Illinois senator Stephen A. Douglas kept it alive. Like Webster, Douglas feared for the Union if the compromise failed. Realizing that it would never pass as a package, he proposed to break it up into its components and hold a separate vote on each. With a handful of senators voting for all parts, and with different sectional blocs supporting one provision or another, Douglas engineered a majority for the compromise, and Fillmore signed it.

Compromise of 1850 The four-step compromise which admitted California as a free state, allowed the residents of the New Mexico and Utah territories to decide the slavery issue for themselves, ended the slave trade in the District of Columbia, and passed a new fugitive slave law.

The **Compromise of 1850** (see Map 14–1) was not a compromise in the sense of each opposing side consenting to certain terms desired by the other. The North gained California but would have done so in any case. Southern leaders looked to the West and saw no slave territories

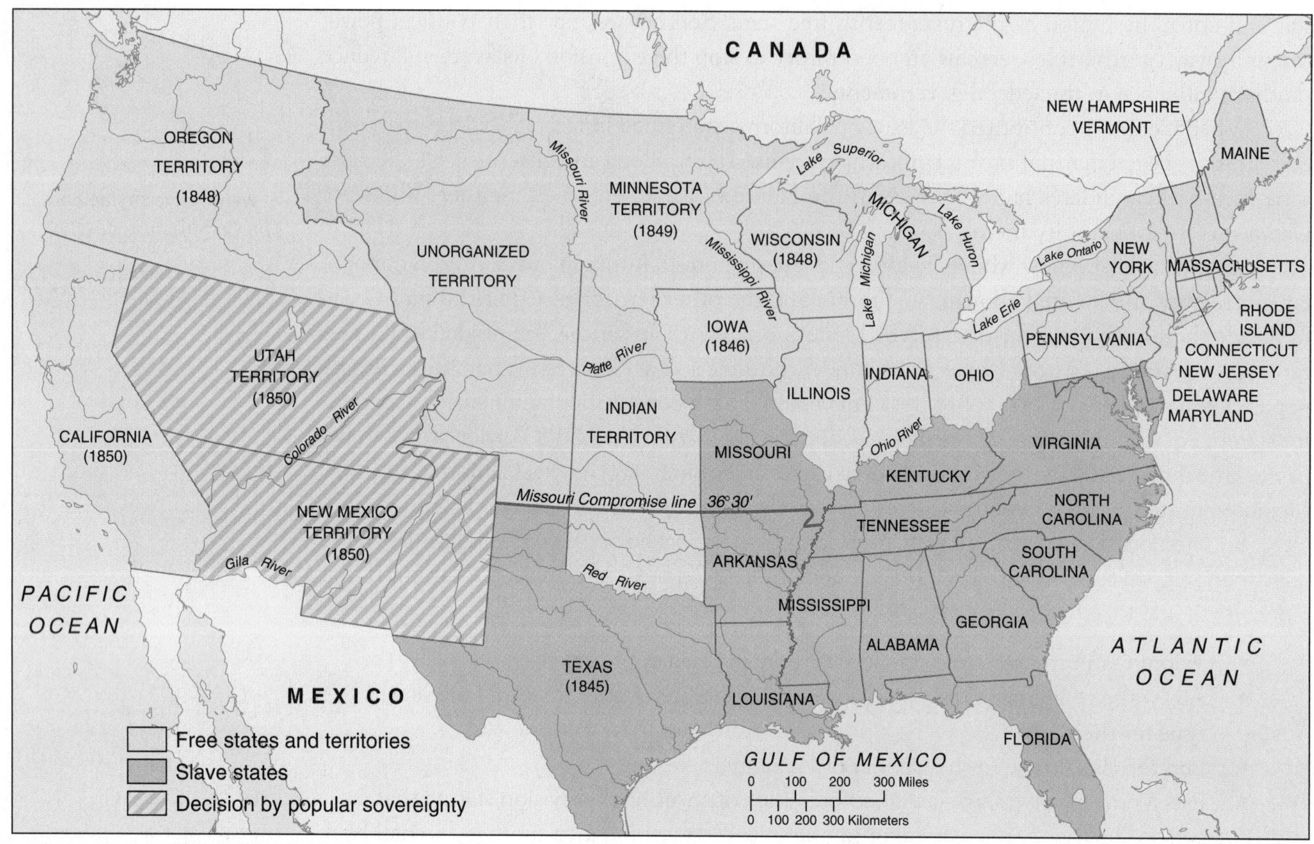

MAP 14–1 The Compromise of 1850 Given the unlikely prospect that any of the western territories would opt for slavery, the compromise sealed the South's minority status in the Union.

What were the results of the Compromise of 1850, and how did the country react to the news of the Compromise?

Fugitive Slave Act Law, part of the Compromise of 1850, that required the authorities in the North to assist southern slave catchers and return runaway slaves to their owners.

awaiting statehood. Their future in the Union appeared to be one of numerical and economic decline, and the survival of their institutions seemed doubtful. They gained the **Fugitive Slave Act,** which reinforced their right to seize and return to bondage slaves who had fled to free territory, but it was slight consolation. And the North's hostile reception to the law made southerners doubt its commitment to the compromise.

Read the Document at **www.myhistorylab.com** *The Fugitive Slave Act (1850)*

Response to the Fugitive Slave Act

The Fugitive Slave Act was ready-made for abolitionist propaganda mills and heartrending stories. A few months after Congress passed it, a Kentucky slaveholder visited Madison, Indiana, and snatched a black man from his wife and children, claiming that the man had escaped nineteen years earlier. Black people living in northern communities feared capture, and some fled across the Canadian border. Several northern cities and states vowed resistance, but except for a few publicized cases, northern authorities typically cooperated with southern slave owners to help them retrieve their runaway property. The effect of the act on public opinion, however, was to polarize North and South even further.

The strongest reaction to the act was in the black communities of the urban North. Previously, black abolitionists in the North had focused on freeing slaves in the South. The Fugitive Slave Act brought the danger of slavery much closer to home. No black person was safe under the new law. Mistaken identity, the support of federal courts for slaveholders' claims, and the presence of informants made reenslavement a real possibility. The lives that 400,000 black northerners had constructed, often with great difficulty, appeared suddenly uncertain.

The Underground Railroad Freedom Center, Cincinnati, Ohio
http://www.freedomcenter.org/

Black northerners formed associations to protect each other and repel, violently if necessary, any attempt to capture and reenslave them. Frederick Douglass, an escaped slave himself, explained the need for such organizations: "We must be prepared . . . see the streets . . . running with blood . . . should this law be put into operation." Some black people left the United States. In October 1850, 200 left Pittsburgh for Ontario, Canada, vowing that "they would die before being taken back into slavery." As many as 20,000 African Americans may have found their way across the border during the 1850s in response to fears over capture and reenslavement.

CAUTION!!

COLORED PEOPLE

OF BOSTON, ONE & ALL,

You are hereby respectfully CAUTIONED and advised, to avoid conversing with the

Watchmen and Police Officers of Boston,

For since the recent ORDER OF THE MAYOR & ALDERMEN, they are empowered to act as

KIDNAPPERS

AND

Slave Catchers,

And they have already been actually employed in KIDNAPPING, CATCHING, AND KEEPING SLAVES. Therefore, if you value your LIBERTY, and the *Welfare of the Fugitives* among you, *Shun* them in every possible manner, as so many *HOUNDS* on the track of the most unfortunate of your race.

Keep a Sharp Look Out for KIDNAPPERS, and have TOP EYE open.

***APRIL* 24, 1851.**

The Fugitive Slave Act threatened the freedom of escaped slaves living in the North, and even of free black northerners. This notice, typical of warnings posted in northern cities, urged Boston's African American population to take precautions.

Uncle Tom's Cabin

Sectional controversy over the Fugitive Slave Act was relatively modest compared to the firestorm ignited by abolitionist writer Harriet Beecher Stowe with the publication of a novel about southern slavery. *Uncle Tom's Cabin*, which first appeared in serial form in 1851, moved many northern white people from the sidelines of the sectional conflict to more active participation.

Uncle Tom's Cabin created a sensation in the United States and abroad. The book sold 10,000 copies in its first week and 300,000 within a year. By the time of the Civil War, it had sold an unprecedented 3 million copies in the United States and tens of thousands more in Europe. Stowe's book gave slavery a face; it changed people's moral perceptions about the institution in an era of deep Protestant piety; it was a Sermon on the Mount for a generation of northerners seeking witness for their Christianity and a crusade on behalf of their faith. It transformed abolitionism, bringing the movement, whose extreme rhetoric many northerners had previously viewed with disapproval, to the edge of respectability, and moving the nation a bit further on its journey to fulfill its founding ideals.

For southerners, *Uncle Tom's Cabin* was a damnable lie, a political tract disguised as literature. Some southerners retaliated with crude plays and books of their own. In these versions of slavery, no slave families were broken up, no slaves were killed, and all masters were models of Christian behavior. Few northerners, however, read these southern responses. The writers penned them more to convince fellow southerners that slavery was necessary and good than to change opinions in the North.

Watch the Video at **www.myhistorylab.com** *Harriet Beecher Stowe and the Making of* Uncle Tom's Cabin

Black northerners embraced *Uncle Tom's Cabin*. Frederick Douglass's National Black Convention resolved that the book was "a work plainly marked by the finger of God" on behalf of black people. Some black people hoped that the book's popularity would highlight the hypocrisy of white northerners who were quick to perceive evil in the South but were often blind to discrimination against African Americans in the North. Despite reactions to Stowe's book, however, black northerners continued to face voting restrictions, segregation, and official harassment.

The Election of 1852

While the nation was reading and reacting to *Uncle Tom's Cabin*, a presidential election campaign took place. The Compromise of 1850 had divided the Whigs deeply. Northern Whigs perceived it as a capitulation to southern slaveholding interests and refused to support the renomination of President Millard Fillmore. Many southern Whigs, angered by the suspicions and insults of their erstwhile northern colleagues, abandoned the party. Although the Whigs

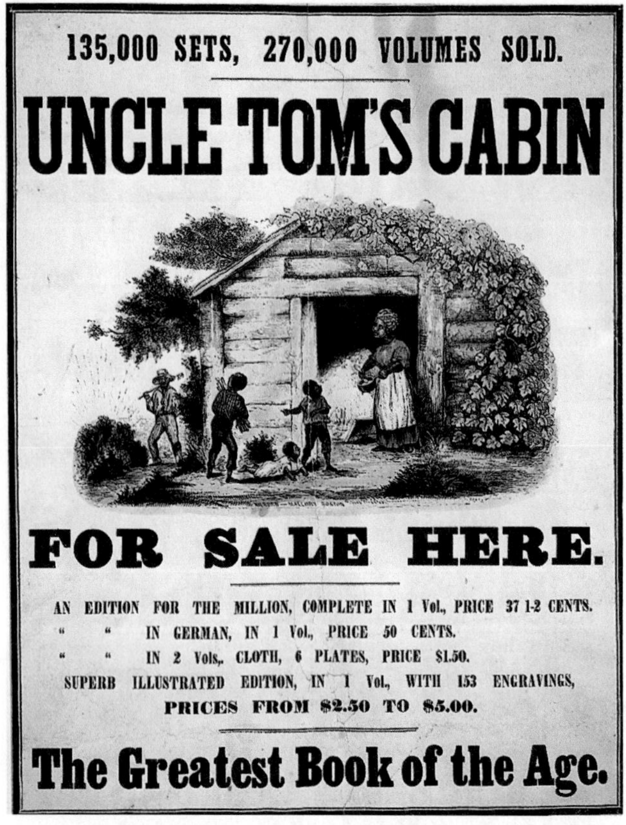

An advertisement for *Uncle Tom's Cabin.* The book became a worldwide best-seller illuminating the tragedy of slavery in its corruption of family, human dignity, and Christianity.

nominated Mexican War hero and Virginian Winfield Scott for president, few southern Whigs viewed the nonslaveholding general as a friend of their region.

The Democratic Party entered the campaign more united. Despite reservations, the northern and southern wings of the party both announced their support for the Compromise of 1850. Southern Democrats viewed the party's nominee, Franklin Pierce of New Hampshire, as safe on the slavery issue despite his New England heritage. Pierce satisfied northerners as a nationalist devoted to the idea of Manifest Destiny. He belonged to Young America, a mostly Democratic group that advocated extending American influence into Central and South America and the Caribbean with an aggressive foreign policy. His service in the Mexican War and his good looks and charm won over doubters from both sections.

Given the disarray of the Whigs and the relative unity of the Democrats, the election results were predictable. Pierce won overwhelmingly with 254 electoral votes to Scott's 42. But Pierce's landslide victory could not obscure the deep fissures in the American party system. The Whigs, although they would continue to run local candidates through the rest of the 1850s, were finished as a national party. And the Democrats, despite their electoral success, emerged frayed from the election. In the Lower South, conflicts within the party between supporters and opponents of the Compromise of 1850 had overshadowed the contests between Democrats and Whigs. Southern Democrats had wielded great influence at the party's nominating convention and dominated party policy, clouding its prospects in the North. During the election, much of the party's support in the North had come from the first-time votes of mainly Catholic immigrants. But the growing political influence of Catholics alarmed evangelical Protestants of both parties, thus adding religious bigotry to the divisive issues undermining the structure of the national parties.

POLITICAL REALIGNMENT

WHAT FACTORS contributed to the Republicans' rise to political prominence?

The conflicts over slavery and religion wrecked the Second American Party system. The Whigs disintegrated, though remnants persisted in several states and localities, and the Democrats became more southern and more closely identified with immigrants, especially Roman Catholics. The Republicans, a new party, combined the growing antislavery and antisouthern sentiment in the North with religious nativism. Whether America would dissolve into warring factions over slavery or sectarian strife was anyone's guess in the mid-1850s. Eventually, the issue of slavery overwhelmed ethnic and religious concerns.

Franklin Pierce hoped to duck the slavery issue by focusing on Young America's dreams of empire. But his attempts to forge national sentiment around an aggressive foreign policy failed. And his administration's inept handling of a new territorial controversy in Kansas forced him to confront the slavery debate.

Young America's Foreign Misadventures

Pierce's first missteps occurred in pursuit of Young America's foreign ambitions. The administration turned a greedy eye toward Spanish-ruled Cuba, just 90 miles off the coast of Florida. Spanish authorities were harassing American merchants exporting sugar from Cuba and the American naval vessels protecting the merchants' ships. Southerners supported an aggressive

Cuba policy, seeing the island as a possible new slave state. And nationalists saw great virtue in replacing what they perceived as a despotic colonial regime with a democratic government under the guidance of the United States.

In October 1854, three American diplomats met in Ostend, Belgium, to discuss Cuba. It is not clear whether Pierce approved or even knew of their meeting, but the diplomats believed that they had the administration's blessing. One of them, the American minister to Spain, Pierre Soulé of Louisiana, was especially eager for the United States to acquire Cuba. The group composed a document on Cuba called the **Ostend Manifesto** that claimed that the island belonged "naturally to the great family of states of which the Union is the Providential Nursery." The implication was that Spain's control of Cuba was unnatural. The United States would offer to buy Cuba from Spain, but if Spain refused to sell, the authors warned, "by every law, human and Divine, we shall be justified in wresting it from Spain."

Ostend Manifesto Message sent by U.S. envoys to President Pierce from Ostend, Belgium, in 1854, stating that the United States had a "divine right" to wrest Cuba from Spain.

The Ostend Manifesto caused an uproar and embarrassed the Pierce administration when it became public. Other nations quickly denounced it as a "buccaneering document" and a "highwayman's plea." It provoked a similar reaction in the United States, raising suspicions in the North that the South was willing to provoke a war with Spain to expand the number of slaveholding states.

QUICK REVIEW

The Ostend Manifesto (1854)

- Pierce administration coveted Cuba.
- Manifesto claimed that Cuba naturally belonged in a family of states with the United States.
- Public revelation of the manifesto produced criticism and embarrassment for the administration.

While Pierce fumbled in the area of foreign policy, Senator Stephen A. Douglas of Illinois was developing a national project that also promised to draw the country together, the construction of a transcontinental railroad and the settling of the land it traversed. The result was worse conflict and the first outbreak of sustained sectional violence.

Stephen Douglas's Railroad Proposal

Douglas, like many westerners, wanted a transcontinental railroad. He himself had a personal stake in railroad building in that he owned some Chicago real estate and speculated in western lands. But beyond personal gain, Douglas, the supreme nationalist, understood that a transcontinental railroad would enhance the nation's journey toward becoming a continental empire. Not only would it physically link East and West, it would also help spread American democracy.

Douglas had in mind a transcontinental route extending westward from Chicago through the Nebraska Territory. Unfortunately for his plans, Indians already occupied this region, many of them on land the U.S. government had set aside as Indian Territory and barred to white settlement. Removing the "Indian barrier" and establishing white government were "first steps," in the senator's view, toward a "tide of emigration and civilization."

Once again, and not for the last time, the federal government responded by reneging on earlier promises and forcing Indians to move. In 1853, President Pierce sent agents to convince the Indians in the northern part of the Indian Territory to cede land for the railroad.

With the Indian "obstacle" removed, Douglas sought congressional approval to establish a government for the Nebraska Territory. But southern senators defeated his proposal. They objected to it not only because it called for a northern rather than southern route for the transcontinental railroad but also because the new territory lay above the Missouri Compromise line and would enter the Union as yet another free state. Bowing to southern pressure, Douglas rewrote his bill and resubmitted it in January 1854. He predicted that the new bill would "raise a hell of a storm." He was right.

The Kansas-Nebraska Act

Douglas's Kansas-Nebraska Bill split the Nebraska Territory into two territories, Kansas and Nebraska, with the implicit understanding that Kansas would become a slave state and Nebraska a free state. Consistent with Douglas's belief in popular sovereignty, it left the actual decision on slavery to the residents of the territories. But because it allowed southerners to bring slaves into an area formerly closed to slavery, it repealed the Missouri Compromise.

QUICK REVIEW

Kansas-Nebraska Act

- Split Nebraska Territory into Kansas and Nebraska.
- Left the decision on slavery to residents of the territories.
- Allowed southerners to bring slaves into an area closed to slavery under the Missouri Compromise.

Northerners of all parties were outraged. The Missouri Compromise had endured for thirty-four years as a basis for sectional accord on slavery. Now it was threatened, northern leaders charged, by the South's unquenchable desire to spread slavery and expand its political power. President Pierce, however, backed the bill, ensuring the support of enough northern Democrats to secure it a narrow victory. The **Kansas-Nebraska Act** was law.

Kansas-Nebraska Act Law passed in 1854 creating the Kansas and Nebraska Territories but leaving the question of slavery open to residents, thereby repealing the Missouri Compromise.

"Bleeding Kansas"

Because of its fertile soil, favorable climate, and location adjacent to the slave state of Missouri, Kansas was the most likely of the new territories to support slavery. As a result, both southerners and antislavery northerners began an intensive drive to recruit settlers and establish a majority there.

As proslavery residents of Missouri poured into Kansas, antislavery organizations funded and armed their own migrants. In March 1855, proslavery forces, relying on the ineligible votes of Missouri residents, fraudulently elected a territorial legislature. This legislature promptly passed a series of harsh measures, including a law mandating the death penalty for aiding a fugitive slave and another making it a felony to question slaveholding in Kansas. For good measure, the proslavery majority expelled the few free-staters elected to the assembly. In response, free-staters established their own government in Topeka and vowed to make Kansas white.

A sporadic civil war erupted in Kansas in November 1855 and reached a climax in the spring of 1856. Journalists dubbed the conflict **"Bleeding Kansas."** On May 21, a group of proslavery officials attacked the free-state stronghold of Lawrence, subjecting it to a heavy artillery barrage. No one was killed, but the town suffered substantial damage. Eastern newspapers, exaggerating the incident, called it "the sack of Lawrence." Three days later, antislavery agitator John Brown, originally from Connecticut, went with several sympathizers to Pottawatomie Creek south of Lawrence in search of proslavery settlers. Armed with razor-sharp broadswords, they split the skulls and hacked the bodies of five men.

"Bleeding Kansas" Violence between pro- and antislavery forces in Kansas Territory after the passage of the Kansas-Nebraska Act in 1854.

The memory of the failed revolutions in Europe remained fresh in the minds of Americans concerned about their own fragile democratic institutions. The disintegration of law and order on the Plains brought a foreboding recognition to many Americans. The double outrage of a fraudulent election followed by severe legislation resembled more the despotism of restored regimes in Europe than the extension of American democracy.

See the **Map**
at **www.myhistorylab.com**
The Compromise of 1850 and the Kansas-Nebraska Act

Kansans were not the only Americans bleeding over slavery. Five days before the "sack of Lawrence," Massachusetts senator Charles Sumner delivered a longwinded diatribe, "The Crime Against Kansas," full of personal insults against several southerners, especially elderly South Carolina senator Andrew P. Butler. Two days after Sumner's outburst, and a day after the story of the sack of Lawrence appeared in the newspapers, Butler's cousin, South Carolina congressman Preston Brooks, entered the mostly vacant Senate chamber, where Sumner sat working on a speech. Seeking to defend his cousin's honor, Brooks raised his walking cane and beat Sumner over the head. Bloody and unconscious, the senator slumped to the floor. He recovered but did not return to the Senate for over three years. His empty chair offered northerners' mute confirmation of their growing conviction that southerners were despotic. Southerners showered Brooks with new walking canes.

Armed Missourians cross the border into Kansas to vote illegally for a proslavery government in 1855.

Know-Nothings and Republicans: Religion and Politics

The Sumner incident, along with the Kansas-Nebraska Bill and the civil war in Kansas, further polarized North and South, widening sectional divisions within the political parties. Some northern Democrats distanced themselves from their party and looked for political alternatives; northern Whigs seized on changing public opinion to form new coalitions; and free-soil advocates gained new adherents. From 1854 to 1856, northerners moved into new political parties that altered the national political landscape and sharpened sectional conflict.

Although the slavery issue was mainly responsible for the party realignment in the North, other factors played a role as well. Nearly 3.5 million immigrants entered the United States between 1848 and 1860, the greatest influx in American history in proportion to the total population. Some of these newcomers, especially the Germans, were escaping failed democratic revolutions in Europe. They were predominantly middle-class Protestants who, along with the smaller number of German Catholics and Jews, settled mostly in the cities, where they established shops and other businesses. More than 1 million of the immigrants, however, were poor Irish Roman Catholics, fleeing their homeland to avoid starvation.

One of Thomas Nast's vitriolic comments on the separation between Church (i.e., the Roman Catholic church) and State.

The Irish immigrants made their homes in northern cities, which were in the midst of Protestant revivals and reform. They also competed for jobs with native-born Protestant workers. Because the Irish would work for lower wages, the job competition bred animosity and sometimes violence. But it was their Roman Catholic religion that most concerned some urban Protestants, who associated Catholicism with despotism and immorality, the same evils they attributed to southerners. For their part, the Irish made it clear that they had little use for Protestant reform, especially temperance and abolitionism. The clash of cultures would soon further disturb a political environment increasingly in flux over the slavery issue.

Read the **Document** at **www.myhistorylab.com** ***From Then to Now Online: Religion and Politics***

New parties emerged from this cauldron of religious, ethnic, and sectional strife. Anti-immigrant, anti-Catholic sentiment gave rise to the **Know-Nothing Party,** which began as a secret organization in July 1854. Its name derived from the reply that members gave when asked about the party: "I know nothing." Although strongest in the North, Know-Nothing chapters blossomed in several southern cities that had experienced some immigration since 1848, among them Richmond, Louisville, New Orleans, and Savannah. The party's members in both North and South were mostly former Whigs. In addition to their biases against Catholics and foreigners, the Know-Nothings shared a fear that the slavery issue could destroy the Union. But because attempts to solve the issue seemed only to increase sectional tensions, the Know-Nothings hoped to ignore it.

Know-Nothing Party Anti-immigrant party formed from the wreckage of the Whig Party and some disaffected northern Democrats in 1854.

Know-Nothing candidates fared surprisingly well in local and congressional elections during the fall of 1854, carrying 63 percent of the statewide vote in Massachusetts and making strong showings in New York and Pennsylvania. In office, Know-Nothings achieved some notable reforms. In Massachusetts, where they pursued an agenda similar to that of the Whigs in earlier years, they secured administrative reforms and supported public health and public education programs.

The Know-Nothings' anti-Catholicism, however, overshadowed their reform agenda. In several states and cities, they passed legislation barring Catholics from public office and unsuccessfully sought to increase the time required for an immigrant to become a citizen from one year to 21 years. The Know-Nothings also fostered anti-Catholic violence, such as the bloody election day riot that erupted in Louisville, Kentucky, in 1855.

Republican Party Party that emerged in the 1850s in the aftermath of the bitter controversy over the Kansas-Nebraska Act, consisting of former Whigs, some northern Democrats, and many Know-Nothings.

Ethnic and religious bigotry were weak links to hold together a national party. Southern and northern Know-Nothings soon fell to quarreling over slavery despite their vow to avoid it, and the party split. Many northern Know-Nothings soon found a congenial home in the new **Republican Party.** The Republican Party formed in the summer of 1854 from a coalition of antislavery Conscience Whigs and Democrats disgusted with the Pierce administration's Kansas policy. Like the Know-Nothings, the Republicans advocated strong state and federal governments to promote economic and social reforms. But the new party did not espouse the Know-Nothings' anti-Catholic and anti-immigrant positions. The overriding bond among Republicans was their opposition to the extension of slavery in the territories.

Reflecting its opposition to slavery, the Republican Party was an antisouthern sectional party. Northern Whig merchants and entrepreneurs who joined the party were impatient with southern obstruction in Congress of federal programs for economic development, such as a transcontinental railroad, harbor and river improvements, and high tariffs to protect American industries (located mostly in the North) from foreign competition. In a bid to keep slavery out of the territories, the Republicans favored limiting homesteads in the West to 160 acres. Not incidentally, populating the territories with northern whites would ensure a western base for the new party.

QUICK REVIEW

Republican Values

- Supporters of reform.
- Opposed to slavery.
- Antisouthern sectional party.

Heightened sectional animosity laced with religious and ethnic prejudice fueled the emergence of new parties and the weakening of old political affiliations in the early 1850s. Accompanying the political realignment were diverging views on the proper role of government. As the nation prepared for the presidential election of 1856, the Democrats had become a party top-heavy with southerners; the Know-Nothings splintered along sectional lines; some Whigs remained active under the old party name, mainly on the state and local levels in North and South; and the Republican Party was becoming an important political force in the North and, to southerners, the embodiment of evil.

The Election of 1856

The presidential election of 1856 proved to be one of the strangest in American history. The Know-Nothings and the Republicans faced a national electorate for the first time while the Democrats were deeply divided over the Kansas issue.

The upstart Republicans held their convention in Philadelphia in mid-July. The platform condemned the "twin relics of barbarism"—slavery and polygamy. There was no epidemic, current or pending, of men and women seeking multiple partners. But, as everyone understood at the time, the Mormons in Utah Territory espoused, though did not require, polygamy. Memories of Mormon settlements in the Midwest and the turmoil they generated remained fresh in the minds of residents in a region where Republicans hoped to pick up significant support. While antisouthern sentiment varied, few voters were sympathetic to the Mormons.

The Republicans passed over their most likely candidate, the New York senator and former Whig William H. Seward. Instead, they followed a tried-and-true Whig precedent and nominated a military hero, John C. Frémont, a handsome, dark-haired soldier of medium height and medium intelligence. His wife, Jessie Benton, the daughter of Missouri senator Thomas Hart Benton, was his greatest asset. In effect, she ran the campaign and wisely encouraged her husband to remain silent. The Know-Nothings split into "South Americans" and "North Americans." The South Americans nominated Millard Fillmore, although he was not a Know-Nothing. The North Americans eventually and reluctantly embraced Frémont, despite the widespread but mistaken belief that he was a Roman Catholic.

The Democrats, facing a northern revolt and southern opposition to any candidate who did not support the extension of slavery, turned to Pennsylvania's James Buchanan whose greatest virtue was that he had been out of the country the previous four years as ambassador to Great Britain. Southerners accepted him as electable and sensitive to slavery. Northern Democrats hoped for the best.

Democratic Party strategy in the North focused on shoring up its immigrant base by connecting the Republicans to the Know-Nothings and simultaneously appealing to evangelical Protestants by intimating that Frémont had received a Catholic education, had studied for the priesthood, or was himself a Roman Catholic secretly attending Mass and "going through all the crosses and gyrations, eating wafers," take your pick. Democratic papers cried out that Frémont was "*the instrument of vice, and the foe of God and of Freedom.*"

The importance of evangelical imagery in the political campaigns of the major parties was especially evident among the Republicans. A participant in the party convention likened the party platform to "God's revealed Word," and a minister supporting the Republican ticket saw the election "as a decisive struggle . . . between freedom and Slavery, truth and falsehood, justice and oppression, God and the devil."

Away from the pulpit, Republican campaigners sometimes found tough going in the North, indicating how much the slavery extension debate had overtaken sectarian issues. A portion of the northern electorate viewed the Republican Party as a gilded version of the radical antislavery parties of the 1840s, promoting racial equality and emancipation to the detriment of whites.

James Buchanan emerged victorious. The only national party had won a national election. The Democrats did it by holding the lower North as Pennsylvania, New Jersey, Illinois, Indiana, and California voted for Buchanan, and sweeping the Lower South. But "Old Buck's" victory was narrow in these northern states; the Republicans performed remarkably well considering it was the first time they had fielded a presidential candidate. They had achieved a "victorious defeat," making Buchanan the first candidate to win without carrying the North since 1828. Republicans eagerly looked forward to the next presidential contest and the good prospects of prying at least Pennsylvania, Indiana, and Illinois from the Democratic column. For the first time ever, an avowedly antislavery party had carried eleven free states.

The South had not yet lapsed into one-party politics. Millard Fillmore garnered 40 percent of the popular vote in the South, but won only the state of Maryland. He fared poorly in the Lower South. The states that had the greatest stake in the slave economy voted solidly Democratic.

Buchanan, who brought more than a generation of political experience to the presidency, would need every bit and more. He had scarcely settled into office when two major crises confronted him: a Supreme Court decision that challenged the right of Congress to regulate slavery in the territories and renewed conflict over Kansas.

The Dred Scott Case

Dred Scott was a slave owned by an army surgeon based in Missouri. In the 1830s and early 1840s, he had traveled with his master to the state of Illinois and the Wisconsin Territory before returning to Missouri. In 1846, Scott sued his master's widow for freedom on the grounds that the laws of Illinois and the Wisconsin Territory barred slavery. After a series of appeals, the case reached the Supreme Court. Chief Justice Roger Taney of Maryland, joined by five other justices of the nine-member Supreme Court (five of whom came from slave states), dismissed Scott's suit two days after Buchanan's inauguration in March 1857.

Read the **Document**
at **www.myhistorylab.com**
Opinion of the Supreme Court for Dred Scott v. Sanford *(1857)*

Taney's opinion contained two bombshells. First, he argued that black people were not citizens of the United States. Because Scott was not a citizen, he could not sue. The framers, according to Taney, respected a long-standing view that slaves were "beings of an inferior order . . . so far inferior that they had no rights which the white man was bound to respect."

Second, Taney held that even if Scott had standing in court, his residence in the Wisconsin Territory did not make him a free man. This was because the Missouri Compromise, which was still in effect in the 1840s, was, in Taney's view, unconstitutional. (The Wisconsin Territory lay above the compromise line.) The compromise, the chief justice explained, deprived citizens

Dred Scott and his wife, Harriet, are portrayed here with their children as an average middle-class family, an image that fueled northern opposition to the Supreme Court's 1857 decision that denied Scott's freedom and citizenship.

of their property (slaves) without the due process of law granted by the Fifth Amendment to the U.S. Constitution. In effect, Taney ruled that Congress could not bar slavery from the territories.

The **Dred Scott decision** was especially unsettling to the tens of thousands of free blacks throughout the country, especially in the South. The Court, in stripping their citizenship, made them vulnerable to reenslavement or expulsion. The case also accelerated restrictions on the southern free black population as its legal recourse vanished with the decision. Several cities, including Charleston, experimented with requirements that free blacks purchase and wear badges identifying them as free. For African Americans, the enemy was no longer the slaveholder, but the very government from which they had hoped for redress.

The decision also shocked Republicans. The right of Congress to ban slavery from the territories, which Taney had apparently voided, was one of the party's central tenets. Republicans responded by ignoring the implications of the decision for the territories while promising to abide by it so far as it affected Dred Scott himself. Once in office, Republicans vowed, they would seek a reversal. This position allowed them to attack the decision without appearing to defy the law.

The *Dred Scott* decision boosted Republican fortunes in the North even as it seemed to undercut the party. Fears of a southern Slave Power conspiracy now seemed ever more justified. If Congress could not ban slavery from the territories, Republicans asked, how secure was the right of states to ban slavery within their borders? A small group of slaveholders, they charged, was holding nonslaveholding white people hostage to the institution of slavery.

The Lecompton Constitution

Establishing a legitimate government in Kansas was the second major issue to bedevil the Buchanan administration. The president made a good start, sending his friend and fellow Pennsylvanian Robert Walker (then a resident of Mississippi) to Kansas as territorial governor to oversee the election of a constitutional convention in June 1857.

Dred Scott decision Supreme Court ruling, in a lawsuit brought by Dred Scott, a slave demanding his freedom based on his residence in a free state and a free territory with his master, that slaves could not be U.S. citizens and that Congress had no jurisdiction over slavery in the territories.

The violence had subsided in Kansas, and prospects had grown for a peaceful settlement. But free-staters, fearing that the slavery forces planned to stuff the ballot box with fraudulent votes, announced a boycott of the June election. As a result, proslavery forces dominated the constitutional convention, which was held in Lecompton. And Walker, although a slaveholder, let it be known that he thought Kansas would never be a slave state. He thus put himself at odds with proslavery residents from the outset.

Walker persuaded the free-staters to vote in October to elect a new territorial legislature. The returns gave the proslavery forces a narrow victory, but Walker discovered irregularities. Walker threw out the fraudulent returns, and the free-staters took control of the territorial legislature for the first time.

Lecompton Constitution Proslavery draft written in 1857 by Kansas territorial delegates elected under questionable circumstances; it was rejected by two governors, supported by President Buchanan, and decisively defeated by Congress.

Undeterred, the proslavery forces drafted a proslavery constitution at the constitutional convention in Lecompton. Buchanan, who had promised southerners a proslavery government in Kansas, dismissed Walker before he could rule on the Lecompton Constitution, then ignored the recommendation of Walker's successor that he reject it. He submitted the **Lecompton Constitution** to the Senate for approval even though it clearly sidestepped the popular sovereignty requirement of the Kansas-Nebraska Act.

Like the Kansas-Nebraska Act, the Lecompton Constitution outraged many northerners. Northern Democrats facing reelection refused to support a president of their own party, and, though the constitution passed in the Senate, Democratic opposition killed it in the House. Congress would eventually admit Kansas to the Union as a free state in January 1861.

The *Dred Scott* decision and Buchanan's support of the Lecompton Constitution helped the Republicans and hurt northern Democrats in the 1858 congressional elections. The **Panic of 1857,** a severe economic recession that lingered into 1858, also worked to the advantage of the Republicans.

Panic of 1857 Banking crisis that caused a credit crunch in the North; it was less severe in the South, where high cotton prices spurred a quick recovery.

The Democratic administration did nothing as unemployment rose; starvation stalked the streets of northern cities, and homeless women and children begged for food and shelter. Republicans claimed that government intervention, specifically, Republican-sponsored legislation to raise certain tariffs, give western land to homesteaders, and fund transportation projects, if passed by Congress, could have prevented the panic. The Democrats' inaction, they said, reflected the southern Slave Power's insensitivity to northern workers.

Southerners disagreed. The panic had scarcely touched them. Cotton prices were high, and few southern banks failed. Cotton seemed indeed to be king. The financial crisis in the North reinforced the southern belief that northern society was corrupt and greedy. The Republicans' proposed legislative remedies, in their view, would enrich the North and beggar the South.

The Religious Revival of 1857–1858

In the midst of economic depression and sectional controversy, a religious revival swept across the nation's cities in the winter of 1857–1858. Beginning with lunchtime prayer meetings among businessmen in New York City, the phenomenon spread throughout the country, though concentrating in the larger urban centers of the Northeast. The sectional crisis and the economic downturn had a part in bringing urban middle-class men into churches and meeting halls at the noon hour, but the gatherings emphasized prayer and personal reflection, avoiding political discussion and focusing on individual redemption. Sectional strife had diverted attention from personal salvation, and the financial panic served as a reminder that wealth and possessions could be fleeting, but the soul was everlasting. Ministers and lay leaders of the movement encouraged men to turn away from the reform "isms" of the era—feminism, abolitionism, and socialism among them. Men, they suggested, should not worship secular ideologies, but should make the Bible the foundation of their behavior and thought. And they should reestablish their leadership both in spiritual and family matters.

Religion provided not only solace but also explanations for a time beset by increasing uncertainty. The revival, which peaked in early 1858, did not change society dramatically any more than it pulled the nation out of the economic doldrums. But now with each turn in the political arena many more people, not only the fervent evangelicals, came to understand that these mere events held transcendent meaning.

Some feared that the growing integration of religion and politics could harm the nation's religious life and burden the political process with sharper divisions than were necessary. But by 1858, it became increasingly difficult to distinguish the political from the spiritual. The Illinois senatorial contest between Democrat Stephen A. Douglas and Abraham Lincoln of the Republican Party proved a case in point. Their debates underscored the moral dimensions of political questions and the resulting difficulties of effecting compromises.

The Lincoln-Douglas Debates

Douglas faced a forceful opponent in his 1858 reelection campaign. The Republicans had nominated Abraham Lincoln, a 49-year-old lawyer and former Whig congressman. The Kentucky-born Lincoln had risen from modest circumstances to become a prosperous lawyer in the Illinois state capital of Springfield. After one term in Congress from 1847 to 1849, he returned to his law practice but maintained his interest in politics. Strongly opposed to the extension of slavery into the territories, he considered joining the Republican Party after the passage of the Kansas-Nebraska Act. Most Illinois voters opposed the extension of slavery into the territories, although generally not out of concern for the slaves. Illinois residents, like most northerners, wanted to keep the territories free for white people. Few voters would support dissolving the Union over the slavery issue. Douglas, who knew his constituents well, branded Lincoln a dangerous radical for warning, in a biblical paraphrase, that the United States, like "a house divided against itself," could not "endure permanently half slave and half free."

Read the **Document** at **www.myhistorylab.com** *The Lincoln-Douglas Debates of 1858*

Lincoln could not allow the charge of radicalism to go unanswered. So, in July 1858, he challenged Douglas to a series of debates across the state. Douglas was reluctant to provide exposure for his lesser-known opponent, but he could not reject Lincoln's offer outright, lest voters think he was dodging his challenger. He agreed to debates in seven of the state's nine congressional districts.

Lincoln-Douglas debates Series of debates in the 1858 Illinois senatorial campaign during which Douglas and Lincoln staked out their differing opinions on the issue of slavery.

The **Lincoln-Douglas debates** were a defining event in American politics. For Douglas, slavery was not a moral issue. What mattered was what white people wanted. If they wanted slavery, fine; if they did not, fine also. Lincoln and many Republicans had a very different view. For them, slavery was a moral issue. As such, it was independent of what the residents of a territory wanted.

Lincoln not only identified the cause of the Republican Party with the forces of liberty and freedom all over the world, but also framed the debate as a contest between good and evil. Evangelical rhetoric had pervaded political discourse for nearly two decades. But coming on the heels of a national religious revival, Lincoln's assertion reinforced the perception that the nation was approaching a crossroads, not only a secular divide, but a battle that could determine the future of mankind for eternity: "As I view the contest, it is not less than a contest for the advancement of the kingdom of Heaven or the kingdom of Satan."

Lincoln tempered his moralism with practical politics. He took care to distance himself from the abolitionists, asserting that he abided by the Constitution and did not seek to interfere in places where slavery existed. Moreover, Lincoln, like most Republicans, hated the institution of slavery, but held ambivalent views about African Americans. These views would change in time, sometimes prodded by events, other times by thought and prayer. About slavery, there was little ambiguity in his position, even if he tried to project a moderate image on the campaign trail. Privately, he hoped for its demise. To Lincoln, slavery was immoral, but inequality was not. The Republican Party was antislavery, but it did not advocate racial equality.

Abraham Lincoln making a point at Coles County (Illinois) Fairgrounds, 1858. His U.S. Senate opponent, Stephen A. Douglas, sitting at Lincoln's right, waits his turn. The Lincoln-Douglas debates captivated Illinois voters, who turned out in great numbers to witness the rhetorical fireworks.

Illinois voters retained a narrow Democratic majority in the state legislature, which reelected Douglas to the U.S. Senate. (State legislatures elected senators until 1913, when the Seventeenth Amendment provided for direct election by the people.) But Douglas alienated southern Democrats with his strong defense of popular sovereignty and lost whatever hope he had of becoming the standard-bearer of a united Democratic Party in 1860. Lincoln lost the senatorial contest but won national respect and recognition.

Despite Lincoln's defeat in Illinois, the Republicans made a strong showing in the 1858 congressional elections across the North. The increased Republican presence and the sharpening sectional divisions among Democrats portended a bitter debate over slavery in the new Congress. Americans, more than ever before, were viewing issues and each other in sectional terms. *Northern* and *southern* took on meanings that expressed a great deal more than geography.

THE ROAD TO DISUNION

WHY WERE southerners so alarmed by the election of Abraham Lincoln in 1860?

The unsatisfying Compromise of 1850, "Bleeding Kansas" and "Bleeding Sumner," the *Dred Scott* case, and Lecompton convinced many northerners that southerners were conspiring with the federal government to restrict their political and economic liberties. Southerners saw these same events as evidence of a northern conspiracy to reduce the South's political and economic influence. There were no conspiracies, but with so little goodwill on either side, hostility predominated. Slavery, above all, accounted for the growing divide.

In 1859 abolitionist John Brown, who had avenged the "sack of Lawrence" in 1856, led a raid against a federal arsenal at Harpers Ferry, Virginia, in the vain hope of sparking a slave revolt. This event brought the frustrations of both sides of the sectional conflict to a head. The presidential election campaign of 1860 began before the uproar over the raid had subsided. In the course of that contest, one of the last nationally unifying institutions, the Democratic Party, broke apart. The election of Abraham Lincoln, an avowedly sectional candidate, triggered a crisis that defied peaceful resolution.

Although the crisis spiraled into a civil war, this outcome did not signal the triumph of sectionalism over nationalism. Ironically, in defending their stands, both sides appealed to time-honored nationalist and democratic sentiments. Southern secessionists believed they were the true keepers of the ideals that had inspired the American Revolution. They were merely re-creating a more perfect Union. It was not they, but the Republicans, who had sundered the old Union by subverting the Constitution's guarantee of liberty. Lincoln similarly appealed to nationalist themes, telling northerners that the United States was "the last best hope on earth."

Northerners and southerners both appealed to nationalism and democracy but applied different meanings to these concepts. The differences underscored how far apart the sections had grown. When southerners and northerners looked at each other, they no longer saw fellow Americans; they saw enemies. The reason was slavery.

Slavery and its corollary, white supremacy, lay at the core of the sectional crisis that prompted secession and the bloody civil war that followed. For many white southerners, the journey from the ideals of the American Revolution led naturally to a Slave Republic: Enslavement of blacks guaranteed the freedom and equality of whites. Many northerners believed that slavery represented a tragic detour from the nation's founding principles, especially as articulated in the Declaration of Independence. Contemporaries understood that these fundamentally different views of slavery led directly to the breakup of the Union.

North-South Differences

Slavery accounted for or played a role in creating distinctions between North and South that transcended their shared heritage.

Economic differences. Behind the ideological divide that separated North and South lay real and growing social and economic differences (see the Overview table, South and North Compared in 1860). As the North became increasingly urban and industrial, the South remained primarily rural and agricultural. The urban population of the free states increased from 10 to 26 percent between 1820 and 1860. In the South, in the same period, it increased only from 5 to 10 percent. Likewise the proportion of the northern workforce in agriculture declined from 68 percent to 40 percent between 1800 and 1860, whereas in the South it increased from 82 percent to 84 percent. Northern farmers made up for the decline in farm workers by relying on machinery. In 1860, the free states had twice the value of farm machinery per worker as the slave states.

The demand for farm machinery in the North reflected the growing demand for manufactured products in general. The need of city-dwellers for ready-to-wear shoes and clothing, household iron products, processed foods, homes, workplaces, and public amenities boosted industrial production in the North. In contrast, in the South, the slower rate of urbanization, the

QUICK REVIEW

Economic Differences

- Rapid urbanization in the North not seen in the South.
- Southern industrialization inhibited by slavery.
- Northern industrialization fueled technological innovation.

lower proportion of immigrants, and the region's labor-intensive agriculture kept industrial development modest. The proportion of U.S. manufacturing capital invested in the South declined from 31 to 16 percent between 1810 and 1860. In 1810, per capita investment in industrial enterprises was 2.5 times greater in the North than in the South; in 1860, it was 3.5 times greater.

These economic developments generated communities of innovation in the North, especially in the rapidly expanding cities, where people traded ideas and technical information and skills. One of the most important innovations of the era was the telegraph, pioneered by Samuel F. B. Morse, who convinced the government to subsidize a line from Washington, DC, to Baltimore, Maryland, in 1843 and then electrified his patrons with instantaneous reports from the political party conventions of 1844. As information became a valuable currency for a new age, such improvements in communications and transportation tended to reinforce the economic dominance of the Northeast.

Social and religious differences. More subtle distinctions between North and South became evident as well by midcentury. The South had a high illiteracy rate, nearly three times greater than the North, eight times greater if black southerners are included. Northerners supported far more public schools and libraries than southerners. In the South, education was barred by law to slaves and limited for most white people. Many white leaders viewed education more as a privilege for the well-to-do than a right for every citizen.

Evangelical Protestantism attracted increasing numbers in both North and South, but its character differed in the two regions. In the North, evangelical Protestants viewed social reform as a prerequisite for the Second Coming of Christ. As a result, they were in the forefront of most reform movements. Southern evangelicals generally defended slavery.

The effects of slavery. Slavery permeated southern society. Investment in land and slaves limited investment in manufacturing and railroads. The availability of a large slave labor force reduced the need for farm machinery and limited the demand for manufactured products. Slaves were relatively immobile. They did not migrate to cities in massive numbers as did northern farmers. Nor could they quickly fill the labor demands of an expanding urban economy. Agriculture usually took precedence.

Slavery also divided northern from southern churches. And it accounted for the contrast between the inward, otherworldly emphasis of southern theology and the reformist theology of northern evangelicals. Southerners associated black slavery with white freedom; northerners associated it with white degradation.

Slavery contributed to the South's martial tradition and its lukewarm attitude toward public education. Fully 95 percent of the nation's black population lived in the South in 1860, and 90 percent of these were slaves. As a result, the South was often a region on edge. Fearful of revolt, especially in the 1850s, when rumors of slave discontent ran rampant, white people felt compelled to maintain patrols and militias in constant readiness. The South was also determined to keep slaves as ignorant as possible. Educated slaves would be susceptible to abolitionist propaganda and more inclined to revolt.

QUICK REVIEW

The Effects of Slavery on the South

- Slavery accounted for many of the differences between North and South.
- Investment in land and slaves limited investment in manufacturing.
- Slavery contributed to the South's martial tradition and attitude toward public education.

The South's defense of slavery and the North's attack on it fostered an array of stereotypes that exaggerated the real differences between the sections. Like all stereotypes, these reduced individuals to dehumanized categories. They encouraged the people of each section to view those of the other less as fellow Americans than as aliens in their midst.

Ironically, although slavery increasingly defined the character of the South in the 1850s, a growing majority of white southerners did not own slaves. Slavery nonetheless implicated nonslaveholders in ways that ensured their support for it. By satisfying the demand for labor on large plantations, it relieved many rural white southerners from serving as farmhands and enabled them to work their own land. Slaveholders also recruited nonslaveholders to suppress slave violence or rebellion. It was nonslaveholders, for example, who often manned patrols and militia companies. Some nonslaveholders hoped to purchase slaves someday. Many dreamed of migrating westward to the next cotton frontier where they might find greater opportunity to own land and slaves. Finally, regardless of a white man's social or economic status, he shared an important feature with the largest slaveholder: As long as racial slavery existed, the color of his skin made him a member of a privileged class that could never be enslaved.

While white southerners were more united on slavery than on other issues, their defense of slavery presented them with a major dilemma. By the 1850s, most Western nations had condemned and abolished the institution. And because northerners controlled the flow of information through the popular newspapers and the national network of communications, credit, and commerce, southerners were likely to find themselves increasingly isolated. A minority in their own country and a lonely voice for a despised institution that was for them a significant source of wealth, southerners were understandably jittery.

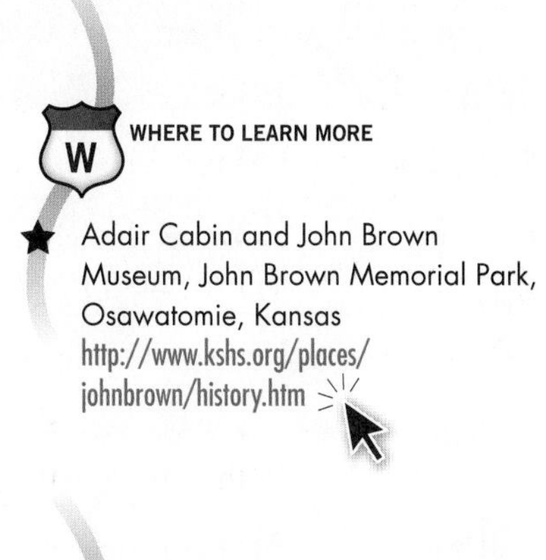

W
WHERE TO LEARN MORE
Adair Cabin and John Brown Museum, John Brown Memorial Park, Osawatomie, Kansas
http://www.kshs.org/places/johnbrown/history.htm

WHERE TO LEARN MORE

Harpers Ferry National Historical Park, West Virginia
http://www.nps.gov/hafe/index.htm

John Brown's Raid

Shortly after he completed his mayhem at Pottawatomie Creek, John Brown left Kansas and approached several New England abolitionists for funds to continue his private war in the territory. But when Brown returned to Kansas in late 1857, he discovered that peace had settled over that troubled territory. Residents now cared more about making money than about making war. Leaving Kansas for the last time, he went east with a new plan. He proposed to attack and capture the federal arsenal at Harpers Ferry, Virginia, a small town near the Maryland border. The assault, Brown imagined, would spark a slave uprising that would eventually spread to the rest of the state. With funds from his New England friends, he equipped a few dozen men and hired an English army officer to train them.

Brown and his "army" moved to a Maryland farmhouse in the summer of 1859 to train and complete planning for the raid. On the night of October 16, 1859, he and 22 followers captured the federal arsenal at Harpers Ferry and waited for the slaves to rally to his banner. Meanwhile, the townspeople alerted outside authorities. The Virginia militia and a detachment of United States Marines under the command of Colonel Robert E. Lee arrived and put a quick end to **John Brown's Raid.** They wounded Brown and killed or captured most of his force.

John Brown's Raid New England abolitionist John Brown's ill-fated attempt to free Virginia's slaves with a raid on the federal arsenal at Harpers Ferry, Virginia, in 1859.

Brown had launched the operation without provisions and at a site from which escape was impossible. Although the primary goal of the attack had been to inspire a slave insurrection, no one had bothered to inform the local slaves. And despite the secret nature of the expedition, Brown had left behind a mountain of documents at the Maryland farmhouse. Was he crazy? As the *Boston Post* editorialized after the raid, "John Brown may be a lunatic, [but if so] then one-fourth of the people of Massachusetts are madmen."

Although the *Post* may have exaggerated, the editorial reflected an article of faith among many abolitionists that, given the signal, slaves would immediately throw off their chains, slaughter their masters, and join a rebellion. But even those slaves in the area who knew of the raid understood the odds against Brown and had the good sense not to join him.

John Brown on trial for treason and murder at Charlestown, Virginia. The image of the wounded and prostrate Brown eloquently defending his actions before his accusers touched many northerners who otherwise condemned his action. Even a few southerners, including Virginia's governor Henry A. Wise, admired his courage.

OVERVIEW South and North Compared in 1860

	South	North
Population	Biracial; 35 percent African American	Overwhelmingly white; less than 2 percent African American
Economy	Growing, though relatively undiversified; 84 percent of workforce in agriculture	Developing through industrialization and urbanization; 40 percent of workforce in agriculture
Labor	Heavily dependent on slave labor, especially in Lower South	Free wage labor
Factories	15 percent of national total	85 percent of national total; concentrated in the Northeast
Railroads	Approximately 10,000 miles of track; primarily shorter lines, with fewer links to trunk lines	Approximately 20,000 miles of track; more effectively linked in trunk lines connecting east and west
Literacy	17 percent illiteracy rate for free population	6 percent illiteracy rate

Read the **Document** at **www.myhistorylab.com** *John Brown, Address before Sentencing (1859)*

The raid, though foolish and unsuccessful, played on southerners' worst fears of slave rebellion, adding a new dimension: Here was an attack engineered not from within the South but from the North. Some southern white people may have dismissed the ability or even the desire of slaves to mount revolts on their own, but they less easily dismissed the potential impact of outside white agitators. The state of Virginia tried Brown on the charge of treason to the state. The trial was swift but fair. The jury sentenced Brown to hang.

The outpouring of northern grief over Brown's death convinced white southerners that the threat to their security was not over. The discovery of Brown's correspondence at his Maryland farmhouse further fueled southern rancor, and southerners increasingly ceased to believe northern disclaimers about the raid. John Brown's Raid significantly changed southern public opinion. However much they defended slavery, most southerners were for the Union. The northern reaction to John Brown's trial and death, however, troubled them. The *Richmond Whig*, a newspaper that reflected moderate Upper South opinion, observed in early 1860 "recent events have wrought almost a complete revolution in the sentiments, the thoughts, the hopes, of the oldest and steadiest conservatives in all the southern states. . . . There are thousands upon . . . thousands of men in our midst who, a month ago, scoffed at the idea of a dissolution of the Union as a madman's dream, but who now hold the opinion that its days are numbered, its glory perished."

Hear the **Audio** at **www.myhistorylab.com** *John Brown: An Address by Frederick Douglass*

It was one thing to condemn slavery in the territories but another to attack it violently where it was long established. Southerners now saw in the Republican Party the embodiment of John Brown's ideals and actions. So, in their view, the election of a Republican president would be a death sentence for the South.

THE ELECTION OF 1860

An atmosphere of mutual sectional distrust and animosity characterized the campaign for the presidential election of 1860. In April, the Democratic Party, the sole surviving national political organization, held its convention in Charleston, South Carolina. Northern Democrats arrived in Charleston united behind Stephen A. Douglas. Although they constituted a majority of the delegates, they could not muster the two-thirds majority necessary to nominate their candidate. Other issues, however, were decided on a simple majority vote, permitting northern Democrats to defeat a platform proposal for a federal slave code in the territories.

Southern extremists who favored secession hoped to disrupt the convention and divide the party. They reasoned that the Republicans would then win the presidency, providing the South with the justification to secede. The platform vote gave them the opportunity they were seeking. Accompanied by spectators' cheers, delegates from five Lower South states, South Carolina, Florida, Mississippi, Louisiana, and Texas, walked out. The Arkansas and Georgia delegations joined them the following day.

Still without a nominee, the Democrats agreed to reconvene in Baltimore in June. This time, the Upper South delegations marched out when Douglas Democrats, in a commanding majority, refused to seat the Lower South delegations that had walked out in Charleston. The remaining delegates nominated Douglas for president. The bolters, who included almost all the southern delegates plus a few northerners loyal to President Buchanan, met in another hall and nominated John C. Breckinridge of Kentucky.

The disintegration of the national Democratic Party alarmed those southerners who understood that it would ensure the election of a Republican president in November. The *Memphis Appeal* warned that "the odium of the Black-Republican party has been that it is *Sectional*." Should southerners now allow a group of "restless and reckless or misguided men to destroy the national Democratic party?" the *Appeal* asked. Its emphatic answer was "No!"

The *Appeal* reflected the sentiment of many former Whigs, mainly from the Upper South, who would not support Breckinridge and could not support Douglas. Together with Whig allies in the North who had not defected to the Republican Party, they met in Baltimore in May 1860 to form the **Constitutional Union Party** and nominated John Bell of Tennessee for president.

Constitutional Union Party National party formed in 1860, mainly by former Whigs, that emphasized allegiance to the Union and strict enforcement of all national legislation.

Sensing victory, the Republicans convened in Chicago. If they could hold the states won by Frémont in 1856, add Minnesota (a new Republican-leaning state), and win Pennsylvania and one of three other Lower North states, Illinois, Indiana, or New Jersey, their candidate would win. These calculations dictated a platform and a candidate who could appeal to the four Lower North swing states, where antislavery sentiment was not so strong.

In selecting an appropriate presidential nominee, the Republicans faced a dilemma. Senator William H. Seward came to Chicago as the leading candidate. But his immoderate condemnation of southerners and slavery worried moderate northern voters—precisely the voters the party needed for victory.

Reservations about Seward benefited Abraham Lincoln. Lincoln's lieutenants at the convention stressed their candidate's moderation and morality, distancing him from both the abolitionists and Seward. Moreover, Chicago was Lincoln's home turf, and he had many friends working for him at the convention. When Seward faltered, Lincoln rose and won the Republican nomination.

The presidential campaign of 1860 actually comprised two campaigns. In the South, the contest was between Breckinridge and Bell; in the North, it was Lincoln against Douglas. Breckinridge and Bell had scattered support in the North, as did Douglas in the South, but in the main this was a sectional election. Lincoln did not even appear on the ballot in most southern states.

Lincoln became the nation's sixteenth president, with 40 percent of the popular vote (see Map 14–2). Douglas, though second after Lincoln in the popular balloting, won the undivided electoral vote of only one state, Missouri.

Lincoln took most northern states by significant margins and won all the region's electoral votes except three in New Jersey. This gave him a substantial majority of 180 electoral votes. Breckinridge won eleven southern states but received a majority of the popular

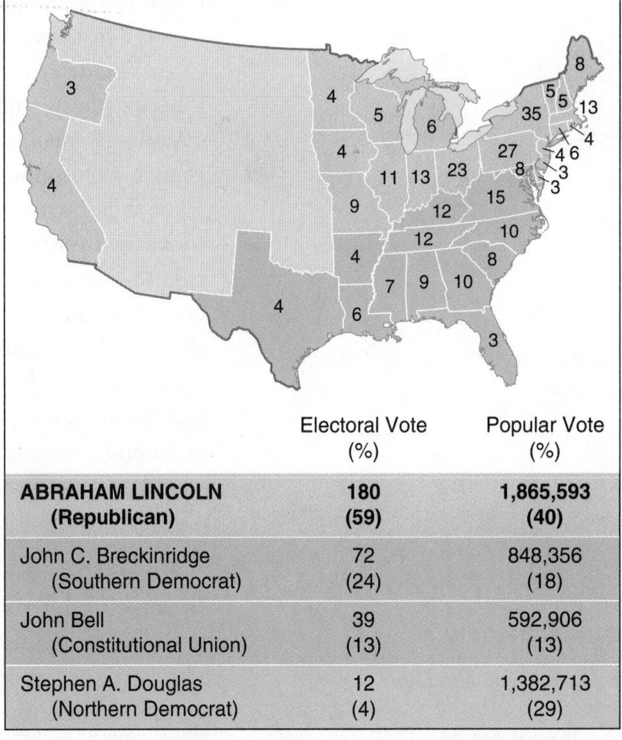

	Electoral Vote (%)	Popular Vote (%)
ABRAHAM LINCOLN (Republican)	**180 (59)**	**1,865,593 (40)**
John C. Breckinridge (Southern Democrat)	72 (24)	848,356 (18)
John Bell (Constitutional Union)	39 (13)	592,906 (13)
Stephen A. Douglas (Northern Democrat)	12 (4)	1,382,713 (29)

MAP 14–2 **The Election of 1860** The election returns from 1860 vividly illustrate the geography of sectionalism.

Based on the geographic sectionalism shown in this map, what issues were important to voters in the election of 1860?

vote in just four. In the South as a whole, his opponents, Bell and Douglas, together reaped 55 percent of the popular vote, confirming Republicans' skepticism about southern determination to secede.

Secession and Slavery

The events following Lincoln's election demonstrated how wildly mistaken were those who dismissed southern threats of secession. Four days after Lincoln's victory, the South Carolina legislature called on the state's citizens to elect delegates to a convention to consider secession. Meeting on December 20, the delegates voted unanimously to leave the Union. By February 1, six other states had all held similar conventions and decided to leave the Union. Representatives from the seven seceding states met to form a separate country, the **Confederate States of America.** On February 18, Jefferson Davis was sworn in as its president.

Confederate States of America Nation proclaimed in Montgomery, Alabama, in February 1861, after the seven states of the Lower South seceded from the United States.

The swiftness of secession in the Lower South obscured the divisions in most southern states over the issue. Secessionists barely secured a majority in the Georgia and Louisiana conventions. In Mississippi, Florida, and Alabama, the secessionist majority was more comfortable, but pro-Union candidates polled a significant minority of votes. With Lincoln headed for the White House, the greatest support for secession came from large landowners in counties in which slaves comprised a majority of the population. Support for secession was weakest among small, nonslaveholding farmers.

The secessionists mounted an effective propaganda campaign, deftly using the press to persuade voters to elect their delegates to the state conventions. Framing the issue as a personal challenge to every southern citizen, they argued that it would be cowardly to remain in the Union, a submission to despotism and enslavement. Most of all, secessionists focused on the threat to the institution of slavery as the primary cause for leaving the Union. (See American Views, The Cause of the Civil War.)

The delegates who voted to take Texas out of the Union, for example, charged that a Lincoln administration would result in "the abolition of negro slavery" and "the recognition of political equality between the white and negro races." South Carolina delegates justified secession by alleging that northerners "have encouraged and assisted thousands of our slaves to leave their homes; and those who remain, have been incited by emissaries, books and pictures to servile insurrection." Leaders in Georgia and Mississippi issued similar declarations. Just in case there was any doubt as to what the Confederate States of America stood for, Vice President Alexander Stephens proclaimed the "cornerstone" of the new government "rests upon the great truth that the negro is not equal to the white man; that slavery, subordination to the superior race, is his natural and moral condition." Slavery thus defined the South, and any attempt to lure the errant slave states back into the Union required unprecedented negotiating skills and a willingness to compromise. Neither the outgoing nor incoming administrations would possess these attributes.

Presidential Inaction

QUICK REVIEW

Buchanan and Secession

- Buchanan had to deal with secession crisis in the months between Lincoln's election and inauguration.
- Buchanan failed to work with Congress to find a solution.
- Buchanan hoped waiting would bring the South to its senses.

Because Lincoln would not take office until March 4, 1861, the Buchanan administration had to cope with the secession crisis during the critical months of December and January. The president's failure to work out a solution with Congress as secession fever swept the Lower South undermined Unionist forces in the seceding states.

When Buchanan lost the support of northern Democrats over the Lecompton Constitution, he turned to the South for support and filled his cabinet with southerners. Now, facing the secession crisis, he proposed holding a constitutional convention to amend the Constitution in ways that would satisfy the South's demands on slavery. This outright surrender to southern demands, however, had no chance of passing in Congress. Buchanan's administration quickly fell apart. As the Lower South states left the Union, their representatives and senators left Washington, and with them went Buchanan's closest advisers and key cabinet officials.

Buchanan, a lame duck, bereft of friends and advisers, did little more than condemn secession. He was reluctant to take action that would limit the options of the incoming administration or, worse, tip the balance in the Upper South toward secession. He hoped that waiting might bring an isolated Lower South to its senses and give efforts to mediate the sectional rift a chance to succeed.

Peace Proposals

Previous sectional conflicts, dating from the Missouri Compromise of 1820, had brought forth the ingenuity and goodwill of political leaders to effect compromise and draw the Union back from the brink of disintegration. Both ingenuity and goodwill were scarce commodities in the gray secession winter of 1860–1861. The two conflicting sides had little trust in each other, and the word "compromise" was viewed as more a synonym for capitulation than salvation.

Kentucky senator John J. Crittenden chaired a Senate committee that proposed a package of constitutional amendments in December 1860 designed to solve the sectional crisis. The central feature of the Crittenden Plan was the extension of the Missouri Compromise line through the territories all the way to California. The plan was of marginal interest to the South, because it was unlikely to result in any new slave states. And Republicans opposed it because it contradicted one of their basic principles, the exclusion of slavery from the territories.

Meanwhile, ex-president John Tyler emerged from retirement to lead an effort by the Border States, the Upper South and the Lower North, to forge a peace. Delegates from these states met in February 1861, but their plan differed little from Crittenden's, and it, too, got nowhere in Congress.

Lincoln's Views on Secession

President-elect Lincoln monitored the secession of the Lower South states and the attempts to reach a compromise from his home in Springfield. Although he said nothing publicly, he made it known that he did not favor compromises like those proposed by Crittenden and Tyler.

Lincoln counted on Unionist sentiment to keep the Upper South from seceding. Like Buchanan, he felt that the longer the Lower South states remained isolated, the more likely they would be to return to the fold. For a while, events seemed to bear him out.

One by one, Upper South states registered their support for the Union. North Carolinians went to the polls in February and turned down the call for a secession convention. Also in February, Virginians elected Unionists to their convention by a five-to-one margin. In Missouri, not one secessionist won election to the state convention. In Kentucky, the legislature adjourned without taking action on a convention or a statewide referendum on secession. And the Maryland legislature, already out of session, showed no inclination to reconvene.

A closer look, however, reveals that there were limits to the Upper South's Unionism. Most voters in the region went to the polls assuming that Congress would eventually reach a compromise based on the Crittenden proposals, Tyler's peace conference, or some other remedy. Leaders in the Upper South saw themselves as peacemakers. As one Virginian explained, "Without submission to the North or desertion of the South, Virginia has that moral position within the Union which will give her power to arbitrate between the sections." But what if arbitration failed? Or what if the Lower South states precipitated a crisis that forced the Upper South to choose sides? It was unlikely that the Upper South would abide the use of federal force against its southern neighbors.

Lincoln believed that the slavery issue had to come to a crisis before the nation could solve it. Although he said in public that he would never interfere with slavery in the slave states, the deep moral revulsion he felt toward the institution left him more ambivalent in private. As he confided to a colleague in 1860, "The tug has to come, and better now, than any time hereafter."

Fort Sumter: The Tug Comes

In his inaugural address on March 4, 1861, Abraham Lincoln denounced secession and vowed to uphold federal law but tempered his firmness with a conciliatory conclusion. Addressing southerners specifically, he assured them, "We are not enemies but friends. . . . Though passion may have strained, it must not break our bonds of affection. The mystic chords of memory, stretching from every battlefield, and patriot grave, to every living heart and hearthstone, all over this broad land, will yet swell the chorus of the Union, when again touched, as surely they will be, by the better angels of our nature."

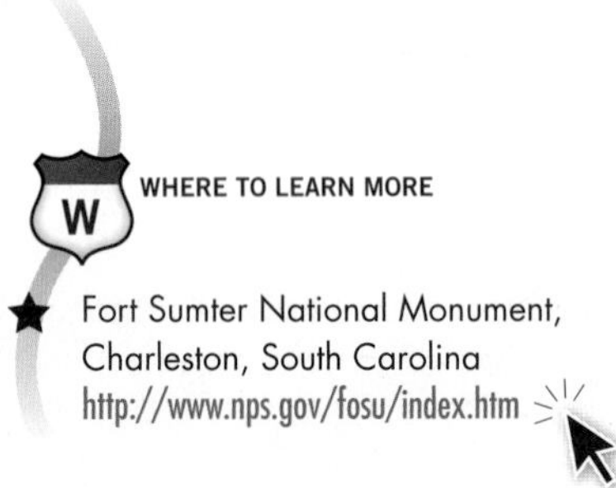

W
WHERE TO LEARN MORE
Fort Sumter National Monument, Charleston, South Carolina
http://www.nps.gov/fosu/index.htm

Southerners wanted concessions, not conciliation, however. The new president said nothing about slavery in the territories, nothing about the constitutional amendments proposed by Crittenden and Tyler, and nothing about the release of federal property in the South to the Confederacy. Even some northerners hoping for an olive branch were disappointed. But Lincoln was hoping for time—time to get the Lower South states quarreling with one another, time to allow Union sentiment to build in the Upper South, and time to convince northerners that the Union needed preserving. He did not get that time.

Fort Sumter Begun in the late 1820s to protect Charleston, South Carolina, it became the center of national attention in April 1861 when President Lincoln attempted to provision federal troops at the fort, triggering a hostile response from on-shore Confederate forces, opening the Civil War.

One day after Lincoln's inauguration, Major Robert Anderson, the commander of **Fort Sumter** in Charleston harbor, informed the administration that he had only four to six weeks' worth of provisions left. Anderson assumed that Lincoln would order him to evacuate the fort. The commanding General of the Army, Winfield Scott, advised the president accordingly, as did many members of his cabinet. Lincoln stalled.

The issue was simple, though the alternatives were difficult: Do not provision Fort Sumter and the garrison would fall to the Confederate government; provision the fort and risk a military confrontation as the Confederate authorities would perceive such action as an act of war. Lincoln had vowed in his inaugural address to uphold the Constitution and "to protect and defend" the country's interests; yet, he had also promised that he would not make any aggressive movements against the South.

at **www.myhistorylab.com**
What Caused the Civil War?

News of Anderson's plight changed the mood in the North. The Slave Power, some said, was holding him and his men hostage. Frustration grew over Lincoln's silence and inaction. The Confederacy's bold resolve seemed to contrast sharply with the federal government's confusion and inertia.

In early April, Lincoln ordered an expedition to provision Fort Sumter. Hoping to avoid a confrontation, the president did not send the troops that Anderson had requested. Instead, he ordered unarmed ships to proceed to the fort, deliver the provisions, and leave. Only if the Confederates fired on them were they to force their way into the fort with the help of armed reinforcements. Lincoln notified South Carolina authorities that he intended to do nothing more than "feed the hungry."

QUICK REVIEW

From Inauguration to War

- Lincoln struck conciliatory tone in inaugural address.
- South wanted concessions, not conciliation.
- Crisis over Fort Sumter sparks the war.

At Charleston, Confederate general P. G. T. Beauregard had standing orders to turn back any relief expedition. But President Davis wanted to take Sumter before the provisions arrived to avoid fighting Anderson and the reinforcements at the same time. He also realized that the outbreak of fighting could compel the Upper South to join the Confederacy. But his impatience to force the issue placed the Confederacy in the position of firing, unprovoked, on the American flag and at Major Anderson, who had become a hero to the North.

AMERICAN VIEWS

The Cause of the Civil War

The matter of causation has become controversial only in subsequent generations. Writers have cited economic differences between the sections, clashing interpretations of the Constitution, the tariff, and states' rights as factors in addition to slavery that brought about the Civil War. This is not surprising. People do not want to ascribe the death of 350,000 young southern men to the cause of human bondage, especially if one can identify an ancestor or two among the fallen. Contemporaries, however, had no need to dissemble about their actions or their society. The following excerpts from prominent southern politicians, a noted physician-writer, and a leading clergyman reflected the broad consensus in the South that secession and the war that would follow centered on the issue of slavery and the consequences of its abolition.

Speech of Henry L. Benning before the Virginia Convention, February 18, 1861

What was the reason that induced Georgia to take the step of secession? This reason may be summed up in one single proposition. It was a conviction, a deep conviction on the part of Georgia, that a separation from the North was the only thing that could prevent the abolition of her slavery.

Source: Addresses delivered before the Virginia state convention by Hon. Fulton Anderson, commissioner from Mississippi, Hon. Henry L. Benning, commissioner from Georgia, and Hon. John S. Preston, commissioner from South Carolina, February 1861. (Richmond: W. M. Elliott, printer, 1861).

Speech of Alexander Stephens, Vice President of the Confederate States of America, Savannah, Georgia, March 21, 1861

The new constitution [of the C.S.A.] has put at rest, forever, all the agitating questions relating to our peculiar institution African slavery as it exists amongst us the proper status of the negro in our form of civilization. . . .

Our new government is founded upon . . . its foundations are laid, its cornerstone rests, upon the great truth that the negro is not equal to the white man; that slavery and subordination to the superior race is his natural and normal condition. This, our new government, is the first, in the history of the world, based upon this great physical, philosophical, and moral truth.

Source: Henry Cleveland, *Alexander H. Stephens, in Public and Private: With Letters and Speeches, Before, During, and Since the War* (Philadelphia: National Publishing Company, 1866): 717–728.

Sermon of Rev. Benjamin M. Palmer, Thanksgiving Day, November 29, 1860, New Orleans, LA

[W]hat, at this juncture, is [our] providential trust? I answer that it is to conserve and to perpetuate the institution of domestic slavery as now existing. . . . Need I pause to show how this system is interwoven with our entire social fabric . . . and sanctioned in the Scriptures of God . . . ? Must I pause to show how it has fashioned our modes of life, and determined all our habits of thought and feeling, and moulded the very type of our civilization? How then can the hand of violence be laid upon it without involving our existence?

Source: Thanksgiving Sermon, Delivered at the First Presbyterian Church, New Orleans, on Thursday, November 29, 1860 (New York: G. F. Hesbit & Co., Printers, 1860).

William H. Holcombe, MD, "The Alternative: A Separate Nationality, or the Africanization of the South," February 1861.

Opposition to slavery, to its existence, its extension and its perpetuation, is the sole cohesive element of the triumphant faction. . . . The question is at length plainly presented: submission or secession. The only alternative left us is this: *a separate nationality or the Africanization of the South.* He has not analyzed this subject aright nor probed it to the bottom, who supposes that the real quarrel between the North and the South is about the Territories, or the decision of the Supreme Court, or even the constitution itself. . . . The division is broader and deeper and more incurable than this. The antagonism is fundamental and ineradicable. The true secret of it lies in the total reversion of public opinion which has occurred in both sections of the country in the last quarter of a century on the subject of slavery.

Source: Southern Literary Messenger, February 1861: 81–88.

- **How** do these excerpts reflect the merger of religion and politics?
- **What** connections do these leaders make between slavery and white supremacy?
- **Given** the views expressed in these excerpts, what could the Lincoln administration have done to restore the Union short of war?

OVERVIEW The Emerging Sectional Crisis

Event	Year	Effect
Wilmot Proviso	1846	Congressman David Wilmot's proposal to ban slavery from territories acquired from Mexico touched off a bitter sectional dispute in Congress.
Compromise of 1850	1850	Law admitted California as a free state, granted the population of Utah and New Mexico Territories the right to decide on slavery, and established a new and stronger Fugitive Slave Act, all of which "solved" the territorial issue raised by the Wilmot Proviso but satisfied neither North nor South and planted the seeds of future conflict.
Election of 1852	1852	Results confirmed demise of the Whig Party, initiating a period of political realignment.
Kansas-Nebraska Act	1854	Law created the Kansas and Nebraska Territories and repealed the Missouri Compromise of 1820 by leaving the question of slavery to the territories' residents. Its passage enraged many northerners, prompting some to form the new Republican Party.
"Bleeding Kansas"	1855–1856	Sometimes violent conflict between pro- and antislavery forces in Kansas further polarized the sectional debate.
Election of 1856	1856	Presidency was won by Democrat James Buchanan of Pennsylvania, but a surprisingly strong showing by the recently formed Republican Party in the North set the stage for the 1860 election.
Dred Scott Case	1857	The Supreme Court ruling that slaves were not citizens and that Congress had no authority to ban slavery from the territories boosted Republican prospects in the North.
Lecompton Constitution	1857	Proslavery document, framed by a fraudulently elected constitutional convention in Kansas and supported by President Buchanan, further convinced northerners that the South was subverting their rights.
John Brown's Raid	1859	Unsuccessful attempt to free the South's slaves, this attack on a federal arsenal in Harpers Ferry, Virginia, increased sectional tension.
Election of 1860	1860	Republican Abraham Lincoln won a four-way race for the presidency. The last major national party, the Democrats, disintegrated. Lower South states seceded.
Fort Sumter	1861	Confederate forces attacked the fort in April 1861, Lincoln called for troops, and several Upper South states seceded. The Civil War was underway.

Black smoke billows from Fort Sumter in the Charleston harbor during the first engagement of the Civil War.

On April 10, Davis ordered Beauregard to demand the immediate evacuation of Fort Sumter. Anderson refused but wondered what the hurry was, considering that his provisions would run out in a few days. The remark gave Beauregard pause and prompted additional negotiations. Anderson did not yield, and as unarmed Federal supply vessels appeared before dawn on April 12, 1861, the first Confederate shell whistled down on the fort. After more than a day of shelling, during which more than 5,000 artillery rounds struck Fort Sumter, Anderson surrendered. Remarkably, neither side suffered any casualties, a deceptive beginning to an exceptionally bloody war.

When the verdict of Fort Sumter reached President Lincoln, he called on the southern states still in the Union to send troops to put down the rebellion. Refusing to make war on South Carolina, the Upper South states of Virginia, North Carolina, Tennessee, and Arkansas seceded, and the Confederacy expanded to eleven states.

CONCLUSION

When David Wilmot submitted his amendment to ban slavery from the territories gained from Mexico, he could not have foreseen that the debate he unleashed would end in civil war just fifteen years later. Northerners and southerners had lived together in one nation for nearly eighty years. During that time, they had reached accommodations on slavery at the Constitutional Convention of 1787, in the Compromises of 1820 and 1850, and on numerous lesser occasions. But by the 1850s the slavery issue had become weighted with so much moral and political freight that it defied easy resolution. Throughout the Western world, attitudes toward slavery were changing. Northern evangelical Protestants in the 1840s and 1850s branded slavery a sin and slaveholders sinners. The overwhelming popularity of *Uncle Tom's Cabin* both tapped and fed this sentiment. America could no longer continue its journey as a nation half slave and half free.

The political conflict over slavery coalesced around northern efforts to curtail southern expansion and power and southern attempts to maintain power and influence in the federal government by planting the institution in the western territories. This conflict eventually helped undo the Compromise of 1850 and turned Stephen A. Douglas's railroad bill into a battle royal over Kansas. Unable to resolve sectional differences over slavery, the Whigs disintegrated, and the Democrats divided into northern and southern factions. The Republican Party was formed from the political debris. Ethnic and religious conflicts further disturbed the political landscape and contributed to party realignment.

Northerners and southerners eventually interpreted any incident or piece of legislation as an attempt by one side to gain moral and political advantage at the other's expense. Northerners viewed the *Dred Scott* decision, the Lecompton Constitution, and the southern reaction to John Brown's Raid as evidence of a Slave Power conspiracy to deny white northerners their constitutional rights. Southerners interpreted the northern reaction to these same events as evidence of a conspiracy to rob them of security and equality within the Union.

Ironically, as Americans in both sections talked of freedom and self-determination, the black men and women in their midst had little of either. Their American journey generated scant recognition. Lincoln went to war to preserve the Union; Davis, to defend a new nation. Slavery was the spark that ignited the conflict, but white America seemed more comfortable embracing abstract ideals than real people. Northerners and southerners would confront this irony during the bloodiest war in American history, but they would not resolve it.

Where to Learn More

The Underground Railroad Freedom Center, Cincinnati, Ohio. The Center provides information on the northern response to the Fugitive Slave Act. See its website at http://www.freedomcenter.org/.

Adair Cabin and John Brown Museum, John Brown Memorial Park, Osawatomie, Kansas. Maintained by the Kansas Historical Society, the cabin (which once belonged to John Brown's sister) and the museum are located on the site of the Battle of Osawatomie, one of the critical events of "Bleeding Kansas." Its website is http://www.kshs.org/places/johnbrown/history.htm.

Harpers Ferry National Historical Park, West Virginia. Exhibits interpret John Brown's Raid and re-create some of the atmosphere and structures of the 1850s village and the federal arsenal. Its website is http://www.nps.gov/hafe/index.htm.

Fort Sumter National Monument, Charleston, South Carolina. This historic site interprets the bombardment of the fort and the events that immediately preceded the Civil War. Go to http://www.nps.gov/fosu/index.htm.

Review Questions

1. How do you account for the great success of Harriet Beecher Stowe's *Uncle Tom's Cabin?*
2. How did the failure of democratic revolutions in Europe affect Americans' perspectives on their own system of government?
3. Discuss the role of evangelical religion in sharpening the sectional conflict between North and South.
4. Between the time he was elected president in November and his inauguration in March, what options did Abraham Lincoln have for resolving the sectional crisis?
5. Northerners and southerners appealed to the same American ideals in support of their respective positions. Could they both have been correct?

Key Terms

"Bleeding Kansas" (p. 374)
Compromise of 1850 (p. 369)
Confederate States of America (p. 386)
Constitutional Union Party (p. 385)
***Dred Scott* decision** (p. 378)
Fort Sumter (p. 388)
Fugitive Slave Act (p. 370)
John Brown's Raid (p. 383)
Kansas-Nebraska Act (p. 374)
Know-Nothing Party (p. 375)
Lecompton Constitution (p. 378)
Lincoln-Douglas debates (p. 380)
Ostend Manifesto (p. 373)
Panic of 1857 (p. 379)
Popular sovereignty (p. 367)
Republican Party (p. 376)
Wilmot Proviso (p. 366)

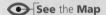

PEARSON myhistorylab Connections

Reinforce what you learned in this chapter by studying the many documents, images, maps, review tools, and videos available at **www.myhistorylab.com.**

Read and Review

Study and Review Study Plan: Chapter 14

Read the Document

Edward Gould Buffum, Six Months in the Gold Mines (1850)

George Fitzhugh, The Blessings of Slavery (1857)

Harriet Beecher Stowe, Uncle Tom's Cabin *(1852)*

A Catechism for Slaves (1854)

An African American Novel Critiques Racism in the North (1859)

Benjamin Drew, from Narratives of Fugitive Slaves in Canada (1855)

John Brown's Address before Sentencing (1859)

John C. Calhoun, Proposal to Preserve the Union (1850)

Opinion of the Supreme Court for Dred Scott v. Sanford *(1857)*

The Compromise of 1850

The Fugitive Slave Act (1850)

The Lincoln-Douglas Debates of 1858

See the Map

Slave Population Patterns, 1790 and 1860

The Compromise of 1850 and the Kansas-Nebraska Act

United States Territorial Expansion in the 1850s

Research and Explore

Read the Document

Personal Journeys Online

From Then to Now Online: Religion and Politics

Hear the Audio *John Brown: An Address by Frederick Douglass*

Watch the Video

Harriet Beecher Stowe and the Making of Uncle Tom's Cabin

What Caused the Civil War?

Hear the Audio

Hear the audio files for Chapter 14 at **www.myhistorylab.com.**

1861-1865

15

Battle Cries and Freedom Songs: The Civil War

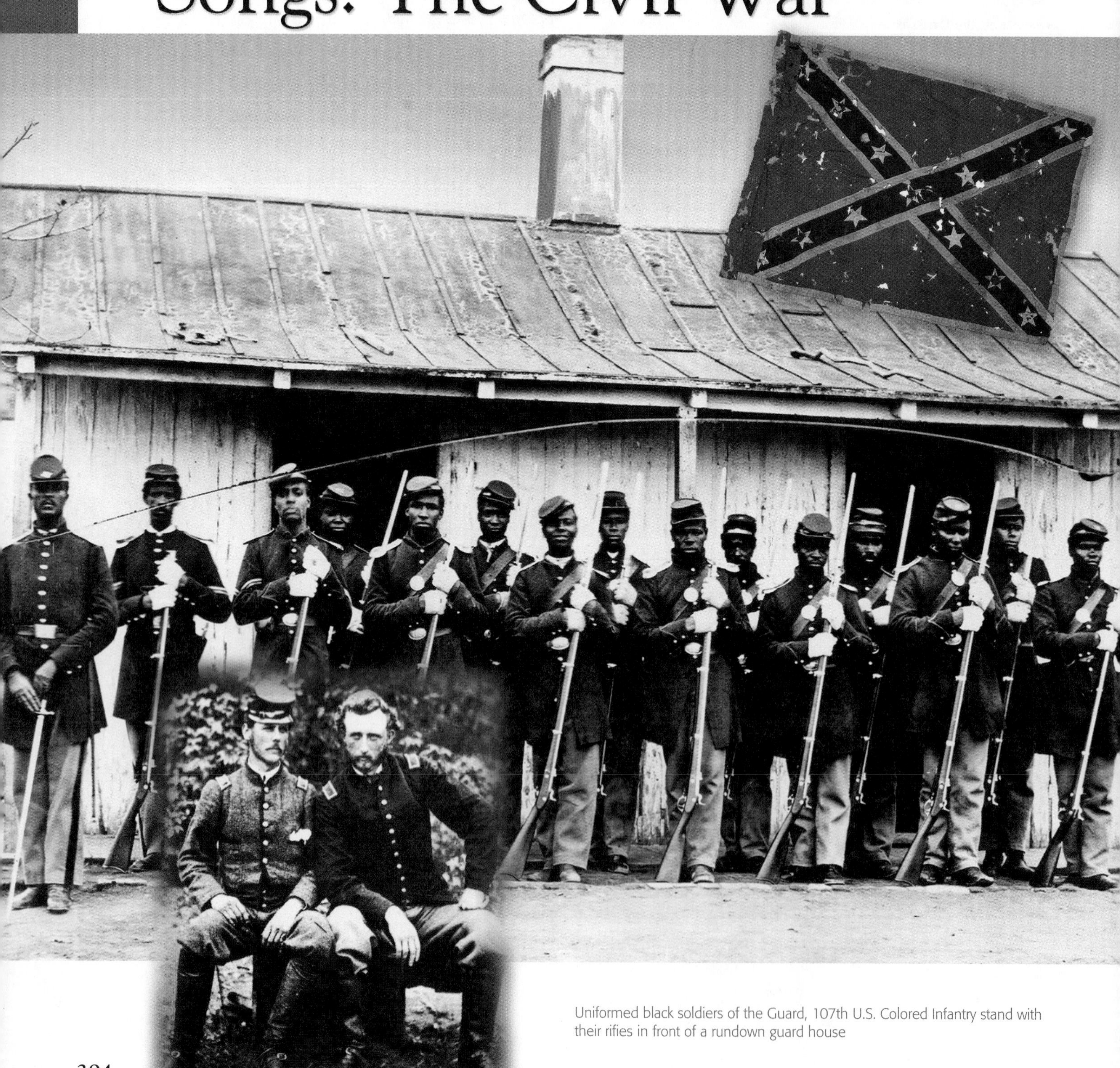

Uniformed black soldiers of the Guard, 107th U.S. Colored Infantry stand with their rifies in front of a rundown guard house

Hear the **Audio**

Hear the audio files for Chapter 15 at **www.myhistorylab.com**.

MOBILIZATION, NORTH AND SOUTH *(page 397)*

WHAT WERE the North's key advantages at the outset of the war?

THE EARLY WAR, 1861–1862 *(page 402)*

HOW DID the two sides' objectives dictate their strategies in the early years of the war?

TURNING POINTS, 1862–1863 *(page 407)*

WHAT CONVINCED Lincoln to issue the Emancipation Proclamation?

WAR TRANSFORMS THE NORTH *(page 417)*

WHAT IMPACT did the war have on the North's economy?

THE CONFEDERACY DISINTEGRATES *(page 420)*

HOW DID the war affect civilian life in the South?

THE UNION PREVAILS, 1864–1865 *(page 423)*

WHAT WAS Grant's strategy for ending the war?

One American Journey

July 14, 1861

Camp Clark, Washington, DC

My very dear Sarah:

The indications are very strong that we shall move in a few days, perhaps tomorrow. And lest I should not be able to write you again I feel impelled to write a few lines that may fall under your eye when I am no more. Our movement may be one of a few days' duration and be full of pleasure. And it may be one of severe conflict and death to me. "Not my will but thine O God be done." If it is necessary that I should fall on the battle-field for my Country I am ready. I have no misgivings about, or lack of confidence in the cause in which I am engaged, and my courage does not halt or falter. I know how American Civilization now leans upon the triumph of the government and how great a debt we owe to those who went before us through the blood and suffering of the Revolution. And I am willing, perfectly willing, to lay down all my joys in this life, to help maintain this government, and to pay that debt. But my dear wife, when I know that with my own joys I lay down nearly all of yours, . . . is it weak or dishonorable that while the banner of my purpose floats calmly and proudly in the breeze, underneath, my unbounded love for you my darling wife children should struggle in fierce though useless contest with my love of country? . . .

Sarah, my love for you is deathless, it seems to bind me with mighty cables that nothing but omnipotence can break; and yet my love of Country comes over me like a strong wind and bears me irresistibly with all those chains to the battle-field.

The memories of the blissful moments I have enjoyed with you come crowding over me, and I feel most deeply grateful to God and you, that I have enjoyed them for so long. And how hard it is for me to give them up and burn to ashes the hopes and future years, when, God willing, we might still have lived and loved together, and see our boys grown up to honorable manhood around us. . . . If I do not [return], my dear Sarah, never forget how much I loved you, nor that when my last breath escapes me on the battle-field, it will whisper your name.

Forgive my many faults, and the many pains I have caused you. How thoughtless, how foolish I have sometimes been! . . .

But, O Sarah, if the dead can come back to this earth and flit unseen around those they love, I shall be with you, in the gladdest days and the darkest nights . . . always, always, and if there be a soft breeze upon your cheek, it shall be my breath[;] as the cool air fans your throbbing temple, it shall be my spirit passing by. Sarah do not mourn me dead; think I am gone and wait for thee, for we shall meet again. . . .

Sullivan

Read the **Document** at **www.myhistorylab.com**

Personal Journeys Online

- **Sam R. Watkins, Co. "Aytch": *A Confederate Memoir of the Civil War,* 1882. A Confederate soldier recounts the horrors of war he witnessed in a southern hospital and on the battlefield.**
- **Ambrose Bierce, "What I Saw of Shiloh," *Civil War Stories,* 1909. Account of a Union soldier's experiences at the Battle of Shiloh.**

CHRONOLOGY

1861 January	Benito Juarez becomes president of Mexico, dedicated to restoring national unity.
March	Tsar Alexander II emancipates Russia's serfs.
	Kingdom of Italy proclaimed.
April	Confederates fire on Fort Sumter; Civil War begins.
July	First Battle of Bull Run.
1862 February	Forts Henry and Donelson fall to Union forces.
March	Peninsula Campaign begins.
	Battle of Glorieta Pass, New Mexico.
April	Battle of Shiloh.
	New Orleans falls to Federal forces.
May	Union captures Corinth, Mississippi.
July	Seven Days' Battles end.
	Congress passes the Confiscation Act.
August	Second Battle of Bull Run.
September	Battle of Antietam.
December	Battle of Fredericksburg.
1863 January	Emancipation Proclamation takes effect.
May	Battle of Chancellorsville; Stonewall Jackson is mortally wounded.
June	French forces capture Mexico City.
July	Battle of Gettysburg.
	Vicksburg falls to Union forces.
	New York Draft Riot occurs.
	Black troops of the 54th Massachusetts Volunteer Infantry Regiment assault Fort Wagner outside Charleston.
September	Battle of Chickamauga.
November	Battle of Chattanooga.
1864 May	Battle of the Wilderness.
June	Battle of Cold Harbor.
	Ferdinand Maximilian Joseph, archduke of Austria, crowned emperor of Mexico with support of French troops.
September	Sherman captures Atlanta.
November	President Lincoln is reelected.
	Sherman begins his march to the sea.
1865 January	Congress passes Thirteenth Amendment to the Constitution, outlawing slavery (ratified December 1865).
February	Charleston surrenders.
March	Confederate Congress authorizes enlistment of black soldiers.
April	Federal troops enter Richmond.
	Lee surrenders to Grant at Appomattox Court House.
	Lincoln is assassinated.

SULLIVAN BALLOU'S letter to his wife on the eve of the First Battle of Bull Run typified the sentiments of the civilian armies raised by both North and South: a clear purpose of the importance of their mission, a sense of foreboding, an appeal and acknowledgment of the guiding hand of God, and, most of all, words of love for family.

Sullivan Ballou took the ultimate journey for his beliefs and his love. The Civil War preserved the Union, abolished slavery, and killed at least 620,000 soldiers, more than in all the other wars the country fought from the Revolution to the Korean conflict combined. To come to terms with this is to try to reconcile the war's great accomplishments with its awful consequences. ✦

MOBILIZATION, NORTH AND SOUTH

WHAT WERE the North's key advantages at the outset of the war?

Neither side was prepared for a major war. The Confederacy lacked a national army. Each southern state had a militia, but by the 1850s, these companies had become more social clubs than fighting units. Aside from privately owned ships and some captured Federal vessels, the Confederacy also lacked a navy. The Union had a regular army of only 16,000 men, most of whom were stationed west of the Mississippi River. Their major responsibility had been to intervene between white settlers and Indians.

Each government augmented these meager military reserves with thousands of new recruits and developed a bureaucracy to mount a war effort. At the same time, the administrations of Presidents Lincoln and Davis secured the loyalty of their civilian populations and devised military strategies for a war of indeterminate duration. How North and South went about these tasks reflected both the different objectives of the two sides and the distinctive personalities of their leaders, Abraham Lincoln and Jefferson Davis.

Watch the Video at **www.myhistorylab.com** *What Caused the Civil War?*

War Fever

The day after Major Robert Anderson surrendered Fort Sumter, President Lincoln moved to enlarge his small, scattered army by mobilizing state militias for 90 days. Four states—Virginia, Arkansas, North Carolina, and Tennessee—refused the call and seceded from the Union. About one-third of the officer corps of the regular army, including some of the highest ranking officers, resigned their commissions to join the Confederacy. Still, Lincoln seemed likely to meet his target of 75,000 troops.

Read the Document at **www.myhistorylab.com** *A Nation Divided: The Civil War*

Lincoln's modest 90-day call-up reflected the general belief, North and South, that the war would end quickly. Not everyone thought the war would be brief. William T. Sherman, who had recently headed a Louisiana military academy and would become one of the Union's few great commanders, wrote in April 1861, "I think it is to be a long war, very long, much longer than any politician thinks."

Northerners closed ranks behind the president after the Confederacy's attack on Fort Sumter. Stephen A. Douglas, a leading Democrat, called on the Republican Lincoln to offer his and his party's support. "There can be no neutrals in this war," Douglas said, "only patriots, or traitors." Residents of New York City, where sympathy for the South had probably been greater than anywhere else in the North, now sponsored huge public demonstrations in support of the war effort.

Southerners were equally eager to support their new nation. Enlistment rallies, wild send-offs at train stations, and auctions and balls to raise money for the troops were staged throughout the Confederacy. As in the North, war fever fired hatred of the enemy.

Appeals to God were commonplace on both sides. The feeling that a holy war was unfolding energized recruits. A Union soldier expressed his feelings in a letter home at the beginning of the war: "I believe our cause to be the cause of liberty and light . . . the cause of God, and holy and justifiable in His sight, and for this reason, I fear not to die in it if need be." Equally convinced of the righteousness of his cause, a Confederate soldier wrote: "Our Cause is Just and God is Just and we shall finally be successful whether I live to see the time or not." As war fever gripped North and South, volunteers on both sides rushed to join, quickly filling the quotas of both armies.

By early spring of 1862, however, the Confederate government was compelled to order the first general draft in American history. It required three years of service for men between 18 and 35 (a range later expanded from 17 to 50). In 1864, the Confederate Congress added a compulsory reenlistment provision. At that point, the only way a recruit could get out of the army was to die or desert.

The Confederate draft law allowed several occupational exemptions. Among them was an infamous provision that allowed one white man on any plantation with more than 20 slaves to be excused from service. The reason for the exemption was to ensure the security and productivity of large plantations, not to protect the privileged, but it led some southerners to conclude that the struggle had become "a rich man's war but a poor man's fight."

The initial flush of enthusiasm faded in the North as well. Responding to a call for additional troops, some northern states initiated a draft during the summer of 1862. In March 1863, Congress passed the Enrollment Act, a draft law that, like the Confederate draft, allowed for occupational exemptions. A provision that allowed a draftee to hire a substitute aroused resentment among working-class northerners. Anger at the draft, as well as poor working conditions, sparked several riots during 1863. But the North was less dependent on conscription than was the South. Only 8 percent of the Union's soldiers were drafted, compared to 20 percent for the Confederacy.

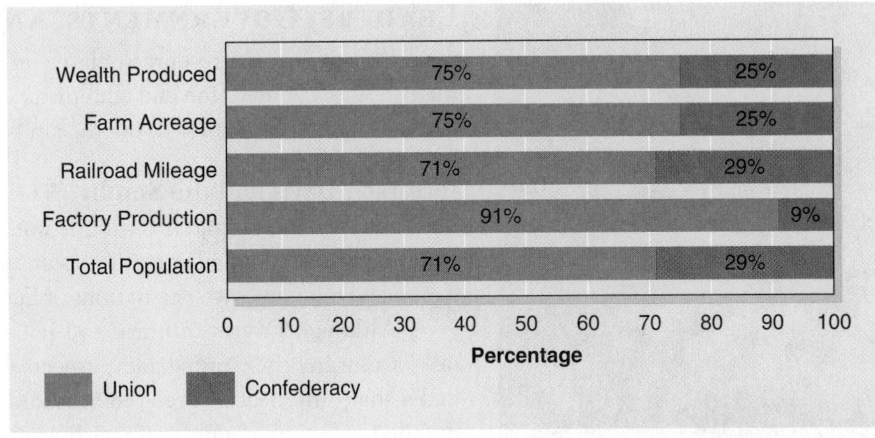

FIGURE 15–1 A Comparison of the Union and Confederate Control of Key Resources at the Outset of the Civil War

THE NORTH'S ADVANTAGE IN RESOURCES

The resources of the North, including its population, industrial and agricultural capacity, and transportation network, greatly exceeded those of the South (see Figure 15–1). The 2.1 million men who fought for the Union represented roughly half the men of military age in the North. The 900,000 men who fought for the Confederacy, by contrast, represented fully 90 percent of its eligible population. Irish and German immigrants continued to flow into the North during the war, although at a slower rate than before, and thousands of them enlisted, often as substitutes for native-born northerners. Nearly 200,000 African Americans, most of them ex-slaves from the South, took up arms for the Union. Not until the last month of the war did the Confederacy consider arming slaves.

At the beginning of the war, the North controlled 90 percent of the nation's industrial capacity. The North had dozens of facilities for producing war matériel; the South had only one munitions plant, the Tredegar Iron Works in Richmond. Northern farms, more mechanized than their southern counterparts, produced record harvests of meat, grain, and vegetables. Southern farms were also productive, but the South lacked the North's capacity to transport and distribute food efficiently. The railroad system in the North was more than twice the size of the South's.

Thanks to the North's abundance of resources, no soldier in any previous American army had ever been outfitted as well as the blue-uniformed Union trooper. The official color of the Confederate uniform was gray, although a dusty brown shade was more common. Most southern soldiers, however, did not wear distinguishable uniforms, especially toward the end of the war. They also often lacked proper shoes or any footwear at all. Still, the South never lost a battle because of insufficient supplies or inadequate weaponry. New foundries opened, and manufacturing enterprises in Augusta, Georgia; Selma, Alabama; and elsewhere joined the Tredegar Iron Works in keeping the Confederate armies equipped.

Unstable finances proved more of a handicap for the Confederacy than its relatively low industrial capacity. The Confederate economy, and its treasury, depended heavily on cotton exports. But a Union naval blockade and the ability of textile manufacturers in Europe to find new sources of supply restricted this crucial source of revenue. The imposition of taxes would have improved the Confederacy's finances, but southerners resisted taxation. The government sold interest-bearing bonds to raise money, but as Confederate fortunes declined, so did bond sales. With few other options, the Confederacy financed more than 60 percent of the $1.5 billion it spent on the war with printing-press money. Inflation spiraled out of control, demoralizing civilians.

The Union had more abundant financial resources than the Confederacy, and the federal government was more successful than the Confederate government at developing innovative ways to meet the great cost of the war. Like the Confederacy, the Federal government issued paper money, bills derisively known as "greenbacks," that was not backed by gold or silver. But the Federal government also offset its expenses with the country's first income tax, which citizens could pay in greenbacks, a move that bolstered the value and credibility of the paper currency. These financial measures eliminated the need for wage and price controls and rationing and warded off ruinous inflation in the North.

QUICK REVIEW

Northern Advantages

- Twice the number of soldiers.
- North controlled 90 percent of nation's industrial capacity.
- Naval superiority.

Read the **Document** at **www.myhistorylab.com**
Jefferson Davis, Address to the Provisional Congress (1861)

Jefferson Davis, Confederate president, was born in Kentucky. After attending West Point and serving for seven years in the military, Davis became a gentleman planter. He returned to military service during the Mexican War, became a senator in 1847, and served as secretary of war under President Franklin Pierce, then returned to the Senate in 1857.

Leaders, Governments, and Strategies

Leadership ability, like resources, played an important role in the war. It was up to the leaders of the two sides to determine and administer civilian and military policy, to define war objectives, and to inspire a willingness to sacrifice in both citizens and soldiers.

Jefferson Davis and the South. The Confederate president, Jefferson Davis, had to build a government from scratch during a war. Abraham Lincoln at least had the benefit of an established governmental structure, a standing army, healthy financial resources, and established diplomatic relations with the nations of Europe.

Although Davis's military and political background qualified him for the prodigious task of running the Confederacy, aspects of his character compromised his effectiveness. He had a sharp intellect but related awkwardly to people. Colleagues found him aloof. He was inclined to equate compromise with weakness and interpreted any opposition as a personal attack.

Abraham Lincoln and the North. Northerners, like southerners, needed a convincing reason to endure the prolonged sacrifice of the Civil War. For them, the struggle was a distant one, fought mostly on southern soil. Lincoln and other northern leaders secured support by convincing their compatriots of the importance of preserving the Union. The president viewed the conflict in global terms, its results affecting the hopes for democratic government around the world. He concluded that the war "presents to the whole family of man, the question, whether a constitutional republic . . . can or cannot maintain its territorial integrity, against its own domestic foes."

Lincoln's fight for the border states. The secession of Virginia, Arkansas, North Carolina, and Tennessee left four border slave states, Maryland, Delaware, Kentucky, and Missouri, hanging in the balance. Were Maryland and Delaware to secede, the federal capital at Washington, DC, would be surrounded by Confederate territory. The loss of Kentucky and Missouri would threaten the borders of Iowa, Illinois, Indiana, and Ohio and remove the Deep South from the threat of imminent invasion. Kentucky's manpower, livestock, and waterways were important to both sides.

Lincoln adopted a "soft" strategy to secure the border states, stressing the restoration of the Union as the sole objective of Federal military operations and assuring border residents that his government would not interfere with slavery. Union commanders barred fugitive slaves from their camps during the first year of the war, promising "to keep the war a lily-white crusade," as one officer put it. But early reports from the four states were troubling. The four governors displayed polite indifference or overt hostility to the federal government.

Maryland's strategic location north of Washington, DC, rendered its loyalty to the Union vital. Although a majority of its citizens opposed secession, a mob attack on Union troops passing through Baltimore in April 1861 indicated strong prosouthern sentiment. Lincoln dispatched Federal troops to monitor the fall elections in the state, placed its legislature under military surveillance, and arrested officials who opposed the Union cause, including the mayor of Baltimore. This show of force guaranteed the pro-Union candidate for governor an overwhelming victory and saved Maryland for the Union. Delaware, although nominally a slave state, remained staunchly for the Union.

Missourians settled their indecision by combat. The fighting culminated with a Union victory in March 1862 at the Battle of Pea Ridge, Arkansas. The Union victory was notable for two reasons. First, the Confederate force included 3,500 mounted Indians led by Colonel Stand Watie, a Cherokee, who achieved one of the rare Rebel victories during the two-day battle. The Cherokees joined the Confederate cause in the hopes of securing a better deal than they had received from Washington. The decisive Union victory at Pea Ridge also secured Missouri and northern Arkansas for federal forces, further diminishing Confederate influence in the Upper South.

Kentucky never seceded but attempted to remain neutral at the outset of the war. The legislature was pro-Union, the governor prosouthern. Both sides actively recruited soldiers in the state. In September 1861, when Confederate forces invaded Kentucky and Union forces moved to expel them, the state became one of the war's battlegrounds.

Although Virginia went with the Confederacy, some counties in the western part of the state opposed secession and, as early as the summer of 1861, took steps to establish a pro-Union state. In June 1863, West Virginia became the nation's thirty-fifth state.

Strategies and tactics. To a great extent, the political objectives of each side determined its military strategy. Southerners wanted independence and protection of their institutions; northerners fought to preserve the Union. The North's goal required conquest. Federal forces had to invade the South, destroy its armies, and rout its government, a difficult assignment considering the vast geographic extent of the Confederacy. The Confederacy, for its part, did not need to conquer the North. Fighting a defensive battle in its own territory, the South had only to hang on until growing northern opposition to the war or some decisive northern military mistake convinced the Union to stop fighting.

But the South's strategy had two weaknesses. First, it demanded more patience than the South had shown in impulsively attacking Fort Sumter. Second, the South might not have sufficient resources to draw out the war long enough to swing northern public opinion behind peace. The question was: What would break first, northern support for the war or southern ability to wage it?

The Southern Landscape

The southern landscape played a significant strategic role in the Civil War. The South covered 800,000 square miles, about the size of Spain, Italy, France, Germany, and Poland combined. The region was mostly rural with a 3,500-mile coastline, impenetrable forests and swamps, numerous rivers, a mountain chain, and irregular terrain except on the coast. Union and Confederate officers who had attended West Point learned open field combat with two armies arrayed against each other in close formation, firing weapons with limited range and accuracy. The introduction of rifled muskets and light artillery increased the accuracy, range, and deadliness of weaponry. Attacking entrenched soldiers or troops with commanding geographical positions rarely proved successful and usually resulted in high casualties for the attacking army.

The southern landscape played a major role in the Civil War. The undulating terrain and the obstacles presented by rivers, streams, woods, and cultivated fields are all on display here as Union troops under General Ambrose Burnside take the bridge (today named after the General) over Antietam Creek in September 1862. Rebel forces held the higher ground, however, and pushed the Federals back later in the day.

The dense forests of the South also hampered traditional battle tactics. Bullets and artillery shells often ignited the underbrush, creating an inferno that trapped troops. The dense smoke caused by fire and weapons restricted visibility. Some soldiers became victims of friendly fire as a result.

Then there was the cloying heat and humidity of the South. Most of the major engagements occurred in the late spring, summer, and fall. Wool uniforms exhausted troops, and unsanitary conditions, compounded by the absence of frost until the late fall, heightened the casualties from disease. The moisture and excessive heat also generated sustained and often violent thunderstorms.

Downpours turned roads into mud and gentle streams into raging rivers. The condition of southern roads, never very good even in fine weather, played a role in delaying deployment of troops, the coordination of attacks, and the pursuit of a defeated foe.

The South's uneven terrain also hampered traditional battle tactics. At Antietam, for example, the numerous depressions, or valleys, between hills meant that soldiers disappeared from view every so often. In hilly terrain the artillery echoed off hills, making it difficult for troops to determine the direction of firing.

These environmental idiosyncrasies of the South should have given Confederate troops a significant advantage. They fought on their home turf and they maneuvered among friendly residents. The Confederates, however, like most of their Union counterparts, had rarely ventured beyond their neighborhoods growing up and often found themselves in unfamiliar terrain. Thus, for the most part, the respective commanders adapted to the geography on the fly. The Union's superiority in railroads, steamships, and telegraphy, especially during the last eighteen months of the war, enabled commanders to transcend environmental barriers and the South's immense territory to move troops and information quickly.

THE EARLY WAR, 1861–1862

HOW DID the two sides' objectives dictate their strategies in the early years of the war?

The North's offensive strategy dictated the course of the war for the first two years. In the West, the federal army's objectives were to hold Missouri, Kentucky, and Tennessee, to control the Mississippi River, and eventually to detach the area west of the Appalachians from the rest of the Confederacy. In the East, Union forces sought to capture Richmond, the Confederate capital. The U.S. Navy imposed a blockade along the Confederate coast and pushed into inland waterways to capture southern ports.

The Confederates defended strategic locations throughout their territory or abandoned them when prudence required. Occasionally, taking advantage of surprise or terrain, southern forces ventured out to engage Union armies. Between engagements, each side sniped at, bushwhacked, and trapped the other.

By the end of 1862, the result remained in the balance. Although Union forces had attained some success in the West, the southern armies there remained intact. In the East, where resourceful Confederate leaders several times stopped superior Union forces, the southerners clearly had the best of it.

First Bull Run

QUICK REVIEW

The First Battle of Bull Run

- July 21, 1861: Beauregard (Confederacy) and McDowell (Union) meet at Manassas.
- Confederate troops repulse a strong Union attack.
- Destroyed belief in North that the war would be over quickly.

By July 1861, when the border states appeared more secure for the Union, President Lincoln shifted his attention southward and ordered General Irvin McDowell to move his forces into Virginia to take Richmond (see Map 15–1). Confronting McDowell 20 miles southwest of Washington at Manassas was a Confederate army under General P. G. T. Beauregard. The two armies clashed on July 21 at the First Battle of Bull Run (known to the Confederacy as the First Battle of Manassas). The Union troops seemed at first on the verge of winning. But Beauregard's forces, along with General Joseph E. Johnston's reinforcements, repulsed the assault, scattering not only the Union army but also hundreds of picnickers who had come out from Washington to watch the fight.

Bull Run dispelled some illusions and reinforced others. It boosted southerners' confidence and seemed to confirm their boast that one Confederate could whip ten Yankees, even

GLOBAL CONNECTIONS

The Civil War in Europe

The American Civil War was not, of course, a global conflict. The growing power of the United States during the first half of the nineteenth century, however, ensured that the war would generate considerable interest in Europe. The elite of both Great Britain and France could barely conceal their delight at the possible breakup of a rival nation and one whose government stood as a living rebuke to exclusive religious and political institutions.

The staunchest supporter of the Union cause was Russia. That the most despotic regime on the continent supported the most democratic nation was strictly a matter of geopolitics. The Russians viewed a united America as an effective rival to their perennial enemies, France and England. When the Russian Atlantic and Pacific fleets called on New York and San Francisco, respectively, in 1863, many observers interpreted the maneuver as a signal of support for the federal navy and a warning against British or French intervention. In truth, the tsar wished to remove his fleet from Russia's ice-bound harbors for the winter in case tensions with Great Britain escalated into war.

The British and French positions were of vital interest to the Confederacy. Early in the conflict, both countries recognized the Confederate States of America as a belligerent, which enabled the Davis administration to obtain loans and munitions. When a U.S. naval ship intercepted a British vessel carrying two Confederate envoys and detained them, British authorities threatened retaliation and sent two troop vessels to Canada to support their claim. The Lincoln administration wisely apologized and released the captives. The crisis passed.

The Confederacy was never able to gain recognition from Britain and France as an independent nation. The European powers feared American reprisal and the military situation of the Confederacy deteriorated after the losses at Gettysburg and Vicksburg in July 1863. Also, Europe had experienced a number of short grain crops and now relied increasingly on shipments from the North.

The French would not intrude into the American conflict without the British, though they managed to make trouble elsewhere, invading Mexico in 1862 over the alleged nonpayment of a debt and installing Maximilian of Austria as Emperor. They were confident that the Americans, engaged in a civil war, would not interfere. When the Civil War ended in April 1865, the Lincoln administration massed troops at the Mexican border as a warning, and the French withdrew. Mexican nationalists overthrew Maximilian and established a republic in 1867.

Though the British aristocracy favored the Confederacy, the middle and working classes championed the Union cause, especially once emancipation became a war aim. Even the textile workers who suffered from the cessation of the cotton trade supported the Union cause. A statue of Abraham Lincoln adorns a square in the center of Manchester, England. The inscription on the pedestal reads in part, "This statue commemorates the support that the working people of Manchester gave in their fight for the abolition of slavery during the American Civil War."

- What factor was most important in deterring Great Britain and France from recognizing the independence of the Confederate States of America?

though the opposing armies were of relatively equal strength when the fighting began. The Union rout planted the suspicion in northern minds that perhaps the Confederates were invincible and destroyed the widespread belief in the North that the war would be over quickly.

[See the Map
at www.myhistorylab.com
The Civil War Part I: 1861–1862

The War in the West

Federal forces may have retreated in Virginia, but they advanced in the west. Two Confederate forts on the Tennessee-Kentucky border, Fort Henry on the Tennessee River and Fort Donelson on the Cumberland River, guarded the strategic waterways that linked Tennessee

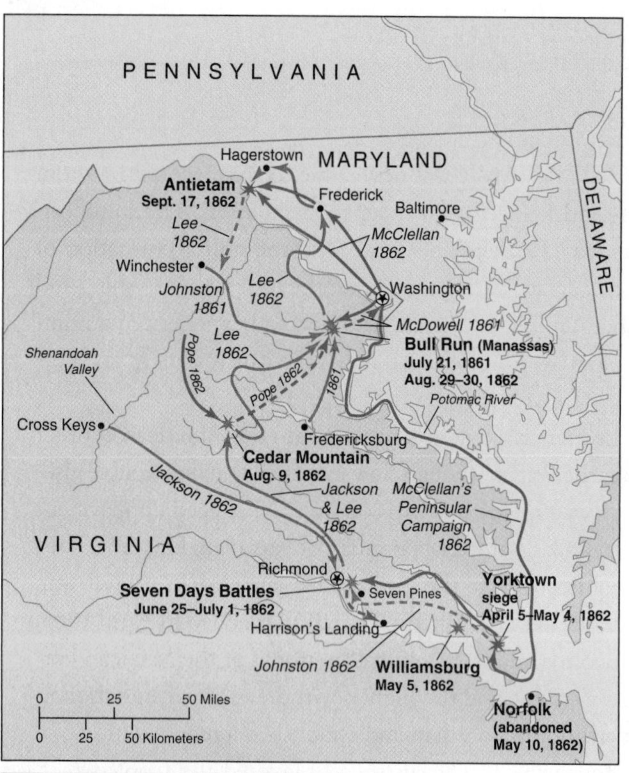

Area controlled by Union
Area controlled by Confederacy
Union advances
Confederate advances
Union retreats
Confederate retreats
Union victories
Confederate victories

MAP 15–1 **From First Bull Run to Antietam: The War in the East, 1861–1862** The early stages of the war demonstrated the strategies of the Confederacy and the Union. Federal troops stormed into Virginia hoping to capture Richmond and bring a quick end to the war. Through a combination of poor generalship and Confederate tenacity, they failed Confederate troops hoped to defend their territory, prolong the war, and eventually win their independence as northern patience evaporated. They proved successful initially, but, with the abandonment of the defensive strategy and the invasion of Maryland in the fall of 1862, the Confederates suffered a political and morale setback at Antietam.

Why did the South abandon its defensive strategy in the fall of 1862?

and Kentucky to the Mississippi Valley. The forts also defended Nashville, the Tennessee state capital (see Map 15–2). In February 1862, Union general Ulysses S. Grant coordinated a land and river campaign against the forts, with Flag Officer Andrew H. Foote commanding a force of ironclad Union gunboats.

Grant appreciated the strategic importance of river systems in the conquest of the western Confederacy. His combined river and land campaign caught the southerners unprepared and outflanked. By February 16, both forts had fallen. The Union victory drove a wedge into southern territory and closed the Confederacy's quickest path to the west from Virginia and the Carolinas. The Confederacy's only safe link across the Appalachians was now through Georgia. The Confederacy never recovered its strategic advantage in the West after the loss of Forts Henry and Donelson.

Grant next moved his main army south to Pittsburgh Landing on the Tennessee River, to prepare for an assault on the key Mississippi River port and rail center of Vicksburg. After blunting a surprise Confederate attack at Shiloh Church near Pittsburgh Landing, Grant pushed the southerners back to Corinth, Mississippi.

Federal forces complemented their victories at Shiloh and Corinth with another important success at New Orleans. Admiral David G. Farragut, who remained a Unionist even though born in Tennessee, blasted the Confederate river defenses protecting New Orleans and sailed a federal fleet to the city in April 1862. With the fall of Memphis to Union forces in June, Vicksburg remained the only major river town still in Confederate hands. The western losses exposed a major problem in the Confederates' defensive strategy: Their military resources were stretched too thin to defend their vast territory.

THE REAL WAR

The fierce fighting at Shiloh wrought unprecedented carnage. More American soldiers were lost at Shiloh than in all of the nation's wars combined up to that time. Each side suffered more than 10,000 casualties. By the time the smoke had cleared, the soldiers' initial enthusiasm and bravado were replaced by the sober realization that death or capture was a likely outcome, and that heroism, courage, and piety did not guarantee survival. "Too shocking, too horrible," a Confederate survivor of Shiloh wrote. "God grant that I may never be the partaker in such scenes again . . . when released from this I shall ever be an advocate of peace."

All wars are bloody, none more so in American history than the Civil War. Old military tactics combined with modern weapons accounted for some of the gore, and primitive medical practice added to the toll. Death and physical wounds were not the only results of battle. The experience of combat and the scenes of human and natural destruction had a profound psychological impact on the soldiers.

Read the **Document** at **www.myhistorylab.com** *Clara Barton, Memoirs about Medical Life at the Battlefield (1862)*

Some soldiers coped with the gore by writing about it, thus distancing themselves from the awful reality. At the brutal battle of Spotsylvania in May 1864, only an earthen parapet separated the two armies firing at close range. A Union soldier wrote, "The dead and wounded were torn to pieces. . . . The mud was half-way to our knees, and by our constant movement the dead were almost buried at our feet." Many men were "nothing but a lump of meat or clot of gore."

Other soldiers were consumed by the death and suffering. The war changed them forever. Union soldier and future U.S. Supreme Court Justice Oliver Wendell Holmes, Jr. wrote to his parents, "Before you get this you will know how immense the butcher's bill has been. [T]hese nearly two weeks have contained all of the fatigue & horror that war can furnish. . . . I am not the same man." The same feeling gripped a young man on the other side, Marion Hill Fitzpatrick of Georgia. "I have changed much in my feelings," he wrote to his parents. "The bombs and balls excite me but little and a battlefield strewed with dead and wounded is an every day consequence."

Yet, after the war many writers presented the conflict as a tableau of flying flags, heroic combatants, noble causes, and triumphal parades. Walt Whitman, who served as a nurse during the conflict, worried that "the real war will never get into the history books." Soldiers understood that once the war was over, memory would sanitize the conflict. The "real war" lives on in their letters and diaries. Daniel Bond of the 1st Minnesota began a diary: "Believing war to be a concentration of all that is wicked; and the most cruel invention of the worst enemy of the human race. And believing that were the real truth with regard to its extreme cruelty known, much would be done at least to soften its horrors . . . I have written this Journal with a view to telling some truths that will not be recorded in its histories." (See American Views: The Costs of War.)

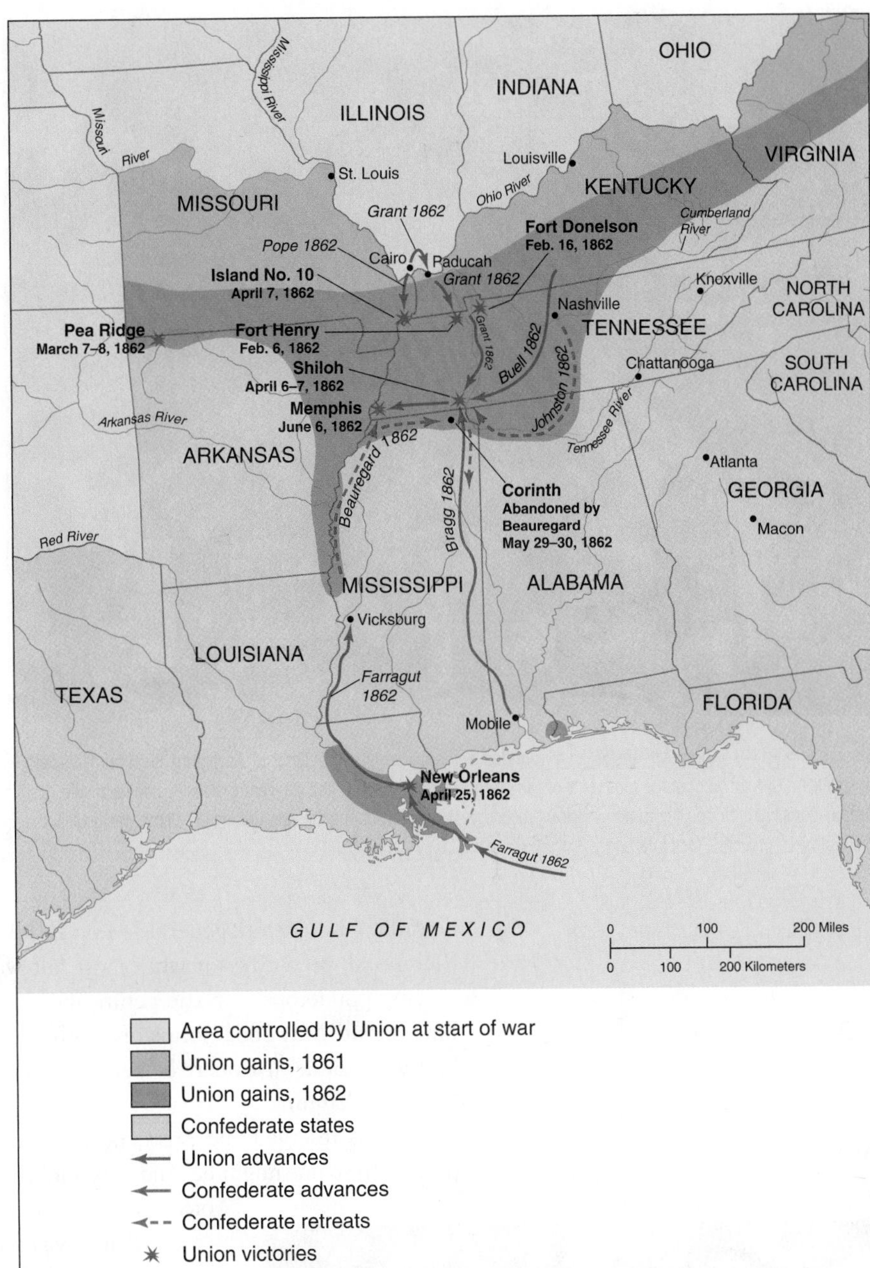

MAP 15–2 **The War in the West, 1861–1862** Because of the early Union emphasis on capturing Richmond, the war in the West seemed less important to northerners. But from a strategic standpoint, the victories at Forts Henry and Donelson, which drove a wedge into southern territory and closed the Confederacy's quickest path to the West from Virginia and the Carolinas, and the capture of New Orleans and its Mississippi River port were crucial and set the stage for greater federal success in the West in 1863.

Based on this map, what was the Union's overall strategy in these campaigns?

The war became more brutal after Shiloh. Civilian populations became fair game, and when Confederate marksmen used severely wounded Union combatants for target practice as they lay below them at Fredericksburg that winter, it was clear that the war was entering a new, more brutal phase. Total war? As far back as the Peloponnesian War, officers had targeted civilians. But the Civil War was the first industrialized war and the impact on combat was devastating. The length of the war contributed to its brutality. The North became more desperate to end the struggle, and the South to prolong it in order to exhaust the patience of northerners. Both

Read the **Document** at **www.myhistorylab.com**
From Then to Now Online: The Soldiers' War

A surgeon prepares to amputate the leg of a wounded Union soldier after the Battle of Gettysburg. Such primitive field hospitals functioned without the rudiments of sanitation and contributed to the staggering casualties on each side. Amputations were the most common surgical procedures performed during the war. Cutting off a limb was usually the first option to prevent a fatal infection.

objectives were prescriptions for tragedy. The journey to war had been easy. The journey out of it would be very hard.

The War in the East

With Grant and Farragut squeezing the Confederacy in the West, Lincoln ordered a new offensive against Richmond in the East that he believed would end the war. Following the defeat at Bull Run, he had shaken up the Union high command and appointed General George B. McClellan to lead what was now called the Army of the Potomac. McClellan was well liked by his soldiers, who referred to him affectionately as "Little Mac." McClellan returned their affection, perhaps too much. A superb organizer, he would prove overly cautious on the field of battle.

In March 1862, at the outset of the Peninsula Campaign, McClellan moved his 112,000-man army out of Washington and maneuvered his forces by boat down the Potomac River and Chesapeake Bay to the peninsula between the York and James rivers southeast of the Confederate capital (see Map 15–1). Union forces took Yorktown, Williamsburg, and Norfolk. Confederate general Joseph E. Johnston withdrew his forces up the peninsula toward Richmond, preparing for what most felt would be the decisive battle of the war. McClellan, moving ponderously up the peninsula, clashed with Johnston's army inconclusively at Seven Pines in late May 1862. Johnston was badly wounded in the clash, and President Davis replaced him with General Robert E. Lee, who renamed the forces under his command the Army of Northern Virginia.

Lee's reserved and aristocratic bearing masked a gambler's disposition. A fellow officer noted, "his name might be Audacity. He will take more chances, and take them quicker than any other general in this country." Under his daring leadership, the Confederacy's defensive strategy underwent an important shift.

Civil War generals Ulysses S. Grant (left) and Robert E. Lee (right).

Lee seized the initiative on June 25, 1862, attacking McClellan's right flank. Although inconclusive, the attack pushed the nervous McClellan into a defensive position. For a week, the armies sparred in a series of fierce engagements known collectively as the Seven Days' Battles. More than 30,000 men were killed or wounded on both sides, the deadliest week of the war so far. Although McClellan prevailed in these contests, the carnage so shocked him that he withdrew to Harrison's Landing on the James River. An exasperated Lincoln replaced McClellan with John Pope. Although Lee had saved Richmond, his troops had suffered frightfully. He had lost one-fourth of his 80,000-man army, but he remained convinced of the wisdom of his offensive-defensive strategy.

Lee went to work to vindicate these tactics. A series of inconclusive skirmishes brought Union and Confederate armies together once more near Manassas Junction. The Second Battle of Bull Run was as much a disaster for the Union as the first had been. Lee's generalship befuddled Pope and again saved Richmond. Lee and the Army of Northern Virginia were developing a reputation for invincibility.

TURNING POINTS, 1862–1863

WHAT CONVINCED Lincoln to issue the Emancipation Proclamation?

The impressive Confederate victories in the East masked the delicate condition of southern fortunes. Lee's offensive-defensive strategy seemed to be working, but it raised the possibility that the Confederacy could exhaust its men and resources before it sealed its independence.

The waning summer months of 1862 brought other concerns to the Davis administration in Richmond. The Union navy was choking the South's commercial link with Europe. Davis looked to the nations of Europe for diplomatic recognition as well as for trade.

Having stymied the Union war machine, Lee contemplated a bold move, a thrust into northern territory to bring the conflict to the North and stoke northerners' rising hostility to the war. President Lincoln also harbored a bold plan. Gradually, during the spring and summer of 1862, the president had concluded that emancipation of the Confederacy's slaves was essential for preserving the Union. But Lincoln was reluctant to take this step before the Union's fortunes on the battlefield improved. As the fall of 1862 approached, the Union and Confederate governments both prepared for the most significant conflicts of the war to date.

THE NAVAL WAR

The Union's naval strategy was to blockade the southern coast and capture its key seaports and river towns. The intention was to prevent arms, clothing, and food from reaching the Confederacy and keep cotton and tobacco from leaving. Destroying the South's ability to carry on trade would prevent the Confederacy from raising money to purchase the goods it needed to wage war. This vital trade brought the Confederacy into contact with European nations, a connection its leaders hoped to reinforce on the diplomatic front.

Neither side had much of a navy at the outset of the war. With more than 3,000 miles of Confederate coastline to cover, the Union blockade was weak at first. As time passed and the number of ships in the Union navy grew, the blockade tightened.

Understandably, the Confederate naval strategy was to break the blockade and defend the South's vital rivers and seaports. The Confederacy built several warships to serve as blockade runners and as privateers to attack Union merchant ships, and they briefly disrupted federal operations before Union vessels regained the advantage. The Confederacy was heavily dependent on the flow of trade and restriction of its flow hurt the southern cause.

QUICK REVIEW

The War at Sea

- Union naval blockade strengthened over time.
- Confederate ships had limited success running the blockade.
- Restriction of trade hurt the southern cause.

ANTIETAM

The alarming arithmetic of the offensive-defensive strategy convinced Lee that the South could not sustain a prolonged conflict. He knew that his army must keep up the pressure on the Union forces and, if possible, destroy them quickly. Union success in the Mississippi Valley threatened to cut the Confederacy in two and deprive it of the resources of a vast chunk of territory. Within a year, the Confederacy might cease to exist west of the Appalachians. He desperately needed a dramatic victory.

In September 1862, Lee crossed the Potomac into Maryland (see Map 15–1). He was on his way to cut the Pennsylvania Railroad at Harrisburg. Lee established camp at Frederick, scattering his army at various sites, convinced that McClellan and the Army of the Potomac would not attack him.

Luck intervened for the North. At an abandoned Confederate encampment, a Union corporal found three wrapped cigars on the ground, evidently tossed away by a careless Confederate officer. To the corporal's amazement, the wrapping was a copy of Lee's orders for the disposition of his army. But even with this information, "Little Mac" moved so cautiously that Lee had time to retreat to defensive positions at Sharpsburg, Maryland, along Antietam Creek. There Lee's army of 39,000 men came to blows with McClellan's army of 75,000.

QUICK REVIEW

Turning Point: Antietam

- Kept Lee from directly threatening the North.
- Prompted Britain and France to abandon plans to recognize the Confederacy.
- Provided Lincoln with the opportunity to announce the Emancipation Proclamation.

The Battle of Antietam saw the bloodiest single day of fighting in American history. About 2,100 Union soldiers and 2,700 Confederates died, and another 18,500, equally divided, were wounded. Although the armies had fought to a tactical draw, the battle was a strategic defeat for the Confederacy. In the battle's aftermath, Lee's troops limped back across the Potomac into Virginia and McClellan did not pursue them.

Antietam marked a major turning point in the war. It kept Lee from directly threatening northern industry and financial institutions. It prompted Britain and France to abandon plans to grant recognition to the Confederacy as an independent nation. And it provided Lincoln with the victory he needed to announce the abolition of slavery.

EMANCIPATION

President Lincoln despised slavery, but he had always maintained that preserving the Union was his primary war goal. "If I could save the Union without freeing any slave I would do it," he wrote to the newspaper editor Horace Greeley in August 1862, "and if I could save it by freeing all the slaves I would do it; and if I could save it by freeing some and leaving others alone, I would also do that." But from the war's outset, the possibility of emancipation as a war objective was considered in the Republican Congress, in the Union army, and among citizens throughout the northern states. As a result, pressure grew within the Union army to declare emancipation as a way of depriving the South and the Confederate army of their labor force.

Lincoln had said in his inaugural address that he had "no purpose, directly or indirectly, to interfere with the institution of slavery in the states where it exists." By March 1862, however, his moral repugnance for slavery, and the military arguments for abolition, led him to propose a resolution, which Congress adopted, supporting the compensated emancipation of slaves. The measure died, however, when Congress failed to appropriate funds for it and slaveholders in the border states expressed no interest in the plan.

Pressure from some northern civilians and Union soldiers and from Congress for some form of emancipation mounted in the spring of 1862. In response, the Republican Congress prohibited slavery in the territories and abolished slavery in the District of Columbia. The act emancipating the district's slaves called for compensating slave owners and colonizing the freed slaves in black republics, such as Haiti and Liberia. Then, in July 1862, Congress passed the **Confiscation Act,** which ordered the seizure of land from disloyal southerners and the emancipation of their slaves.

Confiscation Act Second confiscation law passed by Congress, ordering the seizure of land from disloyal southerners and the emancipation of their slaves.

Although support for emancipation had grown both in the army and among civilians, Lincoln still faced political considerations that dictated against it. Emancipation was still not favored by a majority in the North, especially not in the border states. The thousands of Irish Catholic immigrants who entered the Union army and who had competed with black workers for jobs in northern cities during the 1850s were especially opposed to emancipation, fearing a loss of economic security. But other considerations favored emancipation. Freeing the slaves would appeal to the strong antislavery sentiment in Britain and gain support for the Union cause abroad. And it would weaken the Confederacy's ability to wage war by removing a crucial source of labor.

Emancipation Proclamation Decree announced by President Abraham Lincoln in September 1862 and formally issued on January 1, 1863, freeing slaves in all Confederate states still in rebellion.

The Emancipation Proclamation. By mid-1862, the president had resolved to act on his moral convictions and proclaim emancipation. Taking the advice of Secretary of State Seward, however, he decided to wait for a battlefield victory so that the measure would not appear an act of desperation. Antietam gave the president his opening, narrow though it was, and on September 22, 1862, he announced his intention to issue the **Emancipation Proclamation,** to take

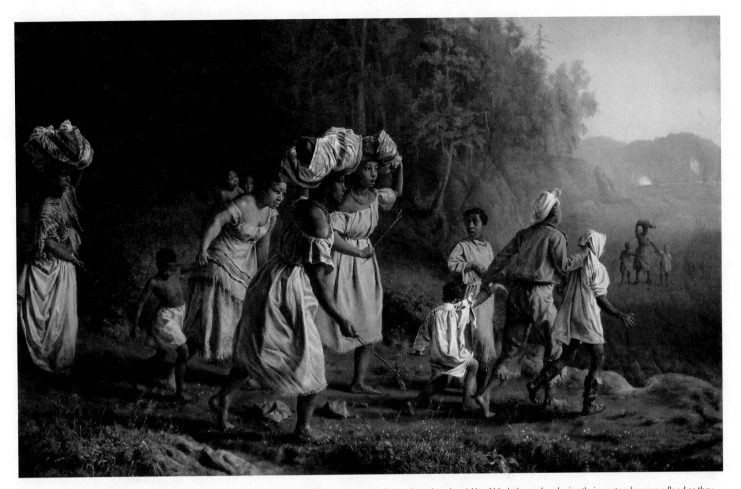

Even before the Emancipation Proclamation, slaves throughout the South "stole" their freedom. After the Proclamation, the trickle of black slaves abandoning their masters became a flood as they sought freedom behind Union lines.

Theodore Kaufman (1814–1896), *On to Liberty,* 1867, Oil on canvas, 36" × 56" (91.4 × 142.2 cm). The Metropolitan Museum of Art. Gift of Erving and Joyce Wolf, 1982 (1982.443.3). Photograph © The Metropolitan Museum of Art/Art Resource, NY

effect January 1, 1863, in all states still in rebellion. The proclamation exempted slaves in the border states loyal to the Union and in areas under Federal occupation. By raising the stakes of the war, President Lincoln hoped to shorten it. And, by leaving slaves in the border states untouched, he maintained their loyalty, or at least their neutrality.

Read the **Document** at **www.myhistorylab.com** *The Emancipation Proclamation (1863)*

Southerners reacted to the Emancipation Proclamation with outrage. Some viewed it as an invitation to race war and conjured up fears of freed slaves slaying white women and children while their men were at the battlefront. Jefferson Davis, taking a positive view, thought that the proclamation would invigorate the southern war effort.

Northerners generally approved of the Emancipation Proclamation. Although abolitionists comprised a minority of the northern population, most civilians and soldiers recognized the military advantages of emancipation.

The Emancipation Proclamation represented far more than its qualified words and phrases expressed. "A mighty act," Massachusetts governor John Andrew called it. Lincoln had freed the slaves. He and the Union war effort were now tied to the cause of freedom. What had begun as a war to save the Union was now a holy war of deliverance. Freedom and Union entwined in the public consciousness of the North. As Lincoln noted in his December 1862 message to Congress,

"[I]n giving freedom to the slave, we assure freedom to the free." Emancipation also unified the Republican Party and strengthened the president's hand in conducting the war. America had moved further along in the journey toward fulfilling its founding ideals.

"Stealing" freedom. As word of the Emancipation Proclamation raced through the slave grapevine, slaves rejoiced. But the proclamation only continued a process that had begun when the first Union armies invaded the South. In the months before freedom came, many slaves had run away to Union camps, dug Union trenches, and scouted for Federal troops.

See the Map
at www.myhistorylab.com
Effects of the Emancipation Proclamation

Southern masters fought to deter their slaves by severely punishing the families of black men who fled to the Union lines. They used the courts and slave catchers to reclaim runaways. Some Confederate masters protected their investments by removing slaves to Texas or to areas far from federal forces. And a few slaveowners whipped, sold, and even killed their slaves to prevent them from joining the Union troops.

But in the end, slaveholders could not stem the tide of slaves fleeing toward the Union lines and freedom. The 1862 Confiscation Act included slaves with other Confederate property as "contraband" of war and subject to confiscation. As they helped the Union cause, contrabands also sought to help fellow slaves "steal" their freedom. When Union forces occupied part of the Georgia coast in April 1862, for example, March Haynes, a slave who had worked as a river pilot in Savannah, began smuggling slaves to the Union lines. Federal general Quincy Adams Gilmore provided a fast boat for Haynes's missions. In return, Haynes supplied Gilmore with "exact and valuable information" on the strength and location of Confederate defenses.

QUICK REVIEW

"Stealing" Freedom

- Emancipation Proclamation accelerated process of slaves running away to Union camps.
- "Contrabands" helped fellow slaves to "steal" their freedom.
- Ex-slaves served in increasing numbers in Union army.

The Emancipation Proclamation accelerated the slaves' flight from bondage. After 1863, ex-slaves served in increasing numbers in the Union army.

Black troops in the Union army. More than 80 percent of the roughly 180,000 black soldiers and 20,000 black sailors who fought for the Union were slaves and free black men from the South. For the typical black southerner who joined the army, the passage from bondage to freedom came quickly. Making his escape from his master, he perhaps "stole" his family as well. He typically experienced his first days of freedom behind Union lines, where he may have learned to read and write. Finally, he put on the federal uniform, experiencing, as one black southern volunteer commented, "the biggest thing that ever happened in my life."

Read the Document
at www.myhistorylab.com
Susie King Taylor, Reminiscences of an Army Laundress (1902)

President Lincoln strongly advocated enlisting former slaves. In March 1863, he wrote, with exaggerated enthusiasm, that "the bare sight of 50,000 armed and drilled black soldiers on the banks of the Mississippi would end the rebellion at once." On the contrary, the appearance of black Union troops infuriated the Confederates.

Black Union troops—former slaves—repelling Confederates at New Bern, NC, February 1864. African Americans, both free and slave, fought valiantly and often fiercely for their freedom; the alternative was sometimes execution on the spot or reenslavement.

The Confederate government formally labeled white officers leading black troops as instigators of slave rebellion and punished them accordingly, presumably by hanging. Black soldiers, when captured, were returned to slavery. The Lincoln administration retaliated by suspending prisoner exchanges, which resulted in horrible conditions in Confederate and Union prisons. Roughly 56,000 prisoners died in captivity, a toll that would have been much lower had Confederate authorities treated black prisoners of war the same as whites.

But for black volunteers, the promise of freedom and redemption outweighed the dangers of combat. Black abolitionists campaigned tirelessly for the enlistment of free black men and fugitive slaves in the Union army. Frederick Douglass, whose son Lewis distinguished himself in the all-black 54th Massachusetts Volunteer Infantry Regiment, explained in early 1863, "Once let the black man get upon his person the brass letters, 'U.S.,' let him get an eagle on his buttons and a musket on his shoulder and bullets in his pockets, and there is no power on earth which can deny that he has earned the right to citizenship in the United States."

Although black soldiers were eager to engage the enemy and fought as ably as their white comrades, they received lower pay and performed the most menial duties in camp. Abolitionists and black leaders pressured President Lincoln for more equitable treatment of African American recruits.

Despite discrimination, black soldiers fought valiantly at Port Hudson, Louisiana; near Charleston; and, late in the war, at the siege of Petersburg, Virginia. The most celebrated black encounter with Confederate troops occurred in July 1863, during a futile assault by the 54th Massachusetts Regiment on Fort Wagner outside Charleston. The northern press, previously lukewarm toward black troops, heaped praise on the effort. "Through the cannon smoke of that dark night," intoned a writer in the *Atlantic Monthly*, "the manhood of the colored race shines before many eyes that would not see."

If only President Lincoln could find such gallantry among his generals! George McClellan had failed to follow his advantage at Antietam in September 1862, allowing Lee's army to escape to Virginia and remain a formidable fighting force. And despite Union successes in the West, the Confederate forces massed there remained largely intact.

Read the **Document**
at **www.myhistorylab.com**
"I Hope to Fall with My Face to the Foe": Lewis Douglass Describes the Battle of Fort Wagner (1863)

QUICK REVIEW

Blacks in the Union Army

- 80 percent of black Union soldiers were slaves or free blacks from the South.
- President Lincoln strongly advocated enlisting former slaves.
- Black Union troops infuriated the Confederates.
- Danger and discrimination did not stop blacks from fighting for the Union.

From Fredericksburg to Gettysburg

In late 1862, after Antietam, the president replaced McClellan with General Ambrose E. Burnside. Burnside was shy and insecure. Claiming incompetence, he had twice refused the command. His judgment proved better than Lincoln's.

Fredericksburg. Moving swiftly against Lee's dispersed army in northern Virginia, Burnside reached the Rappahannock River opposite Fredericksburg in November 1862 (see Map 15–3). But the pontoon bridges to ford his 120,000 soldiers across the river arrived three weeks late, giving Lee an opportunity to gather his 78,000 men. On December 13, the Union forces launched a poorly coordinated and foolish frontal assault that the Confederates repelled, inflicting heavy federal casualties. Burnside, having performed to his own expectations, was relieved of command, and Major General Joseph Hooker was installed in his place.

Gettysburg National Military Park, Gettysburg, Pennsylvania
http://www.nps.gov/gett/index.htm

Chancellorsville. The hard-drinking Hooker lacked Burnside's humility but not his incompetence. Resuming the offensive in the spring of 1863, Hooker hoped to outflank Lee. But the Confederate commander surprised Hooker by sending Stonewall Jackson to outflank the Union right. Between May 1 and May 4, Lee's army delivered a series of crushing attacks on Hooker's forces at Chancellorsville. Outnumbered two to one, Lee had pulled off another stunning victory, but at a high cost. Lee lost some 13,000 men, fewer than Hooker's 17,000, but more than the Confederacy could afford.

Lee also lost Stonewall Jackson at Chancellorsville. Nervous Confederate sentries mistakenly shot and wounded him as he returned from a reconnoitering mission, and he died a few days later. Lee recognized the tragedy of Jackson's loss for himself and his country. "Any victory," the Confederate commander wrote, "would be dear at such a price. I know not how to replace him."

Still, Lee appeared invincible. Chancellorsville thrust Lincoln into a bout of despair. "My God!" he exclaimed in agony, "What will the country say! What will the country say!" Meanwhile, Lee, to take advantage of the Confederacy's momentum and the Union's gloom, planned another bold move. On June 3, 1863, the 75,000-man Army of Northern Virginia broke camp and headed north once again.

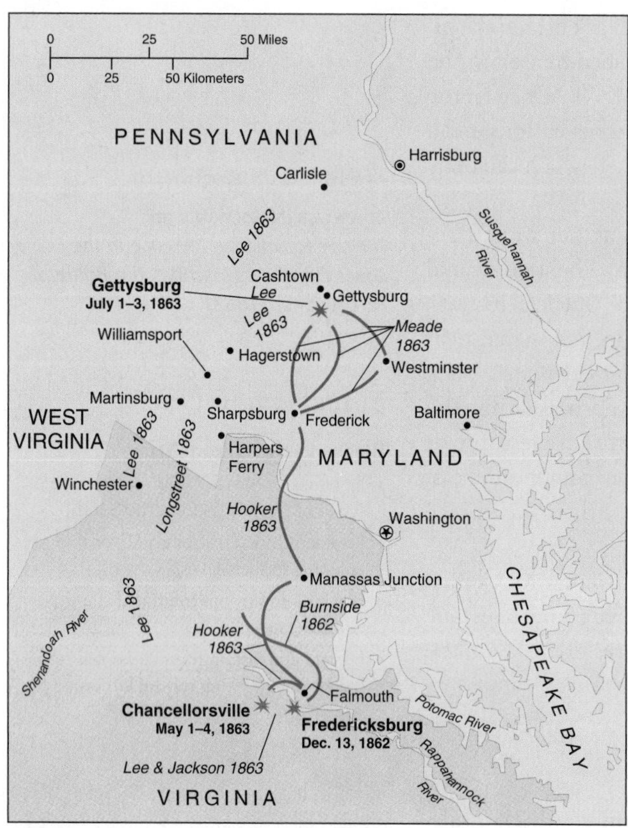

MAP 15–3 **From Fredericksburg to Gettysburg: The War in the East, December 1862–July 1863** By all logic, the increasingly outgunned and outfinanced Confederacy should have been showing signs of faltering by 1863. But bungling by Union generals at Fredericksburg and Chancellorsville sustained southern fortunes and encouraged Robert E. Lee to attempt another invasion of the North.

How was Robert E. Lee able to press on, outgunned and outfinanced, into 1863 and beyond?

See the **Map**
at **www.myhistorylab.com**
The Civil War Part II: 1863–1865

Gettysburg. President Lincoln sent the Union Army of the Potomac after Lee. But General Hooker dallied, requested more troops, and allowed the Confederates to march from Maryland into Pennsylvania. An infuriated Lincoln replaced Hooker with George Gordon Meade.

Lee's Army of Northern Virginia occupied a wide swath of Pennsylvania territory from Chambersburg to Wrightsville along the Susquehanna River, across from the state capital at Harrisburg. When Lee learned of Meade's movements, he ordered his troops to consolidate in a defensive position at Cashtown, 45 miles from Harrisburg. That the greatest battle of the war erupted at nearby Gettysburg was pure chance. A Confederate brigade left Cashtown to confiscate much-needed shoes from a factory in Gettysburg. Meeting federal cavalry resistance near the town, the brigade withdrew. On July 1, 1863, a larger Confederate force advanced toward Gettysburg to disperse the cavalry and seize the shoes. What the Confederates did not realize was that the entire Army of the Potomac was coming up behind the cavalry (see Map 15–4).

During the first day of battle, July 1, the Confederates appeared to gain the upper hand, forcing Union troops back from the town to a new position on Cemetery Hill. On the second day, the entire Union army was in place, but the Confederates took several key locations along Cemetery Ridge before federal forces pushed them back to the previous day's positions. Although the opposing sides had suffered heavy casualties, both armies were intact; and, if anything, Lee had the advantage. On July 3, the third day of the battle, Lee made a fateful error. Believing that the center of Meade's line was weak, he ordered an all-out assault against it.

The next morning, a bright, hot summer day, the Confederates launched an assault on Culp's Hill, only to fall back by noon. The key battle of the day occurred at three in the afternoon at Cemetery Ridge, preceded by a fierce artillery duel. When the Union guns suddenly went silent, the Confederates, thinking they had knocked them out, began a charge led by General George Pickett. As the Confederate infantry marched out with battle colors flying, the Union artillery opened up again and tore apart the charging southerners. The Confederates retreated down the gentle slope strewn with their fallen comrades, the hopes of a southern victory dashed.

After Pickett's charge, Lee rode among his troops and urged them to brace for a final Union assault. The attack never came. Meade allowed Lee to withdraw into Maryland and cross the Potomac to Virginia. Gettysburg was the bloodiest battle of the war. The Union suffered 23,000 casualties; the Confederacy, 28,000. The battle's outcome boosted morale in the North and drained Lee's army of men and material.

The Union victory at Gettysburg lifted the veil of gloom in the North. People exhaled collectively when Union troops foiled the Confederate invasion. President Lincoln, in his address dedicating the cemetery at Gettysburg in November of that year, used the evangelical metaphor of rebirth to comment on the importance of the sacrifice on that battlefield. On this consecrated ground, he declared, from the "honored dead," will come "a new birth of freedom."

While the battle changed the mood in the North, it did not mark the beginning of the end of the Confederacy. But coupled with the loss of Vicksburg on July 4 (see below), it dealt a serious blow to Rebel fortunes. Many Confederate troops considered the Gettysburg campaign a draw or a temporary setback at worst; but there was no doubting the implications of the Vicksburg surrender on the nation's birthday.

AMERICAN VIEWS

The Costs of War

The main character in southern writer Ellen Glasgow's novel The Battle-Ground *(1902) exclaims after his first battle, "I didn't know it was like this. Why, they're no better than mangled rabbits—I didn't know it was like this." Civilians fought the Civil War and nothing in their lives prepared them for the carnage they encountered. The lasting impression from diaries and letters of those who fought is less of grand causes than of horror—of disease, death, and dying. Here is a small sample.*

- **If** the scenes of war were so horrible, why did these writers feel compelled to describe the grisly details?
- **Given** these horrors of war, why did the writers continue to serve?
- **The** Civil War proved the final journey for 620,000 men from both sides. The war solved the issues of secession and slavery. Was the sacrifice worth it?

Private Sam Watkins of the Army of Tennessee encountering a comrade after a battle: I overtook another man walking along. I did not know to what regiment he belonged, but I remember of first noticing his left arm was entirely gone. His face was as white as a sheet. The breast and sleeve of his coat had been torn away, and I could see the frazzled end of his shirt sleeve, which appeared to be sucked into the wound. I looked at it pretty close and I said "Great God!" for I could see his heart throb, and the respiration of his lungs. I was filled with wonder and horror at the sight. He was walking along, when all at once he dropped down and died without a struggle or a groan.

Source: Reprinted with the permission of Scribner, a Division of Simon & Schuster, Inc., from "CO. AYTCH" by Sam R. Watkins. (NY: Simon & Schuster, Inc., 1997).

Robert Goldthwaite Carter of the 22nd Massachusetts describes his walk across the Gettysburg battlefield the night after the battle ended:

In every direction, among the bodies was the debris of battle—haversacks, canteens, hats, caps, sombreros, blankets of every shade and hue, bayonets, cartridge boxes. . . . Corpses strewed the ground at every step. Arms, legs, heads, and parts of dismembered bodies were scattered all about, and sticking among the rocks, and against the trunks of trees, hair, brains, entrails and shreds of human flesh still hung, a disgusting, sickening, heart-rending spectacle to our young minds.

Source: Robert Goldthwaite Carter, *Four Brothers in Blue: A Story of the Great Civil War from Bull Run to Appomattox* (Norman, OK: University of Oklahoma Press, 1999; original edition, 1913), p. 324.

Kate Cumming, a Scottish immigrant to Mobile, Alabama, became a Confederate nurse ministering to the wounded and ill in all manner of temporary facilities. Here she describes the operating "room" in one of the makeshift hospitals:

I was compelled to pass the place, and the sight I there beheld made me shudder and sick at heart. A stream of blood ran from the table into a tub in which was the arm. It had been taken off at the socket, and the hand . . . was hanging over the edge of the tub, a lifeless thing. I often wish I could become as callous as many seem to be, for there is no end to these horrors. . . . The passage to the kitchen leads directly past the amputating room below stairs, and many a time I have seen the blood running in streams from it.

Source: Richard Barksdale Harwell, ed., *Kate: The Journal of a Confederate Nurse* (Baton Rouge: Louisiana State University Press, 1987), p. 25.

Ambrose Bierce fought for the 9th Indiana Volunteers. Like Walt Whitman, the sanitizing of the war after the fact infuriated him. The stories he wrote after the war based on his battle experiences stressed the physical and psychological impact of the war on the civilian soldiers. Here he describes "What I Saw at Shiloh."

. . . the bodies, half buried in ashes; some in the unlovely looseness of attitude denoting sudden death by the bullet, but by far the greater number in postures of agony that told of the tormenting flame. Their clothing was half burnt away – their hair and beard entirely; the rain had come too late to save their nails. Some were swollen to double girth; others shriveled to manikins. According to degree of exposure, their faces were bloated and black or yellow and shrunken. The contraction of muscles which had given them claws for hands had cursed each countenance with a hideous grin.

Source: Reprinted with the permission of Scribner, a Division of Simon & Schuster, Inc., from "CO. AYTCH" by Sam R. Watkins. (NY: Simon & Schuster, Inc., 1997).

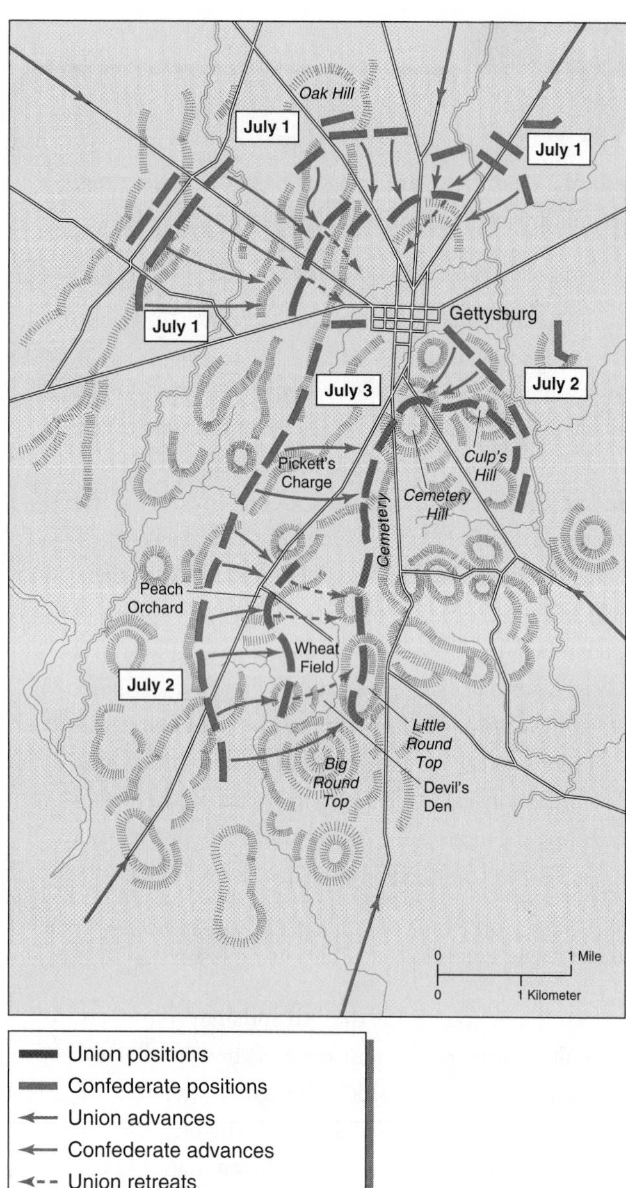

MAP 15–4 **The Battle of Gettysburg, July 1–3, 1863** In a war that lasted four years, it is difficult to point to the decisive battle. But clearly, the outcome during those July days at Gettysburg set the tone for the rest of the war. The result was unclear until the final day of battle, and even then it might have gone either way. Winning by a whisker was enough to propel Union armies to a string of victories over the next year and to throw Confederate forces back on their defenses among an increasingly despairing population. Gettysburg marked the last major southern invasion of the North.

Why was the Battle of Gettysburg so crucial?

Read the **Document**
at **www.myhistorylab.com**
Abraham Lincoln, The Gettysburg Address (1863)

Vicksburg, Chattanooga, and the West

As Union forces thwarted Confederate dreams in Pennsylvania, other federal troops bore down on strategic Rebel strongholds in the western theater of the war. Union military success in the West would seriously compromise the South's ability to move goods and men across rail lines and over waterways and leave vulnerable the ultimate western prize, the Confederate bread basket, Georgia.

Vicksburg. On July 4, one day after Pickett's charge at Gettysburg, the city of Vicksburg, the last major Confederate stronghold on the Mississippi, surrendered to Ulysses S. Grant. Grant had demonstrated an ability to use his forces creatively, swiftly, and with a minimum loss of life in his campaigns in the western Confederacy, but Vicksburg presented him with several strategic obstacles (see Map 15–5). In 1862, the formidable defenses on the city's western edge, which overlooked and controlled the Mississippi, had thwarted a Union naval assault, and the labyrinth of swamps, creeks, and woods protecting the city from the north had foiled General Sherman. The only feasible approaches appeared to be from the south and east.

By March 1863, Grant had devised a brilliant plan to take Vicksburg that called for rapid maneuvering and expert coordination that worked with rather than against the area's geography. Grant had his 20,000 Union troops ferried across the Mississippi from the Louisiana side at a point south of Vicksburg. Then he marched them quickly into the interior of Mississippi. They moved northeastward, captured the Mississippi state capital at Jackson, and turned west toward Vicksburg. On May 22, 1863, Grant settled down in front of the city, less than 600 yards from Confederate positions. Grant's tight siege and the Union navy's bombardment from the river cut the city off completely. As food stores dwindled, residents were forced to eat mules and rats to survive. Their situation hopeless, General John Pemberton and his 30,000-man garrison surrendered on July 4.

Chattanooga. As Grant was besieging Vicksburg in June 1863, Union general William S. Rosecrans, commanding the Army of the Cumberland, advanced against Confederate general Braxton Bragg, whose Army of Tennessee held Chattanooga, a "doorway" on the railroad that linked Richmond to the lower South. The capture of the city would complete the uncoupling of the West from the eastern Confederacy.

Bragg lacked confidence in his men and consistently overestimated the force and cunning of his enemy. At Rosecrans's approach, he abandoned Chattanooga and took up positions above nearby Chickamauga Creek. When the two armies clashed at Chickamauga on September 19, Bragg pushed Rosecrans back to Chattanooga. Bragg seized the railroad leading into Chattanooga and bottled up Rosecrans there, much as Grant had confined Pemberton at Vicksburg. Both sides had suffered heavily. Suddenly, the Union's careful strategy for the conquest of the western Confederacy seemed in jeopardy.

The Confederate position on the heights overlooking Chattanooga appeared impregnable. But the Confederate camp was plagued by dissension, with some officers openly questioning Bragg's ability. President Davis considered replacing him but had no one else available with Bragg's experience. Instead, Davis ordered General James Longstreet (along with one-third

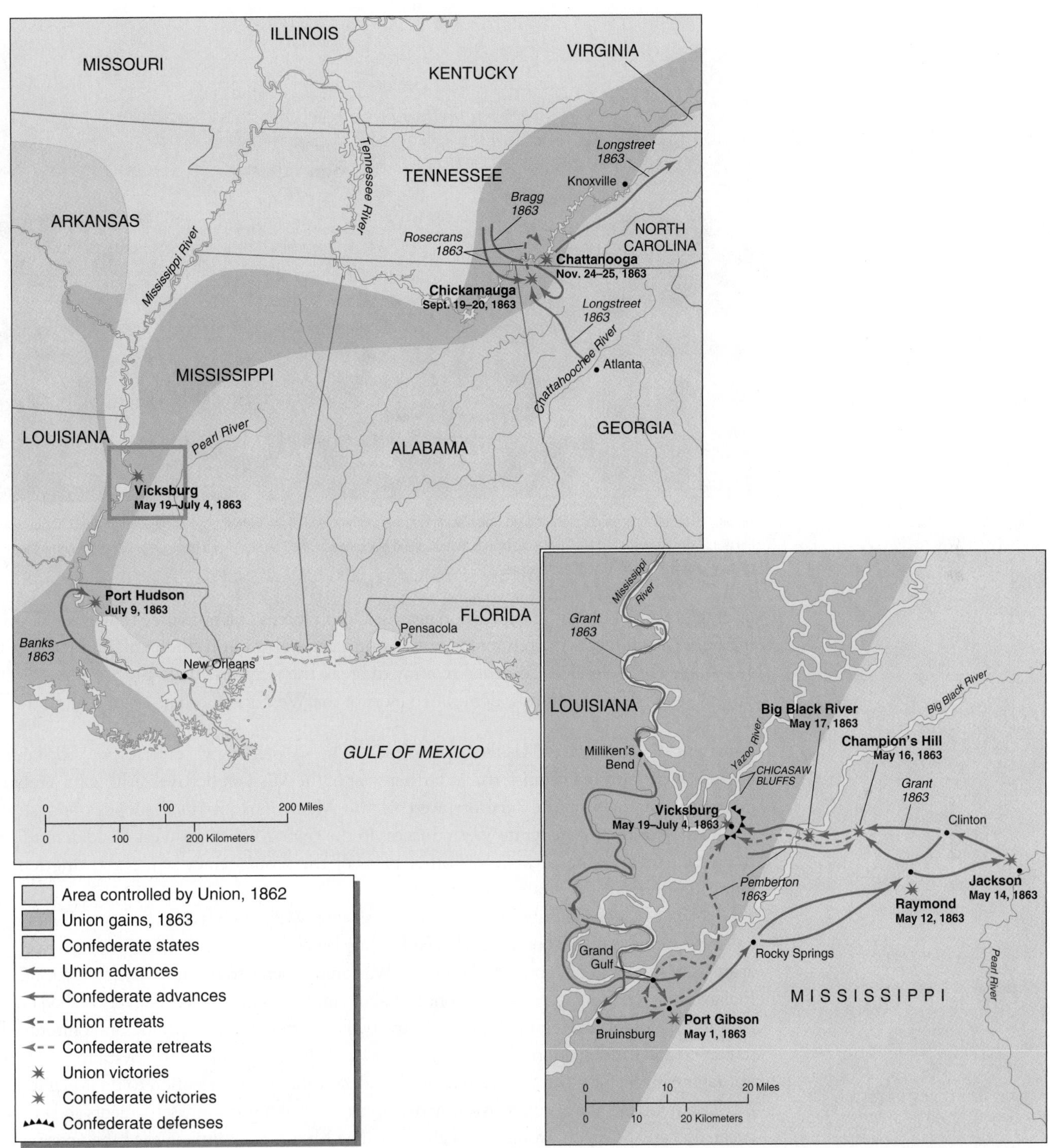

MAP 15–5 **Vicksburg and Chattanooga: The War in the West, 1863** Devising a brilliant strategy, Union general Ulysses S. Grant took the last major Mississippi River stronghold from Confederate hands on July 4, 1863, dealing a significant economic and morale blow to the South. Coupled with the defeat at Gettysburg a day earlier, the fall of Vicksburg portended a bitter finale to hopes for southern independence. Grant completed his domination of the West by joining forces with several Union generals to capture Chattanooga and push Confederate forces into Georgia, setting the stage for the capture of that key southern state in 1864.

What key military decisions enabled Grant to force the surrender of Vicksburg?

Timothy H. O'Sullivan's photograph of dead Union soldiers at the southern end of the Gettysburg battlefield, July 2, 1863. O'Sullivan titled the work "The Harvest of Death." Note the bodies bloodied and blackened by the July heat. Such photographs brought home the carnage of the war in vivid detail to northern civilians.

of Bragg's army) on a futile expedition against Union forces at Knoxville, Tennessee. Converging on Chattanooga with reinforcements, Union generals Grant, Sherman, and Hooker took advantage of the divided Confederate army to break the siege and force Bragg's army to retreat into Georgia. The Union now dominated most of the West and faced an open road to the East.

The war in the trans-Mississippi West. The Confederacy's reverses at Vicksburg and Chattanooga mirrored its misfortunes farther west of the Mississippi River. Although a relatively minor theater of war, the territory west of the Mississippi provided supplies and strategic advantages for the Confederate West. Success in the trans-Mississippi West could divert Federal troops and relieve the pressure on other parts of the Confederacy while allowing food and munitions to reach desperate southern armies.

Native American tribes in the trans-Mississippi West, such as the Navajos, Dakotas, and Lakotas, spent a good deal of the Civil War battling Federal troops for territory and resources, quite apart from the sectional conflict. The Civil War drew federal troops from the frontier, affording Indians an opportunity to press their concerns about tardy and incomplete delivery of food and supplies and the loss of lands granted to them by treaty. The Eastern Sioux in Minnesota confronted both starvation and the migration of whites onto their lands during the fall of 1862. With the white man's war raging in the East, the Sioux struck in the fall of 1862 to call attention to their plight. About 200 Eastern Sioux rampaged across southern Minnesota, striking at white settlements and killing between 350 and 800 men, women, and children. The Minnesota militia quelled the uprising. More than three hundred Sioux were tried and condemned to death, though President Lincoln pardoned all but thirty-eight. Federal authorities removed the remainder of the Eastern Sioux to a desolate area in the Dakota Territory and extinguished all of their remaining land rights in Minnesota.

Texas, however, was the focus of the trans-Mississippi campaign. The state was critical to Confederate fortunes, both as a source of supply for the East and as a base for the conquest of the Far West. Texas was far from secure. It suffered from internal dissent and violence on its borders. Not all Texans supported secession. On the state's western border, Comanches raided homesteaders at will until late 1864. In the east and along the southern frontier in the lower Rio Grande Valley, Union gunboats and troops disrupted Confederate supply lines. By 1864, with the Union in control of the Mississippi, and Federal troops along the Mexican border, Texas had lost its strategic importance.

WAR TRANSFORMS THE NORTH

WHAT IMPACT did the war have on the North's economy?

The Union successes in 1863 had a profound impact on both sides. For the North, hopes of victory and reunion increased. The federal government expanded its bureaucracy to wage war efficiently, and a Republican-dominated Congress passed legislation that broadened federal power and furthered the war effort. Boosted by federal economic legislation and wartime demand, the northern economy boomed. Women entered the workforce in growing numbers. But labor unrest and class and racial tensions suggested that prosperity had a price.

WARTIME LEGISLATION AND POLITICS

Before the Civil War, the federal government rarely affected citizens' lives directly. But raising troops, protecting territory, and mobilizing the economy for war required a strong and active central government. With the departure of the South from the Union, Republicans dominated all branches of the federal administration. This left them in a position to test the constitutional limits of federal authority.

Suppressing dissent. President Lincoln began almost immediately to use executive authority to suppress opposition to the war effort in the North. In one of his most controversial actions, he issued a temporary suspension of the writ of habeas corpus, the constitutional protection against illegal imprisonment. Suspending it allowed the government to arrest suspected Confederate agents and hold them indefinitely, a procedure sanctioned by the Constitution "when in cases of rebellion or invasion the public safety may require it." The suspension became permanent in September 1862 and was used primarily in the border states to detain those suspected of trading with the enemy, defrauding the War Department, or evading the draft.

Executive sanctions fell particularly hard on the Democratic Party. Although many Democrats opposed secession and supported the Union, they challenged the president on the conduct of the war, on emancipation, and on his coolness toward peace initiatives. A few had ties with Confederate agents. Republicans called these dissenters **"Copperheads,"** after the poisonous snake.

Copperheads A term Republicans applied to northern war dissenters and those suspected of aiding the Confederate cause during the Civil War.

Despite the suspension of habeas corpus, Lincoln compiled a fairly good record for upholding basic American civil liberties. Although the authorities shut down a handful of newspapers temporarily, the administration made no attempt to control the news or subvert the electoral process. Two major elections were held during the war. In the first, the off-year election in 1862, Republicans retained control of Congress but lost several seats to Democrats. In the presidential election of 1864, Lincoln won reelection in a hard-fought contest.

While fellow Republicans sometimes chastised the president for violating civil liberties, mismanaging military command assignments, or moving too slowly on emancipation, they rarely threatened to disrupt the party. But there was dissent in the Republican Party, and it had an effect on national policy. **Radical Republicans** hounded Lincoln from early in his administration, establishing the Joint Committee on the Conduct of the War to examine and monitor military policy. Some of them accused Democratic generals, including McClellan, of deliberately subverting the war effort with their poor performance. They also pressed Lincoln for quicker action on emancipation, though they supported the president on most crucial matters.

Radical Republicans A shifting group of Republican congressmen, usually a substantial minority, who favored the abolition of slavery from the beginning of the Civil War and later advocated harsh treatment of the defeated South.

Creating a national economy. Lincoln likewise supported his party on an array of initiatives in Congress. Republicans used the federal government to enhance individual opportunities, especially in the West. The **Homestead Act,** passed in May 1862, granted 160 acres free to any settler in the territories who agreed to improve the land (by cultivating it and erecting a house) within five years of the grant. The act was also a boon for railroad companies.

Homestead Act Law passed by Congress in May 1862 providing homesteads with 160 acres of free land in exchange for improving the land within five years of the grant.

Other legislation to boost the nation's economy and the fortunes of individual manufacturers and farmers included the **Land Grant College Act** of 1862, a protective tariff that same year, and the National Banking Act of 1863. The Land Grant Act awarded the proceeds from the sale

Land Grant College Act Law passed by Congress in July 1862 awarding proceeds from the sale of public lands to the states for the establishment of agricultural and mechanical colleges.

Read the **Document**
at **www.myhistorylab.com**
The Homestead Act of 1862

of public lands to the states for the establishment of colleges offering instruction in "agriculture and mechanical arts." The tariff legislation protected northern industry from foreign competition while raising revenue for the Union. The National Banking Act of 1863 replaced the bank notes of individual states, which were often backed by flimsy reserves and subject to wild fluctuations in value, with a uniform national currency.

Through such initiatives, the Republican-dominated Congress forged a national economy that connected citizens to the fortunes of the national government. Construction began on a transcontinental railroad that, together with the Homestead Act, would help settle the West and bind the nation together in fact. A high protective tariff not only generated revenue for the government, it bolstered northern manufacturing. Through the sale of securities to the general public to help fund the war, hundreds of thousands of citizens now had a stake in the government's survival and success. A federal income tax bound Americans even closer to the government in Washington. A national currency fueled a national economy. Businesses, aided by government-subsidized efficiencies in transportation and communication, became national rather than regional enterprises. Farmers benefited from the Land Grant College Act that offered the latest labor-saving efficiencies for a scientific agriculture. The Constitution of the United States did not explicitly sanction any of these measures. Operating under the broad mandate of the "war powers" allowed the Congress to support the government and protect the citizenry in times of insurrection. The results were a more powerful nation and a more centralized government.

Read the **Document**
at **www.myhistorylab.com**
"If It Were Not for My Trust in Christ I Do Not Know How I Could Have Endured It": Testimony from Victims of New York's Draft Riots (1863)

These measures helped sustain the Union war effort and enjoyed widespread support. The expansion of government into other areas, however, aroused opposition in some quarters, none more than the draft laws.

Conscription and the draft riots. Congress passed the first national conscription law in 1863. Almost immediately, evasion, obstruction, and weak enforcement threatened to undermine it. As military authorities began arresting draft dodgers and deserters, secret societies formed to harbor draftees and instruct them on evasion.

Conflicts between citizens and federal officials over the draft sometimes erupted in violence. The worst draft riot occurred in New York City in July 1863. Competition with blacks for jobs, the use of blacks as strikebreakers, and the feeling that were it not for the Emancipation Proclamation, the war would be over made the Irish population of the city adamant about avoiding fighting and

The lynching of a black New Yorker during the Draft Riot in July 1863. The violence against black people during the riot reflected decades of racial tension, especially between Irish immigrants and black residents, over jobs and housing.

dying for a cause they reviled. The fact that more affluent New Yorkers could buy their way out of the draft by hiring a substitute for $300 made this also a class issue for the mostly working-class and poor Irish residents of the city.

The racial and class issues were apparent in the **New York Draft Riot.** After a mostly Irish mob had destroyed the draft office at the federal marshal's headquarters, it launched an indiscriminate attack on the city's black population and institutions, including burning the Colored Orphan Asylum to the ground and hanging two black New Yorkers who wandered into their path. The rioters also sacked the mayor's house, tore up railroad tracks, looted the Brooks Brothers clothing store, and destroyed commercial and residential property on fashionable Fifth Avenue, crying "Down with the rich!" City officials and the police stood by, unable or unwilling to stem the riot. Army units fresh from Gettysburg, along with militia and naval units, quelled the riot.

New York Draft Riot A mostly Irish-immigrant protest against conscription in New York City in July 1863 that escalated into class and racial warfare that had to be quelled by federal troops.

QUICK REVIEW

The Draft Riots

- 1863: Congress passed national conscription law.
- New York, July 1863: Mostly Irish mob burns federal marshal's headquarters.
- Racial and class antagonisms fueled riot.

The Northern Economy

After an initial downturn during the uncertain months preceding the war, the northern economy picked up quickly. High tariffs and massive federal spending soon made up for the loss of southern markets and the closing of the Mississippi River. Profits skyrocketed for some businesses. New industries boomed, and new inventions increased manufacturing efficiency, as in the sewing machine industry, which was first commercialized in the 1850s. Technological advances there greatly increased the output of the North's garment factories. Production of petroleum, used as a lubricant, increased from 84,000 gallons to 128 million gallons during the war.

Despite the loss of manpower to the demands of industry and the military, the productivity of northern agriculture grew during the war.

Trade unions and strikebreakers. Working people should have benefited from wartime prosperity. With men off to war and immigration down, labor was in short supply. Although wages increased, prices rose more. Declining real wages led to exploitation, especially of women in garment factories. The trade union movement, which suffered a serious setback in the depression of 1857, revived. Local unions of shoemakers, carpenters, and miners emerged in 1862 across the North, and so did a few national organizations. By 1865, more than 200,000 northern workers belonged to labor unions.

Employers struck back at union organizing by hiring strikebreakers, usually African Americans, who were available because until the war's midpoint, they were unwelcome for military service. Labor conflicts between striking white workers and black strikebreakers sparked riots in New York City and Cincinnati. The racial antagonism accounted in part for workers' opposition to Lincoln's Emancipation Proclamation and for the continued strength of the Democratic Party in northern cities.

Profiteers and corruption. The promise of enormous profits bred greed and corruption as well as exploitation. Illicit trade between North and South was inevitable and profiteers not only defied the government to trade with the enemy but also sometimes swindled the government outright. Some merchants reaped high profits supplying the army with shoddy goods at inflated prices.

Deep social and ethical problems were emerging in northern society and would become more pronounced in the decades after the Civil War. For the time being, the benefits of economic development for the Union cause outweighed its negative consequences. The thriving northern economy fed, clothed, and armed the Union's soldiers and kept most civilians employed and well fed. Prosperity and the demands of a wartime economy also provided northern women with unprecedented opportunities.

QUICK REVIEW

The Northern Economy

- Tariffs and federal spending made up for loss of southern markets.
- Profits skyrocketed in some businesses.
- New industries emerged and new technologies increased efficiency.
- Wages failed to keep up with rising prices.

Northern Women and the War

More than 100,000 northern women took jobs in factories, sewing rooms, classrooms, hospitals, and arsenals during the Civil War. Stepping in for their absent husbands, fathers, and sons, they often performed tasks previously reserved for men but at lower pay. The expanding bureaucracy in Washington also offered opportunities for many women. The United States Treasury alone employed 447 women in the war years. And unlike private industry, the federal government paid women and men equally for the same work.

The new economic opportunities the war created for women left northern society more open to a broader view of women's roles. One indication of this change was the admission of women to eight previously all-male state universities after the war. Like the class and racial tensions that surfaced in northern cities, the shifting role of women during the Civil War hinted at the promises and problems of postwar life. The changing scale and nature of the American economy, the expanded role of government, and the shift in class, racial, and gender relations are all trends that signaled what historians call the "modernization" of American society. Many of these trends began before the war, but the war highlighted and accelerated them.

THE CONFEDERACY DISINTEGRATES

HOW DID the war affect civilian life in the South?

Even under the best of conditions, the newly formed political and economic institutions of the Confederacy would have had difficulty maintaining control over the country's class and racial tensions. But as battlefield losses mounted, the Confederacy disintegrated.

After 1863, defeat infected Confederate politics, ruined the southern economy, and eventually invaded the hearts and minds of the southern people. Disillusionment against the Confederate government did not erode support for Lee and his army. The South pinned its waning hopes on its defensive military strategy. If it could prolong the conflict a little longer, perhaps a war-weary North would replace Lincoln and the Republicans in the 1864 elections with a Democratic president and Congress inclined to make peace.

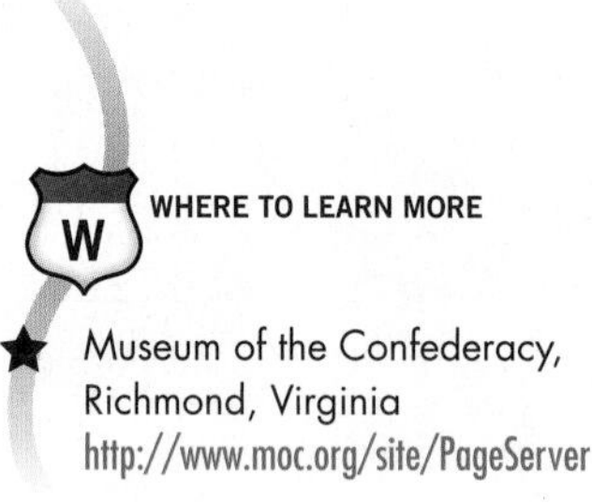

WHERE TO LEARN MORE

Museum of the Confederacy, Richmond, Virginia
http://www.moc.org/site/PageServer

SOUTHERN POLITICS

As the war turned against the Confederacy, southerners increasingly turned against each other. Some joined peace societies, which emerged as early as 1861. North Carolinians opposed to the war formed the Order of the Heroes of America, whose members not only demonstrated for peace but also took control of the Piedmont and mountain sections of the state. Other southerners preferred quieter dissent. They refused to join the army, pay taxes, or obey laws prohibiting trade with the enemy.

States' rights proved an obstacle to the Davis administration's efforts to exert central authority. The governors of Georgia and North Carolina gave the Richmond government particular difficulty, hoarding munitions, soldiers, supplies, food, and money. Even cooperative governors refused to allow state agents to collect taxes for the Confederacy.

Several parts of the South began clamoring for peace during the fateful summer of 1863. By November 1864, the Confederacy was suffering as much from internal disaffection as from the attacks of Union armies. Confederate authorities could not suppress civilian unrest in Virginia, North Carolina, and Tennessee, and Union spies operated openly in Mobile, Wilmington, and Richmond.

Davis and other Confederate leaders might have averted some of these political problems had they succeeded in building a strong sense of Confederate nationalism among soldiers and civilians. They tried several strategies to do so. For example, Davis tried to identify the Confederacy's fight for independence with the American Revolution of 1776. But egalitarian revolutionary ideals quickly lost their appeal in the face of poverty, starvation, and defeat. Davis also tried to cast the Confederacy as a bastion of freedom standing up to Lincoln's despotic abuse of executive authority, but he, too, eventually invoked authority similar to

Lincoln's. Confederate religious leaders sought to distinguish their new nation from the North by referring to southerners as God's "chosen people." But when Confederate military fortunes declined, religious leaders drew back from such visions of collective favor and stressed the need for individual salvation.

Southern Faith

In a devout society convinced it was fighting a holy war, some southerners sought to attribute their mounting losses to a moral failing. Some identified slavery as the culprit. But most Confederates held steadfast to the notion that God was on their side and that battlefield losses represented His temporary displeasure, not abandonment. They asked, as it is written in Judges 6:13, "If the Lord be with us, why then is all this befallen us?" They answered by drawing comfort from the Old Testament account of Job's suffering: "Though he slay me, yet will I trust him."

For black southerners, the Bible held other confirmations. The war was indeed becoming the fulfillment of a biblical prophecy. They turned to the Book of Daniel for its explicit explanation:

> For the king of the north shall return, and shall set forth a multitude greater than the former, and shall certainly come after certain years with a great army and with much riches.
>
> And in those times there shall many stand up against the king of the south: also the robbers of thy people shall exalt themselves to establish the vision; but they shall fall.

The Southern Economy

By 1863, the Confederacy was having a difficult time feeding itself. Destruction of farms by both sides and growing Union control of waterways and rail lines restricted the distribution of food. Speculators held certain commodities off the market to drive up prices, making shortages of food, cloth, and medicines worse. Bread riots erupted in Mobile, Atlanta, and Richmond.

Southern soldiers had marched off to war in neat uniforms with shiny buttons, many leaving behind self-sustaining families. But in August 1863, diarist Mary Chesnut, wife of a Confederate official in Richmond, watched 10,000 men marching near Richmond and commented, "Such rags and tags as we saw now. Most garments and arms were . . . taken from the enemy." The soldiers' families were threadbare as well. In the devastated areas near battle sites, civilians survived by selling fragments of dead soldiers' clothing stripped off their bodies and by collecting spent bullets and selling them for scrap.

The predations of both Union and Confederate soldiers further threatened civilians in the South. The women and children left alone on farms and plantations were vulnerable to stragglers and deserters from both armies who sometimes robbed, burned houses, raped, and murdered. Southerners also feared that slaves on isolated plantations would rise up against their masters. Most slaves, however, were more intent on escape than revenge.

As Confederate casualties mounted, more and more southern women and children, like their northern counterparts, faced the pain of grief. Funeral processions became commonplace in the cities and black

Wartime food shortages, skyrocketing inflation, and rumors of hoarding and price-gouging drove women in several southern cities to protest violently. Demonstrations like the 1863 food riot shown here reflected a larger rending of southern society as Confederate losses and casualties mounted on the battlefield. Some southern women placed survival and providing for their families ahead of boosting morale and silently supporting a war effort that had taken their men away. Their defection hurt the Confederate cause.

Read the **Document**
at **www.myhistorylab.com**
Mary Boykin Chesnut, A Confederate Lady's Diary (1861)

the color of fashion. With little food, worthless money, and a husband, son, or father gone forever, the future looked bleak.

Southern Women and the War

In the early days of the Civil War, southern white women continued to live their lives according to antebellum conventions. Magazine articles urged them to preserve themselves as models of purity for men debased by the violence of war.

Women flooded newspapers and periodicals with patriotic verses and songs. A major theme of these works, illustrated by the following example from the *Richmond Record* in September 1863, was the need to suppress grief and fear for the good of the men at the front:

> The maid who binds her warrior's sash
> And smiling, all her pain dissembles,
> The mother who conceals her grief
> [had] shed as sacred blood as e'er
> Was poured upon the plain of battle.

A Virginia woman confided to her diary, "We must learn the lesson which so many have to endure, to struggle against our feelings."

By the time of the Civil War, such emotional concealment had become second nature to planters' wives. They had long had to endure their anguish over their husbands' nocturnal visits to the slave quarters. They were used to the condescension of men who assumed them to be intellectually inferior. And they accepted in bitter, self-sacrificing silence the contradiction between the myth of the pampered leisure they were presumed to enjoy and the hard demands their lives actually entailed. But some southern women chafed at their supporting role and, as Confederate manpower and matériel needs became acute, took on new productive responsibilities. Initially, they did so within the domestic context: Women formed clubs to sew flags and uniforms. To raise money for the war effort, they held benefits and auctions and collected jewelry and other valuables.

QUICK REVIEW

Confederate Women

- As war dragged on, southern women took more active role at home and in the workplace.
- Some served as spies and nurses.
- Near the end of the war, many women helped their husbands desert.

Soon, however, the needs of the Confederacy drew women outside the home to fill positions vacated by men. They managed plantations. They worked in the fields alongside slaves. They worked in factories to make uniforms and munitions. They worked in government offices as clerks and secretaries. They taught school. A few, like Belle Boyd and Rose O'Neal Greenhow, spied for the Confederacy. And many, like their northern counterparts, served as nurses. Eventually, battlefield reverses and economic collapse undermined all these roles, leaving women and men alike struggling simply to survive.

White family "refugeeing." In advance of Union armies, tens of thousands of southern families fled to safer locales, a bitter exodus that fulfilled the Federals' vow to bring the war to the South's civilian population.

As the war dragged on and the southern economy and social order deteriorated, even the patriots suffered from resentment and doubt. By 1864, many women were helping their deserting husbands or relatives elude Confederate authorities.

By 1864, many southern white women had tired of the war. What had begun as a sacred cause had disintegrated into a nightmare of fear and deprivation. Uprooted from their homes, some women wandered through the war-ravaged South, exposed to violence, disease, and hunger and seeking shelter where they could find it. Those women fortunate enough to remain in their homes turned to work, others to protest, and many to religion. Some devoutly religious women concluded that it was God, not the Yankees, who had brought destruction on the South for its failure to live up to its responsibilities to women and children. Others blamed their men. Women greeted defeated troops retreating from Vicksburg with shouts of "We are disappointed in you!" However, despite hardship and privation, support for the Confederacy persisted among some women, stoked by fierce hatred of the enemy.

THE UNION PREVAILS, 1864–1865

WHAT WAS Grant's strategy for ending the war?

Despite the Union's dominant military position after Vicksburg and Gettysburg and the Confederacy's mounting homefront problems, three obstacles to Union victory remained. Federal troops under General William T. Sherman controlled Chattanooga and the gateway to Georgia, but the Confederate Army of Tennessee, now commanded by Joseph E. Johnston, was still intact, blocking Sherman's path to Atlanta. Robert E. Lee's formidable Army of Northern Virginia still protected Richmond. And the Confederacy still controlled the rich Shenandoah Valley, which fed Lee's armies and supplied his cavalry with horses. In March 1864, President Lincoln brought General Ulysses S. Grant to Washington and appointed him commander of all Union armies. Grant set about devising a strategy to overcome these obstacles.

Grant's Plan to End the War

Grant brought two innovations to the final campaign. First, he coordinated the Union war effort. Before, the Union's armies in Virginia and the West had operated independently, giving Confederate leaders the opportunity to direct troops and supplies to whichever arena most needed them. Now Grant proposed to deprive them of that option. The Union's armies in Virginia and the Lower South would attack at the same time, keeping steady pressure on all fronts. Second, Grant changed the tempo of the war. Before, long periods of rest had intervened between battles. Grant, with the advantage of superior numbers, proposed nonstop warfare.

Although Grant's strategy ultimately worked, several problems and miscalculations undermined its effectiveness. With Sherman advancing in Georgia, Grant's major focus was Lee's army in Virginia. But Grant underestimated Lee. The Confederate general thwarted him for almost a year and inflicted horrendous casualties on his army. Confederate forces under Jubal Early drove Union forces from the Shenandoah Valley in June 1864, depriving Grant of troops and allowing the Confederates to maintain their supply lines. And the incompetence of General Benjamin Butler, charged with advancing up the James River to Richmond in May 1864 to relieve Lee's pressure on Grant, further eroded Grant's plan. Finally, Grant had to contend with disaffection in his officer corps. Many of his officers felt enduring loyalty to General George McClellan, whom Lincoln had dismissed in 1862, and considered Grant a mediocrity who had triumphed in the West only because his opposition there had been third-rate.

Lee's only hope was to make Grant's campaign so costly and time-consuming that the northern general would abandon it before the southerners ran out of supplies and troops. But despite problems and setbacks, Grant kept relentless pressure on Lee. Tied down in Virginia, the Confederate general was unable to send troops to help slow Sherman's advance in Georgia.

QUICK REVIEW

Grant's Strategy

- Better coordination of Union effort and the application of steady pressure.
- The waging of nonstop warfare.
- Grant's plan worked in the long run, but at a high cost.

From the Wilderness to Cold Harbor. Grant and General George Meade began their campaign against Lee in May 1864, crossing the Rapidan River near Fredericksburg, Virginia, and marching toward an area known as the Wilderness (see Map 15–6). Lee attacked the Army of the Potomac, which outnumbered his forces 118,000 to 60,000, in the thickets of the Wilderness on May 5 and 6 before it could reach open ground. The densely wooded terrain reduced the Union army's advantage in numbers and artillery. Much of the fighting involved fierce hand-to-hand combat. Exchanges of gunfire at close range set the dry underbrush ablaze.

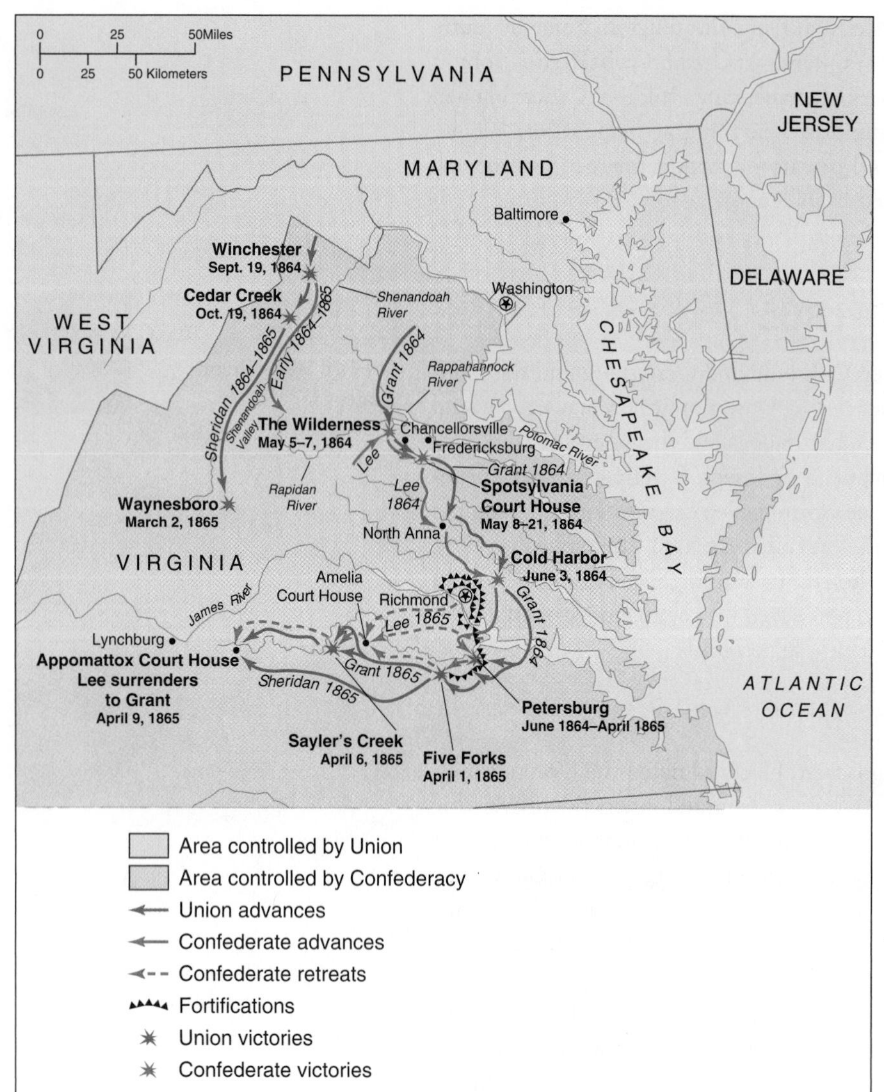

MAP 15–6 **Grant and Lee in Virginia, 1864–1865** The engagements in Virginia from May 1864 to April 1865 between the two great generals proved decisive in ending the Civil War. Although Lee fared well enough in the Wilderness, Spotsylvania, and Cold Harbor campaigns, the sheer might and relentlessness of Grant and his army wore down the Confederate forces. When Petersburg fell after a prolonged siege on April 2, 1865, Richmond, Appomattox, and dreams of southern independence soon fell as well.

What happened at Cold Harbor? What did this battle reveal about the Union's population advantage over the Confederacy?

Wounded soldiers, trapped in the fires, begged their comrades to shoot them before they burned to death. The toll was frightful, 18,000 casualties on the Union side, 10,000 for the Confederates. Other Union commanders would have pulled back and rested after such an encounter. But Grant, relentless in the pursuit of the enemy, startled Lee's army by pushing on, and Lee's offensive in the Battle of the Wilderness was his last. From then on, his army was on the defensive against Grant's relentless pursuit.

Marching and fighting, his casualties always higher than Lee's, Grant continued southward. Attacking the entrenched Confederate army at Spotsylvania, his army suffered another 18,000 casualties to the Confederates' 11,000. Undeterred, Grant moved on toward Cold Harbor, where Lee's troops again awaited him in entrenched positions. Flinging his army against withering Confederate fire on June 3, he lost 7,000 men in eight minutes.

In less than a month of fighting, the Army of the Potomac had lost 55,000 men. The slaughter undermined Grant's support in northern public opinion and led peace advocates to renew their quest for a ceasefire. With antiwar sentiment growing in the North as the presidential elections approached in November, Lee's defensive strategy seemed to be working.

Grant decided to change his tactics. Abandoning his march on Richmond from the north, he shifted his army south of the James River to approach the Confederate capital from the rear. Wasting no time, he crossed his army over the James and, on June 17, 1864, surprised the Confederates with an attack on Petersburg, a critical rail junction 23 miles south of Richmond. It was a brilliant maneuver, but the hesitant actions of Union corps commanders gave Lee time to reinforce the town's defenders. Both armies dug in for a lengthy siege.

Atlanta. While Grant engaged Lee in Virginia, Union forces under William T. Sherman in Georgia engaged in a deadly dance with the Army of Tennessee under the command of Joseph E. Johnston as they began the campaign to take Atlanta. Hoping to lure Sherman into a frontal assault, Johnston settled his forces early in May at Dalton, an important railroad junction in Georgia 25 miles south of Chattanooga and 75 miles north of Atlanta. The wily Union general declined to attack and instead made a wide swing around the Confederates, prompting Johnston to abandon Dalton, rush south, and dig in again at Resaca to prevent Sherman from cutting the railroad. Again Sherman swung around without an assault, and again Johnston rushed south to cut him off, this time at Cassville.

Read the **Document** at **www.myhistorylab.com**
William T. Sherman, The March Through Georgia (1875)

This waltz continued for two months, until Johnston had retreated to a strong defensive position on Kennesaw Mountain, barely 20 miles north of Atlanta. At this point, early in July, Sherman decided to attack, with predictably disastrous consequences. The Union suffered 3,000 casualties, the Confederates only 600. Sherman would not make such a mistake again. He resumed his maneuvering and by mid-July had forced Johnston into defensive positions on Peachtree Creek just north of Atlanta. President Davis feared that Johnston would let Sherman take Atlanta without a fight and "dance" with the Union general until the sea stopped them both. Davis dismissed Johnston and installed John Bell Hood of Texas in his place. This was a grave error. Hood, in the opinion of those who fought for him, had a "lion's heart" but a "wooden head."

In late July, Hood began a series of attacks on Sherman, beginning at Peachtree Creek on July 20, and was thrown back each time with heavy losses. Sherman launched a series of flanking maneuvers around the city in late August that left Hood in danger of being surrounded. The Confederate general had no choice but to abandon Atlanta and save his army. On the night of September 1, Hood evacuated the city, burning everything of military value.

The loss of Atlanta was a severe blow to the Confederacy. Several of the South's major railroads converged at the city, and its industries helped arm and clothe the armies. Atlanta's fall also left Georgia's rich farmland at the mercy of Sherman's army. Most significant, the fall of Atlanta revived the morale of the war-weary North and helped ensure Lincoln's reelection in November. The last hope of the Confederacy, that a peace candidate would replace Lincoln and end the war, had faded.

The Election of 1864 and Sherman's March

Before Sherman's victory at Atlanta, northern dismay over Grant's enormous losses and his failure to take Richmond raised the prospect of a Democratic election victory. Nominating George B. McClellan, the former commander of the Union's armies, as their presidential candidate, the Democrats appealed to voters as the party of peace. They also appealed to the anti-emancipation sentiment that was strong in some parts of the North.

The fall of Atlanta and the suddenly improved military fortunes of the Union undermined Democratic prospects. Another Union victory three weeks before the elections gave Lincoln a further boost and diminished McClellan's chances. Since September, Union forces under General Philip H. Sheridan had been on the offensive in the Shenandoah Valley (see Map 15–6). In a decisive battle on October 19, they overwhelmed the valley's Confederate defenders. Lee had now been deprived of a vital source of supply.

The Republican victory. In the voting on November 8, Lincoln captured 55 percent of the popular vote, losing only New Jersey, Delaware, and Kentucky. Republicans likewise swept the congressional elections, retaining control of both the Senate and the House of Representatives.

The Republican victory reinforced the Union commitment to emancipation. A proposed constitutional amendment outlawing slavery everywhere in the United States, not just those areas still in rebellion, passed Congress and was ratified as the **Thirteenth Amendment** to the U.S. Constitution in 1865. All the earlier amendments related to government powers and functions; this was the first to outlaw a domestic institution previously protected by the Constitution and state law.

Thirteenth Amendment
Constitutional amendment ratified in 1865 that freed all slaves throughout the United States.

Sherman's march to the sea. After Sherman took Atlanta, he proposed to break Confederate resistance once and for all by marching his army to the sea and destroying everything in its path. Sherman's March got underway on November 15. His force of

General Ulysses S. Grant had the pews from a local church moved to a grove of trees where he and his officers planned the following day's assault on Confederate troops at Cold Harbor, Virginia. Grant appears at the left of the photograph, leaning over a bench and studying a map.

60,000 men, encountering little resistance, entered Savannah on December 22, 1864. Just a few weeks earlier, Union forces in Tennessee had routed Hood's army at the Battle of Franklin and then crushed it entirely at the Battle of Nashville. Hood's defeat removed any threat to Sherman's rear.

Sherman resumed his march in February 1865, heading for South Carolina, the heart of the Confederacy and the state where the Civil War had begun. South Carolinians sent taunting messages promising stiff resistance, but these served only to further provoke Sherman's troops. They pushed aside the small force that assembled to oppose them, wreaked greater destruction in South Carolina than they had in Georgia, and burned the state capitol at Columbia. Sherman sent the colonel of a black regiment to receive the surrender of Charleston and ordered black troops to be the first to take possession of the city. The soldiers marched in singing "John Brown's Body," to the cheers of the city's black population.

Sherman ended his march in Goldsboro, North Carolina, in March 1865 after repelling a surprise Confederate attack at Bentonville led by the restored Joseph E. Johnston and the remnants of the Army of Tennessee. Behind the Union army lay a barren swath 425 miles long from Savannah to Goldsboro.

Lincoln's second inaugural. When Abraham Lincoln took the oath of office for a second time on March 4, 1865, the result of the war was a foregone conclusion even if the precise date of its end was not. In a brief but inspirational address, the president provided the spiritual blueprint for reconciliation, though it disappointed some in the crowd who hoped for a declaration of victory, a promise of retribution against the rebel traitors, or at least an acknowledgment that God was clearly on the side of the Union. Instead, Lincoln declared that God had cursed both sides and had visited a destructive war on the nation because of the sin of slavery, a sin, he stressed, that was national, not regional.

Read the **Document** at **www.myhistorylab.com** *Abraham Lincoln, Second Inaugural Address (1865)*

Nor was the president prepared to proclaim victory, despite its inevitability. In fact, the war could continue for some indeterminate time: "Fondly do we hope—fervently do we pray—that this mighty scourge of war may speedily pass away. Yet, if God wills that it continue, until all the wealth piled by the bond-man's two hundred and fifty years of unrequited toil shall be sunk, and until every drop of blood drawn with the lash, shall be paid by another drawn with the sword, as was said three thousand years ago, so still it must be said 'the judgments of the Lord, are true and righteous altogether.'"

And once the bloody conflict ends, Lincoln intoned, let reconciliation rather than retribution inform the national policy: "With malice toward none; with charity for all; with firmness in the right, as God gives us to see the right, let us strive on to finish the work we are in; to bind up the nation's wounds; to care for him who shall have borne the battle, and for his widow, and his orphan—to do all which may achieve and cherish a just, and a lasting peace, among ourselves, and with all nations." In the meantime, the bitter struggle would continue.

Arming the Confederacy's slaves. In March 1865, in a move reflecting their desperation, Confederate leaders revived a proposal that they had previously rejected: to arm and free slaves. President Davis hoped this action would gain the Confederacy not only a military benefit but also diplomatic recognition from countries that had balked because of slavery.

On March 13, 1865, a reluctant Confederate Congress passed a bill to enlist black soldiers, but without offering them freedom. Ten days later, President Davis and the War Office issued a general order that promised immediate freedom to slaves who enlisted. The war ended before the order could have any effect. The irony was that in the summer of 1864, a majority of northerners probably would have accepted reunion without emancipation had the Confederacy abandoned its fight.

The Road to Appomattox and the Death of Lincoln

With Sherman's triumph in Georgia and the Carolinas and Sheridan's rout of the Confederates in the Shenandoah Valley, Lee's army remained the last obstacle to Union victory. On April 1, Sheridan's cavalry seized a vital railroad junction on Lee's right flank, forcing Lee to abandon Petersburg and the defense of Richmond. Lee tried a daring run westward toward Lynchburg, hoping to secure much-needed supplies and to join Johnston's Army of Tennessee in North Carolina to continue the fight.

President Davis fled Richmond with his cabinet and headed toward North Carolina. Union troops occupied the Confederate capital on April 3, and two days later, President Lincoln

Generals Robert E. Lee and Ulysses S. Grant surrounded by officers in the McLean House at Appomattox Court House, Virginia.

walked through its streets to the cheers of his army and an emotional reception from thousands of black people. "I know I am free," shouted one black spectator, "for I have seen Father Abraham and felt him."

The surrender at Appomattox. Grant's army of 60,000 outran Lee's diminishing force of 35,000 and cut off his escape at Appomattox Court House, Virginia, on April 7. Convinced that further resistance was futile, the Confederate commander met Grant on April 9, 1865, in the McLean house at Appomattox to sign the documents of surrender. The Union general offered generous terms, allowing Lee's men to go home unmolested and to take with them horses or mules "to put in a crop."

WHERE TO LEARN MORE

Appomattox Court House, Appomattox, Virginia
http://www.nps.gov/apco/index.htm

Though some southerners entertained fleetingly the idea of launching a guerrilla campaign against Union forces, most were sick of the war. One Confederate leader, traveling through the stricken South in April 1865, reported that soldiers and civilians alike considered any continuation of the conflict "madness." Joseph E. Johnston surrendered to Sherman near Durham, North Carolina, on April 26. On May 10, Union cavalry captured President Davis in southern Georgia. On May 26, Texas general Kirby Smith surrendered his trans-Mississippi army, and the Civil War came to an end.

The death of Lincoln. Washington greeted the Confederate surrender at Appomattox with predictable and raucous rejoicing, torchlight parades, cannon salutes, and crowds spontaneously bellowing "The Star-Spangled Banner." On April 11, President Lincoln addressed a large crowd from the White House balcony and spoke briefly of his plans to reconstruct the South with the help of persons loyal to the Union, including recently freed slaves. At least one listener found the speech disappointing. A sometime actor and full-time Confederate patriot, John Wilkes Booth, muttered to a friend in the throng, "That means nigger citizenship. Now, by God, I'll put him through. That is the last speech he will ever make."

On the evening of April 14, Good Friday, the president went to Ford's Theatre in Washington to view a comedy, *Our American Cousin*. During the performance, Booth shot the president, wounding him mortally, then jumped from Lincoln's box to the stage shouting "*Sic semper tyrannis*" ("Thus ever to tyrants") and fled the theater. Union troops tracked him down to a barn in northern Virginia and killed him. Investigators arrested eight accomplices who

OVERVIEW Major Battles of the Civil War, 1861–1865

Battle or Campaign	Date	Outcome and Consequences
First Bull Run	July 21, 1861	Confederate victory, destroyed the widespread belief in the North that the war would end quickly, fueled Confederate sense of superiority
Forts Henry and Donelson	February 6–16, 1862	Union victory, gave the North control of strategic river systems in the western Confederacy and closed an important link between the eastern and western Confederacy
Shiloh Church	April 6–7, 1862	Union victory, high casualties transformed attitudes about the war on both sides
Seven Days' Battles	June 25–July 1, 1862	Standoff, halted McClellan's advance on Richmond in the Peninsula Campaign
Second Bull Run	August 29–30, 1862	Confederate victory, reinforced Robert E. Lee's reputation for invincibility
Antietam	September 17, 1862	Standoff halted Lee's advance into the North, eliminated Confederacy's chance for diplomatic recognition, encouraged Lincoln to issue the Emancipation Proclamation
Fredericksburg	December 13, 1862	Confederate victory, revived morale of Lee's army
Chancellorsville	May 2–6, 1863	Confederate victory, Stonewall Jackson killed, encouraged Lee to again invade North
Gettysburg	July 1–3, 1863	Union victory, halted Confederate advance in the North, major psychological blow to Confederacy
Vicksburg	November 1862–July 1863	Union victory; closed the key Confederate port on the Mississippi, also dealt a severe blow to Confederate cause
Chattanooga	August–November 1863	Union victory, solidified Union dominance in the West
Wilderness and Cold Harbor	May and June 1864	Two Confederate victories, inflicted huge losses on Grant's army; turned public opinion against Grant but failed to force him to withdraw
Atlanta	May–September 1864	Union victory; Confederacy lost key rail depot and industrial center
Sherman's March	November 1864–March 1865	Nearly unopposed, Sherman's army cut a path of destruction through Georgia and South Carolina, breaking southern morale
Battles of Franklin and Nashville	November and December 1864	Union victories in Tennessee; effectively destroyed Army of Tennessee
Siege of Petersburg	June 1864–April 1865	Long stalemate ended in Union victory; led to fall of Richmond and surrender of Lee's army at Appomattox Court House

had conspired with Booth to murder other high officials in addition to Lincoln. Four of the accomplices were hanged.

Southerners reacted to Lincoln's assassination with surprisingly mixed emotions. Many saw some slight hope of relief for the South's otherwise bleak prospects. But General Johnston and others like him were aware of Lincoln's moderating influence on the radical elements in the Republican Party that were pressing for harsh terms against the South. The president's death, Johnston wrote, was "the greatest possible calamity to the South."

CONCLUSION

Watch the Video at **www.myhistorylab.com** *The Meaning of the Civil War for Americans*

Just before the war, William Sherman had warned a friend from Virginia, "You people of the South don't know what you are doing. This country will be drenched in blood. . . . [W]ar is a terrible thing." He was right. More than 365,000 Union soldiers died during the war, 110,000 in battle, and more than 256,000 Confederate soldiers, 94,000 in battle. Total casualties on both sides, including wounded, were more than 1 million.

The southern armies suffered disproportionately higher casualties than the northern armies. One in four Confederate soldiers died or endured debilitating wounds, compared to one in ten federal soldiers. Compounding the suffering of the individuals behind these gruesome statistics was the incalculable suffering, in terms of grief, fatherless children, women who never married, families never made whole, of the people close to them.

The war devastated the South. The region lost one-fourth of its white male population between the ages of 20 and 40. It also lost two-fifths of its livestock and half its farm machinery. Union armies destroyed many of the South's railroads and shattered its industry. Between 1860 and 1870, the wealth of the South declined by 60 percent, and its share of the nation's total wealth dropped from more than 30 percent to 12 percent. The wealth of the North, in contrast, increased by half in the same period.

The Union victory solved the constitutional question about the right of secession and sealed the fate of slavery. The issue that dominated the prewar sectional debate had vanished. Now, when politicians intoned Independence Day orations or campaign speeches about the ideals of democracy and freedom, the glaring reality of human bondage would no longer mock their rhetoric.

The Civil War stimulated societal changes that grew more significant over time. It did not make the Union an industrial nation, but it taught the effectiveness of centralized management, new financial techniques, and the coordination of production, marketing, and distribution. Entrepreneurs would apply these lessons to create the expanding corporations of the postwar American economy. Likewise, the war did not revolutionize gender relations in American society, but by opening new opportunities to women in fields such as nursing and teaching, it helped lay the foundation for the woman's suffrage movement of the 1870s and 1880s.

For many Americans, especially black and white southerners, the war was the most important event in their lives, but it was not responsible for every postwar change in American society, and it left many features of American life intact. The experience of pulling together in a massive war effort, for example, did not soften class antagonisms. Capitalism, not labor, triumphed during the war. And it was industrialists and entrepreneurs, not working people, who most benefited from the war's bonanza.

For black southerners, emancipation was the war's most significant achievement. The war to end slavery changed some American racial attitudes, especially in the North. When Lincoln broadened the war's objectives to include the abolition of slavery, he connected the success of the Union to freedom for the slave. At the outset of the Civil War, only a small minority of northerners considered themselves abolitionists. After the Emancipation Proclamation, every northern soldier became a liberator. The courage of black troops and the efforts of African American leaders to link the causes of reunion and freedom were influential in bringing about this shift.

Most white southerners did not experience a similar enlightenment. Some were relieved by the end of slavery, but most greeted it with fear, anger, and regret.

If the Civil War resolved the sectional dispute of the 1850s by ending slavery and denying the right of the southern states to secede, it created two new equally troubling problems: how to reunite South and North and how to deal with the legacy of slavery. At his last cabinet meeting on April 14, Lincoln seemed inclined to be conciliatory, cautioning against reprisals on Confederate leaders and noting the courage of General Lee and his officers.

America's greatest crisis had closed. In its wake, former slaves tested their new freedom, and the nation groped for reconciliation. The struggle to preserve the Union and abolish slavery had renewed and vindicated the nation's ideals. It was time to savor the hard-fought victories before plunging into the uncertainties of Reconstruction.

Where to Learn More

Museum of the Confederacy, Richmond, Virginia. This museum has rotating exhibits on various aspects of the Confederate effort during the Civil War, both on the home front and on the battlefield. The Confederate White House, which is open to the public, is next door to the museum. Visit its website at http://www.moc.org/site/PageServer.

Gettysburg National Military Park, Gettysburg, Pennsylvania. An excellent and balanced interpretation awaits the visitor at this national park. See its website, http://www.nps.gov/gett/index.htm.

National Museum of the History of Medicine, Washington, DC. For those interested in the grisly details of Civil War medicine, the museum's permanent exhibit is "To Bind Up the Nation's Wounds: Medicine During the Civil War." The museum also has a long-running exhibit, "Abraham Lincoln: The Final Casualty of the War," which includes the bullet that ended his life. http://nmhm.washingtondc.museum

Appomattox Court House, Appomattox, Virginia. What historian Bruce Catton termed "a stillness at Appomattox" can be felt at the McLean house in this south-central Virginia town. The house is much as it was when General Robert E. Lee surrendered his forces to General Ulysses S. Grant on April 9, 1865. An almost reverential solitude covers the house and the well-maintained grounds today. Its website is at http://www.nps.gov/apco/index.htm.

Review Questions

1. How did the Union and the Confederacy compare in terms of resources, leadership, and military strategies in the period 1861–1863? What impact did these factors have on the course of the war?
2. What was the significance of the battles of Antietam and Gettysburg? In what ways were they turning points in the Civil War?
3. Given that the federal government was fighting a civil war, why did not European powers, other than France, take advantage of that distraction and meddle in Latin American affairs?
4. What effects did the Emancipation Proclamation have on the Union and Confederate causes?
5. Compare and contrast the roles played by women in the North and in the South during the Civil War, and explain how their actions and activities aided or hindered the war effort of their respective nations.
6. Sullivan Ballou made the ultimate sacrifice for his cause. Why did he fight?

Key Terms*

Confiscation Act (p. 408)
Copperheads (p. 417)
Emancipation Proclamation (p. 408)
Homestead Act (p. 417)
Land Grant College Act (p. 417)
New York Draft Riot (p. 419)
Radical Republicans (p. 417)
Thirteenth Amendment (p. 425)

*See the Overview table, on p. 429 for important battles of the Civil War.

PEARSON myhistorylab Connections

Reinforce what you learned in this chapter by studying the many documents, images, maps, review tools, and videos available at **www.myhistorylab.com**.

Read and Review

Study and Review **Study Plan: Chapter 15**

Read the Document

Clara Barton, Memoirs about Medical Life at the Battlefield (1862)

Jefferson Davis, Address to the Provisional Congress (1861)

Mary Boykin Chesnut, A Confederate Lady's Diary (1861)

Susie King Taylor, Reminiscences of an Army Laundress (1902)

The Homestead Act of 1862

Abraham Lincoln, Second Inaugural Address (1865)

Abraham Lincoln, The Gettysburg Address (1863)

"I Hope to Fall with My Face to the Foe": Lewis Douglass Describes the Battle of Fort Wagner (1863)

"If It Were Not for My Trust in Christ I Do Not Know How I Could Have Endured It": Testimony from Victims of New York's Draft Riots (1863)

J. Horace Lacy, "Lee at Fredericksburg" (1886)

The Emancipation Proclamation (1863)

William T. Sherman, The March Through Georgia (1875)

See the Map

The Civil War Part I: 1861–1862

The Civil War Part II: 1863–1865

Effects of the Emancipation Proclamation

Research and Explore

Read the Document

Personal Journeys Online

From Then to Now Online: The Soldiers' War

A Nation Divided: The Civil War

Hear the Audio

When This Cruel War Is Over

Battle Hymn of the Republic

Watch the Video

What Caused the Civil War?

The Meaning of the Civil War for Americans

Hear the Audio

Hear the audio files for Chapter 15 at **www.myhistorylab.com.**

1865-1877

16 Reconstruction

An elderly man reads a newspaper with the headline "Presidential Proclamation, Slavery," which refers to the January 1863 Emancipation Proclamation in this painting by Henry Louis Stephens (1824–1882).

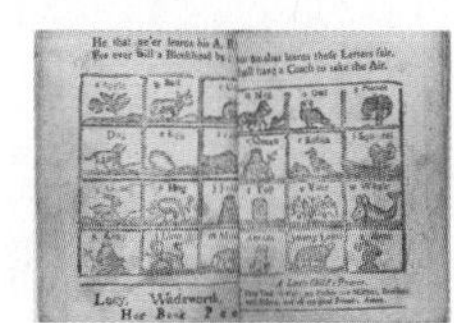

Hear the Audio
Hear the audio files for Chapter 16 at **www.myhistorylab.com**.

WHITE SOUTHERNERS AND THE GHOSTS OF THE CONFEDERACY, 1865 *(page 438)*

HOW DID southerners remember the war? How did it shape their response to Reconstruction?

MORE THAN FREEDOM: AFRICAN AMERICAN ASPIRATIONS IN 1865 *(page 439)*

WHAT WERE African Americans' hopes for Reconstruction?

FEDERAL RECONSTRUCTION, 1865–1870 *(page 444)*

HOW DID Presidential Reconstruction differ from Congressional Reconstruction?

COUNTER-RECONSTRUCTION, 1870–1874 *(page 452)*

WHAT ROLE did violence play in Counter-Reconstruction?

REDEMPTION, 1874–1877 *(page 455)*

WHY DID the federal government abandon African Americans after 1872?

MODEST GAINS *(page 459)*

HOW AND why did Reconstruction end?

One American Journey

An Appeal to the American People (1871)

When a dark and fearful strife
Raged around the nation's life,
And the traitor plunged his steel
Where your quivering hearts could feel,
When your cause did need a friend,
We were faithful to the end.

With your soldiers, side by side,
Helped we turn the battle's tide,
Till o'er ocean, stream and shore,
Wave the rebel flag no more,
And above the rescued sod
Praises rose to freedom's God.

But to-day the traitor stands
With crimson on his hands,
Scowling 'neath his brow of hate,
On our weak and desolate,
With the blood-rust on the knife
Aimed at the nation's life.

Asking you to weakly yield
All we won upon the field,
To ignore, on land and flood,
All the offerings of our blood,
And to write above our slain
"They have fought and died in vain."

Source: Maryemma Graham, ed., *Complete Poems of Frances E. W. Harper* (New York: Oxford University Press, 1988), pp. 81–83.

Read the **Document** at **www.myhistorylab.com**

Personal Journeys Online

- **N. J. Bell, *Southern Railroad Man*, 1865. A railroad conductor recalls the aftermath of the Civil War and its impact on a white family in Wilmington, NC.**
- **Adelbert Ames, "Letter from the Republican Governor of Mississippi," 1875. Letter to his wife expressing frustration at the violence against black voters in his state and his hope for federal intervention.**

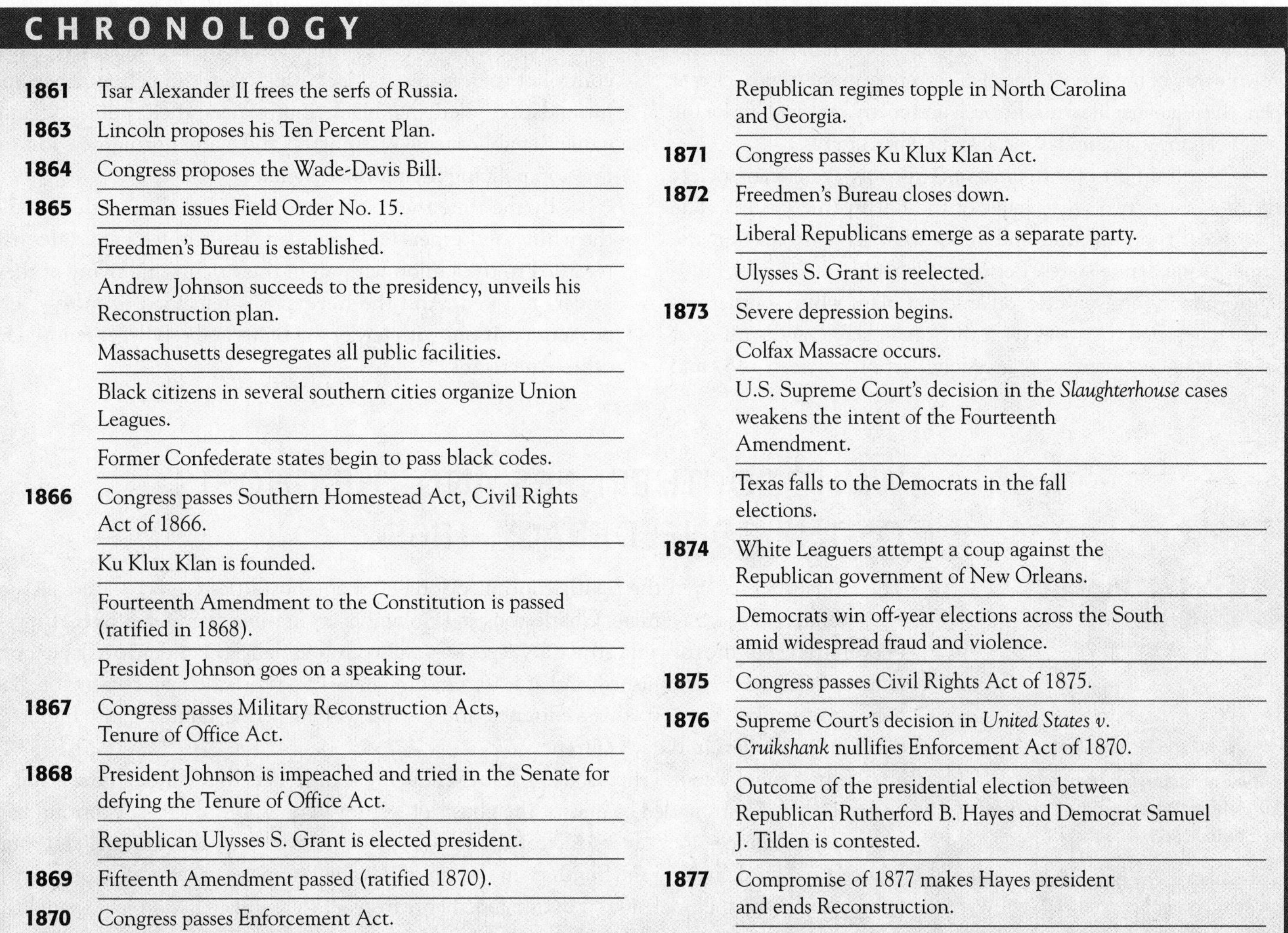

CHRONOLOGY

1861	Tsar Alexander II frees the serfs of Russia.
1863	Lincoln proposes his Ten Percent Plan.
1864	Congress proposes the Wade-Davis Bill.
1865	Sherman issues Field Order No. 15.
	Freedmen's Bureau is established.
	Andrew Johnson succeeds to the presidency, unveils his Reconstruction plan.
	Massachusetts desegregates all public facilities.
	Black citizens in several southern cities organize Union Leagues.
	Former Confederate states begin to pass black codes.
1866	Congress passes Southern Homestead Act, Civil Rights Act of 1866.
	Ku Klux Klan is founded.
	Fourteenth Amendment to the Constitution is passed (ratified in 1868).
	President Johnson goes on a speaking tour.
1867	Congress passes Military Reconstruction Acts, Tenure of Office Act.
1868	President Johnson is impeached and tried in the Senate for defying the Tenure of Office Act.
	Republican Ulysses S. Grant is elected president.
1869	Fifteenth Amendment passed (ratified 1870).
1870	Congress passes Enforcement Act.
	Republican regimes topple in North Carolina and Georgia.
1871	Congress passes Ku Klux Klan Act.
1872	Freedmen's Bureau closes down.
	Liberal Republicans emerge as a separate party.
	Ulysses S. Grant is reelected.
1873	Severe depression begins.
	Colfax Massacre occurs.
	U.S. Supreme Court's decision in the *Slaughterhouse* cases weakens the intent of the Fourteenth Amendment.
	Texas falls to the Democrats in the fall elections.
1874	White Leaguers attempt a coup against the Republican government of New Orleans.
	Democrats win off-year elections across the South amid widespread fraud and violence.
1875	Congress passes Civil Rights Act of 1875.
1876	Supreme Court's decision in *United States v. Cruikshank* nullifies Enforcement Act of 1870.
	Outcome of the presidential election between Republican Rutherford B. Hayes and Democrat Samuel J. Tilden is contested.
1877	Compromise of 1877 makes Hayes president and ends Reconstruction.

Frances Ellen Watkins Harper, the author of this poem, pleaded with northerners not to abandon African Americans in their quest for full equality. She appealed both to their sense of fairness—that African Americans had fought side-by-side and laid down their lives for the Union cause—and to their self-interest to not allow their winning the war, and the sacrifices that entailed, to be betrayed by losing the peace.

At the time, 1871, Reconstruction was under full assault in the South by white paramilitary groups associated with the Democratic Party. Though violence against the freedmen and their aspirations had been persistent since the end of the Civil War, the growing political power of blacks in the South after 1867 provoked more organized and violent assaults on blacks and some of their white colleagues. The federal government attempted to quell these disturbances with troops and legislation, but these measures were largely ineffective. While a majority of northern whites had opposed slavery, a majority also opposed racial equality. By 1871, a consensus emerged in the North to allow southern whites a free hand in dealing with their political problems. Harper's appeal, therefore, fell on deaf ears. The nation's journey toward a more just society took a major detour in the decade after the Civil War.

Frances Harper's personal journey was more rewarding. She was born into a free black family in Maryland, a slave state, in 1825. Orphaned at the age of 3 and raised by her aunt and uncle, she attended a noted school for free blacks in Baltimore. By the time she was 25, she had become the first woman professor at a seminary in Ohio which later became Wilberforce University. In 1853, Harper moved to Philadelphia where she worked in the Underground Railroad and became one of the few black women lecturers on abolition. In 1860, she married Fenton Harper, and had a daughter with him. When he died in 1864, she took her daughter and resumed lecturing, becoming one of the first women of color to travel throughout the South in the days after emancipation, helping to educate former slaves.

Although she arrived in the South with considerable hope, Harper left after five frustrating years. Violence against African Americans and their white allies had escalated and threatened to reduce the former slaves to a permanent category of second-class citizenship. Her poem was one of her last attempts to reach a northern public already grown weary of the periodic racial disturbances in the South. Harper spent the rest of her life writing novels and poetry, and working for the causes of temperance and of racial and women's rights.

The position of African Americans in American society was one of the two great issues of the Reconstruction era. The other great issue was how and under what terms to readmit the former Confederate states. Between 1865 and 1867, under President Andrew Johnson's Reconstruction plan, white southerners pretty much had their way with the former slaves and with their own state governments. Congressional action between 1867 and 1870 attempted to balance black rights and home rule, with mixed results. After 1870, white southerners gradually regained control of their states and localities, often through violence and intimidation, denying black southerners their political gains while Republicans in Washington and white northerners lost interest in policing their former enemies.

By the time the last federal troops left the South in 1877, the white southerners had prevailed. The Confederate states had returned to the Union with all of their rights and many of their leaders restored. And the freed slaves remained in mostly subservient positions with few of the rights and privileges enjoyed by other Americans. ✦

WHITE SOUTHERNERS AND THE GHOSTS OF THE CONFEDERACY, 1865

HOW DID southerners remember the war? How did it shape their response to Reconstruction?

Read the **Document** at **www.myhistorylab.com** *Carl Schurz, Report on the Condition of the South (1865)*

Lost Cause The phrase many white southerners applied to their Civil War defeat. They viewed the war as a noble cause but only a temporary setback in the South's ultimate vindication.

The casualties of war in the South continued long after the hostilities ceased. Cities such as Richmond, Atlanta, Savannah, Charleston, and Columbia lay in ruins; farmsteads were stripped of everything but the soil; infrastructure, especially railroads, was damaged or destroyed; factories and machinery were demolished; and at least 5 million bales of cotton, the major cash crop, had gone up in smoke. Add a worthless currency, and the loss was staggering, climbing into hundreds of billions of dollars in today's currency.

Their cause lost and their society destroyed, white southerners lived through the summer and fall of 1865 surrounded by ghosts, the ghosts of lost loved ones, joyful times, bountiful harvests, self-assurance, and slavery. Defeat shook the basic tenets of their religious beliefs. Some praised God for delivering the South from the sin of slavery. But many other white southerners refused to accept their defeat as a divine judgment. Instead, they insisted, God had spared the South for a greater purpose. They came to view the war as the **Lost Cause** and interpreted it, not as a lesson in humility, but as an episode in the South's journey to salvation. White southerners transformed the bloody struggle into a symbol of courage against great odds and piety against sin. Eventually, they believed, redemption would come.

This engraving shows southerners decorating the graves of rebel soldiers at Hollywood Memorial Cemetery in Richmond, Virginia, in 1867. Northerners and southerners alike honored their war dead. But in the South, the practice of commemorating fallen soldiers became an important element in maintaining the myth of the Lost Cause that colored white southerners' view of the war.

The Lost Cause would not merely exist as a memory, but also as a three-dimensional depiction of southern history, in rituals and celebrations, and as the educational foundation for future generations. The statues of the Confederate common soldier erected typically on the most important site in a town, the courthouse square; the commemorations of Confederate Memorial Day, the birthdays of prominent Confederate leaders, and the reunions of veterans, all marked with flourishing oratory, brass bands, parades, and related spectacles; and the textbooks implanting the white history of the South in young minds and carrying the legacy down through the generations—all of these ensured that the Lost Cause would not only be an interpretation of the past, but also the basic reality of the present and the foundation for the future.

Most white southerners approached the great issues of freedom and reunification with unyielding views. They saw African Americans as adversaries whose attempts at self-improvement were a direct challenge to white people's belief in their own racial superiority. White southerners saw outside assistance to black southerners as another invasion. The Yankees might have destroyed their families, their farms, and their fortunes, but they would not destroy the racial order. The war may have ended slavery, but white southerners were determined to preserve strict racial boundaries.

W
WHERE TO LEARN MORE
Beauvoir, Biloxi, Mississippi
http://www.beauvoir.org

MORE THAN FREEDOM: AFRICAN AMERICAN ASPIRATIONS IN 1865

WHAT WERE African Americans' hopes for Reconstruction?

Black southerners had a quite different perspective on the Civil War and Reconstruction, seeing the former as a great victory for freedom and the latter as a time of great possibility. To black southerners the Civil War was a war of liberation, not a Lost Cause. The response of southern whites to black aspirations still stunned African Americans, who believed, naively perhaps, that what they sought—education, land, access to employment, and equality in law and politics—were basic rights and modest objectives. The former slaves did not initially even dream of social equality; far less did they plot murder and mayhem, as white people feared. They did harbor two potentially contradictory aspirations. The first was to be left alone, free of white supervision. But the former slaves also wanted land, voting and civil rights, and education. To secure these, they needed the intervention and support of the white power structure.

Hear the Audio at **www.myhistorylab.com** *Free At Last*

In 1865, African Americans had reason to hope that their dreams of full citizenship might be realized. They enjoyed a reservoir of support for their aspirations among some Republican leaders. The first step Congress took beyond emancipation was to establish the Bureau of Refugees, Freedmen, and Abandoned Lands in March 1865. Congress envisioned the **Freedmen's Bureau,** as it came to be called, as a multipurpose agency to provide social, educational, and economic services, advice, and protection to former slaves and destitute white southerners. The bureau marked the federal government's first foray into social welfare legislation. Congress also authorized the bureau to rent confiscated and abandoned farmland to freedmen in 40-acre plots, with an option to buy. This auspicious beginning belied the great disappointments that lay ahead.

Freedmen's Bureau Agency established by Congress in March 1865 to provide social, educational, and economic services, advice, and protection to former slaves and destitute whites; lasted seven years.

Read the Document at **www.myhistorylab.com** *The Freedmen's Bureau Bill (1865)*

Education

The greatest success of the Freedmen's Bureau was in education. The bureau coordinated more than fifty northern philanthropic and religious groups, which, in turn, established 3,000 freedmen's schools in the South, serving 150,000 men, women, and children.

Initially, single young women from the Northeast comprised much of the teaching force. By 1871, black teachers outnumbered white teachers in the "colored" schools. The financial troubles of northern missionary societies and white northerners' declining interest in the freedmen's condition opened opportunities for black teachers. Support for them came from black churches, especially the African Methodist Episcopal (AME) Church.

Watch the Video at **www.myhistorylab.com** *The Schools that the Civil War and Reconstruction Created*

At the end of the Civil War, only about 10 percent of black southerners were literate, compared with more than 70 percent of white southerners. Within a decade, black literacy had risen above 30 percent. Joseph Wilson, a former slave, attributed the rise to "this longing of ours for freedom of the mind as well as the body."

Some black southerners went on to one of the thirteen colleges established by the American Missionary Association and black and white churches. Between 1860 and 1880 more than 1,000 black southerners earned college degrees at institutions still serving students today, such as Howard University in Washington, DC, Fisk University in Nashville, Hampton Institute (now University), Tuskegee Institute, and Biddle Institute (now Johnson C. Smith University) in Charlotte.

QUICK REVIEW

Freedom and Education

- The Freedmen's Bureau established 3,000 freedmen's schools.
- 1865–1875: Black literacy rises from 10 to 30 percent.
- 1860–1880: 1,000 black southerners earn college degrees.

The Freedmen's Bureau, northern churches, and missionary societies established more than 3,000 schools, attended by some 150,000 men, women, and children in the years after the Civil War. At first, mostly young white women from the Northeast staffed these schools.

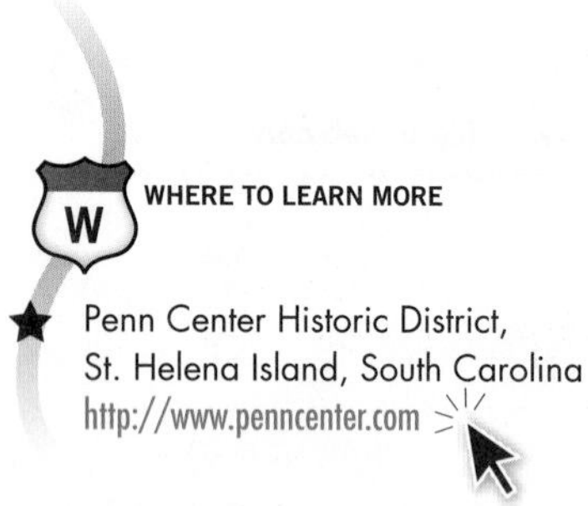

WHERE TO LEARN MORE

Penn Center Historic District, St. Helena Island, South Carolina
http://www.penncenter.com

Pursuing freedom of the mind involved challenges beyond those of learning to read and write. Many white southerners condemned efforts at "Negro improvement." They viewed the time spent on education as wasted, forcing the former slaves to catch their lessons in bits and pieces between work, often by candlelight or on Sundays. White southerners also harassed white female teachers, questioning their morals and threatening people who rented rooms to them. After the Freedmen's Bureau folded in 1872 and many of the northern societies that supported freedmen's education collapsed or cut back their involvement, education for black southerners became more haphazard.

Read the **Document**

at **www.myhistorylab.com**
Charlotte Forten, Life on the Sea Islands

"Forty Acres and a Mule"

Although education was important to the freed slaves in their quest for civic equality, land ownership offered them the promise of economic independence. For generations, black people had worked southern farms and had received nothing for their labor.

An overwhelmingly agricultural people, freedmen looked to farm ownership as a key element in their transition from slavery to freedom. "Gib us our own land and we take care of ourselves," a Charleston freedman asserted to a northern visitor in 1865. "But without land, de ole massas can hire or starve us, as dey please." Even before the war's end, rumors circulated through black communities in the South that the government would provide each black family with 40 acres and a mule. These rumors were fueled by General William T. Sherman's **Field Order No. 15** in January 1865, which set aside a vast swath of abandoned land along the South Atlantic coast from the Charleston area to northern Florida for grants of up to 40 acres. The Freedmen's Bureau likewise raised expectations when it was initially authorized to rent 40-acre plots of confiscated or abandoned land to freedmen.

Field Order No. 15 Order by General William T. Sherman in January 1865 to set aside abandoned land along the southern Atlantic coast for forty-acre grants to freedmen, rescinded by President Andrew Johnson later that year.

By June 1865, about 40,000 former slaves had settled on Sherman land along the southeastern coast. In 1866, Congress passed the **Southern Homestead Act,** giving black people preferential access to public lands in five southern states. Two years later, the Republican government of South Carolina initiated a land-redistribution program financed by the sale of state bonds. The state used proceeds from the bond sales to purchase farmland, which it then resold to freedmen, who paid for it with state-funded long-term low-interest loans. By the late 1870s, more than 14,000 African American families had taken advantage of this program.

Southern Homestead Act Largely unsuccessful law passed in 1866 that gave black people preferential access to public lands in five southern states.

Land ownership did not ensure financial success. Most black-owned farms were small and on marginal land. The value of these farms in 1880 was roughly half that of white-owned farms. Black farmers also had trouble obtaining credit to purchase or expand their holdings. A lifetime of fieldwork left some freedmen without the managerial skills to operate a farm. The hostility of white neighbors also played a role in thwarting black aspirations.

The vast majority of former slaves, however, especially those in the Lower South, never fulfilled their dreams of land ownership. Rumors to the contrary, the federal government never intended to implement a land-redistribution program in the South. General Sherman viewed his field order as a temporary measure to support freedmen for the remainder of the war. President Andrew Johnson nullified the order in September 1865, returning confiscated land to its former owners. Even Republican supporters of black land ownership questioned the constitutionality of seizing privately owned real estate. Most of the land-redistribution programs that emerged after the war, including government-sponsored programs, required black farmers to have capital. But in the impoverished postwar economy of the South, it was difficult for them to acquire it.

Republican Party rhetoric of the 1850s extolled the virtues and dignity of free labor over the degradation of slave labor. Free labor usually meant working for a wage or under some other contractual arrangement. After the war, many white northerners envisioned former slaves assuming the status of free laborers, not necessarily of independent landowners.

Most of the officials of the Freedmen's Bureau shared these views and therefore saw reviving the southern economy as a higher priority than helping former slaves acquire farms. They wanted both to get the crop in the field and start the South on the road to a free labor system. Thus, they encouraged freedmen to work for their former masters under contract and to postpone their quest for land.

Read the **Document** at **www.myhistorylab.com**
Clinton B. Fisk, "Plain Counsels for Freedmen" (1865)

At first, agents of the Freedmen's Bureau supervised labor contracts between former slaves and masters. But after 1867, bureau surveillance declined. Agents assumed that both black laborers and white landowners had become accustomed to the mutual obligations of contracts. The bureau, however, underestimated the power of white landowners to coerce favorable terms or to ignore those they did not like. Contracts implied a mutuality that most planters could not accept in their relations with former slaves.

Read the **Document** at **www.myhistorylab.com**
A Sharecrop Contract (1882)

By the late 1870s, most former slaves in the rural South had been drawn into a subservient position in a new labor system called **sharecropping.** The premise of this system was relatively simple: The landlord furnished the sharecroppers with a house, a plot of land to work, seed, some farm animals, and farm implements and advanced them credit at a store the landlord typically owned. In exchange, the sharecroppers promised the landlord a share of their crop, usually one-half. The croppers kept the proceeds from the sale of the other half to pay off their debts at the store and save or spend as they and their families saw fit. In theory, a sharecropper could save enough to secure economic independence.

sharecropping Labor system that evolved during and after Reconstruction whereby landowners furnished laborers with a house, farm animals, and tools and advanced credit in exchange for a share of the laborers' crop.

But white landlords perceived black independence as both contradictory and subversive. With landlords keeping the accounts at the store, black sharecroppers found that the proceeds from their share of the crop never left them very far ahead. Some found themselves in perpetual debt and worked as virtual slaves. Not all white landlords cheated their tenants, but given the sharecroppers' innocence regarding accounting methods and crop pricing, the temptation to do so was great.

W
WHERE TO LEARN MORE
Levi Jordan Plantation, Brazoria County, Texas
http://www.webarchaeology.com

Migration to Cities

Even before the hope of land ownership faded, African Americans looked for alternatives to secure their personal and economic independence. Before the war, the city had offered slaves and free black people a measure of freedom unknown in the rural South. After the war, African Americans moved to cities to find families, seek work, escape the tedium and supervision of farm life, or simply to test their right to move about.

Between 1860 and 1870, the African American population in every major southern city rose significantly. In Atlanta, for example, black people accounted for one in five residents in 1860 and nearly one in two by 1870.

Once in the city, freedmen had to find a home and a job. They usually settled on the outskirts of town, where building codes did not apply. Rather than developing one large ghetto, as happened in many northern cities, black southerners lived in small concentrations in and around cities. Sometimes armed with a letter of reference from their former masters, black people went door to door to seek employment. Many found work serving white families, as guards, laundresses, or maids, for very low wages. Both skilled and unskilled laborers found work rebuilding war-torn cities like Atlanta.

Most rural black southerners, however, worked as unskilled laborers. In both Atlanta and Nashville, black people comprised more than 75 percent of the unskilled workforce in 1870. Their wages were at or below subsistence level. A black laborer in Richmond admitted to a journalist in 1870 that he had difficulty making ends meet on $1.50 a day. "It's right hard," he reported. "I have to pay $15 a month rent, and only two little rooms." His family survived because his wife took in laundry, while her mother watched the children. Considering the laborer's struggle, the journalist wondered, "Were not your people better off in slavery?" The man replied, "Oh, no sir! We're a heap better off now. . . . We're men now, but when our masters had us we was only change in their pockets."

The black church was the center of African American life in the postwar urban South. Most black churches were founded after the Civil War, but some, such as the First African Baptist Church in Richmond, shown here in an 1874 engraving, traced their origins to before 1861.

Faith and Freedom

Religious faith framed and inspired the efforts of African Americans to test their freedom on the farm and in the city. White southerners used religion to transform the Lost Cause from a shattering defeat to a premonition of a greater destiny. Black southerners, in contrast, saw emancipation in biblical terms as the beginning of an exodus from bondage to the Promised Land.

Some black churches in the postwar South had originated during the slavery era, but most split from white-dominated congregations after the war. White churchgoers deplored the expressive style of black worship, and black churchgoers were uncomfortable in congregations that treated them as inferiors. A separate church also reduced white surveillance.

The church became a primary focus of African American life. It gave black people the opportunity to hone skills in self-government and administration that white-dominated society denied them. Within the supportive confines of the congregation, they could assume leadership positions, render important decisions, deal with financial matters, and engage in politics. The church also operated as an educational institution. Local governments, especially in rural areas, rarely constructed public schools for black people; churches often served that function.

GLOBAL CONNECTIONS

Emancipation and Freedom in the United States and Russia

Tsar Alexander II (1855–1881) freed Russia's serfs in 1861, two years before Abraham Lincoln's Emancipation Proclamation. Although Russian serfs had more rights than American slaves, both were tied to the land and to their landlords/masters. The liberation of the serfs was part of a broader reform plan designed to help modernize Russia.

On becoming tsar in 1855, Alexander II had relaxed the speech, travel, and press restrictions imposed by his predecessors, resulting in an influx of Western ideas into Russia. These ideas helped create widespread public support for the liberation of the serfs. The tsar couched his emancipation proclamation in the ideals of God and country, but its origin lay primarily in Russia's economic aspirations and the tsar's political strategy. While most Americans perceived their liberated slaves as forming an agricultural working class, Alexander made land ownership one of the major attractions of emancipation. The government divided farms equally between the landlords and the former serfs, compensating the owners for the divided property.

In theory at least, Russian serfs seemed in a better position than the southern freedmen to secure economic independence, given the land they received. One Russian official exulted, "The people are erect and transformed; the look, the walk, the speech, everything is changed." But the Russian serfs found their economic situation little improved. The land chosen for redistribution was marginal, and redistribution came with a major catch: The former serfs were required to repay the state on the installment plan. Given the quality of the land, the relatively high interest rates attached to the loans, and the vast numbers of serfs and their families, repayment was unrealistic even in the long term. To ensure that the former serfs would pay up, the tsar allowed local governments to keep the peasants on their land until they fulfilled their financial obligations. In other words, they were as much tied to the land after emancipation as before. And, as a method to improve the quality of agricultural cultivation, the multiplicity of small plots and impoverished peasants was also a failure.

As in the United States, violence marred the transition from bondage to freedom. Rebellions flared in several parts of Russia, but the tsar's armies put these uprisings down quickly. Some of the former serfs managed to escape to towns and cities and become part of the growing laboring class, much as freedmen went to southern cities. In the cities, both former serfs and slaves came closer to the free-labor ideal posited but not supported by their respective governments. In rural areas, reform broke down through a lack of planning and a failure of will.

- After emancipation, did the Russian serf or the American slave have a better opportunity to establish economic independence?

QUICK REVIEW

Black Churches

- Many African Americans found inspiration and courage in their religious faith.
- Most black churches split from white-dominated congregations after the war.
- Black churches created a variety of organizations that served the black community.

The desire to read the Bible inspired thousands of former slaves to attend the church school. The church also spawned other organizations that served the black community, such as burial societies, Masonic lodges, temperance groups, trade unions, and drama clubs. African Americans took great pride in their churches, which became visible measures of their progress. The church and the congregation were a cohesive force in black communities.

The efforts of former slaves in the classroom, on the farm, in cities, and in the churches reflect the enthusiasm and expectations with which black southerners greeted freedom, raising the hopes of those who came to help them, such as Frances Harper. But the majority of white southerners were unwilling to see those expectations fulfilled. For this reason, African Americans could not secure the fruits of their emancipation without the support and protection of the federal government. The issue of freedom was therefore inextricably linked to the other great issue of the era, the rejoining of the Confederacy to the Union, as expressed in federal Reconstruction policy.

FEDERAL RECONSTRUCTION, 1865–1870

HOW DID Presidential Reconstruction differ from Congressional Reconstruction?

When the Civil War ended in 1865, no acceptable blueprint existed for reconstituting the Union. President Lincoln believed that a majority of white southerners were Unionists at heart, and that they could and should undertake the task of reconstruction. He favored a conciliatory policy toward the South in order, as he put it in one of his last letters, "to restore the Union, so as to make it . . . a Union of hearts and hands as well as of States." He counted on the loyalists to be fair with respect to the rights of the former slaves.

As early as 1863, Lincoln had proposed to readmit a seceding state if 10 percent of its prewar voters took an oath of loyalty to the Union, and it prohibited slavery in a new state constitution. But this Ten Percent Plan did not require states to grant equal civil and political rights to former slaves, and many Republicans in Congress thought it was not stringent enough. In 1864, a group of them responded with the Wade-Davis Bill, which required a majority of a state's prewar voters to pledge their loyalty to the Union and demanded guarantees of black equality before the law. The bill was passed at the end of a congressional session, but Lincoln kept it from becoming law by refusing to sign it (an action known as a "pocket veto"). Lincoln, of course, died before he could implement a Reconstruction plan.

QUICK REVIEW

Johnson's Reconstruction Plan

- Johnson extended pardons and property rights to southerners who swore an oath of allegiance.
- Prominent Confederates and the very wealthy had to appeal to the president for a pardon.
- His plan had nothing to say about the voting and civil rights of former slaves.

The controversy over the plans introduced during the war reflected two obstacles to Reconstruction that would continue to plague the ruling Republicans after the war. First, neither the Constitution nor legal precedent offered any guidance on whether the president or Congress should take the lead on Reconstruction policy. Second, there was no agreement on what that policy should be. Proposals requiring various preconditions for readmitting a state, loyalty oaths, new constitutions with certain specific provisions, guarantees of freedmen's rights, all provoked vigorous debate.

President Andrew Johnson, some conservative Republicans, and most Democrats believed that because the Constitution made no mention of secession, the southern states had been in rebellion but had never left the Union, and therefore that there was no need for a formal process to readmit them. Moderate and radical Republicans disagreed, arguing that the defeated states had forfeited their rights. Moderates and radicals parted company, however, on the conditions necessary for readmission to the Union. The radicals wanted to treat the former Confederate states as territories, or "conquered provinces," subject to congressional legislation. Moderates wanted to grant the seceding states more autonomy and limit federal intervention in their affairs while they satisfied the conditions of readmission. Neither group held a majority in Congress, and legislators sometimes changed their positions (see the Overview table, Contrasting Views of Reconstruction).

PRESIDENTIAL RECONSTRUCTION, 1865–1867

When the Civil War ended in April 1865, Congress was not in session and would not reconvene until December. Thus, the responsibility for developing a Reconstruction policy initially fell on Andrew Johnson, who succeeded to the presidency upon Lincoln's assassination. Most northerners, including many Republicans, approved Johnson's Reconstruction plan when he unveiled it in May 1865. Johnson extended pardons and restored property rights, except in slaves, to southerners who swore an oath of allegiance to the Union and the Constitution. Southerners who had held prominent posts in the Confederacy, however, and those with more than $20,000 in taxable property, had to petition the president directly for a pardon. The plan said nothing about the voting rights or civil rights of former slaves.

Northern Democrats applauded the plan's silence on these issues and its promise of a quick restoration of the southern states to the Union. They expected the southern states to favor their party and expand its political power. Republicans approved the plan because it restored property rights to white southerners, although some wanted it to provide for black suffrage. Republicans also hoped that Johnson's conciliatory terms might attract some white southerners to the Republican Party.

On the two great issues of freedom and reunion, white southerners quickly demonstrated their eagerness to reverse the results of the Civil War. Although most states accepted President Johnson's modest requirements, several objected to one or more of them. Mississippi and Texas refused to ratify the Thirteenth Amendment, which abolished slavery. Alabama accepted only parts of the amendment. South Carolina declined to nullify its secession ordinance. No southern state authorized black voting. When Johnson ordered special congressional elections in the South in the fall of 1865, the all-white electorate returned many prominent Confederate leaders to office.

Watch the **Video** at **www.myhistorylab.com** *Reconstruction in Texas*

In late 1865, the newly elected southern state legislatures revised their antebellum slave codes. The updated **black codes** allowed local officials to arrest black people who could not document employment and residence or who were "disorderly" and sentence them to forced labor on farms or road crews. The codes also restricted black people to certain occupations, barred them from jury duty, and forbade them to possess firearms. Apprenticeship laws permitted judges to take black children from parents who could not, in the judges' view, adequately support them. Given the widespread poverty in the South in 1865, the law could apply to almost any freed black family. Northerners looking for contrition in the South found no sign of it. Worse, President Johnson did not seem perturbed about this turn of events.

black codes Laws passed by states and municipalities denying many rights of citizenship to free blacks after the Civil War.

The Republican-dominated Congress reconvened in December 1865 in a belligerent mood. When the radicals, who comprised nearly half of the Republican Party's strength in Congress, could not unite behind a program, their moderate colleagues took the first step toward a congressional Reconstruction plan. The moderates shared the radicals' desire to protect the former slaves' civil rights. But they would not support land-redistribution schemes or punitive measures against prominent Confederates, and disagreed on extending voting rights to the freedmen. The moderates' first measure, passed in early 1866, extended the life of the Freedmen's Bureau and authorized it to punish state officials who failed to extend equal civil rights to black citizens. But President Johnson vetoed the legislation.

Read the **Document** at **www.myhistorylab.com** *The Mississippi Black Code (1865)*

Undeterred, Congress passed the Civil Rights Act of 1866 in direct response to the black codes. The act specified the civil rights to which all U.S. citizens were entitled. In creating a category of national citizenship with rights that superseded state laws, the act changed federal-state relations (and in the process overturned the *Dred Scott* decision). President Johnson vetoed the act, but it became law when Congress mustered a two-thirds majority to override his veto, the first time in American history that Congress passed major legislation over a president's veto.

Read the **Document** at **www.myhistorylab.com** *The Civil Rights Act of 1866*

To keep freedmen's rights safe from presidential vetoes, state legislatures, and federal courts, the Republican-dominated Congress moved to incorporate some of the provisions of the 1866 Civil Rights Act into the Constitution. The **Fourteenth Amendment,** which Congress passed in June 1866, addressed the issues of civil and voting rights. It guaranteed every citizen equality before the law. The two key sections of the amendment prohibited states from violating the civil rights of their citizens, thus outlawing the black codes, and gave states the choice of enfranchising black people or losing representation in Congress. Some radical Republicans expressed

Fourteenth Amendment Passed by Congress in 1866, guaranteed every citizen equality before the law by prohibiting states from violating the civil rights of their citizens, thus outlawing the black codes.

"Selling a Freeman to Pay His Fine at Monticello, Florida." *This 1867 engraving shows how the black codes of the early Reconstruction era reduced former slaves to virtually their pre–Civil War status. Scenes like this convinced northerners that the white South was unrepentant and prompted congressional Republicans to devise their own Reconstruction plans.*

Read the **Document**
at **www.myhistorylab.com**
The Fourteenth Amendment (1868)

disappointment that the amendment, in a reflection of northern ambivalence, failed to give the vote to black people outright.

The amendment also disappointed advocates of woman suffrage, for the first time using the word *male* in the Constitution to define who could vote. Susan B. Anthony, who had campaigned for the abolition of slavery before the war and helped mount a petition drive that collected 400,000 signatures for the Thirteenth Amendment, founded the American Equal Rights Association in 1866 with her colleagues to push for woman suffrage at the state level.

The Fourteenth Amendment had little immediate impact on the South. Although enforcement of black codes diminished, white violence against black people increased. In the 1870s, several decisions by the U.S. Supreme Court weakened the amendment's provisions. Eventually, however, it would play a major role in securing the civil rights of African Americans.

President Johnson encouraged southern white intransigence by openly denouncing the Fourteenth Amendment. In August 1866, at the start of the congressional election campaign, he undertook an unprecedented tour of key northern states to sell his message of sectional

AMERICAN VIEWS

Mississippi's 1865 Black Codes

White southerners, especially landowners and business owners, feared that emancipation would produce a labor crisis; freedmen, they expected, would either refuse to work or strike hard bargains with their former masters. White southerners also recoiled from the prospect of having to treat their former slaves as full social equals. Thus, beginning in late 1865, several southern states, including Mississippi, enacted laws designed to control black labor, mobility, and social status. Northerners responded to the codes as a provocation, a bold move to deny the result of the war and its consequences.

- **How** did the black codes fit into President Andrew Johnson's Reconstruction program?
- **Some** northerners charged that the black codes were a backdoor attempt at reestablishing slavery. Do you agree?
- **If** southern states enacted black codes to stabilize labor relations, how did the provisions below effect that objective?

From an Act to Confer Civil Rights on Freedmen, and for Other Purposes

Section 1. All freedmen, free negroes and mulattoes may sue and be sued, implead and be impleaded, in all the courts of law and equity of this State, and may acquire personal property, and choose in action, by descent or purchase, and may dispose of the same in the same manner and to the same extent that white persons may: Provided, That the provisions of this section shall not be so construed as to allow any freedman, free negro or mulatto to rent or lease any lands or tenements except in incorporated cities or towns, in which places the corporate authorities shall control the same.

Section 7. Every civil officer shall, and every person may, arrest and carry back to his or her legal employer any freedman, free negro, or mulatto who shall have quit the service of his or her employer before the expiration of his or her term of service without good cause; and said officer and person shall be entitled to receive for arresting and carrying back every deserting employee aforesaid the sum of five dollars, and ten cents per mile from the place of arrest to the place of delivery; and the same shall be paid by the employer, and held as a set off for so much against the wages of said deserting employee: Provided, that said arrested party, after being so returned, may appeal to the justice of the peace or member of the board of police of the county, who, on notice to the alleged employer, shall try summarily whether said appellant is legally employed by the alleged employer, and has good cause to quit said employer. Either party shall have the right of appeal to the county court, pending which the alleged deserter shall be remanded to the alleged employer or otherwise disposed of, as shall be right and just; and the decision of the county court shall be final.

From an Act to Amend the Vagrant Laws of the State

Section 2. All freedmen, free negroes and mulattoes in this State, over the age of eighteen years, found on the second Monday in January, 1866, or thereafter, with no lawful employment or business, or found unlawfully assembling themselves together, either in the day or night time, and all white persons assembling themselves with freedmen, Free negroes or mulattoes, or usually associating with freedmen, free negroes or mulattoes, on terms of equality, or living in adultery or fornication with a freed woman, freed negro or mulatto, shall be deemed vagrants, and on conviction thereof shall be fined in a sum not exceeding, in the case of a freedman, free negro or mulatto, fifty dollars, and a white man two hundred dollars, and imprisonment at the discretion of the court, the free negro not exceeding ten days, and the white man not exceeding six months.

Source: "Laws in Relation to Freedmen," 39 Congress, 2 Session, Senate Executive Document 6, Freedmen's Affairs, 182–86.

reconciliation to the public. Although listeners appreciated Johnson's desire for peace, they questioned his claims of southern white loyalty to the Union. The president's diatribes against the Republican Congress won him followers in those northern states with a reservoir of opposition to black suffrage. But the tone and manner of his campaign offended many as undignified. In the November elections, the Democrats suffered embarrassing defeats in the North as Republicans managed better than two-thirds majorities in both the House and Senate, sufficient to override presidential vetoes. Radical Republicans, joined by moderate colleagues buoyed by the election results and revolted by the president's and the South's intransigence, seized the initiative when Congress reconvened.

Congressional Reconstruction, 1867–1870

Congressional Reconstruction Name given to the period 1867–1870 when the Republican-dominated Congress controlled Reconstruction era policy.

Tenure of Office Act Passed by the Republican controlled Congress in 1867 to limit presidential interference with its policies, the act prohibited the president from removing certain officeholders without the Senate's consent. President Andrew Johnson, angered at what he believed an unconstitutional attack on presidential authority, deliberately violated the act by firing Secretary of War Edwin M. Stanton. The House responded by approving articles of impeachment against a president for the first time in American history.

The radicals' first salvo in their attempt to take control of Reconstruction occurred with the passing over President Johnson's veto of the Military Reconstruction Acts. The measures, passed in March 1867, inaugurated a period known as **Congressional Reconstruction** or Radical Reconstruction. With the exception of Tennessee, the only southern state that had ratified the Fourteenth Amendment and been readmitted to the Union, Congress divided the former Confederate states into five military districts, each headed by a general (see Map 16–1). The commanders' first order of business was to conduct voter-registration campaigns to enroll black people and bar white people who had held office before the Civil War and supported the Confederacy. The eligible voters would then elect delegates to a state convention to write a new constitution that guaranteed universal manhood suffrage. Once a majority of eligible voters ratified the new constitution and the Fourteenth Amendment, their state would be eligible for readmission to the Union.

The Reconstruction Acts fulfilled the radicals' three major objectives. First, they secured the freedmen's right to vote. Second, they made it likely that southern states would be run by Republican regimes that would enforce the new constitutions, protect former slaves' rights, and maintain the Republican majority in Congress. Finally, they set standards for readmission that required the South to accept the preeminence of the federal government and the end of slavery. These measures seemed appropriate in view of the war's outcome and the freedmen's status, but white southerners, especially those barred from participation, perceived the state and local governments constructed upon the new basis as illegitimate. Many southern whites would never acknowledge the right of these governments and their officials to rule over them.

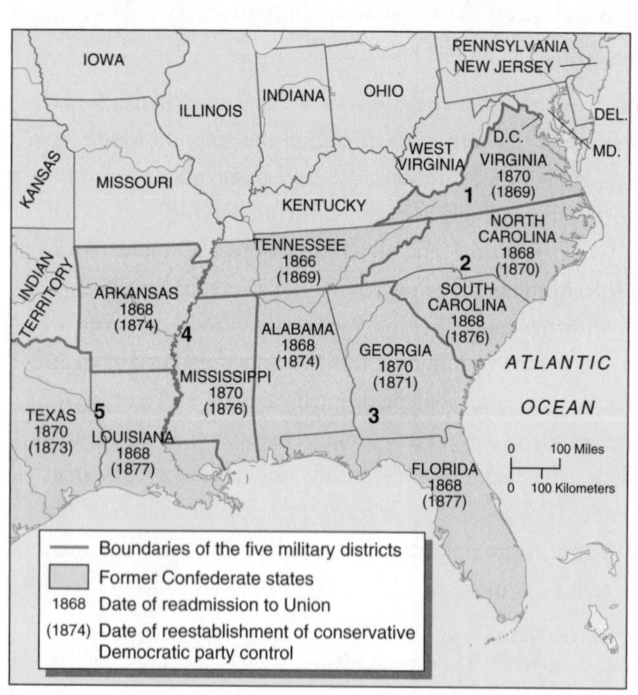

MAP 16–1 **Congressional Reconstruction, 1865–1877** When Congress wrested control of Reconstruction policy from President Andrew Johnson, it divided the South into the five military districts depicted here. The commanding generals for each district held the authority both to hold elections and to decide who could vote.

What does the division of the South into military districts that included more than one state tell us about how northern Republicans saw the former Confederacy?

To limit presidential interference with their policies, Republicans passed the **Tenure of Office Act**, prohibiting the president from removing certain officeholders without the Senate's consent. Johnson, angered at what he believed was an unconstitutional attack on presidential authority, deliberately violated the act by firing Secretary of War Edwin M. Stanton, a leading radical, in February 1868. The House responded by approving articles of impeachment against a president for the first time in American history. That set the stage for the next step prescribed by the Constitution: a Senate trial to determine whether the president should be removed from office.

Johnson had indeed violated the Tenure of Office Act, a measure of dubious constitutionality even to some Republicans, but enough Republicans felt that his actions fell short of the "high crimes and misdemeanors" standard set by the Constitution for dismissal from office. Seven Republicans deserted their party, and Johnson was acquitted. The seven Republicans who voted against their party did so not out of respect for Johnson but because they feared that a conviction would damage the office of the presidency and violate the constitutional separation of powers. The outcome weakened the radicals and eased the way for Grant, a moderate Republican, to gain the party's nomination for president in 1868.

The Republicans viewed the 1868 presidential election as a referendum on Congressional Reconstruction. They supported black suffrage in the South but equivocated on allowing African Americans to vote in the North. Black northerners could vote in only eight of the twenty-two northern states, and between 1865 and 1869, white northerners rejected equal suffrage referendums in eight of eleven states. Republicans "waved the bloody shirt," reminding voters of Democratic disloyalty, the sacrifices of war, and the peace only Republicans could redeem. Democrats denounced Congressional Reconstruction as federal tyranny and, in openly racist appeals, warned white voters that a Republican victory would mean black rule. Grant won the election, but his margin of victory was uncomfortably narrow. Reflecting growing ambivalence in the North over issues of race and federal authority, New York's Horatio Seymour, the Democratic presidential nominee, probably carried a majority of the nation's white vote. Black voters' overwhelming support for Grant probably provided his margin of victory.

The Republicans retained a strong majority in both houses of Congress and managed to pass another major piece of Reconstruction legislation, the **Fifteenth Amendment,** in February 1869. In response to growing concerns about voter fraud and violence against freedmen, the amendment guaranteed the right of American men to vote, regardless of race. Although the amendment provided a loophole allowing states to restrict the right to vote based on literacy or property qualifications, it was nonetheless a milestone. It made the right to vote perhaps the most distinguishing characteristic of U.S. citizenship.

The Fifteenth Amendment allowed states to keep the franchise a male prerogative, angering many in the woman suffrage movement more than had the Fourteenth Amendment. The resulting controversy severed the ties between the movement and Republican politics. Susan B. Anthony broke with her abolitionist colleagues and opposed the amendment. In an appeal brimming with ethnic and racial animosity, Elizabeth Cady Stanton warned that "if you do not wish the lower orders of Chinese, African, Germans and Irish, with their low ideas of womanhood to make laws for you and your daughters . . . awake to the danger . . . and demand that woman, too, shall be represented in the government!" Such language created a major rift in the nascent women's movement.

The Democratic Party ran an openly racist presidential campaign in 1868. This pro-Republican drawing by noted cartoonist Thomas Nast includes three Democratic constituencies: former Confederate soldiers (note the "CSA" on the belt buckle); the Irish or immigrant vote (note the almost simian depiction of the Irishman), and the well-dressed Democratic presidential candidate, Horatio Seymour, sporting a "5th Avenue" button and waving a wallet full of bills, a reference to the corrupt Democratic politics in New York City. The three have their feet on an African American soldier. In the background note the "colored orphan asylum" and "southern school" ablaze, and the lynching of black children.

Southern Republican Governments, 1867–1870

Away from Washington, the first order of business for the former Confederacy was to draft state constitutions. The documents embodied progressive principles new to the South. They mandated the election of numerous local and state offices. Self-perpetuating local elites could no longer appoint themselves or cronies to powerful positions. The constitutions committed southern states, many for the first time, to public education. Lawmakers enacted a variety of reforms, including social welfare, penal reform, legislative reapportionment, and universal manhood suffrage.

The Republican regimes that gained control in southern states promoted vigorous state government and the protection of civil and voting rights. Three Republican constituencies supported these governments: native whites, native blacks, and northern transplants. The small native white group was mostly made up of yeomen farmers. Residing mainly in the upland regions

Fifteenth Amendment Passed by Congress in 1869, guaranteed the right of American men to vote, regardless of race.

QUICK REVIEW

Radical Republican Objectives

- Secure freedmen's right to vote.
- Make it likely that southern states would have Republican governments.
- Require the South to accept preeminence of the federal government and the end of slavery.

OVERVIEW Contrasting Views of Reconstruction: President and Congress

Politician or Group	Policy on Former Slaves	Policy on Readmission of Former Confederate States
President Johnson	Opposed to black suffrage	Maintained that rebellious states were already readmitted
	Silent on protection of black civil rights Opposed to land redistribution	Granted pardons and restoration of property to all who swore allegiance to the United States
Radical Republicans	Favored black suffrage	Favored treating rebellious states as territories and establishing military districts*
	Favored protection of black civil rights Favored land redistribution	Favored limiting franchise to black people and loyal white people
Moderate Republicans	Favored black suffrage*	Favored some restrictions on white suffrage**
	Favored protection of civil rights	Favored requiring states to meet various requirements before being readmitted*
	Opposed land redistribution	Split on military rule

*After 1866.
**True of most but not all members of the group.

QUICK REVIEW

The Tenure of Office Act and Johnson's Impeachment

- Act prohibited the president from removing certain officeholders without the Senate's consent.
- Johnson deliberately violated the act in February 1868.
- Johnson escaped impeachment by one vote.

scalawags Southern whites, mainly small landowning farmers and well-off merchants and planters, who supported the southern Republican Party during Reconstruction.

carpetbaggers Northern transplants to the South, many of whom were Union soldiers who stayed in the South after the war.

Read the **Document**

at **www.myhistorylab.com**
From Then to Now Online: African American Voting Rights in the South

Read the **Document**

at **www.myhistorylab.com**
"Address of the Colored Citizens of Norfolk, Virginia" (1865)

of the South and long ignored by lowland planters and merchants in state government, they were left devastated by the war. They struggled to keep their land and hoped for an easing of credit and for debt-stay laws to help them escape foreclosure. They wanted public schools for their children and good roads to get their crops to market. Some urban merchants and large planters also called themselves Republicans. They were attracted to the party's emphasis on economic development, especially railroad construction, and would become prominent in Republican leadership after 1867, forming a majority of the party's elected officials. Collectively, opponents called these native white southerners **scalawags.**

Northern transplants, or **carpetbaggers,** as many southern whites called them, constituted a second and smaller group of southern Republicans. Thousands of northerners came south during and after the war. Many were Union soldiers who simply enjoyed the climate and perhaps married a local woman. Most were drawn by economic opportunity. Land was cheap and the price of cotton high. Although most carpetbaggers had supported the Republican Party before they moved south, few became politically active until the cotton economy nosedived in 1866. Financial concerns were not all that motivated carpetbaggers to enter politics; some hoped to aid the freedmen.

Carpetbaggers never comprised more than 2 percent of any state's population. Most white southerners viewed them as an alien presence, instruments of a hated occupying force. Because many of them tended to support extending political and civil rights to black southerners, carpetbaggers were also often at odds with their fellow white Republicans, the scalawags.

African Americans constituted the Republican Party's largest southern constituency. In three states, South Carolina, Mississippi, and Louisiana, they also constituted the majority of eligible voters. They viewed the franchise as the key to civic equality and economic opportunity and demanded an active role in party and government affairs.

Black people began to take part in southern politics even before the end of the Civil War, especially in cities occupied by Union forces. In February 1865, black people in Norfolk, Virginia, gathered to demand a say in the new government that Union supporters were forming in that portion of the state. In April, they created the Colored Monitor Union club, modeled after regular Republican Party organizations in northern cities, called **Union Leagues.** They demanded "the right of universal suffrage" for "all loyal men, without distinction of color." Black people in other southern cities held similar meetings, seeking inclusion in the democratic process to protect their freedom. Despite white threats, black southerners thronged to Union League meetings in 1867, even forging interracial alliances in states such as North Carolina and Alabama. Focusing on political education and recruitment, the leagues successfully mobilized black voters. In 1867, more than 90 percent of eligible black voters across the South turned out for elections. Black women, even though they could not vote, also played a role. During the 1868 presidential campaign, for example, black maids and cooks in the South wore buttons touting the candidacy of the Republican presidential nominee, Ulysses S. Grant.

Union Leagues Republican Party organizations in northern cities that became an important organizing device among freedmen in southern cities after 1865.

See the **Map**
at **www.myhistorylab.com**
Congressional Reconstruction

Black southerners were not content just to vote; they also demanded political office. White Republican leaders in the South often took the black vote for granted. But on several occasions after 1867, black people threatened to run independent candidates, support rival Democrats, or simply stay home unless they were represented among Republican nominees. These demands brought them some success. The number of southern black congressmen in the U.S. House of Representatives increased from two in 1869 to seven in 1873, and more than 600 African Americans, most of them former slaves from plantation counties, were elected to southern state legislatures between 1867 and 1877.

White fears that black officeholders would enact vengeful legislation proved unfounded. African Americans generally did not promote race-specific legislation. Rather, they supported measures such as debt relief and state funding for education that benefited all poor and working-class people. Like all politicians, however, black officials in southern cities sought to enact measures beneficial to their constituents, such as roads and sidewalks.

During the first few years of Congressional Reconstruction, Republican governments walked a tightrope, attempting to lure moderate Democrats and unaffiliated white voters into the party without slighting the black vote. They used the lure of patronage power and the attractive salaries that accompanied public office. In 1868, for example, Louisiana's Republican governor, Henry C. Warmoth, appointed white conservatives to state and local offices, which he divided equally between Confederate veterans and black people, and repealed a constitutional provision disfranchising former Confederate officials.

Republicans also gained support by expanding the role of state government to a degree unprecedented in the South. Southern Republican administrations appealed to hard-pressed upland white constituents by prohibiting foreclosure and passing stay laws that allowed farm owners additional time to repay debts. They undertook building programs that benefited black and white citizens, erecting hospitals, schools, and orphanages. Stepping further into social policy than most northern states at the time, Republican governments in the South expanded women's property rights, enacted legislation against child abuse, and required child support from fathers of

"Time Works Wonders." This Thomas Nast cartoon has Jefferson Davis, former president of the Confederacy, dressed as Iago in William Shakespeare's play *Othello*, declaring with considerable anguish, "For that I suspect the Lusty moor [Othello] hath leap'd into my seat: the thought where of doth like a poisonous mineral gnaw my inwards." Indeed, Hiram Revels occupies Davis's old seat in the U.S. Senate representing the state of Mississippi in 1870.

mulatto children. In South Carolina, the Republican government provided medical care for the poor; in Alabama, it provided free legal aid for needy defendants.

Despite these impressive policies, southern Republicans were unable to hold their diverse constituency together. The excesses of some state governments, high taxes, contests over patronage, and conflicts over the relative roles of white and black party members opened rifts in Republican ranks. Patronage triggered intraparty warfare. Every office secured by a Democrat created a disappointed Republican. Class tensions erupted in the party as economic development policies sometimes superseded relief and social service legislation supported by small farmers. The failure of Alabama Republicans to deliver on promises of debt relief and land redistribution eroded the party's support among up-country white voters. There were differences among black voters too. In the Lower South, divisions that had developed in the prewar era between urban, lighter-skinned free black people and darker, rural slaves persisted into the Reconstruction era. In many southern states, black clergy, because of their independence from white support and their important spiritual and educational role, became leaders. But most preached salvation in the next world rather than equality in this one, conceding more to white people than their rank-and-file constituents.

COUNTER-RECONSTRUCTION, 1870–1874

WHAT ROLE did violence play in Counter-Reconstruction?

Republicans might have survived battles over patronage, policy, expenditures, and taxes. But they could not overcome racism and the violence it generated. Racism killed Republican rule in the South because it deepened divisions within the party, encouraged white violence, and eroded support in the North. Southern Democrats discovered that they could use race baiting and racial violence to create solidarity among white people that overrode their economic and class differences. Unity translated into election victories.

Northerners responded to the persistent violence in the South, not with outrage, but with a growing sense of tedium. They came to accept the arguments of white southerners that it was folly to allow black people to vote and hold office, especially since most northern whites would not extend the franchise to African Americans in their own states.

By 1874, Americans were concerned with an array of domestic problems that overshadowed Reconstruction. A serious economic depression left them more preoccupied with survival than racial justice. Corruption convinced many that politics was part of the nation's problems, not a solution to them. With the rest of the nation thus distracted and weary, white southerners reclaimed control of the South.

THE USES OF VIOLENCE

at **www.myhistorylab.com**
Hannah Irwin Describes Ku Klux Klan Ride (Late 1860s)

Racial violence preceded Republican rule. As African Americans moved about, attempted to vote, haggled over labor contracts, and carried arms as part of the occupying Union forces, they tested the patience of white southerners, to whom any black assertion of equality seemed threatening. African Americans were the face of whites' defeat, of their world turned upside down. If the war was about slavery, then here was the visible proof of the Confederacy's defeat. Many white southerners viewed the term "free black" less as a status than as an oxymoron. The restoration of white supremacy meant the restoration of order and civilization, an objective southern whites would pursue with vengeance.

White paramilitary groups were responsible for much of the violence directed against African Americans. Probably the best-known of these groups was the **Ku Klux Klan.** Founded in Tennessee by six Confederate veterans in 1866, the Klan was initially a social club. Within a year, the Klan had spread throughout the South. In 1867, when black people entered politics in large numbers, the Klan unleashed a wave of terror against them. The Klan directed much of its violence toward subverting the electoral process. One historian has estimated that roughly 10 percent of all black

Ku Klux Klan Perhaps the most prominent of the vigilante groups that terrorized black people in the South during the Reconstruction era, founded by Confederate veterans in 1866.

delegates to the 1867 state constitutional conventions in the South became victims of political violence during the next decade.

By 1868, white paramilitary organizations permeated the South. Violence was particularly severe in election years in Louisiana, which had a large and active black electorate. The most serious example of political violence in Louisiana, occurred in Colfax in 1873, when a white Democratic mob attempted to wrest control of local government from Republicans. For three weeks, black defenders held the town against the white onslaught. When the white mob finally broke through, they massacred the remaining black defenders, including those who had surrendered and laid down their weapons. It was the bloodiest peacetime massacre in nineteenth-century America.

The Klan directed violence at African Americans primarily for engaging in political activity. Here, a black man, John Campbell, vainly begs for mercy in Moore County, North Carolina, in August 1871.

Racial violence and the combative reaction it provoked both among black people and Republican administrations energized white voters. Democrats regained power in North Carolina, for example, after the state's Republican governor enraged white voters by calling out the militia to counter white violence during the election of 1870. That same year, the Republican regime in Georgia fell as well.

The federal government responded with a variety of legislation. One example was the Fifteenth Amendment. Another was the Enforcement Act of 1870, which authorized the federal government to appoint supervisors in states that failed to protect voting rights. When violence and intimidation persisted, Congress followed with a second, more sweeping measure, the Ku Klux Klan Act of 1871. This law permitted federal authorities, with military assistance, if necessary, to arrest and prosecute members of groups that denied a citizen's civil rights if state authorities failed to do so. The Klan Act was not successful in curbing racial violence, as the Colfax Massacre in 1873 made vividly clear. But with it, Congress, by claiming the right to override state authority to bring individuals to justice, established a new precedent in federal-state relations.

Read the **Document** at **www.myhistorylab.com**
Albion W. Tourgée, Letter on Ku Klux Klan Activities (1870)

QUICK REVIEW

The Legislative Responses to Political Violence in the South

- 15th Amendment guaranteed the right to vote.
- Enforcement Act of 1870 authorized federal supervision of elections in states that failed to support voting rights.
- Ku Klux Klan Act of 1871 permitted federal prosecution of members of groups that denied citizen's civil rights if state authorities failed to act.

Northern Indifference

The success of political violence after 1871 reflected both a declining commitment on the part of northern Republicans to support southern Republican administrations and a growing indifference of northerners to the major issues of Reconstruction. That northern base grew increasingly skeptical about Reconstruction policy in general and assistance to the freedmen in particular. Northern Republicans looked around their cities and many saw the local political scene infested with unqualified immigrant voters and corruption. New York City's Democratic boss William M. Tweed and his associates bilked the city of an astounding $100 million. When white southerners charged that unqualified blacks and grasping carpetbaggers corrupted the political process in the South, northerners recognized the argument.

Changing perceptions in the North also indicated a convergence of racial views with white southerners. As a radical Republican congressman from Indiana, George W. Julian, admitted in 1865, white northerners "*hate the negro*." They expressed this hatred in their rejection of black suffrage, racial segregation of their African American population, and periodic violence against black residents, such as during the New York Draft Riots of 1863. Northerners' views were bolstered by prevailing scientific theories of race that "proved" blacks' limited capacities and, therefore, unfitness for either the ballot or skilled occupations.

By the early 1870s, northern public opinion had shifted greatly with respect to black suffrage, in part because of the growing concern about the immigrant vote in northern cities; whereas in the late 1860s cartoons and the press depicted newly enfranchised African Americans nobly, later representations were hostile as this caricature of the South Carolina legislature by Thomas Nast demonstrates.

Northerners also grew increasingly wary of federal power. The emerging scandals of the Grant administration, fueled, it seemed, by government subsidies to railroads and other private businesses, demanded a scaling back of federal power and discretion. When white southerners complained about federal meddling, again, they found resonance in the North.

The excesses and alleged abuses of federal power inspired a reform movement among a group of northern Republicans and some Democrats. In addition, business leaders decried the ability of wealthy lobbyists to influence economic decisions. An influential group of intellectuals and opinion makers lamented the inability of politicians to understand "natural" laws, particularly those related to race. And some Republicans joined the reform movement out of fear that Democrats would capitalize on the turmoil in the South and the political scandals in the North to reap huge electoral victories in 1872.

QUICK REVIEW

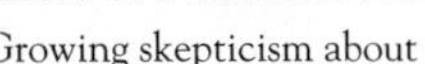

Sources of Northern Indifference

- Growing skepticism about the potential of Reconstruction.
- Convergence of racial views of whites in the North and the South.
- Increased distrust of federal power.

Liberal Republicans and the Election of 1872

Liberal Republicans, as the reformers called themselves, put forward an array of suggestions to improve government and save the Republican Party. They advocated civil service reform to reduce reliance on patronage and the abuses that accompanied office seeking. To limit government and reduce artificial economic stimuli, the reformers called for tariff reduction and an end to federal land grants to railroads. For the South, they recommended a general amnesty for white people and a return to "local self-government" by men of "property and enterprise."

When the Liberals failed to convince other Republicans to adopt their program, they broke with the party. Taking advantage of this split, the Democrats forged an alliance with the Liberals. Together, they nominated journalist Horace Greeley to challenge Ulysses S. Grant for the presidency in the election of 1872. Grant won resoundingly, helped by high turnout among black voters in the South, his continued popularity as a war hero, and Greeley's inept campaign.

Economic Transformation

After 1873, the Republican Party in the South became a liability for the national party, especially as Americans fastened on to economic issues. The major story of the decade would not be equal rights for African Americans, but the changing nature of the American economy. An overextended banking and credit system generated the Panic of 1873 and caused extensive suffering, particularly among working-class Americans. But the depression masked a remarkable economic transformation as the nation moved toward a national industrial economy.

The depression and the economic transformation occupied center stage in the American mentality of the mid-1870s, at least in the North. Most Americans had mentally forsaken Reconstruction long before the Compromise of 1877 made its abandonment a political fact. The sporadic violence against black and white Republicans in the South, and the cries of help from freedmen as their rights and persons were abused by white Democrats, became distant echoes from another era, the era of the Civil War, now commemorated and memorialized, but no longer an active part of the nation's present and future. Of course, for white southerners, the past was not yet past. There was still work to do.

REDEMPTION, 1874–1877

WHY DID the federal government abandon African Americans after 1872?

For southern Democrats, the Republican victory in 1872 underscored the importance of turning out larger numbers of white voters and restricting the black vote. They accomplished these goals over the next four years with a surge in political violence, secure in the knowledge that federal authorities would rarely intervene against them. Preoccupied with corruption and economic crisis and increasingly indifferent, if not hostile, to African American aspirations, most Americans looked the other way. The elections of 1876 confirmed the triumph of white southerners.

Redeemers Southern Democrats who wrested control of governments in the former Confederacy, often through electoral fraud and violence, from Republicans, beginning in 1870.

In a religious metaphor that matched their view of the Civil War as a lost crusade, southern Democrats called their victory "Redemption" and depicted themselves as **Redeemers,** holy warriors who had saved the South from the hell of black Republican rule. Generations of American boys and girls would learn this interpretation of the Reconstruction era, and it would affect race relations for nearly a century.

The Democrats' Violent Resurgence

The violence between 1874 and 1876 differed in several respects from earlier attempts to restore white government by force. Attackers operated more openly and more closely identified themselves with the Democratic Party. Mounted, gray-clad ex-Confederate soldiers flanked Democratic candidates at campaign rallies and "visited" black neighborhoods afterward to discourage black men from voting. With black people intimidated and white people already prepared to vote, election days were typically quiet.

Democrats swept to victory across the South in the 1874 elections. "A perfect reign of terror" redeemed Alabama for the Democrats. The successful appeal to white supremacy inspired a massive white turnout to unseat Republicans in Virginia, Florida (legislature only), and Arkansas. Texas had fallen to the Democrats in 1873. Only South Carolina, Mississippi, and Louisiana, states with large black populations, survived the debacle. But the relentless tide of terror would soon overwhelm them as well.

Democratic leaders in those states announced a "white line" policy, inviting all white men, regardless of party affiliation, to "unite" and redeem the states. They all had the same objective: to eliminate African Americans as a political factor by any means. Black Republicans not only feared for their political future, but also for their lives.

A bold assault occurred in New Orleans in September 1874 when 8,500 White League troops, many of them leading citizens and Confederate veterans, attempted a coup to oust Republican Governor William P. Kellogg and members of his administration. The New Orleans Leaguers overwhelmed the city's racially mixed Metropolitan Police Force under the command of former Confederate general James B. Longstreet. The timely arrival of federal troops, ordered to the scene by President Grant, prevented the takeover. The League was more successful in the Louisiana countryside in the weeks preceding the Democratic victory in November 1874. League troops overthrew or murdered Republican officials in eight parishes.

The Democratic victory in Louisiana encouraged white paramilitarists in Mississippi. Blacks dominated the Warren County government headquartered in Vicksburg. Liners demanded the resignations of all black officials including the sheriff, Peter Crosby, a black Union veteran. Republican Governor Adelbert Ames, a native of Maine, ordered the Liners to disperse and granted Crosby's request to raise a protective militia to respond to future threats.

Peter Crosby's efforts to gather a militia force were too successful. An army of several hundred armed African Americans marched in three columns from the surrounding countryside to Vicksburg. Whites responded to the challenge, firing on the militia and tracking down and terrorizing blacks in the city and county over the next ten days. White Liners (as the Mississippi paramilitarists called themselves) killed at least twenty-nine blacks and wounded countless more. Democrats gained control of the county government.

The Vicksburg incident was a rehearsal for Democratic victories in statewide elections in 1875. Liners focused on the state's majority black counties and vowed to "overawe the negroes and exhibit to them the ocular proof of our power."

The intimidation worked and the Democrats swept to victory in Mississippi. They would not allow Governor Ames to finish his term, threatening him with impeachment. Fearing for his safety, Ames resigned and fled the state. The South's second war of independence was reaching its climax.

July Fourth, 1876. America's one-hundredth birthday. A modest celebration unfolded in Hamburg, South Carolina, a small town in Edgefield County across the Savannah River from Augusta, Georgia. Blacks comprised more than 75 percent of the town's population. They held most of the political offices. An altercation occurred concerning the right of way between the black militia parading in the street and a passing wagon carrying several prominent white residents. When the aggrieved parties met four days later, more than 1,000 armed whites were milling in front of the wooden "armory" where one hundred black militiamen had taken refuge. A shot rang out and shattered a second-floor window and soon a pitched battle was raging. The white attackers fired a cannon that turned most of the building into splinters. As blacks fled, whites tracked them down. The white men also burned homes and shops and robbed residents of the town.

Hamburg was part of a larger pattern of violence and intimidation in the state. In May 1876, South Carolina Democrats drafted *The Plan of the Campaign of 1876*, a manual on how to redeem the state. Some of the recommended strategies included: "Every Democrat must feel honor bound to control the vote of at least one negro, by intimidation, purchase, keeping him away or as each individual may determine how he may best accomplish it. Treat them as to show them, you are the superior race and that their natural position is that of subordination to the white man."

The November election went off in relative calm. In Edgefield County, out of 7,000 potential voters, 9,200 ballots were cast. Similar frauds occurred throughout the state. Still, the result hung in the balance. Both Democrats and Republicans claimed victory and set up rival governments. The following April after a deal brokered in Washington between the parties,

"Declaration of Equality: Justice: 'Five More Wanted.'" An outraged "Justice" in this Thomas Nast cartoon demands the execution of an equal number of white men to balance the six blacks whom whites captured in the aftermath of the Hamburg massacre in July 1876 and then executed. On the pillar to her right are posters with the names of white terrorist groups, the "K.K.K.," the "White League," and the "White Liners," as well as a notice, "Negroes Shot in Cold Blood at Hamburg, S.C." The Hamburg massacre provoked temporary outrage in the North, but little response from the Grant administration. By the fall, widespread violence against blacks in South Carolina generated little comment in the North.

federal troops were withdrawn from South Carolina and a Democratic government installed in Columbia. The victorious Democrats expelled twenty-four Republicans from the state legislature and elected Matthew C. Butler to the U.S. Senate. Butler had led the white attackers at Hamburg.

The Weak Federal Response

When Governor Daniel H. Chamberlain could no longer contain the violence in South Carolina in 1876, he asked the president for help. Grant acknowledged the gravity of Chamberlain's situation but would offer him only the lame hope that South Carolinians would exercise "better judgment and cooperation" and assist the governor in bringing offenders to justice "without aid from the federal Government."

QUICK REVIEW

Civil Rights Act of 1875

- Did not address voting rights.
- Prohibited discrimination in public accommodations.
- Overturned by the U.S. Supreme Court in 1883.

Congress responded to blacks' deteriorating status in the South with the Civil Rights Act of 1875. The act prohibited discrimination against black people in public accommodations, such as theaters, parks, and trains, and guaranteed freedmen's rights to serve on juries. It had no provision for voting rights, which Congress presumed the Fifteenth Amendment protected. Most judges, however, either interpreted the law narrowly or declared it unconstitutional. In 1883, the U.S. Supreme Court agreed and overturned the act, declaring that only the states, not Congress, could redress "a private wrong, or a crime of the individual."

The Election of 1876 and the Compromise of 1877

Reconstruction officially ended with the presidential election of 1876, in which the Democrat Samuel J. Tilden ran against the Republican Rutherford B. Hayes. When the ballots were counted, it appeared that Tilden, a conservative New Yorker respectable enough for northern voters and Democratic enough for white southerners, had won. But despite a majority in the popular vote, disputed returns in three southern states left him with only 184 of the 185 electoral votes needed to win. The three states—Florida, South Carolina, and Louisiana—were the last in the South still to have Republican administrations.

Both camps maneuvered intensively in the following months to claim the disputed votes. Congress appointed a 15-member commission to settle the issue. Because the Republicans controlled Congress, they held a one-vote majority on the commission.

Compromise of 1877 The Congressional settling of the 1876 election which installed Republican Rutherford B. Hayes in the White House and gave Democrats control of all state governments in the South.

Southern Democrats wanted Tilden to win, but they wanted control of their states more. They were willing to deal. Hayes intended to remove federal support from the remaining southern Republican governments anyway. It thus cost him nothing to promise to do so in exchange for the contested electoral votes. The so-called **Compromise of 1877** installed Hayes in the White House and gave Democrats control of every state government in the South. Southern Democrats emerged the major winners from the Compromise of 1877. President Hayes and his successors into the next century left the South alone. In practical terms, the Compromise signaled the revocation of civil rights and voting rights for black southerners. The Fourteenth and Fifteenth Amendments would be dead letters in the South until well into the twentieth century. On the two great issues confronting the nation at the end of the Civil War, reunion and freedom, the white South had won. It reentered the Union largely on its own terms with the freedom to pursue a racial agenda consistent with its political, economic, and social interests.

The Memory of Reconstruction

Southern Democrats used the memory of Reconstruction to help maintain themselves in power. Reconstruction joined the Lost Cause as part of the glorious fight to preserve the civilization of the Old South. As white southerners elevated Civil War heroes into saints and battles into holy struggles, they equated Reconstruction with Redemption. White Democrats had rescued the South from a purgatory of black rule and federal oppression. The southern view of

Reconstruction permeated textbooks, films, and standard accounts of the period. By the early 1900s, professional historians at the nation's finest institutions concurred in this view, ignoring contrary evidence and rendering the story of African Americans invisible. By that time, therefore, most Americans believed that the policies of Reconstruction had been misguided and had brought great suffering to the white South. The widespread acceptance of this view allowed the South to maintain its system of racial segregation and exclusion without interference from the federal government.

Memorialists did not deny the Redeemers' use of terror and violence. To the contrary; they praised it as necessary. South Carolina senator Benjamin R. Tillman, a participant in the Hamburg massacre, stood in front of his Senate colleagues in 1900 and asserted, "We were sorry we had the necessity forced upon us, but we could not help it, and as white men we are not sorry for it, and we do not propose to apologize for anything we have done in connection with it. We took the government away from them [African Americans] in 1876. We did take it. . . . We of the South have never recognized the right of the negro to govern white men, and we never will." The animosity of southern whites toward Republican governments had much less to do with alleged corruption and incompetence than the mere fact of African Americans casting ballots and making laws.

The national historical consensus grew out of a growing national reconciliation concerning the war, a mutual agreement that both sides had fought courageously and that it was time to move on. Hidden in all the goodwill was the tacit agreement between southern and northern whites that the South was now free to work out its own resolution to race relations. Reconstruction rested on a national consensus of African American inferiority.

MODEST GAINS

HOW AND why did Reconstruction end?

If the overthrow of Reconstruction elicited a resounding indifference from most white Americans, black southerners greeted it with frustration. Their dreams of land ownership faded as a new labor system relegated them to a lowly position in southern agriculture. Redemption reversed their economic and political gains and deprived them of most of the civil rights they had enjoyed under Congressional Reconstruction. Although they continued to vote into the 1890s, they had by 1877 lost most of the voting strength and political offices they held. Rather than becoming part of southern society, they were increasingly set apart from it, valued only for their labor.

Watch the Video
at **www.myhistorylab.com**
The Promise and Failure of Reconstruction

Still, the former slaves were better off in 1877 than in 1865. They were free, however limited their freedom. Some owned land; some held jobs in cities. They raised their families in relative peace and experienced the spiritual joys of a full religious life. They socialized freely with relatives and friends, and they moved about. The Reconstruction amendments to the Constitution guaranteed an array of civil and political rights, and eventually these guarantees would form the basis of the civil rights revolution after World War II. But that outcome was long, too long, in the future.

Interpreting the Past
Realities of Freedom (pp. 464–465)

Black southerners experienced some advances in the decade after the Civil War, but these owed little to Reconstruction. Black families functioned as economic and psychological buffers against unemployment and prejudice. Black churches played crucial roles in their communities. Self-help and labor organizations offered mutual friendship and financial assistance. All of these institutions had existed in the slavery era, although on a smaller scale. And some of them, such as black labor groups, schools, and social welfare associations, endured because comparable white institutions excluded black people.

Read the Document
at **www.myhistorylab.com**
Exploring America: Did Reconstruction Work for the Freed People?

Read the Document
at **www.myhistorylab.com**
Thirteenth, Fourteenth, and Fifteenth Amendments

Black people also scored some modest economic successes during the Reconstruction era, mainly from their own pluck. In the Lower South, black per capita income increased 46 percent between 1857 and 1879, compared with a 35 percent decline in white per capita income.

OVERVIEW Constitutional Amendments and Federal Legislation of the Reconstruction Era

Amendment or Legislation	Purpose	Significance
Thirteenth Amendment (passed and ratified in 1865)	Prevented southern states from reestablishing slavery after the war	Final step toward full emancipation of slaves
Freedmen's Bureau Act (1865)	Oversight of resettlement, labor for former slaves	Involved the federal government directly in relief, education, and assisting the transition from slavery to freedom; worked fitfully to achieve this objective during its seven-year career
Southern Homestead Act (1866)	Provided black people preferential access to public lands in five southern states	Lack of capital and poor quality of federal land thwarted the purpose of the act
Civil Rights Act of 1866	Defined rights of national citizenship	Marked an important change in federal-state relations, tilting balance of power to national government
Fourteenth Amendment (passed 1866; ratified 1868)	Prohibited states from violating the rights of their citizens	Strengthened the Civil Rights Act of 1866 and guaranteed all citizens equality before the law
Military Reconstruction Acts (1867)	Set new rules for the readmission of former Confederate states into the Union and secured black voting rights	Initiated Congressional Reconstruction
Tenure of Office Act (1867)	Required congressional approval for the removal of any official whose appointment had required Senate confirmation	A congressional challenge to the president's right to dismiss cabinet members; led to President Andrew Johnson's impeachment trial
Fifteenth Amendment (passed 1869; ratified 1870)	Guaranteed the right of all American male citizens to vote regardless of race	The basis for black voting rights
Civil Rights Act of 1875	Prohibited racial discrimination in jury selection, public transportation, and public accommodations	Rarely enforced; Supreme Court declared it unconstitutional in 1883

QUICK REVIEW

Advances

- Black families and institutions played a crucial role in Reconstruction era.
- Fourteenth Amendment guaranteed equality before the law.
- Fifteenth Amendment protected the right to vote.

***Slaughterhouse* cases** Group of cases resulting in one sweeping decision by the U.S. Supreme Court in 1873 that contradicted the intent of the Fourteenth Amendment by decreeing that most citizenship rights remained under state, not federal, control.

Sharecropping, oppressive as it was, represented an advance over forced and gang labor. Collectively, black people owned more than $68 million worth of property in 1870, a 240 percent increase over 1860, but the average worth of each piece of property was only $408.

The Fourteenth and Fifteenth Amendments to the Constitution are among the few bright spots in Reconstruction's otherwise dismal legacy. But the benefits of these two landmark amendments did not accrue to African Americans until well into the twentieth century. White southerners effectively nullified the Reconstruction amendments, and the U.S. Supreme Court virtually interpreted them, and other Reconstruction legislation, out of existence.

In the ***Slaughterhouse* cases** (1873), the Supreme Court contradicted the intent of the Fourteenth Amendment by decreeing that most citizenship rights remained under state, not federal, control. In ***United States v. Cruikshank*** (1876), the Court overturned the convictions of some of those responsible for the Colfax Massacre, ruling that the Enforcement Act applied only to violations of black rights by states, not individuals. Within the next two decades, the Supreme Court would uphold the legality of racial segregation and black disfranchisement, in effect declaring that the Fourteenth and Fifteenth Amendments did not apply to African Americans.

CONCLUSION

White southerners robbed black southerners of their gains and sought to reduce them again to servitude and dependence, if not to slavery. But in the process, the majority of white southerners lost as well. Yeoman farmers missed an opportunity to break cleanly from the Old South and establish a more equitable society. Instead, they allowed the old elites to regain power and gradually ignore their needs. They preserved the social benefit of a white skin at the cost of almost everything else. Many lost their farms and sank into tenancy. Few had a voice in state legislatures or the U.S. Congress. A new South, rid of slavery and sectional antagonism, had indeed emerged—redeemed, regenerated, and disenthralled. But the old South lingered on.

The journey toward equality after the Civil War had aborted. Reconstruction had not failed. It was overthrown. In the weeks and months after Appomattox, white southerners launched a war against the freedmen and their allies to return white Democrats to power and African Americans to a position of permanent subordination in southern society. The indifferent and often hostile attitudes of white northerners toward blacks played a role in limiting the federal response and ensuring the success of the white South in prosecuting this war. As with the Civil War, the overthrow of Reconstruction was a national tragedy. By 1877, the "golden moment," an unprecedented opportunity for the nation to live up to its ideals by extending equal rights to all its citizens, black and white alike, had passed.

United States v. Cruikshank Supreme Court ruling of 1876 that overturned the convictions of some of those responsible for the Colfax Massacre, ruling that the Enforcement Act applied only to violations of black rights by states, not individuals.

Where to Learn More

Penn Center Historic District, St. Helena Island, South Carolina. The Penn School was a sea-island experiment in the education of free black people established by northern missionaries Laura Towne and Ellen Murray in 1862. They operated it until their deaths in the early 1900s. The Penn School became Penn Community Services in 1948, serving as an educational institution, health clinic, and a social service agency. See its website at http://www.penncenter.com.

***Harper's Magazine* selected articles and cartoons on Reconstruction.** This website includes numerous articles and illustrations that appeared in *Harper's* during the Reconstruction era. This collection is especially good in documenting the violence against African Americans in the South during this era. Go to http://blackhistory.harpweek.com/4Reconstruction/reconlevelone.htm.

Beauvoir, Biloxi, Mississippi. The exhibits at Beauvoir, the home of Jefferson Davis, evoke the importance of the Lost Cause for the white survivors of the Confederacy. Especially interesting is the Jefferson Davis Soldiers Home on the premises and the Confederate Veterans Cemetery. Davis spent his retirement at Beauvoir. Go to http://www.beauvoir.org.

Levi Jordan Plantation, Brazoria County, Texas. This site provides an excellent depiction and interpretation of the lives of sharecroppers and tenants during and immediately after the Reconstruction era. The site is especially valuable for demonstrating the transition from slavery to sharecropping. Go to http://www.webarchaeology.com.

Review Questions

1. Both Russia and America hoped to develop a free-labor agricultural class after their respective emancipations. Why didn't these governments follow through on their own objectives?
2. Given the different perspectives on the Civil War's outcome and what the social structure of a postwar South should be, was there any common ground between southern white and southern black on which to forge a Reconstruction policy?
3. Black people did achieve some notable gains during Reconstruction, despite its overall failure. What were those gains?
4. What prompted Frances Harper to write her pleading poem in 1871?

Key Terms

Black codes (p. 445)
Carpetbaggers (p. 450)
Compromise of 1877 (p. 458)
Congressional Reconstruction (p. 448)
Field Order No. 15 (p. 440)
Fifteenth Amendment (p. 449)
Fourteenth Amendment (p. 445)
Freedmen's Bureau (p. 439)
Ku Klux Klan (p. 452)
Lost Cause (p. 438)
Redeemers (p. 456)
Scalawags (p. 450)
Sharecropping (p. 441)
***Slaughterhouse* cases** (p. 460)
Southern Homestead Act (p. 441)
Tenure of Office Act (p. 448)
Union Leagues (p. 451)
United States v. Cruikshank (p. 461)

myhistorylab Connections

Reinforce what you learned in this chapter by studying the many documents, images, maps, review tools, and videos available at **www.myhistorylab.com.**

Read and Review

Study and Review **Study Plan: Chapter 16**

Read the Document

A Sharecrop Contract (1882)

Carl Schurz, Report on the Condition of the South *(1865)*

Clinton B. Fisk, "Plain Counsels for Freedmen" (1865)

Albion W. Tourgée, Letter on Ku Klux Klan Activities (1870)

"Address of the Colored Citizens of Norfolk, Virginia" (1865)

Address of the Colored State Convention to the People of the State of South Carolina (1865)

Charlotte Forten, Life on the Sea Islands

Hannah Irwin Describes Ku Klux Klan Ride (Late 1860s)

Jourdon Anderson to His Former Master (1865)

President Johnson's Veto of the Civil Rights Act 1866

The Civil Rights Act of 1866

The Fourteenth Amendment (1868)

The Freedmen's Bureau Bill (1865)

The Mississippi Black Code (1865)

Thirteenth, Fourteenth, and Fifteenth Amendments

See the Map *Congressional Reconstrction*

Research and Explore

Read the Document

Personal Journeys Online

From Then to Now Online: African American Voting Rights in the South

Exploring America: Did Reconstruction Work for the Freed People?

Hear the Audio

Free At Last

Remembering Slavery #2

Watch the Video

The Promise and Failure of Reconstruction

Reconstruction in Texas

The Schools that the Civil War and Reconstruction Created

Trials of Racial Identity in Nineteenth-Century America

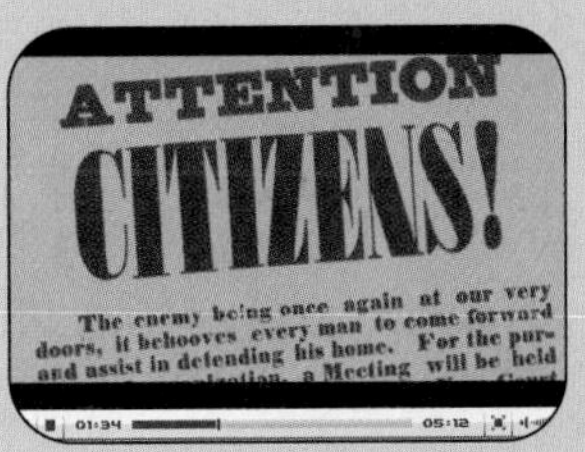

Hear the Audio

Hear the audio files for Chapter 16 at **www.myhistorylab.com.**

INTERPRETING the PAST

Realities of Freedom

FOLLOWING emancipation, what economic and social opportunities actually existed for African Americans in the United States? How did these various opportunities available to freedmen improve their life and that of their families after the official end to slavery?

The Freedmen's Bureau established in 1865 by Congress provided freedmen with clothing, temporary shelter, food, and a series of freedmen's schools across the South. Southern response was to fall into the use of terror to deter blacks from becoming economically independent, using the agencies of groups like the Ku Klux Klan. Sharecropping was an insidious economic arrangement that also placed both whites and blacks in a form of economic slavery to large landholders in the South of the post–Civil War era.

Sharecropping, tenant farming, and peonage were new forms of slavery adopted in the South following the Civil War. The story of African Americans after the end of slavery is complex and varied. Some blacks attempted to seek out better places to establish their new lives while others remained in the security of the only home they had known as slaves.

After slavery we had to get in before night . . .

An Act to Establish a Bureau for the Relief of Freedmen and Refugees, 1865

BE IT ENACTED, That there is hereby established in the War Department, to continue during the present war of rebellion, and for one year thereafter, a bureau of refugees, freedmen, and abandoned lands, to which shall be committed, as hereinafter provided, the supervision and management of all abandoned lands, and the control of all subjects relating to refugees and freedmen from rebel states, or from any district of country within the territory embraced in the operations of the army, under such rules and regulations as may be prescribed by the head of the bureau and approved by the President. The said bureau shall be under the management and control of a commissioner to be appointed by the President, by and with the advice and consent of the Senate . . .

This illustration depicts former slaves outside their sharecropper cabin in Virginia, ca. 1870.

"When We Worked on Shares, We Couldn't Make Nothing"

After slavery we had to get in before night too. If you didn't, Ku Klux would drive you in. They would come and visit you anyway. . . . When he got you good and scared he would drive on away. They would whip you if they would catch you out in the night time. . . .

I've forgot who it is that told us that we was free. Somebody come and told us we're free now. I done forgot who it was.

After freedom, we worked on shares a while. Then we rented. When we worked on shares, we couldn't make nothing, just overalls and something to eat. Half went to the other man and you would destroy your half if you weren't careful. A man that didn't know how to count would always lose. He might lose anyhow. They didn't give no itemized statement. No, you just had to take their word. They never give you no details. They just say you owe so much. No matter how good account you kept, you had to go by their account and now, Brother, I'm tellin' you the truth about this. It's been that way for a long time. You had to take the white man's work on note, and everything. Anything you wanted, you could git if you were a good hand. You could git anything you wanted as long as you worked. If you didn't make no money, that's all right;

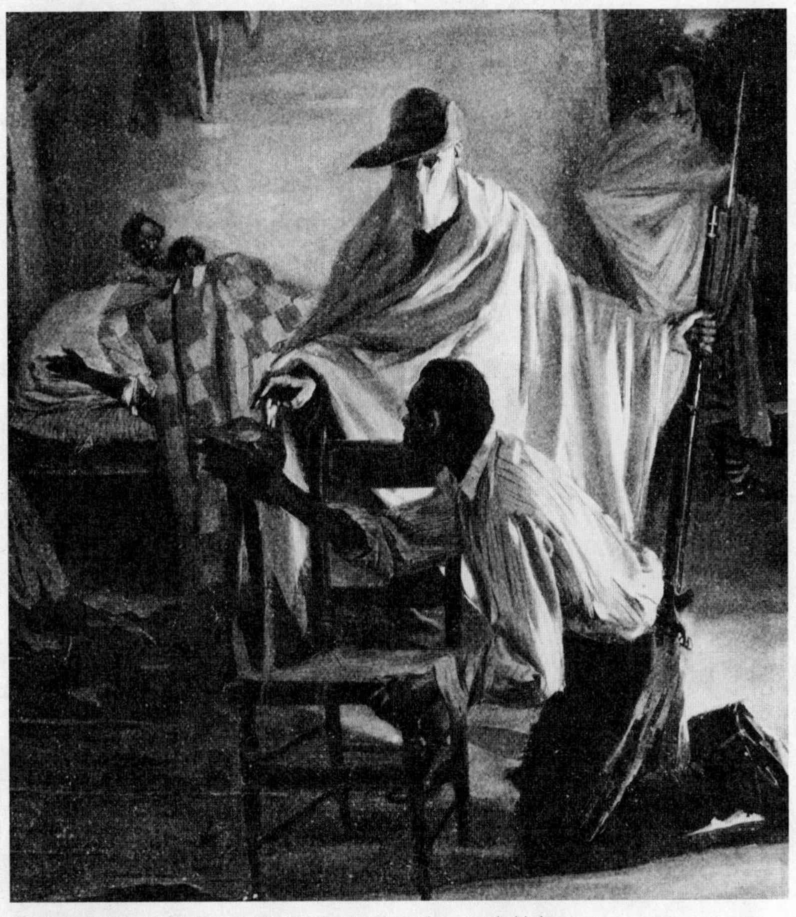

KKK members, wrapped in sheets like ghosts, threaten a free man in his home.

they would advance you more. But you better not leave him, you better not try to leave and get caught. They'd keep you in debt. They were sharp. Christmas come, you could take up twenty dollar, in somethin' to eat and much as you wanted in whiskey. You could buy a gallon of whiskey. Anything that kept you a slave because he was always right and you were always wrong if there was difference. If there was an argument, he would get mad and there would be a shooting take place.

Excerpts from a Sharecropper Contract, 1882

To every one applying to rent land upon shares, the following conditions must be read, and agreed to.

To every 30 or 35 acres, I agree to furnish the team, plow, and farming implements, except cotton planters, and I do not agree to furnish a cart to every cropper. The croppers are to have half of the cotton, corn and fodder (and peas and pumpkins and potatoes if any are planted. . .).

Croppers are to have no part or interest in the cotton seed raised from the crop planted and worked by them. No vine crops of any description, that is, no watermelons, muskmelons, . . . squashes or anything of that kind, except peas and pumpkins, and potatoes, are to be planted in the cotton or corn. All must work under my direction. All plantation work to be done by the croppers. . . .

No cropper to work off the plantation when there is any work to be done on the land he has rented, or when his work is needed by me or other croppers. Trees to be cut down on Orchard, House field & Evanson fences, leaving such as I may designate. . . .

. . . a bureau of refugees, freedmen, and abandoned lands . . .

1877-1900

17

A New South: Economic Progress and Social Tradition

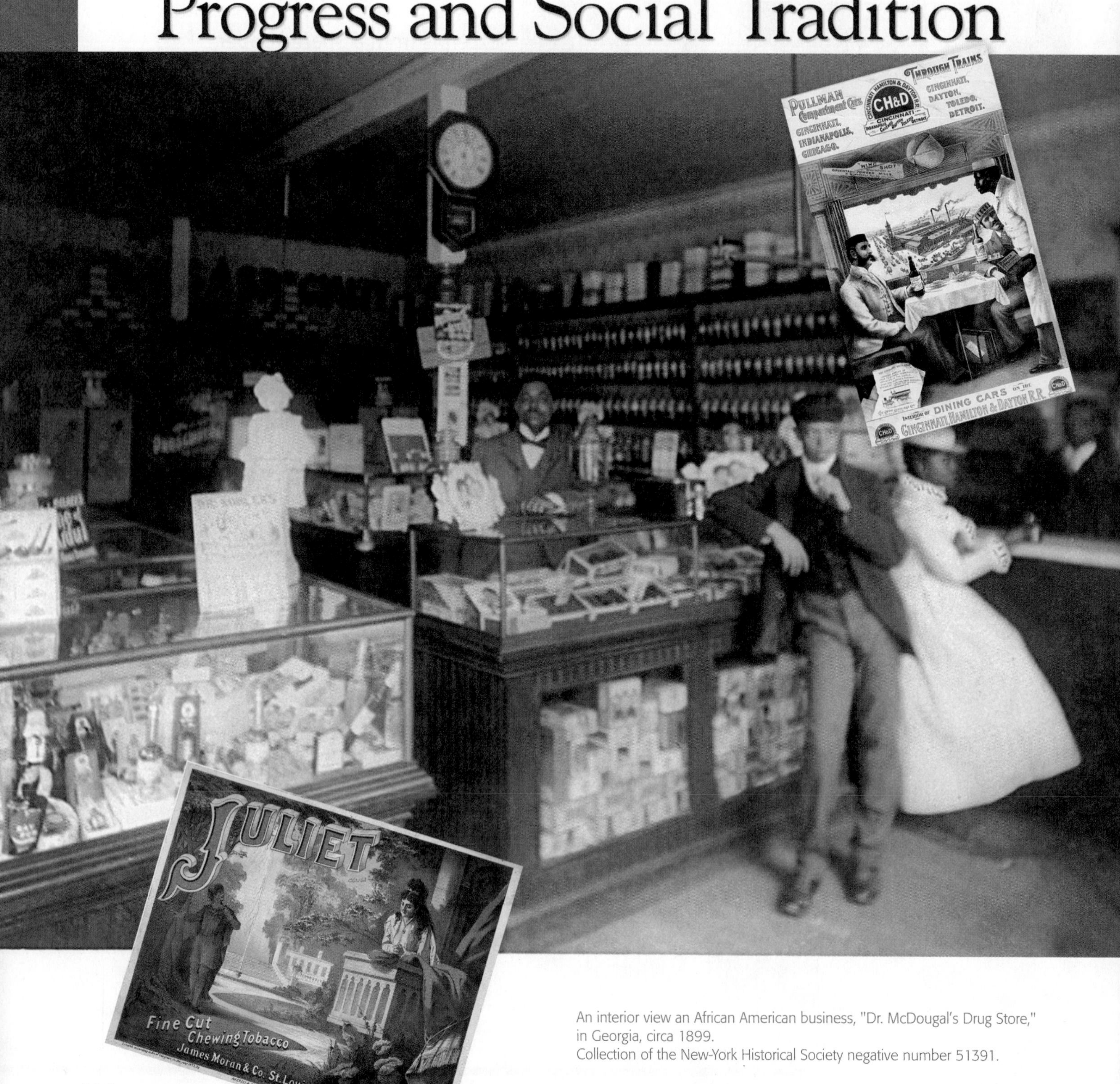

An interior view an African American business, "Dr. McDougal's Drug Store," in Georgia, circa 1899.
Collection of the New-York Historical Society negative number 51391.

Hear the Audio

Hear the audio files for Chapter 17 at **www.myhistorylab.com**.

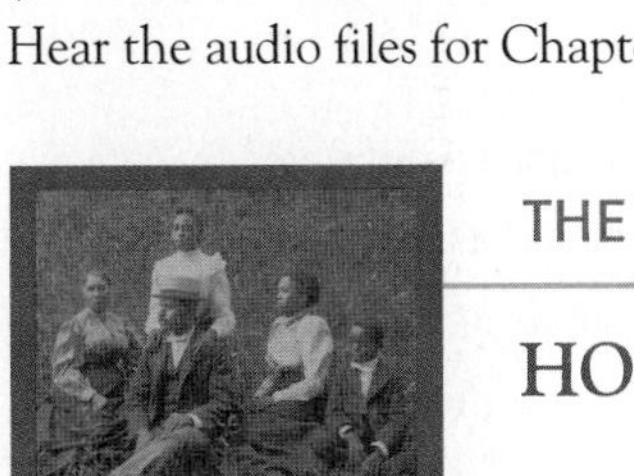

THE "NEWNESS" OF THE NEW SOUTH *(page 469)*

HOW NEW was the New South?

THE SOUTHERN AGRARIAN REVOLT *(page 475)*

WHAT WERE the origins and nature of southern Populism?

WOMEN IN THE NEW SOUTH *(page 477)*

HOW DID traditional gender roles shape the opportunities available to women in the New South?

SETTLING THE RACE ISSUE *(page 480)*

WHAT STEPS did southerners take in the late nineteenth century to limit the freedom of African Americans?

One American Journey

The colored woman of to-day occupies . . . a unique position in this country. . . . She is confronted by both a woman question and a race problem. . . . While the women of the white race can with calm assurance enter upon the work they feel by nature appointed to do [including reform efforts both inside and outside the home], while their men give loyal support and appreciative countenance to [these] efforts, recognizing in most avenues of usefulness the propriety and the need of woman's distinctive co-operation, the colored woman too often finds herself hampered and shamed by a less liberal sentiment . . . on the part of those for whose opinion she cares most. . . .

You do not find the colored woman selling her birthright for a mess of pottage. . . . It is largely our women in the South to-day who keep the black men solid in the Republican Party. The black woman can never forget, however lukewarm the party may to-day appear, that it was a Republican president who struck the manacles from her own wrists and gave the possibilities of manhood to her helpless little ones; and to her mind a Democratic Negro is a traitor and a time-server.

To be a woman in a . . . [new] age carries with it a privilege and an opportunity never implied before. But to be a woman of the Negro race in America, and to be able to grasp the deep significance of the possibilities of the crisis, is to have a heritage, it seems to me, unique in the ages. In the first place, the race is young and full of the elasticity and hopefulness of youth. All its achievements are before it. . . . Everything to this race is new and strange and inspiring. There is a quickening of its pulses and a glowing of its self-consciousness. Aha, I can rival that! I can aspire to that! I can honor my name and vindicate my race! Something like this, it strikes me, is the enthusiasm which stirs the genius of young Africa in America; and the memory of past oppression and the fact of present attempted repression only serve to gather momentum for its irrepressible power. . . . What a responsibility then to have the sole management of the primal lights and shadows! Such is the colored woman's office. She must stamp weal or woe on the coming history of this people. May she see her opportunity and vindicate her high prerogative.

Anna J. Cooper,
A Voice from the South, 1892

Anna Julia Cooper, *A Voice from the South* (Xenia, OH: Aldine Printing House, 1892): pp. 134–135, 138–140, 142–145. The book may be accessed from the Internet: http://docsouth.unc.edu/church/cooper/cooper.html

Read the **Document** at **www.myhistorylab.com**

Personal Journeys Online

- **Booker T. Washington, *Atlanta Compromise Address*, 1895. Speech in which Washington accepts segregation and disfranchisement of southern blacks in return for white southerners' economic assistance.**
- **W. E. B. Du Bois, *Of Mr. Booker T. Washington and Others*, 1903. Du Bois declares that Washington's compromise places African Americans in the South on a journey to failure.**

ANNA J. COOPER undertook an incredible journey that took her from slavery at her birth in Raleigh, North Carolina, in 1858 to a doctoral degree at the Sorbonne in Paris, France, and to a prominent career as an educator. Throughout her life she remained a firm believer in the role women, especially black women, should play in striking down both white supremacy and male domination. In 1892, Dr. Cooper published *A Voice from the South*, excerpted here. The book appeared at a time when the first African American generation raised in freedom generated a relatively prosperous, educated middle class intent on challenging the

CHRONOLOGY

1872	Texas and Pacific Railway connects Dallas to eastern markets.
1880	First southern local of the Women's Christian Temperance Union is formed in Atlanta.
1881	Booker T. Washington establishes Tuskegee Institute.
1882	Agricultural Wheel is formed in Arkansas.
1883	Laura Haygood founds the home mission movement in Atlanta.
1884	James B. Duke automates his cigarette factory.
1886	Dr. John Pemberton creates Coca-Cola.
	Southern railroads conform to national track gauge standards.
1887	Charles W. Macune expands the Southern Farmers' Alliance from its Texas base to the rest of the South.
1888	The Southern Farmers' Alliance initiates a successful boycott of jute manufacturers.
1890	Mississippi becomes the first state to restrict black suffrage with literacy tests.
1892	The Populist Party forms.
1894	United Daughters of the Confederacy is founded.
1895	Booker T. Washington delivers his "Atlanta Compromise" address.
1895	Publication of Theodor Herzl's *The Jewish State* outlining his ideas for a Jewish homeland in Palestine in response to rising anti-Semitism in Europe.
1896	In *Plessy v. Ferguson*, the Supreme Court permits segregation by law.
1897	First Zionist Congress meets in Switzerland.
1898	North Carolina Mutual Life Insurance is founded.
1899	Publication of *Die Grundlagen des neunzehnten Jahrhunderts* ["The Foundations of the Nineteenth Century"] by British scientist Houston Stewart Chamberlain, promoting the superiority of the German "race."
1903	W.E.B. Du Bois publishes *The Souls of Black Folk*.
1905	James B. Duke forms the Southern Power Company.
	Thomas Dixon publishes *The Clansman*.
1906	Bloody race riots break out in Atlanta.
1907	Pittsburgh-based U.S. Steel takes over Birmingham's largest steel producer.

limits of race in the New South. The assertiveness of this generation alarmed their white counterparts, who launched a campaign of violence and repression, mainly directed at black men.

By the early 1900s, Cooper was living in Washington, DC, and had immersed herself in the woman suffrage movement and the promotion of female education. She would live to see the dawn of a new racial and gender era in the South and in America, but the journey would take many years and many lives. Cooper died at the age of 106 in 1964.

THE "NEWNESS" OF THE NEW SOUTH

HOW NEW was the New South?

Anna J. Cooper's journey looked forward to a brighter, if elusive, future for African Americans, women in particular. White southerners marched backward toward an idealized past whose elements they hoped to restore as faithfully as possible, especially those related to race and gender. At the same time, they projected an image of progress, touting economic and technological advances, welcoming investment, and promoting benign race relations and a docile labor force. The progress was genuine, but only within the framework of white supremacy. When the idea of white supremacy proved insufficient to sustain order, white southerners resorted to legislation and violence. The New South, as one observer noted, was merely "the Old South under new conditions." By the early 1900s, the South had traveled further away from the American journey than at any time in its history.

Read the **Document** at www.myhistorylab.com *The Nation, "The State of the South" (1872)*

On the surface, this did not seem to be the case. Southerners did what other Americans were doing between 1877 and 1900; they built railroads, erected factories, and moved to towns and cities, only on a smaller scale and with more modest results. But the factories did not dramatically alter the South's rural economy, and the towns and cities did not make it an urban region. The changes, nonetheless, brought political and social turmoil, emboldening black people like Cooper to assert their rights, encouraging women to work outside the home and pursue public careers, and frightening some white men. The backlash would be significant.

The New South's "newness" was to be found primarily in its economy, not in its social relations, although the two were complementary. After Reconstruction, new industries absorbed tens of thousands of first-time industrial workers from impoverished rural areas. Southern cities grew faster than those in any other region of the country. A burst of railroad construction linked these cities to one another and to the rest of the country, giving them increased commercial prominence. Growing in size and taking on new functions, cities extended their influence into the countryside with newspapers, consumer products, and new values. But this urban influence had important limits. It did not bring electricity, telephones, public health services, or public schools to the rural South. It did not greatly broaden the rural economy with new jobs. And it left the countryside without the daily contact with the outside world that fostered a broader perspective.

The Democratic Party dominated southern politics after 1877, significantly changing the South's political system. Through various deceits, Democrats purged most black people and some white people from the electoral process and suppressed challenges to their leadership. The result was the emergence by 1900 of the **Solid South,** a period of white Democratic Party rule that lasted into the 1950s.

Solid South The one-party (Democratic) political system that dominated the South from the 1890s to the 1950s.

Although most southern women remained at home or on the farm, piecing together families shattered by war, some enjoyed new options after 1877. Middle-class women in the cities, both white and black, became increasingly active in civic work and reform. Tens of thousands of young white women from impoverished rural areas found work in textile mills, in city factories, or as servants. These new options posed a challenge to prevailing views about the role of women but ultimately did not change them.

QUICK REVIEW

Southern Women: 1877–1900

- Most southern women remained at home or on the farm.
- Middle-class women increasingly active in civic work and reform.
- Young white women found work in mills, factories, and as servants.

The status of black southerners changed significantly between 1877 and 1900. The members of the first generation born after emancipation sought more than just freedom as they came of age. They also expected dignity and self-respect and the right to work, to vote, to go to school, and to travel freely. White southerners responded to the new challenge in the same manner they had responded immediately after the war, with violence and restrictive legislation. By 1900, black southerners found themselves more isolated from white southerners and with less political power than at any time since 1865. Despite these setbacks, they succeeded, especially in the cities, in building a rich community life and spawning a vibrant middle class, albeit in a restricted environment.

AN INDUSTRIAL AND URBAN SOUTH

Southerners manufactured very little in 1877, less than 10 percent of the national total. By 1900, however, they boasted a growing iron and steel industry, textile mills that rivaled those of New England, a world-dominant tobacco industry, and a timber-processing industry that helped make the South a leading furniture-manufacturing center. A variety of regional enterprises also rose to prominence, among them the maker of what would become the world's favorite soft drink, Coca-Cola.

W WHERE TO LEARN MORE

Sloss Furnaces National Historical Landmark, Birmingham, Alabama http://www.slossfurnaces.com

Read the **Document** at **www.myhistorylab.com**
John Hill, Testimony on Southern Textile Industry (1883)

Steel mills and textiles. Birmingham, barely a scratch in the forest in 1870, exemplified one aspect of what was new about the New South. Within a decade, its iron and steel mills were belching the smoke of progress across the northern Alabama hills. By 1889, Birmingham had surpassed the older southern iron center of Chattanooga, Tennessee, and was preparing to challenge Pittsburgh, the nation's preeminent steelmaking city.

The southern textile industry also experienced significant growth during the 1880s. Although the South had manufactured cotton products since the early decades of the nineteenth century, chronic shortages of labor and capital kept the industry small. In the 1870s, however, several factors drew local investors into textile enterprises. The population of the rural South was rising, but farm income was low, ensuring a steady supply of cheap labor. Cotton was plentiful and cheap. Mixing profit and southern patriotism, entrepreneurs promoted a strong textile industry as a way to make the South less dependent on northern manufactured products and capital. By 1900, the South had surpassed New England to become the nation's foremost textile-manufacturing center.

The face of southern industry. By the early 1900s, the South had become a national leader in textile production, relying on cheap labor, especially women and young children, such as this young girl in a Lewis Hine photograph at the Globe Cotton Mill in Augusta, Georgia, 1909. She stands in a grimy dress between two large looms. The floor is littered with cotton lint that is harmful to the lungs. Hine took such photographs to call attention to the evil of children labor. To hard-pressed southern families who could not sustain themselves on the farm, these industrial jobs were literally lifesaving, but at a terrible cost to the health, education, and welfare of their children.

Tobacco and Coca-Cola. The South's tobacco industry, like its textile industry, predated the Civil War. Virginia was the dominant producer, and its main product was chewing tobacco. The discovery of bright-leaf tobacco, a strain suitable for smoking in the form of cigarettes, changed Americans' tobacco habits. In 1884, James B. Duke installed the first cigarette-making machine in his Durham, North Carolina, plant. By 1900, Duke's American Tobacco Company controlled 80 percent of all tobacco manufacturing in the United States.

Although not as important as textiles or tobacco in 1900, a soft drink developed by an Atlanta pharmacist, Dr. John Pemberton, eventually became the most renowned southern product worldwide. He called his concoction Coca-Cola. By the mid-1890s, Coca-Cola enjoyed a national market.

QUICK REVIEW

Southern Industries

- Iron and steel.
- Textiles.
- Tobacco.
- Timber.

Railroads and growth. Southern railroad construction boomed in the 1880s, outpacing the rest of the nation. Overall, southern track mileage doubled between 1880 and 1890, with the greatest increases in Texas and Georgia (see Map 17–1). In 1886, the southern railroads agreed to conform to a national standard for track width, firmly linking the region into a national transportation network and ensuring quick and direct access for southern products to the booming markets of the Northeast.

The railroads connected many formerly isolated small southern farmers to national and international agricultural markets. At the same time, it gave them access to a whole new range of products, from fertilizers to fashions. Drawn into commercial agriculture, the farmers were now subject to market fluctuations, their fortunes rising and falling with the market prices for their crops. To an extent unknown before the Civil War, the market now determined what farmers planted, how much credit they could expect, and on what terms. The railroad also opened new areas of the South to settlement and economic development.

QUICK REVIEW

Railroads and the South

- Connected small southern farmers to national and international markets.
- Opened new areas in the South to settlement and development.
- Gave southerners access to a host of new products.

The Limits of Industrial and Urban Growth

These economic developments implied that the South was traveling on a new road. In fact, the journey was back to a very old place. Rapid as it was, urban and industrial growth in the South barely kept pace with that in the booming North (see Chapter 18). A weak agricultural economy

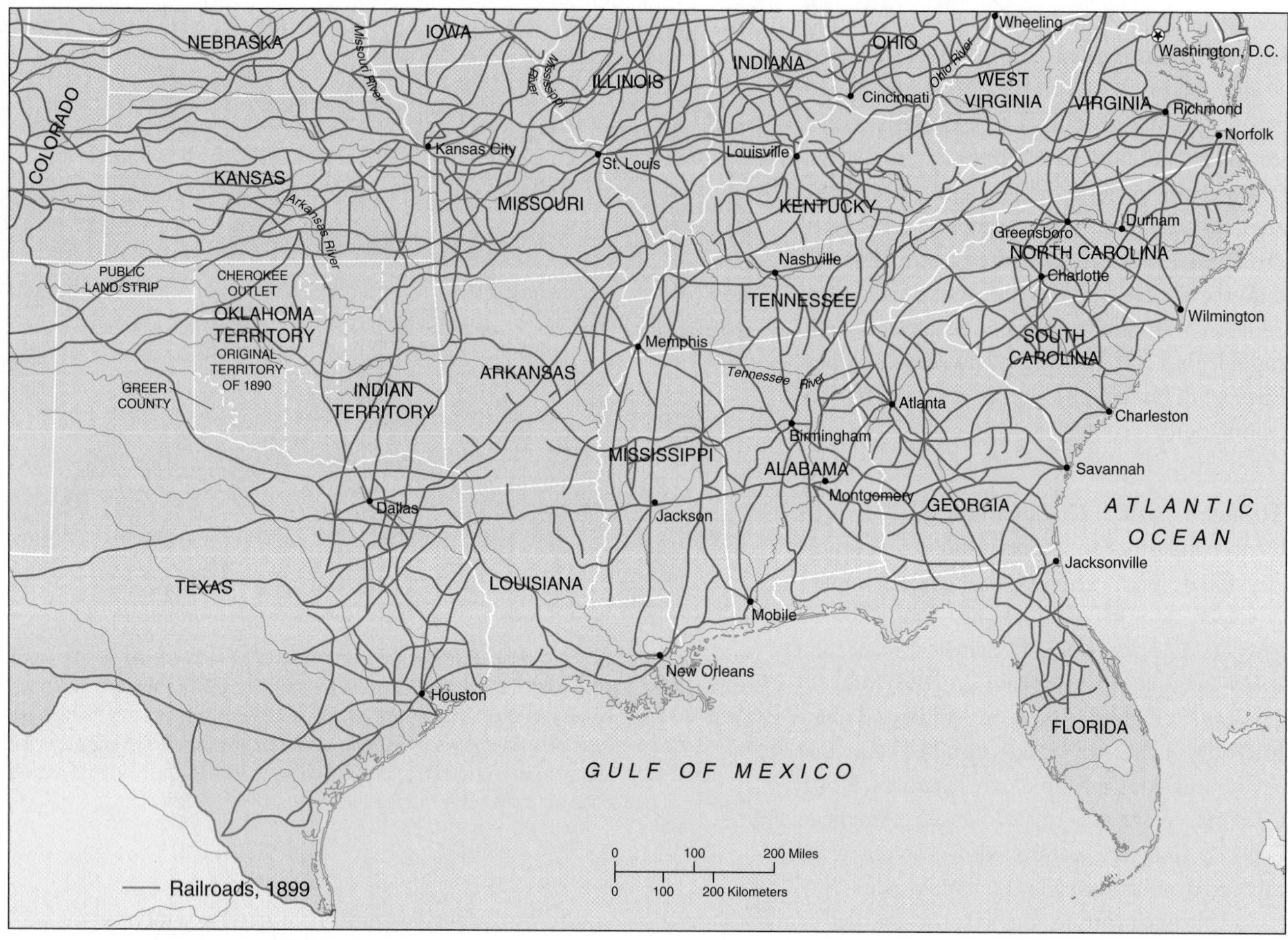

MAP 17–1 **Railroads in the South, 1859 and 1899** A postwar railroad construction boom promoted commercial agriculture and industry in the South. Unlike the railroads of the prewar South, uniform gauges and connections to major trunk lines in the North linked southerners to the rest of the nation. Northern interests, however, owned the major southern railroads in 1899, and most of the products flowing northward were raw materials to be processed by northern industry or shipped elsewhere by northern merchants.

and a high rural birthrate depressed wages in the South. Southern industrial workers earned roughly half the national average manufacturing wage during the late nineteenth century (see Figure 17–1). Business leaders promoted the advantages of this cheap labor to northern investors. In 1904, a Memphis businessman boasted that his city "can save the northern manufacturer . . . who employs 400 hands, $50,000 a year on his labor bill."

Effects of low wages. Despite their attractiveness to industrialists, low wages undermined the southern economy in several ways. Poorly paid workers did not buy much, keeping consumer demand low and limiting the market for southern manufactured goods. They also could not provide much tax revenue, restricting the southern states' ability to fund services like public education. As a result, investment in education lagged in the South. Per-pupil expenditure in the region was at least 50 percent below that of the rest of the nation in 1900.

Finally, low wages kept immigrants, and the skills and energy they brought with them, out of the South. Between 1860 and 1900, during one of the greatest waves of immigration the United States has yet experienced, the foreign-born population of the South actually declined from about 10 percent to less than 2 percent.

Limited capital. Why did the South not do better? Why did it not benefit more from the rapid expansion of the national economy in the last three decades of the nineteenth century?

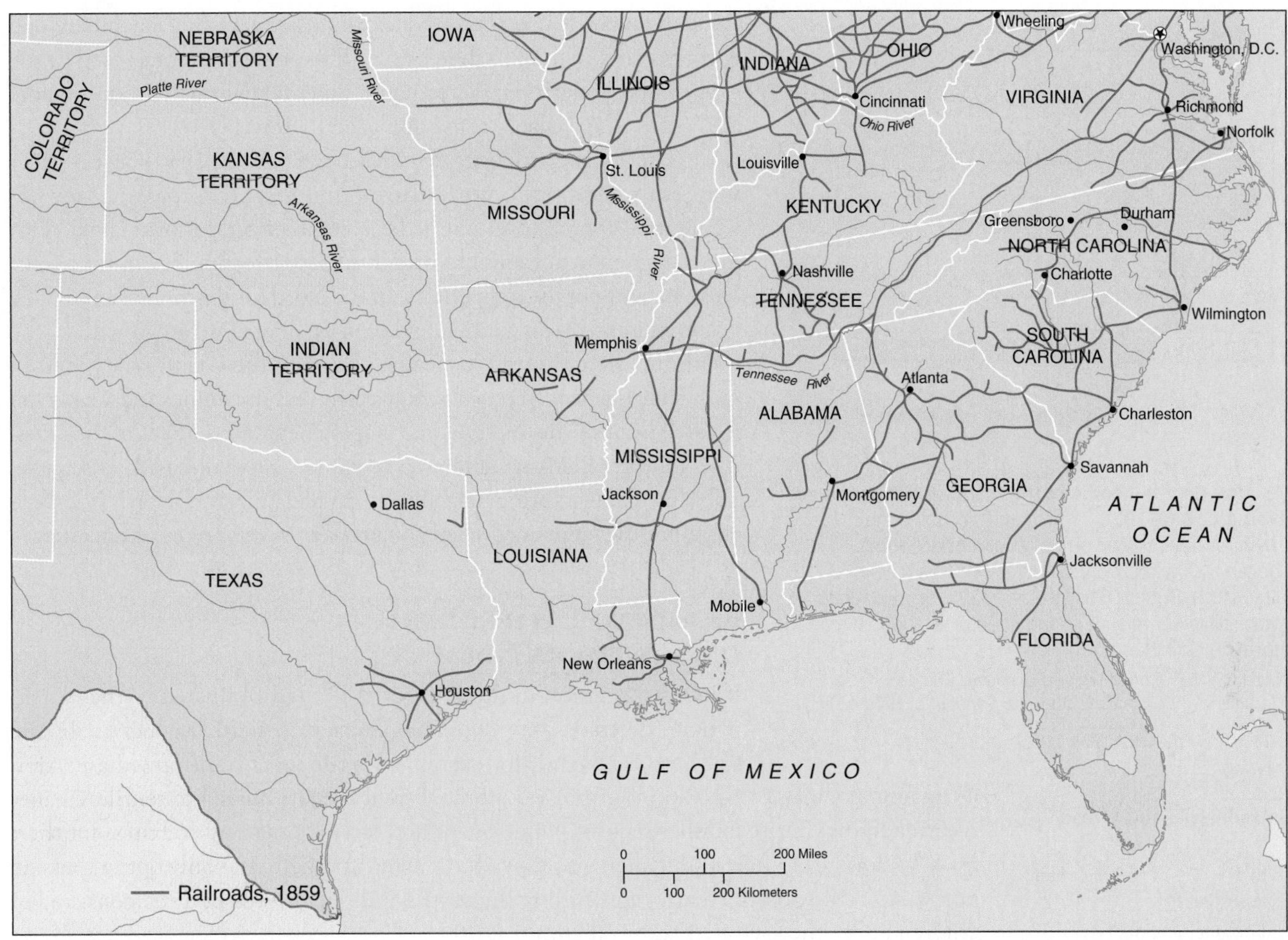

MAP 17–1 **(Continued)**

Compare and contrast railroads in the South in 1859 and 1899. Besides the obvious increase in the number of lines, what other changes do you note in the southern railroad system? What larger trends do these changes reflect?

The simple answer is that, despite its growing links to the national economy, the South remained a region apart.

The Civil War had wiped out the South's capital resources, leaving it, in effect, an economic colony of the North. Northern goods flowed into the South, but northern capital, technology, and people did not. Northern-based national banks emerged in the wake of the Civil War to fund northern economic expansion. The South, in contrast, had few banks, and they lacked sufficient capital reserves to fuel an equivalent expansion. In 1880, Massachusetts alone had five times as much bank capital as the entire South.

With limited access to other sources of capital, the South's textile industry depended on thousands of small investors in towns and cities. These investors avoided risk and shunned innovation. Most textile operations remained small-scale. The average southern firm in 1900 was capitalized at $11,000, compared with an average of $21,000 elsewhere.

The lumber industry, the South's largest, typified the shortcomings of southern economic development in the late nineteenth century. It also reflected the lack of concern about the natural environment. As a nascent conservation movement took hold in the North, southerners continued to view the natural environment as a venue for economic exploitation. The lumber industry required little capital, relied on unskilled labor, and processed its raw materials on site. After clear-cutting (i.e., felling all the trees) in one region, sawmills moved quickly to the next

QUICK REVIEW

Southern Industry

- Textile industry depended on thousands of small investors.
- Lumber industry typified the shortcomings of southern industry.
- Tobacco industry avoided problems that plagued other southern enterprises.

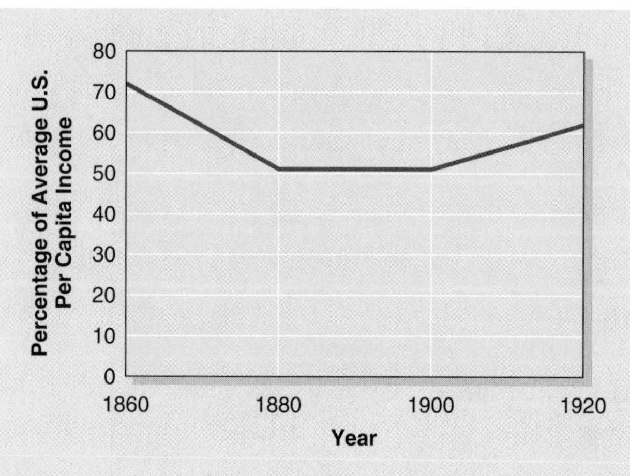

FIGURE 17–1 **Per Capita Income in the South as a Percentage of the U.S. Average, 1860–1920** This graph illustrates the devastating effect of the Civil War on the southern economy. Southerners began a slow recovery during the 1880s that accelerated after 1900. But even as late as 1920, per capita income in the South was still lower relative to the country as a whole than it had been before the Civil War.

Data Source: Richard A. Easterlin, "Regional Economic Trends, 1840–1950," in *American Economic History,* ed. Seymour E. Harris (1961).

stand of timber, leaving behind a bare landscape, rusting machinery, and a workforce no better off than before. This process, later repeated by the coal-mining industry, inflicted environmental damage on once remote areas such as Appalachia, and displaced their residents.

The tobacco industry, avoided the problems that plagued other southern enterprises. James B. Duke's American Tobacco Company was so immensely profitable that he became, in effect, his own bank. With more than enough capital to install the latest technology in his plants, Duke bought out his competitors. In the North, industrialization usually occurred in an urban context and promoted rapid urban growth. In the South, textile mills were typically located in the countryside, often in mill villages where employers could easily recruit families and keep them isolated from the distractions and employment alternatives of the cities. The timber industry similarly remained a rural-based enterprise. Tobacco manufacturing helped Durham and Winston, North Carolina, grow, but they remained small compared to northern industrial cities.

QUICK REVIEW

Restraints on Industrial and Urban Growth

- Weak agricultural economy and high rural birthrate depressed wages.
- Low wages limited consumption, development of skilled workforce, and immigration into the South.
- Limited access to capital hampered industrial innovation and expansion.

Levine Museum of the New South, Charlotte, North Carolina
http://www.museumofthenewsouth.org

Farms to Cities: Impact on Southern Society

If industrialization in the South was limited compared to the North, it nonetheless had an enormous impact on southern society. In the southern Piedmont, for example, textile mills transformed a portion of the farm population into an industrial workforce. Failed farmers moved to textile villages to earn a living. Entire families secured employment and often a house in exchange for their labor. Widows and single young men also moved to the mills, usually the only option outside farm work in the South. Nearly one-third of the textile-mill labor force by 1900 consisted of children under the age of 14 and women.

In 1880, southern towns often did not differ much from the countryside in appearance, economy, religion, and outlook. Over the next twenty years, the gap between town and country widened. By 1900, a town in the New South would boast a business district and more elegant residences than before. It would have a relatively prosperous economy and more frequent contact with other parts of the country. Its influence would extend into the countryside. Mail, the telegraph, the railroad, and the newspaper brought city life to the attention of farm families. In turn, farm families visited nearby towns and cities more often.

The urban South drew the region's talented and ambitious young people. White men moved to cities to open shops or take jobs as bank clerks, bookkeepers, merchants, and salesmen. White women worked as retail clerks, telephone operators, and office personnel. Black women filled the growing demand for laundresses and domestic servants. And black men also found prospects better in towns than on the farm, despite a narrow and uncertain range of occupations available to them. The excitement that drew some southerners to their new cities repelled others. To them, urbanization and the emphasis on wealth, new technology, and display represented a second Yankee conquest. The cities, they feared, threatened to infect the South with northern values, undermining southern grace, charm, faith, and family.

White southerners in town and country, who not long before had lived similar lives, grew distant. Small landholding white farmers and their families had fallen on hard times. The market that lured them into commercial agriculture threatened to take away their independence. They faced the loss of their land and livelihood. Their way of life no longer served as the standard for the South. New South spokesmen promoted cities and industries and ordered farmers to get on board the train of progress before it left the station without them.

THE SOUTHERN AGRARIAN REVOLT

WHAT WERE the origins and nature of southern Populism?

Even more than before the Civil War, cotton dominated southern agriculture between 1877 and 1900. And the economics of cotton brought despair to cotton farmers. The size of the cotton crop continued to set annual records after 1877. Fertilizers revived supposedly exhausted soils in North and South Carolina, turning them white with cotton. The railroad opened new areas for cultivation in Mississippi and eastern Texas. But the price of cotton fell while the price of fertilizers, agricultural tools, food, and most other necessities went up (see Figure 17–2). As a result, the more cotton the farmers grew, the less money they made.

Cotton and Credit

The solution to this agrarian dilemma seemed simple: Grow less cotton. But that course was not possible for several reasons. In a cash-poor economy, credit ruled. Cotton was the only commodity instantly convertible into cash and thus the only commodity accepted for credit. Food crops generated less income per acre than cotton. Local merchants, themselves bound in a web of credit to merchants in larger cities, accepted cotton as collateral. As cotton prices plummeted, the merchants required their customers to grow more cotton to make up the difference. Trapped in debt by low cotton prices and high interest rates, small landowning farmers lost their land in record numbers. Just after the Civil War, less than one-third of white farmers in the South were tenants or sharecroppers. By the 1890s, nearly half were.

Grange The National Grange of the Patrons of Husbandry, a national organization of farm owners formed after the Civil War.

Southern Farmers Organize, 1877–1892

As their circumstances deteriorated, southern farmers fought back. They had lived a communal life of church, family, and kin. Now they would widen the circle of their community to include other farmers sharing the same plight. These were not naive country folk; most owned their own land and participated in the market economy. They just wanted to make the market fairer, to lower interest rates and ease credit, to regulate railroad freight rates, and to keep the prices of necessities in check.

But these goals required legislation that neither the federal government nor southern state governments were inclined to support. Therefore, southern farmers joined their colleagues nationwide to address common grievances related to pricing, credit, and tax policies. Although some of the southern farmers' problems resulted from conditions peculiar to the South, agricultural distress became widespread after 1870. By 1875, nearly 250,000 southern landowners had joined the National Grange of the Patrons of Husbandry or, more popularly, simply the **Grange** (see Chapter 20). The leaders of the Grange, however, were large landowners. They did not have the same interests as the small farmers who made up the organization's rank and file.

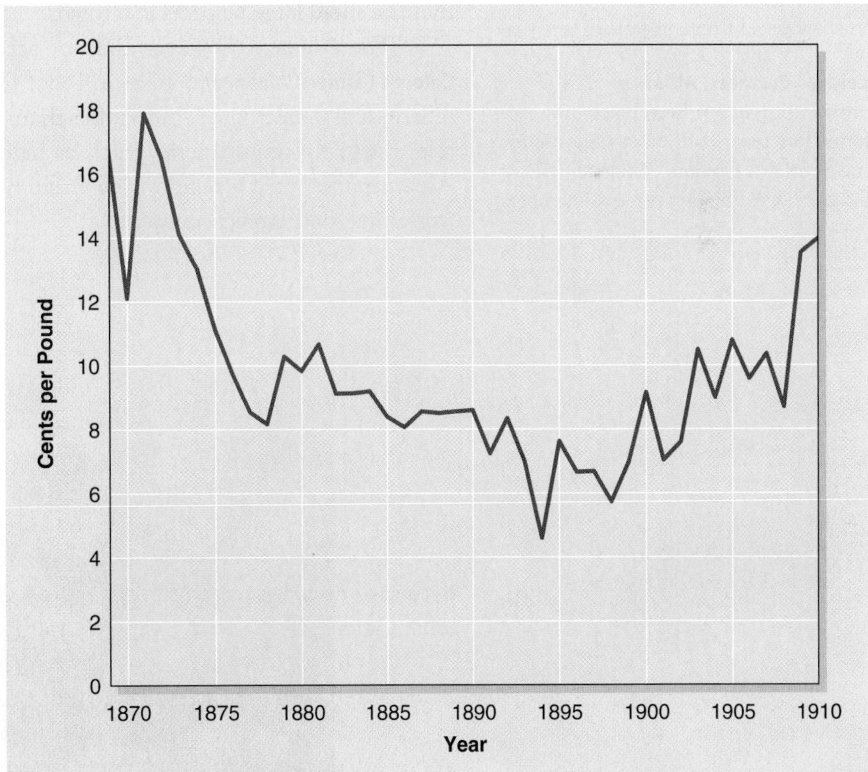

FIGURE 17–2 **The Price of Cotton, 1869–1910** The steadily declining price of cotton after the Civil War, from 18 cents a pound to 5 cents a pound by the early 1890s, reflected extreme overproduction. Behind the numbers lay an impoverished rural South.

Data Source: U.S. Department of Commerce, *Historical Statistics of the United States: Colonial Times to 1957.*

Southern Farmers' Alliance The largest of several organizations that formed in the post-Reconstruction South to advance the interests of beleaguered small farmers.

Salvation and cooperation. The most powerful agricultural reform organization, the **Southern Farmers' Alliance,** originated in Texas in the late 1870s. Alliance-sponsored farmers' cooperatives provided their members with discounts on supplies and credit. Members also benefited from marketing their cotton crops collectively.

The Alliance was still very much a Texas organization in 1887 when Charles W. Macune, a Wisconsin native, became its driving force. Macune sent a corps of speakers to create a network of southern cooperatives. Within two years, the Alliance had spread throughout the South and into the North and West. By 1890, it claimed more than a million members. With the exception of a few large landowners and some tenant farmers, almost all were small farmers who owned their own land. The success of the Alliance reflected both the desperate struggle of these small farmers to keep their land and the failure of other organizations to help them.

The Alliance operated like a religious denomination. Its leaders preached a message of salvation through cooperation to audiences of as many as 20,000 people at huge revival-like rallies. Qualifications for membership included a belief in the divinity of Jesus and the literal truth of the Bible. Alliance speakers, many of them rural ministers, often held meetings in churches. In their talks, they stressed the importance of doing good as much as good farming. The Alliance lobbied state legislatures to fund rural public schools. To increase the sense of community, the Alliance sponsored picnics, baseball games, and concerts.

The Alliance became for many small farmers a surrogate government and church in a region where public officials and many mainline Protestant ministers ignored their needs. It imposed strict morality on its members, prohibiting drinking, gambling, and sexual misconduct. Alliance leaders criticized the many Baptist, Methodist, and Presbyterian ministers who had strayed from the traditional emphasis on individual salvation and were defending a status quo that benefited large planters and towns.

Colored Farmers' Alliance An organization of southern black farmers formed in Texas in 1886 in response to the Southern Farmers' Alliance, which did not accept black people as members.

The Alliance, however, did not accept black members. Black farmers formed the first **Colored Farmers' Alliance** in Texas in 1886. The Colored Alliance had fewer landowners and more tenants and sharecroppers in its ranks than the white organization. It concerned itself with issues relevant to this constituency, such as higher wages for cotton pickers. In 1891, the Colored Alliance attempted a region-wide strike over farm wages but was unable to enforce it in the worsening southern economy.

Black sharecroppers in Georgia cotton fields, 1898; the scene is reminiscent of the slavery era. Southern agriculture contradicted New South rhetoric both in social and economic terms.

The white Alliance had better results with a protest over price fixing. To protect cotton shipped to market, farmers wrapped it in a burlap-like material called jute. In 1888, jute manufacturers combined to raise the price from 7 cents to as much as 14 cents a yard. The Alliance initiated a jute boycott throughout the South, telling farmers to use cotton bagging as an alternative. The protest worked, forcing the chastened jute manufacturers to offer farmers their product at a mere 5 cents per yard.

Storing cotton. This success encouraged Macune to pursue a more ambitious project. Low cotton prices and a lack of cash kept farmers poor. To address these problems, Macune proposed his **subtreasury plan.** Alliance members were to store their crops in a subtreasury (i.e., warehouse), keeping their cotton off the market until the price rose. In the meantime, the government would loan the farmers up to 80 percent of the value of the stored crops at a low interest rate of 2 percent per year. This arrangement would free farmers from merchants' high interest rates and crop liens. Macune urged Alliance members to endorse political candidates who supported the subtreasury scheme. Many Democratic candidates for state legislatures throughout the South did endorse it and were elected, with Alliance backing, in 1890. Once in office, however, they failed to deliver.

subtreasury plan A program promoted by the Southern Farmers' Alliance in response to low cotton prices and tight credit. Farmers would store their crop in a warehouse until prices rose, in the meantime borrowing up to 80 percent of the value of the stored crops from the government at a low interest rate.

The failure of the subtreasury plan, combined with a steep drop in cotton prices after 1890, undermined the Alliance. Alliance membership declined by two-thirds in Georgia that year. Desperate Alliance leaders merged their organization with a new national political party in 1892, the People's Party, better known as the **Populist Party.** The Populists appropriated the Alliance program and challenged Democrats in the South and Republicans in the West. The merger reflected desperation more than calculation. As we will see in Chapter 20, the Populists stirred up national politics between 1892 and 1896. In the South, they challenged the Democratic Party, sometimes courting Republicans, including black voters.

Populist Party A major third party of the 1890s, formed on the basis of the Southern Farmers' Alliance and other organizations, mounting electoral challenges against Democrats in the South and the Republicans in the West.

WOMEN IN THE NEW SOUTH

HOW DID traditional gender roles shape the opportunities available to women in the New South?

Because the antebellum reform movements included abolitionism, they had made little headway in the South. As a result, southern women had a meager reform tradition to build on. The war also left them ambivalent about independence. With husbands, fathers, and brothers dead or incapacitated, many women had to care for themselves and their families in the face of defeat and deprivation. Some determined never again to depend on men. Others, responding to the stress of running a farm or business, would have preferred less independence.

The response of southern white men to the war also complicated women's efforts to improve their status. Southern men had been shaken by defeat. They had lost the war and placed their families in peril. Many responded with alcoholism and violence. To regain their self-esteem, they recast the war as a noble crusade rather than a defeat. And they imagined southern white women as paragons of virtue and purity who required men to defend them. Demands for even small changes in traditional gender roles would threaten this image. Southern women understood this and never mounted an extensive reform campaign like their sisters in the North. Some middle-class women were openly hostile to reform, and others adopted conservative causes more inclined to reinforce the role of men in southern society than to challenge it.

at **www.myhistorylab.com**
The Lives of Southern Women

Despite such limitations, middle-class southern women found opportunities to broaden their social role and enter the public sphere in the two decades after 1880. They found these opportunities primarily in the cities, where servants, stores, and schools freed them of many of the productive functions, such as making clothing, cooking, and childcare, that burdened their sisters in the country and kept them tied to the home.

QUICK REVIEW

Southern Women and Reform

- Southern women played an active role in the public arena.
- The movement to found home mission societies led by single white women.
- Lily Hammond opened settlement houses in Atlanta in the 1890s.

Church Work and Preserving Memories

Southern women waded warily into the public arena, using channels men granted them as natural extensions of the home, such as church work. By the 1880s, evangelical Protestant churches had become prominent in many aspects of southern life. Women took advantage of the church's prominence to build careers using the moral gravity of church affiliation to political advantage. Most of the major reform efforts in the South during this era emanated from the church, and from the women for whom church work was an approved role for their gender.

The movement to found home mission societies, for example, was led by single white women in the Methodist Church. Home missions promoted industrial education among the poor and helped working-class women become self-sufficient. The home mission movement reflected an increased interest in missionary work in white southern evangelical churches. Lily Hammond extended the mission concept when she opened settlement houses in black and white neighborhoods in Atlanta in the 1890s. **Settlement houses,** pioneered in New York in the 1880s, promoted middle-class values in poor neighborhoods and provided them with a permanent source of services. In the North, they were privately sponsored. In the South, they were supported by the Methodist Church and known as Wesley Houses, after John Wesley, the founder of Methodism.

Settlement house A multipurpose structure in a poor neighborhood that offered social welfare, educational, and homemaking services to the poor or immigrants, usually under private auspices and directed by middle-class women.

Religion also prompted southern white women to join the **Women's Christian Temperance Union (WCTU).** Temperance reform, unlike other church-inspired activities, involved women directly in public policy. WCTU members visited schools to educate children about the evils of alcohol, addressed prisoners, and blanketed men's meetings with literature. As a result, they became familiar with the South's abysmal school system and its archaic criminal justice system. They soon began advocating education and prison reform as well as legislation against alcohol.

Women's Christian Temperance Union (WCTU) Women's organization whose members visited schools to educate children about the evils of alcohol, addressed prisoners, and blanketed men's meetings with literature.

By the 1890s, many WCTU members realized that they could not achieve their goals unless women had the vote. Rebecca Latimer Felton, an Atlanta suffragist and WCTU member, reflected the frustration of her generation of southern women in an address to workingwomen in 1892: "But some will say, you women might be quiet, you can't vote, you can't do anything! Exactly so, we have kept quiet for nearly a hundred years hoping to see relief come to the women of this country, and it hasn't come."

Rebecca Felton's own career highlighted the essentially conservative nature of the reform movement among middle-class white women in the New South. She fought for childcare facilities and sex education, as well as compulsory school attendance, and she pushed for the admission of women to the University of Georgia. But she strongly supported textile operators over textile workers and defended white supremacy. She had no qualms about the lynching of black men, executing them without trial "a thousand times a week if necessary" to preserve the purity of white women. In 1922, she became the first woman member of the U.S. Senate. By any definition, Felton was a reformer, but like most middle-class southern women, she had no interest in challenging the class and racial inequities of the New South.

The dedication of southern women to commemorating the memory of the Confederate cause also indicates the conservative nature of middle-class women's reform in the New South. Ladies' Memorial Associations formed after the war to ensure the proper burial of Confederate soldiers and suitable markings for their graves. The associations joined with men to erect monuments to Confederate leaders and, by the 1880s, to the common soldier. These activities reinforced white solidarity and constructed a common heritage for all white southerners regardless of class or location.

Southern white women played a major role in memorializing the Civil War and Confederate veterans. Here, a float prepared for a Confederate veterans parade includes the major symbols of the Lost Cause, including the prominent pictures of Robert E. Lee, Thomas "Stonewall" Jackson, and Jefferson Davis, as well as the Confederate Battle Flag. The sponsorship of a casket company affords some irony to the photograph.

Women's Clubs

A broader spectrum of southern middle-class women joined women's clubs than joined church-sponsored organizations or memorial associations. Most women's clubs began in the 1880s as literary or self-improvement societies that had little interest in reform. By 1890, most towns and cities boasted at least several women's clubs and perhaps a federated club organization. But by that time, some clubs and their members had also begun to discuss political issues, such as child labor reform, educational improvement, and prison reform.

The activities of black women's clubs paralleled those of white women's clubs. Most African American women in southern cities worked as domestics or laundresses. Black women's clubs supported daycare facilities for working mothers and settlement houses in poor black neighborhoods modeled after those in northern cities. Atlanta's Neighborhood Union, founded by Lugenia Burns Hope in 1908, provided playgrounds and a health center and obtained a grant from a New York foundation to improve black education in the city. Black women's clubs also established homes for single black working women to protect them from sexual exploitation, and they worked for woman suffrage.

Only rarely, however, as at some meetings of the Young Women's Christian Association (YWCA) or occasional meetings in support of prohibition, did black and white club members interact. Some white clubwomen expressed sympathy for black women privately, but publicly they maintained white solidarity. Most were unwilling to sacrifice their own reform agenda to the cause of racial reconciliation.

GLOBAL CONNECTIONS

THE RACE "PROBLEM" IN EUROPE

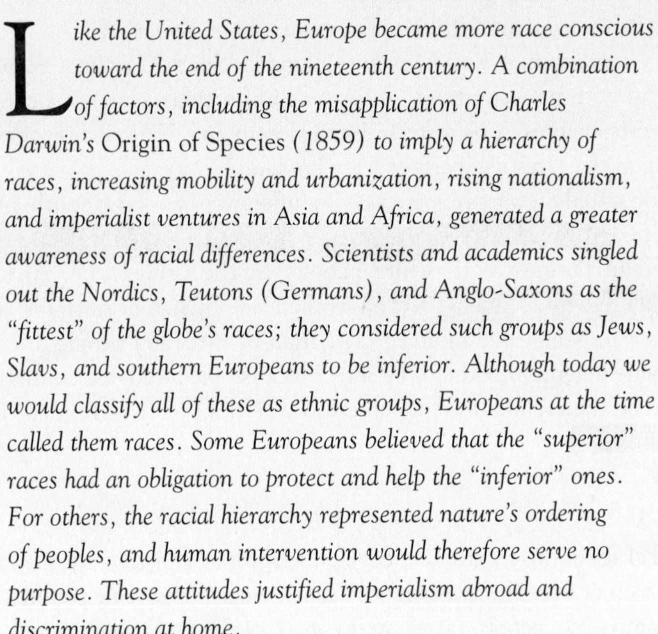

Like the United States, Europe became more race conscious toward the end of the nineteenth century. A combination of factors, including the misapplication of Charles Darwin's Origin of Species *(1859) to imply a hierarchy of races, increasing mobility and urbanization, rising nationalism, and imperialist ventures in Asia and Africa, generated a greater awareness of racial differences. Scientists and academics singled out the Nordics, Teutons (Germans), and Anglo-Saxons as the "fittest" of the globe's races; they considered such groups as Jews, Slavs, and southern Europeans to be inferior. Although today we would classify all of these as ethnic groups, Europeans at the time called them races. Some Europeans believed that the "superior" races had an obligation to protect and help the "inferior" ones. For others, the racial hierarchy represented nature's ordering of peoples, and human intervention would therefore serve no purpose. These attitudes justified imperialism abroad and discrimination at home.*

These racial attitudes emerged at a time when many European nations had already granted Jewish citizens full legal equality. Freed from occupational, educational, and residential restrictions, the Jewish population flourished as never before, rising and assimilating into European society. Their ascension troubled some Europeans, much as contemporary southern whites felt threatened by African American mobility. During the 1880s and 1890s, Germany and Austria founded right-wing parties that utilized anti-Semitism to win votes among groups that were wary of modern trends such as urbanization and industrialization. For such people, newly enfranchised Jews were a natural target of hatred and fear. By the 1890s, Europe had a "Jewish problem" that resembled the American South's "Negro problem."

In 1895, Theodor Herzl, an Austrian Jewish journalist, posed an answer to the problem: the voluntary removal of Europe's Jews to Palestine. Surveying the rising tide of European anti-Semitism, Herzl proposed a Jewish nation-state. "Palestine is our ever memorable historic home . . . the great symbol of the solution of the Jewish Question after eighteen centuries of Jewish suffering."

The first Zionist Congress met in Switzerland in 1897, declaring its aim to create a "home in Palestine secured by public law" for world Jewry. Between 1904 and 1914, about 3,000 Jews per year migrated to the Holy Land. Throughout the first half of the twentieth century, Jewish migration to Palestine was restricted, first by the Ottoman Turks and then by the British. Large numbers of Jews settled instead in the northern cities of the United States.

Blacks in the American South also contemplated separate homelands, either in Africa or in the United States. Back-to-Africa movements appeared periodically in the decades after the Civil War. But as with European Jews, the greatest number of migrants went to the cities of the North, especially after the turn of the twentieth century.

- Why did most blacks in the American South and Jews in Europe during the late nineteenth century decide against migrating to a separate homeland?

SETTLING THE RACE ISSUE

WHAT STEPS did southerners take in the late nineteenth century to limit the freedom of African Americans?

The assertiveness of a new generation of African Americans in the 1880s and 1890s, especially in urban areas, provided the impetus and opportunity for white leaders to secure white solidarity. To counter black aspirations, white leaders enlisted the support of young white southerners, convincing them that the struggle for white supremacy would place them beside the larger-than-life heroes of the Civil War generation. African Americans resisted the resulting efforts to deprive them of their remaining freedoms. Although some left the South, many more built new lives and communities within the restricted framework white southerners allowed them.

The Fluidity of Southern Race Relations, 1877–1890

Race relations remained remarkably fluid in the South between the end of Reconstruction and the early 1890s. Despite the departure of federal troops and the end of Republican rule, many black people continued to vote and hold office. Some Democrats even courted the black electorate. Although segregation ruled in churches, schools, and in some organizations and public places after the Civil War, black people and white people continued to mingle, do business with each other, and often maintain cordial relations.

In 1885, T. McCants Stewart, a black journalist from New York, traveled to his native South Carolina, expecting a rough reception once his train headed south from Washington, DC. To his surprise, the conductor allowed him to remain in his seat while white riders sat on baggage or stood. He provoked little reaction among white passengers when he entered the dining car. Some of them struck up a conversation with him. In Columbia, South Carolina, Stewart found that he could move about with no restrictions. "I can ride in first-class cars. . . . I can go into saloons and get refreshments even as in New York. I can stop in and drink a glass of soda and be more politely waited upon than in some parts of New England."

Other black people corroborated Stewart's experiences in different parts of the South. During the 1880s, black people joined interracial labor unions and continued to be active in the Republican Party. They engaged in business with white people. In the countryside, African Americans and white people hunted and fished together, worked side by side at sawmills, and traded with each other. Cities were segregated more by class than by race, and people of both races sometimes lived in the same neighborhoods. To be sure, black people faced discrimination in employment and voting and random retaliation for perceived violations of racial barriers. But the barriers were by no means fixed.

The White Backlash

The black generation that came of age in this environment demanded full participation in American society. For many in the generation of white southerners who came of age in the same period, this assertiveness rankled. These young white people, raised on the myth of the Lost Cause, were continually reminded of the heroism and sacrifice of their fathers during the Civil War. For them, black people replaced the Yankees as the enemy; they saw it as their mission to preserve white purity and dominance. The South's deteriorating rural economy and the volatile politics of the late 1880s and early 1890s exacerbated the growing tensions between assertive black people and threatened white people. So too did the growth of industry and cities in the South. In the cities, black and white people came into close contact, competing for jobs and jostling each other for seats on streetcars and trains. Racist rhetoric and violence against black people accelerated in the 1890s.

Hear the Audio at **www.myhistorylab.com** *Lynch Law in Georgia*

Lynch Law

In 1892, three prominent black men, Tom Moss, Calvin McDowell, and William Stewart, opened a grocery on the south side of Memphis, an area with a large African American population. The People's Grocery prospered, while a white-owned store across the street struggled.

Lynching became a public spectacle, a ritual designed to reinforce white supremacy. Note the matter-of-fact satisfaction of the spectators at this gruesome murder of a black man.

The proprietor of the white-owned store, W. H. Barrett, was incensed. He obtained an indictment against Moss, McDowell, and Stewart for maintaining a public nuisance. Outraged black community leaders called a protest meeting at the grocery, during which two people made threats against Barrett. Barrett learned of the threats, notified the police, and warned the gathering at the People's Grocery that white people planned to attack and destroy the store. Nine sheriff's deputies, all white, approached the store to arrest the men who had threatened Barrett. Fearing Barrett's threatened white assault, the people in the grocery fired on the deputies, unaware who they were, and wounded three. When the deputies identified themselves, thirty black people surrendered, including Moss, McDowell, and Stewart, and were imprisoned. Four days later, deputies removed the three owners from jail, took them to a deserted area, and shot them dead.

The men at the People's Grocery had violated two of the unspoken rules that white southerners imposed on black southerners to maintain racial barriers: They had prospered, and they had forcefully challenged white authority. During 1892, a year of political agitation and economic depression, 235 **lynchings** occurred in the South. White mobs lynched nearly 2,000 black southerners between 1882 and 1903. Most lynchers were working-class whites with rural roots, who were struggling in the depressed economy of the 1890s and enraged at the fluidity of urban race relations. The most common justification for lynching was the presumed threat posed by black men to the sexual virtue of white women. Sexual "crimes" could include remarks, glances, and gestures. Yet only 25 percent of the lynchings that took place in the thirty years after 1890 had an alleged sexual connection. Certainly, the men of the People's Grocery had committed no sex crime. Lynchers did not carry out their grisly crimes to end a rape epidemic; they killed to keep black men in their place and to restore their own sense of manhood and honor.

lynching Execution, usually by a mob, without trial.

QUICK REVIEW

Lynching

- 1882–1903: nearly 2,000 black southerners lynched.
- Lynching justified by alleged threat of black male sexuality to white female virtue.
- Ida B. Wells took the lead in campaigning against lynchings.

Ida B. Wells, who owned a black newspaper in Memphis, used her columns to publicize the People's Grocery lynchings. The great casualty of the lynchings, she noted, was her faith that education, wealth, and upright living guaranteed black people the equality and justice they had long sought. The reverse was true. The more black people succeeded, the greater was their threat to white people. She investigated other lynchings, countering the claim that they were the result of assaults on white women. When she suggested that, on the contrary, perhaps some white women were attracted to black men, the white citizens of Memphis destroyed her press and office. Exiled to Chicago, Wells devoted herself to the struggle for racial justice.

What is striking about this carnival of lynching from the 1890s onward was its orchestrated cruelty and the involvement of large segments of the white community. Postcards and bootlegged photographs of the events showed men, women, and even children gathering as if for a Sunday picnic, surrounding the mutilated corpse. The elevation of white men as the protector for weak women was one reason for the spectacle, but, more important, lynching reinforced white solidarity and reiterated (especially to blacks) that white supremacy ruled the South with impunity. (See American Views: An Account of a Lynching.)

Read the Document at **www.myhistorylab.com**
Ida B. Wells-Barnett, from A Red Record *(1895)*

SEGREGATION BY LAW

segregation A system of racial control that separated the races, initially by custom but increasingly by law, during and after Reconstruction.

disfranchisement The use of legal means to bar individuals or groups from voting.

Southern white lawmakers sought to cement white solidarity and ensure black subservience in the 1890s by instituting **segregation** by law and the **disfranchisement** of black voters. Racial segregation restricting black Americans to separate and rarely equal public facilities had prevailed nationwide before the Civil War. After 1870, the custom spread rapidly in southern cities.

During the same period, many northern cities and states, often in response to protests by African Americans, were ending segregation. Roughly 95 percent of the nation's black population, however, lived in the South. Integration in the North, consequently, required white people to give up very little to black people. And as African American aspirations increased in the South during the 1890s while their political power waned, they became more vulnerable to segregation by law at the state level. At the same time, migration to cities, industrial development, and technologies such as railroads and elevators increased the opportunities for racial contact and muddled the rules of racial interaction.

Much of the new legislation focused on railroads, a symbol of modernity and mobility in the New South. Local laws and customs could not control racial interaction on interstate railroads. White passengers objected to black passengers' implied assertion of economic and social equality when they sat with them in dining cars and first-class compartments. Black southerners, by contrast, viewed equal access to railroad facilities as a sign of respectability and acceptance. When southern state legislatures required railroads to provide segregated facilities, black people protested.

Segregation laws required the railroads to provide "separate but equal" accommodations for black passengers. Railroads balked at the expense involved in doing so and provided black passengers with distinctly inferior facilities. Many lines refused to sell first-class tickets to black people and treated them roughly if they sat in first-class seats or tried to eat in the dining car. In 1890, Homer Plessy, a black Louisianan, refused to leave the first-class car of a railroad traveling through the state. Arrested, he filed suit, arguing that his payment of the first-class fare entitled him to sit in the same first-class accommodations as white passengers.

Read the Document at **www.myhistorylab.com**
Opinion of the Supreme Court for Plessy v. Ferguson *(1896)*

Plessy v. Ferguson Supreme Court decision holding that Louisiana's railroad segregation law did not violate the Constitution as long as the railroads or the state provided equal accommodations.

The U.S. Supreme Court ruled on the case, ***Plessy v. Ferguson,*** in 1896. In a seven-to-one decision, the Court held that Louisiana's railroad segregation law did not violate the Constitution as long as the railroads or the state provided equal accommodations for black passengers. The decision left unclear what "equal" meant. In the Court's view, "Legislation is powerless to eradicate racial instincts," meaning that segregation of the races was natural and transcended constitutional considerations. The only justice to vote against the decision was John Marshall Harlan, a Kentuckian and former slave owner. He predicted that the decision would result in an all-out assault on black rights.

Harlan's was a prophetic dissent. Both northern and southern states enacted new segregation laws in the wake of *Plessy v. Ferguson*. In practice, the separate facilities for black people these laws required, if provided at all, were rarely equal.

Jim Crow laws Segregation laws that became widespread in the South during the 1890s.

The segregation statutes came to be known collectively as **Jim Crow laws,** after the blackface stage persona of Thomas Rice, a white northern minstrel-show performer in the 1820s. Reflecting white stereotypes of African Americans, Rice had caricatured Crow as a foolish, elderly, lame slave who spoke in an exaggerated dialect. The purpose of these laws was not only to separate the races, but also to humiliate blacks and reinforce white supremacy. Separation was never equal.

Economic segregation followed social segregation. Before the Civil War, black men had dominated such crafts as carpentry and masonry. By the 1890s, white men were replacing them in these trades and excluding them from new ones, such as plumbing and electrical work. Trade unions, composed primarily of craft workers, began systematically to exclude African Americans. Although the steel and tobacco industries hired black workers, most other manufacturers turned them away. Confined increasingly to low or unskilled positions in railroad construction, the timber industry, and agriculture, black people underwent deskilling, a decline in workforce expertise, after 1890. With lower incomes from unskilled labor, they faced reduced opportunities for better housing and education.

Ida B. Wells, an outspoken critic of lynching, fled to Chicago following the People's Grocery lynchings in Memphis in 1892 and became a national civil rights leader.

DISFRANCHISEMENT

With economic and social segregation came political isolation. The authority of post-Reconstruction Redeemer governments had rested on their ability to limit and control the black vote. Following the political instability of the late 1880s and the 1890s, however, white leaders determined to disfranchise black people altogether, thereby reinforcing white solidarity and eliminating the need to consider black interests. Support for disfranchisement was especially strong among large landowners in the South's plantation districts, where heavy concentrations of black people threatened their political domination. Urban leaders, especially after the turmoil of the 1890s, looked on disfranchisement as a way to stabilize politics and make elections more predictable.

The movement to reduce or eliminate the black vote in the South began in the 1880s and continued through the early 1900s (see Overview, The March of Disfranchisement Across the South, 1889–1908). Democrats enacted a variety of measures to attain their objectives without violating the letter of the Fifteenth Amendment. They complicated the registration and voting processes. States enacted **poll taxes,** requiring citizens to pay to vote. They adopted the secret ballot, which confused and intimidated illiterate black voters accustomed to using ballots with colors to identify parties. States set literacy and educational qualifications for voting or required prospective registrants to "interpret" a section of the state constitution. To avoid disfranchising poor, illiterate white voters with these measures, states enacted **grandfather clauses,** granting the vote automatically to anyone whose grandfather could have voted prior to 1867 (the year Congressional Reconstruction began). The grandfathers of most black men in the 1890s had been slaves, ineligible to vote.

Hear the Audio at **www.myhistorylab.com** *A Republican Textbook for Colored Voters*

poll taxes Taxes imposed on voters as a requirement for voting.

grandfather clause Rule that required potential voters to demonstrate that their grandfathers had been eligible to vote; used in some southern states after 1890 to limit the black electorate.

Lawmakers sold white citizens on franchise restrictions with the promise that they would apply only to black voters and would scarcely affect white voters. This promise proved untrue. Alarmed by the Populist uprising, Democratic leaders used disfranchisement to gut dissenting parties. During the 1880s, minority parties in the South consistently polled an average of 40 percent of the statewide vote; by the mid-1890s, the figure had diminished to 30 percent despite the Populist insurgency. Turnout dropped even more dramatically. In Mississippi, for example, voter turnout in gubernatorial races during the 1880s averaged 51 percent; during the 1890s, it was 21 percent. Black turnout in Mississippi, which averaged 39 percent in the 1880s, plummeted to near zero in the 1890s. Overall turnout, which averaged 64 percent during the 1880s, fell to only 30 percent by 1910.

Black people protested disfranchisement vigorously. When 160 South Carolina delegates gathered to amend the state constitution in 1895, the six black delegates among them mounted a passionate but futile defense of their right to vote. Black delegate W. J. Whipper noted the irony

"JIM CROW" CARS

For Virginia Afro-Americans, as Well as Those of Kentucky, Tennessee and Several Other Southern States.

An Attempt to Extend the Provisions of the Outrageous Law to Street Cars.

The Constitutionality of the Law to be Attacked in the Courts by an Electric Street Car Company and Prominent Virginia Afro-Americans.

Richmond, Va.—Since Sunday week, July 1, the "Jim Crow" car law passed by the Virginia legislature last January, and signed by Gov. Tyler in spite of the remonstrance of nearly every influential colored man in Virginia, has been in force. It requires every railroad and, some attorneys say, every street car company in the state to provide separate cars for the exclusive use of colored people. Negroes are not allowed to ride on the cars intended for the use of the whites, and vice versa; but any Negro forcing himself upon a car for whites, and refusing to leave when requested to do so, may be forcibly ejected

Segregation by law accelerated after the 1896 *Plessy v. Ferguson* decision, but public conveyances often failed to abide by the "equal" portion of the separate-but-equal ruling. African Americans in the South fought racial separation and exclusion vigorously, as this excerpt from a black newspaper in Cleveland attests. July 14, 1900.

Read the **Document**
at www.myhistorylab.com
From Then to Now Online: The Confederate Battle Flag

of white people clamoring for supremacy when they already held the vast majority of the state's elected offices. Robert Smalls, the state's leading black politician, urged delegates not to turn their backs on the state's black population. Such pleas fell on deaf ears.

History and Memory

Whites codified white supremacy in laws, enforced it with violence, and institutionalized it on the landscape and in the history books. History not only immortalized the Lost Cause and the Redemption, but it also served a more contemporary purpose. It endorsed white supremacy and justified actions carried out in its name. By the early 1900s, a statue of a Confederate soldier stood guard over courthouse squares throughout the South, silent witness to sacrifice and restoration. In Richmond, the capital of the Confederacy became a shrine. Down the wide boulevard of Monument Avenue, the statues of the war heroes marched. By 1900, only three monuments paid tribute to black soldiers—none in the South. African Americans were as absent in the landscape as they were in the textbooks.

A National Consensus on Race

White southerners openly segregated, disfranchised, and lynched African Americans, and twisted the historical record beyond recognition without a national outcry for the same reasons they were able to overthrow Reconstruction. The majority of Americans in the 1890s subscribed to the notion that black people were inferior to white people and deserved to be treated as second-class citizens. Contemporary depictions of black people show scarcely human stereotypes: black men with bulbous lips and bulging eyes, fat black women wearing turbans and smiling vacuously, and black children contentedly eating watermelon or romping with jungle animals. Among the widely read books of the era was *The Clansman*, a glorification of the rise of the Ku Klux Klan. D. W. Griffith transformed *The Clansman* into an immensely popular motion picture epic under the title *Birth of a Nation*.

Intellectual and political opinion in the North bolstered southern policy. So-called scientific racism purported to establish white superiority and black inferiority on biological grounds. Northern-born professional historians reinterpreted the Civil War and Reconstruction in the white South's favor. Respected national journals openly supported disfranchisement and segregation. The *New York Times*, summarizing this national consensus in 1903, noted that "practically the whole country" supported the "southern solution" to the race issue, because "there was no other possible settlement."

These views permeated Congress, which made no effort to block the institutionalization of white supremacy in the South after 1890, and the courts, which upheld discriminatory legislation. As the white consensus on race emerged, the status of African Americans slipped in the North as well as the South. Although no northern states threatened to deny black citizens the right to vote, they did increase segregation. The booming industries of the North generally did not hire black workers. Antidiscrimination laws on the books since the Civil War went unenforced. In 1904, 1906, and 1908, race riots erupted in

OVERVIEW The March of Disfranchisement across the South, 1889–1908

Year	State	Strategies
1889	Florida	Poll tax
1889	Tennessee	Poll tax
1890	Mississippi	Poll tax, literacy test, understanding clause
1891	Arkansas	Poll tax
1893, 1901	Alabama	Poll tax, literacy test, grandfather clause
1894, 1895	South Carolina	Poll tax, literacy test, understanding clause
1894, 1902	Virginia	Poll tax, literacy test, understanding clause
1897, 1898	Louisiana	Poll tax, literacy test, grandfather clause
1899, 1900	North Carolina	Poll tax, literacy test, grandfather clause
1902	Texas	Poll tax
1908	Georgia	Poll tax, literacy test, understanding clause, grandfather clause

Springfield, Ohio; Greensburg, Indiana; and Springfield, Illinois, matching similar disturbances in Wilmington, North Carolina; and Atlanta, Georgia.

Read the **Document**
at **www.myhistorylab.com**
Exploring America: Racism in America

Response of the Black Community

American democracy had, it seemed, hung out a "whites only" sign. How could African Americans respond to the growing political, social, and economic restrictions on their lives? Given white America's hostility, protest proved ineffective, even dangerous. African

The offices of the North Carolina Mutual Life Insurance Company, around 1900. Founded by John Merrick, C. C. Spaulding, and Dr. A. M. Moore (all of whom appear in the picture), this Durham-based insurance company became one of the most successful black enterprises in the country.

AMERICAN VIEWS

An Account of a Lynching

Luther Holbert allegedly murdered a white plantation owner in Doddsville, Mississippi, in February 1904 after he refused the owner's demand to leave the property. Holbert and his wife fled, but a mob of 1,000 whites tracked them down. Although there was no evidence to link Holbert's wife to the crime, she was taken into custody as well. Six hundred people gathered, fortified by deviled eggs, lemonade, and whiskey. Following is an account from a local newspaper of what happened next.

- **What** was the purpose of visiting such extreme cruelty upon the victims?
- **The** lynching occurred without a proper trial. Do you think any of the perpetrators were ever arrested or tried for the lynching?
- **Why** did a party atmosphere prevail?

They were tied to trees, and while the funeral pyres were being prepared they were forced to suffer the most fiendish tortures. The blacks were forced to hold out their hands while one finger at a time was chopped off. The fingers were distributed as souvenirs. The ears of the murderers were cut off. Holbert was beaten severely, his skull was fractured, and one of his eyes, knocked with the stick, hung by a shred from the socket. . . . The most excruciating form of punishment consisted in the use of a large corkscrew in the hands of some of the mob. This instrument was bored into the flesh of the man and woman, in the arms, legs, and body, and then pulled out, the spirals tearing out big pieces of raw, quivering flesh every time it was withdrawn.

Source: Vicksburg Evening Post, February 8, 1904.

Americans organized more than a dozen boycotts of streetcar systems in the urban South between 1896 and 1908 in an effort to desegregate them, but not one succeeded. The Afro-American Council, formed in 1890 to protest the deteriorating conditions of black life, accomplished little and disbanded in 1908. W. E. B. Du Bois organized an annual Conference on Negro Problems at Atlanta University beginning in 1896, but it produced no effective plan of action.

A few black people chose to leave the South. Most black people who moved in the 1890s stayed within the South, settling in places like Mississippi, Louisiana, and Texas, where they could find work with timber companies or farming new lands that had opened to cotton and rice cultivation.

An urban middle class. More commonly, black people withdrew to develop their own rich community life within the restricted confines white society permitted them. Particularly in the cities of the South, they could live relatively free of white surveillance and even white contact. In 1890, fully 70 percent of black city dwellers lived in the South; and between 1860 and 1900, the proportion of black people in the cities of the South rose from one in six to more than one in three. The institutions, businesses, and families that black people had begun painstakingly building during Reconstruction continued to grow, and in some cases flourish, after 1877.

QUICK REVIEW

Responses to Segregation

- Desegregation efforts in the South failed.
- A few black people chose to leave the South.
- Most black people withdrew into their own communities.

By the 1880s, a new black middle class had emerged in the South. Urban-based, professional, business-oriented, and serving a primarily black clientele, its members fashioned an interconnected web of churches, fraternal and self-help organizations, families, and businesses. Black Baptists, AME, and AME Zion churches led reform efforts that sought to eliminate drinking, prostitution, and other vices in black neighborhoods.

African American fraternal and self-help groups, led by middle-class black people, functioned as surrogate welfare organizations for the poor. Fraternal orders also served as the

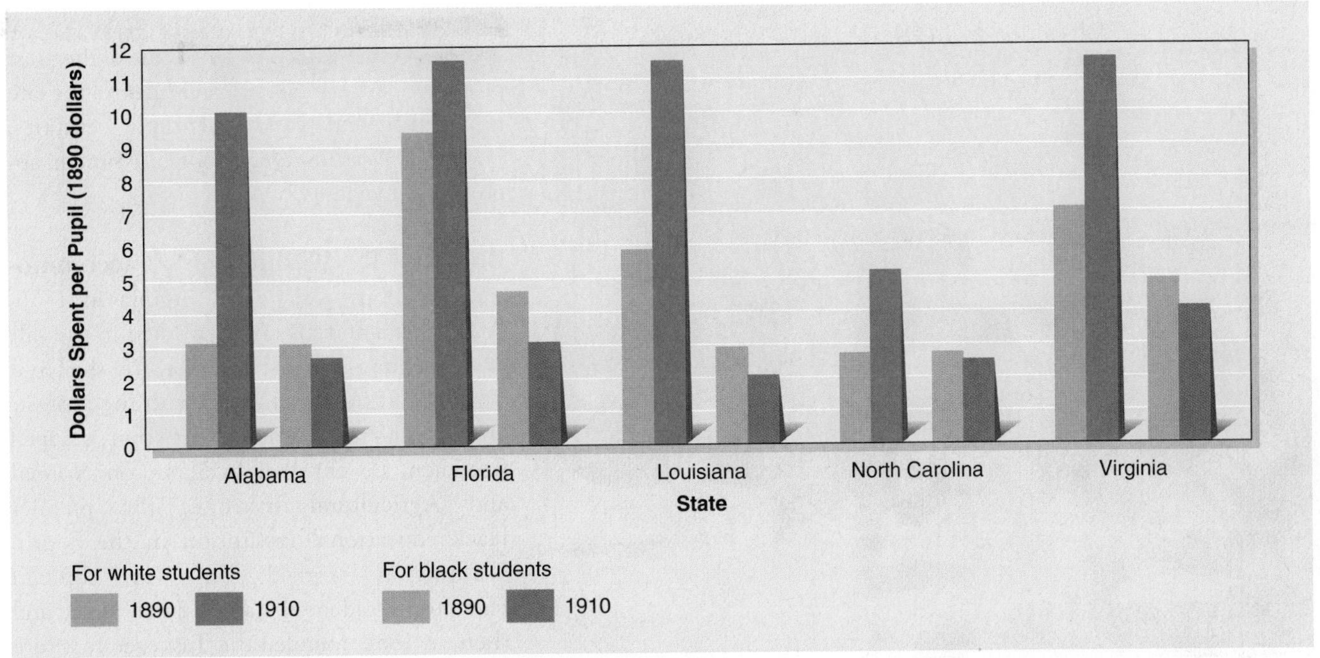

FIGURE 17–3 **Disfranchisement and Educational Spending in the South, 1890–1910** By barring black people from the political process, franchise restrictions limited their access to government services. Educational expenditures, which increased for white people but decreased for black people following disfranchisement, provide one measure of the result.

Data Source: Robert A. Margo, "Disfranchisement, School Finance, and the Economics of Segregated Schools in the United States South, 1890–1910," Ph.D. diss., Harvard University, 1982.

seedbed for such business ventures as the North Carolina Mutual Life Insurance Company, founded in Durham in 1898. Within two decades, North Carolina Mutual became the largest black-owned business in the nation and helped transform Durham into the "capital of the black middle class." Durham's thriving black business district included several black-owned insurance firms, banks, and a textile mill. Most southern cities boasted active black business districts by the 1890s.

The African American middle class worked especially hard to improve black education (see Figure 17–3). Declining black political power encouraged white leaders to reduce funding for black public education. Black students in cities had only makeshift facilities; those in the countryside had almost no facilities. By the early 1900s, the student-teacher ratio in Nashville's segregated school system was 33 to one for white schools but 71 to one for black schools. To improve these conditions, black middle-class leaders solicited educational funds from northern philanthropic organizations.

Black women's roles. After disfranchisement, middle-class black women assumed an even more pivotal role in the black community. They often used their relations with prominent white women and organizations such as the WCTU and the Young Women's Christian Association (YWCA) to press for public commitments to improve the health and education of African Americans. Absent political pressure from black men, and given the danger of African American males asserting themselves in the tense racial climate after 1890, black women became critical spokespersons for their race.

The extension of black club work into rural areas of the South, where the majority of the African American population lived, to educate families about hygiene, nutrition, and childcare, anticipated similar efforts among white women after 1900. But unlike their white counterparts, these middle-class black women worked with limited resources in a context of simmering racial hostility and political and economic impotence. In response, they nurtured a

Hear the **Audio** at **www.myhistorylab.com**
Address at the Atlanta Exposition by Booker T. Washington

Booker T. Washington at his desk, Tuskegee Institute, 1902.

self-help strategy to improve the conditions of the people they sought to help. One of the most prominent African American leaders of the late nineteenth and early twentieth centuries, Booker T. Washington, adopted a similar approach to racial uplift.

Booker T. Washington's accommodation. Born a slave in Virginia in 1856, Washington and his family worked in the salt and coal mines of West Virginia after the Civil War. Ambitious and flushed with the postwar enthusiasm for advancement that gripped freedmen, he enrolled in Hampton Normal and Agricultural Institute, the premier black educational institution in the South. Washington worked his way through Hampton, graduated, taught for a time, and then, in 1881, founded the Tuskegee Institute for black students in rural Alabama. Washington thought that his students would be best served if they learned a trade and workplace discipline. By learning industrial skills, he maintained, black people could acquire self-respect and economic independence. As a result, Tuskegee emphasized vocational training over the liberal arts.

Atlanta Compromise Booker T. Washington's policy accepting segregation and disfranchisement for African Americans in exchange for white assistance in education and job training.

QUICK REVIEW

Booker T. Washington

- Born a slave in Virginia in 1856.
- Founded Tuskegee Institute in 1881.
- Advocated the Atlanta Compromise.

Washington argued that African Americans should accommodate themselves to segregation and disfranchisement until they could prove their economic worth to American society. In exchange for this accommodation, however, white people should help provide black people with the education and job training they would need to gain their independence. Washington articulated this position, known as the **Atlanta Compromise,** in a speech at the Atlanta Cotton States and International Exposition in 1895. Despite his conciliatory public stance, Washington secretly helped to finance legal challenges to segregation and disfranchisement. The social and economic realities of the South, meanwhile, frustrated his educational mission. Increasingly, black people were shut out of the kinds of jobs for which Washington hoped to train them. Facing a depressed rural economy and growing racial violence, they had little prospect of advancement.

National Association for the Advancement of Colored People (NAACP) Interracial organization cofounded by W. E. B. Du Bois in 1910 dedicated to restoring African American political and social rights.

QUICK REVIEW

W. E. B. Du Bois

- Born in Massachusetts in 1868.
- First African American to earn a doctorate at Harvard.
- Promoted self-help, education, and black pride.
- Opponent of Washington's Atlanta Compromise.

W. E. B. Du Bois attacks the Atlanta Compromise. Another prominent African American leader, W. E. B. Du Bois, challenged Washington's acceptance of black social inequality. Born in Massachusetts in 1868, Du Bois was the first African American to earn a doctorate at Harvard. Du Bois promoted self-help, education, and black pride. In *The Souls of Black Folk*, published in 1903, he described the strengths of black culture and attacked Washington's Atlanta Compromise. Du Bois was a cofounder, in 1910, of the **National Association for the Advancement of Colored People (NAACP),** an interracial organization dedicated to restoring African American political and social rights.

Despite their differences, which reflected their divergent backgrounds, Washington and Du Bois agreed on many issues. Both had reservations about allowing illiterate black people to vote, and both believed that black success in the South required some white assistance. But it became apparent to Du Bois that white people did not care to elevate black southerners. In 1906, after a bloody race riot in Atlanta, Du Bois left the South, a decision millions of black southerners would make over the next two decades.

CONCLUSION

On the surface, the South was more like the rest of the nation in 1900 than at any other time since 1860. Southern cities hummed with activity, and industries from textiles to steel dotted the southern interior. Young men and women migrated to southern cities to pursue opportunities unavailable to their parents. Advances in the production and marketing of cigarettes and soft drinks would soon make southern entrepreneurs and their products household names. Southerners ordered fashions from Sears, Roebuck catalogs and enjoyed electric lights, electric trolleys, and indoor plumbing as much as other urban Americans.

Watch the Video at www.myhistorylab.com *The Conflict between Booker T. Washington and W.E.B. Du Bois*

Watch the Video at www.myhistorylab.com *Moonlight and Magnolias: Creating the Old South*

Americans idealized the South—not the urban industrial South, but a mythical South of rural grace and hospitality. National magazines and publishers rushed to print stories about this land of moonlight and magnolias, offering it as a counterpoint to the crowded, immigrant-infested, factory-fouled, money-grubbing North. It was this fantasy South that white people in both the North and the South imagined as they came to a common view on race and reconciled their differences. White southerners cultivated national reconciliation but remained fiercely dedicated to preserving the peculiarities of their region: a one-party political system, disfranchisement of African Americans, and segregation by law. The region's urban and industrial growth, impressive from the vantage of 1865, paled before that of the North. The South remained a colonial economy characterized more by deep rural poverty than urban prosperity.

How one viewed the New South depended on one's vantage point. White northerners accepted at face value the picture white southerners painted for them of a chastened and prosperous, yet still attractive, region. Middle-class white people in the urban South enjoyed the benefits of a national economy and a secure social position. Middle-class white women enjoyed increased influence in the public realm, but not to the extent of their northern sisters. And the institutionalization of white supremacy gave even poor white farmers and factory workers a place in the social hierarchy a rung or two above the bottom.

For black people, the New South proved a crueler ruse than Reconstruction. No one now stepped forward to support their cause and stem the erosion of their economic independence, political freedom, and civil rights. Yet they did not give up the American dream, nor did they give up the South for the most part. They built communities and worked as best they could to challenge restrictions on their freedom.

The New South was thus both American and southern. It shared with the rest of the country a period of rapid urban and industrial growth. But the legacy of war and slavery still lay heavily on the South, manifesting itself in rural poverty, segregation, and black disfranchisement. The burdens of this legacy would limit the attainments of both black and white southerners for another half-century, until Americans finally rejected racial inequality as an affront to their national ideals. America allowed the South to take another path and the South took the nation on a long detour until the despised African righted the way.

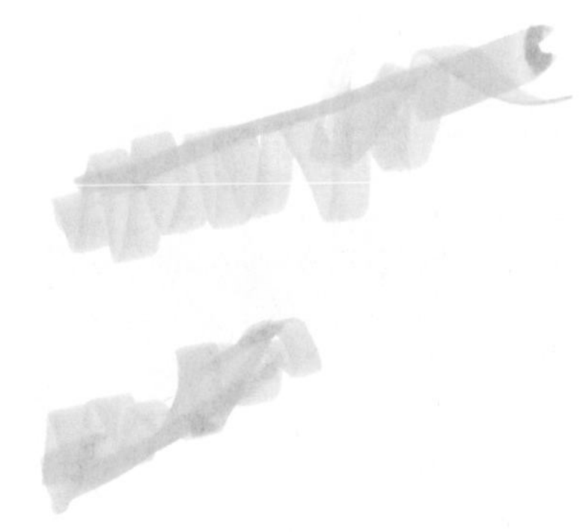

Where to Learn More

Levine Museum of the New South, Charlotte, North Carolina. The museum has exhibits on various New South themes and a permanent exhibit on the history of Charlotte and the Carolina Piedmont. http://www.museumofthenewsouth.org.

Without Sanctuary: Photographs and Postcards of Lynching in America. An exceptional collection of lynching memorabilia with detailed explanations, many of which have been shown in museums throughout the country. The collection emphasizes lynching as a community activity that included a representative cross-section of white society. Many of the images are graphic. http://www.withoutsanctuary.com.

Sloss Furnaces National Historical Landmark, Birmingham, Alabama. The site recalls the time when Birmingham challenged Pittsburgh as the nation's primary steel-producing center. http://www.slossfurnaces.com.

Review Questions

1. In what ways did the growing activism of white middle-class women, the increasing assertiveness of young urban black people, and the persistence of the agricultural depression affect the politics of the South in the late 1880s and early 1890s?
2. We associate segregation and disfranchisement with reactionary political and social views. Yet many white people who promoted both seriously believed them to be reforms. How could white people hold such a view?
3. What strategies did black southerners employ in response to the narrowing of economic and political opportunities in the New South?
4. What accounted for Anna J. Cooper's optimism for African American women in the South at a time when southern whites were beginning an extensive legal and physical assault on black civil rights?
5. Why did racial "problems" emerge as a major issue in Europe and the United States in the late nineteenth century?

Key Terms

Atlanta Compromise (p. 488)
Colored Farmers' Alliance (p. 476)
Disfranchisement (p. 482)
Grandfather clause (p. 483)
Grange (p. 475)
Jim Crow laws (p. 482)
Lynching (p. 481)
National Association for the Advancement of Colored People (NAACP) (p. 488)
Plessy v. Ferguson (p. 482)
Poll taxes (p. 483)
Populist Party (p. 477)
Segregation (p. 482)
Settlement house (p. 478)
Solid South (p. 470)
Southern Farmers' Alliance (p. 476)
Subtreasury plan (p. 477)
Women's Christian Temperance Union (WCTU) (p. 478)

myhistorylab Connections

Reinforce what you learned in this chapter by studying the many documents, images, maps, review tools, and videos available at **www.myhistorylab.com**.

Read and Review

Study and Review **Study Plan: Chapter 17**

Read the Document

The Nation, "The State of the South" (1872)

John Hill, Testimony on Southern Textile Industry (1883)

Anna Julia Cooper, From A Voice from the South: By a Black Woman of the South (1892)

Ida B. Wells-Barnett, False Accusations (1895)

Opinion of the Supreme Court for Plessy v. Ferguson *(1896)*

Booker T. Washington, Atlanta Exposition Address (1895)

The New Slavery in the South—An Autobiography (1904)

Ida B. Wells-Barnett, from A Red Record *(1895)*

Research and Explore

Read the Document

Personal Journeys Online

From Then to Now Online: The Confederate Battle Flag

Exploring America: Racism in America

Hear the Audio

Lynch Law in Georgia

A Republican Textbook for Colored Voters

Address at the Atlanta Exposition by Booker T. Washington

Watch the Video

The Lives of Southern Women

Moonlight and Magnolias: Creating the Old South

The Conflict between Booker T. Washington and W. E. B. Du Bois

Hear the Audio

Hear the audio files for Chapter 17 at **www.myhistorylab.com**.

18 Industry, Immigrants, and Cities

Chinese Primary Public School, 920 Clay St., Chinatown, San Francisco

A young boy is at work amid shabby equipment in a dingy glass factory.

((•—Hear the Audio

Hear the audio files for Chapter 18 at **www.myhistorylab.com**.

NEW INDUSTRY *(page 496)*

HOW DID workers respond to the changing demands of the workplace in the late nineteenth century?

NEW IMMIGRANTS *(page 505)*

WHAT KINDS of communities did new immigrants create in America?

NEW CITIES *(page 513)*

HOW DID the new cities help create the new middle class?

ONE AMERICAN JOURNEY

We were homeless, houseless, and friendless in a strange place. We had hardly money enough to last us through the voyage for which we had hoped and waited for three long years. We had suffered much that the reunion we longed for might come about; we had prepared ourselves to suffer more in order to bring it about, and had parted with those we loved, with places that were dear to us in spite of what we passed through in them, never again to see them, as we were convinced, all for the same dear end. With strong hopes and high spirits that hid the sad parting, we had started on our long journey. And now we were checked so unexpectedly but surely. . . . When my mother had recovered enough to speak, she began to argue with the gendarme, *telling him our story and begging him to be kind. The children were frightened and all but I cried. I was only wondering what would happen. . . . Here we had been taken to a lonely place; . . . our things were taken away, our friends separated from us; a man came to inspect us, as if to ascertain our full value; strange-looking people driving us about like dumb animals, helpless and unresisting; children we could not see crying in a way that suggested terrible things; ourselves driven into a little room where a great kettle was boiling on a little stove; our clothes taken off, our bodies rubbed with a slippery substance that might be any bad thing; a shower of warm water let down on us without warning. . . . We are forced to pick out our clothes from among all the others, with the steam blinding us; we choke, cough, entreat the women to give us time; they persist, "Quick! Quick!, or you'll miss the train!", Oh, so we really won't be murdered! They are only making us ready for the continuing of our journey, cleaning us of all suspicions of dangerous sickness. Thank God! . . .*

Oh, what solemn thoughts I had! How deeply I felt the greatness, the power of the scene! The immeasurable distance from horizon to horizon; . . . the absence of any object besides the one ship; . . . I was conscious only of sea and sky and something I did not understand. And as I listened to its solemn voice, I felt as if I had found a friend, and knew that I loved the ocean.

Mary Antin

Mary Antin, *The Promised Land* (Boston: Houghton Mifflin Co., 1912), chap. VIII.

Read the Document at **www.myhistorylab.com**

Personal Journeys Online

- ***Young Chinese immigrant memoir,* 1882. A Chinese immigrant recalls his migration to America and his early days in San Francisco.**
- ***Letters of Negro Migrants,* 1917. Letters back home from southern black migrants to the North.**

MARY ANTIN, a 13-year-old Jewish girl describes her family's perilous journey from persecution in tsarist Russia to the ship that would take her from Hamburg, Germany, to faraway America. In 1894, Mary and her mother and sisters set out from their village to join her father in Boston.

Millions of European immigrants made similar journeys across the Atlantic (as did Chinese and Japanese immigrants, across the Pacific), a trip fraught with danger, unpredictable detours, occasional heartbreak, the sundering of family ties, and the fear of the unknown. So powerful was the promise of American life for the migrants that they willingly risked these obstacles to come to the United States.

For Mary, America did indeed prove to be *The Promised Land*, as she titled her emigration memoir, published in 1912. At the age of 15, she published her first poem in the *Boston Herald* and, after attending Barnard College in New York City, she wrote on immigrant issues, lectured widely, and worked for Theodore Roosevelt's Progressive Party. She fought against

CHRONOLOGY

1869	The Knights of Labor is founded in Philadelphia.
1870	John D. Rockefeller organizes the Standard Oil Company.
	Congress passes the Naturalization Act barring Asians from citizenship.
1871	Unification of Germany in the wake of rising nationalism following the Franco-Prussian War.
1876	The Centennial Exposition opens in Philadelphia.
	Beginning of the rule of dictator Porfirio Diaz in Mexico, whose regime is ended by the Mexican Revolution.
1877	Execution of ten Molly Maguires in Pennsylvania.
	The Great Uprising railroad strike, the first nationwide work stoppage in the United States, provokes violent clashes between workers and federal troops.
1879	Thomas Edison unveils the electric light bulb.
1880	Founding of the League of American Wheelmen helps establish bicycling as one of urban America's favorite recreational activities.
1881	Assassination of Tsar Alexander II begins a series of pogroms that triggers a wave of Russian Jewish immigration to the United States.
1882	Congress passes the Chinese Exclusion Act.
	First country club in the United States founded in Brookline, Massachusetts.
1883	National League merges with the American Association and opens baseball to working-class fans.
1884	Berlin Conference on Africa to set rules for competing European powers annexing African territory.
1886	The Neighborhood Guild, the nation's first settlement house, opens in New York City.
	Riot in Chicago's Haymarket Square breaks the Knights of Labor.
	American Federation of Labor is formed.
1887	Anti-Catholic American Protective Association is formed.
1888	Wanamaker's department store introduces a "bargain room," and competitors follow suit.
1889	Jane Addams opens Hull House, the nation's most celebrated settlement house, in Chicago.
1890	Jacob A. Riis publishes *How the Other Half Lives*.
1891	African American Chicago physician Daniel Hale Williams establishes Provident Hospital, the nation's first interracially staffed hospital.
1892	General Electric opens the first corporate research and development division in the United States.
	Strike at Andrew Carnegie's Homestead steelworks fails.
1894	Pullman Sleeping Car Company strike fails.
	Immigration Restriction League is formed.
1895	American-born Chinese in California form the Native Sons of the Golden State to counter nativism.
1897	George C. Tilyou opens Steeplechase Park on Coney Island in Brooklyn, New York.
	First Zionist Congress meets in Switzerland, proclaiming its aim to create a home in Palestine for the Jewish people.
1898	Congress passes the Erdman Act to provide for voluntary mediation of railroad labor disputes.

immigration-restriction legislation and promoted public education as the main channel of upward mobility for immigrants.

Mary and her family were part of a major demographic and economic transformation in the United States between 1870 and 1900. Rapid industrial development changed the nature of the workforce and the workplace. Large factories staffed by semiskilled laborers displaced the skilled artisans and small shops that had dominated American industry before 1870. Industrial development also accelerated urbanization. Between the Civil War and 1900, the proportion of the nation's population living in cities, swelled by migrants from the countryside and immigrants from Europe and Asia, increased from 20 to 40 percent, a rate of growth twice that of the population as a whole. During the 1880s alone, more than 5 million immigrants came to the United States, twice as many as in any previous decade.

The changes in American life were exhilarating for some, tragic for others. New opportunities opened as old opportunities disappeared. Vast new wealth was created, but poverty increased. New technologies eased life for some but left others untouched. It would be the great dilemma of early-twentieth-century America to reconcile these contradictions and satisfy the American quest for a decent life for all within the new urban industrial order.

Late-nineteenth-century America is often called the **Gilded Age.** The term is taken from the title of a novel by Mark Twain that satirizes the materialistic excesses of the day. It serves as a shorthand description of the shallow worship of wealth, and the veneer of respectability and prosperity covering deep economic and social divisions, that characterized the period. Even so, an array of opportunities opened for more Americans than at any previous time in the nation's history. ✦

NEW INDUSTRY

HOW DID workers respond to the changing demands of the workplace in the late nineteenth century?

Gilded Age Term applied to late-nineteenth-century America that refers to the shallow display and worship of wealth characteristic of that period.

Read the **Document** at **www.myhistorylab.com** *Mark Twain, from The Gilded Age (1873)*

Between 1870 and 1900, the United States transformed itself from an agricultural nation, a nation of farmers, merchants, and artisans, into the world's foremost industrial power, producing more than one-third of the world's manufactured goods. By the early twentieth century, factory workers made up one-fourth of the workforce, and agricultural workers had dropped from a half to less than a third (see Figure 18–1).

Although the size of the industrial workforce increased dramatically, the number of firms in any given industry shrank. Mergers, changes in corporate management and the organization of the workforce, and a compliant government left a few companies in control of vast segments of the American economy. Workers, reformers, and eventually government challenged this concentration of economic power.

1870 Total Labor Force = 12,920,000

Agriculture 50%
Other 14%
Mining 2%
Commerce 11%
Manufacturing and Construction 23%

1910 Total Labor Force = 36,730,000

Other 18%
Agriculture 31%
Mining 3%
Commerce 19%
Manufacturing and Construction 29%

FIGURE 18–1 **Changes in the American Labor Force, 1870–1910** The transformation of the American economy in the late nineteenth century changed the nature and type of work. By 1910, the United States was an urban, industrial nation with a matching workforce that toiled in factories and commercial establishments (including railroads) and, less frequently, on farms.

INVENTING TECHNOLOGY: THE ELECTRIC AGE

Technology played a major role in transforming factory work and increasing the scale of production. Steam engines and, later, electricity, freed manufacturers from dependence on water power. Factories no longer had to be located by rivers. Technology also enabled managers to substitute machines for workers, skewing the balance of power in the workplace toward employers. And it transformed city life, making available a host of new conveniences. By the early twentieth century, electric lights, appliances, ready-made clothing, and store-bought food eased middle-class life. Electric trolleys whisked clerks, salespeople, bureaucrats, and bankers to new urban and suburban subdivisions. Electric streetlights lit up city streets at night.

For much of the nineteenth century, the United States was dependent on the industrial nations of Europe for technological innovation. In the late nineteenth century, the United States changed from a technology borrower to a technology innovator. By 1910, a million patents had been issued in the United States, 900,000 of them after 1870.

Nothing represented this shift better than Thomas A. Edison's development of a practical electric light bulb and electric generating system. Edison's invention transformed electricity into a new and versatile form of industrial energy. It also reflected a change in the relationship between science and technology. Until the late nineteenth century, advances in scientific theory usually followed technological innovation, rather than the other way around. Techniques for making steel, for example, developed before scientific theories emerged to explain how they worked. In contrast, scientists had developed a theoretical understanding of electricity long before Edison unveiled his light bulb in 1879. Edison's research laboratory at Menlo Park, New Jersey, also established a model for corporate-sponsored research and development that would rapidly increase the pace of technological innovation.

Edison's initial success touched off a wave of research and development in Germany, Austria, Great Britain, France, and the United States. Whoever could light the world cheaply and efficiently held the key to an enormous fortune. Ultimately, the prize fell not to Edison but to Elihu Thomson. Thomson purchased Edison's General Electric Company in 1892 and established the country's first corporate research and development division. His scientists produced what was then the most efficient light bulb design, and by 1914, General Electric was producing 85 percent of the world's light bulbs.

Following this precedent, other American companies established research and development laboratories. Standard Oil, U.S. Rubber, the chemical giant Du Pont, and the photographic company Kodak all became world leaders in their respective industries because of innovations their laboratories developed.

The process of invention that emerged in the United States gave the country a commanding technological lead. But the modernization of industry that made the United States the world's foremost industrial nation after 1900 reflected organizational as well as technological innovation. As industries sought efficient ways to apply technology and expand their markets within and beyond national borders, their workforces expanded, and their need for capital mounted. Coping with these changes required significant changes in corporate management.

WHERE TO LEARN MORE

Edison National Historic Site, West Orange, New Jersey
http://www.nps.gov/edis

Read the **Document**
at **www.myhistorylab.com**
Thomas Edison, The Success of the Electric Light (1880)

The Corporation and Its Impact

The modern corporation provided the structural framework for the transformation of the American economy. A corporation is an association of individuals that is legally authorized to act as a fictional "person" and thus relieves its individual members of certain legal liabilities. A key feature of a corporation is the separation of ownership from management. A corporation can raise capital by selling ownership shares, or stock, to people who have no direct role in running it.

The corporation had two major advantages over other forms of business organization that made it attractive to investors. First, unlike a partnership, which dissolves when a partner dies, a corporation can outlive its founders. This durability permits long-term planning. Second, a corporation's officials and shareholders are not personally liable for its debts. If it goes bankrupt, they stand to lose only what they have invested in it.

As large corporations emerged in major American industries, they had a ripple effect on the economy. To build plants, merge with or acquire other companies, develop new technology, and hire workers, large corporations needed huge supplies of capital. They turned to the banks to help meet these needs, and the banks grew in response. The corporations stimulated technological change as they looked for ways to speed production, improve products, and lower costs. As they grew, they generated jobs.

Large industrial corporations also changed the nature of work. By the early twentieth century, control of the workplace was shifting to managers, and semiskilled and unskilled workers were replacing skilled artisans. These new workers, often foreign-born, performed repetitive tasks for low wages.

Because corporations usually located factories in cities, they stimulated urban growth. Large industrial districts sprawled along urban rivers and rail lines. By 1900, fully 90 percent of all manufacturing occurred in cities.

Two organizational strategies, vertical integration and horizontal integration, helped successful corporations reduce competition and dominate their industries. **Vertical integration** involved the consolidation of all functions related to a particular industry, from the extraction and transport of raw materials to manufacturing and finished-product distribution and sales. Vertical integration reduced a company's dependence on outside suppliers, cutting costs and delays.

Horizontal integration involved the merger of competitors in the same industry. John D. Rockefeller's Standard Oil Company pioneered horizontal integration in the 1880s. He began

QUICK REVIEW

Corporations

- Corporation: an association with legal rights and liabilities separate from those of its members.
- Became a significant factor with the growth of railroads in the 1850s.
- Key feature of the corporation is the separation of ownership and management.

vertical integration The consolidation of numerous production functions, from the extraction of the raw materials to the distribution and marketing of the finished products, under the direction of one firm.

horizontal integration The merger of competitors in the same industry.

Electricity conquered space and the night. The yellow glow of incandescent bulbs, the whiz of trolleys, and the rumble of elevated railways energize the Bowery, an emerging entertainment district in lower Manhattan at the end of the nineteenth century.

W. Louis Sonntag, Jr., *The Bowery at Night*, watercolor, 1895. Copyright Museum of the City of New York. 32.275.2

investing in Cleveland oil refineries by his mid-twenties and formed Standard Oil in 1870. Using a variety of tactics, including threats, deceit, and price wars, Rockefeller rapidly acquired most of his competitors. Supported by investment bankers like J. P. Morgan, Standard Oil controlled 90 percent of the nation's oil refining by 1890. Acquiring oil fields and pipelines as well as refineries, it achieved both vertical and horizontal integration.

QUICK REVIEW

Captains of Industry

- John D. Rockefeller (oil).
- James B. Duke (tobacco).
- Andrew Carnegie (steel).

Other entrepreneurs achieved similar dominance in other industries and amassed similarly enormous fortunes. The concentration of industry in the hands of a few powerful corporate monopolies or **trusts,** as they came to be known, alarmed many Americans. Giant corporations set prices, influenced politicians, and threatened to restrict opportunities for small entrepreneurs like the shopkeepers, farmers, and artisans who abounded at midcentury. Impersonal and governed by profit, the modern corporation challenged the ideal of the self-made man and the belief that success and advancement would reward hard work. These concerns eventually prompted the federal and state governments to respond with antitrust and other regulatory laws (see Chapters 20 and 21).

trusts A combination of corporations cooperating in order to reduce competition and control prices.

The entrepreneurs operated in an environment that allowed them free rein. They had access to capital, markets, and technology. And when they did not, they created it. Above all, they were innovators. The integration of the nation's transportation and communication infrastructure, the managerial revolution that rationalized the operation of geographically distant units and large and diverse work forces, and the application of continuous flow production pioneered in flour mills long before Henry Ford adapted it to car manufacturing, were a few of the innovations entrepreneurs devised to make their operations more efficient and profitable in the postwar years.

The large corporation changed how Americans lived their daily lives. People moved to cities in unprecedented numbers. They purchased goods that did not exist or that had limited distribution prior to the Civil War. They worked in an environment where management and labor became ever more distinct. And they established new consumption patterns in purchasing and furnishing their dwellings and in their leisure activities. Their lives revolved around family, work, and leisure. They were modern Americans.

The Changing Nature of Work

The growth of giant corporations was a mixed blessing. The corporations provided abundant jobs, but they firmly controlled working conditions, especially for those who worked with their hands instead of their brains.

As late as the 1880s, shops of skilled artisans were responsible for most manufacturing in the United States. Since the midcentury, however, industrialists had been introducing ways to simplify manufacturing processes so that they could hire low-skilled workers. This deskilling process accelerated in the 1890s in response to new technologies, new workers, and workplace reorganization.

QUICK REVIEW

Factory Life

- Job conditions were often dangerous.
- Factory workers worked ten hours a day, six days a week.
- Workers lived as close to factories as possible to reduce travel time.

Mechanization and technological innovation did not reduce employment, although they did eliminate some jobs, most of them skilled. On the contrary, the birth of whole new industries—steel, automobiles, electrical equipment, cigarettes, food canning, and machine tools—created a huge demand for workers. Innovations in existing industries, like railroads, similarly spurred job growth.

Ironically, it was a shortage of skilled workers as much as other factors that encouraged industrialists to mechanize. Unskilled workers cost less than the scarce artisans. And with massive waves of immigrants arriving from Europe and Asia between 1880 and 1920 (joined after 1910 by migrants from the American South), the supply of unskilled workers seemed limitless.

Low salaries and long hours. The new workers shared little of the wealth generated by industrial expansion and enjoyed few of the gadgets and products generated by the new manufacturing. Nor did large corporations put profits into improved working conditions. In 1881, on-the-job accidents maimed or killed 30,000 railroad workers. Safety equipment existed that could have prevented many of these injuries, but the railroads refused to purchase it. At a U.S. Steel plant in Pittsburgh, injuries or death claimed one out of every four workers between 1907 and 1910.

Factory workers typically worked 10 hours a day, six days a week in the 1880s. Steel workers put in 12 hours a day. The mills operated around the clock, so once every two weeks, when the workers changed shifts, one group had to take a "long turn" and stay on the job for 24 hours.

Long hours affected family life. By Sunday, most factory workers were too tired to do more than sit around home. During the week, they had time only to eat and sleep. Workers lived as close to the factory as possible, to reduce the time and expense of getting to work.

Big factories were not characteristic of all industries after 1900. In some, like the "needle," or garment, trade, operations remained small scale. But salaries and working conditions in these industries were, if

Smoke belching from Pittsburgh steel mills in the 1890s. Smoke from these mills periodically turned day into night. To some, these stacks represented progress and employment; to others, threats to health and the environment. An environmental survey conducted in the late 1890s called Pittsburgh "hell with a lid off." It was not until 1941 that Pittsburgh passed a smoke abatement ordinance.

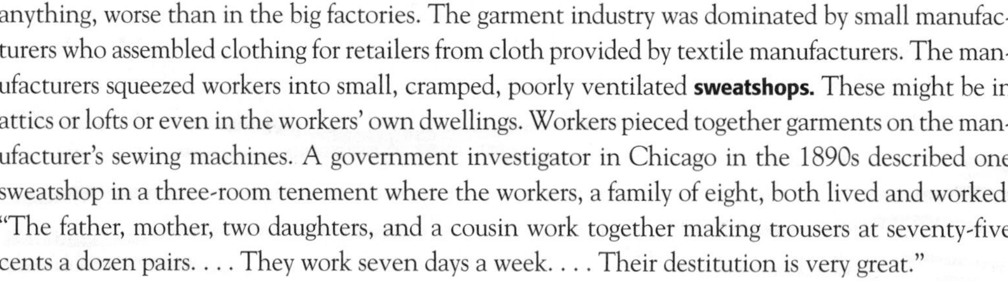

anything, worse than in the big factories. The garment industry was dominated by small manufacturers who assembled clothing for retailers from cloth provided by textile manufacturers. The manufacturers squeezed workers into small, cramped, poorly ventilated **sweatshops.** These might be in attics or lofts or even in the workers' own dwellings. Workers pieced together garments on the manufacturer's sewing machines. A government investigator in Chicago in the 1890s described one sweatshop in a three-room tenement where the workers, a family of eight, both lived and worked: "The father, mother, two daughters, and a cousin work together making trousers at seventy-five cents a dozen pairs. . . . They work seven days a week. . . . Their destitution is very great."

sweatshops Small, poorly ventilated shops or apartments crammed with workers, often family members, who pieced together garments.

Child Labor

Child labor was common in the garment trade and other industries. Industries that employed many children were often dangerous, even for adults. In the gritty coal mines of Pennsylvania, breaker boys, youths who stood on ladders to pluck waste matter from coal tumbling down long chutes, breathed harmful coal dust all day. Girls under 16 made up half the workforce in the silk mills of Scranton and Wilkes-Barre, Pennsylvania. Girls with missing fingers from mill accidents were a common sight in those towns.

By 1900, under pressure from reformers, Pennsylvania and a few other states had passed legislation regulating child labor, but enforcement of these laws was lax. Parents desperate for income often lied about their children's age, and government officials were usually sympathetic toward mill or mine owners, who paid taxes and provided other civic benefits.

Working Women

Women accompanied children into the workforce outside the home in increasing numbers after 1870. The comparatively low wages of unskilled male workers often required women family members to work as well. Between 1870 and 1920, the number of women and children in the workforce more than doubled.

Like child labor, the growing numbers of women in the workforce alarmed middle-class reformers. They worried about the impact on family life and on the women themselves. Streets in working-class districts teemed with unsupervised children. Working-class men were also concerned. The trend toward deskilling favored women. Employers, claiming that women worked only for supplemental money, paid them less than men. In one St. Louis factory in 1896, women received $4 a week for work for which men were paid $16 a week.

Most women worked out of economic necessity. In 1900, fully 85 percent of wage-earning women were unmarried and under the age of 25. They supported siblings and contributed to their parents' income. A typical female factory worker earned $6 a week in 1900. On this wage, a married woman might help pull her family up to subsistence level. For a single woman on her own, however, it allowed little more, in the writer O. Henry's words, "than marshmallows and tea." Her lodging rarely consisted of more than one room.

Noted urban and labor photographer Lewis Hine's crusade against child labor included this photo of breaker boys at a Pennsylvania coal mine, 1910. The boys worked in a constant cloud of coal dust picking out refuse from coal coming down chutes. Note the overseer with a stick at right.

Over time, more work options opened to women, but low wages and poor working conditions persisted. Women entered the needle trades after widespread introduction of the sewing machine in the 1870s. Factories gradually replaced sweatshops in the garment industry after 1900, but working conditions improved little.

On the factory floor, young women had less room for negotiation because the customer was far removed from the manufacturing process, but they banded together, sometimes in labor unions after 1900, to demand and receive concessions from management. Working women, no less than working men, refused to be inanimate recipients of bosses' decrees and working conditions. And if a young woman could obtain some basic skills, other opportunities loomed as well.

The introduction of the typewriter transformed office work, dominated by men until the 1870s, into a female preserve. Women were alleged to have the dexterity and tolerance for repetition that the new technology required. But they earned only half the salary of the men they replaced. Middle-class parents saw office work as clean and honorable compared with factory or sales work. Consequently, clerical positions drew growing numbers of native-born women into the urban workforce after 1890.

By the turn of the century, women were gaining increased access to higher education. Coeducational colleges were rare, but by 1900 there were many women-only institutions. By 1910, women comprised 40 percent of all American college students, compared to 20 percent in 1870. Despite these gains, many professions, including those of physician and attorney, remained closed to women. Men still accounted for more than 95 percent of all doctors in 1900. Women also were rarely permitted to pursue doctoral degrees.

Most women college graduates found employment in such "nurturing" professions as nursing, teaching, and library work. Between 1900 and 1910, the number of trained women nurses increased sevenfold. In response to the growing problems of urban society, a relatively new occupation, social work, opened to women. There were 1,000 women social workers in 1890 and nearly 30,000 by 1920. Reflecting new theories on the nurturing role of women, school boards after 1900 turned exclusively to female teachers for the elementary grades. Despite these gains, women's work remained segregated. More than 90 percent of all wage-earning women in 1900 worked at occupations in which women comprised the great majority of workers. Some reforms meant to improve working conditions for women reinforced this state of affairs. Protective legislation restricted women to "clean" occupations and limited their ability to compete with men in other jobs.

QUICK REVIEW

Working Women in 1900

- 85 percent of wage-earning women unmarried and under 25.
- Typical female factory worker earned $6 per week.
- Even as new opportunities opened up for women, low wages and poor working conditions persisted.

Women also confronted negative stereotypes. Most Americans in 1900 believed a woman's proper role was to care for home and family. The single working woman faced doubts about her virtue. The system of "treating" on dates reinforced stories about loose salesgirls, flirtatious secretaries, and easy factory workers. Newspapers and magazines published exposés of working girls descending into prostitution. These images encouraged sexual harassment at work, which was rarely punished. Still, for a girl growing up after the Civil War, many more possibilities were open to her than before. Louisa May Alcott's *Little Women* appeared in 1868 and became the biggest selling novel since Harriet Beecher Stowe's *Uncle Tom's Cabin*. If any indicator summarized the difference between the overheated 1850s with its imagery of sin and salvation and the postwar era of promise and economic prosperity, it was the transition from Stowe to Alcott. Of the four March girls in Alcott's novel, Josephine, who preferred the masculine-sounding "Jo," became a writer. Meg, a governess, dreamed of acting; Amy, a schoolgirl, hoped to become a great painter. Beth, the only March girl who did not imagine a career outside the home, died prematurely of unknown causes.

QUICK REVIEW

Stereotypes

- Most Americans believed that a woman's proper role was to care for her home and her family.
- Stereotypes reinforced notion that working women were promiscuous.
- Sexual harassment at work was rarely punished.

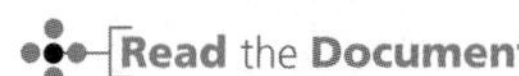

at **www.myhistorylab.com**
Jacob A. Riis, The Battle with the Slum (1902)

Responses to Poverty and Wealth

Concerns about working women merged with larger anxieties about the growing numbers of impoverished workers in the nation's cities during the 1890s and the widening gap between rich and poor. While industrial magnates flaunted their fabulous wealth, working men and women led hard lives on meager salaries and in crowded dwellings.

The new industrial age created great wealth and abject poverty, and the city became the stage upon which these hard economic lessons played out. Here a "modest" Fifth Avenue mansion in turn-of-the-century New York City; farther downtown, Jacob Riis found this tenement courtyard.

22 Baxter Street Court. The Jacob A. Riis Collection, Museum of the City of New York

tenements Four- to six-story residential dwellings, once common in New York, built on tiny lots without regard to providing ventilation or light.

QUICK REVIEW

Settlement Houses

- Effort to moderate effects of poverty through neighborhood reconstruction.
- Neighborhood Guild (1886) in New York was first settlement house in the United States.
- Jane Addams's Hull House (1889) in Chicago was most famous settlement house.

Hull House Chicago settlement house that became part of a broader neighborhood revitalization project led by Jane Addams.

Gospel of Wealth Thesis that hard work and perseverance lead to wealth, implying that poverty is a character flaw.

Inadequate housing was the most visible badge of poverty. Crammed into four- to six-story buildings on tiny lots, **tenement** apartments in urban slums were notorious for their lack of ventilation and light. Authorities did nothing to enforce laws prohibiting overcrowding for fear of leaving people homeless.

One early attempt to deal with these conditions was the settlement house. The settlement house movement, which originated in England, sought to moderate the effects of poverty through neighborhood reconstruction. New York's Neighborhood Guild, established in 1886, was the first settlement house in the country; Chicago's **Hull House,** founded in 1889 by Jane Addams, a young Rockford (Illinois) College graduate, became the most famous. Addams had visited settlement houses in England and thought the idea would work well in American cities.

The Gospel of Wealth. Late-nineteenth-century political ideology discouraged more comprehensive efforts to remedy urban poverty until the Progressive Era (discussed in Chapter 21). According to the **Gospel of Wealth,** a theory popular among industrialists, intellectuals, and some politicians, any intervention on behalf of the poor was of doubtful benefit. Hard work and perseverance, in this view, led to wealth. Poverty, by implication, resulted from the faulty character of the poor.

A flawed attempt to apply Charles Darwin's theory of biological evolution to human society emerged as a more common justification than the Gospel of Wealth for the growing gap between rich and poor. According to the theory of **Social Darwinism,** the human race evolves only through competition. The fit survive, the weak perish, and humanity moves forward. Wealth

OVERVIEW Workers Organize

Organization	History	Strategies
Knights of Labor	Founded in 1869; open to all workers; declined after 1886	Disapproved of strikes; supported an array of labor reforms, including cooperatives; favored broad political involvement
American Federation of Labor	Founded in 1886; open only to craft workers and organized by craft; hostile to blacks and women; became the major U.S. labor organization after 1880s	Opposed political involvement; supported a limited number of labor reforms; approved of strikes

reflects fitness; poverty, weakness. For governments or private agencies to interfere with this natural process is futile. Thus, Columbia University president Nicholas Murray Butler, claiming that "nature's cure for most social and political diseases is better than man's," warned against charity for the poor in 1900.

Social Darwinism The application of Charles Darwin's theory of biological evolution to society, holding that the fittest and wealthiest survive, the weak and the poor perish, and government action is unable to alter this "natural" process.

Workers Organize

Wild swings in the business cycle, the fluctuation between periods of growth and contraction in the economy, aggravated tensions between labor and management. Two prolonged depressions, one beginning in 1873 and the other in 1893, threw as many as 2 million laborers out of work. Skilled workers, their security undermined by deskilling, were hit particularly hard. Their hopes of becoming managers or starting their own businesses disappearing, they saw the nation "drifting," as a carpenter put it in 1870, "to that condition of society where a few were rich, and the many very poor."

See the Map at **www.myhistorylab.com** *Organizing American Labor in the Late Nineteenth Century*

Beginning after the Civil War and continuing through World War I, workers fought their loss of independence to industrial capital by organizing and striking (see the Overview table, Workers Organize). Violence often accompanied these actions.

Such was the case with the railroad strike of 1877, sometimes referred to as the **Great Uprising.** The four largest railroads, in the midst of a depression and in the wake of a series of pay cuts over the preceding four years, agreed to slash wages yet again. When Baltimore & Ohio Railroad workers struck in July to protest the cut, President Rutherford B. Hayes dispatched federal troops to protect the line's property. The use of federal troops infuriated railroad workers throughout the East and Midwest, and they stopped work. Violence erupted in Pittsburgh when the state militia opened fire on strikers and their families, killing 25, including a woman and three children. As news of the violence spread, so did the strike, as far as Galveston, Texas, and San Francisco. Over the next two weeks, police and federal troops continued to clash with strikers. By the time this first nationwide work stoppage in American history ended, more than 100 had been killed. The wage cuts remained.

Great Uprising Unsuccessful railroad strike of 1877 to protest wage cuts and the use of federal troops against strikers; the first nationwide work stoppage in American history.

The **Knights of Labor,** a union of craft workers founded in Philadelphia in 1869, grew dramatically after the Great Uprising under the leadership of Terence V. Powderly. Reflecting the views of many skilled workers, the Knights saw "an inevitable . . . conflict between the wage system of labor and [the] republican system of government." Remarkably inclusive for its time, the Knights welcomed black workers and women to its ranks. Victories in several small railroad strikes in 1884 and 1885 boosted its membership to nearly 1 million workers by 1886.

Knights of Labor Labor union founded in 1869 that included skilled and unskilled workers irrespective of race or gender.

In that year, the Knights led a movement for an eight-hour workday. Ignoring the advice of the national leadership to avoid strikes, local chapters staged more than 1,500 strikes involving more than 340,000 workers. Employers fought back. They persuaded the courts to order strikers back to work and used local authorities to arrest strikers for trespassing or obstructing traffic. In early May 1886, police killed four unarmed workers during a skirmish with strikers in Chicago.

Read the Document at **www.myhistorylab.com** *George Engel, Address by a Condemned Haymarket Anarchist (1886)*

During the Great Uprising of 1877, federal troops clashed with striking workers. Here the Maryland militia fires at strikers in Baltimore, killing 12. As Reconstruction ended, government attention shifted from the South to quelling labor unrest.

Rioting broke out when a bomb exploded at a meeting in Haymarket Square to protest the slayings. The bomb killed seven policemen and four strikers and left 100 people wounded. Eight strike leaders were tried for the deaths, and despite the lack of evidence linking them to the bomb, four were executed.

The Haymarket Square incident, and a series of disastrous walkouts that followed it, weakened the Knights of Labor. By 1890, it had fewer than 100,000 members. Thereafter, the **American Federation of Labor (AFL),** founded in 1886, became the major organizing body for skilled workers.

The AFL was much less ambitious, and less inclusive, than the Knights of Labor. Led by a British immigrant, Samuel Gompers, it emphasized **collective bargaining,** negotiations between management and union representatives, to secure workplace concessions. The AFL also discouraged political activism. With this business unionism, the AFL proved more effective than the Knights of Labor at meeting the needs of skilled workers, but it left out the growing numbers of unskilled workers, black workers, and women workers, to whom the Knights had given a glimmer of hope.

American Federation of Labor (AFL) Union formed in 1886 that organized skilled workers along craft lines and emphasized a few workplace issues rather than a broad social program.

collective bargaining Representatives of a union negotiating with management on behalf of all members.

Read the **Document** at **www.myhistorylab.com** *Andrew Carnegie, Wealth and Its Uses (1907)*

Rather than including all workers in one large union, the AFL organized skilled workers by craft. It then focused on a few basic workplace issues important to each craft. The result was greater cohesion and discipline. In 1889 and 1890, more than 60 percent of AFL-sponsored strikes were successful, a remarkable record in an era when most strikes failed. Responding to this success, employers determined to break the power of craft unions just as they had destroyed the Knights. In 1892, Andrew Carnegie dealt the steelworkers' union a major setback in the Homestead strike. Carnegie's manager, Henry Clay Frick, announced to workers at Carnegie's Homestead plant in Pennsylvania that he would not renew the union's collective bargaining contract. Expecting a strike, Frick locked the union workers out of the plant and hired 300 armed guards to protect the nonunion ("scab") workers he planned to hire in their place. Union workers, with the help of their families and unskilled workers, seized control of Homestead's roads and utilities. In a bloody confrontation, they drove back Frick's forces. Nine strikers and seven guards died. But Pennsylvania's governor called out the state militia to open the plant and protect the nonunion workers. After four months, the union capitulated. With this defeat, skilled steelworkers lost their power on the shop floor. Eventually, mechanization cost them their jobs.

In 1894, workers suffered another setback in the Pullman strike, against George Pullman's Palace Sleeping Car Company. The strike began when the company cut wages for workers at its plant in the "model" suburb it had built outside Chicago, without a corresponding cut in the rent it charged workers for their company-owned housing. When Pullman rejected their demands, the workers appealed for support to the American Railway Union (ARU), led by Eugene V. Debs. On behalf of the Pullman strikers, Debs ordered a boycott of any trains with Pullman cars, disrupting train travel in several parts of the country. The railroads claimed to be innocent victims of a local dispute, and with growing public support, they fired workers who refused to handle trains with Pullman cars. Debs called for all ARU members to walk off the job, crippling rail travel nationwide. When Debs refused to honor a federal court injunction against the strike, President Cleveland, at the railroads' request, ordered federal troops to enforce it. Debs was arrested, and the strike and the union were broken.

These setbacks, and the depression that began in 1893, left workers and their unions facing an uncertain future. But growing public opposition to the use of troops, the high-handed tactics of industrialists, and the rising concerns of Americans about the power of big business sustained the unions. Workers would call more than 22,000 strikes over the next decade, the majority of them union-sponsored. Still, no more than 7 percent of the American workforce was organized by 1900. By that time, a dramatic change in the industrial workforce was afoot. As the large factories installed labor- and time-saving machinery, unskilled foreign-born labor flooded onto the shop floor. Immigrants transformed not only the workplace, but also the cities where they settled and the nation many eventually adopted. In the process, they changed themselves.

QUICK REVIEW

Pullman Strike

- 1894 strike against Pullman's Palace Sleeping Car Company.
- Pullman workers sought solidarity with Eugene Debs's American Railway Union.
- President Cleveland ordered federal troops to enforce injunction against strike.

NEW IMMIGRANTS

WHAT KINDS of communities did new immigrants create in America?

The late nineteenth century was a period of unprecedented worldwide population movements. The United States was not the only New World destination for the migrants of this period. Many also found their way to Brazil, Argentina, and Canada. The scale of overseas migration to the United States after 1870, however, dwarfed all that preceded it. Between 1870 and 1910, the country received more than 20 million immigrants. Before the Civil War, most immigrants came from northern Europe. Most of the new immigrants, by contrast, came from southern and eastern Europe. Swelling their ranks were migrants from Mexico and Asia, as well as internal migrants moving from the countryside to American cities (see Map 18–1 and Figure 18–2).

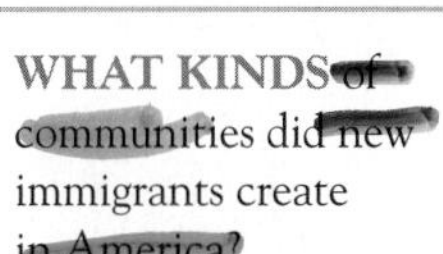

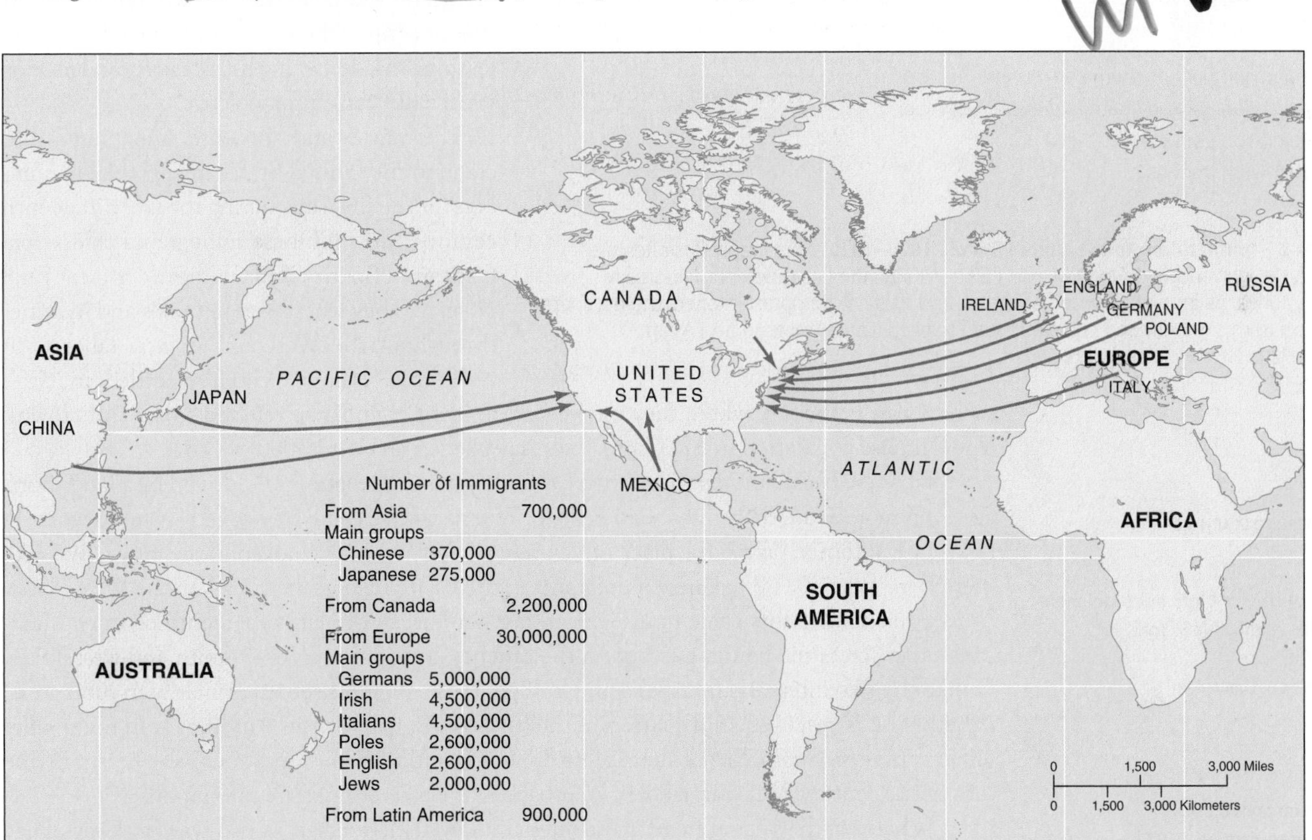

MAP 18–1 **Patterns of Immigration, 1820–1914** The migration to the United States was part of a worldwide transfer of population that accelerated with the industrial revolution and the accompanying improvement in transportation.

What forces propelled so many people to emigrate from European countries? How did conditions in the United States in the late nineteenth century differ from those in south and central Europe?

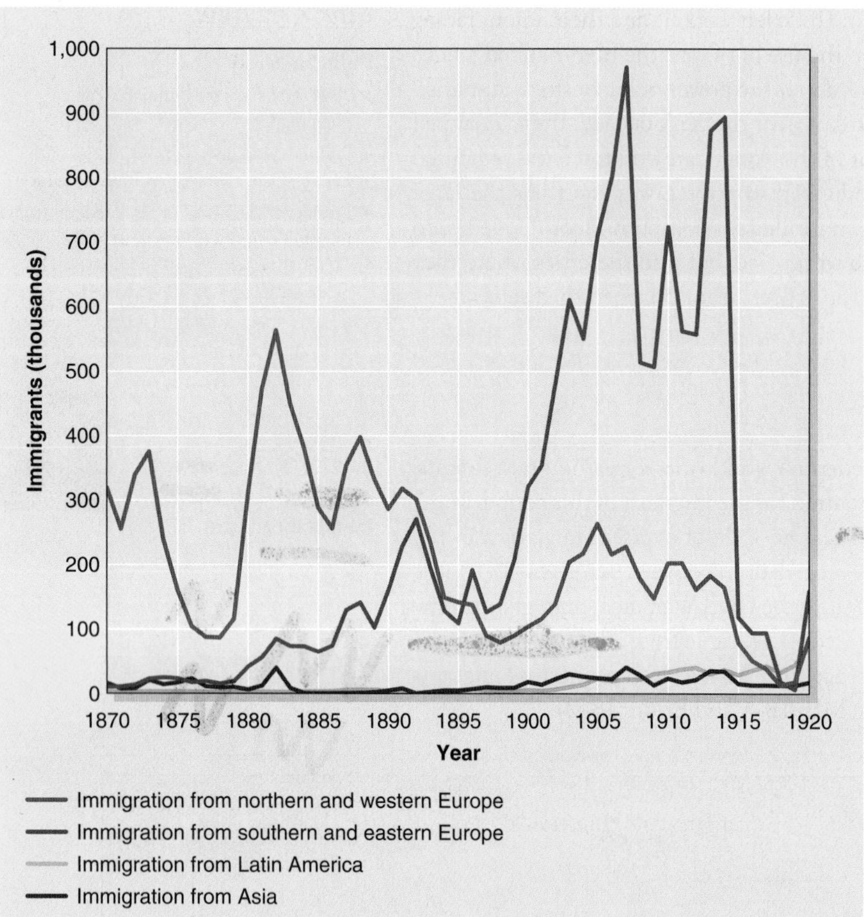

FIGURE 18–2 **Immigration to the United States, 1870–1920** The graph illustrates the dramatic change in immigration to the United States during the late nineteenth and early twentieth centuries. As immigration from northern and western Europe slackened, the numbers of newcomers from southern and eastern Europe swelled. Latin American and Asian immigration also increased during this period.

Old World Backgrounds

The people of southern and eastern Europe had long been accustomed to migrating within Europe on a seasonal basis to find work to support their families. In the final quarter of the nineteenth century, however, several factors drove migrants beyond the borders of Europe and into the Western Hemisphere.

A growing rural population combined with unequal land distribution to create economic distress in late-nineteenth-century Europe. With land ownership concentrated in increasingly fewer hands, more and more people found themselves working ever smaller plots as laborers rather than owners.

For Russian Jews, religious persecution compounded economic hardship. After the assassination of Tsar Alexander II in 1881, which was falsely blamed on Jews, the government sanctioned a series of violent attacks on Jewish settlements; these attacks were known as **pogroms.** At the same time, the government forced Jews into fewer towns, deepening their poverty and making them easier targets for violence.

Chinese and Japanese immigrants also came to the United States in appreciable numbers for the first time during the late nineteenth century. Most Chinese immigrants came from Canton in South China, a region of great rural poverty. They worked on railroads and in mines throughout the West and as farm laborers in California. Many eventually settled in cities such as San Francisco, where they established residential enclaves referred to as Chinatowns. The Chinese population in the United States peaked at about 125,000 in 1882.

Japanese began immigrating to the United States in the late 1880s, driven by a land shortage even more acute than the one in Europe. The first wave came by way of Hawaii to work on farms in California, taking the place of Chinese workers who had moved to the cities. By 1900, there were some 50,000 Japanese immigrants in the United States, nearly all on the West Coast.

Some immigrants came from right on our borders. In the late nineteenth century, Mexicans came across the border to work on the ranches and cotton farms of south and west Texas. Unlike their counterparts from Asia and Europe, these migrants settled primarily in rural areas. Whether on farms, in squalid quarters in the *barrios* of El Paso or San Antonio, or in the smaller urban centers in South Texas, such as Laredo, living and working conditions were harsh. By the turn of the century, Mexican laborers in urban areas began to organize into unions.

Wherever they came from, most migrants saw their route as a two-way highway. They intended to stay only a year or two, long enough to earn money to buy land or, more likely, to start a business back home and improve life for themselves and their families. Roughly half of all immigrants to the United States between 1880 and World War I returned to their country of origin. Some made several round trips. Jews, unwelcome in the lands they left, were the exception. No more than 10 percent of Jewish immigrants returned to Europe, and very few Jews from Russia, who accounted for almost 80 percent of Jewish immigrants after 1880, went back home.

W
WHERE TO LEARN MORE
Statue of Liberty National Monument and Ellis Island, New York, New York
http://www.nps.gov/stli

Watch the **Video**
at **www.myhistorylab.com**
Ellis Island Immigrants, 1903

pogroms Government-directed attacks against Jewish citizens, property, and villages in tsarist Russia beginning in the 1880s; a primary reason for Russian Jewish migration to the United States.

Most of the newcomers were young men. (Jews, again, were the exception: Reflecting their intention to stay in their new home, they tended to migrate in families.) Immigrants easily found work in the nation's booming cities. The quickest way to make money was in the large urban factories, with their voracious demands for unskilled labor. Except for the Japanese, few immigrants came to work on farms after 1880.

By 1900, women began to equal men among all immigrant groups as young men who had decided to stay sent for their families. In a few cases, entire villages migrated, drawn by the good fortune of one or two compatriots, a process called **chain migration.** The success of Francesco Barone, a Buffalo tavern owner, induced 8,000 residents of his former village in Sicily to migrate to that city, many arriving on tickets Barone purchased.

Immigrants tended to live in neighborhoods among people from the same homeland. The desire of the new immigrants to retain their cultural traditions led contemporary observers to doubt their ability to assimilate into American society. Even sympathetic observers, such as social workers, marveled at the utterly foreign character of immigrant districts.

See the Map at **www.myhistorylab.com** *Foreign-Born Population, 1890*

chain migration Process common to many immigrant groups whereby one family member brings over other family members, who in turn bring other relatives and friends and occasionally entire villages.

Hear the Audio at **www.myhistorylab.com** *Hungarian Rag*

Cultural Connections in a New World

Immigrants maintained their cultural traditions through the establishment of religious and communal institutions. Charitable organizations were frequently connected to religious institutions. The church or synagogue became the focal point for immigrant neighborhood life. Much more than a place of worship, it was a school for transmitting Old World values and language to American-born children. The church or synagogue also functioned as a recreational facility and a gathering place for community leaders. In Jewish communities, associations called *landsmanshaften* arranged for burials, jobs, housing, and support for the sick, poor, and elderly. Because religious institutions were so central to their lives, immigrant communities insisted on maintaining control over them.

Religious institutions played a less formal role among Chinese and Japanese neighborhoods. For them, the family functioned as the source of religious activity and communal organization. Chinatowns were organized in clans of people with the same surname. An umbrella organization called the Chinese Consolidated Benevolent Association emerged; it functioned like the Jewish *landsmanshaften*. A similar association, the Japanese Association of America, governed the Japanese community in the United States. This organization was sponsored by the Japanese government, which was sensitive to mistreatment of its citizens abroad and anxious that immigrants set a good example. The Japanese Association, unlike other ethnic organizations, actively encouraged assimilation and stressed the importance of Western dress and learning English.

Ethnic newspapers, theaters, and schools supplemented associational life for immigrants. These institutions reinforced Old World culture while informing immigrants about American ways. Thus, the *Jewish Daily Forward*, first published in New York in 1897, reminded readers of the importance of keeping the Sabbath while admonishing them to adopt American customs.

QUICK REVIEW

Maintenance of Cultural Traditions

- Religious and communal institutions played a key role in maintaining immigrants' cultural traditions.
- Churches were often the focal point of immigrant life.
- The family was the most important institution in Chinese and Japanese communities.

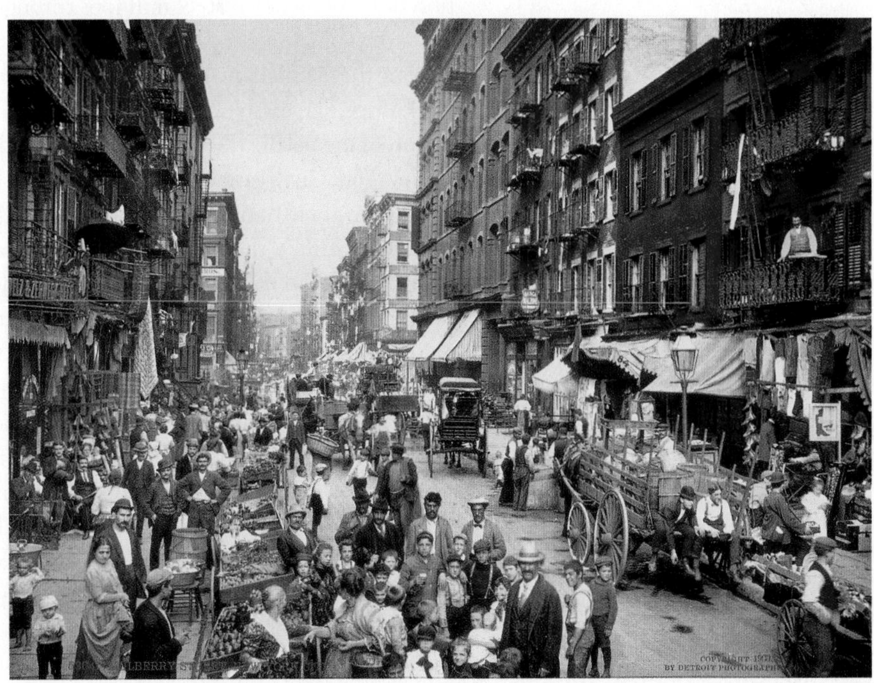

Mulberry Street, New York, 1905. The vibrant, predominantly Russian-Jewish Lower East Side of New York at first reflected more the culture of the homeland than of the United States. Language, dress, and ways of doing business, keeping house, and worshiping, all followed Old World patterns. Gradually, thanks especially to the influence of school-age children, a blend of Russian Jewish and American traditions emerged.

The Job

If immigrant culture provided newcomers with a supportive environment, work offered the ultimate reward for coming to America. All immigrants perceived the job as the way to independence and as a way out, either back to the Old World or into the larger American society.

Immigrants typically got their first job with the help of a countryman. Italian, Chinese, Japanese, and Mexican newcomers worked with contractors who placed them in jobs. These middlemen often provided housing, loans, and other services for recent arrivals. Other immigrant groups, such as Poles and Russian Jews, often found work through their ethnic associations or village or family connections. Family members sometimes exchanged jobs with one another.

Read the **Document** at **www.myhistorylab.com** *Lee Chew, "Life of a Chinese Immigrant" (1903)*

The type of work available to immigrants depended on their skills, the local economy, and local discrimination. Mexican migrants to southern California, for example, concentrated in railroad construction. Mostly unskilled, they replaced Chinese laborers when the federal government prohibited Chinese immigration after 1882. Mexicans built the interurban rail lines of Los Angeles in 1900 and established communities at their construction camps. Los Angeles businessmen barred Mexicans from other occupations. Similarly, Chinese immigrants were confined to work in laundries and restaurants within the boundaries of Los Angeles's Chinatown.

The Japanese who came to Los Angeles around 1900 were forced into sectors of the economy that native-born white people had either shunned or failed to exploit. The Japanese turned this discrimination to their benefit when they transformed the cultivation of market-garden crops into a major agricultural enterprise. By 1904, Japanese farmers owned more than 50,000 acres in California.

Stereotypes also channeled immigrants' work options, sometimes benefiting one group at the expense of another. Jewish textile entrepreneurs, for example, sometimes hired only Italians because they thought them less prone to unionization than Jewish workers. Other Jewish bosses hired only Jewish workers, hoping that ethnic loyalty would overcome the lure of the unions. Pittsburgh steelmakers preferred Polish workers to the black workers who began arriving in northern cities in appreciable numbers after 1900. This decision began the decades-long tradition of handing down steel mill jobs through the generations in Polish families.

Jews, alone among European ethnic groups, found work almost exclusively with one another. Among the factors contributing to this pattern may have been the discrimination Jews faced in eastern Europe, the existence of an established Jewish community when they arrived, and their domination of the needle trades. Jews comprised three-quarters of the more than a half-million workers in New York City's garment industry in 1910. Jews were also heavily concentrated in the retail trade.

Like their native-born counterparts, few married immigrant women worked outside the home, but unlike the native-born, many Italian and Jewish women did piecework for the garment industry in their apartments. Unmarried Polish women often worked in factories or as domestic servants. Japanese women, married and single, worked with their families on farms. Until revolution in China in 1911 began to erode traditional gender roles, married Chinese immigrant women typically remained at home.

The paramount goal for many immigrants was to work for themselves rather than for someone else. Most new arrivals, however, had few skills, and no resources beyond their wits, with which to realize their dreams. Major banks at the time were unlikely to extend even a small business loan to a budding ethnic entrepreneur. Family members and small ethnic-based community banks provided the initial stake for most immigrant businesses.

Immigrants could not fully control their own destinies in the United States, any more than native-born Americans could. The vagaries of daily life, including death, disease, and bad luck, thwarted many immigrants' dreams. Hard work did not always ensure success. Add to these the difficulty of cultural adjustment to an unfamiliar environment, and the newcomer's confident hopes could fade quickly. Almost all immigrants, however, faced an obstacle that white native-born Americans did not: the antiforeign prejudice of American nativism.

Read the **Document** at **www.myhistorylab.com** *Exploring America: The Unwelcome Mat*

Nativism

Despite the openness of America's borders in the nineteenth century, and contrary to the nation's reputation as a refuge from foreign persecution and poverty, immigrants did not always receive a warm reception. From the 1830s to 1860, nativist sentiment, directed mainly at Irish Catholic immigrants, expressed itself in occasional violence and job discrimination. Anti-immigrant sentiment gave rise to an important political party, the Know-Nothings, in the 1850s.

When immigration revived after the Civil War, so did antiforeign sentiment. But late-nineteenth-century **nativism** differed in two ways from its antebellum predecessor. First, the target was no longer Irish Catholics, but the even more numerous Catholics and Jews of southern and eastern Europe, people whose languages and usually darker complexions set them apart from the native-born majority. Second, late-nineteenth-century nativism had a pseudoscientific underpinning. As we saw in Chapter 17, the "scientific" racism of the period maintained that some people are inherently inferior to others. Social Darwinism, which justified the class hierarchy, reinforced scientific racism.

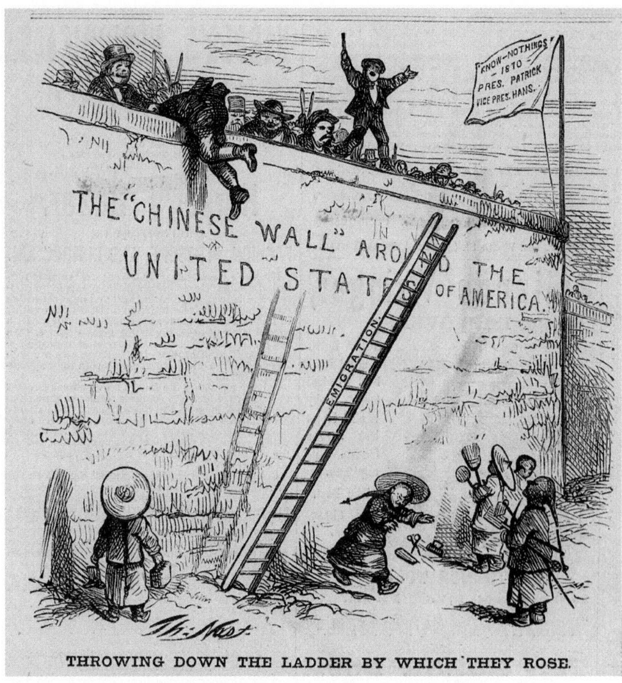

"Throwing Down the Ladder by Which They Rose," Thomas Nast's 1870 attack on nativism. White workers, many of them immigrants themselves, objected to labor competition from Chinese immigrants and eventually helped to persuade Congress to pass the Chinese Exclusion Act in 1882.

When the "inferior" races began to arrive in the United States in significant numbers after 1880, nativists sounded the alarm. A prominent Columbia University professor wrote in 1887 that Hungarians and Italians were "of such a character as to endanger our civilization." Nine years later, the director of the U.S. census warned that eastern and southern Europeans were "beaten men from beaten races. They have none of the ideas and aptitudes which fit men to take up readily and easily the problem of self-care and self-government." The result of unfettered migration would be "race suicide."

nativism Favoring the interests and culture of native-born inhabitants over those of immigrants.

The popular press translated these scientific pronouncements into blunter language. In the mid-1870s, a Chicago newspaper described recently arrived immigrants from Bohemia (the present-day Czech Republic) as "depraved beasts, harpies, decayed physically and spiritually, mentally and morally, thievish and licentious." The rhetoric of the scientific press was scarcely less extreme. *Scientific American* magazine warned immigrants to "assimilate" quickly or "share the fate of the native Indians" and face "a quiet but sure extermination."

WHERE TO LEARN MORE

Angel Island State Park, San Francisco Bay
http://www.Angelisland.org

Such sentiments generated proposals to restrict foreign immigration. The treatment of the Chinese provided a precedent. Chinese immigrants had long worked for low wages, under harsh conditions, in mining and railroad construction in the West. Their different culture and their willingness to accept low wages provoked resentment among native- and European-born workers. Violence against Chinese laborers increased during the 1860s and 1870s. In 1870, the Republican-dominated Congress passed the Naturalization Act, which limited citizenship to "white persons and persons of African descent." The act was specifically intended to prevent Chinese from becoming citizens, a ban not lifted until 1943, but it affected other Asian groups also. The Chinese Exclusion Act of 1882, passed following another decade of anti-Chinese pressure, made the Chinese the only ethnic group in the world that could not immigrate freely into the United States.

Labor competition also contributed to the rise of new anti-immigrant organizations. A group of skilled workers and small businessmen formed the American Protective Association (APA) in 1887 and claimed half a million members a year later. The APA sought to limit Catholic civil rights in the United States to protect the jobs of Protestant workingmen.

The Immigration Restriction League (IRL), formed in 1894 in the midst of a depression, took a more modest and indirect approach. The IRL proposed to require prospective immigrants to pass a literacy test that most southern and eastern Europeans would presumably fail. The IRL

AMERICAN VIEWS

 Tenement Life 

In 1890, the Danish immigrant Jacob A. Riis published How the Other Half Lives, *an exposé of living conditions among immigrants in New York City's Lower East Side neighborhood. The book, complete with vivid photographs, caused a sensation. At a time when newspapers and magazines competed for readers with lurid tales of urban life, Riis's detailed and gruesome depictions shocked readers and provided an impetus for housing reform in New York and, eventually, across the urban nation. Riis's scientific tone, devoid of sensationalism, rendered the scenes that much more dramatic. For a nation that valued family life and the sanctity of childhood, Riis's accounts of how the environment, inside and outside the tenement, destroyed young lives provided moving testimony that for some and perhaps many immigrants, the "promise" had been taken out of the Promised Land.*

- **What** is Jacob Riis's attitude toward the tenement dwellers?
- **Considering** the destitute character of the family Riis describes, what sort of assistance do you think they receive?
- **Why** do you suppose the authorities were reluctant to enforce sanitary, capacity, and building regulations in these neighborhoods?

Look into any of these houses, everywhere the same piles of rags, of malodorous bones and musty paper all of which the sanitary police flatter themselves they have banished. . . . Here is a "parlor" and two pitch-dark coops called bedrooms. Truly, the bed is all there is room for. The family teakettle is on the stove, doing duty for the time being as a wash-boiler. By night it will have returned to its proper use again, a practical illustration of how poverty . . . makes both ends meet. One, two, three beds are there, if the old boxes and heaps of foul straw can be called by that name; a broken stove with crazy pipe from which the smoke leaks at every joint, a table of rough boards propped up on boxes, piles of rubbish in the corner. The closeness and smell are appalling. . . .

Well do I recollect the visit of a health inspector to one of these tenements on a July day when the thermometer outside was climbing high in the nineties; but inside, in that awful room, with half a dozen persons washing, cooking, and sorting rags, lay the dying baby alongside the stove, where the doctor's thermometer ran up to 115 degrees! Perishing for the want of a breath of fresh air in this city of untold charities! . . .

A message came one day last spring summoning me to a Mott Street tenement in which lay a child dying from some unknown disease. With the "charity doctor" I found the patient on the top floor, stretched upon two chairs in a dreadfully stifling room. She was gasping in the agony of peritonitis [abdominal infection] that had already written its death-sentence on her wan and pinched face. The whole family, father, mother, and four ragged children, sat around looking on with the stony resignation of helpless despair that had long since given up the fight against fate as useless. A glance around the wretched room left no doubt as to the cause of the children's condition. "Improper nourishment," said the doctor, which translated to suit the place, meant starvation. The father's hands were crippled from lead poisoning. He had not been able to work for a year. A contagious disease of the eyes, too long neglected, had made the mother and one of the boys nearly blind. The children cried with hunger. . . . For months the family had subsisted on two dollars a week from the priest, and a few loaves and a piece of corned beef which the sisters sent them on Saturday. The doctor gave direction for the treatment of the child, knowing that it was possible only to alleviate its sufferings until death should end them, and left some money for food for the rest. An hour later, when I returned, I found them feeding the dying child with ginger ale, bought for two cents a bottle at the pedlar's cart down the street. A pitying neighbor had proposed it as the one thing she could think of as likely to make the child forget its misery.

Source: Jacob A. Riis, *How the Other Half Lives: Studies Among the Tenements of New York* (New York: Charles Scribner's Sons, 1890).

ultimately failed to have its literacy requirement enacted. The return of prosperity and the growing preference of industrialists for immigrant labor put an end to calls for formal restrictions on immigration for the time being. Less than 30 years later, however, Congress would enact major restrictive legislation aimed at southern and eastern European immigrants. In the meantime, IRL propaganda encouraged northern universities to establish quotas limiting the admission of new immigrants, especially Jews.

Immigrants and their communal associations fought attempts to restrict immigration. The Japanese government even hinted at violent retaliation if Congress ever enacted restrictive legislation on Japanese similar to that imposed on the Chinese. But most immigrants believed that the more "American" they became, the less prejudice they would encounter. Accordingly, leaders of immigrant groups stressed the importance of assimilation.

Assimilation connotes the loss of one culture in favor of another. The immigrant experience of the late nineteenth and early twentieth centuries might better be described as a process of adjustment between old ways and new. It was a dynamic process that resulted in entirely new cultural forms. The Japanese, for example, had not gone to Los Angeles to become truck farmers, but circumstances led them to that occupation, and they used their cultural heritage of hard work, strong family ties, and sober living to make a restricted livelihood successful. Sometimes economics and the availability of alternatives resulted in modifications of traditions that nonetheless maintained their spirit. In the old country, Portuguese held *festas* every Sunday honoring a patron saint. In New England towns, they confined the tradition to their churches instead of parading through the streets. And instead of baking bread themselves, Portuguese immigrant women were happy to buy all the bread they needed from local bakers.

Despite the antagonism of native-born white people toward recent immigrants, the greatest racial divide in America remained that between black and white. Newcomers quickly caught on to this distinction and sought to assert their "whiteness" as a common bond with other European immigrant groups and a badge of acceptance into the larger society. For immigrants, therefore, becoming "white," distancing themselves from African American culture and people, was often part of the process of adjusting to American life, especially as increasing numbers of black southerners began moving to northern cities.

QUICK REVIEW

The Naturalization Act of 1870

- Limited citizenship to "white persons and persons of African descent."
- Act intended to bar Chinese from becoming citizens.
- Subsequent Chinese Exclusion Act of 1882 made Chinese the only group that could not immigrate freely to the United States.

Roots of the Great Migration

Nearly 90 percent of African Americans still lived in the South in 1900, most in rural areas. Between 1880 and 1900, however, black families began to move into the great industrial cities of the Northeast and Midwest. They were drawn by the same economic promise that attracted overseas migrants and were pushed by growing persecution in the South. Job opportunities probably outweighed all other factors in motivating what became known as the **Great Migration.**

Great Migration The mass movement of African Americans from the rural South to the urban North, spurred especially by new job opportunities during World War I and the 1920s.

In most northern cities in 1900, black people typically worked as common laborers or domestic servants. They competed with immigrants for jobs, and in most cases they lost. Immigrants even claimed jobs that black workers had once dominated, such as barbering and service work in hotels, restaurants, and transportation.

Black women had very few options in the northern urban labor force outside of domestic service, although they earned higher wages than they had for similar work in southern cities. The retail and clerical jobs that attracted young working-class white women remained closed to black women. Employers rejected them for any job involving direct contact with the public.

Watch the **Video** at **www.myhistorylab.com** *The Great Migration*

The lack of options black migrants confronted in the search for employment matched similar frustrations in their quest for a place to live. Even more than foreign immigrants, they were restricted to segregated urban ghettos. Small black ghettos existed in antebellum northern cities. As black migration to northern cities accelerated after 1900, the pattern of residential isolation became more pronounced. The black districts in northern cities were more diverse than

GLOBAL CONNECTIONS

 THE ERA OF GLOBAL MIGRATIONS 

The massive wave of immigration from Europe and Asia to the United States was part of a worldwide migration in the late nineteenth century. Italian peasants, for example, migrated to major cities in their newly unified country, to Berlin and London, to South America, and to Canada and Australia as well as to the United States. A major objective of the migrants was to improve their lot so that they and their families would have a better life. Countries undergoing industrialization, particularly those in the Western Hemisphere, provided opportunities that did not exist in China, Japan, Italy, and eastern Europe.

In Italy, too little land, too many people, and the lack of educational and social opportunities aided the migration stream. Italy experienced a sudden surge in fertility in the 1880s. That, combined with a declining mortality rate, resulted in sharply reduced resources and land, especially in the mostly rural regions of southern Italy and Sicily. It was a region where tax policies favored the wealthy landlords. High tariffs protected northern Italian industry but not southern enterprises, resulting in high unemployment. Adding to the misery, a blight eradicated vineyards in southern Italy, and, in 1905, a series of earthquakes rattled the region. In 1908, a tsunami in the Straits of Messina between Sicily and the Italian mainland leveled the city of Messina. None of these economic, political, and natural misfortunes by themselves caused people to pull up roots in a very rooted society. But in combination, their effect was powerful.

The same combination spurred immigration from other countries. Economic policies that ruined farm workers in southern China touched off migrations to the West Coast of the United States. In Japan, soaring inflation and unemployment during the 1870s and 1880s, worsened by a destructive typhoon in 1884, prompted nearly 30,000 Japanese to leave for Hawaii. Russian Jewish migrants feared not only for their livelihoods but their lives. Emigration was more of a necessity than a choice in these cases.

While opportunities provided the attraction, and economic, political, and religious oppression at home provided the push, technology enhanced the means to get to far-flung places. The migration of labor was something that had gone on since ancient times. But by the late nineteenth century, the advent of railroads and steamships shrunk the world, making jobs accessible anywhere. These new modes of transportation, combined with inexpensive newspapers, letters from countrymen, and the telegraph, also spread information quickly and more widely than ever before. As Mary Antin wrote about her Russian town in the early 1890s, "America was in everybody's mouth."

- Why did such massive immigration occur in the late nineteenth century?

those in southern cities. Migration brought rural southerners, urban southerners, and West Indians together with the black northerners already living there. People of all social classes lived in these districts.

The difficulties that black families faced to make ends meet paralleled in some ways those of immigrant working-class families. Restricted job options, however, limited the income of black families, even with black married women five times more likely to work than married white women. In black families, moreover, working teenage children were less likely to stay home and contribute their paychecks to the family income.

Popular culture reinforced the marginalization of African Americans. Vaudeville and minstrel shows, popular urban entertainments around 1900, featured songs belittling black people and black characters with names like Useless Peabody and Moses Abraham Highbrow. Immigrants frequented these shows and absorbed the culture of racism from them. The new medium of film perpetuated the negative stereotypes.

In the North as in the South, African Americans sought to counter the hostility of the larger society by building their own communal institutions. An emerging middle-class leadership sought to develop black businesses. Despite these efforts, chronic lack of capital kept black businesses mostly small and confined to the ghetto. Immigrant groups often pooled extended-family capital resources or tapped ethnic banks. With few such resources at their disposal, black businesses failed at a high rate. Most black people worked outside the ghetto for white employers. Economic marginalization often attracted unsavory businesses—dance halls, brothels, and bars—to black neighborhoods. One recently arrived migrant from the South complained that in his Cleveland neighborhood, his family was surrounded by loafers, "gamblers [and] pocket pickers; I can not raise my children here like they should be."

Other black institutions proved more lasting than black businesses. In Chicago in 1891, black physician Daniel Hale Williams established Provident Hospital, the nation's first interracially staffed hospital, with the financial help of wealthy white Chicagoans. Although it failed as an interracial experiment, the hospital thrived, providing an important training ground for black physicians and nurses.

Black branches of the Young Men's and Young Women's Christian Association provided living accommodations, social facilities, and employment information for black young people. Many black migrants to northern cities, perhaps a majority, were single, and the Y provided them with guidance and a "home." White people funded many black Y projects but did not accept black members in their chapters. By 1910, black settlement houses modeled on the white versions appeared in several cities.

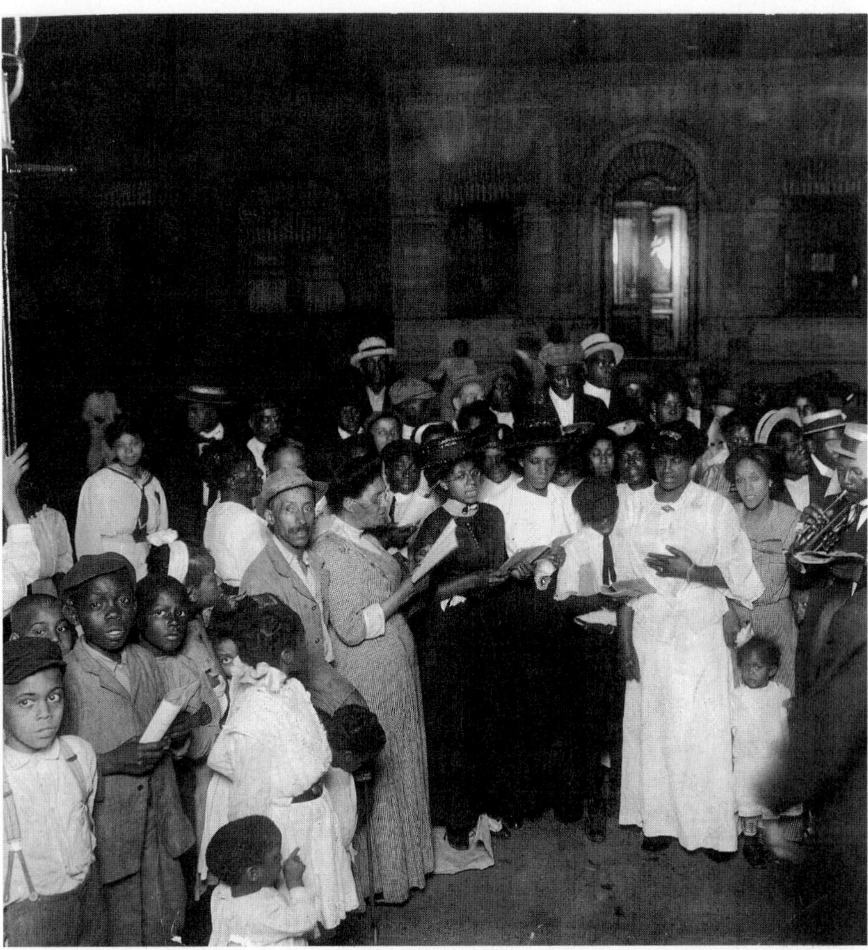

An African American religious meeting, New York City, early 1900s. Black migrants from the South found vibrant communities in northern cities typically centered around black churches and their activities. Like immigrants from Asia and Europe, who sought to transplant the culture of their homelands within the urban United States, black migrants reestablished southern religious and communal traditions in their new homes.

NEW CITIES

HOW DID the new cities help create the new middle class?

Immigration from abroad and migration from American farms to the cities resulted in an urban explosion during the late nineteenth century (see Map 18–2). In 1850, six cities had a population exceeding 100,000; by 1900, thirty-eight did. In 1850, only 5 percent of the nation's population lived in cities of more than 100,000 inhabitants; by 1900, the figure was 19 percent. The nation's population tripled between 1860 and 1920, but the urban population increased ninefold.

In Europe, a few principal cities, such as Paris and Berlin, absorbed most of the urban growth during this period. In the United States, by contrast, growth was more evenly distributed among many cities. Despite the relative evenness of growth, a distinctive urban system had emerged by 1900, with New York and Chicago anchoring an urban-industrial core extending in a crescent from New England to the cities bordering the Great Lakes. This region included nine of the nation's ten largest cities in 1920. Western cities like Denver, San Francisco, and Los Angeles emerged as dominant urban places in their respective regions but did not challenge the urban core for supremacy. Southern cities, limited in growth by low consumer demand, low wages, and weak capital formation, were drawn into the orbit of the urban core (see Chapter 17).

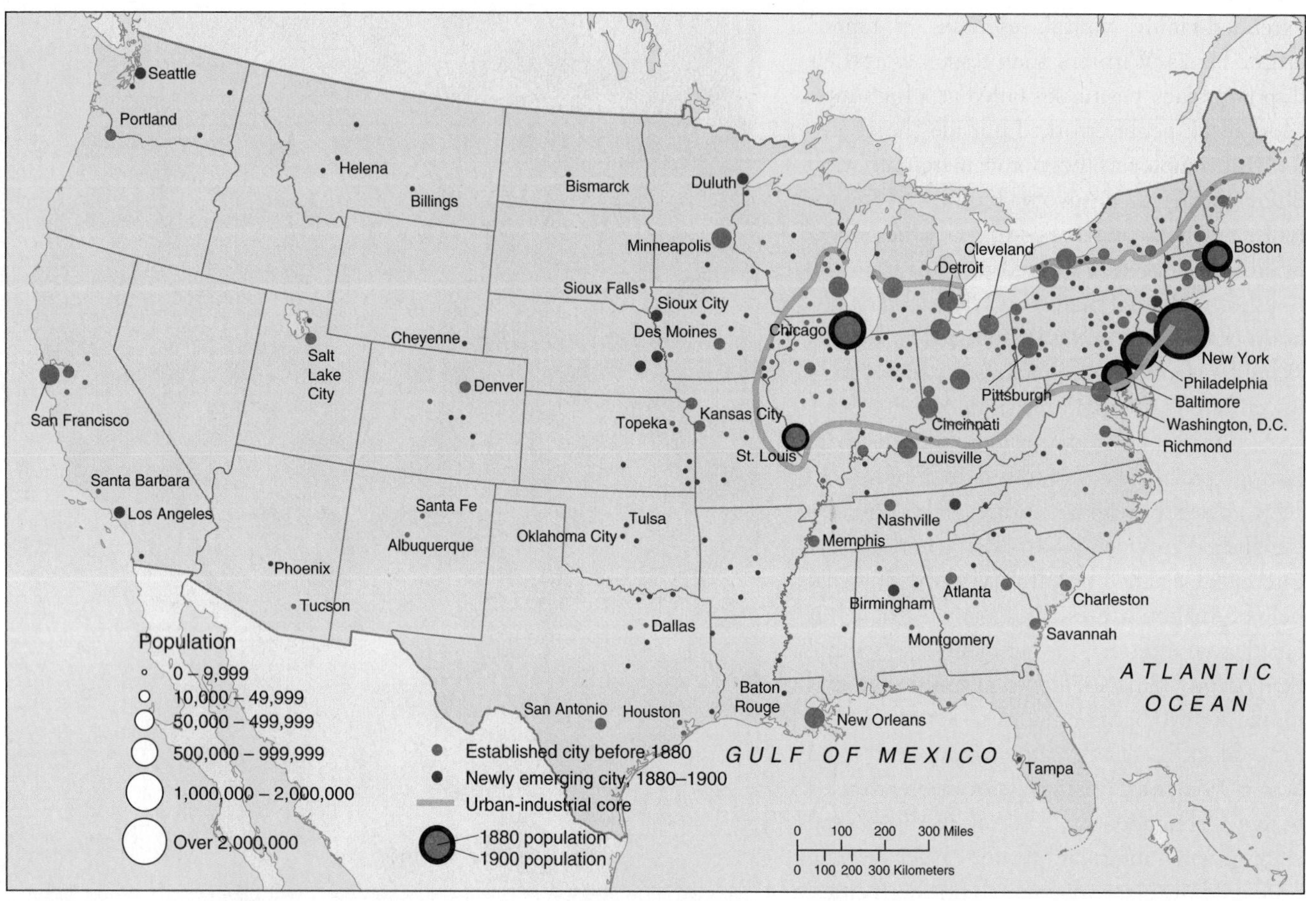

MAP 18–2 **The Growth of American Cities, 1880–1900** Several significant trends stand out on this map. First is the development of an urban-industrial core, stretching from New England to the Midwest, where the largest cities were located. And second is the emergence of relatively new cities in the South and West, reflecting the national dimensions of innovations in industry and transportation.

What were the economic forces that contributed to the growth of some cities and the decline of others?

Urban growth highlighted the growing divisions in American society. The crush of people and the emergence of new technologies expanded the city outward and upward as urban dwellers sorted themselves by social class and ethnic group. While the new infrastructure of water and sewer systems, bridges, and trolley tracks kept steel mills busy, it also fragmented the urban population by allowing settlements well beyond existing urban boundaries. The way people satisfied their needs for food, clothing, and shelter stimulated the industrial economy while distinguishing one class from another. Although urban institutions emerged to counter these divisive trends, they could not overcome them completely.

Centers and Suburbs

The centers of the country's great cities changed in scale and function in this era, achieving a prominence they would eventually lose in the twentieth century. Downtowns expanded up and out as tall buildings arose, monuments to business and finance, creating towering urban skylines. Residential neighborhoods were pushed out, leaving the center dominated by corporate headquarters and retail and entertainment districts.

Corporate heads administered their empires from downtown, even if their factories were located on the urban periphery or in other towns and cities. Banks and insurance companies clustered in such financial centers. Department stores and shops clustered in retail districts in strategic locations along electric trolley lines.

As retail and office uses crowded out dwellings from the city center, a new phenomenon emerged: the residential neighborhood. Advances in transportation technology, first the horse-drawn street railway and, by the 1890s, the electric trolley, eased commuting for office workers. Some in the growing and increasingly affluent middle class left the crowded, polluted city altogether to live in new residential suburbs. These people did not abandon the city; they still looked to it for its jobs, schools, libraries, and entertainment, but they rejected it as a place to live, leaving it to the growing ranks of working-class immigrants and African Americans.

The suburb emerged as the preferred place of residence for the urban middle class after 1870. As early as 1873, Chicago boasted nearly 100 suburbs with a combined population of more than 50,000. The ideals that had promoted modest suburban growth earlier in the nineteenth century—privacy, aesthetics, and home ownership—became increasingly important to the growing numbers of middle-class families after 1880. Consider the Russells of Short Hills, New Jersey. Short Hills lay 18 miles by railroad from New York City. William Russell; his wife, Ella Gibson Russell; and their six children moved there from Brooklyn in the late 1880s, seeking a "pleasant, cultured people whose society we could enjoy" and a cure for Russell's rheumatism. Russell owned and managed a small metal brokerage in New York. Ella Russell cared for their six children with the help of a servant and also found time for several clubs and charities.

The design of the Russell home reflected the principles Catharine Beecher and Harriet Beecher Stowe outlined in their suburban home bible, *American Woman's Home* (1869). The kitchen, according to Beecher and Stowe, should be organized for expedience and hygiene. The home's utilities should be confined to a central core, freeing wall areas for other functions. The new technology of central heating made it unnecessary to divide a house into many small rooms, each with its own fireplace or stove. Taking advantage of this change, Beecher and Stowe recommended that a home's ground floor have fewer but larger rooms, to encourage the family to pursue their individual activities in a common space. Parlors and reception rooms disappeared, along with such former standards as the children's wing, the male "smoking room," and the female parlor.

The once-prevailing view that women were too frail for vigorous exercise was changing. Thus, the entire Russell family was to be found enjoying the tennis, swimming, and skating facilities at the Short Hills Athletic Club. Because the community bordered on undeveloped woodland traversed by trails, "wheel clubs" appeared in the 1880s to organize families for bicycle outings. The emphasis on family togetherness also reflected the changing role of men in late-nineteenth-century society. Women's roles also broadened, as Ella Russell's club work attested.

Suburbs differed, not only from the city, but also from one another. With the growth after 1890 of the electric trolley, elevated rail lines, and other relatively inexpensive forms of commuter travel, suburbs became accessible to a broader spectrum of the middle class. The social structure, architecture, and amenities of suburbs varied, depending on the rail service and distance from the city. The commuter railroad remained popular among people like the Russells who could afford the time and expense of commuting to and from the city center.

The suburb underscored the growing fragmentation of life in and around American cities in the late nineteenth century. Residence, consumer habits, and leisure activities reflected growing social and class divisions. Yet, at the same time, the growing materialism of American society promised a common ground for its disparate ethnic, racial, and social groups.

The New Middle Class

From the colonial era, America's urban middle class had included professionals, physicians, lawyers, ministers, educators, editors, as well as merchants, shopkeepers, and skilled artisans (until they dropped from the middle class in the late nineteenth century). In the late nineteenth century, industrial technology and urban growth expanded the urban middle class to include

QUICK REVIEW

The New Middle Class

- Middle class expanded to include new "white-collar" workers, such as salespeople, managers, and technicians.
- Affluent middle class lived in suburbs.
- Less wealthy middle-class workers remained in cities.
- New middle class set trends in residential patterns, consumption, and leisure.

salespeople, factory supervisors, managers, civil servants, technicians, and a broad range of "white-collar" office workers, such as insurance agents, bank tellers, and legal assistants. This newer middle class set national trends in residential patterns, consumption, and leisure.

The more affluent members of the new middle class, like the Russells, repaired to new subdivisions within and outside the city limits. Simple row houses sheltered the growing numbers of clerks and civil servants who remained in the city. These dwellings contrasted sharply with the crowded one- or two-room apartments that confined the working class. Rents for these apartments ran as much as $3 a week, at a time when few workers made more than $9 or $10.

A Consumer Society

The new middle class transformed America into a consumer society. In earlier times, land had been a symbol of prestige. Now it was consumer goods. And the new industries obliged with a dazzling array of merchandise and technologies. By 1910, the new middle class lived in all-electric homes with indoor plumbing. A typical kitchen might include an electric coffeepot, a hot plate, a chafing dish, and a toaster. The modern city dweller worked by the clock, not by the sun. Eating patterns changed: Cold packaged cereals replaced hot meats at breakfast; fast lunches of Campbell's soup, "a meal in itself," or canned stews weaned Americans from the heavy lunch.

The middle class liked anything that saved time: trolleys, trains, electric razors, vacuum cleaners. The telephone replaced the letter for everyday communication; it was quicker and less formal. By 1900, some 1.4 million phones were in service, and many middle-class homes had one. Observers wondered if the telephone would eventually make written communication obsolete.

The middle class liked its news in an easy-to-read form. Urban tabloids multiplied after 1880, led by Joseph Pulitzer's *New York World* and William Randolph Hearst's *New York Journal*. The newspapers organized the news into topical sections, used bold headlines and graphics to catch the eye, ran human interest stories to capture the imagination, inaugurated sports pages to attract male readers, and offered advice columns for women. And they opened their pages to a wide range of attractive advertising, much of it directed to women, who did about 90 percent of the shopping in American cities by 1900.

As the visual crowded out the printed in advertising, newspapers, and magazines, these materials became accessible to a wider urban audience. Although mainly middle class in orientation, the tabloid press drew urban society together with new features such as the comic strip, which first appeared in the 1890s, and heart-rending personal sagas drawn from real life. Immigrants, who might have had difficulty reading small-type newspapers, received their initiation into the mainstream of American society through the tabloids.

In a similar manner, the department store, essentially a middle-class retail establishment, became one of the city's most democratic forums and the focus of the urban downtown after 1890. Originating in the 1850s and 1860s with the construction of retail palaces such as Boston's Jordan Marsh, Philadelphia's Wanamaker & Brown, New York's Lord & Taylor, and Chicago's Marshall Field, the department store came to epitomize the bounty of the new industrial capitalism. They exuded limitless abundance with their extensive inventories, items for every budget, sumptuous surroundings, and efficient, trained personnel.

At first, most department-store customers were middle-class married women. Not expected to work and with disposable income and flexible schedules, these women had the means and time to wander department store aisles. The stores catered to their tastes, and the current emphasis on home and domesticity, with such items as prefabricated household furnishings, ready-made clothing, toys, and stationery. Department stores maintained consumers' interest with advertising campaigns arranged around holidays like Easter and Christmas, the seasons, and the school calendar. Each event required new clothing and accessories, and the ready-made clothing industry changed fashions accordingly.

Soon the spectacle and merchandise of the department store attracted shoppers from all social strata, not just the middle class. Although many less affluent women came merely to "window-shop," some came to buy. After 1890, department stores increasingly hired young immigrant women to cater to their growing foreign-born clientele.

The department store, the turn-of-the-century shopping mall, provided inexpensive amusement for young working-class people, especially immigrants. Mary Antin recalled how she and her teenage friends and sister would spend their Saturday nights patrolling "a dazzlingly beautiful palace called a 'department store.'" It was there that Mary and her sister "exchanged our hateful homemade European costumes . . . for real American machine-made garments, and issued forth glorified in each other's eyes."

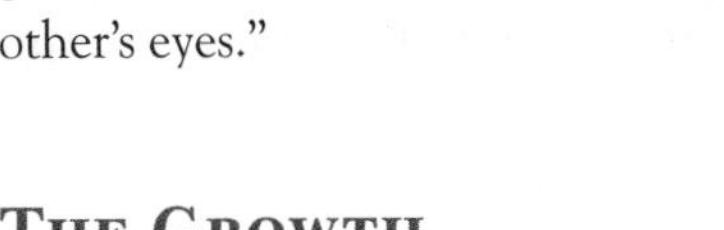

Window shopping at Marshall Field's department store, Chicago, 1909. The department store led the transformation of downtown to retail and office space. Large window displays directed their advertising primarily to women, who comprised most of the shoppers by the early 1900s.

The Growth of Leisure Activities

By 1900, department stores had added sporting goods and hardware sections and were attracting customers from a wide social spectrum. The expanding floor space devoted to sporting goods reflected the growth of leisure in urban society. And like other aspects of that society, leisure and recreation both separated and cut across social classes. The leisure activities of the wealthy increasingly removed them from the rest of urban society. As such sports as football became important extracurricular activities at Harvard, Yale, and other elite universities, intercollegiate games became popular occasions for the upper class to congregate and, not incidentally, to discuss business. The elite also gathered at the athletic clubs and country clubs that emerged as open spaces disappeared in the city. High fees and strict membership criteria kept these clubs exclusive. The clubs offered a suburban retreat, away from the diverse middle- and working-class populations, where the elite could play in privacy.

Middle-class urban residents could not afford country clubs, but they rode electric trolleys to the end of the line to enjoy suburban parks and bicycle and skating clubs. Reflecting the emphasis on family togetherness in late-nineteenth-century America, both men and women participated in these sports. Bicycling in particular became immensely popular.

If college football was the rage among the elite, baseball was the leading middle-class spectator sport. Organized baseball originated among the urban elite before the Civil War. The middle class took over the sport after the war. Baseball epitomized the nation's transition from a rural to an urban industrial society. Reflecting rural tradition, it was played on an expanse of green, usually on the outskirts of the city. It was leisurely; unlike other games, it had no time limit. Reflecting industrial society, however, it had clearly defined rules and was organized into leagues. Professional leagues were profit-making enterprises, and, like other enterprises, they frequently merged. Initially, most professional baseball games were played on weekday afternoons, making it hard for working-class spectators to attend. After merging with the American Association in 1883, the National League adopted some of its innovations to attract more fans, including beer sales, cheap admission, and, despite the objections of Protestant churches, Sunday games.

QUICK REVIEW

Department Stores

- Originated in the 1850s and 1860s.
- First customers were married, middle-class women.
- By 1900 department stores attracted customers from a wide social spectrum.

The tavern, or saloon, was the workingman's club. Typically an all-male preserve, the saloon provided drink, cheap food, and a place to read a newspaper, socialize, and learn about job opportunities. Alcoholism was a severe problem in cities, especially, though not exclusively, among working-class men, fueling the prohibition movement of the late nineteenth century.

Amusement parks, with their mechanical wonders, were another hallmark of the industrial city. Declining trolley fares made these parks accessible to the working class around 1900. Unlike taverns, they provided a place for working-class men and women to meet and date.

Read the **Document** at **www.myhistorylab.com** *Richard K. Fox, from Coney Island Frolics (1883)*

The most renowned of these parks was Brooklyn's Coney Island. In 1897, George C. Tilyou opened Steeplechase Park on Coney Island. Together with such attractions as mechanical horses and 250,000 of Thomas Edison's light bulbs, Steeplechase dazzled patrons with its technological wonders. It was quickly followed by Luna Park and Dreamland, and the Coney Island attractions became collectively known as "the poor man's paradise." Immigrant entrepreneurs, seeing a good thing, flocked to Coney Island to set up sideshows, pool halls, taverns, and restaurants.

After 1900, the wonders of Coney Island began to lure people from all segments of an increasingly diverse city. Sightseers came from around the world. In much the same manner, baseball was becoming a national pastime as games attracted a disparate crowd of people with little in common but their devotion to the home team.

Increasing materialism had revealed great fissures in American urban society by 1900. Yet places like department stores, baseball parks, and amusement parks provided democratic spaces for some interaction. Newspapers and schools also offered diverse groups the vicarious opportunity to share similar experiences.

The Ideal City

For all its problems, the American city was undeniably the locus of the nation's energy; in some ways, with the passing of the frontier, it competed with the West in the national imagination as the environment where possibility was boundless. John Dewey, on his first encounter with Chicago in 1894, sensed this energy, writing to his wife back home, "Chicago is the place to make you appreciate at every turn the absolute opportunity which chaos affords. . . . I had no conception that things could be so much more phenomenal & objective than they are in a country village." This sense of limitless energy and innovation appeared most notably in urban skylines where skyscrapers reached heavenward as graceful cathedrals of commerce. The tall buildings bespoke a confidence that declared even the sky was not the limit.

Read the **Document** at **www.myhistorylab.com** *From Then to Now Online: Green Cities*

There was great interest in creating clean cities, harmonious with nature, and with aesthetic and cultural amenities. The advent of planned towns with these qualities coincided with a growing conservation movement that also included protecting the natural environment from the sprawl of urban growth. Few landscapes expressed this new urban ideal better than the 1893 World's Columbian Exposition in Chicago, a World's Fair to celebrate the 400th anniversary of the European discovery of America. The fair demonstrated how with foresight, planning, and copious funds, it was possible to create a safe and aesthetic urban environment, quite different from the gritty industrial city just beyond its borders. Dubbed the White City, the exposition epitomized cleanliness, grandeur, beauty, and order in its architecture. That it was sheer fantasy, a temporary respite from the reality beyond the gates, did not faze the millions who attended. The White City represented the possibility, and in America, anything was possible.

CONCLUSION

The new industrial order, the changing nature of work, the massive migrations of populations from the countryside and abroad, and the rise of great cities changed the American landscape in the late nineteenth century. By 1900, the factory worker and the department store clerk were more representative of the new America than the farmer and small shopkeeper. Industry and technology had created thousands of new jobs, but they also eliminated the autonomy many workers had enjoyed and limited their opportunities to advance. The individual journey from farms and small towns to large cities, and from Europe, Asia, and Latin America to the United States, became a collective journey, moving America further toward becoming a modern urban and industrial nation, with all of the accompanying ills, but also with all of its possibilities.

Immigrants thronged to the United States to realize their dreams of economic and religious freedom. They found both to varying degrees but also discovered a darker side to the promise of American life. The great cities thrilled newcomers with their possibilities and their abundance of goods and activities. But the cities also bore witness to the growing divisions in American society. As the new century dawned, the prospects for urban industrial America seemed limitless, yet the stark contrasts that had appeared so vividly inside and outside the Centennial Exposition persisted and deepened.

Still, it would be wrong to depict the nation in 1900 as merely a larger and more divided version of what it had been in 1876. Although sharp ethnic, racial, and class differences persisted, the nation seemed better poised to address them in 1900 than it had a quarter-century earlier. Labor unions, ethnic organizations, government legislation, and new urban institutions promised ways to remedy the worst abuses of the new urban, industrial economy.

Where to Learn More

Edison National Historic Site, West Orange, New Jersey. The site contains the Edison archives, including photographs, sound recordings, and industrial and scientific machinery. Its 20 historic structures dating from the 1880–1887 period include Edison's home and laboratory. http://www.nps.gov/edis.

The Tenement Museum. An excellent presentation of the living conditions and lives of five immigrant families who resided at 97 Orchard Street in Manhattan's Lower East Side from 1863 to the early decades of the twentieth century. Enter the tenement and enter their world. It is not always pleasant, but it is always fascinating. http://www.tenement.org.

Angel Island State Park, San Francisco Bay. Angel Island served as a detention center from 1910 to 1940 for Asian immigrants who were kept there for days, months, and, in some cases, years while immigration officials attempted to ferret out illegal entries. Exhibits depict the era through pictures and artifacts. http://www.Angelisland.org.

Statue of Liberty National Monument and Ellis Island, New York, New York. More than 12 million immigrants were processed at Ellis Island between 1892 and 1954. The exhibits provide a fine overview of American immigration history during this period. There is an ongoing oral history program as well. http://www.nps.gov/stli.

Review Questions

1. Were there ways to achieve the benefits of industrialization without its social costs, or did the nation's political and economic systems make that impossible?
2. How did working-class women respond to the new economy? How did their participation and responses differ from that of working-class men?
3. What factors accounted for immigration becoming a global phenomenon during the late nineteenth century?
4. The growing fragmentation of urban life reflected deep divisions in modern urban industrial society. At the same time, there were forces that tended to overcome these divisions. What were these forces, and were they sufficient to bridge the divisions?
5. How did Old World conditions influence Mary Antin's adjustment to American life? Would individuals from other immigrant groups have expressed similar sentiments, or was Mary's reaction specific to her Jewish background?

Key Terms

American Federation of Labor (p. 504)
Chain migration (p. 507)
Collective bargaining (p. 504)
Gilded Age (p. 496)
Gospel of Wealth (p. 502)
Great Migration (p. 511)
Great Uprising (p. 503)
Horizontal integration (p. 497)
Hull House (p. 502)
Knights of Labor (p. 503)
Nativism (p. 509)
Pogroms (p. 506)
Social Darwinism (p. 503)
Sweatshops (p. 500)
Tenements (p. 502)
Trusts (p. 498)
Vertical integration (p. 497)

myhistorylab Connections

Reinforce what you learned in this chapter by studying the many documents, images, maps, review tools, and videos available at **www.myhistorylab.com**.

Read and Review

Study and Review **Study Plan: Chapter 18**

Read the Document

Mark Twain, from The Gilded Age (1873)

Thomas Edison, The Success of the Electric Light (1880)

Upton Sinclair, The Jungle *(1906)*

Andrew Carnegie, Wealth and Its Uses (1907)

George Engel, Address by a Condemned Haymarket Anarchist (1886)

Lee Chew, "Life of a Chinese Immigrant" (1903)

Chinese Exclusion Act (1882)

Richard K. Fox, from Coney Island Frolics (1883)

William Graham Sumner, from What the Social Classes Owe to Each Other (1883)

See the Map

Foreign-Born Population, 1890

Organizing American Labor in the Late Nineteenth Century

Jacob A. Riis, The Battle with the Slum (1902)

Research and Explore

Read the Document

Personal Journeys Online

From Then to Now Online: Green Cities

Exploring America: The Unwelcome Mat

Hear the Audio *Hungarian Rag*

Watch the Video

The Great Migration

Ellis Island Immigrants, 1903

Hear the Audio

Hear the audio files for Chapter 18 at **www.myhistorylab.com.**

1865-1890

19 Transforming the West

This idealized 1875 engraving presents a harmonious image of western expansion and railroad construction that belies a more complex and disruptive reality, particularly for Native Americans.

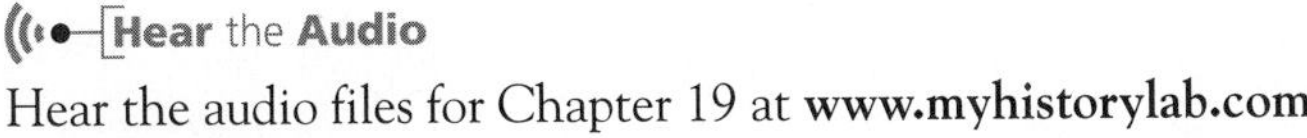

Hear the Audio

Hear the audio files for Chapter 19 at **www.myhistorylab.com**.

SUBJUGATING NATIVE AMERICANS *(page 525)*

WHAT WERE the main objectives of federal Indian policy in the late nineteenth century?

EXPLOITING THE MOUNTAINS: THE MINING BONANZA *(page 531)*

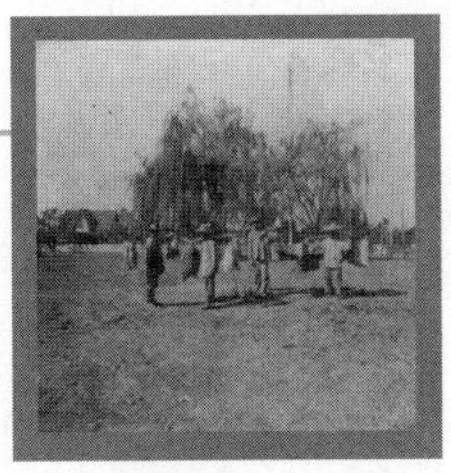

HOW DID mining in the West change over the course of the second half of the nineteenth century?

USING THE GRASS: THE CATTLE KINGDOM *(page 536)*

WHAT FACTORS contributed to the development of the range cattle industry?

WORKING THE EARTH: HOMESTEADERS AND AGRICULTURAL EXPANSION *(page 539)*

HOW DID new technology contribute to the growth of western agriculture?

ONE AMERICAN JOURNEY

After a pleasant ride of about six miles we attained a very high elevation, and, passing through a gorge of the mountains, we entered a level, circular valley, about three miles in diameter, surrounded on every side by mountains. The track is on the eastern side of the plain, and at the point of junction extends in nearly a southwest and northeast direction. Two lengths of rails are left for today's work. . . . At a quarter to nine A.M. *the whistle of the C.P. [Central Pacific Railroad] is heard, and soon arrives, bringing a number of passengers. . . . Two additional trains arrive from the East. At a quarter to eleven the Chinese workmen commenced leveling the bed of the road with picks and shovels, preparatory to placing the ties. . . . At 12 M. the rails were laid, and the iron spikes driven. The last tie . . . is of California laurel, finely polished, and is ornamented with a silver escutcheon bearing the following inscription: "The last tie laid on the Pacific Railroad, May 10th, 1869." . . .*

The point of contact is 1,085 4/5 miles from Omaha, leaving 690 miles for the C.P. portion of the work. The engine Jupiter, of the C.P., and engine 119, of the U.P.R.R. [Union Pacific Railroad] moved up within thirty feet of each other. . . . Three cheers were given for the Government of the United States, for the railroad, for the President, for the Star Spangled Banner, for the laborers, and for those who furnished the means respectively. The four spikes, two gold and two silver, were furnished by Montana, Idaho, California, and Nevada. Dr. Harkness, of Sacramento, on presenting to Governor Stanford a spike of pure gold, delivered a short and appropriate speech. The Hon. F.A. Tuttle, of Nevada, presented Dr. Durant with a spike of silver, saying: 'To the iron of the East, and the gold of the West, Nevada adds her link of silver to span the continent and wed the oceans.' . . . The two locomotives then moved up until they touched each other, . . . and at one P.M., under an almost cloudless sky . . . the completion of the greatest railroad on earth was announced.

Andrew J. Russell, "The Completion of the Pacific Railroad," *Frank Leslie's Illustrated Newspaper,* June 5, 1869.

Read the **Document** at **www.myhistorylab.com**

Personal Journeys Online

- **Eugene Chihuahua, *Leaving the West,* 1885. An Apache's account of being forced from his home into imprisonment.**
- **Emma Hill, *Settling in Kansas,* 1873. A woman's account of pioneer hardships.**
- **Carl and Fredrik Bergman, *Times Look Quite Promising,* 1884–1893. Swedish immigrants describe their experiences in Texas.**

ANDREW J. RUSSELL'S short journey on the morning of May 10, 1869, from Ogden to Promontory Summit, Utah, enabled him, in his capacity as the official Union Pacific photographer, to document what he called "the completion of the greatest work of the age, by which this vast continent is spanned, from ocean to ocean, by the iron path of travel and commerce." The construction of the transcontinental railroad set a precedent for western development. The two railroads that met in a desolate sagebrush basin were huge corporate enterprises, not individual efforts, and corporations would dominate western growth as much as they did eastern industrialization. The crowd of onlookers had good reason to give three cheers for the federal government, for it played a crucial role in railroad construction, as in virtually all aspects of western development. Congress had authorized the Union Pacific and Central Pacific to build the railroad link, given them the right-of-way for their tracks, and provided huge land grants and financial subsidies.

The railroads' dependence on capital investment, engineering knowledge, technological innovations, and labor skills also typified western development. Their labor forces both reflected and reinforced the region's racial and ethnic diversity. European immigrants,

CHRONOLOGY

1858	Gold is discovered in Colorado, Nevada, and British Columbia.
1860	Gold is discovered in Idaho.
1862	Homestead Act is passed.
	Gold is discovered in Montana.
1864	Militia slaughters Cheyennes at Sand Creek, Colorado.
1867	Cattle drives make Abilene the first cow town.
1868	Fort Laramie Treaty is signed.
1869	First transcontinental railroad is completed.
1872	Canada enacts homestead law.
1874	Gold is discovered in the Black Hills.
	Turkey Red wheat is introduced in Kansas.
	Barbed wire is patented.
1876	Indians devastate U.S. troops in the Battle of the Little Bighorn.
1879	Defeat of Araucanian Indians opens the pampas to settlement in Argentina.
	"Exodusters" migrate to Kansas.
1885	Chinese massacred at Rock Springs, Wyoming.
1887	Dawes Act is passed.
1890	Government troops kill 200 Sioux at Wounded Knee, South Dakota.
1892	Mining violence breaks out at Coeur d'Alene, Idaho.
1893	Western Federation of Miners is organized.

Mexicans, Paiute Indians, both male and female, and especially Chinese, recruited in California and Asia, chiseled the tunnels through the mountains, built the bridges over the gulches, and laid the ties and rails across the plains. But Russell had the Chinese workers step back so as not to appear in the famous photographs he took at Promontory, an indication of the racism that marred so many western achievements.

Laying track as quickly as possible to collect the subsidies awarded by the mile, the railroad corporations adopted callous and reckless construction tactics, resulting in waste, deaths (perhaps as many as a thousand Chinese), and environmental destruction, all consequences that would similarly characterize other forms of economic development in the West. And as with most American undertakings in the West, the construction provoked conflict with the Cheyenne, Sioux, and other tribes.

The most important feature of the railroad, however, was that traffic moved in both directions. The transcontinental and subsequent railroads helped move soldiers, miners, cattle raisers, farmers, merchants, and other settlers into the West, but they also enabled the West to send precious metals, livestock, lumber, and wheat to the growing markets in the East. Thus the railroad both integrated the West into the rest of the nation and made it a crucial part of the larger economic revolution that transformed America after the Civil War.

SUBJUGATING NATIVE AMERICANS

WHAT WERE the main objectives of federal Indian policy in the late nineteenth century?

The initial obstacle to exploiting the West was the people already living there, who used its resources in their own way and held different concepts of progress and civilization. As whites pressed westward, they attempted to subjugate the Indians, displace them from their lands, and strip them of their culture.

Tribes and Cultures

Throughout the West, Indians had adapted to their environment, developing subsistence economies ranging from simple gathering to complex systems of irrigated agriculture. Each activity encouraged their sensitivity to the natural world, and each had social and political implications.

W
WHERE TO LEARN MORE
Golden Spike National Historic Site, near Promontory, Utah
http://www.nps.gov/gosp

In the Northwest, abundant food from rich waters and dense forests gave rise to complex and stable Indian societies. Tillamooks, Chinooks, and other tribes developed artistic handicrafts, elaborate social institutions, and a satisfying religious life. At the opposite environmental

This photograph, taken by A. J. Russell, records the celebration at the joining of the Central Pacific and Union Pacific railroads on May 10, 1869, at Promontory Summit, Utah. Railroads transformed the American West, linking the region to outside markets, spurring rapid settlement, and threatening Indian survival.

extreme, in the dry and barren Great Basin of Utah and Nevada, Shoshones and Paiutes ate grasshoppers and other insects to supplement their diet of rabbits, mice, and other small animals. Such harsh environments restricted the size, strength, and organizational complexity of societies. In the Southwest, the Pueblos dwelled in permanent towns of adobe buildings and practiced intensive agriculture. Because tribal welfare depended on maintaining complex irrigation systems, the Zunis, Hopis, and other Pueblos emphasized community solidarity rather than individual ambition. Town living encouraged social stability and the development of effective governments, elaborate religious ceremonies, and creative arts.

The most numerous Indian groups lived on the Great Plains. The largest of these tribes were the Lakotas, or Sioux, who ranged from western Minnesota through the Dakotas; the Cheyennes and Arapahos, who controlled much of the central plains between the Platte and Arkansas rivers; and the Comanches, preeminent on the southern plains. Two animals dominated the lives of these peoples: the horse, which enabled them to move freely over the plains and to use the energy stored in the valuable grasses, and the buffalo, which provided meat, hides, bones and horns for tools, and a focus for spiritual life.

W WHERE TO LEARN MORE

National Museum of the American Indian, Smithsonian Institution, Washington, DC
http://www.nmai.si.edu

QUICK REVIEW

Indians in the West

- Desert tribes had to contend with a harsh environment.
- The cultures of many Southwest tribes emphasized communal solidarity.
- The most numerous Indian groups in the West lived on the Great Plains.

Clashing values. Despite their diversity, all tribes emphasized community welfare over individual interest. They based their economies on subsistence rather than profit. They tried to live in harmony with nature to ward off sickness, injury, death, or misfortune. And they were intensely religious, absorbed with the need to establish proper relations with supernatural forces that linked human beings with all other living things. These connections also shaped Indians' attitude toward land, which they regarded, like air and water, as part of nature to be held and used communally, not as an individual's personal property from which others could be excluded.

White and Indian cultural values were incompatible. Disdaining Native Americans and their religion, white people condemned them as "savages" to be converted or exterminated. Rejecting the concept of communal property, most settlers demanded land for the exclusive use of ambitious individuals. Ignoring the need for natural harmony, they followed their own culture's goal of extracting wealth from the land for a market economy.

Federal Indian Policy

The government had in the 1830s adopted the policy of separating whites and Indians (see Chapter 10). Eastern tribes were moved west of Missouri and resettled on land then scorned as "the Great American Desert," unsuitable for white habitation and development. This division presumed a permanent frontier with perpetual Indian ownership of western America. It collapsed in the 1840s, when the United States acquired Texas, California, and Oregon, and migrants crossed Indian lands to reach the West Coast. Rather than curbing white entry into Indian country, the government built forts along the overland trails and ordered the army to punish Indians who threatened travelers.

White migration devastated the Indians, already competing among themselves for the limited resources of the Plains. Migrants' livestock destroyed crucial timber and pastures along streams in the semiarid region; trails disrupted buffalo grazing patterns and eliminated buffalo from tribal hunting ranges. The Plains Indians also suffered from diseases the white migrants introduced. Smallpox, cholera, measles, whooping cough, and scarlet fever, for which Indians had no natural immunity, swept through the tribes, killing up to 40 percent of their population. Emigrants along the Platte River routes came across "villages of the dead."

QUICK REVIEW

White Migration and the Plains Indians

- Livestock destroyed timber and pastures.
- Migrant trails disrupted buffalo grazing patterns.
- New diseases killed as much as 40 percent of some Indian groups.

By the early 1850s, white settlers sought to occupy Indian territory. Recognizing that the Great Plains could support agriculture, they demanded the removal of the Indians. Simultaneously, railroad companies developed plans to lay tracks across the plains. To promote white settlement, the federal government decided to relocate the tribes to separate specific reserves. In exchange for accepting such restrictions, the tribes were promised annual payments of livestock, clothing, and other materials. To implement this policy, the government negotiated treaties extinguishing Indian rights to millions of acres (see Map 19–1) and ordered the army to keep Indians on their assigned reservations.

But the treaties, often coerced or misleading, so disadvantaged the tribes that one historian has termed them "instruments of chicanery and weapons of aggression." White negotiators sometimes omitted from the formal documents provisions that Indians had insisted upon, or included others specifically rejected, and at times Congress sharply reduced the annual payments or the size of the reservations promised in the treaties.

Read the **Document** at **www.myhistorylab.com** *Helen Hunt Jackson, From* A Century of Dishonor *(1881)*

Warfare and Dispossession

Most smaller tribes accepted the government's conditions, realizing that their survival depended upon accommodation to American power. Many larger tribes resisted. From the 1850s to the 1880s, warfare engulfed the advancing frontier. Indians sometimes initiated conflict, especially in the form of small raids, but invading Americans bore ultimate responsibility for these wars. As General Philip Sheridan declared of the Indians: "We took away their country and their means of support, broke up their mode of living, their habits of life, introduced disease and decay among them, and it was for this and against this that they made war. Could anyone expect less?"

One notorious example of white aggression occurred in 1864, at Sand Creek, Colorado. Gold discoveries had attracted a flood of white settlers onto land only recently guaranteed to the Cheyennes and Arapahos. Rather than enforcing the Indians' treaty rights, however, the government compelled the tribes to relinquish their lands, except for a small tract designated as the Sand Creek reservation. But white settlers wanted to eliminate the Indian presence altogether. John Chivington, a Methodist minister who had organized Denver's first Sunday school, led a militia force to the Sand Creek camp of a band of Cheyennes under Black Kettle, an advocate of peace and accommodation. The militia attacked Black Kettle's sleeping camp without warning. With howitzers and rifles, the soldiers fired into the camp and then assaulted any survivors with swords and knives. One white trader later described the helpless Indians: "They were scalped, their brains knocked out; the [white] men used their knives, ripped open women, clubbed little children, knocked them in the head with their guns, beat their brains out, mutilated their bodies in every sense of the word."

The **Sand Creek Massacre** appalled many easterners. The Cheyennes, protested the commissioner of Indian affairs, were "butchered in cold blood by troops in the service of the United States." Westerners, however, justified the brutality as a means to secure their own opportunities. One western newspaper demanded, "Kill all the Indians that can be killed. Complete extermination is our motto."

Sand Creek Massacre The near annihilation in 1864 of Black Kettle's Cheyenne band by Colorado troops under Colonel John Chivington's orders to "kill and scalp all, big and little."

Other tribes were more formidable. None was more powerful than the Sioux, whose military skills had been honed in conflicts with other tribes. An army offensive against the Sioux in 1866

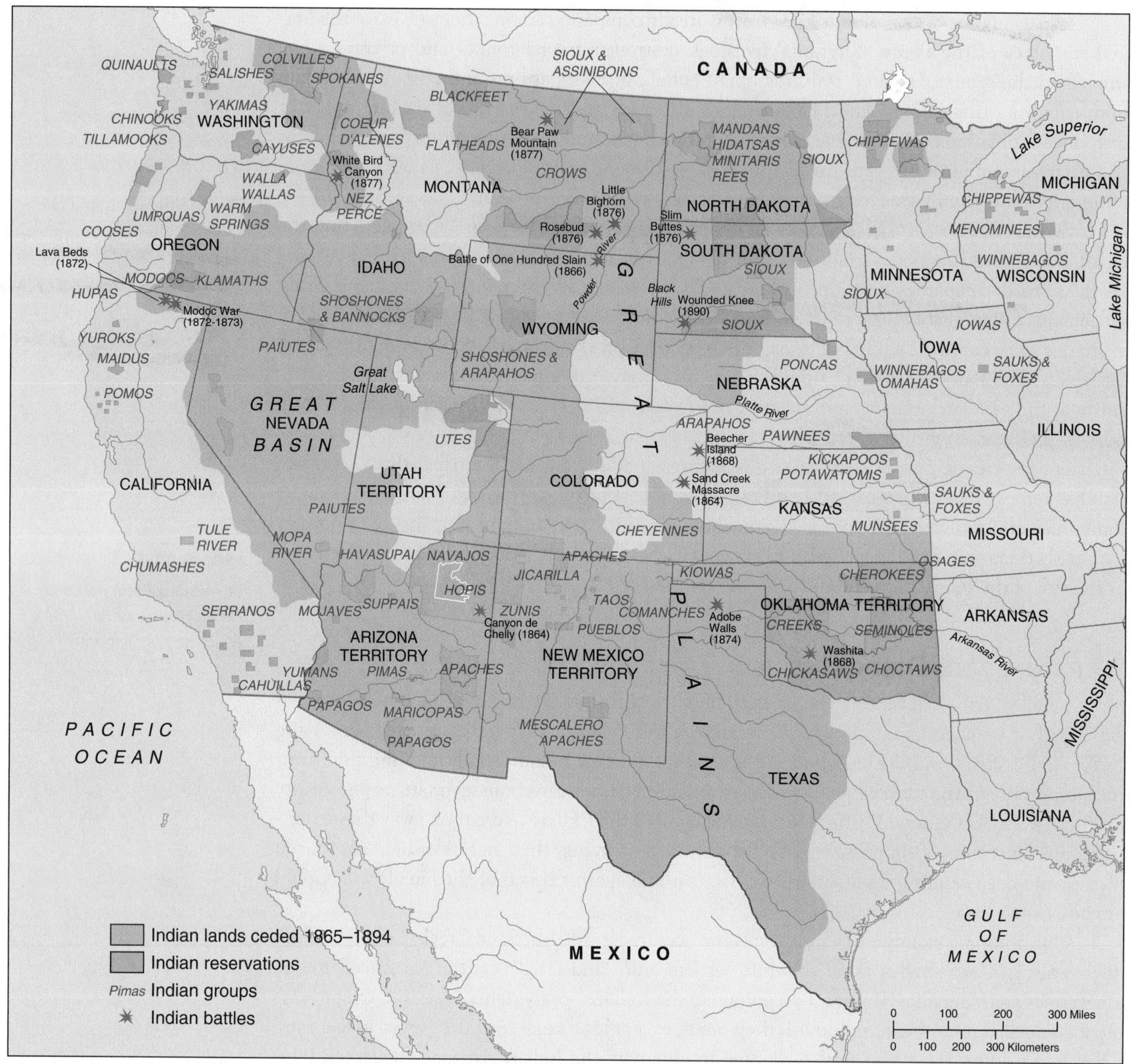

MAP 19–1 Indian Land Cessions, 1860–1894 As white people pushed into the West to exploit its resources, Indians were steadily forced to cede their lands. By 1900 they held only scattered parcels, often in areas considered worthless by white people. Restricted to these reservations, tribes endured official efforts to suppress Indian customs and values.

What does this map tell you about federal Indian policy in the decades after the Civil War? What forces shaped post–Civil War policy?

failed completely. Entire units deserted in fear and frustration; others were crushed by the Sioux. General William T. Sherman, who had marched through Georgia against Confederates, knew that the odds were different in the West. Fifty Plains Indians, he declared, could "checkmate" 3,000 soldiers. General Philip Sheridan calculated that the army suffered proportionately greater losses fighting Indians than either the Union or the Confederacy had suffered in the Civil War.

With the army unable to defeat the Sioux and their allies, and with many easterners shocked by both the military's indiscriminate aggression and the expense of the fighting, the government sued for peace. Describing white actions as "uniformly unjust," a federal peace commission in 1868 negotiated the **Treaty of Fort Laramie,** in which the United States abandoned the Bozeman Trail and other routes and military posts on Sioux territory, one of the few times Indians forced whites to retreat. The United States also guaranteed the Sioux permanent ownership of the western half of South Dakota and the right to inhabit and hunt in the Powder River country in Wyoming and Montana, an area to be henceforth closed to all white people.

Treaty of Fort Laramie The treaty acknowledging U.S. defeat in the Great Sioux War in 1868 and supposedly guaranteeing the Sioux perpetual land and hunting rights in South Dakota, Wyoming, and Montana.

The army was a key institution in developing the West. It built roads, undertook scientific activities, distributed rations and clothing to destitute settlers, settled civil disputes, and even supervised the earliest national parks. Government contracts to supply military posts with food, building materials, uniforms, grain, and horses promoted freight companies, commercial development, and agriculture.

But the army's primary role was military, and its leaders were bitter about the Sioux victory. Turning to the southern plains, they adopted a devastating new strategy: winter campaigns directed at villages. Winter impaired Indian mobility by depleting food sources for both people and ponies, while the army could draw upon stocks of supplies, equipment, and animals. And attacks on villages, inevitably causing heavy casualties among women and children, might demoralize warriors. The Seventh Cavalry initiated the strategy in a surprise attack on a Cheyenne winter camp on the Washita River in Oklahoma. Colonel George A. Custer reported that his troops killed 103 men and, "in the excitement," many women and children as well. They then destroyed the tribe's 875 horses, its lodges and clothing, and its "whole supply" of food. Any survivors would be impoverished and starving in the bitter weather. By such offensives, the army secured the southern plains by 1875.

Momentum soon shifted on the northern plains as well. Peace had prevailed for several years after the Fort Laramie treaty, but in 1872, the Northern Pacific Railroad began to build westward on a route that would violate Sioux territory. Rather than stopping the railroad, the government sent an army to protect the surveyors. Sherman drew up plans for the war that he expected the construction to provoke. He regarded railroad expansion as the most important factor in defeating the Indians, for it would allow troops to travel as far in a day as they could march in weeks. Other technological developments, from the telegraph to rapid-fire weapons, also undercut the skills of the Indian warrior.

The destruction of the buffalo also threatened Native Americans. From 1872 to 1874, white hunters killed 4 million buffalo. Railroad survey and construction parties disrupted grazing areas, and hunters working for the railroads killed hordes of buffalo, both to feed construction crews and to prevent the animals from obstructing rail traffic. Hide hunters slaughtered even more of the beasts for their skins, leaving the bodies to rot. Federal officials encouraged the buffalo's extermination because it would destroy the Indians' basis for survival.

The climactic provocation of the Sioux began in 1874, when Colonel George A. Custer led an invasion to survey the Black Hills for a military post and to confirm the presence of gold. Thousands of white miners then illegally poured onto Sioux land. Ignoring Sioux demands that the government enforce the Fort

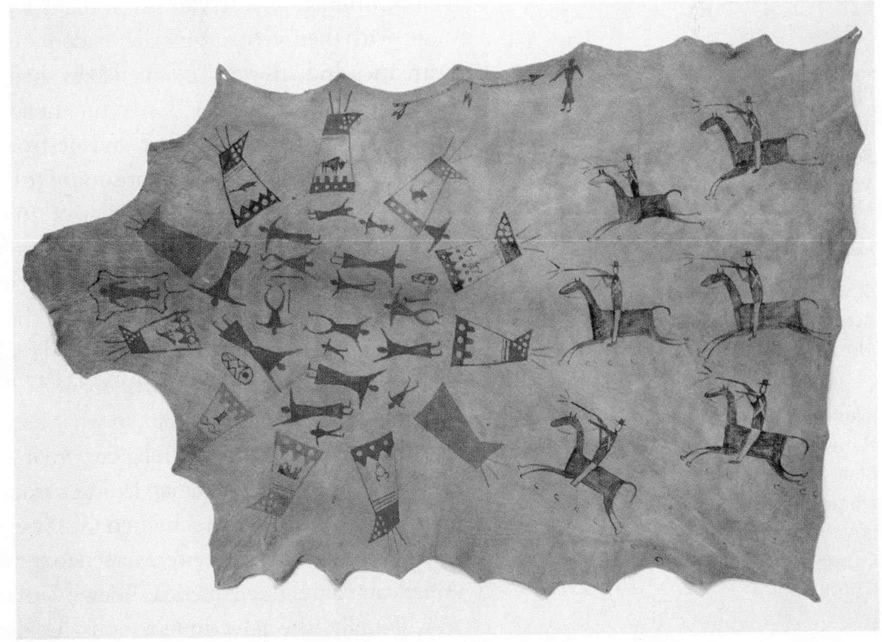

A hide painting depicting the army's 1872 winter attack on an unsuspecting Piegan village on the Marias River in Montana. The army killed 173 people, mostly women and children, in this massacre of a "friendly" village; its intended target was another Indian village, seventeen miles away.

Read the **Document** at **www.myhistorylab.com** *Exploring America: Dakota Sioux Conflict*

Laramie treaty, the army insisted that the Indians leave their Powder River hunting grounds. When the Sioux refused, the army attacked. The Oglala Sioux under Crazy Horse repulsed one prong of this offensive at the Battle of the Rosebud in 1876 and then joined a larger body of Sioux under Sitting Bull and their Cheyenne and Arapaho allies to overwhelm a second American column, under Custer, at the **Battle of the Little Bighorn.**

W
WHERE TO LEARN MORE
Little Bighorn Battlefield National Monument, Crow Agency, Montana
http://www.nps.gov/libi/

But the Indians could not follow up their dramatic victory. They had to divide their forces to find fresh grass for their horses and to hunt for food. Not similarly handicapped but supplied and equipped by an industrializing nation, the U.S. Army relentlessly pursued the separate bands to exhaustion. In the end, the conquest of the northern plains came, not through any decisive victory, but through attrition and the inability of the traditional Indian economy to support resistance to the technologically and numerically superior white forces.

In the Southwest, the Navajos and the Comanches were subdued, as the Sioux had been, by persistent pursuit that prevented them from obtaining food. The last to submit were the Apaches, under Geronimo. In 1886, he and 36 followers, facing 5,000 U.S. troops, finally surrendered. Geronimo and other Apaches were sent to a military prison in Florida; the tribes were herded onto barren reservations. The Oglala chief Red Cloud concluded of the white invasion: "They made us many promises, more than I can remember, but they never kept but one. They promised to take our land, and they took it."

Battle of the Little Bighorn Battle in which Colonel George A. Custer and the Seventh Cavalry were defeated by the Sioux and Cheyennes under Sitting Bull and Crazy Horse in Montana in 1876.

Life on the Reservation: Americanization

Conquering the tribes and seizing their land were only the initial objectives of government policy. The next goal was to require Indians to adopt white ways, instilled by education and religion and enforced when necessary by the military. This goal did not involve assimilation but merely "Americanization," an expression of cultural conquest.

Read the **Document** at **www.myhistorylab.com** *From Then to Now Online: The Legacy of Americanization*

The government received aid from many Christian denominations, which had long proposed nonviolent methods of controlling Indians. Reformers wanted to change Indian religious and family life, train Indian children in Protestant beliefs, and force Indians to accept private ownership and market capitalism.

Confined to reservations, Indians were a captive audience for white reformers. Furthermore, with their very survival dependent on government rations and annual payments stipulated by treaties, Indians were "compelled by sheer necessity," as one federal official said, to accept government orders "or starve." Government agents of the Bureau of Indian Affairs used their power to undermine tribal authority and destroy traditional Indian government, prohibiting tribal councils from meeting and imprisoning tribal leaders.

Read the **Document** at **www.myhistorylab.com** *Secretary of Interior's Congressional Report on Indian Affairs (1887)*

Read the **Document** at **www.myhistorylab.com** *Accounts of the Wounded Knee Massacre (1890s)*

White activists sought to destroy Indian religion because it was "pagan" and because it helped Indians resist assimilation. Protestant religious groups persuaded the Bureau of Indian Affairs to frame a criminal code prohibiting tribal religious practices. Established in 1884, the code remained in effect until 1933. To enforce the ban, the government withheld rations and disrupted the religious ceremonies that transmitted traditional values. In 1890, to suppress the Ghost Dance religion, the army even used artillery and killed at least 200 Sioux men, women, and children at Wounded Knee, South Dakota, in what became known as the **Wounded Knee Massacre.**

Wounded Knee Massacre The U.S. Army's brutal winter massacre in 1890 of at least two hundred Sioux men, women, and children as part of the government's assault on the tribe's Ghost Dance religion.

The government and religious groups also used education to eliminate Indian values and traditions. They isolated Indian children from tribal influences at off-reservation boarding schools. Troops often seized Indian children for these schools, where they were confined until after adolescence. The schoolchildren were forced to speak English, attend Christian services, and profess white American values (see American Views: Zitkala-Sa's View of Americanization).

Finally, the government and the religious reformers imposed the economic practices and values of white society on Indians. Government agents taught Indian men how to farm and distributed agricultural implements, but Indians could not farm successfully on reservation lands that whites had already rejected as unproductive. Whites, however, believed that the real

Dressed in their school uniforms, Indian children sit under the U.S. flag. Government and missionary schools sought to promote "Americanization" and suppress native cultures. Such education, said one member of Congress, "is the solution of the vexed Indian problem."

Western History Collections, University of Oklahoma Library, "Phillips #436."

obstacle to economic prosperity for the Indians was their rejection of private property. The Indians' communal values, the reformers argued, inhibited the pursuit of personal success that lay at the heart of capitalism.

To force such values on Indians, Congress in 1887 passed the **Dawes Act,** which divided tribal lands among individual Indians. Western settlers who had no interest in the Indians supported the law because it provided that reservation lands not allocated to individual Indians would be opened to white settlers. Under this "reform," the amount of land held by Indians declined by more than half by 1900. White acquisition and exploitation of Indian land seemed to be the only constant in the nation's treatment of Native Americans.

Certainly assimilation scarcely succeeded. Some Indians did accept Christianity, formal education, and new job skills in attempting to adapt to their changing world. But often they employed such knowledge in another strategy of resistance, lecturing and lobbying to reform Indian policies or working to curtail the economic exploitation of their tribes. Other Indians, when they returned from school to their reservations, simply went "back to the blanket," as disgusted white critics called their reversion to traditional ways. Most Indians resented assimilationist efforts, clinging to their own values and rejecting as selfish, dishonorable, and obsessively materialistic those favored by whites. As Big Bear, a chief of the Otoe-Missouria, defiantly declared, "You cannot make white men of us. That is one thing you can't do." But if it was not yet clear what place Native Americans would have in America, it was at least clear by 1900 that they would no longer stand in the way of western development.

Dawes Act An 1887 law terminating tribal ownership of land and allotting some parcels of land to individual Indians with the remainder opened for white settlement.

Watch the Video
at **www.myhistorylab.com**
Sioux Ghost Dance

QUICK REVIEW

Americanization

- Government policy required Indians to adopt white values and beliefs.
- Protestant reformers played an active role in the implementation of this policy.
- A variety of coercive methods were used to achieve "Americanization."
- These efforts at forced assimilation largely failed.

EXPLOITING THE MOUNTAINS: THE MINING BONANZA

In the late nineteenth century, the West experienced several stages of economic development that transformed the environment, produced economic and social conflict, and integrated the region into the modern national economy. The first stage of development centered on mining, which attracted eager prospectors into the mountains and deserts in search of gold and silver. They founded communities, stimulated the railroad construction that brought

HOW DID mining in the West change over the course of the second half of the nineteenth century?

AMERICAN VIEWS

Zitkala-Sa's View of Americanization

Zitkala-Sa, or Red Bird, was an 8-year-old Sioux girl when she was taken from her South Dakota reservation in 1884 and placed in a midwestern missionary school, where she encountered what she called the "iron routine" of the "civilizing machine." Here she recalls her first day at the school.

- **What** lessons were the missionaries trying to teach Zitkala-Sa by their actions?
- **What** lessons did Zitkala-Sa learn?

Soon we were being drawn rapidly away by the white man's horses. When I saw the lonely figure of my mother vanish in the distance, a sense of regret settled heavily upon me. . . . I no longer felt free to be myself, or to voice my own feelings. The tears trickled down my cheeks, and I buried my face in the folds of my blanket. Now the first step, parting me from my mother, was taken, and all my belated tears availed nothing. . . . Trembling with fear and distrust of the palefaces . . . I was as frightened and bewildered as the captured young of a wild creature. . . .

[At the missionary school,] the constant clash of harsh noises, with an undercurrent of many voices murmuring an unknown tongue, made a bedlam within which I was securely tied. And though my spirit tore itself in struggling for its lost freedom, all was useless. . . .

We were placed in a line of girls who were marching into the dining room. . . . A small bell was tapped, and each of the pupils drew a chair from under the table. Supposing this act meant they were to be seated, I pulled out mine and at once slipped into it from one side. But when I turned my head, I saw that I was the only one seated, and all the rest at our table remained standing. Just as I began to rise, looking shyly around to see how chairs were to be used, a second bell was sounded. All were seated at last, and I had to crawl back into my chair again. I heard a man's voice at one end of the hall, and I looked around to see him. But all others hung their heads over their plates. As I glanced at the long chain of tables, I caught the eyes of a paleface woman upon me. Immediately I dropped my eyes, wondering why I was so keenly watched by the strange woman. The man ceased his mutterings, and then a third bell was tapped. Every one picked up his knife and fork and began eating. I began crying instead, for by this time I was afraid to venture anything more.

But this eating by formula was not the hardest trial in that first day. Late in the morning, my friend Judewin gave me a terrible warning. Judewin knew a few words of English; and she had overheard the paleface woman talk about cutting our long, heavy hair. Our mothers had taught us that only unskilled warriors who were captured had their hair shingled by the enemy. Among our people, short hair was worn by mourners, and shingled hair by cowards!

. . . I remember being dragged out, though I resisted by kicking and scratching wildly. In spite of myself, I was carried downstairs and tied fast in a chair. I cried aloud, shaking my head all the while until I felt the cold blades of the scissors against my neck, and heard them gnaw off one of my thick braids. Then I lost my spirit. . . . My long hair was shingled like a coward's. In my anguish I moaned for my mother, but no one came to comfort me. Not a soul reasoned quietly with me, as my own mother used to do; for now I was only one of many little animals driven by a herder. . . .

I blamed the hard-working, well-meaning, ignorant [missionary] woman who was inculcating in our hearts her superstitious ideas. Though I was sullen in all my little troubles, as soon as I felt better I was . . . again actively testing the chains which tightly bound my individuality like a mummy for burial. . . .

Many specimens of civilized peoples visited the Indian school. The city folks with canes and eyeglasses, the countrymen with sunburnt cheeks and clumsy feet, forgot their relative social ranks in an ignorant curiosity. Both sorts of these Christian palefaces were alike as at seeing the children of savage warriors so docile and industrious. . . .

In this fashion many [whites] have passed idly through the Indian schools during the last decade, afterward to boast of their charity to the North American Indian. But few there are who have paused to question whether real life or long-lasting death lies beneath this semblance of civilization.

Source: Zitkala-Sa, "The School Days of an Indian Girl" (1900). Reprinted in *American Indian Stories* (Glorieta, NM: Rio Grande Press, 1976).

further development, and contributed to the disorderly heritage of the frontier. But few gained the wealth they expected.

See the Map
at www.myhistorylab.com
Resources and Conflict in the West

Rushes and Mining Camps

The first important gold rush in the Rocky Mountains came in Colorado in 1859. More than 100,000 prospectors crowded into Denver and nearby mining camps. Simultaneously, the discovery of the famous Comstock Lode in Nevada produced an eastward rush of miners from California and booming mining camps like Virginia City. Strikes in the northern Rockies followed in the 1860s. The last of the frontier gold rushes came in 1874 on the Sioux reservation in the Black Hills of South Dakota, where the roaring mining camp of Deadwood flourished. Later, other minerals shaped frontier development: silver in Nevada, silver and lead in Colorado and Idaho, silver and copper in Arizona and Montana.

Mining camps were often isolated by both distance and terrain. They frequently consisted only of flimsy shanties, saloons, crude stores, dance halls, and brothels, all hastily built by entrepreneurs. Such towns reflected the speculative, exploitive, and transitory character of mining. And yet they did contribute to permanent settlement by encouraging agriculture, industry, and transportation in the surrounding areas.

The camps had an unusual social and economic structure. Their population was overwhelmingly male. In 1860, for example, about 2,300 men and only 30 women lived in the Nevada camps of Virginia City and Gold Hill. Women found far fewer economic opportunities than men did on the mining frontier. Some became prospectors, but most stayed within conventional domestic spaces. Several opened lodging houses or hotels. Those with less capital worked as seamstresses and cooks and took in washing. The few married women often earned more than their husbands by boarding other miners willing to pay for the trappings of family life.

Prostitution. But the largest source of paid employment for women was prostitution, a flourishing consequence of the gender imbalance and the limited economic options for women. Many who entered brothels already suffered from economic hardship or a broken family. Some Chinese women were virtually sold into prostitution. By the 1890s, as men gained control of the vice trade from the madams, violence, suicide, alcoholism, disease, drug addiction, and poverty overcame most prostitutes.

Public authorities showed little concern for the abuse and even murder of prostitutes, although they fined and taxed "sporting women" to raise revenue. Condemning such moral indifference, middle-class Protestant women in Denver and other cities established "rescue homes" to protect or rehabilitate prostitutes and dance-hall girls from male vice and violence. But their attempts to impose piety and purity had little success; male community leaders valued social order less than they did economic opportunity.

QUICK REVIEW

Prostitution

- Largest source of paid employment for women in western mining camps.
- Most women entered prostitution as a result of economic or familial hardship.
- Authorities showed little interest in welfare of prostitutes.

Saloon society. The gender imbalance in the mining camps also made saloons prevalent among local businesses. An 1879 business census of Leadville, Colorado, reported 10 dry-goods stores, 4 banks, and 4 churches, but 120 saloons, 19 beer halls, and 118 gambling houses. Saloons were social centers in towns where most miners lived in crowded and dirty tents and rooming houses.

The male-dominated saloon society of the mining camps generated social conflict. Disputes over mining claims could become violent, adding to the disorder. The California mining town of Bodie experienced 29 killings between 1877 and 1883, a homicide rate higher than that of any U.S. city a century later. But such killings occurred only within a small group of males, young, single, surly, and armed, who were known as the Badmen of Bodie. Daily life for most people was safe.

Collective violence. Indeed, personal and criminal violence, which remains popularly associated with the West, was less pervasive than collective violence. This, too, affected mining camps and was aggravated by their ethnic and racial diversity. Irish, Germans, English, Chinese, Australians, Italians, Slavs, and Mexicans, among others, rushed into the mining regions. In many camps, half the population was foreign-born. The European immigrants who sometimes encountered nativist hostility in the East experienced less animosity in the West, but nonwhite minorities often suffered. Whites frequently drove Mexicans and Chinese from their claims or refused to let them work in higher-paid occupations in the mining camps. The Chinese had originally migrated to the California gold fields and thereafter spread to the new mining areas of the Rockies and the Great Basin, where they worked in mining when possible, operated laundries and restaurants, and held menial jobs like hauling water and chopping wood. In 1870, more than a quarter of Idaho's population and nearly 10 percent of Montana's was Chinese. Where they were numerous, the Chinese built their own communities and maintained their customs.

QUICK REVIEW

Chinese Miners and Anti-Chinese Violence

- Chinese originally migrated to California gold fields and then moved on to mining fields in the Rockies and Great Basin.
- 1870: Chinese make up more than 25 percent of Idaho's population and 10 percent of Montana's population.
- Racism and fear of economic competition sparked anti-Chinese violence.

But racism and fear of economic competition sparked hostility and violence against the Chinese almost everywhere. The worst anti-Chinese violence occurred in Rock Springs, Wyoming, in 1885 when whites killed 28 Chinese workers and drove away all 700 residents from the local Chinatown. Although the members of the mob were well known, the grand jury, speaking for the white majority, found no cause for legal action. Such community sanction for violence against racial minorities made mob attacks one of the worst features of the mining camps.

Labor and Capital

New technology had dramatic consequences for both miners and the mining industry. Initially, mining was an individual enterprise in which miners used simple tools, such as picks, shovels, and wash pans, to work shallow surface deposits known as placers. Placer mining attracted prospectors with relatively little capital or expertise, but surface deposits were quickly exhausted. More complex and expensive operations were needed to reach the precious metal buried in the earth.

Read the **Document** at **www.myhistorylab.com** *John Lester, "Hydraulic Mining" (1873)*

Hydraulic mining, for example, required massive capital investment to build reservoirs, ditches, and troughs to power high-pressure water cannons that would pulverize hillsides and uncover the mineral deposits. Quartz, or lode, mining, sometimes called hard-rock mining, required still more money, technology, and time to sink a shaft into the earth, timber underground chambers and tunnels, install pumps to remove underground water and hoists to lower men and lift out rock, and build stamp mills and smelters to treat the ore.

Opening restaurants and boarding houses, some women earned money from their domestic skills in the mining camps.

Such complex, expensive, and permanent operations necessarily came under corporate control. Often financed with eastern or British capital, the new corporations integrated the mining industry into the larger economy. Hard-rock mining produced more complex ores than could be treated in remote mining towns. With the new railroad network, they were shipped to smelting plants as far away as Kansas City and St. Louis and then to refineries in eastern cities. Western ores thus became part of national and international business.

QUICK REVIEW

Technology and Mining

- Mining began as an individual enterprise.
- Deeper mining required expensive equipment.
- As mining became more complex and costly, it came under corporate control.

Effects of corporate mining. Although corporate mining helped usher the mining frontier into a more stable period, it had disturbing effects. Its impact on the environment was horrendous. Hydraulic mining washed away hillsides, depositing debris in canyons and valleys to a depth of 100 feet or more, clogging rivers and causing floods, and burying thousands of acres of farmland. Such damage provoked an outcry and eventually led to government regulation. Fewer westerners worried about sterile slag heaps or the toxic fumes that belched from smelters and killed vegetation. They were the signs of progress. "The thicker the fumes," declared one proud Butte newspaper, "the greater our financial vitality."

Corporate mining also hurt miners, transforming them into wageworkers with restricted opportunities. Miners' status declined as new machinery, such as power drills, reduced the need for skilled laborers and enabled employers to hire cheaper workers from eastern and southern Europe. Mining corporations, moreover, did little to protect miners' health or safety. Miners died in cave-ins, explosions, and fires or from the great heat and poisonous gases in underground mines. Others contracted silicosis, lead poisoning, or other diseases or were crippled or killed by machines.

Unions and union busting. To protect themselves, miners organized unions. These functioned as benevolent societies, aiding injured miners or their survivors, establishing hospitals and libraries, and providing an alternative to the saloons with union halls serving as social and educational centers. Unions also promoted miners' interests by striking against wage cuts and campaigning for mine safety. They convinced states to pass mine safety laws and, beginning in the 1880s, to appoint mine inspectors. The chief role of these state officials was, in the words of a Colorado inspector, to decide "How far should an industry be permitted to advance its material welfare at the expense of human life?"

The industry itself, however, often provided the answer to this question, for mining companies frequently controlled state power and used it to crush unions. Thus, in 1892, in the Coeur d'Alene district of Idaho, mining companies locked out strikers and imported a private army, which battled miners in a bloody gunfight. Management next persuaded the governor and the president to send in the state militia and the U.S. Army. State officials then suppressed the strike and the union by confining all union members and their sympathizers in stockades.

Strikes, union busting, and violence continued for years. When mining companies in Utah, Colorado, and Montana pursued the same aggressive tactics of lockouts and wage cuts, the local miners' unions in the West united for

Chinese miners in Idaho operate the destructive water cannons used in hydraulic mining. One startled observer described the environmental devastation of such work: "It is impossible to conceive of anything more desolate, more utterly forbidding, than a region which has been subjected to this hydraulic mining treatment."

Chinese mining laborers, Idaho, 76–119. 2/A Idaho State Historical Society.

strength and self-protection. In 1893, they formed one of the nation's largest and most militant unions, the Western Federation of Miners.

Violence and conflict were attributable not to frontier lawlessness but to the industrialization of the mines. Both management's tactics—blacklisting union members, locking out strikers, obtaining court injunctions against unions, and using soldiers against workers—and labor's response mirrored conditions in the industrial East. In sum, western mining, reflecting the industrialization of the national economy, had been transformed from a small-scale prospecting enterprise characterized by individual initiative and simple tools into a large-scale corporate business characterized by impersonal management, outside capital, advanced technology, and wage labor.

QUICK REVIEW

Miners' Unions

- Paid benefits to injured miners or their survivors.
- Provided social and educational centers.
- Promoted miners' interests on the job.

USING THE GRASS: THE CATTLE KINGDOM

WHAT FACTORS contributed to the development of the range cattle industry?

The development of the range-cattle industry opened a second stage of exploitation of the late-nineteenth-century West. It reflected the needs of an emerging eastern urban society, the economic possibilities of the grasslands of the Great Plains, the technology of the expanding railroad network, and the requirements of corporations and capital. It also brought "cow towns" and urban development to the West. The fabled cowboy, though essential to the story, was only a bit player.

Cattle Drives and Cow Towns

The cattle industry originated in southern Texas, where the Spanish had introduced cattle in the eighteenth century. Developed by Mexican ranchers, "Texas longhorns" proved well adapted to the plains grasslands. By the 1860s, they numbered about 5 million head. As industrial expansion in the East and Midwest enlarged the urban market for food, the potential value of Texas steers increased. And the extension of the railroad network into the West opened the possibility of tapping that market. The key was to establish a shipping point on the railroads west of the settled farming regions, a step first taken in 1867 by Joseph McCoy, an Illinois cattle shipper. McCoy selected Abilene, Kansas. Abilene was the western railhead of the Kansas Pacific Railroad and was ringed by lush grasslands for cattle. Texans opened the **Chisholm Trail** through Indian Territory to drive their cattle northward to Abilene. Within three years, a million and a half cattle reached Abilene, divided into herds of several thousand, each directed by a dozen cowhands on a "long drive" taking two to three months.

Read the **Document** at **www.myhistorylab.com** *Joseph G. McCoy, Historic Sketches of the Cattle Trade of the West and Southwest (1874)*

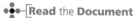

Chisholm Trail The route followed by Texas cattle raisers driving their herds north to markets at Kansas railheads.

Cow town life. The cattle trade attracted other entrepreneurs who created a bustling town. As both railroads and settlement advanced westward, a series of other cow towns—Ellsworth, Wichita, Dodge City, Cheyenne—attracted the long drives, cattle herds, and urban development.

Read the **Document** at **www.myhistorylab.com** *Perspectives on the American Cowboy (1884, 1886)*

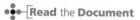

As with the mining camps, the cow towns' reputation for violence was exaggerated. They adopted gun-control laws, prohibiting the carrying of handguns within city limits, and established police forces to maintain order. The primary duties of law officers were arresting drunks, fixing sidewalks, and collecting fines. The cow towns regulated, rather than prohibited, prostitution and gambling, for merchants viewed these vices as necessary to attract the cattle trade. Thus, the towns taxed prostitutes and gamblers and charged high fees for liquor licenses. By collecting such "sin taxes," Wichita was able to forgo general business taxes, thereby increasing its appeal to prospective settlers.

Not all cow towns became cities like Wichita; most, like Abilene, dwindled into small towns serving farm populations. But cow towns, again like mining camps, contributed to the growth of an urban frontier. Railroads often determined the location and growth of western cities, providing access to markets for local products, transporting supplies and machinery for residents, and attracting capital for commercial and industrial development. The West, in fact, had become the most urban region in the nation by 1890, with two-thirds of its population living in communities of at least 2,500 people.

Rise and Fall of Open-Range Ranching

The significance of the long drive to the cow towns faded as cattle raising expanded beyond Texas. Indian removal and extension of the railroads opened land for ranching in Kansas, Nebraska, Wyoming, Colorado, Montana, and the Dakotas. Cattle reaching Kansas were increasingly sold to stock these northern ranges rather than for shipment to the packinghouses. Ranches soon spread across the Great Plains and into the Great Basin, the Southwest, and even eastern Oregon and Washington. This expansion was helped by the initially low investment that ranching required. Calves were cheap, labor costs low, and grazing lands the open range of the public domain.

By the early 1880s, the high profits from this enterprise and an expanding market for beef attracted speculative capital and reshaped the industry. Eastern and European capital flooded the West, with British investors particularly prominent. Some investors went into partnership with existing ranchers, providing capital in exchange for expertise and management. On a larger scale, British and American corporations acquired, expanded, and managed huge ranches.

QUICK REVIEW

Cattle Ranching

- Indian removal and the arrival of the railroad opened land for ranching.
- High profits in the industry attracted speculative capital and large companies.
- The industry collapsed in the 1880s due to overgrazing.

Effects of corporate control. Large companies soon dominated the industry, just as they had gained control of mining. Cattle companies often worked together to enhance their power, especially by restricting access to the range and by intimidating small competitors. Some large companies illegally enclosed the open range, building fences to exclude newcomers and minimize labor costs by reducing the number of cowboys needed to control the cattle. One Wyoming newspaper complained: "Some morning we will wake up to find that a corporation has run a wire fence about the boundary lines of Wyoming, and all within the same have been notified to move."

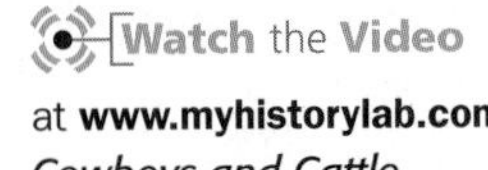

at **www.myhistorylab.com**
Cowboys and Cattle

Such tensions sometimes exploded in instances of social violence as serious as those that disrupted the mining frontier. Attempts by large ranchers to fence off public lands in Texas provoked the Fence-Cutters War of 1883–84. Montana's largest cattlemen organized an armed force known as "Stuart's Stranglers" and, in America's worst vigilante violence, killed over a hundred people they viewed as challenging their power.

The corporate cattle boom overstocked the range and threatened the industry itself. Overgrazing replaced nutritious grasses with sagebrush, Russian thistle, and other plants that livestock found unpalatable. Droughts in the mid-1880s further withered vegetation and enfeebled the animals. Millions of cattle starved or froze to death in terrible blizzards in 1886 and 1887. These ecological and financial disasters destroyed the open-range cattle industry. The surviving ranchers reduced their operations, restricted the size of their herds, and tried to ensure adequate winter feed by growing hay. To

Cowboys gather around the chuck wagon at the XIT Ranch in Texas. Poor pay and arduous work defined the lives of most cowboys.

GLOBAL CONNECTIONS

 The West Abroad 

Americans have always liked to think of the American West as a distinctive region whose prospectors, cowboys, and homesteaders helped shape an exceptional national experience. In fact, however, other countries also experienced comparable developments in the late nineteenth century. While the United States and other countries romanticized their frontier experiences, common environmental, economic, and social forces diminished their distinctiveness.

An obvious demonstration that the frontier was not uniquely American was the interlocking western development in the United States and Canada. The mining frontier crossed the border and included gold rushes in British Columbia from 1858 to 1867 and the Yukon in the 1890s. Canadian goldfields imported California's mining regulations and also followed the pattern of corporate supplanting placer mining. As for cattle raising, one Alberta rancher said in 1884: "We adopted pretty much the same system as was carried on across the border." Ranchers used Canada's public domain for pasture, while cowboys had familiar clothing, work, and wages. Stock associations developed to safeguard ranchers' interests, and gradually big eastern Canadian and British firms dominated the industry.

Like its American counterpart, the Canadian government promoted the construction of a transcontinental railroad, the Canadian Pacific, with land grants and subsidies. It enacted a homestead law providing free land in 1872. It encouraged European immigrants to settle and then witnessed land booms, commercial wheat production, and falling crop prices.

Canada experienced less violence and disorder than the United States, largely because of its Indian policy. Although it too established reservations, Canada treated Indians with respect, created a system of incorruptible agents, and used the North West Mounted Police to prevent the exploitation of Indians by settlers. The Mounted Police also maintained law and order on the mining and ranching frontiers.

While Canada most closely paralleled the American experience, Australia, too, had similarities. Its gold rush began in 1851, attracted miners, technology, and capital from California, and saw violence against Chinese. As in North America, corporate mining soon replaced the original "diggers." In 1861 Australia enacted homestead-type laws to assist small farmers who eventually developed into major wheat producers. And in the 1870s a large-scale pastoral economy, though based on sheep, not cattle, emerged in its vast arid region.

Argentina had no mining frontier, but after suppressing the Araucanian Indians in 1879 to open the pampas to settlement, it developed first a cattle ranching and then an agricultural frontier. Argentine gauchos, like American cowboys, came to symbolize the national character, though they too soon became ranch hands dependent on wages. The government promoted railroad construction in the 1880s, and European immigration helped people the prairies, spurring wheat production and the adoption of the new farming technologies.

- How might transnational factors such as economic, technological, and demographic changes contribute to understanding the development of the American West in the late nineteenth century?

further reduce their dependence on natural vegetation, they introduced drought-resistant sorghum and new grasses; to reduce their dependence on rainfall, they drilled wells and installed windmills to pump water.

Cowhands and Capitalists

One constant in the cattle industry was the cowboy, but his working conditions and opportunities changed sharply over time and corresponded little to the romantic image of a dashing individual free of social constraints. Cowboys' work was hard, dirty, seasonal, tedious, sometimes dangerous, and poorly paid. Many early cowboys were white southerners unwilling or unable to return home after the Civil War. Black cowhands made up perhaps 25 percent of the trail-herd outfits. Many others, especially in Texas and the Southwest, were Mexicans. Indeed, Mexicans developed most of the tools, techniques, and trappings that characterized the cattle industry, from boots, chaps, and the "western" saddle to roundups and roping. As the industry expanded northward, more cowboys came from rural Kansas, Nebraska, and neighboring states.

Initially, in the frontier-ranching phase dominated by the long drive, cowboys were seasonal employees who worked closely with owners. Often the sons or neighbors of ranchers, they frequently expected to become stock raisers themselves. They typically enjoyed the rights to "maverick" cattle, or put their own brand on unmarked animals they encountered, and to "run a brand," or to own their own cattle while working for a ranch. These informal rights provided opportunities to acquire property and move up the social ladder.

As ranching changed with the appearance of large corporate enterprises, so did the work and work relationships of cowhands. The power and status of employer and employees diverged, and the cowboys' traditional rights disappeared. Employers redefined mavericking as rustling and prohibited cowhands from running a brand of their own. One cowboy complained that these restrictions deprived a cowhand of his one way "to get on in the world." But that was the purpose: Cowboys were to be workers, not potential ranchers and competitors. To increase labor efficiency, some companies prohibited their cowboys from drinking, gambling, and carrying guns.

W WHERE TO LEARN MORE

★ National Cowboy Hall of Fame, Oklahoma City, Oklahoma
http://www.cowboyhalloffame.org/

Unions and strikes. Cowboys sometimes responded to these structural transformations the same way skilled workers in the industrial East did, by forming unions and striking. The first strike occurred in Texas in 1883, when the Panhandle Stock Association, representing large operators, prohibited ranch hands from owning their own cattle and imposed a standard wage. More than 300 cowboys struck seven large ranches for higher wages and the right to brand mavericks for themselves and to run small herds on the public domain. Ranchers evicted the cowboys, hired scabs, and used the Texas Rangers to drive the strikers from the region.

Other strikes also failed because corporate ranches and their stock associations had great influence and cowhands faced long odds in their efforts to organize. They were isolated across vast spaces and had little leverage in the industry. After asking employers for "what we are worth after many years' experience," they conceded, "We are dependent on you."

The transformation of the western cattle industry and its integration into a national economy dominated by corporations thus made the cherished image of cowboy independence and rugged individualism more myth than reality. One visitor to America in the late 1880s commented: "Out in the fabled West, the life of the 'free' cowboy is as much that of a slave as is the life of his Eastern brother, the Massachusetts mill-hand. And the slave-owner is in both cases the same, the capitalist."

WORKING THE EARTH: HOMESTEADERS AND AGRICULTURAL EXPANSION

HOW DID new technology contribute to the growth of western agriculture?

Even more than ranching and mining, agricultural growth boosted the western economy and bound it tightly to national and world markets. In this process, the government played a significant role, as did the railroads, science and technology, eastern and foreign capital, and the dreams and hard work of millions of rural settlers. The development of farming produced remarkable economic growth, but it left the dreams of many unfulfilled.

Settling the Land

To stimulate agricultural settlement, Congress passed the most famous land law, the **Homestead Act** of 1862 (see the Overview table, Government Land Policy). The measure offered 160 acres of land free to anyone who would live on the plot and farm it for five years. The act promised opportunity and independence to ambitious farmers.

Homestead Act 1862 law providing 160 acres of land to anyone who would live on and farm the land for five years.

Read the Document at www.myhistorylab.com *The Homestead Act of 1862*

Limits of the Homestead Act. Despite the apparently liberal land policy, however, prospective settlers found less land open to public entry than they expected. Federal land laws did not apply in much of California and the Southwest, where Spain and Mexico had previously transferred land to private owners. Elsewhere, the government had given away millions of acres to railroads or authorized selling millions more for educational and other purposes. Moreover, other laws provided for easy transfer of public lands to cattle companies, to other corporations exploiting natural resources, and to land speculators.

Read the Document at www.myhistorylab.com *Frederick Jackson Turner, "The Significance of the Frontier in American History" (1893)*

Thus, settlers in Kansas, Nebraska, Minnesota, and the Dakotas in the late 1860s and early 1870s often found most of the best land unavailable for homesteading and much of the rest remote from transportation facilities and markets. Although 375,000 farms were claimed by 1890 through the Homestead Act, a success by any measure, most settlers had to purchase their land.

The Homestead Act also reflected traditional eastern conceptions of the family farm, which were inappropriate in the West. A farm of 160 acres would have suited conditions in eastern Kansas or Nebraska, but farther west, larger-scale farming was necessary. And the law ignored the need for capital—for machinery, buildings, livestock, and fencing—that was required for successful farming.

Promoting settlement. Nevertheless, many interests promoted settlement. Newspaper editors trumpeted the prospects of their region. Land companies, eager to sell their speculative holdings, sent agents through the Midwest and Europe to encourage migration. Steamship companies, hoping to sell transatlantic tickets, advertised the opportunities in the American West across Europe. Religious and ethnic groups encouraged immigration.

Most important, railroad advertising and promotional campaigns attracted people to the West. Promotion of the West was in the railroads' financial interest. Not only would they profit from selling their huge land reserves to settlers, but a successful agricultural economy would produce crops to be shipped east and a demand for manufactured goods to be shipped west on their lines. The railroads therefore advanced credit to prospective farmers, provided transportation assistance, and extended technical and agricultural advice.

Mexican-American ranch family, Mora Valley, New Mexico Territory, 1895. Anglo-dominated development often displaced such families from their traditional lands and turned them into wage-laborers.

Courtesy: Photographic Archives, Palace of the Governors, Museum of New Mexico, Santa Fe, New Mexico /DCA Negative No: 22468.

Thus encouraged, migrants poured into the West, occupying and farming more acres between 1870 and 1900 than Americans had in the previous 250 years (see Figure 19–1). Farmers settled in every region. Most, however, streamed into the Great Plains states, from the Dakotas to Texas.

White migrants predominated in the mass migration, but African Americans initiated one of its most dramatic episodes, a millenarian folk movement they called the Exodus. Seeking to escape the misery and repression of the post-Reconstruction South, these poor "Exodusters" established several dozen black communities in 1879 in Kansas and Nebraska on the agricultural frontier.

Many of the new settlers came from Europe, bringing with them not only their own attitudes toward the land but also special crops, skills, settlement patterns, and

OVERVIEW Government Land Policy

Legislation	Result
Railroad land grants (1850–1871)	Granted 181 million acres to railroads to encourage construction and development
Homestead Act (1862)	Gave 80 million acres to settlers to encourage settlement
Morrill Act (1862)	Granted 11 million acres to states to sell to fund public agricultural colleges
Other grants	Granted 129 million acres to states to sell for other educational and related purposes
Dawes Act (1887)	Allotted some reservation lands to individual Indians to promote private property and weaken tribal values among Indians and offered remaining reservation lands for sale to whites (by 1906, some 75 million acres had been acquired by whites)
Various laws	Permitted direct sales of 100 million acres by the Land Office

agricultural practices. Peasants from Norway, Sweden, and Denmark flocked to Minnesota. Germans, Russians, and Irish put down roots across Texas, Kansas, Nebraska, and the Dakotas. French, Germans, and Italians developed vineyards, orchards, and nurseries in California, where laborers from Japan and Mexico arrived to work in fields and canneries. Many Mexicans also entered Texas, some as temporary harvest labor, others as permanent residents. By 1890, many western states had substantial foreign-born populations; North Dakota's exceeded 40 percent, California's was nearly as high. Immigrants often settled together in separate ethnic communities, held together by their church, and attempted to preserve their language and customs rather than be assimilated.

QUICK REVIEW

Westward Migration

- The Homestead Act, promoters, and the railroads prompted migration.
- Migrants poured into the West between 1870 and 1900.
- Most migrants were whites, but African American communities were established in Kansas and Nebraska.

Hispanic losses. Migrants moved into the West in search of opportunity, which they sometimes seized at the expense of others already there. In the Southwest, Hispanics had long lived in village communities largely outside a commercial economy, farming small tracts of irrigated land and herding sheep on communal pastures. As Anglos, or white Americans, arrived, their political and economic influence undermined traditional Hispanic society. Congress restricted the original Hispanic land grants to only the villagers' home lots and irrigated fields, throwing open most of their common lands to newcomers. Hispanic title was confirmed to only 2 million of the 37.5 million acres at stake. Anglo ranchers and settlers manipulated the federal land system to control these lands.

Spanish Americans resisted these losses in court or through violence. One militant group, organized as *Las Gorras Blancas* ("the White Caps"), staged night raids to cut fences erected by Anglo ranchers and farmers and to attack the property of railroads, the symbol of the encroaching new order. Such resistance, however, had little success.

As their landholdings shrank, Hispanic villagers could not maintain their pastoral economy. Few turned to homesteading, for that would have required dispersed settlement and abandoning the village and its church, school, and other cultural institutions. Thus many Hispanics became seasonal wage laborers in the Anglo-dominated economy, sometimes working as stoop labor in the commercial sugar-beet fields that emerged in the 1890s, sometimes working on the railroads or in the

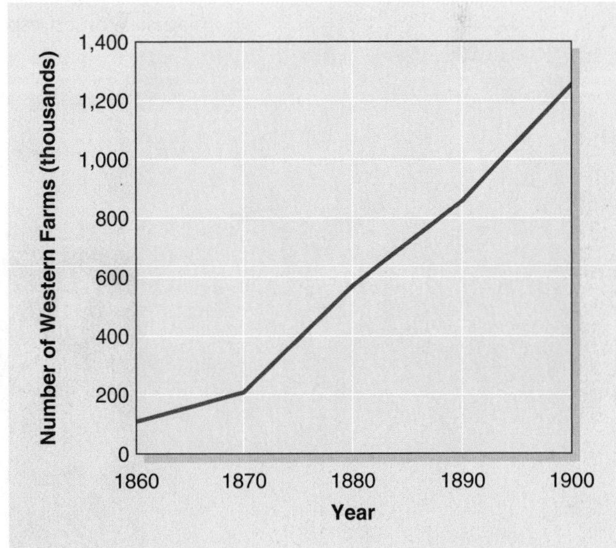

FIGURE 19–1 **The Growth of Western Farming, 1860–1900**
Indian removal, railroad expansion, and liberal land policies drew farm families into the West from much of Europe as well as the East. Technological innovations like barbed wire and farm machinery soon enabled them to build farms, but economic, social, and environmental challenges remained.
Data Source: Historical Statistics of the United States (1975).

mines. Such seasonal labor enabled Hispanics to maintain their villages and provided sufficient income to adopt some Anglo technology, such as cook stoves and sewing machines. But if Hispanics retained some cultural autonomy, they had little influence over the larger processes of settlement and development that restricted their opportunities and bound them to the western and national economy.

Home on the Range

In settling the West, farm families encountered many difficulties, especially on the Great Plains, where they had to adapt to a radically new environment. The scarcity of trees on the plains meant that there was little wood for housing, fuel, and fencing. Until they had reaped several harvests and could afford to import lumber, pioneer families lived in houses made of sod. Though inexpensive and sturdy, sod houses were also dark and dirty. Snakes, mice, and insects often crawled out of the walls and roofs.

Read the **Document** at **www.myhistorylab.com** *Advice on Keeping Children on the Farm (1881)*

Women's work. Within these rough houses, women worked to provide food, clothing, and medicine to ensure the family's survival. Their efforts were greatly constrained by the harsh environment. For fuel, families often had to rely on buffalo or cattle "chips," dried dung. The scarcity of water also complicated women's domestic labor. They often had to transport water over long distances, pulling barrels on "water sleds" or carrying pails on neck yokes. They melted snow for wash water and used the same water over again for different chores. Where possible, they also helped to dig wells by hand.

Some women farmed the land themselves. Single women could claim land under the Homestead Act, and in some areas, women claimants made up 18 percent of the total and succeeded more frequently than men in gaining final title. At times, married women operated the family farm by themselves while their husbands worked elsewhere to earn the money needed for seeds, equipment, and building supplies.

Isolation and community. Isolation and loneliness troubled many early settlers on the plains. Women especially suffered because they frequently had less contact with other people

Sunday school meeting in Custer County, Nebraska, in 1888. Sunday schools were important social as well as religious institutions on the Great Plains, where, as one newspaper reported, rural families often felt like "strangers in a strange land."

than farm men, who conducted their families' business in town and participated in such public activities as political meetings.

Over time, conditions improved. As population increased, women in particular worked to bind isolated households into communities by organizing social activities and institutions. They held fairs, dances, and picnics and established churches, schools, and libraries, thereby gaining both companionship and a sense of purpose.

Churches, in turn, also promoted community. Indeed, many were "union" churches, open to people of all denominations. In addition to holding religious services, revivals, and camp meetings, churches were often the center of social life, especially by sponsoring socials and children's organizations. Nondenominational Sunday schools helped bind together differing nationalities and church preferences, and because they did not require the services of an ordained minister they often enabled women to initiate and lead community activities.

Other institutions also encouraged community action. Rural families created their own agricultural cooperatives and other economic and social organizations, like local Grange lodges. External developments also served the rural population. Rural Free Delivery, for example, eventually brought letters, newspapers, magazines, and advertisements to farm families' doorsteps; mail-order companies made available to farm people such helpful goods as stoves, sewing machines, and shoes. Such changes helped incorporate westerners into the larger society.

QUICK REVIEW

Farm Families in the West

- A harsh environment complicated farm life.
- Women's labor was critical to family survival.
- Isolation made life difficult for many.
- The growth of community institutions improved conditions.

Farming the Land

Pioneer settlers had to make daunting adjustments to develop the agricultural potential of their new land. Advances in science, technology, and industry made such adjustments possible. The changes not only reshaped the agricultural economy but also challenged traditional rural values and expectations.

Growing crops. Fencing was an immediate problem, for crops needed protection from livestock. But without timber, farmers could not build wooden fences. Barbed wire, developed in the mid-1870s, solved the problem. By 1900, farmers were importing nearly 300 million pounds of barbed wire each year from eastern and midwestern factories.

The aridity of most of the West also posed difficulties. In California, Colorado, and a few other areas, settlers used streams fed by mountain snow packs to irrigate land. Elsewhere, enterprising farmers developed variants of the "dry farming" practices that the Mormons had introduced in Utah to maximize the limited rainfall. Some farmers erected windmills to pump underground water. The scarce rainfall also discouraged the cultivation of many of the crops that supported traditional general agriculture and encouraged farmers to specialize in a single cash crop for market. Government agencies and agricultural colleges contributed to the success of such adaptations, and private engineers and inventors also fostered agricultural development. Related technological advancements included grain elevators that would store grain for shipment and load it into rail cars mechanically and mills that used corrugated, chilled-iron rollers rather than millstones to process the new varieties of wheat.

Mechanization and technological innovations made possible the large-scale farming practiced in semiarid regions. Farmers required special plows to break the tough sod, new harrows to prepare the soil for cultivation, grain drills to plant the crop, and harvesting and threshing machines to bring it in. Thanks to more and better machines, agricultural efficiency and productivity shot up. By the 1890s, machinery permitted the farmer to produce 18 times more wheat than hand methods had. Nearly 1,000 corporations were manufacturing agricultural machinery to meet the demands of farmers, who purchased implements in steadily mounting quantities.

Growing tensions. These developments reflected both the expansion of agriculture and its increasing dependence on the larger society. Western commercial farmers needed the high demand of eastern and midwestern cities and the expanding world market. The rail network

Farm workers harvested grain with a horse-drawn Marsh harvester, manufactured by a Chicago company. Such machinery increased farm productivity but made farming more expensive.

provided essential transportation for their crops; the nation's industrial sector produced necessary agricultural machinery. Banks and loan companies extended the credit and capital that allowed farmers to take advantage of mechanization and other new advances; and many other businesses graded, stored, processed, and sold their crops. In short, because of its market orientation, mechanization, and specialization, western agriculture relied on other people or impersonal forces as it was incorporated into the national and international economy.

When conditions were favorable—good weather, good crops, and good prices—western farmers prospered. Too often, however, they faced adversity. The early years of settlement were unusually wet, but even then periodic droughts brought crop failures. Other natural hazards also disrupted production. Especially alarming were plagues of grasshoppers. Grasshoppers ate crops, clothing, and bedding; they attacked sod houses and chewed woodwork and furniture.

In the late 1880s, drought coincided with a slump in crop prices. The large European market that had encouraged agricultural expansion in the 1870s and early 1880s contracted after 1885, when several nations erected trade barriers to U.S. commodities. More important, America's production competed with that from Argentina, Canada, Australia, and Russia, and a world surplus of grain drove prices steadily downward.

Squeezed between high costs for credit, transportation, and manufactured goods and falling agricultural prices, western farmers faced disaster. They responded by lashing back at their points of contact with the new system. They especially condemned the railroads, believing that the companies charged excessive and discriminatory freight rates.

Farmers censured the grain elevators in the local buying centers. Often owned by eastern corporations, including the railroads, elevators allegedly exploited their local monopoly to cheat farmers by fixing low prices or misrepresenting the quality of wheat. A Minnesota state investigation found that systematic fraud by elevators cost farmers collectively a massive sum. Farmers also denounced the bankers and mortgage lenders who had provided the credit for them to acquire land, equipment, and machinery. Much of the money had come from eastern investors seeking the higher interest rates in the West. With failing crops and falling prices, however, the debt burden proved calamitous for many farmers. Beginning in 1889, many western farms were foreclosed.

Stunned and bitter, western farmers concluded that their problems arose because they had been incorporated into the new system, an integrated economy directed by forces beyond their control. And it was a system that did not work well. "There is," one of them charged, "something radically wrong in our industrial system. There is a screw loose."

CONCLUSION

The farmers' complaints indicted the major processes by which the West was developed and exploited in the late nineteenth century. Railroad expansion, population movements, eastern investment, corporate control, technological innovations, and government policies had incorporated the region fully into the larger society. Indians experienced this incorporation most thoroughly and most tragically, losing their lands, their traditions, and often their lives.

Cowboys and miners also learned that the frontier merely marked the cutting edge of eastern industrial society. Both groups were wageworkers, often for corporations controlled by eastern capital, and if industrial technology directly affected miners more than cowhands, neither could escape integration into the national economy by managerial decisions, transportation links, and market forces. Most settlers in the West were farmers, but they too learned that their distinctive environment did not insulate them from assimilation into larger productive, financial, and marketing structures.

Western developments, in short, reflected and interacted with those of eastern industrial society. The processes of incorporation drained away westerners' hopes along with their products, and many of the discontented would demand a serious reorganization of relationships and power. Led by angry farmers, they turned their attention to politics and government, where they encountered new obstacles and opportunities.

Where to Learn More

Little Bighorn Battlefield National Monument, Crow Agency, Montana. The site of Custer's crushing defeat includes a monument to the Seventh Cavalry atop Last Stand Hill. A newly authorized Indian Memorial will include sacred texts, artifacts, and pictographs of the Plains Indians. http://www.nps.gov/libi/.

Sand Creek Massacre National Historic Site, near Eads, Colorado. Dedicated in 2007, the newest addition to the National Park System marks the forlorn scene of the 1864 massacre of Black Kettle's Cheyenne band. Historical and environmental context available online at http://www.nps.gov/sand/.

National Museum of the American Indian, Smithsonian Institution, Washington, DC. This spectacular museum opened in 2004 and reflects the world view of Native Americans, with exhibits on spirituality and identity, performances of traditional dances, and important lecture series. http://www.nmai.si.edu.

National Cowboy Hall of Fame, Oklahoma City, Oklahoma. This large institution contains an outstanding collection of western art, displays of cowboy and Indian artifacts, and both kitschy exhibitions of the mythic Hollywood West and serious galleries depicting the often hard realities of the cattle industry. Its many public programs also successfully combine fun with learning. http://www.cowboyhalloffame.org/.

Golden Spike National Historic Site, near Promontory, Utah. The completion of the transcontinental railroad here in 1869 is reenacted from May to October, using reproductions of the original locomotives. Visitors can drive the route of the railroad, now a National Backway Byway through abandoned mining and railroad towns, from Promontory to Nevada. Virtual tour, history, and tourist links at http://www.nps.gov/gosp.

Review Questions

1. Why was the completion of the first transcontinental railroad, described by Andrew J. Russell, celebrated from Boston to San Francisco? How did western railroads shape the settlement and development of the West and affect the East as well?
2. What factors were most influential in the subjugation of American Indians?
3. What were the major goals of federal Indian policy, and how did they change?
4. How did technological developments affect Indians, miners, and farmers in the West?
5. How did the federal government help transform the West?
6. In what ways did European investors, markets, and migrants influence the development of the American West?

Key Terms

Battle of the Little Bighorn (p. 530)
Chisholm Trail (p. 536)
Dawes Act (p. 531)
Homestead Act (p. 539)
Sand Creek Massacre (p. 527)
Treaty of Fort Laramie (p. 529)
Wounded Knee Massacre (p. 530)

myhistorylab Connections

Reinforce what you learned in this chapter by studying the many documents, images, maps, review tools, and videos available at **www.myhistorylab.com**.

Read and Review

Study and Review **Study Plan: Chapter 19**

Read the Document

Helen Hunt Jackson, From A Century of Dishonor (1881)

Accounts of the Wounded Knee Massacre (1890s)

John Lester, "Hydraulic Mining" (1873)

Joseph G. McCoy, Historic Sketches of the Cattle Trade of the West and Southwest (1874)

Perspectives on the American Cowboy (1884, 1886)

Advice on Keeping Children on the Farm (1881)

Frederick Jackson Turner, Rise of the New West (1906)

Secretary of Interior's Congressional Report on Indian Affairs (1887)

The Homestead Act of 1862

Frederick Jackson Turner, "The Significance of the Frontier in American History" (1893)

See the Map *Resources and Conflict in the West*

Research and Explore

Read the Document

Personal Journeys Online

From Then to Now Online: The Legacy of Americanization

Exploring America: Dakota Sioux Conflict

Exploring America: Americanization

Watch the Video

The Real West Is an Urban West

Sioux Ghost Dance

Cowboys and Cattle

Hear the Audio

Hear the audio files for Chapter 19 at **www.myhistorylab.com**.

1877-1900

20 Politics and Government

In the late nineteenth century, parades like this Republican one in Canton, Ohio, in 1896 were popular features of a participatory political culture dominated by political parties and intense partisanship.

Hear the Audio

Hear the audio files for Chapter 20 at **www.myhistorylab.com**.

THE STRUCTURE AND STYLE OF POLITICS *(page 551)*

HOW DID parties shape late-nineteenth-century politics?

THE LIMITS OF GOVERNMENT *(page 556)*

WHAT EXPLAINS the weakness and inefficiency of late-nineteenth-century government?

PUBLIC POLICIES AND NATIONAL ELECTIONS *(page 558)*

HOW EFFECTIVE was government in addressing the problems of America's industrializing economy?

THE CRISIS OF THE 1890s *(page 562)*

WHAT FACTORS contributed to the rise and fall of the Populist Party?

One American Journey

The largest political procession of the season in Fort Wayne, so far, was that of the Republicans Saturday night. They turned out in very large numbers and paraded on the principal streets preparatory to the speaking which came later at the Rifles' armory. The following were in line:

First Regiment Band

Railroad Men's Club

Soldiers' and Sons' Union Club

Tippecanoe Club

Chase Club

Lincoln Club

McKinley Club

Colored Drum Corps

Colored Republicans' Club

Republican Voters

The McKinley Club wore tin hats and the Tippecanoe club carried torches that spouted fire at intervals. One of the prettiest illuminations was the railroad lantern light of the Railroad Men's Republican club. The numerous lights of the colors used in the railway service make as pretty a sight as can be seen anywhere.

Most of the clubs were in fine uniforms and made a grand appearance. Numerous banners and transparencies announcing mottoes of the campaign were carried. One banner bore the words, "Cleveland's record—Glad Lincoln was shot—Pronounced the war a failure."

The great parade was viewed by thousands of people who thronged the streets all along the line of march.

The hall was crowded and the meeting was most enthusiastic. Music was furnished by the band and Emerson quartette of Huntington. . . . The quartette just took the cake. Anything more enjoyable and mirth-provoking than their glees rendered as they render them would be hard to find. After music by the quartette, which was enthusiastically encored, Dr. Stemen, the presiding officer, introduced the speaker of the evening, Hon. L. R. Stookey, of Warsaw, Ind. Mr. Stookey is a ready and rapid speaker. He paid a glowing tribute to the soldiers, and referred in scathing terms to Grover Cleveland's treatment of them and his insulting vetoes of pension bills. He spoke . . . [of a law providing for election supervisors at the polls] and what we ask is that it shall apply without limitation north and south whenever there is an attempt or danger of attempt, to deny equal rights of all to cast their free ballot and have it counted as cast.

When he concluded the Emerson quartette gave another selection and responded to an encore. The audience then began to call loudly for "You," "You." Mr. A. J. You, our candidate for congress, was then introduced and made a stirring address. Mr. You has been speaking nearly every day and evening and is holding out first rate and proving himself one of the most popular candidates in the field.

He was repeatedly and enthusiastically cheered during his speech. Another selection by the quartette, and the house resounded with calls for "Brown," "Brown." Rev. W. H. Brown, for years the pastor of the A. M. E. church, of this city, took the platform and though he protested that the hour was too late to permit another speech made it clearly evident in the course of a twenty minute speech that the colored people of the country understand the situation and intend to stand by the party that broke the chains and gave freedom to the slave. The meeting then adjourned to music by the Glee club.

Source: Fort Wayne (Ind.) *Weekly Gazette,* October 20, 1892.

Read the **Document** at **www.myhistorylab.com**

Personal Journeys Online

- **Susan B. Anthony, *Speech to the National American Woman Suffrage Association,* 1894. Asking Congress for political justice.**
- **Henry Vincent, *Marching Through Iowa,* 1894. The journey of Kelly's "industrial army."**
- **William Jennings Bryan, 1896. Campaigning across America.**

THE *FORT WAYNE WEEKLY GAZETTE,* a fiercely Republican newspaper, proudly reported on the activities of the local Republicans in Indiana during the political campaign in 1892. The pageantry and hoopla made politics a major source of popular entertainment for Republicans and Democrats alike. But the extreme campaign rhetoric and outright misrepresentation of opponents indicated the intensity of partisan emotions. So did the military-style campaign, with uniformed marchers organized into companies, brigades, and divisions; with signs, slogans, and speeches referring to soldiers and the Civil War; with rallies held in armories. These campaign features also pointed to the enduring importance of the Civil War as a basis for partisan divisions and loyalties and marked electoral politics as a rough-and-tumble masculine business.

At the same time, contemporary issues did matter. Stookey's stump appeal for election supervisors to protect voters' rights at the polls pointed to an important policy issue while hinting at the sometimes violent nature of elections, including the suppression of voters. It also emphasized that suffrage was often a contested issue.

The prominent role of Rev. Brown, the content of his speech, and the participation of the Colored Drum Corps and the Colored Republicans' Club in the parade show that partisan divisions in the United States overlapped with racial, religious, and other social divisions. Black voters, for instance, would "stand by the party that broke the chains and gave freedom to the slave."

While the *Gazette* lavished praise on the Republican campaign, its Democratic counterpart, the *Fort Wayne Sentinel,* extolled the success of the Democratic campaign. Such partisanship permeated journalism as well as nearly all aspects of public life, including government agencies.

These features of late-nineteenth-century politics would eventually be transformed in significant ways. But while they endured, they shaped not only campaigns and elections but also the form and role of government. Only a national crisis in the 1890s would finally cause some Americans to demand more of their political leaders and institutions. ✦

THE STRUCTURE AND STYLE OF POLITICS

HOW DID parties shape late-nineteenth-century politics?

Politics in the late nineteenth century was an absorbing activity. Campaigns and elections expressed social values as they determined who held the reins of government. Political parties dominated political life. They organized campaigns, controlled balloting, and held the unswerving loyalty of most of the electorate. While the major parties worked to maintain a sense of unity and tradition among their followers, third parties sought to activate those the major parties left unserved. Other Americans looked outside the electoral arena to achieve their political goals.

CAMPAIGNS AND ELECTIONS

Political campaigns and elections generated remarkable public participation and enthusiasm. They constituted a major form of entertainment at a time when recreational opportunities were limited. Attending party meetings and conventions, listening to lengthy speeches appealing to

CHRONOLOGY

1867	Patrons of Husbandry (the Grange) is founded.
1869	Massachusetts establishes the first state regulatory commission.
1873	Silver is demonetized in the "Crime of '73."
1874	Woman's Christian Temperance Union is organized.
1875	U.S. Supreme Court, in *Minor v. Happersett*, upholds denial of suffrage to women.
1876	Greenback Party runs presidential candidate.
1877	Rutherford B. Hayes becomes president after disputed election.
	Farmers' Alliance is founded.
	Supreme Court, in *Munn v. Illinois*, upholds state regulatory authority over private property.
1878	Bland-Allison Act requires the government to buy silver.
1880	James A. Garfield is elected president.
1881	Garfield is assassinated; Chester A. Arthur becomes president.
1883	Pendleton Civil Service Act is passed.
1884	Grover Cleveland is elected president.
1886	Supreme Court, in *Wabash v. Illinois*, rules that only the federal government, not the states, can regulate interstate commerce.
1887	Interstate Commerce Act is passed.
1888	Benjamin Harrison is elected president.
1890	Sherman Antitrust Act is passed.
	McKinley Tariff Act is passed.
	Sherman Silver Purchase Act is passed.
	National American Woman Suffrage Association is organized.
	Wyoming enters the Union as the first state with woman suffrage.
1892	People's Party is organized.
	Cleveland is elected to his second term as president.
1893	Depression begins.
	Sherman Silver Purchase Act is repealed.
1894	Coxey's Army marches to Washington.
	Pullman strike ends in violence.
1895	Supreme Court, in *Pollock v. Farmers' Loan and Trust Company*, invalidates the federal income tax.
	Supreme Court, in *United States v. E. C. Knight Company*, limits the Sherman Antitrust Law to commerce, excluding industrial monopolies.
1896	William Jennings Bryan is nominated for president by Democrats and Populists.
	William McKinley is elected president.
1900	Currency Act puts U.S. currency on the gold standard.

group loyalties and local pride, gathering at the polls to watch the voting and the counting, celebrating victory and drowning the disappointment of defeat—all these provided social enjoyment and defined popular politics.

Virtually all men participated in politics. In many states, even immigrants not yet citizens were eligible to vote and flocked to the polls. African Americans voted regularly in the North and irregularly in the South before being disfranchised at the end of the century. Overall, turnout was remarkably high, averaging nearly 80 percent of eligible voters in presidential elections between 1876 and 1900, a figure far greater than ever achieved thereafter (see Figure 20–1).

Political parties mobilized this huge electorate. With legal regulations and public machinery for elections negligible, parties dominated the campaigns and elections. Until the 1890s, most states had no laws to ensure secrecy in voting, and balloting often took place in open rooms or on sidewalks. Election clerks and judges were not public officials but partisans chosen by the political parties.

QUICK REVIEW

Elections and Campaigns

- Major form of entertainment.
- Virtually all men participated in politics.
- Political parties mobilized the electorate.
- Elections provided men a forum to demonstrate commitment to party and its values.

Nor did public authorities issue official ballots. Instead voters used party tickets—strips of paper printed by the parties—listing only the names of the candidates of the party issuing them and varying in size and color. Casting a ballot thus revealed the voter's party allegiance. Fighting and intimidation were so commonplace at the polls that one state supreme court ruled in 1887 that they were "acceptable" features of elections.

As the court recognized, the open and partisan aspects of the electoral process did not necessarily lead to election fraud, however much they shaped the nature of political participation. In these circumstances, campaigns and elections provided opportunities for men to demonstrate publicly their commitment to their party and its values, thereby reinforcing their partisan loyalties.

Although not permitted to vote, women, too, often exhibited their partisanship in this exciting political environment. Women wrote partisan literature and gave campaign speeches. Sometimes they acted together with men; other times they worked through separate women's organizations. In these partisan groups women discussed and circulated party literature and devised plans to influence elections.

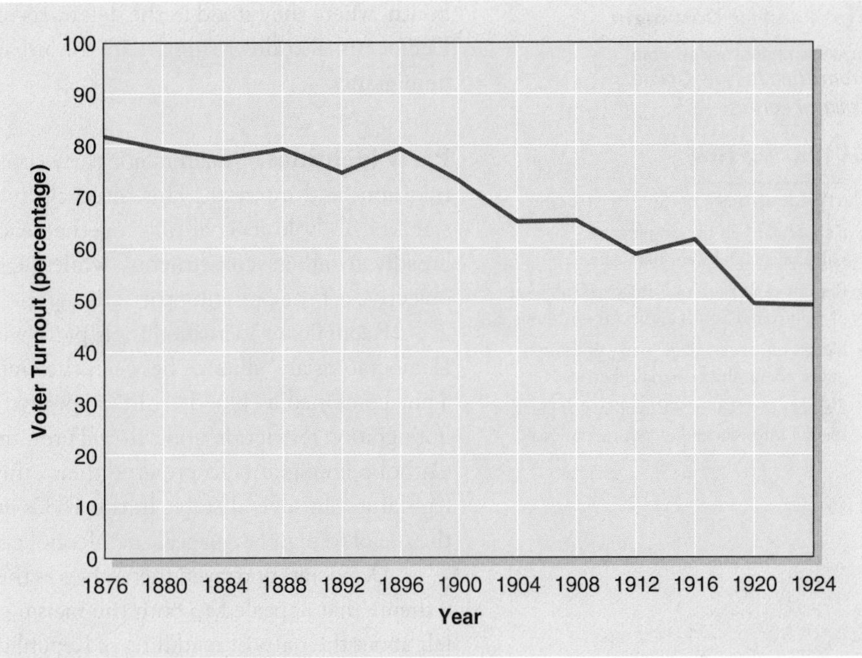

FIGURE 20–1 **Voter Turnout in Presidential Elections, 1876–1924** The exciting partisan politics of the late nineteenth century produced very high voter turnouts, but as party competition declined and states enacted more restrictive voter regulations, popular participation in elections fell in the twentieth century.

PARTISAN POLITICS

A remarkably close balance prevailed between the two major parties in the elections of this era. Democrats and Republicans had virtually the same level of electoral support, one reason they worked so hard to get out the vote (see Map 20–1). Control of the presidency and Congress shifted back and forth. Rarely did either party control both branches of government at once.

The party balance gave great influence to New York, New Jersey, Ohio, and Indiana, whose evenly divided voters controlled electoral votes that could swing an election either way. Both parties tended to nominate presidential and vice presidential candidates from those states to woo their voters. The parties also concentrated campaign funds and strategy on the swing states.

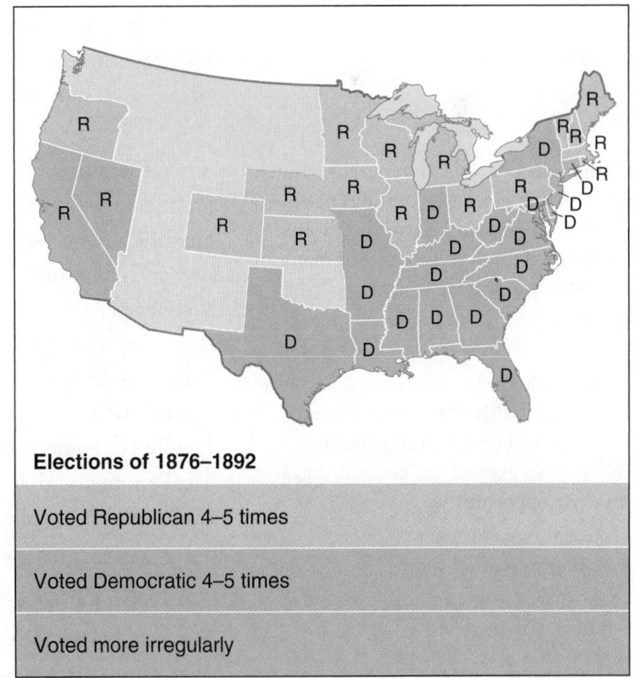

MAP 20–1 **The Two-Party Stalemate of the Late Nineteenth Century** Strong parties, staunch loyalties, and an evenly divided electorate made for exciting politics but often stalemated government in the late nineteenth century. Most states voted consistently for one of the major parties, leaving the few swing states like New York and Indiana the scenes of fierce partisan battles.

Party loyalty. Interrelated regional, ethnic, religious, and local factors determined the party affiliations of most Americans. Economic issues, although important to the politics of the era, generally did not decide party ties. Farmers, for example, despite their many shared economic concerns, affiliated with both major parties. Like religious belief and ethnic identity, partisan loyalty was largely a cultural trait passed from parents to children, a situation that helps to explain the electoral stability of most communities.

Republicans were strongest in the North and Midwest, where they benefited from their party's role as the defender of the Union in the Civil War. But not all northerners voted for the Grand Old Party, or GOP. The Republican Party appealed primarily to old-stock Americans and other Protestants, including those of German and Scandinavian descent. African Americans, loyal to the party that had emancipated and enfranchised the slaves of the South, also supported the GOP where they could vote. Democrats were strongest in the

Read the Document
at **www.myhistorylab.com**
From Then to Now Online: Political Parties

QUICK REVIEW

Party Identities

- Republican self-image: party of nationalism and national unity.
- Republican vision of Democrats: alliance of embittered South and northern slums.
- Democratic self-image: party of limited government and personal liberties.
- Democratic vision of Republicans: party of special interests and meddling nativists.

South, where they stood as the defenders of the traditions of the region's white population. But Democrats also drew support in the urban Northeast, especially from Catholics and recent immigrants.

Party identities. Each major party consisted of a complex coalition of groups with differing traditions and interests. This internal diversity often provoked conflict and threatened party stability. To hold its coalition together, each party identified itself with a theme that appealed broadly to all its constituents, while suggesting that it was menaced by the members and objectives of the opposing party.

Republicans identified their party with nationalism and national unity and attacked the Democrats as an "alliance between the embittered South and the slums of the northern cities." They combined a "bloody shirt" appeal to the memories of the Civil War with campaigns for immigration restriction and cultural uniformity. Seeing a threat to American society in efforts by Catholic immigrants to preserve their ethnic and cultural traditions, for example, Republican legislatures in several states in the 1880s and 1890s enacted laws regulating parochial schools, the use of foreign languages, and alcohol consumption.

Democrats portrayed themselves as the party of limited government and "personal liberties," a theme that appealed to both the racism of white southerners and the resentment immigrants felt about the nativist meddling of Republicans. The Democrats' commitment to personal liberties had limits. They supported the disfranchisement of African Americans, the exclusion of Chinese immigrants, and the dispossession of American Indians. Nevertheless, their emphasis on traditional individualism and localism proved popular.

The partisan politics of both major parties culminated in party machines, especially at the local level. Led by powerful bosses, the machines controlled not only city politics but also municipal government. Party activists used well-organized ward clubs to mobilize working-class voters, who were rewarded with municipal jobs and baskets of food or coal doled out by the machine. Such assistance was often necessary, given the lack of public welfare systems, but to buy votes the machine also sold favors. Public contracts and franchises were peddled to businesses whose high bids covered kickbacks to the machine.

Prohibition Party A venerable third party still in existence that has persistently campaigned for the abolition of alcohol but has also introduced many important reform ideas into American politics.

Greenback Party A third party of the 1870s and 1880s that garnered temporary support by advocating currency inflation to expand the economy and increase opportunity.

Populist Party A major third party of the 1890s formed on the basis of the Farmers' Alliance and other reform organizations.

Granger laws State laws enacted in the Midwest in the 1870s that regulated rates charged by railroads, grain elevator operators, and other middlemen.

Third parties. The partisan politics of the era left room for several third parties, organized around specific issues or groups. The **Prohibition Party** persistently championed the abolition of alcohol but also supported electoral reforms such as woman suffrage, economic reforms such as railroad regulation and income taxes, and social reforms including improved race relations. The **Greenback Party** of the 1870s denounced "the infamous financial legislation which takes all from the many to enrich the few." Its policies of labor reform and currency inflation (to stimulate and democratize the economy) attracted supporters from Maine to Texas. Other significant third parties included the Anti-Monopoly Party, the Union Labor Party, and, most important, the People's or **Populist Party** of the 1890s. Although third parties often won temporary success at the local or regional level, they never permanently displaced the major parties or undermined traditional voter allegiances.

Associational Politics

Much political activity was neither partisan nor electoral. Associations of like-minded citizens, operating as pressure groups, played an increasingly important role in late-nineteenth-century politics. These organizations worked to achieve public policies beneficial to their members. Farmers organized many such groups, most notably the Patrons of Husbandry, known familiarly as the Grange (see Chapter 17). Its campaign for public regulation of the rates charged by railroads and grain elevators helped convince midwestern states to pass the so-called **Granger laws.**

Industrialists also formed pressure groups. Organizations such as the American Iron and Steel Association and the American Protective Tariff League lobbied Congress for high tariff laws and made campaign contributions to friendly politicians of both parties. At the state level, business groups used their political clout to block the reform efforts of farmers and workers, sometimes in the legislatures but otherwise in the courts.

A small group of conservative reformers known derisively as **Mugwumps** (the term derives from the Algonquian word for "chief") devoted most of their effort to campaigning for honest and efficient government through civil service reform. Other pressure groups focused on cultural politics. The rabidly anti-Catholic American Protective Association, for example, agitated for laws restricting immigration, taxing church property, and inspecting Catholic religious institutions.

Christian lobbyists committed their political energies to demanding laws imposing their view of personal moral behavior. They campaigned to require Bible reading in schools, restrict divorces, and prohibit gambling and other "sinful" practices. Their greatest success was the Comstock Law, passed by Congress in 1873, which outlawed the possession or sale of "obscene" materials, including any contraceptive information or devices. Directly affecting the lives of many Americans, the Comstock Law clearly revealed the importance of this type of political activism.

The Grange rejected partisanship but not politics. This sympathetic cartoon shows a Granger trying to warn Americans blindly absorbed in partisan politics of the dangers of onrushing industrialization.

Mugwumps Elitist and conservative reformers who favored sound money and limited government and opposed tariffs and the spoils system.

National American Woman Suffrage Association The organization, formed in 1890, that coordinated the ultimately successful campaign to achieve women's right to vote.

Women as activists. Women also sought power and influence through associational politics. The **National American Woman Suffrage Association** lobbied Congress and state legislatures for constitutional amendments extending the vote to women. Despite the opposition of male politicians of both major parties, suffragists succeeded by the mid-1890s in gaining full woman suffrage in four western states, Wyoming, Colorado, Idaho, and Utah, and partial suffrage (the right to vote in school elections) in several other states, east and west.

Other women shaped public issues through social service organizations. Although the belief that women belonged in the domestic sphere limited their involvement in electoral politics, it furnished a basis for political action focused on welfare and moral reform. With petition campaigns, demonstrations, and lobbying, women's social service organizations sought to remedy poverty and disease, improve education and recreation, and provide day nurseries for the children of working women.

Women combined domesticity and politics in the temperance movement. Alcoholism, widespread in U.S. society, was regarded as a major cause of crime, wife abuse, and broken homes. The temperance movement thus invoked women's presumed moral superiority to address a real problem that fell within their accepted sphere. The Woman's Christian Temperance Union (WCTU) gained a massive membership by campaigning for restrictive liquor laws.

Women lobbying a congressional committee to support woman suffrage. Susan B. Anthony noted with regret that "to all men women suffrage is only a side issue."

Under the leadership of Frances Willard, the WCTU built on traditional women's concerns to develop an important critique of American society. Reversing the conventional view, Willard argued that alcohol abuse was a result, not a cause, of poverty and social disorder. Under the slogan of "Home Protection," the WCTU inserted domestic issues into the political sphere with a campaign for social and economic reforms far beyond temperance. It pushed for improved health conditions, reached out to the Knights of Labor to support workplace reforms, and lobbied for federal aid to education, particularly as a means to provide schooling for black children in the South. It eventually supported woman suffrage as well, on the grounds that women needed the vote to fulfill their duty to protect home, family, and morality.

THE LIMITS OF GOVERNMENT

WHAT EXPLAINS the weakness and inefficiency of late-nineteenth-century government?

laissez-faire The doctrine that government should not intervene in the economy, especially through regulation.

Despite the popular enthusiasm for partisan politics and the persistent pressure of associational politics, government in the late nineteenth century was neither active nor productive by present standards. The receding governmental activism of the Civil War and Reconstruction years coincided with a resurgent belief in localism and **laissez-faire** policies. In addition, a Congress and presidency divided between the two major parties, a small and inefficient bureaucracy, and judicial restraints joined powerful private interests to limit the size and objectives of the federal government.

THE WEAK PRESIDENCY

The presidency was a weak and restricted institution. The impeachment of President Johnson at the outset of Reconstruction had undermined the office. President Grant clearly subordinated it to the legislative branch by deferring to Congress on appointments and legislation. Other factors contributed as well. The men who filled the office between 1877 and 1897 were all honest and generally capable. Each had built a solid political record at the state or federal level. But they were all conservatives, with a narrow view of the presidency, and proposed few initiatives. The presidents of this era viewed their duties as chiefly administrative. They made little effort to reach out to the public or to exert legislative leadership. The presidency was also hampered by its limited control over bureaus and departments, which responded more directly to Congress, and by its small staff, consisting of no more than a half-dozen secretaries, clerks, and telegraphers.

THE INEFFICIENT CONGRESS

Congress was the foremost branch of the national government. It exercised authority over the federal budget, oversaw the cabinet, debated public issues, and controlled legislation. Its members were often state and national party leaders, who were strong-willed and, as one senator conceded, "tolerated no intrusion from the President or from anybody else."

But Congress was scarcely efficient. Its chambers were noisy and chaotic, and members rarely devoted their attention to the business at hand. The repeated shifts in party control impeded effective action. So, too, did the loss of experienced legislators to rapid turnover. In some Congresses, a majority of members were first-termers. Procedural rules, based on precedents from a simpler time and manipulated by determined partisans, hindered congressional action. Some rules restricted the introduction of legislation; others prevented its passage. The most notorious rule required that a quorum be not only present but voting. When the House was narrowly divided along party lines, the minority could block all business simply by refusing to answer when the roll was called.

But as a nationalizing economy required more national legislation, the amount of business before Congress grew relentlessly (see Figure 20–2). The expanding scale of congressional work prompted a gradual reform of procedures and the centralization of power in the Speaker of the House and the leading committees. These changes did not, however, create a coherent program for government action.

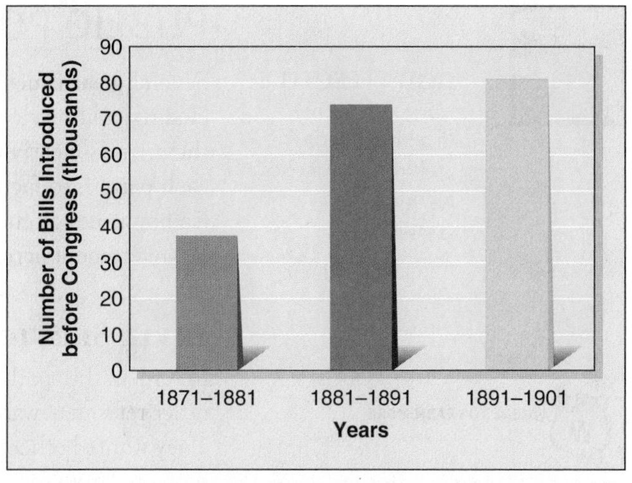

FIGURE 20–2 **Increase in Congressional Business, 1871–1901** Industrialization, urbanization, and western expansion brought increased demands for government action, but the party stalemate, laissez-faire attitudes, and inefficient public institutions often blocked effective responses.

The Federal Bureaucracy and the Spoils System

Reflecting presidential weakness and congressional inefficiency, the federal bureaucracy remained small and limited in the late nineteenth century. There were little more than 50,000 government employees in 1871, and three-fourths of them were local postmasters scattered across the nation.

The system for selecting and supervising federal officials had developed gradually in the first half of the century. Known as the spoils system, its basic principle was that victorious politicians awarded government jobs to party workers, often with little regard for qualifications, and ousted the previous employees. The spoils system played a crucial role in all aspects of politics. It enabled party leaders to strengthen their organizations, reward loyal party service, and attract the political workers needed to mobilize the electorate. Supporters described it as a democratic system that offered opportunities to many citizens and prevented the emergence of an entrenched bureaucracy.

Critics, however, charged that the system was riddled with corruption, abuse, and inefficiency. Rapid turnover bred instability; political favoritism bred incompetence. Certainly, the spoils system was ineffective for filling positions that required special clerical skills or scientific expertise. Even worse, the spoils system absorbed the president and Congress in unproductive conflicts over patronage.

QUICK REVIEW

The Late-Nineteenth-Century Presidency

- Weak and subordinated to Congress.
- Presidents between 1877 and 1897 were conservative and offered few initiatives.
- Presidents of this era made little effort to reach out to public.

Inconsistent State Government

State governments were more active than the federal government. Considered closer and more responsible to the people, they had long exercised police power and regulatory authority. They collected taxes for education and public works, and they promoted private enterprise and public health. Still, they did little by today's standards. Few people thought it appropriate for government at any level to offer direct help to particular social groups. Some state governments contracted in the 1870s and 1880s, following the wartime activism of the 1860s, and new state constitutions restricted the scope of public authority.

Nonetheless, state governments gradually expanded their role in response to the stresses produced by industrialization. Following the lead of Massachusetts in 1869, most states had by the turn of the century created commissions to investigate and regulate industry. Public intervention in other areas of the economy soon followed. In Minnesota, for example, the state helped farmers by establishing a dairy commission, prohibiting the manufacture or sale of margarine, creating a bureau of animal industry, and employing state veterinarians.

Not all such agencies and laws were effective, nor were all state governments as diligent as Minnesota's. Southern states, especially, lagged, and one midwesterner complained that his legislature "meets in ignorance, sits in corruption, and dissolves in disgrace every two years." Still, the widening scope of state action represented a growing acceptance of public responsibility for social welfare and economic life and laid the foundation for more effective steps in the early twentieth century.

QUICK REVIEW

The Spoils System

- Fifty thousand federal employees in 1871.
- Politicians awarded government jobs to party loyalists.
- Critics charged that the system was corrupt.

PUBLIC POLICIES AND NATIONAL ELECTIONS

HOW EFFECTIVE was government in addressing the problems of America's industrializing economy?

Several great issues dominated the national political arena in the late nineteenth century, including civil service reform, tariffs, and business and financial regulation. Rarely, however, did these issues clearly and consistently separate the major political parties. Instead, they divided each party into factions along regional, interest, and economic lines. As a consequence, these leading issues often played only a small role in determining elections and were seldom resolved by government action.

Civil Service Reform

WHERE TO LEARN MORE

Rutherford B. Hayes Presidential Center, Fremont, Ohio
http://www.rbhayes.org/hayes/

Reform of the spoils system emerged as a prominent issue during the 1870s. The Mugwumps and other reformers wanted a professional civil service, based on merit and divorced from politics. They wanted officeholders to be selected on the basis of competitive written examinations and protected from removal on political grounds. They expected such a system to promote efficiency, economy, and honesty in government. But they also expected it to increase their own influence and minimize that of "mere politicians."

President Rutherford B. Hayes favored civil service reform but did not fully renounce the spoils system. He rewarded those who had helped to elect him, permitted party leaders to name or veto candidates for the cabinet, and insisted that his own appointees contribute funds to Republican election campaigns. But he rejected the claims of some machine leaders and office seekers and struck a blow for change when he fired Chester A. Arthur from his post as New York customs-house collector after an investigation pronounced Arthur's patronage system "unsound in principle, dangerous in practice," and characterized by "ignorance, inefficiency, and corruption."

The weakness of the civil service reformers was dramatically underscored in 1880 when the Republicans, to improve their chances of carrying the crucial state of New York, nominated Chester A. Arthur for vice president on a ticket headed by James Garfield of Ohio. They won, and Garfield immediately found himself enmeshed in the demands of the unreformed spoils system. Within a few months of his inauguration in 1881, Garfield was assassinated by a disappointed and crazed office seeker, and Arthur became president.

Pendleton Civil Service Act A law of 1883 that reformed the spoils system by prohibiting government workers from making political contributions and creating the Civil Service Commission to oversee their appointment on the basis of merit rather than politics.

Public dismay over this tragedy finally spurred changes in the spoils system. In 1883 Congress passed the **Pendleton Civil Service Act,** prohibiting federal employees from soliciting or receiving political contributions from government workers and creating the Civil Service Commission to administer competitive examinations to applicants for government jobs. The act gave the commission jurisdiction over only about 10 percent of federal positions but provided that presidents could extend its authority. A professional civil service free from partisan politics gradually emerged, strengthening the executive branch's ability to handle its increasing administrative responsibilities.

The new emphasis on merit and skill rather than party ties opened new opportunities to women. Federal clerks were nearly exclusively male as late as 1862, but by the early 1890s, women held a third of the clerical positions in the executive departments in Washington. These workers constituted the nation's first substantial female clerical labor force. Their work in public life challenged the conventional belief that a woman's ability and personality limited her to the domestic sphere.

Read the **Document** at **www.myhistorylab.com**
Pendleton Civil Service Act (1883)

The Political Life of the Tariff

Americans debated heatedly over tariff legislation throughout the late nineteenth century. This complex issue linked basic economic questions to partisan, ideological, and regional concerns. Tariffs on imported goods provided revenue for the federal government and protected American industry from European competition. They promoted industrial growth but often allowed favored industries to garner high profits. By the 1880s, tariffs covered 4,000 items and generated more revenue than the government needed to carry on its limited operations.

Reflecting its commitment to industry, the Republican Party vigorously championed protective tariffs. Party leaders also claimed that American labor benefited from tariff protection. Most Democrats, by contrast, favored tariff reduction, a position that reflected their party's relatively laissez-faire outlook. They argued that lower tariffs would encourage foreign trade and, by reducing the treasury surplus, minimize the temptation for the government to pursue activist policies. They pointed out the discriminatory effects of high tariffs, which benefited some interests, such as certain manufacturers, but hurt others, such as some farmers, while raising the cost of living for all (see the Overview, Arguments in the Tariff Debates).

Political divisions over public policies often occurred within rather than between the major parties. Here the platform of the Democratic Party ("Democracy") is splintering because of conflicting interests.

The differences between the parties, however, were often more rhetorical than substantial. They disagreed only about how high tariffs should be and what interests they should protect. Congressmen of both parties voted for tariffs that would benefit their districts.

In the 1884 campaign, the Republican presidential candidate, James G. Blaine, maintained that prosperity and high employment depended on high tariffs. The Democrats' platform endorsed a lowered tariff, but their candidate, New York governor Grover Cleveland, generally ignored the issue. Unable to address this and other important issues, both parties resorted to scandal mongering. One observer called the election "a more bitter, personal, and disgusting campaign than we have ever seen."

Cleveland continued to avoid the tariff issue for three years after his election, until the growing treasury surplus and rising popular pressure for tariff reduction prompted him to act. He devoted his entire 1887 annual message to attacking the "vicious, inequitable, and illogical" tariff, apparently making it the dominant issue of his 1888 reelection campaign. Once again, however, the distinctive political attribute of the period—intense and organized campaigning between closely balanced parties—forced both Democrats and Republicans to blur their positions. Cleveland proposed a Democratic platform that ignored his recent message and did not even use the word *tariff*. Cleveland won slightly more popular votes than his Republican opponent, Benjamin Harrison of Indiana, but Harrison carried the electoral college, indicating the decisive importance of strategic campaigning, local issues, and large campaign funds rather than great national issues.

WHERE TO LEARN MORE

President Benjamin Harrison's Home, Indianapolis, Indiana http://www.presidentbenjaminharrison.org

The triumphant Republicans raised tariffs to prohibitive levels with the McKinley Tariff Act of 1890. William McKinley praised the law as "protective in every paragraph and American on every page," but it provoked a popular backlash that helped return the Democrats to power. Still, the Democrats made little effort to push tariff reform.

The Beginnings of Federal Regulation

While business leaders pressed for protective tariffs and other public policies that promoted their interests, they otherwise used their great political influence to ensure governmental laissez-faire. Popular pressure nonetheless compelled Congress to take the first steps toward the regulation of business with the passage of the Interstate Commerce Act in 1887 and the Sherman Antitrust Act in 1890.

Popular concern focused first on the railroads, the preeminent symbol of big business. Both farm groups and business shippers complained of discriminatory rates levied by railroads. Consumers condemned the railroads' use of pooling arrangements to suppress competition and raise rates. The resulting pressure was responsible for the Granger laws enacted in several midwestern states in the 1870s to regulate railroad freight and storage rates. At first, the Supreme Court upheld this legislation, ruling in *Munn v. Illinois* (1877) that state governments had the right to regulate private property when it was "devoted to a

QUICK REVIEW

Tariffs and Politics

- Tariffs provided revenues and protected American industries from competition.
- Republicans were strong supporters of protective tariffs.
- Congressmen voted for tariffs that benefited their home districts.

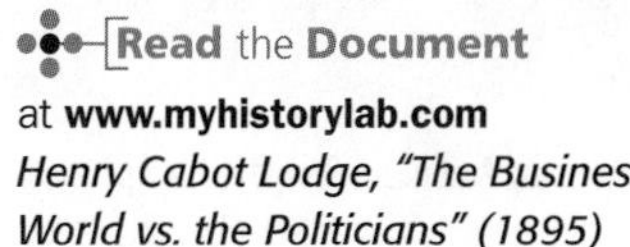

Read the **Document** at **www.myhistorylab.com**
Henry Cabot Lodge, "The Business World vs. the Politicians" (1895)

OVERVIEW Arguments in the Tariff Debates

Area Affected	High-Tariff Advocates	Low-Tariff Advocates
Industry	Tariffs promote industrial growth.	Tariffs inflate corporate profits.
Employment	Tariffs stimulate job growth.	Tariffs restrict competition.
Wages and prices	Tariffs permit higher wages.	Tariffs increase consumer prices.
Government	Tariffs provide government revenue.	Tariffs violate the principle of laissez-faire and produce revenues that tempt the government to activism.
Trade	Tariffs protect the domestic market.	Tariffs restrict foreign trade.

Interstate Commerce Act The 1887 law that prohibited pooling and discriminatory rates by railroads and established the first federal regulatory agency, the Interstate Commerce Commission.

Interstate Commerce Commission (ICC) The first federal regulation agency, established in 1887 to oversee railroad practices.

Sherman Antitrust Act The first federal antitrust measure, passed in 1890; sought to promote economic competition by prohibiting business combinations in restraint of trade or commerce.

public use." But in 1886, the Court ruled in *Wabash, St. Louis, and Pacific Railway Company v. Illinois* that only the federal government could regulate interstate commerce. This decision effectively ended state regulation of railroads but simultaneously increased pressure for congressional action. With the support of both major parties, Congress in 1887 passed the **Interstate Commerce Act.**

The act prohibited rebates, discriminatory rates, and pooling and established the **Interstate Commerce Commission (ICC)** to investigate and prosecute violations. The ICC was the first federal regulatory agency. But its powers were too limited to be effective. Railroads continued their objectionable practices and frustrated the commission by refusing to provide required information and endlessly appealing its orders to a conservative judiciary. In its first 15 years, only one court case was decided in favor of the ICC.

Many people saw railroad abuses as indicative of the dangers of corporate power in general and demanded a broader federal response. As with railroad regulation, the first antitrust laws—laws intended to break up or regulate corporate monopolies—were passed by states. Exposés of the monopolistic practices of such corporations as Standard Oil forced both major parties to endorse national antitrust legislation during the campaign of 1888. In 1890, Congress enacted the **Sherman Antitrust Act** with only a single vote in opposition. But this near unanimity concealed real differences over the desirability and purpose of the law. Although it emphatically prohibited any combination in restraint of trade (any attempt to restrict competition), the law was vaguely written and too weak to prevent abuses. The courts further weakened the act, and presidents of both parties made little effort to enforce it. Essentially still unfettered, large corporations remained a threat in the eyes of many Americans.

In the 1880s many Americans feared that corporate power had too much influence in government and was endangering popular liberty. The question, as posed by this cartoon, was "What are you going to do about it?"

THE MONEY QUESTION

Persistent wrangling over questions of currency and coinage made monetary policy the most divisive political issue. Despite the sometimes arcane and difficult nature of the money question, millions of Americans adopted positions on it and defended them with religious ferocity.

Creditors, especially bankers, as well as conservative economists and many business leaders favored limiting the money supply. They called this a **sound money** policy and insisted that it would ensure economic stability, maintain property values, and retain investor confidence. Farmers and other debtors complained that this deflationary monetary policy would depress already low crop prices, drive debtors further into debt, and restrict economic opportunities. They favored expanding the money supply to match the country's growing population and economy. They expected this inflationary policy to raise prices, stimulate the economy, reduce debt burdens, and increase opportunities.

The conservative leadership of both major parties supported the sound money policy, but their rank-and-file membership, especially in the West and the South, included many inflationists. As a result, the parties avoided confronting each other on the money issue.

The conflict between advocates of sound money and inflation centered on the use of paper money, or "greenbacks," and silver coinage. In 1875, sound money advocates in Congress enacted a deflationary law that withdrew some greenbacks from circulation and required that the remainder be convertible into gold after 1878. This action forced the money issue into electoral politics. Outraged inflationists organized the Greenback Party. The Greenbackers polled more than a million votes in 1878 and elected 14 members of Congress, nearly gaining the balance of power in the House. As the depression faded, however, so did interest in the greenback issue, and the party soon withered.

QUICK REVIEW

Interstate Commerce Commission (ICC)

- Established by Interstate Commerce Act (1887).
- Commission was first federal regulatory agency.
- In first fifteen years, only one court case was decided in favor of the ICC.

Read the Document at **www.myhistorylab.com** *Workingman's Amalgamated Sherman Anti-Trust (1893)*

sound money Misleading slogan that referred to a conservative policy of restricting the money supply and adhering to the gold standard.

Interpreting the Past *Currency Reform* (pp. 574–575)

The silver issue. Inflationists then turned to the silver issue, which would prove more enduring and disruptive. Historically, the United States had been on a bimetallic standard, using both gold and silver as the basis of its currency. But after the 1840s, the market price of silver rose above the currency value assigned to it by the government. Silver miners and owners began to sell the metal for commercial use rather than to the government for coinage, and little silver money circulated. In 1873, Congress passed a law "demonetizing" silver, thereby making gold the only standard for U.S. currency. Gold-standard supporters hoped that the law would promote international trade by aligning U.S. financial policy with that of Great Britain, which insisted on gold-based currency. But they also wanted to prevent new silver discoveries in the American West from expanding the money supply.

Indeed, silver production soon boomed, flooding the commercial market and dropping the value of the metal. Dismayed miners wanted the Treasury Department to purchase their surplus silver on the old terms and demanded a return to the bimetallic system. More important, the rural debtor groups seeking currency inflation joined in this demand, seeing renewed silver coinage as a means to reverse the long deflationary trend in the economy. (See Global Connections: The Money Issue and the World.)

Again, both major parties equivocated. Eastern conservatives of both parties denounced silver; southerners and westerners demanded **free silver,** meaning unlimited silver coinage. By 1878, a bipartisan coalition succeeded in passing the Bland-Allison Act. This compromise measure required the government to buy and coin at least $2 million of silver a month. However, the government never exceeded the minimum, and the law had little inflationary effect.

free silver Philosophy that the government should expand the money supply by purchasing and coining all the silver offered to it.

After hard times hit rural regions in the late 1880s, inflationists secured passage of the Sherman Silver Purchase Act of 1890. The Treasury now had to buy a larger volume of silver and pay for it with treasury notes redeemable in either gold or silver. But this, too, produced little inflation, because the government did not coin the silver it purchased, redeemed the notes only with gold, and, as western silver production increased further, had to spend less and less to buy the stipulated amount of silver. Debtors of both parties remained convinced that the government favored the "classes rather than the masses." Gold-standard advocates (again, of both parties) were even less happy with the law and planned to repeal it at their first opportunity. The division between the two groups was deep and bitter.

QUICK REVIEW

The Money Question

- Bimetallic standard: use of both gold and silver as basis of currency, practice of United States prior to 1873.
- Advocates of "gold standard" hoped to promote international trade and economic stability.
- Advocates of "free silver" hoped to stimulate economy, reduce debt, and create opportunity.

GLOBAL CONNECTIONS

 THE MONEY ISSUE AND THE WORLD 

Although the money issue dominated American politics in the late nineteenth century, it was deeply connected to international developments over which ordinary Americans had little influence.

Governments, companies, and individuals engaged in international trade or investment required a common standard to measure commodities, payments, and credit. Conventional wisdom (now discredited) held that gold and silver, metals with "intrinsic" value, provided that required standard, and they served as the basis of national money systems. The United States, France, and several other countries had a bimetallic standard, basing their money supply on both gold and silver. Great Britain had adopted the gold standard in 1816, while Russia, Austria, Japan, India, and other nations relied on a silver standard.

This diversity of money standards posed little difficulty as long as national economies were somewhat independent. But industrialization and advances in transportation and communication produced new patterns of trade and investment and increasingly linked different countries together economically in an early form of globalization. Pressure developed for a uniform monetary standard. British investors in American railroads, mines, and western land, for example, feared that currency fluctuation would devalue their property. Beginning in 1867 a series of international monetary conferences were held. Britain, the world's dominant economic power, insisted upon the gold standard, and under such pressure (and for other reasons often peculiar to themselves) most other countries gradually followed suit. Germany, for instance, adopted the gold standard in 1871 at least in part to help unify its previously separate states. Sweden and the Netherlands switched from silver to gold in 1872. France, Austria, Russia, and Japan followed thereafter.

The American "demonetization" of silver in 1873, although also prompted by other political and economic developments peculiar to the United States, fit into this international context. American policy makers agreed with European leaders that silver and bimetallism—to say nothing of the heresy of greenback paper money—threatened business stability, investor confidence, and public credit. Gold, declared Treasury officials, was "a universal currency," while silver coinage would align the United States with "inferior nations" like Mexico rather than with "the great commercial nations of the world."

The gold standard, championed by the creditor interests in all industrialized nations, did attract necessary foreign investment in the United States and facilitate the nation's foreign trade, but it often imposed great hardships on farmers and workers, who with some reason denounced the influence of "international bankers" on the monetary policy of the United States. One sympathetic member of Congress complained of Britain: "The powers that rule us are the monopoly that has made a hell of Ireland and India."

THE CRISIS OF THE 1890s

WHAT FACTORS contributed to the rise and fall of the Populist Party?

In the 1890s, social, economic, and political pressures created a crisis for both the political system and the government. A third-party political challenge generated by agricultural discontent disrupted traditional party politics. A devastating depression spawned social misery and labor violence. Changing public attitudes led to new demands on the government and a realignment of parties and voters. These developments, in turn, set the stage for important political, economic, and social changes in the new century.

FARMERS PROTEST INEQUITIES

The agricultural depression that engulfed the Great Plains and the South in the late 1880s brought misery and despair to millions of rural Americans. Falling crop prices and rising debt overwhelmed many people already exhausted from overwork and alarmed by the new corporate order. "At the age of 52 years, after a long life of toil, economy, and self-denial, I find myself and family virtual paupers," lamented one Kansan. His family's farm, rather than being "a house of refuge for our declining years, by a few turns of the monopolistic crank has been rendered valueless." To a large extent, the farmers' plight stemmed from bad weather and international overproduction of farm products. Seeking relief, however, the farmers naturally focused on the inequities of railroad discrimination, tariff favoritism, a restrictive financial system, and apparently indifferent political parties.

Credit inequities. Angry farmers particularly singled out the systems of money and credit that worked so completely against agricultural interests. Government rules for national banks directed credit into the urbanized North and East at the expense of the rural South and West and prohibited loans on farm property and real estate. As a result, farmers had to turn to other sources of credit and pay higher interest rates. In the West, farmers borrowed from mortgage companies to buy land and machinery, but declining crop prices made it difficult for them to pay their debts, and mortgage foreclosures then crushed the hopes of many. In the South, the credit shortage interacted with the practices of cotton marketing and retail trade to create the sharecropping system, which trapped more and more farmers, black and white, in a vicious pattern of exploitation. Moreover, the government's policies of monetary deflation worsened the debt burden for all farmers.

Freight rates and tariffs. Farmers protested other features of the nation's economic system as well. Railroad freight rates were two or three times higher in the West and South than in the North and East. The near-monopolistic control of grain elevators and cotton brokerages in rural areas left farmers feeling exploited. Protective tariffs on agricultural machinery and other manufactured goods further raised their costs. The failure of political parties and the government to devise effective regulatory and antitrust measures or to correct the inequities in the currency, credit, and tariff laws capped the farmers' anger. By the 1890s, many were convinced that the nation's economic and political institutions were aligned against them.

Farmers organize. In response, farmers turned to the **Farmers' Alliance,** the era's greatest popular movement of protest and reform. Originating in Texas, the Southern Farmers' Alliance spread throughout the South and across the Great Plains to the Pacific coast. African American farmers organized the Colored Farmers' Alliance. The Northwestern Farmers' Alliance reached westward and northward from Illinois to Nebraska and Minnesota. In combination, these groups constituted a massive grassroots movement committed to economic and political reform.

Farmers' Alliance A broad mass movement in the rural South and West during the late nineteenth century, encompassing several organizations and demanding economic and political reforms.

The Farmers' Alliance restricted membership to men and women of the "producing class" and urged them to stand "against the encroachments of monopolies and in opposition to the growing corruption of wealth and power." At first, the Alliance organized farmers' cooperatives to market crops and purchase supplies. Although some co-ops worked well, most soon failed because of the opposition of established business interests. In Leflore County, Mississippi, when members of the Colored Farmers' Alliance shifted their trade to an Alliance store, local merchants provoked a conflict in which state troops killed 25 black farmers, including the local leaders of the Colored Alliance.

The Alliance also developed ingenious proposals to remedy rural credit and currency problems. In the South, the Alliance pushed the subtreasury system, which called on the government to warehouse farmers' cotton and advance them credit based on its value (see Chapter 17). In the West, the Alliance proposed a system of federal loans to farmers, using land as security. These proposals were immensely popular among farmers, but the major parties and Congress rejected them. The Alliance also took up earlier calls for free silver, government control of railroads, and banking reform, again to no avail.

The People's Party

In the West, discontented agrarians organized independent third parties to achieve reforms the major parties had ignored. State-level third parties appeared in the elections of 1890 under many names. All eventually adopted the labels "People's" or "Populist," which were first used by a Kansas party formed by members of the Farmers' Alliance, the Knights of Labor, the Grange, and the old Greenback Party. The new party's campaign, marked by grim determination and fierce rhetoric, set the model for Populist politics.

Read the **Document**
at **www.myhistorylab.com**
The People's Party Platform (1892)

The Populist parties proved remarkably successful. They gained control of the legislatures of Kansas and Nebraska and won congressional elections in Kansas, Nebraska, and Minnesota. Their victories came at the expense of the Republicans, who had traditionally controlled politics in these states, and contributed to a massive defeat of the GOP in the 1890 midterm elections. Thereafter, Populists won further victories throughout the West. In the mountain states, where their support came more from miners than from farmers, they won governorships in Colorado and Montana. On the Pacific coast, angry farmers found allies among urban workers in Seattle, Tacoma, Portland, and San Francisco, where organized labor had campaigned for reform since the 1880s. The Populists elected a governor in Washington, congressmen in California, and legislators in all three states.

With their new political power, farmers enacted reform legislation in many western states. New laws regulated banks and railroads and protected debtors by capping interest rates and restricting mortgage foreclosures. Others protected unions and mandated improved workplace conditions. Still others made the political system more democratic. Populists were instrumental, for example, in winning woman suffrage in Colorado and Idaho, although the united opposition of Democrats and Republicans blocked their efforts in other states.

In the South, the angry farmers did not initially form third parties but instead attempted to seize control of the dominant Democratic Party by forcing its candidates to pledge support to the Alliance platform. The rural southern electorate then swept these "Alliance Democrats" into office. But most of these Democrats then repudiated their Alliance pledges and remained loyal to their party and its traditional opposition to governmental activism. Betrayed again by the political system, disgruntled Alliance members began organizing their own Populist parties, but they faced obstacles that western farmers did not. A successful challenge to the entrenched Democrats would require the political cooperation of both white and black farmers, but that would expose Populists to demagogic attacks from Democrats for undermining white supremacy, frightening away potential white supporters.

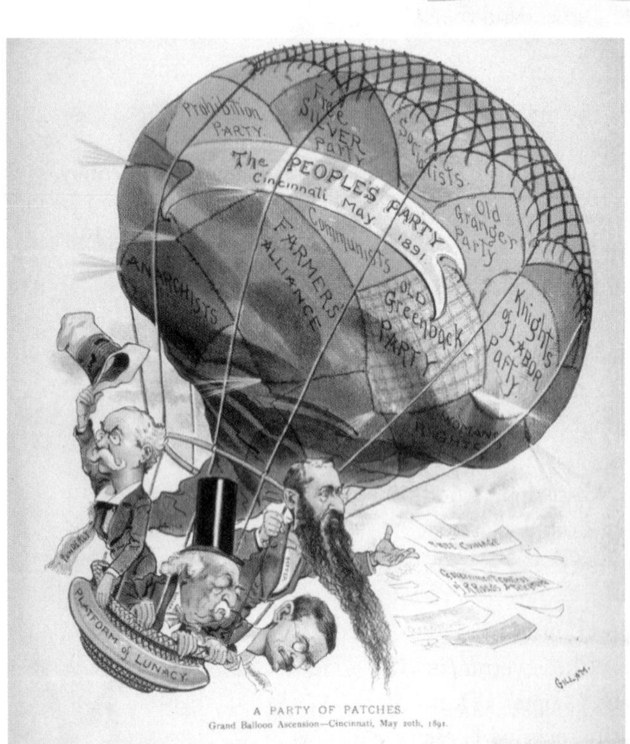

Established interests ridiculed the Populists unmercifully. This hostile cartoon depicts the People's Party as an odd assortment of radical dissidents committed to a "Platform of Lunacy."

Some southern Populists, black and white, did appeal for racial cooperation in political if not social action. In Georgia, the Populist leader Tom Watson supported a biracial party organization and counseled white people to accept black people as partners in their common crusade. "You are kept apart," Watson told black and white southerners, "that you may be separately fleeced of your earnings. You are made to hate each other because upon that hatred is rested the keystone of the arch of financial despotism which enslaves you both."

But steeped in racism, most white southerners recoiled from the prospect of interracial unity. And for their part, most black people remained loyal to the Republican Party for its role in abolishing slavery and for the few patronage crumbs the party still threw their way. Moreover, primarily tenants and farm laborers, their interests were not identical to those of white landowning farmers who formed the core of the Populist Party. Unwilling or unable to mobilize black voters and largely unsuccessful in dislodging white voters from the Democratic Party,

Populists in the South achieved but limited political success, making significant inroads only in the legislatures of Texas, Alabama, and Georgia, and sending Tom Watson to Congress.

National action. Populists soon realized that successful reform would require national action. They met in Omaha, Nebraska, on July 4, 1892, to organize a national party and nominated former Greenbacker James B. Weaver for president. The party platform, known as the **Omaha Platform,** rejected the laissez-faire policies of the old parties: It demanded government ownership of the railroads and the telegraph and telephone systems, a national currency issued by the government rather than by private banks, the subtreasury system, free silver, a graduated income tax, and the redistribution to settlers of land held by railroads and speculative corporations. Accompanying resolutions endorsed the popular election of senators, the secret ballot, and other electoral reforms to make government more democratic and responsive to popular wishes.

The Populists left Omaha to begin an energetic campaign. Weaver toured the western states and with movement leader Mary Lease invaded the Democratic stronghold of the South where some Populists tried to mobilize black voters. Southern Democrats, however, used violence and fraud to intimidate Populist voters and cheat Populist candidates out of office. Some local Populist leaders were murdered, and Weaver was driven from the South. Southern Democrats also appealed effectively to white supremacy, undermining the Populist effort to build a biracial reform coalition.

Elsewhere, too, Populists met disappointment. Midwestern farmers unfamiliar with Alliance ideas and organization ignored Populist appeals and stood by their traditional political allegiances. So did most eastern working-class voters, who learned little of the Populist program beyond its demand for inflation, which they feared would worsen their own conditions.

The Populists lost the election but showed impressive support. They garnered more than a million votes, carried several western states, and won hundreds of state offices throughout the West and in pockets of the South. Populist leaders immediately began working to expand their support, to the alarm of both southern Democrats and northern Republicans.

QUICK REVIEW

Populist Reforms

- Regulation of banks and railroads.
- Protection for debtors.
- Protection for unions.
- Regulation of workplace safety.
- Creation of a more democratic political system.

Omaha Platform The 1892 platform of the Populist Party repudiating laissez-faire and demanding economic and political reforms to aid distressed farmers and workers.

THE CHALLENGE OF THE DEPRESSION

The emergence of a significant third-party movement was but one of many developments that combined by the mid-1890s to produce a national political crisis. A harsh and lengthy depression began in 1893, cruelly worsening conditions not only for farmers but for most other Americans. Labor unrest and violence engulfed the nation, reflecting workers' distress but frightening more comfortable Americans. The persistent failure of the major parties to respond to serious problems contributed mightily to the growing popular discontent. Together these developments constituted an important challenge to America's new industrial society and government.

Although the Populists lost in 1892, the election nonetheless reflected the nation's spreading dissatisfaction. Voters decisively rejected President Harrison and the incumbent Republicans in Congress, putting the Democrats in control of Congress and Grover Cleveland back in the White House. But the conservative Cleveland was almost oblivious to the mounting demand for reform. He delivered an inaugural address championing laissez-faire and rejecting government action to solve social or economic problems.

Cleveland's resolve was immediately tested when the economy collapsed in the spring of 1893. Railroad overexpansion, a weak banking system, tight credit, and plunging agricultural prices all contributed to the disaster. So too did a depression in Europe, which reduced American export markets and prompted British investors to sell their American investments for gold. Hundreds of banks closed, and thousands of businesses, including the nation's major railroads, went bankrupt. By winter, 20 percent of the labor force was unemployed, and the jobless scavenged for food in a country that had no public unemployment or welfare programs.

QUICK REVIEW

The Depression of 1893

- Harsh and lengthy depression began in 1893.
- By winter 1893, 20 percent of the labor force was unemployed.
- Most state governments offered little relief.

Churches, local charity societies, and labor unions tried to provide relief but were overwhelmed. Most state governments offered little relief beyond encouraging private charity to the homeless.

Appeals for federal action. If Cleveland and Congress had no idea how the federal government might respond to the depression, other Americans did. Jacob Coxey, a Populist businessman from Ohio, proposed a government public-works program for the unemployed to be financed with paper money. This plan would improve the nation's infrastructure, create jobs for the unemployed, and provide an inflationary stimulus to counteract the depression's deflationary effects. In short, Coxey advocated positive government action to combat the depression.

Coxey organized a march of the unemployed to Washington as "a petition with boots on" to support his ideas. **Coxey's Army** of the unemployed, as the excited press dubbed it, marched through the industrial towns of Ohio and Pennsylvania and into Maryland, attracting attention and support. Other armies formed in eastern cities from Boston to Baltimore, and some of the largest organized in the western cities of Denver, San Francisco, and Seattle. All set out for the capital.

Coxey's Army A protest march of unemployed workers, led by Populist businessman Jacob Coxey, demanding inflation and a public works program during the depression of the 1890s.

Read the **Document**

at **www.myhistorylab.com**
Jacob S. Coxey, "Address of Protest" (1894)

The sympathy and assistance with which Americans greeted these industrial armies reflected more than anxiety over the depression and unemployment. As one economist noted, what distinguished the Populists and Coxeyites from earlier reformers was their appeal for federal action. Their substantial public support suggested a deep dissatisfaction with the failure of the government to respond to social and economic needs.

Nonetheless, the government acted to suppress Coxey. When he reached Washington with 600 marchers, police and soldiers arrested him and his aides, beat sympathetic bystanders in a crowd of 20,000, and herded the marchers into detention camps. Unlike the lobbyists for business and finance, Coxey was not permitted to reach Congress to deliver his statement urging the government to assist "the poor and oppressed."

Protecting big business. The depression also provoked labor turmoil. In 1894, there were some 1,400 industrial strikes, involving nearly 700,000 workers, the largest number of strikers in any year in the nineteenth century. Cleveland had no response except to call for law and order. One result was the government's violent suppression of the Pullman strike (see Chapter 18).

In a series of decisions in 1895, the Supreme Court strengthened the bonds between business and government. First, it upheld the use of a court-ordered injunction to break the Pullman strike. As a result, injunctions became a major weapon for courts and corporations against labor unions, until Congress finally limited their use in 1932. Next, in *United States v. E. C. Knight Company*, the Court gutted the Sherman Antitrust Act by ruling that manufacturing, as opposed to commerce, was beyond the reach of federal regulation. Finally, the Court invalidated an income tax that agrarian Democrats and Populists had maneuvered through Congress. Not until 1913, and then only with an amendment to the Constitution, would it be possible to adopt an equitable system of taxation.

Surveying these developments, farmers and workers increasingly concluded that the government protected powerful interests while ignoring the plight of ordinary Americans. Certainly the callous treatment shown workers contrasted sharply with Cleveland's concern for bankers as he managed the government's monetary policy in the depression. Cleveland blamed the economic collapse on the Sherman Silver Purchase Act, which he regarded as detrimental to business confidence and a threat to the nation's gold reserve. He persuaded Congress in 1893 to repeal the law, enraging southern and western members of his own party. These Silver Democrats condemned Cleveland for betraying the public good to "the corporate interests."

Cleveland's policy failed to end the depression. By 1894, the Treasury began borrowing money from Wall Street to bolster the gold reserve. These transactions benefited a syndicate of

Jacob Coxey's "Army" of the unemployed marches to Washington, DC, in 1894. Many such "industrial armies" were organized during the depressed 1890s, revealing dissatisfaction with traditional politics and limited government.

bankers headed by J. P. Morgan. It seemed to critics that an indifferent Cleveland was helping rich bankers profit from the nation's economic agony.

The Battle of the Standards and the Election of 1896

The government's unpopular actions, coupled with the unrelenting depression, alienated workers and farmers from the Cleveland administration and the Democratic Party. In the off-year elections of 1894, the Democrats suffered the greatest loss of congressional seats in American history. Populists increased their vote by 42 percent, making especially significant gains in the South. But the real beneficiaries of the popular hatred of Cleveland and his policies were the Republicans. They gained solid control of Congress as well as state governments across the North and West. All three parties began to plan for the presidential election of 1896.

As hard times persisted, the silver issue came to overshadow all others. Some Populist leaders, hoping to broaden the party's appeal, began to emphasize silver rather than the more radical but divisive planks of the Omaha Platform. Many southern and western Democrats, who had traditionally favored silver inflation, also decided to stress the issue, both to undercut the Populists and to distance themselves and their party from the despised Cleveland.

McKinley and the Republicans. William McKinley, governor of Ohio and author of the McKinley Tariff Act of 1890, emerged as the front-runner of a crowd of hopeful Republican presidential candidates. The Republicans nominated McKinley on the first ballot at their 1896 convention. Their platform called for high tariffs but also endorsed the gold standard, placating eastern delegates but prompting several western Silver Republicans to withdraw from the party.

William Jennings Bryan in 1896. A powerful orator of great human sympathies, Bryan was adored by his followers as "the majestic man who was hurling defiance in the teeth of the money power." Nominated three times for the presidency by the Democrats, he was never elected.

Bryan and the Silverites. When the Democratic convention met, embattled supporters of the gold standard soon learned that the silver crusade had made them a minority in the party. With a fervor that conservatives likened to "scenes of the French Revolution," the Silver Democrats revolutionized their party. They adopted a platform repudiating Cleveland and his policies and endorsing free silver, the income tax, and tighter regulation of trusts and railroads. A magnificent speech supporting this platform by William Jennings Bryan helped convince the delegates to nominate him for president.

Holding their convention last, the Populists faced a terrible dilemma. The Democratic nomination of Bryan on a silver platform undercut their hopes of attracting disappointed reformers from the major parties. Bryan, moreover, had already worked closely with Nebraska Populists, who now urged the party to endorse him rather than split the silver vote and ensure the victory of McKinley and the gold standard. Other Populists argued that fusing—joining with the Democrats—would cost the Populists their separate identity and subordinate their larger political principles to the issue of free silver. After anguished discussion, the Populists nominated Bryan for president.

Money and oratory. The campaign was intense and dramatic, with each side demonizing the other. Eastern financial and business interests contributed millions of dollars to McKinley's campaign. Standard Oil alone provided $250,000, about the same amount as the Democrats' total national expenses. Republicans used these funds to organize an unprecedented campaign. Shifting the emphasis from parades to information, they issued 250 million campaign documents in a dozen languages, warning of economic disaster should Bryan be elected and the bimetallic standard be restored, but promising that McKinley's election

AMERICAN VIEWS

A Populist Views American Government

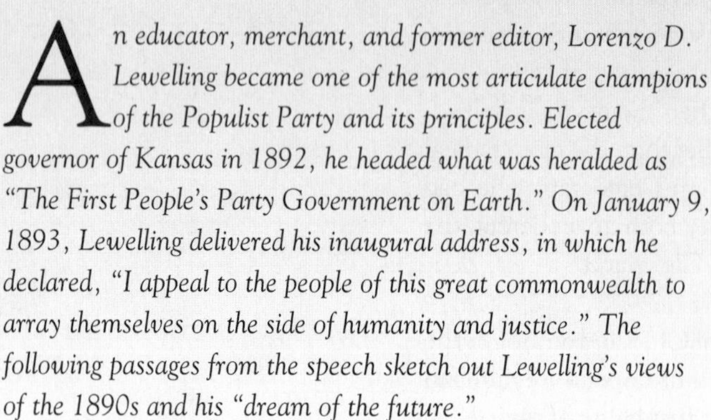

An educator, merchant, and former editor, Lorenzo D. Lewelling became one of the most articulate champions of the Populist Party and its principles. Elected governor of Kansas in 1892, he headed what was heralded as "The First People's Party Government on Earth." On January 9, 1893, Lewelling delivered his inaugural address, in which he declared, "I appeal to the people of this great commonwealth to array themselves on the side of humanity and justice." The following passages from the speech sketch out Lewelling's views of the 1890s and his "dream of the future."

- **How** does Lewelling's rhetoric reflect the deep divisions of the 1890s?
- **What** is Lewelling's view of the proper role of government?
- **For what** does Lewelling criticize the government of the 1890s?
- **What** does Lewelling mean by his statement that "the rich have no right to the property of the poor"?

The survival of the fittest is the government of brutes and reptiles, and such philosophy must give place to a government which recognizes human brotherhood. It is the province of government to protect the weak, but the government today is resolved into a struggle of the masses with the classes for supremacy and bread, until business, home, and personal integrity are trembling in the face of possible want in the family.

Feed a tiger regularly and you tame and make him harmless, but hunger makes tigers of men. If it be true that the poor have no right to the property of the rich let it also be declared that the rich have no right to the property of the poor.

It is the mission of Kansas to protect and advance the moral and material interests of all its citizens. It is its especial duty at the present time to protect the producer from the ravages of combined wealth. National legislation has for twenty years fostered and protected the interests of the few, while it has left the South and West to supply the products with which to feed and clothe the world, and thus to become the servants of wealth.

The demand for free coinage has been refused. The national banks have been permitted to withdraw their circulation, and thus the interests of the East and West have been diverged until the passage of the McKinley bill culminated in their diversement. The purchasing power of the dollar has become so great [that] corn, wheat, beef, pork, and cotton have scarcely commanded a price equal to the cost of production.

The instincts of patriotism have naturally rebelled against these unwarranted encroachments of the power of money. Sectional hatred has also been kept alive by the old powers, the better to enable them to control the products and make the producer contribute to the millionaire; and thus, while the producer labors in the field, the shop, and the factory, the millionaire usurps his earnings and rides in gilded carriages with liveried servants. . . .

The problem of today is how to make the State subservient to the individual, rather than to become his master. Government is a voluntary union for the common good. It guarantees to the individual life, liberty, and the pursuit of happiness. The government then must make it possible for the citizen to enjoy liberty and pursue happiness. If the government fails of these things, it fails in its mission. . . . If old men go to the poor-house and young men go to prison, something is wrong with the economic system of the government.

What is the State to him who toils, if labor is denied him and his children cry for bread? What is the State to the farmer who wearily drags himself from dawn till dark to meet the stern necessities of the mortgage on the farm? What is the State to him if it sanctions usury and other legal forms by which his home is destroyed and his innocent ones become a prey to the fiends who lurk in the shadow of civilization? What is the State to the business man, early grown gray, broken in health and spirit by successive failures; anxiety like a boding owl his constant companion by day and the disturber of his dreams by night? How is life to be sustained, how is liberty to be enjoyed, how is happiness to be pursued under such adverse conditions as the State permits if it does not sanction? Is the State powerless against these conditions?

This is the generation which has come to the rescue. Those in distress who cry out from the darkness shall not be heard in vain. Conscience is in the saddle. We have leaped the bloody chasm and entered a contest for the protection of home, humanity, and the dignity of labor.

The grandeur of civilization shall be emphasized by the dawn of a new era in which the people shall reign, and if found necessary they will "expand the powers of government to solve the enigmas of the times." The people are greater than the law or the statutes, and when a nation sets its heart on doing a great and good thing it can find a legal way to do it.

I have a dream of the future. I have the evolution of an abiding faith in human government, and in the beautiful vision of a coming time I behold the abolition of poverty. A time is foreshadowed when the withered hand of want shall not be outstretched for charity; when liberty, equality, and justice shall have permanent abiding places in the republic.

Source: People's Party Paper (Atlanta), January 20, 1893.

would finally end the depression. Republicans were aided by a national press so completely sympathetic that many newspapers not only shaped their editorials but distorted their news stories to Bryan's disadvantage. Lacking the Republicans' superior resources, the Democrats relied on Bryan's superb speaking ability and youthful energy. Bryan was the first presidential candidate to campaign systematically, speaking hundreds of times to millions of voters. But as the Democratic candidate, Bryan was, ironically, burdened with the legacy of the hated Cleveland administration.

Read the **Document** at **www.myhistorylab.com** *William Jennings Bryan, "Cross of Gold" Speech (1896)*

The intense campaign brought a record voter turnout, but McKinley won decisively by capturing the East and Midwest as well as Oregon and California (see Map 20–2). Bryan carried

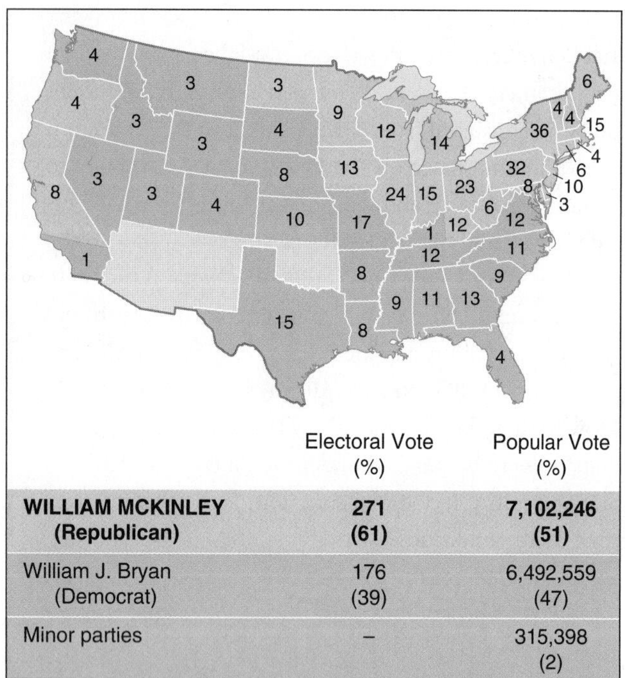

	Electoral Vote (%)	Popular Vote (%)
WILLIAM MCKINLEY (Republican)	**271 (61)**	**7,102,246 (51)**
William J. Bryan (Democrat)	176 (39)	6,492,559 (47)
Minor parties	–	315,398 (2)

MAP 20–2 **The Election of 1896** William Jennings Bryan carried most of the rural South and West, but his free silver campaign had little appeal to more urban and industrial regions, which swung strongly to Republican candidate William McKinley.

Was the election of 1896 closer than the electoral vote would suggest?

the traditionally Democratic South and the mountain and plains states, where Populists and silverites dominated. He failed to gain support in either the Midwest or the cities of the East, where his silver campaign had little appeal to industrial workers.

The elections of 1894 and 1896 ended the close balance between the major parties. Cleveland's failures, coupled with an economic recovery in the wake of the election of 1896, gained the Republicans a reputation as the party of prosperity and industrial progress, firmly establishing them in power for years to come. By contrast, the Democratic Party receded into an ineffectual sectional minority dominated by southern conservatives, despite Bryan's liberal views.

The People's Party simply dissolved. Demoralized by fusion with the Democrats, who had earlier violently repressed them, many southern Populists dropped out of politics. The Democrats' disfranchisement laws, directed at discontented poor white southerners as well as poor black southerners, further undermined the Populists in the South. In the West, the silver tide of 1896 carried many Populists into office, but with their party collapsing, they had no hope of reelection. By 1898, the Populist Party had virtually disappeared. Its reform legacy, however, proved more enduring. The issues it raised would continue to shape state and national politics.

McKinley plunged into his presidency. Unlike his predecessors, he had a definite, if limited, program, consisting of tariff protection, sound money, and overseas expansion. He worked actively to see it through Congress and to shape public opinion, thereby helping establish the model of the modern presidency. He had promised prosperity, and it returned, although not because of the record high tariff his party enacted in 1897 or the Currency Act of 1900, which firmly established the gold standard. Prosperity returned, instead, because of reviving markets and a monetary inflation that resulted from the discovery of vast new deposits of gold in Alaska, Australia, and South Africa. The silverites had recognized that an expanding industrial economy required an expanding money supply. Ironically, the new inflation was greater than the inflation that would have resulted from free silver. With the return of prosperity and the decline of social tensions, McKinley easily won reelection in 1900, defeating Bryan a second time.

CONCLUSION

In late-nineteenth-century America, politics and government often seemed at cross-purposes. Political contests were exciting events, absorbing public attention, attracting high voter turnout, and often raising issues of symbolic or substantive importance. Closely balanced political parties commanded the zealous support of their constituents and wielded power and influence. The institutions of government, by contrast, were limited in size, scope, and responsibility. A weakened presidency and an inefficient Congress, hampered by a restrictive judiciary, were often unable to resolve the very issues that were so dramatically raised in the political arena. The persistent disputes over tariff and monetary policy illustrate this impasse. But the issue that most reflected it was civil service reform. The patronage system provided the lifeblood of politics but also disrupted government business.

Localism, laissez-faire, and other traditional principles that shaped both politics and government were becoming increasingly inappropriate for America's industrializing society. New challenges were emerging that state and local governments could not effectively solve on their own. The national nature of the railroad network, for example, finally brought the federal government into the regulatory arena, however imperfectly, with the Interstate Commerce Act of 1887. Both the depression of the 1890s and the popular discontent articulated most clearly by the Populist rejection of laissez-faire underscored the need for change and discredited the limited government of the Cleveland administration.

By the end of the decade, the political system had changed. The Republicans had emerged as the dominant party, ending the two-party stalemate of previous decades. Campaign hoopla in local communities, like the elaborate parade and ceremonies in Fort Wayne described at the beginning of this chapter, had given way to information-based campaigns directed by and through national organizations. A new, activist presidency was emerging. And the disruptive currency issue faded with the hard times that had brought it forth. Still greater changes were on the horizon. The depression and its terrible social and economic consequences undermined traditional ideas about the responsibilities of government and increased public support for activist policies. The stage was set for the Progressive Era.

Where to Learn More

Rest Cottage, Evanston, Illinois. Frances Willard's home, from which she directed the Woman's Christian Temperance Union, is carefully preserved as a museum. The Willard Memorial Library contains more memorabilia and papers of Willard and the WCTU. http://www.wctu.org/house.html.

President Benjamin Harrison's Home, Indianapolis, Indiana. President Harrison's brick Italianate mansion, completed in 1875, has been completely restored with the family's furniture and keepsakes. The former third-floor ballroom serves as a museum with exhibits of many artifacts of the Harrisons' public and private lives. http://www.presidentbenjaminharrison.org.

Susan B. Anthony House National Historic Landmark, Rochester, New York. This modest house was the home of the prominent suffragist and contains Anthony's original furnishings and personal photographs. http://www.susanbanthonyhouse.org/index.php.

Rutherford B. Hayes Presidential Center, Fremont, Ohio. This complex contains President Hayes's home, office, and extensive grounds together with an excellent library and museum holding valuable collections of manuscripts, artifacts, and photographs illustrating his personal interests and political career. http://www.rbhayes.org/hayes/.

Review Questions

1. What social and institutional factors shaped the disorderly nature of elections in the late nineteenth century? How did they operate in U.S. politics?
2. What social and institutional factors determined the role of government? How and why did the role of government change during this period?
3. What factors determined the party affiliation of American voters? Why did so many third parties develop during this era?
4. How might the planks of the Omaha Platform have helped solve farmers' troubles?
5. What factors shaped the conduct and outcome of the election of 1896? How did that contest differ from earlier elections?

Key Terms

Coxey's Army (p. 566)
Farmers' Alliance (p. 563)
Free silver (p. 561)
Granger laws (p. 554)
Greenback Party (p. 554)
Interstate Commerce Act (p. 560)
Interstate Commerce Commission (ICC) (p. 560)
Laissez-faire (p. 556)
Mugwumps (p. 555)
National American Woman Suffrage Association (p. 555)
Omaha Platform (p. 565)
Pendleton Civil Service Act (p. 558)
Populist Party (p. 554)
Prohibition Party (p. 554)
Sherman Antitrust Act (p. 560)
Sound money (p. 561)

PEARSON myhistorylab Connections

Reinforce what you learned in this chapter by studying the many documents, images, maps, review tools, and videos available at **www.myhistorylab.com**.

Read and Review

Study and Review **Study Plan: Chapter 20**

Read the Document

Pendleton Civil Service Act (1883)

Workingman's Amalgamated Sherman Anti-Trust (1893)

William Jennings Bryan, "Cross of Gold" Speech (1896)

The People's Party Platform (1892)

Henry Cabot Lodge, "The Business World vs. the Politicians" (1895)

Proceedings of the Thirteenth Session of the National Grange of the Patrons of Husbandry (1879)

Jacob S. Coxey, "Address of Protest" (1894)

Research and Explore

Read the Document

Personal Journeys Online

From Then to Now Online: Political Parties

Hear the Audio

Hear the audio files for Chapter 20 at **www.myhistorylab.com.**

Currency Reform

EXPLAIN AND DESCRIBE the powerful political lure of currency reform in American presidential campaigns between 1876 and 1900. Where did various political groups and candidates stand on this issue and to whom did they attempt to appeal?

In the late nineteenth century, farmers became dependent upon a complex credit system that generally worked to their disadvantage. In the West, they had to borrow money to finance their purchases of land and machinery; in the South, they were enmeshed in the sharecropping system. Falling crop prices drove them deeper into debt, threatening both their farms and their families. Many favored currency reform to improve their conditions, reasonably regarding inflation as a means of raising crop prices and reducing their debt burden. But government financial policies, restricting paper and silver money and maintaining the gold standard, tended in the opposite direction and seemed to benefit the wealthy classes ("bankers and bondholders") rather than the producing masses. "The wicked financial system of our government," cried Farmers' Alliance leader L.L. Polk of North Carolina, had made agriculture "the helpless victim of the rapacious greed and tyrannical power of gold." Some agrarians supported the subtreasury as a means of creating a democratic paper currency; more remained convinced that money required a metal base and favored free silver coinage. Either policy, combined with banking reform, would mean government regulation of the financial structure to ensure economic opportunity and equal rights for all classes and sections. Supporters of the gold standard were no less fiercely convinced of their own righteousness, dismissing currency reform ideas as "popular delusions, vagaries, and quackeries" and condemning William Jennings Bryan for appealing "to the base instincts of the ignorant or to the misery of the distressed."

We demand a national currency . . .

Populist Platform, 1892

Silver, which has been accepted as coin since the dawn of history, has been demonetized to add to the purchasing power of gold by decreasing the value of all forms of property as well as human labor, and the supply of currency is purposely abridged to fatten usurers, bankrupt enterprise, and enslave industry. A vast conspiracy against mankind has been organized on two continents, and it is rapidly taking possession of the world. If not met and overthrown at once it forebodes terrible social convulsions, the destruction of civilization, or the establishment of an absolute despotism.

We demand a national currency, safe, sound, and flexible issued by the general government only, a full legal tender for all debts, public and private. . . . We demand free and unlimited coinage of silver and gold at the present legal ratio of 16 to 1.

William H. Harvey, *Coin's Financial School, 1893*

It is proposed by the bimetallists to remonetize silver, and add it to the quantity of money that is to be used for measuring the value of all other property. . . .

You increase the value of all property by adding to the number of money units in the land. You make it possible for the debtor to pay his debts; business to start anew, and revivify all the industries of the country, which must remain paralyzed so long as silver as well as all other property is measured by a gold standard. . . .

The money lenders in the United States, who own substantially all our money, have a selfish interest in maintaining the gold standard. They, too, will not yield. . . .

With silver remonetized, and gold at a premium, not one-tenth the hardships could result that now afflict us. . . . The bimetallic standard will make the United States the most prosperous nation on the globe.

This Republican campaign poster of 1896 depicts William McKinley standing on sound money and promising a revival of prosperity. The depression of the 1890s shifted the electorate into the Republican column.

William Jennings Bryan, "Cross of Gold Speech," Democratic National Convention, July 9, 1896

You come to us and tell us that the great cities are in favor of the gold standard. I tell you that the great cities rest upon these broad and fertile prairies. Burn down your cities and leave our farms, and your cities will spring up again as if by magic. But destroy our farms and the grass will grow in the streets of every city in the country. . . .

If they dare to come out in the open field and defend the gold standard as a good thing, we shall fight them to the uttermost, having behind us the producing masses of the nation and the world. Having behind us the commercial interests and the laboring interests and all the toiling masses, we shall answer their demands for a gold standard by saying to them, you shall not press down upon the brow of labor this crown of thorns. You shall not crucify mankind upon a cross of gold.

The *Chicago Tribune* for the Gold Standard, 1896

The enemies of the gold standard are those who do not own any money and have no desire to earn any. Prominent among them are the shiftless, the drunkards, the incurably lazy, the bankrupts, and the debtors who would rather repudiate an obligation than work to pay it. These enemies of the gold standard whom Bryan is rallying under his standard are the enemies also of good government and of law and order.

Bryan asks if the Nation which won its independence from Great Britain must become, a century later, the abject slave of that country by adopting its financial policy of a gold standard. His resort to [such] wretched claptrap appeals to ignorance, prejudice, and passion is evidence of his lack of knowledge or of his contempt for moral decency. He talks as if he did not know that gold has become the international money of mankind and that its use is a badge of civilization, and not an acknowledgement of English supremacy.

The world is full of degenerates of all kinds. It would not be surprising to find among them financial degenerates—men who believe sincerely that the faulty, clumsy currencies of benighted, medieval days are better than any modern civilization can devise. The man who wants the silver standard for its own sake and not in order to cheat someone with it must be a degenerate or an exceedingly ignorant fellow, who does not know that after giving the silver standard a trial for centuries the commercial nations one by one cast it aside for a better standard—gold.

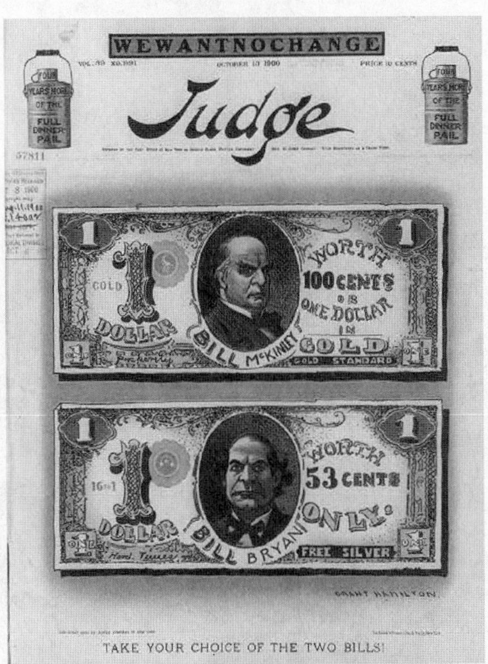

Cartoonist Grant Hamilton emphasizes the free silver issue in this cartoon, criticizing the silver dollar advocated by William Jennings Bryan as "worth 53 cents."

Burn down your cities . . .

21 The Progressive Era

Women march in support of Mother Jones in Trinidad, Colorado. Dramatic tactics and careful organizing like those that marked this parade often helped secure reform in the Progressive Era.

Hear the Audio

Hear the audio files for Chapter 21 at **www.myhistorylab.com**.

THE FERMENT OF REFORM *(page 580)*

WHAT VALUES and beliefs bound progressives together?

REFORMING SOCIETY *(page 586)*

HOW DID progressives respond to the social challenges of industrializing America?

REFORMING POLITICS AND GOVERNMENT *(page 592)*

HOW DID progressives change American politics and government?

THEODORE ROOSEVELT AND THE PROGRESSIVE PRESIDENCY *(page 595)*

HOW DID Theodore Roosevelt envision the power of the president?

WOODROW WILSON AND PROGRESSIVE REFORM *(page 598)*

HOW DID Woodrow Wilson's vision of reform differ from Theodore Roosevelt's?

ONE AMERICAN JOURNEY

In the spring of 1903 I went to Kensington, Pennsylvania, where 75,000 textile workers were on strike. Of this number at least 10,000 were little children. The workers were striking for more pay and shorter hours. Every day little children came into Union Headquarters, some with their hands off, some with the thumb missing, some with their fingers off at the knuckle. They were stooped little things, round shouldered and skinny. Many of them were not over ten years of age. . . .

We assembled a number of boys and girls one morning in Independence Park and from there we arranged to parade with banners to the court house where we would hold a meeting.

A great crowd gathered in the public square in front of the city hall. I put the little boys with their fingers off and hands crushed and maimed on a platform. I held up their mutilated hands and showed them to the crowd and made the statement that Philadelphia's mansions were built on the broken bones, the quivering hearts, and drooping heads of these children. . . .

I [then] decided to go with the children to see President Roosevelt to ask him to have Congress pass a law prohibiting the exploitation of childhood. I thought that President Roosevelt might see these mill children and compare them with his own little ones spending the summer at the seashore at Oyster Bay. . . .

Everywhere [en route] we had meetings, showing with little children the horrors of child labor. . . . [In New York City] I told an immense crowd of the horrors of child labor in the mills . . . and I showed them Gussie Rangnew, a little girl from whom all the childhood had gone. Her face was like an old woman's. Gussie packed stockings in a factory, eleven hours a day for a few cents a day. . . . [I said,] "Fifty years ago there was a cry against slavery and men gave up their lives to stop the selling of black children on the block. Today the white child is sold for two dollars a week to the manufacturers."

. . . We marched down to Oyster Bay but the president refused to see us and he would not answer my letters. But our march had done its work. We had drawn the attention of the nation to the crime of child labor. And while the strike of the textile workers in Kensington was lost and the children driven back to work, not long afterward the Pennsylvania legislature passed a child labor law that kept thousands of children home from the mills.

The Autobiography of Mother Jones, 3rd ed. (Chicago: Kerr Publishing Co., 1977).

Read the **Document** at **www.myhistorylab.com**

Personal Journeys Online

- **Alice Hamilton, *Investigating Industrial Health,* 1943. Hamilton's recollection of her pioneering efforts in Chicago to investigate and improve industrial health conditions.**
- **Al Smith, *Enacting Reform Legislation,* 1929. Smith's account of overcoming opposition to reform laws in the wake of the Triangle Fire in 1911.**

THE SWEET-FACED, WHITE-HAIRED "MOTHER" JONES was nearly 70 years old when she led "the children's crusade" in 1903. Born Mary Harris in Ireland, she had survived famine, emigration, hard labor, and the horrible deaths of her husband and their four children. Indomitable, she had become a celebrated union organizer and powerful orator against what she saw as the economic injustices of America.

The journey of Mother Jones, with Gussie Rangnew and other maimed children, from Kensington, Pennsylvania, to Oyster Bay, New York, was thus just part of her legendary life journey. But it also illustrated critical features of life in the **Progressive Era.** Important movements challenged traditional relationships and attitudes—here involving working conditions, unregulated industrial development, concepts of opportunity and childhood

CHRONOLOGY

1893–1898	Depression grips the nation.
1893	New Zealand establishes woman suffrage.
1894	New Zealand establishes maximum hours and compulsory arbitration.
1898	South Dakota adopts initiative and referendum.
	New Zealand initiates old age pensions.
	National Consumers' League is organized.
1899	Anti-Cigarette League of America is established.
1900	Robert La Follette is elected governor of Wisconsin.
1901	United States Steel Corporation is formed.
	President William McKinley is assassinated; Theodore Roosevelt becomes president.
	Socialist Party of America is organized.
	New York Tenement House Law is enacted.
	Galveston, Texas, initiates the city commission plan.
1902	Antitrust suit is filed against Northern Securities Company.
	McClure's initiates muckraking journalism.
	Mississippi enacts the first direct-primary law.
	National Reclamation Act is passed.
	Roosevelt intervenes in coal strike.
1903	Women's Trade Union League is organized.
1904	National Child Labor Committee is formed.
	Roosevelt is elected president.
1905	Industrial Workers of the World is organized.
1906	Hepburn Act strengthens the Interstate Commerce Commission.
	Meat Inspection Act extends government regulation.
	Pure Food and Drug Act is passed.
1908	*Muller v. Oregon* upholds maximum workday for women.
	William Howard Taft is elected president.
1910	National Association for the Advancement of Colored People is organized.
	Ballinger-Pinchot controversy erupts.
1912	Children's Bureau is established.
	Progressive Party organizes and nominates Roosevelt.
	Woodrow Wilson is elected president.
1913	Sixteenth and Seventeenth Amendments are ratified.
	Underwood-Simmons Tariff Act establishes an income tax.
	Federal Reserve Act creates the Federal Reserve System.
1914	Federal Trade Commission is established.
	Harrison Act criminalizes narcotics.
1915	National Birth Control League is formed.
1916	Keating-Owen Act prohibits child labor.
1917	Congress enacts literacy test for immigrants.
1918	Woman Suffrage is adopted in England.
1919	Eighteenth Amendment is ratified.
1920	Nineteenth Amendment is ratified.

itself—and often met strong resistance and only limited success. "Progressives" seeking change investigated problems, proposed solutions, organized their supporters, and attempted to mobilize public opinion—just as Mother Jones sought to do. And rather than rely only on traditional partisan politics, reformers adopted new political techniques, including lobbying and demonstrating as nonpartisan pressure groups. Reform work begun at the local and state levels—where the campaign against child labor had already met some success—inexorably moved to the national level as the federal government expanded its authority and became the focus of political interest. Finally, Mother Jones's march reveals the exceptional diversity of the progressive movement, for she and her followers were marching, in part, against the seemingly indifferent Theodore Roosevelt, perhaps the most prominent progressive.

The issue of child labor, then, did not define progressivism. Indeed, in a sense, there was no "progressive movement," for progressivism had no unifying organization, central leadership, or consensus on objectives. Instead, it represented the coalescing of different and sometimes even contradictory movements that sought changes in the nation's social, economic, and political life. But reformers did share certain convictions. They believed that industrialization and urbanization had produced serious social disorders, from city slums to corporate abuses. They believed that new ideas and methods were required to correct these problems. In particular, they rejected the ideology of individualism in favor of broader concepts of social responsibility, and they sought to achieve social order through organization and efficiency. Finally, most progressives believed that government itself, as the organized agent of public responsibility, should address social and economic problems.

THE FERMENT OF REFORM

WHAT VALUES and beliefs bound progressives together?

The diversity of progressivism reflected the diverse impulses of reform. Reformers responded to the tensions of industrialization and urbanization by formulating programs according to their own interests and priorities. Nearly every movement for change encountered fierce opposition. But in raising new issues and proposing new ideas, progressives helped America grapple with the problems of industrial society. (See Overview, Major Progressive Organizations and Groups.)

Progressive Era An era in the United States (roughly between 1900 and 1917) in which important movements challenged traditional relationships and attitudes.

The Context of Reform: Industrial and Urban Tensions

The origins of progressivism lay in the crises of the new urban-industrial order that emerged in the late nineteenth century. The severe depression and mass suffering of the 1890s, the labor violence and industrial armies, the political challenges of Populism and an obviously ineffective government shattered the complacency many middle-class Americans had felt about their nation and made them aware of social and economic inequities that rural and working-class families had long recognized. Many Americans began to question the validity of Social Darwinism and the laissez-faire policies that had justified unregulated industrial growth. They began to reconsider the responsibilities of government and, indeed, of themselves for social order and betterment.

Read the **Document**
at **www.myhistorylab.com**
Mother Jones, "The March of the Mill Children" (1903)

Read the **Document**
at **www.myhistorylab.com**
Herbert Croly, Progressive Democracy (1914)

By 1900, returning prosperity had eased the threat of major social violence, but the underlying problems intensified. Big business, which had disrupted traditional economic relationships in the late nineteenth century, suddenly became bigger in a series of mergers between 1897 and 1903, resulting in huge new business combinations. Such gigantic corporations threatened to squeeze opportunities for small firms and workers, dominate markets, and raise social tensions. They also inspired calls for public control.

QUICK REVIEW

Triangle Shirtwaist Fire
- 1911: Fire kills 146 workers.
- Managers had locked the exits.
- The United States had the highest rate of industrial accidents in the world.

Industrial growth affected factory workers most directly. Working conditions were difficult and often dangerous. Wages were minimal; an economist in 1905 calculated that 60 percent of all adult male breadwinners made less than a living wage. Family survival, then, often required women and children to work, often in the lowest paid, most exploited positions. Poor ventilation, dangerous fumes, open machinery, and the absence of safety programs threatened not only workers' health but their lives as well. Such conditions were gruesomely illustrated in 1911, when a fire killed 146 workers, most of them young women, trapped inside the factory of the Triangle Shirtwaist Company in New York because management had locked the exits. The United States had the highest rate of industrial accidents in the world. Half a million workers were injured and 30,000 killed at work each year. These terrible conditions cried out for reform.

Overcome with grief, families of the victims of the Triangle Shirtwaist fire later received from the factory owners $75 for each life lost. Still mourning, family members asked, "Justice, what justice?"

Other Americans saw additional social problems in the continuing flood of immigrants who were transforming America's cities. From 1900 to 1917, more than 14 million immigrants entered the United States. Most of the arrivals were so-called new immigrants from southern and eastern Europe, rather than the British, Irish, Germans, and Scandinavians who had arrived earlier. Several hundred thousand Japanese also arrived, primarily in California, as did increasing numbers of Mexicans. Crowding into urban slums, immigrants overwhelmed municipal sanitation, education, and fire protection services.

OVERVIEW Major Progressive Organizations and Groups

Group	Activity
Social Gospel movement	Urged churches and individuals to apply Christian ethics to social and economic problems
Muckrakers	Exposed business abuses, public corruption, and social evils through investigative journalism
Settlement House movement	Attempted through social work and public advocacy to improve living and working conditions in urban immigrant communities
National Consumers' League (1898)	Monitored businesses to ensure decent working conditions and safe consumer products
Women's Trade Union League (1903)	United workingwomen and their middle-class allies to promote unionization and social reform
National Child Labor Committee (1904)	Campaigned against child labor
Country Life movement	Attempted to modernize rural social and economic conditions according to urban-industrial standards
National American Woman Suffrage Association	Led the movement to give women the right to vote
Municipal reformers	Sought to change the activities and structure of urban government to promote efficiency and control
Conservationists	Favored efficient management and regulation of natural resources rather than uncontrolled development or preservation

Church and Campus

Many groups, drawing from different traditions and inspirations, responded to these economic and social issues. Reform-minded Protestant ministers were especially influential, creating the **Social Gospel movement,** which sought to introduce religious ethics into industrial relations and appealed to churches to meet their social responsibilities. Washington Gladden, a Congregational minister in Columbus, Ohio, was one of the earliest Social Gospelers. Shocked in 1884 by a bloody strike crushed by wealthy members of his own congregation, Gladden began a ministry in working-class neighborhoods that most churches ignored. He endorsed unions and workers' rights and proposed replacing a cruelly competitive wage system with profit sharing.

Social Gospel movement Movement created by reform-minded Protestant ministers seeking to introduce religious ethics into industrial relations and appealing to churches to meet their social responsibilities.

The Social Gospel was part of an emerging liberal movement in American religion. Scholars associated with this movement discredited the literal accuracy of the Bible and emphasized instead its general moral and ethical lessons. As modernists, they abandoned theological dogmatism for a greater tolerance of other faiths and became more interested in social problems. By linking reform with religion, the Social Gospel movement gave progressivism a powerful moral drive that affected much of American life.

The Social Gospel movement provided an ethical justification for government intervention to improve the social order. Scholars in the social sciences also gradually helped turn public attitudes in favor of reform by challenging the laissez-faire views of the Social Darwinists and traditional academics. In *Applied Sociology* (1906), Lester Ward called for social progress through rational planning and government intervention rather than through unrestrained and unpredictable competition. Economists rejected laissez-faire principles in favor of state action to accomplish social evolution. Industrialization, declared economist Richard T. Ely, "has brought to the front a vast number of social problems whose solution is impossible without the united efforts of church, state, and science."

muckraking Journalism exposing economic, social, and political evils, so named by Theodore Roosevelt for its "raking the muck" of American society.

Watch the **Video**

at **www.myhistorylab.com**
Punching the Clock

Read the **Document**

at **www.myhistorylab.com**
Frederick W. Taylor, The Principles of Scientific Management (1911)

QUICK REVIEW

Scientific Management

- Progressive leaders praised the "gospel of efficiency."
- Promoted application of scientific management to government, society, and industry.
- Saw application of scientific method as the key to reform.

QUICK REVIEW

Unions

- American Federation of Labor recruited skilled workers, particularly native-born white males.
- International Ladies Garment Workers Union and Amalgamated Clothing Workers organized garment trades.
- Industrial Workers of the World used innovative tactics and sought to organize a diverse set of workers.

MUCKRAKERS

Journalists also spread reform ideas by developing a new form of investigative reporting known as **muckraking.** Technological innovations had recently made possible the mass circulation of magazines, and editors competed to attract an expanding urban readership. Samuel S. McClure sent his reporters to uncover political and corporate corruption for *McClure's Magazine*. Sensational exposés sold magazines, and soon *Cosmopolitan, Everybody's,* and other journals began publishing investigations of business abuses, dangerous working conditions, and the miseries of slum life.

Muckraking novels also appeared. *The Octopus* (1901), by Frank Norris, dramatized the Southern Pacific Railroad's stranglehold on California's farmers, and *The Jungle* (1906), by Upton Sinclair, exposed the nauseating conditions in Chicago's meatpacking industry. Such muckraking aroused indignant public demands for reform.

THE GOSPEL OF EFFICIENCY

Many progressive leaders believed that efficiency and expertise could control or resolve the disorder of industrial society. President Theodore Roosevelt praised the "gospel of efficiency." Like many other progressives, he admired the success of corporations in applying management techniques to guide economic growth. Drawing from science and technology as well as from the model of the corporation, many progressives attempted to manage or direct change efficiently. They used scientific methods to collect extensive data and relied on experts for analysis and recommendations. "Scientific management," a concept often used interchangeably with "sound business management," seemed the key to eliminating waste and inefficiency in government, society, and industry.

Business leaders especially advocated efficiency, order, and organization. Industrialists were drawn to the ideas of Frederick Taylor, a proponent of scientific management, for cutting factory labor costs. Taylor proposed to increase worker efficiency through imposed work routines, speedups, and mechanization. Workers, Taylor insisted, should "do what they are told promptly and without asking questions. . . . It is absolutely necessary for every man in our organization to become one of a train of gear wheels." By assigning workers simple and repetitive tasks on machines, Taylorization made their skills expendable and enabled managers to control the production, pace of work, and hiring and firing of personnel. Stripped of their influence and poorly paid, factory workers shared little of the wealth generated by industrial expansion and scientific management.

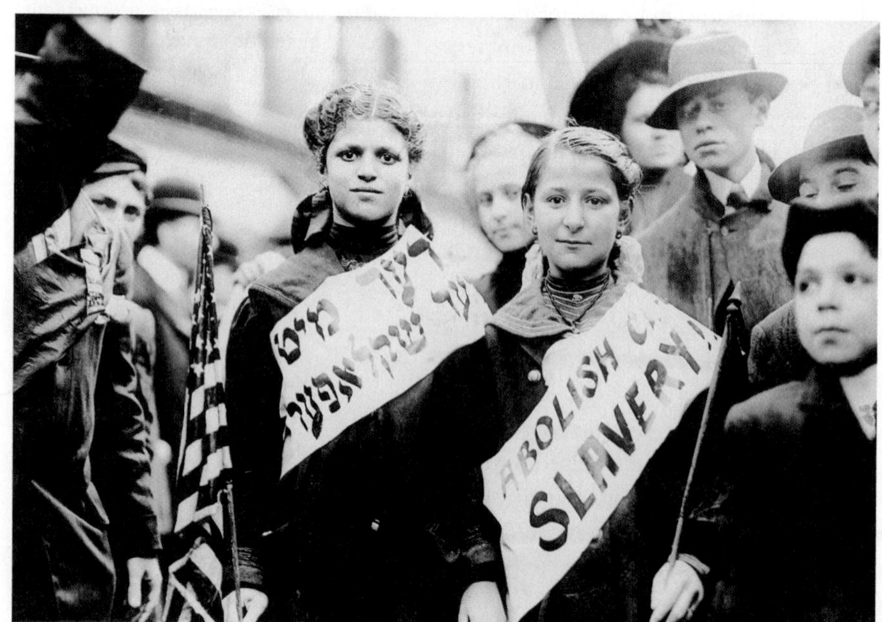

The campaign against child labor attracted passionate support from many Americans. Here two girls, wearing "Abolish Child Slavery" banners in Yiddish and English, participate in a labor parade in New York City on May 1, 1909.

Sophisticated managers of big business saw some forms of government intervention as another way to promote order and efficiency. In particular, they favored regulations that could bring about safer and more stable conditions in society and the economy. Government regulations, they reasoned, could reassure potential consumers, open markets, mandate working conditions that smaller competitors could not provide, or impose systematic procedures that competitive pressures would otherwise undercut.

Labor Demands Its Rights

Industrial workers with different objectives also hastened the ferment of reform. Workers resisted the new rules of efficiency experts and called for improved wages and working conditions and reduced work hours. They and their middle-class sympathizers sought to achieve some of these goals through state intervention, demanding laws to compensate workers injured on the job, curb child labor, and regulate the employment of women.

Workers also organized unions to improve their lot. The American Federation of Labor (AFL) claimed 4 million members by 1920, recruiting mainly skilled workers, particularly native-born white males. New unions organized the factories and sweatshops where most immigrants and women worked. Despite strong employer resistance, the International Ladies Garment Workers Union (1900) and the Amalgamated Clothing Workers (1914) organized the garment trades, developed programs for social and economic reforms, and led their members—mostly young Jewish and Italian women—in spectacular strikes.

A still more radical union tried to organize miners, lumberjacks, and Mexican and Japanese farm workers in the West, black dockworkers in the South, and immigrant factory hands in New England. Founded in 1905, the Industrial Workers of the World (IWW), whose members were known as **"Wobblies,"** used sit-down strikes, sit-ins, and mass rallies, tactics adopted by other industrial unions in the 1930s and the civil rights movement in the 1960s.

Watch the Video
at **www.myhistorylab.com**
Women in the Workplace, 1904

Wobblies Popular name for the members of the Industrial Workers of the World (IWW).

QUICK REVIEW

The Changing Role of Women

- More women working outside the home than ever before.
- In 1910, 25 percent of all workers were women.
- Importance of women in the workplace challenged traditional views of "natural" gender roles.

Extending the Woman's Sphere

Women reformers and their organizations played a key role in progressivism. Women responded not merely to the human suffering caused by industrialization and urbanization but also to related changes in their own status and role. By the early twentieth century, more women than before were working outside the home—in the factories, mills, and sweatshops of the industrial economy and as clerks in stores and offices. In 1910, more than one-fourth of all workers were women, increasing numbers of them married. Their importance in the workforce and participation in unions and strikes challenged assumptions that woman's "natural" role was to be a submissive housewife.

The women's clubs that had begun multiplying in the late nineteenth century became seed-beds of progressive ideas in the early twentieth century. Often founded for cultural purposes, women's clubs soon adopted programs for social reform and gave their members a route to public influence.

Women also joined or created other organizations that pushed beyond the limits of traditional domesticity. "Woman's place is in the home," observed one progressive, but "no longer is the home encompassed by four walls." By threatening healthy and happy homes, urban problems required that women become "social housekeepers" in the community.

Although most progressive women stressed women's special duties and responsibilities as social housekeepers, others began to demand women's equal rights. In 1914, for example, critics of New York's policy of dismissing women teachers who married formed a group called the Feminist Alliance and demanded "the removal of all social, political, economic and other discriminations which are based upon sex, and the award of all rights and duties in all fields on the basis of individual capacity alone." With these new organizations and ideas, women gave important impetus and direction to the reform sentiments of the early twentieth century.

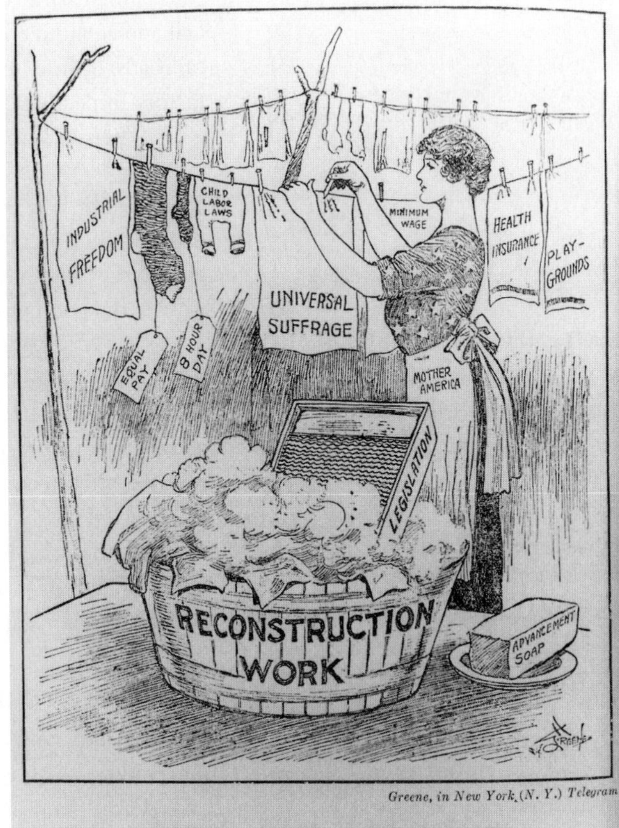

Women's activism was critically important in reconstructing American life during the Progressive Era. Busily engaged in social housekeeping, Mother America uses corrective legislation to clean the dirty laundry of industrialization and injustice.

Transatlantic Influences

A major source of America's progressive impulse lay outside its borders. European nations were already grappling with many of the problems that stemmed from industrialization and urbanization, and they provided guidance, examples, and possible solutions. Progressive reformers soon learned that America's political, economic, and social structures made it necessary to modify, adapt, or even abandon these imported ideas, but their influence was obvious.

International influences were especially strong in the Social Gospel movement, symbolized by William T. Stead, a British social evangelist, whose idea of a "Civic Church" (a partnership of churches and reformers) captured great attention in the United States. Muckrakers not only exposed American problems but looked for foreign solutions. *Everybody's* sent Charles E. Russell around the world in 1905 to describe the social advances in Europe and New Zealand. (See Global Connections, The New Zealand Way.)

By 1912, American consumer activists, trade unionists, factory inspectors, and feminists regularly participated in international conferences on labor legislation, child welfare, social insurance, and housing reform and returned home with new ideas and strategies. State governments organized commissions to analyze European policies and agencies for lessons that might be applicable in the United States.

Socialism

The growing influence of socialist ideas also promoted the spirit of progressivism. Socialism never attracted a large following in the United States, but its criticism of the industrial economy gained increasing attention in the early twentieth century. American socialists condemned social and economic inequities, criticized limited government, and demanded public ownership of railroads, utilities, and communications. They also campaigned for tax reforms, better housing, factory inspections, and recreational facilities for all.

The most prominent socialist was the dynamic and engaging Eugene V. Debs. An Indiana labor leader who had converted to socialism while imprisoned for his role in the 1894 Pullman strike, Debs had evangelical energy and a generous spirit. He decried what he saw as the dehumanization produced by industrial capitalism and hoped for an egalitarian society where everyone would have the opportunity "to develop the best there is in him for his own good as well as the good of society."

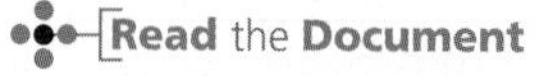
Read the **Document**
at **www.myhistorylab.com**
Eugene V. Debs, "The Outlook for Socialism in America" (1900)

Hear the **Audio**
at **www.myhistorylab.com**
The Speech That Sent Debs to Jail

In 1901, Debs helped organize the Socialist Party of America; thereafter, he worked tirelessly to attract followers to a vision of socialism deeply rooted in American political and religious traditions. In the next decade, the party won many local elections, especially in Wisconsin and New York, where it drew support from German and Russian immigrants, and in Oklahoma, where it attracted poor tenant farmers.

Most progressives considered socialist ideas too drastic. Nevertheless, socialists contributed importantly to the reform ferment, not only by providing support for reform initiatives but often also by prompting progressives to push for changes to undercut increasingly attractive radical alternatives.

Opponents of Reform

fundamentalists Religious conservatives who believe in the literal accuracy and divine inspiration of the Bible.

Not all Americans supported progressive reforms. Social Gospelers faced opposition from Protestant traditionalists emphasizing what they termed fundamental beliefs. Particularly strong among evangelical denominations with rural roots, these **fundamentalists** stressed personal salvation rather than social reform. Indeed, the urban and industrial crises that inspired Social Gospelers to preach reform drove many evangelical leaders to endorse social and political conservatism. The evangelist Billy Sunday condemned the Social Gospel as "godless social service nonsense."

Business interests, angered by exposés of corporate abuse and corruption, attacked the muckrakers. Business groups such as the American Bankers' Association accused muckrakers of

GLOBAL CONNECTIONS

The New Zealand Way

In its very name, the Progressive Era seems characteristically American, but its major developments were actually part of a worldwide phenomenon in which the peoples of many different nations promoted significant reforms, especially through the expansion of government responsibility and power. While Europeans provided an important range of reform ideas and models for Americans, it was often New Zealand, described by one muckraker as the "practical utopia of the South Seas," that "blazed the world's way" in social and economic reforms.

Small, rural, sparsely populated, only slightly industrialized, and still a colony of Great Britain, New Zealand might seem an unlikely candidate to lead progressive reform, but one American minister predicted in 1900 that "we fool Americans will go on for fifty or seventy-five years before we . . . undertake what they have already achieved in New Zealand." New Zealanders were less driven by a desire to correct the evils of industrialization and urbanization—poverty, sweatshops, slums, labor exploitation, social conflict—than by a determination to prevent their emergence in the first place. As the charismatic Liberal leader Richard Seddon declared, "If we deal with [these problems] now, the curse of the older countries will never come to New Zealand."

With the election of a Liberal government in 1891, New Zealand launched two decades of reform. It began the serious regulation of working conditions in 1891. In 1894 the General Assembly mandated regular factory inspections and established maximum hours, first for women and then for men, and prohibited child labor in factories. Other laws in the 1890s established minimum wages for women. The Industrial Conciliation and Arbitration Act of 1894 both encouraged unionization and required compulsory arbitration to deal with industrial disputes and ensure social peace and progress. A model system of workers' compensation was established in 1901.

New Zealand also pioneered in political and social reform. In 1893 it became the first country to establish woman suffrage in national elections. With one member of the parliament reasoning that "it is the duty of the State to make proper provision for the aged," New Zealand initiated old age pensions in 1898. Early in the twentieth century it expanded state-funded, rather than contributory, pensions to cover widows with children, injured miners, and other groups. Beginning in 1905, it developed public housing programs, providing first rental housing for low-income families and then government loans for the purchase of homes. The Public Health Act of 1900 initiated a series of laws expanding government responsibility for proper sanitation, safe water, vaccinations, and the regulation of food and drugs.

New Zealand reformers urged the United States to follow the "New Zealand Way" and adopt these and other reforms, and many American progressives did look to that small country for guidance. "If a British colony dares to lead," noted one progressive journalist, "surely it is not visionary to expect our Republic to fall in line."

- What economic, social, and political factors might explain why progressive reform emerged more slowly and less completely in the United States than in New Zealand?

promoting socialism. Major corporations like Standard Oil created public relations bureaus to improve their image and identify business, not its critics, with the public interest. Advertising boycotts discouraged magazines from running critical stories, and credit restrictions forced some muckraking journals to suspend publication. By 1910, the heyday of muckraking was over.

Labor unions likewise encountered resistance. Led by the National Association of Manufacturers, business groups denounced unions as corrupt and radical, hired thugs to disrupt them, organized strikebreaking agencies, and used blacklists to eliminate union activists. The antiunion campaign peaked in Ludlow, Colorado, in 1914, when John D. Rockefeller's Colorado Fuel and Iron Company used armed guards and the state militia to shoot and burn striking workers and their families. The courts aided employers by issuing injunctions against strikes and prohibiting unions from using boycotts, one of their most effective weapons.

Progressives campaigning for government intervention and regulation also met stiff resistance. Many Americans objected to what they considered unwarranted interference in private economic matters. Again, the courts often supported these attitudes. In *Lochner v. New York*

QUICK REVIEW

Opponents of Reform

- Protestant fundamentalists.
- Business interests.
- Antiunion forces.

(1905), the Supreme Court even overturned a maximum-hours law on the grounds that it deprived employers and employees of their "freedom of contract." Progressives continually struggled against such opponents, and progressive achievements were limited by the persistence and influence of their adversaries.

REFORMING SOCIETY

HOW DID progressives respond to the social challenges of industrializing America?

With their varied motives and objectives, progressives worked to transform society by improving living conditions, educational opportunities, family life, and social and industrial relations. (See Overview, Major Laws and Constitutional Amendments of the Progressive Era.) They sought what they called social justice, but their plans for social reform sometimes also smacked of social control. Organized women dominated the movement to reform society, but they were supported, depending on the goal, by Social Gospel ministers, social scientists, urban immigrants, labor unions, and even some conservatives eager to regulate personal behavior.

W WHERE TO LEARN MORE

Hull House, Chicago, Illinois
http://www.uic.edu/jaddams/hull/

Settlement Houses and Urban Reform

The spearheads for social reform were settlement houses—community centers in urban immigrant neighborhoods. Reformers created 400 settlement houses, largely modeled after Hull House in Chicago, founded in 1889 by Jane Addams. Most were led and staffed primarily by middle-class young women, seeking to alleviate poverty and do useful professional work when most careers were closed to them. Settlement work did not immediately violate prescribed gender roles because it initially focused on the "woman's sphere"—family, education, domestic skills, and cultural "uplift."

However, settlement workers soon saw that the root problem for immigrants was widespread poverty that required more than changes in individual behavior. Unlike earlier reformers, they regarded many of the evils of poverty as products of the social environment rather than of moral weakness. Thus, settlement workers campaigned for stricter building codes to improve slums, better urban sanitation systems to enhance public health, public parks to revive the urban environment, and laws to protect women and children.

Their crusades for sanitation and housing reform demonstrated the impact that social reformers often had on urban life. Settlement worker Mary McDowell became known as the "Garbage Lady" for her success in improving Chicago's massive environmental problems. Similarly, Lawrence Veiller was convinced by his work at the University Settlement in New York City that "the improvement of the homes of the people was the starting point for everything." Based on the findings of settlement workers, Veiller drafted a new housing code limiting the size of tenements and requiring toilet facilities, ventilation, and fire protection. In 1901, the New York Tenement House Law became a model for other cities.

Julia Lathrop, Jane Addams, and Mary McDowell in Washington, DC, in 1913. Important figures in Chicago settlement houses, these women gained national influence by expanding their activities to encompass a wide range of reform efforts.

Protective Legislation for Women and Children

While settlement workers initially undertook private efforts to improve society, many reformers eventually concluded that only government intervention could achieve social justice. The National Child Labor Committee, organized in 1904, led the campaign to curtail child labor (see Figure 21–1). Reformers documented the problem with extensive investigations and also benefited from the public outrage stirred by Mother Jones's "children crusade" and by socialist John Spargo's muckraking book *The Bitter Cry*

OVERVIEW Major Laws and Constitutional Amendments of the Progressive Era

Legislation	Effect
New York Tenement House Law (1901)	Established a model housing code for safety and sanitation
Newlands Act (1902)	Provided for federal irrigation projects
Hepburn Act (1906)	Strengthened the Interstate Commerce Commission
Pure Food and Drug Act (1906)	Regulated the production and sale of food and drug products
Meat Inspection Act (1906)	Authorized federal inspection of meat products
Sixteenth Amendment (1913)	Authorized a federal income tax
Seventeenth Amendment (1913)	Mandated the direct popular election of senators
Underwood-Simmons Tariff Act (1913)	Lowered tariff rates and levied the first regular federal income tax
Federal Reserve Act (1913)	Established the Federal Reserve System to supervise banking and provide a national currency
Federal Trade Commission Act (1914)	Established the FTC to oversee business activities
Harrison Act (1914)	Regulated the distribution and use of narcotics
Smith-Lever Act (1914)	Institutionalized the county agent system
Keating-Owen Act (1916)	Indirectly prohibited child labor
Eighteenth Amendment (1919)	Instituted prohibition
Nineteenth Amendment (1920)	Established woman suffrage

of the Children (1906). In 1900, most states had no minimum working age; by 1914, every state but one had such a law. Effective regulation, however, required national action, for many state laws were weak or poorly enforced.

Social reformers also lobbied for laws regulating the wages, hours, and working conditions of women and succeeded in having states from New York to Oregon pass maximum-hours legislation. After the Supreme Court upheld such laws in *Muller v. Oregon* (1908), 39 states enacted new or stronger laws on women's maximum hours between 1909 and 1917. Eight midwestern and western states authorized commissions to set minimum wages for women, but few other states followed.

Protective legislation for women posed a troubling issue for reformers. In California, for example, middle-class clubwomen favored protective legislation on the grounds of women's presumed weakness. They wanted to preserve "California's potential motherhood." More radical progressives, as in the socialist-led Women's Trade Union League of Los Angeles, supported such legislation to help secure economic independence and equality in the labor market for women, increase the economic strength of the working class, and serve as a precedent for laws improving conditions for all workers.

Progressive Era lawmakers adopted the first viewpoint. They limited protective legislation to measures reflecting the belief that

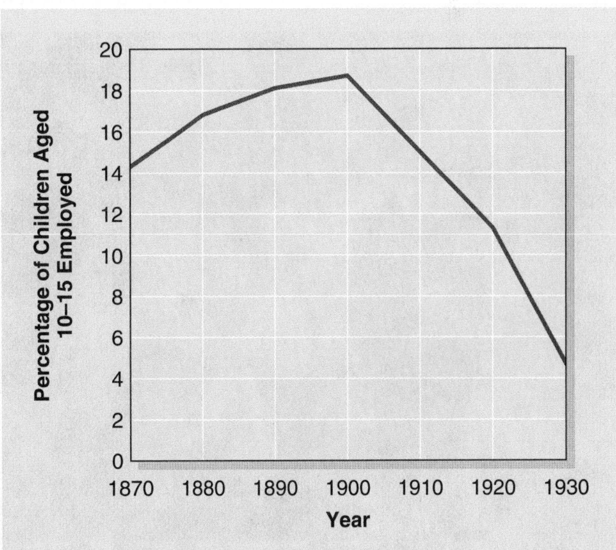

FIGURE 21–1 **Child Labor, 1870–1930** Nearly 2 million children worked in factories and fields in 1900, twice as many as in 1870. Progressives' efforts to curtail child labor through laws for compulsory education and a minimum working age encountered resistance, and change came slowly.

Data Source: U.S. Bureau of the Census.

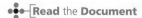

Read the Document
at **www.myhistorylab.com**
Jane Addams, from Twenty Years at Hull House (1910)

women needed paternalist protection, even by excluding them from certain occupations. Laws establishing a minimum wage for women, moreover, usually set a wage level below subsistence rates. Rather than ensuring women's economic independence, then, protective legislation in practice reinforced women's subordinate place in the labor force.

Social justice reformers forged the beginnings of the welfare state in further legislation. Prompted by both humanitarian and paternalistic urgings, many states began in 1910 to provide "mothers' pensions" to indigent widows with dependent children. Twenty-one states, led by Wisconsin in 1911, enacted workers' compensation programs, ending the custom of holding workers themselves liable for injuries on the job.

Compared to the social insurance programs in western Europe, however, these were feeble responses to the social consequences of industrialization. Proposals for health insurance, unemployment insurance, and old-age pension programs went nowhere. Business groups and other conservative interests curbed the movement toward state responsibility for social welfare.

Reshaping Public Education

Watch the Video
at **www.myhistorylab.com**
What Was the Progressive Education Movement?

Concerns about child labor overlapped with increasing attention to the public schools. The rapid influx of immigrants, as well as the demands of the new corporate workplace, generated interest in education not only as a means of advancement but also as a tool for assimilation and the training of future workers.

Between 1880 and 1920, compulsory school attendance laws, kindergartens, age-graded elementary schools, professional training for teachers, vocational education, parent-teacher associations, and school nurses became standard elements in American education. School reformers believed these measures to be both educationally sound and important for countering slum environments. Others supported the kindergarten as "the earliest opportunity to catch the little Russian, the little Italian, the little German, Pole, Syrian, and the rest and begin to make good American citizens of them."

QUICK REVIEW

Public Education

- Concern about child labor overlapped with attention to public education.
- Widespread reforms carried out between 1880 and 1920.
- Public education in the South lagged behind the North.

Public education in the South lagged behind the North. Northern philanthropy and southern reformers brought some improvements after 1900, as per capita expenditures for education doubled, school terms were extended, and high schools spread across the region. But the South frittered away its limited resources on a segregated educational system that shortchanged both races. Black southerners particularly suffered, for the new programs increased the disparity in funding for white and black schools. South Carolina spent 12 times as much per white pupil as per black pupil.

The famous photographer Lewis Hine used his camera to document child labor. The 11-year-old boys at this North Carolina textile mill in 1908 earned sixty cents a day.

Racism also underlay important changes in the schooling of Native Americans. The earlier belief that education would promote equality and facilitate assimilation gave way to a conviction that Indians were inferior and fit merely for manual labor. Educators now rejected the notion of a common school education for Indian children in favor of manual training that would enable Indians to fill menial jobs and whites to "turn their attention to more intellectual employments." Educators also renounced the practice of integrating Indian children into previously all-white classrooms, a policy begun in 1891.

Challenging Gender Restrictions

Most reformers held fairly conservative, moralistic views about sexuality and gender roles, but a small group of influential women sharply challenged conventional ideas about the social role of women. In critiquing women's subordinate status in society and articulating the case for full female equality, these women began self-consciously to refer to themselves as "feminists."

Read the **Document** at **www.myhistorylab.com** *Charlotte Perkins Gilman, "If I Were a Man" (1914)*

In *Women and Economics* (1898) and subsequent writings, Charlotte Perkins Gilman maintained that a communally organized society, with cooperative kitchens, nurseries, laundries, and housekeeping run by specialists, would free women from domestic drudgery and enable them to fulfill productive roles in the larger society while being happier wives and better mothers.

Read the **Document** at **www.myhistorylab.com** *Emma Goldman, Anarchism and Other Essays (1917)*

Emma Goldman, a Russian immigrant, was more of an activist in seeking woman's emancipation. A charismatic speaker (and celebrated anarchist), she delivered lectures attacking marriage as legalized prostitution rather than a partnership of independent equals and advocating birth control as a means to willing and "healthy motherhood and happy child-life."

Margaret Sanger succeeded where Goldman could not in establishing the modern birth control movement. A public-health nurse and an IWW organizer, she soon made the struggle for reproductive rights her personal crusade. Sanger saw in New York's immigrant neighborhoods the plight of poor women worn out from repeated pregnancies or injured or dead from self-induced knitting-needle abortions. Despite federal and state laws against contraceptives, Sanger began promoting birth control as a way to avert such tragedies. Prohibiting contraceptives meant "enforced motherhood," Sanger declared. "Women cannot be on an equal footing with men until they have full and complete control over their reproductive function."

QUICK REVIEW

Margaret Sanger

- Crusader for reproductive rights.
- Argued that reproductive rights were essential to goal of equality for women.
- Forced to leave country after indictment for distributing information about contraception.

Sanger's crusade attracted support from many women's and labor groups, but it also infuriated those who regarded birth control as a threat to the family and morality. Indicted for distributing information about contraception, Sanger fled to Europe. Other women took up the cause, forming the National Birth Control League in 1915 to campaign for the repeal of laws restricting access to contraceptive information and devices.

Reforming Country Life

Although most progressives focused on the city, others sought to reform rural life, both to modernize its social and economic conditions and to integrate it more fully into the larger society. They worked to improve rural health and sanitation, to replace inefficient one-room schools with modern consolidated ones under professional control, and to extend new roads and communication services into the countryside. To further these goals, President Theodore Roosevelt created the Country Life Commission in 1908. The country lifers had a broad program for social and economic change, involving expanded government functions, activist government agencies staffed by experts, and the professionalization of rural social services.

Agricultural scientists, government officials, and many business interests also sought to promote efficient, scientific, and commercial agriculture. A key innovation was the county-agent system: The U.S. Department of Agriculture and business groups placed an agent in each county to teach farmers new techniques and to encourage changes in the rural social values that had previously spawned the Populist radicalism that most progressives decried. Few farmers, however, welcomed these efforts. Most farmers believed that their problems stemmed, not from rural life, but from industrial society and its nefarious trusts, banks, and middlemen. Rural Americans did not want their lives revolutionized.

Even so, rural people were drawn into the larger urban-industrial society during the Progressive Era. Government agencies, agricultural colleges, and railroads and banks steadily tied farmers to urban markets. Telephones and rural free delivery of mail lessened countryside isolation but quickened the spread of city values. Improved roads and the coming of the automobile eliminated many rural villages and linked farm families directly with towns and cities. Consolidated schools wiped out the social center of rural neighborhoods and carried children out of their communities, eventually encouraging an ever-growing migration to the city.

Moral Crusades and Social Control

Moral reform movements, although often appearing misguided or unduly coercive today, generally reflected the progressive hope to protect people in a debilitating environment. In practice, however, these efforts to shape society tended toward social control. Moreover, these efforts often meshed with the restrictive attitudes that conservative Americans held about race, religion, immigration, and morality. The result was widespread attempts to restrict certain groups and control behavior.

QUICK REVIEW

Opposition to Immigration

- Nativists in California wanted to restrict the entry of Japanese and Mexicans.
- The national debate focused on immigrants from southern and eastern Europe.
- Some nativists demanded the "Americanization" of immigrants.

Controlling immigrants. Many Americans wanted to limit immigration for racist reasons. Nativist agitation in California prompted the federal government to secure restrictions on Japanese immigration in 1907. Californians, including local progressives, also hoped to curtail the migration of Mexicans.

Nationally, public debate focused on restricting the flow of new immigrants from southern and eastern Europe. Some labor leaders believed that immigration held down wages and impeded unionization; many sociologists thought it created serious social problems; other Americans disliked the newcomers on religious, cultural, or ethnic grounds. Many backed their prejudice with a distorted interpretation of Darwinism, labeling the Slavic and Mediterranean peoples "inferior races."

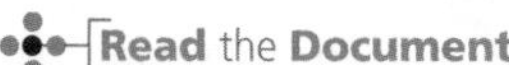

at **www.myhistorylab.com**
Exploring America: Americanization

Other nativists demanded the "Americanization" of immigrants already in the country. The Daughters of the American Revolution sought to inculcate loyalty, patriotism, and conservative values. Settlement workers and Social Gospelers promoted a gentler kind of Americanization through English classes and home mission campaigns, but they too attempted to transfer their own values to the newcomers.

prohibition A ban on the production, transportation and sale of liquor, achieved temporarily through state laws and the Eighteenth Amendment.

Prohibition. Closely linked to progressives' worries about immigrants was their campaign for **prohibition.** This movement engaged many of the progressives' basic impulses. Social workers saw liquor as a cause of crime, poverty, and family violence; employers blamed it for causing industrial accidents and inefficiency; Social Gospel ministers condemned the "spirit born of hell" because it impaired moral judgment and behavior. But also important was native-born Americans' fear of new immigrants—"the dangerous classes, who are readily dominated by the saloon." Many immigrants, in fact, viewed liquor and the neighborhood saloon as vital parts of daily life, and so prohibition became a focus of nativist hostility, cultural conflict, and Americanization pressures. In the South, racism also figured prominently. Alexander McKelway, the southern secretary for the National Child Labor Committee, endorsed prohibition as a way to maintain social order and white supremacy.

Protestant fundamentalists also stoutly supported prohibition, working through the Anti-Saloon League, founded in 1893. Their nativism and antiurban bias surfaced in demands for prohibition to prevent the nation's cities from lapsing into "raging mania, disorder, and anarchy."

With these varied motivations, prohibitionists campaigned for local and state laws against the manufacture and sale of alcohol. Beginning in 1907, they proved increasingly successful, especially in the South, Midwest, and Far West. By 1917, 26 states had prohibition laws. Congress then approved the **Eighteenth Amendment,** which made prohibition the law of the land by 1920.

Eighteenth Amendment Constitutional revision, adopted in 1919, that prohibited the production and sale of alcohol in the United States.

Less controversial were drives to control or prohibit narcotics and cigarettes. Patent (over-the-counter) medicines commonly contained opium, heroin, and cocaine (popularly used for hay fever), and physicians known as "dope doctors" openly dispensed drugs to paying customers. Fears that addiction was spreading in "the fallen and lower classes"—and particularly among black people and immigrants—prompted Congress in 1914 to pass the Harrison Act, prohibiting the distribution and use of narcotics for other than medicinal purposes. The Anti-Cigarette League of America, organized in 1899 and having 300,000 members by 1901, led the charge against cigarettes. Many states soon restricted cigarettes, but such laws were rarely enforced and often repealed within a few years.

The Flanner House, a black settlement house in Indianapolis, provided the black community with many essential services, including health care. In addition to this baby clinic, pictured in 1918, it established a tuberculosis clinic at a time when the city's public hospitals refused to treat black citizens afflicted with the disease.

Suppressing prostitution. Reformers also sought to suppress the "social evil" of prostitution. Like crowded slums, sweatshops, and child labor, the "vice districts" where prostitution flourished were seen as part of the exploitation and disorder in the industrial cities. Women's low wages as factory workers and domestic servants explained some of the problem, as a muckraking article entitled "The Daughters of the Poor" pointed out. But nativism spurred public concern, as when New York officials insisted that most prostitutes and brothel owners, some of whom "have been seducers of defenseless women all their lives," were foreign-born.

The response to prostitution was typical of progressivism: investigation and exposure, a reliance upon experts—boards of health, medical groups, clergy—for recommendations, and enactment of new laws. The progressive solution emerged in state and municipal action abolishing the "red light" districts previously tolerated and in a federal law, the Mann Act of 1910, prohibiting the interstate transport of women "for immoral purposes."

For Whites Only?

Racism permeated the Progressive Era. In the South, progressivism was built on black disfranchisement and segregation. Like most white southerners, progressives believed that racial control was necessary for social order and that it enabled reformers to address other social problems. Such reformers also invoked racism to gain popular support for their objectives. In Georgia, for instance, child labor reformers warned that while white children worked in the Piedmont textile mills, black children were going to school: Child labor laws and compulsory school attendance laws were necessary to maintain white supremacy.

Governors Hoke Smith of Georgia and James Vardaman, "the White Chief," of Mississippi typified the link between racism and reform in the South. These men supported progressive reforms but also viciously attacked black rights. Their racist demagogy incited antiblack violence throughout the South.

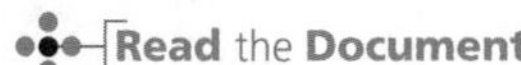

Read the Document
at **www.myhistorylab.com**
Platform Adopted by the National Negro Committee (1909)

Even in the North, race relations deteriorated. Civil rights laws went unenforced, restaurants and hotels excluded black customers, and schools were segregated. A reporter in Pennsylvania found that "this disposition to discriminate against Negroes has greatly increased within the past decade." Antiblack race riots exploded in New York in 1900 and in Springfield, Illinois—Abraham Lincoln's hometown—in 1908.

Hear the Audio
at **www.myhistorylab.com**
The Progress of Colored Women by Mary Church Terrell

Black activism. Although most white progressives promoted or accepted racial discrimination, and most black southerners had to adapt to it, black progressive activism was growing. Even in the South, some African Americans struggled to improve conditions. In Atlanta, for example, black women created progressive organizations and established settlement houses, kindergartens, and daycare centers.

Hear the Audio
at **www.myhistorylab.com**
Crisis Magazine by W.E.B. Du Bois

In the North, African Americans more openly criticized discrimination and rejected Booker T. Washington's philosophy of accommodation. Ida Wells-Barnett, the crusading journalist who had fled the South for Chicago (see Chapter 17), became nationally prominent for her militant protests. She fought fiercely against racial injustices, especially school segregation, agitated for woman suffrage, and organized kindergartens and settlement houses for Chicago's black migrants.

Niagara Movement African American group organized in 1905 to promote racial integration, civil and political rights, and equal access to economic opportunity.

Read the Document at **www.myhistorylab.com** *The Niagara Movement, Declaration of Principles (1905)*

Still more important was W. E. B. Du Bois, who campaigned tirelessly against all forms of racial discrimination. In 1905, Du Bois and other black activists met in Niagara Falls, Canada, to make plans to promote political and economic equality. In 1910, this **Niagara Movement** joined with a small group of white reformers, including Jane Addams, to organize the National Association for the Advancement of Colored People. The NAACP sought to overthrow segregation and establish equal justice and educational opportunities. As its director of publicity and research, Du Bois launched an influential magazine, *The Crisis*, to shape public opinion. "Agitate," he counseled, "protest, reveal the truth, and refuse to be silenced." By 1918, the NAACP had 44,000 members in 165 branches.

REFORMING POLITICS AND GOVERNMENT

HOW DID progressives change American politics and government?

Progressives of all kinds worked to reform politics and government. But their political activism was motivated by different concerns, and they sometimes pursued competing objectives. Many wanted to change procedures and institutions to promote greater democracy and responsibility. Others hoped to improve the efficiency of government, eliminate corruption, or increase their own influence. All justified their objectives as necessary to adapt the political system to the nation's new needs.

Read the Document at **www.myhistorylab.com** *Helen M. Todd, "Getting Out the Vote" (1911)*

Woman Suffrage

One of the most important achievements of the era was woman suffrage. The movement had begun in the mid-nineteenth century, but suffragists had been frustrated by the prevailing belief that women's proper sphere was the home and the family. Males dominated the public sphere, including voting. Woman suffrage, especially when championed as a step toward women's equality, seemed to challenge the natural order of society, and it generated much opposition, not only among men but among traditionalist-minded women as well.

Carrying ballot boxes on a stretcher to ridicule American pretensions to a healthy democracy without woman suffrage, these activists marched in a dramatic parade in New York City in 1915. Combining such tactics with traditional appeals to patriotism and women's moral purity, woman suffragists eventually achieved the greatest democratic reform of the Progressive Era.

Most women progressives viewed suffrage as the key issue of the period. Already taking active leadership in broad areas of public affairs—especially by confronting and publicizing social problems and then lobbying legislators and other officials to adopt their proposed solutions—they thought it ridiculous to be barred from the ballot box. But most of all, the vote meant power, both to convince politicians to take seriously their demands for social reforms and to participate fully in electoral as in other forms of politics, thereby advancing the status of women.

In the early twentieth century, suffragists began to outflank their traditional opposition. Under a new generation of leaders, such as Carrie Chapman Catt and Harriot Stanton Blatch, they adopted activist tactics, including parades, mass meetings, and "suffrage tours" by automobile. They also organized by political districts and attracted workingwomen and labor unions. By 1917, the National American Woman Suffrage Association had over 2 million members.

Some suffrage leaders adopted new arguments to gain more support. Rather than insisting on the justice of woman suffrage or emphasizing equal rights, they spoke of the special moral and maternal instincts women could bring to politics if allowed to vote. Many suffragists, particularly among working-class groups, remained committed to the larger possibilities they saw in suffrage, but the new image of the movement increased public support by appealing to conventional views of women.

Gradually, the suffrage movement began to prevail (see Map 21–1). In 1910, Washington became the first state since the mid-1890s to approve woman suffrage, followed by California in 1911 and Arizona, Kansas, and Oregon in 1912. Suffragists also mounted actions to revive interest in a federal constitutional amendment to grant women the vote, and women sent petitions and organized pilgrimages to Washington from across the country. By 1919, thirty-nine states had established full or partial woman suffrage, and Congress finally approved an amendment. Ratified by the states in 1920, the **Nineteenth Amendment** marked a critical advance in political democracy.

Read the Document at **www.myhistorylab.com** *Jane Addams, "Ballots Necessary for Women" (1906)*

QUICK REVIEW

Votes for Women

- Woman suffrage movement began in the mid-nineteenth century.
- Early-twentieth-century leaders adopted activist tactics.
- Nineteenth Amendment ratified in 1920.

Nineteenth Amendment Constitutional revision that in 1920 established women citizens' right to vote.

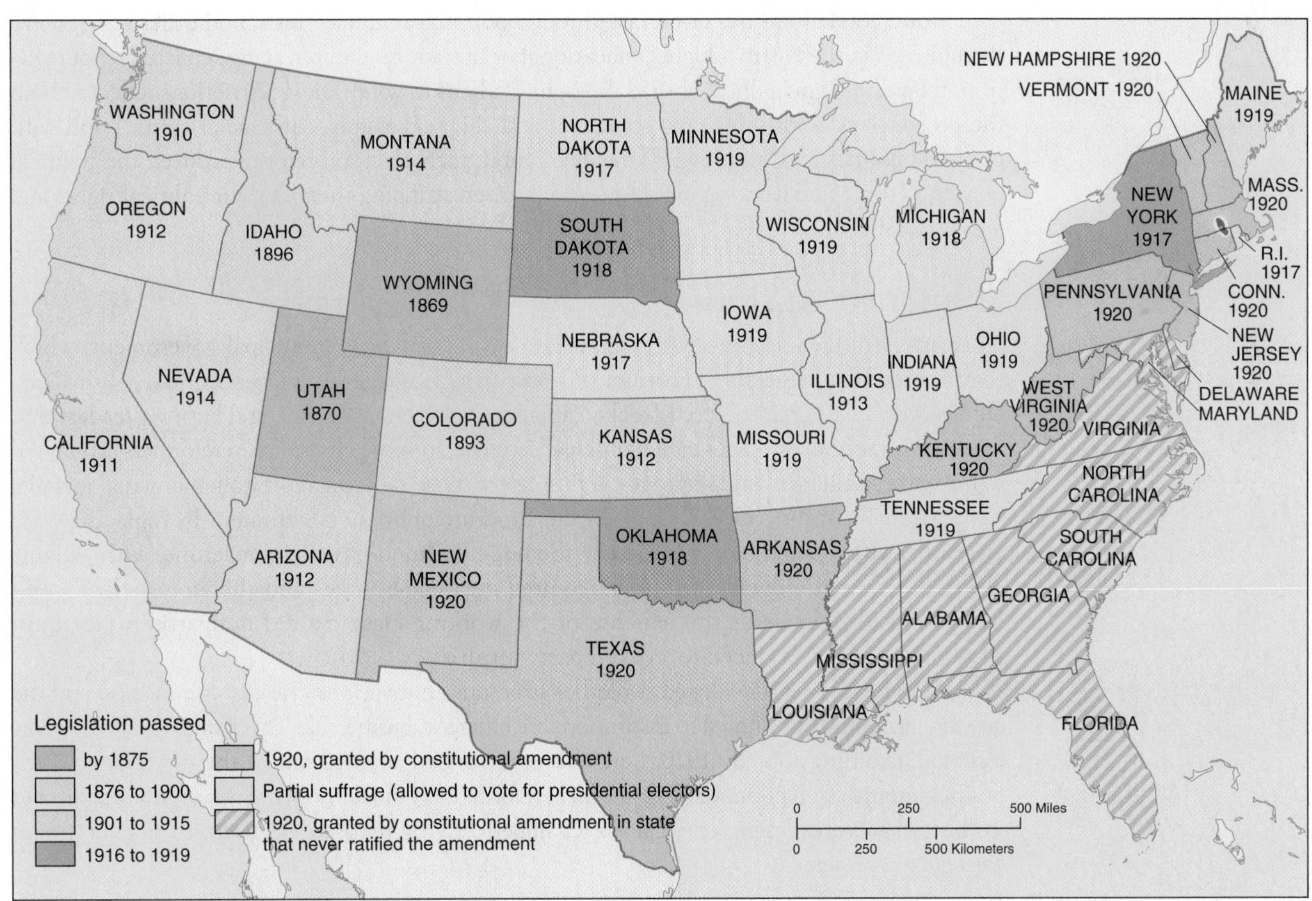

MAP 21–1 **Woman Suffrage in the United States before the Ratification of the Nineteenth Amendment** Beginning with Wyoming in 1869, woman suffrage slowly gained acceptance in the West, but women in the South and much of the East got the ballot only when the Nineteenth Amendment was ratified in 1920.

How might you explain the relatively early dates at which women in the West got the right to vote? Why was woman suffrage slower in coming to the East and South?

ELECTORAL REFORM

Australian ballot Secret voting and the use of official ballots rather than party tickets.

Other electoral reforms changed the election process and the meaning of political participation. The so-called **Australian ballot** adopted by most states during the 1890s provided for secret voting, freeing voters from intimidation and discouraging vote buying and other corruption.

Government responsibility for the ballot soon led to public regulation of other parts of the electoral process previously controlled by parties. Beginning with Mississippi in 1902, nearly every state provided for direct primaries to remove nominations from the boss-ridden caucus and convention system. Many states also reformed campaign practices.

These reforms weakened the influence of political parties. Their decreasing ability to mobilize voters was reflected in a steady decline in voter participation, from 79 percent in 1896 to 49 percent in 1920 (see Figure 20–1). These developments had ominous implications, for parties and voting had traditionally linked ordinary Americans to their government. As parties slowly contracted, nonpartisan organizations and pressure groups, promoting narrower objectives, gained influence. Many of these special-interest groups represented the same middle- or upper-class interests that had led the attack on parties. Their organized lobbying would steadily give them greater influence over government and contribute to the declining popular belief in the value of voting or participation in politics.

Disfranchisement more obviously undermined American democracy. In the South, Democrats—progressive and conservative alike—eliminated not only black voters but also many poor white voters from the electorate through poll taxes, literacy tests, and other restrictions. Republicans in the North adopted educational or literacy tests in ten states, enacted strict registration laws, and gradually abolished the right of aliens to vote. These restrictions reflected both the progressives' anti-immigrant prejudices and their obsessions with social control and with purifying politics and "improving" the electorate. Such electoral reforms reduced the political power of ethnic and working-class Americans, often stripping them of their political rights and means of influence.

QUICK REVIEW

Municipal Reform

- Urban reformers sought to break alliances between city bosses and business leaders.
- Urban reformers developed the concept of the city commission and the city manager.
- Business groups often promoted such structural reforms.

MUNICIPAL REFORM

Antiparty attitudes also affected progressives' efforts to reform municipal government, which they regarded as inefficient and corrupt, at least partly because of the power of urban political machines. Muckrakers had exposed crooked alliances between city bosses and business leaders that resulted in wasteful or inadequate municipal services. In some cities, urban reformers attempted to break these alliances and improve conditions for those suffering most from municipal misrule.

More elitist progressives changed the structure of urban government by replacing ward elections, which could be controlled by the neighborhood-based city machine, with at-large elections. To win citywide elections required greater resources and therefore helped swell middle-class influence at the expense of the working class. So did nonpartisan elections, which reformers introduced to weaken party loyalties.

Urban reformers developed two other structural innovations: the city commission and the city manager. Both attempted to institutionalize efficient, businesslike government staffed by professional administrators. By 1920, hundreds of cities had adopted one of the new plans, which business groups often promoted. Again, then, reform often shifted political power from ethnic and working-class voters, represented however imperfectly by partisan elections, to smaller groups with greater resources.

PROGRESSIVE STATE GOVERNMENT

Progressives also reshaped state government. Some tried to democratize the legislative process, regarding the legislature—the most important branch of state government in the nineteenth century—as ineffective and even corrupt, dominated by party bosses and corporate influences. The Populists had first raised such charges in the 1890s and proposed two novel solutions. The

initiative enabled reformers to propose legislation directly to the electorate, bypassing an unresponsive legislature; the **referendum** permitted voters to approve or reject legislative measures. South Dakota Populists established the first system of "direct legislation" in 1898, and progressives adopted these innovations in 20 other states between 1902 and 1915.

Other innovations also expanded the popular role in state government. The **Seventeenth Amendment,** ratified in 1913, provided for the election of U.S. senators directly by popular vote instead of by state legislatures. Beginning with Oregon in 1908, ten states adopted the **recall,** enabling voters to remove unsatisfactory public officials from office.

As state legislatures and party machines were curbed, dynamic governors such as Robert La Follette in Wisconsin, Charles Evans Hughes in New York, and Hiram Johnson in California pushed progressive programs into law. Elected governor in 1900, "Fighting Bob" La Follette turned Wisconsin into "the laboratory of democracy." Overcoming fierce opposition from "stalwart" Republicans, La Follette established direct primaries, railroad regulation, the first state income tax, workers' compensation, and other important measures before being elected to the U.S. Senate in 1906. La Follette also stressed efficiency and expertise. The Legislative Reference Bureau that he created to advise on public policy was staffed by university professors. He used regulatory commissions to oversee railroads, banks, and other interests. Most states followed suit, and expert commissions became an important feature of state government, gradually gaining authority at the expense of elected local officials.

initiative Procedure by which citizens can introduce a subject for legislation, usually through a petition signed by a specific number of voters.

referendum Submission of a law, proposed or already in effect, to a direct popular vote for approval or rejection.

Seventeenth Amendment Constitutional change that in 1913 established the direct popular election of U.S. senators.

recall The process of removing an official from office by popular vote, usually after using petitions to call for such a vote.

THEODORE ROOSEVELT AND THE PROGRESSIVE PRESIDENCY

HOW DID Theodore Roosevelt envision the power of the president?

When an anarchist assassinated William McKinley in 1901, Theodore Roosevelt entered the White House, and the progressive movement gained its most prominent leader. The son of a wealthy New York family, Roosevelt had pursued a career in Republican politics, serving as a New York legislator, U.S. civil service commissioner, and assistant secretary of the navy. After his exploits in the Spanish-American War (see Chapter 22), he was elected governor of New York in 1898 and vice president in 1900. Roosevelt's flamboyance and ambitions made him the most popular politician of the time and enabled him to dramatize the issues of progressivism and to become the first modern president.

TR and the Modern Presidency

Roosevelt rejected the limited role of Gilded Age presidents. He believed that the president could do anything to meet national needs that the Constitution did not specifically prohibit. Indeed, the expansion of government power and its consolidation in the executive branch were among his most significant accomplishments.

Rather than defer to Congress, Roosevelt exerted legislative leadership. He spelled out his policy goals in more than 400 messages to Congress, sent drafts of bills to Capitol Hill, and intervened to win passage of "his" measures. Roosevelt generally avoided direct challenges to the conservative Old Guard Republicans who controlled Congress, but his activities helped shift the balance of power within the national government.

Roosevelt also reorganized the executive branch. He believed in efficiency and expertise, which he attempted to institutionalize in special commissions and administrative procedures. To promote rational policymaking and public management, he staffed the expanding federal bureaucracy with able professionals.

Finally, Roosevelt encouraged the development of a personal presidency by exploiting the public's interest in their exuberant young president. He established the first White House press room and skillfully handled the mass media. His endless and well-reported activities, from playing with his children in the White House to wrestling, hiking, and horseback-riding with

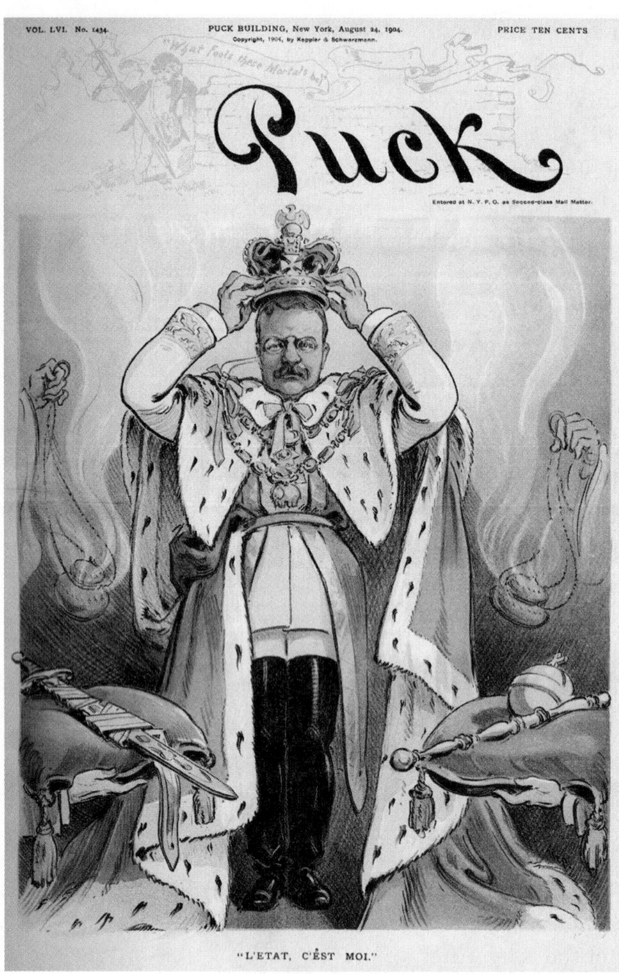

Fearing that Roosevelt was expanding presidential power and usurping congressional authority, critics depicted him as assuming a monarchical role.

various notables, made him a celebrity, known as TR or Teddy. The publicity not only kept TR in the spotlight but also enabled him to mold public opinion.

Roosevelt and Labor

One sign of TR's vigorous new approach to the presidency was his handling of a coal strike in 1902. Members of the United Mine Workers Union walked off their jobs, demanding higher wages, an eight-hour day, and recognition of their union. The mine owners closed the mines and waited for the union to collapse. But led by John Mitchell, the strikers held their ranks. The prospect of a freezing winter frightened consumers. Management's stubborn arrogance contrasted with the workers' orderly conduct and willingness to negotiate and hardened public opinion against the owners.

Although his legal advisers told him that the government had no authority to intervene, Roosevelt invited both the owners and the union leaders to the White House and declared that the national interest made government action necessary. Mitchell agreed to negotiate with the owners or to accept an arbitration commission appointed by the president. The owners, however, refused even to speak to the miners and demanded that Roosevelt use the army to break the union, as Cleveland had done in the Pullman strike in 1894.

Roosevelt was not a champion of labor, and he had favored shooting the Pullman strikers. But as president, he believed his role was to mediate social conflict for the public good. Roosevelt announced that he would use the army to seize and operate the mines, not to crush the union. Reluctantly, the owners accepted the arbitration commission they had previously rejected. The commission gave the miners a 10 percent wage increase and a nine-hour day, but not union recognition, and permitted the owners to raise coal prices by 10 percent. Roosevelt's intervention set important precedents for an active government role in labor disputes and a strong president acting as a steward of the public.

Managing Natural Resources

Federal land policy had helped create farms and develop transportation, but it had also ceded to speculators and business interests much of the nation's forests, mineral deposits, waterpower sites, and grazing lands. Reckless exploitation of these resources alarmed a new generation that believed the public welfare required the **conservation** of natural resources through efficient and scientific management. Conservationists achieved early victories in the Forest Reserve Act (1891) and the Forest Management Act (1897), which authorized the federal government to withdraw timberlands from development and to regulate grazing, lumbering, and hydroelectric sites in the forests.

conservation The efficient management and use of natural resources, such as forests, grasslands, and rivers, as opposed to preservation or uncontrolled exploitation.

Roosevelt built on these beginnings and on his friendship with Gifford Pinchot to make conservation a major focus of his presidency. Appointed in 1898 to head the new Division of Forestry (renamed the Forest Service in 1905), Pinchot brought rational management and regulation to resource development. With his advice, TR used presidential authority to triple the size of the forest reserves to 150 million acres, set aside another 80 million acres valuable for minerals and petroleum, and establish dozens of wildlife refuges. In 1908, Roosevelt held a White House conference of state and federal officials that led to the creation of the National Conservation Commission, 41 state conservation commissions, and widespread public support for the conservation movement.

Read the Document at **www.myhistorylab.com** *Gifford Pinchot, The Fight for Conservation (1910)*

Not everyone, of course, agreed with TR's conservationist policies. Some favored **preservation,** hoping to set aside land as permanent wilderness, whereas Roosevelt favored a scientific and efficient rather than uncontrolled use of resources. Preservationists won some

preservation Protecting forests, land, and other features of the natural environment from development or destruction, often for aesthetic appreciation.

victories, saving a stand of California's giant redwoods and helping create the National Park Service in 1916, but more Americans favored the utilitarian emphasis of the early conservationists.

Other interests opposed conservation completely. While some of the larger timber and mineral companies supported conservation as a way to guarantee long-run profits, smaller western entrepreneurs often cared only about quick returns. Many westerners, moreover, resented having easterners make key decisions about western growth and saw conservation as a perpetuation of this colonial subservience.

But westerners were happy to take federal money for expensive irrigation projects that private capital would not underwrite. They favored the 1902 National Reclamation Act, which established what became the **Bureau of Reclamation.** Its engineers were to construct dams, reservoirs, and irrigation canals, and the government was to sell the irrigated lands in tracts no larger than 160 acres. With massive dams and networks of irrigation canals, it reclaimed fertile valleys from the desert, but by not enforcing the 160-acre limitation it helped create powerful corporate farms in the West.

Westerners also welcomed Roosevelt's conservationist emphasis on rational development when it restricted Indian control of land and resources. He favored policies breaking up many reservations to open the land to whites for "efficient" development and diverting Indian waters to growing cities like Phoenix. Tribal protests were ignored.

Theodore Roosevelt and John Muir, here on a 1903 camping trip in Yosemite, championed public responsibility for the nation's scenic and other natural resources.

Corporate Regulation

Nothing symbolized Roosevelt's active presidency better than his popular reputation as a "trust buster." TR regarded the formation of large business combinations favorably, but he realized he could not ignore the public anxiety about corporate power. Rather than invoking "the foolish antitrust law," he favored government regulation to prevent corporate abuses and defend the public interest. "Misconduct," not size, was the issue.

But Roosevelt did file lawsuits against some "bad trusts," including the Northern Securities Company, a holding company organized by J. P. Morgan to control the railroad network of the Northwest. For TR, this suit was an assertion of government power that reassured a worried public and encouraged corporate responsibility. In 1904, the Supreme Court ordered the dissolution of the Northern Securities Company. Ultimately, Roosevelt brought 44 antitrust suits against business combinations, but except for a few like Standard Oil, he avoided the giant firms. Many of the cases had inconclusive outcomes, but Roosevelt was more interested in establishing a regulatory role for government than in breaking up big businesses.

Elected president in his own right in 1904 over the colorless and conservative Democratic candidate, Judge Alton B. Parker, Roosevelt responded to the growing popular demand for reform by pushing further toward a regulatory government. In 1906, Congress passed the Hepburn Act to extend the authority of the Interstate Commerce Commission over railroads, the Pure Food and Drug Act, and the Meat Inspection Act. All three were compromises between reformers seeking serious government control of the industries involved and political defenders and lobbyists of the industries themselves.

Despite the compromises and weaknesses in the three laws, TR contended that they marked "a noteworthy advance in the policy of securing federal supervision and control over corporations." In 1907 and 1908, he pushed for an eight-hour workday, stock market regulation, and inheritance and income taxes. Republican conservatives in Congress blocked such reforms, and tensions increased between the progressive and conservative wings of the party.

John Muir National Historic Site, Martinez, California
http://www.nps.gov/jomu

Bureau of Reclamation Federal agency established in 1902 providing public funds for irrigation projects in arid regions.

Read the **Document**

at **www.myhistorylab.com**
From Then to Now Online: The Environmental Movement

Taft and the Insurgents

TR handpicked his successor as president: a loyal lieutenant, William Howard Taft. If Roosevelt thought that Taft would be a successful president, continuing his policies and holding the

Republican Party together, he was wrong. Taft's election in 1908, over Democrat William Jennings Bryan in his third presidential campaign, led to a Republican political disaster.

Taft did preside over important progressive achievements. His administration pursued a more active and successful antitrust program than Roosevelt's. He supported the Mann-Elkins Act (1910), which extended the ICC's jurisdiction to telephone and telegraph companies. Taft set aside more public forest lands and oil reserves than Roosevelt had. He also supported a constitutional amendment authorizing an income tax, which went into effect in 1913 under the **Sixteenth Amendment.** One of the most important accomplishments of the Progressive Era, the income tax would provide the means for the government to expand its activities and responsibilities.

Sixteenth Amendment Constitutional revision that in 1913 authorized a federal income tax.

Nevertheless, Taft soon alienated progressives and floundered into a political morass. His problems were twofold. First, the Republicans were divided. Midwestern reform Republicans, led by La Follette, clashed with conservative Republicans, led by Senator Nelson Aldrich of Rhode Island. Second, Taft was politically inept. He was unable to mediate between the two Republican factions, and the party split apart.

Reformers wanted to restrict the power of the Speaker of the House, "Uncle Joe" Cannon, a reactionary who systematically blocked progressive measures and loudly declared, "I am goddamned tired of listening to all this babble of reform." After seeming to promise support, Taft backed down when conservatives threatened to defeat important legislation. The insurgents in Congress eventually restricted the speaker's powers, but they never forgave what they saw as Taft's betrayal. The tariff also alienated progressives from Taft. He had campaigned in 1908 for a lower tariff to curb inflation, but when they introduced tariff reform legislation, the president failed to support them, and Aldrich's Senate committee added 847 amendments, many of which raised tariff rates. Progressives concluded that Taft had sided with the Old Guard against real change.

This perception solidified when Taft stumbled into a controversy over conservation. Gifford Pinchot had become embroiled in a complex struggle with Richard Ballinger, Taft's secretary of the interior. Ballinger, who was closely tied to western mining and lumbering interests, favored private development of public lands. When Pinchot challenged Ballinger's role in a questionable sale of public coal lands in Alaska to a J. P. Morgan syndicate, Taft upheld Ballinger and fired Pinchot. Progressives concluded that Taft had repudiated Roosevelt's conservation policies.

The progressives determined to replace Taft, whom they now saw as an obstacle to reform. In 1911, the National Progressive League organized to champion La Follette for the Republican nomination in 1912. Roosevelt rejected an appeal for support, convinced that a challenge to the incumbent president was both doomed and divisive. Besides, his own position was closer to Taft's than to what he called "the La Follette type of fool radicalism." But Taft's political blunders increasingly angered Roosevelt. Condemning Taft as "disloyal to our past friendship," TR began to campaign for the Republican nomination himself. In 13 state primaries, he won 278 delegates, to only 46 for Taft. But most states did not then have primaries; as a result, Taft was able to dominate the Republican convention and win renomination. Roosevelt's forces formed a third party—the Progressive Party—and nominated the former president. The Republican split almost guaranteed victory for the Democratic nominee, Woodrow Wilson.

WOODROW WILSON AND PROGRESSIVE REFORM

HOW DID Woodrow Wilson's vision of reform differ from Theodore Roosevelt's?

The pressures for reform called forth many new leaders. The one who would preside over progressivism's culmination, and ultimately its collapse, was Woodrow Wilson. Elected president in 1912 and 1916, he mediated among differing progressive views to achieve a strong reform program, enlarge the power of the executive branch, and make the White House the center of national politics.

The Election of 1912

Despite the prominence of Roosevelt and La Follette, progressivism was not simply a Republican phenomenon. As the Republicans quarreled during Taft's administration, Democrats pushed progressive remedies and achieved major victories in the state and congressional elections of 1910. To improve the party's chances in 1912, William Jennings Bryan announced that he would step aside. The Democratic spotlight shifted to the governor of New Jersey, Woodrow Wilson.

Wilson first entered public life as a conservative, steeped in the limited-government traditions of his native South. As president of Princeton University, beginning in 1902, he became a prominent representative of middle-class respectability and conservative causes. In 1910, New Jersey's Democratic bosses selected him for governor to head off the progressives. But once in office, Wilson championed popular reforms and immediately began to campaign as a progressive for the party's 1912 presidential nomination.

Read the **Document** at **www.myhistorylab.com** *Theodore Roosevelt, "The New Nationalism" (1910)*

A strong president, Wilson led Congress to enact sweeping and significant legislation.

New Nationalism Theodore Roosevelt's 1912 program calling for a strong national government to foster, regulate, and protect business, industry, workers, and consumers.

New Freedom Woodrow Wilson's 1912 program for limited government intervention in the economy to restore competition by curtailing the restrictive influences of trusts and protective tariffs, thereby providing opportunities for individual achievement.

Read the Document at **www.myhistorylab.com**
Woodrow Wilson, from The New Freedom (1913)

Underwood-Simmons Tariff Act The 1913 reform law that lowered tariff rates and levied the first regular federal income tax.

Wilson's progressivism differed from that of Roosevelt in 1912. TR emphasized a strong government to promote economic and social order. He defended big business as inevitable and healthy provided that government control ensured that it would benefit the entire nation. Roosevelt called this program the **New Nationalism,** reflecting his belief in a powerful state and a national interest. He also supported demands for social welfare, including workers' compensation and the abolition of child labor.

Wilson was horrified by Roosevelt's vision. His **New Freedom** program rejected what he called TR's "regulated monopoly." Wilson wanted "regulated competition," with the government's role limited to breaking up monopolies through antitrust action and preventing artificial barriers like tariffs from blocking free enterprise. Wilson opposed social-welfare legislation as paternalistic, reaching beyond the proper scope of the federal government, which he hoped to minimize.

Roosevelt's endorsement of social legislation attracted many women into political action. As Jane Addams observed, "their long concern for the human wreckage of industry has come to be considered politics." The Progressive Party also endorsed woman suffrage, accepted women as convention delegates, and pledged to give women equal representation on party committees. (See American Views: The Need for Woman Suffrage.)

Despite his personal popularity, however, TR was unable to add progressive Democrats to the Republicans who followed him into the Progressive Party, and thus was doomed to defeat. Other reform voters embraced the Socialist candidate, Eugene V. Debs, who captured 900,000 votes—6 percent of the total. Taft played little role in the campaign.

Wilson won an easy electoral college victory, though he received only 42 percent of the popular vote and fewer popular votes than Bryan had won in any of his three campaigns (see Map 21–2). Roosevelt came in second, Taft third. The Democrats also gained control of Congress, giving Wilson the opportunity to enact his New Freedom program.

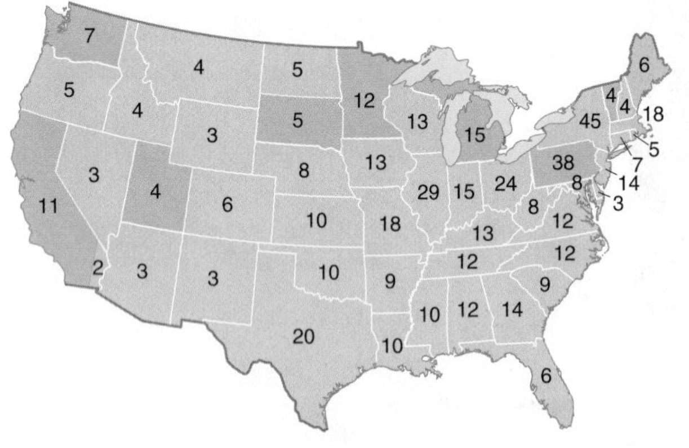

	Electoral Vote (%)	Popular Vote (%)
WOODROW WILSON (Democrat)	**435 (82)**	**6,296,547 (42)**
Theodore Roosevelt (Progressive)	88 (17)	4,118,571 (27)
William Taft (Republican)	8 (1)	3,486,720 (23)
Eugene Debs (Socialist)	–	900,672 (6)

MAP 21–2 **The Election of 1912** The split within the Republican Party enabled Woodrow Wilson to carry most states and become president even though he won only a minority of the popular vote.

How is it possible that Woodrow Wilson received 82 percent of the electoral vote but only 42 percent of the popular vote?

Implementing the New Freedom

As president, Wilson built on Roosevelt's precedent to strengthen executive authority. He proposed a full legislative program and worked forcefully to secure its approval. When necessary, he appealed to the public for support, ruthlessly used patronage, or compromised with conservatives. With such methods and a solid Democratic majority, Wilson gained approval of important laws.

Wilson turned first to the traditional Democratic goal of reducing the high protective tariff, the symbol of special privileges for industry. He forced through the **Underwood-Simmons Tariff Act** of 1913, the first substantial reduction in duties since before the Civil War. The act also levied the first income tax under the recently ratified Sixteenth Amendment. Conservatives condemned the "revolutionary" tax, but it was designed simply to compensate for lower tariff rates. The top tax rate paid by the wealthiest was a mere 7 percent.

Wilson next reformed the nation's banking and currency system, which was inadequate for a modernizing economy. Wilson skillfully maneuvered a compromise measure through Congress, balancing the demands of agrarian progressives for government control with the bankers' desires for private control. The **Federal Reserve Act** of 1913 created 12 regional Federal Reserve banks that, although privately controlled, were to be supervised by the Federal Reserve Board, appointed by the president. The law also provided for a flexible national currency and improved access to credit.

Wilson's third objective was new legislation to break up monopolies. Initially, he supported the Clayton antitrust bill, which prohibited

AMERICAN VIEWS

The Need for Woman Suffrage

The movement for woman suffrage was one of the most important components of progressivism, and it gained increasing numbers of adherents, who created new organizations, adopted new tactics, and crafted new arguments for the reform. The task remained the same: persuading first legislative committees and then electorates to approve a fundamental change in the political system. In 1912 Caroline A. Lowe, of Kansas City, Missouri, delivered the following remarks to a hearing of a joint committee formed by the Judiciary Committee and the Woman Suffrage Committee of the U.S. Senate.

- **What** arguments does Lowe advance to support the need for woman suffrage?
- **How** does Lowe attempt to counteract objections to the reform?
- **How** does Lowe's rhetoric reflect the varied impulses underlying progressive reform?

Gentlemen of the committee, it is as a wage earner and on behalf of the 7,000,000 wage-earning women in the United States that I wish to speak.

I entered the ranks of the wage earners when 18 years of age. Since then I have earned every cent of the cost of my own maintenance, and for several years was a potent factor in the support of my widowed mother.

The need of the ballot for the wage-earning women is a vital one. No plea can be made that we have the protection of the home or are represented by our fathers and brothers. We need the ballot that we may broaden our horizon and assume our share in the solution of the problems that seriously affect our daily lives. . . .

We need the ballot for the purpose of self-protection. . . . Does the young woman cashier in Marshall Field's need any voice in making the law that sets the hours of labor that shall constitute a day's work?. . . . Has the young woman whose scalp was torn from her head at the Lawrence mill any need of a law demanding that safety appliances be placed upon all dangerous machinery? And what of the working girls who, through unemployment, are denied the opportunity to sell the labor of their hands and are driven to the sale of their virtue?

. . . . We wage earners know it to be almost universal that the men in the industries receive twice the wage granted to us, although we may be doing the same work and should have the same pay. We women work side by side with our brothers. We are children of the same parents, reared in the same homes, educated in the same schools, ride to and fro on the same early morning and late evening streetcars, work together the same number of hours in the same shops, and we have equal need of food, clothing, and shelter. But at 21 years of age our brothers are given a powerful weapon for self-defense, a larger means for growth and self-expression. We working women, even because we are women and find our sex not a source of strength but a source of weakness and offering a greater opportunity for exploitation, are denied this weapon.

Gentlemen of the committee, is there any justice underlying such a condition? If our brother workingmen are granted the ballot with which to protect themselves, do you not think that the working women should be granted this same right?

What of the working girl and her employer? Why is the ballot given to him while it is denied to us? Is it for the protection of his property, that he may have a voice in the governing of his wealth, of his stocks and bonds and merchandise?

The wealth of the working woman is of far greater value to the State. From nature's raw products the working class can readily replace all of the material wealth owned by the employing class, but the wealth of the working woman is the wealth of flesh and blood, of all her physical, mental, and spiritual powers. It is the wealth, not only of today, but that of future generations, that is being bartered away so cheaply. Have we no right to a voice in the disposal of our wealth, the greatest wealth that the world possesses—the priceless wealth of its womanhood?

Is it not the cruelest injustice that the man whose material wealth is a source of strength and protection to him and of power over us should be given the additional advantage of an even greater weapon which he can use to perpetuate our condition of helpless subjection?

. . . Mr. Chairman and gentlemen of the committee, the time is ripe for the extension of the franchise to women. We do not

(continued)

come before you to beg you to grant us a favor; we come presenting to you a glorious opportunity to place yourselves abreast of the current of this great evolutionary movement. You can refuse to accept this opportunity, and you may, for a moment, delay the movement, but only as the old woman who, with her tiny broom, endeavored to sweep back the incoming tide from the sea.

If today, taking your places as men of affairs in the world's progress, you step out in unison with the eternal upward trend toward true democracy, you will support the suffrage amendment now before your committee.

Source: U.S. Congress, Senate, Joint Committee, 62nd Cong., 2nd sess., S. Document 601, pp. 16–19.

Read the **Document**

at **www.myhistorylab.com**
Louis Brandeis, Other People's Money and How the Bankers Use It (1913)

Federal Reserve Act The 1913 law that revised banking and currency by extending limited government regulation through the creation of the Federal Reserve System.

Federal Trade Commission Government agency established in 1914 to provide regulatory oversight of business activity.

unfair trade practices and sharply restricted holding companies. But when business leaders and other progressives strenuously objected, Wilson reversed himself. Opting for continuous federal regulation rather than for the dissolution of trusts, Wilson endorsed the creation of the **Federal Trade Commission** (FTC) to oversee business activity and prevent illegal restrictions on competition.

The Federal Trade Commission Act of 1914 dismayed many of Wilson's early supporters because it embraced the New Nationalism's emphasis on positive regulation. Roosevelt's 1912 platform had proposed a federal trade commission; Wilson now accepted what he had earlier denounced as a partnership between trusts and the government that the trusts would dominate. Indeed, Wilson's conservative appointments to the FTC ensured that the agency would not seriously interfere with business, and by the 1920s, the FTC had become virtually a junior partner of the business community.

The fate of the Clayton antitrust bill after Wilson withdrew his support reflected his new attitude toward big business. Congressional conservatives gutted the bill with crippling amendments before permitting it to become law in 1914.

These measures indicate the limited nature of Wilson's vision of reform. In fact, he now announced that no further reforms were necessary—astonishing many progressives whose objectives had been completely ignored. Wilson refused to support woman suffrage and helped kill legislation abolishing child labor and expanding credits to farmers. He demonstrated his indifference to issues of social justice by supporting the introduction of racial segregation within the government itself. Government offices, shops, restrooms, and restaurants were all segregated; employees who complained were fired. Federal officials in the South discharged black employees.

The Expansion of Reform

Wilson had won in 1912 only because the Republicans had split. By 1916, Roosevelt had returned to the GOP, and Wilson realized that he had to attract some of TR's former followers. Wilson therefore abandoned his opposition to social and economic reforms and promoted measures he had previously condemned. But he had also grown in the White House and now recognized that some problems could be resolved only by positive federal action.

To assist farmers, Wilson in 1916 convinced Congress to pass the Federal Farm Loan Act. This law, which Wilson himself had earlier rejected twice, provided farmers with federally financed long-term agricultural credits. The Warehouse Act of 1916 improved short-term agricultural credit. The Highway Act of 1916 provided funds to construct and improve rural roads through the adoption of the dollar-matching principle by which the federal government would expand its power over state activities in the twentieth century.

Wilson and the Democratic Congress also reached out to labor. Wilson signed the Keating-Owen Act prohibiting the interstate shipment of products made by child labor. In 1902, Wilson had denounced Roosevelt's intervention in the coal strike, but in 1916 he broke a labor-management impasse and averted a railroad strike by helping pass the Adamson Act establishing an eight-hour day for railroad workers. Wilson also pushed the Kern-McGillicuddy Act, which achieved the progressive goal of a workers' compensation system for federal employees. Together, these laws marked an important advance toward government regulation of the labor market.

Wilson also promoted activist government when he nominated Louis Brandeis to the Supreme Court. Known as "the people's lawyer," Brandeis had successfully defended protective labor legislation before the conservative judiciary. The nomination outraged conservatives, including William Howard Taft and the American Bar Association. Brandeis was the first Jew nominated to the court, and anti-Semitism motivated some of his opponents. Wilson overcame a vicious campaign against Brandeis and secured his confirmation.

By these actions, Wilson brought progressivism to a culmination of sorts and consolidated reformers behind him for a second term. Less than a decade earlier, Wilson the private citizen had assailed government regulation and social legislation; by 1916, he had guided an unprecedented expansion of federal power. His own personal and political journey symbolized the development of progressivism.

CONCLUSION

Progressivism had its ironies and paradoxes. It called for democratic reforms—and did achieve woman suffrage, direct legislation, and popular election of senators—but helped disfranchise black southerners and northern immigrants. It advocated social justice but often enforced social control. It demanded responsive government but helped create bureaucracies largely removed from popular control. It endorsed the regulation of business in the public interest but forged regulatory laws and commissions that tended to aid business.

Both the successes and the failures of progressivism revealed that the nature of politics and government had changed significantly. Americans had come to accept that government action could resolve social and economic problems, and the role and power of government expanded accordingly. The emergence of an activist presidency, capable of developing programs, mobilizing public opinion, directing Congress, and taking forceful action, epitomized this key development.

These important features would be crucial when the nation fought World War I, which brought new challenges and dangers to the United States. The Great War would expose many of the limitations of progressivism and the naiveté of the progressives' optimism.

Where to Learn More

John Muir National Historic Site, Martinez, California. The architecture and furnishings of this 17-room house reflect the interests of John Muir, the writer and naturalist who founded the Sierra Club and led the preservationists in the Progressive Era. http://www.nps.gov/jomu.

Sewall-Belmont House National Historic Site, Washington, DC. Headquarters of the National Woman's Party, this 200-year-old house on Capitol Hill has memorabilia of the woman suffrage movement, including posters, flags, and photographs of the early marches, and an extensive feminist library focused on the struggle for equal suffrage. Beginning in 1923 Alice Paul campaigned from this building for the Equal Rights Amendment. http://www.sewallbelmont.org.

Hull House, Chicago, Illinois. This pioneering settlement house is now a museum on the campus of the University of Illinois, Chicago. http://www.uic.edu/jaddams/hull/.

Lower East Side Tenement Museum, New York City, New York. A six-story tenement building containing 22 apartments, this museum vividly illustrates the congested and unhealthy living conditions of urban immigrants from the 1870s to the early twentieth century. See http://www.tenement.org for a virtual tour.

Review Questions

1. How and why did the presidency change during the Progressive Era?
2. How did the progressive concern for efficiency affect social reform efforts, public education, government administration, and rural life?
3. How and why did the relationship between business and government change during this time?
4. Why did social reform and social control often intermingle in the Progressive Era? Can such objectives be separate?
5. What factors, old and new, stimulated the reform movements of progressivism?
6. How did the role of women change during the Progressive Era? How did the changes affect progressivism?
7. Why did the demand for woman suffrage provoke such determined support and such bitter opposition?

Key Terms

Australian ballot (p. 594)
Bureau of Reclamation (p. 597)
Conservation (p. 596)
Eighteenth Amendment (p. 590)
Federal Reserve Act (p. 602)
Federal Trade Commission (p. 602)
Fundamentalists (p. 584)
Initiative (p. 595)
Muckraking (p. 582)
New Freedom (p. 600)
New Nationalism (p. 600)
Niagara Movement (p. 592)
Nineteenth Amendment (p. 593)
Preservation (p. 596)
Progressive Era (p. 580)
Prohibition (p. 590)
Recall (p. 595)
Referendum (p. 595)
Seventeenth Amendment (p. 595)
Sixteenth Amendment (p. 598)
Social Gospel movement (p. 581)
Underwood-Simmons Tariff Act (p. 600)
Wobblies (p. 583)

PEARSON myhistorylab Connections

Reinforce what you learned in this chapter by studying the many documents, images, maps, review tools, and videos available at **www.myhistorylab.com**.

Read and Review

Study and Review **Study Plan: Chapter 21**

Read the Document

Herbert Croly, Progressive Democracy (1914)

Charlotte Perkins Gilman, "If I Were a Man" (1914)

Emma Goldman, Anarchism and Other Essays (1917)

Eugene V. Debs, "The Outlook for Socialism in America" (1900)

Frederick W. Taylor, The Principles of Scientific Management (1911)

Jane Addams, from Twenty Years at Hull House (1910)

Gifford Pinchot, The Fight for Conservation (1910)

Helen M. Todd, "Getting Out the Vote" (1911)

Jane Addams, "Ballots Necessary for Women" (1906)

Louis Brandeis, Other People's Money and How the Bankers Use It (1913)

Mary Church Terrell, The Progress of Colored Women (1898)

Mother Jones, "The March of the Mill Children" (1903)

Platform Adopted by the National Negro Committee (1909)

The Niagara Movement, Declaration of Principles (1905)

Theodore Roosevelt, "The New Nationalism" (1910)

Woodrow Wilson, from The New Freedom (1913)

See the Map *Woman Suffrage before the Nineteenth Century*

Research and Explore

Read the Document

Personal Journeys Online

From Then to Now Online: The Environmental Movement

Exploring America: Americanization

Hear the Audio

Crisis Magazine by W.E.B. Du Bois

The Primary Needs of the Negro Race by Kelly Miller

The Progress of Colored Women by Mary Church Terrell

The Speech That Sent Debs to Jail

Watch the Video

Bull Moose Campaign Speech

Punching the Clock

Women in the Workplace, 1904

What Was the Progressive Education Movement?

Hear the Audio

Hear the audio files for Chapter 21 at **www.myhistorylab.com.**

1865-1917

22

Creating an Empire

A jubilant Uncle Sam celebrates victory in the Spanish-American War and anticipates the building of an American empire. This cover of an American magazine, 1898, commemorates the country's swift victory in the war.

Hear the Audio

Hear the audio files for Chapter 22 at **www.myhistorylab.com**.

THE ROOTS OF IMPERIALISM *(page 610)*

WHAT ARGUMENTS were made in favor of American expansion in the late nineteenth century?

FIRST STEPS *(page 612)*

WHAT STEPS did the United States take to expand its global influence in the decades before the Spanish-American War?

THE SPANISH-AMERICAN WAR *(page 616)*

WHAT WERE the most important consequences of the Spanish-American War?

Library of Congress

IMPERIAL AMBITIONS: THE UNITED STATES AND EAST ASIA, 1899–1917 *(page 620)*

WHAT WAS the nature of U.S. involvement in Asia?

IMPERIAL POWER: THE UNITED STATES AND LATIN AMERICA, 1899–1917 *(page 624)*

HOW DID Latin Americans respond to U.S. intervention in the region?

ENGAGING EUROPE: NEW CONCERNS, OLD CONSTRAINTS *(page 630)*

WHY DID the United States take a larger role in Europe at the beginning of the twentieth century?

One American Journey

Havana, Cuba October 1901

When the Spanish-American war was declared the United States . . . assumed a position as protector of the interests of Cuba. It became responsible for the welfare of the people, politically, mentally, and morally. The mere fact of freeing the island from Spanish rule has not ended the care which this country should give. . . . The effect will be to uplift the people, gaining their permanent friendship and support and greatly increasing our own commerce. At present there are two million people requiring clothing and food, for but a small proportion of the necessaries of life are raised on the island. It is folly to grow food crops when sugar and tobacco produce such rich revenues in comparison. The United States should supply the Cubans with their breadstuffs, even wine, fruit, and vegetables, and should clothe the people. . . . The money received for their crops will be turned over in a great measure in buying supplies from the United States. . . .

Naturally the manufacturers of the United States should have precedence in furnishing machinery, locomotives, cars, and rails, materials for buildings and bridges, and the wide diversity of other supplies required, as well as fuel for their furnaces. With the present financial and commercial uncertainty at an end the people of the island will . . . come into the American market as customers for products of many kinds.

The meeting of the Constitutional Convention on November 5th will be an event in Cuban history of the greatest importance, and much will depend upon the action and outcome of this convention as to our future control of the island. . . . I considered it unwise to interfere, and I have made it a settled policy to permit the Cubans to manage every part of their constitution-making. This has been due to my desire to prevent any possible charge of crimination being brought against the United States in the direction of their constitutional affairs. . . .

There is no distrust of the United States on the part of the Cubans, and I know of no widespread antipathy to this country, its people, or its institutions. There are, of course, a handful of malcontents, as there must be in every country. . . .

I could not well conceive how the Cubans could be otherwise than grateful to the United States for its efforts in their behalf. . . . In the brief time since the occupation of the island by American troops the island has been completely rehabilitated—agriculturally, commercially, financially, educationally, and governmentally. This improvement has been so rapid and so apparent that no Cuban could mistake it. To doubt in the face of these facts that their liberators were not still their faithful friends would be impossible.

Major-General Leonard Wood, "The Future of Cuba," *The Independent* 54 (January 23, 1902): 193–194; idem, "The Cuban Convention," *The Independent* 52 (November 1, 1900): 265–266.

Read the **Document** at **www.myhistorylab.com**

Personal Journeys Online

- **Josiah Strong, *Our Country,* 1885. An appeal for Anglo-Saxon imperialism by an American minister.**
- **Charles Denby, *Shall We Keep the Philippines?,* 1898. An argument for an economic empire by an American diplomat.**
- **Vincent F. Howard, *Imperialism,* 1900. A poem denouncing the imperialist journey.**

CHRONOLOGY

1861–1869	Seward serves as secretary of state.
1867	United States purchases Alaska from Russia.
1870	Annexation of the Dominican Republic is rejected.
1879	France conquers Algeria.
1881	Naval Advisory Board is created.
1882	Great Britain occupies Egypt.
1887	United States gains naval rights to Pearl Harbor.
1890	Alfred Thayer Mahan publishes *The Influence of Sea Power upon History*.
1893	Harrison signs but Cleveland rejects a treaty for the annexation of Hawaii.
1893–1897	Depression increases interest in economic expansion abroad.
1894–1895	Sino-Japanese War is fought.
1895	United States intervenes in Great Britain–Venezuelan boundary dispute.
	Cuban insurrection against Spain begins.
1896	William McKinley is elected president on an imperialist platform.
1898	Spanish-American War is fought.
	Hawaii is annexed.
	Anti-Imperialist League is organized.
	Treaty of Paris is signed.
1899–1902	Filipino-American War is fought.
1899	Open Door note is issued.
	First Hague Peace Conference creates Court of Arbitration.
1900	Boxer Rebellion against foreign influence breaks out in China.
1901	Theodore Roosevelt becomes president.
1903	Platt Amendment restricts Cuban autonomy.
	Panama "revolution" is abetted by the United States.
1904	United States acquires the Panama Canal Zone.
	Roosevelt Corollary is announced.
1904–1905	Russo-Japanese War is fought.
1905	Treaty of Portsmouth ends the Russo-Japanese War through U.S. mediation.
1906–1909	United States occupies Cuba.
1907–1908	Gentlemen's Agreement restricts Japanese immigration.
1909	United States intervenes in Nicaragua.
1912–1933	United States occupies Nicaragua.
1914	Panama Canal opens.
1914–1917	United States intervenes in Mexico.
1915–1934	United States occupies Haiti.
1916–1924	United States occupies the Dominican Republic.
1917	Puerto Ricans are granted U.S. citizenship.
1917–1922	United States occupies Cuba.

General Leonard Wood's reports on Cuba, then under his control as military governor, captured the complex mixture of attitudes and motives that underlay the journey of the United States from a developing nation to a world power. Plans for economic expansion, a belief in national mission, a sense of responsibility to help others, scarcely hidden religious impulses and racist convictions—all combined in an uneasy mixture of self-interest and idealism.

The tension between what a friend of Wood's called the "righteous" and the "selfish" aspects of expanding American influence lay beneath the surface in Wood's reports. His claim that he was not interfering with Cuba's constitutional convention was disingenuous, for he had already undertaken to limit those who could participate as voters or delegates and was even then devising means to restrict the convention's autonomy. And in his repeated insistence that the Cubans were grateful for the intervention of "their faithful friends," the Americans, Wood obviously protested too much: Cubans, as well as Filipinos, Puerto Ricans, and others, rarely perceived American motives or American actions as positively as did Wood and other proponents of American expansion. Victory in the Spanish-American War had provided the United States with an extensive empire, status as a world power, and opportunities and problems that would long shape U.S. foreign policy. ✦

THE ROOTS OF IMPERIALISM

WHAT ARGUMENTS were made in favor of American expansion in the late nineteenth century?

imperialism The policy and practice of exploiting nations and peoples for the benefit of an imperial power either directly through military occupation and colonial rule or indirectly through economic domination of resources and markets.

The United States had a long-established tradition of expansion across the continent. Indeed, by the 1890s, Republican Senator Henry Cabot Lodge of Massachusetts boasted that Americans had "a record of conquest, colonization, and territorial expansion unequalled by any people in the nineteenth century." Lodge now urged the country to build an overseas empire, emulating the European model of **imperialism** based on the acquisition and exploitation of colonial possessions. Other Americans favored a less formal empire, in which United States interests and influence would be ensured through extensive trade and investments rather than through military occupation. Still others advocated a cultural expansionism in which the nation exported its ideals and institutions. All such expansionists could draw from many sources to support their plans. (see Overview, Rationales for Imperialism).

Ideological and Religious Arguments

Scholars, authors, politicians, and religious leaders provided interlocking ideological arguments for the new imperialism. Some intellectuals, for example, invoked Social Darwinism, maintaining that the United States should engage in a competitive struggle for wealth and power with other nations. "The survival of the fittest," declared one writer, was "the law of nations as well as a law of nature." As European nations expanded into Asia and Africa in the 1880s and 1890s, seeking colonies, markets, and raw materials, these advocates argued, the United States had to adopt similar policies to ensure national success.

Read the **Document** at **www.myhistorylab.com** *Rudyard Kipling, "The White Man's Burden" (1899)*

Related to Social Darwinism was a pervasive belief in racial inequality and in the superiority of people of English, or Anglo-Saxon, descent. To many Americans, the industrial progress, military strength, and political development of England and the United States were proof of an Anglo-Saxon superiority that carried with it a responsibility to extend the blessings of their rule to less able people. As a popular expression put it, colonialism was the "white man's burden," carrying with it a duty to aid and uplift other peoples. Such attitudes led some expansionists to favor imposing American ideas and practices on other cultures regardless of their own values and customs.

Reflecting this aggressiveness, as well as Darwinian anxieties, some Americans endorsed expansion as consistent with their ideals of masculinity. Forceful expansion would be a manly course, relying upon and building strength and honor among American males. Men who confronted the challenges of empire would thereby improve their ability to compete in the international arena. "Pride of race, courage, manliness," predicted one enthusiast, would be both the causes and the consequences of an assertive foreign policy.

W
WHERE TO LEARN MORE
Mission Houses, Honolulu, Hawaii
http://www.missionhouses.org

American missionaries also promoted expansionist sentiment. Hoping to evangelize the world, American religious groups increased the number of Protestant foreign missions sixfold from 1870 to 1900. Women in particular organized foreign missionary societies and served in the missions. Missionaries publicized their activities throughout the United States, generating interest in foreign developments and support for what one writer called the "imperialism of righteousness." Abroad they pursued a religious transformation that often resembled a cultural conversion, for they promoted trade, developed business interests, and encouraged westernization through technology and education as well as religion. Sometimes, as in the Hawaiian Islands, American missionaries even promoted annexation by the United States.

Indeed, the American religious press endlessly repeated the themes of national destiny, racial superiority, and religious zeal. Missionaries contributed to the imperial impulse by describing their work in terms of the conquest of enemy territory. Thus, while missionaries were motivated by what they considered to be idealism and often brought real benefits to other lands, especially in education and health, religious sentiments reinforced the ideology of American expansion.

OVERVIEW Rationales for Imperialism

Category	Beliefs
Racism and Social Darwinism	The conviction that Anglo-Saxons were racially superior and should dominate other peoples, either to ensure national success, establish international stability, or benefit the "inferior" races by imposing American ideas and institutions on them
Righteousness	The conviction that Christianity, and a supporting American culture, should be aggressively spread among the benighted peoples of other lands
Mahanism	The conviction, following the ideas advanced by Alfred Thayer Mahan, that U.S. security required a strong navy and economic and territorial expansion
Economics	A variety of arguments holding that American prosperity depended on acquiring access to foreign markets, raw materials, and investment opportunities

Strategic Concerns

Other expansionists were motivated by strategic concerns, shaped by what they saw as the forces of history and geography. America's location in the Western Hemisphere, its coastlines on two oceans, and the ambitions and activities of other nations, particularly Germany and Britain, convinced some Americans that the United States had to develop new policies to protect and promote its national security and interests. Alfred Thayer Mahan, president of the Naval War College, emphasized the importance of a strong navy for national greatness in his book *The Influence of Sea Power upon History*. To complement the navy, Mahan proposed that the United States build a canal across the isthmus of Panama to link its coasts, acquire naval bases in the Caribbean and the Pacific to protect the canal, and annex Hawaii and other Pacific islands to promote trade and service the fleet.

at **www.myhistorylab.com**
Alfred Thayer Mahan, The Interest of America in Sea Power (1897)

Mahanism found a receptive audience. President Benjamin Harrison declared in 1891 that "as to naval stations and points of influence, we must look forward to a departure from the too conservative opinions which have been held heretofore." Still more vocal advocates of Mahan's program were a group of nationalistic Republicans, predominantly from the Northeast. They included politicians like Henry Cabot Lodge and Theodore Roosevelt, journalists like Whitelaw Reid and Albert Shaw, and diplomats and lawyers like John Hay and Elihu Root.

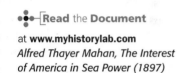

Mahanism The ideas advanced by Alfred Thayer Mahan, stressing U.S. naval, economic, and territorial expansion.

Emily Hartwell, an American missionary, and her Chinese converts ("Bible Women") in the Foochow Mission in 1902. American missionaries wanted to spread the Gospel abroad but inevitably spread American influence as well. Hartwell used the ethnocentric and militant rhetoric of the imperialism of righteousness in appealing to Americans for money and prayers for her "picket duty on the very outskirts of the army of the Lord."

Even so, Mahan was not solely responsible for the large-navy policy popular among imperialists. Its origins went back to 1881, when Congress established the Naval Advisory Board, which successfully lobbied for larger naval appropriations. An extensive program to replace the navy's obsolete wooden ships with modern cruisers and battleships was well under way by 1890, when Mahan's book appeared. The United States soon possessed the formidable navy the expansionists wanted. This larger navy, in turn, demanded strategic bases and coaling stations.

Economic Designs

One reason for the widespread support for a larger navy was its use to expand and protect America's international trade. Nearly all Americans favored economic expansion through foreign trade. Such a policy promised national prosperity: more markets for manufacturers and farmers, greater profits for merchants and bankers, more jobs for workers. Far fewer favored the acquisition of colonies that was characteristic of European imperialism. (See Global Connections: European Colonial Imperialism.)

The United States had long aggressively fostered American trade, especially in Latin America and East Asia. As early as 1844, the United States had negotiated a trade treaty with China, and ten years later a squadron under Commodore Matthew Perry had forced the Japanese to open their ports to American products. In the late nineteenth century, the dramatic expansion of the economy caused many Americans to favor more government action to open foreign markets to American exports.

Exports, especially of manufactured goods, which grew ninefold between 1865 and 1900, did increase greatly in the late nineteenth century. Still, periodic depressions fed fears of overproduction. The massive unemployment and social unrest that accompanied these economic crises also provided social and political arguments for economic relief through foreign trade.

In the depression of the 1890s, with the secretary of state seeing "symptoms of revolution" in the Pullman strike and Coxey's Army of unemployed workers (see Chapter 20), the interest in foreign trade became obsessive. More systematic government efforts to promote trade seemed necessary, a conclusion strengthened by new threats to existing American markets. In that tumultuous decade, European nations raised tariff barriers against American products, and Japan and the European imperial powers began to restrict commercial opportunities in the areas of China that they controlled. Many American leaders decided that the United States had to adopt decisive new policies or face economic catastrophe.

FIRST STEPS

WHAT STEPS did the United States take to expand its global influence in the decades before the Spanish-American War?

Despite the growing ideological, strategic, and economic arguments for imperialism, the government only fitfully interested itself in foreign affairs before the mid-1890s. It did not pursue a policy of isolationism from international affairs, for the nation maintained normal diplomatic and trade ties and at times vigorously intervened in Latin America and East Asia. But in general the government deferred to the initiative of private interests, reacted haphazardly to outside events, and did little to create a professional foreign service. In a few bold if inconsistent steps, however, the United States moved to expand its influence.

Seward and Blaine

Two secretaries of state, William H. Seward, secretary under Presidents Abraham Lincoln and Andrew Johnson (1861–1869), and James G. Blaine, secretary under Presidents James Garfield and Benjamin Harrison (1881, 1889–1892), laid the foundation for a larger and more aggressive U.S. role in world affairs. Seward possessed an elaborate imperial vision, based on his understanding of commercial opportunities, strategic necessities, and national destiny. His interest in opening East Asia to American commerce and establishing American hegemony over the Caribbean anticipated the subsequent course of American expansion. Seward purchased Alaska from Russia in 1867, approved the navy's occupation of the Midway Islands in the Pacific, pushed American trade on a reluctant Japan, and repeatedly tried to acquire Caribbean naval bases (see Map 22–1).

Blaine was an equally vigorous, if inconsistent, advocate of expansion. He worked to extend what he called America's "commercial empire" in the Pacific. In an effort to induce Latin American nations to import manufactured products from the United States rather than Europe, Blaine proposed a customs union to reduce trade barriers, expecting it to strengthen U.S. control of hemispheric markets. Wary of economic subordination to the colossus of the north, however, the Latin American nations rejected Blaine's plan but did agree to establish what eventually came to be known as the **Pan American Union.** Based in Washington, it helped to promote hemispheric understanding and cooperation.

If U.S. officials were increasingly assertive toward Latin America and Asia, however, they remained little involved in Europe and wholly indifferent to Africa, which the European powers were then carving up into colonies. In short, despite some important precedents for the future, much of American foreign policy remained undeveloped, sporadic, and impulsive.

Pan American Union International organization originally established as the Commercial Bureau of American Republics by Secretary of State James Blaine's first Pan-American Conference in 1889 to promote cooperation among nations of the Western Hemisphere through commercial and diplomatic negotiations.

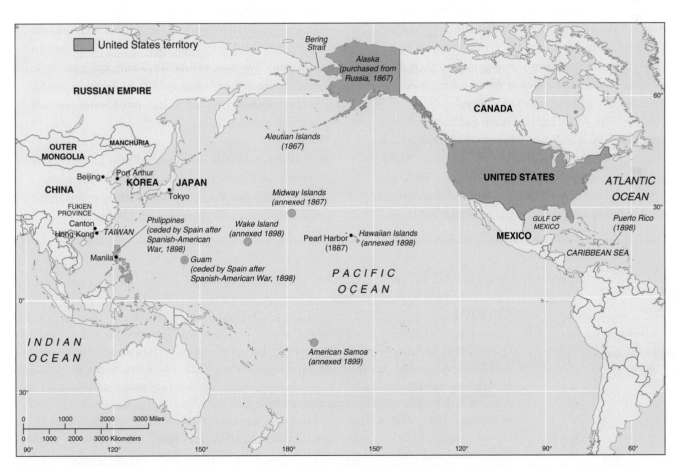

MAP 22–1 **United States Expansion in the Pacific, 1867–1899** Pursuing visions of a commercial empire in the Pacific, the United States steadily expanded its territorial possessions as well as its influence there in the late nineteenth century.

How did a desire to expand American economic activity in China motivate and shape U.S. expansion in the Pacific? What light does this map shed on this question?

GLOBAL CONNECTIONS

 EUROPEAN COLONIAL IMPERIALISM 

The United States was not alone in expanding its role in the world. Beginning in the 1870s, leading European nations engaged in a competitive struggle to partition much of Africa and Asia in pursuit of their imperial ambitions. Like Americans, Europeans advanced many justifications for imperialism. Many favored colonies to acquire markets, resources, and investment opportunities; others saw in colonies strategic advantages or international prestige. Some interwove racist and religious attitudes to justify European empire building as "an instrument for the good of humanity."

But advanced industrialization, more than the questionable blessings of religion and race, accounted for European success. Railroads, steamships, and ocean cables facilitated transportation and communication, and modern weaponry easily overcame native resistance. In the Battle of Omdurman in 1898, a British expedition armed with machine guns massacred 11,000 Sudanese tribesmen trying to defend their independence while itself suffering only 28 casualties. Said one observer: "It was not a battle but an execution."

Before the 1870s Africa had largely escaped European colonialism, but within 30 years European powers had divided much of the continent. France gained most of northwestern Africa, conquering Algeria in 1879, occupying Tunisia in 1881, and dividing Morocco with Spain. Britain acquired territory from the Mediterranean Sea to the Cape. To control the area around the Suez Canal, viewed as the empire's lifeline to India, the British occupied Egypt in 1882 and then seized the Sudan. With unimaginable brutality, Belgium's King Leopold colonized the Congo in central Africa. Germany established colonies in southwestern Africa and, like Italy, in East Africa.

European powers also advanced on Asia. To its earlier control of India, Great Britain added Burma and Malaya. France extended its authority over Indochina in the 1880s and 1890s by gaining control of Vietnam and Laos. Russia expanded its empire into contiguous territories, securing Turkestan in Central Asia and then reaching toward East Asia, particularly the Manchurian region of China. Other nations also sought spheres of influence in China, acquiring ports, naval stations, and railroad and mining concessions.

Competitive imperialism risked conflict, between expansive nations as well as with colonized peoples, but such risks did not deter aspiring imperialists. In 1887 the Japanese foreign minister insisted: "We have to establish a new, European-style empire on the edge of Asia." And in 1895 an American leader declared of European imperialism: "The United States must not fall out of the line of march."

- While many Americans distinguished their foreign policy goals from European imperialism, how might the nation's expansion into the American West and its treatment of Native Americans correspond to such colonialism?

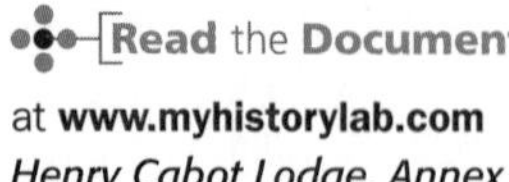

at **www.myhistorylab.com**
Henry Cabot Lodge, Annex of Hawaii (1895)

HAWAII

Blaine regarded Hawaii as "indispensably" part of "the American system." As early as 1842, the United States had announced its opposition to European control of Hawaii, a key waystation in the China trade and where New England missionaries and whalers were already active. Although Hawaii continued to be ruled by native monarchs, American influence grew, particularly as other Americans arrived to establish sugar plantations and eventually dominate the economy. Treaties in 1875 and 1887 integrated the islands into the American economy and gave the United States control over Pearl Harbor on the island of Oahu. In 1887, the United States rejected a proposal from Britain and France for a joint guarantee of Hawaii's independence and endorsed a new Hawaiian constitution that gave political power to wealthy white residents. The obvious next step was U.S. annexation, which Blaine endorsed in 1891.

A combination of factors soon impelled American planters to bid for annexation. The McKinley Tariff Act of 1890 effectively closed the U.S. market to Hawaiian sugar producers, threatening their economic ruin. At the same time, Queen Liliuokalani moved to restore native control of Hawaiian affairs. To ensure market access and protect their political authority, the American planters decided to seek annexation to the United States. In 1893, they overthrew the queen. John Stevens, the American diplomatic representative, ordered U.S. marines to help the rebels and then declared an American protectorate over the new Hawaiian government. A delegation from the new provisional government, which did not include any native Hawaiians, went to Washington to draft a treaty for annexation. President Harrison signed the pact but could not get Senate approval before the new Cleveland administration took office.

Grover Cleveland immediately called for an investigation of the whole affair. Soon convinced that "the undoubted sentiment of the people is for the Queen, against the provisional Government, and against annexation," Cleveland apologized to the queen for the "flagrant wrong" done her by the "reprehensible conduct" of U.S. diplomats and troops. But the American-dominated provisional government refused to step down, and Cleveland's rejection of annexation set off a noisy debate in the United States.

Many Republicans strongly supported annexation, which they regarded as merely part of a larger plan of expansion. Democrats generally opposed annexation. They doubted, as Missouri senator George Vest declared, whether the United States should desert its traditional principles and "venture upon the great colonial system of the European powers." The Hawaiian episode of 1893 thus foreshadowed the arguments over imperialism at the end of the century and emphasized the policy differences between Democrats and the increasingly expansionist Republicans.

As other imperial powers look on, the United States abandons its traditional principles to rush headlong into world affairs. Uncle Sam would not always find it a smooth ride.

Chile and Venezuela

American reactions to developments in other countries in the 1890s also reflected an increasingly assertive national policy and excitable public opinion. In 1891, American sailors on shore leave in Chile became involved in a drunken brawl that left two of them dead, 17 injured, and dozens in jail. Encouraged by a combative navy, President Harrison threatened military retaliation against Chile, provoking an outburst of bellicose nationalism in the United States. Harrison relented only when Chile apologized and paid an indemnity.

A few years later, the United States again threatened war over a minor issue but against a more formidable opponent. In 1895, President Cleveland intervened in a boundary dispute between Great Britain and Venezuela over British Guiana. Cleveland was motivated not only by the long-standing U.S. goal of challenging Britain for Latin American markets but also by ever more expansive notions of the Monroe Doctrine and the authority of the United States. Secretary of State Richard Olney sent Britain a blunt note demanding arbitration of the disputed territory and stoutly asserting American supremacy in the Western Hemisphere. Cleveland urged Congress to establish a commission to determine the boundary and enforce its decision by war if necessary. As war fever swept the United States, Britain agreed to arbitration, recognizing the limited nature of the issue that so convulsed Anglo-American relations.

Cleveland's assertion of U.S. hemispheric dominance angered Latin Americans, and their fears deepened when the United States decided arbitration terms with Britain without consulting Venezuela, which protested before bowing to American pressure. The United States had intervened less to protect Venezuela from the British bully than to advance its own hegemony. The further significance of the Venezuelan crisis, Captain Mahan noted, lay in its "awakening of our countrymen to the fact that we must come out of our isolation . . . and take our share in the turmoil of the world."

THE SPANISH-AMERICAN WAR

WHAT WERE the most important consequences of the Spanish-American War?

The forces pushing the United States toward imperialism and international power came to a head in the Spanish-American War. Cuba's quest for independence from the oppressive colonial control of Spain activated Americans' long-standing interest in the island. Many sympathized with the Cuban rebels' yearning for freedom, others worried that disorder in Cuba threatened their own economic and political interests, and some thought that intervention would increase the influence of the United States in the Caribbean and along key Pacific routes to Asian markets. But few foresaw that the war that finally erupted in 1898 would dramatically change U.S. relationships with the rest of the world and give the United States a colonial empire.

THE CUBAN REVOLUTION

The last major European colony in Latin America, Cuba held an economic potential that attracted American business interests and a strategic significance for any Central American canal. In the late nineteenth century, American investors expanded their economic influence in Cuba, while Cubans themselves rebelled repeatedly but unsuccessfully against increasingly harsh Spanish rule. Cuban discontent erupted again in 1895, when the Cuban patriot José Martí launched another revolt.

The rebellion was a classic guerrilla war, with the rebels controlling the countryside and the Spanish army the towns and cities. American economic interests were seriously affected, for both Cubans and Spaniards destroyed American property and disrupted American trade. But the brutality with which Spain attempted to suppress the revolt promoted American sympathy for the Cuban insurgents. Determined to cut the rebels off from their peasant supporters, the Spanish herded most civilians into "reconcentration camps," where tens of thousands died of starvation and disease.

yellow press A deliberately sensational journalism of scandal and exposure designed to attract an urban mass audience and increase advertising revenues.

American sympathy was further aroused by the sensationalist **yellow press.** To attract readers and boost advertising revenues, the popular press of the day adopted bold headlines, fevered editorials, and real or exaggerated stories of violence, sex, and corruption. A circulation war helped stimulate interest in a Cuban war. Failure to intervene to protect the innocent from Spanish lust and cruelty, insisted the yellow journalists, would be dishonorable and cowardly.

QUICK REVIEW

The Press and Cuba

- Yellow press stimulated interest in Cuba.
- Newspapers emphasized violence, sex, and corruption.
- Much of America's religious press advocated American intervention.

The nation's religious press, partly because it reflected the prejudice of many Protestants against Catholic Spain, also advocated American intervention. The *Catholic Herald* of New York sarcastically referred to the "bloodthirsty preachers" of the Protestant churches, but such preachers undeniably influenced American opinion against Spain.

As the Cuban rebellion dragged on, more and more Americans advocated intervention to stop the carnage, protect U.S. investments, or uphold various principles. In the election of 1896, both major parties endorsed Cuban independence.

GROWING TENSIONS

In his 1897 inaugural address, President William McKinley outlined an expansionist program ranging from further enlargement of the navy to the annexation of Hawaii and the construction of a Central American canal in Nicaragua, but his administration soon focused on Cuba. McKinley's principal complaint was that chronic disorder in Cuba disrupted American investments and agitated public opinion. Personally opposed to military intervention, McKinley first used diplomacy to press Spain to adopt reforms that would settle the rebellion. In late 1897, Spain modified its brutal military tactics and offered limited autonomy to Cuba. But Cubans insisted on complete independence, a demand that Spain rejected.

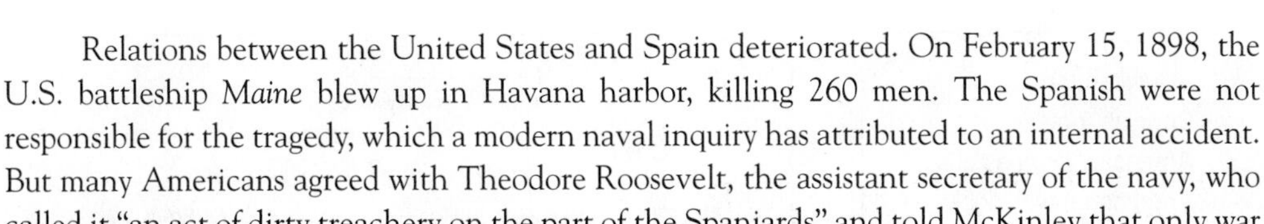

Relations between the United States and Spain deteriorated. On February 15, 1898, the U.S. battleship *Maine* blew up in Havana harbor, killing 260 men. The Spanish were not responsible for the tragedy, which a modern naval inquiry has attributed to an internal accident. But many Americans agreed with Theodore Roosevelt, the assistant secretary of the navy, who called it "an act of dirty treachery on the part of the Spaniards" and told McKinley that only war was "compatible with our national honor."

QUICK REVIEW

Pressure on McKinley to Go to War

- Spain was reluctant to modify oppressive policies in Cuba.
- Destruction of the *Maine* inflamed public opinion.
- Political advisers warned of election defeats if action were not taken.

Popular anger was inflamed, but the sinking of the *Maine* by itself did not bring war, though it did restrict McKinley's options and pressure him to be more assertive toward Spain. Other pressures soon began to build on the president. Increasingly, business interests favored war as less disruptive than a volatile peace that threatened their investments. Further, McKinley feared that a moderate policy would endanger Republican congressional candidates.

At the end of March 1898, McKinley sent Spain an ultimatum. He demanded an armistice in Cuba, an end to the reconcentration policy, and the acceptance of American arbitration, which implied Cuban independence. Again, Spain made concessions, abolishing reconcentration and declaring a unilateral armistice. But McKinley had already begun war preparations. He submitted a war message to Congress on April 11, asking for authority to use force against Spain. Congress declared war on Spain on April 25, 1898.

Read the **Document** at **www.myhistorylab.com** *The Teller Amendment (1898)*

A few national leaders welcomed the war as a step toward imperialism, but there was little popular support for an imperialist foreign policy. Most interventionists were not imperialists, and Congress added the **Teller Amendment** to the war resolution, disclaiming any intention of annexing Cuba and promising that Cubans would govern themselves. Congress also refused to approve either a canal bill or the annexation of Hawaii. Nevertheless, the Spanish-American War did turn the nation toward imperialism.

Teller Amendment A congressional resolution adopted in 1898 renouncing any American intention to annex Cuba.

War and Empire

Read the **Document** at **www.myhistorylab.com** *William McKinley, "Decision on the Philippines"* (1900)

The decisive engagement of the war took place not in Cuba but in another Spanish colony, the Philippines, and it involved the favored tool of the expansionists, the new navy (see Map 22–2). Once war was declared, Commodore George Dewey led the U.S. Asiatic squadron into Manila Bay and destroyed the much weaker Spanish fleet on May 1, 1898. This dramatic victory galvanized expansionist sentiment in the United States. With Dewey's triumph, exulted one expansionist, "We are taking our proper rank among the nations of the world. We are after markets, the greatest markets now existing in the world." To expand this foothold in Asia, McKinley ordered troops to the Philippines, postponing the military expedition to Cuba itself.

Dewey's victory also precipitated the annexation of Hawaii, which had seemed unlikely only weeks before. Annexationists now pointed to the islands' strategic importance as stepping stones to Manila. In July, Congress approved annexation, a decision welcomed by Hawaii's white minority. Native Hawaiians solemnly protested this step taken "without reference to the consent of the people of the Hawaiian Islands." Filipinos would soon face the same American imperial impulse.

Military victory also came swiftly in Cuba, once the U.S. Army finally landed in late June. Victory came despite bureaucratic bungling in the War Department, which left the American army poorly led, trained, and supplied. More than 5,000 Americans died of diseases and accidents brought on by such mismanagement; only 379 were killed in battle. State militias supplemented the small regular army, as did volunteer units, such as the famous Rough Riders, a cavalry regiment of cowboys and eastern dandies organized by Leonard Wood and Theodore Roosevelt.

QUICK REVIEW

Dewey's Victory

- May 1, 1898: Dewey's squadron destroys Spanish fleet in Manila Bay.
- Expansionists saw victory as an opportunity for greater U.S. presence in the region.
- McKinley followed up Dewey's victory by sending troops to the Philippines.

While the Rough Riders captured public attention, other units were more effective. The 10th Negro Cavalry, for example, played the crucial role in capturing San Juan Hill, a

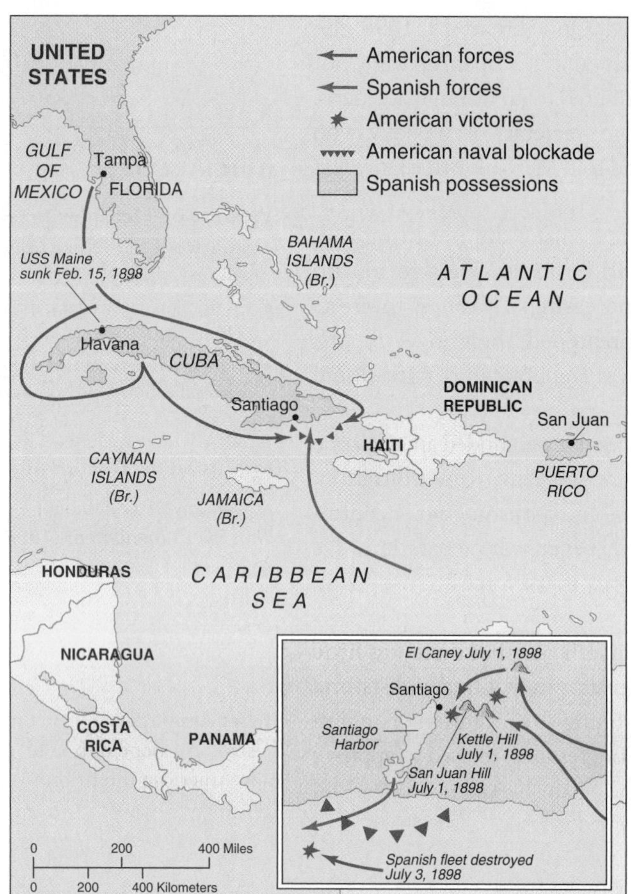

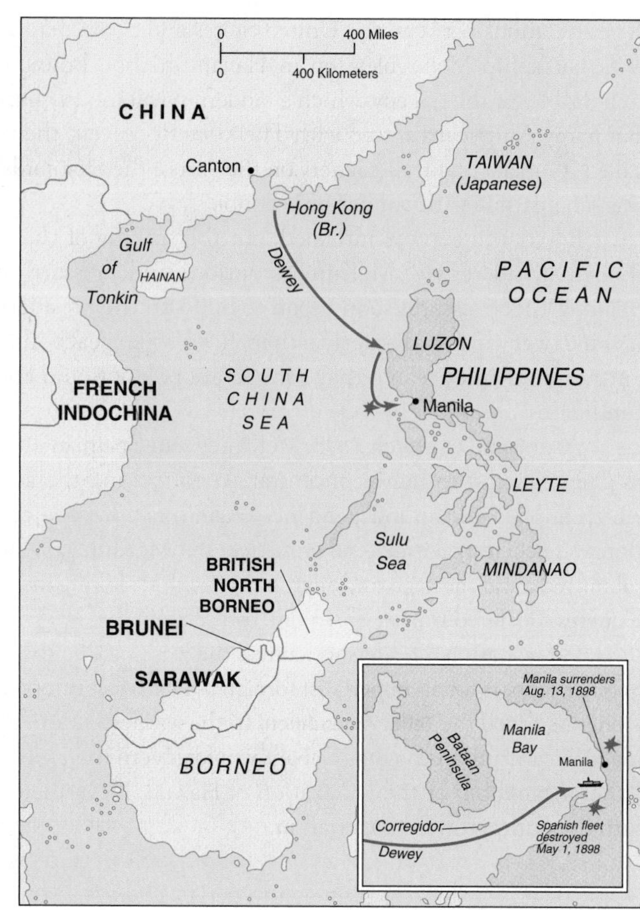

MAP 22–2 **The Spanish-American War** The United States gained quick victories in both theaters of the Spanish-American War. Its naval power proved decisive, with Commodore Dewey destroying one enemy fleet in the Philippines, and a second U.S. naval force cutting off the Spanish in Cuba.

How did the Philippines become part of a war that began in Cuba? What does the American attack on the Philippines tell you about the goals of American officials during the Spanish-American War?

battle popularly associated with the Rough Riders. Nevertheless, the Rough Riders gained the credit, thanks in part to Roosevelt's self-serving and well-promoted account of the conflict.

U.S. naval power again proved decisive. In a lopsided battle on July 3, the Spanish squadron in Cuba was destroyed, isolating the Spanish army and guaranteeing its defeat. U.S. forces then seized the nearby Spanish colony of Puerto Rico without serious opposition. Humbled, Spain signed an armistice ending the war on August 12.

The Treaty of Paris

Read the **Document** at **www.myhistorylab.com** *Mark Twain, "Incident in the Philippines" (1924)*

Watch the **Video** at **www.myhistorylab.com** *Roosevelt's Rough Riders*

The armistice required Spain to accept Cuban independence, cede Puerto Rico and Guam (a Pacific island between Hawaii and the Philippines) to the United States, and allow the Americans to occupy Manila, pending the final disposition of the Philippines at a formal peace conference. The acquisition of Puerto Rico and Guam indicated the expansionist nature the conflict had assumed for the United States. So did the postponement of the Philippine issue. McKinley knew that delay would permit the advocates of expansion to build public support for annexation.

McKinley defended his decision to acquire the Philippines with self-righteous imperialist rhetoric, promising to extend Christian influence and American values. But he was motivated primarily by a determination to use the islands to strengthen America's political and commercial position in East Asia. Moreover, he believed the Filipinos poorly suited to self-rule, and he feared that Germany or Japan might seize the Philippines if the United States did not. Meeting in Paris in December, American and Spanish negotiators settled the final terms for peace. Spain agreed—despite Filipino demands for independence—to cede the Philippines to the United States.

Uncle Sam considers the expansionist menu offered by President McKinley. The Sandwich Islands (Hawaii) was only the appetizer.

The decision to acquire the Philippines sparked a dramatic debate over the ratification of the Treaty of Paris. Imperialists invoked the familiar arguments of economic expansion, national destiny, and strategic necessity, while asserting that Americans had religious and racial responsibilities to advance civilization by uplifting backward peoples.

Opponents of the treaty raised profound questions about national goals and ideals (see American Views: A Southern Senator Opposes Annexation). Opponents included such prominent figures as the civil service reformer Carl Schurz, the steel baron Andrew Carnegie, the social reformer Jane Addams, the labor leader Samuel Gompers, and the author Mark Twain. Their organizational base was the Anti-Imperialist League, which campaigned against the treaty, distributing pamphlets, petitioning Congress, and holding rallies. The League's criticisms reflected a conviction that imperialism was a repudiation of the moral and political traditions embodied in the Declaration of Independence. The acquisition of overseas colonies, they argued, conflicted with the nation's commitment to liberty and its claim to moral superiority.

But other arguments were less high-minded. Many anti-imperialists objected to expansion on the racist grounds that Filipinos were inferior and unassimilable. Gompers feared that cheap Asian labor would undercut the wages and living standards of American workers. The *San Francisco Call,* representing California-Hawaiian sugar interests, wanted no competition from the Philippines.

Finally, on February 6, 1899, the Senate narrowly ratified the treaty. All but two Republicans supported the pact; most Democrats opposed it, although several voted in favor after William Jennings Bryan suggested that approval was necessary to end the war and detach the Philippines from Spain. Thereafter, he hoped, a congressional resolution would give the Filipinos their independence. But by a single vote, the Republicans defeated a Democratic proposal for Philippine independence once a stable government had been established; the United States would keep the islands.

Republicans countered William Jennings Bryan's attempt to make imperialism an issue in 1900 by wrapping themselves in patriotism and the American flag. "Take Your Choice," a cartoon from Judge, posed President McKinley raising Old Glory over the Philippines with a disheveled and frantic Bryan chopping down the symbol of American pride and power.

Bryan attempted to make the election of 1900 a referendum on "the paramount issue" of imperialism, promising to free the Philippines if the Democrats won. But other issues determined the outcome. Some of the most ardent anti-imperialists were conservatives who remained loyal to McKinley

AMERICAN VIEWS

A Southern Senator Opposes Annexation

In the Senate's debate over the ratification of the Treaty of Paris, ending the Spanish-American War and ceding the Philippines to the United States, both supporters and opponents appealed to noble ideals, invoked base motives, and expressed anxiety for the future. Senator James H. Berry, a conservative Democrat from Arkansas, delivered a particularly forceful attack upon the treaty. The following passages from his speech outline some of his views of what he termed President McKinley's "wild scheme of colonization and acquisition of territory."

- **In** what ways did Berry regard the treaty as a repudiation of the war itself?
- **What** were the dangers that Berry saw for the United States in approving the treaty?
- **What** forces did Berry believe were directing the development of American foreign policy?

When the protocol for peace was signed on the 12th day of last August, I think it could have been truthfully said that there had never been a time since the organization of the Government when the American Republic commanded so much respect from the nations of the world, and never a time when its own citizens felt for that Republic so much love, so much devotion, and so much admiration. Less than six months have passed and there are thousands and tens of thousands of intelligent and patriotic citizens who sincerely believe that the danger of the destruction and overthrow of our institutions has never been so great as it is today.

What has been the cause of the remarkable change in the policy of our Government? What has been the mighty influence that has caused us to depart from the teachings of our fathers and to enter upon a course of action directly opposed to all that we have professed? . . .

The cause for the universal rejoicing of our people at the close of the war can be easily understood. . . . The pride and glory that the American people felt in the Army and Navy was greatly enhanced by the fact that all felt and knew that the war had been waged by us from unselfish and disinterested motives. We had fought to make others free as we ourselves were free; we had fought to enable the Cuban people to throw off their colonial dependence upon Spain and establish a free and independent government for themselves; we had disclaimed, in the act declaring war, any intention of acquiring territory in the island. The President

QUICK REVIEW

The Anti-Imperialist League

- Central to campaign against the Treaty of Paris (ratified 1899).
- League members saw treaty as a repudiation of American moral and political traditions.
- Many anti-imperialists objected to expansion on racist grounds.

because they could not tolerate Bryan's economic policies. Republicans also benefited from the prosperity the country experienced under McKinley after the hard 1890s, and they played on the nationalist emotions evoked by the war, especially by nominating the "hero of San Juan Hill," Theodore Roosevelt, for vice president. Bryan lost again, as in 1896, and under Republican leadership, the United States became an imperial nation.

IMPERIAL AMBITIONS: THE UNITED STATES AND EAST ASIA, 1899–1917

WHAT WAS the nature of U.S. involvement in Asia?

In 1899, as the United States occupied its new empire, Assistant Secretary of State John Bassett Moore observed that the nation had become "a world power. . . . Where formerly we had only commercial interests, we now have territorial and political interests as well." American policies to promote these expanded interests focused first on East Asia and Latin America, where the Spanish-American War had provided the United States with both opportunities and challenges. In Asia, the first issue concerned the fate of the Philippines, but looming beyond it were American ambitions in China, where other imperial nations had their own goals.

himself had said that the forcible acquisition of territory would not be tolerated by the American people, and that such an attempt would be criminal aggression. The American people were proud because they had done a brave and generous and unselfish deed, which would be a gratification to them and to their children in all the years to come.

They had no thought then that the great combinations of wealth and greed would be able thereafter to unite and bring to bear such a mighty influence as would control the public press, to a large extent public sentiment, the President, and the Senate of the United States, and secure the adoption of a policy that would hereafter forever dim and obscure the glory that they had fairly won. We fought Spain in order to free the Cubans from her control. We can not, in my opinion, without placing a blot upon the fair name of the Republic, without dishonor to ourselves, fight the inhabitants of the Philippine Islands in order to subject them to our control. But such is the proposition made to us today.

. . . We are told that we must conquer these people in the interest of humanity and for their own good, that we must entail enormous expense upon our own people, that we must drag our youth to that far-off land, and kill and slaughter hundreds and, it may be, thousands of these people in order that we may civilize and Christianize the remainder. . . .

[But] the plea of humanity is not the true cause of this movement. It doubtless has controlled the judgment of many, but the all-powerful force behind it is the desire of extending trade and commerce. It is the desire for gain, and not to relieve suffering. . . .

But it is not the people of these far-off islands that concern me most; it is the effect upon our own country, our own Government, and our own institutions; . . . it is the regret that I feel for the great demoralization of our people which must come when all their ideals are shattered and when we adopt a line of action which we have for more than a hundred years denounced as unjust and wicked. . . .

We are entering upon a dangerous field. We are doing it on the pretense, it may be, of humanity and Christianity, but behind it all, I repeat, is the desire for trade and commerce; and whenever and wherever considerations of money making are placed above the honor and fair fame of this Republic, the men who are doing it are undermining the very foundations of the Government under which we live.

Source: Congressional Record, 55th Cong., 3rd sess., pp. 1297–99 (January 31, 1899).

The Filipino-American War

Filipino nationalists, like the Cuban insurgents, were already fighting Spain for their independence before the sudden American intervention. The Filipino leader, Emilio Aguinaldo, welcomed Dewey's naval victory as the sign of a *de facto* alliance with the United States; he then issued a declaration of independence and proclaimed the Philippine Republic. His own troops captured most of Luzon, the Philippines' major island, before the U.S. Army arrived. When the Treaty of Paris provided for U.S. ownership rather than independence, Filipinos felt betrayed. Mounting tensions erupted in a battle between American and Filipino troops outside Manila on February 4, 1899, sparking a long and brutal war.

Read the **Document**
at **www.myhistorylab.com**
William Graham Sumner, "On Empire and the Philippines" (1898)

Ultimately, the United States used nearly four times as many soldiers to suppress the Filipinos as it had to defeat Spain in Cuba and, in a tragic irony, employed many of the same brutal methods for which it had condemned Spain. U.S. military commanders adopted ever harsher measures, often directed at civilians, who were crowded into concentration camps in which perhaps 200,000 died. American troops often made little effort to distinguish between soldiers and noncombatants, viewing all Filipinos with racial antagonism. After reporting one massacre of a thousand men, women, and children, an American soldier declared, "I am in my glory when I can sight my gun on some dark skin and pull the trigger."

A California newspaper defended such actions with remarkable candor: "There has been too much hypocrisy about this Philippine business. . . . Let us all be frank. WE DO NOT WANT THE FILIPINOS. WE DO WANT THE PHILIPPINES. All of our troubles in this annexation matter have been caused by the presence in the Philippine Islands of the Filipinos. . . . The more of them killed the better. It seems harsh. But they must yield before the superior race."

Other Americans denounced the war. The Anti-Imperialist League revived, citing the war as proof of the corrosive influence of imperialism on the nation's morals and principles. Women figured prominently in mass meetings and lobbying efforts to have the troops returned, their moral stature further undercutting the rationale for colonial wars. By 1902, the realities of imperial policy—including American casualties far exceeding those of the Spanish-American War—disillusioned most of those who had clamored to save Cuba.

By that time, however, the American military had largely suppressed the rebellion, and the United States had established a colonial government headed by an American governor general appointed by the president. Filipino involvement in the government was limited on educational and religious grounds. Compared to the brutal war policies, U.S. colonial rule was relatively benign, though paternalistic. William Howard Taft, the first governor general, launched a program that brought the islands new schools and roads, a public health system, and an economy tied closely to both the United States and a small Filipino elite. Independence would take nearly half a century.

China and the Open Door

America's determined involvement in the Philippines reflected its preoccupation with China. By the mid-1890s, other powers threatened prospects for American commercial expansion in China. Japan, after defeating China in 1895, annexed Formosa (Taiwan) and secured economic privileges in the mainland province of Fukien (Fujian); the major European powers then competed aggressively to claim other areas of China as their own **spheres of influence.**

spheres of influence Regions dominated and controlled by an outside power.

These developments alarmed the American business community. It was confident that, given an equal opportunity, the United States would prevail in international trade because of its efficient production and marketing systems. But the creation of exclusive spheres of influence limited the opportunity to compete. In early 1898, business leaders organized the Committee on American Interests in China to lobby Washington to promote American trade in the shrinking Chinese market. The committee persuaded the nation's chambers of commerce to petition the McKinley administration to act. This campaign influenced McKinley's interest in acquiring the Philippines, but the Philippines, in the words of Mark Hanna, were only a "foothold"; China was the real target.

QUICK REVIEW

Filipino-American War

- Filipinos felt betrayed by Treaty of Paris.
- February 4, 1899: fighting between American and Filipino troops sparked war.
- 1902: U.S. colonial rule is established after a brutal war.

In 1899, the government moved to advance American interests in China. Without consulting the Chinese, Secretary of State John Hay asked the imperial powers to maintain an **Open Door** for the commercial and financial activities of all nations within their Chinese spheres of influence. Privately, Hay had already approved a plan to seize a Chinese port for the United States, if necessary to join in the partition of China, but equal opportunity for trade and investment would serve American interests far better. It would avoid the expense of military occupation, avert further domestic criticism of U.S. imperialism, and guarantee a wider sphere for American business.

Open Door American policy of seeking equal trade and investment opportunities in foreign nations or regions.

The other nations replied evasively, except for Russia, which rejected the Open Door concept. In 1900, an antiforeign Chinese nationalist movement known as the Boxers laid siege to the diplomatic quarter in Beijing. The defeat of the Boxer Rebellion by a multinational military force, to which the United States contributed troops, again raised the prospect of a division of China among the colonial powers. Hay sent a second Open Door note, reaffirming "the principle of equal and impartial trade" and respect for China's territorial integrity.

Despite Hay's notes, China remained a tempting arena for imperial schemes. But the Open Door became a cardinal doctrine of American foreign policy in the twentieth century, a means by which the United States sought to dominate foreign markets. The United States promoted an informal or economic empire, as opposed to the traditional territorial colonial empire identified with European powers. Henceforth, American economic interests expected the U.S. government to oppose any developments that threatened to close other nations' economies to American penetration and to advance "private enterprise" abroad.

Rivalry with Japan and Russia

At the turn of the twentieth century, both the Japanese and the Russians were more deeply involved in East Asia than was the United States. Japan and Russia expressed little support for the Open Door, which they correctly saw as favoring American interests over their own. But in pursuing their ambitions in China, the two countries came into conflict with each other. Alarmed at the threat of Russian expansion in Manchuria and Korea, Japan in 1904 attacked the Russian fleet at Port Arthur and defeated the Russian army in Manchuria.

American sympathies in the Russo-Japanese War lay with Japan, for the Russians were attempting to close Manchuria to foreign trade. President Theodore Roosevelt privately complained that a reluctant American public opinion meant that "we cannot fight to keep Manchuria open." He welcomed the Japanese attack in the belief that "Japan is playing our game." But he soon began to fear that an overwhelming Japanese victory would threaten American interests as much as Russian expansionism did, so he skillfully mediated an end to the war. In the Treaty of Portsmouth in 1905, Japan won control of Russia's sphere of influence in Manchuria, half the Russian island of Sakhalin, and recognition of its domination of Korea.

The treaty marked Japan's emergence as a great power, but, ironically, it worsened relations with the United States. Anti-American riots broke out in Tokyo. The Japanese people blamed Roosevelt for obstructing further Japanese gains and blocking a Russian indemnity that would have helped Japan pay for the war. Tensions were further aggravated by San Francisco's decision in 1906 to segregate Asian and white schoolchildren. Japan regarded this as a racist insult, and Roosevelt worried that "the infernal fools in California" would provoke war. Finally, he persuaded the city to rescind the school order in exchange for his limiting Japanese immigration, which lay at the heart of California's hostility. Under the **Gentlemen's Agreement,** worked out through a series of diplomatic notes in 1907 and 1908, Japan agreed to deny passports to workers trying to come to the United States, and the United States promised not to prohibit Japanese immigration overtly or completely.

The United States and Japan entered into other agreements aimed at calming their mutual suspicions in East Asia but failed to mend the deteriorating relationship. Increasingly, Japan began to exclude American trade from its territories in East Asia and to press for further control over China. General Leonard Wood complained that the Japanese "intend to dominate Asia as we do the Americas." Elihu Root, Roosevelt's secretary of state, insisted that the Open Door and American access had to be maintained but asserted also that the

Gentlemen's Agreement A diplomatic agreement in 1907 between Japan and the United States curtailing but not abolishing Japanese immigration.

QUICK REVIEW

Trade with China

- American business interests lobbied for access to China's markets.
- 1899: Secretary of State John Hay calls for an Open Door policy.
- Open Door became a central doctrine of American foreign policy.

A FAIR FIELD AND NO FAVOR.
UNCLE SAM: "I'm out for commerce, not conquest."

The United States usually preferred the "annexation of trade" to the annexation of territory. The Open Door policy promised to advance American commercial expansion, but Uncle Sam had to restrain other imperialists with colonial objectives.

United States did not want to be "a protagonist in a controversy in China with Russia and Japan or with either of them." The problem was that the United States could not sustain the Open Door without becoming a protagonist in China. This paradox, and the unwillingness to commit military force, would plague American foreign policy in Asia for decades.

IMPERIAL POWER: THE UNITED STATES AND LATIN AMERICA, 1899–1917

HOW DID Latin Americans respond to U.S. intervention in the region?

In Latin America, where no major powers directly challenged American objectives as Japan and Russia did in Asia, the United States was more successful in exercising imperial power (see Map 22–3). In the two decades after the Spanish-American War, the United States intervened militarily in Latin America no fewer than 20 times to promote its own strategic and economic interests (see Overview, U.S. Interventions in Latin America, 1891–1933). Intervention at times achieved American goals, but it often ignored the wishes and interests of Latin Americans, provoked resistance and disorder, and aroused lasting ill will.

U.S. RULE IN PUERTO RICO

Military invasion during the Spanish-American War and the Treaty of Paris brought Puerto Rico under American control, with mixed consequences. A military government improved transportation and sanitation and developed public health and education. But to the dismay of Puerto Ricans, who had been promised that American rule would bestow "the advantages and blessings of enlightened civilization," their political freedoms were curtailed.

QUICK REVIEW

U.S. Rule in Puerto Rico

- Insular Cases (1901): U.S. Supreme Court upholds Puerto Rico's inferior status as "unincorporated territory."
- Economic development of island favors American investors.
- Puerto Ricans leave island in growing numbers to seek work in United States.

In 1900, the United States established a civil government, but it was under U.S. control, with popular participation even less than under Spain. In the so-called Insular Cases (1901), the Supreme Court upheld the authority of Congress to establish an inferior status for Puerto Rico as an "unincorporated territory" without promise of statehood. Disappointed Puerto Ricans pressed to end this colonial status, some advocating independence, others statehood or merely greater autonomy. This division would continue for decades to come. In 1917, the United States granted citizenship and greater political rights to Puerto Ricans, but their island remained an unincorporated territory under an American governor appointed by the president.

Economic development also disappointed most islanders, for American investors quickly gained control of the best land and pursued large-scale sugar production for the U.S. market. The landless peasants struggled to survive as workers on large plantations. Increasingly, Puerto Ricans left their homes to seek work in the United States.

CUBA AS A U.S. PROTECTORATE

Despite the Teller Amendment, the Spanish-American War did not leave Cuba independent. McKinley opposed independence and distrusted the Cuban rebels. Accordingly, a U.S. military government was established in the island. Only in 1900, when the Democrats made an issue of imperialism, did the McKinley administration move toward permitting a Cuban government and withdrawing American troops. McKinley summoned a Cuban convention to draft a constitution under the direction of the American military governor, General Leonard Wood. Reflecting the continuing U.S. fear of Cuban autonomy, the constitution restricted suffrage on the basis of property and education, leaving few Cubans with the right to vote.

Even so, before removing its troops, the United States wanted to ensure its control over Cuba. It therefore made U.S. withdrawal contingent on Cuba's adding to its constitution

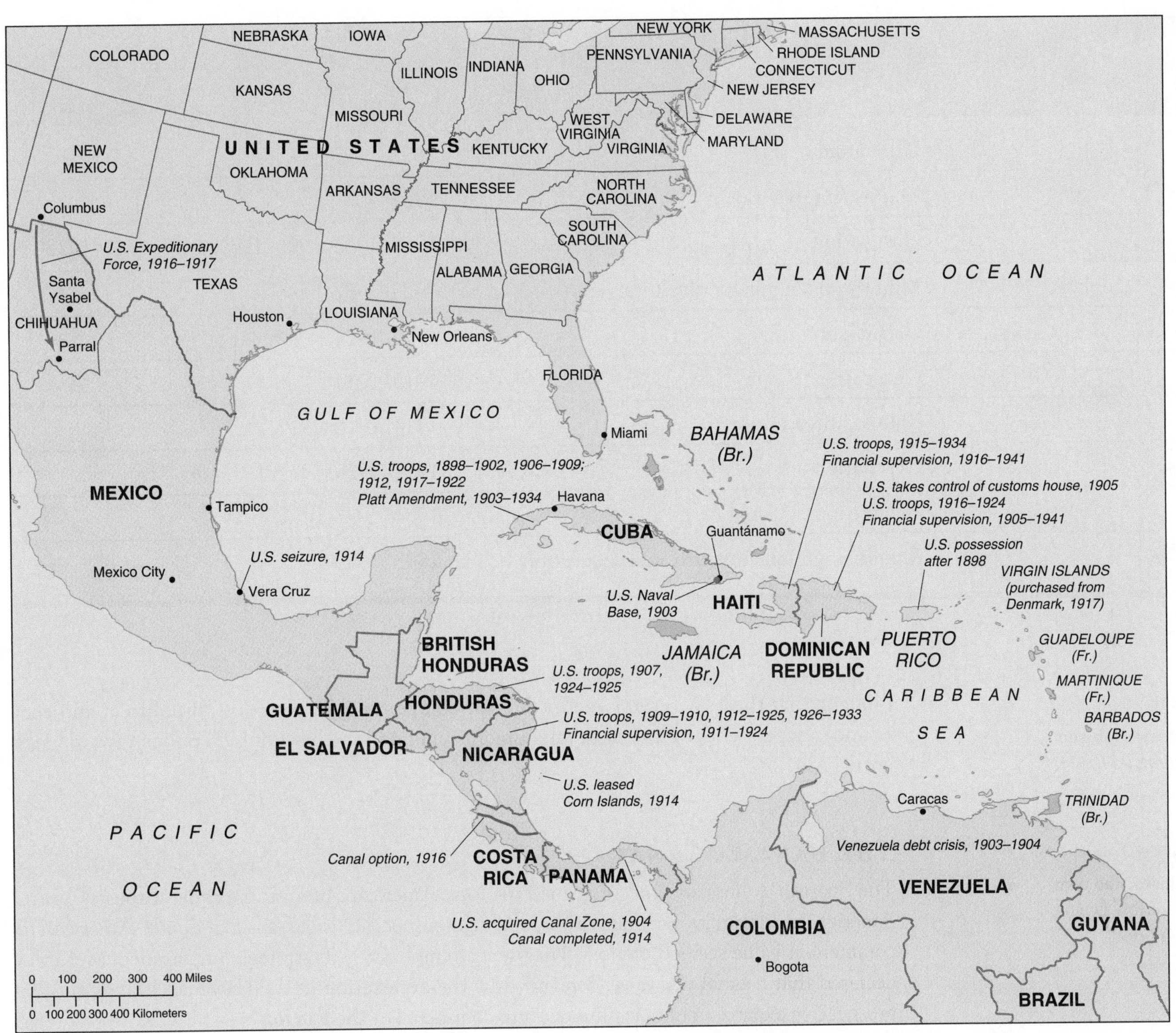

MAP 22–3 **The United States in the Caribbean** For strategic and economic reasons, the United States repeatedly intervened in the Caribbean in the first three decades of the twentieth century. Such interventions protected the U.S. claim to dominance but often provoked great hostility among Latin Americans.

What does this map tell you about the attitudes of American policymakers toward the Caribbean and Central America?

the provisions of the **Platt Amendment,** drawn up in 1901 by the U.S. secretary of war. The Platt Amendment restricted Cuba's autonomy in diplomatic relations with other countries and in internal financial policies, required Cuba to lease naval bases to the United States, and most important, authorized U.S. intervention to maintain order and preserve Cuban independence. As General Wood correctly observed, "There is, of course, little or no independence left Cuba under the Platt Amendment."

Platt Amendment A stipulation the United States had inserted into the Cuban constitution in 1901 restricting Cuban autonomy and authorizing U.S. intervention and naval bases.

To preserve American influence, the United States sent troops into Cuba three times between 1906 and 1917. During their occupations of Cuba, the Americans modernized its financial system, built roads and public schools, and developed a public-health and sanitation program that eradicated the deadly disease of yellow fever. But most Cubans

OVERVIEW U.S. Interventions in Latin America, 1891–1933

Country	Type of Intervention	Year
Chile	Ultimatum	1891–1892
Colombia	Military intervention	1903
Cuba	Occupation	1898–1902, 1906–1909, 1912, 1917–1922
Dominican Republic	Military and administrative intervention	1905–1907
	Occupation	1916–1924
Haiti	Occupation	1915–1934
Mexico	Military intervention	1914, 1916–1917
Nicaragua	Occupation	1912–1925, 1927–1933
Panama	Acquisition of Canal Zone	1904
Puerto Rico	Military invasion and territorial acquisition	1898

Read the Document at www.myhistorylab.com *Platt Amendment (1901)*

thought that these material benefits did not compensate for their loss of political and economic independence. The Platt Amendment remained the basis of U.S. policy toward Cuba until 1934.

Read the Document at www.myhistorylab.com *From Then to Now Online: The Panama Canal*

The Panama Canal

The Spanish-American War intensified the long American interest in a canal through Central America to eliminate the lengthy and dangerous ocean route around South America. Its commercial value seemed obvious, but the war emphasized its strategic importance. McKinley declared that a canal was now "demanded by the annexation of the Hawaiian Islands and the prospective expansion of our influence and commerce in the Pacific."

Theodore Roosevelt moved quickly to implement McKinley's commitment to a canal after becoming president in 1901. First, Roosevelt persuaded Britain to renounce its treaty right to a joint role with the United States in any canal venture. Where to build the canal was a problem. One possibility was Nicaragua, where a sea-level canal could be built. Another was Panama, then part of Colombia. A canal through Panama would require an elaborate system of locks. But the French-owned Panama Canal Company had been unsuccessfully trying to build a canal in Panama and was now eager to sell its rights to the project before they expired in 1904.

Read the Document at www.myhistorylab.com *Theodore Roosevelt, Panama Canal Message to Congress (1903)*

In 1902, Congress directed Roosevelt to purchase the French company's claims for $40 million and build the canal in Panama if Colombia ceded a strip of land across the isthmus on reasonable terms. Otherwise, Roosevelt was to negotiate with Nicaragua for the alternative route. In 1903, Roosevelt pressed Colombia to sell a canal zone to the United States for $10 million and an annual payment of $250,000. Colombia, however, rejected the proposal, fearing the loss of its sovereignty in Panama and hoping for more money.

Roosevelt was furious. After threatening "those contemptible little creatures" in Colombia, he began writing a message to Congress proposing military action to seize the isthmus of Panama. Instead of using direct force, however, Roosevelt worked with Philippe Bunau-Varilla, a French official of the Panama Canal Company, to exploit long-smoldering

Panamanian discontent with Colombia. Roosevelt ordered U.S. naval forces to Panama; from New York, Bunau-Varilla coordinated a revolt against Colombian authority directed by officials of the Panama Railroad, owned by Bunau-Varilla's canal company. The bloodless "revolution" succeeded when U.S. forces prevented Colombian troops from landing in Panama, although the United States was bound by treaty to maintain Colombian sovereignty in the region. Bunau-Varilla promptly signed a treaty accepting Roosevelt's original terms for a canal zone and making Panama a U.S. protectorate, which it remained until 1939. Panamanians themselves denounced the treaty for surrendering sovereignty in the zone to the United States, but the United States took formal control of the canal zone in 1904 and completed construction of the Panama Canal in 1914.

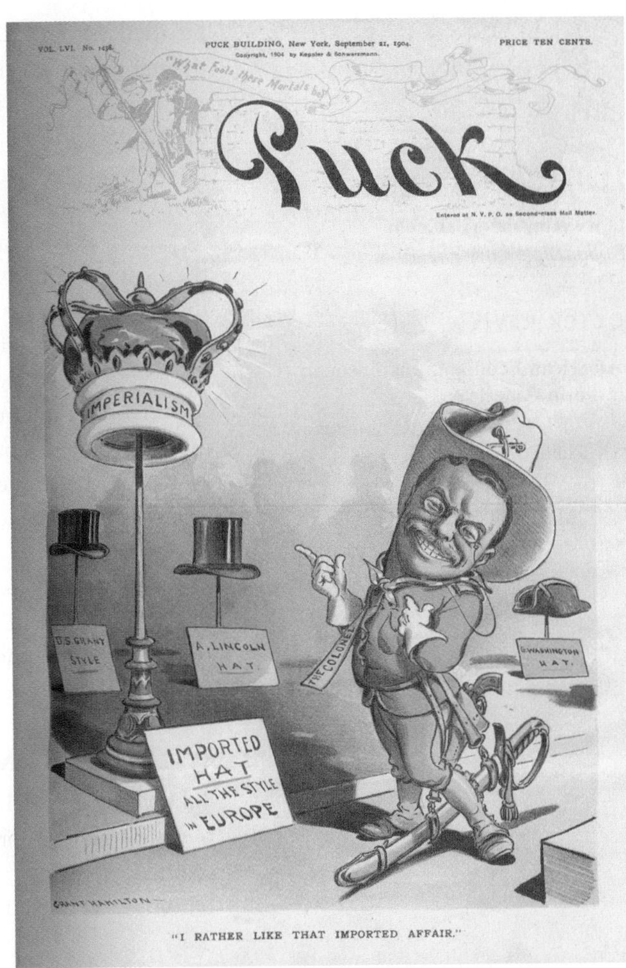

The *Puck* cartoonist criticizes Theodore Roosevelt's aggressive foreign policy by depicting him in his Rough Rider uniform and indicating his preference for the crown of European imperialism over the simple American hats of previous presidents.

The Roosevelt Corollary

To protect the security of the canal, the United States increased its authority in the Caribbean. The objective was to establish conditions there that would both eliminate any pretext for European intervention and promote American control over trade and investment. The inability of Latin American nations to pay their debts to foreign lenders raised the possibility of European intervention, as evidenced by a German and British blockade of Venezuela in 1903 to secure repayment of debts to European bankers. "If we intend to say hands off to the powers of Europe," Roosevelt concluded, "then sooner or later we must keep order ourselves."

Toward that end, in 1904, Roosevelt announced a new policy, the so-called **Roosevelt Corollary** to the Monroe Doctrine. "Chronic wrongdoing," he declared, would cause the United States to exercise "an international police power" in Latin America. The Monroe Doctrine had expressed American hostility to European intervention in Latin America; the Roosevelt Corollary attempted to justify U.S. intervention and authority in the region. Roosevelt invoked his corollary immediately, imposing American management of the debts and customs duties of the Dominican Republic in 1905. Commercial rivalries and political intrigue in that poor nation had created disorder, which Roosevelt suppressed for both economic and strategic reasons. Financial insolvency was averted, popular revolution prevented, and possible European intervention forestalled.

Latin Americans vigorously resented the United States' unilateral claim to authority. By 1907, the so-called Drago Doctrine (named after Argentina's foreign minister) was incorporated into international law, prohibiting armed intervention to collect debts. Still, the United States would continue to invoke the Roosevelt Corollary to advance its interests in the hemisphere.

QUICK REVIEW

Acquisition of the Canal Zone

- Possible canal sites were located in Nicaragua and Panama (then part of Colombia).
- 1903: Colombia rejects Roosevelt's offer to purchase canal zone in Panama.
- 1903–1904: U.S. forces support Panamanian rebellion against Colombia and take control of canal zone.

Roosevelt Corollary President Theodore Roosevelt's policy asserting U.S. authority to intervene in the affairs of Latin American nations; an expansion of the Monroe Doctrine.

dollar diplomacy The U.S. policy of using private investment in other nations to promote American diplomatic goals and business interests.

Dollar Diplomacy

Roosevelt's successor as president, William Howard Taft, hoped to promote U.S. interests in less confrontational ways. He proposed "substituting dollars for bullets"—using government action to encourage private American investments in Latin America to supplant European interests, promote development and stability, and earn profits for American bankers. Under this **dollar diplomacy,** American investments in the Caribbean increased dramatically during Taft's presidency from 1909 to 1913, and the State Department helped arrange for American bankers to establish financial control over Haiti and Honduras.

But Taft did not shrink from employing military force to protect American property or to establish the conditions he thought necessary for American investments. In fact, Taft intervened more frequently than Roosevelt had, with Nicaragua a major target. In 1909, Taft sent U.S. troops there to aid a revolution fomented by an American mining corporation and to seize the Nicaraguan customs houses. Under the new government, American bankers then gained control of Nicaragua's national bank, railroad, and customs service. To protect these arrangements, U.S. troops were again dispatched in 1912. To control popular opposition to the American client government, the marines remained in Nicaragua for two decades.

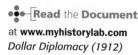

Read the Document at **www.myhistorylab.com** *Dollar Diplomacy (1912)*

QUICK REVIEW

American Economic Involvement in Latin America

- 1913: U.S. investment in region reaches 1.5 billion.
- Americans captured large share of Latin America's foreign trade.
- American investment failed to improve conditions for most Latin Americans.

Dollar diplomacy increased American power and influence in the Caribbean and tied underdeveloped countries to the United States economically and strategically. By 1913, American investments in the region reached $1.5 billion, and Americans had captured more than 50 percent of the foreign trade of Costa Rica, Cuba, the Dominican Republic, Guatemala, Haiti, Honduras, Nicaragua, and Panama. But this policy failed to improve conditions for most Latin Americans. U.S. officials remained primarily concerned with promoting American control and extracting American profits from the region. Not surprisingly, dollar diplomacy proved unpopular in Latin America.

Wilsonian Interventions

Taking office in 1913, the Democrat Woodrow Wilson repudiated the interventionist policies of his Republican predecessors. He promised that the United States would "never again seek one additional foot of territory by conquest" but would instead work to promote "human rights, national integrity, and opportunity" in Latin America.

The Big Stick in the Caribbean Sea.
The Roosevelt Corollary proclaimed the intention of the United States to police Latin America. Enforcement came, as this cartoon shows, with Roosevelt and subsequent presidents sending the U.S. Navy to one Caribbean nation after another.

Nonetheless, Wilson soon became the most interventionist president in American history. Convinced that the United States had to expand its exports and investments abroad and that U.S. dominance of the Caribbean was strategically necessary, he also held the racist belief that Latin Americans were inferior and needed paternalistic guidance from the United States. In providing that guidance, through military force if necessary, Wilson came close to assuming that American principles and objectives were absolutes, and that different cultural traditions and national aspirations were simply wrong.

Caribbean interventions. In 1915, Wilson ordered U.S. marines to Haiti to preserve "gravely menaced" American interests. The United States saved and even enhanced those interests by establishing a protectorate over Haiti and drawing up a constitution that increased U.S. property rights and commercial privileges. The U.S. Navy selected a new Haitian president, granting him nominal authority over a client government. Real authority, however, rested with the American military, which controlled Haiti until 1934, protecting the small elite who cooperated with American interests and exploited their own people.

See the **Map**
at **www.myhistorylab.com**
Activities of the United States in the Caribbean, 1898–1930s

QUICK REVIEW

Woodrow Wilson and Mexico

- Initially supported Venustiano Carranza and the Constitutionalists.
- Switched to support of Francisco "Pancho" Villa when Carranza proved too independent.
- Ended up fighting both Villa and Carranza.
- Extended full recognition to Carranza's government in January 1917.

Wilson also intervened elsewhere in the Caribbean. In 1916, when the Dominican Republic refused to cede control of its finances to U.S. bankers, Wilson ordered the marines to occupy the country. The marines ousted Dominican officials, installed a military government to rule "on behalf of the Dominican government," and ran the nation until 1924. In 1917, the United States intervened in Cuba, which remained under American control until 1922.

Interfering with Mexico. Wilson also involved himself in the internal affairs of Mexico. The lengthy dictatorship of Porfirio Díaz had collapsed in 1911 in revolutionary disorder. The popular leader Francisco Madero took power and promised democratic and economic reforms that alarmed both wealthy Mexicans and foreign investors, particularly Americans. In 1913, General Victoriano Huerta seized control in a brutal counterrevolution backed by the landed aristocracy and foreign interests. Appalled by the violence of Huerta's power grab and aware that opponents had organized to reestablish constitutional government, Wilson refused to recognize the Huerta government.

Wilson authorized arms sales to the Constitutionalist forces led by Venustiano Carranza, pressured Britain and other nations to deprive Huerta of foreign support, and blockaded the Mexican port of Veracruz. In 1914 Wilson exploited a minor incident to have the marines attack and occupy Veracruz. This assault damaged his image as a promoter of peace and justice, and even Carranza and the Constitutionalists denounced the American occupation as unwarranted aggression. After Carranza toppled Huerta, Wilson shifted his support to Francisco ("Pancho") Villa, who seemed more susceptible to American guidance. But Carranza's growing popular support in Mexico and Wilson's preoccupation with World War I in Europe finally led the United States to grant de facto recognition to the Carranza government in 1915.

Villa then began terrorizing New Mexico and Texas, hoping to provoke an American intervention that would undermine Carranza. In 1916, Wilson ordered troops under General John J. Pershing to pursue Villa into Mexico, leading Carranza to fear a permanent U.S. occupation of northern Mexico. Soon the American soldiers were

Racist attitudes about the "white man's burden" underlay many of Wilson's interventions in Mexico and elsewhere in Latin America.

fighting the Mexican army rather than Villa's bandits. On the brink of full-fledged war, Wilson finally ordered U.S. troops to withdraw in January 1917 and extended full recognition to the Carranza government. Wilson lamely defended these steps as showing that the United States had no intention of imposing on Mexico "an order and government of our own choosing." That had been Wilson's original objective, however. His aggressive tactics had not merely failed but also embittered relations with Mexico.

ENGAGING EUROPE: NEW CONCERNS, OLD CONSTRAINTS

WHY DID the United States take a larger role in Europe at the beginning of the twentieth century?

While the United States expanded its power in Latin American and strove to increase its influence in Asia in the early twentieth century, it also took a larger role in Europe. Its traditional policy of noninvolvement, however, remained popular with many Americans and constituted an important restraint upon the new imperial nation.

Responding to the lopsided outcome of the Spanish-American War, European nations immediately began to adjust their policies to take into account the evident power of the United States. German officials even considered seeking an alliance in order to strengthen Germany in Europe. But Germany's rival, Great Britain, moved quickly to resolve all possible disputes with the United States and thereby establish a basis for long-term cooperation. Britain's support for the American annexation of the Philippines and its decision in 1901 to accede to American control of the projected Panama Canal were early examples of this policy. By 1905, only a decade after Britain and the United States seemed on the verge of war over Venezuela, British and American diplomats agreed that their nations' interests were "absolutely identical and that the more closely we can work together, the better it will be for us and the world at large."

Roosevelt also cautiously intervened in European affairs. The great European powers were aligning themselves into rival blocs: the Entente of Britain and France (and sometimes Russia) and the Alliance of Germany and Austria-Hungary (and sometimes Italy). When France and Germany quarreled over the control of Morocco in 1906, Roosevelt helped arrange an international conference at Algeciras, Spain, to resolve the crisis. While placating Germany, American diplomats then helped uphold France's claims, upon its pledge to maintain an open door in Morocco, a pledge the United States would later use to insist upon securing petroleum and commercial opportunities. Roosevelt had helped preserve the balance of power in Europe while advancing what he saw as America's own interests.

Eager to ensure stability, American leaders also engaged Europeans in efforts to promote arbitration of international disputes. In 1899, the United States participated in the First Hague Peace Conference, which created the Permanent Court of Arbitration. Roosevelt helped arrange a second Hague conference in 1907. It did not accept American proposals for compulsory arbitration, but it led to another conference in 1909 which issued the Declaration of London codifying international law for maritime war and establishing the rights of neutral nations. And Roosevelt, Taft, and Wilson negotiated dozens of arbitration or conciliation treaties providing for submitting international disputes to the Hague Court.

However, public opinion and Senate opposition, rooted in older perspectives toward involvement in world affairs, persistently restricted the effectiveness of these efforts. Although the treaties themselves had broad loopholes, the Senate insisted upon further restricting the possible questions to be arbitrated and reserved for itself the right to approve every particular decision to arbitrate. These restrictive views, grumbled Roosevelt and Taft, rendered the treaties ineffective; they would shortly cause Wilson still greater difficulty.

CONCLUSION

By the time of Woodrow Wilson's presidency, the United States had been expanding its involvement in world affairs for half a century. Several themes had emerged from this activity: increasing American domination of the Caribbean, continuing interest in East Asia, the creation of an overseas empire, and the evolution of the United States into a major world power. Underlying these developments was an uneasy mixture of ideas and objectives. The American involvement in the world reflected a traditional, if often misguided, sense of national rectitude and mission. Generous humanitarian impulses vied with ugly racist prejudices as Americans sought both to help other peoples and to direct them toward U.S. concepts of religion, sanitation, capitalist development, and public institutions. American motives ranged from ensuring national security and competing with European colonial powers to the conviction that the United States had to expand its economic interests abroad. But if imperialism, both informal and at times colonial, brought Americans greater wealth and power, it also increased tensions in Asia and contributed to anti-American hostility and revolutionary ferment in Latin America. It also entangled the United States in the Great Power rivalries that would ultimately result in two world wars.

Where to Learn More

Mission Houses, Honolulu, Hawaii. Built between 1821 and 1841, these buildings were homes and shops of missionaries sent to Hawaii by the American Board of Commissioners for Foreign Missions. Their exhibits include furnishings and memorabilia of a group important in developing American ties with Hawaii. http://www.missionhouses.org.

Funston Memorial Home, Iola, Kansas. Operated as a museum by the Kansas State Historical Society, this is the boyhood home of General Frederick Funston, prominent in the Spanish-American War and the Filipino-American War. For a virtual tour, together with military information, political cartoons, Roosevelt correspondence, and Funston links, see http://skyways.lib.ks.us/museums/funston.

James G. Blaine House, Augusta, Maine. The Executive Mansion of Maine's governor since 1919, this house was formerly Blaine's home and still contains his study and furnishings from the time he served as secretary of state and U.S. senator. http://www.blainehouse.org.

Review Questions

1. After the Spanish-American War, General Leonard Wood asserted that Cubans believed that their American "liberators" were "still their faithful friends." Why might Cubans not have agreed with Wood?
2. What factors, old and new, shaped American foreign policy in the late nineteenth century? How were they interrelated?
3. How were individual politicians and diplomats able to affect America's foreign policy? How were they constrained by governmental institutions, private groups, and public opinion?
4. To what extent was the United States' emergence as an imperial power a break from, as opposed to a culmination of, its earlier policies and national development?
5. How effective were U.S. interventions in Latin America? What were the objectives and consequences?
6. In what ways did the policies of other nations shape the development of American foreign policy?

Key Terms

Dollar diplomacy (p. 627)
Gentlemen's Agreement (p. 623)
Imperialism (p. 610)
Mahanism (p. 611)
Open Door (p. 622)
Pan American Union (p. 613)
Platt Amendment (p. 625)
Roosevelt Corollary (p. 627)
Spheres of influence (p. 622)
Teller Amendment (p. 617)
Yellow press (p. 616)

myhistorylab Connections

Reinforce what you learned in this chapter by studying the many documents, images, maps, review tools, and videos available at **www.myhistorylab.com**.

Read and Review

Study and Review **Study Plan: Chapter 22**

Read the Document

The Teller Amendment (1898)

William Graham Sumner, "On Empire and the Philippines" (1898)

William McKinley, "Decision on the Philippines" (1900)

Rudyard Kipling, "The White Man's Burden" (1899)

Dollar Diplomacy (1912)

Carl Schurz, Platform of the American Anti-Imperialist League (1899)

Alfred Thayer Mahan, The Interest of America in Sea Power (1897)

Henry Cabot Lodge, Annex of Hawaii (1895)

Platt Amendment (1901)

Mark Twain, "Incident in the Philippines" (1924)

Theodore Roosevelt, Panama Canal Message to Congress (1903)

See the Map *Activities of the United States in the Caribbean, 1898–1930s*

Research and Explore

Read the Document

Personal Journeys Online

From Then to Now Online: The Panama Canal

Exploring America: White Man's Burden

Watch the Video *Roosevelt's Rough Riders*

Hear the Audio

Hear the audio files for Chapter 22 at **www.myhistorylab.com.**

1914-1920

23 America and the Great War

Women war workers in an engineering shop, 1917.

Hear the Audio

Hear the audio files for Chapter 23 at **www.myhistorylab.com**.

WAGING NEUTRALITY *(page 637)*

WHY WERE Americans so reluctant to get involved in World War I?

WAGING WAR IN AMERICA *(page 642)*

HOW DID the war effort threaten civil liberties?

WAGING WAR AND PEACE ABROAD *(page 647)*

WHAT HOPES did Wilson have for the Treaty of Versailles?

WAGING PEACE AT HOME *(page 651)*

WHAT CHALLENGES did America face in the aftermath of the war?

One American Journey

Property can be paid for; the lives of peaceful and innocent people cannot be. The present German submarine warfare against commerce is a warfare against mankind. . . . It is a war against all nations. . . . Each nation must decide for itself how it will meet it. . . . There is one choice we cannot make, we are incapable of making: we will not choose the path of submission and suffer the most sacred rights of our nation and our people to be ignored or violated. . . . Neutrality is no longer feasible or desirable where the peace of the world is involved and the freedom of its peoples, and the menace to that peace and freedom lies in the existence of autocratic governments backed by organized force which is controlled wholly by their will, not the will of the people. The world must be made safe for democracy. Its peace must be planted upon the tested foundations of political liberty.

. . . It is a fearful thing to lead this great peaceful people into war, into the most terrible and disastrous of all wars, civilization itself seeming to be in the balance. But the right is more precious than the peace, and we shall fight for the things which we have always carried nearest our hearts. . . . To such a task we can dedicate our lives and our fortunes, everything that we are and everything that we have, with the pride of those who know that the day has come when America is privileged to spend her blood and her might for the principles that gave her birth and happiness and the peace she has treasured.

Excerpted from President Woodrow Wilson's Request for Declaration of War, April 2, 1917. Woodrow Wilson Presidential Library

Read the **Document** at **www.myhistorylab.com**

Personal Journeys Online

- **Jane Addams, *Peace and Bread in Time of War,* 1922. Describing the transition of President Wilson from an advocate of peace to one of war.**
- **Letter from former president Theodore Roosevelt to Sir Edward Grey, 1915 promoting American preparedness and support of the Allies.**

ESCORTED BY THE U.S. CAVALRY on the evening of April 2, 1917, Woodrow Wilson drove through a misty rain eerily illuminated by searchlights down Pennsylvania Avenue to Capitol Hill to deliver his war address. Throughout the day, the Emergency Peace Federation had frantically lobbied Congress, but sentiment in both houses was growing for war. When Wilson promised to make the world "safe for democracy," many members of Congress, waving small American flags, broke into cheers, and pro-war Senator Henry Cabot Lodge personally congratulated Wilson.

On April 4, Senator Robert La Follette delivered a three-hour speech denouncing the president's call for war as a dangerous and reckless journey for the American nation. But La Follette's well-known oratorical talents proved unable to sway the forces for war in Congress. Indeed, his speech aroused such anger in the Senate chamber that he was handed a noose as he exited the room. Both the Senate and the House overwhelmingly supported Wilson's request and the United States entered the war on April 6. Denounced in the press, Senator La Follette and his family were ostracized for his antiwar views, providing a sobering indication of the treatment Americans would face who dared to oppose the war against Germany.

Two years later on July 10, 1919, Wilson made the same journey down Pennsylvania Avenue to Capitol Hill. He asked the Senate to ratify a peace treaty that most Americans favored and that he promised would prevent future wars. But Wilson's reception in the Senate was chilly; some even refused to stand when he entered the room and many others received the address in silence. The Senate ultimately rejected the treaty and Wilson's peace.

Between these two presidential appearances, Americans experienced the horrors of the Great War, confronting and overcoming

CHRONOLOGY

1914	World War I begins in Europe.
	President Woodrow Wilson declares U.S. neutrality.
1915	Germany begins submarine warfare.
	Lusitania is sunk.
	Woman's Peace Party is organized.
1916	Sussex Pledge is issued.
	Preparedness legislation is enacted.
	Woodrow Wilson is reelected president.
1917	Germany resumes unrestricted submarine warfare.
	March uprisings end the tsarist regime in Russia.
	The United States declares war on Germany.
	Selective Service Act establishes the military draft.
	Espionage Act is passed.
	Committee on Public Information, War Industries Board, Food Administration, and other mobilization agencies are established.
	American Expeditionary Force arrives in France.
	East St. Louis race riot erupts.
	Bolshevik Revolution occurs in Russia.
1918	Wilson announces his Fourteen Points.
	Sedition Act is passed.
	Eugene Debs is imprisoned.
	The United States intervenes militarily in Russia.
	Armistice ends World War I.
1919	Paris Peace Conference is held.
	Steel, coal, and other strikes occur.
	Red Scare breaks out.
	Prohibition amendment is adopted.
	Wilson suffers a massive stroke.
1920	Palmer Raids round up radicals.
	League of Nations is defeated in the U.S. Senate.
	Woman suffrage amendment is ratified.
	U.S. troops are withdrawn from Russia.
	Warren Harding is elected president.
1921	United States signs a separate peace treaty with Germany.

challenges but also sacrificing some of their national ideals and aspirations. Not only was the war the United States' first major military conflict on foreign soil, but it also changed American life.

Many of the changes, from increased efficiency to Americanization, reflected prewar progressivism, and the war years did promote some reforms. But the war also diverted reform energies into new channels, subordinated generous impulses to attitudes that were more coercive, and strengthened the conservative opposition to reform. The results were often reactionary and contributed to a postwar mood that not only curtailed further reform but also helped defeat the peace treaty upon which so much had been gambled. ✦

WAGING NEUTRALITY

WHY WERE Americans so reluctant to get involved in World War I?

Few Americans were prepared for the Great War that erupted in Europe in August 1914, but fewer still foresaw that their own nation might become involved in it. With near unanimity, they supported neutrality. But American attitudes, decisions, and actions, both public and private, undercut neutrality, and the policies of governments in Berlin, London, and Washington drew the United States into the war.

The Origins of Conflict

There had been plenty of warning. Since the 1870s, the competing imperial ambitions of the European powers had led to economic rivalries, military expansion, diplomatic maneuvering, and international tensions. A complex system of alliances divided the continent into two opposing blocs. In central Europe, the expansionist Germany of Kaiser Wilhelm II allied itself with the multinational Austro-Hungarian Empire. Confronting them, Great Britain and France entered into alliances with tsarist Russia. A succession of crises threatened this precarious balance of power, and in May 1914, an American diplomat reported anxiously, "There is too much hatred, too many jealousies." He predicted "an awful cataclysm."

Central Powers Germany and its World War I allies in Austria, Turkey, and Bulgaria.

Allies In World War I, Britain, France, Russia, and other nations fighting against the Central Powers but not including the United States.

QUICK REVIEW

The Outbreak of War

- June 28, 1914: Archduke Franz Ferdinand assassinated.
- July 28, 1914: Austria declares war on Serbia with German support.
- Chain reaction draws all European powers into the war.

The cataclysm began a month later. On June 28, a Serbian terrorist assassinated Archduke Franz Ferdinand, the heir to the Austro-Hungarian throne, in Sarajevo. With Germany's support, Austria declared war on Serbia on July 28. Russia then mobilized its army against Austria to aid Serbia, its Slavic client state. To assist Austria, Germany declared war on Russia and then on Russia's ally, France. Hoping for a quick victory, Germany struck at France through neutral Belgium; in response, Britain declared war on Germany on August 4. Soon Turkey and Bulgaria joined Germany and Austria to form the **Central Powers.** The **Allies**—Britain, France, and Russia—were joined by Italy and Japan.

Mass slaughter enveloped Europe as huge armies battled to a stalemate. The British and French faced the Germans along a line of trenches stretching across France and Belgium from the English Channel to Switzerland. Little movement occurred despite great efforts and terrible casualties from artillery, machine guns, and poison gas. The belligerents subordinated their economies, politics, and cultures to military demands. The Great War, said one German soldier, had become "the grave of nations."

AMERICAN ATTITUDES

Although the United States had also competed for markets, colonies, and influence, few Americans had expected this calamity. Most believed that the United States had no vital interest in the war and would not become involved. President Wilson issued a proclamation of neutrality and urged Americans to be "neutral in fact as well as in name . . . impartial in thought as well as in action."

However, neither the American people nor their president stayed strictly neutral. German Americans often sympathized with Germany, and many Irish Americans hoped for a British defeat that would free Ireland from British rule. But most Americans sympathized with the Allies. Ethnic, cultural, and economic ties bound most Americans to the British and French. Politically, too, most Americans felt a greater affinity for the democratic Western Allies—tsarist Russia repelled them—than for Germany's more authoritarian government and society.

Wilson himself admired Britain's culture and government and distrusted Germany's imperial ambitions. Like other influential Americans, Wilson believed that a German victory would threaten America's economic, political, and perhaps even strategic interests. Secretary of State William Jennings Bryan was genuinely neutral, but most officials favored the Allies. Robert Lansing, counselor of the State Department; Walter Hines Page, the ambassador to England; and Colonel Edward House, Wilson's closest adviser on foreign affairs—all assisted British diplomats, undercut official U.S. protests against British violations of American neutrality, and encouraged Wilson's suspicions of Germany.

QUICK REVIEW

Ties to the Allies

- Ethnic, cultural, and economic ties bound most Americans to the British and French.
- Americans felt affinity for Western democracies.
- Sympathy with Allies did not mean Americans favored intervention.

British propaganda bolstered American sympathies. British writers, artists, and lecturers depicted the Allies as fighting for civilization against a brutal Germany that mutilated nuns and babies. Although German troops, like most other soldiers, did commit outrages, they were not guilty of the systematic barbarity claimed by Allied propagandists. Britain, however, shaped America's view of the conflict.

Sympathy for the Allies, however, did not mean that Americans favored intervention. Indeed, few Americans doubted that neutrality was the appropriate course and peace the proper goal. The carnage in France solidified their convictions. Wilson was determined to pursue peace as long as his view of national interests allowed.

The Economy of War

Economic issues soon threatened American neutrality. International law permitted neutral nations to sell or ship war matériel to belligerents, and with the economy mired in a recession when the war began, many Americans looked to war orders to spur economic recovery. But the British navy prevented trade with the Central Powers. Only the Allies could buy American goods. Some Americans worried that this one-sided war trade undermined genuine neutrality. Congress even considered an embargo on munitions. But few Americans supported the idea.

A second economic issue complicated matters. To finance their war purchases, the Allies borrowed from American bankers. Initially, Secretary of State Bryan persuaded Wilson to prohibit loans to the belligerents as "inconsistent with the true spirit of neutrality." But as the importance of the war orders to both the Allies and the American economy became clear, Wilson ended the ban. By April 1917, American loans to the Allies exceeded $2 billion, nearly a hundred times the amount lent to Germany. These financial ties, like the war trade they underwrote, linked the United States to the Allies and convinced Germany that American neutrality was only a formality.

The Diplomacy of Neutrality

The same imbalance characterized American diplomacy. Wilson insisted on American neutral rights but acquiesced in British violations of those rights, while sternly refusing to yield on German actions.

When the war began, the United States asked belligerents to respect the 1909 **Declaration of London** on neutral rights. Germany agreed to do so; the British refused. Instead, skirting or violating established procedures, Britain blockaded Germany, mined the North Sea, and forced neutral ships into British ports to search their cargoes and confiscate material deemed useful to the German war effort. Wilson branded Britain's blockade illegal and unwarranted, but by October he had conceded many of America's neutral rights in order to avoid conflict with Britain.

Declaration of London Statement drafted by an international conference in 1909 to clarify international law and specify the rights of neutral nations.

The British then prohibited food and other products that Germany had imported during peacetime, thereby interfering further with neutral shipping. Even the British admitted that these steps had no legal justification. But when the Wilson administration finally protested, it undermined its own position by noting that "imperative necessity" might justify a violation of international law. This statement virtually authorized the British to violate American rights. Wilson yielded further by observing that "no very important questions of principle" were involved in the Anglo-American quarrels over ship seizures and that they could be resolved after the war.

Submarine warfare. This policy tied the United States to the British war effort and provoked a German response. With its army stalemated on land and its navy no match for Britain's, Germany decided in February 1915 to use its submarines against Allied shipping in a war zone around the British Isles. Neutral ships risked being sunk by mistake, partly because British ships illegally flew neutral flags. Germany maintained that the blockade and the acquiescence of neutral countries in British violations of international law made submarine warfare necessary.

In May 1915, a German submarine sank a British passenger liner, the *Lusitania*. It had been carrying arms, and the German embassy had warned Americans against traveling on the ship, but the loss of life—1,198 people, including 128 Americans—caused Americans to condemn Germany. Yet only six of a thousand editors surveyed called for war, and even the combative Theodore Roosevelt estimated that 98 percent of Americans still opposed war. Wilson saw that he had to "carry out the double wish of our people, to maintain a firm front in respect of what we demand of Germany and yet do nothing that might by any possibility involve us in the war."

QUICK REVIEW

Submarine Warfare

- 1915: U.S. gives tacit support to British naval blockade of Germany.
- Germany responds by initiating submarine warfare.
- May 1915: German submarine sinks the *Lusitania*.
- Americans demanded a tough stand against Germany, but did not want to be drawn into the war.

This was a difficult stance. Wilson demanded that Germany abandon its submarine campaign. His language was so harsh that Bryan resigned, warning that by requiring more of Germany than of Britain, the president violated neutrality and threatened to draw the nation into war. Bryan protested Britain's use of American passengers as shields to protect contraband cargo and proposed prohibiting Americans from traveling on belligerent ships. His proposal gained support in the South and West and was introduced as a resolution in both the Senate and the House in February 1916.

Wilson moved to defeat the resolutions, insisting that they impinged on presidential control of foreign policy and on America's neutral rights. In truth, the resolutions abandoned no vital national interest and offered to prevent another provocative incident. Moreover, neither law nor tradition gave Americans the right to travel safely on belligerent ships. Wilson's assertion of such a right committed him to a policy that could only lead to conflict.

Sussex Pledge Germany's pledge during World War I not to sink merchant ships without warning, on the condition that Britain also observe recognized rules of international laws.

Arguments over submarine warfare climaxed in April 1916. A German submarine torpedoed the French ship *Sussex*, injuring four Americans. Wilson threatened to break diplomatic relations if Germany did not abandon unrestricted submarine warfare against all merchant vessels, enemy as well as neutral. This threat implied war. Germany promised not to sink merchant ships without warning but made its ***Sussex* Pledge** contingent on the United States' requiring Britain also to adhere to "the rules of international law universally recognized before the war." Peace for America would depend on the British adopting a course they had already rejected. Wilson's diplomacy had left the nation's future at the mercy of others.

The Battle over Preparedness

preparedness Military buildup in preparation for possible U.S. participation in World War I.

The threat of war sparked a debate over military policy. Theodore Roosevelt and a handful of other politicians, mostly northeastern Republicans convinced that Allied victory was in the national interest, advocated what they called **preparedness,** a program to expand the armed forces and establish universal military training. Conservative business groups also joined the agitation. The National Security League, consisting of eastern bankers and industrialists, combined demands for preparedness with attacks on progressive reforms.

But most Americans, certain that their nation would not join the bloody madness, opposed expensive military preparations. Many supported the peace movement. Most opponents agreed that military spending would undermine domestic reform and raise taxes while enriching arms merchants and financiers.

Wilson also opposed preparedness initially, but he reversed his position when the submarine crisis with Germany intensified. He also began to champion military expansion lest Republicans accuse him in the 1916 election of neglecting national defense.

A preparedness parade winds its way down Pennsylvania Avenue in Washington, DC. By 1916, President Wilson, invoking the spirit of patriotism, had given his support to the preparedness program of military expansion.

The Election of 1916

Wilson's preparedness plans stripped the Republicans of one issue in 1916, and his renewed support of progressive reforms (see Chapter 21) helped to hold Bryan Democrats in line. Wilson continued his balancing act in the campaign itself, at first stressing Americanism and preparedness but then emphasizing peace. The slogan "He Kept Us Out of War" appealed to the popular desire for peace, and the Democratic campaign became one long peace rally.

The Republicans were divided. They had hoped to regain their progressive members after Roosevelt urged the Progressive Party to follow him back into the GOP. But many joined the Democratic camp instead, including several Progressive Party leaders, who endorsed Wilson for having enacted the party's demands of 1912. Roosevelt's frenzied interventionism had alienated many midwestern Republicans opposed to preparedness and cost him any chance of gaining the nomination for himself. Instead, the GOP nominated Charles Evans Hughes, a Supreme Court justice and former New York governor. The platform denounced Wilson's "shifty expedients" in foreign policy and promised "strict and honest neutrality." Unfortunately for Hughes, Roosevelt's attacks on Wilson for not pursuing a war policy persuaded many voters that the GOP was a war party.

Watch the Video
at **www.myhistorylab.com**
Charles E. Hughes 1916 Presidential Campaign Speech

self-determination The right of a people or a nation to decide its own political allegiance or form of government without external influence.

The election was the closest in decades (see Map 23–1). When California narrowly went for Wilson, it decided the contest. The results reflected sectional differences, with the South and West voting for Wilson and most of the Northeast and Midwest for Hughes. The desire for peace, all observers concluded, had determined the election.

QUICK REVIEW

The Zimmermann Note

- Proposed alliance between Germany and Mexico in event of war between Germany and United States.
- Mexico would recover territory in Texas, New Mexico, and Arizona.
- Publication of note increased support for American intervention.

Descent into War

Still, Wilson knew that war loomed, and he made a last effort to avert it. In 1915 and 1916, he had tried to mediate the European conflict, using Colonel House as a secret intermediary. Now he again appealed for an end to hostilities. In January 1917, he sketched out the terms of what he called a "peace without victory." Anything else, he warned, would only lead to another war. The new world order should be based on national equality and **self-determination,** arms reductions, freedom of the seas, and an international organization to ensure peace. It was a distinctly American vision.

Neither the Allies nor the Central Powers were interested. Each side had sacrificed too much to settle for anything short of outright victory. To break the deadlock, Germany resumed unrestricted submarine warfare. German generals believed that even if the United States declared war, it could do little more in the short run to injure Germany than it was already doing. German submarines, they hoped, would end the war by cutting the Allies off from U.S. supplies before the United States could send an army to Europe. On January 31, Germany announced its decision to unleash its submarines in a broad war zone.

Wilson commits to war. Wilson was now virtually committed to a war many Americans opposed. He broke diplomatic relations with Germany and asked Congress to arm American merchant vessels. When the Senate refused, Wilson invoked an antipiracy law of 1819 and armed the ships anyway. Although no American ships had yet been sunk, he also ordered the naval gun crews to fire at submarines on sight. The secretary of the navy warned Wilson that these actions violated international law and were a step toward war; Wilson called his policy "armed neutrality." Huge rallies across America demanded peace.

Several developments soon shifted public opinion. On March 1, Wilson released an intercepted message from the German foreign minister, Arthur Zimmermann, to the German minister in Mexico. It proposed that in the event of war between the United States and Germany, Mexico should ally itself with Germany; in exchange, Mexico would recover its "lost territory in Texas, New Mexico, and Arizona." The Zimmermann note produced a wave of hostility toward Germany and increased support

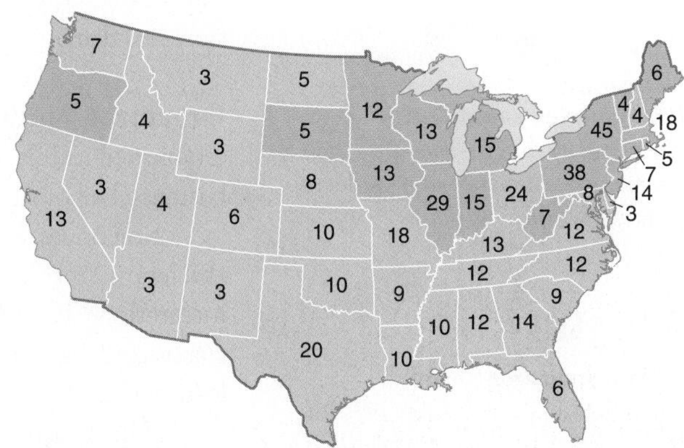

	Electoral Vote (%)	Popular Vote (%)
WOODROW WILSON (Democrat)	**277 (52)**	**9,127,695 (49.4)**
Charles E. Hughes (Republican)	254 (48)	8,533,507 (46.2)
A. L. Benson (Socialist)	–	585,113 (3.2)
Other parties (Socialist Labor, Prohibition)	–	233,909 (1.3)

MAP 23–1 **The Election of 1916** Woodrow Wilson won reelection in 1916, despite a reunified Republican Party, by sweeping the South and West on campaign appeals to peace and progressive reform.

How was Woodrow Wilson able to win reelection in 1916 despite the reunification of the Republican Party?

for intervention in the war, especially in the Southwest, which had opposed involvement. When submarines sank four American freighters in mid-March, anti-German feeling broadened.

On April 2, 1917, Wilson delivered his war message, declaring that neutrality was no longer possible, given Germany's submarine "warfare against mankind." To build support for joining a war that most people had long regarded with revulsion and as alien to American interests, Wilson set forth the nation's war goals as simple and noble. The United States would not fight for conquest or domination but for "the ultimate peace of the world and for the liberation of its peoples." After vigorous debate, the Senate passed the war resolution 82 to 6 and the House 373 to 50. On April 6, 1917, the United States officially entered the Great War.

WAGING WAR IN AMERICA

HOW DID the war effort threaten civil liberties?

Mobilizing for military intervention was a massive undertaking. The government reorganized the economy to emphasize centralized management, developed policies to control public opinion and suppress dissent, and transformed the role of government itself.

Managing the War Economy

To harness the nation's economic power for the war, federal and state governments developed a complex structure of agencies and controls for every sector of the economy, from industry and agriculture to transportation and labor (see Overview, Major Government Wartime Agencies). Supervised by the Council of National Defense, these agencies shifted resources to war-related enterprises, increased production of goods and services, and improved transportation and distribution.

War Industries Board (WIB) The federal agency that reorganized industry for maximum efficiency and productivity during World War I.

QUICK REVIEW

The War Industries Board

- Promoted business interests.
- Helped suspend antitrust laws.
- Guaranteed huge profits.

Organizing industry. The most important agency was the **War Industries Board (WIB),** established in July 1917 to set industrial priorities, coordinate military purchasing, and supervise business. Led by financier Bernard Baruch, the WIB exercised unprecedented power over industry by setting prices, allocating scarce materials, and standardizing products and procedures to boost efficiency. Yet Baruch was not an industrial dictator; he aimed at business-government integration. The WIB promoted major business interests, helped suspend antitrust laws, and guaranteed huge corporate profits. Some progressives began to see the dangers, and business leaders the advantages, of government economic intervention.

The Railroad Administration also linked business ambitions to the war economy. Under William McAdoo, it operated the nation's railroads as a unified system to move supplies and troops efficiently. Centralized management eliminated competition, permitted improvements in equipment, and brought great profits to the owners but higher prices to the general public.

Ensuring food supplies. Equally effective and far more popular was the Food Administration, headed by Herbert Hoover. Hoover had organized relief supplies for war-torn Belgium and now controlled the production and distribution of food for the United States and its allies. He persuaded millions of Americans to accept meatless and wheatless days, so that the Food Administration could feed military and foreign consumers. Half a million women went door to door to secure food-conservation pledges from housewives. City residents planted victory gardens in parks and vacant lots, and President Wilson even pastured sheep on the White House lawn.

Hoover also worked closely with agricultural processors and distributors, ensuring profits in exchange for cooperation. Farmers profited from the war, too. To encourage production, Hoover established high prices for commodities, and agricultural income rose by 30 percent. State and federal governments provided commercial farmers with sufficient farm labor despite the military draft and competition from high-wage war industries.

OVERVIEW Major Government Wartime Agencies

Agency	Purpose
War Industries Board	Reorganized industry to maximize wartime production
Railroad Administration	Modernized and operated the nation's railroads
Food Administration	Increased agricultural production, supervised food distribution and farm labor
National War Labor Board	Resolved labor-management disputes, improved labor conditions, and recognized union rights as means to promote production and efficiency
Committee on Public Information	Managed propaganda to build public support for the war effort

Overseeing labor relations. The National War Labor Board supervised labor relations. In exchange for labor's cooperation, this agency guaranteed the rights of unions to organize and bargain collectively. With such support, unions sharply increased their membership. The labor board also encouraged improved working conditions, higher wages, and shorter hours. War contracts stipulated an eight-hour day, and by the end of the war, nearly half the nation's workers had achieved the 48-hour week. Wages rose, too, but often only as fast as inflation. These improvements limited labor disputes during the war, and Secretary of War Baker praised labor as "more willing to keep in step than capital." But when such unions as the Industrial Workers of the World did not keep in step, the government suppressed them.

QUICK REVIEW

National War Labor Board

- Supervised labor relations.
- Guaranteed the rights of unions to organize and bargain collectively.
- Labor unions sharply increased their membership under this protection.

Although these and other government regulatory agencies were dismantled when the war ended, their activities reinforced many long-standing trends in the American economy, from the consolidation of business to the commercialization of agriculture and the organization of labor. They also set a precedent for governmental activism that would prove valuable during the crises of the 1930s and 1940s.

WOMEN AND MINORITIES: NEW OPPORTUNITIES, OLD INEQUITIES

Women and war work. The reorganization of the economy also had significant social consequences, especially for women and African Americans. In response to labor shortages, public officials and private employers exhorted women to join the work force. Women now took jobs previously closed to them. More than 100,000 women worked in munitions plants and 40,000 in the steel industry. Women constituted 20 percent or more of all workers making electrical machinery, leather and rubber goods, and food. They operated drills and lathes, controlled cranes in steel mills, and repaired equipment in machine shops.

Many working women simply shifted to other jobs, where their existing skills earned better wages and benefits. The reshuffling of jobs among white women opened new vacancies for black women in domestic, clerical, and industrial employment. As black women replaced white women in the garment and textile industries, social reformers spoke of "a new day for the colored woman worker" and African American women themselves celebrated their long-awaited industrial employment. But their optimism was unwarranted and their gains short-lived. Racial as

With women's labor crucial for the war effort, both government agencies and private industry recruited women for factory work. Here, four women, wearing "womanall" worksuits, pause at their jobs at the Westinghouse Electric Company in 1918.

Hagley Museum and Library, Wilmington, Delaware.

Black women work in a brickyard for wartime construction. Mobilization opened new jobs for women, but racial subordination and segregation persisted. Black women often performed the hardest and least desirable work.

well as gender segregation continued to mark employment. Federal efforts to prevent pay inequities and sexual harassment in the workplace were halfhearted and subordinated to the goals of efficiency and productivity. The policies of the government and employers ensured that women would be unable to sustain their wartime advances in the workplace. (See American Views: Reconstruction and the Colored Woman, January 1919.)

Woman suffrage and prohibition. The war did help middle-class women reformers achieve two long-sought objectives: woman suffrage and prohibition. Women's support for the war effort prompted more Americans to support woman suffrage. Congress approved the suffrage amendment, which was ratified in 1920. Convinced that abstaining from alcohol would save grain and make workers and soldiers more efficient, Congress also passed the Prohibition amendment, which was ratified in 1919.

QUICK REVIEW

Women and the War

- The war opened jobs in industry for women.
- New job opportunities appeared for black women.
- Reformers achieved two objectives: woman suffrage and prohibition.

African Americans and war work. The war also changed the lives of African Americans. The demand for industrial labor caused a huge migration of black people from the rural South, where they had little opportunity, few rights, and no hope. In northern cities, they worked in shipyards, steel mills, and packing houses. Half a million African Americans moved north during the war, doubling and tripling the black populations of Chicago, Detroit, and other industrial cities.

Unfortunately, blacks often encountered the kind of racial discrimination and violence in the North that they had hoped to leave behind in the South. Fearful and resentful whites started race riots in northern cities. In East St. Louis, Illinois, where thousands of black southerners sought defense work, a white mob, in July 1917, murdered at least 39 black people, sparing, as an investigating committee reported, "neither age nor sex in their blind lust for blood."

Financing the War

To finance the war, the government borrowed money and raised taxes. Business interests favored the first course, but southern and western progressives argued that taxation was more efficient and equitable and would minimize war profiteering. Despite conservative and business opposition to progressive taxation, the tax laws of 1917 and 1918 established a graduated tax structure with higher taxes on large incomes, corporate profits, and wealthy estates. Conservative opposition, however, would frustrate progressives' hopes for permanent tax reforms.

Liberty Bonds Interest-bearing certificates sold by the U.S. government to finance the American World War I effort.

The government raised two-thirds of the war costs by borrowing. Most of the loans came from banks and wealthy investors, but the government also campaigned to sell **Liberty Bonds** to the general public. Celebrities went to schools, churches, and rallies to persuade Americans to buy bonds as their patriotic duty. Using techniques of persuasion and control from advertising and mass entertainment, the Wilson administration thus enlisted the emotions of loyalty, fear, patriotism, and obedience for the war effort.

Conquering Minds

The government also tried to promote a war spirit among the American people by establishing propaganda agencies and enacting legislation to control social attitudes and behavior. This

AMERICAN VIEWS

Reconstruction and the Colored Woman, January 1919

In 1917, commentators throughout America noted the "mass exodus" of African Americans from the South to the North. Adversely affected by an agricultural depression in the South and attracted to wartime employment opportunities in the North, 500,000 blacks moved into northern cities. Black migrants made the journey to what they called the "promised land." And although conditions were better than they had endured in the South, they encountered white hostility and even violence at home and at work. Still, wartime mobilization required thousands of new workers, and even African American women found new opportunities as railroad workers and general laborers in a variety of fields. As railroad worker Helen Ross explained, "All the colored women like this work and want to keep it. . . . Of course we should like easier work than this if it were open to us, but this pays well and is no harder than other work open to us." Grateful for even the least desirable jobs, these black women workers were, however, ultimately forced to return to their former jobs after the war.

Black social worker Forrester B. Washington of the Detroit Urban League wrote frequently about the injustices faced by black migrants, pointing up the particular hardships suffered by African American women.

- **What** kinds of work did African American women do during the war?
- **How** did the experiences faced by African American women at home correspond to the nation's wartime goals abroad?
- **How** would you describe the impact of the Great War on African American women?

The history of the experiences of colored women in the present war should make fair-minded Americans blush with shame. They have been universally the last to be employed. They were the marginal workers of industry all through the war. They have been given, with few exceptions, the most undesirable and lowest paid work, and now the war is over they are the first to be released.

It is especially significant that Chicago, which now has the third largest negro population in the country, should be the most inconsiderate in its treatment of the colored woman worker. As a matter of fact, the country as a whole has not treated the colored working woman according to the spirit of democracy. The essential difference between Chicago and elsewhere is that in other cities the colored woman made some little progress into the skilled and so-called semi-skilled industries. In Chicago, while she did get into many occupations in which she had never gained entrance before, they were only the marginal occupations. She became the bus girl in the dairy lunches, the elevator girl, the ironer in the laundry, etc. Now she is being discharged from even these menial and low-paid positions. . . .

Detroit, perhaps, stands foremost among the cities of the country in the industrial opportunities offered colored women during the war. Here they were found working on machines in many of the big auto plants. . . . Colored women were also employed in Detroit as assemblers, inspectors and shippers in auto plants, as core makers and chippers in foundries, as shell makers in munition factories, as plate makers in dental laboratories, as garment makers and as armature winders in insulated wire factories. . . .

The American employer in his treatment of colored women wage-earners should square himself with the democratic ideal of which he made so much during the war. During those perilous times white and black women looked alike in the factory when they were striving to keep the industry of the country up to 100 per cent production, just as white and black soldiers looked alike going over the top to preserve the honor of the country. . . .

If either the American employer or the American laborer continues to deny the colored woman an opportunity to make a decent living, the Bolshevik cannot be blamed for proclaiming their affirmation of democratic principles a sham.

Source: Life and Labor, vol. 9 (January 1919): 3–7.

program drew from the restrictive side of progressivism: its impulses toward social control, behavior regulation, and nativism. It also reflected the interests of more conservative forces. The Wilson administration adopted this program of social mobilization because many Americans opposed the war.

Committee on Public Information (CPI) Government agency during World War I that sought to shape public opinion in support of the war effort through newspapers, pamphlets, speeches, films, and other media.

Government propaganda. To rally Americans behind the war effort, Wilson established the **Committee on Public Information (CPI)** under journalist George Creel. Despite its title, the CPI sought to manipulate, not inform, public opinion. The CPI flooded the country with press releases, advertisements, cartoons, and canned editorials. The CPI made newsreels and war movies to capture public attention. It scheduled 75,000 speakers, who delivered a million speeches to 400 million listeners. It hired artists to design posters, professors to write pamphlets in 23 languages, and poets to compose war poems for children.

Other government agencies launched similar campaigns. The Woman's Committee of the Council of National Defense established the Department of Educational Propaganda and Patriotic Education. The agency worked to win over women who opposed the war, particularly in the rural Midwest, West, and South. It formed women's speakers bureaus, developed programs for community meetings at country schools, and distributed millions of pamphlets.

Government propaganda had three themes: national unity, the loathsome character of the enemy, and the war as a grand crusade for liberty and democracy. Obsessed with national unity and conformity, Creel promoted fear, hatred, and prejudice in the name of a triumphant Americanism. Germans were depicted as brutal, even subhuman, rapists and murderers. The campaign suggested that any dissent was unpatriotic, if not treasonous, and dangerous to national survival. This emphasis on unreasoning conformity helped prompt hysterical attacks on German Americans, radicals, and pacifists.

Read the Document at **www.myhistorylab.com**
Boy Scouts of America, "Support the War Effort" (1917)

Read the Document at **www.myhistorylab.com**
The Espionage Act (1917)

Suppressing Dissent

The Wilson administration also suppressed dissent, now officially branded disloyalty. For reasons of their own, private interests helped shape a reactionary repression that tarnished the nation's professed idealistic war goals. The campaign also established unfortunate precedents for the future.

Espionage Act Law whose vague prohibition against obstructing the nation's war effort was used to crush dissent and criticism during World War I.

Sedition Act of 1918 Broad law restricting criticism of America's involvement in World War I or its government, flag, military, taxes, or officials.

Congress rushed to stifle antiwar sentiment. The **Espionage Act** provided heavy fines and up to 20 years in prison for obstructing the war effort, a vague phrase but "omnipotently comprehensive," warned an Idaho senator who opposed the law. In fact, the Espionage Act became a weapon to crush dissent and criticism. Eventually, Congress passed the still more sweeping **Sedition Act of 1918,** which provided severe penalties for speaking or writing against the draft, bond sales, and war production and for criticizing government personnel or policies.

Postmaster General Albert Burleson banned antiwar or radical newspapers and magazines from the mail. Even more zealous in attacking radicals and presumed subversives was the reactionary attorney general, Thomas Gregory, who made little distinction between traitors and pacifists, war critics, and radicals. Eugene Debs was sentenced to ten years in prison for a "treasonous" speech in which he declared it "extremely dangerous to exercise the right of free speech in a country fighting to make democracy safe in the world." By war's end, a third of the Socialist Party's national leadership was in prison, leaving the party in a shambles.

Read the Document at **www.myhistorylab.com**
Eugene Debs, Critique of World War I (1918)

Gregory also enlisted the help of private vigilantes, including the several hundred thousand members of the reactionary American Protective League, which sought to purge radicals and reformers from the nation's economic and political life. They wiretapped telephones, intercepted private mail, burglarized union offices, broke up German-language newspapers, harassed immigrants, and staged mass raids, seizing thousands of people who they claimed were not doing enough for the war effort.

Read the Document at **www.myhistorylab.com**
Newton D. Baker, "The Treatment of German-Americans" (1918)

State and local authorities also suppressed what they saw as antiwar, radical, or pro-German activities. They established 184,000 investigative and enforcement agencies, known as councils of defense or public-safety committees. They encouraged Americans to spy on one another, required people to buy Liberty Bonds, and prohibited teaching German in schools or using the language in religious services and telephone conversations. Indeed, suppression of all things German reached extremes. Germanic names of towns, streets, and people were changed; sauerkraut became liberty cabbage, and the hamburger the liberty sandwich.

"Beat Back the Hun," a poster to induce Americans to buy Liberty Bonds, demonizes the enemy in a raw, emotional appeal. Liberty bond drives raised the immense sum of $23 billion.

Members of the business community exploited the hysteria to promote their own interests at the expense of farmers, workers, and reformers. On the Great Plains from Texas to North Dakota, the business target was the Nonpartisan League, a radical farm group demanding state control or ownership of banks, grain elevators, and flour mills. Although the League supported the war, oversubscribed bond drives, and had George Creel affirm its loyalty, conservatives depicted it as seditious to block its advocacy of political and economic reforms, including the confiscation of large fortunes to pay for the war. Nebraska's council of defense barred League meetings. Public officials and self-styled patriots broke up the League's meetings and whipped and jailed its leaders.

In the West, business interests targeted labor organizations, especially the Industrial Workers of the World. In Arizona, for example, the Phelps-Dodge Company broke a mine strike in 1917 by depicting the Wobblie miners as bent on war-related sabotage. A vigilante mob, armed and paid by the mining company, seized 1,200 strikers, many of them Wobblies and one-third of them Mexican Americans, and herded them into the desert without food or water.

The government itself assisted the business campaign. It used the army to break loggers' support for the IWW in the Pacific Northwest, and it raided IWW halls across the country in September 1917. The conviction of nearly 200 Wobblies on charges of sedition in three mass trials in Illinois, California, and Kansas crippled the nation's largest industrial union.

In the end, the government was primarily responsible for the war hysteria. It encouraged suspicion and conflict through inflammatory propaganda, repressive laws, and violation of basic civil rights, by supporting extremists who used the war for their own purposes, and by tolerating mob violence against German Americans. This ugly mood would infect the postwar world.

WAGING WAR AND PEACE ABROAD

WHAT HOPES did Wilson have for the Treaty of Versailles?

While mobilizing the home front, the Wilson administration undertook an impressive military effort to help the Allies defeat the Central Powers. Wilson also struggled to secure international acceptance for his plans for a just and permanent peace.

The War to End All Wars

When the United States entered the war, the Allied position was dire. The losses from three years of trench warfare had sapped military strength and civilian morale. French soldiers mutinied and refused to continue an assault that had cost 120,000 casualties in five days; the German submarine campaign was devastating the British. On the eastern front, the Russian army had collapsed, and the Russian government had gradually disintegrated after the overthrow of the tsarist regime.

WHERE TO LEARN MORE

Wisconsin Veterans Museum, Madison, Wisconsin
http://museum.dva.state.wi.us

Selective Service Act of 1917 The law establishing the military draft for World War I.

In May, Congress passed the **Selective Service Act of 1917,** establishing conscription. More than 24 million men eventually registered for the draft, and nearly 3 million entered the army when their numbers were drawn in a national lottery. Almost 2 million more men volunteered, as did more than 13,000 women, who served in the navy and marines. Nearly one-fifth of America's soldiers were foreign-born (Europeans spoke of the "American Foreign Legion"); 367,000 were black. Many Native Americans served with distinction as well; in recognition, Indian veterans were made citizens in 1919, a status extended to all Indians five years later.

WHERE TO LEARN MORE

National Infantry Museum, Columbus, Georgia
http://www.nationalinfantrymuseum.com/

Hear the Audio at www.myhistorylab.com
Immigrants and the Great War

Civilians were transformed into soldiers in hastily organized training camps, operated according to progressive principles. Prohibition prevailed in the camps; the poorly educated and largely working-class recruits were taught personal hygiene; worries about sin and inefficiency produced massive campaigns against venereal disease; and immigrants were taught English and American history. Some units were ethnically segregated: At Camp Gordon, Georgia, Italians and Slavs had separate units, with their own officers.

Racial segregation was more rigid, not only in training camps and military units but in assignments as well. The navy assigned black sailors to menial positions, and the army similarly used black soldiers primarily as gravediggers and laborers. But one black combat division was created, and four black regiments fought under French command. France decorated three of these units with its highest citations for valor. White American officers urged the French not to praise black troops, treat black officers as equals, or permit fraternization. But white racism could not diminish the extraordinary record of one of the most famous of the black units in France—the 369th Infantry Regiment, also known as the "Harlem Hellfighters." The 369th spent 191 days in combat and was the first Allied unit to reach the Rhine.

Read the Document at www.myhistorylab.com
From Then to Now Online: Women and War

Read the Document at www.myhistorylab.com
Eugene Kennedy, A "Doughboy" Describes the Fighting Front (1918)

Women were recruited as noncombatant personnel, such as clerks, translators, and switchboard operators, thereby enabling more men to be assigned to combat duty. The navy awarded them equal rank with males performing the same tasks, and they were eligible after the war for veterans benefits. The army was a different story. Although they served in uniform and under military discipline, women had no formal military status, were ineligible for benefits, and often had their skills and contributions devalued.

Into action in France. The first American troops, the American Expeditionary Force (AEF), landed in France in June 1917. Months of training, under French direction, then followed as the Americans learned about trench warfare: using bayonets, grenades, and machine guns and surviving poison-gas attacks. Finally in October, the 1st Division, the Big Red One, moved into the trenches.

WHERE TO LEARN MORE

Sgt. Alvin C. York Homeplace and State Historic Site, Pall Mall, Tennessee
http://www.state.tn.us/environment/parks/SgtYork/

Full-scale American intervention began in the late spring of 1918 (see Map 23–2). In June, the fresh American troops helped the French repulse a German thrust toward Paris at Château-Thierry. Further savage fighting at Belleau Wood blocked the Germans again, prompting a French officer to declare, "You Americans are our hope, our strength, our life." In July, the AEF helped defeat another German advance, at Rheims. The influx of American troops had tipped the balance toward Allied victory. By July 18, the German chancellor later acknowledged, "even the most optimistic among us knew that all was lost. The history of the world was played out in three days."

The Russian front. In July, Wilson also agreed to commit 15,000 American troops to intervene in Russia. Russia's provisional government had collapsed when the radical **Bolshevik** faction of the communist movement had seized power in November 1917. Under V. I. Lenin, the Bolsheviks signed an armistice with Germany in early 1918, which freed German troops for the summer offensive in France. The Allied interventions were initially designed to reopen the eastern front and later to help overthrow the Bolshevik government.

Bolshevik Member of the Communist movement in Russia that established the Soviet government after the 1917 Russian Revolution.

Lenin's call for the destruction of capitalism and imperialism alarmed the Allied leaders. One Wilson adviser urged the "eradication" of the Russian government. Soon, American and British troops were fighting Russians in an effort to influence Russia's internal affairs. U.S. forces remained in Russia even after Germany surrendered in 1918. They did not leave until 1920. These military interventions failed, but they contributed to Russian distrust of the West.

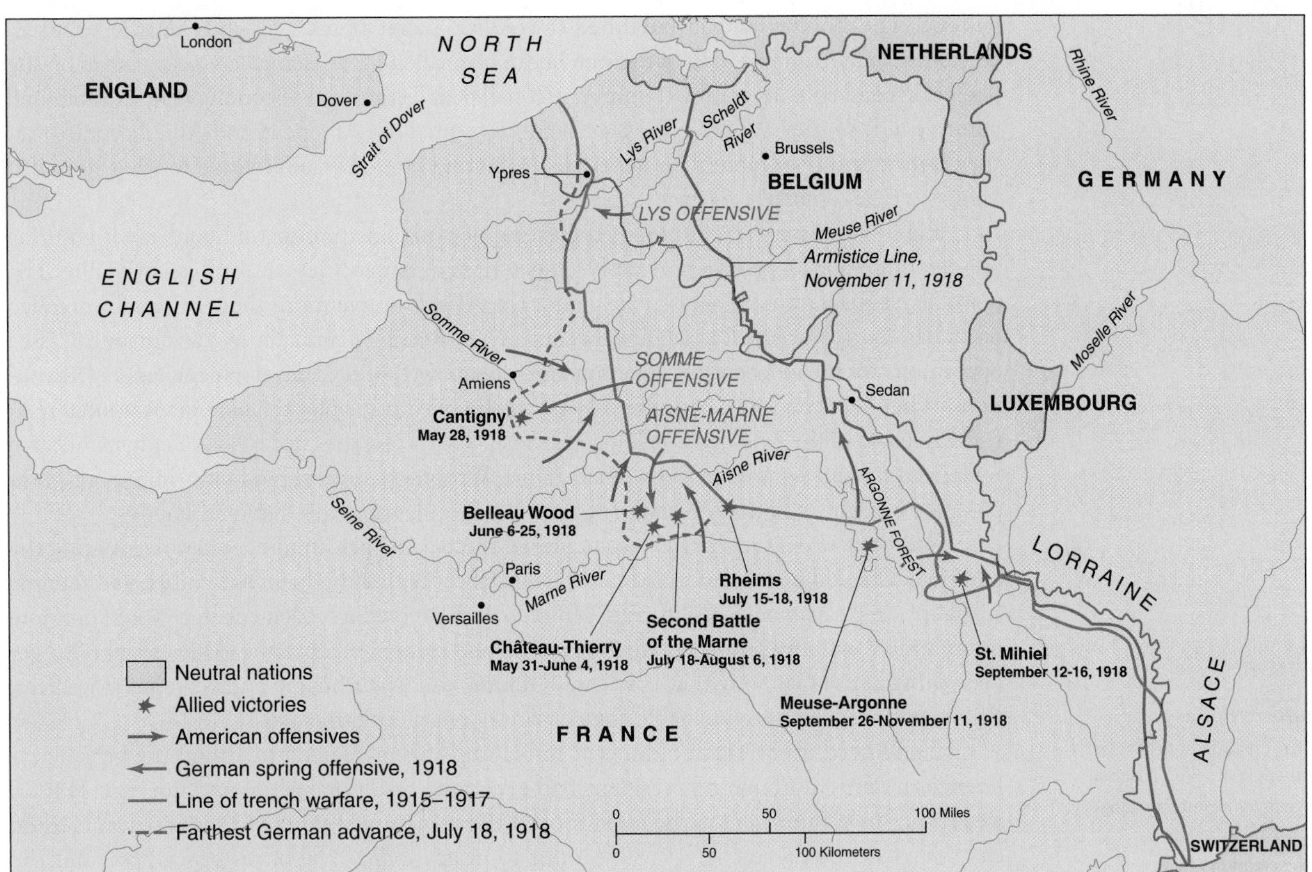

MAP 23–2 **The Western Front, 1918** After three years of trench warfare, the arrival of large numbers of American troops in 1918 enabled the Allies to launch an offensive that drove back the Germans and forced an armistice.

How did the entry of American troops turn the tide of war on the western front?

The western front. The Allies were more successful on the western front. Having stopped the German offensive in July, they launched their own advance. The decisive battle began in late September when an American army over 1 million strong attacked German trenches in the Argonne Forest. Many Americans were still inexperienced; some had been drafted only in July and had spent more time traveling than training. Nevertheless, they advanced steadily, despite attacks with poison gas and heavy artillery.

The battle for the Argonne raged for weeks. A German general reported that his exhausted soldiers faced Americans who "were fresh, eager for fighting, and brave." But he found their sheer numbers most impressive. Eventually, this massive assault overwhelmed the Germans. Despite severe casualties, the AEF had helped the British and French to defeat the enemy. With its allies surrendering, its own army in retreat, and revolution breaking out among the war-weary residents of its major cities, Germany asked for peace. On November 11, 1918, an armistice ended the Great War. More than 115,000 Americans were among the 8 million soldiers and 7 million civilians dead.

THE FOURTEEN POINTS

The armistice was only a step toward final peace. President Wilson had already enunciated America's war objectives on January 8, 1918, in a speech outlining what became known as the Fourteen Points. In his 1917 war message, Wilson had advocated a more democratic world system, and this new speech spelled out how to achieve it. But Wilson also had a political

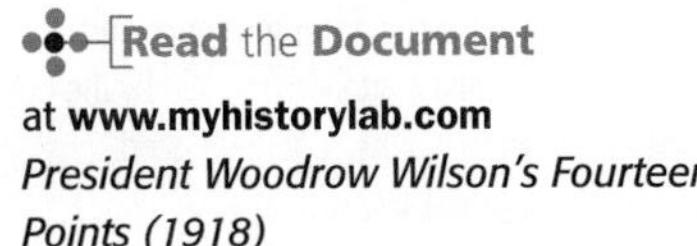

at **www.myhistorylab.com**
President Woodrow Wilson's Fourteen Points (1918)

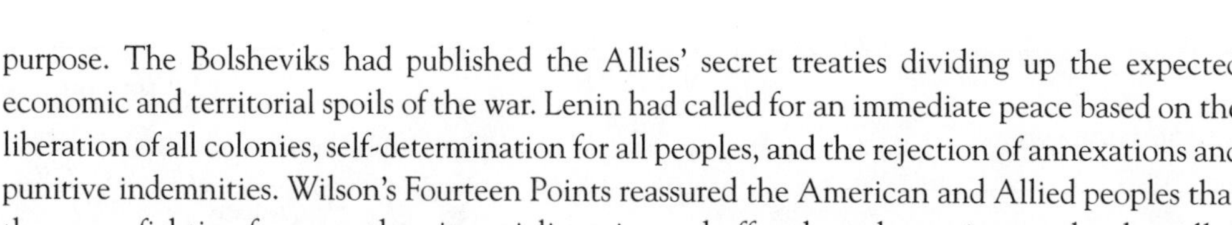

purpose. The Bolsheviks had published the Allies' secret treaties dividing up the expected economic and territorial spoils of the war. Lenin had called for an immediate peace based on the liberation of all colonies, self-determination for all peoples, and the rejection of annexations and punitive indemnities. Wilson's Fourteen Points reassured the American and Allied peoples that they were fighting for more than imperialist gains and offered an alternative to what he called Lenin's "crude formula" for peace.

Eight of Wilson's points proposed creating new nations, shifting old borders, or ensuring self-determination for peoples previously subject to the Austrian, German, or Russian empire. The point about Russia would haunt Wilson after the Allied interventions there began, for it called on all nations to evacuate Russian territory and permit Russia "an unhampered and unembarrassed opportunity for the independent determination of her own political development" under "institutions of her own choosing." Another five points invoked principles to guide international relations: freedom of the seas, open diplomacy instead of secret treaties, reduction of armaments, free trade, and the fair settlement of colonial claims. Wilson's fourteenth and most important point proposed a league of nations to carry out these ideals and ensure international stability.

Wilson and the German government had these principles in mind when negotiating the armistice. The Allies, however, had never explicitly accepted the Fourteen Points, and framing a final peace treaty would be difficult. While Wilson favored a settlement that would promote international stability and economic expansion, he recognized that the Allies sought "to get everything out of Germany that they can." Indeed, after their human and economic sacrifices, Britain and France wanted tangible compensation, not pious principles.

QUICK REVIEW

Wilson's Fourteen Points

- Advocated the creation of new nations under the principle of self-determination.
- Outlined principles for international relations.
- Called for the creation of a League of Nations.

Convinced of the righteousness of his cause, Wilson decided to attend the peace conference in Paris, although no president had ever gone to Europe while in office. But Wilson weakened his position before he even set sail. First, he urged voters to support Democratic candidates in the November 1918 elections to indicate approval of his peace plan. But the electorate, responding primarily to domestic problems like inflation, gave the Republicans control of both houses of Congress. This meant that any treaty would have to be approved by Senate Republicans angry that Wilson had tried to use war and peace for partisan purposes. Second, Wilson refused to consult with Senate Republicans on plans for the peace conference and failed to name important Republicans to the Paris delegation. It was going to be Wilson's treaty, and Republicans would feel no responsibility to approve it.

American soldiers advancing through smoke and shattered trees of the Argonne Forest in October 1918. The Great War was a conflict of relentless attrition, marked by the horrors of poison gas, artillery bombardment, pandemic disease, and what one American called the "unburied dead."

U.S. Army Signal Corps. National Archives III-SC 94980.

The Paris Peace Conference

The peace conference opened on January 18, 1919. Meeting at the Palace of Versailles, the delegations were dominated by the principal Allied leaders: Wilson of the United States, David Lloyd George of Britain, Georges Clemenceau of France, and Vittorio Orlando of Italy. The Central Powers and Bolshevik Russia were excluded. The treaty would be one-sided except to the extent that Wilson could insist on the liberal terms of the Fourteen Points against French and British intransigence.

For months, the conference debated Wilson's other goals and the Allies' demands for compensation and security. Lloyd George later commented, with reference to the self-righteous Wilson and the assertive Clemenceau, "I think I did as well as might be expected, seated as I was between Jesus Christ and Napoleon Bonaparte." Under protest, Germany signed the **Treaty of Versailles** on June 28, 1919. Its terms were far more severe than Wilson had proposed or Germany had anticipated. Germany had to accept sole responsibility for starting the war, a stipulation that all Germans bitterly resented. It was required to pay huge reparations to the Allies, give up land to France, Poland, Belgium, and Denmark, cede its colonies, limit its army and navy to small self-defense forces, destroy military bases, and promise not to manufacture or purchase armaments.

Treaty of Versailles The treaty ending World War I and creating the League of Nations.

Wilson gained some acceptance of self-determination. As the German, Austro-Hungarian, Turkish, and Russian empires had collapsed at the end of the war, nationalist groups had proclaimed their independence. On one hand, the peace settlement formally recognized these new nation-states: Poland, Finland, Estonia, Latvia, and Lithuania in eastern Europe and Austria, Hungary, Czechoslovakia, and Yugoslavia in central Europe. On the other hand, France, Italy, Romania, and Japan all annexed territory regardless of the wishes of the inhabitants. Germans were placed under Polish control in Silesia and Czech control in Bohemia. Austria was not allowed to merge with Germany. And the conference sanctioned colonialism by establishing a trusteeship system that enabled France, Britain, and Japan to take over German colonies and Turkish territory.

The Allied leaders endorsed the changes in eastern Europe in part because the new states there were anticommunist and would constitute a barrier against Bolshevism. Communist movements in early 1919 in Germany, Austria, and Hungary caused the Allies to fear that "the Russian idea was still rising in power," and they hoped to isolate and weaken Bolshevik Russia. Allied armies were in Russia during the peace conference, and Wilson and the other leaders agreed to provide further aid to fight the Bolsheviks. This hostility to Russia, like the punitive terms for Germany and the concessions to imperial interests, boded ill for a stable and just postwar order. (See Global Connections, War and Revolution: The Bolsheviks and the International Community.)

But Wilson hoped that the final section of the Versailles treaty would resolve the flaws of the agreement by establishing his great international organization to preserve peace: the **League of Nations.** The Covenant, or constitution, of the League was built into the treaty. Its crucial feature, Article Ten, bound the member nations to guarantee each other's independence—a provision that was Wilson's concept of collective security. "At least," he told an aide, "we are saving the Covenant, and that instrument will work wonders, bring the blessing of peace, and then when the war psychosis has abated, it will not be difficult to settle all disputes that baffle us now."

League of Nations International organization created by the Versailles Treaty after World War I to ensure world stability.

WAGING PEACE AT HOME

WHAT CHALLENGES did America face in the aftermath of the war?

Wilson was determined to defeat the opposition to the peace treaty. But many Americans were engaged in their own struggles with the new conditions of a nation suddenly at peace but driven by economic, social, and political conflict. Wilson's battle for the League of Nations would fail tragically. The other conflicts would rage until the election of 1920 restored a normalcy of sorts.

Battle over the League

Most Americans favored the Versailles treaty. A survey of 1,400 newspapers found fewer than 200 opposed. Thirty-three governors and 32 state legislatures endorsed the League of Nations. But when Wilson called for the Senate to accept "the moral leadership . . . and confidence of the world" by ratifying the treaty, he met resistance. Some Republicans wanted to prevent the Democrats from campaigning in 1920 as the party responsible for a victorious war and a glorious peace. But most Republican opponents of the treaty raised serious questions, often reflecting national traditions in foreign relations. Nearly all Democrats favored the treaty, but they were a minority; some Republicans would have to be converted for the treaty to be approved.

With the defeat of Germany, Americans wanted their soldiers home. And although many returning African American soldiers were denied celebratory homecomings and would face discrimination and hostility, their role in World War I brought fresh confidence and respect to the African American community. Few units stirred the patriotism and pride as did the valiant 369th Infantry Regiment, decorated by the French government for heroism and "gallantry under fire." Here African American friends and families turn out to welcome home the "Men of Bronze," as they were also called.

Progressive Republican senators, such as Robert La Follette and Hiram Johnson, led one group of opponents. Called the **Irreconcilables,** they opposed participation in the League of Nations, which they saw as designed to perpetuate the power of imperialist countries. Article Ten, they feared, would require the United States to help suppress rebellions in Ireland against British rule or to enforce disputed European borders. Most of the Irreconcilables gave priority to restoring civil liberties and progressive reform at home. Many progressives also criticized the treaty's compromises on self-determination, reparations, and colonies. Linking these failures with Wilson's domestic policies, one former supporter concluded, "The administration has become reactionary, and deserves no support from any of us."

A larger group of opponents had reservations about the treaty's provisions. These **Reservationists** were led by Henry Cabot Lodge, the chair of the Senate Foreign Relations Committee. They regarded Article Ten as eroding congressional authority to declare war. They also fretted that the League might interfere with domestic questions, such as immigration laws.

Lodge's opposition was further shaped by both partisanship and deep personal hostility. Wilson reciprocated, and when Lodge proposed reservations or amendments to the treaty, Wilson refused to compromise. He proposed "a direct frontal attack" on his opponents. If they wanted war, he said, he would "give them a belly full." In early September 1919, Wilson set out across the country to win popular support for the League. In three weeks, he traveled 8,000 miles and delivered 37 speeches.

Irreconcilables Group of U.S. senators opposed to ratification of the Treaty of Versailles after World War I.

Reservationists Group of U.S. senators opposing approval of the Treaty of Versailles, without significant amendments.

In poor health following a bout with influenza, Wilson collapsed in Pueblo, Colorado. Taken back to Washington, Wilson on October 2 suffered a massive stroke that paralyzed his left side and left him psychologically unstable and temporarily blind. Wilson's physician and his wife, Edith Galt Wilson, kept the nature of his illness secret from the public, Congress, and even the vice president and cabinet. Rumors circulated that Edith Wilson was running the administration, but she was not. Instead, it was immobilized.

By February 1920, Wilson had partially recovered, but he remained suspicious and quarrelsome. Bryan and other Democratic leaders urged him to accept Lodge's reservations to gain ratification of the treaty. Wilson refused. Isolated and inflexible, he ordered Democratic senators to vote with the Irreconcilables against the treaty as amended by Lodge. On March 19, 1920, the Senate killed the treaty.

QUICK REVIEW

Defeat of the Treaty

- Most Democrats favored the treaty.
- Republicans led by Henry Cabot Lodge wanted amendments.
- Wilson's refusal to compromise doomed the treaty.

Economic Readjustment and Social Conflict

The League was not the only casualty of the struggle to conclude the war. Grave problems shook the United States in 1919 and early 1920. An influenza epidemic had erupted in Europe in 1918 among the massed armies. It now hit the United States, killing perhaps 700,000 Americans, far more than had died in combat. Frightened officials closed public facilities and banned public meetings in futile attempts to stop the contagion.

Meanwhile, the Wilson administration had no plans for an orderly reconversion of the wartime economy, and chaos ensued. The government canceled war contracts and dissolved the regulatory agencies. Noting that "the war spirit of cooperation and sacrifice" had disappeared

War and Revolution: The Bolsheviks and the International Community

An uneasy amalgam of distinctive nationalities, the Russian Empire at the start of World War I covered vast territories and included 178 million people. A poor, agrarian country, Russia suffered from autocratic tsarist rule. Long-standing economic problems and political aspirations, especially among land-starved peasants, combined to make Russia a cauldron of tensions inflamed by its involvement in the Great War. The Russian army reflected the discontent that plagued the empire; 400,000 soldiers were killed during the first six months of war, and thereafter desertion became a significant problem.

Food shortages provoked protests among peasants and workers—all challenging tsarist rule. Uprisings in March 1917 immobilized Petrograd, the capital, persuaded the military to mutiny, and ended the Romanov dynasty. A Provisional Government dominated by liberal reformers came to power. Despite recognition and financial aid from its Allies—the United States, France, and Britain—the new government was politically vulnerable and unable to solve the country's pressing problems.

As frustrations mounted, support for the Bolshevik faction of the Communist Party grew. The Bolsheviks envisioned a world without classes or war—a vision that appealed to a war-weary society with a disintegrating economy. In November 1917, the Provisional Government collapsed and the Bolsheviks came to power.

Promising peace, land, and workers' control, the Bolsheviks were led by V. I. Lenin, a lawyer who had worked for a socialist revolution in Russia since the turn of the century. On March 3, 1918, Russia and Germany signed the Treaty of Brest-Litovsk, an armistice that cost Russia significant territory. But Lenin defended the treaty because Germany still occupied large parts of Russia and the counterrevolutionary, or "White," forces were gathering momentum.

The Allies decried both the Bolshevik revolution and the separate peace with Germany, which enabled Germany to strengthen its forces on the western front. Russia's withdrawal from the war emboldened the "Whites," the opponents of the Bolshevik "Reds," and encouraged the Allies to assist them with financial support and troops. But the Allied invasions of Russia were failures, serving only to convince Lenin that the Allies were imperialists bent on overthrowing the world's only socialist state. In the tumultuous postwar period, Lenin's call for workers to overthrow their governments, European and American leaders believed, fed the postwar labor unrest that wracked industrialized nations. Woodrow Wilson fumed that the "poison" of Bolshevism was "running through the veins of the world." Wilson feared that returning African American troops would serve as the "greatest medium in conveying bolshevism to America," but other policymakers targeted aliens, immigrants, and labor activists, culminating in the "Red Scare."

The fears stirred by the Bolshevik Revolution, however, did not provoke similar governmental extremism in either Great Britain or France, both of which would recognize the Soviet Union by 1924. But America, as the British ambassador noted, was singularly "frightened" of the revolution, and the United States would withhold recognition until 1933.

- What was the impact of the Bolshevik revolution on the war and peace? How did the Allies respond to the Bolsheviks who came to power in Russia in 1917?

with the Armistice, Bernard Baruch decided to "turn industry absolutely free" and abolished the War Industries Board as of January 1, 1919. Other agencies followed in such haste that turmoil engulfed the economy.

The government also demobilized the armed forces. With no planning or assistance, veterans were hustled back into civilian life. There they competed for scarce jobs with workers recently discharged from the war industries.

As unemployment mounted, the removal of wartime price controls brought runaway inflation. The cost of food, clothing, and other necessities more than doubled over prewar rates. The return of the soldiers caused a serious housing shortage, and rents skyrocketed. Democratic leaders urged Wilson to devote less time to the League of Nations and more to the cost of living and the tensions it unleashed. Farmers also suffered from economic readjustments. Net farm income declined by 65 percent between 1919 and 1921. Farmers who had borrowed money for machinery and land to expand production for the war effort were left impoverished and embittered.

Postwar battles: gender and race. Women also lost their wartime economic advances. Returning soldiers took away their jobs. Male trade unionists insisted that women go back to being housewives. At times, male workers struck to force employers to fire women and barred women from unions in jobs where union membership was required for employment. Indeed, state legislatures passed laws prohibiting women from working in many of the occupations they had successfully filled during the war. By 1919, half of the women newly employed in heavy industry during the war were gone; by 1920, women constituted a smaller proportion of the workforce than they had in 1910.

The postwar readjustments also left African Americans disappointed. During the war, they had agreed with W. E. B. Du Bois to "forget our special grievances and close our ranks shoulder to shoulder with our own white fellow citizens." Participation in the war effort, they had hoped, might be rewarded by better treatment thereafter. Now, the meagerness of their reward became clear.

QUICK REVIEW

Labor Unrest

- Efforts to roll back war-time gains angered workers.
- 4 million workers launched 3,600 strikes in 1919.
- The largest strike involved efforts to organize steelworkers.

Housing shortages and job competition interacted with racism in 1919 to produce race riots in 26 towns and cities, resulting in at least 120 deaths. In Chicago, 38 people were killed and more than 500 injured in a five-day riot that began when white thugs stoned to death a black youth swimming too near "their" beach. White rioters then fired a machine gun from a truck hurtling through black neighborhoods. But black residents fought back, no longer willing, the *Chicago Defender* reported, "to move along the line of least resistance as did their sires." The new militancy reflected both their experiences in the military and in industry and their exposure to propaganda about freedom and democracy. Racial conflict was part of a postwar battle between Americans hoping to preserve the new social relations fostered by the war effort and those wanting to restore prewar patterns of power and control.

Strikers crowd outside the employment office of the Skinner & Eddy shipyard where the Seattle General Strike began in 1919. The strike shut down the city for five days and anti-Bolshevik hysteria led to a government crackdown on the strike.

Fighting for industrial democracy. Even more pervasive discontents roiled as America adjusted to the postwar world. More than 4 million angry workers launched a wave of 3,600 strikes in 1919. They were reacting not only to the soaring cost of living, which undermined the value of their wages, but also to employers' efforts to reassert their authority and destroy the legitimacy labor had won by its participation in the war effort. The abolition of government controls on industry enabled employers not only to raise prices but also to rescind their recognition of unions and reimpose objectionable working conditions. Employers also protected their rising profits by insisting that wages remain fixed. In response, strikers demanded higher wages, better conditions, and recognition of unions and the right of collective bargaining.

The greatest strike involved the American Federation of Labor's attempt to organize steelworkers, who endured dangerous conditions and 12-hour shifts. When the steel companies refused to recognize the union or even discuss issues, 365,000 workers went out on strike in September 1919. Employers hired thugs to beat the strikers, used strikebreakers to take their jobs, and exploited ethnic and racial divisions. To undercut support for the workers, management portrayed the strikers as disruptive radicals influenced by Bolshevism. After four months, the strike failed.

Employers used the same tactic to defeat striking coal miners, whose wages had fallen behind the cost of living. Refusing to negotiate with the United Mine Workers, coal operators claimed that Russian Bolsheviks had financed the strike to destroy the American economy. Attorney General A. Mitchell Palmer secured an injunction against the strike under the authority of wartime legislation. Because the government no longer controlled coal prices or enforced protective labor rules, miners complained bitterly that the war had ended for corporations but not for workers.

Two municipal strikes in 1919 also alarmed the public when their opponents depicted them as revolutionary attacks on the social order. In Seattle, the Central Labor Council called a general strike to support 35,000 shipyard workers striking for higher wages and shorter hours. When 60,000 more workers from 110 local unions also walked out, the city ground to a halt. The strikers behaved peacefully and protected public health and safety by operating garbage and fire trucks and providing food, water, and electricity. Nevertheless, Seattle's mayor, business leaders, and newspapers attacked them as Bolsheviks and anarchists. Threatened with military intervention, the labor council called off the strike, but not before it had caused a public backlash against unions across the nation.

Red Scare Post–World War I anti-Bolshevik hysteria in the United States directed against labor activists, radical dissenters, and some ethnic groups.

In Boston, the police commissioner fired police officers for trying to organize a union to improve their inadequate pay. In response, the police went on strike. As in Seattle, Boston newspapers, politicians, and business leaders attributed the strike to Bolshevism. Massachusetts Governor Calvin Coolidge gained nationwide acclaim when he mobilized the National Guard to break the strike. The entire police force was fired; many of their replacements were war veterans.

The Red Scare

The strikes contributed to an anti-Bolshevik hysteria that swept the country in 1919. The **Red Scare** reflected fears that the Bolshevik revolution in Russia might spread to the United States. Steeped in the antiradical propaganda of the war years, many Americans were appalled by Russian Bolshevism, described by the *Saturday Evening Post* as a "compound of slaughter, confiscation, anarchy, and universal disorder." But the Red Scare also reflected the willingness of antiunion employers, ambitious politicians, sensational journalists, zealous veterans, and racists to exploit the panic to advance their own purposes.

Fed by misleading reports about Russian Bolshevism and its influence in the United States, the Red Scare reached panic levels by mid-1919. Bombs mailed anonymously to several prominent people on May Day seemed proof enough that a Bolshevik conspiracy threatened America. The Justice Department, Congress, and patriotic organizations like the American Legion joined with business groups to suppress radicalism, real and

At the peak of the Red Scare, few major newspapers questioned the wholesale assault on civil liberties and instead placed fears of Bolshevism above rights of individuals, especially workers, immigrants, and radicals. In this 1919 cartoon, the *Philadelphia Inquirer*, using the American flag as a protective cover, registers its support for the exile of radical immigrants and ideas.

imagined. Wilson and Attorney General Palmer called for more stringent laws and refused to release political prisoners jailed during the war. State governments harassed and arrested hundreds.

Palmer created a new agency, headed by J. Edgar Hoover, to suppress radicals and impose conformity. Its war on radicalism became the chief focus of the Justice Department. As an ambitious and ruthless bureaucrat, Hoover had participated in the government's assault on aliens and radicals during the war. Now he collected files on labor leaders and other "radical agitators" from Senator Robert La Follette to Jane Addams, issued misleading reports on communist influence in labor strikes and race riots, and contacted all major newspapers "to acquaint people like you with the real menace of evil-thinking, which is the foundation of the Red Movement."

In November 1919, Palmer and Hoover began raiding groups suspected of subversion. A month later, they deported 249 alien radicals, including the anarchist Emma Goldman, to Russia. In January 1920, Palmer and Hoover rounded up more than 4,000 suspected radicals in 33 cities. Often without warrants, they broke into union halls, club rooms, and private homes, assaulting and arresting everyone in sight. People were jailed without access to lawyers; some were beaten into signing false confessions. The *Washington Post* declared, "There is no time to waste on hairsplitting over infringement of liberty."

Other Americans began to recoil from the excesses and illegal acts. Support for the Red Scare withered. Palmer's attempt to inflame public emotion backfired. When his predictions of a violent attempt to overthrow the government on May 1, 1920, came to naught, most Americans realized that no menace had ever existed. They agreed with the *Rocky Mountain News:* "We can never get to work if we keep jumping sideways in fear of the bewhiskered Bolshevik." But if the Red Scare faded in mid-1920, the hostility to immigrants, organized labor, and dissent it reflected would endure for a decade.

Jailed for her antiwar speeches, Lithuanian-born anarchist and birth control advocate Emma Goldman (1869–1940) was deported to the Soviet Union on the *SS Buford*, known as the Red Ark. Her autobiography, entitled *Living My Life* (1931), traces her political activism from her arrival in the United States in 1885.

The Election of 1920

The Democratic coalition that Wilson had cobbled together on the issues of progressivism and peace came apart after the war. Workers resented the administration's hostility to the postwar strikes. Ethnic groups brutalized by the Americanization of the war years blamed Wilson for the war or condemned his peace settlement. Farmers grumbled about wartime price controls and postwar falling prices. Wartime taxes and the social and economic turmoil of 1919–1920 alienated the middle class. Americans were weary of great crusades and social sacrifices; in the words of Kansas journalist William Allen White, they were "tired of issues, sick at heart of ideals, and weary of being noble." They yearned for what the Republican presidential candidate, Warren Harding of Ohio, called "normalcy."

The Republican ticket in 1920 symbolized the reassurance of simpler times. Harding was a genial politician who devoted more time to golf and poker than to public policy. An Old Guard conservative, he had stayed with the GOP when Theodore Roosevelt led the progressives out in 1912. His running mate, Calvin Coolidge, governor of Massachusetts, owed his nomination to his handling of the Boston police strike.

Wilson called the election of 1920 "a great and solemn referendum" on the League of Nations, but such lofty appeals fell flat. Harding was ambiguous about the League, and the Democratic national platform endorsed it but expressed a willingness to accept amendments or reservations. The Democratic nominees, James Cox, former governor of Ohio, and the young Franklin D. Roosevelt, Wilson's assistant secretary of the navy, favored the League, but it was not a decisive issue in the campaign.

Harding won in a landslide reflecting the nation's dissatisfaction with Wilson and the Democratic Party. Not even his closest backers considered Harding qualified for the White House, but, as Lippmann said, the nation's "public spirit was exhausted" after the war years. The election of 1920 was "the final twitch" of America's "war mind."

CONCLUSION

Participation in the war had changed the U.S. government, economy, and society. Some of these changes, including the centralization of the economy and an expansion of the regulatory role of the federal government, were already under way; some offered opportunities to implement progressive principles or reforms. Woman suffrage and prohibition gained decisive support because of the war spirit. But other consequences of the war betrayed both progressive impulses and the democratic principles the war was allegedly fought to promote. The suppression of civil liberties, manipulation of human emotions, repression of radicals and minorities, and exploitation of national crises by narrow interests helped disillusion the public. The repercussions of the Great War would linger for years, at home and abroad.

WHERE TO LEARN MORE

National Infantry Museum, Columbus, Georgia. This sprawling collection of weapons, uniforms, and equipment includes exhibits on World War I. http://www.nationalinfantrymuseum.com/.

General John J. Pershing Boyhood Home, Laclede, Missouri. Maintained by the Missouri State Park Board, Pershing's restored nineteenth-century home exhibits some of his personal belongings and papers. http://www.mostateparks.com/pershing site.htm.

Sgt. Alvin C. York Homeplace and State Historic Site, Pall Mall, Tennessee. The home of America's greatest military hero of World War I contains fascinating artifacts, including York's letters written in the trenches. http://www.state.tn.us/environment/parks/SgtYork/.

Wisconsin Veterans Museum, Madison, Wisconsin. The most stunning museum of its size in the United States, this large building combines impressive collections of artifacts ranging from uniforms to tanks, with substantive exhibits and video programs based on remarkable historical research. It both documents and explains the participation of Wisconsin soldiers in the nation's wars, including the Spanish-American War and World War I. http://museum.dva.state.wi.us.

REVIEW QUESTIONS

1. Why did Senator Robert La Follette oppose the war against Germany? How did many Americans regard the war and possible U.S. intervention?
2. What were the major arguments for and against U.S. entry into the Great War? What position do you find most persuasive? Why?
3. How and why did the United States shape public opinion in World War I? What were the consequences, positive and negative, of the propaganda of the Committee on Public Information, the Food Administration, and other government agencies?
4. How did the war affect women and minorities?
5. Evaluate the role of Woodrow Wilson at the Paris Peace Conference. What obstacles did he face? How successful was he in shaping the settlement?
6. Discuss the arguments for and against American ratification of the Treaty of Versailles.

KEY TERMS

Allies (p. 638)
Bolshevik (p. 648)
Central Powers (p. 638)
Committee on Public Information (CPI) (p. 646)
Declaration of London (p. 639)
Espionage Act (p. 646)
Irreconcilables (p. 652)
League of Nations (p. 651)
Liberty Bonds (p. 644)
Preparedness (p. 640)
Red Scare (p. 655)
Reservationists (p. 652)
Sedition Act of 1918 (p. 646)
Selective Service Act of 1917 (p. 648)
Self-determination (p. 641)
***Sussex* Pledge** (p. 640)
Treaty of Versailles (p. 651)
War Industries Board (WIB) (p. 642)

myhistorylab Connections

Reinforce what you learned in this chapter by studying the many documents, images, maps, review tools, and videos available at **www.myhistorylab.com**.

Read and Review

Study and Review **Study Plan: Chapter 23**

Read the Document

Letter from William Jennings (1915)

Newton D. Baker, "The Treatment of German-Americans" (1918)

The Espionage Act (1917)

Eugene V. Debs, Critique of World War I (1918)

Eugene Kennedy, A "Doughboy" Describes the Fighting Front (1918)

President Woodrow Wilson's Fourteen Points (1918)

Henry Cabot Lodge's Objections to Treaty of Versailles (1919)

F. J. Grimke, Address to African American Soldiers (1919)

Boy Scouts of America, "Support the War Effort" (1917)

Research and Explore

Read the Document

Personal Journeys Online

From Then to Now Online: Women and War

Hear the Audio

Immigrants and the Great War

The Speech That Sent Debs to Jail

If We Must Die; poem and reading by Claude McKay

Watch the Video

American Entry into World War I

Charles E. Hughes 1916 President ial Campaign Speech

Hear the Audio

Hear the audio files for Chapter 23 at **www.myhistorylab.com.**

24 Toward a Modern America

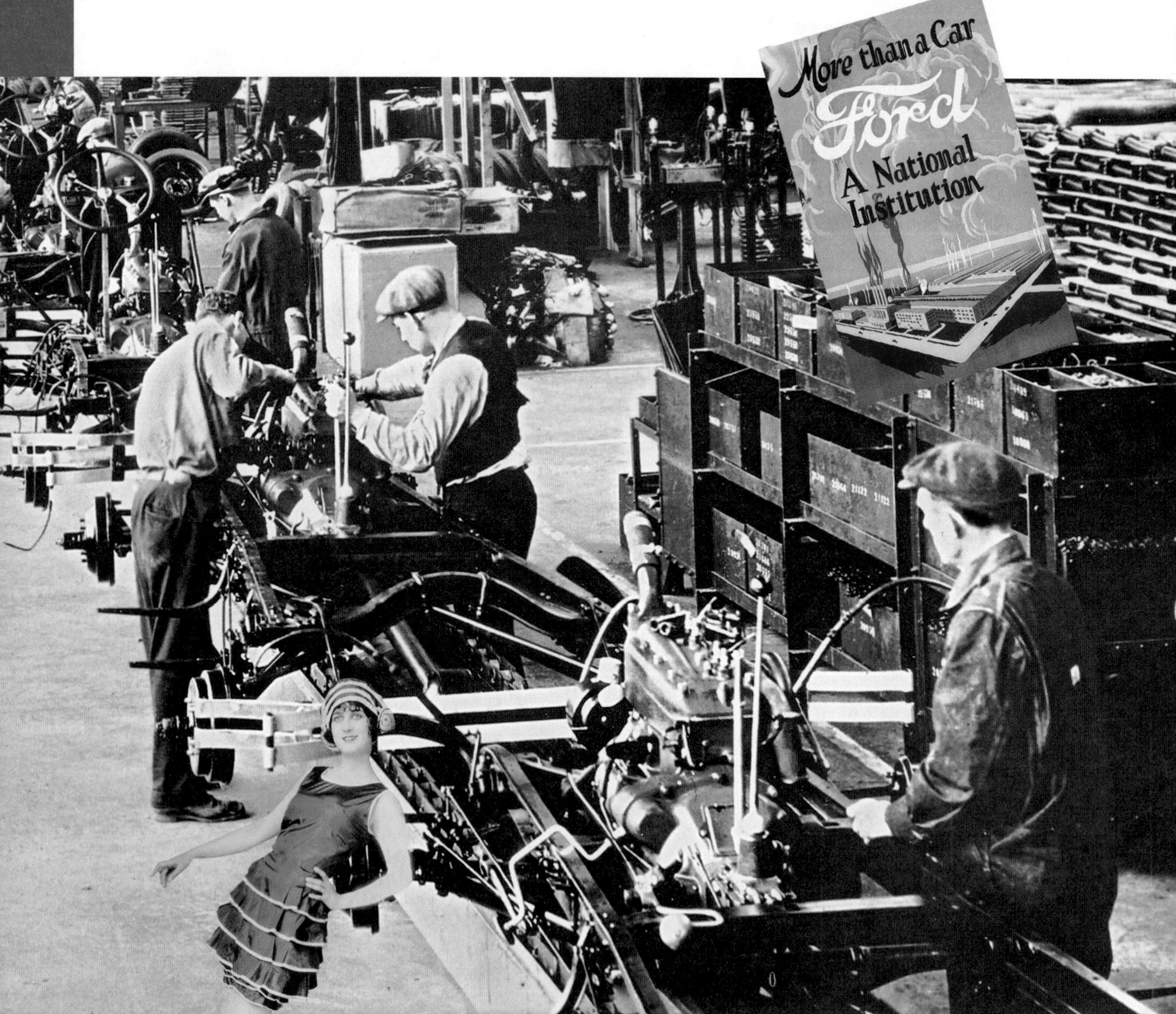

An assembly line in the Rouge Plant of the Ford Motor Company.

Hear the Audio

Hear the audio files for Chapter 24 at **www.myhistorylab.com**.

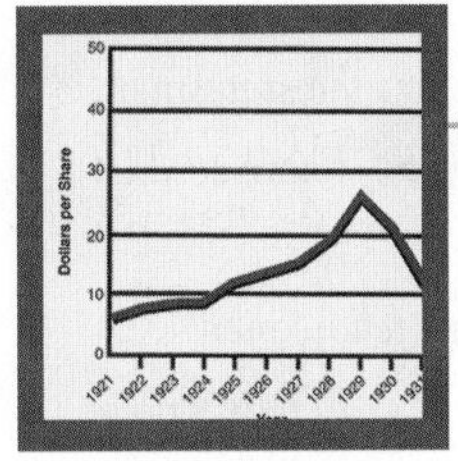

THE ECONOMY THAT ROARED *(page 663)*

WHAT CONTRIBUTED to the economic boom of the 1920s?

THE BUSINESS OF GOVERNMENT *(page 667)*

WHAT WAS the relationship between big business and government in the 1920s?

CITIES AND SUBURBS *(page 669)*

WHAT FACTORS contributed to the growth of America's cities and suburbs in the 1920s?

MASS CULTURE IN THE JAZZ AGE *(page 672)*

HOW DID new systems of distribution, marketing, and mass communication shape American culture?

CULTURE WARS *(page 675)*

WHAT FORCES fueled the culture wars of the 1920s?

A NEW ERA IN THE WORLD? *(page 680)*

WHAT ROLE did the United States play in international diplomacy in the decade after World War I?

HERBERT HOOVER AND THE FINAL TRIUMPH OF THE NEW ERA *(page 682)*

WHAT FACTORS contributed to Herbert Hoover's victory in 1928 over his Democratic opponent, Alfred E. Smith? In what ways did Hoover epitomize the policies of the New Era?

ONE AMERICAN JOURNEY

Happy times were here again. American industry, adopting Henry Ford's policy of mass production and low prices, was making it possible for everybody to have his share of everything. The newspapers, the statesmen, the economists, all agreed that American ingenuity had solved the age-old problem of poverty. There could never be another depression. . . .

The war had done something to Henry, it had taught him a new way to deal with his fellow men. . . . He became more abrupt in his manner, more harsh in his speech. "Gratitude?" he would say. "There's no gratitude in business. Men work for money." . . . From now on he was a business man, and held a tight rein on everything. This industry was his, he had made it himself, and what he wanted of the men he hired was that they should do exactly as he told them. . . .

Every worker had to be strained to the uttermost limit, every one had to be giving the last ounce of energy he had in his carcass. . . . They were tired when they started in the morning, and when they quit they were grey and staggering with fatigue, they were empty shells out of which the last drop of juice had been squeezed. . . .

Henry Ford was now getting close to his two million cars a year goal. . . . From the moment the ore was taken out of the ship at the River Rouge plant [in Detroit], through all the processes turning it into steel and shaping it into automobile parts with a hundred-ton press, and putting five thousand parts together into a car which rolled off the assembly line under its own power—all those processes were completed in less than a day and a half!

Some forty-five thousand different machines were now used in the making of Ford cars, in sixty establishments scattered over the United States. . . . Henry Ford was remaking the roads of America, and in the end he would remake the roads of the world—and line them all with filling stations and hot-dog stands of the American pattern.

Upton Sinclair, *The Flivver King: A Story of Ford-America* (Chicago: Charles H. Kerr, 1999).

Read the **Document** at **www.myhistorylab.com**

Personal Journeys Online

- ***Chicago Daily Tribune*, "Capt. Charles Lindbergh, Lone U.S. Flyer, Wings Way from New York to Paris in 33 Hours 29 Minutes," 1927. Photographic essay of Lindbergh's accomplishment.**
- **Elsie Johnson McDougald, "The Double Task: The Struggle of Negro Women for Sex and Race Emancipation," 1925. Article attacks racial stereotypes and discusses the diversity among African American women in New York City.**

UPTON SINCLAIR, one of America's most famous muckraking journalists, won his greatest recognition with the 1906 publication of his novel *The Jungle*, which graphically depicted the wretched conditions endured by Chicago's immigrant meatpacking workers. In *The Flivver King*, Sinclair demonstrates his extraordinary ability to weave together the dramatic and historical journey of industrial America, as embodied in the rise of the automobile industry and the revolutionizing vision of Henry Ford, the entrepreneur who captured the American mind and symbolized modern America to the world.

"Machinery," proclaimed Henry Ford, "is the new Messiah." Ford had introduced the assembly line at his automobile factory on the eve of World War I, and by 1925 it was turning out a Model T car every ten seconds. The term "mass production" originated in Henry Ford's 1926 description of the system of flow-production techniques popularly called "Fordism." The system

CHRONOLOGY

1915	Ku Klux Klan is founded anew.
1919	Volstead Act is passed.
1920	Urban population exceeds rural population for the first time.
	Warren Harding is elected president.
	Prohibition takes effect.
	First commercial radio show is broadcast.
	Sinclair Lewis publishes *Main Street*.
1921	Sheppard-Towner Maternity and Infancy Act is passed.
	Washington Naval Conference limits naval armaments.
1922	Fordney-McCumber Act raises tariff rates.
	Sinclair Lewis publishes *Babbitt*.
	Country Club Plaza in Kansas City opens.
1923	Harding dies; Calvin Coolidge becomes president.
1924	National Origins Act sharply curtails immigration.
	Coolidge is elected president.
1925	Scopes trial is held in Dayton, Tennessee.
	F. Scott Fitzgerald publishes *The Great Gatsby*.
1927	Charles A. Lindbergh flies solo across the Atlantic.
1928	Kellogg-Briand Pact is signed.
	Herbert Hoover is elected president.
1929	Ernest Hemingway publishes *A Farewell to Arms*.

symbolized the nation's booming economy: in the 1920s, Europeans used the word *Fordize* as a synonym for *Americanize*.

Henry Ford was conflicted about the progress he championed—the changes he saw and had helped facilitate. Launching a crusade against the new direction America was headed, Ford decided, according to Sinclair, that "what America needed was to be led back to its past." Embracing nativism and Protestantism, Ford, an ardent anti-Semite, targeted Jewish Americans in his diatribes, blaming them for radicalism and labor organization, and he singled out the "International Jew" for allegedly controlling the international financial community.

Henry Ford and Fordism reflected the complexity of the 1920s. Economic growth and technological innovation were paired with social conflict as traditions were destroyed, values were displaced, and new people were incorporated into a society increasingly industrialized, urbanized, and dominated by big business. Industrial production and national wealth soared, buoyed by new techniques and markets for consumer goods. Business values pervaded society, and government promoted business interests.

But not all Americans prospered. Many workers were unemployed, and the wages of still more were stagnant or falling. Farmers endured grim conditions and worse prospects. Social change brought pleasure to some and deep concern to others. City factories like the Ford Works attracted workers from the countryside, increasing urbanization; rapid suburbanization opened other horizons. Leisure activities flourished, and new mass media promoted modern ideas and stylish products. Workers would have to achieve personal satisfaction through consumption and not production. But such experiences often proved unsettling, and some Americans, like Ford, sought reassurance by imposing their cultural or religious values on everyone around them. ✦

THE ECONOMY THAT ROARED

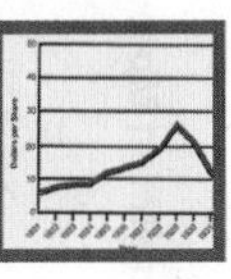

WHAT CONTRIBUTED to the economic boom of the 1920s?

Following a severe postwar depression in 1920 and 1921, the American economy boomed through the remainder of the decade. Gross domestic product soared nearly 40 percent; output per worker-hour, or productivity, rose 72 percent in manufacturing; average per capita income increased by a third. Although the prosperity was not evenly distributed and some sectors of the economy were deeply troubled, most Americans welcomed the industrial expansion and business principles of the New Era.

BOOM INDUSTRIES

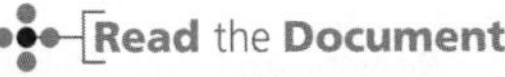

Read the Document at **www.myhistorylab.com** *Edward Earle Purinton, "Big Ideas from Big Business" (1921)*

Many factors spurred the economic expansion of the 1920s. The huge wartime and postwar profits provided investment capital that enabled business to mechanize. Mass production spread quickly in American industry; machine-made standardized parts and the assembly line increased efficiency and production. Businesses steadily adopted the scientific management principles of Frederick W. Taylor (see Chapter 21). The nation more than doubled its capacity to generate electricity during the decade, further bolstering the economy.

WHERE TO LEARN MORE

Henry Ford Museum and Greenfield Village, Dearborn, Michigan http://www.hfmgv.org

The automobile industry drove the economy. Its productivity increased constantly, and sales rose from about 1.9 million vehicles in 1920 to nearly 5 million by 1929, when 26 million vehicles were on the road (see Figure 24–1). The automobile industry also employed one of every 14 manufacturing workers and stimulated other industries, from steel to rubber and glass. It created a huge new market for the petroleum industry and fostered oil drilling in Oklahoma, Texas, and Louisiana. It launched new businesses, from service stations (over 120,000 by 1929) to garages. It also encouraged the construction industry, a mainstay of the 1920s economy. Large increases in road building and residential housing, prompted by growing automobile ownership and migration to cities and suburbs, provided construction jobs, markets for lumber and other building materials, and profits.

Watch the Video at **www.myhistorylab.com** *The Rise and Fall of the Automobile Economy*

The Great War also stimulated the chemical industry. The government confiscated chemical patents from German firms that had dominated the field and transferred them to U.S. companies like DuPont. With this advantage, DuPont in the 1920s became one of the nation's largest industrial firms, a chemical empire producing plastics, finishes, dyes, and organic chemicals. Led by such successes, the chemical industry became a $4 billion giant employing 300,000 workers by 1929.

The new radio and motion picture industries also flourished. Commercial broadcasting began with a single station in 1920. By 1927, there were 732 stations, and Congress created the Federal Radio Commission to prevent wave-band interference. The rationale for this agency, which was reorganized as the Federal Communications Commission (FCC) in 1934, was that the airwaves belong to the American people and not to private interests. Nevertheless, corporations quickly dominated the new industry.

oligopoly An industry, such as steel making or automobile manufacturing, that is controlled by a few large companies.

The motion-picture industry became one of the nation's five largest businesses, with 20,000 movie theaters selling 100 million tickets a week. Hollywood studios were huge factories, hiring directors, writers, camera crews, and actors to produce films on an assembly-line basis. While Americans watched Charlie Chaplin showcase his comedic genius in such films as *The Gold Rush* (1925), corporations like Paramount were integrating production with distribution and exhibition to maximize control and profit and eliminate independent producers and theaters. The advent of talking movies later in the decade brought still greater profits and power to the major studios, which alone could afford the increased engineering and production costs.

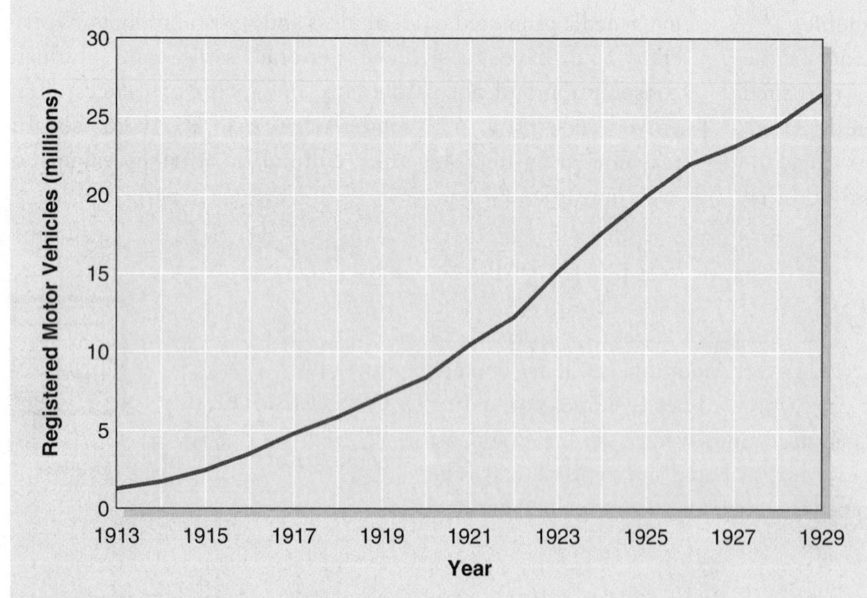

FIGURE 24–1 **Registered Motor Vehicles, 1913–1929** The rapid adoption of automobiles shaped the 1920s, stimulating demand for steel and gasoline, encouraging the use of credit, facilitating urbanization, promoting tourism, and suggesting new cultural horizons.
Data Source: U.S. Bureau of Public Roads.

Corporate Consolidation

A wave of corporate mergers, rivaling the one at the turn of the century, swept over the 1920s economy. Great corporations swallowed up thousands of small firms. Particularly significant was the spread of **oligopoly**—the control of an entire industry by a few giant firms. The number of automobile manufacturers dropped from 108 to 44, while only three companies—Ford, General Motors, and Chrysler—produced 83 percent of the nation's cars. In the electric light and power industry, nearly 4,000 local utility companies were merged into a dozen holding companies. By 1929, the nation's 200 largest corporations controlled nearly half of all nonbanking corporate wealth.

Open Shops and Welfare Capitalism

Business also launched a vigorous assault on labor. In 1921, the National Association of Manufacturers organized an **open-shop** campaign to break union-shop contracts, which required all employees to be union members. Denouncing collective bargaining as un-American, businesses described the open shop, in which union membership was not required and usually prohibited, as the "American plan." They forced workers to sign so-called **yellow-dog contracts** that bound them to reject unions to keep their jobs. Business also used boycotts to force employers into a uniform antiunion front. Bethlehem Steel, for example, refused to sell steel to companies employing union labor. Where unions existed, corporations tried to crush them, using spies or hiring strikebreakers.

open shop Factory or business employing workers whether or not they are union members; in practice, such a business usually refuses to hire union members and follows antiunion policies.

yellow-dog contracts Employment agreements binding workers not to join a union.

welfare capitalism A paternalistic system of labor relations emphasizing management responsibility for employee well-being.

Some companies advocated a paternalistic system called **welfare capitalism** as an alternative to unions. Eastman Kodak, General Motors, U.S. Steel, and other firms provided medical services, insurance programs, pension plans, and vacations for their workers and established employee social clubs and sports teams. These policies were designed to undercut labor unions and persuade workers to rely on the corporation. Welfare capitalism, however, covered scarcely 5 percent of the workforce and often benefited only skilled workers already tied to the company through seniority.

Corporations in the 1920s also promoted company unions, management-sponsored substitutes for labor unions. But company unions were usually forbidden to handle wage and hour issues. Their function was to implement company policies and undermine real unionism.

Partly because of these pressures, membership in labor unions fell from 5.1 million in 1920 to 3.6 million in 1929. But unions also contributed to their own decline. Conservative union leaders neglected ethnic and black workers in mass-production industries. Nor did they try to organize women, by 1930 nearly one-fourth of all workers. And they failed to respond effectively to other changes in the labor market. The growing numbers of white-collar workers regarded themselves as middle class and beyond the scope of union action.

With increasing mechanization and weak labor unions, workers suffered from job insecurity and stagnant wages. Unemployment reached 12 percent in 1921 and remained a persistent concern of many working-class Americans during the decade. And despite claims to the contrary, hours were long: The average workweek in manufacturing remained more than 50 hours.

The promise of business to pay high wages proved hollow. Real wages (purchasing power) did improve, but most of the improvement came before 1923 and reflected falling prices more than rising wages. The failure to raise wages when productivity was increasing threatened the nation's long-term prosperity. In short, rising national income largely reflected salaries and dividends, not wages.

Ford Motor Company's assembly line at the River Rouge plant in Detroit. The increasing mechanization of work, linked to managerial and marketing innovations, boosted productivity in the 1920s and brought consumer goods within the reach of far more Americans than before.

Some workers fared worse than others. Unskilled workers, especially southern and eastern Europeans, black migrants from the rural South, and Mexican immigrants, saw their already low

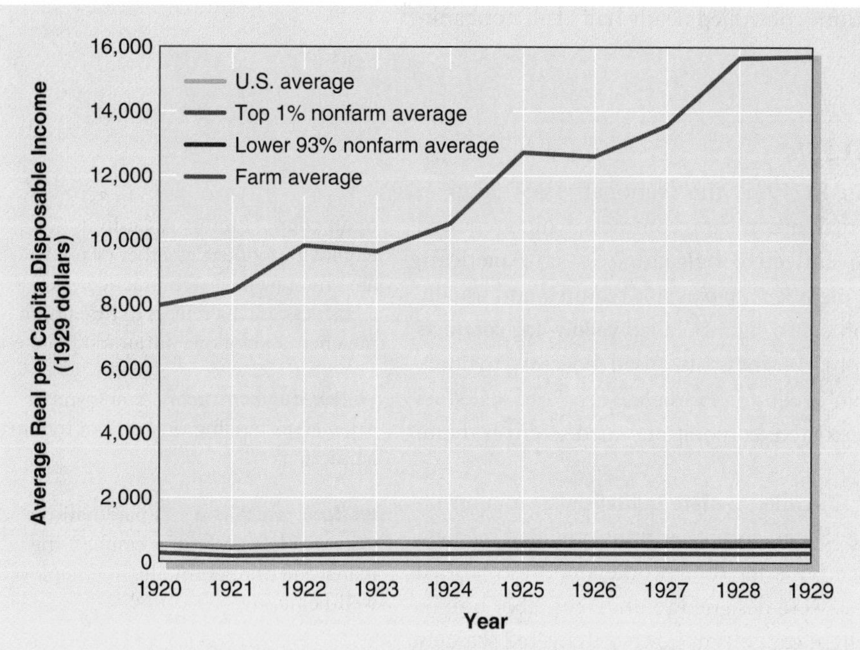

FIGURE 24–2 **Growing Income Inequality in the 1920s** Despite the aura of prosperity in the 1920s, the vast majority of Americans received little or no increase in their real income. Farm families dragged the average down further, while the wealthiest Americans doubled their own incomes.

Data Source: Charles Holt, "Who Benefited from the Prosperity of the Twenties?" *Explorations in Economic History*, 14 (1977).

wages decline relative to those of skilled workers. Southern workers earned much less than northerners, even in the same industry, and women were paid much less than men even for the same jobs. Overall, the gap between rich and poor widened during the decade (see Figure 24–2). By 1929, fully 71 percent of American families earned less than what the U.S. Bureau of Labor Statistics regarded as necessary for a decent living standard. The maldistribution of income meant that eventually Americans would be unable to purchase the products they made.

Consumer credit, rare before the 1920s, expanded during the decade. Credit offered temporary relief by permitting consumers to buy goods on time. General Motors introduced consumer credit on a national basis to create a mass market for expensive automobiles. By 1927, two-thirds of automobiles were purchased on the installment plan. By 1929, providing consumer credit had become the nation's tenth-largest business. Nevertheless, installment loans did not in the long run raise the purchasing power of an income; they simply added interest charges to the price of products.

QUICK REVIEW

Signs of Underlying Economic Weakness

- Unemployment remained high.
- Wages did not rise with increased prosperity.
- The gap between rich and poor grew.
- Consumption fueled by expanding consumer credit.

SICK INDUSTRIES

Despite the general appearance of prosperity, several "sick" industries dragged on the economy. Coal mining, textile and garment manufacturing, and railroads suffered from excess capacity (too many mines and factories), shrinking demand, low returns, and management-labor conflicts. For example, U.S. coal mines had a capacity of a billion tons, but scarcely half of that amount was needed because of increasing use of oil, natural gas, and hydroelectricity. Using company police, strikebreakers, and injunctions, mine operators broke the United Mine Workers and slashed wages by up to one-third. Unemployment in the industry approached 30 percent.

Similarly, the textile industry coped with overcapacity and declining demand by shifting operations from New England to the cheap-labor South, employing girls and young women for 56-hour weeks at 18 cents an hour. Textile companies, aided by local authorities, suppressed strikes in Tennessee and North Carolina. Despite substandard wages and repressive policies, the textile industry remained barely profitable.

QUICK REVIEW

Sick Industries

- Coal mining.
- Textiles.
- Agriculture.

American agriculture never recovered from the 1921 depression. Agricultural surpluses and shrinking demand forced down prices. After the war, foreign markets dried up, and domestic demand for cotton slackened. Moreover, farmers' wartime expansion left them heavily mortgaged in the 1920s. Small farmers, unable to compete with larger, better-capitalized farmers, suffered most. Many lost their land and became tenants or farm hands.

Racial discrimination worsened conditions for black and Hispanic tenants, sharecroppers, and farm workers. In the South, African American sharecroppers trapped in grinding poverty endured segregation, disfranchisement, and violence. Mexican immigrants and Hispanic Americans labored as migrant farm workers in the Southwest and California. Exploited by the contract-labor system pervasive in large-scale agriculture, they suffered from poor wages, miserable living conditions, and racism.

THE BUSINESS OF GOVERNMENT

WHAT WAS the relationship between big business and government in the 1920s?

The Republican surge in national politics also shaped the economy. In the 1920 election, the Republican slogan was "Less government in business, more business in government." By 1924, Calvin Coolidge, the decade's second Republican president, proclaimed, "This is a business country . . . and it wants a business government." Under such direction, the federal government advanced business interests at the expense of other objectives.

REPUBLICAN ASCENDANCY

Republicans in 1920 had retained control of Congress and put Warren Harding in the White House. Harding was neither capable nor bright, but he recognized his own limitations and promised to appoint "the best minds" to his cabinet. Some of his appointees were highly accomplished, and two of them, Secretary of Commerce Herbert Hoover and Secretary of the Treasury Andrew Mellon, shaped economic policy throughout the 1920s.

A self-described progressive dedicated to efficiency, Hoover made the Commerce Department the government's most dynamic office. He cemented its ties with the leading sectors of the economy, expanded its collection and distribution of industrial information, pushed to exploit foreign resources and markets, and encouraged innovation. Hoover's goal was to foster prosperity by making business efficient, responsive, and profitable.

Andrew Mellon had a narrower goal. A wealthy banker and industrialist, he pressed Congress to reduce taxes on businesses and the rich. He argued that lower taxes would enable wealthy individuals and corporations to increase their capital investments, thereby creating new jobs and general prosperity. But Mellon's hope that favoring the rich would cause prosperity to trickle down to the working and middle classes proved ill-founded. Nevertheless, despite the opposition of progressives in Congress, Mellon succeeded in lowering maximum tax rates and eliminating wartime excess-profits taxes in 1921.

The Harding administration promoted business interests in other ways, too. The tariff of 1922 raised import rates to protect industry from foreign competition. But high tariffs made it difficult for European nations to earn the dollars to repay their war debts to the United States. High rates also impeded American farm exports and raised consumer prices.

The Harding administration aided the business campaign against unions and curtailed government regulation. By appointing advocates of big business to the Federal Trade Commission and the Federal Reserve Board, among others, Harding made government the collaborator rather than the regulator of business.

Finally, Harding reshaped the Supreme Court into a still more aggressive champion of business. He named the conservative William Howard Taft as chief justice and matched him with three other justices. All were, as one of them proclaimed, sympathetic to business leaders "beset and bedeviled with vexatious statutes, prying commissions, and government intermeddling of all sorts." The Court struck down much of the government economic regulation adopted during the Progressive Era, invalidated restraints on child labor and a minimum wage law for women, and approved restrictions on labor unions.

W WHERE TO LEARN MORE

★ Warren G. Harding House, Marion, Ohio
http://ohsweb.ohiohistory.org/places/c03/index.shtml

GOVERNMENT CORRUPTION

The green light that Harding Republicans extended to private interests led to corruption and scandals. Harding appointed many friends and cronies who saw public service as an opportunity for graft. Attorney General Harry Daugherty's associates in the Justice Department took bribes in exchange for pardons and government jobs. The head of the Veterans Bureau went to prison for cheating disabled veterans of $200 million. Albert Fall, the secretary of the interior, leased petroleum reserves set aside by progressive conservationists to oil companies in exchange for cash, bonds, and cattle for his New Mexico ranch. Exposed for his role in the Teapot Dome

QUICK REVIEW

The Teapot Dome Scandal

- Corruption and scandals plagued the Harding administration.
- Albert Fall, the secretary of the interior, leased petroleum reserves in exchange for cash and cattle.
- As a result of his part in the Teapot Dome scandal, Fall went to prison.

scandal, named after a Wyoming oil reserve, Fall became the first cabinet officer in history to go to jail. Daugherty escaped a similar fate by destroying records and invoking the Fifth Amendment.

Harding was appalled by the scandals. "My God, this is a hell of a job!" he told William Allen White. "I have no trouble with my enemies. . . . But my damned friends, . . . they're the ones that keep me walking the floor nights!" Harding died shortly thereafter, probably of a heart attack.

Coolidge Prosperity

On August 3, 1923, Vice President Calvin Coolidge was sworn in as president. Coolidge's calm appearance hid a furious temper and a mean spirit. Coolidge supported business with ideological conviction. He opposed the activist presidency of the Progressive Era, cultivating instead a deliberate inactivity calculated to lower expectations of government.

Like Harding, Coolidge installed business supporters in the regulatory agencies. To chair the Federal Trade Commission he appointed an attorney who had condemned the agency as "an instrument of oppression and disturbance and injury instead of help to business." Under this leadership, the FTC described its new goal as "helping business to help itself," which meant approving trade associations and agreements to suppress competition. This attitude, endorsed by the Supreme Court, aided the mergers that occurred after 1925. The *Wall Street Journal* crowed, "Never before, here or anywhere else, has a government been so completely fused with business."

WHERE TO LEARN MORE

Calvin Coolidge Homestead, Plymouth, Vermont
http://www.calvin-coolidge.org/html/the_homestead.html
http://www .historicvermont .org/coolidge/

Read the **Document**
at **www.myhistorylab.com**
Calvin Coolidge, Inaugural Address (1925)

League of Women Voters League formed in 1920 advocating for women's rights, among them the right for women to serve on juries and equal pay laws.

"Coolidge prosperity" determined the 1924 election. The Democrats, hopelessly divided, took 103 ballots to nominate the colorless, conservative Wall Street lawyer John W. Davis. A more interesting opponent for Coolidge was Robert La Follette, nominated by discontented farm and labor organizations that formed a new Progressive Party. La Follette campaigned against "the power of private monopoly over the political and economic life of the American people." The Republicans, backed by immense contributions from business, denounced La Follette as an agent of Bolshevism. The choice, Republicans insisted, was "Coolidge or Chaos." Thus instructed, Americans chose Coolidge, though barely half the electorate bothered to vote.

Championing America as a "business country," President Coolidge (center) poses on the White House lawn with members of the Investment Bankers Association shortly after he assumed office in 1923.

The Fate of Reform

But progressive reform was not completely dead. A small group in Congress, led by La Follette and George Norris, attacked Mellon's regressive tax policies and supported measures regulating agricultural processors, protecting workers' rights, and maintaining public ownership of a hydroelectric dam at Muscle Shoals, Alabama, that conservative Republicans wanted to privatize. Yet the reformers' successes were few and often temporary.

The fate of women's groups illustrates the difficulties reformers faced in the 1920s. At first, the adoption of woman suffrage prompted politicians to champion women's reform issues. In 1920, both major parties endorsed many of the goals of the new **League of Women Voters.** Within a year, many states had granted women the right to serve on juries, several enacted equal-pay laws, and Wisconsin adopted an equal-rights law. Congress passed the **Sheppard-Towner Maternity and Infancy Act,** the first federal social-welfare law, in 1921. It provided federal funds for infant and maternity care, precisely the type of protective legislation that the suffragists had described as women's special interest. Women also ran for political office and by 1922 there were fifteen women mayors of small towns throughout the nation.

Sheppard-Towner Maternity and Infancy Act The first federal social-welfare law, passed in 1921, providing federal funds for infant and maternity care.

But thereafter women reformers gained little. As it became clear that women did not vote as a bloc but according to their varying social and economic backgrounds, Congress lost interest in women's issues. In 1929, Congress killed the Sheppard-Towner Act. Nor could reformers gain ratification of a child-labor amendment after the Supreme Court invalidated laws regulating child labor. Conservatives attacked women reformers as "Bolsheviks."

CITIES AND SUBURBS

The 1920 census was the first to report that more Americans lived in urban than in rural areas. The trend toward urbanization accelerated in the 1920s as millions of Americans fled the depressed countryside for the booming cities. This massive population movement interacted with technological innovations to reshape cities, build suburbs, and transform urban life (see Map 24–1).

WHAT FACTORS contributed to the growth of America's cities and suburbs in the 1920s?

Very strong population growth
Moderate population growth
Population loss
African-American migration

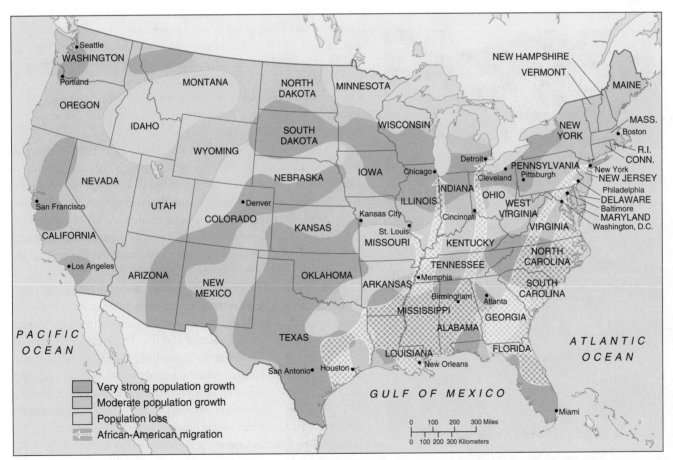

MAP 24–1 **Population Shifts, 1920–1930** Rural Americans fled to the cities during the 1920s, escaping a declining agricultural economy to search for new opportunities. African Americans in particular left the rural South for eastern and midwestern cities, but the urban population also jumped in the West and in the South itself.

Why did certain states and areas gain population during this period and why did others see population decreases?

Expanding Cities

Watch the Video at www.myhistorylab.com *The Great Migration*

Read the Document at www.myhistorylab.com *Letters from the Great Migration (1916–1917)*

See the Map at www.myhistorylab.com *The Expansion of Black Harlem, 1911–1930*

Urbanization affected every region of the country. In absolute terms, the older industrial cities of the Northeast and upper Midwest grew the most, attracting migrants from the rural South and distressed Appalachia. New York remained the nation's foremost metropolis.

Rural southerners also headed for southern cities. In fact, the South was the nation's most rapidly urbanizing region. Migrants from the countryside poured into Atlanta, Birmingham, Memphis, and Houston. Little more than jungle before 1914, Miami became the fastest growing city in the United States during the 1920s—"the Magic City."

In the West, Denver, Portland, and Seattle (each a regional economic hub) and several California cities grew rapidly. Los Angeles grew by 115 percent and by 1930 was the nation's fifth-largest city, with over 1.2 million people.

The population surge transformed the urban landscape. As land values soared, developers built skyscrapers, giving Cleveland, Kansas City, San Francisco, and many other cities modern skylines. By the end of the decade, American cities had nearly 400 skyscrapers taller than 20 stories.

The Great Black Migration

Great Migration The mass movement of African Americans from the rural South to the urban North, spurred especially by new job opportunities during World War I and the 1920s.

A significant feature of the rural-to-urban movement was the **Great Migration** of African Americans from the South. Like other migrants, they were responding chiefly to economic factors. Southern segregation and violence made migration attractive, but job opportunities made it possible. Prosperity created jobs, and with the decline in European immigration, black workers filled the positions previously given to new immigrants. Though generally the lowest paid and least secure jobs, they were better than sharecropping in the rural South. The migrants often found adjustment to their new environment difficult. Southern rural black culture clashed with industrial work rhythms and discipline and with urban living. Still, more than 1.5 million African Americans moved to northern cities in the 1920s.

Zora Neale Hurston, folklorist, anthropologist, and novelist, wrote with wit and verve about the African American South she so closely studied. Part of the dynamic community known as the Harlem Renaissance, Hurston won recognition in 1925 for her short story "Spunk." Her collective work, especially her later novel, *Their Eyes Were Watching God*, both reflected and advanced the creative pulse of what one black intellectual regarded as the first opportunity for African Americans to realize "group expression and self-determination."

There black ghettos usually developed, more because of prejudice than the wishes of the migrants. Although African Americans, like European immigrants, often wanted to live together to sustain their culture, racist restrictions meant that segregation, not congregation, most shaped their urban community. With thousands of newcomers limited to certain neighborhoods, housing shortages developed. High rents and low wages forced black families to share inferior and unsanitary housing that threatened their health and safety.

However, the Great Migration also increased African Americans' racial consciousness, autonomy, and power. In 1928, for instance, black Chicagoans, using the ballot denied to African Americans in the South, elected the first black man to Congress since the turn of the century. Mutual-aid societies and fraternal orders proliferated. Churches were particularly influential. A reporter in 1926 counted 140 black churches in a 150-block area of Harlem.

Another organization also appealed to poor black ghetto dwellers. The Universal Negro Improvement Association (UNIA), organized by Marcus Garvey, a Jamaican immigrant to New York, rejected the NAACP's goal of integration. A black nationalist espousing racial pride, Garvey exhorted black people to migrate to Africa to build a "free, redeemed, and mighty nation." In the meantime, he urged them to support black businesses. UNIA organized many enterprises, including groceries, restaurants, laundries, a printing plant, and the Black Star Steamship Line, intended as a commercial link between the United States, the West Indies, and Africa. UNIA attracted half a million members, the first black mass movement in American history. When Garvey was convicted of mail fraud and deported, however, the movement collapsed.

Racial pride also found expression in the **Harlem Renaissance,** an outpouring of literature, painting, sculpture, and music. Inspired by African American culture and black urban life, writers and artists created works of power and poignancy. The poetry of Langston Hughes reflected the rhythm and mood of jazz and the blues. Other leading authors of the Harlem Renaissance who asserted their independence included Claude McKay, who wrote of the black working class in *Home to Harlem* (1928), Zora Neale Hurston, James Weldon Johnson, and Dorothy West.

Harlem Renaissance A new African American cultural awareness that flourished in literature, art, and music in the 1920s.

Read the **Document**
at **www.myhistorylab.com**
Exploring America
Harlem Renaissance

Watch the **Video**
at **www.myhistorylab.com**
The Harlem Renaissance

Barrios

Hispanic migrants also entered the nation's cities in the 1920s, creating their own communities, or barrios. Fifty thousand Puerto Ricans settled in New York, mostly in East ("Spanish") Harlem, where they found low-paying jobs. Far more migrants arrived from Mexico. Although many worked as migrant farm laborers, they often lived in cities in the off-season. Others permanently joined the expanding urban economy in industrial and construction jobs. The barrios, with their own businesses, churches, and cultural organizations, created a sense of permanency.

These communities enabled the newcomers to preserve their cultural values and build social institutions, such as *mutualistas* (mutual aid societies), that helped them obtain credit, housing, and healthcare. But the barrios also reflected the hostility that Hispanics encountered in American cities. Los Angeles maintained separate schools for Mexicans, and a social worker reported that "America has repulsed the Mexican immigrant in every step he has taken" toward integration. As new migrants streamed in, conditions in the barrios deteriorated, for few cities provided adequate public services for them.

Some Hispanics fought discrimination. La Orden de Hijos de America ("The Order of the Sons of America"), organized in San Antonio in 1921, campaigned against inequities in schools and the jury system. In 1929, it helped launch the larger League of United Latin American Citizens (LULAC), which would help advance civil rights for all Americans.

Making tortillas–the staple of the Mexican diet. These Mexican American women used stone mortars in the 1920s to grind the corn by hand at the El Sol del Mayo tortilla plant in East Los Angeles. Spurned by Anglo society, Mexican Americans found support, jobs, and community in the barrios where they lived and worked. The barrios also enabled some Mexican Americans, like plant owner Maria Zuevedo, to become small business owners. They provided products and services that satisfied the traditional cultural values of the Mexican community.

Security Pacific Collection/Los Angeles Pubic Library.

The Road to Suburbia

As fast as the cities mushroomed in the 1920s, the suburbs grew twice as fast. Automobiles created the modern suburb. Nineteenth-century suburbs were small and linear, stretching along the street railway system. The new developments were sprawling and dispersed, for the automobile enabled people to live in formerly remote areas. A single-family house surrounded by a lawn became the social ideal, a pastoral escape from the overcrowded and dangerous city. Many suburbs excluded African Americans, Hispanics, Jews, and working-class people.

Suburbanization and the automobile brought other changes. The government provided federal money to states to build highways, and by the end of the decade, road construction was the largest single item in the national budget. Autos and suburbs also stimulated the growth of new industries. In 1922, J. C. Nichols opened the Country Club Plaza, the first suburban shopping center, in Kansas City; it provided free off-street parking. Department stores and other large retailers began leaving the urban cores for the suburbs, where both parking and more affluent customers were waiting. Drive-in restaurants began with Royce Hailey's Pig Stand in Dallas in 1921. That same year, the first fast-food franchise chain, White Castle, appeared, with its standardized menu and building, serving hamburgers "by the sack" to Americans in record numbers.

MASS CULTURE IN THE JAZZ AGE

HOW DID new systems of distribution, marketing, and mass communication shape American culture?

The White Castle chain symbolized a new society and culture. Urbanization and the automobile joined with new systems of distributing, marketing, and communications to mold a mass culture of standardized experiences and interests. Not all Americans participated equally in the new culture, however, and some attacked it.

Read the Document at www.myhistorylab.com *Advertisements (1925, 1927)*

ADVERTISING THE CONSUMER SOCIETY

Advertising and its focus on increasing consumption shaped the new society. Advertisers exhorted consumers via newspapers, billboards, streetcar signs, junk mail, radio, movies, and even skywriting. They sought to create a single market where everyone, regardless of region and ethnicity, consumed brand-name products. Advertisers attempted to stimulate new wants by ridiculing previous models or tastes as obsolete, acclaiming the convenience of a new brand, or linking the latest fashion with status or sex appeal.

The home, in particular, became a focus of consumerism. Middle- and upper-class women purchased mass-produced household appliances, such as electric irons, toasters, vacuum cleaners, washing machines, and refrigerators. Working-class women bought packaged food, ready-made clothing, and other consumer goods to lighten their workload. Advertisers attempted to redefine the housewife's role as primarily that of a consumer, purchasing goods for her family.

A shifting labor market also promoted mass consumption. The increasing number of white-collar workers had more time and money for leisure and consumption. Factory workers, whose jobs often provided little challenge, less satisfaction, and no prospect for advancement, found in consumption not only material rewards but, thanks to advertisers' claims, some self-respect and fulfillment as stylish and attractive people worthy of attention.

Under the stimulus of advertising, consumption increasingly displaced the traditional virtues of thrift, prudence, and avoidance of debt. Installment buying became common. By 1928, fully 85 percent of furniture, 80 percent of radios, and 75 percent of washing machines were bought on credit. But with personal debt rising more than twice as fast as incomes, even aggressive advertising and the extension of credit could not indefinitely prolong the illusion of a healthy economy.

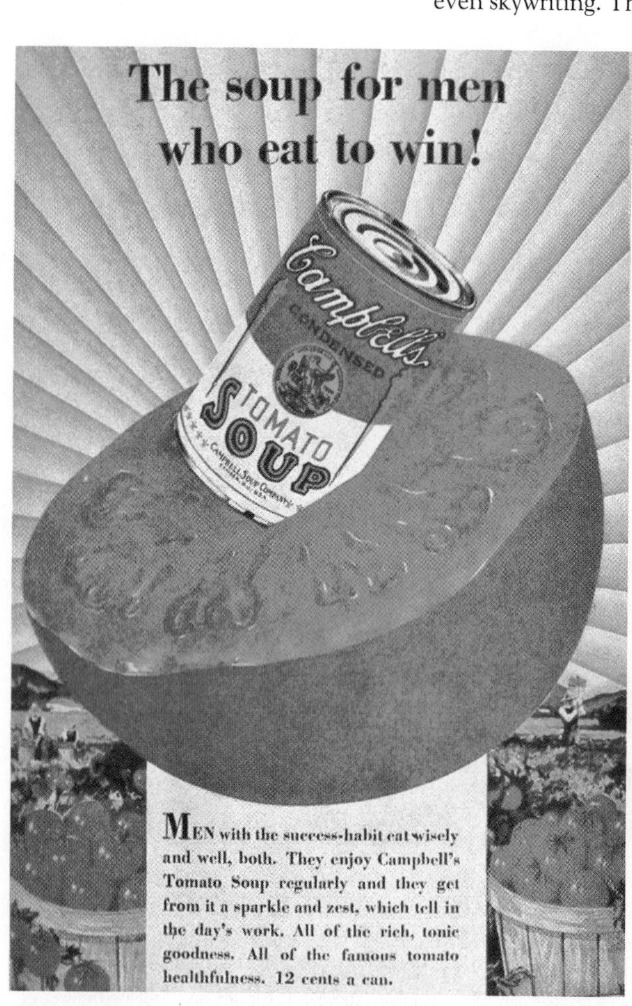

Advertisements for brand-name products, like this 1929 ad for Campbell's tomato soup, often tried to link simple consumption with larger issues of personal success and achievement.

LEISURE AND ENTERTAINMENT

During the 1920s, Americans also spent more on recreation and leisure, important features of the new mass society. Millions of people packed into movie theaters whose ornate style symbolized their social importance.

Movies helped to spread common values and to set national trends in dress, language, and behavior. Studios made films to attract the largest audiences and fit prevailing stereotypes. Cecil B. De Mille titillated audiences while reinforcing conventional standards with religious epics like *The Ten Commandments* (1923) and *The King of Kings* (1927). Set in ancient times, such movies depicted both sinful pleasures and the eventual triumph of moral order.

Radio also helped to mold popular culture. The first radio network, the National Broadcasting Company (NBC), was formed in 1926. Soon it was charging $10,000 to broadcast a commercial to a national market. Networks provided standardized entertainment, personalities, and news to Americans across the nation. Radio incorporated listeners into a national society.

The phonograph, another popular source of entertainment, allowed families to listen to music of their choice in their own homes. The phonograph business boomed. Manufacturers turned out more than 2 million phonographs and 100 million records annually. The popularity of the trumpet player Louis Armstrong and other jazz greats gave the decade its nickname, the **Jazz Age.**

Jazz Age The 1920s, so called for the popular music of the day as a symbol of the many changes taking place in the mass culture.

Jazz derived from African American musical traditions. The Great Migration spread it from New Orleans and Kansas City to cities throughout the nation. Its improvisational and rhythmic characteristics differed sharply from older and more formal music and were often condemned by people who feared that jazz would undermine conventional restraints on behavior. (See Global Connections, The International Journey of Jazz.)

Professional sports also became more commercialized. Millions of Americans, attracted by the popularity of such celebrities as Babe Ruth of the New York Yankees, crowded into baseball parks to follow major league teams. Ruth treated himself as a commercial commodity, hiring an agent, endorsing Cadillacs and alligator shoes, and defending a salary in 1932 that dwarfed that of President Hoover by declaring, "I had a better year than he did."

Large crowds turned out to watch boxers Jack Dempsey and Gene Tunney pummel each other; those who could not get tickets listened to radio announcers describe each blow. College football attracted frenzied followers among people with no interest in higher education. By 1929, the Carnegie Commission noted that the commercialization of college sports had "overshadowed the intellectual life for which the university is assumed to exist."

The New Morality

The promotion of consumption and immediate gratification weakened traditional self-restraint and fed a desire for personal fulfillment. The failure of wartime sacrifices to achieve promised glories deepened Americans' growing disenchantment with traditional values. The social dislocations of the war years and growing urbanization accelerated moral and social change. Sexual pleasure became an increasingly open objective. Popularization of Sigmund Freud's ideas weakened prescriptions for sexual restraint; the growing availability of birth control information enabled women to enjoy sex with less fear of pregnancy. Traditionalists worried as divorce rates, cigarette consumption, and hemlines went up while respect for parents, elders, and clergy went down.

Violinist Carroll Dickerson, at the Sunset Café in 1922, led one of the jazz bands that flourished in Chicago's many clubs, pointing up the central role of African Americans in the Jazz Age. *Variety* magazine dubbed Chicago the "hottest café town" in the United States, but the Illinois Vigilance Association despaired that "in Chicago alone" it had "traced the fall of 1,000 girls to jazz music" in just two years.

Young people seemed to embody the new morality. Rejecting conventional standards,

GLOBAL CONNECTIONS

The International Journey of Jazz

A central part of American culture in the 1920s, jazz expanded its global reach in the decade known for mass production and mass consumerism. Just as Henry Ford sold his Model T cars abroad, jazz musicians took their distinctively American form of music south to Latin America and east to England, France, the Soviet Union, and China.

Jazz caught the imagination of the world. For many at home and abroad, the jarring spontaneity of jazz signaled a new age. It was, according to George Gershwin, the result of "energy stored up in America." For the composer John Alden Carpenter, it represented "the first art innovation originating in America to be accepted seriously in Europe." A German critic could not have agreed more, exclaiming, "Jazz is the expression of a Kultur epoch. . . . Jazz is a musical revelation, a religion, a philosophy of the world, just like Expressionism and Impressionism."

Jazz also had its detractors—both in the United States and abroad. At home, one of the principal architects of mass production, Henry Ford, labeled jazz "musical slush" that encouraged the youth to imitate the "drivel of morons." A noted French poet called jazz "a triumph of barbaric folly," and an English observer worried that jazz—the "aboriginal music of the Negro"—might threaten American music.

Still, the enthusiasm for jazz was so strong that white jazz musicians claimed credit for its origins—at least until the 1930s, when the historical role of African Americans in creating jazz was more fully acknowledged in the United States and Europe. Black musicians had given Europe its first taste of jazz during World War I with James Reese Europe's 369th Division Band. Throughout the 1920s, other African American bands and performers traveled abroad, spreading the international message of jazz while escaping the racism of their home country. Sam Wooding's orchestra toured Europe and the Soviet Union; Herb Flemming's band, the Red Devils, and Benny Peyton's band along with remarkable performers like Josephine Baker dazzled audiences with dance and music in Buenos Aires, Paris, and London.

Jazz underscored to America and the world that an important part of the American heritage derived from an African—not European—heritage. But as the popularity of jazz grew internationally, the music no longer belonged exclusively to Americans, or even African Americans. Other countries appropriated the music and shaped it on their own terms. Still, the origins of jazz—this movement that captured the world's attention—belonged to black musicians who regarded jazz as a special expression of the African American community.

- How did the influence of jazz affect America domestically and internationally?

they embraced the era's frenzied dances, bootleg liquor, smoking, more revealing clothing, and sexual experimentation. They welcomed the freedom from parental control that the automobile afforded. The "flapper"—a frivolous young woman with short hair and a skimpy skirt who danced, smoked, and drank in oblivious self-absorption—was a major obsession in countless articles bearing such titles as "These Wild Young People" and "The Uprising of the Young."

But the new morality was neither as new nor as widespread as its advocates and critics believed. Signs of change had appeared before the Great War in the popularity of new clothing fashions, social values, and public amusements among working-class and ethnic groups. And if it now became fashionable for the middle class to adopt such attitudes and practices, most Americans still adhered to traditional beliefs and values. Moreover, the new morality offered only a limited freedom. It certainly did not promote social equality for women, who remained subject to traditional double standards, with marriage and divorce laws, property rights, and employment opportunities biased against them.

Read the **Document**
at **www.myhistorylab.com**
Margaret Sanger, "Happiness in Marriage" (1926)

The Searching Twenties

Many writers rejected what they considered the materialism, conformity, and provincialism of mass culture. Their criticism made the postwar decade one of the most creative periods in American literature. The brutality and hypocrisy of the war stimulated the critics' disillusionment and alienation. What Gertrude Stein called the Lost Generation considered, in the words of F. Scott Fitzgerald, "all Gods dead, all wars fought, all faiths in man shaken." Ernest Hemingway, wounded as a Red Cross volunteer during the war, rejected idealism in his novel *A Farewell to Arms* (1929), declaring that he no longer saw any meaning in "the words sacred, glorious, and sacrifice."

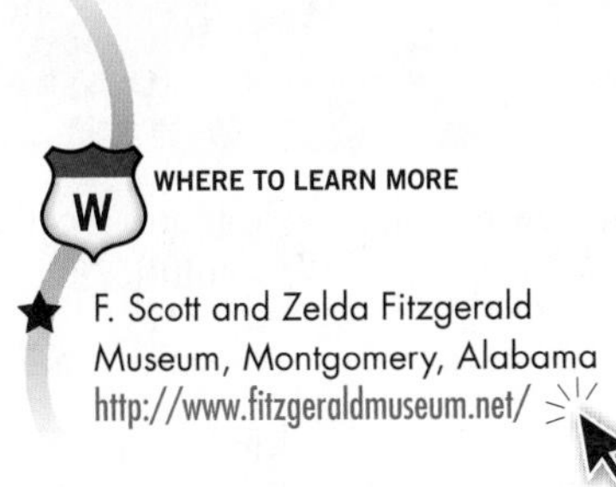

WHERE TO LEARN MORE

F. Scott and Zelda Fitzgerald Museum, Montgomery, Alabama http://www.fitzgeraldmuseum.net/

Novelists also turned their attention to American society. In *The Great Gatsby* (1925), Fitzgerald traced the self-deceptions of the wealthy. Sinclair Lewis ridiculed middle-class society and its narrow business culture in *Babbitt* (1922), whose title character provided a new word applied to the smug and shallow. In 1930, Lewis became the first American to win the Nobel Prize in literature.

Other writers condemned the mediocrity and intolerance of mass society. The critic Harold Stearns edited *Civilization in the United States* (1922), a book of essays. Its depiction of a repressive society sunk in hypocrisy, conformity, and materialism prompted his departure for Paris, where he lived, like Hemingway and Fitzgerald, as an expatriate, alienated from America. H. L. Mencken made his *American Mercury* the leading magazine of cultural dissenters. Conventional and conservative himself, Mencken heaped vitriol on the "puritans," "peasants," and "prehensile morons" he saw everywhere in American life.

CULTURE WARS

WHAT FORCES fueled the culture wars of the 1920s?

Despite the blossoming of mass culture and society in the 1920s, conflicts divided social groups. Some of these struggles involved reactions against the new currents in American life, including technological and scientific innovations, urban growth, and materialism. But movements to restrict immigration, enforce prohibition, prohibit the teaching of evolution, and even sustain the Ku Klux Klan did not have simple origins, motives, or consequences. The forces underlying the culture wars of the 1920s would surface repeatedly in the future (see Overview, Issues in the Culture Wars of the 1920s).

Read the **Document** at **www.myhistorylab.com** *From Then to Now Online: The Culture Wars*

NATIVISM AND IMMIGRATION RESTRICTION

For years, many Americans, from racists to reformers, had campaigned to restrict immigration. In 1917, Congress required immigrants to pass a literacy test. But renewed immigration after the war revived the anti-immigration movement, and the propaganda of the war and the Red Scare years generated public support for more restriction. Depicting immigrants as radicals, racial inferiors, religious subversives, or criminals, nativists clamored for congressional action. The arrests of two Italian-born anarchists, Nicola Sacco and Bartolomeo Vanzetti, in May 1920 fueled the controversy over radicalism and immigration. Charged with armed robbery and murder, they proclaimed their innocence and insisted that they were on trial solely for their political beliefs. Convicted in 1921, they were executed in 1927. Opponents of the verdict saw the trial and execution as a result of public hysteria, but defenders, like evangelist Billy Sunday, championed it as a vindication of American justice.

The passage of the Emergency Quota Act in 1921 responded to popular concerns by reducing immigration by about two-thirds and establishing quotas for nationalities on the basis of their numbers in the United States in 1910. Restrictionists, however, demanded more stringent action, especially against the largely Catholic and Jewish immigrants from southern and eastern Europe. Coolidge himself urged that America "be kept American," by which he meant white, Anglo-Saxon, and Protestant.

Read the **Document** at **www.myhistorylab.com** *1924 Immigration Law*

Congress adopted this racist rationale in the **National Origins Act of 1924,** which proclaimed its objective to be the maintenance of the "racial preponderance" of "the basic strain of our population." This law restricted immigration quotas to 2 percent of the foreign-born population of each nationality as recorded in the 1890 census, which was taken before the mass immigration from southern and eastern Europe. Another provision, effective in 1929, restricted total annual

National Origins Act of 1924 Law sharply restricting immigration on the basis of immigrants' national origins and discriminating against southern and eastern Europeans and Asians.

OVERVIEW Issues in the Culture Wars of the 1920s

Issue	Proponent view	Opponent view
The new morality	Promotes greater personal freedom and opportunities for fulfillment	Promotes moral collapse
Evolutionism	A scientific advance linked to notions of progress	A threat to religious belief
Jazz	Modern and vital	Unsettling, irregular, vulgar, and primitive
Immigration	A source of national strength from ethnic and racial diversity	A threat to the status and authority of old-stock white Protestants
Great Migration	A chance for African Americans to find new economic opportunities and gain autonomy and pride	A threat to traditional white privilege, control, and status
Prohibition	Promotes social and family stability and reduces crime	Restricts personal liberty and increases crime
Fundamentalism	An admirable adherence to traditional religious faith and biblical injunctions	A superstitious creed given to intolerant interference in social and political affairs
Ku Klux Klan	An organization promoting community responsibility, patriotism, and traditional social, moral, and religious values	A group of religious and racial bigots given to violent vigilantism and fostering moral and public corruption
Mass culture	Increases popular participation in national culture; provides entertainment	Promotes conformity, materialism, mediocrity, spectacle, and relaxation
Consumerism	Promotes material progress and higher living standards	Promotes waste, sterility, and self-indulgence

immigration to 150,000, with quotas that nearly eliminated southern and eastern Europeans. The law also completely excluded Japanese immigrants.

Other actions targeted Japanese residents in America. California, Oregon, Washington, Arizona, and other western states prohibited them from owning or leasing land, and in 1922, the Supreme Court ruled that, as nonwhites, they could never become naturalized citizens. Dispirited by the prejudice of the decade, Japanese residents hoped for fulfillment through their children, the ***Nisei,*** who were American citizens by birth.

Nisei U.S. citizens born of immigrant Japanese parents.

Ironically, the Philippines, as a U.S. territory, was not subject to the National Origins Act, and Filipino immigration increased ninefold during the 1920s. Most Filipino newcomers became farm laborers, especially in California, or worked in Alaskan fisheries. Similarly, because the law did not apply to immigrants from the Western Hemisphere, Mexican immigration also grew. Nativists lobbied to exclude Mexicans, but agribusiness interests in the Southwest blocked any restrictions on low-cost migrant labor.

QUICK REVIEW

Restrictions on Immigration

- Emergency Quota Act of 1921 reduced immigration and established quotas for nationalities.
- National Origins Act of 1924 restricted immigration on the basis of national origins.
- Other steps targeted Japanese residents in the West.

THE KU KLUX KLAN

Nativism was also reflected in the popularity of the revived Ku Klux Klan, the goal of which, according to its leader, was to protect "the interest of those whose forefathers established the nation." Founded in Georgia in 1915 and modeled on its Reconstruction predecessor, the new Klan was a national, not only a southern, movement and claimed several million members by the mid-1920s. Admitting only native-born white Protestants, the Klan embodied the fears of a traditional culture threatened by social change. Ironically, its rapid spread owed much to modern business and promotional techniques as hundreds of professional recruiters raked in hefty commissions selling Klan memberships to those hoping to defend their way of life.

In part, the Klan was a fraternal order, providing entertainment, assistance, and community for its members. Its picnics, parades, charity drives, and other social and family-oriented activities—perhaps a half-million women joined the Women of the Ku Klux Klan—sharply distinguished the organization from both the small, secretive Klan of the nineteenth century and the still smaller, extremist Klan of the later twentieth century. Regarding themselves as reformers, Klan members supported immigration restriction and Prohibition.

But the Klan also exploited racial, ethnic, and religious prejudices and campaigned against many social groups and what it called "alien creeds." It attacked African Americans in the South, Mexicans in Texas, Japanese in California, and Catholics and Jews everywhere. A twisted religious impulse ran through much of the Klan's organization and activities. It hired itinerant Protestant ministers to spread its message, erected altars and flaming crosses at its meetings, and sang Klan lyrics to the tunes of well-known hymns. The Klan also resorted to violence. In 1921, for example, a Methodist minister who belonged to the Klan murdered a Catholic priest on his own doorstep, and other Klansmen burned down Catholic churches. The leader of the Oregon Klan insisted that "the only way to cure a Catholic is to kill him."

To the Klan, Catholics and Jews symbolized not merely subversive religions but also the ethnic diversity and swelling urban population that challenged traditional Protestant culture. To protect that culture, the Klan attempted to censor or disrupt "indecent" entertainment, assaulted those it accused of adultery, and terrorized doctors who performed abortions.

While the Klan's appeal seemed rooted in the declining countryside, it also attracted urban residents. Chicago had the largest Klan organization in the nation, with 50,000 members, and Houston, Dallas, Portland, Indianapolis, Denver, and the satellite communities ringing Los Angeles were also Klan strongholds. Urban Klansmen were largely lower or lower middle class, many recently arrived from the country and retaining its attitudes; others were long-term urban residents who feared being marginalized by social changes, especially by competition from immigrants and new ideas.

The Klan also ventured into politics, with some success. But eventually it encountered resistance. In the North, Catholic workers disrupted Klan parades. In the South, too, Klan excesses provoked a backlash. After the Klan in Dallas flogged 68 people in a "whipping meadow" along the Trinity River in 1922, respect turned to outrage. Newspapers demanded that the Klan disband, district attorneys began to prosecute Klan thugs, and in 1924 Klan candidates were defeated by a ticket headed by Miriam "Ma" Ferguson, whose gubernatorial campaign called for anti-Klan laws and for the loss of tax exemptions for churches used for Klan meetings. Elsewhere the Klan was stung by revelations of criminal behavior and corruption by Klan leaders, who had been making fortunes pocketing membership fees and selling regalia to followers. The Klan crusade to purify society had bred corruption and conflict everywhere. By 1930, the Klan had nearly collapsed.

Read the Document at www.myhistorylab.com *Creed of Klanswomen (1924)*

Read the Document at www.myhistorylab.com *Hiram Evans, The Klan's Fight for Americanism (1926)*

QUICK REVIEW

The New Klan

- National movement claiming millions of members.
- Functioned as a fraternal organization providing community activities.
- Focused particularly on hatred of Catholics and Jews.
- Popular backlash contributed to Klan's collapse by 1930.

To entertain families and friends, the KKK held "Klan Day at the Races," pictured here at Denver's Overland Park Race Track.

Prohibition and Crime

Like the Klan, Prohibition both reflected and provoked social tensions in the 1920s. Reformers had long believed that prohibiting the sale of alcohol would improve social conditions, reduce

Volstead Act The 1920 law defining the liquor forbidden under the Eighteenth Amendment and giving enforcement responsibilities to the Prohibition Bureau of the Department of the Treasury.

crime and family instability, increase economic efficiency, and purify politics. They rejoiced in 1920 when the Eighteenth Amendment, prohibiting the manufacture, sale, or transportation of alcoholic beverages, took effect. Congress then passed the **Volstead Act,** which defined the forbidden liquors and established the Prohibition Bureau to enforce the law. But many social groups, especially in urban ethnic communities, opposed Prohibition, and the government could not enforce the law where public opinion did not endorse it.

Evasion was easy. By permitting alcohol for medicinal, sacramental, and industrial purposes, the Volstead Act gave doctors, priests, and druggists a huge loophole through which to satisfy their friends' needs. City-dwellers made "bathtub gin," and rural people distilled "moonshine." Scofflaws frequented the speakeasies that replaced saloons or bought liquor from bootleggers and rumrunners, who imported it from Canada, Cuba, or Mexico. The limited resources of the Prohibition Bureau often allowed bootleggers to operate openly.

The ethics and business methods of bootleggers soon shocked Americans, however. The huge profits encouraged organized crime, which had previously concentrated on gambling and prostitution, to develop elaborate liquor-distribution networks. Operating outside the law, crime "families" used violence to enforce contracts, suppress competition, and attack rivals. In Chicago, Al Capone's army of nearly a thousand gangsters killed hundreds. Using the profits from bootlegging and new tools like the automobile and the submachine gun, organized crime corrupted city governments and police forces.

Hear the Audio at **www.myhistorylab.com** *Prohibition is a Failure*

Gradually, even many "drys"—people who had initially favored Prohibition—dropped their support, horrified by the boost the amendment gave organized crime and worried about the general disrespect for law that it promoted. A 1926 poll found that four-fifths of Americans wanted to repeal or modify Prohibition. Yet it remained in force because it was entangled in party politics and social conflict. Democrats called for repeal in their 1928 and 1932 platforms, and in 1933, 36 states ratified an amendment repealing what Herbert Hoover had called a "noble experiment."

Evangelist Aimee Semple McPherson delivering her "Foursquare Gospel" that offered all sinners salvation.

Old-Time Religion and the Scopes Trial

Religion provided another fulcrum for traditionalists attempting to stem cultural change. Protestant fundamentalism, which emphasized the infallibility of the Bible, including the creation story, emerged at the turn of the century as a conservative reaction to religious modernism and the social changes brought by the mass immigration of Catholics and Jews, the growing influence of science and technology, and the secularization of public education. But the fundamentalist crusade to reshape America became formidable only in the 1920s. Evangelists like Billy Sunday and Aimee Semple McPherson attracted thousands to their revivals across America. (See American Views: Evangelism and the Search for Salvation.)

Fundamentalist groups, colleges, and publications sprang up throughout the nation, especially in the South. The anti-Catholic sentiment exploited by the Klan was but one consequence of fundamentalism's insistence on strict biblical Christianity. A second was the assault on Darwin's theory of evolution, which contradicted literal interpretations of biblical Creation. Fundamentalist legislators tried to prevent the teaching of evolution in public schools in at least 20 states. In 1923, Oklahoma banned textbooks based on Darwinian theory, and Florida's legislature denounced teaching evolution as "subversive." In 1925, Tennessee forbade teaching any idea contrary to the biblical account of human origins.

AMERICAN VIEWS

Evangelism and the Search for Salvation

Aimee Semple McPherson defied traditional roles for women in becoming one of the most famous evangelical leaders in the United States. Traveling in her "Gospel Car," she crisscrossed the nation reminding her followers that "Jesus Is Coming Soon" and advising them to "Get Ready." In 1923, she opened the Angelus Temple in Los Angeles—a white-domed building large enough for 5,000 followers of what McPherson called the "Foursquare Gospel." A lighted rotating cross on top of the dome could be seen from fifty miles away—a beacon for those who journeyed to her center of "spiritual energy." A charismatic orator, McPherson embraced the theatrics of Hollywood to stir her crowds and raised vast sums of money, or "love gifts," to finance the Temple and its activities. Playing upon the phrase shareholder, McPherson sold doll-house chairs for $25 each, enabling purchasers to be "chair-holders" in the Temple. Though tainted by a mysterious disappearance in 1926, she remained extraordinarily popular, attracting crowds of thousands who sought salvation during times of change and uncertainty. McPherson died in 1944 from an accidental overdose of sleeping pills.

In this excerpt from one of her autobiographies, McPherson describes the growth of the Angelus Temple and her pioneering use of radio to advance her "success in soul winning."

- **Why** was Aimee Semple McPherson so popular in the 1920s?
- **What** does her success suggest about the role of religion in American life?
- **How** do you think evangelicals like McPherson might have viewed the cult of business that also characterized the decade?

From the days the doors opened on January 1, 1923, a mighty spiritual revival surged into Angelus Temple with ever-increasing power and fervor. Eight thousand converts knelt at the altars in the first six months and fifteen hundred believers were immersed in the baptistry. Hundreds were healed and baptized with the Holy Spirit. One thousand young people covenanted together to serve as the Angelus Temple Foursquare Crusaders. And as the weeks and months passed, new outreaches commenced.

In February, the Prayer Tower opened, where prayer has not ceased as men gather in two-hour shifts during the night and women pray during the day, bringing God thousands of requests which come by mail, telephone, and telegraph from all over the world.

Then came the challenge of the radio! . . . My soul was thrilled with the possibilities this media offered for the spread of gospel. We secured time on a radio station and began broadcasting a few services. But the thought persisted that if Angelus Temple had her own radio station we could broadcast almost all of the meetings!

And God provided through the love gifts of his people for the radio station. In February 1924, KFSG—Kall Four Square Gospel—went on the air, broadcasting the glorious song, "Give the winds a mighty voice, Jesus saves!" . . . Time and time again converted gamblers, dope addicts, bootleggers, and white-slavery victims rose from knees to send thrilling testimonies out over radio station KFSG as well as to the Temple audience. . . . For three years I stayed close by Angelus Temple, preaching and teaching many times a week, conducting a daily "Sunshine Hour" broadcast, writing, editing, publishing, and praying for the sick. . . . The revival swept on and out. Branch churches sprang up in cities and towns. [And the Foursquare gospel] message has become well known around the world.

Source: Aimee Semple McPherson: The Story of My Life (Waco, TX: Word Books, 1973).

Social or political conservatism, however, was not an inherent part of old-time religion. The most prominent antievolution politician, William Jennings Bryan, continued to campaign for political, social, and economic reforms. Never endorsing the Klan, he served on the American Committee on the Rights of Religious Minorities and condemned anti-Semitism and anti-Catholicism. Bryan feared that Darwinism promoted political and economic conservatism.

The controversy over evolution came to a head when the American Civil Liberties Union (ACLU) responded to Tennessee's violation of the constitutional separation of church and state by offering to defend any teacher who tested the antievolution law. John Scopes, a high school biology teacher in Dayton, Tennessee, did so and was arrested. The Scopes trial attracted

Interpreting the Past
The Scopes Trial as a Harbinger of Change (pp. 686–687)

national attention after Bryan agreed to assist the prosecution and Clarence Darrow, a famous Chicago lawyer and prominent atheist, volunteered to defend Scopes.

Millions of Americans tuned their radios to hear the first trial ever broadcast. The judge, a fundamentalist, sat under a sign urging people to "Read Your Bible Daily." He ruled that scientists could not testify in support of evolution: Because they were not present at the Creation, their testimony would be "hearsay." But he did allow Darrow to put Bryan on the stand as an expert on the Bible. Bryan insisted on the literal truth of every story in the Bible, allowing Darrow to ridicule his ideas and force him to concede that some biblical passages had to be construed symbolically. Though the local jury took only eight minutes to convict Scopes, fundamentalists suffered public ridicule from reporters.

But fundamentalism was hardly destroyed, and antievolutionists continued their campaign. New organizations, such as the Bryan Bible League, lobbied for state laws and an antievolution amendment to the Constitution. Three more states forbade teaching evolution, but by 1929 the movement had faltered. Even so, fundamentalism retained religious influence and would again challenge science and modernism in American life.

A NEW ERA IN THE WORLD?

WHAT ROLE did the United States play in international diplomacy in the decade after World War I?

Abroad and at home, Americans in the 1920s sought peace and economic order. Rejection of the Treaty of Versailles and the League of Nations did not foreshadow isolationism. Indeed, in the 1920s, the United States became more deeply involved in international matters than ever before in peacetime. This involvement both produced important successes and sowed the seeds for serious future problems.

War Debts and Economic Expansion

The United States was the world's dominant economic power in the 1920s, changed by the Great War from a debtor to a creditor nation. The loans the United States had made to its allies during the war troubled the nation's relations with Europe throughout the decade. American insistence on repayment angered Europeans, who saw the money as a U.S. contribution to the joint war effort against Germany. Moreover, high American tariffs blocked Europeans from exporting goods to the United States and earning dollars to repay their debts. Eventually, the United States readjusted the terms for repayment, and American bankers extended large loans to Germany, which used the money to pay reparations to Britain and France, whose governments then used the same money to repay the United States. This unstable system depended on a continuous flow of money from the United States.

multinational corporations Firms with direct investments, branches, factories, and offices in a number of countries.

America's global economic role expanded in other ways as well. Exports, especially of manufactured goods, soared. To expand their markets and avoid foreign tariffs, many U.S. companies became **multinational corporations,** establishing branches or subsidiaries abroad. Ford built assembly plants in England, Japan, Turkey, and Canada. International Telephone and Telegraph owned two dozen factories in Europe and employed more overseas workers than any other U.S. corporation.

Other companies gained control of foreign supply sources. American oil companies invested in foreign oil fields, especially in Latin America, where they controlled more than half of Venezuelan production. The United Fruit Company developed such huge operations in Central America that it often dominated national economies. In Costa Rica, the company had a larger budget than the national government.

Europeans and Latin Americans alike worried about this economic invasion; even Secretary of Commerce Herbert Hoover expressed concerns. Multinationals, he warned, might eventually take markets from American manufacturers and jobs from American workers. Business leaders, however, dismissed such reservations.

Hoover's concerns, moreover, did not prevent him from promoting economic expansion abroad. The government worked to open doors for American businesses in foreign countries, helping them to secure access to trade, investment opportunities, and raw materials. Hoover's Bureau of Foreign Commerce opened 50 offices around the world to boost American business. Hoover also pressed the British to give U.S. corporations access to rubber production in the British colony of Malaya. Secretary of State Charles Evans Hughes negotiated access to Iraqi oil fields for U.S. oil companies. The government also authorized bankers and manufacturers to form combinations, exempt from antitrust laws, to exploit foreign markets.

QUICK REVIEW

America's Economic Power

- U.S. was the world's dominant economic power in the 1920s.
- U.S. wartime loans to European countries were a trouble spot throughout the decade.
- To expand their markets and avoid tariffs, many U.S. companies became multinational corporations.

Rejecting War

Although government officials cooperated with business leaders to promote American strategic and economic interests, they had little desire to use force abroad. Popular reaction against the Great War, strengthened by a strong peace movement, constrained policymakers. Having repudiated collective security as embodied in the League of Nations, the United States nonetheless sought to minimize international conflict and promote its national security. In particular, the State Department sought to restrict the buildup of armaments among nations.

At the invitation of President Harding, delegations from nine nations met in Washington at the Washington Naval Conference in 1921 to discuss disarmament. The conference drafted a treaty to reduce battleship tonnage and suspend the building of new ships for a decade. Japan and the United States also agreed not to fortify their possessions in the Pacific any further and to respect the Open Door in East Asia. Public opinion welcomed the treaty; the U.S. Senate ratified it with only one dissenting vote, and the 1924 Republican platform hailed it as "the greatest peace document ever drawn."

The United States made a more dramatic gesture in 1928, when it helped draft the **Kellogg-Briand Pact.** Signed by 64 nations, the treaty renounced aggression and outlawed war. Without provisions for enforcement, however, it was little more than symbolic. The Senate reserved the right of self-defense, repudiated any responsibility for enforcing the treaty, and maintained U.S. claims under the Monroe Doctrine.

Kellogg-Briand Pact A 1928 international treaty that denounced aggression and war but lacked provisions for enforcement.

Managing the Hemisphere

Senate insistence on the authority of the Monroe Doctrine reflected the U.S. claim to a predominant role in Latin America. The United States continued to dominate the hemisphere to promote its own interests. It exerted its influence through investments, control of the Panama Canal, invocation of the Monroe Doctrine, and, when necessary, military intervention.

In response to American public opinion, the peace movement, and Latin American nationalism, the United States retreated from the extreme gunboat diplomacy of the Progressive Era, withdrawing troops from the Dominican Republic and Nicaragua. But Haiti remained under U.S. occupation throughout the decade, American troops stayed in Cuba and Panama, and the United States directed the financial policies of other Latin American countries. Moreover, it sent the marines into Honduras in 1924 and back to Nicaragua in 1926. Such interventions could establish only temporary stability while provoking further Latin American hostility.

Latin American resentment led to a resolution at the 1928 Inter-America Conference denying the right of any nation "to intervene in the internal affairs of another." The U.S. delegation rejected the measure, but the anger of Latin Americans prompted the Hoover administration to rescind support for the Roosevelt Corollary (see Chapter 22), and J. Reuben Clark, chief legal officer of the State Department, drafted the Clark Memorandum. Not published

QUICK REVIEW

U.S. Policy in Latin America

- United States moved away from gunboat diplomacy.
- Continued to occupy Haiti and intervened when it felt its interests were at stake.
- Such interventions provoked Latin American hostility.

until 1930, this document stated that the Roosevelt Corollary was not a legitimate extension of the Monroe Doctrine and thereby helped prepare the way for the so-called Good Neighbor Policy toward Latin America. Still, the United States did not pledge nonintervention and retained the means, both military and economic, to dominate the hemisphere.

HERBERT HOOVER AND THE FINAL TRIUMPH OF THE NEW ERA

WHAT FACTORS contributed to Herbert Hoover's victory in 1928 over his Democratic opponent, Alfred E. Smith? In what ways did Hoover epitomize the policies of the New Era?

WHERE TO LEARN MORE

Herbert Hoover National Historic Site, West Branch, Iowa
http://www.hoover.archives.gov/

As the national economy steamed ahead in 1928, the Republicans chose as their presidential candidate Herbert Hoover, a man who symbolized the policies of prosperity and the New Era. Hoover was not a politician—he had never been elected to office—but a successful administrator who championed rational and efficient economic development.

The Democrats, by contrast, chose a candidate who evoked the cultural conflicts of the 1920s. Alfred E. Smith, a four-term governor of New York, was a Catholic, an opponent of Prohibition, and a Tammany politician tied to the immigrant constituency of New York City. His nomination plunged the nation into the cultural strife that had divided the Democrats in 1924. Rural fundamentalism, anti-Catholicism, Prohibition, and nativism were crucial factors in the campaign.

But Hoover was, in certain ways, the more progressive candidate. Sympathetic to labor, sensitive to women's issues, hostile to racial segregation, and favorable to the League of Nations, Hoover had always distanced himself from what he called "the reactionary group in the Republican party." By contrast, despite supporting factory reform and state welfare legislation to benefit his urban working-class constituents, Smith was as parochial as his most rural adversaries. He responded to a question about the needs of the states west of the Mississippi by asking, "What states *are* west of the Mississippi?"

Although many Americans voted against Smith because of his social background, the same characteristics attracted others. Millions of urban and ethnic voters, previously Republican or politically uninvolved, voted for Smith and laid the basis for the new Democratic coalition that would emerge in the 1930s. In 1928, however, with the nation still enjoying the economic prosperity so closely associated with Hoover and the Republicans, the Democrats were routed.

CONCLUSION

The New Era of the 1920s changed America. Technological and managerial innovations produced giant leaps in productivity, new patterns of labor, a growing concentration of corporate power, and high corporate profits. Government policies, from protective tariffs and regressive taxation to the relaxation of regulatory laws, reflected and reinforced the triumphs of the business elite over traditional cautions and concerns.

The decade's economic developments, in turn, stimulated social change, drawing millions of Americans from the countryside to the cities, creating an urban nation, and fostering a new ethic of materialism, consumerism, and leisure and a new mass culture based on the automobile, radio, the movies, and advertising. This social transformation swept up many Americans but left others unsettled by the erosion of traditional practices and values. Henry Ford, who as Upton Sinclair observed, remade the "roads of America," was also disturbed by America's new direction and reflected the ambivalence others shared about modern society. The concerns of many traditionalists found expression in campaigns for prohibition and against immigration, the revival of the Ku Klux Klan, and the rise of religious fundamentalism. Intellectuals denounced the materialism and conformity they saw in the new social order and fashioned new artistic and literary trends.

But the impact of the decade's trends was uneven. Mechanization increased the productivity of some workers but cost others their jobs; people poured into the cities while others left for the suburbs; Prohibition, intended to stabilize society, instead produced conflict, crime, and corruption; government policies advanced some economic interests but injured others. Even the notion of a "mass" culture obscured the degree to which millions of Americans were left out of the New Era. With no disposable income and little access to electricity, rural Americans scarcely participated in the joys of consumerism; racial and ethnic minorities were often isolated in ghettos and barrios; and many workers faced declining opportunities. Most ominous was the uneven prosperity undergirding the New Era. Although living standards rose for many Americans and the rich expanded their share of the national wealth, more than 40 percent of the population earned less than $1,500 a year and fell below the established poverty level. The unequal distribution of wealth and income made the economy unstable and vulnerable to a disastrous collapse.

Where to Learn More

F. Scott and Zelda Fitzgerald Museum, Montgomery, Alabama. The novelist and his wife lived a short while in this house in her hometown. http://www.fitzgeraldmuseum.net/.

Herbert Hoover National Historic Site, West Branch, Iowa. Visitors may tour Hoover's birthplace cottage, presidential library, and museum. http://www.hoover.archives.gov/.

Henry Ford Museum and Greenfield Village, Dearborn, Michigan. Among many fascinating exhibits, "The Automobile in American Life" superbly demonstrates the importance of the automobile in American social history. http://www.hfmgv.org.

Warren G. Harding House, Marion, Ohio. Harding's home from 1891 to 1921 is now a museum with period furnishings. http://ohsweb.ohiohistory.org/places/c03/index.shtml.

Calvin Coolidge Homestead, Plymouth, Vermont. Operated by the Vermont Division of Historic Sites, the homestead preserves the exact interiors and furnishings from when Coolidge took the presidential oath of office there in 1923. http://www.calvin-coolidge.org/html/the_homestead.html and http://www.historicvermont.org/coolidge/.

Review Questions

1. How did the automobile industry affect the nation's economy and society in the 1920s? In the excerpt from *The Flivver King*, how does Upton Sinclair illustrate the tension between workers and technology even as they both served Henry Ford's vision of mass production and mass consumerism?
2. What factors characterized the boom industries of the 1920s? The sick industries? How accurate is it to label the 1920s the decade of prosperity?
3. What were the underlying issues in the election of 1924? Of 1928? What role did politics play in the public life of the 1920s?
4. What were the chief points of conflict in the culture wars of the 1920s? What were the underlying issues in these clashes? Why were they so hard to compromise?
5. In what ways did World War I experience shape developments in the 1920s?
6. What were the chief features of American involvement in world affairs in the 1920s? To what extent did that involvement constitute a new role for the United States?

Key Terms

Great Migration (p. 670)
Harlem Renaissance (p. 671)
Jazz Age (p. 673)
Kellogg-Briand Pact (p. 681)
League of Women Voters (p. 668)
Multinational corporations (p. 680)
National Origins Act of 1924 (p. 675)
Nisei (p. 676)
Oligopoly (p. 664)
Open shop (p. 665)
Sheppard-Towner Maternity and Infancy Act (p. 669)
Volstead Act (p. 678)
Welfare capitalism (p. 665)
Yellow-dog contracts (p. 665)

myhistorylab Connections

Reinforce what you learned in this chapter by studying the many documents, images, maps, review tools, and videos available at **www.myhistorylab.com**.

Read and Review

Study and Review **Study Plan: Chapter 24**

Read the Document

Calvin Coolidge, Inaugural Address (1925)

Edward Earle Purinton, "Big Ideas from Big Business" (1921)

Carter G. Woodson, A Century of Negro Migration (1918)

1924 Immigration Law

Advertisements (1925, 1927)

Margaret Sanger, "Happiness in Marriage" (1926)

Court Statements Nicola Sacco and Bartolomeo Vanzetti (1927)

Creed of Klanswomen (1924)

Hiram Evans, The Klan's Fight for Americanism (1926)

Letters from the Great Migration (1916–1917)

Charles S. Johnson, The City Negro (1925)

See the Map

African American Population, 1910 and 1950

The Expansion of Black Harlem, 1911–1930

Research and Explore

Read the Document

Personal Journeys Online

From Then to Now Online: The Culture Wars

Hear the Audio

Prohibition is a Failure

"I Too"; poem and reading by Langston Hughes

Watch the Video

The Great Migration

The Harlem Renaissance

The Rise and Fall of the Automobile Economy

Warren C. Harding

Hear the Audio

Hear the audio files for Chapter 24 at **www.myhistorylab.com**.

INTERPRETING the PAST

The Scopes Monkey Trial as a Harbinger of Change

EXAMINE the history and impact of Tennessee's Butler Act (1925) and the trial of John T. Scopes that followed. Why did the debate over Darwin's *Origin of Species* generate such passionate division? What issues were at stake and why has the debate continued?

The Roaring '20s was a decade of turmoil and change in the United States. Technological and scientific innovation, urban growth, and the blossoming of mass culture and materialism—all challenged deeply rooted convictions of American traditionalists, especially religious fundamentalists. The evangelist T. T. Martin warned in his tract, *Hell and the High Schools*, that "the teaching of Evolution is being drilled into our boys and girls in our High Schools during the most susceptible, dangerous age of their lives." Swayed by such sentiments, John Washington Butler, a farmer and Primitive Baptist who served in the Tennessee legislature, denounced any challenge to the teachings of the Bible and proposed a bill forbidding the teaching of evolution in the schools of Tennessee. Enacted in March 1925, the Butler Act prohibited teaching the origins of man that deviated from the biblical version.

The Act provoked an immediate reaction from the American Civil Liberties Union. To challenge the law, John T. Scopes, a popular general science teacher in Dayton, agreed to be arrested and placed on trial. William Jennings Bryan, a prominent fundamentalist Christian, consented to prosecute the case because he believed in the rights of the majority: if the people of Dayton opposed Darwinism then they should be allowed to prohibit it in the schools. Attracted by the possibility of opposing Bryan in the courtroom, Clarence Darrow, nationally famous criminal lawyer, liberal, and agnostic, offered his services for the defense. The trial that ensued, Scopes later recalled, had "more acts and sideshows and freaks" than the circus.

John T. Scopes was found guilty and fined. William Jennings Bryan, one of the nation's great orators and reformers, was publicly ridiculed as a backward bigot and died several days after the conclusion of the trial. And despite the verdict, Darrow emerged victorious after a crushing cross-examination of Bryan. The sentence was appealed to the Tennessee Supreme Court, which upheld the Dayton sentence, but set the sentence aside on a legal technicality that the jury had not set the fine levied against Scopes. The Butler Act would not be repealed by the Tennessee state legislature until 1967. The U.S. Supreme Court would declare similar laws to be unconstitutional in an Arkansas case in 1968.

Through the historical figures of William Jennings Bryan and Clarence Darrow, the Scopes trial symbolized the cultural battles of the twenties. And when Darrow (leaning against the table) interrogated Bryan on the accuracy of the Bible, the New York Times *called the exchange the "most amazing courtroom scene in Anglo-American history."*

Butler Act, 1925

That it shall be unlawful for any teacher in any of the Universities, Normals and all other public schools of the State which are supported in whole or in part by the public school funds of the State, to teach any theory that denies the story of the Divine Creation of man as taught in the Bible, and to teach instead that man has descended from a lower order of animals.

H. L. Mencken, Aftermath (of the Scopes Trial), *Baltimore Evening Sun*, September 14, 1925

True enough, even a superstitious man has certain inalienable rights. He has a right to harbor and indulge his imbecilities as long as he pleases, provided only he does not try to inflict them upon other men by force. He has a right to argue for them as eloquently as he can, in season and out of season. He has a right to teach them to his children. But certainly he has no right to be protected against the free criticism of those who do not hold them. He has no right to demand that they be treated as sacred. He has no right to preach them without challenge. . . .

The meaning of religious freedom, I fear, is sometimes greatly misapprehended. It is taken to be a sort of immunity, not merely from governmental control but also from public opinion. A dunderhead gets himself a long-tailed coat, rises behind the sacred desk, and emits such bilge as would gag a Hottentot. Is it to pass unchallenged? If so, then what we have is not religious freedom at all, but the most intolerable and outrageous variety of religious despotism. Any fool, once he is admitted to holy orders, becomes infallible. Any half-wit, by the simple device of ascribing his delusions to revelation, takes on an authority that is denied to all the rest of us.

John T. Scopes, a popular science teacher at the high school, indicated after the trial that he believed the Butler Act was "unjust."

Epperson v. Arkansas, 393 U.S. 97 (1968)

In the present case, there can be no doubt that Arkansas has sought to prevent its teachers from discussing the theory of evolution because it is contrary to the belief of some that the Book of Genesis must be the exclusive source of doctrine as to the origin of man. No suggestion has been made that Arkansas' law may be justified by considerations of state policy other than the religious views of some of its citizens. It is clear that fundamentalist sectarian conviction was and is the law's reason for existence. Its antecedent, Tennessee's "monkey law," candidly stated its purpose: to make it unlawful "to teach any theory that denies the story of the Divine Creation of man as taught in the Bible, and to teach instead that man has descended from a lower order of animals." Perhaps the sensational publicity attendant upon the Scopes trial induced Arkansas to adopt less explicit language. It eliminated Tennessee's reference to "the story of the Divine Creation of man" as taught in the Bible, but there is no doubt that the motivation for the law was the same: to suppress the teaching of a theory which, it was thought, "denied" the divine creation of man.

Arkansas' law cannot be defended as an act of religious neutrality. Arkansas did not seek to excise from the curricula of its schools and universities all discussion of the origin of man. The law's effort was confined to an attempt to blot out a particular theory because of its supposed conflict with the Biblical account, literally read. Plainly, the law is contrary to the mandate of the First, and in violation of the Fourteenth, Amendment to the Constitution.

The judgment of the Supreme Court of Arkansas is Reversed.

1929-1939

25 The Great Depression and the New Deal

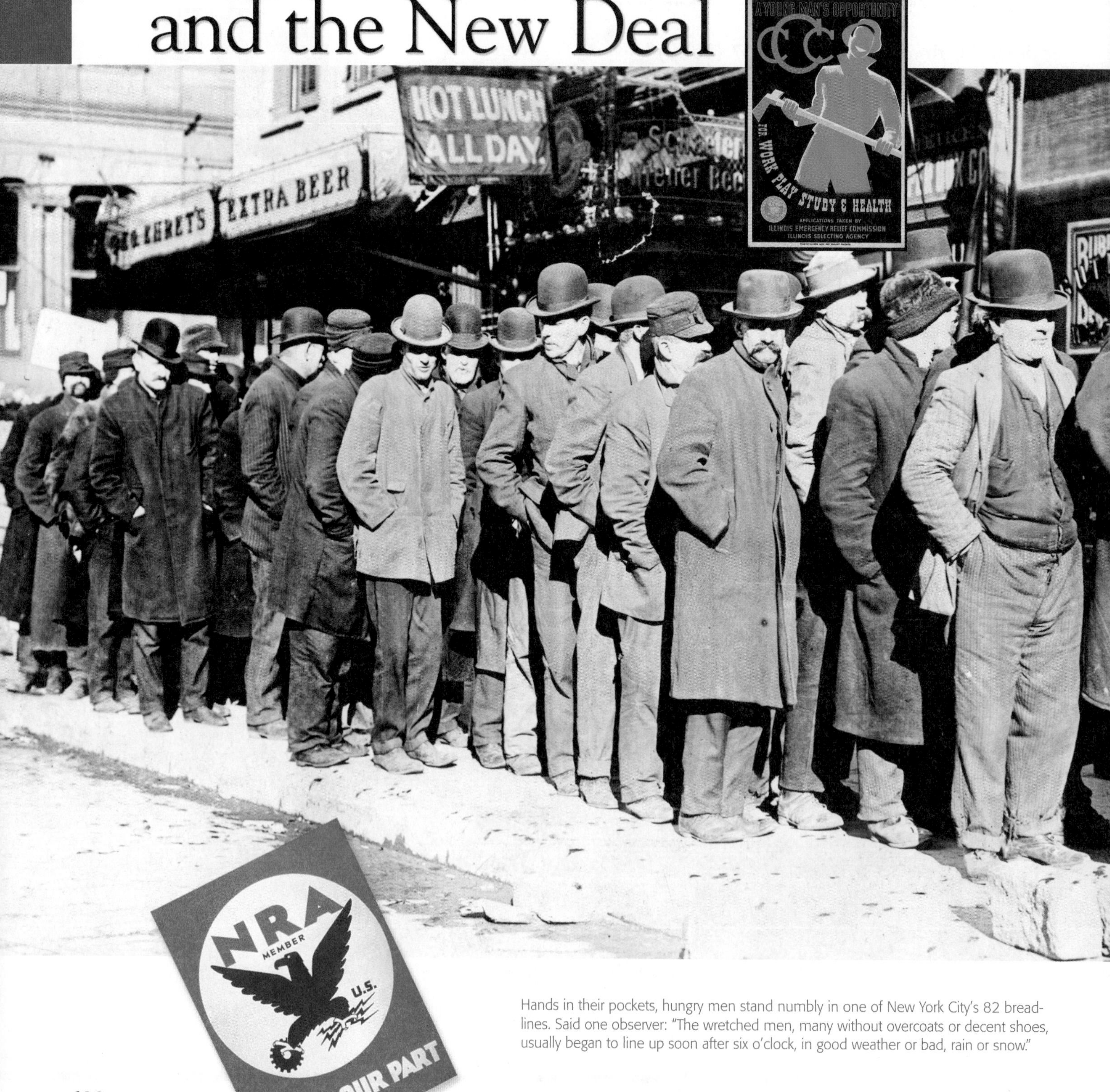

Hands in their pockets, hungry men stand numbly in one of New York City's 82 breadlines. Said one observer: "The wretched men, many without overcoats or decent shoes, usually began to line up soon after six o'clock, in good weather or bad, rain or snow."

Hear the **Audio**
Hear the audio files for Chapter 25 at **www.myhistorylab.com**

HARD TIMES IN HOOVERVILLE *(page 692)*

WHAT TRIGGERED the Great Depression?

HERBERT HOOVER AND THE DEPRESSION *(page 696)*

HOW DID Herbert Hoover respond to the depression? Why did his policies fail?

LAUNCHING THE NEW DEAL *(page 698)*

WHAT WERE the goals of the early New Deal?

CONSOLIDATING THE NEW DEAL *(page 702)*

WHAT WERE the major accomplishments of the Second New Deal?

THE NEW DEAL AND AMERICAN LIFE *(page 705)*

WHAT IMPACT did the New Deal have on American social and economic life?

EBBING OF THE NEW DEAL *(page 711)*

WHY DID the New Deal lose momentum after 1936?

GOOD NEIGHBORS AND HOSTILE FORCES *(page 712)*

HOW DID Roosevelt respond to the rise of fascism in Europe?

ONE AMERICAN JOURNEY

We are bringing order out of the old chaos with a greater certainty of labor at a reasonable wage and of more business at a fair profit. These governmental and industrial developments hold promise of new achievements for the nation.

Our first problem was, of course, the banking situation because, as you know, the banks had collapsed. Some banks could not be saved but the great majority of them, either through their own resources or with government aid, have been restored to complete public confidence. This has given safety to millions of depositors in these banks.

The second step we have taken in the restoration of normal business enterprise has been to clean up thoroughly unwholesome conditions in the field of investment. . . . The country now enjoys the safety of bank savings under the new banking laws, the careful checking of new securities under the Securities Act and the curtailment of rank stock speculation through the Securities Exchange Act. . . .

Those, fortunately few in number, who are frightened by boldness and cowed by the necessity for making decisions, complain that all we have done is unnecessary and subject to great risks. Now that these people are coming out of their storm cellars, they forget that there ever was a storm. [But] nearly all Americans are sensible and calm people. We do not get greatly excited nor is our peace of mind disturbed, whether we be businessmen or workers or farmers, by awesome pronouncements concerning the unconstitutionality of some of our measures of recovery and relief and reform. We are not frightened by reactionary lawyers or political editors. All these cries have been heard before.

I still believe in ideals. I am not for a return to that definition of Liberty under which for many years a free people were being gradually regimented into the service of the privileged few. I prefer and I am sure you prefer that broader definition of Liberty under which we are moving forward to greater freedom, to greater security for the average man than he has ever known before in the history of America.

Excerpted from President Franklin D. Roosevelt's radio address entitled "On Moving Forward to Greater Freedom and Greater Security," September 30, 1934.

Read the **Document** at **www.myhistorylab.com**

Personal Journeys Online

- **Letter from Eleanor Roosevelt to Walter White, 1936. Roosevelt writes against lynching.**
- **Paul Taylor, "Again the Covered Wagon," *Survey Graphic*, July 1935. Article on the migration of "Okies" to California during the Dust Bowl.**

AS PRESIDENT FRANKLIN D. ROOSEVELT acknowledged in this 1934 radio address, the U.S. economy had utterly collapsed. Men, women, children everywhere saw their families and dreams shattered, watched their life savings vanish in faulty banks, and felt the sting of humiliation as they stood in bread lines or begged for clothes or food scraps. The winter of 1932–1933 had been particularly cruel: Unemployment soared and stories of malnutrition and outright starvation made headlines in newspapers throughout the nation.

The election of Franklin D. Roosevelt in 1932 had, however, lifted the spirits and hopes of jobless Americans throughout the nation. They enthusiastically responded to his "new deal for the American people" and particularly embraced his use of the radio to address the nation. In these "fireside chats," the president offered reassurance about the economic crisis, compassionately explaining his decisions and policies, as he did in this 1934 address. And he promised a brighter future, charting a new journey, he predicted, that would restore confidence among despairing

CHRONOLOGY

1929	Stock market crashes.
1931	Japan invades Manchuria.
1932	Farmers' Holiday Association organizes rural protests in the Midwest.
	Reconstruction Finance Corporation is created to assist financial institutions.
	Bonus Army is routed in Washington, DC.
	Franklin D. Roosevelt is elected president.
1933	Adolf Hitler comes to power in Germany.
	Emergency Banking Act is passed.
	The United States recognizes the Soviet Union.
	Agricultural Adjustment Administration (AAA) is created to regulate farm production.
	National Recovery Administration (NRA) is created to promote industrial cooperation and recovery.
	Federal Emergency Relief Act provides federal assistance to the unemployed.
	Civilian Conservation Corps (CCC) is established to provide work relief in conservation projects.
	Public Works Administration (PWA) is created to provide work relief on large public construction projects.
	Civil Works Administration (CWA) provides emergency winter relief jobs.
	Tennessee Valley Authority (TVA) is created to coordinate regional development.
1934	Securities and Exchange Commission (SEC) is established.
	Indian Reorganization Act reforms Indian policy.
	Huey Long organizes the Share-Our-Wealth Society.
	Democrats win midterm elections.
1935	Supreme Court declares NRA unconstitutional.
	Italy attacks Ethiopia.
	National Labor Relations Act (Wagner Act) guarantees workers' rights to organize and bargain collectively.
	Social Security Act establishes a federal social insurance system.
	Banking Act strengthens the Federal Reserve.
	Revenue Act establishes a more progressive tax system.
	Resettlement Administration is created to aid dispossessed farmers.
	Rural Electrification Administration (REA) is created to help provide electric power to rural areas.
	Soil Conservation Service is established.
	Emergency Relief Appropriation Act authorizes public relief projects for the unemployed.
	Works Progress Administration (WPA) is created.
	Huey Long is assassinated.
1936	Supreme Court declares AAA unconstitutional.
	Roosevelt is reelected president.
	Hitler remilitarizes the Rhineland.
	Roosevelt sails to South America as part of Good Neighbor Policy.
	Sit-down strikes begin.
1937	Chicago police kill workers in Memorial Day Massacre.
	FDR tries but fails to expand the Supreme Court.
	Farm Security Administration (FSA) is created to lend money to small farmers to buy and rehabilitate farms.
	National Housing Act is passed to promote public housing projects.
	"Roosevelt Recession" begins.
1938	Congress of Industrial Organizations (CIO) is founded.
	Germany annexes Austria.
	Fair Labor Standards Act establishes minimum wage and maximum hours rules for labor.
	Roosevelt fails to "purge" the Democratic Party.
	Republicans make gains in midterm elections.
	Munich agreement reached, appeasing Hitler's demand for Sudetenland.
	Kristallnacht, violent pogrom against Jews, occurs in Germany.

Americans and provide greater economic security for the nation's citizens. "Among our objectives," Roosevelt insisted, "I place the security of the men, women, and children of the Nation first."

To be sure, FDR's bold rhetoric occasionally outdistanced his legislative agenda, and certain programs hardly worked against what he termed the "privileged few." Moreover, his policies often failed to challenge the racism and sexism that precluded a new deal for all Americans. Still, the unprecedented federal activism of the 1930s, even while achieving neither full recovery nor systematic reform, effectively restored confidence to many Americans and permanently transformed the nation's responsibility for the welfare of its citizens. ✦

HARD TIMES IN HOOVERVILLE

WHAT TRIGGERED the Great Depression?

The prosperity of the 1920s ended in a stock-market crash that revealed the flaws honeycombing the economy. As the nation slid into a catastrophic depression, factories closed, employment and incomes tumbled, and millions lost their homes, hopes, and dignity. Some protested and took direct action; others looked to the government for relief.

CRASH!

The buoyant prosperity of the New Era, more apparent than real by the summer of 1929, collapsed in October, when the stock market crashed. During the preceding two years, the market had hit record highs, stimulated by optimism, easy credit, and speculators' manipulations. But after peaking in September, it suffered several sharp checks, and on October 29, "Black Tuesday," panicked investors dumped their stocks, wiping out the previous year's gains in one day. Confidence in the economy disappeared, and the slide continued for months, and then years. The market hit bottom in July 1932. Much of the paper wealth of America had evaporated, and the nation sank into the **Great Depression.**

Great Depression The nation's worst economic crisis, extending through the 1930s, producing unprecedented bank failures, unemployment, and industrial and agricultural collapse.

The Wall Street crash marked the beginning of the depression, but it did not cause it. The depression stemmed from weaknesses in the New Era economy. Most damaging was the unequal distribution of wealth and income. Workers' wages and farmers' incomes had fallen far behind industrial productivity and corporate profits; by 1929, the richest 0.1 percent of American families had as much total income as the bottom 42 percent (see Figure 25–1). With more than half the nation's people living at or below the subsistence level, there was not enough purchasing power to maintain the economy.

A second factor was that oligopolies dominated American industries. By 1929, the 200 largest corporations (out of 400,000) controlled half the corporate wealth. Their power led to "administered prices," prices kept artificially high and rigid rather than determined by supply and demand. Because it did not respond to purchasing power, this system not only helped bring on economic collapse but also dimmed prospects for recovery.

Weaknesses in specific industries had further unbalanced the economy. Agriculture suffered from overproduction, declining prices, and heavy debt; so did the coal and textile industries. These difficulties left the economy dependent on a few industries for expansion and employment, and these industries could not carry the burden. Banking presented other problems. Poorly managed and regulated, banks had contributed to the instability of prosperity; they now threatened to spread the panic and depression.

International economic difficulties spurred the depression as well. Shut out from U.S. markets by high tariffs, Europeans had depended on American investments to manage their debts and reparation payments from the Great War. The stock market crash dried up the flow of American dollars to Europe, causing financial panics and industrial collapse and making the Great Depression global. In turn, European nations curtailed their imports of American goods and defaulted on their debts, further debilitating the U.S. economy. (See Global Connections, The Worldwide Collapse.)

Government policies also bore some responsibility for the crash and depression. Failure to enforce antitrust laws had encouraged oligopolies and high prices; failure to regulate banking and the stock market

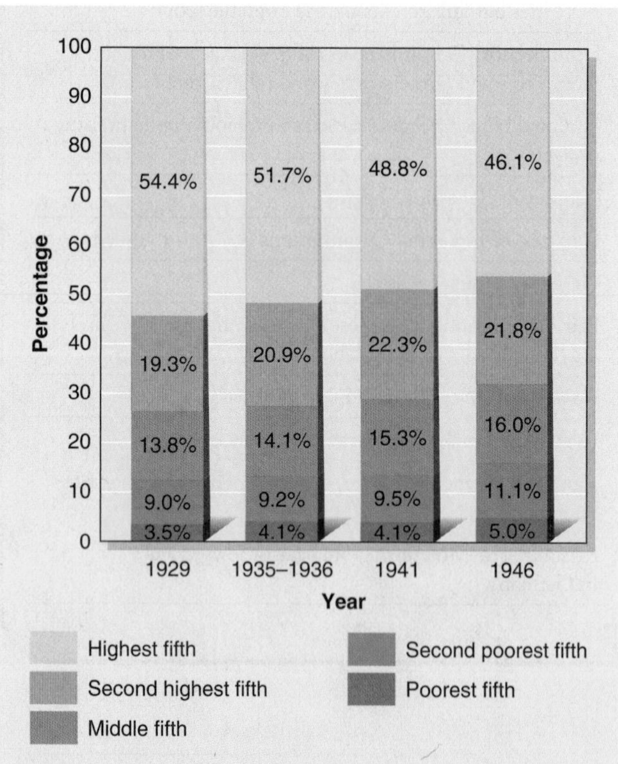

FIGURE 25–1 **Distribution of Income in the United States, 1929–1946** An unequal distribution of income contributed to the Great Depression by limiting purchasing power. Only slight changes occurred until after World War II, but other factors gradually stabilized the national economy.

Data Source: U.S. Bureau of the Census.

had permitted financial recklessness and irresponsible speculation. Reducing tax rates on the wealthy had also encouraged speculation and contributed to the maldistribution of income. Opposition to labor unions and collective bargaining helped keep workers' wages and purchasing power low. The absence of an effective agricultural policy and the high tariffs that inhibited foreign trade and reduced markets for agricultural products hurt farmers. In short, the same governmental policies that shaped the booming 1920s economy also led to economic disaster.

State and local fiscal policies also pointed to economic problems for the 1930s. The expansion of public education and road construction led to higher property taxes in communities throughout the nation, and although per capita tax collection at the federal level actually declined between 1920 and 1929, the tax burden in states and cities increased dramatically. Indeed, state and local taxes rose faster than personal incomes in the 1920s. The real estate industry reported a decline as early as 1926, and homeowners steadily protested their higher property taxes.

But the crash did more than expose the weaknesses of the economy. Business lost confidence and refused to make investments that might have brought recovery. Instead, banks called in loans and restricted credit, and depositors tried to withdraw their savings, which were uninsured. The demand for cash caused banks to fail, dragging the economy down further. And the Federal Reserve Board prolonged the depression by restricting the money supply.

QUICK REVIEW

Causes of the Great Depression

- Unequal distribution of wealth and income.
- Domination of American economy by oligopolies.
- Weakness in important industries.
- International economic problems.
- Government policies.

THE DEPRESSION SPREADS

By early 1930, the effects of financial contraction were painfully evident. Factories shut down or cut back, and industrial production plummeted. By 1932, one-fourth of the labor force was out of work (see Figure 25–2). Personal income dropped by more than half between 1929 and 1932. Moreover, the depression began to feed on itself in a vicious circle: Shrinking wages and employment cut into purchasing power, causing business to slash production again and lay off workers, thereby further reducing purchasing power.

The depression particularly battered farmers. Commodity prices fell by 55 percent between 1929 and 1932, stifling farm income. Unable to pay their mortgages, many farm families lost their homes and fields. The dispossessed roamed the byways, highways, and railways of a troubled country.

See the Map at www.myhistorylab.com *The Great Depression*

Hoovervilles Shantytowns, sarcastically named after President Hoover, in which unemployed and homeless people lived in makeshift shacks, tents, and boxes.

Urban families were also evicted when they could not pay their rent. Some moved in with relatives; others lived in **Hoovervilles**—the name reflects the bitterness directed at the president—shacks where people shivered, suffered, and starved. Oklahoma City's vast Hooverville covered 100 square miles.

Soup kitchens became standard features of the urban landscape, with lines of the hungry stretching for blocks. But charities and local communities could not meet the massive needs, and neither the states nor the federal government had welfare or unemployment compensation programs.

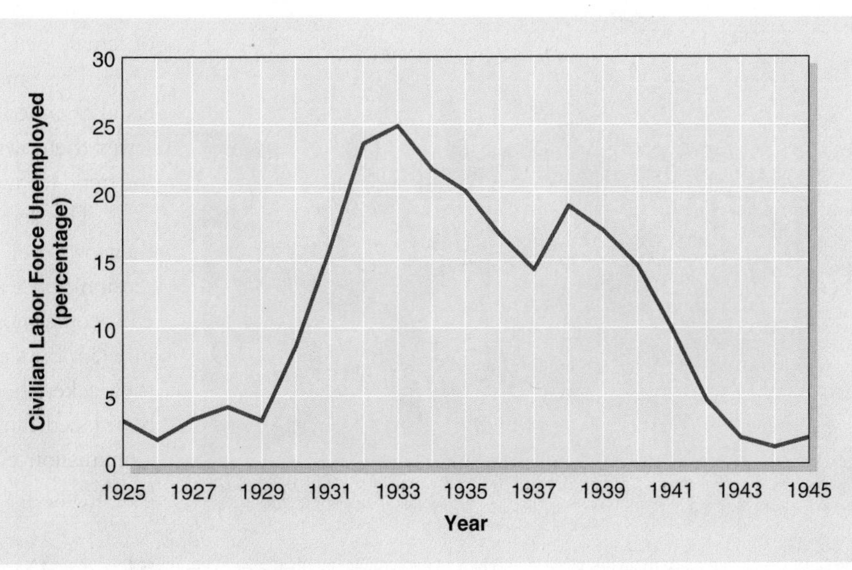

FIGURE 25–2 **Unemployment, 1925–1945** Unemployment soared in the early 1930s, spreading distress and overwhelming charities and local relief agencies. Federal programs improved conditions, but only America's entry into World War II really ended the problem.
Data Source: U.S. Bureau of the Census.

"WOMEN'S JOBS" AND "MEN'S JOBS"

The depression affected wage-earning women in complex ways. Although they suffered 20 percent unemployment by 1932, women were less likely

Homeless Americans gathered in squalid Hoovervilles like this one in Seattle and struggled to survive.

than men to be fired. Gender segregation had concentrated women in low-paid service, sales, and clerical jobs that were less vulnerable than the heavy industries where men predominated. But while traditional attitudes somewhat insulated working women, they also reinforced opposition to female employment, especially that of married women. Three-fourths of the nation's school systems refused to hire married women as teachers, and two-thirds dismissed female teachers who married. Many private employers, especially banks and insurance companies, also fired married women. Nonetheless, the proportion of married women in the workforce increased in the 1930s as women took jobs to help their families survive, and about one-third of working married women provided the sole support for their families.

Families in the Depression

"I have watched fear grip the people in our neighborhood around Hull House," wrote Jane Addams as the depression deepened in 1931 and family survival itself seemed threatened. Divorce declined because it was expensive, but desertion increased, and people postponed marriage. Birthrates fell. Husbands and fathers, the traditional breadwinners, were often humiliated and despondent when laid off from work. Unemployed men, sociologists reported, "lost much of their sense of time and dawdled helplessly and dully about the streets," dreading to return home.

Women's responsibilities, by contrast, often grew. The number of female-headed households increased sharply. Not only did some women become wage earners, but their traditional role as homemakers also gained new significance. To make ends meet, many women sewed their own clothing and raised and canned vegetables, reversing the trend toward consumerism. Some also took on extra work at home.

The depression also affected children. Some parents sacrificed their own well-being to protect their children. But children felt the tension and fear, and many went without food. In New York City, 139 people, most of them children, died of starvation and malnutrition in 1933. Boys and girls stayed home from school and church because they lacked shoes or clothing; others gave up their plans for college. As hope faded, family conflicts increased. The California Unemployment Commission concluded that the depression had left the American family "morally shattered. There is no security, no foothold, no future."

The Great Depression made more desperate the plight of Mexican Americans; they faced discrimination and feared deportation. As migrant laborers, they also struggled with the forces of nature as they traveled from field to field in search of work. This Mexican migrant worker holds his new baby with his wife standing at the door's edge. They live in this shack next to a frozen pea field in California.

"Last Hired, First Fired"

The depression particularly harmed racial minorities. With fewer resources and opportunities, they were less able than other groups to absorb the economic pain. African Americans were caught in a

GLOBAL CONNECTIONS

THE WORLDWIDE COLLAPSE

The Wall Street crash did not immediately provoke widespread alarm at home or abroad. One French observer commented that an "abscess" had been "lanced." British commentators dismissed it as an isolated event and predicted continuing prosperity. President Hoover remained confident well into 1930, even telling a group of religious leaders requesting relief for the unemployed, "You have come sixty days too late. The depression is over."

Still, the stock market collapse did have consequences: It made European borrowing more difficult, especially hurting Germany's failing economy. Without loans from the United States, Germany defaulted on its war debts and faced near bankruptcy. Moreover, the United States accounted for 40 percent of the world's manufactured goods—twice the figure for Germany and England combined in 1929. When the United States slid into depression, the global repercussions were staggering.

The international crisis required global cooperation, but the world's nations responded with various forms of economic nationalism. The United States rejected its role as the lender of the last resort for destitute countries and constructed trade barriers by passing the Smoot-Hawley tariff in 1930. Within months Canada, Mexico, France, Spain, and New Zealand raised their tariffs against American goods. World trade came to a standstill; its volume plummeted by two-thirds between 1929 and 1933.

As the depression deepened, world leaders pointed to external causes and turned to conventional solutions. In the United States, Herbert Hoover claimed that "the hurricane that swept our shores was of European origin" and affirmed the need to balance the budget in hard times. French leaders blamed British monetary policies and blasted the United States for "exporting unemployment" through "mechanization" that replaced workers with machines. The French also regarded a balanced budget as inviolable. In Britain, however, the socialist prime minister, Ramsay MacDonald, faulted capitalism for the collapse, adding "we are not on trial, it is the system under which we live." Britain provided unemployment insurance and public relief. But even MacDonald refused to unbalance the budget to meet the needs of all the jobless. The Japanese finance minister also objected to increased spending for the unemployed.

By 1932, the international crisis had worsened, and the United States and Germany had unemployment rates of 25 and 40 percent, respectively. The German banking system had collapsed in 1931, and the depression helped facilitate the political success of the Nazi Party in 1932. Jobless Germans looted stores and coal yards for food and fuel. As in the United States, working women were targeted as a cause of the depression. One German newspaper declared that "Germany will perish if the women are working and the men are unemployed."

The shockingly high rates of unemployment throughout the world created unprecedented conditions of poverty and despair. And although Americans did not leap from windows during the collapse of the stock market, suicide rates went up in both Germany and the United States during the 1930s. Cases of malnutrition were found in New York, Budapest, and Vienna, among other cities, and relief agencies everywhere were overwhelmed by the needs of the jobless. People lost jobs and homes, creating Hoovervilles in the United States, *bidonvilles* ("tin cities") in France, and the Hungry Mile in Australia. The Great Depression had indeed become global, and, without international cooperation, the unemployed looked to their governments for solutions and support.

- Why did the U.S. depression become a global crisis and how did world leaders respond?

double bind, reported a sociologist at Howard University in 1932: They were "the last to be hired and the first to be fired." Black unemployment rates were more than twice the white rate, reflecting increased job competition and persistent racism.

Racism also limited the assistance African Americans received. Religious and charitable organizations often refused to care for black people. Local and state governments set higher relief eligibility requirements for blacks than for whites and provided them with less aid. Out of work for longer periods of time and without even modest relief assistance, African Americans were forced to crowd together in already cramped apartments, while still paying exorbitant rents to

QUICK REVIEW

Gendered Attitudes about Work

- Women were concentrated in low-paid service, sales, and clerical jobs.
- Hard times reinforced opposition to female employment, particularly of married women.
- Nonetheless, the proportion of married women in the workplace increased in the 1930s.

QUICK REVIEW

African Americans and the Depression

- Black unemployment rates were twice the rate for white people.
- Blacks had less access to state and private aid and relief.
- Blacks faced a bleak economic outlook.

white landlords. By 1932, most African Americans were suffering acute privation. "At no time in the history of the Negro since slavery," reported the Urban League, "has his economic and social outlook seemed so discouraging."

Hispanic Americans also suffered. As mostly unskilled workers, they faced increasing competition for decreasing jobs paying declining wages. They were displaced even in the California agricultural labor force, which they had dominated. By the mid-1930s, they made up only a tenth of the state's migratory labor force, which increasingly consisted of white people who had fled the South and the Great Plains. Other jobs were lost when Arizona, California, and Texas barred Mexicans from public works and highway construction jobs. Vigilantes threatened employers who hired Mexicans rather than white Americans.

Economic woes and racism drove nearly half a million Mexican immigrants and their American-born children from the United States. Local authorities in the Southwest, with the blessing of the Department of Labor, urged all Mexicans, regardless of their citizenship status, to return to Mexico and free up jobs and relief assistance for white Americans. To intimidate Mexican residents, the U.S. Immigration Service conducted several raids, rounding up people and demanding immediate proof of citizenship.

Protest

Bewildered and discouraged, most Americans reacted to the crisis without protest. Influenced by traditional individualism, many blamed themselves for their plight. But others did act, especially to protect their families. Protests ranged from small desperate gestures like stealing food and coal to more dramatic deeds. In Louisiana, women seized a train to call attention to the needs of their families; in New Jersey, in the "bloodless battle of Pleasantville," 100 women held the city council hostage to demand assistance.

Communists, socialists, and other radicals organized more formal protests. Communists led the jobless into "unemployment councils" that staged hunger marches, demonstrated for relief, and blocked evictions. Socialists built similar organizations, including the People's Unemployment League in Baltimore, which had 12,000 members. Groups of this kind provided protection and assistance. However, local officials often suppressed their protests. In 1932, police fired on the Detroit Unemployment Council as it marched to demand food and jobs, killing four marchers and wounding many more.

Rural protests also broke out. Again, communists organized some of them, as in Alabama, where the Croppers' and Farm Workers' Union mobilized black agricultural laborers in 1931 to demand better treatment. In the Midwest, the Farmers' Holiday Association, organized among family farmers in 1932, stopped the shipment of produce to urban markets, hoping to drive up prices. A guerrilla war broke out as farmers blocked roads and halted freight trains, dumped milk in ditches, and fought bloody battles with deputy sheriffs. Midwestern farmers also tried to prevent foreclosure of their farms. In Iowa, farmers beat sheriffs and mortgage agents and nearly lynched a judge conducting foreclosure proceedings; in Nebraska, a Farmers' Holiday leader warned that if the state did not halt foreclosures, "200,000 of us are coming to Lincoln and we'll tear that new State Capitol Building to pieces."

HERBERT HOOVER AND THE DEPRESSION

HOW DID Herbert Hoover respond to the depression? Why did his policies fail?

The Great Depression challenged the optimism, policies, and philosophy that Herbert Hoover had carried into the White House in 1929. The president took unprecedented steps to resolve the crisis but shrank back from the interventionist policies activists urged. His failures, personal as well as political and economic, led to his repudiation and to a major shift in government policies.

The Failure of Voluntarism

Hoover fought economic depression more vigorously than any previous president, but he believed that voluntary private relief was preferable to federal intervention. The role of the national government, he thought, was to advise and encourage the voluntary efforts of private organizations, individual industries, or local communities.

Hoover obtained pledges from business leaders to maintain employment and wage levels. But most corporations soon repudiated these pledges, slashed wages, and laid off workers. Hoover himself said, "You know, the only trouble with capitalism is capitalists; they're too damn greedy." Still, he rejected government action.

Hoover also depended on voluntary efforts to relieve the misery caused by massive unemployment. He created the President's Organization for Unemployment Relief to help raise private funds for voluntary relief agencies. Charities and local authorities, he believed, should help the unemployed; direct federal relief would expand government power and undermine the recipients' character. He vetoed congressional attempts to aid the unemployed.

The depression rendered Hoover's beliefs meaningless. Private programs to aid the unemployed scarcely existed. Only a few unions, such as the Amalgamated Clothing Workers, had unemployment funds, and these were soon spent. Company plans for unemployment compensation covered less than 1 percent of workers, revealing the charade of the welfare capitalism of the 1920s. Private charitable groups like the Salvation Army, church associations, and ethnic societies quickly exhausted their resources.

Nor could local governments cope, and their efforts declined as the depression deepened. By 1932, more than 100 cities made no relief appropriations at all, and the commissioner of charity in Salt Lake City reported that people were sliding toward starvation. Only eight state governments provided even token assistance.

As the depression worsened, Hoover adopted more activist policies. He persuaded Congress to cut taxes to boost consumers' buying power, and he increased the public works budget. The Federal Farm Board lent money to cooperatives and spent millions trying to stabilize crop prices. Unable to control production, however, the board conceded failure by late 1931. More successful was the Reconstruction Finance Corporation (RFC). Established in January 1932, the RFC lent federal funds to banks, insurance companies, and railroads so that their recovery could "trickle down" to ordinary Americans. Hoover still opposed direct aid to the general public, although he finally allowed the RFC to lend small amounts to state and local governments for unemployment relief.

Far more action was necessary, but Hoover remained committed to voluntarism and a balanced budget. Hoover's ideological limitations infuriated Americans who saw him as indifferent to their suffering and a reactionary protector of privileged business interests—an image his political opponents encouraged.

Read the Document at **www.myhistorylab.com**
Dealing with Hard Times: The Great Depression

QUICK REVIEW

The Limits of Voluntarism

- Business leaders failed to live up to pledges to maintain employment and wage levels.
- Private programs to aid the unemployed scarcely existed.
- Local governments were not equipped to deal with the magnitude of the crisis.

Bonus Army Unemployed veterans of World War I gathering in Washington in 1932 to demand payment of service bonuses not due until 1945.

Repudiating Hoover: The 1932 Election

Hoover's treatment of the **Bonus Army** symbolized his unpopularity and set the stage for the 1932 election. In 1932, unemployed veterans of World War I gathered in Washington, demanding payment of service bonuses not due until 1945. Hoover refused to meet with them, and Congress rejected their plan. But 10,000 veterans erected a shantytown at the edge of Washington and camped in vacant public buildings. Hoover decided to evict the veterans, but General Douglas MacArthur exceeded his cautious orders and on July 28 led cavalry, infantry, and tanks against the ragged Bonus Marchers. The troops cleared the buildings and assaulted the shantytown, dispersing the veterans and their families and setting their camp on fire.

Bonus Marchers battling police in Washington, DC, in 1932. Police and military assaults on these homeless veterans infuriated Americans and prompted Democratic presidential nominee Franklin D. Roosevelt to declare, "Well, this will elect me."

This assault provoked widespread outrage. The administration tried to brand the Bonus Marchers as communists and criminals, but subsequent investigations refuted such claims. The incident confirmed Hoover's public image as harsh and insensitive.

In the summer of 1932, with no prospects for victory, Republicans renominated Hoover. Confident Democrats selected Governor Franklin D. Roosevelt of New York, who promised "a new deal for the American people."

New Deal The economic and political policies of the Roosevelt administration in the 1930s.

The 1932 campaign gave scant indication of what Roosevelt's **New Deal** might involve. The Democratic platform differed little from that of the Republicans, and Roosevelt spoke in vague or general terms. Still, observers found clues in Roosevelt's record as governor of New York, where he had created the first state system of unemployment relief and supported social welfare and conservation. More important was his outgoing personality, which radiated warmth and hope in contrast to Hoover's gloom.

QUICK REVIEW

The 1932 Election

- Republicans renominated Hoover.
- The Democratic platform differed little from the Republican platform.
- Franklin D. Roosevelt's victory was a repudiation of Hoover.

FDR carried every state south and west of Pennsylvania. Yet Hoover would remain president for four more months, as the Constitution then required. And in those four months, the depression worsened, spreading misery throughout America. The final blow came in February 1933, when panic struck the banking system. Nearly 6,000 banks had already failed, robbing 9 million depositors of their savings. Desperate Americans rushed to withdraw their funds from the remaining banks, pushing them to the brink. With the federal government under Hoover immobilized, state governments shut the banks to prevent their failure. By March, an eerie silence had descended on the nation. Hoover concluded, "We are at the end of our string."

LAUNCHING THE NEW DEAL

WHAT WERE the goals of the early New Deal?

In the midst of this national anxiety, Franklin D. Roosevelt pushed forward an unprecedented program to resolve the crises of a collapsing financial system, crippling unemployment, and agricultural and industrial breakdown and to promote reform. The early New Deal achieved successes and attracted support, but it also had limitations and generated criticism that suggested the need for still greater innovations.

Read the **Document** at **www.myhistorylab.com**
Franklin D. Roosevelt, First Inaugural Address (1932)

ACTION NOW!

On March 4, 1933, Franklin Delano Roosevelt became president and immediately reassured the American people. He insisted that "the only thing we have to fear is fear itself" and he promised "action, and action now!" Summoning Congress, Roosevelt pressed forward on a broad front. In the first three months of his administration, the famous Hundred Days of the New Deal, the Democratic Congress passed many important laws (see Overview, Major Laws of the Hundred Days).

WHERE TO LEARN MORE

Center for New Deal Studies, Roosevelt University, Chicago, Illinois http://www.roosevelt.edu/newdeal/

Roosevelt's program reflected a mix of ideas, some from FDR himself, some from a diverse group of advisers, including academic experts dubbed the "brain trust," politicians, and social workers. It also incorporated principles from the progressive movement, precedents from the Great War mobilization, and even plans from the Hoover administration. Above all, the New Deal was a practical response to the depression. FDR had set its tone in his campaign when he declared, "The country needs, and, unless I mistake its temper, the country demands bold, persistent experimentation. . . . Above all, try something."

fireside chats Speeches broadcast nationally over the radio in which President Franklin D. Roosevelt explained complex issues and programs in plain language, as though his listeners were gathered around the fireside with him.

Federal Deposit Insurance Corporation (FDIC) Government agency that guarantees bank deposits, thereby protecting both depositors and banks.

FDR first addressed the banking crisis. On March 5, he proclaimed a national bank holiday, closing all remaining banks. Congress then passed his Emergency Banking Act, a conservative measure that extended government assistance to sound banks and reorganized weak ones. Prompt government action, coupled with a reassuring **fireside chat** over the radio by the president, restored popular confidence in the banks. When they reopened on March 13, deposits exceeded withdrawals. In June, Congress created the **Federal Deposit Insurance Corporation (FDIC)** to guarantee bank deposits up to $2,500.

OVERVIEW Major Laws of the Hundred Days

Law	Objective
Emergency Banking Act	Stabilized the private banking system
Agricultural Adjustment Act	Established a farm recovery program based on production controls and price supports
Emergency Farm Mortgage Act	Provided for the refinancing of farm mortgages
National Industrial Recovery Act	Established a national recovery program and authorized a public works program
Federal Emergency Relief Act	Established a national system of relief
Home Owners Loan Act	Protected homeowners from mortgage foreclosure by refinancing home loans
Glass-Steagall Act	Separated commercial and investment banking and guaranteed bank deposits
Tennessee Valley Authority Act	Established the TVA and provided for the planned development of the Tennessee River Valley
Civilian Conservation Corps Act	Established the CCC to provide work relief on reforestation and conservation projects
Farm Credit Act	Expanded agricultural credits and established the Farm Credit Administration
Securities Act	Required full disclosure from stock exchanges
Wagner-Peyser Act	Created a U.S. Employment Service and encouraged states to create local public employment offices

The financial industry was also reformed. The Glass-Steagall Act separated investment and commercial banking to curtail risky speculation. The Securities Act reformed the sale of stocks to prevent the insider abuses that had characterized Wall Street, and in 1934 the **Securities and Exchange Commission (SEC)** was created to regulate the stock market. Two other financial measures in 1933 created the Home Owners Loan Corporation and the Farm Credit Administration, which enabled millions to refinance their mortgages.

Securities and Exchange Commission (SEC) Federal agency with authority to regulate trading practices in stocks and bonds.

Creating Jobs

Roosevelt also provided relief for the unemployed. The Federal Emergency Relief Administration (FERA) furnished funds to state and local agencies. Harry Hopkins, who had headed Roosevelt's relief program in New York, became its director and one of the New Deal's most important members. FERA spent over $3 billion before it ended in 1935, and by then Hopkins and FDR had developed new programs that provided work rather than just cash. Work relief, they believed, preserved both the skills and the morale of recipients. In the winter of 1933–1934, Hopkins spent nearly $1 billion to create jobs for 4 million men and women through the Civil Works Administration (CWA). The CWA hired laborers to build roads and airports, teachers to staff rural schools, and singers and artists to give public performances. The Public Works Administration (PWA) provided work relief on useful projects to stimulate the economy through public expenditures. Directed by Harold Ickes, the PWA spent billions from 1933 to 1939 to build schools, hospitals, courthouses, dams, and bridges.

One of FDR's personal ideas, the Civilian Conservation Corps (CCC), combined work relief with conservation. Launched in 1933, the CCC employed 2.5 million young men to work on reforestation and flood-control projects, build roads and bridges in national forests and parks, restore Civil War battlefields, and fight forest fires.

Helping Some Farmers

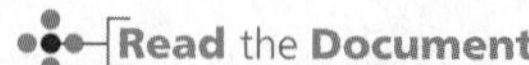

at www.myhistorylab.com
An Attack on New Deal Farm Policies (1936)

Besides providing relief, the New Deal promoted economic recovery. In May 1933, Congress established the Agricultural Adjustment Administration (AAA) to combat the depression in agriculture caused by crop surpluses and low prices. The AAA subsidized farmers who agreed to restrict production. The objective was to boost farm prices to parity, a level that would restore farmers' purchasing power to what it had been in 1914.

Agricultural conditions improved. Farm prices rose from 52 percent of parity in 1932 to 88 percent in 1935, and gross farm income rose by 50 percent. Not until 1941, however, would income exceed the level of 1929, a poor year for farmers. Moreover, some of the decreased production and increased prices stemmed from devastating droughts and dust storms on the Great Plains. The AAA itself harmed poor farmers while aiding larger commercial growers. As southern planters restricted their acreage, they dismissed tenants and sharecroppers, and with AAA payments, they bought new farm machinery, reducing their need for farm labor.

The Flight of the Blue Eagle

QUICK REVIEW

The National Recovery Administration (NRA)

- Sought to halt the slide in prices, wages, and employment.
- Tended to help business, often at the expense of labor.
- Declared unconstitutional in 1935.

The New Deal attempted to revive U.S. industry with the National Industrial Recovery Act (NIRA), which created the National Recovery Administration (NRA). The NRA sought to halt the slide in prices, wages, and employment by suspending antitrust laws and authorizing industrial and trade associations to draft codes setting production quotas, price policies, wages and working conditions, and other business practices. The codes promoted the interests of business generally and big business in particular, but Section 7a of the NIRA guaranteed workers the rights to organize unions and bargain collectively—a provision that John L. Lewis of the United Mine Workers called an Emancipation Proclamation for labor.

Hugh Johnson became director of the NRA. He persuaded business leaders to cooperate in drafting codes and the public to patronize participating companies. The NRA Blue Eagle insignia and its slogan "We Do Our Part" covered workplaces, storefronts, and billboards. Blue Eagle parades marched down the nation's main streets and climaxed in a massive demonstration in New York City.

A coal miner greeting Franklin D. Roosevelt in West Virginia in 1932. Roosevelt's promise of a New Deal revived hope among millions of Americans trapped in hard times.

Support for the NRA waned, however. Corporate leaders used it to advance their own goals and to discriminate against small producers, consumers, and labor. Businesses also violated the labor rights specified in Section 7a. Defiant employers viewed collective bargaining as infringing their authority. Employers even used violence to smother unions. The NRA did little to enforce Section 7a, and Johnson, strongly probusiness, denounced all strikes. Workers felt betrayed. Roosevelt tried to reorganize the NRA, but the act remained controversial until the Supreme Court declared it unconstitutional in 1935.

Critics Right and Left

The early New Deal did not end the depression. Recovery was fitful and uneven; millions of Americans remained unemployed. Nevertheless, the New Deal's efforts to grapple with problems, its successes in reducing suffering and fear, and Roosevelt's own skills carried the Democratic Party to victory in the 1934 elections. But New Deal policies also provoked criticism, from both those convinced that too little had been achieved and those alarmed that too much had been attempted.

Despite the early New Deal's probusiness character, conservatives complained that the expansion of government activity and its regulatory role weakened the autonomy of American business. They also condemned the efforts to aid nonbusiness groups as socialistic, particularly the "excessive" spending on unemployment relief and the "instigation" of labor organizing. These critics attracted little popular support, however, and their selfishness antagonized Roosevelt.

New Deal agricultural programs stabilized the farm economy, but not all farmers benefited. Landowners who received AAA payments evicted these black sharecroppers huddled in a makeshift roadside camp in Missouri in 1935.

More realistic criticism came from the left. In 1932, FDR had campaigned for "the forgotten man at the bottom of the economic pyramid," and some radicals argued that the early New Deal had forgotten the forgotten man. Communists and socialists focused public attention on the poor, especially in the countryside. In California, communists organized Mexican, Filipino, and Japanese farm workers into the Cannery and Agricultural Workers Union; in Arkansas and Tennessee, socialists in 1934 helped organize sharecroppers into the Southern Tenant Farmers Union, protesting the "Raw Deal" they had received from the AAA. Even without the involvement of socialists or communists, labor militancy in 1934 pressed Roosevelt. The number of workers participating in strikes leaped from 325,000 in 1932 (about the annual average since 1925) to 1.5 million in 1934.

Watch the Video
at **www.myhistorylab.com**
Responding to the Great Depression: Whose New Deal?

Read the Document
at **www.myhistorylab.com**
E. E. Lewis, Black Cotton Farmers and the AAA (1935)

Rebuffing FDR's pleas for fair treatment, employers moved to crush the strikes, often using complaisant police and private strikebreakers. In Minneapolis, police shot 67 teamsters, almost all in the back, as they fled an ambush arranged by employers; in Toledo, company police and National Guardsmen attacked autoworkers with tear gas, bayonets, and rifle fire; in the textile strike, police killed six picketers in South Carolina, and soldiers wounded another 50 in Rhode Island. Against such powerful opponents, workers needed help to achieve their rights. Harry Hopkins and other New Dealers realized that labor's demands could not be ignored.

Four prominent individuals mobilized popular discontent to demand government action to assist groups neglected by the New Deal. Representative William Lemke of North Dakota, an agrarian radical leader of the Nonpartisan League, called attention to rural distress. Lemke objected to the New Deal's limited response to farmers crushed by the depression. In his own state, nearly two-thirds of the farmers had lost their land through foreclosures.

Francis Townsend, a California physician, proposed to aid the nation's elderly, many of whom were destitute. The Townsend Plan called for a government pension to every American over the age of 60, provided that the recipient retired from work and spent the entire pension. This scheme promised to extend relief to the elderly, open jobs for the unemployed, and stimulate economic recovery. Over 5,000 Townsend Clubs lobbied for government action to help the elderly poor.

Father Charles Coughlin, a Catholic priest in the Detroit suburb of Royal Oak, threatened to mobilize another large constituency against the limitations of the early New Deal. Thirty million Americans listened eagerly to his weekly radio broadcasts, which mixed religion with anti-Semitism and demands for social justice and financial reform. Coughlin had condemned Hoover for assisting banks but ignoring the unemployed, and initially he welcomed the New Deal as "Christ's Deal." But after concluding that FDR's policies favored "the virile viciousness of business and finance," Coughlin organized the National Union for Social Justice to lobby for

QUICK REVIEW

Critique of the New Deal

- Conservative critics of the expansion of government gained little support.
- Many on the left saw the early New Deal as a "Raw Deal."
- Popular pressure mounted for more aggressive policies.

his goals. With support among lower-middle-class, heavily Catholic, urban ethnic groups, Coughlin posed a real challenge to Roosevelt's Democratic Party.

Roosevelt found Senator Huey P. Long of Louisiana still more worrisome. Alternately charming and autocratic, Long had modernized his state with taxation and educational reforms and an extensive public-works program after his election as governor in 1928. Moving to the Senate and eyeing the White House, Long proposed more comprehensive social-welfare policies than the New Deal had envisaged. In 1934, he organized the Share-Our-Wealth Society. His plan to end poverty and unemployment called for confiscatory taxes on the rich to provide every family with a decent income, health coverage, education, and old-age pensions. Long's appeal was enormous. Within months, his organization claimed more than 27,000 clubs and 7 million members.

These dissident movements raised complex issues and simple fears. They built on concerns about the New Deal, both demanding government assistance and fretting about government intrusion. Their programs were often ill-defined or impractical—Townsend's plan would cost more than half the national income; and some of the leaders, like Coughlin and Long, approached demagoguery. Nevertheless, their popularity warned Roosevelt that government action was needed to satisfy reform demands and ensure his reelection in 1936.

CONSOLIDATING THE NEW DEAL

WHAT WERE the major accomplishments of the Second New Deal?

Responding to the persistence of the depression and political pressures, Roosevelt in 1935 undertook economic and social reforms that some observers have called the Second New Deal. The new measures shifted government action more toward reform even as they still addressed relief and recovery. Nor did FDR's interest in reform simply reflect cynical politics. He had frequently championed progressive measures in the past, and many of his advisers had deep roots in reform movements. After the 1934 elections gave the president an even more Democratic Congress, Harry Hopkins exulted: "Boys—this is our hour. We've got to get everything we want—a works program, social security, wages and hours, everything—now or never."

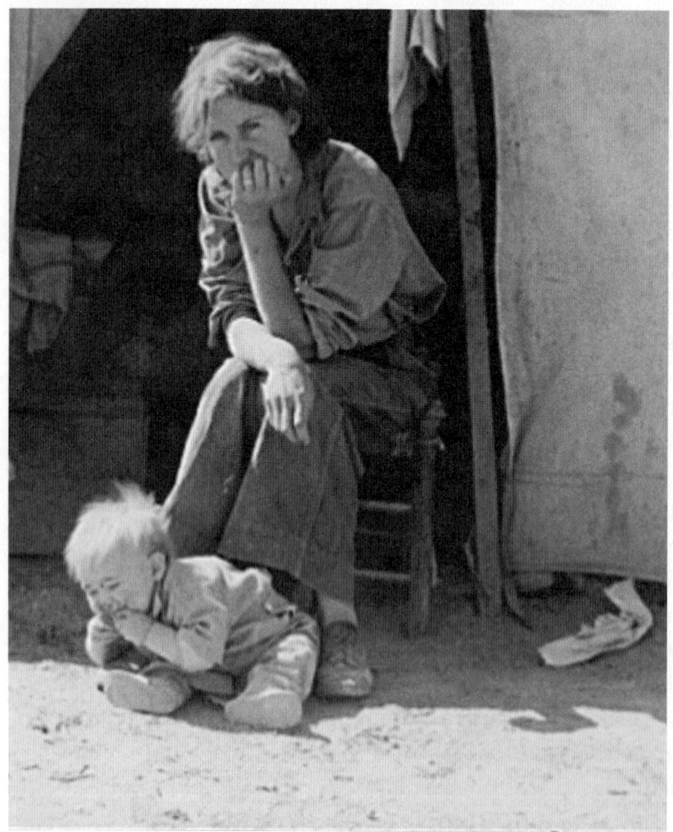

The New Deal enabled photographers and artists to take to the road to capture images of the nation's dispossessed. This photograph by Dorothea Lange of an 18-year-old mother and her child in a migrant labor camp in 1937 illustrates both despair and detachment and conveys the hardship of homelessness and deprivation in the Great Depression.

WEEDING OUT AND LIFTING UP

"In spite of our efforts and in spite of our talk," Roosevelt told the new Congress in 1935, "we have not weeded out the overprivileged and we have not effectively lifted up the underprivileged." To do so, he developed "must" legislation. One of the new laws protected labor's rights to organize and bargain collectively. The Wagner National Labor Relations Act, dubbed "Labor's Magna Carta," guaranteed workers the right to organize unions and prohibited employers from adopting unfair labor practices, such as firing union activists and forming company unions. The law also set up the National Labor Relations Board (NLRB) to enforce these provisions, protect workers from coercion, and supervise union elections.

Social security. Of greater long-range importance was the Social Security Act. Other industrial nations had established national social-insurance systems much earlier, but only the Great Depression moved the United States to accept the idea that the federal government should protect the poor and unemployed. Even so, the law was a compromise, framed by a nonpartisan committee of business, labor, and public representatives and then weakened by congressional conservatives. It provided unemployment compensation, old-age pensions, and aid for dependent mothers and children and the blind.

The conservative nature of the law appeared in its stingy benefit payments, its lack of health insurance, and its exclusion of more than one-fourth of all workers, including many in desperate need of protection, such as farm laborers and domestic servants. Moreover, unlike in other nations, the old-age pensions were financed through a regressive payroll tax on both employees and employers rather than through general tax revenues. Thus the new system was more like a compulsory insurance program.

Despite its weaknesses, the Social Security Act was one of the most important laws in American history and Roosevelt was justifiably proud. It provided, he pointed out, "at least some measure of protection to the average citizen and to his family against the loss of a job and against poverty-ridden old age." Moreover, by establishing federal responsibility for social welfare, it inaugurated a welfare system that subsequent generations would expand.

Read the **Document**
at www.myhistorylab.com
From Then to Now Online: Social Security

QUICK REVIEW

The Social Security Act

- Provided unemployment compensation, old-age pensions, and aid for dependent mothers and children and the blind.
- The law excluded more than a fourth of all workers and did not include health insurance.
- Funded by a regressive payroll tax.

Read the **Document**
at www.myhistorylab.com
Exploring America: The Dust Bowl

Money, tax, and land reform. Another reform measure, the Banking Act of 1935, increased the authority of the Federal Reserve Board over the nation's currency and credit system and decreased the power of the private bankers whose irresponsible behavior had contributed to the depression and the appeal of Father Coughlin. The Revenue Act of 1935 provided for graduated income taxes and increased estate and corporate taxes. Opponents called it the Soak the Rich Tax, but with its many loopholes, it was scarcely that and was certainly not a redistributive measure such as Huey Long had proposed. Nevertheless, it set a precedent for progressive taxation and attracted popular support.

The Second New Deal also responded belatedly to the environmental catastrophe that had turned much of the Great Plains from Texas to the Dakotas into a Dust Bowl (see Map 25–1). Since World War I, farmers had stripped marginal land of its native grasses to plant wheat. When drought and high winds hit the plains in 1932, crops failed, and nothing was left to hold the soil. Dust storms blew away millions of tons of topsoil, despoiling the land and darkening the sky a thousand miles away. Families abandoned their farms in droves. Many of these poor "Okies" headed for California, their plight captured in John Steinbeck's novel, *The Grapes of Wrath* (1939).

In 1935, Roosevelt established the Resettlement Administration to focus on land reform and help poor farmers. Under Rexford Tugwell, this agency initiated soil erosion projects and attempted to resettle impoverished farmers on better land, but the problem exceeded its resources. Congress moved to save the land, if not its people, by creating the Soil Conservation Service in 1935.

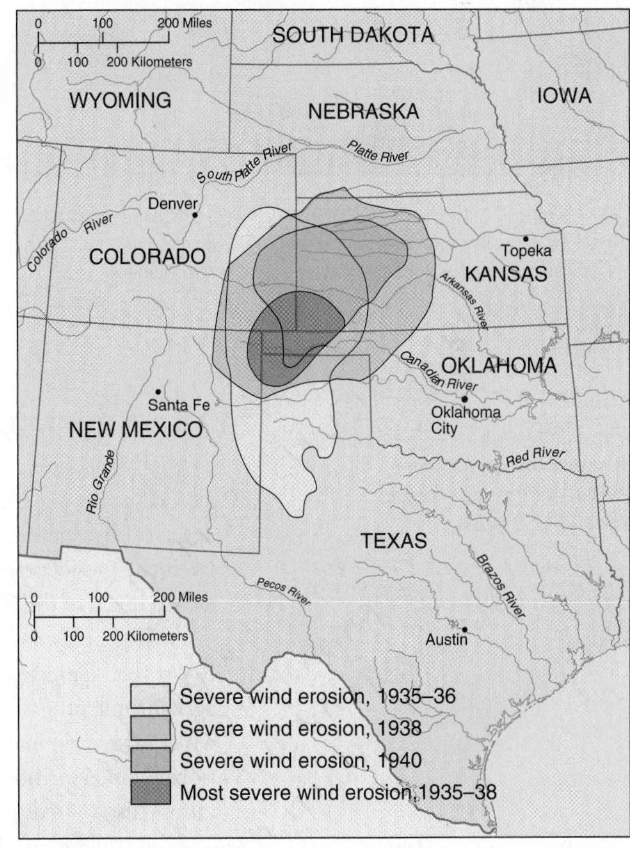

MAP 25–1 **The Dust Bowl** Years of overcultivation, drought, and high winds created the Dust Bowl, which most severely affected the southern Great Plains. Federal relief and conservation programs provided assistance, but many residents fled the area, often migrating to California.

Why were farmers on the Great Plains particularly vulnerable to environmental disaster?

Expanding Relief

If reform gained priority in the Second New Deal, relief remained critical. With millions still unemployed, Roosevelt pushed through Congress in 1935 the Emergency Relief Appropriation Act, authorizing $5 billion—at the time the largest single appropriation in American history—for emergency public employment. Roosevelt created the Works Progress Administration (WPA) under Hopkins, who set up work relief programs to assist the unemployed and boost the economy. Before its end in 1943, the WPA gave jobs to 9 million people (more than a fifth of the labor

Eleanor Roosevelt campaigns with FDR in Fremont, Nebraska, in 1935. A visible activist for social and economic reform, she was also politically important in building the powerful Roosevelt coalition. "Previously," said the journalist Ruby Black, "a President's wife acted as if she didn't know that a political party existed."

force) and spent nearly $12 billion. Three-fourths of its expenditures went on construction projects that could employ manual labor: The WPA built 125,000 schools, post offices, and hospitals; 8,000 parks; nearly 100,000 bridges; and enough roads and sewer systems to circle the earth 30 times. The WPA laid much of the basic infrastructure on which the nation still relies.

The WPA also developed work projects for unemployed writers, artists, musicians, and actors. "Why not?" said FDR. "They are human beings. They have to live." WPA programs allowed people to use their talents while surviving the depression, increased popular access to cultural performances, and established a precedent for federal support of the arts.

The National Youth Administration (NYA), another WPA agency, gave part-time jobs to students, enabling 2 million high school and college students to stay in school, learn skills, and do productive work. At the University of Nebraska, NYA students built an observatory; at Duke University, law student Richard M. Nixon earned 35 cents an hour doing research in the library. Lyndon Johnson, a Texas NYA official, believed that "if the Roosevelt administration had never done another thing, it would have been justified by the work of this great institution for salvaging youth."

Watch the Video
at **www.myhistorylab.com**
President Roosevelt Focuses on America's Youth

The Roosevelt Coalition and the Election of 1936

The 1936 election gave Americans an opportunity to judge FDR and the New Deal. Conservatives alarmed at the expansion of government, businesspeople angered by regulation and labor legislation, and wealthy Americans furious with tax reform decried the New Deal. But they were a minority. Even the presidential candidate they supported, Republican Governor Alf Landon of Kansas, endorsed much of the New Deal, criticizing merely the inefficiency and cost of some of its programs.

The programs and politicians of the New Deal had created an invincible coalition behind Roosevelt. Despite ambivalence about large-scale government intervention, the New Deal's agricultural programs reinforced the traditional Democratic allegiance of white southerners while attracting many western farmers. Labor legislation clinched the active support of the nation's workers. Middle-class voters, whose homes had been saved and whose hopes had been raised, also joined the Roosevelt coalition.

So did urban ethnic groups, who had benefited from welfare programs and appreciated the unprecedented recognition Roosevelt's administration gave them. African Americans voted overwhelmingly Democratic for the first time. Women, too, were an important part of the Roosevelt coalition, and Eleanor Roosevelt often attracted their support as much as Franklin did.

This political realignment produced a landslide. Roosevelt polled 61 percent of the popular vote and the largest electoral vote margin ever recorded, 523 to 8. Democrats also won huge majorities in Congress. Roosevelt's political coalition reflected a mandate for himself and the New Deal; it would enable the Democrats to dominate national elections for three decades.

THE NEW DEAL AND AMERICAN LIFE

WHAT IMPACT did the New Deal have on American social and economic life?

The landslide of 1936 revealed the impact of the New Deal on Americans. Industrial workers mobilized to secure their rights, women and minorities gained increased, if still limited, opportunities to participate in American society, and southerners and westerners benefited from government programs they turned to their own advantage. Government programs changed daily life, and ordinary people often helped shape the new policies.

Labor on the March

The labor revival in the 1930s reflected both workers' determination and government support. Workers wanted to improve their wages and benefits as well as to gain union recognition and union contracts that would allow them to limit arbitrary managerial authority and achieve some control over the workplace. This larger goal provoked opposition from employers and their allies and required workers to organize, strike, and become politically active. Their achievement was remarkable.

The Second New Deal helped. By guaranteeing labor's rights to organize and bargain collectively, the Wagner Act sparked a wave of labor activism. But if the government ultimately protected union rights, the unions themselves had to form locals, recruit members, and demonstrate influence in the workplace.

At first, those tasks overwhelmed the American Federation of Labor (AFL). Its reliance on craft-based unions and reluctance to organize immigrant, black, and women workers left it unprepared for the rush of industrial workers seeking unionization. More progressive labor leaders saw that industry-wide unions were more appropriate for unskilled workers in mass-production industries. Forming the Committee for Industrial Organization (CIO) within the AFL, they campaigned to unionize workers in the steel, auto, and rubber industries, all notoriously hostile to unions. AFL leaders insisted that the CIO disband and then in 1937 expelled its unions. The militants reorganized as the separate **Congress of Industrial Organizations.** (In 1955, the two groups merged as the AFL-CIO.)

Congress of Industrial Organizations (CIO) An alliance of industrial unions that spurred the 1930s organizational drive among the mass-production industries.

The split roused the AFL to increase its own organizing activities, but it was primarily the new CIO that put labor on the march. It inspired workers previously neglected by organized labor. The CIO's interracial union campaign in the Birmingham steel mills, said one organizer, was "like a second coming of Christ" for black workers, who welcomed the union as a chance for social recognition as well as economic opportunity. The CIO also employed new and aggressive tactics, particularly the sit-down strike, in which workers, rather than picketing outside the factory, simply sat inside the plant, thereby blocking both production and the use of strikebreakers.

The CIO won major victories despite bitter opposition from industry and its allies. The issue was not wages but labor's right to organize and bargain with management. Sit-down strikes paralyzed General Motors in 1937 after it refused to recognize the United Auto Workers. GM tried to force the strikers out of its Flint, Michigan, plants by turning off the heat, using police and tear gas, threatening strikers' families, and obtaining court orders to clear the plant by military force. But the governor refused to order National Guardsmen to attack, and the strikers held out, aided by the Women's Emergency Brigade, working-class women who picketed the building, heckled the police, and smuggled food to the strikers. After six weeks, GM signed a contract with the UAW. Chrysler soon followed suit. Ford refused to recognize the union until 1941, often violently disrupting organizing efforts.

QUICK REVIEW

A New Deal for Labor

- The Wagner Act stimulated labor activism.
- The CIO organized workers in the steel, auto, and rubber industries.
- Union membership rose from 3 million in 1932 to 9 million in 1939.

Steel companies also used violence against unionization. In the Memorial Day Massacre in Chicago in 1937, police guarding a plant of the Republic Steel Company fired on strikers and their families, killing ten people as they tried to flee. A Senate investigation found that Republic and other companies had hired private police to attack workers seeking to unionize, stockpiled weapons and tear gas, and corrupted officials. Federal court orders finally forced the companies to bargain collectively.

New Deal labor legislation, government investigations and court orders, and the federal refusal to use force against strikes helped the labor movement secure basic rights for American workers. Union membership leaped from under 3 million in 1932 to 9 million by 1939, and workers won higher wages, better working conditions, and more economic democracy.

Women and the New Deal

New Deal relief programs had a mixed impact on working women. Formal government policy required equal consideration for women and men, but local officials flouted this requirement. Women on relief were restricted to women's work—more than half worked on sewing projects, regardless of their skills—and were paid scarcely half what men received. WPA training programs also reinforced traditional ideas about women's work; black women, for example, were trained to be maids, dishwashers, and cooks. Although women constituted nearly one-fourth of the labor force, they obtained only 19 percent of the jobs created by the WPA, 12 percent of those created by the FERA, and 7 percent of those created by the CWA. The CCC excluded women altogether. Still, relief agencies provided crucial assistance to women during the depression.

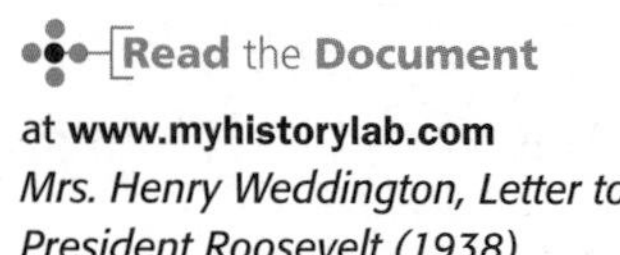

Read the **Document**
at www.myhistorylab.com
Mrs. Henry Weddington, Letter to President Roosevelt (1938)

Other New Deal programs also had mixed benefits for women. Many NRA codes mandated lower wage scales for women than for men, which officials justified as reflecting long-established customs. But by raising minimum wages, the NRA brought relatively greater improvement to women, who were concentrated in the lowest paid occupations, than to male workers. The Social Security Act did not cover domestic servants, waitresses, or women who worked in the home, but it did help mothers with dependent children.

Still more significant, the Social Security Act reflected and reinforced prevailing notions about proper roles for men and women. The system was based on the idea that men should be wage earners and women should stay at home as wives and mothers. Accordingly, if a woman worked outside the home and her husband was eligible for benefits, she would not receive her own retirement pension. And if a woman had no husband but had children, welfare authorities would remove her from work-relief jobs regardless of whether she wanted to continue to work, and would give her assistance from the Aid to Dependent Children (ADC) program, which was also created under the Social Security Act. These new programs, then, while providing much-needed assistance, also institutionalized a modern welfare system that segregated men and women in separate spheres and reaffirmed the then popular belief that the success of the family depended on that separation.

With an appointment in the National Youth Administration, the educator Mary McLeod Bethune was the highest-ranking African American woman in the Roosevelt administration. She advised FDR on all racial matters and envisioned "dozens of Negro women coming after me, filling positions of trust and strategic importance."

Women also gained political influence under the New Deal. Molly Dewson, the director of the Women's Division of the Democratic Party, exercised considerable political power and helped to shape the party's campaigns. Around Dewson revolved a network of women, linked by friendships and experiences in the National Consumers' League, Women's Trade Union League, and other progressive reform organizations. Appointed to many positions in the Roosevelt administration, they helped develop and implement New Deal social legislation. Secretary of Labor Frances Perkins was the first woman cabinet member and a key member of the network; other women were in the Treasury Department, the Children's Bureau, and relief and cultural programs.

Eleanor Roosevelt was their leader. Described by a Washington reporter as "a cabinet member without portfolio," she roared across the social and political landscape of the 1930s, pushing for women's rights, demanding reforms, traveling across the country, writing newspaper columns and speaking on the radio, developing plans to help unemployed miners in West Virginia and abolish slums in Washington, and lobbying both Congress and her husband. FDR used her as his eyes and ears and sometimes his conscience. Indeed, Eleanor Roosevelt had become not merely the most prominent first lady in history but a force in her own right and a symbol of the growing importance of women in public life.

Minorities and the New Deal

Despite the move of African Americans into the Democratic Party, the New Deal's record on racial issues was limited. Although Roosevelt deplored racial abuses, he never pushed for civil rights legislation, fearing to antagonize southern congressional Democrats whose support he needed. For similar reasons, many New Deal programs discriminated against African Americans. And racist officials discriminated in allocating federal relief. Atlanta, for instance, provided average monthly relief checks of $32.66 to white people but only $19.29 to black people.

Nonetheless, disproportionately poor and unemployed African Americans did benefit from the New Deal's welfare and economic programs. W. E. B. Du Bois asserted that "large numbers of colored people in the United States would have starved to death if it had not been for the Roosevelt policies," adding that the New Deal served to sharpen their sense of the value of citizenship by making clear the "direct connection between politics and industry, between government and work, [and] between voting and wages." And key New Dealers campaigned against racial discrimination. Eleanor Roosevelt prodded FDR to appoint black officials, wrote articles supporting racial equality, and flouted segregationist laws. Attacked by white racists, she was popular in the black community. Harry Hopkins and Harold Ickes also promoted equal rights. As black votes in northern cities became important, pragmatic New Dealers also began to pay attention to black needs.

QUICK REVIEW

Impact of the New Deal on Women

- Despite their numbers in the workforce, women received proportionately fewer New Deal jobs than men.
- The increase in the minimum wage brought relatively greater improvements to workers in the lowest-paying jobs, most of whom were women.
- Women gained political influence under the New Deal.

QUICK REVIEW

African Americans and the New Deal

- Many New Deal programs discriminated against African Americans.
- Key New Dealers campaigned against discrimination.
- African Americans pressed for reforms.
- The New Deal improved economic and social conditions for many African Americans.

African Americans themselves pressed for reforms. Civil rights groups protested discriminatory policies, including the unequal wage scales in the NRA codes and the CCC's limited enrollment of black youth. African Americans demonstrated against racial discrimination in hiring and their exclusion from federally financed construction projects.

In response, FDR took more interest in black economic and social problems. He prohibited discrimination in the WPA in 1935, and the NYA adopted enlightened racial policies. Roosevelt also appointed black people to important positions, including the first black federal judge. Many of these officials began meeting regularly at the home of Mary McLeod Bethune of the National Council of Negro Women. Dubbed the Black Cabinet, they worked with civil rights organizations, fought discrimination in government, influenced patronage, and stimulated black interest in politics.

The New Deal improved economic and social conditions for many African Americans. Black illiteracy dropped because of federal education projects, and the number of black college students and graduates more than doubled, in part because the NYA provided student aid to black colleges. New Deal relief and public health programs reduced black infant mortality rates and raised life expectancy rates. Conditions for black people continued to lag behind those for white people, and discrimination persisted, but the black switch to the Roosevelt coalition reflected the New Deal's benefits.

Native Americans also benefited from the New Deal. The depression had imposed further misery on a group already suffering from poverty, wretched health conditions, and the nation's lowest educational level. Many New Deal programs had limited applicability to Indians, but the CCC appealed to their interests and skills. More than 80,000 Native Americans received training in agriculture, forestry, and animal husbandry, along with basic academic subjects. CCC projects, together with those undertaken by the PWA and the WPA, built schools, hospitals, roads, and irrigation systems on reservations.

New Deal officials also refocused government Indian policy, which had undermined tribal authority and promoted assimilation by reducing Indian landholding and attacking Indian culture. Appointed commissioner of Indian affairs in 1933, John Collier prohibited interference with Native American religious or cultural life, directed the Bureau of Indian Affairs to employ more Native Americans, and prevented Indian schools from suppressing native languages and traditions.

Collier also persuaded Congress to pass the Indian Reorganization Act of 1934, often called the Indians' New Deal. The act guaranteed religious freedom, reestablished tribal self-government, and halted the sale of tribal lands. It also provided funds to expand Indian land-holdings, support Indian students, and establish tribal businesses. But social and economic problems persisted on the isolated reservations, and white missionaries and business interests attacked Collier's reforms as atheistic and communistic. And not all Native Americans supported Collier's reforms, asserting that he, too, stereotyped Indians and their culture, and labeling his efforts as "back-to-the-blanket" policies designed to make Native American cultures historical commodities. (See American Views, The Commissioner of the Bureau of Indian Affairs on the New Deal for Native Americans.)

Read the **Document**
at **www.myhistorylab.com**
Caroline Manning, The Immigrant Woman and Her Job (1930)

Hispanic Americans received less assistance from the New Deal. Relief programs aided many Hispanics in California and the Southwest but ignored those who were not citizens. Moreover, local administrators often discriminated against Hispanics, especially by providing higher relief payments to Anglos. Finally, by excluding agricultural workers, neither the Social Security Act nor the Wagner Act gave Mexican Americans much protection or hope. Farm workers remained largely unorganized, exploited, and at the mercy of agribusinesses.

The New Deal: North, South, East, and West

"We are going to make a country," President Roosevelt declared, "in which no one is left out." And with that statement, along with his belief that the federal government must take the lead in building a new "economic constitutional order," FDR ensured that his New Deal programs and policies fanned out throughout the nation.

The New Deal in the South. The New Deal's agricultural program boosted farm prices and income more in the South than any other region. By controlling cotton production, it also promoted diversification; its subsidies financed mechanization. The resulting modernization helped replace an archaic sharecropping system with an emergent agribusiness. The rural poor were displaced, but the South's agricultural economy advanced.

The New Deal also improved southern cities. FERA and WPA built urban sewer systems, airports, bridges, roads, and harbor facilities. Whereas northern cities had already constructed such facilities themselves—and were still paying off the debts these had incurred—the federal government largely paid for such modernization in the South, giving its cities an economic advantage.

Federal grants were supposed to be awarded to states in proportion to their own expenditures, but while southern politicians welcomed New Deal funds, they refused to contribute their share of the costs. Nationally, the federal proportion of FERA expenditures was 62 percent; in the South, it was usually 90 percent and never lower than 73 percent.

Federal money enabled southern communities to balance their budgets, preach fiscal orthodoxy, and maintain traditional claims of limited government. Federal officials complained about the South's "parasitic" behavior in accepting aid but not responsibility, and even southerners acknowledged the hypocrisy of the region's invocation of states' rights. "We recognize state boundaries when called on to give," noted the *Houston Press*, "but forget them when Uncle Sam is doing the giving."

Tennessee Valley Authority Federal regional planning agency established to promote conservation, produce electric power, and encourage economic development in seven southern states.

The federal government had a particularly powerful impact on the South with the **Tennessee Valley Authority (TVA),** launched in 1933 (see Map 25–2). Coordinating activities across seven states, the TVA built dams to control floods and generate hydroelectric power, produced fertilizer, fostered agricultural and forestry development, encouraged conservation, improved

AMERICAN VIEWS

The Commissioner of the Bureau of Indian Affairs on the New Deal for Native Americans

John Collier, reformer and social worker, served as commissioner of the Bureau of Indian Affairs (BIA) from 1933 until 1945. During his tenure, he radically transformed the agency—long known to be corrupt and hostile to Native Americans—into an organization committed to the preservation of tribal cultures and the restoration of Indian lands. Like other New Dealers, Collier attempted to use the power of the federal government to protect those with limited political power and economic influence—in this case Native Americans.

Collier was extraordinarily successful in promoting the restoration of tribal rights and autonomy and helped ensure that future generations of Indians could reclaim their lands. Yet he was frustrated by Congress's unwillingness to fund the programs he believed necessary for a genuine New Deal for Native Americans. In his 1938 annual report, he calls for greater economic support, arguing that it would be a good investment for the nation. Most important, even as he acknowledges that real changes have occurred since 1933, he points out that there is still much to be done to achieve political autonomy and economic self-sufficiency for American Indians.

- **How** did Collier describe the treatment of Native Americans, and why did white Americans regard Indians as a "problem" to be eliminated?
- **What** were the new goals of the Bureau of Indian Affairs?
- **How** did Collier regard the role of land in Native American society? Why?
- **What** was the greatest challenge Collier saw for Native Americans in 1938?

For nearly 300 years white Americans, in our zeal to carve out a nation made to order, have dealt with the Indians on the erroneous, yet tragic, assumption that the Indians were a dying race—to be liquidated. We took away their best lands; broke treaties, promises; tossed them the most nearly worthless scraps of a continent that had once been wholly theirs. But we did not liquidate their spirit. The vital spark which kept them alive was hardy. So hardy, indeed, that we now face an astounding and heartening fact.

Actually, the Indians, on the evidence of federal census rolls of the past eight years, are increasing almost twice the rate of the population as a whole.

With this fact before us, our whole attitude toward the Indians has necessarily undergone a profound change. Dead is the centuries-old notion that the sooner we eliminate this doomed race, preferably humanely, the better. . . . No longer can we naively talk of or think of the "Indian problem."

We, therefore, define our Indian policy somewhat as follows: So productively to use the moneys appropriated by the Congress for Indians as to enable them, on good, adequate land of their own, to earn decent livelihoods and lead self-respecting, organized lives in harmony with their own aims and ideals, as an integral part of American life. This will not happen tomorrow; perhaps not in our lifetime; but with the revitalization of Indian hope due to the actions and attitudes of this government during the last few years, that aim is a probability, and a real one. . . . So intimately is all of Indian life tied up with the land and its utilization that to think of Indians is to think of land. The two are inseparable. Upon the land and its intelligent use depends the main future of the American Indian.

The Indian feels toward his land, not a mere ownership but a devotion and veneration befitting that what is not only a home but a refuge. . . . Not only does the Indian's major source of livelihood derive from the land but his social and political organizations are rooted in soil.

Since 1933, the Indian Service has made a concerted effort—an effort which is as yet but a mere beginning—to help the Indian to build back his landholdings to a point where they will provide an adequate basis for a self-sustaining economy, a self-satisfying social organization.

Source: John Collier. Annual Report of the Secretary of the Interior for the Fiscal Year Ended June 30, 1938. From http://historymatters.gmu.edu/.

navigation, and modernized school and health systems. Private utility companies denounced the TVA as socialistic, but most southerners supported it. Its major drawback was environmental damage that only became apparent later. Over a vast area of the South, it provided electricity for the first time.

Read the **Document**
at www.myhistorylab.com
Tennessee Valley Authority Act (1933)

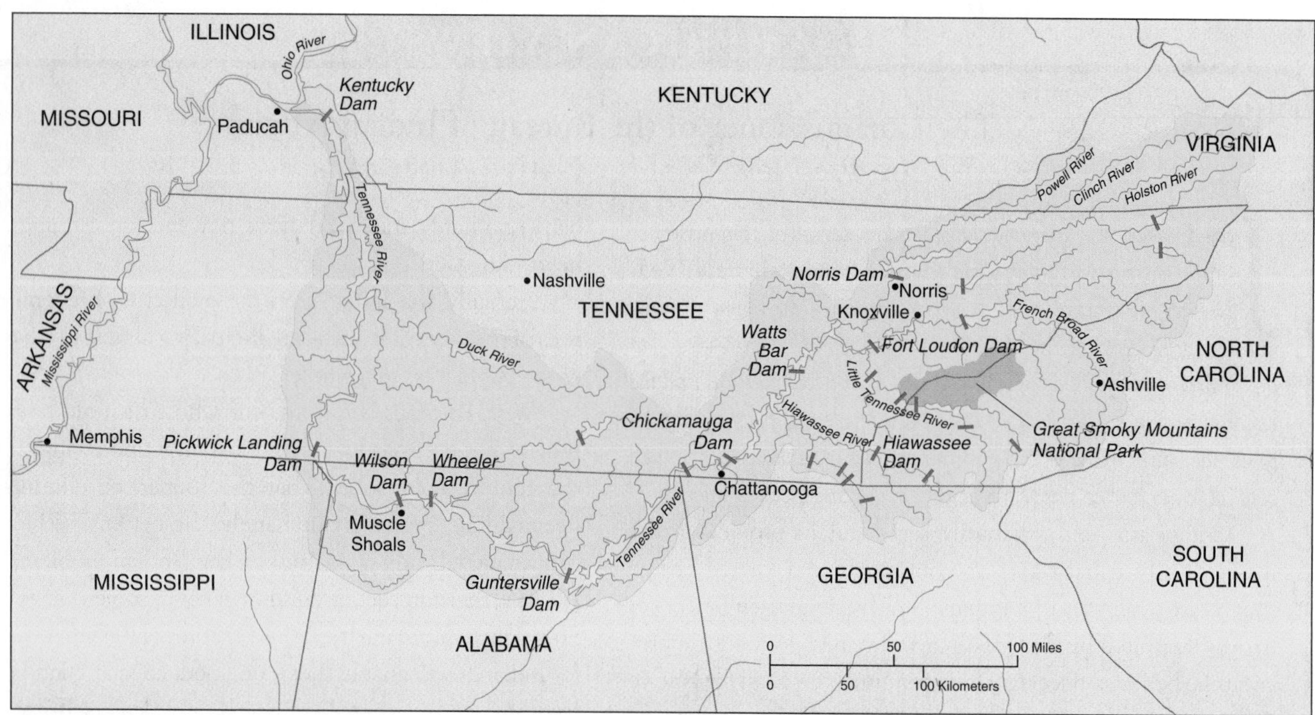

MAP 25–2 **The Tennessee Valley Authority** By building dams and hydroelectric power plants, the TVA controlled flooding and soil erosion and generated electricity that did much to modernize a large region of the Upper South.

Which states benefited the most from the activities of the Tennessee Valley Authority? Why was federal intervention so important in the modernization of this region?

The New Deal further expanded access to electricity by establishing the Rural Electrification Administration (REA) in 1935. Private companies had refused to extend power lines into the countryside because it was not profitable, consigning 90 percent of the nation's farms to drudgery and darkness. The REA revolutionized farm life by sponsoring rural nonprofit electric cooperatives. By 1941, 35 percent of American farms had electricity; by 1950, 78 percent.

The New Deal in the West. The New Deal also changed the West. Westerners received the most federal money per capita in welfare, relief projects, and loans. Like southerners, they accepted federal aid and clamored for more.

The Bureau of Reclamation, established in 1902, emerged as one of the most important government agencies in the West. It built huge dams to control the western river systems and promote large-scale development. By furnishing capital and expertise, the government subsidized and stimulated western economic development, particularly the growth of agribusiness.

Westerners welcomed such assistance but rarely shared the federal goals of rational resource management. Instead, they often wanted to continue to exploit the land and resented federal supervision as colonial control. In practice, however, the government worked in partnership with the West's agribusinesses and timber and petroleum industries.

The New Deal and Public Activism

Despite Hoover's fear that government responsibility would discourage local initiative, the 1930s witnessed an upsurge in activism. New Deal programs, in fact, often encouraged or empowered groups to shape public policy. Moreover, because the administration worried about centralization, some federal agencies fostered what New Dealers called "grassroots democracy." The AAA set up committees that ultimately included more than 100,000 people to implement agricultural policy and held referendums on crop controls; local advisory committees guided the various federal arts projects; federal management of the West's public grasslands mandated cooperation with associations of livestock raisers.

At times, local administration of national programs enabled groups to exploit federal policy for their own advantage. Wealthy planters shaped AAA practices at the expense of poor tenant farmers; local control of TVA projects excluded black people. But federal programs often allowed previously unrepresented groups to contest traditionally dominant interests. Often seeing greater opportunities for participation and influence in federal programs than in city and state governments, community groups campaigned to expand federal authority. In short, depression conditions and New Deal programs actually increased citizen involvement in public affairs.

EBBING OF THE NEW DEAL

WHY DID the New Deal lose momentum after 1936?

After his victory in 1936, Roosevelt committed himself to further reforms. But determined opponents, continuing economic problems, and the president's own misjudgments blocked his reforms and deadlocked the New Deal.

Challenging the Court

Roosevelt regarded the Supreme Court as his most dangerous opponent. During his first term, the Court had declared several important measures unconstitutional. Indeed, most of the justices were elderly conservatives, appointed by Republicans and unsympathetic to an activist federal government. It seemed that the Court would also strike down the Second New Deal.

Emboldened by the 1936 landslide, Roosevelt decided to restructure the federal judiciary. In early 1937, he proposed legislation authorizing the president to name a new justice for each one serving past the age of 70. Additional justices, he said, would increase judicial efficiency. But his real goal was to appoint new justices more sympathetic to the New Deal.

His Court plan led to a divisive struggle. The proposal was perfectly legal: Congress had the authority, which it had used repeatedly, to change the number of justices on the Court. But Republicans and conservative Democrats attacked the plan as a scheme to "pack" the Court and subvert the separation of powers among the three branches of government. Some conservatives called the president a dictator, but even many liberals expressed reservations about the plan or FDR's lack of candor in proposing it.

The Court itself undercut support for FDR's proposal by upholding the Social Security and Wagner acts and minimum-wage legislation. Moreover, the retirement of a conservative justice allowed Roosevelt to name a sympathetic successor. Congress rejected Roosevelt's plan.

Roosevelt's challenge to the Court hurt the New Deal. It worried the public, split the Democratic Party, and revived conservatives. Opponents promptly attacked other New Deal policies, from support for unions to progressive taxation. Henceforth, a conservative coalition of Republicans and southern Democrats in Congress blocked FDR's reforms.

More Hard Times

A sharp recession, beginning in August 1937, added to Roosevelt's problems. The New Deal's deficit spending had reflected his desire to alleviate suffering, not a conviction that it would stimulate economic recovery. As the economy improved in 1936, Roosevelt decided to cut federal expenditures and balance the budget. But private investment and employment remained stagnant, and the economy plunged.

In 1938, Roosevelt reluctantly increased spending. New appropriations for the PWA and other government programs revived the faltering economy, but neither FDR nor Congress would spend what was necessary to end the depression. Only the vast expenditures for World War II would bring full recovery.

Political Stalemate

The recession interrupted the momentum of the New Deal and strengthened its opponents. In late 1937, their leaders in Congress issued a "conservative manifesto" decrying New Deal fiscal, labor, and regulatory policies. Holding seniority in a Congress malapportioned in their favor, they blocked most of Roosevelt's reforms. None of his must legislation passed a special session of Congress in December. In 1938, Congress rejected tax reforms and reduced corporate taxes. The few measures that passed were heavily amended.

To protect the New Deal, Roosevelt turned again to the public, with whom he remained immensely popular. In the 1938 Democratic primaries, he campaigned against the New Deal's conservative opponents. But FDR could not transfer his personal popularity to the political newcomers he supported. What his foes attacked as a purge failed. Roosevelt lost further political leverage when the Republicans gained 75 seats in the House and seven in the Senate and 13 governorships.

The 1938 elections did not repudiate the New Deal, for the Democrats retained majorities in both houses of Congress. But the Republican revival and the survival of the conservative southern Democrats guaranteed that the New Deal had gone as far as it ever would. With Roosevelt in the White House and his opponents controlling Congress, the New Deal ended in political stalemate.

GOOD NEIGHBORS AND HOSTILE FORCES

HOW DID Roosevelt respond to the rise of fascism in Europe?

Even before FDR's conservative opponents derailed the New Deal, the president felt their impact in the area of foreign policy. Isolationists in Congress counseled against any U.S. involvement in world affairs and appealed to the growing national disillusionment with America's participation in the Great War to support their position. Moreover, Roosevelt himself, although not an isolationist, believed that the gravity of the nation's economic depression warranted a primary focus on domestic recovery, and in the early years of his presidency, took few international initiatives.

The actions he did take related directly to salvaging America's desperate economy. As the depression worsened in 1933, American businesses searched for new markets throughout the world, and key business leaders informed FDR that they would welcome the opportunity to expand trade to the Soviet Union. Moscow was also eager to renew ties to the United States, and President Roosevelt extended formal recognition of the Soviet Union in November 1933.

Enhancing trade opportunities and rescuing the economy from the damage wrought by high tariffs figured prominently in Roosevelt's policies in the Western Hemisphere. In large measure, Roosevelt merely extended the Good Neighbor policy begun by his predecessor. Hoover had abandoned the U.S. policy of interventionism, and by the time he left office in March 1933, all U.S. troops had been removed from Latin America. Still, the Great Depression strained U.S.-Latin American relations, sending economic shock waves throughout Central and South America and, in several instances, helping propel to power ruthless dictators who ruled with iron fists and U.S. support.

To symbolize that the United States was a "good neighbor," FDR visited the Caribbean in 1934, receiving an enthusiastic reception, and in 1936, he broke new ground by becoming the first U.S. president to sail to South America. He also worked to encourage trade by reducing tariffs.

Neutrality and Fascism

Outside the hemisphere, during his first term as president, Roosevelt generally followed the policy of avoiding involvement in Europe's political, economic, and social problems. But the aggressive actions of Adolf Hitler in Germany ultimately led Roosevelt to a different position, and in the latter part of the decade, he faced the task of educating the American public, still resentful of U.S. participation in World War I, about the fascist danger that was spreading in Europe.

Hitler came to power in 1933, shortly before FDR entered the White House, and he pledged to restore German pride and nationalism in the aftermath of the Versailles Treaty. As the leader of the National Socialist Workers Party, or Nazis, Hitler established a **fascist government**—a one-party dictatorship closely aligned with corporate interests, committed to a "biological world evolution," and determined to establish a new empire, the Third Reich. He vowed to eliminate Bolshevik radicalism and purify the German "race" through the elimination of those he deemed undesirable, especially targeting Jews, the group Hitler blamed for most, if not all, Germany's ills.

fascist government A government subscribing to a philosophy of dictatorship that merges the interests of the state, armed forces, and big business.

Others aided the spread of fascism. Italian leader Benito Mussolini, who had assumed power in 1922 and envisaged emulating the power and prestige of the Roman Empire, brutally attacked Ethiopia in 1935. The following year, a young fascist military officer, Francisco Franco, led an uprising in Spain, and with the assistance of Italy and Germany, successfully ousted the Spanish Republic and its loyalist supporters by 1939 to create an authoritarian government. Meanwhile, Hitler implemented his plan of conquest: He remilitarized the Rhineland in 1936, and in 1938 he annexed Austria.

Watch the Video at **www.myhistorylab.com** *Jesse Owens and the 1936 Olympics*

The aggressive actions of Germany and Italy failed to eclipse U.S. fears of becoming involved in another European war. Congress passed Neutrality Acts designed to continue America's trade with its world partners but prohibit the president from taking sides in the mounting European crisis.

Appeasement and more neutrality. After annexing Austria, Hitler pushed again in 1938 when he demanded the Sudetenland from Czechoslovakia. The French and the British refused to stand up to Hitler, following instead a policy of appeasement. Meeting in Munich in September 1938, the leaders of England and France abandoned their security obligations to the Czechs, yielding the Sudetenland to Hitler in exchange for a weak promise of no more annexations. In America, too, the sentiment was for peace at all costs, and isolationism permeated the halls of Congress.

Isolationism compounded by anti-Semitism and by the divisions between the leaders of the American Jewish community combined to ensure that the United States would not become a haven for Jews suffering under Nazi brutality. News of Nazi atrocities against Austrian Jews in 1938 shocked the American press, and Hitler's violent pogrom, known as *Kristallnacht* ("Night of the Broken Glass"), conducted against Jews throughout Germany in November 1938, added fresh proof of Nazi cruelty. Although the United States recalled its ambassador from Berlin to protest the pogrom (in response, Germany recalled its ambassador from Washington), it did not alter its restrictive immigration-quota system, the 1924 National Origins Act, to provide refuge for German Jews.

As Europe edged closer to war, the relationship between the United States and Japan, periodically tense in the twentieth century, became more strained. Japan resented U.S. economic interests in East Asia and was offended by the policy of excluding Japanese immigrants. The United States regarded Japan's desires for empire as threatening but also needed Japan as a trading partner, especially in the economically depressed 1930s. Consequently, in September 1931, when Japan seized Manchuria, the United States did little more than denounce the action. Again in 1937, after Japanese troops attacked Chinese forces north of Beijing and outright war began between Japan and China, the United States merely condemned the action.

Edging toward Involvement

After the Munich agreement, President Roosevelt moved away from domestic reform toward preparedness for war, fearful that conflict in Europe was unavoidable and determined to revise the neutrality laws. In his State of the Union address in January 1939, FDR explained that

On November 9, 1938, Nazi Germany launched an attack on Jews, destroying their businesses and burning their synagogues. This street scene in Berlin shows the shattered windows of Jewish businesses. Nazi leader Joseph Goebbels recorded the event, known as Kristallnacht, in his diary: "Yesterday: Berlin. There, all proceeded fantastically. One fire after another. It is good that way. . . . 100 dead. But no German property damaged."

America's neutrality laws might "actually give aid to an aggressor and deny it to the victim." By the fall of that year, he had won support for changes in the laws that would enable the United States to provide important assistance to Britain and France in the winter of 1939–1940. Hitler's defiance of the Munich agreement in Czechoslovakia, overrunning Prague by March 1939, merely anticipated his next move toward Poland and also convinced the British and the French that war was imminent.

CONCLUSION

The Great Depression and the New Deal mark a major divide in American history. The depression cast doubt on the traditional practices, policies, and attitudes that underlay not only the nation's economy but also its social and political institutions and relationships. The New Deal brought only partial economic recovery. However, its economic policies, from banking and securities regulation to unemployment compensation, farm price supports, and minimum wages, created barriers against another depression. The gradual adoption of compensatory spending policies expanded the government's role in the economy. Responding to the failures of private organizations and state and local governments, the federal government assumed the obligation to provide social welfare.

Roosevelt also expanded the role of the presidency. As his White House took the initiative for defining public policy, drafting legislation, lobbying Congress, and communicating with the nation, it became the model for all subsequent presidents. Not only was the president's power increased, but Roosevelt made the federal government, rather than state or local governments, the focus of public interest and expectations.

By the end of the 1930s, as international relations deteriorated, FDR was already considering a shift, as he later said, from Dr. New Deal to Dr. Win-the-War. Reluctant to move beyond public opinion that did not want war and limited by neutrality legislation, FDR cautiously led the nation toward war—this time against an enemy far more threatening than the Great Depression. Ironically, only then would President Roosevelt end the depression that had ravaged the nation for nearly a decade.

WHERE TO LEARN MORE

Center for New Deal Studies, Roosevelt University, Chicago, Illinois. The center contains political memorabilia, photographs, papers, and taped interviews dealing with Franklin D. Roosevelt and the New Deal; it also sponsors an annual lecture series about the Roosevelt legacy. http://www.roosevelt.edu/newdeal/.

Franklin D. Roosevelt Home and Presidential Library, Hyde Park, New York. The Roosevelt home, furnished with family heirlooms, and the spacious grounds, where FDR is buried, personalize the president and provide insights into his career. The nearby library has displays and exhibitions about Roosevelt's presidency, and the Eleanor Roosevelt Wing is dedicated to her career. http://www.fdrlibrary.marist.edu.

Eleanor Roosevelt National Historic Site, Hyde Park, New York. These two cottages, where Eleanor Roosevelt worked and, after 1945, lived, contain her furniture and memorabilia. Visitors can also watch a film biography of ER and tour the grounds of this retreat where she entertained personal friends and world leaders. http://www.nps.gov/elro/.

New Deal Network. A valuable guide to the study of the Great Depression and the New Deal with a rich collection of photographs and documents. http://www.newdeal.feri.org.

REVIEW QUESTIONS

1. Why did President Hoover's emphasis on voluntarism fail to resolve the problems of the Great Depression in the United States?
2. Describe the relief programs of the New Deal. What were they designed to accomplish? What were their achievements and their limitations?
3. What were the major criticisms of the early New Deal? How accurate were those charges?
4. How did the policies of the New Deal shape the constituency and the prospects of the Democratic Party in the 1930s?
5. Describe the conflict between management and labor in the 1930s. What were the major issues and motivations? How did the two sides differ in resources and tactics, and how and why did these factors change over time?
6. How did the role of the federal government change in the 1930s? What factors were responsible for the changes?

KEY TERMS

Bonus Army (p. 697)
Congress of Industrial Organizations (CIO) (p. 705)
Fascist government (p. 713)
Federal Deposit Insurance Corporation (FDIC) (p. 698)
Fireside chat (p. 698)
Great Depression (p. 692)
Hoovervilles (p. 693)
New Deal (p. 698)
Securities and Exchange Commission (SEC) (p. 699)
Tennessee Valley Authority (TVA) (p. 708)

myhistorylab Connections

Reinforce what you learned in this chapter by studying the many documents, images, maps, review tools, and videos available at **www.myhistorylab.com**.

Read and Review

Study and Review **Study Plan: Chapter 25**

Read the Document

Franklin D. Roosevelt, First Inaugural Address (1932)

Luther C. Wandall, A Negro in the CCC (1935)

Tennessee Valley Authority Act (1933)

E. E. Lewis, Black Cotton Farmers and the AAA (1935)

An Attack on New Deal Farm Policies (1936)

Frances Perkins and the Social Security Act (1935, 1960)

Caroline Manning, The Immigrant Woman and Her Job (1930)

Richard Wright, Are We Solving America's Race Problem? (1945)

Mrs. Henry Weddington, Letter to President Roosevelt (1938)

See the Map

The Great Depression

The Tennessee Valley Authority

Research and Explore

Read the Document

Personal Journeys Online

From Then to Now Online: Social Security

Dealing with Hard Times: The Great Depression

Exploring America: The Dust Bowl

Hear the Audio

"I've Known Rivers"; poem and reading by Langston Hughes

FDR's First Inaugural Address

Watch the Video

Dorothea Lange and Migrant Mother

Responding to the Great Depression: Whose New Deal?

President Roosevelt Focuses on America's Youth

Jesse Owens and the 1936 Olympics

Hear the Audio

Hear the audio files for Chapter 25 at **www.myhistorylab.com**.

1939-1945

26

World War II

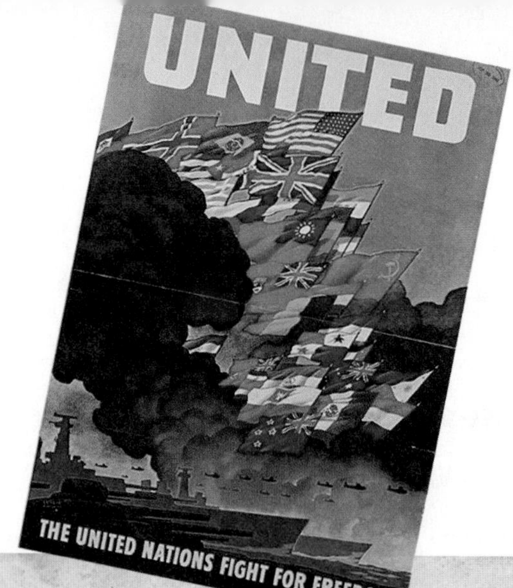
UNITED
THE UNITED NATIONS FIGHT FOR FREEDOM

American soldiers landing on the coast of France at Normandy on June 6, 1944 (D-Day).

Hear the Audio
Hear the audio files for Chapter 26 at **www.myhistorylab.com**.

THE DILEMMAS OF NEUTRALITY *(page 722)*

WHY WERE most Americans reluctant to get involved in World War II?

HOLDING THE LINE *(page 727)*

HOW DID the Allies fare in 1941 and 1942?

MOBILIZING FOR VICTORY *(page 731)*

WHAT STEPS did the U.S. government take to organize the economy for war?

THE HOME FRONT *(page 733)*

HOW DID the war alter American society?

WAR AND PEACE *(page 738)*

WHY DID the Allies win the war?

ONE AMERICAN JOURNEY

December, 1942

The scene [under the stadium] at The University of Chicago would have been confusing to an outsider, if he could have eluded the security guards and gained admittance. He would have seen only what appeared to be a crude pile of black bricks and wooden timbers. . . .

Finally, the day came when we were ready to run the experiment. We gathered on a balcony about 10 feet above the floor of the large room in which the structure had been erected. Beneath us was a young scientist, George Weil, whose duty it was to handle the last control rod that was holding the reaction in check. . . .

Finally, it was time to remove the control rods. Slowly, Weil started to withdraw the main control rod. On the balcony, we watched the indicators which measured the neutron count and told us how rapidly the disintegration of the uranium atoms under their neutron bombardment was proceeding.

At 11:35 A.M., the counters were clicking rapidly. Then, with a loud clap, the automatic control rods slammed home. The safety point had been set too low. . . .

At 2:30, Weil pulled out the control rod in a series of measured adjustments. Shortly after, the intensity shown by the indicators began to rise at a slow but ever-increasing rate. At this moment we knew that the self-sustaining [nuclear] reaction was under way.

The event was not spectacular, no fuses burned, no lights flashed. But to us it meant that release of atomic energy on a large scale would be only a matter of time.

Enrico Fermi, in *The First Reactor* (Washington, DC: U.S. Department of Energy, 1982).

Read the **Document** at **www.myhistorylab.com**

Personal Journeys Online

- **Patricia Cain Koehler, writing in the *Oregon Historical Quarterly* (Fall 1990), recounted her experiences as a young woman helping to build aircraft carriers during World War II.**
- **Leon Overstreet was a construction worker who helped to build Manhattan Project facilities. He was interviewed for S. L. Sanger, *Working on the Bomb: An Oral History of World War II Hanford* (1995).**
- **Bill Mauldin explains the origins of his cartoon G.I.s Willie and Joe. From Studs Terkel, *The Good War* (1985).**

ENRICO FERMI was describing the first controlled nuclear chain reaction—the critical experiment from which atomic weapons and atomic power would soon develop. Fermi had emigrated to escape the growing political repression of Fascist Italy. In 1942, after the United States joined the ongoing global conflict of World War II, Fermi was put in charge of nuclear fission research at the University of Chicago and played a leading role in efforts to develop an atomic bomb. The following year found Fermi, other atomic scientists, and their families at Los Alamos, a science city that the government built hurriedly on a high plateau in northern New Mexico, where isolation was supposed to ensure secrecy and help the United States win the race with Nazi Germany to develop atomic weapons.

The Fermis were not the only family to give Los Alamos a multinational flavor. Laura remembered that it was "all one big family and all one big accent. . . . Everybody in science was there, both from the United States and from almost all European countries." The internationalism of Los Alamos mirrored the larger war effort. Japan's attack on Pearl Harbor in December 1941 thrust the United States into a war that spanned the globe. America's allies against Japan in the Pacific and East Asia included Great Britain, Australia, and China. In Europe, its allies against Nazi Germany and Fascist Italy included Great Britain, the Soviet

CHRONOLOGY

1931	Japan invades Manchuria.
1933	Hitler takes power in Germany.
1935	Congress passes first of three neutrality acts.
	Italy invades Ethiopia.
1936	Germany and Italy form the Rome-Berlin Axis.
	Civil war erupts in Spain.
1937	Japan invades China.
1938	Germany absorbs Austria.
	Munich agreement between Germany, Britain, and France.
1939	Germany and the Soviet Union sign a nonaggression pact.
	Germany absorbs Czechoslovakia.
	Germany invades Poland; Great Britain and France declare war on Germany.
1940	Germany conquers Denmark, Norway, Belgium, the Netherlands, and France.
	Japan, Germany, and Italy sign the Tripartite Pact.
	Germany bombs England in the Battle of Britain.
	The United States begins to draft men into the armed forces.
	Franklin Roosevelt wins an unprecedented third term.
1941	The United States begins a lend-lease program to make military equipment available to Great Britain and later the Soviet Union.
	The Fair Employment Practices Committee is established.
	Germany invades the Soviet Union.
	Roosevelt and Churchill issue the Atlantic Charter.
	Japan attacks U.S. military bases in Hawaii.
1942	American forces in the Philippines surrender to Japan.
	President Roosevelt authorizes the removal and internment of Japanese Americans living in four western states.
	Naval battles in the Coral Sea and off the island of Midway blunt Japanese expansion. U.S. forces land in North Africa.
	Soviet forces encircle a German army at Stalingrad.
	The first sustained and controlled nuclear chain reaction takes place at the University of Chicago.
1943	U.S. and British forces invade Italy, which makes terms with the Allies.
	Race conflict erupts in riots in Detroit, New York, and Los Angeles.
	The landing of Marines on Tarawa initiates the island-hopping strategy.
	U.S. war production peaks.
	Roosevelt, Churchill, and Stalin confer at Tehran.
1944	Allied forces land in Normandy.
	The U.S. Navy destroys Japanese sea power in the battles of the Philippine Sea and Leyte Gulf.
	The Battle of the Bulge is the last tactical setback for the Allies.
1945	Roosevelt, Stalin, and Churchill meet at Yalta to plan the postwar world.
	The United States takes the Pacific islands of Iwo Jima and Okinawa.
	Franklin Roosevelt dies; Harry S. Truman becomes president.
	Germany surrenders to the United States, Great Britain, and the Soviet Union.
	The United Nations is organized at an international meeting in San Francisco.
	Potsdam Conference.
	Japan surrenders after the detonation of atomic bombs over Hiroshima and Nagasaki.

Union, and more than 20 other nations. The scientists racing to perfect the atomic bomb knew that victory was far from certain. Germany and Japan had piled one conquest on another since the late 1930s, and they continued to seize new territories in 1942. Allied defeat in a few key battles could have resulted in a standoff or an Axis victory. A new weapon might end the war more quickly or make the difference between victory and defeat.

The war's domestic impacts were as profound as its international consequences. The race to build an atomic bomb was only one part of a vast effort to harness the resources of the United States to the war effort. The war highlighted racial inequalities, gave women new opportunities, and fostered growth in the South and West. By devastating the nation's commercial rivals, compelling workers to retrain and factories to modernize, World War II left the United States dominant in the world economy. It also increased the size and scope of the federal government and built an alliance among the armed forces, big business, and science that helped shape postwar America. ✦

WHY WERE most Americans reluctant to get involved in World War II?

THE DILEMMAS OF NEUTRALITY

Americans in the 1930s wanted no part of another overseas war. Despite two years of German victories and a decade of Japanese aggression against China, opinion polls in the fall of 1941 showed that a majority of voters still hoped to avoid war. President Roosevelt's challenge was to lead the United States toward rearmament and support for Great Britain and China without alarming a reluctant public.

THE ROOTS OF WAR

The roots of World War II can be found in the aftereffects of World War I. The peace settlement created a set of small new nations in eastern Europe that were vulnerable to aggression by their much larger neighbors, Germany and the Soviet Union (more formally, the Union of Soviet Socialist Republics, or USSR). Italy and Japan thought that the Treaty of Versailles had not recognized their stature as world powers. Many Germans were convinced that Germany had been betrayed rather than defeated in 1918. In the 1930s, economic crisis undermined an already shaky political order. Economic hardship and political instability fueled the rise of right-wing dictatorships that offered territorial expansion by military conquest as the way to redress old rivalries, dominate trade, and gain access to raw materials.

Japanese nationalists believed that the United States, Britain, and France had treated Japan unfairly after World War I, despite its participation against Germany. They believed that Japan should expel the French, British, Dutch, and Americans from Asia and create a **Greater East Asia Co-Prosperity Sphere,** in which Japan gave the orders and other Asian peoples complied. Seizing the Chinese province of Manchuria to expand an East Asian empire that already included Korea and Taiwan emboldened Japan's military in 1931. A full-scale invasion of China followed in 1937. Japan took many of the key cities and killed tens of thousands of civilians in the "rape of Nanking," but failed to dislodge the government of Jiang Jieshi (Chiang Kai-shek) and settled into a war of attrition.

Greater East Asia Co-Prosperity Sphere Japanese nationalists believed that Japan should expel the French, British, Dutch, and Americans from Asia and create this sphere in which Japan would give the orders and other Asian peoples would comply.

Italian aggression embroiled Africa and the Mediterranean. The Fascist dictator Benito Mussolini had sent arms and troops to aid General Francisco Franco's right-wing rebels in Spain. The three-year civil war, which ended with Franco's victory in 1939, became a bloody testing ground for new German military tactics and German and Italian ambitions against democratic Europe.

QUICK REVIEW

The Roots of War

- Roots of war found in aftermath of World War I.
- Peace settlement created small new nations vulnerable to aggression.
- Germany and Japan were angry and unsatisfied with Treaty of Versailles.
- Economic hardship and political instability gave rise to right-wing dictatorships.

In Germany, Adolf Hitler mixed the desire to reassert national pride and power after the defeat of World War I with an ideology of racial hatred. Coming to power by constitutional means in 1933, Hitler quickly consolidated his grip by destroying opposition parties and made himself the German Führer, or absolute leader. Proclaiming the start of a thousand-year Reich ("empire"), he combined the historic German interest in eastward expansion with a long tradition of racialist thought about German superiority.

Special targets of Nazi hatred were the Jews, who were prominent in German business and professional life but soon faced persecution aimed at driving them from the country. In 1935, the Nuremberg Laws denied civil rights to Jews and the campaign against them intensified. On November 9, 1938, in vicious attacks across Germany that became known as *Kristallnacht* ("Night of the Broken Glass"), Nazi thugs rounded up, beat, and murdered Jews, smashed property, and burned synagogues. The Nazi government began expropriating Jewish property and excluded Jews from most employment.

Germany and Italy formed the Rome-Berlin Axis in October 1936 and the Tripartite Pact with Japan in 1940, leading to the term **Axis Powers** to describe the aggressor nations. Hitler's Germany was the most repressive. The Nazi concentration camp began as a device for political terrorism, where socialists and other dissidents and "antisocials"—homosexuals and beggars—could be separated from "pure" Germans. Soon the systematic discrimination and concentration camps would evolve into massive forced-labor camps and then into hellish extermination camps.

Axis Powers The opponents of the United States and its allies in World War II.

Hitler's War in Europe

After annexing Austria through a coup and seizing and slicing up Czechoslovakia, Germany demonstrated the worthlessness of the Munich agreement by invading Poland on September 1, 1939. Britain and France, Poland's allies, declared war on Germany but could not stop the German war machine. Western journalists covering the three-week conquest of Poland coined the term ***Blitzkrieg,*** or "lightning war," to describe the German tactics. Armored divisions with tanks and motorized infantry punched holes in defensive positions and raced forward 30 or 40 miles per day.

Blitzkrieg German war tactic in World War II ("lightning war") involving the concentration of air and armored firepower to punch and exploit holes in opposing defensive lines.

Hitler's greatest advantage was the ability to attack when and where he chose. From September 1939 to October 1941, Germany marched from victory to victory (see Map 26–1). Striking from a central position against scattered enemies, Hitler chose the targets and timing of each new front: eastward to smash Poland in September 1939; northward to conquer Denmark and Norway in April and May 1940; westward to defeat the Netherlands, Belgium, and France in May and June 1940, an attack that Italy also joined; southward into the Balkans, enlisting Hungary, Romania, and Bulgaria as allies and conquering Yugoslavia and Greece in April and May 1941. Hitler also launched the Battle of Britain in the second half of 1940. German planes bombarded Britain mercilessly, in an unsuccessful effort to pound the British into submission.

Hitler gambled once too often in June 1941. Having failed to knock Britain out of the war, he invaded the Soviet Union. The attack caught the Red Army off guard. Germany and the USSR had signed a nonaggression pact in 1939, and the Soviets had helped to dismember Poland. Hitler hoped that smashing the USSR and seizing its vast resources would make Germany invincible. Before desperate Soviet counterattacks and a bitter winter stopped the German columns, they had reached the outskirts of Moscow and expected to finish the job in the spring.

QUICK REVIEW

Germany Conquers Europe

- September 1939: Poland.
- April and May 1940: Denmark and Norway.
- May and June 1940: Netherlands, Belgium, and France.
- April and May 1941: Yugoslavia and Greece.

Trying to Keep Out

For more than two years after the invasion of Poland, strong sentiment against intervention shaped public debate and limited President Roosevelt's ability to help Britain and its allies. Much of the emotional appeal of neutrality came from disillusionment with the American crusade in World War I, which had failed to make the world safe for democracy. Many opponents of intervention wanted the United States to protect its traditional spheres of interest in Latin America and the Pacific. Noninterventionists spanned the political spectrum from left-leaning labor unions to conservative business tycoons like Henry Ford. The country's ethnic variety also complicated U.S. responses. Nazi aggression ravaged the homelands of Americans of Polish, Czech, Greek, and Norwegian ancestry. More than 5 million German Americans remembered the anti-German sentiment of World War I, while many of the 4.6 million Italian Americans admired Mussolini. Any move to intervene in Europe had to take these different views into account, meaning that Roosevelt had to move slowly and carefully in his effort to align the United States on the side of Britain.

The raspy-voiced Adolf Hitler had a remarkable ability to stir the German people. He and his inner circle made skillful use of propaganda, exploiting German resentment over the country's defeat in World War I and, with carefully staged mass rallies, such as this event in 1938, inspiring an emotional conviction of national greatness.

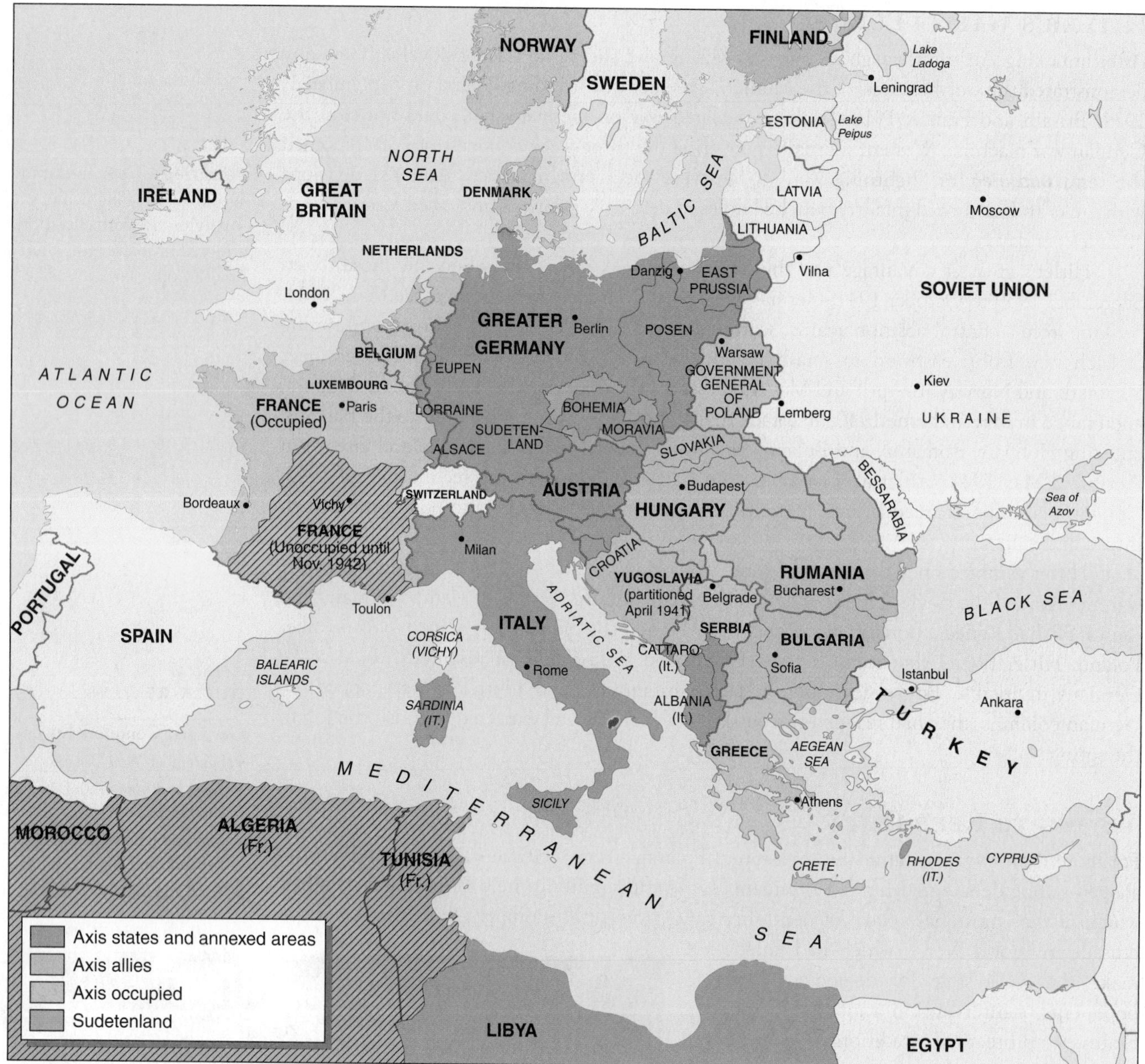

MAP 26–1 **Axis Europe, 1941, on the Eve of Hitler's Invasion of the Soviet Union** After almost two years of war, the Axis Powers controlled most of Europe, from the Atlantic Ocean to the Soviet border through annexation, military conquest, and alliances. Failure to force Britain to make peace caused Hitler to look eastward in 1941 to attempt the conquest of the Soviet Union.

How was Germany's central location in Europe both a strength and a weakness?

Edging toward Intervention

Still, Roosevelt's appeals to democratic values gained support in 1939 and 1940. Radio broadcasts from England describing London under German bombing heightened the sense of imperiled freedom. The importance of open markets also bolstered interventionism. U.S. business leaders had little doubt that Axis victories would bring economic instability and require crushing defense budgets to protect Fortress America.

Watch the **Video** at **www.myhistorylab.com** *Hitler and Roosevelt*

Because 85 percent of the American people agreed that the nation should fight only if it was directly attacked, Roosevelt had to chip away at neutrality, educating, arguing, and taking one step at a time. The first step came in October 1939. A month-long congressional debate inspired millions of letters and telegrams in favor of keeping an arms embargo in place against warring nations. Nevertheless, the lawmakers reluctantly allowed arms sales to belligerent nations on a "cash-and-carry" basis, to avoid expanding European debts. In control of the Atlantic, France and Britain were the only expected customers.

Isolationism and anti-Semitism help to explain why the United States accepted only a few thousand Jewish refugees. American law strictly limited the numbers of Europeans who could enter the United States, and Congress in 1939 declined to authorize the entry outside the quotas of 20,000 Jewish children. Bureaucrats at the State Department blocked entry to "undesirables," such as left-wing opponents of Hitler, and were unsympathetic to Jewish refugees. In 1939, officials turned the passenger ship *St. Louis* away from Miami and forced its 950 German Jewish refugees back to Europe. The consequences of these restrictions would prove tragic later in the war, as the Nazis began systematic genocide of European Jews.

The collapse of France and U.S. rearmament. Despite the efforts of noninterventionists, in 1940 the United States edged closer to involvement in the war. In May, the Roosevelt administration established the National Defense Advisory Commission and the Council of National Defense to deal with strategic planning for war. The sudden defeat of France, which had survived four years of German attacks in World War I, made the new war seem far more serious. The United States no longer had the option of standing on the sidelines while European nations fought to a standstill. In the summer of 1940, Congress voted to expand the army to 2 million men, build 19,000 new warplanes, and add 150 ships to the navy. Lawmakers approved the nation's first peacetime draft in September, requiring 16.5 million men between the ages of 21 and 35 to register for military service on October 16.

In the same month, the United States concluded a destroyer deal with Britain. The British were desperate for small, maneuverable warships to guard imports of food and war materials against German submarines. The Americans had long wanted additional air and naval bases to guard the approaches to North America. Roosevelt met both needs by trading 50 old destroyers for the use of bases on British territories in the Caribbean, Bermuda, and Newfoundland.

The election of 1940. In the presidential election of 1940, the big campaign issue was whether FDR's unprecedented try for a third term represented arrogance or a legitimate concern for continuity in a time of peril. The election was tighter than in 1932 or 1936, but Roosevelt received 55 percent of the vote. The president pledged that no Americans would fight in a foreign war. But if the United States were attacked, he said privately, the war would no longer be "foreign."

Read the **Document** at **www.myhistorylab.com** *Charles Lindbergh, Radio Address (1941)*

The Brink of War

After the election, FDR and his advisers edged the United States toward stronger support of Britain and put pressure on Japan. In January 1941, Roosevelt proposed the lend-lease program, which allowed Britain to "borrow" military equipment for the duration of the war.

The **Lend-Lease Act** triggered intense political debate. Charles Lindbergh, the spokesperson for the America First Committee, protested that the United States should not give away weapons it might need to defend itself. Congress finally passed the measure in March 1941, authorizing the president to lease, lend, or otherwise dispose of arms and other equipment to any country whose defense was considered vital to the security of the United States. The program proved invaluable in aiding Great Britain and later in assisting the Soviet Union.

Lend-Lease Act Program begun in 1941 through which the U.S. transferred military equipment to Britain and other World War II allies.

FDR soon began an undeclared war in the North Atlantic, instructing the navy to report sightings of German submarines to the British. In September, the U.S. destroyer *Greer* clashed with a German submarine. Portraying the incident as German aggression, Roosevelt proclaimed a "shoot on sight" policy for German subs and ordered American ships to escort British convoys to within 400 miles of Britain. In reply, German submarines torpedoed the

QUICK REVIEW

Undeclared War

- March 1941: Lend-lease program approved by Congress.
- FDR ordered Navy to offer support to Britain.
- August 1941: Atlantic Charter lays out British and American war aims.

Atlantic Charter Statement of common principles and war aims developed by President Franklin Roosevelt and British Prime Minister Winston Churchill at a meeting in August 1941.

destroyer *Kearny* on October 17 and sank the destroyer *Reuben James*, with the loss of more than 100 lives, on October 30. The United States was now approaching outright naval war with Germany.

The Atlantic Charter. With U.S. ships on a war footing in the North Atlantic, Roosevelt and the British prime minister, Winston Churchill, met secretly off Newfoundland in August 1941 to map out military strategy and postwar goals. They agreed that the defeat of Germany was their first priority, and Japan was secondary. Their joint proclamation, known as the **Atlantic Charter,** provided a political umbrella for American involvement in the war. Echoing Woodrow Wilson, Roosevelt insisted on a commitment to oppose territorial conquest, support self-government, promote freedom of the seas, and create a system of economic collaboration. Churchill signed to keep Roosevelt happy, but the document papered over sharp differences between U.S. and British expectations about the future of world trade and European colonial possessions.

Events in the Pacific. The final shove came in the Pacific rather than the Atlantic. In 1940, as part of its rearmament program, the United States decided to build a "two-ocean navy." This decision antagonized Japan, prodding it toward a war that most U.S. leaders hoped to postpone or avoid. Through massive investment and national sacrifice, Japan had achieved roughly 70 percent of U.S. naval strength by late 1941. However, America's buildup promised to reduce the ratio to only 30 percent by 1944. Furthermore, the United States was restricting Japan's vital imports of steel, iron ore, and aluminum in an effort to curb its military aggression. In July 1941, after Japan occupied French Indochina, Roosevelt froze Japanese assets in the United States, blocked shipments of petroleum products, and began to build up U.S. forces in the Philippines. These actions caused Japan's rulers to consider war against the United States while Japan still had a petroleum reserve. Both militarily and economically, it looked in Tokyo as if 1942 was Japan's last chance for victory.

Japanese war planners never seriously considered an invasion of the United States or expected a decisive victory. They hoped that attacks on American Pacific bases would shock the United States into letting Japan have its way in Asia or at least win time to create impenetrable defenses in the central Pacific.

DECEMBER 7, 1941

On December 7, 1941, the Japanese navy launched a surprise attack on American bases in Hawaii. The Japanese fleet sailed a 4,000-mile loop through the empty North Pacific, avoiding merchant shipping and American patrols. Before dawn on December 7, six Japanese aircraft carriers launched 351 planes in two bombing strikes against Pearl Harbor. When the smoke cleared, Americans counted their losses: eight battleships, eleven other warships, and nearly all military aircraft damaged or destroyed, and 2,403 people killed. They could also count their good fortune. Dockyards, drydocks, and oil storage tanks remained intact because the Japanese admiral had refused to order a third attack. And the American aircraft carriers, at sea on patrol, were unharmed. They proved far more important than battleships as the war developed. Within hours, the Japanese attacked U.S. bases at Guam, Wake Island, and in the Philippines.

W
WHERE TO LEARN MORE
National Museum of the Pacific War, Fredericksburg, Texas
http://www.nimitz-museum.org

Hear the Audio at **www.myhistorylab.com**
Pearl Harbor performed by New York, Georgia Singers

Speaking to Congress the following day, Roosevelt proclaimed December 7, 1941, "a date which will live in infamy." He asked for and got a declaration of war against Japan. Hitler and Mussolini declared war on the United States on December 11, supporting their Tripartite Pactally. On January 1, 1942, the United States, Britain, the Soviet Union, and 23 other nations subscribed to the principles of the Atlantic Charter and pledged not to negotiate a separate peace.

GLOBAL CONNECTIONS

 RATIONING IN BRITAIN 

When World War II broke out, Britain depended on imports for the basic necessities of life—two-thirds of its food, all of its petroleum, all of its rubber, all of its tea.

The British government began to ration gasoline in September 1939 and added butter, sugar, meat, and paper to the list of rationed products early in 1940. By the end of the war, half of all foodstuffs were on strict rationing. The Ministry of Food encouraged Britons to make do with foods that could be grown at home, such as potatoes and carrots, "bright treasure dug from the good British earth." One Ministry of Food advertisement tried to put a good light on shortages:

> The fishermen are saving lives
> By sweeping seas for mines,
> So you'll not grumble, 'What no fish?'
> When you have read these lines.

Clothing was also controlled because cotton was an import and wool was needed for military uniforms. Styles became simpler by government decree. To save cloth, there would be no wide lapels or turned-up cuffs. Skirts became narrower and shorter.

Shortages continued even after the Allies won the Battle of the Atlantic in 1943 and pushed German submarines away from the vital convoy routes. Until the last year of the war, the average German had a better standard of living than the average Briton. At the same time, many members of the British working class welcomed rationing because it equalized consumption among rich and poor and ensured that the wealthy would not monopolize resources.

Because World War II exhausted the British economy, rationing remained in force long after victory. Clothing came off the list in 1949, but meat only in 1954—a year after the coronation of Queen Elizabeth II ushered in a new era in British history and long after the American economy was launched into a postwar boom.

- Rationing in the United States was a way to fine-tune the war economy and engage everyday Americans in the war effort, but in Britain it was a necessity for survival. How might this difference have affected the ways in which the two nations approached the postwar world?

HOLDING THE LINE

HOW DID the Allies fare in 1941 and 1942?

Japan's armies quickly conquered most of Southeast Asia; its navy forced the United States onto the defensive in the central Pacific. As it turned out, Japan's conquests reached their limit after six months, but in early 1942, this was far from clear. At the same time, in Europe, Allied fortunes went from bad to worse. Again, no one knew that German and Italian gains would peak at midyear. Decisive turning points did not come until November 1942, a year after the United States entered the war, and not until the middle of 1943 could the **Allies**—the United States, Britain, the Soviet Union, China, and other nations at war with Germany, Japan, and Italy—begin with confidence to plan for victory.

Allies In World War I, these were Britain, France, Russia, and other belligerent nations (but not the United States, which insisted upon being merely an associated nation) fighting against the Central Powers. In World War II, the Allies fighting the Axis Powers included the United States as well as the Soviet Union, Great Britain, France, China, and other nations.

STOPPING GERMANY

In December 1941, the United States plunged into a truly global war that was being fought on six distinct fronts. In North Africa, the British were battling Italian and German armies that were trying to seize the Suez Canal, a critical transportation link to Asia. Along the 1,000-mile **Eastern Front,** Soviet armies held defensive positions as German forces, pushing deeply into Soviet territory, reached the outskirts of Moscow and Leningrad (now St. Petersburg). In the North Atlantic, German submarines stalked merchant ships carrying supplies to Britain. In China, Japan controlled the most productive provinces but could not crush Chinese resistance. In Southeast Asia, Japanese troops attacked the Philippines, the Dutch East Indies (now Indonesia), New Guinea, Malaya, and Burma. In the central Pacific, the Japanese fleet confronted the U.S. Navy. With the nation facing

Eastern Front The area of military operations in World War II located east of Germany in eastern Europe and the Soviet Union.

danger across both the Atlantic and Pacific oceans, Roosevelt helped Americans understand the global nature of the conflict by calling it the "second world war."

Despite the popular desire for revenge against Japan, the Allies had already decided to defeat Germany first. The reasoning was simple: Germany was far stronger than Japan. Defeat of Japan would not ensure the defeat of Germany, especially if the Germans crushed the Soviet Union or starved Britain into submission. By contrast, a strategy that helped the Soviets and British survive and then destroyed German military power would doom Japan.

The Eastern Front and the Battle of Stalingrad. The Eastern Front held the key to Allied hopes in Europe. In 1941, Germany had seized control of 45 percent of the Soviet population, 47 percent of its grain production, and more than 60 percent of its coal, steel, and aluminum industries. Hitler next sought to destroy the Soviet capacity to wage war, targeting

The Japanese attack on Pearl Harbor shocked the American people. Images of burning battleships confirmed the popular image of Japan as sneaky and treacherous and stirred a desire for revenge. The attack rendered the United States incapable of resisting Japanese aggression in Southeast Asia in early 1942, but it failed to achieve its goal of destroying U.S. naval power in the Pacific.

southern Russia, an area rich in grain and oil. The German thrust in 1942 was also designed to eliminate the British from the Middle East.

The turning point of the war in Europe came at Stalingrad (present-day Volgograd), an industrial center on the western bank of the Volga River. After initially aiming at the city, German armies turned south toward the Russian oil fields, leaving a dangerous strongpoint on their flank that the German command decided to capture. In September and October 1942, German, Italian, and Romanian soldiers fought their way house by house into the city. For both Hitler and Stalin, the city became a test of will that outweighed even its substantial military importance.

The Red Army delivered a counterstroke on November 18 that cut off 290,000 Axis soldiers. Airlifts kept the Germans fighting for more than two additional months, but they surrendered in February 1943. This was the first German mass capitulation, and it came at immense human cost to both sides. The Soviet army suffered more deaths in this battle than the United States did in the entire war.

Behind the victory was an extraordinary revival of the Soviet capacity to make war. In the desperate months of 1941, the Soviets dismantled nearly 3,000 factories and rebuilt them far to the east of the German advance in the midst of Siberian winter. By the time the two armies clashed at Stalingrad, the Soviets were producing four times as many tanks and warplanes as the Germans, portending the outcome of the battles to come.

QUICK REVIEW

December 1941: War on Six Fronts

- North Africa: British battled Italian and German armies.
- Eastern Front: Soviet armies held defensive positions.
- North Atlantic: Merchant ships threatened by German submarines.
- China: China dominated, but not defeated, by Japan.
- Southeast Asia: Japanese forces on the move throughout the region.
- Central Pacific: Japanese fleet faced the U.S. Navy.

The Survival of Britain

After the failure of German air attacks in 1940, the British struggled to save their empire and supply themselves with food and raw materials. In World War I, German submarines (known as U-boats, from *Unterseeboot*) had nearly isolated Great Britain. In 1940 and 1941, they tried again. Through the end of 1941, German "tonnage warfare" sank British, Allied, and neutral merchant vessels faster than they could be replaced.

The Battle of the Atlantic.

The British fought back in what came to be known as the **Battle of the Atlantic.** Between 1939 and 1944, planning and rationing cut Britain's need for imports in half. At sea, the British organized protected convoys. Merchant ships sailing alone were defenseless against submarines. Grouping the merchant ships with armed escorts "hardened" the targets and made them more difficult to find in the wide ocean. Roosevelt's destroyer deal of 1940 and U.S. naval escorts in the western Atlantic in 1941 contributed directly to Britain's survival.

Battle of the Atlantic The long struggle between German submarines and the British and U.S. navies in the North Atlantic from 1940 to 1943.

Nevertheless, German submarines dominated the Atlantic in 1942. The balance shifted only when Allied aircraft began to track submarines with radar, spot them with searchlights as they maneuvered to the surface, track them with new sonar systems, and attack them with depth charges. By the spring of 1943, American shipyards were launching ships faster than the Germans could sink them.

QUICK REVIEW

Britain under Siege

- 1940–1941: German submarines sink British ships faster than it they could be replaced.
- Britain was forced to reduce its dependence on imports.
- New tactics and military technologies allowed the Allies to turn the tide.
- By 1943 the Allies were producing new ships faster than the Germans could sink them.

North Africa.

British ground fighting in 1942 centered in North Africa, where the British operated out of Egypt and the Italians and Germans from the Italian colony of Libya. By October 1942, Field Marshal Erwin Rommel's German and Italian forces were within striking distance of the Suez Canal. At El Alamein, however, General Bernard Montgomery forced the enemy to retreat in early November and lifted the danger to the Middle East.

Retreat and Stabilization in the Pacific

Reports from eastern Asia after Pearl Harbor were appalling. The Japanese attack on the Philippines (see Map 26–2) had been another tactical surprise that destroyed most American air power on the ground and isolated U.S. forces. In February, a numerically inferior Japanese force seized British Singapore, until then considered an anchor of Allied strength, and then pushed the British out of Burma. In a three-month siege, they overwhelmed Filipino and U.S. defensive positions on the

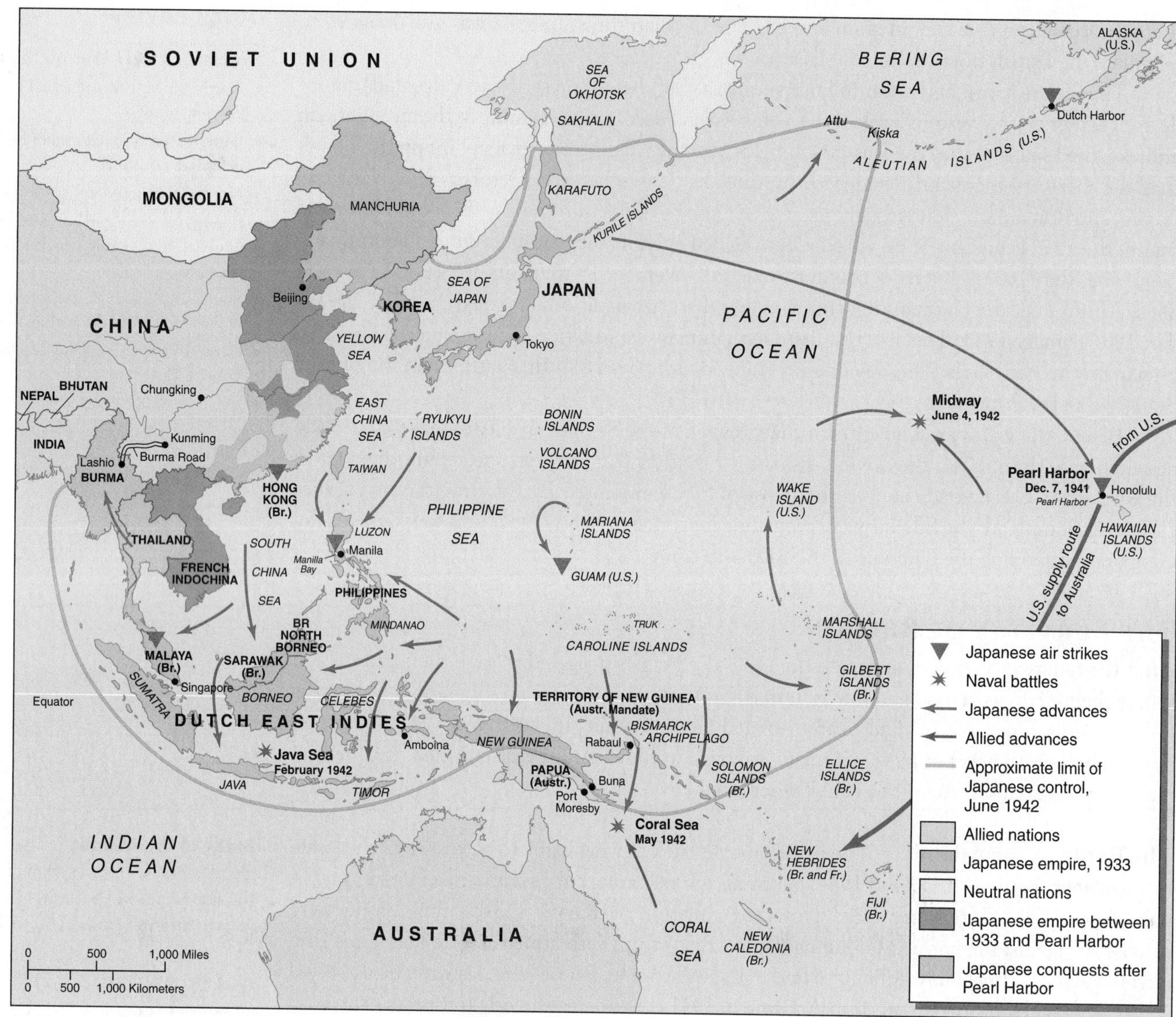

MAP 26–2 **World War II in the Pacific, from Pearl Harbor to Midway** The first six months after the Japanese attack on Pearl Harbor brought a string of Japanese victories and conquests in the Pacific, the islands southeast of Asia, and the British colonies of Malaya and Burma. Japan's advance was halted by a standoff battle in the Coral Sea, a decisive U.S. naval victory at Midway, and the length and vulnerability of Japanese supply lines to the most distant conquests.

What challenges did Japan face as it attempted to hold onto control of the eastern Pacific? How did the geography of the region aid the Allies and shape their strategy?

Bataan peninsula outside Manila; thousands of their captives died of maltreatment on their way to prisoner-of-war camps in what is remembered as the Bataan Death March. On May 6, the last American bastion, the island fortress of Corregidor in Manila Bay, surrendered. The Japanese fleet was virtually undamaged at the end of April, and the Japanese army was triumphant in its conquest of European and American territories in Southeast Asia.

The Battles of the Coral Sea and Midway. The first check to Japanese expansion came on May 7–8, 1942, in the Battle of the Coral Sea, where U.S. aircraft carriers halted a Japanese thrust toward Australia and confirmed that the U.S. Navy could fight effectively. In June, the Japanese struck at the island of Midway, 1,500 miles northwest of Honolulu. Their goal was to destroy American carrier forces. Having cracked Japanese radio codes, U.S. forces were aware of the plan. On the morning of June 4, the Japanese and American carrier fleets faced off across 175 miles of ocean, each sending planes to search out the other. U.S. Navy dive bombers found the Japanese fleet and sank or crippled three aircraft carriers in five minutes; another damaged Japanese carrier sank later in the day. The Battle of Midway ended Japanese efforts to expand in the Pacific.

QUICK REVIEW

Government and the Economy

- War brought a huge expansion of the federal government.
- Office of Price Administration (OPA) oversaw price controls and rationing.
- Under government pressure, industry shifted to defense production.

MOBILIZING FOR VICTORY

War changed the lives of most Americans. Millions of men and women served in the armed forces, and millions more worked in defense factories. In order to keep track of this staggering level of activity, the number of civilian employees of the federal government quadrupled to 3.8 million, a much greater increase than during the New Deal. The breadth of involvement in the war effort gave Americans a common purpose that softened the divisions of region, class, and national origin while calling attention to continuing inequalities of race.

WHAT STEPS did the U.S. government take to organize the economy for war?

Hear the **Audio** at **www.myhistorylab.com** *Obey the Ration Laws*

Manhattan Project The effort, using the code name Manhattan Engineer District, to develop an atomic bomb under the management of the U.S. Army Corps of Engineers during World War II.

Organizing the Economy

The need to fight a global war brought a huge expansion of the federal government. Congress authorized the president to reorganize existing government departments and create new agencies. The War Manpower Commission allocated workers among vital industries and the military. The War Production Board invested $17 billion for new factories and managed $181 billion in war-supply contracts, favoring existing corporations because they had experience in large-scale production.

The Office of Price Administration (OPA) fought inflation with price controls and rationing. By slowing price increases, the OPA helped convince Americans to buy the war bonds that financed half the war spending. Americans also felt the bite of the first payroll deductions for income taxes as the government secured a steady flow of revenues and soaked up some of the high wages that would have pushed inflation. In total, the federal budget in 1945 was $98 billion, eleven times as large as in 1939, and the national debt had increased more than sixfold.

Industry had reluctantly begun to convert from consumer goods to defense production in 1940 and 1941. Existing factories retooled to make war equipment, and huge new facilities turned out thousands of planes and ships.

Most defense contracts went to such established industrial states as Michigan, New York, and Ohio, but the relative impact was greatest in the South and West, where the war marked the takeoff of what Americans would later call the Sunbelt. Millions of Americans moved back and forth across the country to war jobs. Washington, DC, teemed with staff officers, stenographers, and other office workers who helped to coordinate the war effort. Local leaders in cities from Charlotte to Fort Worth to Phoenix saw the war as an economic opportunity and campaigned for defense factories and military bases.

The output of America's war industries was staggering (see Figure 26–1). One historian estimates that 40 percent of the world's military production was coming from the United States by 1944. Equally impressive is the 30 percent increase in the productivity of U.S. workers between 1939 and 1945. Surging farm income pulled

Children in the East Harlem neighborhood of New York clean and flatten tin cans as their contribution to the war effort early in 1942. Thousands of other children participated in similar scrap metal drives around the nation.

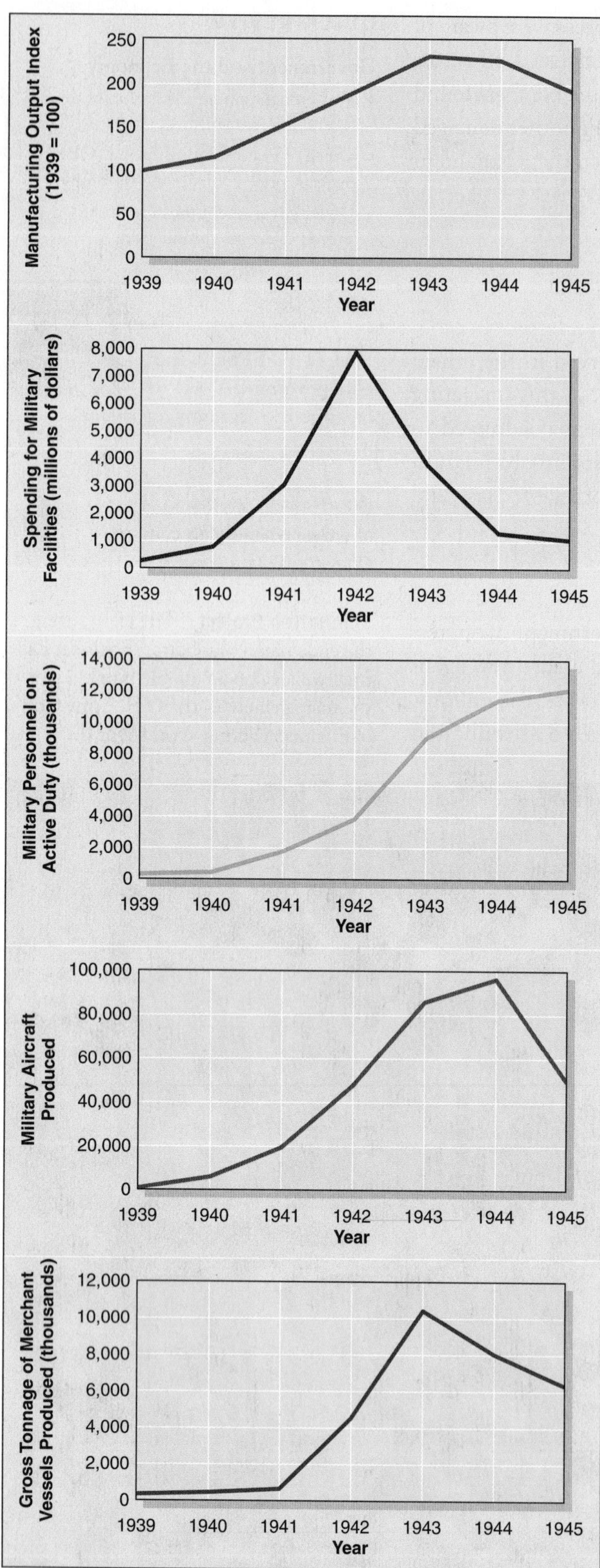

FIGURE 26–1 **Making War: The United States Mobilizes, 1939–1945** The U.S. economic mobilization for World War II reached its peak in 1943, the year in which the Allies prepared for the offensives against Germany and Japan that they hoped would end the war. The number of men and women in uniform continued to grow until 1945.

agriculture out of its long slump. Organized labor offered a no-strike pledge for the duration, ensuring that no one could accuse unions of undermining the war effort but limiting the economic gains of some workers and damping the militancy of the CIO. Nevertheless, overall per capita income doubled, and the poorest quarter of Americans made up some of the ground lost during the Great Depression.

The Enlistment of Science

The war reached into scientific laboratories as well as shops and factories. At the center of the scientific enterprise was Vannevar Bush, former dean at the Massachusetts Institute of Technology. As head of the newly established Office of Scientific Research and Development, Bush guided spending to develop new drugs such as antibiotics, blood-transfusion procedures, weapons systems, radar, sonar, and dozens of other military technologies. The scale of research and development dwarfed previous scientific work and set the pattern of massive postwar federal support for science.

The most costly scientific effort was the development of radar, or radio detection and ranging devices. Building on British research on microwaves, the United States put $3 billion into the Radiation Laboratory at MIT. Increasingly compact and sophisticated radar systems helped to defeat the German and Japanese navies and to give the Allies control of the air over Europe. Radar research and engineering laid the basis for microwave technology, transistors, and integrated circuits after the war.

In the summer of 1945, *Time* magazine planned a cover story on radar as the weapon that won the war. However, the *Time* story was upstaged by the atomic bomb, the product of the war's other great scientific effort. As early as 1939, Albert Einstein had written to FDR about the possibility of such a weapon and the danger of falling behind the Germans. In late 1941, Roosevelt established the **Manhattan Project.** By December 2, 1942, scientists proved that it was possible to create and control a sustained nuclear reaction.

The Manhattan Project moved from theory to practice in 1943. The physicist J. Robert Oppenheimer directed the young scientists at Los Alamos in designing a nuclear-fission bomb. The Manhattan Project ushered in the age of atomic energy. The first bomb was tested on July 16, 1945. The explosion astonished even the physicists; Oppenheimer quoted from Hindu scriptures in trying to comprehend the results: "Now I am become Death, destroyer of worlds."

Men and Women in the Military

World War II required a more than thirtyfold expansion of the U.S. armed forces from their 1939 level of 334,000 soldiers, sailors, and Marines. By 1945, 8.3 million men and women were on active duty in the army and army air forces and 3.4 million in the navy and Marine Corps, totals exceeded only by the Soviet Union. In total, some 350,000 women and more than 16 million men served in the armed forces; 292,000 died in battle, 100,000 survived prisoner-of-war camps, and 671,000 returned wounded.

Native Americans in the military. Twenty-five thousand American Indians served in the armed forces. Most were in racially integrated units, and Harvey Natcheez, of the Ute tribe, was the first American to reach the center of conquered Berlin. Because the Navajo were one of the few tribes that had not been studied by German anthropologists, the Army Signal Corps decided that their language would be unknown to the Axis armies. Roughly 400 members of the tribe were "code-talkers" who served in Marine radio combat-communication teams in the Pacific theater, transmitting vital information in Navajo.

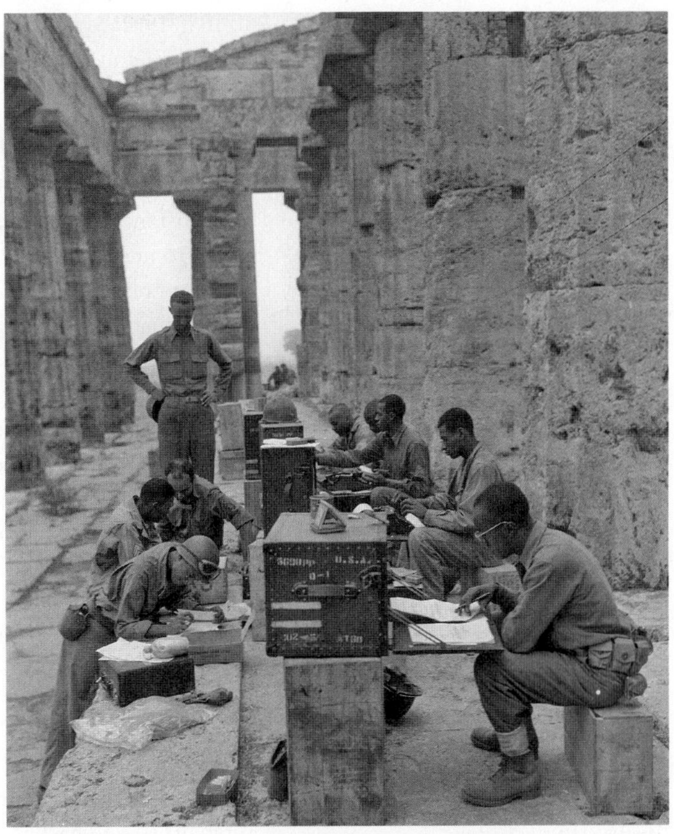

African Americans served in the military in large numbers during World War II. Here a signals company has set up operations in the ruins of an ancient temple in southern Italy.

African Americans in the military. Approximately 1 million African Americans served in the armed forces during World War II. African American leaders had pressed for a provision in the Selective Service Act to bar discrimination "against any person on account of race or color." But as it had since the Civil War, the army organized black soldiers in segregated units and often assigned them to the menial jobs, such as construction work, and excluded them from combat until manpower shortages forced changes in policy.

The average black soldier encountered discrimination on and off the base. Towns adjacent to army posts were sometimes open to white soldiers but off-limits to blacks. At some southern bases, German prisoners of war watched movies from the first rows along with white GIs while African American soldiers watched from the back. Military courts were quick to judge and harshly punish black GIs. It took racially based riots at army bases in North Carolina and Georgia to open up equal (although segregated) access to base recreation facilities.

Despite the obstacles, all-black units, such as the 761st Tank Battalion and the 99th Pursuit Squadron, earned distinguished records. More broadly, the war experience helped to invigorate postwar efforts to achieve equal rights, as had also been true after World War I.

Women in the military. The nation had a different—but also mixed—reaction to the women who joined the armed forces as army and navy nurses and as members of the WACS (Women's Army Corps), WAVES (Navy), SPARS (Coast Guard), and Marine Corps Women's Reserve. The armed services tried not to change established gender roles. Military officials told Congress that women in uniform could free men for combat. Many of the women hammered at typewriters, worked switchboards, inventoried supplies. Others, however, worked close to combat zones as photographers, code analysts, weather forecasters, radio operators, and nurses. WAC officers battled the tendency of the popular press to call females in the service "girls" rather than "women" or "soldiers" yet emphasized that military service promoted "poise and charm."

W
WHERE TO LEARN MORE
Bradbury Science Museum, Los Alamos, New Mexico
http://www.lanl.gov/museum

Read the **Document**
at **www.myhistorylab.com**
Albert Einstein, Letter to President Roosevelt (1939)

THE HOME FRONT

HOW DID the war alter American society?

The war inexorably penetrated everyday life. Residents in war-production cities had to cope with throngs of new workers. Especially in 1941 and 1942, many were unattached males—young men waiting for their draft call and older men without their families. Military and defense officials worried about sexually transmitted diseases and pressured cities to shut down their vice districts. At the same time, college officials scrambled to fill their classrooms, especially after the draft age dropped to 18 in 1942. Many colleges and universities responded to federal requests with special training programs for future officers and engineering and technical training for military personnel.

Families in Wartime

Many Americans put their lives on fast forward. Men ad women often decided to beat the clock with instant matrimony. Couples who had postponed marriage because of the depression could afford to marry as the economy picked up. War intensified casual romances and heightened the appeal of marriage as an anchor in troubled times. Altogether, the war years brought 1.2 million "extra" marriages, compared to the rate for the period 1920–1939.

The war's impact on families was gradual. The draft started with single men, then called up married men without children, and finally tapped fathers in 1943. Left at home were millions of "service wives," whose compensation from the government was $50 per month.

The war had mixed effects on children. "Latchkey children" of working mothers often had to fend for themselves, but middle-class kids whose mothers stayed home could treat the war as an interminable scout project, with salvage drives and campaigns to sell war bonds. In the rural Midwest children picked milkweed pods to stuff life jackets; in coastal communities, they participated in blackout drills. Seattle high schools set aside one class period a day for the High School Victory Corps, training boys as messengers for air-raid wardens, while girls knitted sweaters and learned first aid.

Read the **Document**
at **www.myhistorylab.com**
Exploring America: Propaganda

Learning about the War

The federal government tried to keep civilians of all ages committed to the war. It encouraged scrap drives and backyard victory gardens and created colorful posters to warn against espionage, inspire women to join the effort, and promote rationing and car-pooling. The government also managed news about the fighting. Censors screened soldiers' letters. Early in the war, they blocked publication of most photographs of war casualties, although magazines such as *Life* were full of strong and haunting images. Worried about flagging commitment, censors later authorized photographs of enemy atrocities to motivate the public.

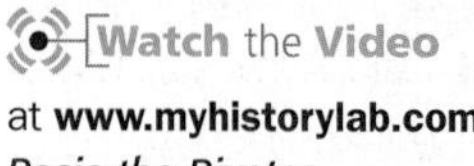

Watch the **Video**
at **www.myhistorylab.com**
Rosie the Riveter

War films revealed the nation's racial attitudes, often drawing distinctions between "good" and "bad" Germans but uniformly portraying Japanese as subhuman and repulsive. The most successful films dramatized the courage of the Allies.

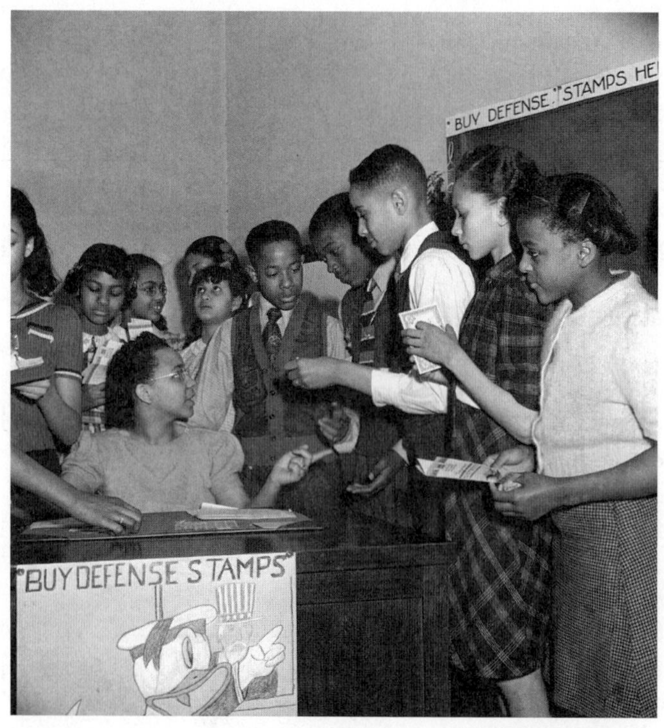

Students at a Washington, DC, high school buy defense stamps in March 1942. Defense stamps were small-denomination versions of war bonds, designed to involve young people in the home front effort.

Women in the Workforce

As draft calls took men off the assembly line, women changed the composition of the industrial workforce. The war gave them new job opportunities that were embodied in the image of Rosie the Riveter. Women made up one-quarter of West Coast shipyard workers and nearly half of Dallas and Seattle aircraft workers. Most women in the shipyards were clerks and general helpers. The acute shortage of welders and other skilled workers, however, opened thousands of lucrative journeyman positions to them. Aircraft companies, which compounded the labor shortage by stubborn "whites only" hiring, developed new power tools and production techniques to accommodate the smaller average size of women workers, increasing efficiency for everyone on the production line.

By July 1944, 19 million women held paid jobs, up 6 million in four years. Women's share of government jobs increased from 19 to

38 percent; they typed and filed in offices, but they also wrote propaganda for the Office of War Information and analyzed intelligence data for the office of Strategic Service. Women's share of manufacturing jobs went from 22 to 33 percent, many of them as W.O.W.s or Woman Ordnance Workers. Mirroring the sequence in which the military draft took men, employers recruited single women before turning to married women in 1943 and 1944. The federal government assisted female entry into the labor force by funding daycare programs that served 600,000 children. Some women worked out of patriotism. Many others, however, needed to support their families and already had years of experience in the workforce. As one of the workers recalled of herself and a friend, "We both had to work, we both had children, so we became welders, and if I might say so, damn good ones."

Americans did not know how to respond to the growing numbers of working women. The country needed their labor, but many worried that their employment would undermine families. Employment recruitment posters showed strong, handsome women with rolled-up sleeves and wrenches in hand, but *Life* magazine reassured readers that women in factories could retain their sex appeal. Men and women commonly assumed that women would want to return to the home after victory.

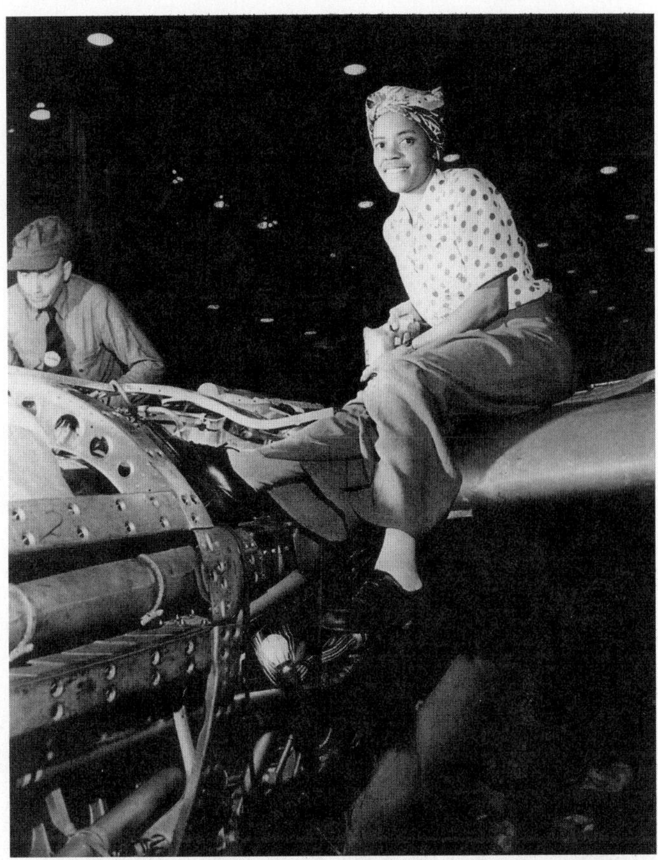

As millions of men entered the armed forces, millions of women went to work. By 1943, federal agencies were actively recruiting women workers. Those who took production-line jobs received the greatest attention, like this worker at the Lockheed Aircraft Corporation plant in Burbank, California, which produced thousands of P-38 "Lightning" fighter planes.

Ethnic Minorities in the War Effort

Mexican American workers made special contributions to the war effort. As defense factories and the military absorbed workers, western farms and railroads faced an acute shortage of workers. In the 1930s, western states had tried to deport Mexican nationals who were competing for scarce jobs. In 1942, however, the United States and Mexico negotiated the *bracero* program, under which the Mexican government recruited workers to come to the United States on six-to-twelve month contracts. More than 200,000 Mexicans worked on U.S. farms under the program, and more than 100,000 worked for western railroads. Although *bracero* workers still faced discrimination, the U.S. government tried to improve working conditions because it wanted to keep public opinion in Latin America favorable to the Allied cause.

The war was a powerful force for the assimilation of Native Americans. Forty thousand moved to off-reservation jobs; they were a key labor force for military supply depots throughout the West. The average cash income of Indian households tripled during the war. Many stayed in cities at its end. The experience of the war accelerated the fight for full civil rights. Congress had made Indians citizens in 1924, in part to recognize their contributions in World War I, but several states continued to deny them the vote. Activists organized the National Congress of American Indians in 1944 and began the efforts that led the U.S. Supreme Court in 1948 to require states to grant voting rights.

African Americans, too, found economic advancement through war jobs. Early in the mobilization, labor leader A. Philip Randolph of the Brotherhood of Sleeping Car Porters worked with Walter White of the NAACP to plan a "Negro March on Washington" to protest racial discrimination by the federal government. To head off a major embarrassment, Roosevelt issued Executive Order 8802 in June 1941, barring racial discrimination in defense contracts and creating the **Fair Employment Practices Committee (FEPC);** the order coined a phrase that reverberated powerfully through the coming decades: "No discrimination on grounds of race, color, creed, or national origin."

The FEPC's small staff resolved fewer than half of the employment-discrimination complaints, and white resistance to black coworkers remained strong. In Mobile, New Orleans, and Jacksonville,

QUICK REVIEW

Rosie the Riveter

- Demand for labor drew women into the workplace.
- Companies opened positions for women in nontraditional jobs.
- Government funded daycare programs to help women enter the workforce.

Read the **Document**
at **www.myhistorylab.com**
A. Philip Randolph, "Why Should We March" (1942)

Read the **Document**
at **www.myhistorylab.com**
Executive Order 8802 (1941)

Fair Employment Practices Committee (FEPC) Federal agency established in 1941 to curb racial discrimination in war production jobs and government employment.

AMERICANOS TODOS
LUCHAMOS POR LA VICTORIA
AMERICANS ALL
LET'S FIGHT FOR VICTORY

The government worked hard to encourage Hispanics to support the war effort, both for their contributions and to maintain good relations with Mexico and other Latin American nations.

agreements between shipyards and segregated unions blocked skilled black workers from high-wage jobs. Nevertheless, African American membership in labor unions doubled, and wartime prosperity raised the average black income from 41 percent of the white average in 1939 to 61 percent by 1950, particularly because labor shortages raised farm wages.

Outside the workplace, African American women found that many voluntary service groups were racially segregated. In response, they formed the Women's Army for National Defense. They did their part by selling war bonds, helping with civil defense, and organizing USO clubs for black soldiers.

Many African Americans saw themselves as engaged in a "Double V" effort for victory against tyranny abroad and victory over racism at home. Economic gains helped. So did the fact that many were able to vote for the first time, either because they had moved to northern states where voting was not racially limited or because they were servicemen serving overseas. The economic and political changes helped to build a base for the civil rights movement that gained momentum in the postwar decades.

Clashing Cultures

As men and women migrated in search of work, they also crossed or collided with traditional boundaries of religion, region, and race. Some of the most troublesome conflicts arose from the acceleration of African American migration out of the South in the early 1940s. Many of the migrants headed for well-established black neighborhoods in northern cities. Others created new African American neighborhoods in western cities. White southerners and black northerners with different ideas of racial etiquette found themselves side by side in West Coast shipyards. In the Midwest, black migrants from the South and white migrants from Appalachia crowded into cities such as Cincinnati and Chicago, competing for the same high-wage jobs and scarce apartments.

Tensions between black and white residents exploded in at least 50 cities in 1943 alone. New York's Harlem neighborhood erupted in a riot after rumors of attacks on black servicemen. In Detroit, the issue was the boundary between white and black territory. In June 1943, an argument over the use of Detroit's Belle Isle Park set off three days of violence: Twenty-five black people and nine white people died in the most serious racial riot of the war.

Watch the Video
at **www.myhistorylab.com**
The Desegregation of the Military and Blacks in Combat

Tensions were simultaneously rising between Mexican Americans and Anglos. As the Mexican community in Los Angeles swelled to an estimated 400,000, newspapers published anti-Mexican articles. On June 6, 1943, off-duty sailors and soldiers attacked Latinos on downtown streets and invaded Mexican American neighborhoods. The main targets were so-called *pachucos*—young Chicanos who wore flamboyant "zoot suits" with long, wide-shouldered jackets and pleated, narrow-cuffed trousers, whom the rioters considered delinquents or draft dodgers. The attacks dragged on for a week of sporadic violence against black people and Filipinos as well as Latinos. The assaults were poignantly ironic because 750,000 Mexican Americans served in the armed forces and were the most decorated group relative to their numbers.

QUICK REVIEW

Race Riots

- 1943: Violent confrontations between blacks and whites in at least fifty cities.
- Detroit, June 1943: Most serious riot of the war results in thirty-four deaths.
- Los Angeles, June 6, 1943: Sailors and soldiers attack young Chicanos.

Internment of Japanese Americans

On February 19, 1942, President Roosevelt authorized the secretary of war to define restricted areas and remove civilian residents who were threats to national security. The primary targets were 112,000 Japanese Americans in California and parts of Washington, Oregon, and Arizona. Japanese immigrants and their children in the western states had experienced 40 years of hostility because of racial prejudice, fear of the growing power of Japan, and jealousy of their business success. The outbreak of war triggered anti-Japanese hysteria and gave officials an excuse to take action against enemy aliens (immigrants who retained Japanese citizenship) and their American-born children.

Most West Coast Japanese were unable to leave because of ties to families and businesses. At the end of April 1942, Japanese in the coastal states were given a week to organize their affairs and report to assembly centers at fairgrounds and armories, where they were housed for several weeks before being moved again to ten internment camps in isolated locations in the western interior (see American Views: Internment of Japanese Americans in 1942). Here, they were housed in tarpaper barracks, hemmed in by barbed-wire fences, and guarded by military police. The victims reacted to the hardship and stress of their forced journeys in different ways. Several thousand second-generation Japanese Americans renounced their citizenship in disgust. But many others demonstrated their loyalty by cooperating with the authorities, finding sponsors who would help them move to other parts of the country, or joining the 442nd Regimental Combat Team, the most decorated American unit in the European war.

Although the U.S. Supreme Court sanctioned the removals in *Korematsu v. United States* (1944), the nation officially recognized its liability for lost property with the Japanese Claims Act of 1948. The nation acknowledged its broader moral responsibility in 1988, when Congress approved redress payments to each of the 60,000 surviving evacuees.

The internment of West Coast Japanese contrasted with the situation of German Americans and Italian Americans. The government interned approximately 11,000 German nationals and German Americans who were explicitly seen as individual threats. Until November 1942, it imposed curfews and travel restrictions on Italians and Italian Americans on the West Coast, but it interned fewer than 2,000. Both numbers were tiny fractions of the total populations.

The End of the New Deal

Roosevelt's New Deal ran out of steam in 1938. The war had reinvigorated his political fortunes by focusing national energies on foreign policy, over which presidents have the greatest power. After the 1942 election left Congress in the hands of Republicans and conservative southern Democrats, lawmakers ignored proposals that war emergency housing be used to improve the nation's permanent housing stock, abolished the National Resources Planning Board, curtailed rural electrification, and crippled the Farm Security Administration. Roosevelt himself declared, at a 1943 press conference, that "Dr. Win-the-War" had replaced "Dr. New Deal."

The presidential election of 1944 raised few new issues of substance. The Republicans nominated Governor Thomas Dewey of New York, who had made his reputation as a crime-fighting district attorney. The Democrats renominated Roosevelt for a fourth term. Missouri Senator Harry S Truman, a tough investigator of American military preparedness, replaced liberal New Dealer Henry Wallace as

In 1942, the federal government removed Japanese Americans from parts of four western states and interned them in isolated camps scattered through the West.

Roosevelt's running mate. The move appeased southern Democrats and moved the ticket toward the political center.

The most important issue was a fourth term for Roosevelt. Supporters argued that the nation could not afford to change leaders in the middle of a war, but Dewey's vigor and relative youth (he was 20 years younger than FDR) pointed up the president's failing health and energy. Voters gave Roosevelt 432 electoral votes to 99, but the narrowing gap in the popular vote—54 percent for Roosevelt and 46 percent for Dewey—made the Republicans eager for 1948.

WAR AND PEACE

WHY DID the Allies win the war?

In January 1943, the U.S. War Department completed the world's largest office building, the Pentagon. The building housed 23,000 workers along 17.5 miles of corridors. The building provided the space in which military planners could coordinate the tasks of raising and equipping the armed forces that would strike directly at Germany and Japan. Indeed, while Congress was chipping away at federal programs, the war effort was massively expanding the government presence in American life. The gray walls of the Pentagon symbolized a U.S. government that was outgrowing its prewar roots.

Turning the Tide in Europe

The unanswered military question of 1942 and 1943 was when the United States and Britain would open a second front against Germany by attacking across the English Channel. U.S. leaders wanted to justify massive mobilization with a war-winning campaign and to strike across Europe to occupy the heart of Germany. Stalin needed a full-scale invasion of western Europe to divert German forces from the Eastern Front, where Soviet troops were inflicting 90 percent of German battle casualties.

The Allies spent 1943 hammering out war aims and strategies. Meeting in Casablanca in January 1943, Roosevelt and Churchill demanded the unconditional surrender of Italy, Germany, and Japan. The phrase meant that there would be no deals that kept the enemy governments or leaders in power and was an effort to avoid the mistake of ending World War I with Germany intact. Ten months later, the Allied leaders huddled again. At Tehran, the United States and Britain promised to invade France within six months. "We leave here," said the three leaders, "friends in fact, in spirit, in purpose."

QUICK REVIEW

Allied Collaboration

- 1943: U.S. and Soviet leaders prepare for a full-scale invasion of Europe.
- Soviet advances made possible by U.S. equipment and materials.
- November 1943: Allied leaders leave Tehran with a timetable for invasion of Europe.

The superficial harmony barely survived the end of the war. The Soviets had shouldered the brunt of the war for nearly two and a half years, suffering millions of casualties and seeing their nation devastated. Stalin and his generals scoffed at the small scale of early U.S. efforts. Roosevelt's ideal of self-determination for all peoples, embodied in the Atlantic Charter, seemed naive to Churchill, who wanted the major powers to carve out realistic spheres of influence in Europe. Stalin wanted control of eastern Europe to protect the Soviet Union against future invasions and assumed that realistic statesmen would understand.

The campaign in North Africa. The United States entered the ground war in Europe with Operation TORCH. Soon after the British victory at El Alamein, British and American troops under General Dwight Eisenhower landed in French Morocco and Algeria on November 8, 1942, against little opposition (see Map 26–3). These were territories that the Germans had left under a puppet French government after the French military collapse in 1940. German troops that remained in North Africa taught U.S. forces hard lessons in tactics and leadership, but their stubborn resistance ended in May 1943, leaving all of Africa in Allied hands.

The invasion of Italy. The central Mediterranean remained the focus of U.S. and British action for the next year, despite the fact that the hard-pressed Soviets were desperate for their allies to attack the heart of German power in northern Europe. However, the British feared

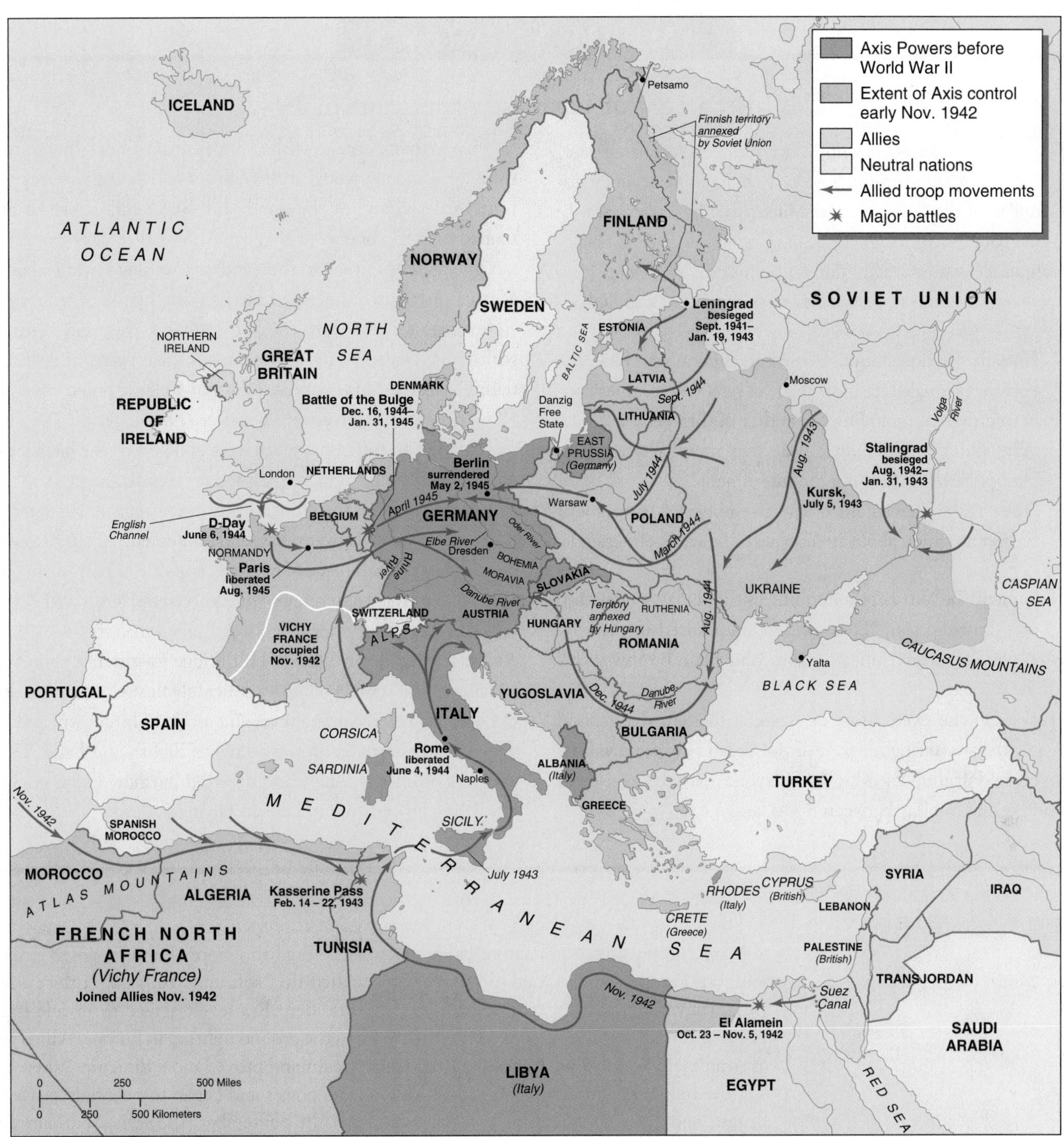

MAP 26–3 **World War II in Europe, 1942–1945** Nazi Germany had to defend its conquests on three fronts. Around the Mediterranean, American and British forces pushed the Germans out of Africa and southern Italy, while guerrillas in Yugoslavia pinned down many German troops. On the Eastern Front, Soviet armies advanced hundreds of miles to drive the German Army out of the Soviet Union and eastern Europe. In June 1944, U.S. and British landings opened the Western Front in northern France for a decisive strike at the heart of Germany.

What were the turning points in the war in Europe?

AMERICAN VIEWS

The Internment of Japanese Americans in 1942

In the spring of 1942, the U.S. army ordered Japanese Americans in four western states relocated to internment camps distant from the Pacific Coast. Monica Itoi Sone describes the experience of her Seattle family as they were transferred to temporary quarters—at the state fairgrounds, renamed "Camp Harmony" by the military—before they were moved again to Idaho.

- **How** do the expectations of *issei* (immigrants who had been born in Japan) differ from those of *nisei* (their American-born children, including the author of this memoir)?
- **Why** did the U.S. army wait five months after Pearl Harbor before beginning the internment?
- **Does** the management of the assembly and internment suggest anything about stereotypes of Japanese Americans?

General DeWitt kept reminding us that E day, evacuation day, was drawing near. "E day will be announced in the very near future. If you have not wound up your affairs by now, it will soon be too late."

. . . On the twenty-first of April, a Tuesday, the general gave us the shattering news. "All the Seattle Japanese will be moved to Puyallup by May 1. Everyone must be registered Saturday and Sunday between 8 A.M. and 5 P.M."

Up to that moment, we had hoped against hope that something or someone would intervene for us. Now there was no time for moaning. A thousand and one details must be attended to in this one week of grace. Those seven days sputtered out like matches struck in the wind, as we rushed wildly about. Mother distributed sheets, pillowcases and blankets, which we stuffed into seabags. Into the two suitcases, we packed heavy winter overcoats, plenty of sweaters, woolen slacks and skirts, flannel pajamas and scarves. Personal toilet articles, one tin plate, tin cup and silverware completed our luggage. The one seabag and two suitcases apiece were going to be the backbone of our future home, and we planned it carefully.

Henry went to the Control Station to register the family. He came home with twenty tags, all numbered "10710," tags to be attached to each piece of baggage, and one to hang from our coat lapels. From then on, we were known as Family #10710. [On the day set for relocation] we climbed into the truck. . . . As we coasted down Beacon Hill bridge for the last time, we fell silent, and stared out at the delicately flushed, morning sky of Puget Sound. We drove through bustling Chinatown, and in a few minutes arrived on the corner of Eighth and Lane. This area was ordinarily lonely and deserted but now it was gradually filling up with silent, labeled Japanese. . . .

military disaster from a premature landing across the English Channel and proposed strikes in southern Europe, which Churchill inaccurately called the "soft underbelly" of Hitler's empire. U.S. Army Chief of Staff George Marshall and President Roosevelt agreed to invade Italy in 1943, in part so that U.S. troops could participate in the ground fighting in Europe. Allied forces overran Sicily in July and August, but the Italian mainland proved more difficult. When Sicily fell, the Italian king and army forced Mussolini from power and began to negotiate peace with Britain and America (but not the Soviet Union). In September, the Allies announced an armistice with Italy, and Eisenhower's troops landed south of Naples on September 9. Germany responded by occupying the rest of Italy.

Just as American military planners had feared, the Italian campaign soaked up Allied resources. The mountainous Italian peninsula was one long series of defensive positions, and the Allies repeatedly bogged down. The Allies only managed to gain control of two-thirds of Italy before German resistance crumbled in the final weeks of the war.

Soviet advances and the Battle of Kursk. Meanwhile, the Soviets recruited, rearmed, and upgraded new armies, despite enormous losses. They learned to outfight the Germans in tank warfare and rebuilt munitions factories beyond German reach. They also made good use of 17.5 million tons of U.S. lend-lease assistance. As Soviet soldiers recaptured western Russia and

Finally at ten o'clock, a vanguard of Greyhound busses purred in and parked themselves neatly along the curb. The crowd stirred and murmured. The bus doors opened and from each, a soldier with rifle in hand stepped out and stood stiffly at attention by the door. . . .

Newspaper photographers with flash-bulb cameras pushed busily through the crowd. One of them rushed up to our bus, and asked a young couple and their little boy to step out and stand by the door for a shot. They were reluctant, but the photographers were persistent and at length they got out of the bus and posed, grinning widely to cover their embarrassment. We saw the picture in the newspaper shortly after and the caption underneath it read, "japs good-natured about evacuation." Our bus quickly filled to capacity. . . . The door closed with a low hiss. We were now the Wartime Civil Control Administration's babies.

About noon we crept into a small town . . . and we noticed at the left of us an entire block filled with neat rows of low shacks, resembling chicken houses. Someone commented on it with awe, "Just look at those chicken houses. They sure go in for poultry in a big way here." Slowly the bus made a left turn, drove through a wire-fenced gate, and to our dismay, we were inside the oversized chicken farm. . . .

The apartments resembled elongated, low stables about two blocks long. Our home was one room, about 18 by 20 feet, the size of a living room. There was one small window in the wall opposite the one door. It was bare except for a small, tinny wood-burning stove crouching in the center. . . .

I stared at our little window, unable to sleep. I was glad Mother had put up a makeshift curtain on the window for I noticed a powerful beam of light sweeping across it every few seconds. The lights came from high towers placed around the camp where guards with Tommy guns kept a twenty-four hour vigil. I remembered the wire fence encircling us, and a knot of anger tightened in my breast. What was I doing behind a fence like a criminal? If there were accusations to be made, why hadn't I been given a fair trial? Maybe I wasn't considered an American anymore. My citizenship wasn't real, after all. Then what was I? I was certainly not a citizen of Japan as my parents were. On second thought, even Father and Mother . . . had little tie with their mother country. In their twenty-five years in America, they had worked and paid their taxes to their adopted government as any other citizen.

Of one thing I was sure. The wire fence was real. I no longer had the right to walk out of it. It was because I had Japanese ancestors. It was also because some people had little faith in the ideas and ideals of democracy.

Source: Monica Itoi Sone, *Nisei Daughter* (Seattle: University of Washington Press, 1979).

Ukraine, they marched in 13 million pairs of American-made boots and ate U.S. rations. They traveled in 78,000 jeeps and 350,000 Studebaker, Ford, and Dodge trucks.

The climactic battle of the German-Soviet war erupted on July 5, 1943. The Germans sent 3,000 tanks against the Kursk salient, a huge wedge that the Red Army had pushed into their lines. In 1941 and 1942, such a massive attack would have forced the Soviets to retreat, but now Soviet generals had prepared a defense with 3,000 tanks of their own. With 1 million men actively engaged on each side for more than two weeks, Kursk was the largest pitched battle of the war. It marked the end of the last great German offensive, leaving Germany capable of a fighting retreat but too weak to have any hope of winning the war and expecting an American and British attack across the English Channel.

QUICK REVIEW

The Beginning of the End

- Allies gained footholds in North Africa.
- Allies took control of much of Italy.
- Germany's last offensive in Russia was turned back.

Operation OVERLORD

On **D-Day**—June 6, 1944—American, British, and Canadian forces landed on the coast of Normandy in northwestern France. The landings were the largest amphibious operation ever staged. Six divisions went ashore from hundreds of attack transports carrying 4,000 landing craft. Dozens of warships and 12,000 aircraft provided support. One British and two American airborne divisions dropped behind German positions. When the sun set on the "longest day," the Allies had a tenuous toehold in France.

D-Day June 6, 1944, the day of the first paratroop drops and amphibious landings on the coast of Normandy, France, in the first stage of Operation OVERLORD during World War II.

Operation OVERLORD U.S. and British invasion of France in June 1944 during World War II.

The next few weeks brought limited success. The Allies secured their beachheads and poured more than a million men and hundreds of thousands of vehicles ashore in the first six weeks. Although the Germans had concentrated forces further north where they expected the attack, the German defenders kept the Allies pinned for weeks along a narrow coastal strip. **Operation OVERLORD,** the code name for the entire campaign across northern France, met renewed success in late July and August. U.S. troops improved their fighting skills through "experience, sheer bloody experience." They finally broke through the German lines around the town of St.-Lô and then drew a ring around the Germans that slowly closed on the town of Falaise. The Germans lost a quarter of a million troops.

The German command chose to regroup closer to Germany rather than fight in France. The Allies liberated Paris on August 25; Free French forces (units that had never surrendered to the Nazis) led the entry. The drive toward Germany was the largest U.S. operation of the war. The only impediments appeared to be winter weather and pushing forward enough supplies for the rapidly advancing armies.

The story was similar on the Eastern Front, where the Soviets relentlessly battered one section of the German lines after another. By the end of 1944, the Red Army had entered the Balkans and reached central Poland. The Soviets had suffered as many as 24 million military and civilian deaths and sustained by far the heaviest burden in turning back Nazi tyranny (see Table 26–1).

Table 26-1

Military and Civilian Deaths in World War II

24 million	Soviet Union
10–20 million	China
6–7 million	Germany and Austria
5.8 million	Poland
3–4 million	Indonesia
2.7 million	Japan
1–2 million	French Indochina (Vietnam, Laos, Cambodia)
	India
	Yugoslavia
500,000–1 million	France
	Greece
	Hungary
	Philippines
	Romania
300,000–500,000	Czechoslovakia
	Great Britain
	Italy
	Korea
	Lithuania
	The Netherlands
	United States

Victory and Tragedy in Europe

See the Map at www.myhistorylab.com *World War II, European Theater*

In the last months of 1944, massive air strikes finally began to reduce German war production, which had actually increased during 1943 and much of 1944. The Americans flew daylight raids from air bases in Britain with heavily armed B-17s ("Flying Fortresses") and B-24s ("Liberators") to destroy factories with precision bombing. On August 17, 1943, however, Germans shot down or damaged 19 percent of the bombers that attacked the aircraft factories of Regensburg and the ball-bearing factories of Schweinfurt. The Americans had to seek easier targets.

Gradually, however, the balance shifted. P-51 escort fighters helped B-17s overfly Germany in relative safety after mid-1944. Thousand-bomber raids on railroads and oil facilities began to cripple the German economy. The raids forced Germany to devote 2.5 million workers to air defense and damage repair and to divert fighter planes from the front lines. The air raids cut German military production by one-third through 1944 and destroyed the transportation system.

The Battle of the Bulge and the collapse of Germany. Even as the air bombardment intensified, Hitler struck a last blow. Stripping the Eastern Front of armored units, he launched 25 divisions against thinly held U.S. positions in the Ardennes Forest of Belgium on December 16, 1944. He hoped to split U.S. and British forces by capturing the Belgian port of Antwerp. The attack surprised the Americans, and taking advantage of snow and fog that grounded Allied aircraft, the Germans drove a 50-mile bulge into U.S. lines. Although the Americans took substantial casualties, the German thrust literally ran out of gas beyond the town of Bastogne. The Battle of the Bulge never seriously threatened the outcome of the war, but pushing the Germans back through the snow-filled forest gave GIs a taste of the conditions that marked the war in the Soviet Union.

One of the war's most controversial actions came in February 1945, when British and American bombers attacked the historic city of Dresden. The raid triggered a firestorm that killed 25,000 people, many of them civilian refugees displaced by the Soviet advance. Because the Soviet army was less than a hundred miles from Berlin but the western allies had yet to cross the Rhine, critics have seen the raid as a purely political gesture by the British and Americans against a nonmilitary target. However, Dresden did have suburban factories producing for the military, and the city was a junction of major rail and telephone lines whose disruption created another obstacle to Germany's last-ditch resistance.

The Nazi empire collapsed in the spring of 1945. American and British divisions crossed the Rhine in March and enveloped Germany's industrial core. The Soviets drove through eastern Germany toward Berlin. On April 25, American and Soviet troops met on the Elbe River. Hitler committed suicide on April 30 in his concrete bunker deep under devastated Berlin, which surrendered to the Soviets on May 2. The Nazi state formally capitulated on May 8.

W
WHERE TO LEARN MORE
United States Holocaust Memorial Museum, Washington, DC
http://www.ushmm.org

The Holocaust. The defeat of Germany revealed appalling evidence of the evil at the heart of the Nazi ideology of racial superiority. After occupying Poland in 1939, the Nazis had transformed concentration camps into forced-labor camps, where overwork, starvation, and disease killed hundreds of thousands of Jews, Gypsies, Poles, Russians, and others the Nazis classed as subhuman. As many as 7 million labor conscripts from eastern and western Europe provided forced labor in fields, factories, mines, and repair crews, often dying on the job from overwork and starvation.

The "final solution" to what Hitler thought of as the "Jewish problem" went far beyond slave labor. The German army in 1941 had gained practice with death by slaughtering hundreds of thousands of Jews and other civilians as it swept across Russia. In the fall of that year, Hitler decided on the total elimination of Europe's Jews. The elite SS, Hitler's personal army within the Nazi Party, in 1942 set out to do his bidding. At Auschwitz, Treblinka, and several other death camps, the SS organized the efficient extermination of up to 6 million Jews and 1 million Poles, Gypsies, and others who failed to fit the Nazi vision of the German master race. Prisoners arrived

The Nazi regime sent slave laborers too weak to continue working on its V-2 rocket project to the Nordhausen concentration camp to die of starvation. When U.S. troops liberated the camp in April 1945, they found more than 3,000 corpses.

by forced marches and cattle trains. Those who were not worked or starved to death were herded into gas chambers and then incinerated in huge crematoriums.

The evidence of genocide—systematic racial murder—is irrefutable. Allied officials had begun to hear reports of mass murder midway through the war, but memories of the inaccurate propaganda about German atrocities in World War I made many skeptical. Moreover, the camps were located in the heart of German-controlled territory, areas that Allied armies did not reach until 1945. At Dachau in southwestern Germany, American forces found 10,000 bodies and 32,000 prisoners near death through starvation. Soviet troops who overran the camps in Poland found even more appalling sights—gas chambers as big as barns, huge ovens, the dead stacked like firewood. For more than half a century, the genocide that we now call the **Holocaust** has given the world its most vivid images of inhumanity.

Holocaust The systematic murder of millions of European Jews and others deemed undesirable by Nazi Germany.

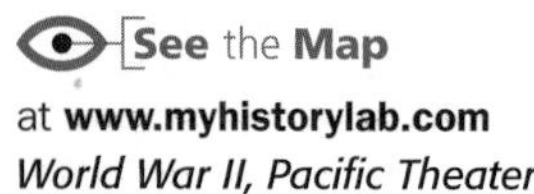

at **www.myhistorylab.com**
World War II, Pacific Theater

National Museum of the Pacific War, Fredericksburg, Texas
http://www.nimitz-museum.org

Island hopping The Pacific campaigns of 1944 that were the American naval versions of the *Blitzkrieg*.

The Pacific War

In the Pacific, as in Europe, the United States used 1943 to probe enemy conquests and to build better submarines, bigger aircraft carriers, and superior planes. Washington divided responsibilities in the Pacific theater. General Douglas MacArthur operated in the islands that stretched between Australia and the Philippines. Admiral Chester Nimitz commanded in the central Pacific. The Allies planned to isolate Japan from its southern conquests. The British moved from India to retake Burma. The Americans advanced along the islands of the southern Pacific to retake the Philippines. With Japan's army still tied down in China, the Americans then planned to bomb Japan into submission.

Racial hatred animated both sides in the Pacific war and fueled a "war without mercy." Americans often characterized Japanese soldiers as vermin. Political cartoons showed Japanese as monkeys or rats, and some Marines had "Rodent Exterminator" stenciled on their helmets. In turn, the Japanese depicted themselves as the "leading race" with the duty to rule the rest of Asia. Japan treated Chinese, Filipinos, and other conquered peoples with contempt and brutality, and the record of Japanese atrocities is substantial. Japanese viewed Americans as racial mongrels and called them demons. Each side expected the worst of the other and frequently lived up to expectations.

The Pacific campaigns of 1944 are often called **island hopping.** Planes from American carriers controlled the air, allowing the navy and land forces to isolate and capture the most strategically located Japanese-held islands while bypassing the rest.

MacArthur used a version of the bypass strategy in the Solomon Islands and New Guinea, leapfrogging past Japanese strong points. The invasion of the Philippines repeated the approach by landing on Leyte, in the middle of the island chain. The Philippine campaign also destroyed the last offensive capacity of the Japanese fleet in the Battle of Leyte Gulf. The Japanese home islands were left with no defensive screen against an expected invasion.

During 1943 and 1944, the United States also savaged the Japanese economy. Submarines choked off food, oil, and raw materials bound for Japan and island bases. By 1945, imports to Japan were one-eighth of the 1940 level. Heavy bombing of Japan began in early 1944, using the new long-range B-29. Japan's dense wooden cities were more vulnerable than their German counterparts, and

Japanese air defenses were much weaker. A fire-bomb raid on Tokyo on the night of March 9, 1945, killed 124,000 people and left 1 million homeless; it was perhaps the single biggest mass killing of all time. Overall, conventional bombing destroyed 42 percent of Japan's industrial capacity. By the time the United States captured the islands of Iwo Jima and Okinawa in fierce fighting (April–June 1945) and neared the Japanese home islands, Japan's position was hopeless.

Searching for Peace

At the beginning of 1945, the Allies sensed victory. Conferring from February 4 to 11 in the Ukrainian town of Yalta, Roosevelt, Stalin, and Churchill planned for the postwar world. The most important American goal was to enlist the Soviet Union in finishing off the Pacific war. Americans hoped that a Soviet attack on Manchuria would tie down enough Japanese troops to reduce U.S. casualties in invading Japan. Stalin repeated his intent to declare war on Japan within three months of victory in Europe, in return for a free hand in Manchuria.

In Europe, the Allies had decided in 1944 to divide Germany and Austria into French, British, American, and Soviet occupation zones and to share control of Berlin. The Red Army already controlled Bulgaria, Romania, and Hungary, countries that had helped the Germans; Soviet officials were installing sympathetic regimes there. Soviet armies also controlled Poland. The most that Roosevelt could coax from Stalin was a vague pledge to allow participation of non-communists in coalition governments in eastern Europe. Stalin also agreed to join a new international organization, the United Nations (UN), whose foundations were laid at a conference in San Francisco in the spring of 1945. The new organization was intended to correct the mistakes of World War I, when the United States had stayed aloof from the League of Nations and had relied on international treaties without mechanisms of enforcement. American leaders wanted the UN to provide a framework through which the United States could coordinate collective security against potential aggressors while retaining its own military strength as the primary means to preserve the peace.

Conservative critics later charged that the western powers "gave away" eastern Europe at the **Yalta Conference.** In fact, the Soviet Union gained little that it did not already control. In East Asia as well, the Soviets could seize the territories the agreement granted them. Roosevelt may have overestimated his ability to charm Stalin, but the Yalta agreements were realistic diplomacy that could not undo the results of four years of fighting by the Soviet Army.

Yalta Conference Meeting of U.S. President Franklin Roosevelt, British Prime Minister Winston Churchill, and Soviet Premier Joseph Stalin held in February 1945 to plan the final stages of World War II and postwar arrangements.

Truman and Potsdam. On April 12, two months after Yalta, Roosevelt died of a cerebral hemorrhage. Harry Truman, the new president, was a shrewd politician, but his experience was limited; Roosevelt had not even told him about the Manhattan Project. Deeply distrustful of the Soviets, Truman first ventured into personal international diplomacy in July 1945 at a British-Soviet-American conference at Potsdam, near Berlin. Most of the sessions debated the future of Germany. The leaders endorsed the expulsion of ethnic Germans from eastern Europe and moved the borders of Poland 100 miles west into historically German territory. Truman also made it clear that the United States expected to dominate the occupation of Japan. Its goal was to democratize the Japanese political system and reintroduce Japan into the international community, a policy that succeeded. The **Potsdam Declaration** on July 26 summarized U.S. policy and gave Japan an opening for surrender. However, the declaration failed to guarantee that Emperor Hirohito would not be tried as a war criminal. The Japanese response was so cautious that Americans read it as rejection.

QUICK REVIEW

Preparations for Victory

- February 1945: Allies debate plans for postwar world at Yalta.
- Soviets solidified their hold on eastern Europe.
- July 26, 1945: Potsdam Declaration fails to produce a definitive response from Japan.

Potsdam Declaration Statement issued by the United States during a meeting of U.S. President Harry Truman, British Prime Minister Winston Churchill, and Soviet Premier Joseph Stalin in which the United States declared its intention to democratize the Japanese political system and reintroduce Japan into the international community.

The atomic bomb. Secretary of State James Byrnes now urged Truman to use the new atomic bomb, tested just weeks earlier. Japan's ferocious defense of Okinawa had confirmed American fears that the Japanese would fight to the death. Thousands of suicide missions by kamikaze pilots who tried to crash their planes into U.S. warships seemed additional proof of Japanese fanaticism. Prominent Americans were wondering if unconditional surrender was worth another six or nine months of bitter fighting. In contrast, using the bomb to end the conflict quickly would ensure that the United States could occupy Japan without Soviet participation, and the bomb might intimidate

Watch the **Video**
at **www.myhistorylab.com**
Atomic Bomb at Hiroshima

The ruins of Hiroshima in the aftermath of the atomic bomb. Atomic bombs, dropped first on Hiroshima and then on Nagasaki in August 1945, instantly destroyed most of each city. Now one airplane could wreak the kind of devastation that massive fire-bombing raids had inflicted on cities such as Hamburg and Tokyo, adding new terror to the idea of total war.

Stalin (see Overview, The Decision to Use the Atomic Bomb). In short, a decision not to use atomic weapons was never a serious alternative in the summer of 1945.

In early August, the United States dropped two of the three available nuclear bombs on Japan. On August 6, at Hiroshima, the first bomb killed at least 80,000 people and poisoned thousands more with radiation. A second bomb, three days later at Nagasaki, took another 40,000 lives. Japan ceased hostilities on August 14 and surrendered formally on September 2. The world has wondered ever since whether the United States might have defeated Japan without resorting to atomic bombs, but recent research shows that the bombs were the shock that allowed the emperor and peace advocates to overcome military leaders who wanted to fight to the death.

How the Allies Won

The Allies won with economic capacity, technology, and military skill. The ability to outproduce the enemy made victory certain in 1944 and 1945, but it was the ability to outthink and outmaneuver the Axis powers that staved off defeat in 1942 and 1943.

WHERE TO LEARN MORE

National Museum of the U.S. Air Force, Dayton, Ohio
http://www.nationalmuseum.af.mil/

In the spring of 1942, an unbroken series of conquests had given the Axis powers control of roughly one-third of the world's production of industrial raw materials, up from only 5 percent in 1939. But while Germany and Japan struggled to turn these resources into military strength, the Soviet Union accomplished wonders in relocating and rebuilding its manufacturing capacity after the disasters of 1941. The United States, meanwhile, rearmed with astonishing swiftness, accomplishing in one year what Germany had thought would take three. By 1944, the United States was outproducing all of its enemies combined; over the course of the war, it manufactured two-thirds of all the war materials used by the Allies.

The United States and the Soviet Union not only built more planes and tanks than the Axis nations, but they also built better ones. The Soviets developed and mass-produced the T-34, the world's most effective tank. American aircraft designers soon jumped ahead of the Germans. The United States and Britain gained the lead in communication systems, radar, code-breaking capability, and, of course, atomic weapons. Even behind the lines the Allies had the technical advantage. The U.S. and British forces that invaded France were fully motorized, and Soviet forces increasingly so, while the German army still depended on horses to draw supply wagons and artillery.

The Allies learned hard lessons from defeat and figured out how to outfight the Axis. Hitler's generals outsmarted the Soviet military in 1941, Japan outmaneuvered the British and Americans in the first months of the Pacific war, and the German navy came close to squeezing the life from Great Britain in 1942. In 1943 and 1944, the tables were turned. The Russians reexamined every detail of their military procedures and devised new tactics that kept the vast German armies off guard and on the defensive. New ways to fight U-boats in the Atlantic devastated the German submarine service and staved off defeat. Americans in the Pacific utilized the full capacity of aircraft carriers, while Japanese admirals still dreamed of confrontations between lines of battleships.

Finally, the Allies had the appeal of democracy and freedom. The Axis nations were clearly the aggressors. Germany and Japan made bitter enemies by exploiting and abusing the people of the

OVERVIEW The Decision to Use the Atomic Bomb

Americans have long argued about whether the use of atomic bombs on the Japanese cities of Hiroshima and Nagasaki was necessary to end the war. Several factors probably influenced President Truman's decision to use the new weapon.

Military necessity	After the war, Truman argued that the use of atomic bombs was necessary to avoid an invasion of Japan that would have cost hundreds of thousand of lives. Military planners expected Japanese soldiers to put up the same kind of suicidal resistance in defense of the home islands as they had to American landings in the Philippines, Iwo Jima, and Okinawa. More recently, historians have argued that the Japanese military was near collapse and an invasion would have met far less resistance than feared.
Atomic diplomacy	Some historians believe that Truman used atomic weapons to overawe the Soviet Union and induce it to move cautiously in expanding its influence in Europe and East Asia. Truman and his advisers were certainly aware of how the bomb might influence the Soviet leadership.
Domestic politics	President Roosevelt and his chief military advisers had spent billions on the secret atomic bomb project without the full knowledge of Congress or the American public. The managers of the Manhattan Project may have believed that only proof of its military value would quiet critics and justify the huge cost.
Momentum of war	The United States and Britain had already adopted wholesale destruction of German and Japanese cities as a military tactic. Use of the atomic bomb looked like a variation on fire bombing, not the start of a new era of potential mass destruction. In this context, some historians argue, President Truman's choice was natural and expected.

countries they conquered, from Yugoslavia and France to Malaya and the Philippines, and incited local resistance movements. The Allies were certainly not perfect, but they fought for the ideals of political independence and were welcomed as liberators as they pushed back the Axis armies.

Read the **Document** at **www.myhistorylab.com** *From Then to Now Online: Nuclear Weapons*

CONCLUSION

The United States ended the war as the world's overwhelming economic power. It had put only 12 percent of its population in uniform, less than any other major combatant. For every American who died, 20 Germans and dozens of Soviets perished. Having suffered almost no direct destruction, the United States was able to dictate a postwar economic trading system that favored its interests.

Nevertheless, the insecurities of the war years influenced the United States for decades. A nation's current leaders are often shaped by its last war. Churchill had directed strategy, and Hitler, Mussolini, and Truman had all fought in World War I and carried its memories into World War II. The lessons of World War II would similarly influence the thinking of presidents from Dwight Eisenhower in the 1950s to George H. W. Bush in the 1990s. Even though the United States ended 1945 with the world's mightiest navy, biggest air force, and only atomic bomb, memories of the instability that had followed World War I made its leaders nervous about the shape of world politics.

One result in the postwar era was conflict between the United States and the Soviet Union, whose only common ground had been a shared enemy. After Germany's defeat, their wartime alliance gave way to hostility and confrontation in the Cold War. At home, international tensions fed the pressure for social and political conformity. The desire to enjoy the fruits of victory after 15 years of economic depression and sacrifice made the postwar generation sensitive to perceived threats to steady jobs and stable families. For the next generation, the unresolved business of World War II would haunt American life.

Where to Learn More

National Museum of the U.S. Air Force, Dayton, Ohio. Visitors can walk among World War II fighter planes and bombers, including the B-29 that dropped the atomic bomb on Nagasaki, and learn about the role of aviation in the war. http://www.nationalmuseum.af.mil/.

National Museum of the Pacific War, Fredericksburg, Texas. In the birthplace of Admiral Chester Nimitz, this new museum is an excellent introduction to the war with Japan. http://www.nimitz-museum.org.

Bradbury Science Museum, Los Alamos, New Mexico. The museum traces the origins of atomic energy for military and civilian uses. Nearby is the Los Alamos County Historical Museum, which gives the feel of everyday life in the atomic town. http://www.lanl.gov/museum.

United States Holocaust Memorial Museum, Washington, DC. The Holocaust Museum gives visitors a deeply moving depiction of the deadly impact of Nazi ideas in the 1930s and 1940s. The museum's website at http://www.ushmm.org also explores virtually every facet of the Holocaust experience for Jews during World War II.

World War II Valor in the Pacific National Monument, Hawaii, Alaska, and California. Created in 2008, this national monument includes sites in the Aleutian Islands of Alaska, the Tule Lake Internment Center in California, and the *USS Arizona* Memorial and Visitor Center at Pearl Harbor, Hawaii. http://home.nps.gov/pwr/customcf/apps/ww2ip/dsp_monuments.cfm.

Review Questions

1. What motivated German, Italian, and Japanese aggression in the 1930s? How did Great Britain, the USSR, and other nations respond to the growing conflict?
2. What arguments did Americans make against involvement in the war in Europe, and how deep was anti-intervention sentiment? Why did President Roosevelt and many others believe it necessary to block German and Japanese expansion? What steps did Roosevelt take to increase U.S. involvement short of war?
3. What was the military balance in early 1942? What were the chief threats to the United States and its allies? Why did the fortunes of war turn in late 1942?
4. Assess how mobilization for World War II altered life in the United States. How did the war affect families? How did it shift the regional balance of the economy? What opportunities did it open for women?
5. Did World War II help or hinder progress toward racial equality in the United States? How did the experiences of Japanese Americans, African Americans, and Mexican Americans challenge American ideals?
6. What factors were decisive in the defeat of Germany? How important were Soviet efforts on the Eastern Front, the bomber war, and the British-American landings in France?
7. What was the U.S. strategy against Japan, and how well did it work? What lay behind President Truman's decision to use atomic bombs against Japanese cities?
8. What role did advanced science and technology play in World War II? How did the scientific lead of the United States affect the war's outcome?

Key Terms

Allies (p. 727)
Atlantic Charter (p. 726)
Axis Powers (p. 722)
Battle of the Atlantic (p. 729)
Blitzkrieg (p. 723)
D-Day (p. 741)
Eastern Front (p. 727)
Fair Employment Practices Committee (FEPC) (p. 735)
Greater East Asia Co-Prosperity Sphere (p. 722)
Holocaust (p. 744)
Island hopping (p. 744)
Lend-Lease Act (p. 725)
Manhattan Project (p. 731)
Operation OVERLORD (p. 742)
Potsdam Declaration (p. 745)
Yalta Conference (p. 745)

myhistorylab Connections

Reinforce what you learned in this chapter by studying the many documents, images, maps, review tools, and videos available at **www.myhistorylab.com**.

Read and Review

Read the Document

A. Philip Randolph, "Why Should We March" (1942)

Albert Einstein, Letter to President Roosevelt (1939)

Charles Lindbergh, Radio Address (1941)

Executive Order 8802 (1941)

Jim Crow in the Army Camps, 1940 and Jim Crow Army (1941)

Manhattan Project Notebook (1945)

See the Map

World War II, European Theater

World War II, Pacific Theater

Research and Explore

Read the Document

Personal Journeys Online

From Then to Now Online: Nuclear Weapons

Exploring America: Propaganda

Hear the Audio

Pearl Harbor performed by New York, Georgia Singers

War Song

Obey the Ration Laws

Watch the Video

Hitler and Roosevelt

Atomic Bomb at Hiroshima

Atomic Age Begins

The Desegregation of the Military and Blacks in Combat

Truman on the End of World War II

Rosie the Riveter

Hear the Audio

Hear the audio files for Chapter 26 at **www.myhistorylab.com**.

1946–1952

27 The Cold War at Home and Abroad

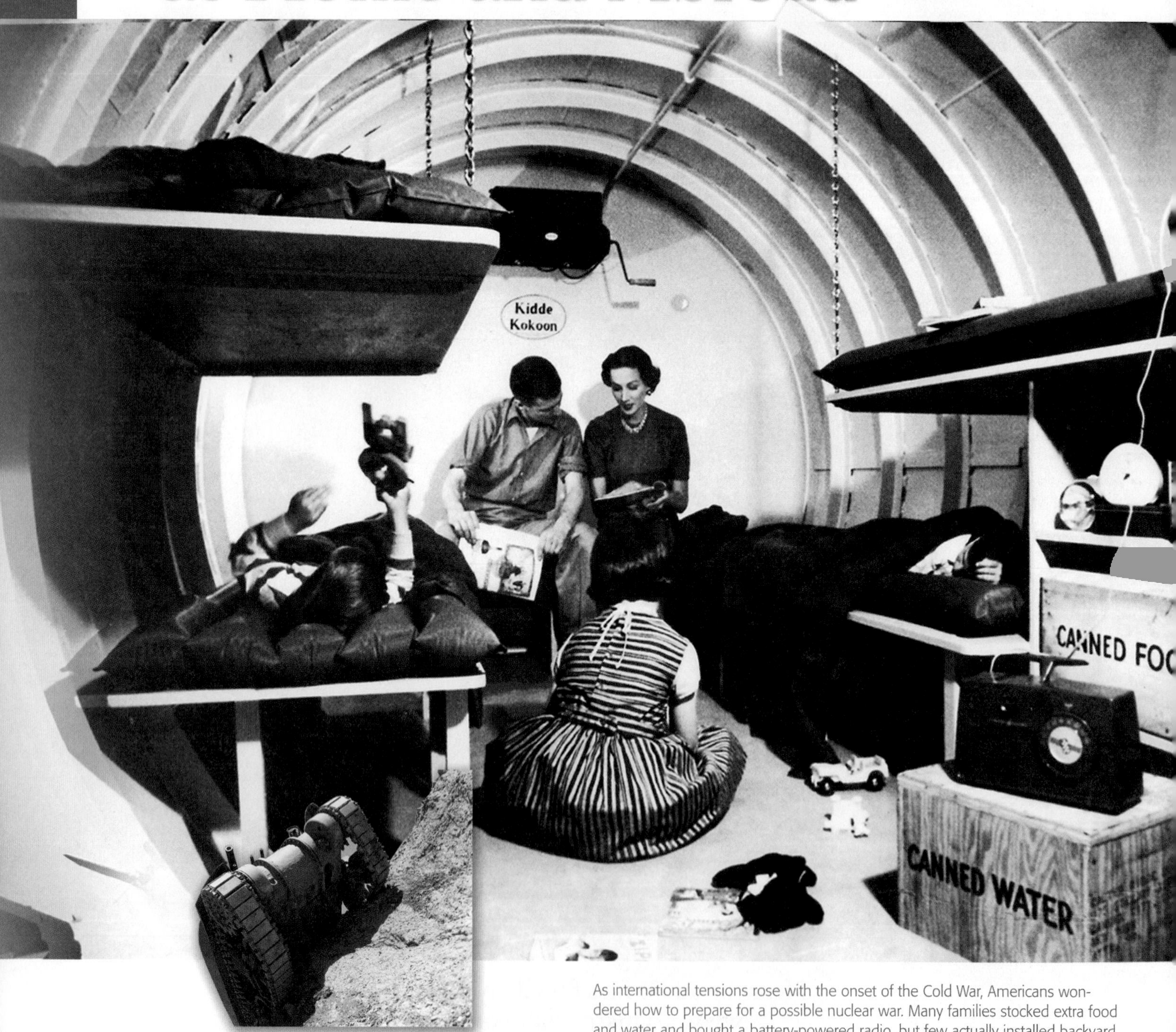

As international tensions rose with the onset of the Cold War, Americans wondered how to prepare for a possible nuclear war. Many families stocked extra food and water and bought a battery-powered radio, but few actually installed backyard bomb shelters like the one being tested by this family in a Long Island suburb.

Hear the Audio

Hear the audio files for Chapter 27 at **www.myhistorylab.com**.

LAUNCHING THE GREAT BOOM *(page 752)*

WHAT WAS the catalyst for the economic boom that began in 1947?

TRUMAN, REPUBLICANS, AND THE FAIR DEAL *(page 757)*

HOW WAS Harry Truman able to win the 1948 presidential election?

CONFRONTING THE SOVIET UNION *(page 760)*

WHAT WERE the origins of the Cold War?

COLD WAR AND HOT WAR *(page 764)*

HOW DID the Korean War shape American domestic politics?

THE SECOND RED SCARE *(page 768)*

WHY DID fear of Communism escalate in the years following World War II?

ONE AMERICAN JOURNEY

Veterans wake up! Your dream home is here.

Dreaming of the good life? Beautiful Lakewood is more than owning a home . . . It is a new and better way of living.

Advertisements like these for the new Los Angeles County community of Lakewood in 1950 aimed at families hungry for a place of their own after the privations of World War II. "Owning your own home . . . to have a place of our own was very, very special," remembered Jackie Rynerson.

The ads tried to make it sound easy, showing a young boy saying: We just bought a slick two-bedroom home for $43 a month and NO DOWN PAYMENT because Pop's a veteran! Even so, June Tweedy recalled that it was still a big step to become a suburban homeowner. "When you put your little check down for your down payment, it was like signing away your life. It seemed like a lot in those days."

City of Lakewood, CA

Read the **Document** at **www.myhistorylab.com**

Personal Journeys Online

- **"This Is How I Keep House," *McCalls*, April 1949. The routine of a typical Levittown housewife.**
- **Eric Hodgins, *Mr. Blandings Builds His Dream House* (1946). A fictional New York advertising agent buys a house in the far edge of suburbia.**
- **Atlanta Housing Council, "Proposed Areas for Expansions of Negro Housing in Atlanta, Georgia," Papers of the Atlanta Urban League, Atlanta University Center, Atlanta, Georgia. Reprinted in Andrew Wiese and Becky Nicolaides, *The Suburb Reader* (2006). Atlanta Housing Council, suggests ways to continue residential segregation in a growing city.**

LAKEWOOD'S NEW FAMILIES were moving into one of the most successful of the giant subdivisions that blossomed in the postwar decade. Like Levittown, New York in the same years, it attracted a flood of buyers desperate for a home of their own On the first day of sales on Palm Sunday, 1950, 25,000 people lined up in front of the sales office, and 7200 houses sold in the first ten months, most before they were actually built.

Lakewooders were part of the first wave in the suburbanization of postwar America. Over the next decades, the families who made the journey from city neighborhoods to thousands of new subdivisions would start the baby boom and rekindle the economy with their purchases of automobiles, appliances, and televisions.

This compelling desire to enjoy the promise of American life after years of sacrifice helps explain why Americans reacted so fiercely to new challenges and threats. They watched as congressional conservatives and President Truman fought over the fate of New Deal programs. More worrisome was the confrontation with the Soviet Union that was soon being called the **Cold War.** Triggered by the Soviet Union's imposition of Communist regimes throughout eastern Europe, the Cold War grew into a global contest in which the United States tried to counter Soviet influence around the world. The Cold War would shape the United States and the world for a generation. ✦

LAUNCHING THE GREAT BOOM

WHAT WAS the catalyst for the economic boom that began in 1947?

When World War II ended, Americans feared that demobilization would bring a rerun of the inflation and unemployment that had followed World War I. Indeed, in the first 18 months of peace, rising prices, strife between labor and management, and shortages of everything from meat to automobiles confirmed their anxiety. But in fact, 1947 and 1948 ushered in an economic expansion that lasted for a quarter-century. The resulting prosperity would finance a military

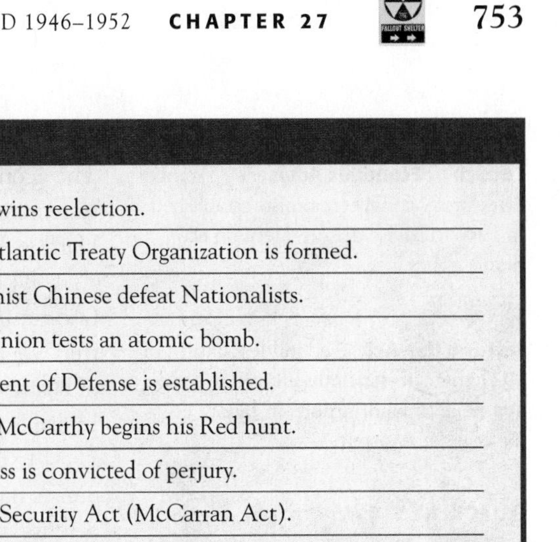

CHRONOLOGY

1944	Servicemen's Readjustment Act (GI Bill) is passed.
1945	United Nations is established.
1946	Employment Act creates Council of Economic Advisers.
	George Kennan sends his "long telegram."
	Winston Churchill delivers his "iron curtain" speech.
1947	Truman Doctrine is announced.
	Truman establishes a federal employee loyalty program.
	Kennan explains containment policy in an anonymous article in *Foreign Affairs*.
	Marshall Plan begins providing economic aid to Europe.
	HUAC holds hearings on Hollywood.
	Taft-Hartley Act rolls back gains of organized labor.
	National Security Act creates National Security Council and Central Intelligence Agency.
1948	Communists stage coup in Czechoslovakia.
	Berlin airlift overcomes Soviet blockade.
	Truman orders desegregation of the armed forces.
	Selective Service is reestablished.
	Truman wins reelection.
1949	North Atlantic Treaty Organization is formed.
	Communist Chinese defeat Nationalists.
	Soviet Union tests an atomic bomb.
	Department of Defense is established.
1950	Senator McCarthy begins his Red hunt.
	Alger Hiss is convicted of perjury.
	Internal Security Act (McCarran Act).
	NSC-68 is drafted and accepted as U.S. policy.
	Korean War begins.
1951	Senate Internal Security Subcommittee begins hearings.
	Truman relieves MacArthur of his command.
	Julius and Ethel Rosenberg are convicted of conspiring to commit espionage.
	Truce talks begin in Korea.
1952	United States tests the hydrogen bomb.
	Eisenhower is elected president.

buildup and an activist foreign policy. It also supported continuity in domestic politics from the late 1940s to the mid-1960s.

Cold War The political and economic confrontation between the Soviet Union and the United States that dominated world affairs from 1946 to 1989.

Reconversion Chaos

Japan's sudden surrender took the United States by surprise. The Pentagon, already scaling back defense spending, canceled $15 billion in war contracts in the first two days after the Japanese surrender. Public pressure demanded that the military release the nation's 12 million service personnel as rapidly as possible. GIs in Europe and the South Pacific waited impatiently for their turn on slow, crowded troop ships. Even at the rate of 25,000 discharges a day, it took a year to get all of them back to civilian life.

Veterans came home to shortages of food and consumer goods. High demand and short supply meant inflationary pressure, checked temporarily by continuing the Office of Price Administration until October 1946. Meanwhile, producers, consumers, and retailers scrambled to evade price restrictions and scarcities.

A wave of strikes made it hard to retool factories for civilian products. Inflation squeezed factory workers, who had accepted wage controls during the war effort. Since 1941, prices had risen twice as fast as base wages. In the fall of 1945, more and more workers went on strike to redress the balance; the strikes interrupted the output of products from canned soup to copper wire. By January 1946, some 1.3 million auto, steel, electrical, and packinghouse workers were off the job. Strikes in these basic industries shut other factories down for lack of supplies. Presidential committees crafted settlements that allowed steel and auto workers to make up ground lost during the war, but they also allowed corporations to pass on higher costs to consumers.

QUICK REVIEW

Postwar Economic Problems

- Military spending and military service came to an abrupt halt.
- Veterans came home to shortages in food and consumer goods.
- Inflation contributed to labor unrest.

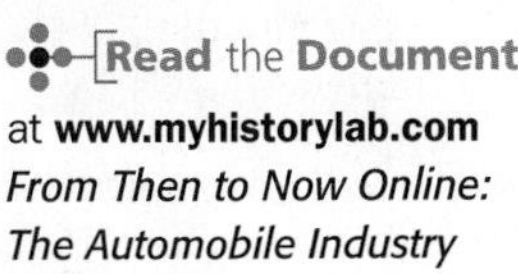

Read the **Document**
at **www.myhistorylab.com**
From Then to Now Online: The Automobile Industry

Economic Policy

Council of Economic Advisers Board of three professional economists established in 1946 to advise the president on economic policy.

Taft-Hartley Act Federal legislation of 1947 that substantially limited the tools available to labor unions in labor-management disputes.

QUICK REVIEW

The Taft-Hartley Act (1947)

- Effort to reverse gains made by labor in the 1930s.
- Public anger over strikes made passage of the act possible.
- Many middle-class Americans believed labor had gone too far.

GI Bill of Rights Legislation in June 1944 that eased the return of veterans into American society by providing educational and employment benefits.

The economic turmoil of 1946 set the stage for two major and contradictory efforts to deal more systematically with peacetime economic readjustment. The Employment Act of 1946 and the Taft-Hartley Act of 1947 represented liberal and conservative approaches to the peacetime economy.

The Employment Act was an effort by congressional liberals to ward off economic crisis by fine-tuning government taxation and spending. It started as a proposal for a full-employment bill that would ensure everyone's "right to a useful and remunerative job." Watered down in the face of business opposition, it still defined economic growth and high employment as national goals. It also established the **Council of Economic Advisers** to assist the president.

In the short term, the Employment Act aimed at a problem that did not materialize. Economists had predicted that the combination of returning veterans and workers idled by canceled defense work would bring depression-level unemployment of 8 to 10 million. In fact, more than 2 million women provided some slack by leaving the labor force outright. In addition, a savings pool of $140 billion in bank accounts and war bonds created a huge demand for consumer goods and workers to produce them. Total employment rose rather than fell with the end of the war, and unemployment in 1946–1948 stayed below 4 percent.

From the other end of the political spectrum, the **Taft-Hartley Act** climaxed a ten-year effort by conservatives to reverse the gains made by organized labor in the 1930s. The act passed in 1947 because of anger about continuing strikes. Many middle-class Americans were convinced that organized labor needed to be curbed.

In November 1946, Republicans capitalized on the problems of reconversion chaos, labor unrest, and dissatisfaction with Truman. Their election slogan was simple: "Had enough?" The GOP won control of Congress for the first time since the election of 1928, continuing the political trend toward the right that had been apparent since 1938.

Adopted by the now firmly conservative Congress, the Taft-Hartley Act was a serious counterattack by big business against large unions. It outlawed several union tools as "unfair labor practices." It barred the closed shop (the requirement that all workers hired in a given company or plant be union members) and blocked secondary boycotts (strikes against suppliers or customers of a targeted business). The federal government could postpone a strike by imposing a cooling-off period, which gave companies time to stockpile their products. Officers of national unions had to swear that they were not Communists or Communist sympathizers, even though corporate executives had no similar obligation. The bill passed over Truman's veto.

With the flood of veterans seeking college degrees after World War II, universities had to improvise to find adequate housing. On this Rhode Island campus, war surplus quonset huts made do as housing for married students.

The GI Bill

Another landmark law for the postwar era passed Congress without controversy. The Servicemen's Readjustment Act of 1944 was designed to ease veterans back into the civilian mainstream. Popularly known as the **GI Bill of Rights,** it was one of the federal government's most successful public assistance programs. Rather than pay cash bonuses to veterans, as after previous wars, Congress tied benefits to specific public goals. The GI Bill guaranteed loans of up to $2,000 for buying a house or farm or starting a business, a substantial sum at a time when a new house cost $6,000. The program encouraged veterans to attend college with money for tuition and books plus monthly stipends.

The GI Bill democratized American higher education by making college degrees accessible to men with working-class backgrounds. It brought far more students into higher education than could otherwise have enrolled. In the peak year of 1947, veterans made up half of all college students. Veterans helped convert the college degree, once available primarily to the socially privileged, into a basic business and professional credential. However, the GI tide unfortunately crowded women out of classrooms. Women's share of bachelor's degrees dropped from 40 percent in 1940 to 25 percent in 1950.

QUICK REVIEW

Housing Shortages

- Americans faced housing shortages after the war.
- The VA mortgage program allowed veterans to purchase homes without a down payment.
- Builders responded with mass-produced housing.

Assembly-Line Neighborhoods

Americans faced a housing shortage after the war. In 1947, fully 3 million married couples were unable to set up their own households. Most doubled up with relatives while they waited for the construction industry to respond. Hunger for housing was fierce. Eager buyers lined up for hours and paid admission fees to tour model homes or to put their names in drawings for the opportunity to buy.

The solution started with the federal government and its Veterans Administration (VA) mortgage program. By guaranteeing repayment, the VA allowed veterans to get home-purchase loans from private lenders without a down payment. Neither the VA program nor the New Deal–era Federal Housing Administration (FHA) mortgage insurance program, however, could do any good unless there were houses to buy. Eyeing the mass market created by the federal programs, innovative private builders devised their own solution. In 1947, William Levitt, a New York builder who had developed defense housing projects, built 2,000 houses for veterans on suburban Long Island. His basic house had 800 square feet of living space in two bedrooms, living room, kitchen, and bath, a 60-by-100-foot lot, and an unfinished attic waiting for the weekend handyman. There were 6,000 Levittown houses by the end of 1948 and more than 17,000 by 1951.

Redlining The withholding of home purchase loans and insurance coverage from inner-city older neighborhoods by federal housing agencies and private industry.

See the Map at **www.myhistorylab.com** *Population Shifts, 1940–1950*

Other successful builders worked on the same scale. They bought hundreds of acres of land, put in utilities for the entire tract, purchased materials by the carload, and kept specialized workers busy on scores of identical houses.

From 1946 through 1950, the federal government backed $20 billion in VA and FHA loans, approximately 40 percent of all home-mortgage debt. Housing starts neared 2 million in the peak year of 1950. By the end of the 1940s, 55 percent of American households owned their homes. The figure continued to climb until the 1980s, broadening access to the dream of financial security for many families. All during this time, the suburban population grew much faster than the population of central cities, and the population outside of metropolitan areas actually declined (see Figure 27–1).

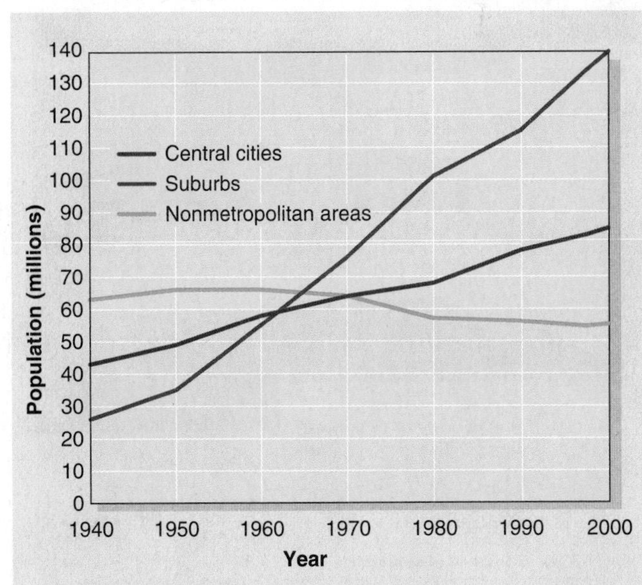

FIGURE 27–1 **The Suburbanizing Nation** In the decades after World War II, Americans moved in unprecedented numbers to new communities surrounding established cities. In the early 1960s, the combined population of suburban areas passed the populations of large central cities and of smaller towns and rural areas.

Isolation and discrimination. Unfortunately, the suburban solution to the housing shortage came with costs. The vast new housing tracts tended to isolate women and children from traditional community life. Moreover, they were of little benefit to African Americans. As the migration of black workers and their families to northern and western cities continued after the war, discrimination excluded them from new housing. Federal housing agencies and private industry worsened the problem by **redlining** older neighborhoods, which involved withholding home-purchase loans and insurance coverage from inner-city areas that were deemed too risky as investments.Thus public and private actions kept African Americans in deteriorating inner-city ghettos.

Jackie Robinson, the first black player in modern major league baseball, joined the Brooklyn Dodgers in 1947. He was both personally courageous and an outstanding player. Here he steals home against the Chicago Cubs in 1952.

Steps toward Civil Rights

The urgent need for decent housing helped to motivate African Americans to demand full rights as citizens. The wartime experience of fighting for freedom abroad while suffering discrimination at home steeled a new generation of black leaders to close the gap between America's ideal of equality and its performance. As had also been true after World War I, some white Americans held the opposite view, hoping to reaffirm racial segregation. A wave of racist violence surged across the South after the war; special targets were black veterans who tried to register to vote. However, many white Americans felt uneasy about the contradiction between a crusade for freedom abroad and racial discrimination at home.

In this era of rapid change and racial tension, the Truman administration recognized the importance of upholding civil rights for all Americans. Caught between pressure from black leaders and the fear of alienating southern Democrats, the president in 1946 appointed the Committee on Civil Rights, whose report developed an agenda for racial justice that would take two decades to put into effect. The NAACP had already begun a campaign of antisegregation lawsuits, which the Justice Department now began to support. The administration ordered federal housing agencies to modify their racially restrictive policies and prohibited racial discrimination in federal employment. Federal committees began to push for desegregation of private facilities in the symbolically important city of Washington, DC. In an important decision in the case of *Shelley v. Kraemer* (1948), the Supreme Court held that clauses in real estate deeds that forbid selling or renting to minorities could not be enforced in the courts.

You'll Be Sure of the Finest When You Plan Your New American KITCHEN STYLED IN STEEL

60 Great Features

No Other Kitchen Equipment Offers Them All!

American KITCHENS STYLED IN STEEL

When You Buy American You Buy the BEST!

AMERICAN CENTRAL

Americans were eager to enjoy the most modern appliances and houses. Manufacturers promoted streamlined kitchens to make life easier for housewives and their families.

The president also ordered "equality of treatment and opportunity" in the armed services in July 1948. The army in particular dragged its feet, hoping to limit black enlistees to 10 percent of the total. Manpower needs and the record of integrated units in the war in Korea from 1950 to 1953 persuaded the reluctant generals. Over the next generation, African Americans would find the military an important avenue for career opportunities.

Changes in national policy were important for ending racial discrimination, but far more Americans were interested in lowering racial barriers in professional team sports. Americans had applauded individual black champions, such as boxer Joe Louis and sprinter Jesse Owens, but team sports required their members to travel, practice, and play together. The center of attention was Jack Roosevelt ("Jackie") Robinson, a gifted African American athlete, who opened the 1947 baseball season as a member of the Brooklyn Dodgers. Robinson broke the color line that had reserved the modern major leagues for white players. His ability to endure taunting and hostility and still excel on the ballfield opened the door for other African Americans and Latinos. In the segregated society of the 1940s, Robinson found himself a powerful symbol of racial change.

Consumer Boom and Baby Boom

The housing boom was a product of both pent-up demand and a postwar "family boom." Americans celebrated the end of the war with weddings; the marriage rate in 1946 surpassed even its wartime high. Many women who left the labor force opted for marriage, and at increasingly younger ages. By 1950, the median age at which women married would be just over 20 years—lower than at any previous time in the twentieth century. The United States ended the 1940s with 7 million more married couples than at the decade's start.

New marriages jumpstarted the "baby boom," as did already married couples who decided to catch up after postponing childbearing during the war. In the early 1940s, an average of 2.9 million children per year were born in the United States; in 1946–1950, the average was 3.6 million. Those 3.5 million "extra" babies needed diapers, swing sets, lunch boxes, bicycles, and schoolrooms (see Figure 27–2).

Fast-growing families also needed to stock up on household goods. Out of an average household income of roughly $4,000 in 1946 and 1947, a family of four had $300 to $400 a year for furnishings and appliances. A couple might equip its new suburban kitchen with a Dripolator coffee maker for $2.45 and a Mirro-Matic pressure cooker for $12.95. The thrifty family could get along with a Motorola table radio for under $30; for $100, it could have a massive radio-phonograph combination in a 4-foot console as the centerpiece of a well-equipped living room.

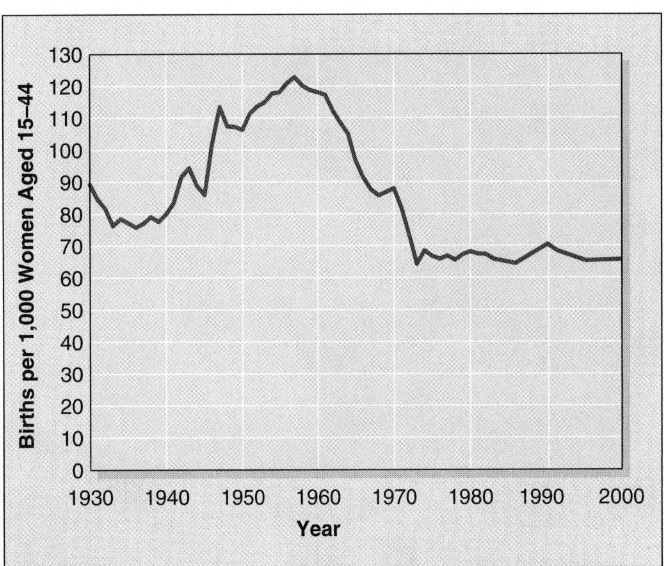

FIGURE 27–2 **The Postwar Baby Boom: The U.S. Birthrate 1930–2000** The baby boom after World War II was the product of high marriage rates and closely spaced children. The generation of Americans born between 1945 and 1960 has strongly affected American society and politics as its members went to school and college, entered the workforce, started their own families, and now have begun to plan for retirement in the twenty-first century.

Read the **Document**
at **www.myhistorylab.com**
Executive Order 9981: Desegregation of the Armed Forces (1948)

TRUMAN, REPUBLICANS, AND THE FAIR DEAL

HOW WAS Harry Truman able to win the 1948 presidential election?

From new products to new homes to new jobs, the economic gains of the postwar years propelled Americans toward the political center. After 15 years of economic crisis and world war, they wanted to enjoy prosperity.

Recognizing this attitude, Harry Truman and his political advisers tried to define policies acceptable to moderate Republicans as well as to Democrats. This meant creating a bipartisan coalition to block Soviet influence in Western Europe and defending the core of the New Deal's social and economic agenda at home.

This political package is known as the strategy of the "vital center," after the title of a 1949 book by Arthur Schlesinger, Jr. The book linked anti-Communism in foreign policy with efforts to enact inclusive social and economic policies to extend freedom abroad and at home. The vital center reflected the political reality of the Cold War years, when Democrats had to prove that they were tough on Communism before they could enact domestic reforms. The approach defined the heart of the Democratic Party for 20 years and found full expression in the administrations of John Kennedy (1961–1963) and Lyndon Johnson (1963–1969).

QUICK REVIEW

Truman and Civil Rights

- A new generation of African American leaders fought for civil rights.
- Presidential Committee on Civil Rights set federal civil rights agenda.
- Truman ordered "equality of treatment and opportunity" in the armed services.

Truman's Opposition

Truman had unexpected luck in his campaign for a full term as president in 1948. Besides the Republicans, he faced new fringe parties on the far right and far left that allowed him to position himself in the moderate center.

Harry Truman greets supporters and railroad workers in Pittsburgh at the start of an 18-state campaign tour in June 1948. Truman's grassroots campaign and down-home style helped him pull out an unexpected victory in November 1948.

Truman's opponents represented the left-leaning American Progressive Party, the **Dixiecrats** (officially the States' Rights Democrats), and the Republicans. The Progressive candidate was Henry Wallace, who had been FDR's vice president from 1941 to 1945, before being dumped in favor of Truman; more recently, he had been Truman's secretary of commerce. The Dixiecrat, Governor Strom Thurmond of South Carolina, had bolted the Democratic Party over civil rights. The most serious challenger was the Republican, Thomas Dewey, who had run against Roosevelt in 1944.

Tom Dewey had a high opinion of himself. He had been an effective governor of New York and represented the moderate eastern establishment within the Republican Party. Fortunately for Truman, Dewey lacked the common touch. Smooth on the outside, he alienated people who should have been his closest supporters. He was a bit of a snob and was an arrogant campaigner, refusing to interrupt his morning schedule to talk to voters.

Dewey was also saddled with the results of the Republican-controlled "do-nothing" 80th Congress (1947–1948). Truman used confrontation with Congress to rally voters who had supported the New Deal. He introduced legislation that he knew would be ignored, and he used his veto even when he knew Congress would override it. All the while he was building a list of campaign issues by demonstrating that the Republicans were obstructionists. Vote for me, Truman argued, to protect the New Deal, or vote Republican to bring back the days of Herbert Hoover.

WHERE TO LEARN MORE

Harry S. Truman National Historical Site, Library, and Museum, Independence, Missouri
http://www.nps.gov/hstr/

Dixiecrats States' Rights Democrats.

Whistle-Stopping across America

The 1948 presidential campaign mixed old and new. For the last time, a major candidate crisscrossed the nation by rail and made hundreds of speeches from the rear platforms of trains. For the first time, national television broadcast the two party conventions, although the primitive cameras showed the handful of viewers little more than talking heads.

Truman ran on both character and issues. He was a widely read and intelligent man who cultivated the image of a backslapper. He covered 31,700 miles in his campaign train and gave ten speeches a day. Republicans belittled the small towns and cities he visited, calling them "whistle stops." Democrats made the term a badge of pride for places like Laramie, Wyoming, and Pocatello, Idaho.

Truman brought the campaign home to average Americans. He tied Dewey to inflation, housing shortages, and fears about the future of Social Security (an issue that Democrats would

GLOBAL CONNECTIONS

Gunnar Myrdal, Race Relations, and Cold War Leadership

In 1938, the Swedish social scientist Gunnar Myrdal came to the United States at the invitation of the Carnegie Foundation to study relations between white and black Americans—what people at the time called the "Negro problem." Six years later, he published An American Dilemma, *a 1,000-page volume with hundreds of additional pages of supporting data. Studying the problems of race relations as a stranger, Myrdal was struck by the basic national values derived from English law and Christian belief, values and opportunities that he termed the "American Creed."*

> Not since Reconstruction has there been more reason to anticipate fundamental changes in American race relations, changes which will involve a development toward the American ideals. . . . America, relative to all the other branches of Western civilization, is moralistic and "moral-conscious." . . .
>
> America feels itself to be humanity in miniature. When in this crucial time the international leadership passes to America, the great reason for hope is that this country has a national experience of united racial and cultural diversity and a national theory, if not a consistent practice, of freedom and equality for all. What America is constantly reaching for is democracy at home and abroad. The main trend in its history is the gradual realization of the American Creed.
>
> In this sense the Negro problem is not only America's greatest failure but also America's incomparably great opportunity for the future. If America should follow its own deepest convictions, its well-being at home would be increased directly. At the same time, America's prestige and power would be increased directly. . . . America can demonstrate that justice, equality and cooperation are possible between white and colored people.

Myrdal's challenge is an important example of the way in which ideas have traveled back and forth across the Atlantic. It also became an important consideration during the Cold War. Washington policymakers realized that the peoples of Africa, Asia, and Latin America were paying close attention to how the nation's white majority treated its black and Hispanic citizens. This concern for America's global reputation helped make otherwise reluctant leaders into supporters of the black civil rights movement and fair treatment of Mexican migrant workers. The admission of multiracial Hawaii as the fiftieth state in 1959 was a challenge to segregationists and was seen as a "bridge to Asia" that carried the message that the United States was welcoming to all peoples.

Gunnar Myrdal, *An American Dilemma* (New York: McGraw-Hill, 1964), pp. lxi, lxx, 1021. (Originally published in 1944)

- Does the idea of an American Creed help us to understand the international roles of the United States in the twenty-first century?

continue to use into the next century). In industrial cities, he hammered at the Taft-Hartley Act. In the West, he pointed out that Democratic administrations had built dams and helped to turn natural resources into jobs. He called the Republicans the party of privilege and arrogance. The Democrats, he said, offered opportunity for farmers, factory workers, and small business owners.

Truman got a huge boost from Dewey's unwillingness to fight. Going into the fall with a huge lead in the public opinion polls, Dewey sought to avoid mistakes. Wallace and Thurmond each took just under 1.2 million votes. Dewey received nearly 22 million popular votes and 189 electoral votes, but Truman won more than 24 million popular votes and 303 electoral votes (see Map 27–1).

QUICK REVIEW

1948: Candidates for President
- Harry Truman (Democrat).
- Thomas Dewey (Republican).
- Henry Wallace (Progressive).
- Strom Thurmond (States' Rights Democrat, or Dixiecrat).

Truman's Fair Deal

Truman hoped to build on the gains of the New Deal. In his State of the Union address in January 1949, he called for a Fair Deal for all Americans. He promised to extend the New Deal and ensure "greater economic opportunity for the mass of the people." Over the next four years, however,

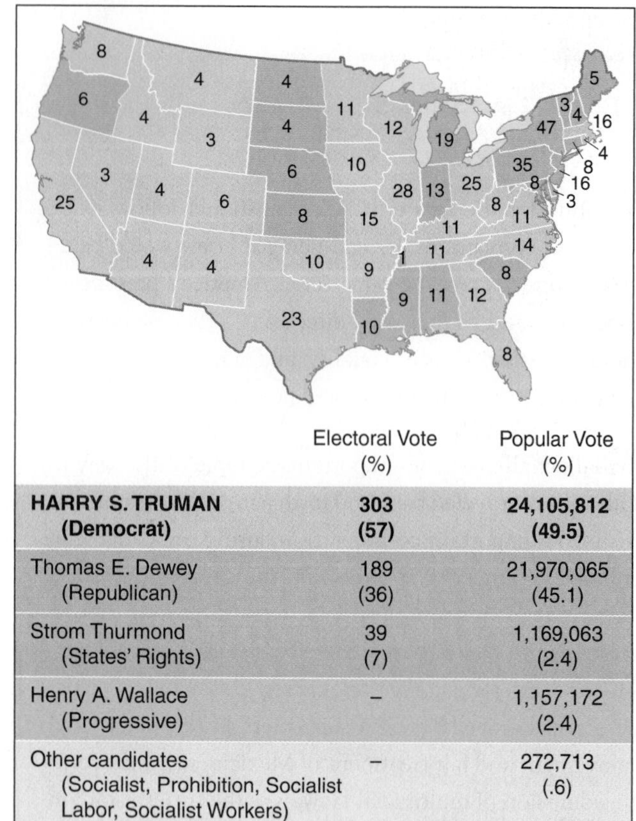

	Electoral Vote (%)	Popular Vote (%)
HARRY S. TRUMAN (Democrat)	**303 (57)**	**24,105,812 (49.5)**
Thomas E. Dewey (Republican)	189 (36)	21,970,065 (45.1)
Strom Thurmond (States' Rights)	39 (7)	1,169,063 (2.4)
Henry A. Wallace (Progressive)	–	1,157,172 (2.4)
Other candidates (Socialist, Prohibition, Socialist Labor, Socialist Workers)	–	272,713 (.6)

MAP 27–1 **The Election of 1948** Harry Truman won a narrow victory in the presidential election of 1948 by holding many of the traditionally Democratic states of the South and West and winning key industrial states in the Middle West. His success depended on the coalition of rural and urban interests that Franklin Roosevelt had pulled together in the 1930s.

Why do you think industrial states in the Midwest supported Harry S. Truman in the 1948 presidential election?

conservative Republicans and southern Democrats forced Congress to choose carefully among Truman's proposals, accepting those that expanded existing programs but rejecting new departures. The result was a set of disconnected measures rather than the consistent program that Truman had advocated.

With the Housing Act of 1949, the federal government reaffirmed its concern about families who had been priced out of the private market. The act provided money for local housing agencies to buy, clear, and resell land for housing. The intent was to clear "substandard and blighted areas" and replace them with affordable modern apartments. The program never worked as intended because of scanty appropriations, poor design of the replacement housing, and local decisions that concentrated public housing in segregated minority neighborhoods, but it established the goal of decent housing for all Americans.

In 1950, Congress revitalized the weak Social Security program. Benefits went up by an average of 80 percent, and 10.5 million additional people received old-age and survivors' insurance. Most of the new coverage went to rural and smalltown people, thus consolidating the broad support that has made it politically difficult to change Social Security ever since, even in the face of projected shortages in the twenty-first century.

Congress rejected other Fair Deal proposals that would remain on the national agenda for decades. A Senate filibuster killed a permanent Fair Employment Practices Commission to fight racial discrimination in hiring, halting progress toward civil rights. The medical establishment blocked a proposal for national health insurance as "socialistic," leaving the issue to be revisited in the 1960s with the passage of Medicare and Medicaid, in the 1990s with Bill Clinton's failed proposals for healthcare reform, and with the Obama administration's long and ultimately successful fight to expand health insurance coverage in 2009–2010. The overall message from Truman's second term was clear: Americans liked what the New Deal had given them but were hesitant about new initiatives.

CONFRONTING THE SOVIET UNION

WHAT WERE the origins of the Cold War?

In 1945, the United States and the Soviet Union were allies, victorious against Germany and planning the defeat of Japan. By 1947, they were engaged in a diplomatic and economic confrontation and soon came close to war over the city of Berlin. The business tycoon and presidential adviser Bernard Baruch characterized the conflict in April 1947 as a "cold war," and newspaper columnist Walter Lippmann quickly popularized the term.

Over the next 40 years, the United States and the Soviet Union contested for economic, political, and military influence around the globe. The heart of Soviet policy was to control eastern Europe as a buffer zone against Germany. The centerpiece of American policy was to link the United States, Western Europe, and Japan into an alliance of overwhelming economic power. For the United States, the Cold War was simultaneously an effort to promote democracy in Europe, maintain a favorable military position in relation to the Soviet Union, and preserve its leadership of the world economy.

Read the **Document** at **www.myhistorylab.com**
Kenneth MacFarland, "The Unfinished Work" (1946)

Each side in the Cold War thought the worst of the other. Behind the conflicts were Soviet insecurity about an aggressive West and American fear of Communist expansionism. Americans and Soviets frequently interpreted each other's actions in the most threatening terms, turning miscalculations and misunderstandings into crises. A U.S. public that had suffered through nearly two decades of economic depression and war reacted to international problems with frustration and anger. The emotional burdens of the Cold War warped and narrowed a generation of American political life around the requirements of anti-Communism.

The End of the Grand Alliance

The Yalta Conference of February 1945 had recognized military realities by marking out rough spheres of influence. The Western allies had the better of the bargain. Defeated Italy and Japan, whose reconstruction was firmly in Western hands, had far greater economic potential than Soviet-controlled Bulgaria, Romania, or Hungary. In addition, the Allies had divided Germany into four occupation zones. The British, French, and American zones in western Germany held more people and industrial potential than the Russian zone in eastern Germany.

As the victorious powers tried to put their broad agreements into operation, they argued bitterly about Germany and eastern Europe. Was the Soviet Union to dominate eastern Europe as its protective buffer, or was the region to be open to Western economic and political influence? For Poland, Truman and his advisers claimed that Yalta had assumed open elections on the American model. The Soviet Union claimed that Yalta had ensured that any Polish government would be friendly to Soviet interests and acted to guarantee that this would be so.

W **WHERE TO LEARN MORE**

★ United Nations Headquarters, New York, New York
http://www.un.org

Facing Soviet intransigence over eastern Europe, Truman decided that the United States should "take the lead in running the world in the way the world ought to be run." One technique was economic pressure. The State Department "mislaid" a Soviet request for redevelopment loans. The United States and Britain objected to Soviet plans to take industrial equipment and raw materials from the western occupation zones in Germany, compensation that the Soviets thought they had been promised.

The United States also tried to involve the Soviet Union and eastern Europe in new international organizations. The Senate approved American membership in the newly organized United Nations (UN) with only two opposing votes, a sharp contrast to its rejection of the League of Nations in 1920. The Washington-based **International Monetary Fund (IMF)** and the **World Bank** were designed to revive international trade. The IMF stabilized national currencies against the short-term pressures of international trade. The World Bank drew on the resources of member nations to make economic development loans to governments for such projects as new dams or agricultural modernization. These organizations ensured that the reviving world economy would revolve around the industrial and technological power of the United States, and they continue to dictate the economic policy of many developing nations into the twenty-first century.

International Monetary Fund (IMF) International organization established in 1945 to assist nations in maintaining stable currencies.

World Bank Designed to revive postwar international trade, it drew on the resources of member nations to make economic development loans to governments for such projects as new dams or agricultural modernization.

In 1946, the United States presented a plan in the United Nations to control atomic energy. Bernard Baruch suggested that an international agency should oversee all uranium production and research on atomic explosives. The Baruch plan emphasized enforcement and inspections that would have opened the Soviet nuclear effort to American interference, an unacceptable prospect for a nation trying to catch up with the United States by building its own atomic bombs.

QUICK REVIEW

New International Organizations

- United Nations.
- International Monetary Fund (IMF).
- World Bank.

While UN delegates debated the future of atomic energy, American leaders were becoming convinced of Soviet aggressiveness. In February 1946, George Kennan, a senior American diplomat in Moscow, sent a "long telegram" to the State Department. He depicted a Soviet Union driven by expansionist Communist ideology. The Soviets, he argued, would constantly probe for weaknesses in the capitalist world. The best response was firm resistance to protect the Western heartlands.

Read the Document at **www.myhistorylab.com**
George F. Kennan, "The Long Telegram" (1946)

The British encouraged the same tough stand. Lacking the strength to shape Europe on its own, Great Britain repeatedly nudged the United States to block Soviet influence. Speaking at Westminster College in Missouri in March 1946, Winston Churchill warned that the Soviet Union had dropped an "iron curtain" across the middle of Europe and urged a firm Western response.

Churchill's speech matched the mood in official Washington. Truman's foreign-policy advisers shared the belief in an aggressive Soviet Union, and the president himself saw the world as a series of either-or choices. Added to military apprehension were worries about political and economic competition. Communist parties in war-ravaged Europe and Japan were exploiting discontent. In Asia and Africa, the allegiance of nationalists who were fighting for independence from European powers remained in doubt. America's leaders worried that much of the Eastern Hemisphere might fall under Soviet control.

Were Truman and his advisers right about Soviet intentions? The evidence is mixed. In their determination to avoid another Munich, Truman and his foreign-policy circle ignored examples of Soviet caution and conciliation. The Soviets withdrew troops from Manchuria in northern China and acquiesced in America's control of defeated Japan. They allowed a neutral but democratic government in Finland and technically free elections in Hungary and Czechoslovakia (although it was clear that Communists would do well there). They demobilized much of their huge army and reduced their forces in eastern Europe.

However, the Soviet regime also acted to justify American fears. The Soviet Union could not resist exerting influence in the Middle East. It pressured Turkey to give it partial control of the exit from the Black Sea. It retained troops in northern Iran until warned out by the United States. The Soviets were ruthless in support of Communist control in eastern Europe in 1946 and 1947; they aided a Communist takeover in Bulgaria, backed a coup in Romania, and undermined the last non-Communist political opposition in Poland. U.S. policymakers read these Soviet actions as a rerun of Nazi aggression and determined not to let a new totalitarian threat undermine Western power.

The Truman Doctrine and the Marshall Plan

Whatever restraint the Soviet Union showed was too late or too little. Early in 1947, Truman and his advisers acted decisively. The British could no longer afford to back the Greek government that was fighting a civil war against Communists, and U.S. officials feared that a Communist takeover in Greece would threaten the stability of Italy, France, and the Middle East. Truman coupled his case for intervention in Greece with an appeal for aid to neighboring Turkey, which lived under the shadow of the Soviet Union. On March 12, he told Congress that the United States faced a "fateful hour" and requested $400 million to fight Communism in Greece and Turkey and secure the free world. Congress agreed, and the United States became the dominant power in the eastern Mediterranean.

Read the **Document**
at **www.myhistorylab.com**
Truman Doctrine (1947)

Truman Doctrine President Harry Truman's statement in 1947 that the United States should assist other nations that were facing external pressure or internal revolution.

Framing the specific request was a sweeping declaration that became known as the **Truman Doctrine.** The president pledged to use U.S. economic power to help free nations everywhere resist internal subversion or aggression. "It must be the policy of the United States," he said, "to support free peoples who are resisting attempted subjugation by armed minorities or by outside pressures. . . . I believe that our help should be primarily through economic and financial aid, which is essential to economic stability and orderly political processes."

Read the **Document**
at **www.myhistorylab.com**
George Marshall, The Marshall Plan (1947)

Meanwhile, Europe was sliding toward chaos. Germany was close to famine after the bitter winter of 1946–1947. Western European nations were bankrupt and unable to import raw materials for their factories. Overstressed medical systems could no longer control tuberculosis and other diseases. Communist parties had gained in Italy, France, and Germany.

Marshall Plan Secretary of State George C. Marshall's European Recovery Plan of June 5, 1947, committing the United States to help in the rebuilding of post-World War II Europe.

The U.S. government responded with unprecedented economic aid. Secretary of State George C. Marshall announced the European Recovery Plan on June 5, 1947. What the press quickly dubbed the **Marshall Plan** committed the United States to help rebuild Europe. The United States invited Soviet and eastern European participation, but under terms that would have reduced Moscow's control over its satellite economies. The Soviets refused, fearing that the United States wanted to undermine its influence, and instead organized their eastern European satellites in their own association for Mutual Economic Assistance, or Comecon, in 1949. In Western Europe, the Marshall Plan was a success. Aid totaled $13.5 billion over four years. It met many of Europe's economic needs and quieted class conflict. The Marshall Plan expanded American influence through cooperative efforts. Because Europeans spent much of the aid on U.S. goods and machinery, and because economic recovery promised markets for U.S. products, business and labor both supported it. In effect, the Marshall Plan created an "empire by invitation," in which Americans and Europeans jointly planned Europe's recovery.

U.S. policy in Japan followed the pattern set in Europe. As supreme commander of the Allied Powers, General Douglas MacArthur acted as Japan's postwar dictator. He tried to change the values of the old war-prone Japan through social reform, democratization, and demilitarization. At the end of 1947, however, the United States decided that democracy and pacifism could go too far. Policymakers were fearful of economic collapse and political chaos, just as in Europe. The "reverse course" in occupation policy aimed to make Japan an economic magnet for other nations in East Asia, pulling them toward the American orbit and away from the Soviet Union.

George Kennan summed up the new American policies in the magazine *Foreign Affairs* in July 1947. Kennan argued that the Soviet leaders were committed to a long-term strategy of expanding Communism. The proper posture of the United States, he said, should be an equally patient commitment to "firm and vigilant **containment** of Russian expansive tendencies." Kennan warned that the emerging Cold War would be a long conflict, with no quick fixes.

General Douglas MacArthur Memorial, Norfolk, Virginia
http://www.macarthurmemorial.org

QUICK REVIEW

Postwar Foreign Policy

- Truman launched the nation into a global battle against Communism.
- The U.S. pledged to help countries that faced external pressure or internal revolution.
- The U.S. played a decisive role in the rebuilding of Europe.

Soviet Reactions

The bold American moves in the first half of 1947 put the Soviet Union on the defensive. In response, Soviet leaders orchestrated strenuous opposition to the Marshall Plan by French and Italian Communists. East of the Iron Curtain, Hungarian Communists expelled other political parties from a coalition government. Bulgarian Communists shot opposition leaders. Romania, Bulgaria, and Hungary signed defense pacts with the Soviet Union.

In early 1948, the Soviets targeted Czechoslovakia. For three years, a neutral coalition government there on the model of Finland had balanced trade with the West with a foreign policy friendly to the Soviet Union. In February 1948, while Russian forces assembled on the Czech border, local Communists took advantage of political bumbling by other members of the governing coalition. Taking control through a technically legal process, they pushed aside Czechoslovakia's democratic leadership and turned the nation into a dictatorship and Soviet satellite within a week.

The climax of the Soviet reaction came in divided Berlin, located 110 miles inside the Soviet Union's East German occupation zone. The city was divided into four sectors: one controlled by the Soviets and the others by the United States, Britain, and France. On June 4, 1948, Soviet troops blockaded surface traffic into Berlin, cutting off the U.S., British, and French sectors. The immediate Soviet aim was to block Western plans to merge their three German occupation zones into an independent federal republic (West Germany). Rather than abandon 2.5 million Berliners or shoot their way through, the Western nations responded to the **Berlin blockade** by airlifting supplies to the city. Stalin decided not to intercept the flights. After 11 months, the Soviets abandoned the blockade, making the Berlin airlift a triumph of American resolve.

Read the **Document** at **www.myhistorylab.com**
George F. Kennan, "Containment" (1947)

containment The policy of resisting further expansion of the Soviet bloc through diplomacy and, if necessary, military action, developed in 1947–1948.

Berlin blockade Three-hundred-day Soviet blockade of land access to United States, British, and French occupation zones in Berlin, 1948–1949.

American Rearmament

The coup in Czechoslovakia and the Berlin blockade shocked American leaders and backfired on the Soviets. The economic assistance strategy of 1947 now looked inadequate. Congress responded in 1948 by reinstating the military draft and increasing defense spending.

The United States had already begun to modernize and centralize its national security apparatus, creating the institutions that would run foreign policy in the second half of the century. The National Security Act of July 1947 created the **Central Intelligence Agency (CIA)** and the **National Security Council (NSC).** The CIA handled intelligence gathering and covert operations. The NSC assembled top diplomatic and military advisers in one committee. In 1949, legislation also created the Department of Defense to oversee the army, navy, and air force (independent

Central Intelligence Agency (CIA) Agency established in 1947 that coordinates the gathering and evaluation of military and economic information on other nations.

National Security Council (NSC) The formal policymaking body for national defense and foreign relations, created in 1947 and consisting of the president, the secretary of defense, the secretary of state, and others appointed by the president.

from the army since 1947). The civilian secretary of defense soon began to exercise influence on foreign policy equal to that of the secretary of state.

North Atlantic Treaty Organization (NATO) Organization of ten European countries, Canada, and the United States whom together formed a mutual defense pact in April, 1949.

In April 1949, ten European nations, the United States, and Canada signed the North Atlantic Treaty as a mutual defense pact. American commitments to the **North Atlantic Treaty Organization (NATO)** included military aid and the deployment of U.S. troops in Western Europe. After 1955, its counterpart would be the Warsaw Pact for mutual defense among the Soviet Union and its European satellites.

Two years later, the United States signed similar but less comprehensive agreements in the western Pacific: the ANZUS Pact with Australia and New Zealand and a new treaty with the Philippines. Taken together, peacetime rearmament and mutual defense pacts amounted to a revolution in American foreign policy.

COLD WAR AND HOT WAR

HOW DID the Korean War shape American domestic politics?

The first phase of the Cold War reached a crisis in the autumn of 1949. Two key events seemed to tilt the world balance against the United States and its allies. In September, Truman announced that the Soviet Union had tested its own atomic bomb. A month later, the Communists under Mao Zedong (Mao Tse-tung) took power in China. The following summer, civil war in Korea sucked the United States into a fierce war with Communist North Korea and China.

Berlin was still a devastated city in 1948. When the Soviet Union closed off ground access to the British, French, and American occupation zones, the city became a symbol of the West's Cold War resolve. Allied aircraft lifted in food, fuel, and other essentials for West Berliners for nearly a year until the Soviets ended the blockade.

The Nuclear Shadow

Experts in Washington had known that the Soviets were working on an A-bomb, but the news dismayed the average citizen. As newspapers and magazines scared their readers with artists' renditions of the effects of an atomic bomb on New York or Chicago, the shock tilted U.S. nuclear policy toward military uses. In 1946, advocates of civilian control had won a small victory when Congress established the Atomic Energy Commission (AEC). The AEC tried to balance research on atomic power with continued testing of new weapons. Now Truman told the AEC to double the output of fissionable uranium and plutonium for "conventional" nuclear weapons. A more momentous decision soon followed. Truman decided in January 1950 to authorize work on the "super" bomb—the thermonuclear fusion weapon that would become the hydrogen bomb (H-bomb).

Nuclear weapons proliferated in the early 1950s. The United States repeatedly tested nuclear fission weapons in Nevada and exploded the first hydrogen bomb in the South Pacific in November 1952. Releasing 100 times the energy of the Hiroshima bomb, the detonation tore a mile-long chasm in the ocean floor. Great Britain became the third nuclear power in the same year. The Soviet Union tested its own hydrogen bomb only nine months after the United States.

The nuclear arms race and the gnawing fear of nuclear war multiplied the apprehensions of the Cold War. Under the guidance of the Federal Civil Defense Administration, Americans learned that they should always keep a battery-powered radio and tune to 640 or 1240 on the AM dial for emergency information when they heard air raid sirens. Schoolchildren learned to hide under their desks when they saw the blinding flash of a nuclear detonation.

More insidiously, nuclear weapons development generated new environmental and health problems. Soldiers were exposed to posttest radiation with minimal protection. Nuclear tests in the South Pacific dusted fishing boats with radioactivity and forced islanders to abandon contaminated homes. Las Vegas promoted tests in southern Nevada as tourist attractions, but radioactive fallout contaminated large sections of the West and increased cancer rates among "downwinders" in Utah. Weapons production and atomic experiments contaminated vast tracts in Nevada, Washington, and Colorado and left huge environmental costs for later generations.

QUICK REVIEW

Nuclear Proliferation in the Early 1950s

- U.S. repeatedly tested nuclear weapons in Nevada.
- November 1952: U.S. explodes first hydrogen bomb in the South Pacific.
- August 1953: Soviet Union tests its own hydrogen bomb.

THE COLD WAR IN ASIA

Communist victory in China's civil war was as predictable as the Soviet nuclear bomb but no less controversial. The collapse of Jiang Jieshi's Nationalist regime was nearly inevitable, given its corruption and narrow support. Nevertheless, Americans looked for a scapegoat when Jiang's anti-Communist government and remnants of the Nationalist army fled to the island of Taiwan off China's southern coast.

Advocates for Jiang, mostly conservative Republicans from the Midwest and West, were certain that Truman's administration had done too little. Critics looked for scapegoats. Foreign Service officers who had honestly analyzed the weakness of the Nationalists were accused of Communist sympathies and hounded from their jobs. The results were tragedy for those unfairly branded as traitors and damage to the State Department, a weakness that would haunt the United States as it became entangled in Southeast Asia in the 1950s and 1960s.

Mao's victory expanded a deep fissure in U.S. foreign policy. During and after World War II, the United States had made Europe its first priority. Strong voices, however, had argued that America's future lay with China, Japan, and the Pacific nations. Influential senators claimed that the "loss of China" was the disastrous result of putting the needs of England and France above the long-term interests of the United States.

NSC-68 AND AGGRESSIVE CONTAINMENT

The turmoil of 1949 led to a comprehensive statement of American strategic goals. In April 1950, the State Department prepared a sweeping report known as **National Security Council Paper 68 (NSC-68).** The document described a world divided between the forces of "slavery" and "freedom" and assumed that the Soviet Union was actively aggressive, motivated by greed for territory and a "fanatic faith" in Communism. To defend civilization itself, said the experts, the United States should use as much force as needed to resist Communist expansion anywhere and everywhere.

The authors of NSC-68 intended to extend the Truman Doctrine and convince Americans of the threat of the Cold War. They also thought in terms of military solutions. In the original containment policy, Truman and his advisers had hoped to contain the Soviets by diplomacy and by integrating the economies of Europe and Japan with that of the United States. Now that the Soviets had the atomic bomb, however, the American atomic shield might be neutralized. Instead, NSC-68 argued that the United States needed to press friendly nations to rearm and make its former enemies into military allies. It also argued that the nation needed expensive conventional forces to defend Europe on the ground and to react to crises as a "world policeman." NSC-68 thus advocated nearly open-ended increases in the defense budget (which, in fact, tripled between 1950 and 1954).

Read the Document at **www.myhistorylab.com** *National Security Council Memorandum Number 68 (1950)*

National Security Council Paper 68 (NSC-68) Policy statement that committed the United States to a military approach to the Cold War.

QUICK REVIEW

American Strategy

- U.S. experts believed that America needed to use force to oppose Communism around the world.
- They argued that the U.S. should pressure allies to rearm.
- They argued for the introduction of conventional forces in Europe.

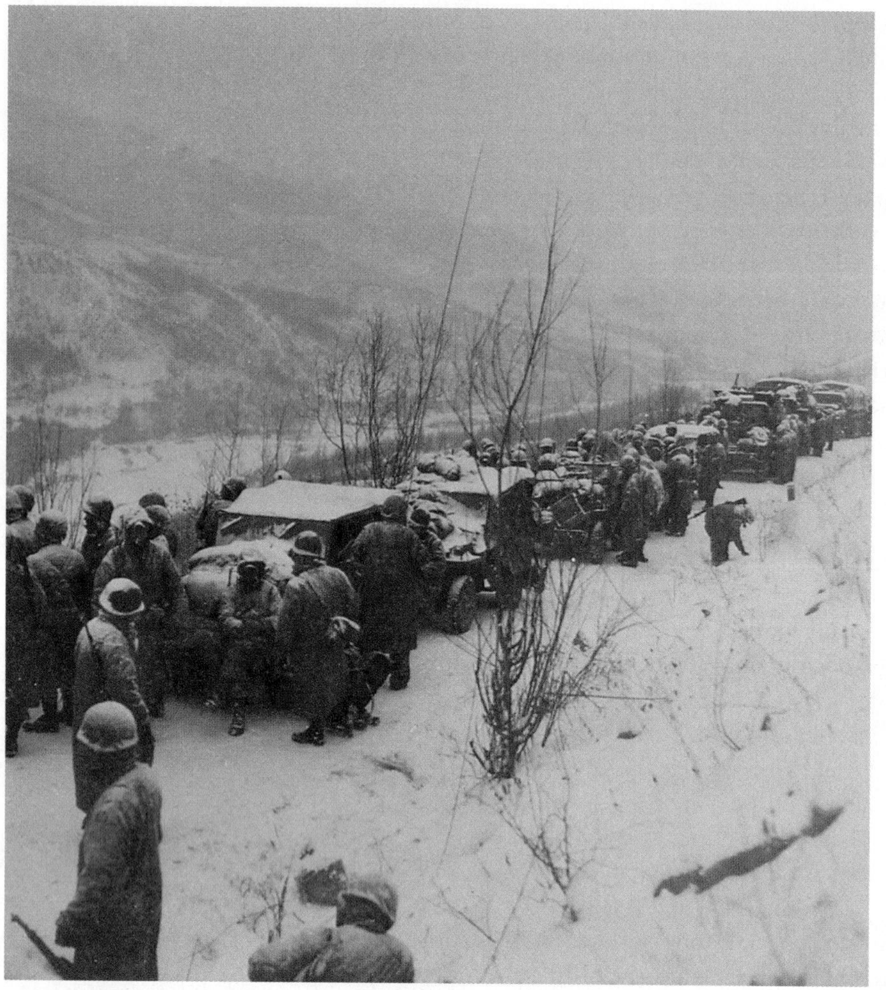

United Nation forces in Korea fought the weather as well as Communist North Koreans and Chinese. Baking summer heat alternated with fierce winters. Snow and cold were a major help to the Chinese when they surprised United States forces in November 1950 and drove American troops such as these southward.

The thinking behind the report led the United States to approach the Cold War as a military competition and to view political changes in Africa and Asia as parts of a Soviet plan. The need for a flexible military response became the centerpiece of a U.S. policy of active intervention that led eventually to the jungles of Vietnam in the 1960s. And the report's implied strategy of bankrupting the Communists through competitive defense spending helped destroy the Soviet Union at the end of the 1980s.

War in Korea, 1950–1953

The success of Mao and the Chinese Communists forced the Truman administration to define national interests in eastern Asia and the western Pacific. Most important was Japan, still an industrial power despite its devastating defeat. The United States had denied the Soviet Union any part in the occupation of Japan in 1945 and had shaped a more democratic nation that would be a strong and friendly trading partner. Protected by American armed forces, Japan would be part of a crescent of offshore strong points that included Alaska, Okinawa, the Philippines, Australia, and New Zealand.

Two questions remained at the start of 1950. One was the future of Taiwan and the remnants of Jiang's regime. Some American policymakers wanted to defend Jiang against the Communists. Others assumed that his tattered forces would collapse and allow Mao to complete the Communist takeover of Chinese territory. The other question was Korea, whose own civil war would soon bring the world to the brink of World War III.

The Korean peninsula is the closest point on the Asian mainland to Japan. With three powerful neighbors—China, Russia, and Japan—Korea had always had to fight for its independence. From 1910 to 1945, it was an oppressed colony of the Japanese Empire. As World War II ended, Soviet troops moved down the peninsula from the north and American forces landed in the south, creating a situation similar to that in Germany. The 38th parallel, which Russians and Americans set as the dividing line between their zones of occupation, became a *de facto* border. The United States in 1948 recognized an independent South Korea, with its capital at Seoul, under a conservative government led by Syngman Rhee. Rhee's support came from large landowners and from a police force trained by the Japanese before 1945. The Soviets recognized a separate North Korea, whose Communist leader, Kim Il Sung, advocated radical social and political change. Both leaders saw the 38th parallel as a temporary barrier and hoped to unify all Koreans under their own rule. Each crushed political dissent and tried to undermine the other with economic pressure and commando raids.

As early as 1947, the United States had decided that Korea was not essential to American military strategy. Planners assumed that U.S. air power in Japan could neutralize unfriendly forces on the Korean peninsula. In January 1950, Secretary of State Dean Acheson carefully excluded Korea from the primary "defensive perimeter" of the United States but kept open the possibility of international guarantees for Korean security.

On June 25, 1950, North Korea, helped by Soviet equipment and Chinese training, attacked South Korea. The invasion began the **Korean War,** which lasted until 1953 (see Map 27–2). Truman and Acheson believed that Moscow lay behind the invasion. In fact, Kim originated the invasion plan because he seemed to be losing the civil war in the south, and he spent a year persuading Stalin to agree to it. Stalin hoped that the conquest of South Korea would force Japan to sign a favorable treaty with the USSR.

American leaders thought that the explosion of a hot war after five years of world tension demanded a military response. As the South Korean army collapsed, Truman committed American ground troops from Japan on June 30. The United States also had the good fortune of securing an endorsement from the United Nations. Because the Soviet Union was boycotting the UN (hoping to force the seating of Mao's People's Republic of China in place of Jiang's government), it could not use its veto when the Security Council asked UN members to help South Korea. The Korean conflict remained officially a United Nations action. Although U.S. generals Douglas MacArthur, Matthew Ridgway, and Mark Clark ran the show as the successive heads of the UN command, 21 other nations committed military resources in a true multinational coalition.

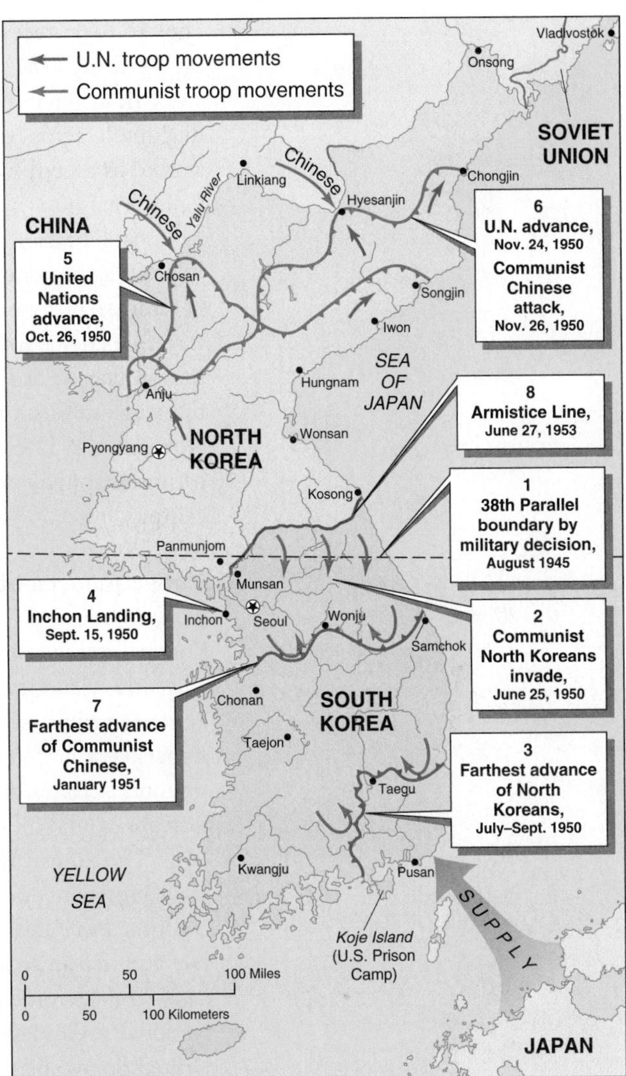

MAP 27–2 **The Korean War** After rapid reversals of fortune in 1950 and early 1951, the war in Korea settled into stalemate. Most Americans agreed with the need to contain Communist expansion but found it deeply frustrating to fight for limited objectives rather than total victory.

Was a stalemate the inevitable end to the Korean War? Why or why not?

The Politics of War

Fortunes in the first year of the Korean conflict seesawed three times. The first U.S. combat troops were outnumbered, outgunned, and poorly trained. They could not stop the North Koreans. By early August, the Americans clung to a narrow toehold around the port of Pusan on the tip of the Korean peninsula. As reinforcements arrived, however, MacArthur transformed the war with a daring amphibious counterattack at Inchon, 150 miles behind North Korean lines. The North Korean army was already overextended and exhausted. It collapsed and fled north.

The temptation to push across the 38th parallel and unify the peninsula under Syngman Rhee was irresistible. MacArthur and Washington officials disregarded warnings by China that it would enter the war if the United States tried to reunite Korea by force. U.S. and South Korean troops rolled north, drawing closer and closer to the boundary between North Korea and China.

Korean War Pacific war started on June 25, 1950, when North Korea, helped by Soviet equipment and Chinese training, attacked South Korea.

Chinese forces attacked MacArthur's command in late October but then disappeared. MacArthur dismissed the attacks as a token gesture. In fact, they were a final warning. On November 26, the Chinese struck the overextended American columns. They had massed 300,000 troops without detection by American aviation. Their assault drove the UN forces into a two-month retreat that again abandoned Seoul.

Despite his glaring mistake, MacArthur remained in command until he publicly contradicted national policy. In March 1951, with the UN forces again pushing north, Truman prepared to offer a ceasefire that would have preserved the separate nations of South and North Korea. MacArthur tried to preempt the president by demanding that China admit defeat or suffer the consequences. He then published a direct attack on the administration's policy of limiting the Asian war to ensure the security of Europe. President Truman had no choice. To protect civilian control of the armed forces, he relieved MacArthur of his command on April 11, 1951.

In Korea itself, U.S. and South Korean forces stabilized a strong defensive line that cut diagonally across the 38th parallel. Here the conflict settled into trench warfare. What had started as a civil war was now an international conflict between the two sides in the larger Cold War.

Stabilization of the Korean front ushered in two years of truce negotiations beginning in July 1951, for none of the key actors wanted a wider war. Negotiations stalled over thousands of Chinese prisoners of war who might not want to return to China. The political decision to turn free choice for POWs into a symbol of resistance to Communism left Truman's administration bogged down in a grinding war. Nearly half of the 140,000 U.S. casualties came after the truce talks started. The war was a decisive factor behind the Republican victory in the November 1952 elections and dragged on until June 1953, when an armistice returned the peninsula roughly to its prewar political division, a situation that endured into the twenty-first century.

Consequences of the Korean War. The war in Korea was a preview of Vietnam 15 years later. American leaders propped up an undemocratic regime to defend democracy. Both North Koreans and South Koreans engaged in savage political reprisals as the battlefront shifted back and forth. American soldiers found it hard to distinguish between allied and enemy Koreans. American emphasis on massive firepower led U.S. forces to demolish entire villages to kill single snipers. The air force tried to break North Korean resistance by pouring bombs on cities, power stations, factories, and dams; General Curtis LeMay estimated that the bombings killed a million Koreans.

The Korean War had global consequences. It helped to legitimize the United Nations and set a precedent for its peacekeeping role in places like the Middle East. In Washington, it confirmed the ideas underlying NSC-68, with its call for the United States to expand its military and to lead an anti-Communist alliance. Two days after the North Korean invasion, President Truman ordered the Seventh Fleet to interpose between mainland China and the Nationalist Chinese on Taiwan, a decision that guaranteed 20 years of hostility between the United States and China. In the same month, the United States began to aid France's struggle to retain control over its Southeast Asian colony of Indochina, which included Laos, Cambodia, and Vietnam.

In Europe, the United States now pushed to rearm West Germany as part of a militarized NATO and sent troops to Europe as a permanent defense force. It increased military aid to European governments and secured a unified command for the national forces allocated to NATO, a step that made West German rearmament acceptable to other nations of Western Europe that remembered 1940. Rearmament also stimulated German economic recovery and bound West Germany to the political and economic institutions of the North Atlantic nations. In 1952, the European Coal and Steel Community marked an important step toward economic cooperation that would evolve into the European Union by the end of the century. Dwight Eisenhower, who had led the Western allies in the invasion of France and Germany, became the new NATO commander in April 1951; his appointment symbolized the American commitment to Western Europe.

QUICK REVIEW

Impact of the Korean War

- Preview of American involvement in Vietnam 15 years later.
- Helped legitimize the UN.
- Confirmed the analysis of NSC-68 in the minds of many American officials.

THE SECOND RED SCARE

WHY DID fear of Communism escalate in the years following World War II?

The Korean War reinforced the second Red Scare, an assault on civil liberties that stretched from the mid-1940s to the mid-1950s and dwarfed the Red Scare of 1919–1920. The Cold War fanned fears of Communist subversion on American soil. Legitimate concerns about espionage mixed with suspicions that Communist sympathizers in high places were helping Stalin and

AMERICAN VIEWS

Integrating the Army in Korea

Racial integration of the armed forces became official policy in 1948, but President Truman's directive was not fully implemented until after the war in Korea. Two veterans of that war—white G.I. Harry Summers and black officer Beverly Scott—recall some of the steps toward integration.

- **What** do these recollections say about the pervasiveness of racism in midcentury American life?
- **How** has the experience of minority soldiers changed from the 1950s to the 1990s?

Harry Summers: When they first started talking about integration, white soldiers were aghast. They would say, How can you integrate the army? How do you know when you go to the mess hall that you won't get a plate or a knife or a spoon that was used by a Negro? Or when you go to the supply room and draw sheets, you might get a sheet that a Negro had slept on? . . .

I remember a night when your rifle company was scheduled to get some replacements. I was in a three-man foxhole with one other guy, and they dropped this new replacement off at our foxhole. The other guy I was in the foxhole with was under a poncho, making coffee. It was bitterly cold. And pitch dark. He got the coffee made, and he gave me a drink, and he took a drink, and then he offered some to this new replacement, who we literally couldn't see, it was that dark.

And the guy said, "No, I don't want any."

"What the hell are you talking about, you don't want any? You got to be freezing to death. Here, take a drink of coffee."

"Well," he said, "you can't tell it now, but I'm black. And tomorrow morning when you find out I was drinking out of the same cup you were using, you ain't gonna be too happy."

Me and this other guy kind of looked at each other.

"You silly son of a bitch," we told him, "here, take the goddam coffee."

Beverly Scott: The 24th Regiment was the only all-black regiment in the division, and as a black officer in an all-black regiment commanded by whites I was always super sensitive about standing my ground. Being a man. Being honest with my soldiers. . . .

Most of the white officers were good. Taken in the context of the times, they were probably better than the average white guy in civilian life. But there was still that patronizing expectation of failure. White officers came to the 24th Regiment knowing or suspecting or having been told that this was an inferior regiment.

[In September 1951, members of the regiment were integrated into other units.]

I was transferred to the 14th [Regiment] and right away I experienced some problems. People in the 14th didn't want anybody from the 24th. I was a technically qualified communications officer, which the 14th said they needed very badly, but when I got there, suddenly they didn't need any commo officers.

Then their executive officer said, "We got a rifle platoon for you. Think you can handle a rifle platoon?"

What the hell do you mean, can I handle a rifle platoon? I was also trained as an infantry officer. He know that. I was a first lieutenant, been in the army six years. . . . If I had been coming in as a white first lieutenant the question never would have been asked.

Source: Rudy Tomedi, *No Bugles, No Drums: An Oral History of the Korean War* (New York: John Wiley, 1993).

Mao. The scare was also a weapon that the conservative wing of the Republican Party used against the men and women who had built Roosevelt's New Deal (see Overview, The Second Red Scare).

Efforts to root out suspected subversives operated on three tracks. National and state governments established loyalty programs to identify and fire suspect employees. The courts punished members of suspect organizations. Congressional and state legislative investigations followed the whims of committee chairs. Anti-Communist crusaders often relied on dubious evidence and eagerly believed the worst. They also threatened basic civil liberties.

The Communist Party and the Loyalty Program

The Communist Party in the United States was in rapid decline as a political factor after World War II. The CIO and United Auto Workers froze Communists out of leadership positions, bringing industrial unions into the American mainstream. Nevertheless, Republicans used Red-baiting as a campaign tactic. In 1946, Republican campaigners told the public that the basic choice was "between Communism and Republicanism." Starting a 30-year political career, a young navy veteran named Richard Nixon won a southern California congressional seat by hammering on his opponent's connections to supposedly Communist-dominated organizations.

Watch the Video at **www.myhistorylab.com** *President Truman and the Threat of Communism*

President Truman responded to the Republican landslide with Executive Order 9835 in March 1947, initiating a loyalty program for federal employees. It authorized the attorney general to prepare a list of "totalitarian, Fascist, Communist, or subversive" organizations and made membership or even "sympathetic association" with such groups grounds for dismissal. The loyalty program applied to approximately 8 million Americans working for the federal government or defense contractors; similar state laws affected another 5 million.

Federal employees worked under a cloud of fear. Would the cooperative store they had once patronized or the protest group they had joined in college suddenly appear on the attorney general's list? Would someone complain that they had disloyal books on their shelves? Loyalty boards asked about religion, racial equality, and a taste for foreign films. They also tried to identify homosexuals, who were thought to be targets for blackmail by foreign agents. The loyalty program resulted in 1,210 firings and 6,000 resignations under Truman and comparable numbers during Dwight Eisenhower's first term from 1953 to 1956.

Naming Names to Congress

Congress was even busier than the executive branch. The congressional hunt for subversives had its roots in 1938, when Congressman Martin Dies, a Texas Democrat, created the Special Committee on Un-American Activities. Originally intended to ferret out pro-Fascists, the Dies committee evolved into the permanent **House Un-American Activities Committee (HUAC)** in 1945. It investigated "un-American propaganda" that attacked constitutional government.

House Un-American Activities Committee (HUAC) Originally intended to ferret out pro-Fascists, it later investigated "un-American propaganda" that attacked constitutional government.

One of HUAC's juiciest targets was Hollywood. Hollywood's reputation for loose morals, foreign-born directors, Jewish producers, and left-leaning writers aroused the suspicions of many congressmen. HUAC sought to make sure that no un-American messages were being peddled through America's most popular entertainment.

Read the Document at **www.myhistorylab.com** *Ronald Reagan, Testimony before the House Un-American Activities Committee (1947)*

When the hearings opened in October 1947, studio executives Jack Warner of Warner Brothers and Louis B. Mayer of MGM assured HUAC of their anti-Communism. So did the popular actors Gary Cooper and Ronald Reagan. By contrast, eight screenwriters and two directors—the so-called Hollywood Ten—refused to discuss their past political associations, citing the free-speech protections of the First Amendment to the Constitution. HUAC countered with citations for contempt of Congress. The First Amendment defense failed when it reached the Supreme Court, and the Ten went to jail in 1950. Other actors, writers, and directors found themselves on the Hollywood blacklist, banned from jobs where they might insert Communist propaganda into American movies.

At the start of 1951, the new Senate Internal Security Subcommittee went into action. The McCarran Committee, named for the Nevada senator who chaired it, targeted diplomats, labor union leaders, professors, and schoolteachers. Both committees turned their investigations into rituals. The real point was not to force personal confessions from witnesses but to badger them into identifying friends and associates who might have been involved in suspect activities.

OVERVIEW The Second Red Scare

Type of Anti-Communist Effort	Key Tools	Results
Employee loyalty programs	U.S. attorney general's list of subversive organizations Executive orders by Truman and Eisenhower	Thousands of federal and state workers fired, careers damaged
Congressional investigations	HUAC McCarran Committee Army-McCarthy hearings	Employee blacklists, investigation of writers and intellectuals, Hollywood Ten
Criminal prosecutions	Trials for espionage and conspiracy to advocate violent overthrow of the U.S. government	Convictions of Communist Party leaders (1949), Alger Hiss (1950), and Rosenbergs (1951)
Restrictions on Communist Party	Internal Security Act (1950) Communist Control Act (1954)	Marginalizing of far left in politics and labor unions

State legislatures imitated Congress by searching for "Reducators" among college faculty in such states as Oklahoma, Washington, and California. Harvard apparently used its influence to stay out of the newspapers, cutting a deal in which the FBI fed it information about suspect faculty, whom the university quietly fired. More common was the experience of the economics professor fired from the University of Kansas City after testifying before the McCarran Committee. He found it hard to keep any job once his name had been in the papers. A local dairy fired him because it thought its customers might be uneasy having a radical handle their milk bottles.

Subversion Trials

In 1948, the Justice Department indicted the leaders of the American Communist Party under the Alien Registration Act of 1940. Eleven men and women were convicted in 1949 of conspiring to advocate the violent overthrow of the United States government through their speech and publications.

The case of Alger Hiss soon followed. In 1948, a former Communist, Whittaker Chambers, named Hiss as a Communist with whom he had associated in the 1930s. Hiss, who had held important posts in the State Department, first denied knowing Chambers but then admitted to having known him under another name. He continued to deny any involvement with Communists and sued Chambers for slander. As proof, Chambers revealed microfilms that he had hidden inside a pumpkin on his Maryland farm, and Congressman Richard Nixon quickly announced the discovery. Tests seemed to show that the "pumpkin papers" were State Department documents that had been copied on a typewriter Hiss had once owned. With the new evidence, the Justice Department indicted Hiss for perjury—lying under oath. A first perjury trial ended in deadlock, but a second jury convicted Hiss in January 1950.

Hiss was a potent symbol as well as a spy. To his opponents, he stood for every wrong turn the nation had taken since 1932. His supporters found a virtue in every trait his enemies hated, from his refined tastes to his degree from Harvard Law School. Many supporters believed he had been framed. However, the weight of evidence from Soviet archives and American intelligence intercepts confirms that he did indeed spy for the Soviets.

Another important case was that of Julius and Ethel Rosenberg. In 1950, the British arrested nuclear physicist Klaus Fuchs, who confessed to passing atomic secrets to the Soviets when he worked at Los Alamos in 1944 and 1945. The "Fuchs spy ring" soon implicated the

American State Department official Alger Hiss taking an oath before the House Committee on Un-American Activities in Washington in 1948. Hiss denied he was a member of a Communist cell, but was later convicted of perjury in 1950.

Rosenbergs, New York radicals of strong beliefs but limited sophistication. Convicted in 1951 on the vague charge of conspiring to commit espionage, they were sent to the electric chair in 1953 after refusing to buy a reprieve by naming other spies.

As with Alger Hiss, the government had a plausible but not airtight case. After their trial, the Rosenbergs became a cause for international protest. Their small children became pawns and trophies in political demonstrations, an experience recaptured in E. L. Doctorow's novel *The Book of Daniel* (1971). There is no doubt that Julius Rosenberg was part of a successful Soviet spy ring, but Ethel Rosenberg's involvement was limited. In the words of FBI director J. Edgar Hoover, the government charged her "as a lever" to pressure her husband into naming his confederates.

Read the **Document** at **www.myhistorylab.com** *Joseph R. McCarthy, from Speech Delivered to the Women's Club of Wheeling, West Virginia (1950)*

Read the **Document** at **www.myhistorylab.com** *Senator Joseph McCarthy's telegram to President Truman following the Wheeling [W. Va.] Speech (1950)*

Senator McCarthy on Stage

The best-remembered participant in the second Red Scare was Senator Joseph McCarthy of Wisconsin. Crude, sly, and ambitious, McCarthy had ridden to victory in the Republican landslide of 1946. He burst into national prominence on February 9, 1950. In a rambling speech in Wheeling, West Virginia, he latched onto the issue of Communist subversion. Although no transcript of the speech survives, he supposedly stated, "I have here in my hand a list of 205 that were known to the Secretary of State as being members of the Communist Party and who, nevertheless, are still working and shaping the policy of the State Department." In the following days, the 205 Communists changed quickly to 57, to 81, to 10, to 116. McCarthy's rise to fame climaxed with an incoherent six-hour speech to the Senate. Over the next several years, his speeches were aimed at moving targets, full of multiple untruths. He threw out so many accusations, true or false, that the facts could never catch up.

The Senate disregarded McCarthy, but the public heard only the accusations, not the lack of evidence. Senators treated McCarthy as a crude outsider in their exclusive club, but voters in 1950 turned against his most prominent opponents. Liberal politicians ran for cover; conservatives were happy for McCarthy to attract media attention away from HUAC and the McCarran Committee. In 1951, McCarthy even called George Marshall, then serving as secretary of defense, an agent of Communism. The idea was ludicrous. Marshall was one of the most upright Americans of his generation, the architect of victory in World War II, and a key contributor to the stabilization of Europe. Nevertheless, McCarthy was so popular that the Republicans featured him at their 1952 convention and their presidential candidate, Dwight Eisenhower, conspicuously failed to defend Marshall, who had been chiefly responsible for Eisenhower's fast-track career.

Richard Nixon (right) and the chief investigator for the House Committee on Un-American Activities inspect microfilm of the "pumpkin papers." Hidden inside a pumpkin on the Maryland farm of committee informant Whittaker Chambers, the papers helped convict Alger Hiss of perjury. Nixon's role in pursuing Hiss launched a political career that took him to the White House.

McCarthy's personal crudeness made him a media star but eventually undermined him. Given control of the Senate Committee on Government Operations in 1953, he investigated dozens of agencies from the Government Printing Office to the Army Signal Corps. Early in 1954, he investigated an army dentist with a supposedly subversive background. The back-and-forth confrontation led to two months of televised hearings. The cameras brought political debates into living rooms and put McCarthy's bullying style on trial. "Have you no decency?" asked the army's lawyer, Joseph Welch, at one point.

Hear the **Audio** at **www.myhistorylab.com** *Joseph P. McCarthy Speech*

The end came quickly. McCarthy's "favorable" rating in the polls plummeted. The U.S. Senate finally voted 67 to 22 in December 1954 to condemn McCarthy for conduct "unbecoming a Member of the Senate." When he died in 1957, he had been repudiated by the Senate and ignored by the media that had built him up.

Read the **Document** at **www.myhistorylab.com** *Senate Resolution 301: Censure of Senator Joseph McCarthy (1954)*

Understanding McCarthyism

The antisubversive campaign that everyone now calls **McCarthyism,** however, died a slower death. It had actually originated with the Truman administration, and laws, such as the Internal Security Act (1950) and the Immigration and Nationality Act (1952), remained as tools of political control during the Eisenhower administration. HUAC continued to mount investigations as late as the 1960s.

McCarthyism Anti-Communist attitudes and actions associated with Senator Joe McCarthy in the early 1950s, including smear tactics and innuendo.

In retrospect, at least four factors made Americans afraid of Communist subversion. One was the legitimate concern about atomic spies. The Soviet Union had developed an extensive espionage network in the early 1940s. More than a few U.S. officials passed on secret information, although there was not the vast interlocking conspiracy that some critics feared. A second was an undercurrent of anti-Semitism and nativism, for many labor organizers and

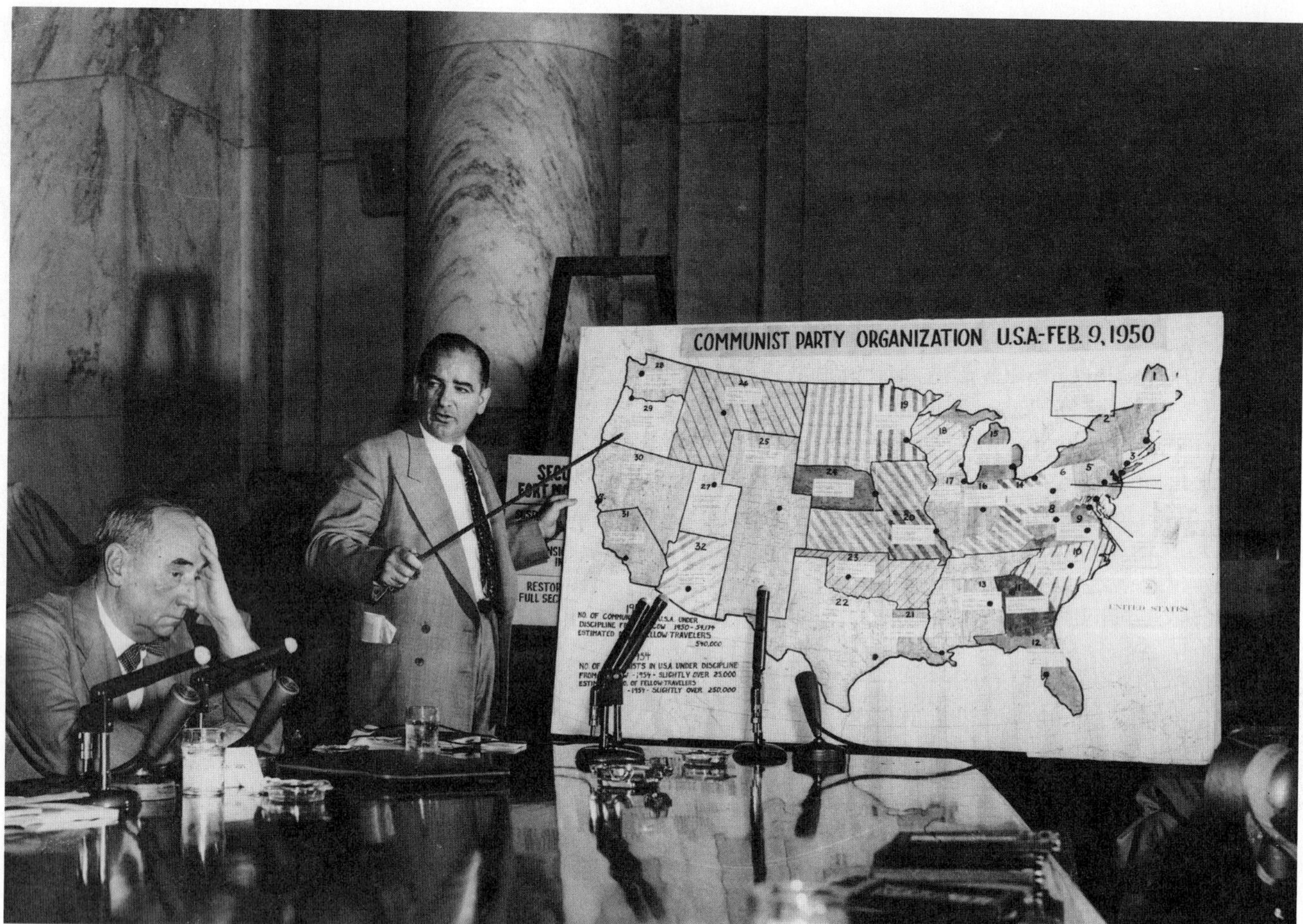

Senator Joe McCarthy used press releases and carefully managed congressional committee hearings to attack suspected Communists, although he had almost no hard information. At the Army-McCarthy hearings in June 1954, he clashed with attorney Joseph Welch. Here Welch listens as McCarthy points to Oregon on a map that supposedly showed Communist Party organization in the United States.

Communist Party members (like the Rosenbergs) had Jewish and eastern European backgrounds. Third was southern and western resentment of the nation's Ivy League elite. Most general, finally, was a widespread fear that the world was spinning out of control. Many people sought easy explanations for global tensions. It was basically reassuring if Soviet and Chinese Communist successes were the result of American traitors rather than of Communist strengths.

Partisan politics mobilized the fears and resentments into a political force. From 1946 through 1952, the conservative wing of the Republican Party used the Red Scare to attack New Dealers and liberal Democrats. HUAC, the McCarran Committee, and McCarthy were all tools for bringing down the men and women who had been moving the United States toward a more active government at home and abroad. The Republican elite used McCarthy until they won control of the presidency and Congress in 1952, and then abandoned him.

The broader goal of the second Red Scare was conformity of thought. Many of the professors and bureaucrats targeted for investigation had indeed been Communists or interested in Communism, usually in the 1930s and early 1940s. Most saw it as a way to increase social justice, and they sometimes excused the failures of Communism in the Soviet Union. Unlike the handful of real spies, however, they were targeted not for actions but for ideas. The investigations and loyalty programs were efforts to ensure that Americans kept any left-wing ideas to themselves.

CONCLUSION

The United States emerged from the Truman years remarkably prosperous despite the turmoil and injustice of the second Red Scare and deep worries about nuclear war. It was also more secure from international threats than many nervous Americans appreciated. The years from 1946 to 1952 set the themes for a generation that believed that the United States could do whatever it set its mind to: end poverty, land an astronaut on the moon, thwart Communist revolutions in other countries. There was a direct line from Harry Truman's 1947 declaration that the United States would defend freedom around the world to John Kennedy's 1961 promise that the nation would bear any burden necessary to protect free nations from Communism. As the world moved slowly toward greater stability in the 1950s, Americans were ready for a decade of confidence.

Where to Learn More

Harry S. Truman National Historical Site, Library, and Museum, Independence, Missouri. The museum has exhibits on Truman's political career and U.S. history during his administration. Also in Independence is the Harry S. Truman Courtroom and Office, with exhibits on his early career. http://www.nps.gov/hstr/.

General Douglas MacArthur Memorial, Norfolk, Virginia. The MacArthur Memorial in downtown Norfolk commemorates the career of a key figure in shaping the postwar world. http://www.macarthurmemorial.org.

United Nations Headquarters, New York, New York. A tour of the United Nations complex in New York is a reminder of the new organizations for international cooperation that emerged from World War II. http://www.un.org.

Levittown. Building the Suburban Dream. Online exhibit about Levittown, Pennsylvania, sponsored by the State Museum of Pennsylvania. http://web1.fandm.edu/levittown.

Smithsonian Institution, National Museum of American History, Washington, DC. The exhibit "America on the Move" includes reproductions of life in Park Forest, Illinois, and the Sandy Boulevard commercial strip in Portland, Oregon, as of 1949. http://americanhistory.si.edu/onthemove/.

Review Questions

1. As described in the opening of the chapter, what housing choices were available after World War II? How did these choices reshape American cities? How did the postwar readjustment create a suburban society?
2. What were the key differences between Harry Truman and congressional Republicans about the legacy of the New Deal? Why did regulating labor unions become a central domestic issue in the late 1940s? Why did Truman manage to win the presidential election of 1948 despite starting as an underdog?
3. How did the postwar years expand opportunity for veterans and members of the working class? How did they limit opportunities for women? How did they begin to challenge racial inequities in American society?
4. What foreign policy priorities did the United States set after 1945? To what extent did the United States achieve its most basic objectives? How did mutual mistrust fuel and deepen the Cold War?
5. How did the character of the Cold War change in 1949 and 1950? What were key actions by the Soviet Union and China, and how did the United States respond? What was the effect of the chaotic fighting in Korea on U.S. domestic politics and diplomacy?
6. What factors motivated an increasingly frantic fear of domestic subversion in the late 1940s and early 1950s? Who were the key actors in the second Red Scare? What was its long-term impact on American society?
7. How did the continuation and expansion of the nation's global commitments after 1945 affect life in the United States?

Key Terms

Berlin blockade (p. 763)
Central Intelligence Agency (CIA) (p. 763)
Cold War (p. 753)
Containment (p. 763)
Council of Economic Advisers (p. 754)
Dixiecrats (p. 758)
GI Bill of Rights (p. 754)
House Un-American Activities Committee (HUAC) (p. 770)
International Monetary Fund (IMF) (p. 761)
Korean War (p. 767)
Marshall Plan (p. 762)
McCarthyism (p. 773)
National Security Council (NSC) (p. 763)
National Security Council Paper 68 (NSC-68) (p. 765)
North Atlantic Treaty Organization (NATO) (p. 764)
Redlining (p. 755)
Taft-Hartley Act (p. 754)
Truman Doctrine (p. 762)
World Bank (p. 761)

PEARSON myhistorylab™ Connections

Reinforce what you learned in this chapter by studying the many documents, images, maps, review tools, and videos available at **www.myhistorylab.com**.

Read and Review

Study and Review **Study Plan: Chapter 27**

Read the Document

Kenneth MacFarland, "The Unfinished Work" (1946)

National Security Council Memorandum Number 68 (1950)

Ronald Reagan, Testimony before the House Un-American Activities Committee (1947)

Joseph R. McCarthy, from Speech Delivered to the Women's Club of Wheeling, West Virginia (1950)

Senator Joseph McCarthy's telegram to President Truman following the Wheeling [W. Va.] Speech (1950)

Executive Order 9981: Desegregation of the Armed Forces (1948)

George F. Kennan, "The Long Telegram" (1946)

George Marshall, The Marshall Plan (1947)

Senate Resolution 301: Censure of Senator Joseph McCarthy (1954)

Servicemen's Readjustment Act (1944)

Thurgood Marshall, "The Legal Attack to Secure Civil Rights" (1942)

Truman Doctrine (1947)

George F. Kennan, "Containment" (1947)

See the Map

Population Shifts, 1940–1950

The Korean War, 1950–1953

Research and Explore

Read the Document

Personal Journeys Online

From Then to Now Online: The Automobile Industry

Exploring America: The Truman Doctrine (1947)

Hear the Audio *Joseph P. McCarthy Speech*

Watch the Video

The Desegregation of the Military and Blacks in Combat

President Truman and the Threat of Communism

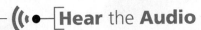

Hear the Audio

Hear the audio files for Chapter 27 at **www.myhistorylab.com**.

1953-1964

28

The Confident Years

Singer Elvis Presley sings "Hillbilly Heartbreak" on stage in Hollywood, California, during a performance in 1956.

Hear the audio files for Chapter 28 at **www.myhistorylab.com**.

A DECADE OF AFFLUENCE *(page 781)*

HOW DID the "Decade of Affluence" alter social and religious life in America?

FACING OFF WITH THE SOVIET UNION *(page 788)*

WHAT IMPACT did Dwight Eisenhower's foreign policy have on U.S. relations with the Soviet Union?

JOHN F. KENNEDY AND THE COLD WAR *(page 793)*

WHAT WAS John F. Kennedy's approach to dealing with the Soviet Union?

RIGHTEOUSNESS LIKE A MIGHTY STREAM: THE STRUGGLE FOR CIVIL RIGHTS *(page 797)*

WHAT WAS the significance of *Brown v. Board of Education of Topeka?*

"LET US CONTINUE" *(page 801)*

HOW DID Lyndon B. Johnson continue the domestic agenda inherited from the Kennedy administration? In what ways did he depart from it?

One American Journey

The first day I was able to enter Central High School [in Little Rock, Arkansas, September 23, 1957, what I felt inside was terrible, wrenching, awful fear. On the car radio I could hear that there was a mob. I knew what a mob meant and I knew that the sounds that came from the crowd were very angry. So we entered the side of the building, very, very fast. Even as we entered there were people running after us, people tripping other people. There has never been in my life any stark terror or any fear akin to that. I'd only been in the school a couple of hours and by that time it was apparent that the mob was just overrunning the school. Policemen were throwing down their badges and the mob was getting past the wooden sawhorses because the police would no longer fight their own in order to protect us. So we were all called into the principal's office, and there was great fear that we would not get out of this building. We were trapped. And I thought, Okay, so I'm going to die here, in school. . . . Even the adults, the school officials, were panicked, feeling like there was no protection. . . . [A] gentleman, who I believed to be the police chief, said . . . "I'll get them out." And we were taken to the basement of this place. And we were put into two cars, grayish blue Fords. And the man instructed the drivers, he said, "Once you start driving, do not stop." And he told us to put our heads down. This guy revved up his engine and he came up out of the bowels of this building, and as he came up, I could just see hands reaching across this car, I could hear the yelling, I could see guns, and he was told not to stop. "If you hit somebody, you keep rolling, 'cause the kids are dead." And he did just that, and he didn't hit anybody, but he certainly was forceful and aggressive in the way he exited this driveway, because people tried to stop him and he didn't stop. He dropped me off at home. And I remember saying, "Thank you for the ride," and I should've said, "Thank you for my life."

Melba Patillo Beals, in Henry Hampton and Steve Frayer, eds., *Voices of Freedom: An Oral History of the Civil Rights Movement from the 1950s through the 1980s* (New York: Bantam, 1990).

Read the **Document** at **www.myhistorylab.com**

Personal Journeys Online

- **Diane Nash, Interview in Mathew Allman, *The New Negro*, 1961. The civil rights sit-in movement in Nashville in 1960.**
- **Suzette Miller, in Staughton Lynd, *Nonviolence in America*, 1966. Grass roots civil rights efforts in Mississippi in 1961.**

MELBA PATTILLO was one of the nine African American students who entered previously all-white Central High in the fall of 1957. Her enrollment in the high school, where she managed to last through a year of harassment and hostility, was a symbolic step in the journey toward greater racial equality in U.S. society.

The struggle for full civil rights for all Americans was rooted in national ideals, but it was also shaped by the continuing tensions of the Cold War. President Dwight Eisenhower acted against his own inclinations and sent federal troops to keep the peace in Little Rock in part because he worried about public opinion in other nations. As the United States and the Soviet Union maneuvered for influence in Africa and Asia, domestic events sometimes loomed large in foreign relations.

Melba Pattillo's life after Little Rock also reveals something about the increasing geographical mobility and economic opportunities available to most Americans. She graduated from San Francisco State University, earned a master's degree from Columbia University, and worked as a television reporter and writer. The prosperous years from 1953 to 1964 spread the economic promise of the 1940s across American society. Young couples could afford large families and new houses. Labor unions grew conservative because cooperation with big business offered immediate gains for their members.

CHRONOLOGY

1953	CIA-backed coup returns Shah Reza Pahlavi to power in Iran.
	Soviet Union detonates hydrogen bomb.
1954	Vietnamese defeat the French; Geneva conference divides Vietnam.
	United States and allies form SEATO.
	Supreme Court decides *Brown v. Board of Education of Topeka*.
	CIA overthrows the government of Guatemala.
	China provokes a crisis over Quemoy and Matsu.
1955	Salk polio vaccine is announced.
	Black citizens boycott Montgomery, Alabama, bus system.
	Soviet Union forms the Warsaw Pact.
	AFL and CIO merge.
1956	Interstate Highway Act is passed.
	Soviets repress Hungarian revolt.
	Israel, France, and Britain invade Egypt.
1957	U.S. Army maintains law and order in Little Rock after violent resistance to integration of Central High School.
	Soviet Union launches *Sputnik*, world's first artificial satellite.
1958	United States and Soviet Union voluntarily suspend nuclear tests.
1959	Fidel Castro takes power in Cuba.
	Nikita Khrushchev visits the United States.
1960	U-2 spy plane shot down over Russia.
	Sit-in movement begins in Greensboro, North Carolina.
1961	Bay of Pigs invasion fails.
	Kennedy establishes the Peace Corps.
	Vienna summit fails.
	Freedom rides are held in the Deep South.
	Berlin crisis leads to construction of the Berlin Wall.
1962	John Glenn orbits the earth.
	Cuban missile crisis brings the world to the brink of nuclear war.
	Michael Harrington publishes *The Other America*.
1963	Civil rights demonstrations rend Birmingham.
	Civil rights activists march in Washington.
	Betty Friedan publishes *The Feminine Mystique*.
	Limited Test Ban Treaty is signed.
	Ngo Dinh Diem is assassinated in South Vietnam.
	President Kennedy is assassinated.
1964	Civil Rights Act is passed.
	Freedom Summer is organized in Mississippi.
	Office of Economic Opportunity is created.
	Gulf of Tonkin Resolution is passed.
	Wilderness Act marks new direction in environmental policy.
1965	Medical Care Act establishes Medicare and Medicaid.
	Elementary and Secondary Education Act extends direct federal aid to local schools.
	Selma-Montgomery march climaxes era of nonviolent civil rights demonstrations.
	Voting Rights Act suspends literacy tests for voting.

Despite challenges at home and abroad, Americans were fundamentally confident during the decade after the Korean War. They expected corporations to use scientific research to craft new products for eager customers and medical researchers to conquer diseases. When the USSR challenged U.S. preeminence and launched the first artificial space satellite in 1957, Americans responded with shock followed by redoubled efforts to regain what they considered their rightful world leadership in science and technology. ✦

A DECADE OF AFFLUENCE

HOW DID the "Decade of Affluence" alter social and religious life in America?

Americans in the 1950s believed in the basic strength of the United States. Television's *General Electric Theater* was third in the ratings in 1956–1957. Every week, its host, Ronald Reagan, a popular Hollywood lead from the late 1930s, stated, "At General Electric, progress is our most important product." It made sense to his viewers. Large, technologically sophisticated corporations were introducing new marvels: Orlon sweaters and Saran Wrap, long-playing records, and Polaroid cameras. As long as the United States defended free enterprise, Reagan told audiences on national speaking tours, the sky was the limit.

What's Good for General Motors

Dwight Eisenhower presided over the prosperity of the 1950s. Both Democrats and Republicans had courted him as a presidential candidate in 1948. Four years later, he picked the Republicans because he wanted to make sure that the party remained committed to NATO and collective security in Europe rather than retreat into isolationism. He easily defeated the Democratic candidate, Adlai Stevenson, the moderately liberal governor of Illinois.

Eisenhower and the politics of the middle. Over the next eight years, Eisenhower claimed the political middle for Republicans. Satisfied with postwar America, Eisenhower accepted much of the New Deal but saw little need for further reform. In a 1959 poll, liberals considered him a fellow liberal and conservatives thought him a conservative. Eisenhower's first secretary of defense, "Engine Charlie" Wilson, had headed General Motors. At his Senate confirmation hearing, he proclaimed, "For years, I thought what was good for the country was good for General Motors and vice versa." Wilson's statement captured a central theme of the 1950s. Not since the 1920s had Americans been so excited about the benefits of big business.

Read the Document
at **www.myhistorylab.com**
Exploring America: The Consumer Society: 1950–1960

The new prosperity. The economy in the 1950s gave Americans much to like. Between 1950 and 1964, output grew by a solid 3.2 percent per year. American workers in the 1950s had more disposable income than ever before. Their productivity, or output per worker, increased steadily. Average compensation per hour of work rose faster than consumer prices in nine of eleven years from 1953 to 1964. Rising productivity made it easy for corporations to share gains with large labor unions. In turn, labor leaders lost interest in making radical changes in American society. In 1955 the older and more conservative American Federation of Labor absorbed the younger Congress of Industrial Organizations. The new AFL CIO positioned itself as a partner in prosperity and a foe of Communism at home and abroad. It was a quiet consensus that seemed to benefit everyone—workers who could afford new consumer goods and corporations that could sell to them. The United States increasingly became a "consumer's republic" that defined mass consumption as the solution to social and economic problems.

For members of minority groups with regular industrial and government jobs, the 1950s could also be economically rewarding. Detroit, Dayton, Oakland, and other industrial cities offered them factory jobs at wages that could support a family. Black people worked through the Urban League, the National Association of Colored Women, and other race-oriented groups to secure fair-employment laws and jobs with large corporations. Many Puerto Rican migrants to New York found steady work in the Brooklyn Navy Yard. Mexican American families in San Antonio benefited from maintenance jobs at the city's military bases. Steady employment allowed black people and Latinos to build strong community institutions and vibrant neighborhood business districts.

QUICK REVIEW

America's Economy in the 1950s

- 1950–1964: U.S. economy grew at a rate of 3.2 percent per year.
- Productivity increased steadily.
- Wages rose faster than consumer prices.

However, there were never enough family-wage jobs for all of the African American and Latino workers who continued to move to northern and western cities. Many Mexican Americans were still migrant farm laborers and workers in nonunionized sweatshops. Minority workers were usually the first to suffer from the erosion of some industrial jobs and the shift of other jobs to new suburban factories that were isolated from minority neighborhoods. Black unemployment crept upward to twice the white rate, laying the seeds of frustration that would burst forth in the 1960s.

Native Americans faced equally daunting prospects. To cut costs and accelerate assimilation, Congress pushed the policy of termination between 1954 and 1962. The government sold tribal land and assets, distributed the proceeds among tribal members, and terminated its treaty relationship with the tribe. Applied to such tribes as the Klamaths in Oregon and the Menominees in Wisconsin, termination gave thousands of Indians one-time cash payments but cut them adrift from the security of tribal organizations.

Reshaping Urban America

Daly City, south of San Francisco, typified the mass-produced suburbs that housed the growing postwar middle class. It was the inspiration for the satirical song, "Little Boxes."

If Eisenhower's administration opted for the status quo on many issues, it nevertheless reshaped U.S. cities around an agenda of economic development. In 1954, Congress transformed the public housing program into urban renewal. Cities used federal funds to replace low-rent businesses and run-down housing on the fringes of their downtowns with new hospitals, civic centers, sports arenas, office towers, and luxury apartments. Urban renewal temporarily revitalized older cities in the Northeast and Midwest that were already feeling the competition of the fast-growing South and West.

Only a decade later, the same cities would be urban crisis spots, in part because of accumulating social costs from urban renewal. The bulldozers often leveled minority neighborhoods in the name of downtown expansion. Urban renewal displaced Puerto Ricans in New York, African Americans in Atlanta and Norfolk, and Mexican Americans in Denver. In Los Angeles, Dodger Stadium replaced a lively Latino community.

The Eisenhower administration also revolutionized American transportation. By the early 1950s, Americans were fed up with roads designed for Model A Fords: They wanted to enjoy their new V-8 engines and the 50 million new cars sold between 1946 and 1955. The solution was the **Federal Highway Act of 1956,** creating a national system of 41,000 miles of interstate and defense highways.

Federal Highway Act of 1956 Measure that provided federal funding to build a nationwide system of interstate and defense highways.

Although the first interstate opened in Kansas in 1956, most of the mileage came into use in the 1960s and 1970s. Interstates halved the time of city-to-city travel. They were good for General Motors, the steel industry, and the concrete industry, requiring the construction equivalent of 60 Panama Canals. The highways promoted long-distance trucking at the expense of railroads. They also wiped out hundreds of homes per mile when they plunged through large cities. As with urban renewal, the bulldozers most often plowed through African American or Latino neighborhoods, where land was cheap and white politicians could ignore protests. Some cities, such as Miami, used the highways as barriers between white and black neighborhoods.

Interstates accelerated suburbanization. The beltways or perimeter highways that began to ring most large cities made it easier and more profitable to develop new subdivisions and factory sites than to reinvest in city centers. Federal grants for sewers and other basic facilities further cut suburban costs. Continuing the pattern of the late 1940s, suburban growth added a million new single-family houses per year.

Comfort on Credit

Prosperity transformed spending habits. The 1930s had taught Americans to avoid debt. The 1950s taught them to buy on credit. The value of consumer debt, excluding home mortgages, tripled from 1952 to 1964.

New forms of marketing facilitated credit-based consumerism. The first large-scale suburban shopping center was Northgate in Seattle, which assembled all the elements of the full-grown mall—small stores facing an interior corridor between anchor department stores and surrounded by parking. By the end of the decade, developers were building malls with 1 million

AMERICAN VIEWS

The Suburban Roots of Environmental Activism

As new subdivisions ate up the rural landscape in the 1950s and 1960s, suburbanites found that they were bringing old environmental problems with them and creating new ones. Leapfrog development often destroyed the very landscapes that attracted people out of cities in the first place. Overburdened roads created traffic jams and air pollution. Septic tanks in high-density developments leaked sewage that fouled rural streams. Orange groves, corn fields, and wooded hills disappeared beneath the blades of bulldozers. Environmentalism was certainly about preserving the wilderness, but it was also about keeping suburbia from fouling its own nest. Journalist William H. Whyte played a leading role in identifying the suburban environmental crisis and making the case for preserving open space and natural areas as metropolitan areas grew.

- **Does** Whyte argue against all suburban growth, or against certain types of growth?
- **How** does knowledge of Whyte's efforts change our understanding of environmentalism?

Over the next three or four years Americans will have a chance to decide how decent a place this country will be to live in, and for generations to come. Already huge patches of once green countryside have been turned into vast, smog-filled deserts that are neither city, suburb, nor country, and each day—at a rate of some 3,000 acres a day—more countryside is being bulldozed under. You can't stop progress, they say, yet much more of this kind of progress and we shall have the paradox of prosperity lowering our real standard of living.

With characteristic optimism, most Americans still assume that there will be plenty of green space on the other side of the fence. But this time there won't be. . . . Flying from Los Angeles to San Bernardino—an unnerving lesson in man's infinite capacity to mess up his environment—the traveler can see a legion of bulldozers gnawing into the last remaining tract of green between the two cities. . . . On the outer edge of the present Philadelphia metropolitan area, where there will be one million new people in the ten years ending 1960, some of the loveliest countryside in the world is being irretrievably fouled, and the main body of suburbanites has yet to arrive. . . .

The problem is the pattern of growth—or, rather, the lack of one. . . . [W]e are ruining the whole metropolitan area of the future. In the townships just beyond today's suburbia there is little planning, and development is being left almost entirely in the hands of the speculative builder. Understandably, he follows the line of least resistance and in his wake is left a hit-or-miss pattern of development. . . .

Sprawl is bad aesthetics; it is bad economics. Five acres are being made to do the work of one, and do it very poorly. This is bad for the farmers, it is bad for communities, it is bad for industry, it is bad for utilities, it is bad for the railroads, it is bad for the recreation groups, it is bad even for developers.

And it is unnecessary. In many suburbs the opportunity has vanished, but it is not too late to lay down sensible guidelines for the communities of the future. Most important of all, it is not too late to reserve open space while there is still some left—land for parks, for landscaped industrial districts, and for just plain scenery and breathing opportunities.

The Editors of *Fortune, The Exploding Metropolis* (Garden City, NY: Doubleday and Co., 1958), pp. 133–135.

square feet of shopping floor. At the start of the 1970s, the universal credit card (Visa, MasterCard) made shopping even easier.

Surrounding the new malls were the servants and symbols of America's car culture. Where cities of the early twentieth century had been built around public transportation—streetcars and subways—those of the 1950s depended on private automobiles. Interstate highways sucked retail business from small-town main streets to interchanges on the edge of town. Nationally franchised motels and fast-food restaurants sprang up along suburban shopping strips. By shopping along highways rather than downtown, suburban whites also opted to minimize contact with people of other races.

The spread of automobiles contributed to increased leisure travel. The tacit pact between large corporations and labor unions meant that more workers had two-week vacations and time to take their families on the road. Between 1954 and 1963, the number of visits to National Parks doubled to more than 100 million and visits to National Forests nearly tripled. On television from 1956 to 1963, variety show hostess Dinah Shore tied the nation's best-selling car to the appeal of vacationing as she belted out the jingle "Drive your Chevrolet through the USA, America's the greatest land of all."

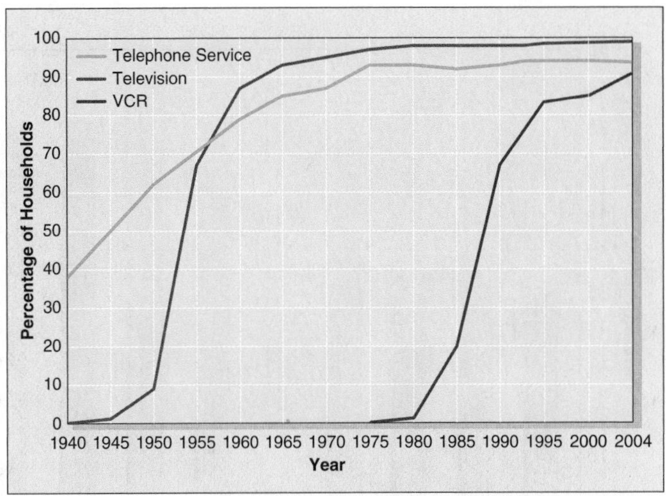

FIGURE 28–1 **Households with Telephones, Televisions, and VCRs** American life in the twentieth century was transformed by a sequence of electronic consumer goods, from telephones to laptop computers. Entertainment items (televisions and videocassette recorders) spread even more rapidly among consumers than did the home telephone.

Data Source: Statistical Abstract of the United States.

The New Fifties Family

Family life in the Eisenhower years departed from historic patterns. Prosperity allowed children to finish school and young adults to marry right after high school. Young women faced strong social pressure to pursue husbands rather than careers. In a decade when the popular press worried about "latent homosexuality," single men were suspect. The proportion of single adults reached its twentieth-century low in 1960. At all social levels, young people married quickly and had an average of three children spaced closely together, adding to the number of baby boomers whose needs would influence American society into the twenty-first century. Strong families, said experts, defended against Communism by teaching American values.

The impact of television. Television was made to order for the family-centered fifties. By 1960, fully 87 percent of households had sets (see Figure 28–1). Popular entertainment earlier had been a communal activity; people saw movies as part of a group, cheered baseball teams as part of a crowd. TV was watched in the privacy of the home.

Situation comedies were the most successful programs. Viewers liked continuing characters who resolved everyday problems in half an hour. Most successful shows depicted the ideal of family togetherness. The families on *The Adventures of Ozzie and Harriet* (1952–1966), *Father Knows Best* (1954–1962), and *Leave It to Beaver* (1957–1962) were white, polite, and happy.

Stay-at-home moms and working women. The 1950s extended the stay-at-home trend of the postwar years. Women gave up some of their earlier educational gains. Their share of new college degrees and professional jobs fell. Despite millions of new electrical appliances, the time spent on housework increased. Magazines proclaimed that proper families maintained distinct roles for dad and mom, and mom was urged to find fulfillment in a well-scrubbed house and children.

In fact, far from allowing women to stay home as housewives, family prosperity in the 1950s often depended on their earnings. The number of employed women reached new highs. By 1960, nearly 35 percent of all women held jobs, including 7.5 million mothers with children under 17 (see Figure 28–2). The pressures of young marriages, large families, and economic needs interacted to erode some of the assumptions behind the idealized family and laid the groundwork for dramatic social changes in the 1960s and 1970s.

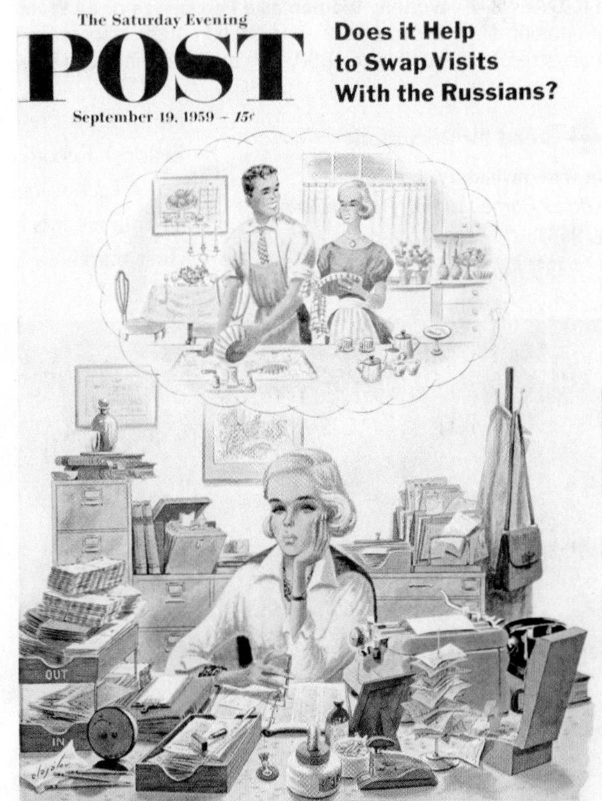

Middle-class women in the 1950s faced conflicting pressures and messages. The popular media idealized the woman whose life revolved around her house and family. As this magazine cover suggests, however, that image was as much a myth as a reality. Despite real limitations on available careers, increasing numbers of women entered the labor force and made necessary contributions to their families' incomes—while daydreaming about getting help with never-ending household tasks.

Day Dreaming by Constantin Alajalov. © 1959 SEPS; Licensed by Curtis Publishing Co., Indianapolis, IN. All rights reserved. www. curtispublishing. com

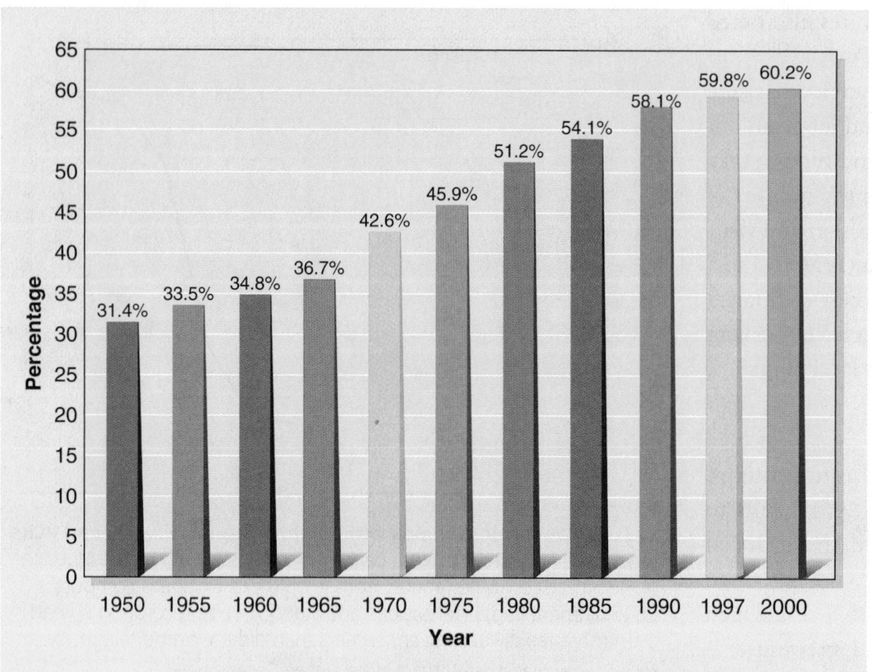

FIGURE 28–2 **Working Women as a Percentage of All Women, 1950–2000** The proportion of American women who are part of the labor force (working or looking for work) has increased steadily since 1950, with the fastest increase between 1965 and 1985.

Inventing Teenagers

Teenagers in the 1950s joined adults as consumers of movies, clothes, and automobiles. Advertisers tapped and expanded the growing youth market by promoting a distinct "youth culture," an idea that became omnipresent in the 1960s and 1970s. Many cities matched their high schools to the social status of their students: college-prep curricula for middle-class neighborhoods, vocational and technical schools for future factory workers, and separate schools or tracks for African Americans and Latinos. In effect, the schools trained some children to be doctors and officers and others to be mechanics and enlisted men.

All teenagers shared rock-and-roll, a new music of the mid-1950s that adapted black urban rhythm-and-blues for a white mass market. Rhythm-and-blues was the hard-edged and electrified offspring of traditional blues and gospel music. In turn, rock music augmented its black roots by drawing vitality from poor white southerners familiar with country and western music (Buddy Holly, Elvis Presley), Hispanics (Richie Valens), and, in the 1960s, the British working class (the Beatles). Record producers played up the association between rock music and youthful rebellion.

Read the **Document**
at **www.myhistorylab.com**
Ladies Home Journal, "Young Mother" (1956)

Technological changes helped rock split off from adult pop music. Portable phonographs and 45-rpm records let kids listen to rock-and-roll in their own rooms. Car radios and transistor radios (first marketed around 1956) let disc jockeys reach teenagers outside the home. The result was separate music for young listeners and separate advertising for teenage consumers, the roots of the teenage mall culture of the next generation.

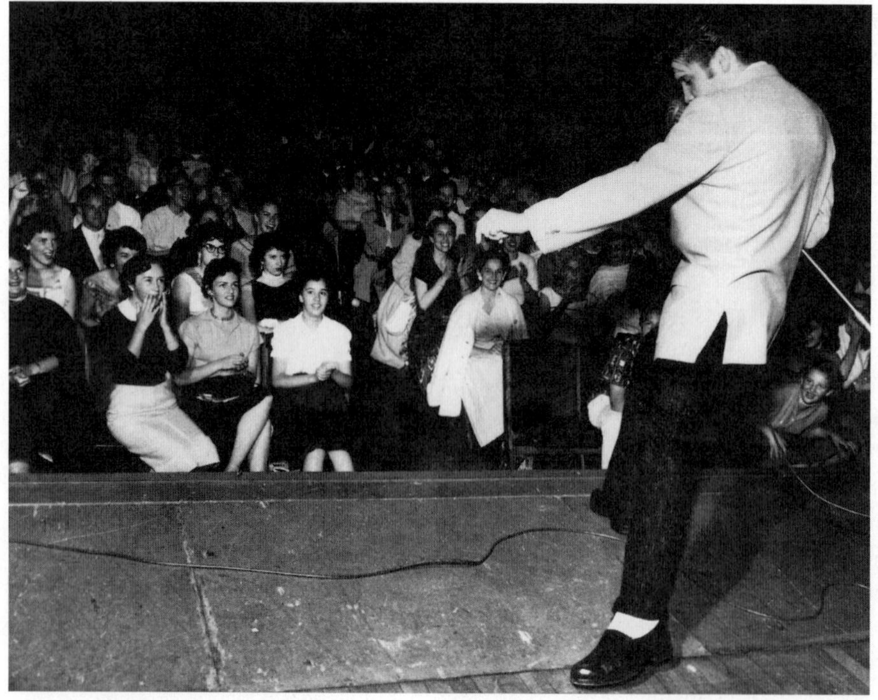

In his first years as a star, Elvis Presley brought new energy to the world of popular music. Frank Driggs/Archive Photos

Turning to Religion

Leaders from Dwight Eisenhower to FBI Director J. Edgar Hoover advocated churchgoing as an antidote for Communism. Regular church attendance grew from 48 percent of the population in 1940 to 63 percent in 1960. *Newsweek* talked about the "vast resurgence of Protestantism," and *Time* claimed that "everybody knows that church life is booming in the U.S."

The situation was more complex. Growing church membership looked impressive at first, but the total barely kept pace with population growth. In some ways, the so-called return to religion was new. Congress created new connections between religion and government when it added "under God" to the Pledge of Allegiance in 1954 and required currency to bear the phrase "In God We Trust" in 1955.

Another strand in the religious revival was found in the revitalized evangelical and fundamentalist churches. During the 1950s, the theologically and socially conservative Southern Baptists passed the Methodists as the largest Protestant denomination. The evangelist Billy Graham continued the grand American tradition of the mass revival meeting.

African American churches were community institutions as well as religious organizations. With limited options for enjoying their success, the black middle class joined prestigious churches. Black congregations in northern cities swelled in the postwar years. Prestigious black churches thrived and often supported extensive social service programs. In southern cities, churches were centers for community pride and training grounds for the emerging civil rights movement.

Other important changes to come in American religion had their roots in the 1950s and early 1960s. Boundaries between many Protestant denominations blurred as church leaders emphasized national unity, paving the way for the ecumenical movement and denominational mergers. Supreme Court decisions sowed the seeds for later political activism among evangelical Christians. In *Engel v. Vitale* (1962), the Court ruled that public schools could not require children to start the school day with group prayer. *Abington Township v. Schempp* (1963) prohibited devotional Bible reading in the schools. Such decisions alarmed many evangelicals; within two decades, school prayer would be a central issue in national politics.

QUICK REVIEW

Family Life

- Women faced pressure to marry early and forgo careers.
- The proportion of single adults reached its twentieth-century low in 1960.
- Young people married early and had an average of three children.

QUICK REVIEW

Teenagers

- Teenagers became consumers in the 1950s.
- Advertisers directed their message at the youth market.
- Teenagers developed a shared culture.

The Gospel of Prosperity

At times in these years, production and consumption outweighed democracy in the American message to the world. Officially, Americans argued that abundance was a natural by-product of a free society. In fact, it was easy to present prosperity as a goal in itself, as Vice President Richard Nixon did when he represented the United States at a technology exposition in Moscow in 1959. The U.S. exhibit included 21 models of automobiles and a complete six-room ranch house. In its "miracle kitchen," Nixon engaged Soviet Communist Party chairman Nikita Khrushchev in a carefully planned "kitchen debate." The vice president claimed that the "most important thing" for Americans was "the right to choose": "We have so many different manufacturers and many different kinds of washing machines so that the housewives have a choice."

The Underside of Affluence

The most basic criticism of the ideology of prosperity was the simplest—that affluence concealed vast inequalities. Michael Harrington had worked among the poor before writing *The Other America* (1962). He reminded Americans about the "underdeveloped nation" of 40 to 50 million poor people who had missed the last two decades of prosperity.

If Harrington found problems at the bottom of U.S. society, C. Wright Mills found dangers in the way that the Cold War distorted American society at the top. *The Power Elite* (1956) described an interlocking alliance of big government, big business, and the military. The losers in a permanent war economy, said Mills, were economic and political democracy. His ideas would reverberate in the 1960s during the Vietnam War.

Other critics targeted the alienating effects of consumerism and the conformity of homogeneous suburbs. Although much of the anti-suburban rhetoric was based on intellectual snobbery rather than research, it represented significant dissent from the praise of affluence.

There was far greater substance to the increasing dissatisfaction among women, who faced conflicting images of the perfect woman in

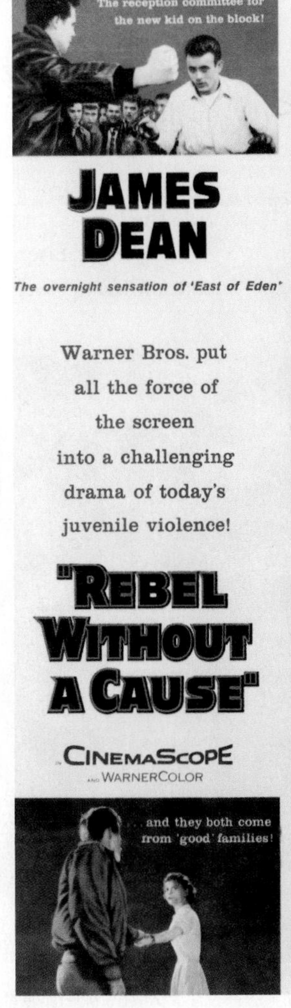

The reception committee for the new kid on the block!
JAMES DEAN
The overnight sensation of 'East of Eden'
Warner Bros. put all the force of the screen into a challenging drama of today's juvenile violence!
"REBEL WITHOUT A CAUSE"
CINEMASCOPE
WARNERCOLOR
...and they both come from 'good' families!

Movie actor James Dean died in an automobile accident shortly after completing *Rebel Without a Cause*. His tragic death and his depiction of alienated youth made him a symbol of dissatisfaction with the middle-class 1950s.

QUICK REVIEW

Critique of the Ideology of Prosperity

- Some critics argued that affluence concealed inequality.
- Others were concerned about the alienating effects of consumerism.
- Many women became dissatisfied with their expected role in society.

the media. On one side was the comforting icon of Betty Crocker, the fictional spokeswoman for General Mills who made housework and cooking look easy. On the other side were sultry sexpots like Marilyn Monroe and the centerfold women of *Playboy* magazine, which first appeared in 1953. Women wondered how to be both Betty and Marilyn. In 1963, Betty Friedan's book *The Feminine Mystique* recognized that thousands of middle-class housewives were seething behind their picture windows. It followed numerous articles in *McCall's*, *Redbook*, and the *Ladies' Home Journal* about the unhappiness of college-educated women who were expected to find total satisfaction in kids and cooking. Friedan repackaged the message of the women's magazines along with the results of a survey of her Smith College classmates, who were then entering their forties. What Friedan called "the problem that has no name" was a sense of personal emptiness.

FACING OFF WITH THE SOVIET UNION

WHAT IMPACT did Dwight Eisenhower's foreign policy have on U.S. relations with the Soviet Union?

Americans got a reassuring new face in the White House in 1953, but not new policies toward the world. As had been true since 1946, the nation's leaders weighed every foreign policy decision for its effect on the Cold War. The United States pushed ahead in an arms race with the Soviet Union, stood guard on the borders of China and the Soviet empire, and judged political changes in Latin America, Africa, and Asia for their effect on the global balance of power.

Why We Liked Ike

at www.myhistorylab.com
Ike for President: Eisenhower Campaign Ad, 1952

In the late twentieth century, few leaders were able to master both domestic policy and foreign affairs. Some presidents, such as Lyndon Johnson, were more adept at social problems than diplomacy. By contrast, Richard Nixon and George H. W. Bush were more interested in the world outside the United States.

Dwight Eisenhower was also a "foreign-policy president." As a general, he had understood that military power should serve political ends. He had helped to hold together the alliance that defeated Nazi Germany and built NATO into an effective force in 1951–1952. He then sought the Republican nomination, he said, to ensure that the United States would keep its international commitments. He sealed his victory in 1952 by emphasizing his foreign-policy expertise, telling a campaign audience that "to bring the Korean war to an early and honorable end . . . requires a personal trip to Korea. I shall make that trip . . . I shall go to Korea."

The U.S. exhibit at a technology exposition in Moscow in 1959 displayed a wide range of American consumer goods, from soft-drink dispensers to sewing machines. It included a complete six-room ranch house with an up-to-date kitchen where, in a famous encounter dubbed the "kitchen debate," Vice President Richard Nixon and Soviet Communist Party chairman Nikita Khrushchev disputed the merits of capitalism and Communism.

What makes Eisenhower's administration hard to appreciate is that many of its accomplishments were things that did not happen. Eisenhower refused to dismantle the social programs of the New Deal. He exerted American political and military power around the globe but avoided war. Preferring to work behind the scenes, he knew how to delegate authority and keep disagreements private.

In his "hidden-hand" presidency, Eisenhower sometimes masked his intelligence. It helped his political agenda if Americans thought of him as a smiling grandfather. He was the first president to have televised news conferences and knew how to manipulate them. The "Ike" whose face smiled from "I Like Ike" campaign buttons and who gave rambling, incoherent answers at White House press conferences knew exactly what he was doing—controlling information and keeping the opposition guessing. He was easily reelected in 1956, when Americans saw no reason to abandon competent leadership.

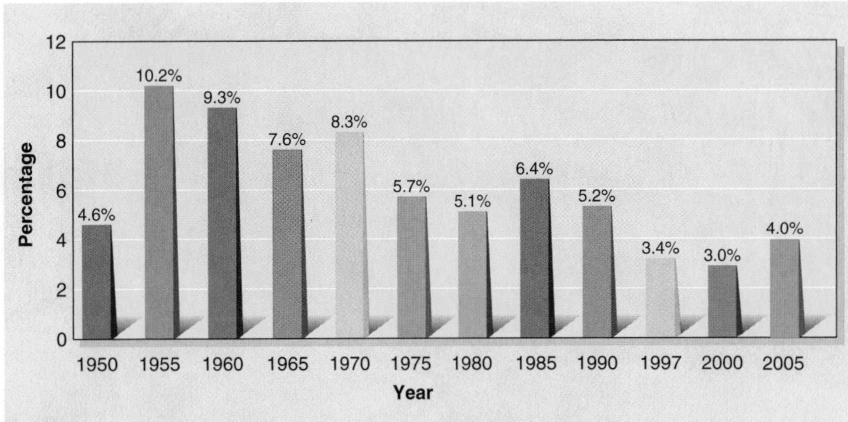

FIGURE 28–3 **Defense Spending as a Percentage of Gross Domestic Product, 1950–2005** Defense spending has been an important force for economic development and innovation. The impact of the defense budget on the domestic economy was greatest in the mid-1950s, at the height of the Cold War. Lesser peaks came during the Vietnam War in the late 1960s and the Reagan administration defense buildup in the early 1980s.

Data Source: Statistical Abstract of the United States.

A Balance of Terror

The backdrop for U.S. foreign policy was the growing capacity for mutual nuclear annihilation. The rivalry between the United States and the USSR was played out within a framework of deterrence, the knowledge that each side could launch a devastating nuclear attack. The old balance of power had become a balance of terror.

The Eisenhower administration's doctrine of **massive retaliation** took advantage of America's superior technology while economizing on military spending. Eisenhower and his advisers worried that matching the land armies of China and the Soviet Union would inflate the role of the federal government in American society (see Figure 28–3). Eisenhower compared uncontrolled military spending to crucifying humankind on a "cross of iron." "Every gun that is fired," he warned, "every warship launched, every rocket fired signifies . . . a theft from those who hunger and are not fed, those who are cold and not clothed." The administration concentrated military spending where the nation already had the greatest advantage—on atomic weapons. In response to any serious attack, the United States would direct maximum force against the homeland of the aggressor.

massive retaliation Popular name for the military doctrine adopted in the 1950s, whereby the United States promised to respond to any attack on itself or its allies with massive force, including nuclear weapons.

The massive-retaliation doctrine treated nuclear weapons as ordinary or even respectable. It put European and American cities on the frontline in the defense of Germany, for it meant that the United States would react to a Soviet conventional attack on NATO by dropping nuclear bombs on the Soviet Union, which would presumably retaliate in kind. The National Security Council in 1953 made reliance on "massive retaliatory damage" by nuclear weapons official policy.

The doctrine grew even more fearful as the Soviet Union developed its own hydrogen bombs. The chairman of the Atomic Energy Commission terrified the American people by mentioning casually that the Soviets could now obliterate New York City. Dozens of nuclear weapons tests in the late 1950s made the atomic threat immediate.

The Soviet Union added to the worries about atomic war by launching the world's first artificial satellite. On the first Sunday of October 1957, Americans discovered that *Sputnik*—Russian for "satellite"—was orbiting the earth. Soviet propagandists claimed that their technological "first" showed the superiority of Communism, and Americans wondered if the United States had lost its edge. Schools beefed up science courses and began to introduce the "new math," Congress passed the National Defense Education Act to expand college and postgraduate education, and the new **National Aeronautics and Space Administration (NASA)** took over the satellite program in 1958.

National Aeronautics and Space Administration (NASA) Federal agency created in 1958 to manage American space flights and exploration.

Containment in Action

Someone who heard only the campaign speeches in 1952 might have expected sharp foreign-policy changes under Eisenhower, but there was more continuity than change. John Foster Dulles, Eisenhower's secretary of state, had attacked the Democrats as defeatists and appeasers. He demanded that the United States liberate eastern Europe from Soviet control and encourage

Schoolchildren in the 1950s regularly practiced taking cover in case of atomic attack. If there was warning, they were to file into interior hallways, crouch against the walls, and cover their heads with their jackets as protection against flying glass. If they saw the blinding flash of an atomic explosion without warning, they were to "duck and cover" under their school desks.

Jiang Jieshi to attack Communist China. Warlike language continued after the election. In 1956, Dulles proudly claimed that tough-minded diplomacy had repeatedly brought the United States to the verge of war. "We walked to the brink and looked it in the face," he famously commented.

In fact, Eisenhower viewed the Cold War in the same terms as Truman. He worried about the "sullen weight of Russia" pushing against smaller nations and saw a world caught between the incompatible values of freedom and Communism, but caution replaced campaign rhetoric about "rolling back" Communism. Around the periphery of the Communist nations, from eastern Asia to the Middle East to Europe, the United States accepted the existing sphere of Communist influence but attempted to block its growth, a policy most Americans accepted.

The U.S. worldview assumed both the right and the need to intervene in the affairs of other nations, especially countries in Latin America, Asia, and Africa. Policymakers saw these nations as markets for U.S. products and sources of vital raw materials. When political disturbances arose in these states, the United States blamed Soviet meddling to justify U.S. intervention. If Communism could not be rolled back in eastern Europe, the CIA could still undermine anti-American governments in the third world. The Soviets themselves took advantage of local revolutions even when they did not instigate them; in doing so they confirmed Washington's belief that the developing world was a game board on which the superpowers carried on their rivalry by proxy.

Watch the Video at www.myhistorylab.com *Duck and Cover*

Along with economic motivations and military concerns, religious belief played an important role in shaping the Cold War. When national leaders decried "godless communism," they were voicing a widely shared concern rather than mouthing a slogan. Roman Catholic leaders and laypeople worried about the restricted freedom of religious practice in Poland, Hungary, and other Soviet satellites. Members of the nation's political elite often had ties or sympathy with missionary work in China, which was effectively halted after 1949, making them deeply suspicious of the new Communist regime. At the top, strong religious convictions influenced the way that Harry Truman, Dwight Eisenhower, and John Foster Dulles viewed the confrontation with China and the USSR in moral as well as practical terms.

Twice during Eisenhower's first term, the CIA subverted democratically elected governments that seemed to threaten U.S. interests. In Iran, which had nationalized British and U.S. oil companies in an effort to break the hold of Western corporations, the CIA in 1953 backed a coup that toppled the government and helped the young shah, as the reigning monarch was called, to gain control. The shah then cooperated with the United States, but his increasingly repressive regime would lead to his overthrow in 1979 and deep Iranian resentment of the United States. In Guatemala, the leftist government was threatening the United Fruit Company. When the Guatemalans accepted weapons from the Communist bloc in 1954, the CIA imposed a regime friendly to U.S. business (see Map 28–1).

For most Americans in 1953, democracy in Iran was far less important than ending the war in Korea and stabilizing relations with China. Eisenhower declined to escalate the Korean War by blockading China and sending more U.S. ground forces. Instead, he positioned atomic bombs

GLOBAL CONNECTIONS

A Decade of Alliances: First World, Second World, Third World

Since the time of George Washington's Farewell Address, the United States had avoided what Thomas Jefferson called "entangling alliances" with other nations, and it entered foreign wars only with great reluctance in 1917 and 1941.

Under the pressures of the Cold War, however, the United States initiated and constructed a series of mutual defense pacts with dozens of other nations in an effort to create a wall of allied states to prevent the expansion of Communism from the Soviet Union and China. First and most important was the North Atlantic Treaty Organization, which bound the United States and Canada to the mutual defense of western Europe in 1949. Quick to follow were alliances with Japan in 1951, with Australia and New Zealand in 1952 (the ANZUS pact), and with South Korea in 1953. The next year the United States, Britain, and France tried to imitate NATO with the Southeast Asia Treaty Organization (SEATO) that included Thailand, the Philippines, and Pakistan (which then included what is now Bangladesh). The Central Treaty Organization (CENTO) came in 1955 with Pakistan, Iran, Iraq, Turkey, the United States, and Britain.

As a counter to both the Western alliances and the Warsaw Pact of the Communist bloc, Indonesia's president Sukarno in 1955 hosted a meeting of Asian and African nations that wanted to remain uncommitted. The nations that attended the meeting at Bandung, Indonesia, called for a "third way" that did not require aligning themselves with either side in the Cold War. In 1961 President Tito of Yugoslavia hosted the first official Non-Aligned Movement Summit, where the key figures were Tito, Sukarno, Prime Minister Nehru of India, President Nasser of Egypt, and President Nkrumah of Ghana. The non-aligned nations were termed the "Third World" in contrast to the First World of the United States and its alliances and the Second World of Communist nations.

Fifty years later, with the Cold War long ended, "Third World" has lost its political meaning and evolved into an imprecise synonym for the "less developed nations" whose economies lag in industrialization and income.

Among U.S. alliances, SEATO and CENTO dissolved in the 1970s but NATO remains a keystone of American foreign policy. Since 1999 it has expanded to include many of the newly democratic nations of central and eastern Europe, for a 2009 total of twenty-eight members. NATO intervened belatedly to halt the genocidal civil war in Bosnia and again in Kosovo (both in the former Yugoslavia in southeastern Europe), and NATO has participated in the war against Al Qaeda and the Taliban in Afghanistan.

- Why was it easier for the United States to maintain an alliance system in Europe than in Asia?

on Okinawa, only 400 miles from China. The nuclear threat, along with the continued cost of the war on both sides, brought the Chinese to a truce that left Korea divided into two nations.

Watch the **Video** at **www.myhistorylab.com** *Eisenhower's Special Message to Congress on the Middle East, 1957*

Halfway around the world, there was a new crisis when three U.S. friends—France, Britain, and Israel—ganged up on Egypt. France was angry at Egyptian support for revolutionaries in French Algeria. Britain was even angrier at Egypt's nationalization of the British-dominated Suez Canal. And Israel wanted to weaken its most powerful Arab enemy. On October 29, 1956, Israel attacked Egypt. A week later, British and French forces attempted to seize the canal.

Although the United States had been the first nation to recognize Israel in 1948, the relationship was much less close than it would become. The United States forced a quick cease-fire, partly to maintain its standing with oil-producing Arab nations. Because Egypt blocked the canal with sunken ships, the war left Britain and France dependent on American oil that Eisenhower would not provide until they left Egypt. Resolution of the crisis involved one of the first uses of peacekeeping troops under the United Nations flag.

In Europe, Eisenhower accepted the status quo because conflicts there could result in nuclear war. In 1956, challenges to Communist rule arose in East Germany, Poland, and Hungary and threatened to break up the Soviet empire. The Soviets replaced liberal Communists in East

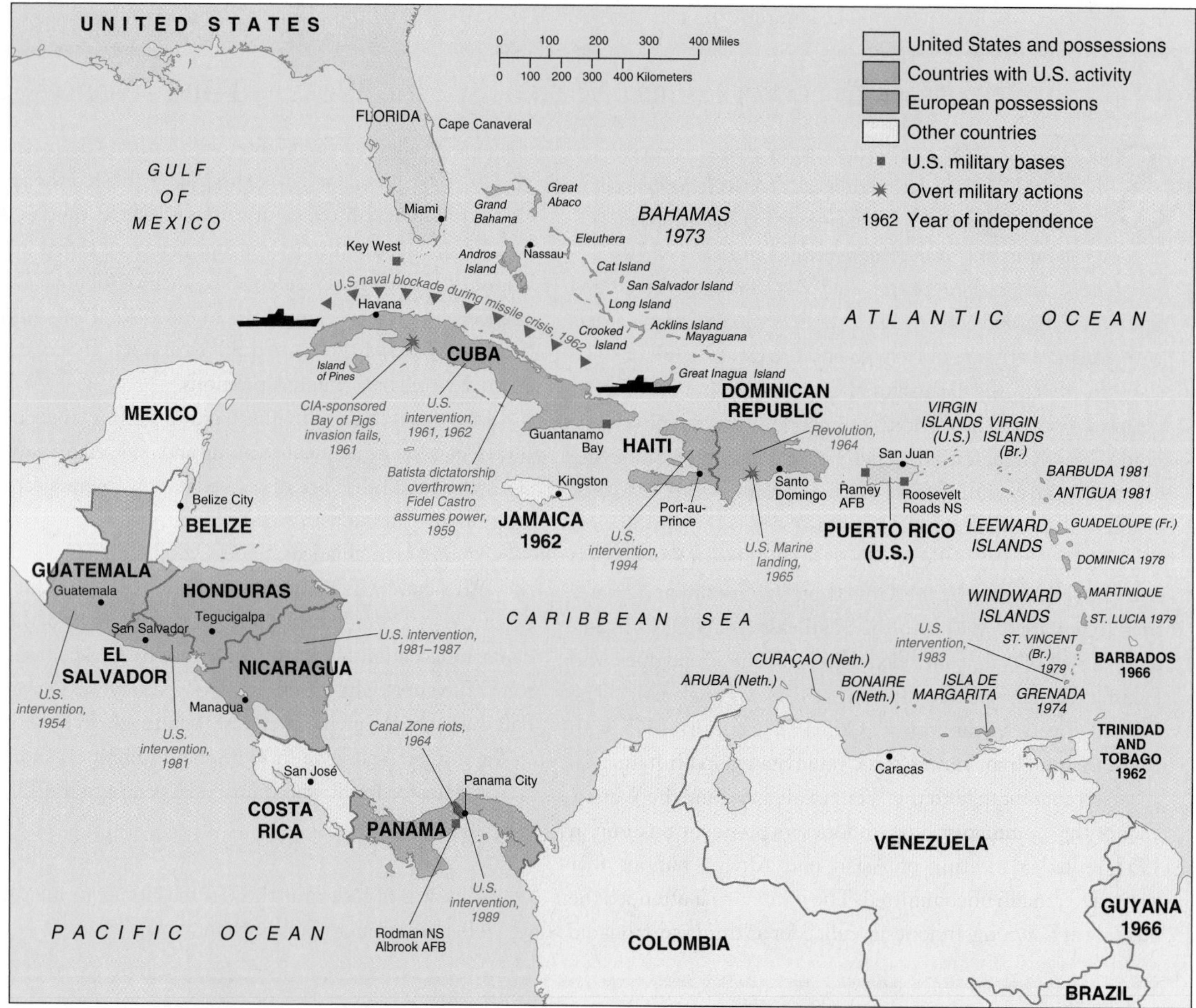

MAP 28–1 **U.S. Intervention around the Caribbean since 1954** The United States has long kept a careful eye on the politics of neighboring nations to the south. In the second half of the twentieth century, the United States frequently used military assistance or force to influence or intervene in Caribbean and Central American nations. The purpose has usually been to counter or undermine left-leaning governments; some interventions, as in Haiti, have been intended to stabilize democratic regimes.

Which countries in the region have been the target of U.S. intervention? How have American policymakers justified such actions?

Germany while accepting a more liberal leader in Poland. In Hungary, however, reformers took the fatal step of proposing to quit the Warsaw Pact. Open warfare broke out when the Soviet army rolled across the border to preserve the Soviet empire. Hungarian freedom fighters in Budapest used rocks and firebombs against Soviet tanks for several days, while pleading in vain for Western aid. NATO would not risk war with the USSR. Tens of thousands of Hungarians died, and 200,000 fled when the Soviets crushed the resistance.

Global Standoff

The Soviet Union, China, and the United States and its allies were all groping in the dark as they maneuvered for influence in the 1950s and 1960s. In one international crisis after another, each player misinterpreted the other's motivations and diplomatic signals. Now that documents from both sides of the Cold War are becoming available, historians have realized what dangerously different meanings the two sides gave to their confrontations between 1953 and 1964.

A good example is the U-2 spy plane affair of 1960, which derailed progress toward nuclear disarmament. The Kremlin was deeply worried that West Germany and China might acquire nuclear bombs. Washington wanted to reduce military budgets and nuclear fallout. Both countries voluntarily suspended nuclear tests in 1958 and prepared for a June 1960 summit meeting in Paris, where Eisenhower intended to negotiate a test ban treaty. But on May 1, 1960, Soviet air defenses shot down an American U-2 aircraft over the heart of Russia and captured the pilot, Francis Gary Powers. The cover story for the U-2 was weather research, but the frail-looking black plane was a CIA operation. Designed to soar above the range of Soviet antiaircraft missiles, U-2s had obtained information that assured American officials there was no missile gap.

When Moscow trumpeted the news of the plane's downing, Eisenhower took personal responsibility in hopes that Khrushchev would accept the U-2 as an unpleasant reality of international espionage. Unfortunately, the planes meant something very different to the Soviets, touching their festering sense of inferiority. They had stopped protesting the flights in 1957, because they saw complaints as demeaning. The Americans thought their silence signaled acceptance. Khrushchev had staked his future on good relations with the United States; when Eisenhower refused to apologize in Paris, Khrushchev stalked out. Disarmament was set back for years because the two sides had such different understandings of the same events.

The most important aspect of Eisenhower's foreign policy was continuity. Despite militant rhetoric, the administration pursued containment as defined under Truman. The Cold War consensus, however, prevented the United States from seeing the nations of the developing world on their own terms. By viewing every independence movement and social revolution as part of the competition with Communism, U.S. leaders created unnecessary problems. In the end, Eisenhower left troublesome and unresolved issues—upheaval in Latin America, civil war in Vietnam, tension in Germany, the nuclear arms race—for his successor, John Kennedy, who wanted to confront international Communism even more vigorously.

Read the Document at **www.myhistorylab.com**
Test Ban Treaty (1962)

QUICK REVIEW

The U-2 Spy Plane Incident

- May 1, 1960: Soviets shot down American U-2 spy plane.
- Eisenhower took responsibility, hoping to reassure the Soviets.
- The Soviets responded with renewed distrust and hostility.
- The incident set back efforts at disarmament for years.

JOHN F. KENNEDY AND THE COLD WAR

John Kennedy was a man of contradictions. A Democrat who promised to get the country moving again, he presided over policies whose direction was set under Eisenhower. Despite stirring rhetoric about leading the nation toward a **New Frontier** of scientific and social progress, he recorded his greatest failures and successes in the continuing Cold War.

WHAT WAS John F. Kennedy's approach to dealing with the Soviet Union?

New Frontier John F. Kennedy's domestic and foreign policy initiatives, designed to reinvigorate a sense of national purpose and energy.

THE KENNEDY MYSTIQUE

Kennedy won the presidency over Richard Nixon in a cliff-hanging election that was more about personality and style than about substance (see Map 28–2). Television was crucial to the outcome. The campaign featured the first televised presidential debates. In the first session, Nixon actually gave better replies, but his nervousness and a bad makeup job turned off millions of viewers, who admired Kennedy's energy. Nixon never overcame the setback, but the race was tight, with tiny margins in crucial states giving Kennedy the victory. His televised inauguration was the perfect setting for an impassioned plea for national unity: "My fellow Americans," he challenged, "ask not what your country can do for you—ask what you can do for your country."

Kennedy brought dash to the White House. His beautiful and refined wife, Jackie, made sure to seat artists and writers next to diplomats and businessmen at White House dinners. Kennedy's staff and large family played touch football, not golf. No president had shown such verve since Teddy Roosevelt. People began to talk about Kennedy's "charisma," his ability to lead by sheer force of personality. In fact, the image of a fit, vigorous man concealed the reality that

WHERE TO LEARN MORE

John F. Kennedy Library and Museum, Boston, Massachusetts
http://www.jfklibrary.org

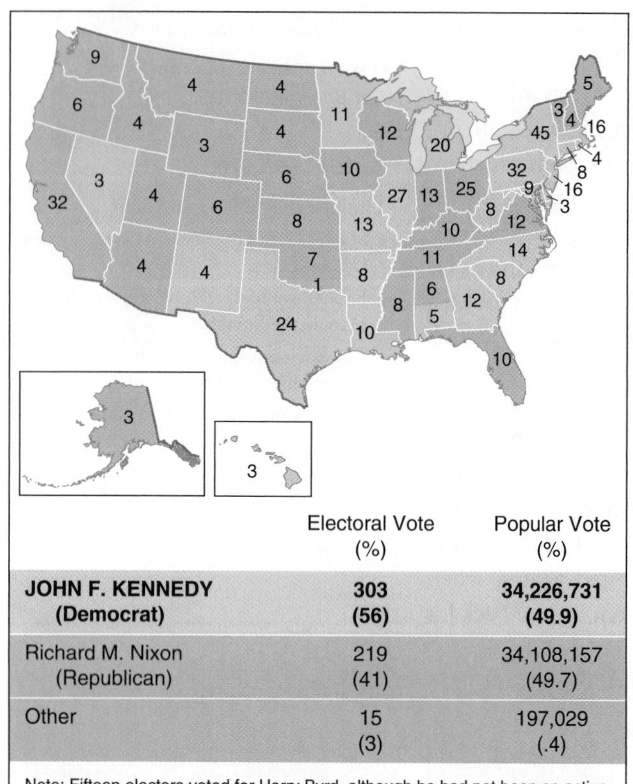

	Electoral Vote (%)	Popular Vote (%)
JOHN F. KENNEDY (Democrat)	**303 (56)**	**34,226,731 (49.9)**
Richard M. Nixon (Republican)	219 (41)	34,108,157 (49.7)
Other	15 (3)	197,029 (.4)

Note: Fifteen electors voted for Harry Byrd, although he had not been an active candidate. Minor party candidates took a tiny percentage of the popular vote.

MAP 28–2 **The Election of 1960** The presidential election of 1960 was one of the closest in American history. John Kennedy's victory depended on his appeal in northern industrial states with large Roman Catholic populations and his ability to hold much of the traditionally Democratic South. Texas, the home state of his vice-presidential running mate, Lyndon Johnson, was vital to the success of the ticket.

In what parts of the country was Kennedy strongest? How does this map help explain Kennedy's tepidness on civil rights once elected president?

he was battling severe physical ailments that demanded constant medical attention and often left him with debilitating pain.

Kennedy's Mistakes

Kennedy and Khrushchev perpetuated similar problems. Talking tough to satisfy their more militant countrymen, they repeatedly pushed each other into a corner, continuing the problems of mutual misunderstanding that had marked the 1950s. When Khrushchev promised, in January 1961, to support "wars of national liberation," he was really fending off Chinese criticism. But Kennedy overreacted in his first State of the Union address by asking for more military spending.

Three months later, Kennedy fed Soviet fears of American aggressiveness by sponsoring an invasion of Cuba. At the start of 1959, Fidel Castro had toppled the corrupt dictator Fulgencio Batista, who had made Havana infamous for Mafia-run gambling and prostitution. Castro then nationalized American investments, and thousands of Cubans fled to the United States.

When 1,400 anti-Castro Cubans landed at Cuba's **Bay of Pigs** on April 17, 1961, they were following a plan prepared by the Eisenhower administration. The CIA had trained and armed the invaders and convinced Kennedy that the landing would trigger spontaneous uprisings. But when Kennedy refused to commit U.S. armed forces to support them, Cuban forces captured the attackers.

Kennedy followed the Bay of Pigs debacle with a hasty and ill-thought-out summit meeting with Khrushchev in Vienna in June. Poorly prepared and nearly incapacitated by agonizing back pain, Kennedy made little headway. Coming after Kennedy's refusal to salvage the Bay of Pigs by military intervention, the meeting left the Soviets with the impression that the president was weak and dangerously erratic.

To exploit Kennedy's perceived vulnerability, the Soviet Union renewed tension over Berlin, deep within East Germany. The divided city served as an escape route from Communism for hundreds of thousands of East Germans. Khrushchev now threatened to transfer the Soviet sector in Berlin to East Germany, which had no treaty obligations to France, Britain, or the United States. If the West had to deal directly with East Germany for access to Berlin, it would have to recognize a permanently divided Germany. Kennedy sounded the alarm: He doubled draft calls, called up reservists, and warned families to build fallout shelters.

Bay of Pigs Site in Cuba of an unsuccessful landing by fourteen hundred anti-Castro Cuban refugees in April 1961.

Berlin Wall Wall erected by East Germany in 1961 that isolated West Berlin from the surrounding areas in Communist-controlled East Berlin and East Germany.

Rather than confront the United States directly, however, the Soviets and East Germans on August 13, 1961, built a wall around the western sectors of Berlin while leaving the access route to West Germany open. The **Berlin Wall** thus isolated East Germany without challenging the Western allies in West Berlin itself. In private, Kennedy accepted the wall as a clever way to stabilize a dangerous situation. However, Berlin remained a point of East-West tension until East German Communism collapsed in 1989 and Berliners tore down the hated wall.

Getting into Vietnam

U.S. involvement in Vietnam, located in Southeast Asia on the southern border of China, dated to 1949–1950. After World War II ended, France had fought to maintain its colonial rule there against rebels who combined Communist ideology with fervor for national independence under the leadership of Ho Chi Minh. Although the United States supported independence of most other European colonies, the triumph of Mao Zedong in China and the Korean War caused policymakers to see Vietnam as another Cold War conflict. The United States picked up three-quarters of the costs. Nevertheless, the French military position collapsed in 1954 after Vietnamese forces overran the French stronghold at Dien Bien Phu. The French had enough, and President Eisenhower was unwilling to join another Asian war. A Geneva peace conference "temporarily" divided Vietnam into a Communist north and a non-Communist south and scheduled elections for a single Vietnamese government.

The United States then replaced France as the supporter of the pro-Western Vietnamese in the south. Washington's client was Ngo Dinh Diem, an anti-Communist from South Vietnam's Roman Catholic elite. U.S. officials encouraged Diem to put off the elections and backed his efforts to construct an independent South Vietnam. Ho meanwhile consolidated the northern half as a Communist state that claimed to be the legitimate government for all Vietnam. The United States further reinforced containment in Asia by bringing Thailand, the Philippines, Pakistan, Australia, New Zealand, Britain, and France together in the **Southeast Asia Treaty Organization (SEATO)** in 1954.

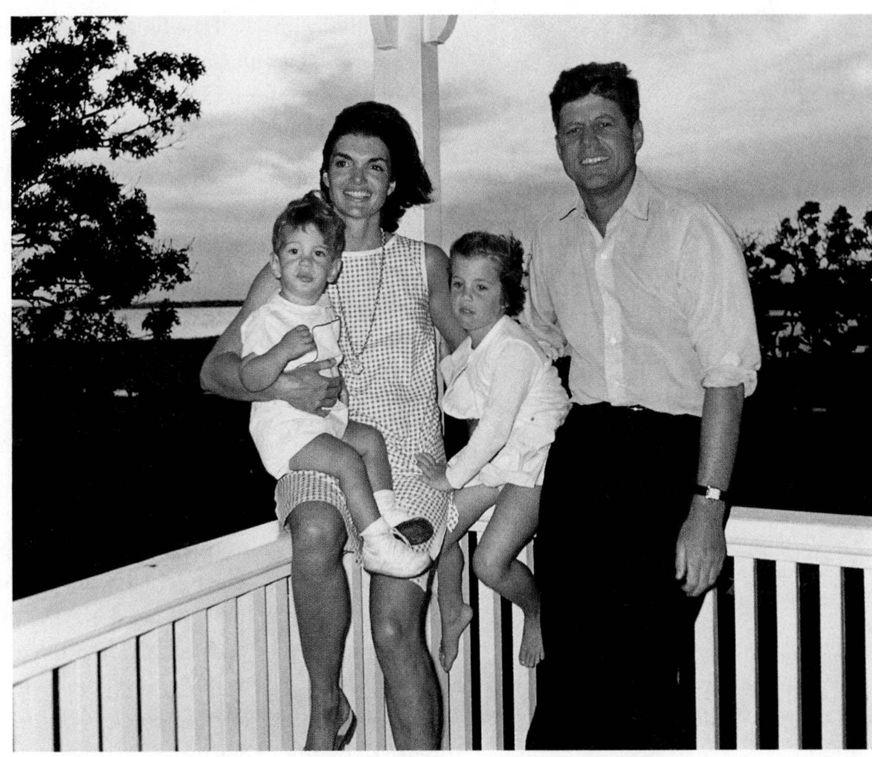

For many Americans in the early 1960s, John and Jacqueline Kennedy and their two children represented the ideal family, although the carefully posed pictures with happy smiles concealed the president's severe health problems and deep rifts in the marriage.

Another indirect consequence of the Vienna summit was the growing U.S. entanglement in South Vietnam, where Kennedy saw a chance to take a firm stand and reassert America's commitment to containment. In the countryside, Communist insurgents known as the **Viet Cong** were gaining strength. Diem controlled the cities with the help of a large army and a Vietnamese elite that had worked with the French. The United States stepped up its supply of weapons and sent advisers (Green Berets).

U.S. aid did not work. Despite overoptimistic reports and the help of 16,000 U.S. troops, Diem's government by 1963 was losing the loyalty—the "hearts and minds"—of many South Vietnamese. North Vietnamese support for the Viet Cong canceled the effect of U.S. assistance. Diem courted a second civil war by violently crushing opposition from Vietnamese Buddhists. Kennedy's administration tacitly approved a coup on November 1 that killed Diem and his brother and installed an ineffective military junta.

Southeast Asia Treaty Organization (SEATO) Mutual defense alliance signed in 1954 by the United States, Britain, France, Thailand, Pakistan, the Philippines, Australia, and New Zealand.

Viet Cong Communist rebels in South Vietnam who fought the pro-American government established in South Vietnam in 1954.

Missile Crisis: A Line Drawn in the Waves

The escalating tensions of 1961 in Southeast Asia, the Caribbean, and Germany were a prelude to the crisis that came closest to triggering a nuclear war. On October 15, 1962, reconnaissance photos revealed Soviets at work on launching sites in Cuba from which nuclear missiles could hit the United States. Top officials spent five exhausting and increasingly desperate days sorting through the options. A full-scale invasion of Cuba was not feasible on short notice, and "surgical" air strikes were technically impossible. Either sort of military operation would kill hundreds of Soviet personnel and force Moscow to react. Secretary of Defense Robert McNamara suggested demanding removal of the missiles and declaring a naval "quarantine" against the arrival of further offensive weapons. A blockade would buy time for diplomacy.

Read the **Document**

at **www.myhistorylab.com**
Executive Discussions on the Cuban Missile Crisis (1962)

Watch the **Video**

at **www.myhistorylab.com**
President John F. Kennedy and the Cuban Missile Crisis

Kennedy imposed the blockade on Monday, October 22. While Khrushchev hesitated, Soviet ships circled outside the quarantine line. On Friday, Khrushchev offered to withdraw the missiles in return for a U.S. pledge not to invade Cuba. On Saturday, a second communication nearly dashed this hopeful opening by raising a new complaint about U.S. missiles on the territory of NATO allies. The letter was the result of pressure by Kremlin hard-liners and Khrushchev's own wavering. Kennedy decided to accept the first letter and ignore the second. The United States pledged not to invade Cuba and secretly promised to remove obsolete Jupiter missiles from Turkey. Khrushchev accepted these terms on Sunday, October 28.

Why did Khrushchev risk the Cuban gamble? One reason was to protect Castro as a symbol of Soviet commitment to anti-Western regimes in the developing world. Kennedy had tried to preempt Castroism in 1961 by launching the **Alliance for Progress,** an economic-development program for Latin America that tied aid to social reform. However, the United States had also orchestrated the Bay of Pigs invasion and funded a CIA campaign to sabotage Cuba. High U.S. officials were not contemplating a full-scale invasion, but Castro and Khrushchev had reason to fear the worst.

Alliance for Progress Program of economic aid to Latin America during the Kennedy administration.

QUICK REVIEW

U.S. Intervention Abroad

- Many Americans assumed the United States had a right to intervene abroad.
- Eisenhower used the CIA to subvert democratically elected governments in Iran and Guatemala.
- The United States replaced France as the supporter of pro-Western Vietnamese in South Vietnam.

Khrushchev also hoped to redress the strategic balance. As Kennedy discovered on taking office, the United States actually led the world in the deployment of strategic missiles. The strategic imbalance had sustained NATO during the Berlin confrontation, but 40 launchers in Cuba with two warheads each would have doubled the Soviet capacity to strike at the United States.

Soviet missiles in Cuba thus flouted the Monroe Doctrine and posed a real military threat. Kennedy and Khrushchev had also backed each other into untenable positions. In September, Kennedy had warned that the United States could not tolerate Soviet offensive weapons in Cuba, never dreaming that they were already there. Had Khrushchev acted openly (as the United States had done when it placed missiles in Turkey), the United States would have been hard pressed to object under international law. By acting in secret and breaking previous promises, the Soviets outsmarted themselves. When the missiles were discovered, Kennedy had to act.

WHERE TO LEARN MORE
W
National Air and Space Museum, Washington, DC
http://www.nasm.si.edu/

In the end, both sides were cautious. Khrushchev backed down rather than fight. Kennedy fended off hawkish advisers who wanted to destroy Castro. The world had trembled, but neither nation wanted war over "the missiles of October."

Science and Foreign Affairs

Read the Document at **www.myhistorylab.com** *Test Ban Treaty (1962)*

The two superpowers competed through science as well as diplomacy. When Kennedy took office, the United States was still playing catch-up in space technology. Kennedy committed the United States to placing a U.S. astronaut on the moon by 1970. The decision narrowed a multifaceted scientific and military program to a massive engineering project that favored the economic capacity of the United States.

The Soviet Union and the United States were also fencing about nuclear weapons testing. After the three-year moratorium, both resumed tests in 1961–1962. Both nations worked on multiple-targetable warheads, antiballistic missiles, and other innovations that might destabilize the balance of terror.

After the missile crisis showed his toughness, however, Kennedy had enough political maneuvering room to respond to pressure from liberal Democrats and groups like Women Strike for Peace and the Committee for a Sane Nuclear Policy by giving priority to disarmament. In July 1963, the United States, Britain, and the USSR signed the **Limited Test Ban Treaty,** which outlawed nuclear testing in the atmosphere, in outer space, and under water, and invited other nations to join in. France and China, the other nuclear powers, refused to sign, and the treaty did not halt weapons development, but it was the most positive achievement of Kennedy's foreign policy and a step toward later disarmament treaties.

Limited Test Ban Treaty Treaty, signed by the United States, Britain, and the Soviet Union, outlawing nuclear testing in the atmosphere, in outer space, and under water.

RIGHTEOUSNESS LIKE A MIGHTY STREAM: THE STRUGGLE FOR CIVIL RIGHTS

WHAT WAS the significance of *Brown v. Board of Education of Topeka?*

Supreme Court decisions are based on abstract principles, but they involve real people. One was Linda Brown of Topeka, Kansas, a third-grader whose parents were fed up with sending her past an all-white public school to attend an all-black school a mile away. The Browns volunteered to help the NAACP challenge Topeka's school segregation by trying to enroll Linda in their neighborhood school, beginning a legal case that reached the Supreme Court. On May 17, 1954, the Court decided ***Brown v. Board of Education of Topeka,*** opening a new civil rights era. Led by the persuasive power of the new chief justice, Earl Warren, the Court unanimously reversed the 1896 case of *Plessy v. Ferguson* by ruling that sending black children to "separate but equal" schools denied them equal treatment under the Constitution.

Brown v. Board of Education of Topeka Supreme Court decision in 1954 that declared that "separate but equal" schools for children of different races violated the Constitution.

Getting to the Supreme Court

The *Brown* decision climaxed a 25-year campaign to reenlist the federal courts on the side of equal rights (see Overview, Civil Rights: The Struggle for Racial Equality). The work began in the 1930s when Charles Hamilton Houston, dean of Howard University's law school, trained a corps of civil rights lawyers. Working on behalf of the NAACP, he hoped to erode *Plessy* by suits focused on interstate travel and professional graduate schools (the least defensible segregated institutions, because states seldom provided alternatives). In 1938, Houston's student Thurgood Marshall, a future Supreme Court justice, took over the NAACP job. He and other NAACP lawyers such as Constance Baker Motley risked personal danger crisscrossing the South to file civil rights lawsuits wherever a local case emerged. In 1949, Motley was the first black lawyer to argue a case in a Mississippi courtroom since Reconstruction.

Read the **Document** at **www.myhistorylab.com** *Brown v. Board of Education of Topeka, Kansas (1954)*

Efforts in the 1940s and early 1950s, often fueled by the experience of World War II soldiers, had important successes. In *Smith v. Allwright* (1944), the Supreme Court invalidated the all-white primary, a decision that led to increased black voter registration in many southern communities. With new political power, and often with the cooperation of relatively progressive white leaders, blacks fought for specific improvements, such as equal pay for teachers or the hiring of black police officers.

The *Brown* case combined lawsuits from Delaware, Virginia, South Carolina, the District of Columbia, and Kansas. In each instance, students and families braved community pressure to demand equal access to a basic public service. Chief Justice Earl Warren brought a divided Court to unanimous agreement. Viewing public education as central for the equal opportunity that lay at the heart of American values, the Court weighed the consequences of segregated school systems and concluded that separate meant unequal. The reasoning fit the temper of a nation that was proud of making prosperity accessible to all.

Brown also built on efforts by Mexican Americans in the Southwest to assert their rights of citizenship. After World War II, Latino organizations such as the League of United Latin American Citizens battled job discrimination and ethnic segregation. In 1946, Mexican American parents sued five Orange County, California, school districts that systematically placed their children in separate schools. In the resulting case of *Mendez v. Westminster*, federal courts prohibited segregation of Mexican-American children in California schools as a violation of the equal protection clause of the Fourteenth Amendment. Eight years later, the Supreme Court forbade Texas from excluding Mexican Americans from juries. These cases provided precedents for the Court's decision in *Brown* and subsequent civil rights cases.

Deliberate Speed

Racial segregation by law was largely a southern problem, the legacy of Jim Crow laws (see Chapter 17). The civil rights movement therefore focused first on the South, allowing Americans elsewhere to think of racial injustice as a regional issue.

OVERVIEW Civil Rights: The Struggle for Racial Equality

Area of Concern	Key Actions	Results
Public school integration	Federal court cases	*Mendez v. Westminster* (1946) *Brown v. Board of Education of Topeka* (1954) Enforcement by presidential action, Little Rock (1957) Follow-up court decisions, including mandatory busing programs in 1970s
Equal access to public facilities	Montgomery bus boycott (1955) Lunch counter sit-ins (1960) Freedom rides (1961) Birmingham demonstrations (1963) March on Washington (1963)	Civil Rights Act of 1964
Equitable voter registration	Voter registration drives, including Mississippi Summer Project (1964) Demonstrations and marches, including Selma to Montgomery march (1965)	Elimination of all-white primary elections with *Smith v. Allwright* Voting Rights Act of 1965 Voting Rights Act Amendments and Extension of 1975

Southern responses to *Brown* revealed regional differences. Few southern communities desegregated schools voluntarily, for to do so undermined the entrenched principle of a dual society. Their reluctance was bolstered in 1955 when the Supreme Court allowed segregated states to carry out the 1954 decision "with all deliberate speed" rather than immediately.

Southern Manifesto A document signed by 101 members of Congress from southern states in 1956 that argued that the Supreme Court's decision in *Brown v. Board of Education of Topeka* itself contradicted the Constitution.

The following year, 101 southern congressmen and senators issued the **Southern Manifesto,** which asserted that the Court decision was unconstitutional. President Eisenhower privately deplored the desegregation decision, which violated his sense of states' rights and upset Republican attempts to gain southern votes. At the same time, many in Washington knew that racial discrimination offered, in the worlds of Dean Acheson, "the most effective kind of ammunition" for Soviet propaganda.

Interpreting the Past
The Quest for African American Equality: Washington, DuBois, and King (pp. 808–809)

Eisenhower's distaste for racial integration left the Justice Department on the sidelines. Courageous parents and students had to knock on schoolhouse doors, often carrying court orders. Responses varied: school districts in border states, such as Maryland, Kentucky, and Oklahoma, desegregated relatively peacefully; farther south, African American children often met taunts and violence.

The first crisis came in Little Rock, Arkansas, in September 1957. The city school board admitted nine African Americans, including Melba Pattillo, to Central High, while segregrationist groups, such as the White Citizens Council, stirred up white fears. Claiming he feared violence, Governor Orval Faubus surrounded Central High with the National Guard and turned the new students away. Under intense national pressure, Faubus withdrew the Guard. The black students entered the school, but a howling mob forced the police to sneak them out after two hours. Fuming at the governor's defiance of federal authority, Eisenhower reluctantly nationalized the National Guard and sent in the 101st Airborne Division to keep order.

Read the Document
at www.myhistorylab.com
Executive Order 10730: Desegregation of Central High School (1957)

Virginians in 1958–1959 tried avoidance rather than confrontation. Massive resistance was a state policy that required local school districts to close rather than accept black students. When court orders to admit 19 black students triggered the shutdown of four high schools and three junior highs in Norfolk, white parents tried to compensate with private

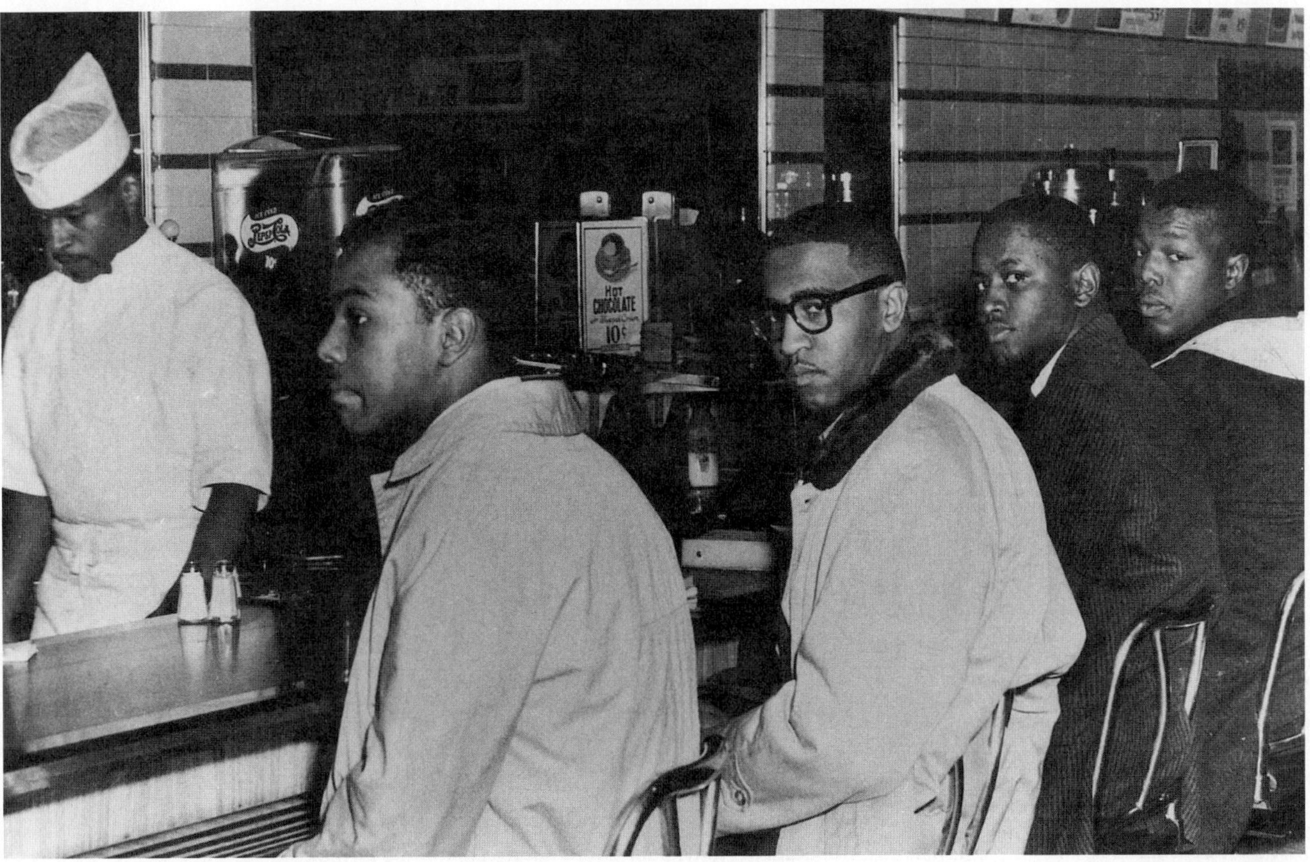

Students from North Carolina A&T, an all-black college, began the lunch-counter sit-in movement in February 1960. Here four students sit patiently in the Greensboro Woolworth's without being served. Participants wore their best clothes and suffered politely through days of verbal and sometimes physical abuse.

academies and tutoring, but it was soon apparent that a modern community could not dismantle public education.

Watch the **Video**
at **www.myhistorylab.com**
How Did the Civil Rights Movement Change American Schools?

The breakthrough in school integration did not come until the end of the 1960s, when the courts rejected further delays, and federal authorities threatened to cut off education funds. As late as 1968, only 6 percent of African American children in the South attended integrated schools. By 1973, the figure was 90 percent. Attention thereafter shifted to northern communities, whose schools were segregated, not by law, but by the divisions between white and black neighborhoods and between white suburbs and multiracial central cities, a situation known as *de facto* segregation.

Public Accommodations

Hear the **Audio**
at **www.myhistorylab.com**
Mass Meeting speech by Martin Luther King, Jr.

The civil rights movement also sought to integrate public accommodations. Most southern states separated the races in bus terminals and movie theaters. They required black riders to take rear seats on buses. They labeled separate restrooms and drinking fountains for "colored" users. Hotels denied rooms to black people, and restaurants refused them service.

The struggle to end segregated facilities started in Montgomery, Alabama. On December 1, 1955, Rosa Parks, a seamstress who worked at a downtown department store, refused to give up her bus seat to a white passenger and was arrested. Parks acted spontaneously, but she was part of a network of civil rights activists who wanted to challenge segregated buses and was the secretary of the Montgomery NAACP. As news of her action spread, the community institutions that enriched southern black life went into action. The Women's Political Council, a group of college-trained black women, initiated a mass boycott of the privately owned bus company.

Read the Document
at **www.myhistorylab.com**
Jo Ann Gibson Robinson, Bus Boycott

Read the Document
at **www.myhistorylab.com**
Julian Bond, Sit-ins and the Origins of SNCC (1960)

Southern Christian Leadership Conference (SCLC) Black civil rights organization founded in 1957 by Martin Luther King Jr. and other clergy.

QUICK REVIEW

The Montgomery Bus Boycott

- December 1, 1955: Rosa Parks refused to give up her bus seat to a white passenger and was arrested.
- The Women's Political Council organized a boycott of the bus company.
- After nearly a year, the Supreme Court ruled the bus segregation law unconstitutional.

Student Nonviolent Coordinating Committee (SNCC) Black civil rights organization founded in 1960 and drawing heavily on younger activists and college students.

Congress of Racial Equality (CORE) Civil rights group formed in 1942 and committed to nonviolent civil disobedience.

Birmingham Civil Rights Institute Museum, Birmingham, Alabama
http://www.bcri.org/index.html

QUICK REVIEW

Civil Rights during the Kennedy Administration

- Kennedy was a tepid supporter of the civil rights movement.
- 1963: activists focused their attention on segregation in Birmingham.
- August 28, 1963: quarter of a million people marched to the Lincoln Memorial in support of civil rights.

Martin Luther King Jr. a 26-year-old pastor, led the boycott. He galvanized a mass meeting with a speech that quoted the biblical prophet Amos: "We are determined here in Montgomery to work and fight until justice runs down like water, and righteousness like a mighty stream."

Montgomery's African Americans organized their boycott in the face of white outrage. A car pool substituted for the buses despite police harassment. As the boycott survived months of pressure, the national media began to pay attention. After nearly a year, the Supreme Court agreed that the bus segregation law was unconstitutional.

Victory in Montgomery depended on steadfast African American involvement. Success also revealed the discrepancy between white attitudes in the Deep South and national opinion. For white southerners, segregation was a local concern best defined as a legal or constitutional matter. For other Americans, it was increasingly an issue of the South's deviation from national moral norms.

The Montgomery boycott won a local victory and made King famous, but it did not propel immediate change. King formed the **Southern Christian Leadership Conference (SCLC)** and sparred with the NAACP about community-based versus court-based civil rights tactics, but four African American college students in Greensboro, North Carolina, started the next phase of the struggle. On February 1, 1960, they put on jackets and ties and sat down at the segregated lunch counter in Woolworth's, waiting through the day without being served. Their patient courage brought more demonstrators; within two days, 85 students packed the store. Nonviolent sit-ins spread throughout the South.

The sit-ins had both immediate and long-range effects. In such comparatively sophisticated border cities as Nashville, Tennessee, sit-ins integrated lunch counters. Elsewhere, they precipitated white violence and mass arrests. King welcomed nonviolent confrontation. SCLC leader Ella Baker, one of the movement's most important figures, helped the students form a new organization, the **Student Nonviolent Coordinating Committee (SNCC).**

The year 1961 brought "freedom rides" to test the segregation of interstate bus terminals. The idea came from James Farmer of the **Congress of Racial Equality (CORE),** who copied a little-remembered 1947 Journey of Reconciliation that had tested the integration of interstate trains. Two buses carrying black and white passengers met only minor problems in Virginia, the Carolinas, and Georgia, but Alabamians burned one of the buses and attacked the riders in Birmingham, where they beat demonstrators senseless and clubbed a Justice Department observer. The governor and police refused to protect the freedom riders. The riders traveled into Mississippi under National Guard protection but were arrested at the Jackson bus terminal. Despite Attorney General Robert Kennedy's call for a cooling-off period, freedom rides continued through the summer. The rides proved that African Americans were in charge of their own civil rights revolution.

The March on Washington, 1963

John Kennedy was a tepid supporter of the civil rights movement and entered office with no civil rights agenda. He appointed segregationist judges to mollify southern congressmen and would have preferred that African Americans stop disturbing the fragile Democratic Party coalition.

In the face of the slow federal response, the SCLC concentrated for 1963 on rigidly segregated Birmingham. April began with sit-ins and marches that aimed to integrate lunch counters, restrooms, and stores and secure open hiring for some clerical jobs. Birmingham's commissioner of public safety, Bull Connor, used fire hoses to blast demonstrators against buildings and roll children down the streets. When demonstrators fought back, his men chased them with dogs. Continued marches brought the arrest of hundreds of children.

The Birmingham demonstrations were inconclusive. White leaders accepted minimal demands on May 10 but delayed enforcing them. Antiblack violence continued, including a bomb that killed four children in a Birmingham church. Meanwhile, the events in Alabama had forced President Kennedy to board the freedom train with an eloquent June 11 speech and to send a civil rights bill to Congress.

On August 28, 1963, a rally in Washington transformed African American civil rights into a national cause. A quarter of a million people, black and white, marched to the Lincoln Memorial. The day gave Martin Luther King Jr. a national pulpit. His call for progress toward Christian and American goals had immense appeal. Television cut away from afternoon programs for his "I Have a Dream" speech.

The March on Washington drew on activism in the North as well as the South. African Americans in northern states and cities did not face the legal segregation of the South, but they had unequal access to jobs and housing because of private discrimination. They fought back with demands for fair housing and fair employment laws, sometimes with success and sometimes triggering white backlash. A New York law against employment discrimination, for example, was one of the factors that had pushed the Brooklyn Dodgers to sign Jackie Robinson.

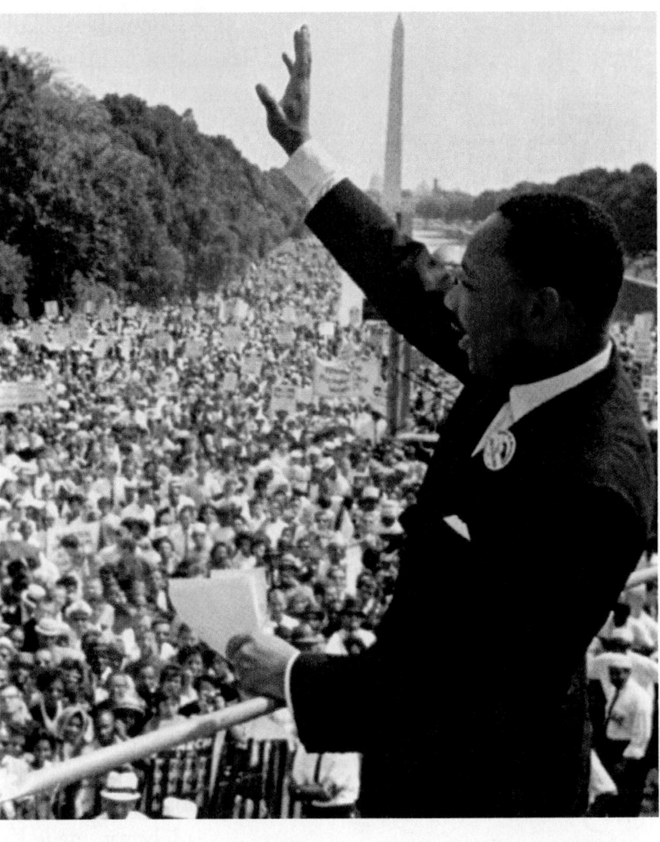

On August 28, 1963, Rev. Martin Luther King Jr. delivered his famous "I Have a Dream" speech to the March on Washington for Jobs and Freedom. The address was a climactic moment in the civil rights movement, encapsulating the optimism of decades of struggle, but the March on Washington also papered over emerging divisions that would become apparent later in the 1960s.

Religious Belief and Civil Rights

Although *Brown* and other civil rights court decisions drew on the secular Constitution, much of the success of the southern civil rights movement came from grassroots Christianity. A century earlier, the abolitionist crusade had drawn much of its power from evangelistic revival movements. Now in the 1950s and 1960s, black southerners drew on prophetic Christianity to forge and act on a vision of a just society. Religious conviction and solidarity provided courage in the face of opposition.

At the same time, most white Christians understood that segregation contradicted the message of the Bible. The two largest religious groups in the South, the Presbyterian Church of the United States and the Southern Baptist Convention, took public stands in favor of desegregation in the mid-1950s. Revival leader Billy Graham shared a pulpit with Martin Luther King Jr. in 1957 and insisted against local laws that his revival services be integrated. The opponents of civil rights thus lacked the moral support of the South's most fundamental cultural institutions.

Watch the Video at **www.myhistorylab.com**
Rev. Dr. Martin Luther King Jr.'s Speech at the March on Washington, August 1963

In this context, it was no accident that black churches were organizing centers for civil rights work. King named his organization the Southern Christian Leadership Conference with clear intent and purpose.

"LET US CONTINUE"

HOW DID Lyndon B. Johnson continue the domestic agenda inherited from the Kennedy administration? In what ways did he depart from it?

The two years that followed King's speech mingled despair and accomplishment. The optimism of the March on Washington shattered with the assassination of John Kennedy in November 1963. In 1964 and 1965, however, President Lyndon Johnson pushed through Kennedy's legislative agenda and much more in a burst of government activism unmatched since the 1930s. Federal legislation brought victory to the first phase of the civil rights revolution, launched the **War on Poverty,** expanded health insurance and aid to education, and opened an era of environmental protection.

War on Poverty Set of programs introduced by Lyndon Johnson between 1963 and 1966 designed to break the cycle of poverty by providing funds for job training, community development, nutrition, and supplementary education.

Dallas, 1963

In November 1963, President Kennedy visited Texas to raise money and patch up feuds among Texas Democrats. On November 22, the president's motorcade took him near the Texas School Book Depository building in Dallas, where Lee Harvey Oswald had stationed himself at a window on the sixth floor. Acting on his own, Oswald fired three shots that wounded Texas Governor

Sixth Floor Museum, Dallas, Texas
http://www.jfk.org

Read the Document
at www.myhistorylab.com
Lyndon Johnson, "The War on Poverty" (1964)

Office of Economic Opportunity (OEO) Federal agency that coordinated many programs of the War on Poverty between 1964 and 1975.

John Connally and killed the president. Vice President Lyndon Johnson took the oath of office as president on Air Force One while the blood-spattered Jacqueline Kennedy looked on. Two days later, as Oswald was being led from one jail cell to another, Jack Ruby, a Texas nightclub owner, killed him with a handgun in full view of TV cameras.

War on Poverty

Five days after the assassination, Lyndon Johnson claimed Kennedy's progressive aura for his new administration. "Let us continue," he told the nation, promising to implement Kennedy's policies. In fact, Johnson was vastly different from Kennedy. He was a professional politician who had reached the top through Texas politics and congressional infighting. As Senate majority leader during the 1950s, he had built a web of political obligations and friendships. Johnson's upbringing in rural Texas shaped a man who was endlessly ambitious, ruthless, and often personally crude, but also deeply committed to social equity. He had entered public life with the New Deal in the 1930s and believed in its principles. Johnson, not Kennedy, was the true heir of Franklin Roosevelt.

Johnson inherited a domestic agenda that the Kennedy administration had defined but not enacted. Kennedy's farthest-reaching initiative was rooted in the acknowledgment that poverty was a persistent U.S. problem. Michael Harrington's study *The Other America* became an unexpected bestseller. As poverty captured public attention, Kennedy's economic advisers devised a community action program that emphasized education and job training, a national service corps, and a youth conservation corps. They prepared a package of proposals to submit to Congress in 1964 that focused on social programs intended to alter behaviors that were thought to be passed from generation to generation, thus following the American tendency to attribute poverty to the personal failings of the poor.

Martin Luther King Jr. National Historical Site, Atlanta, Georgia
http://www.nps.gov/malu/

Johnson made Kennedy's antipoverty package his own. Adopting Cold War rhetoric, he declared "unconditional war on poverty." The core of Johnson's program was the **Office of Economic Opportunity (OEO).** Established under the direction of Kennedy's brother-in-law R. Sargent Shriver in 1964, the OEO operated the Job Corps for school dropouts, the Neighborhood Youth Corps for unemployed teenagers, the Head Start program to prepare poor children for school, and VISTA (Volunteers in Service to America) to send volunteers into America's poorest communities. OEO's biggest effort went to Community Action Agencies. By 1968, more than 500 such agencies provided health and educational services. Despite flaws, the War on Poverty improved life for millions of Americans.

National Civil Rights Museum, Memphis, Tennessee
http://www.civilrightsmuseum.org

Read the Document
at www.myhistorylab.com
Civil Rights Act of 1964

Civil Rights Act of 1964 Federal legislation that outlawed discrimination in public accommodations and employment on the basis of race, skin color, sex, religion, or national origin.

Freedom Summer Voter registration effort in rural Mississippi organized by black and white civil rights workers in 1964.

Civil Rights, 1964–1965

Johnson's passionate commitment to economic betterment accompanied a commitment to civil rights. In Johnson's view, segregation not only deprived African Americans of access to opportunity but also distracted white southerners from their own poverty and underdevelopment.

One solution was the **Civil Rights Act of 1964,** which Kennedy had introduced but which Johnson got enacted. The law prohibited segregation in public accommodations, such as hotels, restaurants, gas stations, theaters, and parks, and outlawed employment discrimination on federally assisted projects. It also created the Equal Employment Opportunity Commission (EEOC) and included gender in the list of categories protected against discrimination, a provision whose consequences were scarcely suspected in 1964.

Even as Congress was debating the 1964 law, **Freedom Summer** moved political power to the top of the civil rights agenda. Organized by SNCC, the Mississippi Summer Freedom Project was a voter-registration drive that sent white and black volunteers to the small towns and back roads of Mississippi. The target was a political system that used rigged literacy tests and intimidation to keep black southerners from voting. In Mississippi in 1964, only 7 percent of eligible black citizens were registered voters. Local black activists had laid the groundwork for a registration effort with years of courageous effort through the NAACP and voter leagues. Now an increasingly militant SNCC took the lead. The explicit goal was to increase the number of African American voters. The tacit intention was to attract national attention by putting middle-class white college students in the line of fire. Freedom Summer gained 1,600 new voters and taught 2,000 children in SNCC-run Freedom Schools at the cost of beatings, bombings, church arson, and the murder of three project workers.

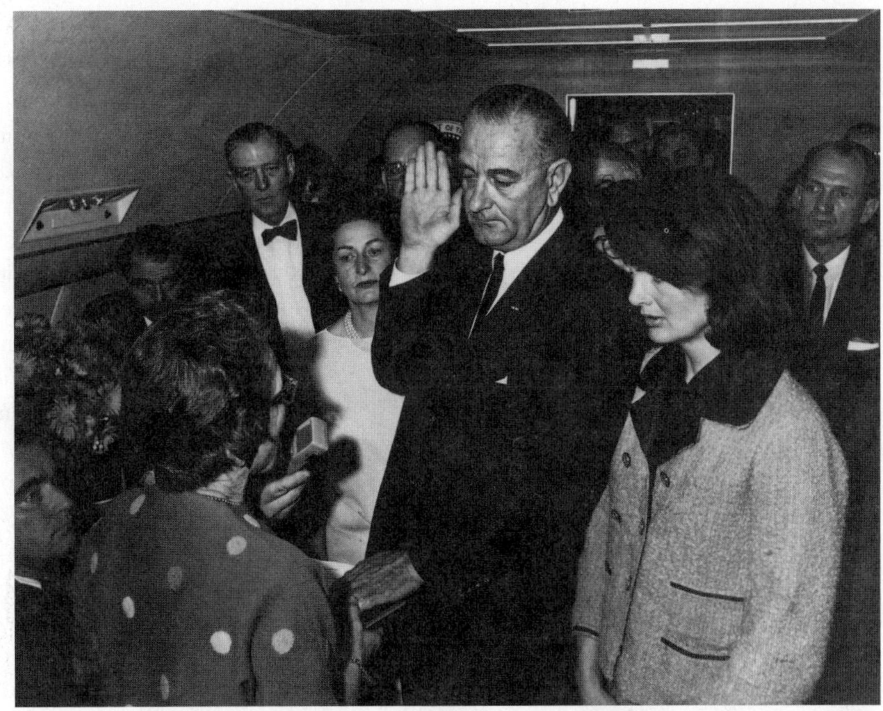

President Lyndon Johnson was a crafty and sometimes ruthless politician, but he also had a deep personal commitment to solving problems of poverty and inequality in American society.

Another outgrowth of the SNCC effort was the Mississippi Freedom Democratic Party (MFDP), a biracial coalition that bypassed Mississippi's all-white Democratic Party, followed state party rules, and sent its own delegates to the 1964 Democratic convention. To preserve party harmony, President Johnson refused to expel the "regular" Mississippi Democrats and offered instead to seat two MFDP delegates and enforce party rules for 1968. The MFDP walked out, seething with anger.

Freedom Summer and political realities both focused national attention on voter registration. Lyndon Johnson and Martin Luther King Jr. agreed on the need for federal voting legislation when King visited the president in December 1964 after winning the Nobel Peace Prize. For King, power at the ballot box would help black southerners to take control of their own communities. For Johnson, voting reform would fulfill the promise of American democracy. It would also benefit the Democratic Party by replacing with black voters the white southerners who were drifting toward the anti-integration Republicans.

Read the **Document**
at www.myhistorylab.com
Fannie Lou Hammer, Voting Rights in Mississippi, 1962–1964

The target for King and the SCLC was Dallas County, Alabama, where only 2 percent of eligible black residents were registered, compared with 70 percent of white residents. Peaceful demonstrations started in January 1965. By early February, jails in the county seat of Selma held 2,600 black people whose offense was marching to the courthouse to demand the vote. The campaign climaxed with a march from Selma to the state capital of Montgomery.

On Sunday, March 7, 500 marchers crossed the bridge over the Alabama River, to meet a sea of state troopers. The troopers gave them two minutes to disperse and then attacked on foot and horseback "as if they were mowing a big field." The attack drove the demonstrators back in bloody confusion while television cameras rolled.

As violence continued, Johnson addressed a joint session of Congress to demand a voting-rights law. By opening the political process to previously excluded citizens, the Voting Rights Act was as revolutionary and far-reaching as the Nineteenth Amendment, which guaranteed women the right to vote, and the Labor Relations Act of 1935, which recognized labor unions as the equals of corporations.

Voting Rights Act Legislation in 1965 that overturned a variety of practices by which states systematically denied voter registration to minorities.

Johnson signed the **Voting Rights Act** on August 6, 1965. The law outlawed literacy tests and provided for federal voting registrars in states where registration or turnout in 1964 was less than 50 percent of the eligible population. It applied initially in seven southern states. Black registration in these states jumped from 27 percent to 55 percent within the first year. In 1975, Congress extended coverage to Hispanic voters in the Southwest. The Act required new moderation from white leaders, who had to satisfy black voters, and it opened the way for black and Latino candidates to win positions at every level of state and local government. In the long run, the Voting Rights Act climaxed the battle for civil rights and shifted attention to the continuing problems of economic opportunity and inequality.

QUICK REVIEW

Voting Rights Act of 1965

- Outlawed literacy tests.
- Provided for federal voting registration in seven southern states.
- Resulted in dramatic increase in black registration in those states.

President Lyndon Johnson signing the Tonkin resolution. This gave him power to escalate the Vietnam War after the Gulf of Tonkin incident in which American vessels had been attacked by the North Vietnamese.

War, Peace, and the Landslide of 1964

Lyndon Johnson was the peace candidate in 1964. Johnson had maintained Kennedy's commitment to South Vietnam. On the advice of such Kennedy holdovers as Defense Secretary Robert McNamara, he stepped up commando raids and naval shelling of North Vietnam, on the assumption that North Vietnam controlled the Viet Cong. On August 2, North Vietnamese torpedo boats attacked the U.S. destroyer *Maddox* in the Gulf of Tonkin while it was eavesdropping on North Vietnamese military signals. Two days later, the *Maddox* and the *C. Turner Joy* reported another torpedo attack (probably false sonar readings). Johnson ordered a bombing raid in reprisal and asked Congress to authorize "all necessary measures" to protect U.S. forces and stop further aggression. Congress passed the **Gulf of Tonkin Resolution** with only two nay votes, effectively authorizing the president to wage undeclared war.

Johnson's militancy paled beside that of his Republican opponent. Senator Barry Goldwater of Arizona represented the new right wing of the Republican Party, which was drawing strength from the South and West. Johnson looked moderate when Goldwater declared that "extremism in the defense of liberty is no vice." In contrast, Johnson pledged not "to send American boys nine or ten thousand miles from home to do what Asian boys ought to be doing for themselves" while Goldwater proposed an all-out war.

The election was a landslide. Johnson's 61 percent of the popular vote was the greatest margin ever recorded in a presidential election. Democrats racked up two-to-one majorities in Congress. For the first time in decades, liberal Democrats could enact their domestic program without begging votes from conservative southerners or Republicans, and Johnson could achieve his goal of a **Great Society** based on freedom and opportunity for all.

The result was a series of measures that Johnson pushed through Congress before the Vietnam War eroded his political standing and distracted national attention. The National Endowment for the Arts and the National Endowment for the Humanities seemed uncontroversial at the time but would later become the focus of liberal and conservative struggles over the character of American life. The Wilderness Act (1964), which preserved 9.1 million acres from development, would prove another political battlefield in the face of economic pressures in the next century.

The goal of increasing opportunity for all Americans stirred the president most deeply. The Elementary and Secondary Education Act was the first general federal aid program for public schools, allocating $1.3 billion for textbooks and special education. The Higher Education Act funded low-interest student loans and university research facilities. The Medical Care Act created **Medicare,** federally funded health insurance for the elderly, and **Medicaid,** which helped states offer medical care to the poor. The Appalachian Regional Development Act funded economic development in the depressed mountain counties of 12 states from Georgia to New York and proved a long-run success.

Gulf of Tonkin Resolution Request to Congress from President Lyndon Johnson in response to North Vietnamese torpedo boat attacks in which he sought authorization for "all necessary measures" to protect American forces and stop further aggression.

Great Society Theme of Lyndon Johnson's administration, focusing on poverty, education, and civil rights.

Read the **Document** at **www.myhistorylab.com**
From Then to Now Online: Medical Research on Polio and AIDS

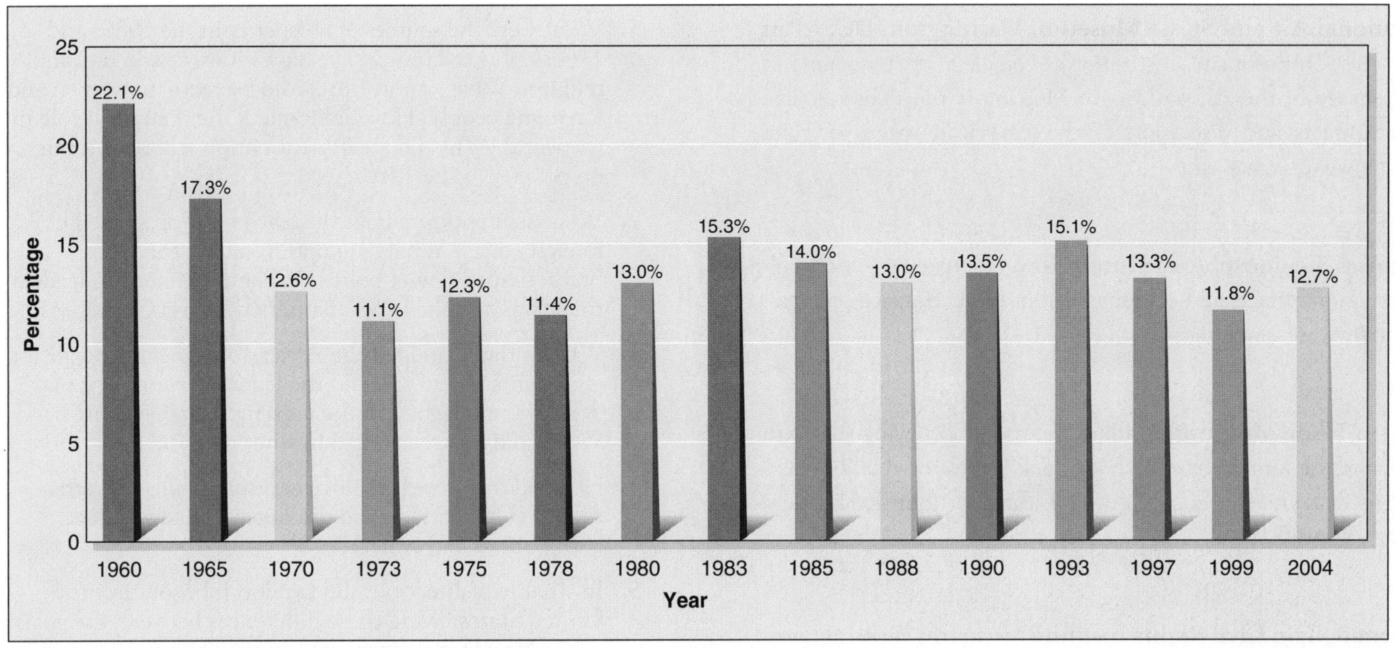

FIGURE 28–4 **Poverty Rate, 1960–2004** With the improvement of federal health insurance, assistance for the elderly, and antipoverty programs, the proportion of Americans living in poverty dropped dramatically in the later 1960s. It began to inch upward again in the 1980s, when the priorities of the federal government shifted.

Data Source: Statistical Abstract of the United States.

It is sometimes said that the United States declared war on poverty and lost. In fact, the nation came closer to winning the war on poverty than it did the war in Vietnam. New or expanded social insurance and income-support programs, such as Medicare, Medicaid, Social Security, and food stamps, cut the proportion of poor people from 22 percent of the American population in 1960 to 13 percent in 1970 (see Figure 28–4). Infant mortality dropped by a third because of improved nutrition and better access to healthcare for mothers and children. Taken together, the political results of the 1964 landslide moved the United States much closer to the vision of an end to poverty and racial injustice.

Medicare Basic medical insurance for the elderly, financed through the federal government; program created in 1965.

Medicaid Supplementary medical insurance for the poor, financed through the federal government; program created in 1965.

QUICK REVIEW

The Great Society

- Reflected Johnson's commitment to reducing poverty.
- Provided federal aid for public schools.
- Established Medicare and Medicaid.
- Reduced percentage of Americans living in poverty.
- Improved health and nutrition of the poor.

CONCLUSION

The era commonly remembered as the 1950s stretched from 1953 to 1964. Consistent goals guided U.S. foreign policy through the entire period, including vigilant anti-Communism and the confidence to intervene in trouble spots around the globe. At home, the Supreme Court's *Brown* decision introduced a decade-long civil rights revolution that reached its emotional peak with the March on Washington and its political climax with the Civil Rights Act (1964) and Voting Rights Act (1965). However, many patterns of personal behavior and social relations remained unchanged. Women faced similar expectations from the early fifties to the early sixties. Churches showed more continuity than change.

But the consistency and stability of the 1950s were fragile. The national consensus would splinter after 1964. What had seemed like a common road to the future soon divided into many different paths. Some members of minority groups turned their backs on integration. Some younger Americans dropped out of mainstream society to join the aptly named counterculture. Others sought the security of religious commitment and community. Perhaps most divisively, "hawks" battled "doves" over Vietnam. If civil rights and Cold War had been the defining issues for the fifties, Vietnam would define the sixties, which stretched from 1965 to 1974.

Where to Learn More

National Air and Space Museum, Washington, DC. Part of the Smithsonian Institution's complex of museums in Washington, the Air and Space Museum is the richest source for artifacts and discussion of the American space program. http://www.nasm.si.edu/.

Kansas Cosmosphere, Hutchinson, Kansas. A rich collection of artifacts and equipment from the U.S. space program. http://www.cosmo.org.

Sixth Floor Museum, Dallas, Texas. Occupying the sixth floor of the former Texas School Book Depository building, exhibits examine the life, death, and legacy of John F. Kennedy. http://www.jfk.org.

Birmingham Civil Rights Institute Museum, Birmingham, Alabama. This museum and archive deal with the background of southern racial segregation, civil rights activism, and the 1963 demonstrations in Birmingham. http://www.bcri.org/ index.html.

Martin Luther King Jr. National Historical Site, Atlanta, Georgia. The birthplace and grave of Reverend King are the nucleus of a park set in the historic black neighborhood of Auburn. http://www.nps.gov/malu/.

National Civil Rights Museum, Memphis, Tennessee. Located in the Lorraine Motel, where Martin Luther King Jr. was killed, the museum traces the participants, background, and effects of key events in the civil rights movement. http://www.civilrightsmuseum.org.

National Afro-American Museum and Cultural Center, Wilberforce, Ohio. The exhibit "From Victory to Freedom: Afro-American Life in the Fifties" looks at home, family, music, and religion. http://ohsweb.ohiohistory.org/places/sw13/index.shtml.

John F. Kennedy Library and Museum, Boston, Massachusetts. Exhibits offer a sympathetic view of Kennedy's life and achievements. http://www.jfklibrary.org.

Review Questions

1. What were the sources of prosperity in the 1950s and 1960s? How did prosperity shape cities, family life, and religion? What opportunities did it create for women and for young people? How did it affect the American role in the world? Why did an affluent nation still need a war on poverty in the 1960s?
2. What assumptions about the Soviet Union shaped U.S. foreign policy? What assumptions about the United States shaped Soviet policy? What did American leaders think was at stake in Vietnam, Berlin, and Cuba?
3. Who initiated and led the African American struggle for civil rights? What role did the federal government play? What were the goals of the civil rights movement? Where did it succeed, and in what ways did it fall short?
4. How did the growth of nuclear arsenals affect international relations? How did the nuclear shadow affect U.S. politics and society?
5. In what new directions did Lyndon Johnson take the United States? Were there differences between the goals of the New Frontier and the Great Society?
6. Why was school integration the focus of such strong conflict? How did the work of Mexican Americans and African Americans support the same goal of equal access to education?
7. How did religious belief shape American society in the Eisenhower and Kennedy years?

Key Terms

Alliance for Progress (p. 796)
Bay of Pigs (p. 794)
Berlin Wall (p. 794)
Brown v. Board of Education of Topeka (p. 797)
Civil Rights Act of 1964 (p. 802)
Congress of Racial Equality (CORE) (p. 800)
Federal Highway Act of 1956 (p. 783)
Freedom Summer (p. 802)
Great Society (p. 804)
Gulf of Tonkin Resolution (p. 804)
Limited Test Ban Treaty (p. 796)
Massive retaliation (p. 789)
Medicaid (p. 805)
Medicare (p. 805)
National Aeronautics and Space Administration (NASA) (p. 789)
New Frontier (p. 793)
Office of Economic Opportunity (OEO) (p. 802)
Southeast Asia Treaty Organization (SEATO) (p. 795)
Southern Christian Leadership Conference (SCLC) (p. 800)
Southern Manifesto (p. 798)
Student Nonviolent Coordinating Committee (SNCC) (p. 800)
Viet Cong (p. 795)
Voting Rights Act (p. 803)
War on Poverty (p. 801)

myhistorylab Connections

Reinforce what you learned in this chapter by studying the many documents, images, maps, review tools, and videos available at **www.myhistorylab.com**.

Read and Review

Study and Review **Study Plan: Chapter 28**

Read the Document

Ladies Home Journal, "Young Mother" (1956)

Brown v. Board of Education of Topeka, Kansas (1954)

Life Magazine Identifies the New Teenage Market (1959)

John F. Kennedy, Cuban Missile Crisis Address (1962)

Student Nonviolent Coordinating Committee, Statement of Purpose (1960)

Test Ban Treaty (1962)

Lyndon Johnson, "The War on Poverty" (1964)

Executive Discussions on the Cuban Missile Crisis (1962)

Executive Order 10730: Desegregation of Central High School (1957)

Fannie Lou Hammer, Voting Rights in Mississippi, 1962–1964

Jo Ann Gibson Robinson, Bus Boycott

Julian Bond, Sit-ins and the Origins of SNCC (1960)

Civil Rights Act of 1964

See the Map *Civil Rights Movement*

Research and Explore

Read the Document

Personal Journeys Online

From Then to Now Online: Medical Research on Polio and AIDS

Exploring America: The Consumer Society: 1950–1960

Hear the Audio *Mass Meeting speech by Martin Luther King, Jr.*

Watch the Video

Ike for President: Eisenhower Campaign Ad, 1952

Duck and Cover

President John F. Kennedy and the Cuban Missile Crisis

How Did the Civil Rights Movement Change American Schools?

Eisenhower's Special Message to Congress on the Middle East, 1957

Rev. Dr. Martin Luther King, Jr.'s Speech at the March on Washington, August, 1963

Hear the Audio

Hear the audio files for Chapter 28 at **www.myhistorylab.com**.

The Quest for African American Equality: Washington, Du Bois, and King

HOW AND IN what manner were the goals of Booker T. Washington and W. E. B. Du Bois like those of Dr. Martin Luther King Jr. during the civil rights movement of the 1950s and 1960s? How do the style and techniques of both men compare to those used by Dr. King?

Booker T. Washington was a leading African American educator in the late 19th century. Washington proposed that African Americans accept the racial separation of Jim Crow laws and the refusal of southern states to grant them voting rights for the time being in exchange for immediate guarantees of economic security and the right to work in industry and agriculture. Against critics angered by his temporary acceptance of Jim Crow, Washington explained that any attempt to challenge segregation would be disastrous for blacks, who could instead enhance their economic status and use that to effect permanent change.

W. E. B. Du Bois was among Washington's strongest critics and a founder of the Niagara Movement. Du Bois was the first black graduate of Harvard University. He was a principal in establishing the National Association for the Advancement of Colored People (NAACP) in 1909 and became its director of publications in 1910. Du Bois argued that segregation should be confronted directly and aggressively and was in complete opposition to a position of accommodation.

The Reverend Dr. Martin Luther King Jr. was the foremost civil rights leader of the twentieth century. King conducted an activist civil rights movement that challenged Jim Crow on both the social and political fronts in the South. King was instrumental in the establishment of a civil rights program that was founded on the philosophy of nonviolent civil disobedience taken from the teachings of both Mahatma Gandhi and Henry David Thoreau.

A white man directs a black woman away from a waiting room for whites only at a bus station in Dallas, Texas. In the South, the law segregated public transportation facilities by race.

Justice John Marshall Harlan, dissenting opinion, *Plessy v. Ferguson* (1896)

If evils will result from the commingling of the two races upon public highways established for the benefit of all, they will be infinitely less than those that will surely come from state legislation regulating the enjoyment of civil rights upon the basis of race. We boast of the freedom enjoyed by our people above all other peoples. But it is difficult to reconcile that boast with a state of the law which, practically, puts the brand of servitude and degradation upon a large class of our fellow citizens,-our equals before the law. The thin disguise of 'equal' accommodations for passengers in railroad coaches will not mislead any one, nor atone for the wrong this day done. . . .

'People of the United States,' for whom, and by whom through representatives, our government is administered. Such a system is inconsistent with the guaranty given by the constitution to each state of a republican form of government, and may be stricken down by congressional action, or by the courts in the discharge of their solemn duty to maintain the supreme law of the land, anything in the constitution or laws of any state to the contrary notwithstanding.

For the reason stated, I am constrained to withhold my assent from the opinion and judgment of the majority.

Booker T. Washington, from *Atlanta Compromise Speech*, 1895

The wisest among my race understand that the agitation of questions of social equality is the extremist folly, and that progress in the enjoyment of all the privileges that will come to us must be the result of severe and constant struggle rather than of artificial forcing. No race that has anything to contribute to the markets of the world is long in any degree ostracized. It is important and right that all privileges of the law be ours, but it is vastly more important that we be prepared for the exercise of these privileges. The opportunity to earn a dollar in a factory just now is worth infinitely more than the opportunity to spend a dollar in an opera-house.

W. E. B. Du Bois, from *Mr. Booker T. Washington and Others* (1903)

The black men of America have a duty to perform, a duty stern and delicate, a forward movement to oppose a part of the work of their greatest leader. So far as Mr. Washington preaches Thrift, Patience, and Industrial Training for the masses, we must hold up his hands and strive with him, rejoicing in his honors and glorying in the strength of this Joshua called of God and of man to lead the headless host. But so far as Mr. Washington apologizes for injustice, North or South, does not rightly value the privilege and duty of voting, belittles the emasculating effects of caste distinctions, and opposes the higher training and ambition of our brighter minds, — so far as he, the South, or the Nation, does this, we must unceasingly and firmly oppose them. By every civilized and peaceful method we must strive for the rights which the world accords to men, . . .

29 Shaken to the Roots

1965-1980

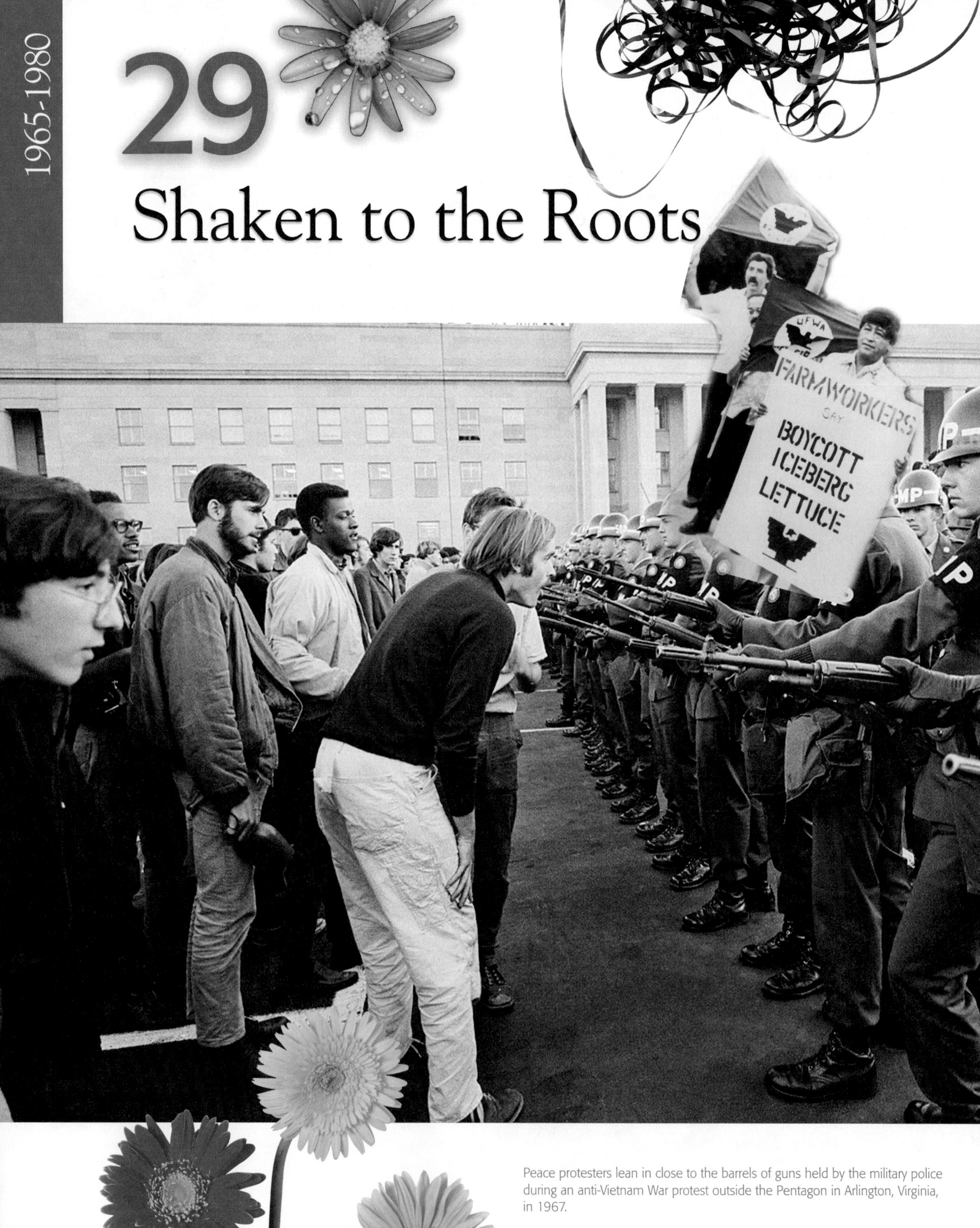

Peace protesters lean in close to the barrels of guns held by the military police during an anti-Vietnam War protest outside the Pentagon in Arlington, Virginia, in 1967.

Hear the Audio

Hear the audio files for Chapter 29 at **www.myhistorylab.com**.

WHY DID the national consensus of the 1950s and early 1960s unravel?

WHAT CHALLENGES did cities face in the late 1960s and 1970s?

HOW DID the Tet Offensive change American public opinion about the war in Vietnam?

WHAT WAS the legacy of Richard Nixon's presidency?

WHAT FACTORS limited Jimmy Carter's effectiveness as president?

ONE AMERICAN JOURNEY

The strike [against California grape growers] broke out in September of 1965. . . . The whole boycott is a nonviolent tool. It's an economic sanction, so to speak but it's a way that people can participate. One thing about nonviolence is that it opens the doors for everyone to participate, the women, the children. And women being involved on the picket lines made it easier for the men then to accept nonviolence. . . . I consider nonviolence to be a very strong spiritual force because it's almost like an energy that goes out and touches people.

Most of them [the farmworkers] were either first generation Mexican-Americans or recent immigrants. To get them to accept the whole philosophy that you can create a movement with nonviolence was not easy. It was not easy. To get them to understand that—and this you could see happening in people, that they would become transformed. They would actually become stronger through practicing nonviolence.

I gave a speech [at Northern Illinois University] and this one young man came up to me afterwards and he said, "My mother works in the fields. She's an onion picker" He says, "and I was always ashamed of my mother until today." . . . We have to get farmworkers the same types of benefits, the same type of wages, the respect that they deserve because they do the most sacred work of all. They feed our nation every day.

Dolores Huerta, interview with Vincent Harding at The Veterans of Hope Project, http://www.veteransofhope.org/show.php?vid=51&tid=46&sid=77

Read the **Document** at **www.myhistorylab.com**

Personal Journeys Online

- ***Easy Rider*, 1969. Fantasies of escape from 1960s America in a popular movie.**
- **Craig McNamara, interview in Joan Morrison and Robert K. Morrison, *From Camelot to Kent State: The Sixties Experience in the Words of Those Who Lived It*, 1987. Antiwar protest and the generation gap in 1968.**
- **Buzz Aldrin and Neil Armstrong land on the moon, July 20, 1969. Edgar Cortright, ed., *Apollo Expeditions to the Moon* (Washington: NASA SP 350, 1975).**
- **Reies Lopez Tijerina, "Letter from the Santa Fe Jail," reprinted in *A Documentary History of the Mexican Americans*, ed. by Wayne Moquin, 1971. A Hispanic civil rights manifesto from 1969.**
- **"Bill Gates and Paul Allen Talk," *Fortune*, 132, October 2, 1995, pp. 69–72. Copyright © 1995 *Fortune*. Microsoft founders recall the early days.**

From the early 1960s, DOLORES HUERTA was a co-worker with Cesar Chavez in organizing the United Farm Workers union (UFW). Her personal journey took her from her birthplace in the state of New Mexico to Stockton, California, where she grew up in a multiracial neighborhood, and then to every corner of the United States as a spokesperson for the UFW. In this interview she reflected on the power of nonviolent approaches such as the national boycott of table grapes that was the UFW's most successful tactic.

Dolores Huerta's story speaks to the importance of grassroots action and to the role of churches as sources of social change, but also to the depth of economic and cultural divisions within the United States in the later 1960s and 1970s. At the same time that groups like the UFW worked to build social movements across ethnic differences, many minority Americans responded to slow progress toward racial equality by advocating separation rather than integration, helping to plunge the nation's cities into crisis, while other Americans began to draw back from some of the objectives of racial integration. The failure to win an easy victory in Vietnam eroded the nation's confidence and fueled bitter divisions about the nation's goals. Stalemate in Southeast Asia, political changes in third-world countries, and an oil supply crisis in the 1970s challenged U.S. influence in the world. Political scandals, summarized in three syllables, "Watergate," undercut faith in government. Fifteen years of turmoil forced a grudging recognition of the limits to American military power, economic capacity, governmental prerogatives, and even the ideal of a single American dream. ✦

CHRONOLOGY

1962	Rachel Carson publishes *Silent Spring*.
	Port Huron Statement launches Students for a Democratic Society.
	Supreme Court limits vocal prayer in schools in *Engel v. Vitale*.
1965	Congress approves Wilderness Act.
	Malcolm X is assassinated.
	Residents of Watts neighborhood in Los Angeles riot.
	Immigration Reform Act allows increased immigration from outside Europe.
1967	African Americans riot in Detroit and Newark.
1968	Viet Cong launches Tet Offensive.
	James Earl Ray kills Martin Luther King Jr.
	Lyndon Johnson declines to run for reelection.
	SDS disrupts Columbia University.
	Sirhan Sirhan kills Robert Kennedy.
	Peace talks start between the United States and North Vietnam.
	Police riot against antiwar protesters during the Democratic National Convention in Chicago.
	Richard Nixon is elected president.
1969	Neil Armstrong and Buzz Aldrin walk on the moon.
1970	United States invades Cambodia.
	National Guard units kill students at Kent State and Jackson State universities.
	Earth Day is celebrated.
	Environmental Protection Agency is created.
1971	*New York Times* publishes the secret Pentagon Papers.
	President Nixon freezes wages and prices.
	Plumbers unit is established in the White House.
1972	Nixon visits China.
	United States and Soviet Union adopt SALT I.
	Operatives for Nixon's reelection campaign break into Democratic headquarters in the Watergate complex in Washington, DC.
1973	Paris accords end direct U.S. involvement in South Vietnamese war.
	United States moves to all-volunteer armed forces.
	Watergate burglars are convicted.
	Senate Watergate hearings reveal the existence of taped White House conversations.
	Spiro Agnew resigns as vice president, is replaced by Gerald Ford.
	Arab states impose an oil embargo after the third Arab-Israeli War.
1974	Nixon resigns as president, is succeeded by Gerald Ford.
1975	Communists triumph in South Vietnam.
	United States, USSR, and European nations sign the Helsinki Accords.
1976	Jimmy Carter defeats Gerald Ford for the presidency.
1978	Carter brings the leaders of Egypt and Israel to Camp David for peace talks.
	U.S. agrees to transfer control of the Panama Canal to Panama.
1979	SALT II agreement is signed but not ratified.
	OPEC raises oil prices.
	Three Mile Island nuclear plant comes close to disaster.
	Iranian militants take U.S. embassy hostages.
1980	Iranian hostage rescue fails.
	Soviet troops enter Afghanistan.
	Ronald Reagan defeats Jimmy Carter for the presidency.

THE END OF CONSENSUS

WHY DID the national consensus of the 1950s and early 1960s unravel?

at www.myhistorylab.com
The Vietnam War

Pleiku is a town in Vietnam 240 miles north of Saigon (now Ho Chi Minh City). In 1965, Pleiku was the site of a South Vietnamese army headquarters and U.S. military base. At 2:00 A.M. on February 7, Viet Cong attacked the U.S. base, killing eight Americans and wounding a hundred. President Johnson ordered retaliatory airstrikes. A month later, Johnson ordered a full-scale air offensive code-named ROLLING THUNDER. The official reason for the bombing was to pressure North Vietnam to negotiate an end to the war. In the back of President Johnson's mind were the need to prove his toughness and the mistaken assumption that China was aggressively backing North Vietnam.

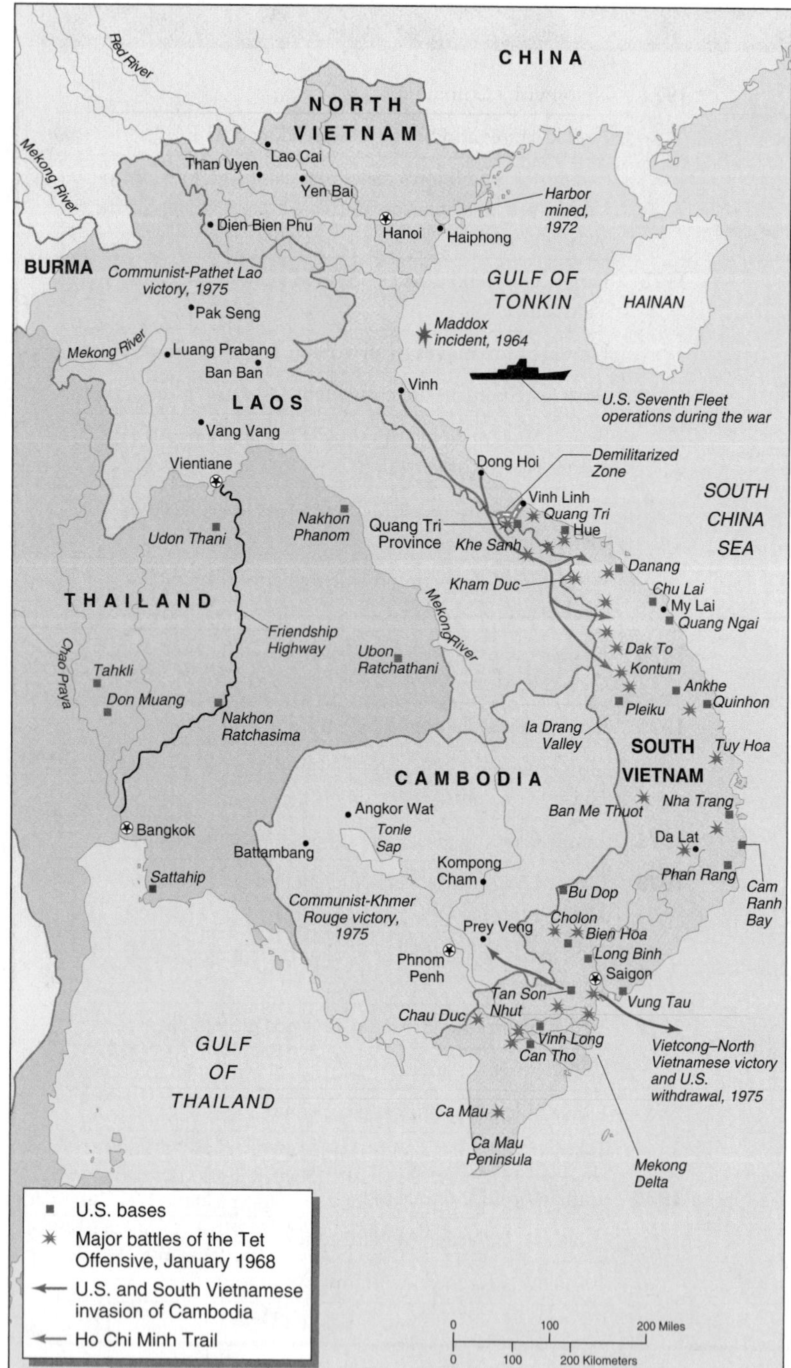

MAP 29–1 **The War in Vietnam** The United States attacked North Vietnam with air strikes but confined large-scale ground operations to South Vietnam and Cambodia. In South Vietnam, U.S. forces faced both North Vietnamese army units and Viet Cong rebels, all of whom received supplies by way of the so-called Ho Chi Minh Trail, named for the leader of North Vietnam. The coordinated attacks on cities and towns throughout South Vietnam during the Tet Offensive in 1968 surprised the United States.

Take a look at the targets of the Tet Offensive. What do the facts that there were so many of them and that they were spread out across South Vietnam tell you about the nature of the war?

The air strikes pushed the United States over the line from propping up the South Vietnamese government to leading the war effort. A president who desperately wanted a way out of Southeast Asia kept adding U.S. forces. Eventually, the war in Vietnam would distract the United States from the goals of the Great Society and drive Johnson from office. It hovered like a shadow over the next two presidents, set back progress toward global stability, and divided the American people.

Deeper into Vietnam

Lyndon Johnson faced limited options in Vietnam (see Map 29–1). The pervasive American determination to contain Communism and Kennedy's previous commitments there hemmed Johnson in. Advisers persuaded him that controlled military escalation—a middle course between withdrawal and all-out war—could secure Vietnam. They failed to understand the extent of popular opposition to the official government in Saigon and the willingness of North Vietnam to sacrifice to achieve national unity.

Rolling Thunder put the United States on the up escalator to war. Because an air campaign required ground troops to protect bases in South Vietnam, U.S. Marines landed on March 8. Over the next four months, William Westmoreland, the commander of U.S. forces in South Vietnam, wore away Johnson's desire to contain U.S. involvement. More bombs, a pause, an offer of massive U.S. aid—nothing brought North Vietnam to the negotiating table. On July 28, he finally gave Westmoreland doubled draft calls and an increase in U.S. combat troops from 75,000 to 275,000 by 1966 (see Figure 29–1). Johnson's decision turned a South Vietnamese war into a U.S. war. At the end of 1967, U.S. forces in South Vietnam totaled 485,000; they reached their maximum of 543,000 in August 1969.

The U.S. strategy on the ground was **search and destroy.** As conceived by Westmoreland, sophisticated surveillance and heavily armed patrols were used to locate enemy detachments, which could then be destroyed by air strikes, artillery, and reinforcements carried in by helicopter. The approach made sense when the opposition consisted of North Vietnamese troops and large Viet Cong units.

However, most opponents were not North Vietnamese divisions but South Vietnamese guerrillas. The Viet Cong avoided set-piece battles. Instead, they forced the United States to make repeated sweeps through farms and villages. The enemy was difficult for Americans to recognize among farmers and workers, making South Vietnamese society itself the target. The U.S. penchant for massive firepower killed thousands of Vietnamese and made millions refugees. Because the South Vietnamese government was unable to secure areas after American sweeps, the Viet Cong often reappeared after the Americans had crashed through a district.

The U.S. air war also had limited results. Pilots dropped a vast tonnage of bombs on the Ho Chi Minh Trail, a network of supply routes from North Vietnam to South Vietnam through the mountains of neighboring Laos. Despite the bombing, thousands of workers converted rough paths into roads that were repaired as soon as they were damaged. The air assault on North Vietnam itself remained "diplomatic," intended to force North Vietnam to stop intervening in the South Vietnamese civil war. Since North Vietnam's leadership considered North and South to be one country, the American goal was unacceptable. Attacking North Vietnam's poorly developed economy, the United States soon ran out of targets.

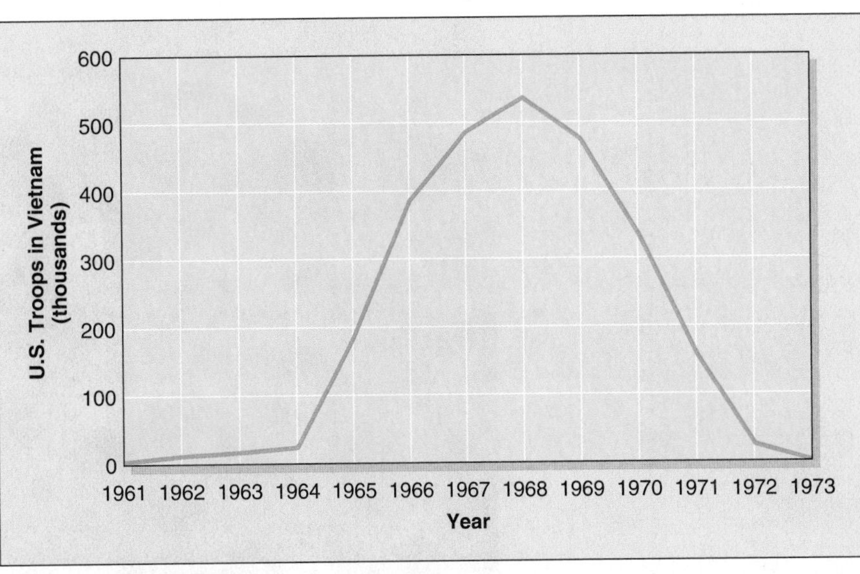

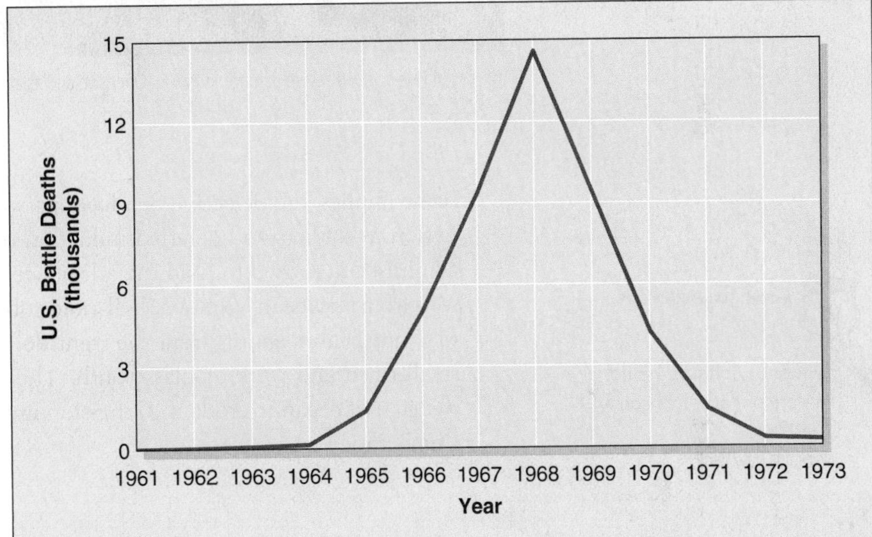

FIGURE 29–1 **The United States in Vietnam** American involvement in Vietnam grew slowly during the Kennedy administration from 1961 to 1963, expanded rapidly under Lyndon Johnson from 1964 to 1968, and fell just as rapidly under Richard Nixon from 1969 to 1973. The Nixon Doctrine tried to substitute American weapons and equipment for American military personnel but failed to prevent a North Vietnamese victory in 1975 after United States withdrawal.

Statistical Abstract of the United States.

Voices of Dissent

At home, protest against the war quickly followed the commitment of U.S. combat forces. The first national antiwar march took place in Washington on April 17, 1965. Twenty-five thousand people picketed the White House, assembled at the Washington Monument for speeches by Senator Ernest Gruening of Alaska (one of the two dissenting votes on the Gulf of Tonkin Resolution) and African American leaders, and walked up the Mall to the Capitol.

Martin Luther King Jr. offered one of the strongest condemnations of the war in a speech at New York's Riverside Church on April 4, 1967. He decried the diversion of resources from domestic programs to the military, the impact of the war on the people of Vietnam, and what he saw as the poisonous effects of warfare on the soul of America. The speech was a deeply Christian argument for policies of negotiation and reconciliation in place of war.

From protest to confrontation. In 1966 and 1967, antiwar activity changed from respectful protest to direct confrontations with what protesters called the war machine. Much of the anger was directed at the military draft administered by the **Selective Service System.** As the

search and destroy U.S. military tactic in South Vietnam, using small detachments to locate enemy units and then massive air, artillery, and ground forces to destroy them.

Selective Service System Federal agency that coordinated military conscription before and during the Vietnam War.

The city of Hue suffered severe damage in the Tet Offensive and its aftermath. Here refugees return to the rubble of bombed-out houses.

name implies, the Selective Service supposedly picked the young men who could best serve the nation as soldiers and deferred induction of those with vital skills. As the war expanded, the administration tried to hold the allegiance of the middle class by finding ways to exempt their sons from service in Vietnam. Full-time college enrollment was good for a deferment; so was the right medical diagnosis from the right doctor. As a result, draftees and enlistees tended to be small-town and working-class youth. The resentment created by the draft was an important wedge that began to erode the long-standing alliance between working-class Americans and the Democratic Party.

WHERE TO LEARN MORE

Lyndon B. Johnson National Historical Park, Johnson City, Texas
www.nps.gov/lyjo

Military service also deepened the gap between blacks and whites. The black community supplied more than its share of combat soldiers. In 1965, when African Americans made up 11 percent of the nation's population, 24 percent of the soldiers who died in Vietnam were black. This disparity forced the Defense Department to revise its combat assignments so that the racial impact was more equal in later years.

Draft resistance provided a direct avenue for protest against the war. Some young men burned the small paper cards that indicated their selective service classification, causing Congress to enact steep penalties for the act. Several thousand moved to Canada, to spend a decade or more in exile. Thousands of others described their religious and ethical opposition to war in applications for conscientious-objector classification. Much smaller numbers went to jail for refusing to cooperate in any way with the Selective Service System.

In October 1967, 100,000 people marched on the Pentagon to protest the war in Vietnam.

New Left and Community Activism

The antiwar movement was part of a growing grassroots activism that took much of its tone from the university-based **Students for a Democratic Society (SDS).** SDS tried to harness youthful disillusionment about consumerism, racism, and imperialism. It wanted to counter the trends that seemed to be turning Americans into tiny cogs in the machinery of big government, corporations, and universities. SDS thought of itself as a "New Left" that was free from the doctrinal squabbles that hampered the old left of the 1930s and 1940s.

Many of the original SDS leaders were also participants in the civil rights movement. The same was true of Mario Savio, founder of the **Free Speech Movement (FSM)** at the University of California at Berkeley in 1964. Savio hoped to build a multi-issue "community of protest" around the idea of "a free university in a free society." FSM protests climaxed with a December sit-in that led to 773 arrests and stirred protest on other campuses.

What SDS wanted to do with its grassroots organizing resembled the federal community-action programs associated with the war on poverty. The **Model Cities Program** (1966) invited residents of poor neighborhoods to write their own plans for using federal funds to improve local housing, education, health services, and job opportunities. Model Cities assemblies challenged the racial bias in programs like urban renewal and helped train community leaders.

In the 1970s and 1980s, when SDS was long gone and the Model Cities Program was fading, the lessons of grassroots reform would still be visible in alternative organizations and political movements that strengthened democracy from the bottom up. Activists staffed food cooperatives, free clinics, women's health groups, and drug-counseling centers across the country. Community-based organization was a key element in self-help efforts by African Americans, Asian Americans, and Latinos. Neighborhood associations and community-development corporations that provided affordable housing and jobs extended the "backyard revolution" into the 1980s and beyond. Social conservatives, such as antiabortionists, used the same techniques on behalf of their own agendas.

Watch the Video
at www.myhistorylab.com
Protests Against the Vietnam War

QUICK REVIEW

Opposition to the War

- Antiwar activists and students challenged the "Cold Warriors."
- In 1966 and 1967 antiwar activity intensified.
- Antiwar activists directed their anger against the Selective Service System.

Students for a Democratic Society (SDS) The leading student organization of the New Left of the early and mid-1960s.

Read the Document
at www.myhistorylab.com
Students for a Democratic Society, The Port Huron Statement (1962)

Free Speech Movement (FSM) Student movement at the University of California, Berkeley, formed in 1964 to protest limitations on political activities on campus.

Youth Culture and Counterculture

The popular context for the serious work of the New Left was the growing youth culture and **counterculture.** Millions of young people in the second half of the 1960s expressed their alienation from American society by sampling drugs or chasing the rainbow of a youth culture. The middle-aged and middle-class dubbed the rebellious young "hippies."

The youth culture took advantage of the nation's prosperity. It was consumerism in a tie-dyed T-shirt. A high point was the 1969 Woodstock rock festival in New York State. But Woodstock was an excursion, not a life-altering commitment. Members of the Woodstock Generation were consumers in a distinct market niche, dressing but not living like social reformers or revolutionaries.

Within the youth culture was a smaller and more intense counterculture that added Eastern religion, social radicalism, and evangelistic

Writer Ken Kesey and the self-defined Merry Pranksters toured the country in a brightly painted bus, parked here in San Francisco's Golden Gate Park. They sometimes threw open parties where they served punch laced with psychedelic drugs in the hope of inciting radical social change.

Model Cities Program Effort to target federal funds to upgrade public services and economic opportunity in specifically defined urban neighborhoods between 1966 and 1974.

counterculture Various alternatives to mainstream values and behaviors that became popular in the 1960s, including experimentation with psychedelic drugs, communal living, a return to the land, Asian religions, and experimental art.

QUICK REVIEW

Youth Culture and Hippies

- Millions of young people expressed their alienation from mainstream American society.
- Youth culture contained a smaller, more intense counterculture.
- A minority devoted themselves to serious social and political change.

belief in the drug LSD. San Francisco's Haight-Ashbury district became a national mecca for hippies in 1967's "Summer of Love," and hippie districts sprang up around university campuses across the country.

The cultural rebels of the late 1950s and early 1960s had been trying to combine personal freedom with new social arrangements. Many hippies were more interested in altering their minds with drugs than with politics or poetry. Serious exploration of societal alternatives was left for the minority who devoted themselves to the political work of the New Left, communal living, women's liberation, and other movements.

Sounds of Change

The youth culture was shaped by films and philosophers, by pot and poets, but above all by music. Many changes in American society are mirrored in the abrupt shift from the increasingly complacent rock-and-roll of the early 1960s to the more provocative albums of mid-decade. The songs were still aimed at popular success, but the musicians were increasingly self-conscious of themselves as artists and social critics.

At the start of the decade, the African American roots of rock-and-roll were unmistakable, but there was no social agenda. Elvis Presley and the Everly Brothers kept the messages personal. Music that criticized American society initially found a much smaller audience through the folk-music revival in a few big cities and university campuses. Singers like Pete Seeger and Joan Baez drew on white country music and old labor-organizing songs to keep alive dissenting voices.

Then, in an artistic revolution, the doors opened to a new kind of rock music. The Beatles capitalized on their immense popularity to begin a career of artistic experimentation. They also opened the way for such hard-edged British bands as the Rolling Stones and The Who to introduce social criticism and class consciousness into rock lyrics. San Francisco's new psychedelic-rock scene took its name from drugs, such as LSD, and centered on shows at the Fillmore Auditorium and performers such as the Grateful Dead, Jefferson Airplane, and Janis Joplin.

Bob Dylan, a folksinger with an acoustic guitar, "went electric" at the Newport, Rhode Island, folk festival in 1965 and further transformed the music scene. Dylan's music was musically exciting and socially critical in a way that expressed much of the discontent of American young people.

Communes and Cults

Out of the half-secular, half-spiritual vision of the counterculture came people who not only dropped out of mainstream institutions but also tried to drop into miniature societies built on new principles. Thousands of Americans in the late 1960s and 1970s formed "intentional communities" or "communes." Upper New England, the Southwest, and the West Coast were commune country where members usually tried to combine individual freedom and spontaneity with cooperative living.

A number of communes were serious endeavors. Some tried to follow spiritual leadings from Christianity or Buddhism. Others studied *The Whole Earth Catalog* (1968) to learn how to live off the land. Thousands of smaller and less conspicuous urban communes whose members occupied large old houses pursued experiments in socialism, environmentalism, or feminism. Such efforts helped to spread the ideas of organic farming, cooperative land ownership, and low-consumption environmentalism that would move into the mainstream.

at www.myhistorylab.com
National Organization for Women, Statement of Purpose (1966)

The Feminist Critique

The growing dissatisfaction of many women with their domestic roles helped set the stage for a revived feminism that was another result of the ferment of the 1960s. Important steps in this revival included the Presidential Commission on the Status of Women in 1961; the addition of

OVERVIEW Why Were We in South Vietnam?

U.S. leaders offered a number of justifications for U.S. military involvement in Vietnam. Here are some of the key arguments, with points that supported or questioned the explanation.

To Prop Up a Domino:	Communist success in South Vietnam would undermine pro-American regimes in adjacent nations, which would topple like a row of dominoes.	
	Pro	The firm U.S. stand contributed to an anti-Communist coup in Indonesia in 1965 and encouraged pro-American interests in Thailand and the Philippines.
	Con	Detailed knowledge of each nation in Southeast Asia shows that their own histories and internal issues were far more important in determining their futures than was American action in Vietnam.
To Contain China:	China's Communist regime wanted to expand its control throughout Asia.	
	Pro	The People's Republic of China was hostile to the United States, as shown in the Korean War, and had a long history of trying to control Vietnam.
	Con	North Vietnam had closer ties to the Soviet Union than to China and played the two Communist nations against each other to preserve its independence from China.
To Defeat Aggression:	South Vietnam was an independent nation threatened by invasion.	
	Pro	The major military threat to South Vietnam after 1965 came from the growing presence of the North Vietnamese army, and U.S. military intervention was necessary to counter that invasion.
	Con	The conflict in South Vietnam originated as a civil war within South Vietnam. Moreover, South and North Vietnam were a single nation, artificially divided in 1954, so that North Vietnam was trying to reunify rather than invade South Vietnam.
To Protect Democracy:	South Vietnam was a democratic nation that deserved U.S. support.	
	Pro	South Vietnam had an emerging middle class and an opportunity to develop democratic institutions.
	Con	South Vietnam was never a true democracy, ruled first by civilian dictator Ngo Dinh Diem and then a series of military strongmen.

gender as one of the categories protected by the Civil Rights Act of 1964 (see Chapter 28), and creation of the National Organization for Women (NOW) in 1966.

Mainstream feminism targeted unequal opportunity in the job market. Throughout the mid-1960s and 1970s, activists battled to open job categories to women and for equal pay for everyone with equal qualifications and responsibilities.

Changes in sexual behavior paralleled efforts to equalize treatment in the workplace. More reliable methods of contraception, especially birth-control pills introduced in the early 1960s, gave women greater control over childbearing. In some ways a replay of ideas from the 1920s, a new sexual revolution eroded the double standard that expected chastity of women but tolerated promiscuity among men. One consequence was a singles culture that accepted sexual activity between unmarried men and women.

More radical versions of the feminist message came from women who had joined the civil rights and antiwar movements only to find themselves working the copy machine and the coffeemaker while men plotted strategy. Radicals caught the attention of the national media with a demonstration against the 1968 Miss America pageant. Protesters crowned a sheep as Miss America and encouraged women to make a statement by tossing their bras and makeup in the trash.

QUICK REVIEW

The Revival of Feminism

- 1961: Presidential Commission on the Status of Women.
- 1964: Gender added to categories covered protected by Civil Rights Act of 1964.
- 1966: Creation of National Organization for Women (NOW).

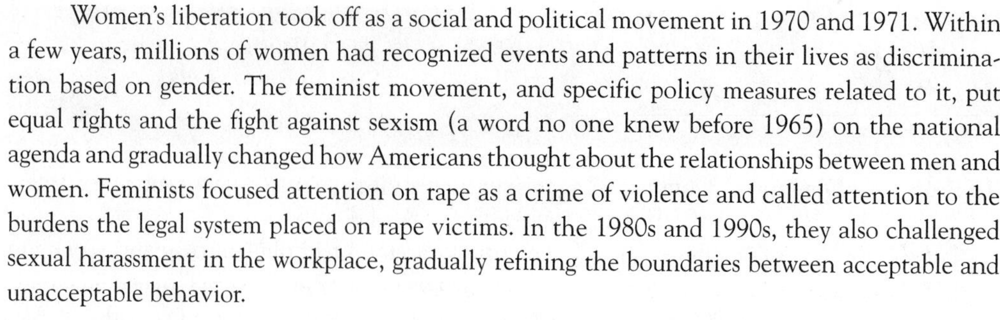

Women's liberation took off as a social and political movement in 1970 and 1971. Within a few years, millions of women had recognized events and patterns in their lives as discrimination based on gender. The feminist movement, and specific policy measures related to it, put equal rights and the fight against sexism (a word no one knew before 1965) on the national agenda and gradually changed how Americans thought about the relationships between men and women. Feminists focused attention on rape as a crime of violence and called attention to the burdens the legal system placed on rape victims. In the 1980s and 1990s, they also challenged sexual harassment in the workplace, gradually refining the boundaries between acceptable and unacceptable behavior.

Coming Out

Read the Document at **www.myhistorylab.com** *The Gay Liberation Front, Come Out (1970)*

The new militancy among gay men and lesbians drew on several of the social changes of the late 1960s and 1970s. Willingness to acknowledge and talk about nonstandard sexual behavior was part of a change in public values. Tactics of political pressure came from the antiwar and civil rights movements.

Gay activism spread from big cities to small communities, from the coasts to Middle America. New York police had long harassed gay bars and their customers. When police raided Manhattan's Stonewall Inn in June 1969, however, patrons fought back in a weekend of disorder. The **Stonewall Rebellion** was a catalyst for homosexuals to assert themselves as a political force. San Francisco also became a center of gay life.

Stonewall Rebellion On June 27, 1969, patrons fought back when police raided the gay Stonewall Inn in New York; the name refers to that event and to the increase in militancy by gay Americans that it symbolizes.

With New Yorkers and San Franciscans as examples, more and more gay men and lesbians "came out," or went public about their sexual orientation. They published newspapers, organized churches, and lobbied politicians for protection of basic civil rights such as equal access to employment, housing, and public accommodations. They staged "gay pride" days and marches. In 1974, the American Psychiatric Association eliminated homosexuality from its official list of mental disorders.

CITIES UNDER STRESS

WHAT CHALLENGES did cities face in the late 1960s and 1970s?

In the confident years after World War II, big cities had an upbeat image. By the 1970s, however, slums and squalid back streets dominated popular imagery. Movies and television reinforced the message that cities had become places of random and frequent violence.

Diagnosing an Urban Crisis

The nation entered the 1960s with the assumption that urban problems were growing pains. Exploding metropolitan areas needed money for streets, schools, and sewers. Politicians viewed the difficulties of central cities as by-products of exuberant suburban growth, which left outmoded downtowns in need of physical redevelopment.

Central cities had a special burden in caring for the domestic poor. Baltimore, for example, had 27 percent of the Maryland population in 1970 but 66 percent of the state's welfare recipients.

Many urban problems were associated with the "second ghettos" created by the migration of 2.5 million African Americans from southern farms to northern and western cities in the 1950s and 1960s. By 1970, one-third of all African Americans lived in the 12 largest cities, crowding into ghetto neighborhoods dating from World War II.

Read the Document at **www.myhistorylab.com** *Toi Derricotte, Black in a White Neighborhood, 1977–1978*

At the end of their journeys, postwar black migrants found systems of race relations that limited their access to decent housing, the best schools, and many unionized jobs. Many families arrived just in time to face the consequences of industrial layoffs and plant closures in the 1970s and 1980s. Already unneeded in the South because of the mechanization of agriculture, the migrants found themselves equally unwanted in the industrial North, caught in decaying neighborhoods and victimized by crime.

Central cities faced additional financial problems unrelated to poverty and race. Many of their roads, bridges, fire stations, and water mains were 50 to 100 years old by the 1960s and 1970s, and they were wearing out. Decay of urban utility and transportation systems was a by-product of market forces and public policy. Private developers often borrowed money saved through northeastern bank accounts, insurance policies, and pension funds to finance new construction in sunbelt suburbs. The defense budget pumped tax dollars from the old industrial cities into the South and West.

QUICK REVIEW

Urban Problems

- Minorities and the poor were concentrated in urban centers.
- Postwar black migrants to the north found themselves with limited access to better houses, schools, and jobs.
- Cities faced decaying infrastructure and high taxes.

Conflict in the Streets

African Americans and Hispanics who rioted in city streets in the mid-1960s were fed up with the lack of job opportunities, with substandard housing, and with crime. Riots in Rochester, Harlem, and Brooklyn in July 1964 opened four years of racial violence. Before they subsided, the riots had scarred most big cities and killed 200 people, most of them African Americans.

The explosion of the Watts neighborhood in Los Angeles fixed the danger of racial unrest in the public mind. Trouble started on August 11, 1965, when a white highway-patrol officer arrested a young African American for drunken driving. Loud complaints drew a crowd, and the arrival of Los Angeles police turned the bystanders into an angry mob that attacked passing cars. The primary targets were symbols of white authority and businesses with reputations for exploiting their customers, a conclusion reached by the National Advisory Commission on Civil Disorders. Rioting, looting, and arson spread through Watts for two days until the National Guard cordoned off the trouble spots and occupied the neighborhood on August 14 and 15. After Watts, Americans expected "long hot summers" and got them. Scores of cities suffered riots in 1966, including a riot by Puerto Ricans in Chicago that protested the same problems blacks faced. The following year, the worst violence was in Newark, New Jersey, and in Detroit, where 43 deaths and blocks of blazing buildings stunned television viewers.

Few politicians wanted to admit that African Americans and Hispanics had serious grievances. Their impulse was to blame riffraff and outside agitators. This theory was wrong. Almost all participants were neighborhood residents. Except that they were younger, they were representative of the African American population, and their violence came from the frustration of rising expectations. Despite the political gains of the civil rights movement, unemployment remained high, and the police still treated all blacks as potential criminals. The urban riots were political actions to force the problems of African Americans onto the national agenda.

Minority Self-Determination

Minority separatism and demands for self-determination tapped the same anger that fueled the urban riots. Drawing on a long heritage of militancy (such as armed resistance during racial riots), activists challenged the central goal of the civil rights movement, which sought full integration and participation in American life. The phrase **Black Power,** popularized by SNCC leader Stokely Carmichael, summed up the new alternative.

Black Power Philosophy emerging after 1965 that real economic and political gains for African Americans could come only through self-help, self-determination, and organizing for direct political influence.

The slogans of Black Power, Brown Power, and Red Power spanned goals that ran from civil rights to cultural pride to revolutionary separatism. They were all efforts by minorities to define themselves through their own heritage and backgrounds, not simply by looking in the mirror of white society.

Read the Document at www.myhistorylab.com
Stokely Carmichael and Charles V. Hamilton, from Black Power: The Politics of Liberation in America (1967)

Nation of Islam Religious movement among black Americans that emphasizes self-sufficiency, self-help, and separation from white society.

Black Panthers Political and social movement among black Americans, founded in Oakland, California, in 1966 and emphasizing black economic and political power.

Expressions of Black Power. Black Power translated many ways—control of one's own community through the voting machine, celebration of the African American heritage, creation of a parallel society that shunned white institutions.

Black Power also meant increased interest in the **Nation of Islam,** or Black Muslims, who combined a version of Islam with radical separatism. They called for self-discipline, support of black institutions and businesses, and total rejection of whites. The Nation of Islam appealed to blacks who saw no future in integration and was strongest in northern cities where it offered an alternative to the life of the streets.

In the early 1960s, Malcolm X emerged as a leading Black Muslim. Growing up as Malcolm Little, he was a street-wise criminal until he converted to the Nation of Islam in prison. After his release, Malcolm preached that blacks should stop letting whites set the terms by which they judged their appearance, communities, and accomplishments. He emphasized the African cultural heritage and economic self-help and proclaimed himself an extremist for black rights. In the last year of his life, however, he returned from a pilgrimage to Mecca willing to consider limited acceptance of whites. Rivals within the movement assassinated him in February 1965, but his ideas lived on in *The Autobiography of Malcolm X*.

The **Black Panthers** pursued similar goals. Bobby Seale and Huey Newton grew up in the Oakland, California, area and met as college students. They saw African American ghettos as internal colonies in need of self-determination and asserted their equality. They shadowed police patrols to prevent mistreatment of African Americans and carried weapons into the California State Legislature in May 1967 to protest gun control. The Panthers also promoted community-based self-help efforts, such as a free-breakfast program for school children and medical clinics, and ran political candidates.

In contrast to the rioters in Watts, the Panthers had a political program, if not the ability to carry it through. Panther chapters imploded when they attracted shakedown artists as well as visionaries. Nevertheless, they survived as a political organization into the 1970s, and former Panther Bobby Rush entered Congress in 1992.

Hispanic activism in the Southwest. Latinos in the Southwest developed their own Brown Power movement in the late 1960s. Led by Reies López Tijerina, Hispanics in rural New Mexico demanded the return of lands that had been lost to Anglo Americans despite the guarantees of the Treaty of Guadalupe Hidalgo in 1848. Mexican Americans in the 1970s organized for political power in southern Texas communities where they were a majority.

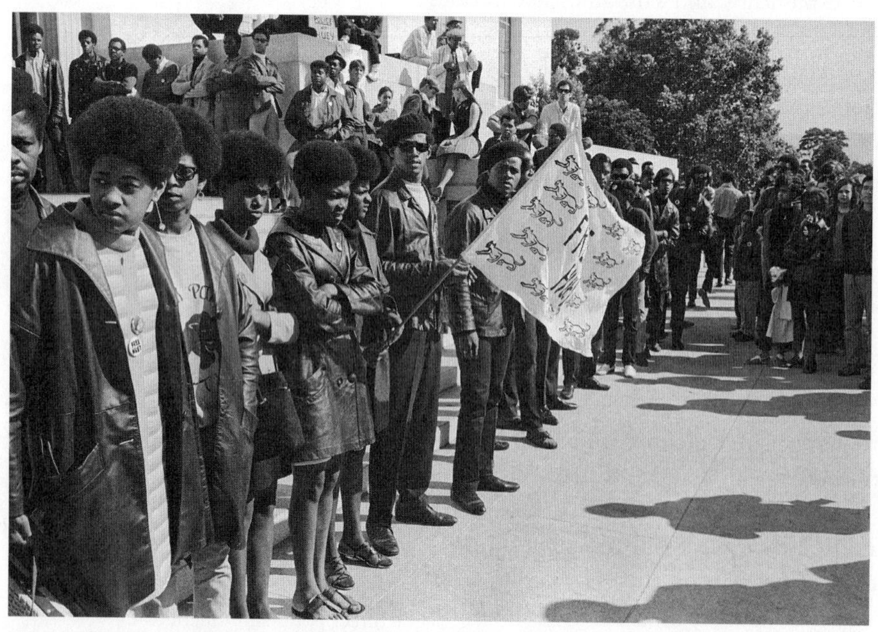

Members of the Black Panthers assemble outside the Alameda County Courthouse in Oakland, California, on July, 15, 1968, as Panther leader Huey Newton goes on trial for killing a police officer.

The best-known Hispanic activism combined social protest with the crusading spirit of earlier labor union organizing campaigns. Cesar Chavez organized the multiracial United Farm Workers (UFW) among Mexican American agricultural workers in California in 1965. Chavez was committed both to nonviolent action for social justice and to the labor movement. UFW demands included better wages and safer working conditions, such as less exposure to pesticides. Because farmworkers were not covered by the National Labor Relations Act, there was no established mechanism to force growers to recognize the union as a bargaining agent. Chavez supplemented work stoppages with national boycotts against table grapes, making *la huelga* ("the strike") a cause for urban liberals.

Native Americans assert their identity. Native Americans also fought both for equal access to American society and to preserve cultural traditions through tribal institutions. Like efforts to secure rights and opportunities for African Americans and Latinos, the "Red Power" movement had deep roots in efforts to reverse the termination policy of the 1950s and to secure economic improvements for reservations. Indians in cities like Los Angeles and Portland came together across tribal lines to develop social and cultural services. One result of this political work came in 1968, when Congress restored the authority of tribal law on reservations. Three years later the Alaska Native Claims Settlement Act granted native Alaskans 44 million acres and $963 million to settle claims for their ancestral lands. Legally sophisticated tribes sued for compensation and enforcement of treaty provisions, such as fishing rights in the Pacific Northwest. Larger tribes established their own colleges, such as Navajo Community College (1969) and Oglala Lakota College (1971).

A second development was media-oriented protests that asserted Red Power. One of the earliest was a series of "fish-ins" in which Indians from Washington state, helped by the multitribal National Indian Youth Council, exercised treaty-based fishing rights in defiance of state regulations. Native American students gained national attention by seizing the abandoned Alcatraz Island for a cultural and educational center (1969–1971). Indians in Minneapolis created the **American Indian Movement (AIM)** in 1968 to increase economic opportunity and stop police mistreatment. AIM participated in the cross-country Broken Treaties Caravan, which climaxed by occupying the Bureau of Indian Affairs in Washington in 1972. AIM also allied with Sioux traditionalists on the Pine Ridge Reservation in South Dakota against the tribe's elected government. In 1973, they took over the village of Wounded Knee, where the U.S. Army in 1890 had massacred 300 Indians. They held out for 70 days before leaving peacefully.

Cesar Chavez and Helen Chavez lead a march in support of striking farmworkers near Delano, California, in April 1966. The Delano strike was a milestone in the struggle of Mexican Americans for economic opportunity. It was also part of a shift in the focus of the labor movement from the old industrial states to the fast-growing West and South.

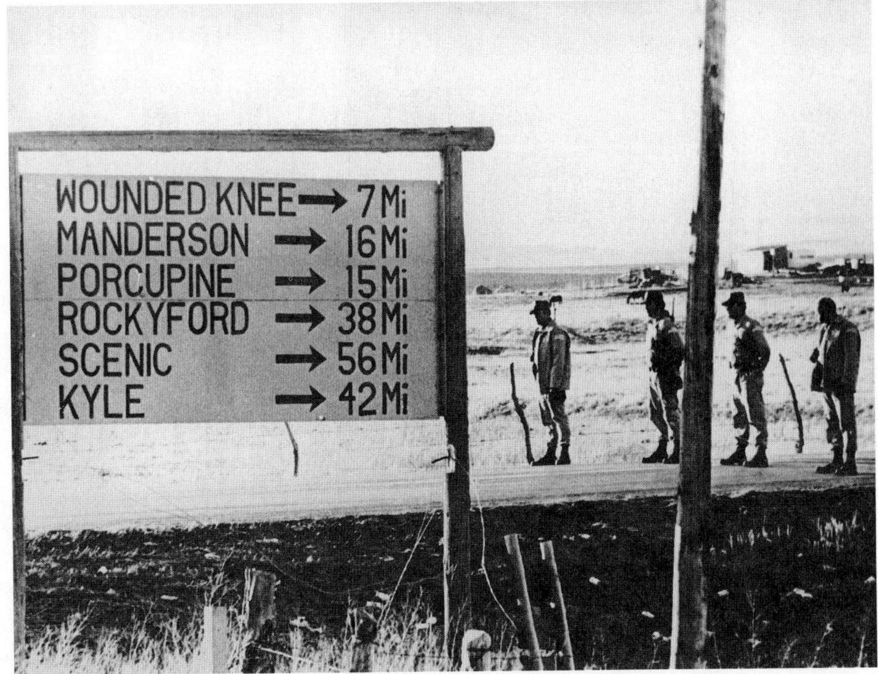

Armed confrontation between militant Indians and state and federal law enforcement at Wounded Knee, South Dakota, in 1973 recalled the decades of warfare between Plains tribes and the U.S. Army in the previous century.

Suburban Independence: The Outer City

In the mid-1960s, the United States became a suburban nation. The 1970 census found more people living in the suburban counties of metropolitan areas (37 percent) than in central cities (31 percent) or in small towns and rural areas (31 percent). Just after World War II, most new suburbs had been bedroom communities that depended on the jobs, services, and shopping of central cities. By the

Read the Document at **www.myhistorylab.com**
Exploring America: The American Indian Movement

American Indian Movement (AIM) Group of Native American political activists who used confrontations with the federal government to publicize their case for Indian rights.

Baker v. Carr U.S. Supreme Court decision in 1962 that allowed federal courts to review the appointment of state legislative districts and established the principle that such districts should have roughly equal populations ("one person, one vote").

Swann v. Charlotte-Mecklenburg Board of Education U.S. Supreme Court decision in 1971 that upheld cross-city busing to achieve the racial integration of public schools.

late 1960s, suburbs were evolving into "outer cities," whose inhabitants had little need for the old central city.

Suburban economic growth and political influence. Suburbs captured most new jobs, leaving the urban poor with few opportunities for employment. In the 15 largest metropolitan areas, the number of central city jobs fell by 800,000 in the 1960s, while the number of suburban jobs rose by 3.2 million. Suburban rings gained a growing share of public facilities intended to serve the entire metropolitan area. As pioneered in California, community colleges served the suburban children of the baby boom.

Suburban political power grew along with economic clout. In 1962, the Supreme Court handed down a landmark decision in the case of ***Baker v. Carr.*** Overturning laws that treated counties or other political subdivisions as the units to be represented in state legislatures, *Baker* required that legislative seats be apportioned on the basis of population. The principle of "one person, one vote" broke the stranglehold of rural counties on state governments, but the big beneficiaries were not older cities, but fast-growing suburbs. By 1975, suburbanites held the largest block of seats in the House of Representatives. Reapportionment in 1982, based on the 1980 census, produced a House that was even more heavily suburban.

School busing controversies. School integration controversies in the 1970s reinforced a tendency for suburbanites to separate themselves from city problems. In ***Swann v. Charlotte-Mecklenburg Board of Education*** (1971), the U.S. Supreme Court held that crosstown busing was an acceptable solution to the *de facto* segregation that resulted from residential patterns within a single school district. When school officials around the country failed to achieve racial balance, federal judges ordered their own busing plans. Although integration through busing occurred peacefully in dozens of cities, many white people resented the practice. Working-class students in cities like Boston who depended on public schools found themselves on the front lines of integration, while many middle-class families switched to private education.

Because the Supreme Court also ruled that busing programs normally stopped at school-district boundaries, suburbs with independent districts escaped school integration. One result was to make busing self-defeating, for it led white families to move out of the integrating school district. Others placed their children in private academies, as happened frequently in the South. The political separation of suburbs from city thus allowed white suburbanites to think of themselves as defending local control rather than privilege.

THE YEAR OF THE GUN, 1968

HOW DID the Tet Offensive change American public opinion about the war in Vietnam?

Some years are turning points that force society to reconsider its basic assumptions. In 1914, the violence of World War I undermined Europe's belief in progress. In 1933, Americans had to rethink the role of government. In 1968, mainstream Americans increasingly turned against the war in Vietnam, student protest and youth counterculture turned ugly, and political consensus shattered.

The Tet Offensive

At the end of 1967, U.S. officials were overconfidently predicting victory. Then, at the beginning of Tet, the Vietnamese New Year, the Viet Cong attacked 36 of 44 provincial capitals and the national capital, Saigon. They hit the U.S. embassy and reached the runways of Tan Son Nhut air base. If the United States was winning, the Tet Offensive should not have been possible.

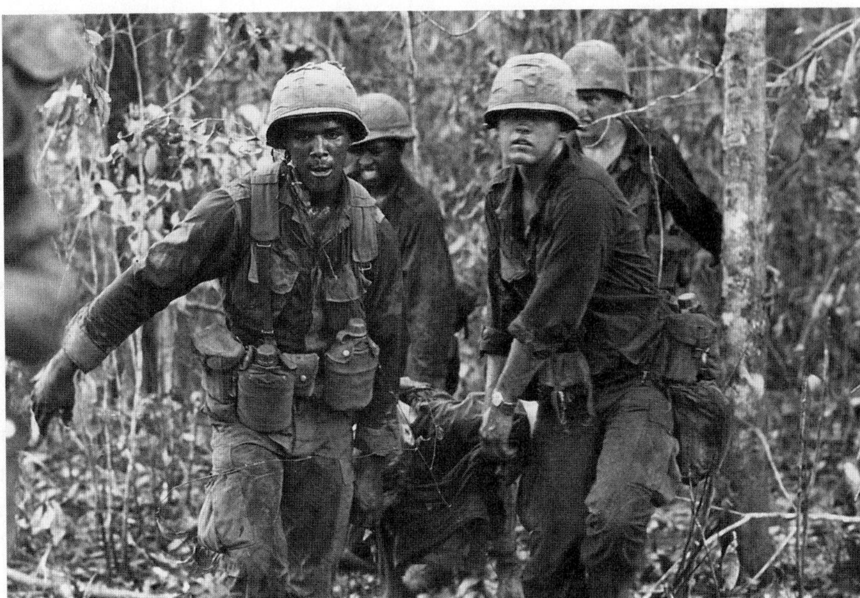
GIs evacuate a wounded comrade from fighting near the border between Vietnam and Cambodia.

As a military effort, the attacks failed. U.S. and South Vietnamese troops repulsed the attacks and cleared the cities. But the offensive was a psychological blow that convinced the American public that the war was quicksand. Television coverage of the Tet battles made the bad publicity worse. At least until Tet, the commentary from network news anchors had supported the U.S. effort, but the pictures undermined civilian morale. A handful of images stayed in people's memories—a Buddhist monk burning himself to death in protest; a child with flesh peeled off by napalm; a South Vietnamese official executing a captive on the streets of Saigon.

In the wake of the Tet crisis, General Westmoreland's request for 200,000 more troops forced a political and military reevaluation. Clark Clifford, a dedicated Cold Warrior, was the new secretary of defense. Now he had second thoughts. Twenty "wise men"—the big names of the Cold War—told the president that the war was unwinnable on terms acceptable to America's allies and to many Americans. The best option, the wise men told LBJ, was disengagement.

QUICK REVIEW

The Tet Offensive

- January 30, 1968: Viet Cong attacked cities across Vietnam.
- As a military effort, the offensive failed.
- The attack shook American confidence that the war was winnable.

LBJ's Exit

The president was already in political trouble. After other prominent Democrats held back, Minnesota's liberal senator Eugene McCarthy had decided to challenge Johnson in the presidential primaries. Because he controlled the party organizations in two-thirds of the states, Johnson did not need the primary states for renomination and ignored the first primary in New Hampshire. McCarthy won a startling 42 percent of the popular vote and 20 of 24 delegates in the New Hampshire primary. The vote was a protest against Johnson's Vietnam policy rather than a clear mandate for peace. Nevertheless, the vote proved that the political middle would no longer hold. By showing Johnson's vulnerability, New Hampshire also drew Robert Kennedy into the race. The younger brother of JFK, Kennedy could be arrogant and abrasive, but he was more successful than other mainstream politicians in touching the hearts of Hispanic and African American voters.

Facing political challenges and an unraveling war, on March 31, 1968, Johnson announced a halt to most bombing of North Vietnam, opening the door for peace negotiations that formally began in May 1969. He then astounded the country by withdrawing from the presidential race. It was a statesmanlike act by a man who had been consumed by a war he did not want, had never understood, and could not end.

Violence and Politics: King, Kennedy, and Chicago

Johnson's dramatic withdrawal was followed by the violent disruption of U.S. politics through assassination and riot. On April 4, 1968, an ex-convict, James Earl Ray, shot and killed Martin Luther King Jr. as he stood on the balcony of a Memphis motel. King was in Memphis to support striking city workers, an example of his increasing emphasis on economic justice and equality as

GLOBAL CONNECTIONS

Red Spring, 1968

Columbia University in New York City was in turmoil in the spring of 1968. Its African American students and its SDS chapter had several grievances. One was the university's cooperation with the Pentagon-funded Institute for Defense Analysis. Another was its plan to build a gymnasium on park land that might better serve the residents of Harlem. Some students wanted changes in university policy, others a confrontation that would recruit new radicals. They occupied five university buildings, including the library and the president's office, for a week in April until police evicted them. A student strike and additional clashes with the authorities lasted until June.

The "battle of Morningside Heights" (the location of Columbia) generated banner headlines in the United States, but it was tame when compared to events in Europe. During the same "red spring," demonstrations and revolts by angry university students and workers created upheaval on both sides of the Iron Curtain. Examples of rebellion traveled back and forth across the Atlantic in news stories and television clips, connecting the unrest as a global phenomenon.

In the months that followed the Tet crisis, much of the industrial world was in ferment. Students rioted in Italy and Berlin over rigid university systems, the Vietnam War, and the power of multinational corporations. Workers and students protested against the Franco regime in Spain. In Paris, student demonstrations against the Vietnam War turned into attacks on the university system and the French government. Students fought police in the Paris streets in the first days of May with the approval of a majority of Parisians. Radical industrial workers called a general strike. The government nearly toppled before the disturbance subsided.

Grassroots rebellion also shook the Soviet grip on eastern Europe. University students in Poland protested the stifling of political discussion. Alexander Dubcek, the new leader of the Czech Communist Party, brought together students and the middle class around reforms that caused people to talk about the "Prague Spring"—a blossoming of democracy inside the Soviet bloc. Here the changes went too far. As Czechs pressed for more and more political freedom, the Soviet Union feared losing control of one of its satellites. On August 21, 500,000 troops from the USSR and other Warsaw Pact nations rolled across the border and forced Czechoslovakia back into line.

- What common factors might help explain student unrest on both sides of the Iron Curtain?

well as civil rights. King's death was the product of pure racial hatred, and it triggered a climactic round of violence in black ghettos. Fires devastated the West Side of Chicago and downtown Washington, DC. The army guarded the steps of the Capitol, ready to protect Congress from its fellow citizens.

The shock of King's death was still fresh when another political assassination stunned the nation. On June 5, Robert Kennedy won California's primary election. He was still behind Vice President Hubert Humphrey in the delegate count but coming on strong. As Kennedy walked out of the ballroom at his headquarters in the Ambassador Hotel in Los Angeles, a Jordanian immigrant named Sirhan Sirhan put a bullet in his brain. Sirhan may have wanted revenge for America's tilt toward Israel in that country's victorious Six-Day War with Egypt and Jordan in 1967.

QUICK REVIEW

The 1968 Democratic Convention

- August 26–29: Democrats meet to nominate Hubert Humphrey.
- Antiwar protesters plan to march on the convention hall.
- Undisciplined police helped precipitate violence between the police and the protesters.

Kennedy's death ensured the Democratic nomination for Humphrey, a liberal who had loyally supported Johnson's war policy. After his nomination, Humphrey faced the Republican Richard Nixon and the Independent George Wallace. Nixon positioned himself as the candidate of the political middle. Wallace appealed to southern whites and working-class northerners who feared black militancy and hated "the ivory-tower folks with pointy heads."

Both got great help from the Democratic Convention, held in Chicago on August 26–29. While Democrats feuded among themselves, Chicago Mayor Richard Daley and his police department monitored antiwar protesters. The National Mobilization Committee to End the War in Vietnam drew from the New Left and from older peace activists—sober and committed people who had fought against nuclear weapons in the 1950s and the Vietnam War throughout the 1960s. They wanted to embarrass the Johnson-Humphrey administration by marching to the convention hall on nomination night. Mixed in were the Yippies, an informal group who planned to attract young people to Chicago with the promise of street theater, media events, and confrontation that would puncture the pretenions of the power structure. To the extent they had a program, it was to use the youth culture to attract converts to radical politics.

The volatile mix was ready for a spark. On August 28, the same night that Democratic delegates were nominating Humphrey, tensions exploded in a police riot. Protesters and Yippies had congregated in Grant Park, across Michigan Avenue from downtown hotels. Undisciplined police waded into the crowds with clubs and tear gas. Young people fought back with rocks and bottles. Television caught the hours of violence that ended when the National Guard separated police from demonstrators. For Humphrey, the convention was a catastrophe, alienating liberal Democrats and associating Democrats with disorder in the public mind.

The election was closer than Humphrey had any right to hope (see Map 29–2). Election day gave Wallace 13.5 percent of the popular vote, Humphrey 42.7 percent of the popular vote and 191 electoral votes, and Nixon 43.4 percent of the popular vote and 301 electoral votes.

The Wallace candidacy was a glimpse of the future. The national media saw Wallace in terms of bigotry and a backlash against civil rights, getting only part of the story. Many of Wallace's northern backers were unhappy with both parties. Liberal on economic issues but conservative on family and social issues, many of these working-class voters evolved into "Reagan Democrats" by the 1980s. In the South, Wallace was a transitional choice for conservative voters who would eventually transfer their allegiance from the Democratic to the Republican Party.

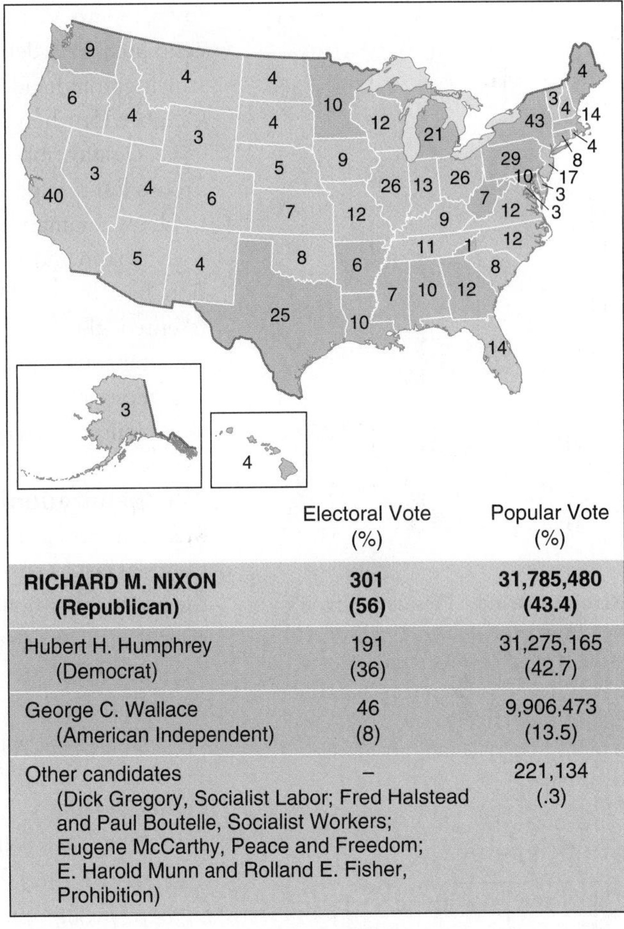

	Electoral Vote (%)	Popular Vote (%)
RICHARD M. NIXON (Republican)	**301 (56)**	**31,785,480 (43.4)**
Hubert H. Humphrey (Democrat)	191 (36)	31,275,165 (42.7)
George C. Wallace (American Independent)	46 (8)	9,906,473 (13.5)
Other candidates (Dick Gregory, Socialist Labor; Fred Halstead and Paul Boutelle, Socialist Workers; Eugene McCarthy, Peace and Freedom; E. Harold Munn and Rolland E. Fisher, Prohibition)	–	221,134 (.3)

MAP 29–2 **The Election of 1968** Richard Nixon won the presidency with the help of George Wallace, the American Independent Party candidate. Wallace won several southern states, offering an alternative to white southerners unhappy with the Democratic Party but not yet prepared to vote Republican. He also drew northern working-class votes away from Hubert Humphrey and thus helped Nixon to take several midwestern states.

How does this map help explain the shift of the South to the Republican Party over the course of the 1970s?

NIXON, WATERGATE, AND THE CRISIS OF THE EARLY 1970s

WHAT WAS the legacy of Richard Nixon's presidency?

The new president was an unlikely politician, ill at ease in public and consumed by a sense of inferiority. His painful public presence and dishonesty have tended to obscure his administration's accomplishments. He reduced tensions in the Cold War. He reluctantly upgraded civil rights enforcement, set goals for minority hiring by federal contractors, and presided over impressive environmental legislation.

GETTING OUT OF VIETNAM, 1969–1975

After 1968, things got worse in Southeast Asia before they got better. Despite his claims during the campaign, Nixon had no secret plan to end the war. Opposition intensified with the revelation that U.S. soldiers in March 1968 had slaughtered hundreds of men, women, and children

at **www.myhistorylab.com**
The Vietnam War

in the South Vietnamese village of My Lai after failing to find any Viet Cong. This crime accentuated the dehumanizing power of war and showed how far the United States was straying from its ideals. Protests at home culminated in 1969 with the Vietnam Moratorium on October 15, when 2 million protesters joined rallies across the country.

Disaffection also mounted in Vietnam. Racial tensions sapped morale on the front lines. Troops lost discipline, took drugs, and hunkered down waiting for their tours of duty to end, and the high command had to adapt its code of justice to keep an army on the job.

Nixon and Vice President Spiro Agnew responded by trying to isolate the antiwar opposition, but Nixon also reduced the role of U.S. ground forces. Nixon claimed that his policies represented "the great silent majority of my fellow Americans." The administration arranged for a "spontaneous" attack by construction workers on antiwar protesters in New York. The hard-hat counterattack was a cynically manipulated symbol, but Nixon and Agnew tapped genuine anger about failure in Asia and rapid change in U.S. society.

"Vietnamization" and the secret war against Cambodia. Nixon's secretary of defense, Melvin Laird, responded to the antiwar sentiment with "Vietnamization," withdrawing U.S. troops as fast as possible without undermining the South Vietnamese government. In July 1969, the president announced the **Nixon Doctrine.** The United States would help other countries fight their wars with weapons and money but not with soldiers. The policy substituted machines for men. Americans rearmed and enlarged the South Vietnamese army and surreptitiously bombed Communist bases in neutral Cambodia.

Nixon Doctrine President Nixon's new American policy (1969) toward Asia in which the United States would honor treaty commitments but would gradually disengage and expect Asian nations to handle military defense on their own.

The secret war against Cambodia culminated on April 30, 1970, with an invasion. The aim was to smash Viet Cong and North Vietnamese bases to allow time to rebuild the South Vietnamese army. Americans who had hoped that the war was fading away were outraged. At Kent State University in Ohio, the National Guard was called in to maintain order. Taunts, tossed bottles, and the recent record of violence put them on edge. On May 4, one unit fired on a group of young people and killed four of them. At Jackson State University in Mississippi, two students were killed when troops fired on their dormitory.

QUICK REVIEW

The Nixon Doctrine

- Nixon responded to antiwar protesters by reducing the role of U.S. ground forces in Vietnam.
- "Vietnamization": The withdrawal of U.S. troops as fast as possible without undermining the South Vietnamese government.
- The Nixon Doctrine substituted weapons and money for troops.

Stalemate and cease-fire. The Cambodian "incursion" extended the military stalemate in Vietnam to U.S. policy. Beginning in December 1969, a new lottery system for determining the order of draft calls by birthdate let two-thirds of young men know they would not be drafted. In December 1970, Congress repealed the Gulf of Tonkin Resolution and prohibited the use of U.S. ground troops outside South Vietnam. Cambodia, however, was already devastated. The U.S. invasion had destabilized its government and opened the way for the bloodthirsty Khmer Rouge, who killed millions of Cambodians in the name of a working-class revolution. Vietnamization continued; only 90,000 U.S. ground troops were still in Vietnam by early 1972. A final air offensive in December smashed Hanoi into rubble and helped to force four and a half years of peace talks to a conclusion.

The cease-fire began on January 27, 1973. It confirmed U.S. withdrawal from Vietnam. North Vietnamese and Viet Cong forces would remain in control of the territory they occupied in South Vietnam, but they were not to be reinforced or substantially reequipped. The United States promised not to increase its military aid to South Vietnam. There were no solid guarantees for the South Vietnamese government. Immediately after coming to terms with North Vietnam, Nixon suspended the draft in favor of an all-volunteer military.

In 1975, South Vietnam collapsed. Only the U.S. presence had kept its political, ethnic, and religious factions together. For the first two years after the Paris agreement, North Vietnam quietly rebuilt its military capacity. In the spring of 1975, it opened an offensive, and South Vietnamese morale evaporated. Resistance crumbled so rapidly that the United States had to evacuate its embassy in Saigon by helicopter while frantic Vietnamese tried to join the flight.

Nixon and the Wider World

To his credit, Richard Nixon took U.S. foreign policy in new directions even while he was struggling to escape from Vietnam and Cambodia. Like Dwight Eisenhower before him, Nixon's reputation as an anti-Communist allowed him to improve relations with China and the Soviet Union. Indeed, he hoped to distract the American people from frustration in Southeast Asia with accomplishments elsewhere.

One of the first triumphs was a legacy from previous administrations. On July 20, 1969, Buzz Aldrin and Neil Armstrong successfully landed on the moon. Their *Apollo 11* expedition combined science and Cold War politics. The American flag that they planted on the lunar surface represented victory in one phase of the space race between the United States and the Soviet Union. The National Aeronautics and Space Administration had been working since 1961 to meet John F. Kennedy's goal of a manned trip to the moon before the end of the decade.

Closer to home, Nixon and Henry Kissinger, his national security adviser (and later secretary of state), shared what they considered a realistic view of foreign affairs. For both men, foreign policy was not about crusades or moral stands. It was about the balance of world economic and military power. With the United States weakened by the Vietnam War and the Soviets worried by the rise of China, the time was ripe to move toward a new balance among the three nations.

Since 1950, the United States had acted as if China did not exist, refusing economic relations and insisting that the Nationalist regime on Taiwan was the legitimate Chinese government. But the People's Republic of China was increasingly isolated within the Communist world. In 1969, it almost went to war with the Soviet Union. Nixon was eager to take advantage of Chinese-Soviet tension. Secret talks led to an easing of the American trade embargo in April 1971 and a tour of China by a U.S. table-tennis team. Henry Kissinger, Nixon's national security adviser, then arranged for Nixon's startling visit to Mao Zedong in Beijing in February 1972.

Strategic Arms Limitation Treaty (SALT) Treaty signed in 1972 by the United States and the Soviet Union to slow the nuclear arms race.

détente (French for "easing of tension") Used to describe the new U.S. relations with China and the Soviet Union in 1972.

Playing the "China card" helped to improve relations with the Soviet Union. The Soviets needed increased trade with the United States and a counterweight to China, the United States was looking for help in getting out of Vietnam, and both countries wanted to limit nuclear armaments. Protracted negotiations led to the **Strategic Arms Limitation Treaty (SALT)** that Nixon signed in Moscow in May 1972. The agreements blocked the creation of extensive antiballistic missiles systems (ABMs) but failed to limit bombers, cruise missiles, or multiple independently targeted warheads on single missiles.

Diplomats used the French word ***détente*** to describe the new U.S. relations with China and the Soviet Union. *Détente* means an easing of tensions, not friendship or alliance. It facilitated travel between the United States and China. It allowed U.S. farmers to sell wheat to the Soviets. More broadly, *détente* implied that the United States and China recognized mutual interests in Asia and that the United States acknowledged the Soviet Union as an equal in world affairs. *Détente* made the world safer.

Richard Nixon and Secretary of State William Rogers on the Great Wall during Nixon's historic visit to China.

Courting Middle America

Nixon designed domestic policy to help him win reelection. His goal was to solidify his "Middle American" support. The strategy targeted the growing populations of the South and the suburbs, as well as blue-collar voters who were ready to abandon the Democrats for law-and-order Republicans.

New Federalism President Richard Nixon's policy to shift responsibilities of government programs from the federal level to the states.

The Nixon White House preferred to ignore troubled big cities. Instead, Nixon tilted federal assistance to the suburbs. The centerpiece of his **New Federalism** was General Revenue Sharing (1972), which passed federal funds directly to local governments with no limits on use. By 1980, it had transferred more than $18 billion to the states and more than $36 billion to local governments. Revenue sharing was a suburban-aid program. Its no-strings grants supplemented the general funds of every full-service government, whether a city of 2 million or a suburban town of 500.

Nixon hoped to move cautiously in enforcing school desegregation, but a task force led by Secretary of Labor George Shultz crafted an approach that allowed substantial desegregation. In this instance, as elsewhere with his domestic policies, Nixon was inflammatory in speeches but moderate in action, increasing the funding of federal civil rights agencies.

Oil, OPEC, and Stagflation

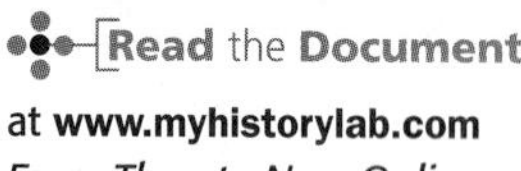
Read the Document at www.myhistorylab.com *From Then to Now Online: Energy Worries*

One of the most troublesome domestic issues was inflation. The cost of living began to outpace wages in the late 1960s. One of the causes was LBJ's decision to fight in Vietnam without tax increases until 1968. An income tax cut in 1969, supported by both parties, made the situation worse. Inflation eroded the value of savings and pensions. It also made U.S. goods too expensive for foreign buyers and generated a trade deficit that placed pressures on the international value of the dollar.

The U.S. economy took another hit from inflation in 1973–1974. The main cause was the sharp increase in the price of energy, an input to every product and service. Angry at U.S. support for Israel in the Arab-Israeli War of October 1973, Arab nations imposed an embargo on oil exports that lasted from October 1973 to March 1974. The shortages eased when the embargo ended, but the **Organization of Petroleum Exporting Countries (OPEC)** had challenged the ability of the industrial nations to dictate world economic policy.

Organization of Petroleum Exporting Countries (OPEC) Cartel of oil-producing nations in Asia, Africa, and Latin America that gained substantial power over the world economy in the mid- to late 1970s by controlling the production and price of oil.

While Nixon searched for short-term political advantage, underlying problems of the U.S. economy went untreated. After 30 years at the top, the United States could no longer dominate the world economy by itself. The newly found power of OPEC was obvious. Just as important was the surging industrial capacity of Germany and Japan, which now had economies as modern as that of the United States. Declining rates of saving and investment in industrial capacity seemed to put the United States in danger of following the British road to economic obsolescence and second-level status. Indeed, a new term entered the popular vocabulary in 1971: *Stagflation* was the painful combination of stagnant economic growth, high unemployment, and inflation that matched no one's economic theory but everyone's daily experience.

QUICK REVIEW

Causes of Inflation in the Early 1970s

- LBJ's decision to fight in Vietnam without tax increases until 1968.
- An income tax cut in 1969.
- Increasing oil prices.

Americans as Environmentalists

In the turbulent 1970s, Americans found one issue they could agree on. In the 1970s, resource conservation grew into a multifaceted environmental movement.

After the booming 1950s, Americans had started to pay attention to "pollution," a catchall for the damage that advanced technologies and industrial production did to natural systems. Rachel Carson's *Silent Spring* in 1962 pushed pollution onto the national agenda. Carson, a well-regarded science writer, described the side effects of DDT and other pesticides on animal life. Her book resonated with many suburbanites, who realized that urban sprawl provided housing and shopping centers at the cost of bulldozed forests and farms, polluted streams, and smog-choked skies. (See American Views: The Suburban Roots of Environmental Activism, Chapter 28.)

Read the Document at www.myhistorylab.com *Exploring America: Rachel Carson*

Tanks full of toxic chemical waste were buried within a stone's throw of homes in the Love Canal neighborhood of Niagara Falls, New York, forcing homeowners to abandon their houses.

Environmentalism gained strength among Americans in 1970. On April 22, 10,000 schools and 20 million other people took part in Earth Day, an occasion first conceived by Wisconsin senator Gaylord Nelson. Earth Day gained a grassroots following in towns and cities across the country. New York closed Fifth Avenue to automobiles for the day. Companies touted their environmental credentials. The event helped to transform the technical field of pollution control into a broadly based movement.

The American establishment had been looking for a safe and respectable crusade to divert the idealism and discontent of the 1960s. Now the mainstream media discovered the ravaged planet. So did a politically savvy president. An expedient proenvironmental stance might attract some of the antiwar constituency. Nixon had already signed the National Environmental Policy Act on January 1, 1970, and later in the year created the **Environmental Protection Agency (EPA)** to enforce environmental laws. The rest of the Nixon administration brought legislation on clean air, clear water, pesticides, hazardous chemicals, and endangered species (see Overview, The Environmental Decades) that made environmental management and protection part of governmental routine.

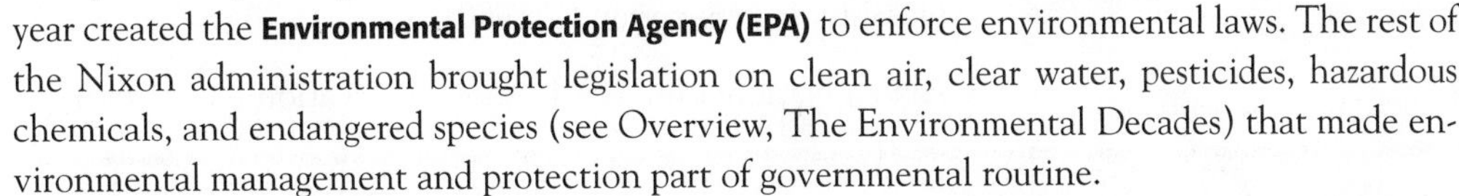

Environmental Protection Agency (EPA) Federal agency created in 1970 to oversee environmental monitoring and cleanup programs.

As Americans became more aware of human-caused environmental hazards, they realized that minority and low-income communities had more than their share of problems. Landfills and waste disposal sites were frequently located near minority neighborhoods. In Buffalo, white working-class residents near the Love Canal industrial site discovered in 1978 that an entire neighborhood was built on land contaminated by decades of chemical dumping. Activists sought to understand the health effects and force compensation, paving the way for Superfund cleanup legislation (see American Views: Grassroots Community Action).

QUICK REVIEW

Environmentalism

- In the 1970s resource conversation grew into an environmental movement.
- Nixon created the Environmental Protection Agency (EPA) in 1970.
- Low-income and minority communities bore a disproportionate share of environmental problems.

From Dirty Tricks to Watergate

The **Watergate** crisis pivoted on Richard Nixon's character. Despite his solid political standing, Nixon saw enemies everywhere and overestimated their strength. Subordinates learned during his first administration that the president would condone dishonest actions—"dirty tricks"—if they stood to improve his political position. In 1972 and 1973, dirty tricks grew from a scandal into a constitutional crisis when Nixon abused the power of his office to cover up wrongdoing and hinder criminal investigations.

Watergate A complex scandal involving attempts to cover up illegal actions taken by administration officials and leading to the resignation of President Richard Nixon in 1974.

The chain of events that undermined Nixon's presidency started with the **Pentagon Papers.** In his last year as secretary of defense, Robert McNamara had commissioned a report on the U.S. road to Vietnam. The documents showed that the country's leaders had planned to expand the war even while they claimed to be looking for a way out. In June 1971, one of the contributors to the report, Daniel Ellsberg, leaked it to the *New York Times*. Its publication infuriated Nixon.

Pentagon Papers Classified Defense Department documents on the history of the United States' involvement in Vietnam, prepared in 1968 and leaked to the press in 1971.

In response, the White House compiled a list of journalists and politicians who opposed Nixon. As one White House staffer, John Dean, put it, the president's men could then "use the available federal machinery [Internal Revenue Service, FBI] to screw our political enemies." Nixon set up a special investigations unit in the White House. Two former CIA employees, E. Howard Hunt and G. Gordon Liddy, became the chief "plumbers," as the group was known because its job was to prevent leaks of information.

OVERVIEW The Environmental Decades

Administration	Focus of Concern	Legislation
Johnson	Wilderness and wildlife	Wilderness Act (1964) National Wildlife Refuge System (1966) Wild and Scenic Rivers Act (1968)
Nixon	Pollution control and endangered environments	National Environmental Policy Act (1969) Environmental Protection Agency (1970) Clean Air Act (1970) Occupational Safety and Health Act (1970) Water Pollution Control Act (1972) Pesticide Control Act (1972) Coastal Zone Management Act (1972) Endangered Species Act (1973)
Ford	Energy and hazardous materials	Toxic Substances Control Act (1976) Resource Conservation and Recovery Act (1976)
Carter	Energy and hazardous materials	Energy Policy and Conservation Act (1978) Comprehensive Emergency Response, Compensation, and Liability Act (Superfund) (1980)
	Parks and wilderness	Alaska National Interest Lands Conservation Act (1980)

Early in 1972, Hunt went to work for CREEP—the Committee to Re-Elect the President—while Liddy took another position on the presidential staff. CREEP had already raised millions and was hatching plans to undermine Democrats with rumors and pranks. Then, on June 17, 1972, five inept burglars hired with CREEP funds were caught breaking into the Democratic National Committee office in Washington's Watergate apartment building. The people involved knew that an investigation would lead back to the White House. Nixon felt too insecure to ride out what would probably have been a small scandal. Instead, he initiated a coverup. On June 23, he ordered his assistant H. R. Haldeman to warn the FBI off the case with the excuse that national security was involved. Nixon compounded this obstruction of justice by arranging a $400,000 bribe to keep the burglars quiet.

The coverup worked in the short run. As mid-level officials from the Justice Department pursued their investigation, the public lost interest in what looked more like slapstick than a serious crime. Nixon's opponent in the 1972 election was South Dakota Senator George McGovern, an impassioned opponent of the Vietnam War. McGovern was honest, intelligent, and well to the left of center on such issues as the defense budget and legalization of marijuana. He did not appeal to the white southerners and blue-collar northerners whom Nixon and Agnew were luring from the Democrats. An assassination attempt that took George Wallace out of national politics also helped Nixon win in a landslide.

The coverup began to come apart with the trial of the Watergate burglars in January 1973. Federal Judge John Sirica used the threat of heavy sentences to pressure one burglar into a statement that implied that higher-ups had been involved. Meanwhile, the *Washington Post* was linking Nixon's people to dirty tricks and illegal campaign contributions. Nixon was aware of many of the actions that his subordinates had undertaken. He now began to coach people on what they should tell investigators, claimed his staff had lied to him, and tried to set up White House Counsel John Dean to take the fall.

In the late spring and early summer, attention shifted to the televised hearings of the Senate's Select Committee on Presidential Campaign Activities. The real questions, it became obvious, were what the president knew and when he knew it. It seemed to be John Dean's word against Richard Nixon's.

A bombshell turned the scandal into a constitutional crisis. A mid-level staffer told the committee that Nixon had made tape recordings of his White House conversations. Both the Senate and the Watergate special prosecutor, Archibald Cox, subpoenaed the tapes. Nixon refused to give them up, citing executive privilege and the separation of powers. In late October, after he failed to cut a satisfactory deal, he fired his attorney general and the special prosecutor. This "Saturday-night massacre" caused a storm of protest, and many Americans thought that it proved that Nixon had something to hide. In April 1974, he finally released edited transcripts of the tapes, with foul language deleted and key passages missing; he claimed that his secretary had accidentally erased crucial material. Finally, on July 24, 1974, the U.S. Supreme Court ruled unanimously that Nixon had to deliver 64 tapes to the new special prosecutor.

Watch the **Video** at **www.myhistorylab.com** *Richard Nixon, "I am not a crook"*

Opposition to the president now spanned the political spectrum from Barry Goldwater to liberal Democrats, and Congress began impeachment proceedings. On July 27, the House Judiciary Committee took up the specific charges. Republicans joined Democrats in voting three articles of impeachment: for hindering the criminal investigation of the Watergate break-in, for abusing the power of the presidency by using federal agencies to deprive citizens of their rights, and for ignoring the committee's subpoena for the tapes. Before the full House could vote on the articles of impeachment and send them to the Senate for trial, Nixon delivered the tapes. One of them contained the "smoking gun," direct evidence that Nixon had participated in the coverup on June 23, 1972, and had been lying ever since. On August 8 he announced his resignation, effective the following day.

Watergate was two separate but related stories. On one level, it was about individuals who deceived or manipulated the American people. Nixon and his cronies wanted to win too badly to play by the rules and repeatedly broke the law. Nixon paid for his overreaching ambition with the end of his political career; more than 20 others paid with jail terms. On another level, the crisis was a lesson about the Constitution. The separation of powers allowed Congress and the courts to rein in a president who had spun out of control. The Ervin Committee hearings in 1973 and the House Judiciary Committee proceedings in 1974 were rituals to assure Americans that the system still worked. Nevertheless, the sequence of political events from 1968 to 1974 disillusioned many citizens.

The Ford Footnote

Gerald Ford was Nixon's appointee to replace Spiro Agnew, who had resigned and pleaded no contest to charges of bribery and income tax evasion in 1973 as Watergate was gathering steam. Ford was competent but unimaginative. His first major act was his most controversial—the pardon of Nixon for "any and all crimes" committed while president. Since Nixon had not yet been indicted, the pardon saved him from future prosecution. To many Americans, the act looked like a payoff.

Ford's administration presided over the collapse of South Vietnam in 1975, but elsewhere in the world, *détente* continued. U.S. diplomats joined the Soviet Union and 30 other European nations in the capital of Finland to sign the **Helsinki Accords.** The agreements called for increased commerce between the Eastern and Western blocs and for human-rights guarantees. They also legitimized the national boundaries that had been set in eastern Europe in 1945. At home, the federal government did little new during Ford's two and a half years in office.

Helsinki Accords Agreement in 1975 among NATO and Warsaw Pact members that recognized European national boundaries as set after World War II and included guarantees of human rights.

Ford beat back Ronald Reagan for the 1976 Republican presidential nomination, but he was clearly vulnerable. His Democratic opponent was a political enigma. James Earl Carter Jr.

AMERICAN VIEWS

Grassroots Community Action

In the 1950s, a major chemical company closed a waste dump in Niagara Falls, New York. The site, known as Love Canal, was soon surrounded by a park, school, and hundreds of modest homes. Residents put up with noxious odors and seepage of chemical wastes until 1978, when they learned that the state health department was concerned about the health effects on small children and pregnant women. Over the next two years, residents battled state and federal bureaucracies and reluctant politicians for accurate information about the risks they faced and then for financial assistance to move from the area (often their homes represented their only savings). In October 1980, President Carter signed a bill to move all of the families permanently from the Love Canal area.

One of the leaders of the grassroots movement was housewife Lois Gibbs. The following excerpts from her story show her increasing sophistication as a community activist, starting by ringing doorbells in 1978 and ending with national television exposure in 1980. Although the Love Canal case itself was unusual, community-based organizations in all parts of the country learned the tactics of effective action in the 1960s and 1970s.

- **What** public programs in the 1960s and 1970s gave citizens experience in grassroots action?
- **How** might the Internet change the tactics of community organizing?

Knocking on Doors

I decided to go door-to-door with a petition. It seemed like a good idea to start near the school, to talk to the mothers nearest it. I had already heard that a lot of the residents near the school had been upset about the chemicals for the past couple of years. I thought they might help me. I had never done anything like this. . . . I was afraid a lot of doors would be slammed in my face, that people would think I was some crazy fanatic. But I decided to do it anyway . . . and knocked on my first door. There was no answer. I just stood there, not knowing what to do. It was an unusually warm June day and I was perspiring. I thought: What am I doing here? I must be crazy. People are going to think I am. Go home, you fool! And that's just what I did.

It was one of those times when I had to sit down and face myself. I was afraid of making a fool of myself, I had scared myself, and I had gone home. When I got there, I sat at the kitchen table with my petition in my hand, thinking. Wait. What if people do slam doors in your face? People may think you're crazy. But what's more important—what people think or your child's health? Either you're going to do something or you're going to have to admit you're a coward and not do it. . . . The next day, I went out on my own street to talk to people I knew. It was a little easier to be brave with them. If I could convince people I knew—friends—maybe it would be less difficult to convince others. . . . I went to the back door, as I always did when I visited a neighbor. Each house took about twenty or twenty-five minutes. . . .

Phil Donahue and Political Action

The *Phil Donahue Show* called. They wanted us to appear on their June 18 show. The reaction in the office was different this time, compared to the show in October 1978. In October, everyone was excited. "Phil Donahue—wow!" Now, residents reacted differently. "Donahue. That's great press. Now we'll get the politicians to move!" . . . Now our people looked at the show as a tool to use in pushing the government to relocate us permanently. By this time we understood how politicians react to public pressure, how to play the political game. We eagerly agreed to go, and found forty other residents to go with us. . . . [After arriving in Chicago] We then planned how we would handle the *Phil Donahue Show*. . . . We had to get the real issues across. Each resident was assigned an issue. One told of the chromosome tests. Another was to concentrate on her multiple miscarriages. Another was to ask for telegrams from across the country to the White House in support of permanent relocation. I coached them to get their point in, no matter the question asked. For example, if Donahue asked what you thought of the mayor, and your assignment was to discuss miscarriages, you should answer: "I don't like the mayor because I have had three miscarriages and other health problems, and he won't help us." Or: "My family is sick, and the mayor won't help us. That's why we need people to send telegrams to the White House for permanent relocation." . . . The residents were great! Each and every one followed through with our plan.

Source: Lois Marie Gibbs, as told to Murray Levine, *Love Canal: My Story* (Albany: State University of New York Press, 1982), pp. 12–13, 161–64.

had been a navy officer, a farmer, and the governor of Georgia. He was one of several new-style politicians who transformed southern politics in the 1970s. Carter and the others left race-baiting behind to talk like modern New Dealers, emphasizing that whites and blacks both needed better schools and economic growth. He appealed to Democrats as someone who could reassemble LBJ's political coalition and return the South to the Democratic Party. In his successful campaign, Carter presented himself as an alternative to party hacks and Washington insiders.

JIMMY CARTER: IDEALISM AND FRUSTRATION IN THE WHITE HOUSE

WHAT FACTORS limited Jimmy Carter's effectiveness as president?

Jimmy Carter took office with little room to maneuver. Watergate bequeathed him a powerful and self-satisfied Congress and a combative press. OPEC oil producers, Islamic fundamentalists, and Soviet generals followed their own agendas. The American people themselves were fractionalized and quarrelsome, uneasy with the new advocacy of equality for women, uncertain as a nation whether they shared the same values and goals.

CARTER, ENERGY, AND THE ECONOMY

Carter's approach to politics reflected his training as an engineer. He liked to break a problem into logical parts and was better at working with details than broad goals. He failed to understand the importance of personalities or the rules of Washington politics, losing friends even in his own party.

The biggest domestic problem remained the economy, which slid into another recession in 1978. Another jump in oil prices helped make 1979 and 1980 the worst years for inflation in the postwar era. Interest rates surged past 20 percent as the Federal Reserve tried to reduce inflation by squeezing business and consumer credit. Carter himself was a fiscal conservative whose impulse was to cut federal spending. This course worsened unemployment and alienated liberal Democrats, who wanted to revive the Great Society.

Read the **Document** at **www.myhistorylab.com** *Jimmy Carter, The "Malaise" Speech (1979)*

Carter simultaneously proposed a comprehensive energy policy. He asked Americans to make energy conservation the moral equivalent of war—to accept individual sacrifices for the common good. Congress created the Department of Energy but refused to raise taxes on oil and natural gas to reduce consumption. However, the Energy Policy and Conservation Act (1978) did encourage alternative energy sources to replace foreign petroleum.

Antinuclear activism blocked one obvious alternative to fossil fuels. The antinuclear movement had started with concern about the ability of the Atomic Energy Commission to monitor the safety of nuclear-power plants and about the disposal of spent fuel rods. In the late 1970s, activists staged sit-ins at the construction sites of nuclear plants. A near-meltdown at the Three Mile Island nuclear plant in Pennsylvania in March 1979 stalemated efforts to expand nuclear-power capacity.

CLOSED FACTORIES AND FAILED FARMS

Ford and Carter both faced massive problems of economic transition that undercut their efforts to devise effective government programs. Industrial decay stalked such "gritty cities" as Allentown, Pennsylvania; Trenton, New Jersey; and Gary, Indiana. Communities whose workers had made products in high volume for a mass market found that technological revolutions made them obsolete. Critics renamed the old manufacturing region of the Northeast and Midwest the Rustbelt in honor of its abandoned factories.

deindustrialization The process of economic change involving the disappearance of outmoded industries and the transfer of factories to new low-wage locations, with devastating effects in the Northeast and Midwest, especially in the 1970s and 1980s.

Stories of **deindustrialization** were similar in small cities like Springfield, Ohio, and large cities like Cleveland. As high-paying jobs in unionized industries disappeared, sagging income undermined small businesses and neighborhoods. Falling tax revenue brought Cleveland to the verge of bankruptcy in 1978; bankers forced public service cuts and tax increases, which meant further job losses.

Plant closures were only one facet of business efforts to increase productivity by substituting machinery for employees. Between 1947 and 1977, American steelmakers doubled output while cutting their workforce from 600,000 to 400,000. High interest rates and a strong dollar made U.S. exports too expensive and foreign imports cheap, forcing American manufacturers to cut costs or perish.

Parallel to the decline of heavy industry was the continuing transformation of American agriculture from small family enterprises to corporate agribusinesses. Agriculture was a national success story in the aggregate, but one accompanied by many human and environmental costs. The early 1970s brought an unexpected boom in farming. Crop failures and food shortages around the world in 1972 and 1973 expanded markets and pushed up prices for U.S. farm products. For a few years, agriculture looked like the best way for the United States to offset the high cost of imported oil. But the boom was over by the 1980s, when global commodity prices slumped. Farmers found themselves with debts they could not cover.

The boom of the 1970s was thus a brief interruption in the long-term transformation of U.S. agriculture. The number of farms slid from 4 million in 1960 to 2.4 million in 1980 and 1.9 million in 2000. Many farmers sold out willingly, glad to escape from drudgery and financial insecurity. Others could not compete in an agricultural system that favored large-scale production by demanding large amounts of capital for equipment and fertilizer. By 2000, fewer than 2 percent of American workers made their living from farming.

Egyptian President Anwar al-Sadat, U.S. President Jimmy Carter, and Israeli Prime Minister Menachem Begin share a symbolic handshake after the signing of a peace treaty between Egypt and Israel on August 26, 1979. The treaty codified the historic agreement that the leaders had hammered out at Camp David, Maryland, in September 1978.

Building a Cooperative World

Despite troubles on the home front, Carter's first two years brought foreign policy successes that reflected a new vision of a multilateral world. As a relative newcomer to international politics, Carter was willing to work with African, Asian, and Latin American nations on a basis of mutual respect. Carter appointed Andrew Young—an African American from Georgia with long experience in the civil rights movement—as ambassador to the United Nations, where he worked effectively to build bridges to third-world nations. Carter convinced the Senate in 1978 to approve treaties to transfer control of the Panama Canal to Panama by 2000, removing a sore point in relations with Latin America.

Carter's strong religious beliefs and moral convictions were responsible for a new concern with human rights around the globe. He criticized the Soviet Union for prohibiting free speech and denying its citizens the right to emigrate, angering Soviet leaders, who did not expect the human rights clauses of the Helsinki Accords to be taken seriously. Carter was also willing to criticize some (but not all) American allies. He withheld economic aid from South Africa, Guatemala, Chile, and Nicaragua, which had long records of human rights abuses. In Nicaragua, the change in policy helped left-wing Sandinista rebels topple the Somoza dictatorship.

Carter had several successes. He completed the Nixon initiative by normalizing diplomatic relations with China. He also risked his reputation and credibility in September 1978 to bring Egyptian President Anwar al-Sadat and Israeli Prime Minister Menachem Begin together at Camp David, the presidential retreat. He refused to admit failure and dissuaded the two leaders from walking out. A formal treaty known popularly as the **Camp David Agreement** was signed in Washington on March 26, 1979. The pact normalized relations between Israel and its most powerful neighbor and led to Israel's withdrawal from the Sinai Peninsula. It was a vital prelude to further progress toward Arab-Israeli peace in the mid-1990s.

Camp David Agreement Agreement to reduce points of conflict between Israel and Egypt, hammered out in 1977 with the help of U.S. President Jimmy Carter.

QUICK REVIEW

Carter's Foreign Policy Successes

- Appointed Andrew Young as ambassador to UN, where he helped build bridges to third-world nations.
- Made human rights a key issue in American policy.
- Facilitated Camp David Agreement between Egypt and Israel.

New Crises Abroad

In the last two years of Carter's administration, the Cold War sprang back to life around the globe and smothered the promise of a new foreign policy. The Soviets ignored the human-rights provisions of the Helsinki Accords. Soviet advisers or Cuban troops intervened in African civil wars. At home, Cold Warriors who had never accepted détente found it easier to attack Carter than Nixon.

The failure of SALT II. Carter inherited negotiations for SALT II—a strategic arms-limitation treaty that would have reduced both the U.S. and Soviet nuclear arsenals—from the Ford administration. SALT II met stiff resistance in the Senate. Opponents claimed it would create a "window of vulnerability" in the 1980s that would invite the Soviets to launch a nuclear first strike. Carter tried to counter criticism by stepping up defense spending, starting a buildup that would accelerate under Ronald Reagan.

Hopes for SALT II vanished on December 24, 1979, when Soviet troops entered Afghanistan, a technically neutral Muslim nation on the southern border of the Soviet Union. A pro-Soviet government had fallen into factional strife, while tribespeople, unhappy with modernization, were mounting increasing resistance. One of the factions invited intervention by the Soviets, who quickly installed a client government. The situation resembled the U.S. involvement in South Vietnam. Similar, too, was the inability of Soviet forces to suppress the Afghan guerrillas, who had American weapons and controlled the mountains. In the end, it took the Soviets a decade to find a way out.

The Iranian hostage crisis. The final blow to Carter's foreign policy came in Iran. Since 1953, the United States had strongly backed Iran's monarch, Shah Reza Pahlavi. The shah modernized Iran's economy, but his feared secret police jailed and tortured political opponents. U.S. aid and oil revenues helped him build a large army, but the Iranian middle class despised his authoritarianism, and Muslim fundamentalists opposed the Westernizing influence of modernization. A revolution toppled the shah at the start of 1979.

The upheaval installed a nominally democratic government, but the Ayatollah Ruhollah Khomeini, a Muslim cleric who hated the United States, exercised real power. Throughout 1979, Iran grew increasingly anti-American. After the United States allowed the exiled shah to seek medical treatment in New York, a mob stormed the U.S. embassy in Tehran on November 4, 1979, and took more than 60 Americans hostage. They demanded that Carter surrender the shah. The administration tried economic pressure and diplomacy, but Khomeini had no desire for accommodation. When Iran announced in April 1980 that the hostages would remain in the hands of the militants rather than be transferred to the government, Carter ordered an airborne rescue. Even a perfectly managed effort would have been difficult. The hostages were held in the heart of a city of 4 million hostile Iranians, hundreds of miles from the nearest aircraft carrier and thousands of miles from U.S. bases. Hampered by lack of coordination among the military services, the attempt turned into a fiasco that added to the national embarrassment and a feeling of powerlessness. The United States and Iran finally reached agreement on the eve of the

The Iran hostage crisis reflected intense anti-American feelings in Iran and provoked an equally bitter anti-Iranian reaction in the United States. Fifty-two of the more than 60 U.S. embassy employees first seized were held for 444 days, giving the United States a painful lesson about the limits on its ability to influence events around the world.

1980 election. The hostages gained their freedom after 444 days, at the moment Ronald Reagan took office as the new president.

The hostage crisis consumed Jimmy Carter the way that Vietnam had consumed Lyndon Johnson. It gripped the public and stalemated other issues. Carter's tragedy was that "his" Iranian crisis was the fruit of policies hatched by the Eisenhower administration and pursued by every president since then, all of whom had overlooked the shah's despotic government because of his firm anti-Communism.

CONCLUSION

In the mid-1970s, Americans encountered real limits to national capacity. From 1945 to 1973, they had enjoyed remarkable prosperity. That ended in 1974. Long lines at gas stations showed that prosperity was fragile. Cities and regions felt the costs of obsolete industries. Environmental damage caused many Americans to reconsider the goal of economic expansion.

The nation also had to recognize that it could not run the world. American withdrawal from Vietnam in 1973 and the collapse of the South Vietnamese government in 1975 were defeats; the United States ended up with little to show for a long and painful war. SALT I stabilized the arms race, but it also recognized that the Soviet Union was an equal. The American nuclear arsenal might help deter a third world war, but it could not prevent the seizure of hostages in Iran.

These challenges came amid deep economic and social changes in the United States. The ways Americans made their livings and the range of opportunities they faced were in flux. Farm laborers had better working conditions, but auto workers had fewer jobs. The nation finished the 1970s more egalitarian than it had been in the early 1960s but also more divided. More citizens had the opportunity to advance economically and to seek political power, but there were deepening fissures between social liberals and cultural conservatives, old and new views about roles for women, rich and poor, whites and blacks. In 1961, John Kennedy had called on his fellow citizens to "bear any burden, pay any price" to defend freedom. By 1980, the nation had neither the economic capacity to pay any price nor the unity to agree on what burdens it should bear.

Where to Learn More

Lyndon B. Johnson National Historical Park, Johnson City, Texas. Johnson's ranch, southwest of Austin, gives visitors a feeling for the open landscape in which Johnson spent his early years. http://www.nps.gov/lyjo/.

Vietnam Veterans Memorial, Washington, DC. A simple wall engraved with the names of the nation's Vietnam War dead is testimony to one of the nation's most divisive wars. http://www.nps.gov/vive.

Richard Nixon Library and Birthplace, Yorba Linda, California. Exhibits trace Nixon's political career and related world events with a sympathetic interpretation. http://nixonfoundation.org/.

Titan Missile Museum, Green Valley, Arizona. The Green Valley complex near Tucson held 18 Titan missiles. They were deactivated after SALT I, and the complex is now open to visitors. http://www.titanmissilemuseum.org/.

Review Questions

1. Why did the United States fail to achieve its objectives in Vietnam? What factors limited President Johnson's freedom of action there? How did the Tet Offensive affect U.S. policy? How did antiwar protests in the United States influence national policy?
2. How did racial relations change between 1965 and 1970? What were the relationships between the civil rights movement and minority separatism? What were the similarities and differences between African American, Latino, and Native American activism?
3. In what ways was 1968 a pivotal year for U.S. politics and society? How was it influenced by global events?
4. What were the implications of *détente?* Why did the Cold War reappear in the late 1970s? How and why did U.S. influence over the rest of the world change during the 1970s?
5. How did Richard Nixon's political strategy respond to the growth of the South and West? How did it respond to the shift of population from central cities to suburbs?
6. How did the backgrounds of Presidents Johnson, Nixon, and Carter shape their successes and failures as national leaders?
7. What political and constitutional issues were at stake in the Watergate scandal? How did it change American politics?
8. Why was the space race important for the United States? How did it strengthen the alliance between American science, government, and industry?

Key Terms

American Indian Movement (AIM) (p. 824)
Baker v. Carr (p. 824)
Black Panthers (p. 822)
Black Power (p. 821)
Camp David Agreement (p. 837)
Counterculture (p. 818)
Deindustrialization (p. 836)
Détente (p. 829)
Environmental Protection Agency (EPA) (p. 831)
Free Speech Movement (FSM) (p. 817)
Helsinki Accords (p. 833)
Model Cities Program (p. 818)
Nation of Islam (p. 822)
New Federalism (p. 830)
Nixon Doctrine (p. 828)
Organization of Petroleum Exporting Countries (OPEC) (p. 830)
Pentagon Papers (p. 831)
Search and destroy (p. 815)
Selective Service System (p. 815)
Stonewall Rebellion (p. 820)
Strategic Arms Limitation Treaty (SALT) (p. 829)
Students for a Democratic Society (SDS) (p. 817)
Swann v. Charlotte-Mecklenburg Board of Education (p. 824)
Watergate (p. 831)

myhistorylab Connections

Reinforce what you learned in this chapter by studying the many documents, images, maps, review tools, and videos available at **www.myhistorylab.com.**

Read and Review

Study and Review Study Plan: Chapter 29

Read the Document

Cesar Chavez, "He Showed Us the Way" (1978)

Donald Wheeldin, "The Situation in Watts Today" (1967)

Stokely Carmichael and Charles V. Hamilton, from Black Power: The Politics of Liberation in America (1967)

Students for a Democratic Society, The Port Huron Statement (1962)

The Gay Liberation Front, Come Out (1970)

Jimmy Carter, The "Malaise" Speech (1979)

Roe v. Wade *(January 22, 1973)*

The Civil Rights Act of 1964

Toi Derricotte, Black in a White Neighborhood, 1977–1978

Voting Literacy Test (1965)

National Organization for Women, Statement of Purpose (1966)

See the Map *Vietnam War*

Research and Explore

Read the Document

Personal Journeys Online

From Then to Now Online: Energy Worries

Exploring America: American Indian Movement

Exploring America: Rachel Carson

Hear the Audio

Angela Davis interview from prison

liberation/poem by Sonia Sanchez

Message to the Grassroots by Malcolm X, excerpt

Watch the Video

Civil Rights March on Washington

Richard Nixon, "I am not a crook"

Malcolm X

The Vietnam War

Protests Against the Vietnam War

Jimmy Carter and the "Crisis of Confidence"

Hear the Audio

Hear the audio files for Chapter 29 at **www.myhistorylab.com.**

1981-1992

30 The Reagan Revolution and a Changing World

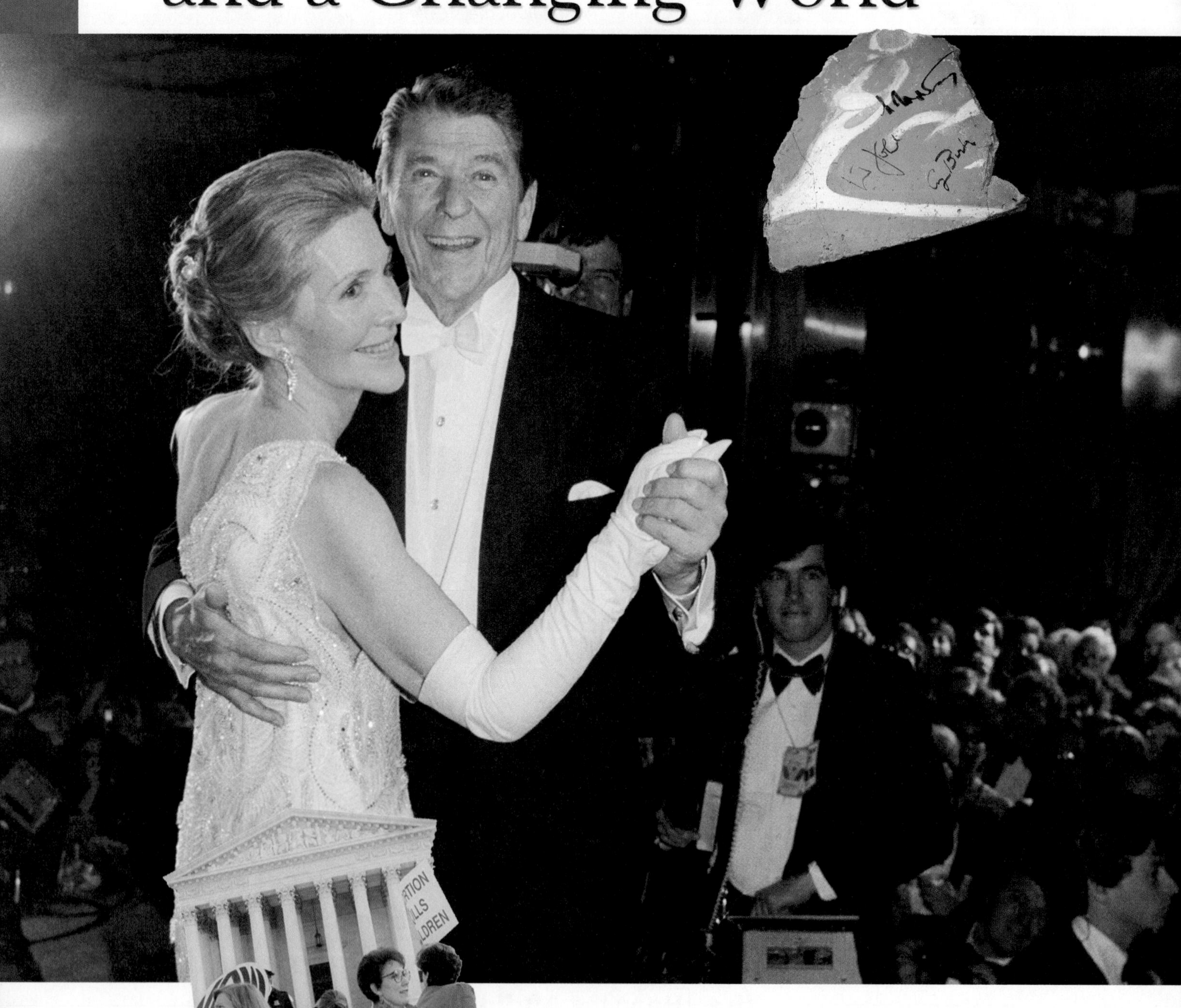
KEEP ABORTION LEGAL
ABORTION KILLS CHILDREN

Ronald Reagan and his wife, Nancy, celebrate his inauguration as president.

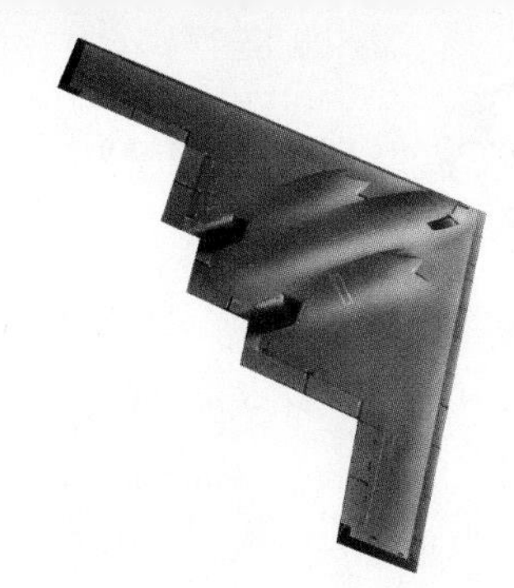

Hear the Audio

Hear the audio files for Chapter 30 at **www.myhistorylab.com**.

REAGAN'S DOMESTIC REVOLUTION *(page 846)*

WHAT WAS revolutionary about the Reagan revolution?

THE CLIMAX OF THE COLD WAR *(page 854)*

HOW AND why did the Cold War come to an end?

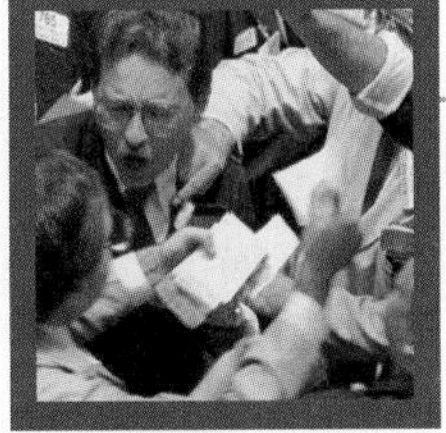

GROWTH IN THE SUNBELT *(page 861)*

HOW DID growth in the Sunbelt shape national politics in the 1980s and 1990s?

VALUES IN COLLISION *(page 865)*

WHAT KEY social and cultural issues divided Americans in the 1980s and 1990s?

One American Journey

I am pursuing the American dream—to have a house of my own, for my family. I try to make my children understand: "You have to help me in the shop, so I can save and buy a small house." But they have their own lives, their own families, other jobs. The money they earn is not that much. So they still need me as much as I need them.

When I became an American citizen a few months ago, it was very emotional for me. I was happy that I could be part of my new country. I do feel loyalty to the United States. I think of myself as both Cambodian and an American citizen. I cannot forget where I came from.

My maiden name was Thann Meng Vann. When I became an American citizen, I took an American name, Celia, and my husband's family name, Noup, because I hope that he will some day return. I lost contact with him when our country was falling in April 1975. The outpost he commanded was surrounded by Khmer Rouge. I have never found out what happened to him after he was captured. Sometimes I have seen him in my dreams, but he never talks to me.

The first time I dreamed about my husband as in a hut where the Khmer Rouge had ordered my family to stay after our city, Phnom Penh, was evacuated. In the dream, I saw him in our bedroom in Phnom Penh. He looked very sad. I woke up in the middle of the night. I shouted. I cried out loud.

The next day, the Communists send an old person to talk with me, to tell me that they heard me in the night. They warned me not to do that any more. For four years they tried to kill me. They tried every trick in the book to catch me breaking their rules.

Now, in my dreams at night, people speak in the Cambodian language. But I never dream about Cambodia. No more. My dreams always take place in a house with my daughters that is unknown to me . It is always the same house, on a streetcorner, three stories high.

On weekdays, I live in the house that my daughter Mealy and her husband rent; it is only five minutes from my shop. On weekends, I live with my daughter Monie and her husband in Torrance. I share the cost of food for the households. Sometimes I buy groceries. And I pay some rent for both Parika and me. I try to help my children as much as I can. I can't take it all with me. [Laughs]

I have four grandchildren, all babies—two years, one year, and a few months. The only time I have for them is on weekends, when my daughters are working at my shop. I babysit the kids while I do bookkeeping. I enjoy their company.

We've been here seven years now. My children still think like Cambodians, but their way of acting is American.

Celia Noup, in Al Santoli, *New Americans: An Oral History* (New York, 1988)

Read the **Document** at **www.myhistorylab.com**

Personal Journeys Online

- **Jubilee Lau, "Chinese and Proud of It," 1996. From Hong Kong to Idaho in the 1980s.**
- **Richard Rodriguez, *Hunger of Memory*, 1982. Learning English in an immigrant household.**
- **Ana Cabellero, 1980s. Mexican American Generations in El Paso. Interview in Al Santoli, *New Americans*, 1988.**

CHRONOLOGY

1973	*Roe v. Wade:* Supreme Court strikes down state laws banning abortion in the first trimester of pregnancy.
1980	Ronald Reagan is elected president.
1981	Economic Recovery and Tax Act, reducing personal income tax rates, is passed.
	Reagan breaks strike by air traffic controllers.
	AIDS is recognized as a new disease.
1982	Nuclear freeze movement peaks.
	United States begins to finance Contra rebels against the Sandinista government in Nicaragua.
	Equal Rights Amendment fails to achieve ratification.
1983	241 Marines are killed by a terrorist bomb in Beirut, Lebanon.
	Strategic Defense Initiative introduced.
	United States invades Grenada.
1984	Reagan wins reelection.
1985	Mikhail Gorbachev initiates economic and political reforms in the Soviet Union.
1986	Tax Reform Act is adopted.
1987	Congress holds hearings on the Iran-Contra scandal.
	Reagan and Gorbachev sign the Intermediate-Range Nuclear Forces Treaty.
1988	George H. W. Bush is elected president.
1989	Communist regimes in eastern Europe collapse; Germans tear down Berlin Wall.
	Financial crisis forces federal bailout of many savings and loans.
	United States invades Panama to capture General Manuel Noriega.
1990	Iraq invades Kuwait; and United States sends forces to the Persian Gulf.
	West Germany and East Germany reunite.
	Americans with Disabilities Act is adopted.
1991	Persian Gulf War: Operation Desert Storm drives the Iraqis from Kuwait.
	Soviet Union dissolves into independent nations.
	Strategic Arms Reduction Treaty (START) is signed.
1992	Acquittal of officers accused of beating Rodney King triggers Los Angeles riots.

CELIA NOUP taught school for 20 years in Cambodia, which borders on South Vietnam. In 1975, after a long civil war, the Communist Khmer Rouge insurgents took over Cambodia's capital, Phnom Penh, and forced its inhabitants into the countryside to work in the fields. Four years later, Noup managed to make her way to a refugee camp in neighboring Thailand and then to the United States. Within a decade, she was working from 5:00 A.M. to 7:00 P.M. in her own donut shop near Los Angeles airport and worrying about helping her children buy houses.

Celia Noup's journey shows some of the ways that new waves of immigration from Asia, Latin America, and Africa have changed the United States over the last generation. Immigrants fueled economic growth in the 1980s and 1990s with their labor and their drive to succeed in business. They revitalized older neighborhoods in cities from coast to coast and changed the ethnic mix of major cities. And they created new racial tensions that found their way into national political debates about immigration and into open conflict in places such as Miami and Los Angeles.

Noup's story is also a reminder of the drawn-out consequences of the U.S. involvement in Vietnam and the long shadow of the Cold War. The Cambodian civil war was fueled by reactions to the Vietnamese war and the U.S. invasion of Cambodia in 1969. American refugee policy was humanitarian but also political, opening the door to people fleeing Communist regimes but holding it shut against refugees from right-wing dictatorships. In Washington, foreign policy decisions in the 1980s started with the desire of a new administration to reaffirm American toughness after failures in Vietnam and ended with the astonishing evaporation of the Cold War.

By the end of Ronald Reagan's presidency (1981–1989), new rules governed domestic affairs as well as international relations. In the 1980s Americans decided to reverse the growth of federal government responsibilities that had marked both Republican and Democratic administrations since the 1930s. By the 1990s, the center of U.S. politics had shifted substantially to the right. The backdrop to the political changes was massive readjustments in the American economy that began in the 1970s with the decline of heavy industry and then continued to shift employment from factory jobs to service jobs in the 1980s. The ideology of unregulated markets celebrated economic success, but masked a troubling reality: a widening gap between the rich and poor. The result by 1992 was a nation that was much more secure in the world than it had been in 1980, but also more divided against itself. ✦

REAGAN'S DOMESTIC REVOLUTION

WHAT WAS revolutionary about the Reagan revolution?

Read the **Document** at **www.myhistorylab.com**
Ronald Reagan, First Inaugural Address (1981)

Political change began in 1980, when Ronald Reagan and his running mate, George H. W. Bush, rode American discontent to a decisive victory in the presidential election (see Map 30–1). Building on a conservative critique of American policies and developing issues that Jimmy Carter had placed on the national agenda, Reagan presided over revolutionary changes in U.S. government and policies. The consequences of his two terms included an altered role for government, powerful but selective economic growth, and a shift of domestic politics away from bread-and-butter issues toward moral or lifestyle concerns.

REAGAN'S MAJORITY

Ronald Reagan reinvented himself several times on his unusual journey to the White House. A product of small-town Illinois, he succeeded in Hollywood in the late 1930s as a romantic lead actor while adopting the liberal politics common at the time. After World War II, he moved rapidly to the political right as a spokesman for big business. He entered politics with a rousing conservative speech at the 1964 Republican convention and then accepted the invitation of wealthy California Republicans to run for governor in 1966, serving two terms in that office.

Some of Reagan's most articulate support came from anti-Communist stalwarts of both parties, who feared that the United States was losing influence in the world. Despite Jimmy Carter's tough actions in 1979 and 1980 and increased defense spending, such conservatives had not trusted him to do enough. Soviet military buildup, charged the critics, was creating a "window of vulnerability," a dangerous period when the Soviet Union might threaten the United States with a first strike by nuclear weapons.

Other Reagan voters directed their anger at government bureaucracies. Wealthy entrepreneurs from the fast-growing South and West believed that Nixon-era federal offices, such as the Environmental Protection Agency and the Occupational Safety and Health Administration, were choking their businesses in red tape. Many of these critics had amassed new fortunes in oil, real estate, and retailing and hated the taxes that funded social programs.

Christian conservatives worried that social activists were using the federal courts to alter traditional values. Jimmy Carter, a member of the Southern Baptist church, had won a clear majority among white evangelical voters in 1976, but Reagan's contrasting position on school prayer and abortion gave him the edge in 1980 and made him the overwhelming preference of conservative Christian voters in 1984.

In many ways the two groups of Reagan supporters were mismatched. Christian moralists had little in common with the high-rollers and Hollywood tycoons with whom Reagan rubbed shoulders. But both shared a distrust of the federal government.

Foreign policy activists and opponents of big government would have been unable to elect Reagan without disaffected blue-collar and middle-class voters who deserted the Democrats. Reagan's campaign hammered on the question "Are you better off than you were four years ago?" Democrats faced a special dilemma with the deepening tension between working-class white voters and black voters, a division that had roots in the expansion of African American populations and neighborhoods in cities like Detroit and Chicago during the 1950s and 1960s. Democrats needed both groups to win but found white blue-collar voters deeply alienated by affirmative action and busing for school integration.

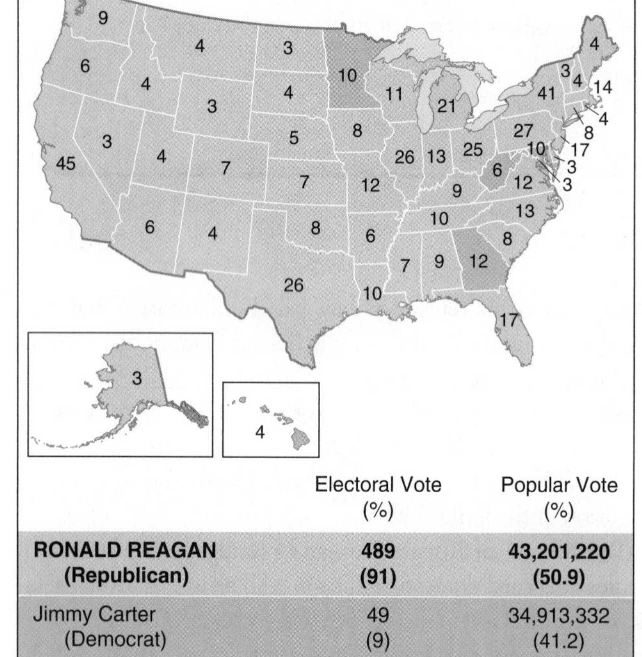

	Electoral Vote (%)	Popular Vote (%)
RONALD REAGAN (Republican)	**489 (91)**	**43,201,220 (50.9)**
Jimmy Carter (Democrat)	49 (9)	34,913,332 (41.2)
John B. Anderson (Independent)	–	5,581,379 (6.6)
Other candidates (Libertarian)	–	921,299 (1.1)

MAP 30–1 **The Election of 1980** Ronald Reagan won in a landslide in 1980. Independent candidate John Anderson took more votes from Jimmy Carter than from Reagan, but Reagan's personal magnetism was a powerful political force. His victory confirmed the shift of the South to the Republican Party.

What political and cultural trends were reflected in Reagan's strong performance in the South and West?

A further Democratic challenge was Ronald Reagan's personal appeal. With a common touch that made him a favorite for a sizable segment of the public, Reagan tapped into the nostalgia for a simpler America. The new president won over many Americans by surviving a 1981 assassination attempt in fine spirits. Reagan's popularity compounded the Democrats' inability to excite younger voters. The mid-1980s consistently showed that roughly two-thirds of people in their twenties and early thirties were choosing the Republicans as the party of energy and new ideas, leaving the Democrats to the middle-aged and elderly.

Ronald Reagan and his wife, Nancy, celebrate Reagan's inauguration as president.

In the election of 1984, Democrats sealed their fate by nominating Walter Mondale, who had been vice president under Carter. Mondale was earnest, honest, and dull. Reagan ran on the theme "It's Morning in America," with the message that a new age of pride and prosperity had begun. Mondale assumed that Americans cared enough about the exploding federal deficit that Reagan's defense spending had produced to accept an across-the-board tax increase. With the economy growing and inflation now in check, most voters did not want Mondale to remind them of long-range financial realities, and Reagan won reelection with 98 percent of the electoral votes. His election confirmed that the American public found conservative ideas increasingly attractive.

WHERE TO LEARN MORE

Ronald Reagan Boyhood Home, Dixon, Illinois
http://www.ronaldreaganhome.com

The New Conservatism

Reagan's approach to public policy drew on conservative intellectuals who offered a coherent critique of the New Deal–New Frontier approach to U.S. government. They feared that the antiwar movement had undermined the anti-Communist stance and that social changes were corrupting mainstream values.

Read the Document at **www.myhistorylab.com**
T. Boone Pickens, "My Case for Reagan" (1984)

Downsizing the Great Society. Worries about big government permeated the critique of domestic policy. Edward Banfield's radical ideas about the failures of the Great Society set the tone of the neoconservative analysis. In *The Unheavenly City* (1968), he questioned the basic idea of public solutions for social problems. He argued that inequality is based on human character and rooted in the basic structure of society; government action can only solve problems that require better engineering, such as pollution control, better highways, or the delivery of explosives to military targets. Government's job, said Banfield, was to preserve public order, not to right wrongs or encourage unrealistic expectations.

Free market utopians. Another strand of conservative argument came from free market utopians. After years of stagflation, Americans were eager to hear that unleashing free markets would trigger renewed prosperity.

The common themes of the conservative critique were simple: Free markets work better than government programs; government intervention does more harm than good; government assistance saps the initiative of the poor. In 1964, three-quarters of Americans had trusted Washington "to do what is right." By 1980, three-quarters were convinced that the federal government wasted tax money. The cumulative effect of the neoconservative arguments was to trash the word "liberal" and convince many Americans that labor unions and minorities were "special interests" but that oil tycoons, defense contractors, and other members of Reagan's coalition were not.

QUICK REVIEW

Central Assertions of the Conservative Critique

- Free markets work better than government programs.
- Government intervention does more harm than good.
- Government assistance saps the initiative of the poor.

Conservative political savvy. Conservatives promoted their ideology with new political tactics. Targeted mailings raised funds and mobilized voters with emotional appeals while bypassing the mass media, with their supposed preference for mainstream or liberal policies. Conservative organizers also knew how to use radio call-in shows to spread their message. Such appeals contrasted with the Democrats' reliance on more traditional ways to get out the vote through personal contacts and labor unions. Through the 1980s, Democrats repeatedly found themselves blindsided by creative Republican campaign tactics.

Reaganomics: Deficits and Deregulation

Economic Recovery and Tax Act of 1981 (ERTA) A major revision of the federal income tax system.

The heart of the 1980s revolution was the **Economic Recovery and Tax Act of 1981 (ERTA),** which reduced personal income tax rates by 25 percent over three years. The explicit goal was to stimulate business activity by lowering taxes overall and slashing rates for the rich. Cutting the government's total income by $747 billion over five years, ERTA meant less money for federal programs and more money in the hands of consumers and investors to stimulate economic growth.

Read the Document at **www.myhistorylab.com** *Paul Craig Roberts, The Supply-Side Revolution (1984)*

Reagan's first budget director, David Stockman, later revealed a second goal. ERTA would lock in deficits by "pulling the revenue plug." Because defense spending and Social Security were untouchable, Congress would find it impossible to create and fund new programs without cutting old ones. If Americans still wanted social programs, they could enact them at the local or state level, but Washington would no longer pay.

deregulation Reduction or removal of government regulations and encouragement of direct competition in many important industries and economic sectors.

The second part of the economic agenda was to free capitalists from government regulations, in the hope of increasing business innovation and efficiency. The **deregulation** revolution built on a head start from the 1970s. A federal antitrust case had split the unified Bell System of AT&T and its subsidiaries into seven regional telephone companies and opened long-distance service to competition. Congress also deregulated air travel in 1978.

Environmental regulation and federal lands. Corporate America used the Reagan administration to attack environmental legislation as "strangulation by regulation." Reagan's new budgets sliced funding for the Environmental Protection Agency. Vice President Bush headed the White House Task Force on Regulatory Relief, which delayed or blocked regulations on hazardous wastes, automobile emissions, and exposure of workers to chemicals on the job.

Most attention, however, went to the controversial appointment of a Colorado lawyer, James Watt, as secretary of the interior. Watt was sympathetic to a western movement known as the **Sagebrush Rebellion,** which wanted the vast federal land holdings in the West transferred to the states for less environmental protection and more rapid economic use. Federal resource agencies sold trees to timber companies at a loss to the Treasury, expanded offshore oil drilling, and expedited exploration for minerals.

Sagebrush Rebellion Political movement in the western states in the early 1980s that called for easing of regulations on the economic issue of federal lands and the transfer of some or all of those lands to state ownership.

Deregulation of the banking industry. The early 1980s also transformed American financial markets. Savings and loans had traditionally been conservative financial institutions that funneled individual savings into safe home mortgages. Under new rules, savings and loans began to compete for deposits by offering high interest rates and reinvesting the money in much riskier commercial real estate. By 1990, the result was a financial crisis in which bad loans destroyed hundreds of S&Ls, especially in the Southwest. American taxpayers were left to bail out depositors to the tune of hundreds of billions of dollars to prevent a collapse of the nation's financial and credit system.

With the deregulation of financial markets, corporate consolidations and mergers flourished. Corporate raiders raised money with "junk bonds"—high-interest, high-risk securities—and snapped up profitable and cash-rich companies that could be milked of profits and assets. The merger mania channeled capital into paper transactions rather than investments in new equipment and products. Another effect was to damage the economies of small and middle-sized communities by transferring control of local companies to outside managers.

QUICK REVIEW

Key Components of Reaganomics

- Lower personal income tax rates.
- Increase defense spending.
- Deregulate industry.

In the short term, the national economy boomed in the mid-1980s. Deregulated credit, tax cuts, and massive deficit spending on defense fueled exuberant growth. The stock market mirrored the overall prosperity; the Dow Jones average of blue-chip industrial stock prices more than tripled from August 1982 to August 1987.

Crisis for Organized Labor

The flip side of the economic boom was another round in the Republican offensive against labor unions. Reagan set the tone when he fired more than 11,000 members of the Professional Air Traffic Controllers Organization for violating a no-strike clause in their hiring agreements. He claimed to be enforcing the letter of the law, but the message to organized labor was clear. For many years, corporations had hesitated to hire permanent replacements for striking workers. With Reagan's example, large companies, such as Hormel and Phelps-Dodge, chose that option, undercutting the strike as an effective union strategy.

Read the **Document**
at **www.myhistorylab.com**
Ronald Reagan, The Air Traffic Controllers Strike (1981)

Decline of union membership and blue-collar jobs. Organized labor counted a million fewer members at the end of Reagan's administration in 1989 than in 1964, even though the number of employed Americans had nearly doubled. As union membership declined and unions struggled to cope with the changing economy, corporations seized the opportunity to demand wage rollbacks and concessions on working conditions as trade-offs for continued employment, squeezing workers in one plant and then using the settlement to pressure another. Workers in the 1970s and 1980s faced the threat that employers might move a factory to a new site elsewhere in the United States or overseas. Or a company might sell out to a new owner, who could close a plant and reopen without a union contract.

Another cause for shrinking union membership was the overall decline of blue-collar jobs, from 36 percent of the American workforce in 1960 to roughly 25 percent at the end of the 1990s. Unionization of white-collar workers made up only part of the loss from manufacturing. Unions were most successful in recruiting government workers, such as police officers, teachers, and bus drivers. By the late 1980s, the American Federation of State, County, and Municipal Employees had twice the membership of the United Steel Workers.

Impact of economic restructuring. In the 1950s and 1960s, increasing productivity, expanding markets for U.S. goods, and strong labor unions had made it possible for factory workers to enter the middle class. In an era of deindustrialization, however, companies replaced blue-collar workers with machinery or shifted production to nonunion plants. The corporate merger mania of the 1980s added to instability when takeover specialists loaded old companies with new debt, triggering efforts to cut labor costs, sell off plants, or raid pension funds for cash to pay the interest. Manufacturing employment in the 1980s declined by nearly 2 million jobs, with the expansion of high-tech manufacturing concealing much higher losses in traditional industries.

The working-class family depicted on the television show *Roseanne* offered viewers a glimpse of the problems facing many Americans in an era of economic change marked by deindustrialization and the rise of service jobs.

An Acquisitive Society

The new prosperity fueled lavish living by the wealthy and a fascination with the "lifestyles of the rich and famous." Prime-time soap operas flourished, bringing to the small screen stories of intrigue among the rich folks. With a few exceptions, even the "middle class" in television sitcoms enjoyed lives available only to the top 20 percent of Americans.

"They're museum quality!"

This 1993 cartoon contrasting a yuppie couple and a family dressed as hippies makes two points. While highlighting the rapid changes in American styles and tastes from the 1970s to the 1990s, it also satirizes the supposed yuppie tendency to value everything as a commodity or "collectible."

The national media in the early 1980s discovered yuppies, or young urban professionals, who were both a marketing category and a symbol of social change. These upwardly mobile professionals supposedly defined themselves by elitist consumerism. Middle-line retailers like Sears had clothed Americans for decades and furnished their homes. With the help of catalog shopping, status-seeking consumers now flocked to such upscale retailers as Neiman-Marcus and Bloomingdale's.

Far richer than even such atypical yuppies were wheeler-dealers who made themselves into media stars of finance capitalism. The autobiography of Lee Iacocca, who had helped revive the fortunes of the Chrysler Corporation, was a best-seller in 1984, portraying the corporate executive as hero. *Forbes* magazine began to publish an annual list of the nation's 400 richest people. Long before his television show, real-estate developer Donald Trump made himself a celebrity with a well-publicized personal life and a stream of projects crowned with his name: office tower, hotel, casino. New movements in popular music reacted to the acquisitive 1980s. Punk rock pared rock-and-roll to its basics, lashing out at the emptiness of 1970s disco sound. Hip-hop originated among African Americans and Latinos in New York, soon adding the angry and often violent lyrics of rap. Rap during the 1980s was about personal power and sex, but it also dealt with social inequities and deprivation and tapped some of the same anger and frustration that had motivated black power advocates in the 1960s. When it crossed into mainstream entertainment, it retained a hard-edged "attitude" that undercut any sense of complacency about an inclusive American society.

Read the **Document**
at www.myhistorylab.com
Patricia Morrisroe, "Yuppies—The New Class" (1985)

Read the **Document**
at www.myhistorylab.com
William Julius Wilson, The Urban Underclass

Mass Media and Fragmented Culture

On June 1, 1980, CNN Cable News Network gave television viewers their first chance to watch news coverage 24 hours a day. CNN made a global reputation with live reporting on the pro-democracy protests of Chinese students in Beijing in 1989. When American bombs began to fall on Baghdad in January 1991, White House officials watched CNN to find out how their war was going.

CNN, MTV, and the rest of cable television reflected both the fragmentation of American society in the 1980s and 1990s and the increasing dependence on instant communication. As late as 1980, ordinary Americans had few choices for learning about their nation and world: virtually identical newscasts on NBC, CBS, and ABC and similar stories in *Time* and *Newsweek* helped to create a common understanding. Fifteen years later, they had learned to surf through dozens of cable channels in search of specialized programs and were beginning to explore the amazing variety of the World Wide Web (see Chapter 31).

Read the **Document**
at www.myhistorylab.com
Exploring America: Growing Inequality

Poverty amid Prosperity

Federal tax and budget changes had different effects on the rich and poor (see Figure 30–1). Those in the top fifth increased their share of after-tax income relative to everyone else during the 1980s, and the richest 1 percent saw their share of all privately held wealth grow from 31 percent to 37 percent. The 1981 tax cuts also came with sharp increases in the Social Security tax, which hit lower-income workers the hardest. The tax changes meant that the average annual income of households in the bottom 20 percent *declined* and that many actually paid higher taxes.

Cities and their residents absorbed approximately two-thirds of the cuts in the 1981–1982 federal budget. Provisions for accelerated depreciation (tax write-offs) of factories and equipment in the 1981 tax act encouraged the abandonment of center-city factories in favor of new facilities in the suburbs. One result was a growing jobs-housing mismatch. There were often plenty of jobs in the suburbs, but the poorer people who most needed the jobs were marooned in city slums and dependent on public transit that seldom served suburban employers.

Federal tax and spending policies in the 1980s decreased the security of middle-class families. As the economy continued to struggle through deindustrialization, average wage rates fell in the 1980s when measured in real purchasing. The squeeze put pressure on traditional family patterns and pushed into the workforce women who might otherwise have stayed home. Many Americans no longer expected to surpass their parents' standard of living.

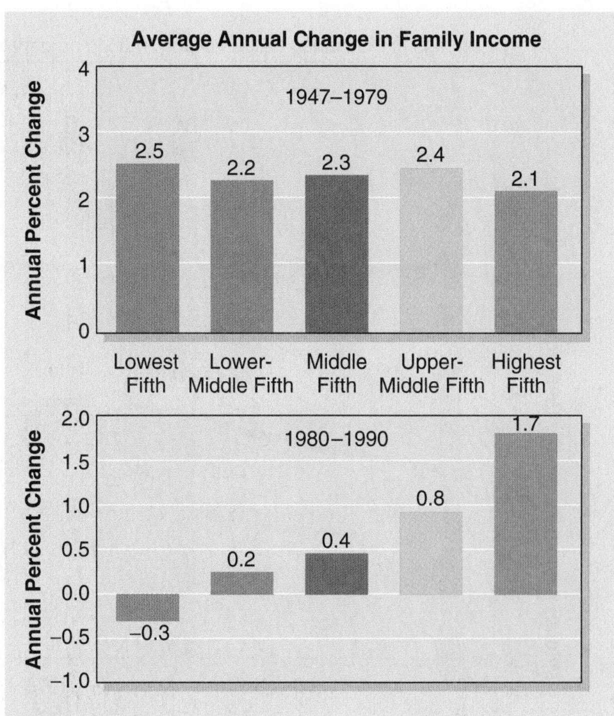

FIGURE 30–1 **Changes in Real Family Income, 1947–1979 and 1980–1990** In the 1980s, the poor got poorer, the middle class made slight gains, and the most affluent 20 percent of the American people did very well. Tax changes that helped well-off households were one factor. Another factor was the erosion of family-wage jobs in manufacturing.

Corporate downsizing and white-collar jobs. Lower-paying office jobs fell under the same sorts of pressure as factory jobs with the increasing reliance of banks, telephone companies, and credit card companies on automation. Increasing numbers of clerical and office workers in organizations of all sorts, from corporations to universities, were "temps" who shifted from job to job. The shift toward temporary and part-time workers not only kept wages low but also allowed less spending on health insurance and other benefits.

The chill of corporate downsizing hit white-collar families most heavily toward the end of the 1980s. Big business consolidations delivered improved profits by squeezing the ranks of middle managers as well as assembly-line workers. With fewer workers to supervise and with new technologies to collect and distribute information, companies could complete their cost cutting by trimming administrators.

Increase in the poverty rate. At the lower end of the economic ladder, the proportion of Americans living in poverty increased. After declining steadily from 1960 to a low of 11 percent in 1973, the poverty rate climbed back to the 13 to 15 percent range. Although the economy in the 1980s created lots of new jobs, half of them paid less than poverty-level wages. Most of the nation's millions of poor people lived in households with employed adults. In 1992, fully 18 percent of all full-time jobs did not pay enough to lift a family of four out of poverty, a jump of 50 percent over the proportion of underpaid jobs in 1981.

The wage gap and the feminization of poverty. Nor could most women, even those working full-time, expect to earn as much as men. In the 1960s and 1970s, the average working woman earned just 60 percent of the earnings of the average man (see Figure 30–2). Only part of the wage gap could be explained by measurable factors, such as education or experience. The gap narrowed in the 1980s and 1990s, with women's earnings rising to 75 percent of men's by 2003. About half of the change was the result of bad news—the decline of earnings among men as high-wage factory jobs disappeared. The other half was the positive result of better-educated younger women finding better jobs. Indeed, women would earn 57 percent of four-year college degrees awarded in 2002 compared to 38 percent in 1960, and they earned 47 percent of first professional degrees, up from 3 percent.

Read the **Document**
at www.myhistorylab.com
From Then to Now Online: Women and Office Work

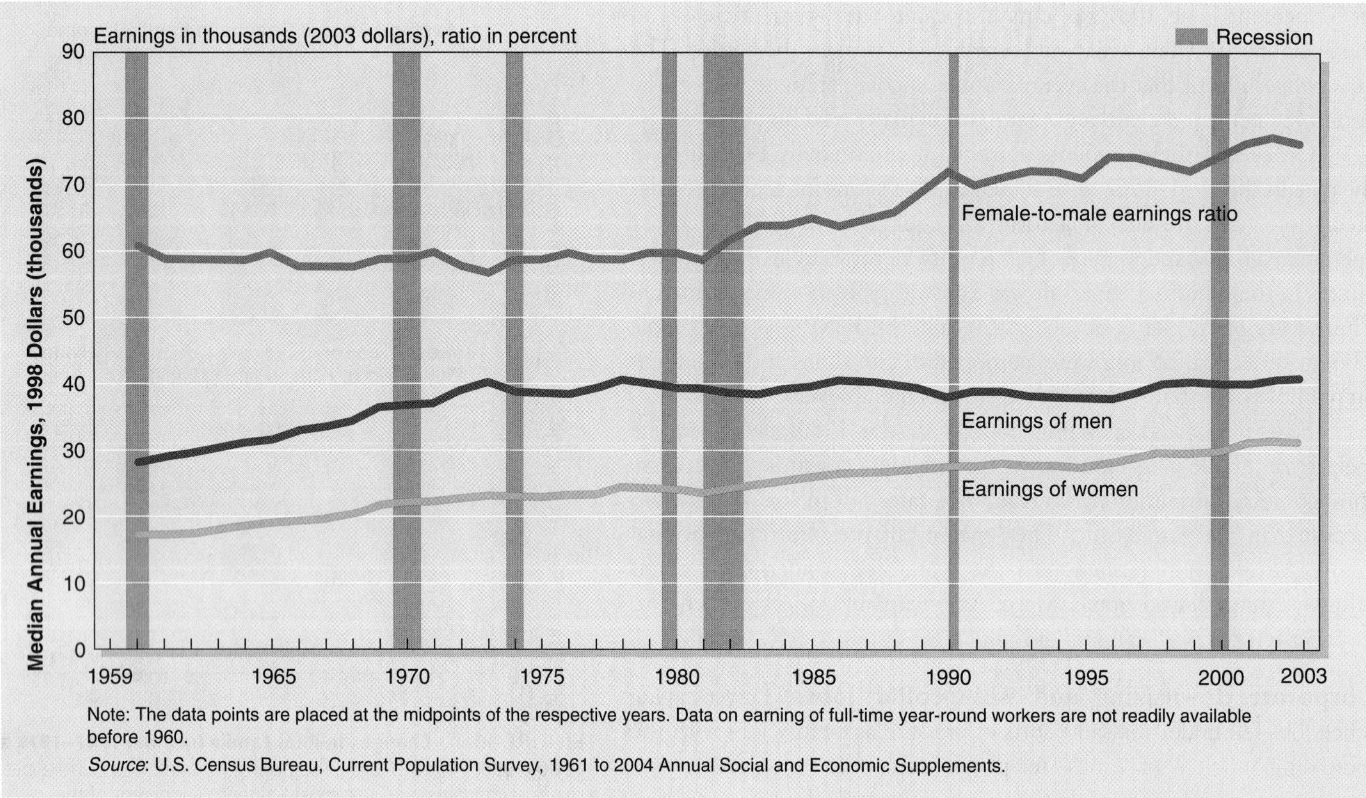

FIGURE 30–2 **Comparison of Men's and Women's Earnings, 1960–2003** U.S. Census data show the median earnings of women who worked full time and year round compared to those of men. Since the 1960s, the gap between women and men has narrowed. One reason is better pay for jobs traditionally held by women, but another has been the declining earning power of men without college educations. Nevertheless, the gender gap in earning power remains an important economic issue.

QUICK REVIEW

The Feminization of Poverty

- At the end of the 1980s, women constituted two-thirds of poor adults.
- 6 percent of married-couple households were below poverty level.
- 32 percent of households headed by a women without a husband present were below poverty level.

Nevertheless, the low earning capacity of women with limited educations meant that women were far more likely than men to be poor. Women constituted nearly two-thirds of poor adults at the end of the 1980s. Only 6 percent of married-couple households were below poverty level, but 32 percent of households headed by a woman without a husband present were poor. The feminization of poverty and American reliance on private support for child rearing also meant that children had a higher chance of living in poverty than adults and that poor American children were worse off than their peers in other advanced nations.

Homelessness in America. Falling below even the working poor were growing numbers of homeless Americans. In the 1980s, several factors made homelessness more visible and pressing. A new approach to the treatment of the mentally ill reduced the population of mental hospitals from 540,000 in 1960 to only 140,000 in 1980. Deinstitutionalized patients were supposed to receive community-based treatment, but many ended up on the streets and in overnight shelters. New forms of self-destructive drug abuse, such as crack addiction, joined alcoholism. A boom in downtown real estate destroyed old skid-row districts with their bars, missions, and dollar-a-night hotels.

These factors tripled the number of permanently homeless people during the early and middle 1980s, from 200,000 to somewhere between 500,000 and 700,000. Twice or three times that many may have been homeless for part of a given year. For every person in a shelter on a given night, two people were sleeping on sidewalks, in parks, in cars, and in abandoned buildings.

Consolidating the Revolution: George Bush

In 1988 George H. W. Bush, Reagan's vice president for eight years, won the presidential election with 56 percent of the popular vote and 40 out of 50 states. Bush's view of national and world politics reflected a background in which personal connections counted. He was raised as part of the New England elite, built an oil business in Texas, and then held a series of high-level federal appointments.

Michael Dukakis, the Democratic nominee in 1988, was a dry-as-dust, by-the-numbers manager who offered the American people "competence." The Bush campaign director, Lee Atwater, looked for hot-button issues that could fit onto a three-by-five card. Pro-Bush advertisements tapped into real worries among the voters—fear of crime, racial tension, eroding social values—and attached them to Dukakis. George Bush, despite his background in prep schools and country clubs, came out looking tough as nails, while the Democrats looked inept.

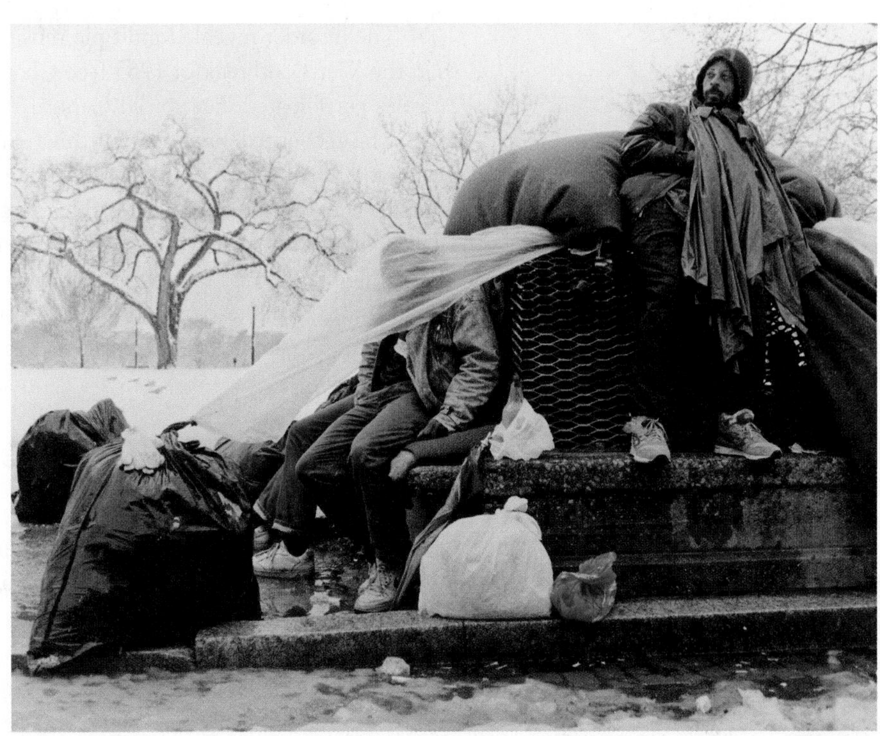
Homeless people huddle over a heating grate outside the Commerce Department building in Washington, waiting until shelters open at night. In the 1980s, rising home prices and the closure of most mental hospitals pushed many Americans onto the streets. Estimates of the number of homeless in the late 1980s ranged from 300,000 to 3 million, depending on the definition of homelessness and the political goals of the estimator.

The ads locked Bush into a rhetorical war on crime and drugs that was his major domestic policy. Americans had good cause to be worried about public safety, but most were generally unaware that the likelihood of becoming the target of a violent crime had leveled off and would continue to fall in the 1990s or that crime was far worse in minority communities than elsewhere, in part due to gang- and drug-related activities. Bush tripled the federal drug control budget and stepped up efforts to stop the flow of illegal drugs across the border. Longer sentences and mandatory jail time meant that half of federal prison inmates in 1990 were in for drug crimes.

Read the **Document** at **www.myhistorylab.com** *George H. W. Bush, Inaugural Address (1989)*

Watch the **Video** at **www.myhistorylab.com** *George Bush Presidential Campaign Ad: The Revolving Door*

George Bush believed that Americans wanted government to leave them alone. He ignored a flood of new ideas from entrepreneurial conservatives, such as HUD Secretary Jack Kemp. The major legislation from the Bush administration was a transportation bill that shifted federal priorities from highway building toward mass transit and the **Americans with Disabilities Act** (1990) to prevent discrimination against people with physical handicaps. In the areas of crime and healthcare, however, Bush's lack of leadership left continuing problems.

Americans with Disabilities Act Legislation in 1992 that banned discrimination against physically handicapped persons in employment, transportation, and public accommodations.

The same attitude produced weak economic policies. The national debt had amounted to 50 percent of personal savings in 1980 but swelled to 125 percent by 1990. The massive budget deficits of the 1980s combined with growing trade deficits to turn the United States from an international creditor to a debtor nation. After pledging no new taxes in his campaign, Bush backed into a tax increase in 1990. A stronger leader might have justified the taxes to the nation, but voters found it hard to forget the president's attempts to downplay the importance of his decision.

The most conspicuous domestic event of the Bush administration—the "Rodney King riot" of April 1992 in Los Angeles—was a reminder of the nation's inattention to the problems of race and poverty. Rodney King was a black motorist who had been savagely clubbed and kicked by police officers while being arrested after a car chase on March 3, 1991. A nearby resident captured the beating on videotape from his apartment. Early the next year, the four officers stood trial for unjustified use of force before a suburban jury. The televised trial and the unexpected verdict of not guilty on April 29 stirred deep anger that escalated into four days of rioting.

The disorder revealed multiple tensions among ethnic groups and was far more complex than the Watts outbreak of 1965 (see Chapter 29). African Americans from south-central Los Angeles participated, but so did Central American and Mexican immigrants in adjacent districts, who accounted for about one-third of the 12,000 arrests. The disorder spread south to Long Beach and north to the edge of upscale neighborhoods in Westwood and Beverly Hills. Rioters assaulted the downtown police headquarters, city hall, and the *Los Angeles Times* building. As in 1965, some targets were white passers-by and symbols of white authority. But members of competing minority groups were also victims as angry black people targeted hundreds of Korean-owned and Vietnamese-owned shops as symbols of economic discrimination. Four days of disorder left 58 people dead, mostly African Americans and Latinos.

THE CLIMAX OF THE COLD WAR

HOW AND why did the Cold War come to an end?

Ronald Reagan entered office determined to reassert U.S. leadership in world affairs and not to lose the Cold War. He considered the Soviet Union not a coequal nation with legitimate world interests but an "evil empire." After the era of *détente*, global tensions had started to mount in the late 1970s. They were soon higher than they had been since the 1960s. But by the end of Reagan's two terms, unexpected changes were rapidly bringing the Cold War to an end, and George Bush faced a radically new set of foreign policy issues.

Confronting the Soviet Union

Who renewed the Cold War after Nixon's diplomacy of *détente* and Carter's early efforts at negotiation? The Soviets had pursued military expansion in the 1970s, triggering the fear that they might stage a nuclear Pearl Harbor. The Soviet Union in 1980 was supporting Marxist regimes in civil wars in Angola, Ethiopia, Nicaragua, and especially Afghanistan, where its 1980 intervention led to a decade of costly and futile military occupation. Were these actions parts of a careful plan? Or did they result from the Cold War inertia of a rudderless nation that reacted to situations one at a time? Given the aging Soviet leadership and the economic weaknesses revealed in the late 1980s, it makes more sense to see the Soviets as muddling along rather than executing a well-planned global strategy.

On the American side, Reagan's readiness to confront "the focus of evil in the modern world" reflected the views of many conservative supporters that the Soviet Union was a monolithic and ideologically motivated foe bent on world conquest. In hindsight, some Reaganites claim that the administration's foreign policy and massive increases in defense spending were part of a deliberate and coordinated scheme to check a Soviet offensive and bankrupt the Soviet Union by pushing it into a new arms race. It is just as likely, however, that the administration's defense and foreign policy initiatives were a set of discrete but effective decisions.

QUICK REVIEW

The New Arms Race

- The Reagan administration reemphasized central Europe as the focus of superpower rivalry.
- Pershing II missiles were placed in Europe in 1983.
- A National Security Directive stated that the U.S. might be able to win a nuclear war.

The Reagan administration reemphasized central Europe as the focus of superpower rivalry, just as it had been in the 1950s and early 1960s. To counter improved Soviet armaments, the United States began to place cruise missiles and mid-range Pershing II missiles in Europe in 1983. NATO governments approved the action, but it frightened millions of their citizens.

Escalation of the nuclear arms race reinvigorated the antiwar and antinuclear movement in the United States as well as Europe. Drawing on the experience of the antiwar movement, the nuclear-freeze campaign caught the imagination of many Americans in 1981 and 1982. It sought to halt the manufacture and deployment of new atomic weapons by the great powers. Nearly a million people turned out for a nuclear-freeze rally in New York in 1982. Hundreds of local communities endorsed the freeze or took the symbolic step of declaring themselves nuclear-free zones.

Strategic Defense Initiative (SDI) President Reagan's program, announced in 1983, to defend the U.S. against nuclear missile attack with untested weapons systems and sophisticated technologies.

In response, Reagan announced the **Strategic Defense Initiative (SDI),** or Star Wars program, in 1983. SDI was to deploy new defenses that could intercept and destroy ballistic missiles as they rose from the ground and arced through space. Few scientists thought that SDI could work. Many arms control experts thought that defensive systems were dangerous and destabilizing, because strong defenses suggested that a nation might be willing to risk a nuclear exchange.

Risky Business: Foreign Policy Adventures

The same administration that sometimes seemed reckless in its grand strategy also took risks to assert U.S. influence in global trouble spots to block or roll back Soviet influence. Reagan asserted America's right to intervene anywhere in the world to support local groups fighting against Marxist governments. The assumption underlying this assertion, which later became known as the **Reagan Doctrine,** was that Soviet-influenced governments in Asia, Africa, and Latin America needed to be eliminated if the United States was to win the Cold War.

Reagan Doctrine The policy assumption that Soviet-influenced governments in Asia, Africa, and Latin America needed to be eliminated if the United States was to win the Cold War.

Nevertheless, Reagan kept the United States out of a major war and backed off in the face of serious trouble. Foreign interventions were designed to achieve symbolic victories rather than change the global balance of power. The exception was the Caribbean and Central America, the "backyard" where the United States had always claimed an overriding interest and where left-wing action infuriated Reagan's conservative supporters.

Intervention and covert activities in Central America. The Reagan administration attributed political turmoil in Central America to Soviet influence and to arms and agitators from Soviet-backed Cuba. Between 1980 and 1983, the United States sent more military aid to conservative governments and groups in Central America than it had during the previous 30 years. Indeed, Central America became the focus of a secret foreign policy operated by the CIA and then by National Security Council (NSC) staff, since a Democratic Congress was not convinced of the danger. The CIA and the NSC engaged not just in espionage but in direct covert operations. The chief target was Nicaragua, the Central American country where leftist Sandinista rebels had overthrown the Somoza dictatorship in 1979. In the early 1980s, Reagan approved CIA plans to arm and organize approximately 10,500 so-called Contras, from the remnants of Somoza's national guard. From bases in Honduras, the Contras harassed the Sandinistas with sabotage and raids.

The Reagan administration bent the law to support its covert effort to overthrow the Sandinista regime. An unsympathetic Congress blocked U.S. funding for the Contras. In response, CIA director William Casey directed Lieutenant Colonel Oliver North of the National Security Council staff to illegally organize aid from private donors. The arms pipeline operated until a supply plane was shot down in 1986. The Contras failed as a military effort, but the civil war and international pressure persuaded the Sandinistas to allow free elections that led to a democratic, centrist government.

The war against drugs. The American war against drugs was simultaneously shaping U.S. policy in the Caribbean and straining relations with Latin America. As president, George Bush parlayed the war on drugs into war on Panama during his first year in office, extending the American tradition of ousting uncooperative governments around the Caribbean. General Manuel Noriega, the Panamanian strongman, had once been on the CIA payroll. He had since turned to international drug sales in defiance of United States antismuggling efforts. On December 20, 1989, American troops invaded Panama, hunted down Noriega, and brought him back to stand trial in the United States on drug-trafficking charges. A handful of Americans and thousands of Panamanians died, many of them civilians caught in the crossfire.

Intervention in the Middle East. If the results of intervention in Nicaragua and Panama were mixed, intervention in the Middle East was a failure. In 1982 Israel invaded Lebanon, a small nation to its north, to clear Palestinian guerrillas from its borders and set up a friendly Lebanese government. The Israeli army bogged down in a civil war between Christian Arabs and

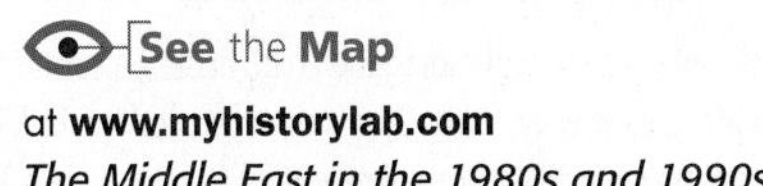

at www.myhistorylab.com
The Middle East in the 1980s and 1990s

Read the Document at www.myhistorylab.com *Ronald Reagan, Iran Contra Address (1987)*

Muslims. Reagan sent U.S. Marines to preserve the semblance of a Lebanese state and provide a face-saving exit for Israel. In October 1983, a terrorist car bomb killed 241 Marines in their barracks. The remainder were soon gone, confirming the Syrian observation that Americans were "short of breath" when it came to Middle East politics. The debacle in Lebanon undermined U.S.-backed peace initiatives in the Middle East.

The Iran-Contra Affair. Even less effective were the Reagan administration's secret efforts to sell weapons to Iran in return for Iranian help in securing the release of Americans held hostage by pro-Iranian Islamic radicals in Lebanon. The United States in 1985 joined Israel in selling 500 antitank missiles to Iran, then embroiled in a long, bitter war with Iraq. The deal followed stern public pronouncements that the United States would never negotiate with terrorists and considered Iran's religious leaders to be backers of international terrorism. It also violated the official trade embargo against Iran, which had been in place since the U.S. embassy seizure in 1979. In May 1986, National Security adviser Robert McFarlane flew to Iran for more arms-for-hostages talks, carrying a chocolate cake and a Bible autographed by Reagan to present to the Iranian leader Ayatollah Khomeini. When the deals came to light in 1986 and congressional hearings were held in the summer of 1987, Americans were startled to learn that Colonel North had funneled millions of dollars from the arms sales to the Nicaraguan Contras in a double evasion of the law.

Watch the Video at www.myhistorylab.com *Oliver North Hearing*

As had been true with Watergate, the Iran-Contra affair was a two-sided scandal. First was the blatant misjudgment of operating a secret, bumbling, and unlawful foreign policy that depended on international arms dealers and ousted Nicaraguan military officers. Second was a concerted effort to cover up the illegal and unconstitutional actions. North shredded relevant documents and lied to Congress. In his final report in 1994, Special Prosecutor Lawrence Walsh found that President Reagan and Vice President Bush were aware of much of what had gone on and had participated in efforts to withhold information and mislead Congress.

Mikhail Gorbachev, holding the child, hosted a summit meeting with President Reagan in Moscow in May 1988. Their smiles ignored the lack of progress toward disarmament beyond the Intermediate-Range Nuclear Forces Treaty of the previous year.

U.S. policy in Asia. American policy in Asia was a refreshing contrast with practices in Central America and the Middle East. In the Philippines, American diplomats helped push corrupt President Ferdinand Marcos out and opened the way for a popular uprising to put Corazon Aquino in office. In South Korea, the United States similarly helped ease out an unpopular dictator by firmly supporting democratic elections that brought in a more popular but still pro-American government.

EMBRACING *PERESTROIKA*

Thaw in the Cold War started in Moscow as Soviet leaders sought to salvage a system under severe economic stress. Mikhail Gorbachev became general secretary of the Communist Party in 1985, when the Soviet Union was trapped in the sixth year of its failed attempt to control Afghanistan. Gorbachev startled Soviet citizens by urging ***glasnost,*** or political openness, with free discussion of issues and relaxation of controls on the press. He followed by setting the goal of ***perestroika,*** or restructuring of the painfully bureaucratic Soviet economy that was falling behind capitalist nations. His hope was that market-oriented reforms would help the Soviet Union keep up with the United States.

Gorbachev decided that he needed to reduce the crushing burden of Soviet defense spending if the Soviet Union was to have any chance of modernizing. During Reagan's second term, the Soviets offered one concession after another in a drive for arms control.

Reagan had the vision (or audacity) to embrace the new Soviet position. He cast off decades of belief in the dangers of Soviet Communism and had the political courage to take Gorbachev seriously. One of his reasons for SDI had been his belief that the abolition of nuclear weapons was better than fine-tuning the balance of terror. Now he was willing to forget his own rhetoric. He frightened his own staff when he met with Gorbachev in the summer of 1986 and accepted the principle of deep cuts in strategic forces. Reagan explained that when he railed against the evil empire, he had been talking about Brezhnev and the bad old days; Gorbachev and *glasnost* were different.

glasnost Russian for "openness," applied to Mikhail Gorbachev's encouragement of new ideas and easing of political repression in the Soviet Union.

perestroika Russian for "restructuring," applied to Mikhail Gorbachev's efforts to make the Soviet economic and political systems more modern, flexible, and innovative.

In the end, Reagan negotiated the **Intermediate-Range Nuclear Forces Treaty (INF)** over the strong objections of the CIA and the Defense Department. INF was the first true nuclear-disarmament treaty (see Overview, Controlling Nuclear Weapons: Four Decades of Effort). Previous agreements had only slowed the growth of nuclear weapons; they were "speed limits" for the arms race. The new pact matched Soviet SS-20s with U.S. cruise missiles as an entire class of weapons that would be destroyed, with on-site inspections for verification.

The wall that divided East from West Berlin from 1962 to 1989 was a hated symbol of the Cold War. When the Communist government of East Germany collapsed in November 1989, jubilant Berliners celebrated the opening of the wall and the reuniting of the divided city.

Crisis and Democracy in Eastern Europe

Reagan's successor, President Bush, acted on his belief in personal diplomacy, basing much of his foreign policy on his changing attitudes toward Mikhail Gorbachev. He started lukewarm, talking tough to please the Republican right wing. Bush feared that Gorbachev, by instituting reforms that challenged the entrenched Communist Party leaders, was being imprudent: one of the worst things he could say about another leader. Before 1989 was over, however, the president had decided that Gorbachev was OK. For the next two years, the United States pushed the prodemocratic transformation of eastern Europe while being careful not to gloat in public or damage Gorbachev's position at home.

The end of Communist regimes in eastern Europe. The people of eastern Europe overcame both U.S. and Soviet caution. Instead of the careful economic liberalization Gorbachev envisioned, the Warsaw Pact system collapsed. Poland held free elections in June 1989, Hungary adopted a democratic constitution in October, and prodemocracy

OVERVIEW Controlling Nuclear Weapons: Four Decades of Effort

Limiting the testing of nuclear weapons	Limited Test Ban Treaty (1963)	Banned nuclear testing in the atmosphere, ocean, and outer space.
	Comprehensive Test Ban Treaty (1996)	Banned all nuclear tests, including underground tests; rejected by U.S. Senate in 1999.
Halting the spread of nuclear weapons	Nuclear Non-Proliferation Treaty (1968)	Pledged five recognized nuclear nations (United States, Soviet Union, Britain, France, China) to pursue disarmament in good faith, and 140 other nations not to acquire nuclear weapons.
	Strategic Arms Limitation Treaty (SALT I, 1972)	Limited the number of nuclear-armed missiles and bombers maintained by the United States and Soviet Union. Closely associated with U.S.-Soviet agreement to limit deployment of antiballistic missile systems to one site each.
	Strategic Arms Limitation Treaty (SALT II, 1979)	Further limited the number of nuclear-armed missiles and bombers. Not ratified but followed by Carter and Reagan administrations.
Reducing the number of nuclear weapons	Intermediate-Range Nuclear Forces Treaty (1987)	Required the United States to eliminate 846 nuclear armed cruise missiles, and the Soviet Union to eliminate 1,846 SS-20 missiles.
	Strategic Arms Reduction Treaty (START I, 1991)	By July 1999, led to reductions of approximately 2,750 nuclear warheads by the United States and 3,725 warheads by the nations of the former USSR. Expired December 2009.
	Strategic Arms Reduction Treaty (START II, 1993)	Set further cuts in nuclear arsenals. Ratified by Russia in April 2000. Russia withdrew in 2002 after the U.S. abandoned the Anti-Ballistic Missile Treaty.
	Strategic Offensive Reductions (2002)	Russia and the United States each agree to deploy no more than 1,700–2,200 strategic nuclear warheads.

Data Source: Arms Control Association.

Intermediate-Range Nuclear Forces Treaty (INF) Disarmament agreement between the U.S. and the Soviet Union under which an entire class of missiles would be removed and destroyed and on-site inspections would be permitted for verification.

demonstrations then forced out Communist leaders in other eastern European countries. When East Germans began to flee westward through Hungary, the East German regime bowed to mounting pressure and opened the Berlin Wall on November 9. By the end of 1989, there were new democratic or non-Communist governments in Czechoslovakia, Romania, Bulgaria, and East Germany. These largely peaceful revolutions destroyed the military and economic agreements that had harnessed the satellites to the Soviet economy (the Warsaw Pact and Comecon). The Soviet Union swallowed hard, accepted the loss of its satellites, and slowly withdrew its army from eastern Europe.

German reunification and the dissolution of the Soviet Union. Events in Europe left German reunification as a point of possible conflict. Soviet policy since 1945 had sought to prevent the reemergence of a strong, united Germany that might again threaten its neighbors. West German Chancellor Helmut Kohl removed one obstacle when he reassured Poland and Russia that Germany would seek no changes in the boundaries drawn after World War II. By July 1990, the United States and the Soviet Union had agreed that a reunited Germany would belong to NATO. The decision satisfied France and Britain that a stronger Germany would still be under the influence of the Western allies. In October, the two Germanies completed their political unification, although it would be years before their mismatched economies functioned as one. Reunification was the last step in the diplomatic legacy of World War II.

The final act in the transformation of the Soviet Union began with a failed coup against Mikhail Gorbachev in August 1991. The Soviet Union had held free elections in 1989. Now Gorbachev scheduled a vote on a new constitution that would decrease the power of the central government. Old-line Communist bureaucrats who feared the change arrested Gorbachev in his vacation house and tried to take over the government apparatus in Moscow. Boris Yeltsin, president of the Russian Republic, organized the resistance. Muscovites flocked to support Yeltsin and defied tank crews in front of the Russian parliament building. Within three days, the plotters themselves were under arrest.

The coup hastened the fragmentation of the Soviet Union. Before the month was out, the Soviet parliament banned the Communist Party. Gorbachev soon resigned. Previously suppressed nationalist feelings caused all 15 component republics of the Soviet Union to declare their independence. The superpower Union of Soviet Socialist Republics ceased to exist. Russia remained the largest and strongest of the new states, followed by Ukraine and Kazakhstan. (See Overview, Why Did the Cold War End?)

QUICK REVIEW

The Fall of Gorbachev and the Soviet Union

- August 1991: old-line Communists attempt a coup against Gorbachev.
- Boris Yeltsin organized the successful resistance to the plotters.
- Gorbachev soon resigned and all fifteen Soviet republics declared their independence.

W
WHERE TO LEARN MORE
The Gulf War
http://archives.cbc.ca/war_conflict/1991_gulf_war/

The Persian Gulf War

On August 2, 1990, President Saddam Hussein of Iraq seized the small neighboring oil-rich country of Kuwait. The quick conquest gave Iraq control of 20 percent of the world's oil production and reserves. President Bush demanded unconditional withdrawal, enlisted European and Arab allies in an anti-Iraq coalition, and persuaded Saudi Arabia to accept substantial U.S. forces to protect it against Iraqi invasion.

The background for Iraq's invasion was a simmering dispute over border oil fields and islands in the Persian Gulf. Iraq was a dictatorship that had just emerged from an immensely costly eight-year war with Iran. Saddam Hussein had depended on help from the United States and Arab nations in this war, but Iraq was now economically exhausted. Kuwait was a small, rich nation whose ruling dynasty enjoyed few friends but plenty of oil royalties. The U.S. State Department had signaled earlier in 1990 that it might support some concessions by Kuwait in its dispute with Iraq. Saddam Hussein read the signal as an open invitation to do what he wanted; having been favored in the past by the United States, he probably expected denunciations but no military response.

See the **Map**
at **www.myhistorylab.com**
The Middle East in the 1980s and 1990s

Read the **Document**
at **www.myhistorylab.com**
George Bush, Allied Military Action in the Persian Gulf (1991)

Watch the **Video**
at **www.myhistorylab.com**
President Bush on the Gulf War

The Iraqis gave George Bush a golden opportunity to assert America's world influence. The Bush administration was concerned that Iraq might target oil-rich Saudi Arabia. The importance of Middle Eastern oil helped to enlist France and Britain as military allies and to secure billions of dollars from Germany and Japan. Iraq had antagonized nearly all its neighbors. The collapse of Soviet power and Gorbachev's interest in cooperating with the United States meant that the Soviets would not interfere with U.S. plans.

Bush and his advisers offered a series of justifications for U.S. actions. First, and most basic, were the desire to punish armed aggression and the presumed need to protect Iraq's other neighbors. In fact, there was scant evidence of Iraqi preparations against Saudi Arabia. The buildup of U.S. air power plus effective economic sanctions would have accomplished both protection and punishment. Sanctions and diplomatic pressure might also have brought withdrawal from most or all of Kuwait. However, additional American objectives—to destroy Iraq's capacity to create nuclear weapons and to topple Saddam's regime—would require direct military action.

Bush probably decided on war in October, eventually increasing the number of American troops in Saudi Arabia to 580,000. The United States stepped up diplomatic pressure by securing a series of increasingly tough United Nations resolutions that culminated in November 1990 with Security Council Resolution 678, authorizing "all necessary means" to liberate Kuwait. The president convinced Congress to agree to military action under the umbrella of the UN. The United States ignored compromise plans floated by France and last-minute concessions from Iraq.

OVERVIEW Why Did the Cold War End?

Commentators have offered a number of explanations for the rapid failure of the USSR and the collapse of Soviet power at the end of the 1980s. All of these factors made contributions to the complex unraveling of the Cold War.

Economic exhaustion:	The United States in the late 1970s embarked on a great modernization and expansion of its military forces. The USSR exhausted its economy and revealed its technical backwardness by trying to keep pace. Gorbachev's policy of *perestroika* was an attempt to reduce the bureaucratic inertia of the economy.
Failure of leadership:	The Soviet Union in the 1970s and early 1980s was governed by unimaginative bureaucrats. A closed elite that thought only of preserving their privileges and authority could not adapt to a changing world. The policy of *glasnost* was an effort to encourage new ideas.
Intervention in Afghanistan:	The disastrous intervention in Afghanistan revealed the limits of Soviet military power. It alienated the large Muslim population of the USSR and brought disillusionment with the incompetence of Soviet leaders.
Triumph of democratic ideas:	As political discussion became more free, the appeal of democratic ideas took on its own momentum, especially in eastern European satellite nations such as East Germany, Czechoslovakia, and Poland.
Power of nationalism:	The collapse of the Soviet empire was triggered by the resurgence of national sentiments throughout the Soviet empire. National sentiments fueled the breakaway of the eastern European satellite nations such as Hungary, Romania, and Poland. Nationalism also broke up the USSR itself as 14 smaller socialist republics declared independence from the Russian-dominated Union.

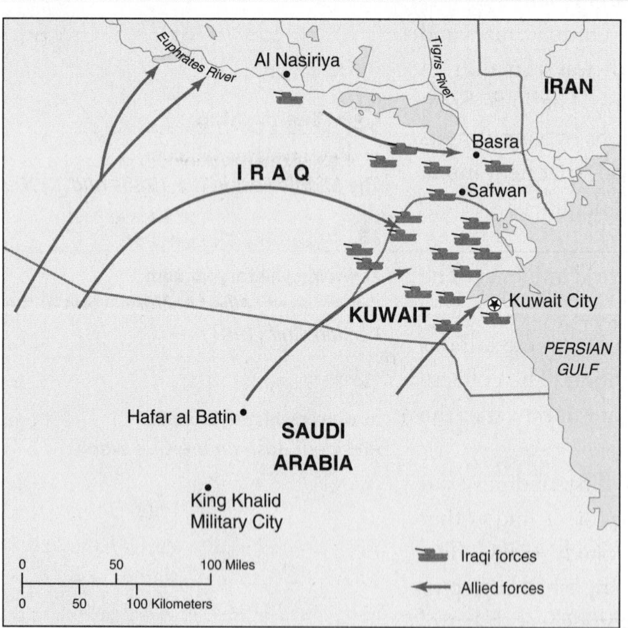

MAP 30–2 **The Persian Gulf War** Ground operations against Iraq in the Persian Gulf War followed six weeks of aerial bombardment. The ground attack, which met quick success, was a multinational effort by the United States, Britain, France, Saudi Arabia, and other Arab nations threatened by an aggressive Iraq. The war freed Kuwait from Iraqi occupation but stopped before forcing a change in Iraq's government.

What was the U.S. strategy in the Persian Gulf War? How was it shaped by America's experience in Vietnam?

The Persian Gulf War began one day after the UN's January 15 deadline for Iraqi withdrawal from Kuwait. Operation Desert Storm opened with massive air attacks on command centers, transportation facilities, and Iraqi forward positions. The air war destroyed 40 to 50 percent of Iraqi tanks and artillery by late February. The attacks also seriously hurt Iraqi civilians by disrupting utilities and food supplies.

The 40-day rain of bombs was the prelude to a ground attack (see Map 30–2). On February 24, 1991, allied forces swept into Iraq. Americans, Saudis, Syrians, and Egyptians advanced directly to liberate Kuwait. A cease-fire came 100 hours after the start of the ground war. Allied forces suffered only 240 deaths in action, compared to perhaps 100,000 for the Iraqis.

Bush directed Desert Storm with the "Vietnam syndrome" in mind, believing that Americans were willing to accept war only if it involved overwhelming U.S. force and ended quickly. The United States hoped to replace Saddam Hussein without disrupting Iraqi society. Instead, the 100-hour war incited armed rebellions against Saddam in southern Iraq by Shiites, a group within the Muslim religion whose adherents comprise a majority in Iraq, and in the north by the ethnically distinct Kurds. Because Bush and his advisers were unwilling to get embroiled in a civil war or commit the United States to occupy all of Iraq, they stood by while Saddam crushed the uprisings. In one sense, the U.S. won the war but not the peace. Saddam Hussein became a hero to many in the Islamic world simply by surviving.

GROWTH IN THE SUNBELT

HOW DID growth in the Sunbelt shape national politics in the 1980s and 1990s?

The rise of the **Sunbelt,** which is anchored by Florida, Texas, and California, reflected the leading economic trends of the 1970s and 1980s, including military spending, immigration from Asia and Latin America, and recreation and retirement spending. Corporations liked the business climate of the South, which had weak labor laws, low taxes, and generally low costs of living and doing business.

Sunbelt The states of the American South and Southwest.

New factories dotted the southern landscape, often in smaller towns rather than cities. General Motors closed factories in Flint, Michigan, but invested in a new Saturn plant in Spring Hill, Tennessee. In contrast to troubled industrial cities in the Northeast and Midwest, cities like Orlando, Charlotte, Atlanta, Dallas, and Phoenix enjoyed headlong prosperity. Houston, with sprawling growth, business spinoffs from NASA, and purring air-conditioners, epitomized the booming metropolitan areas of the South and West.

See the **Map** at **www.myhistorylab.com** *America's Move to the Sunbelt, 1970–1981*

THE DEFENSE ECONOMY

The Vietnam buildup and reinvestment in the military during the Carter (1977–1981) and Reagan (1981–1989) administrations fueled the growth of the Sunbelt. Over the 40 years from the Korean conflict to the Persian Gulf War, the United States made itself the mightiest military power ever known. Military bases and defense contractors remolded the economic landscape, as mild winters and clear skies for training and operations helped the South and West attract more than 75 percent of military payrolls.

Big cities and small depended on defense spending. Southern California thrived on more than 500,000 jobs in the aircraft industry. A thousand miles away, visitors to Colorado Springs could drive past sprawling Fort Carson and visit the new Air Force Academy, opened in 1958. Sunk deep from view was the North American Air Defense Command headquarters beneath Cheyenne Mountain west of the city.

Defense spending underwrote the expansion of American science and technology. Nearly one-third of all engineers worked on military projects. Large universities, such as MIT, the University of Michigan, the California Institute of Technology, and Stanford, were leading defense contractors. The modern electronics business started in New York, Boston, and the San Francisco Bay area with research and development for military uses, such as guided-missile controls. California's Silicon Valley grew with military sales long before it turned to consumer markets. The space component of the aerospace industry was equally reliant on the defense economy, with NASA spending justified by competition with the Soviet Union. NASA's centers were scattered across the South: launch facilities at the Kennedy Space Center in Cape Canaveral, Florida; research labs at Huntsville, Alabama; and Houston's Manned Spacecraft Center as the control center for space exploration.

QUICK REVIEW

The Military and the Economy

- Reinvestment in the military fueled growth in the Sunbelt.
- Communities of all sizes depended on the military.
- Military spending underwrote the expansion of American science and technology.

AMERICANS FROM AROUND THE WORLD

Few Americans anticipated the effects of the **Immigration and Nationality Act of 1965,** which transformed the ethnic mix of the United States and helped to stimulate the Sunbelt boom. The new law initiated a change in the composition of the American people by abolishing the national quota system in effect since 1924. Quotas had favored immigrants from western Europe and limited those from other parts of the world. The old law's racial bias contradicted the self-proclaimed role of the United States as a defender of freedom, and immigration reform was part of the propaganda battle of the Cold War. The new law gave preference to family reunification and welcomed immigrants from all nations equally. The United States also accepted refugees from Communism outside the annual limits.

Immigration and Nationality Act of 1965 Federal legislation that replaced the national quota system for immigration with overall limits of 170,000 immigrants per year from the Eastern Hemisphere and 120,000 per year from the Western Hemisphere.

Immigration reform opened the doors to Mediterranean Europe, Latin America, and Asia. Legal migration to the United States surged from 1.1 million in 1960–1964 to nearly

GLOBAL CONNECTIONS

Disney in Tokyo and Paris

Tokyo Disneyland opened in 1983 as the first Disney theme park outside the United States. Designed by Walt Disney Imagineering, it copied California's original Disneyland and Florida's Walt Disney World. It includes the classic Disneyland features of Adventureland, Westernland, Tomorrowland, and Fantasyland (complete with a Cinderella Castle that looks just like its Florida counterpart).

Tokyo Disney was enormously successful from the start. It has consistently attracted huge crowds. For many years it was the most popular theme park in the world, and developers have added Tokyo DisneySea to keep visitors coming back.

If Japanese immediately took to Tokyo Disneyland, Europeans were much less excited by the Euro Disney Resort that opened east of Paris in 1992. Critics complained about the strict rules for workers. Intellectuals criticized the invasion of American popular culture into the heart of Europe. It took several years, and new attractions like De la Terre à la Lune (Space Mountain), to bring in enough visitors to put the project in the black.

The contrasting experiences demonstrate the close affinities between American and Japanese pop culture. Japanese monster movies of the 1950s, including Godzilla, King of Monsters, and his various opponents, earned money in both Japan and the United States. The huge Japanese animation, or anime, industry that developed after World War II drew on Disney cartoon style. It developed into an economic powerhouse of comic books, TV series, video games, and spinoff toys that made fortunes for Sony, Nintendo, and other companies. Pokemon, which began as a children's game for handheld computers, grew into a marketing phenomenon that made the cover of *Time* magazine.

This exchange of entertainment and consumer products has been part of the increasingly close engagement between the economies of the United States and East Asia. Its roots lie in the democratic revival of Japan after World War II and in the opening of political relations between the United States and the People's Republic of China in the 1970s. It has grown into a huge field of investment and exchange of everything from sneakers to steel, comic book artists to centerfielders.

- What are some reasons for the contrasting ways that Japan and France have responded to Disney theme resorts?

TABLE 30–1

Major Racial and Ethnic Minorities in the United States

	1960 Population (in millions)	Percentage of Total	2000 Population (in millions)	Percentage of Total
American Indians	0.5	0.3	2.5	0.9
Asians and Pacific Islanders	1.1	0.6	10.6	3.7
African Americans	18.9	10.5	34.7	12.3
Hispanics	not available		35.3	12.5

4 million for 1990–1994. Nonlegal immigrants may have doubled the total number of newcomers in the 1970s and early 1980s. Not since World War I had the United States absorbed so many new residents.

Immigration changed the nation's ethnic mix. Members of officially defined ethnic and racial minorities accounted for 25 percent of Americans in 1990 and 30 percent in 2000 (see Table 30–1). Roughly 28 million Americans, or 10.4 percent of the population, had been born in other countries according to the 2000 census.

Read the Document at www.myhistorylab.com *Cecelia Rosa Avila, Third Generation Mexican American (1988)*

The largest single group of new Americans came from Mexico. The long border has facilitated easy movement from south to north. Especially in the border states of Texas, New Mexico, Arizona, and California, permanent immigrants have mingled with tourists, family members on visits, temporary workers, and other workers without legal permission to enter the United States. Mexican Americans were the largest minority group in many southwestern and western states in the later twentieth century.

The East Coast has especially welcomed migrants from the West Indies and Central America. Many Puerto Ricans, who hold U.S. citizenship, came to Philadelphia and New York in the 1950s and 1960s.

Another great immigration has occurred eastward across the Pacific. Chinese, Filipinos, Koreans, Samoans, and other Asians and Pacific Islanders constituted only 6 percent of newcomers to the United States in 1965 but nearly half of all arrivals in 1990. The number of ethnic Chinese in the United States jumped from a quarter of a million in 1965 to 1,645,000 in 1990.

The most publicized Asian immigrants were refugees from Indochina after the Communist victory in 1975. The first arrivals tended to be highly educated professionals who had worked with the Americans. Another 750,000 Vietnamese, Laotians, and Cambodians arrived after 1976 by way of refugee camps in Thailand, as did Celia Noup. Most settled on the West Coast.

In addition to Southeast Asians, political conflicts and upheavals sent other waves of immigrants to the United States. Many Iranians fled the religious regime that took power in their country in the late 1970s, at the same time that Ethiopians were fleeing a nation shattered by drought, civil war, and doctrinaire Marxism. To escape repression in the Soviet Union, Jews and conservative Christians came to the United States in the 1980s, and the collapse of Communism in the Soviet Union opened the door for more Russians, Ukrainians, Romanians, and other eastern Europeans.

Recent immigrants have found both economic possibilities and problems. On the negative side, legal and illegal immigration has added to the number of nonunion workers. By one estimate, two-thirds of the workers in the Los Angeles garment trade were undocumented immigrants. Most worked for small, nonunion firms in basements and storefronts, without health insurance or pensions. But a positive contrast was the abundance of opportunities for talent and ambition in the expanding economy of the mid-1980s and 1990s. The 130,000 Vietnamese immigrants of 1975 now have an average income above the national figure. Asians and Pacific Islanders by 2000 constituted 22 percent of the students in California's public universities. Like earlier European immigrants, many newcomers have opened groceries, restaurants, and other businesses that serve their own group before expanding into larger markets.

QUICK REVIEW

Immigration

- Immigration changed the country's ethnic mix.
- The single largest group of new Americans came from Mexico.
- In 1990 nearly half of all new arrivals were Asians and Pacific Islanders.

Old Gateways and New

The new immigration from Asia, Latin America, and the Caribbean had its most striking effects in coastal and border cities. New York again became a great mixing bowl of the U.S. population. By 1990, some 28 percent of the population of New York City was foreign-born, compared to 42 percent at the height of European immigration in 1910.

Just as important was the transformation of southern and western cities into gateways for immigrants from Latin America and Asia. Los Angeles emerged as "the new Ellis Island" that rivaled New York's historic role in receiving immigrants. The sprawling neighborhoods of East Los Angeles make up the second-largest Mexican city in the world. New ethnic communities appeared in Los Angeles suburbs: Iranians in Beverly Hills, Chinese in Monterey Park, Japanese in Gardena, Thais in Hollywood, Samoans in Carson, Cambodians in Lakewood. One hundred languages are spoken among students entering Los Angeles schools.

New York and Los Angeles are world cities as well as immigrant destinations. Like London and Tokyo, they are capitals of world trade and finance, with international banks and headquarters of multinational corporations. They have the country's greatest concentrations of international lawyers, accounting firms, and business consultants. The deregulation of international finance and the explosive spread of instant electronic communication in the 1980s confirmed their importance as global decision centers (see Table 30–2).

TABLE 30–2

Global Cities

Ranked by Population in 2007 (population in millions)		Ranked as Economic Decision Centers
Tokyo, Japan	35.7	1. London
New York	19.4	2. New York
Ciudad de Mexico	19.0	3. Hong Kong
Mumbai, India	19.0	4. Paris
Sao Paulo, Brazil	18.8	5. Tokyo
Delhi, India	15.9	6. Singapore
Shanghai, China	15.0	7. Chicago
Kolkata, India	14.8	8. Milan
Dhaka, Bangladesh	13.5	9. Los Angeles
Buenos Aires, Argentina	12.8	10. Toronto
Los Angeles	12.5	11. Madrid
Karachi, Pakistan	12.1	12. Amsterdam

Sources: UN Department of Economic and Social Affairs/Population Division, *World Urbanization Prospects*: The 2007 Revision; Peter J. Taylor and Robert Lang, "U.S. Cities in the 'World City Network,' " The Brookings Institution, February 2005.

Similar factors have turned Miami into an economic capital of the Caribbean. A quarter-million Cuban businessmen, white-collar workers, and their families moved to the United States between 1959 and 1962 to escape Castro's socialist government. By the late 1970s Cubans owned about one-third of the area's retail stores and many of its other businesses. Their success in business made Miami a major Latino market and helped to attract millions of Latin American tourists and shoppers. Access to the Caribbean and South America also made Miami an international banking and commercial center with hundreds of offices for corporations engaged in U.S.–Latin American trade.

Cross-border communities in the Southwest, such as El Paso, Texas, and Juarez, Mexico, or San Diego, California, and Tijuana, Mexico, are "Siamese twins joined at the cash register." Employees with work permits commute from Mexico to the United States. American popular culture flows southward. Bargain hunters and tourists pass in both directions.

Both nations have promoted the cross-border economy. The Mexican government in the mid-1960s began to encourage a "platform economy" by allowing companies on the Mexican side of the border to import components and inputs duty-free as long as 80 percent of the items were re-exported and 90 percent of the workers were Mexicans. The intent was to encourage U.S. corporations to locate assembly plants south of the border. Such *maquila* industries were able to employ lower-wage workers and avoid strict antipollution laws (leading to serious threats to public health on both sides of the border). From the Gulf of Mexico to the Pacific Ocean, 1,800 *maquiladora* plants employed half a million workers. North of the border, U.S. factories supplied components under laws that meshed with the Mexican regulations.

QUICK REVIEW

Older Americans

- 2000: 35 million Americans were aged 65 or older.
- Older Americans were a powerful political force.
- Retired Americans changed the social geography of the United States.

The Graying of America

Retirees were another factor contributing to the growth of the Sunbelt. Between 1965 and 2000, the number of Americans aged 65 and over jumped from 18.2 million to 35 million, or 12.4 percent of the population.

Older Americans have become a powerful voice in public affairs. They tend to vote against local taxes but fight efforts to slow the growth of Social Security, even though growing numbers of the elderly are being supported by a relatively smaller proportion of working men and women.

By the 1990s, observers noted increasing resentment among younger Americans, who fear that public policy is biased against the needs of those in their productive years. In turn, the elderly fiercely defend the programs of the 1960s and 1970s that have kept many of them from poverty.

Retired Americans changed the social geography of the United States. Much growth in the South and Southwest has been financed by money earned in the Northeast and Midwest and transferred by retirees. Florida in the 1980s got nearly 1 million new residents aged 60 or older, and California, Arizona, Texas, and the Carolinas also attracted many retirees.

VALUES IN COLLISION

WHAT KEY social and cultural issues divided Americans in the 1980s and 1990s?

In 1988, two very different religious leaders sought a presidential nomination. Pat Robertson's campaign for the Republican nomination tapped deep discontent with the changes in American society since the 1960s. A television evangelist, Robertson used the mailing list from his *700 Club* program to mobilize conservative Christians and push the Republican Party further to the right on family and social issues. Jesse Jackson, a civil rights leader and minister from Chicago, mounted a grassroots campaign with the opposite goal of moving the Democratic Party to the left on social and economic policy. Drawing on his experience in the black civil rights movement, he assembled a "Rainbow Coalition" that included labor unionists, feminists, and others whom Robertson's followers feared.

Read the **Document** at **www.myhistorylab.com** *Jesse Jackson, Common Ground (1988)*

In diagnosing social ills, Robertson pointed to the problems of individual indulgence, while Jackson pointed to racism and economic inequality. Their sharp divergence expressed differences in basic values that divided Americans in the 1980s and beyond. In substantial measure, the conflicts were rooted in the social and cultural changes of the 1960s and 1970s that had altered traditional institutions.

WOMEN'S RIGHTS AND PUBLIC POLICY

The women's liberation movement of the 1960s achieved important gains when Congress wrote many of its goals into law in the early 1970s. Title IX of the Educational Amendments (1972) to the Civil Rights Act prohibited discrimination by sex in any educational program receiving federal aid. The legislation expanded athletic opportunities for women and slowly equalized the balance of women and men in faculty positions. In the same year, Congress sent the Equal Rights Amendment (ERA) to the states for ratification. The amendment read, "Equal rights under the law shall not be denied or abridged by the United States or by any state on account of sex." More than 20 states ratified in the first few months. As conservatives who wanted to preserve traditional family patterns rallied strong opposition, however, the next dozen states ratified only after increasingly tough battles in state legislatures. The ERA then stalled, three states short, until the time limit for ratification expired in 1982.

Read the **Document** at **www.myhistorylab.com** Roe v. Wade *(1973)*

Abortion rights and the conservative backlash. In January 1973, the U.S. Supreme Court expanded the debate about women's rights with the case of ***Roe v. Wade.*** Voting 7 to 2, the Court struck down state laws forbidding abortion in the first three months of pregnancy and set guidelines for abortion during the remaining months. Drawing on the earlier decision of *Griswold v. Connecticut*, which dealt with birth control, the Court held that the Fourteenth Amendment includes a right to privacy that blocks states from interfering with a woman's right to terminate a pregnancy.

Roe v. Wade U.S. Supreme Court decision in 1973 that disallowed state laws prohibiting abortion during the first three months (trimester) of pregnancy and established guidelines for abortion in the second and third trimesters.

These changes came in the context of increasingly sharp conflict over the feminist agenda. Both the ERA and *Roe* stirred impassioned support and equally passionate opposition that pushed the two major political parties in opposite directions. Behind the rhetoric were male fears of increased job competition during a time of economic contraction and concern about changing families. Also fueling the debate was a deep split between the mainstream feminist view of women as fully equal individuals and the contrary conservative belief that women had a special role as anchors of families, an updating of the nineteenth-century idea of separate spheres. The arguments tapped such deep emotion that the two sides could not even agree on a common language, juxtaposing a right to life against rights to privacy and freedom of choice.

Women in the workforce. The most sweeping change in the lives of American women did not come from federal legislation or court cases, but from the growing likelihood that a woman would work outside the home. In 1960, some 32 percent of married women were in the labor force; 40 years later, 61 percent were working or looking for work (along with 69 percent of single women). Federal and state governments slowly responded to the changing demands of work and family with new policies, such as a federal childcare tax credit.

More women entered the workforce as inflation in the 1970s and declining wages in the 1980s eroded the ability of families to live comfortable lives on one income. A second reason for the increase in working women from 29 million in 1970 to 66 million in 2000 was the broad shift from manufacturing to service jobs, reducing demand for factory workers and manual laborers and increasing the need for such "women's jobs" as data-entry clerks, reservation agents, and nurses. Indeed, the U.S. economy still divides job categories by sex. There was some movement toward gender-neutral hiring in the 1970s because of legal changes and the pressures of the women's movement. Women's share of lawyers more than quadrupled, of economists more than tripled, and of police detectives more than doubled. Nevertheless, job types were more segregated by sex than by race in the 1990s.

AIDS (acquired immune deficiency syndrome) A complex of deadly pathologies resulting from infection with the human immunodeficiency virus (HIV).

AIDS and Gay Activism

After the increasing openness about sexual orientation in the 1970s, the character of life in gay communities took an abrupt turn in the 1980s when a new worldwide epidemic emerged. Scientists identified a new disease pattern, **acquired immune deficiency syndrome (AIDS),** in 1981. The name described the symptoms resulting from infection by the human immunodeficiency virus (HIV), which destroys the body's ability to resist disease. HIV is transferred through blood and semen. In the 1980s, the most frequent American victims were gay men and intravenous drug users.

A decade later, it was clear that HIV/AIDS was a national and even global problem. By the end of 2005, AIDS had been responsible for 550,000 deaths in the United States, and transmission to heterosexual women was increasing. The U.S. Centers for Disease Control and Prevention estimated roughly 40,000 new cases of HIV infection per year at the beginning of the twenty-first century, bringing the total of infected Americans to around 1,200,000. Once a problem of big cities, HIV infection had spread to every American community and had helped to change American attitudes about the process of dying through the spread of hospices for the care of the terminally ill. Meanwhile, the toll of AIDS deaths in other parts of the world, particularly eastern Africa, dwarfed that in the United States and made it a world health crisis.

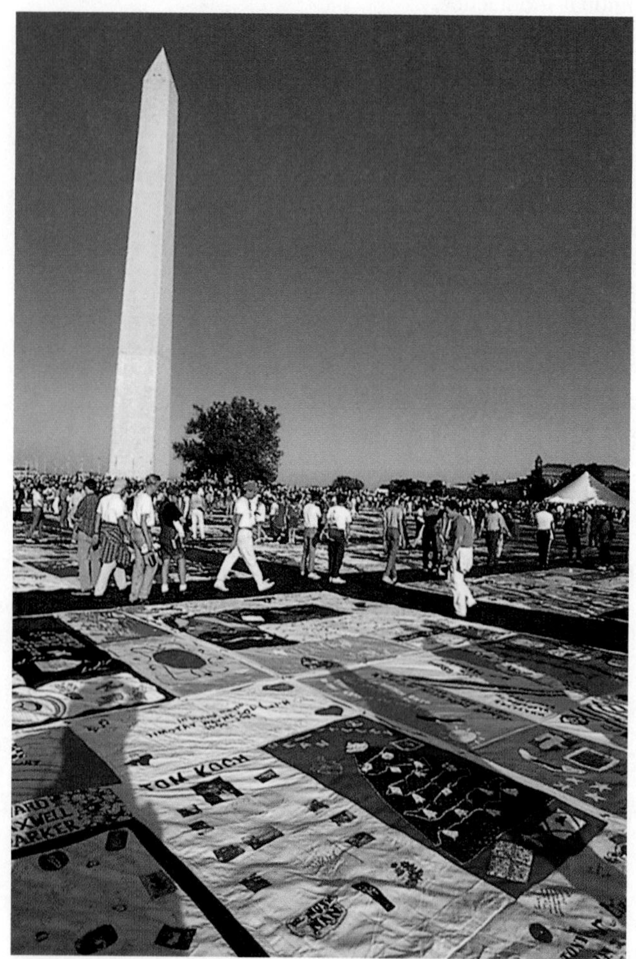

The AIDS Quilt, displayed in Washington in October 1992, combined individual memorials to AIDS victims into a powerful communal statement. The quilt project reminded Americans that AIDS had penetrated every American community.

By the 1990s, Americans were accustomed to open discussion of gay sexuality, if not always accepting of its reality. Television stars and other entertainers could "come out" and retain their popularity. So could politicians in certain districts. On the issue of gays in the military, however, Congress and the Pentagon were more cautious, accepting a policy that made engaging in homosexual acts, though not sexual orientation itself, grounds for discharge.

Churches in Change

Americans take their search for spiritual grounding much more seriously than do citizens of other industrial nations (see Map 30–3). Roughly half of privately organized social activity (such as charity work) is church related. In the mid-1970s, 56 percent of Americans said that religion was "very important" to them, compared to only 27 percent of Europeans. Moreover, religious belief is an important source of political convictions and basis for political action (see American Views: The Religious Imperative in Politics).

Nonetheless, the mainline Protestant denominations that traditionally defined the center of American belief were struggling after 1970. The United Methodist Church, the Presbyterian Church U.S.A., the United Church of Christ, and the Episcopal Church battled internally over the morality of U.S. foreign policy, the role of women in the ministry, and the reception of gay and lesbian members. They were strengthened by an ecumenical impulse that united denominational branches divided by ethnicity or regionalism. However, they gradually lost their position among American churches, perhaps because ecumenism diluted the certainty

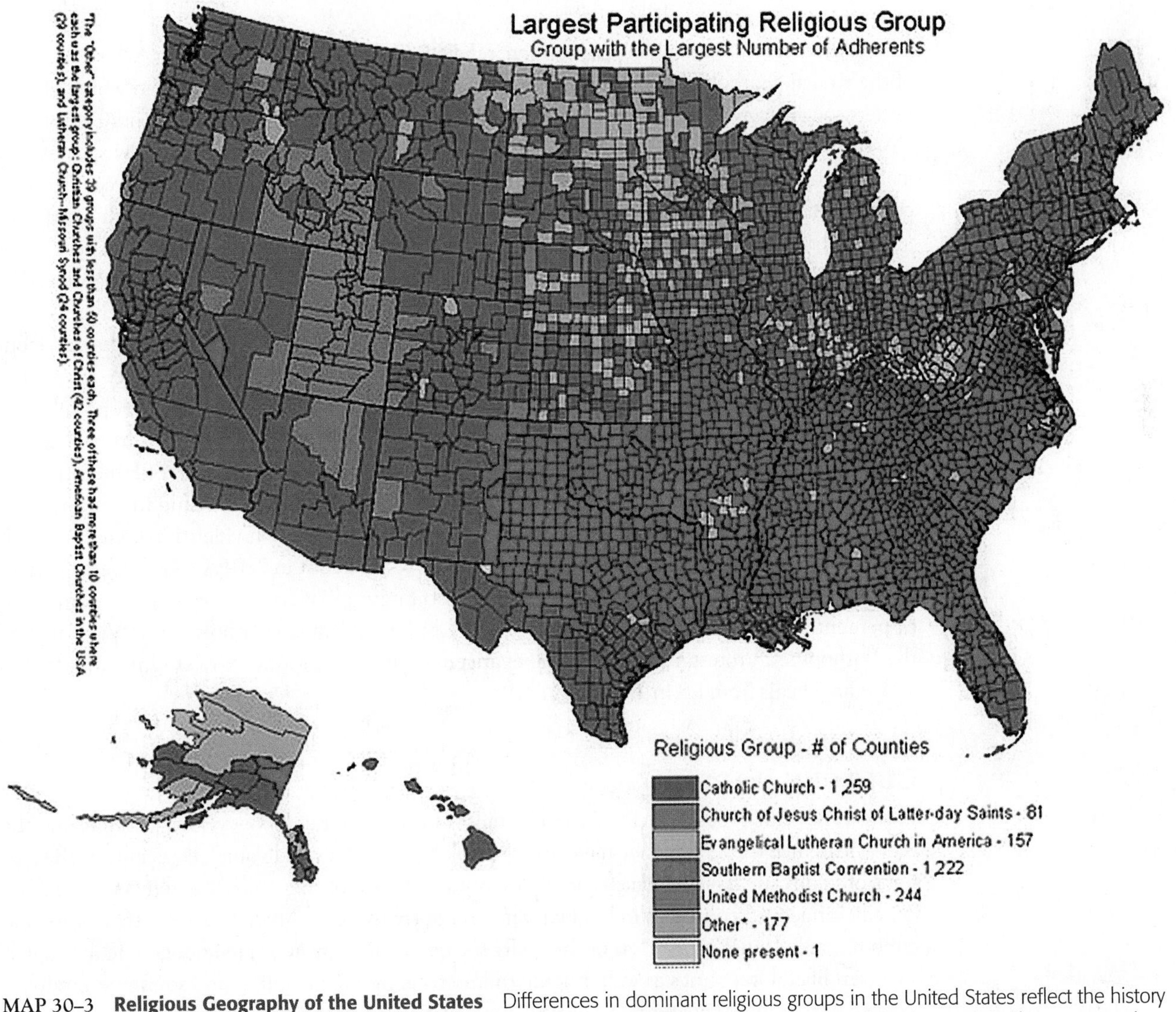

MAP 30–3 **Religious Geography of the United States** Differences in dominant religious groups in the United States reflect the history of immigration (Lutherans in the upper Midwest, Roman Catholics in the Northeast and Southwest), internal migration (the concentration of Mormons in and near Utah), and cultural differences between North and South.

Source: Glenmary Research Institute.

of their message. Liberal Protestantism has historically been strongest in the slow-growing Northeast and Midwest.

By contrast, evangelical Protestant churches have benefited from the direct appeal of their message and from strong roots in the booming Sunbelt. Members of evangelical churches (25 percent of white Americans) now outnumber the members of mainline Protestant churches (20 percent). Major evangelical denominations include Baptists, the Church of the Nazarene, and the Assemblies of God. Fundamentalists, defined by a belief in the literal truth of the Bible, are a subset of evangelicals. So are 8 to 10 million Pentecostals and charismatics, who accept "gifts of the spirit," such as healing by faith and speaking in tongues.

at **www.myhistorylab.com** *Evangelical Religion and Politics, Then and Now*

Outsiders knew evangelical Christianity through "televangelists," such as Oral Roberts and Pat Robertson. Spending on religious television programming rose from $50 million to $600 million by 1980. The "electronic church" built on the radio preaching and professional revivalism of the 1950s. By the 1970s it reached 20 percent of American households.

Evangelical churches emphasized religion as an individual experience focused on personal salvation. Unlike many of the secular and psychological avenues to fulfillment, however, they also offered communities of faith that might stabilize fragmented lives. The conservative nature of their theology and social teaching in a changing society offered certainty that was especially attractive to many younger families.

Another important change in national religious life has been the continuing Americanization of the Roman Catholic Church following the Second Vatican Council in 1965, in which church leaders sought to respond to postwar industrial society. In the United States, Roman Catholicism moved toward the center, helped by the popularity of John Kennedy and by worldly success that made Catholics the economic peers of Protestants. Even as the tight connection between Catholicism and membership in European immigrant communities gradually faded, Asian and Latino immigrants brought new vigor to many parishes, and many inner-city churches have been centers for social action. Church practice lost some of its distinctiveness; celebrating Mass in English rather than Latin was an important move toward modernization, but it also sparked a conservative counter-effort to preserve the traditional liturgy. Traditional and nontraditional Catholics also disagree about whether priests should be allowed to marry and other adaptations to American culture.

The new globalization of American society simultaneously increased the nation's religious diversity and confirmed the dominant position of Christianity. Many immigrants from Asia and Africa have come with their native religious beliefs. There are now hundreds of Hindu temples and thousands of Buddhist centers. More than a million Muslims now worship in mosques that are found in every major city. In total, the proportion of Americans who identify themselves with non-Christian religions grew from 3 percent in 1990 to 4 percent in 2001. Over the same period, however, the proportion identifying with a Christian group or denomination grew from 86 to 87 percent. Indeed, many recent immigrants are Christians: Roman Catholics from Vietnam and the Philippines, Protestants from Korea, evangelicals from the former Soviet Union, Catholics and evangelicals from Latin America.

Culture Wars

In the 1950s and 1960s, Americans argued most often over foreign policy, racial justice, and the economy. Since the 1980s, they have also quarreled over beliefs and values, especially as the patterns of family life have become more varied. In the course of these quarrels, religious belief has heavily influenced politics as individuals and groups try to shape America around their own, and often mutually conflicting, ideas of the godly society. Americans who are undogmatic in religion are often liberal in politics as well, hoping to lessen economic inequities and strengthen individual social freedom. Religious and political conservatism also tend to go together.

The division on social issues is related to theological differences within Protestantism. The "conservative" emphasis on personal salvation and the literal truth of the Bible expresses itself in a desire to restore "traditional" social patterns. Conservatives worry that social disorder occurs when people follow personal impulses and pleasures. In contrast, the "liberal" or "modern" emphasis on the universality of the Christian message restates the Social Gospel with its call to build the Kingdom of God through social justice and may recognize divergent pathways toward truth. Liberals worry that greed in the unregulated marketplace creates disorder and injustice.

The cultural conflict also transcends the historic three-way division of Americans among Protestants, Catholics, and Jews. Instead, the conservative-liberal division now cuts through each group. For example, Catholic reformers, liberal Protestants, and Reform Jews may find agreement on issues of cultural values despite theologies that are worlds apart. The same may be true of conservative Catholics, fundamentalist Protestants, and Orthodox Jews.

Conservatives initiated the culture wars, trying to stabilize what they fear is an American society spinning out of control because of lack of self-discipline and sexual indulgence. In fact, the evidence on the sexual revolution is mixed. Growing numbers of teenagers reported being sexually active in the 1970s, but the rate of increase tapered off in the 1980s. The divorce rate began to drop after 1980. Births to teenagers dropped after 1990, and the number of two-parent families increased. There was, however, an astonishing eagerness to talk about sex in the 1990s, a decade when soap-opera story lines and talk shows covered everything from family violence to exotic sexual tastes.

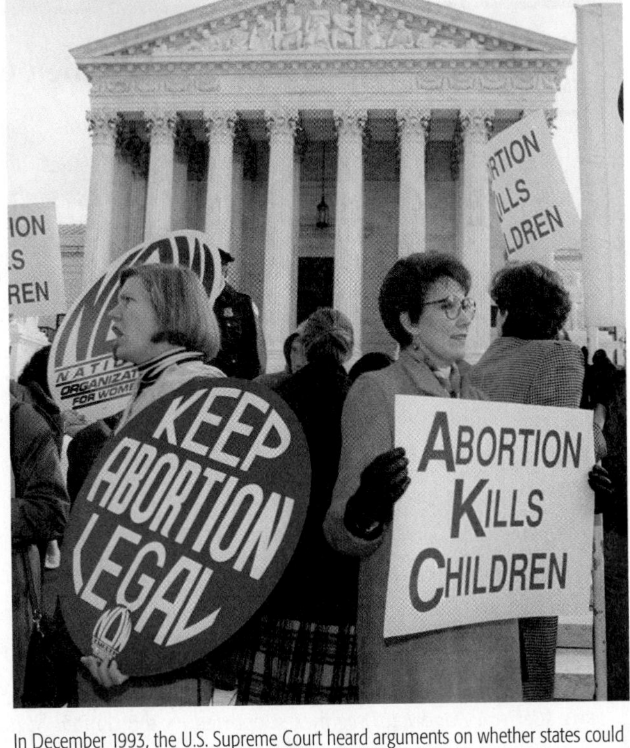
KEEP
ABORTION
LEGAL
ABORTION
KILLS
CHILDREN
In December 1993, the U.S. Supreme Court heard arguments on whether states could require protesters to remain a certain distance from abortion clinics. These antiabortion and proabortion protesters revealed the deep divisions over this and other issues in the culture wars.

The explosion of explicit attention to sexual behavior set the stage for religiously rooted battles over two sets of issues. One cluster revolved around so-called family values, questioning the morality of access to abortion, the acceptability of homosexuality, and the roles and rights of women. A second set of concerns has focused on the supposed role of public schools in undermining morality through sex education, unrestricted reading matter, nonbiblical science, and the absence of prayer. The Supreme Court decisions in 1962 and 1963 that prohibited vocal prayer and devotional Bible reading in public schools were targets for many.

A culturally conservative issue with great popular appeal in the early 1990s was an effort to prevent states and localities from protecting homosexuals against discrimination. Under the slogan "No special rights," antigay measures passed in Cincinnati, Colorado, and communities in Oregon in 1993 and 1994, only to have the Supreme Court overturn the Colorado law in *Romer v. Evans* (1996). It is important to note that public support for lesbian and gay civil rights varies with different issues (strong support for equal employment opportunity, much less for making marriage available to same-sex couples) and whether the issues are framed in terms of specified rights for gays or in terms of the right of everyone to be free from government interference with personal decisions, such as living arrangements and sexual choices.

CONCLUSION

Taken as a whole, the years from 1981 through 1992 brought transformations that redirected the course of American life. Because many changes were associated with national policy choices, it is fair to call this the era of the Reagan revolution. The astonishing collapse of the Soviet Union ended 40 years of Cold War. New political leadership in Washington reversed the 50-year expansion of federal government programs to deal with economic and social inequities. Prosperity alternated with recessions that shifted the balance between regions. Economic inequality

AMERICAN VIEWS

The Religious Imperative in Politics

The strong religious faith of many Americans frequently drives them to different stands on political issues. The first of these two documents, a letter by Jerry Falwell to potential supporters of the Moral Majority, reflects the politically conservative outlook of many evangelical Christians. Falwell was pastor of the Thomas Road Baptist Church in Lynchburg, Virginia. He founded the Moral Majority, a conservative religious lobbying and educational organization, in 1979 and served as its president until 1987, the year he wrote the letter reprinted here. The organization was especially important for voter registration efforts among conservative Christians. The second document, from an open letter issued by the Southside United Presbyterian Church in Tucson in 1982, expresses the conviction of other believers that God may sometimes require civil disobedience to oppose oppressive government actions. The letter explains the church's reasons for violating immigration law to offer sanctuary to refugees from repressive Central American regimes supported by the United States.

- **How** do Falwell and the Southside Presbyterian Church define the problems that demand a religious response?
- **Are** there any points of agreement?
- **How** does each statement balance the claims of God and government?

From the Reverend Jerry Falwell:

I believe that the overwhelming majority of Americans are sick and tired of the way that amoral liberals are trying to corrupt our nation from its commitment to freedom, democracy, traditional morality, and the free enterprise system. And I believe that the majority of Americans agree on the basic moral values which this nation was founded upon over 200 years ago.

Today we face four burning crises as we continue in this Decade of Destiny—the 1980s—loss of our freedom by giving in to the Communists; the destruction of the family unit; the deterioration of the free enterprise system; and the crumbling of basic moral principles which has resulted in the legalizing of abortion, wide-spread pornography, and a drug problem of epidemic proportions.

That is why I went to Washington, D.C., in June of 1979, and started a new organization, The Moral Majority. Right now you may be wondering: "But I thought Jerry Falwell was the preacher on the Old-Time Gospel Hour television program?"

You are right. For over twenty-four years I have been calling the nation back to God from the pulpit on radio and television. But in recent months I have been led to do more than just preach. I have been compelled to take action.

I have made the commitment to go right into the halls of Congress and fight for laws that will save America.

I will still be preaching every Sunday on the Old-Time Gospel Hour and I still must be a husband and father to my precious family in Lynchburg, Virginia.

But as God gives me the strength, I must do more. I must go into the halls of Congress and fight for laws that will protect the grand old flag for the sake of our children and grandchildren.

From Southside United Presbyterian Church:

We are writing to inform you that Southside Presbyterian Church will publicly violate the Immigration and Nationality Act, Section 274 (A).

We take this action because we believe the current policy and practice of the United States Government with regard to Central American refugees is illegal and immoral. We believe our government is in violation of the 1980 Refugee Act and international law by continuing to arrest, detain, and forcibly return refugees to the terror, persecution, and murder in El Salvador and Guatemala.

We believe that justice and mercy require the people of conscience to actively assert our God-given right to aid anyone fleeing from persecution and murder.

We beg of you, in the name of God, to do justice and love mercy in the administration of your office. We ask that "extended voluntary departure" be granted to refugees from Central America and that current deportation proceedings against these victims be stopped.

Until such time, we will not cease to extend the sanctuary of the church. Obedience to God requires this of us all.

Sources: Gary E. McCuen, ed., *The Religious Right* (Hudson, WI, G. E. McCuen, 1989); Ann Crittenden, *Sanctuary* (New York, Weidenfeld & Nicolson, 1988).

increased after narrowing for a generation at the same time that more and more leaders proclaimed that unregulated markets could best meet social needs. Middle-class Latinos and African Americans made substantial gains, while many other minority Americans sank deeper into poverty.

At the same time, it is important to recognize that every revolution has its precursors. Intellectuals have been clarifying the justifications for Reagan administration actions since the 1960s. The Reagan-Bush years extended changes that began in the 1970s, particularly the conservative economic policies and military buildup of the troubled Carter administration. Intervention in the Persian Gulf amplified U.S. policies that had been in place since the CIA intervened in Iran in 1953. The outbreak of violence in Los Angeles after the Rodney King verdict showed that race relations remained tense, complicated by the growing numbers of Latinos and immigrants from Asia who competed with African Americans for economic advancement.

In 1992, the United States stood as the undisputed world power. Its economy was poised for a surge of growth at the same time that rivals such as Japan were mired in economic crisis. It was the leader in scientific research and the development of new technologies. Its military capacities far surpassed those of any rival and seemed to offer a free hand in shaping the world—capacities that would be tested and utilized in the new century.

Where to Learn More

Ronald Reagan Boyhood Home, Dixon, Illinois. The home where Reagan lived from 1920 to 1923 tells relatively little about Reagan himself but a great deal about the small-town context that shaped his ideas. http://www.ronaldreaganhome.com.

The Intermediate-Range Nuclear Forces Treaty (INF). The full-text document of the INF agreement between the United States and the Soviet Union, the first true nuclear-disarmament treaty. http://www.state.gov/www/global/arms/treaties/inf1.html.

The Gulf War. See video clips from the Canadian Broadcasting Cooperation that provide a running narrative of the military crisis and war. http://archives.cbc.ca/war_conflict/1991_gulf_war/.

Review Questions

1. Is it accurate to talk about a Reagan Revolution in U.S. politics? Did Reagan's presidency change the economic environment for workers and business corporations? How did economic changes in the 1980s affect the prospects of the richest and poorest Americans?
2. How did American ideas about the proper role of government change during the 1980s? What was the basis of these changes?
3. What caused the breakup of the Soviet Union and the end of the Cold War? Did U.S. foreign policy under Reagan and Bush contribute significantly to the withdrawal of Soviet power from eastern Europe? Did the collapse of the USSR show the strength of the United States and its allies or the weakness of Soviet Communism?
4. How did the United States use military force during the Reagan and Bush administrations? Did military actions achieve the expected goals?
5. What were some of the important economic trends that shifted American growth toward the Sunbelt (South and West)? How has immigration from other nations affected the different American regions?
6. What changes in family roles and sexual behavior became divisive political issues? How have churches responded to cultural changes? What are some of the ways in which churches and religious leaders have tried to influence political decisions?
7. How did U.S. military involvement in Southeast Asia in the 1960s continue to affect American society for decades to come?

Key Terms

Acquired immune deficiency syndrome (AIDS) (p. 866)
Americans with Disabilities Act (p. 853)
Deregulation (p. 848)
Economic Recovery and Tax Act of 1981 (ERTA) (p. 848)
Glasnost (p. 857)
Immigration and Nationality Act of 1965 (p. 861)
Intermediate-Range Nuclear Forces Treaty (INF) (p. 858)
Perestroika (p. 857)
Reagan Doctrine (p. 855)
Roe v. Wade (p. 865)
Sagebrush Rebellion (p. 848)
Strategic Defense Initiative (SDI) (p. 854)
Sunbelt (p. 861)

PEARSON **myhistorylab** Connections

Reinforce what you learned in this chapter by studying the many documents, images, maps, review tools, and videos available at **www.myhistorylab.com**.

Read and Review

Study and Review **Study Plan: Chapter 30**

Read the Document

George H. W. Bush, Inaugural Address (1989)

Patricia Morrisroe, "Yuppies — The New Class" (1985)

Paul Craig Roberts, The Supply-Side Revolution (1984)

Ronald Reagan, First Inaugural Address (1981)

T. Boone Pickens, "My Case for Reagan" (1984)

George Bush, Allied Military Action in the Persian Gulf (1991)

Cecelia Rosa Avila, Third Generation Mexican American (1988)

Jesse Jackson, Common Ground (1988)

Ronald Reagan, Iran Contra Address (March 4, 1987)

Ronald Reagan, The Air Traffic Controllers Strike (1981)

William Julius Wilson, The Urban Underclass (1980)

Roe v. Wade *(1973)*

See the Map

America's Move to the Sunbelt, 1970–1981

The Middle East in the 1980s and 1990s

Research and Explore

Read the Document

Personal Journeys Online

From Then to Now Online: Women and Office Work

Exploring America: Growing Inequality

Watch the Video

George Bush Presidential Campaign Ad: The Revolving Door

Oliver North Hearing

Evangelical Religion and Politics, Then and Now

President Bush on the Gulf War

Ronald Reagan on the Wisdom of Tax Cuts

Hear the Audio

Hear the audio files for Chapter 30 at **www.myhistorylab.com.**

1993-2010

31

Complacency, Crisis, and Global Reengagement

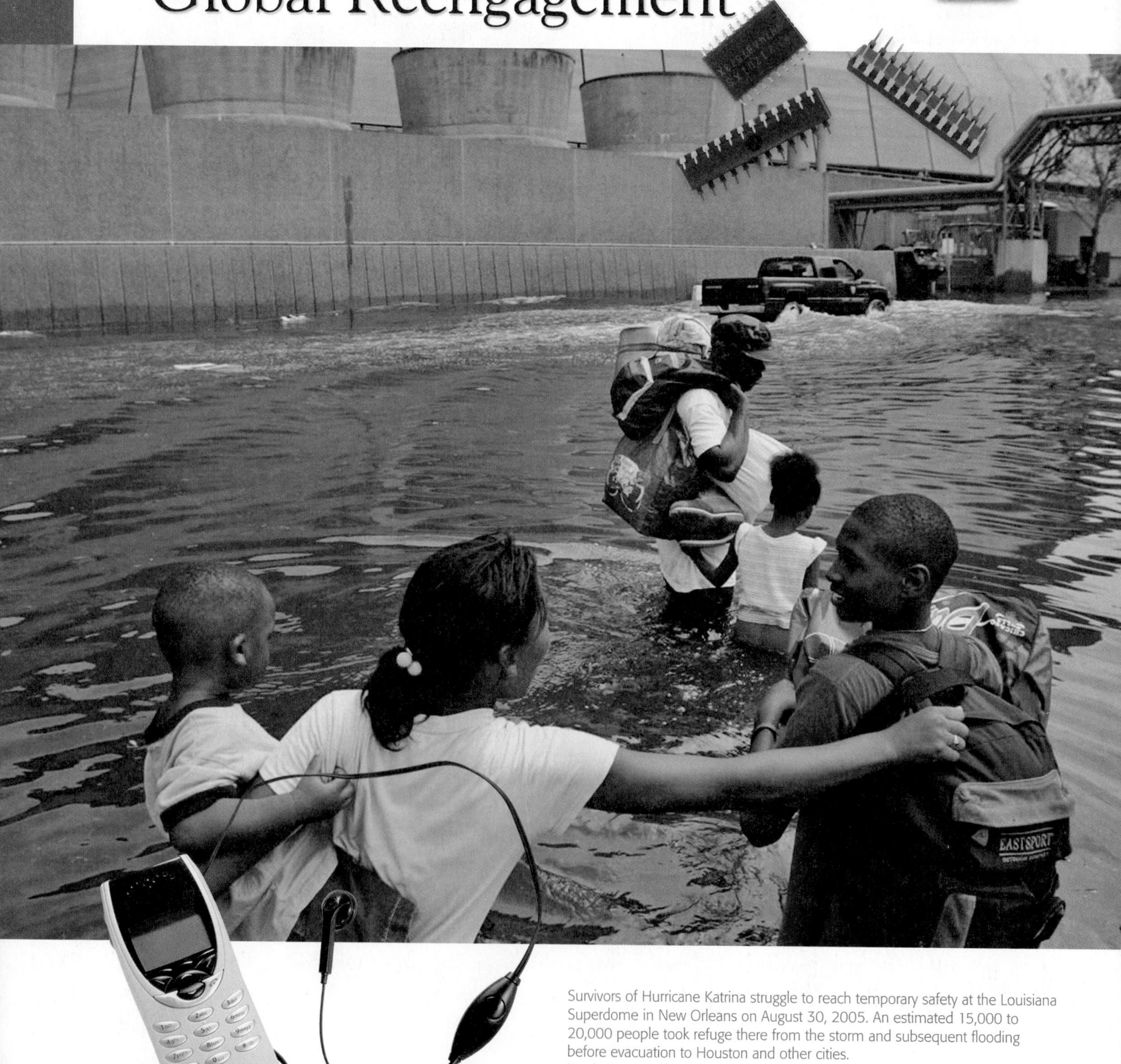

Survivors of Hurricane Katrina struggle to reach temporary safety at the Louisiana Superdome in New Orleans on August 30, 2005. An estimated 15,000 to 20,000 people took refuge there from the storm and subsequent flooding before evacuation to Houston and other cities.
Top image: Stephen Crowley/*The New York Times*

Hear the Audio
Hear the audio files for Chapter 31 at **www.myhistorylab.com**.

POLITICS OF THE CENTER *(page 877)*

WHAT ISSUES did Bill Clinton capitalize on in his 1992 presidential campaign?

A NEW ECONOMY? *(page 882)*

WHAT ROLE did new information technology play in the economic boom of the 1990s?

BROADENING DEMOCRACY *(page 888)*

WHAT GAINS did women and minorities make in national politics in the 1990s?

EDGING INTO A NEW CENTURY *(page 895)*

WHAT WERE the key elements of George W. Bush's agenda?

PARADOXES OF POWER *(page 897)*

HOW DID the government and the American people respond to the enormous challenges of the first decade of the twenty-first century?

One American Journey

When Katrina came and left, we started clapping. . . . I looked out the window and I said, "Lord, look at this here. We got to roll up our sleeves and start cleaning up." . . . I had this little storm tracker radio . . . I'm listening, and I'm looking at our automobile, and it was being submerged every minute that went by. I'm saying, "Something is wrong, because this water should be receding, but it's coming in faster." . . . I heard the man on the radio say, "If you're held up anywhere in New Orleans, you need to try your best to make it to the Superdome or convention center, because the levees have been breached and we can't stop the water."

The Superdome was about half a mile away. . . . we had a few light things like a toothbrush and your driver's license. So we had to walk through the water to about our waist. At the time there was just a lot of stuff from the automobiles like gas, oil, and stuff like that in the water. We saw some dead bodies as we were walking . . . We left about 10:00, and we got there about 11:00 or 12:00.

We thought we was going to a shelter, but it was more of a prison. Outside the Superdome, we was searched by the military. . . . Soon as we got in there, I knew something wasn't right. . . . There wasn't no effort to try and get us out, but they constantly was bringing more people into the Superdome.

You could count the white people in the rest of the Superdome on one hand. I say 99 percent was black and poor. I know everybody else feels like we weren't in a major city in America, our country.

Kevin Owens, in D'Ann R. Penner and Keith C. Ferdinand, *Overcoming Katrina: African American Voices from the Crescent City and Beyond* (Palgrave Macmillan, 2008).

Read the **Document** at **www.myhistorylab.com**

Personal Journeys Online

- **Anthony Fernandez III, "Remembering the Oklahoma City Bombing," 2007. A search and rescue worker describes the background of the picture on page 880.**
- **Dawn Shurmaitis, 2001. Volunteering in the aftermath of the September 11, 2001, attack.**
- **John McNamara, Story #400, The September 11 Digital Archive, 13 April 2002. A New York firefighter describes the day of the World Trade Center attack.**

Kevin Owens was among the tens of thousands of New Orleans residents who were flooded out of their homes in August 2005 when levees failed in the aftermath of Hurricane Katrina. Like many others, his first Katrina journey took him and his family to temporary safety in the Louisiana Superdome, where overcrowding and lack of food and sanitation meant days of misery. His second Katrina journey came when federal officials evacuated Superdome refugees to Texas and his third when he and his family left Texas for a job in Birmingham, Alabama. He has returned to New Orleans to assess the damage to his house and told his interviewer that he'd like to be part of the rebuilding process. He felt in the meanwhile "like I've been robbed of everything I love." As of 2009, the city's population was still down 130,000, 30 percent, from the pre-Katrina total.

The disaster of Hurricane Katrina struck many Americans as proof that the nation was in trouble. It followed the terrorist attacks of September 11, 2001, and a war in Iraq where the United States seemed unable to consolidate its early victories, while the inadequate emergency response in New Orleans showed deep problems at home. The events in these first years of the twenty-first century ended a decade of prosperity at home and complacency about the place of the United States in the world. In the new century Americans struggled to cope with deeply partisan politics, to cope with a fast-changing and troubled economy, and to understand their changing place in the world. ✦

CHRONOLOGY

1969	First version of Internet (ARPAnet) launched.
1980	CNN begins broadcasting.
1991	World Wide Web launched.
1992	Bill Clinton elected president.
1993	Congress approves the North American Free Trade Agreement (NAFTA).
	Congress adopts Family Leave Act.
1994	Independent Counsel Kenneth Starr begins investigation of Bill and Hillary Clinton. Paula Jones files sexual harassment lawsuit against Bill Clinton.
	Republicans sweep to control of Congress.
	Federal government temporarily shuts down for lack of money.
1995	United States sends peacekeeping troops to Bosnia.
1996	Clinton wins a second term as president.
1998	Paula Jones lawsuit dismissed.
	House of Representatives impeaches Clinton.
1999	Senate acquits Clinton of impeachment charges.
	United States leads NATO intervention in Kosovo.
2000	George W. Bush defeats Al Gore in nation's closest presidential election.
2001	Congress passes massive ten-year tax reduction.
	United States refuses to agree to Kyoto Treaty to limit global warming.
	Terrorists crash airliners into World Trade Center and Pentagon.
	U.S. military operations oust Taliban regime in Afghanistan.
	Congress passes U.S. PATRIOT Act to combat domestic terror.
2002	United States and Russia agree to cut number of deployed nuclear warheads.
	Congress creates Department of Homeland Security.
	United Nations Security Council passes resolution requiring Iraq to allow open inspections of weapons systems.
2003	U.S. and British troops invade Iraq and topple government of Saddam Hussein.
	Supreme Court allows limited forms of affirmative action in university admissions.
2004	George W. Bush reelected as president.
2005	Hurricane Katrina devastates New Orleans.
	Iraq adopts new constitution.
2006	Democrats regain narrow edge in Congress.
2008	Barack Obama elected president.
2010	Congress expands health insurance coverage. United States ends formal combat role in Iraq.

POLITICS OF THE CENTER

WHAT ISSUES did Bill Clinton capitalize on in his 1992 presidential campaign?

at **www.myhistorylab.com**
Bill Clinton Sells Himself to America: Presidential Campaign Ad, 1992

In the race for president in 1992, Bill Clinton promised economic leadership and attention to everyday problems. He promised to reduce government bureaucracy and the deficit, touted the value of stable families, and talked about healthcare and welfare reform. His message revealed an insight into the character of the United States in the 1990s. What mattered most were down-to-earth issues, not the distant problems of foreign policy, which seemed to have little urgency after the end of the Cold War. Bill Clinton's election, first term, and reelection in 1996 showed the attraction of pragmatic policies and the political center in a two-party system.

The Election of 1992: A New Generation

The mid-1990s brought a new generation into the political arena. The members of "Generation X" came of voting age with deep worries about the foreclosing of opportunities. They worried that previous administrations had ignored growing economic divisions and let the competitive position of the United States deteriorate. The range of suggested solutions differed widely—individual moral reform, a stronger labor movement, leaner competition in world markets—but the generational concern was clear.

This generational change made 1992 one of the most volatile national elections in decades. A baby boomer and successful governor of Arkansas who was not widely known nationally,

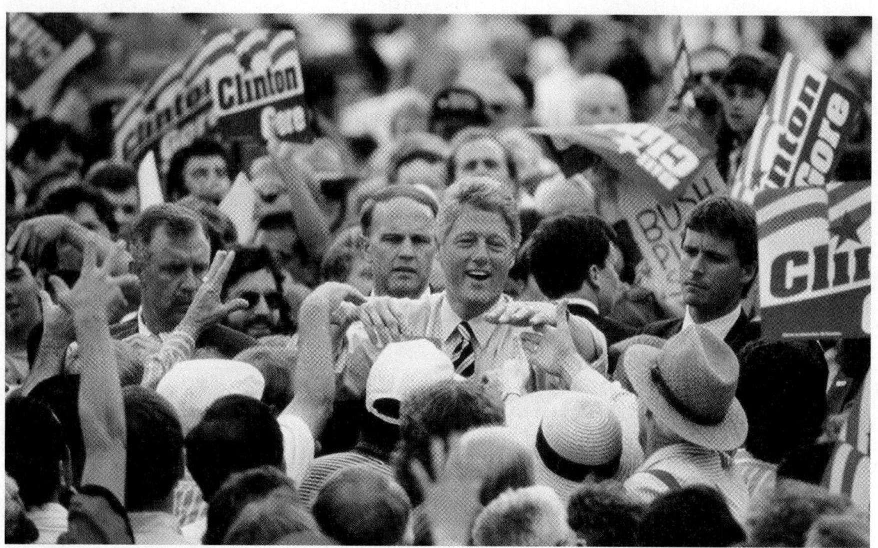

Despite personal flaws, Bill Clinton was enormously effective as a political campaigner.

Democrat Bill Clinton decided that George H. W. Bush was vulnerable when more senior Democrats opted to pass on the contest. Clinton made sure that the Democrats fielded a full baby boomer (and southern) ticket by choosing as his running mate the equally youthful Tennessean Albert Gore Jr.

Bush, the last politician of the World War II generation to gain the White House, won renomination by beating back the archconservative Patrick Buchanan, who claimed that the last 12 years had been a long betrayal of true conservatism. The Republican National Convention in Houston showed how important cultural issues had become to the Republican Party. The party platform conformed to the beliefs of the Christian right.

The wild card was the Texas billionaire Ross Perot, whose independent campaign started with an appearance on a television talk show. Perot loved flip charts, distanced himself from professional politicians, and claimed to talk sense to the American people. He also tried to occupy the political center. In May, Perot outscored both Bush and Clinton in opinion polls, but his behavior became increasingly erratic. He withdrew from the race and then reentered after floating stories that he was the target of dark conspiracies.

Bush campaigned as a foreign policy expert. He expected voters to reward him for the end of the Cold War, but he ignored anxieties about the nation's direction at home. His popularity had surged immediately after the Persian Gulf War, only to fall as the country became mired in a recession. Clinton hammered away at economic concerns, appealing to swing voters, such as suburban independents and blue-collar Reagan Democrats. He presented himself as the leader of new, pragmatic, and livelier Democrats.

Election day gave the Clinton-Gore ticket 43 percent of the popular vote, Bush 38 percent, and Perot 19 percent. Clinton held the Democratic core of northern and midwestern industrial states and loosened the Republican hold on the South and West (see Map 31–1).

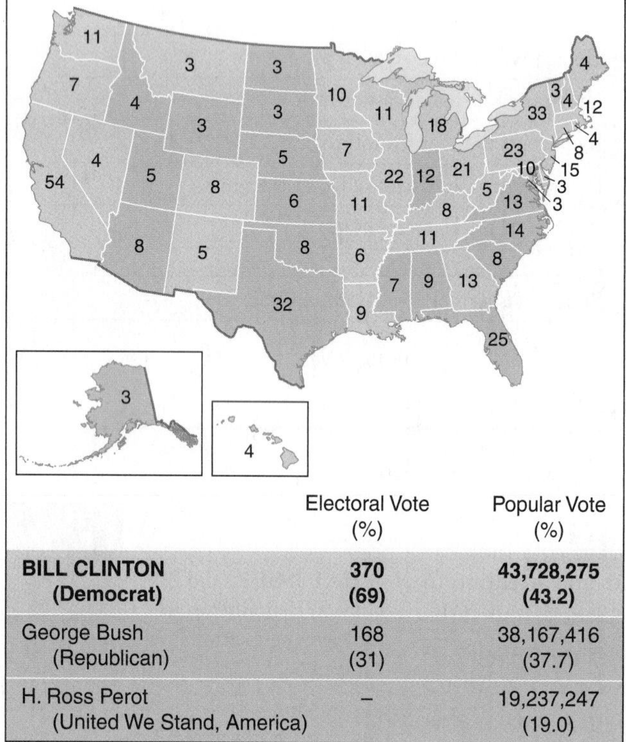

	Electoral Vote (%)	Popular Vote (%)
BILL CLINTON (Democrat)	**370 (69)**	**43,728,275 (43.2)**
George Bush (Republican)	168 (31)	38,167,416 (37.7)
H. Ross Perot (United We Stand, America)	–	19,237,247 (19.0)

MAP 31–1 **The Election of 1992** Bill Clinton defeated George H. W. Bush in 1992 by reviving the Democratic Party in the industrial Northeast and enlisting new Democratic voters in the western states, where he appealed both to Hispanic immigrants and to people associated with fast-growing high-tech industries. He won reelection in 1996 with the same pattern of support. However, the coalition was an unstable combination of "Old Democrats," associated with older industries and labor unions, and "New Democrats," favoring economic change, free trade, and globalization.

What explains Bill Clinton's strength in the South and the West? How would you explain his victories in Georgia and Louisiana?

Policing the World

Although Clinton was much more interested in domestic policies, he inherited a confused expectation that the United States could use its military and economic power to keep the world on an even keel and counter ethnic hatred without incurring serious risks to itself. During the administration's first years, U.S. diplomats helped broker an Israel-PLO accord that gave Palestinians self-government in Gaza and the West Bank, only to watch extremists on both sides undermine the accords and plunge Israel into a near–civil war by 2002. The world also benefited from a gradual reduction of nuclear arsenals and from a 1996 treaty to ban the testing of nuclear weapons.

Bosnia and Kosovo. Clinton reluctantly committed the United States to a multinational effort to end the bloody civil war in ethnically and religiously divided Bosnia in 1995. In the early 1990s, the former Communist nation of Yugoslavia, in southeastern Europe, fragmented into five independent nations: Slovenia, Macedonia, Croatia, Bosnia, and Yugoslavia (the name retained by the predominantly Serbian nation with its capital at Belgrade). Bosnia, divided both ethnically and religiously between Christians and Muslims, erupted in bitter civil war. Christian Serbs, supported by Belgrade, engaged in massacres and deportations of Muslim Bosnians with the goal of creating "ethnically clean" Serbian districts. Too late to stop most bloodshed, NATO troops after 1995 enforced a brittle peace accord and a division of territory into Bosnian and Serb sectors under a shaky federated government.

The U.S. military revisited the same part of Europe in 1999, when the United States and Britain led NATO's intervention in Kosovo. The overwhelming majority of people in this Yugoslav province were ethnic Albanians who had chafed under the control of the Serb-controlled Yugoslav government. When a Kosovar independence movement began a rebellion, Yugoslav president Slobodan Milosevic responded with brutal repression that threatened to drive over 1 million ethnic Albanians out of the province. To protect the Kosovars, NATO in March 1999 began a bombing campaign that targeted Yugoslav military bases and forces in Kosovo. In June, Yugoslavia agreed to withdraw its troops and make way for a multinational NATO peacekeeping force, marking a measured success for U.S. policy.

QUICK REVIEW

Candidates for President in 1992

- Republican George H. W. Bush seeking a second term.
- Democrat Bill Clinton: little-known governor of Arkansas.
- Independent Ross Perot: Texas billionaire and political maverick.

Read the **Document**

at **www.myhistorylab.com**
Exploring America: Globalization

The reinvention of NATO. To satisfy Russia, the peacekeeping force that entered Kosovo in June was technically a U.S. operation, but it was a reinvented NATO that negotiated with Yugoslavia. The new NATO is a product of the new Europe of the 1990s. A key step was expansion into the former Soviet sphere in eastern Europe. In 1999, NATO formally admitted Poland, Hungary, and the Czech Republic over the objections of Russia. Three years later, NATO agreed to give Russia a formal role in discussions about a number of its policy decisions, further eroding the barriers of the Cold War, and it added another nine nations of eastern Europe in 2004 and 2009.

Clinton's neoliberalism. Domestic policy attracted Clinton's greatest interest, and his first term can be divided into two parts. In 1993–1994, he worked with a slim Democratic majority in Congress to modernize the U.S. economy, taking advantage of an economic upturn that lasted for most of the decade. In 1995 and 1996, however, he faced solid Republican majorities, the result of an unanticipated Republican tide in the November 1994 elections.

The heart of Clinton's agenda was an effort to make the United States economy more equitable domestically and more competitive internationally. These goals marked Clinton as a **neoliberal** who envisioned a partnership between a leaner government and a dynamic private sector. Steps to "reinvent" government cut federal employment below Reagan administration levels. A new tax bill reversed some of the inequities of the 1980s by increasing taxes on the weathiest 1.2 percent of households. In early 1993, Clinton pushed through the Family and Medical Leave Act, which provided up to 12 weeks of unpaid leave for workers with newborns or family emergencies and had been vetoed twice by George H. W. Bush.

neoliberal Advocate or participant in the effort to reshape the Democratic Party for the 1990s around a policy emphasizing economic growth and competitiveness in the world economy.

Clinton's biggest setback was the failure of comprehensive healthcare legislation. The goals seemed simple at first: containment of healthcare costs and extension of basic medical insurance from 83 percent of Americans under age 65 to 100 percent. In the abstract, voters agreed that something needed to be done.

Clinton appointed his wife, Hillary Rodham Clinton, to head the healthcare task force. Many found this an inappropriate role for a first lady. The plan that emerged from the White House ran to 1,342 pages of complex regulations, with something for everyone to dislike. Thus the reform effort went nowhere.

QUICK REVIEW

Clinton's Agenda

- Make the U.S. economy more equitable domestically and competitive internationally.
- Reduce the size of government while raising taxes on the wealthy and reducing them on the poor.
- Clinton's biggest setback was the failure of comprehensive healthcare legislation.

Contract with America and the Election of 1996

Read the Document at www.myhistorylab.com *Republican Contract with America (1994)*

Contract with America Platform proposing a sweeping reduction in the role and activities of the federal government on which many Republican candidates ran for Congress in 1994.

Temporary Assistance for Needy Families (TANF) Federal program tying benefits to work requirements and time limits; created in 1996 to replace earlier welfare programs to aid families and children.

Conservative political ideology and personal animosity against the Clintons were both part of the background for an extraordinary off-year election in 1994, in which voters defeated dozens of incumbents and gave Republicans control of Congress. For most of 1995, the new speaker of the House, Newt Gingrich of Georgia, dominated political headlines as he pushed the **Contract with America,** the official Republican campaign platform for the 1994 elections, which called for a revolutionary reduction in federal responsibilities.

Clinton lay low and let the new Congress attack environmental protections, propose cuts in federal benefits for the elderly, and try to slice the capital-gains tax to help the rich. As Congress and president battled over the budget, congressional Republicans refused to authorize interim spending and forced the federal government to shut down for more than three weeks between November 1995 and January 1996. Gingrich was the clear loser in public opinion, both for the shutdowns and for his ideas. Democrats painted Gingrich and his congressional allies as a radical fringe who wanted to gut Medicare and Medicaid, undermine education, punish legal immigrants, and sell off national parks—core values and programs that most Americans wanted to protect.

After the budget confrontations, 1996 brought a series of measures to reward work—a centrist position acceptable to most Americans. The minimum wage increased. Congress made pension programs easier for employers to create and made health insurance portable when workers changed jobs. After tough negotiations, Clinton signed bipartisan legislation to "end welfare as we know it." **Temporary Assistance for Needy Families (TANF)** replaced Aid to Families with Dependent Children (AFDC). TANF had strict requirements that aid recipients be seeking work or be enrolled in schooling, and it set a time limit on assistance. By 2001, the number of public-assistance recipients had declined 58 percent from its 1994 high, but there are doubts that many of the former recipients have found jobs adequate to support their families.

Search and rescue worker Anthony Fernandez and rescue dog Aspen pause during the search through the ruins of the Oklahoma City federal building after its bombing by domestic terrorists in 1995.

Clinton's reelection in 1996 was a virtual replay of 1992. His opponent, Robert Dole, represented the World War II generation of politicians. Because the nation was prosperous and at peace, and because Clinton had claimed the political center and sounded like Dwight Eisenhower, the results were never in doubt. Clinton became the first Democratic president to be elected to a second term since Franklin Roosevelt. The Clinton-Gore ticket took 70 percent of the electoral votes and 49 percent of the popular vote (versus 41 percent for Dole and 9 percent for a recycled Ross Perot). Clinton easily won the Northeast, the industrial Midwest, and the Far West; Hispanic voters alienated by anti-immigrant rhetoric from the Republicans helped Clinton also take the usually Republican states of Florida and Arizona.

The election confirmed that voters liked the pragmatic center. They were cautious about the free-market advocates on the extreme right, showing little interest in having Republicans actually enact the Contract with America. They were equally unimpressed by liberal advocates of entitlements on the European model. What voters wanted was to continue the reduction of the federal role in domestic affairs that had begun in the 1980s without damaging social insurance programs.

The Dangers of Everyday Life

Part of the background for the sometimes vicious politics of mid-decade was a sense of individual insecurity and fear of violence that coexisted with an economy that was booming in some sectors but still leaving many Americans behind.

Random violence and domestic terrorism. One after another, headlines and news flashes in the 1990s proclaimed terrifying random acts of violence. The greatest losses of life came in Waco, Texas, and in Oklahoma City. On April 19, 1993, federal agents raided the fortified compound of the Branch Davidian cult outside Waco after a 51-day siege. The raid triggered a fire, probably set from inside, that killed more than 80 people. On the second anniversary of the Waco raid, Timothy McVeigh packed a rented truck with explosive materials and detonated it in front of the federal office building in downtown Oklahoma City, presumably as revenge against what he considered an oppressive government. The blast collapsed the entire front of the nine-story building and killed 169 people. In April 1999, two high school students in Littleton, Colorado, took rifles and pipe bombs into Columbine High School to kill 12 classmates, a teacher, and themselves; schools in Arkansas and Oregon experienced similar terror from gun-wielding students.

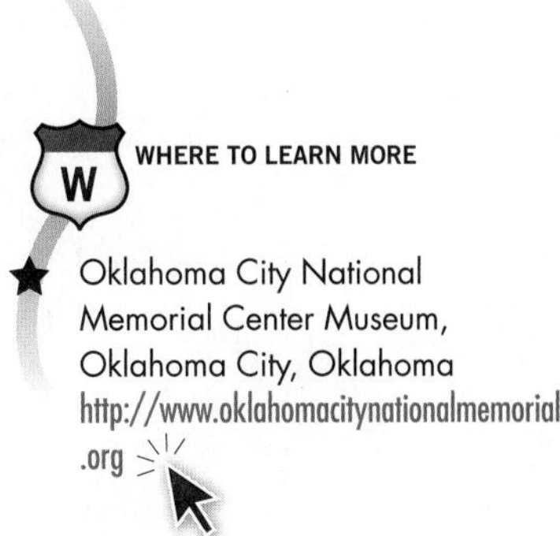

Oklahoma City National Memorial Center Museum, Oklahoma City, Oklahoma
http://www.oklahomacitynationalmemorial.org

Read the Document
at **www.myhistorylab.com**
U.S. v. Timothy James McVeigh (1997)

Gun control. Workplace assassins, schoolroom murders, and domestic terrorism invigorated efforts to monitor access to firearms. The Brady Handgun Violence Prevention Act, passed in 1994, took its name from James Brady, President Reagan's first press secretary, who was seriously injured in the 1981 attempt to kill the president. The act set up a waiting period and background checks for purchases of firearms from retailers, pawnshops, and licensed firearm dealers.

Gun control was political dynamite, for Americans have drastically differing understandings of the Second Amendment, which states: "A well regulated militia, being necessary to the security of a free State, the right of the people to keep and bear arms, shall not be infringed." The powerful National Rifle Association, the major lobby for gun owners and manufacturers, now argued that the amendment establishes an absolute individual right. Federal courts for many decades interpreted the Second Amendment to apply to the possession of weapons in connection with citizen service in a government-organized militia. In June 2008, however, the Supreme Court in *District of Columbia v. Heller* struck down the ban in Washington, DC, on the ownership or possession of handguns. The majority in the 5-4 decision argued that the Second Amendment implied an individual right to own firearms. At the same time, it left most state and federal firearms laws intact by allowing restrictions on individual categories of weapons and regulations on acquisition and use that fall short of prohibitions.

Crime and the war on drugs. Conservatives, including many gun-ownership advocates, put their faith in strict law enforcement as the best route to public security. The 1990s saw numerous states adopt "three-strike" measures that drastically increased penalties for individuals convicted of a third crime. The number of people serving sentences of a year or longer in state and federal prisons grew from 316,000 in 1980 to 740,000 in 1990 and 1,422,000 in 2004, with another 714,000 being held for shorter periods in local jails. By 2007, more than one in every 100 adults was behind bars.

The war on drugs, begun in the 1980s, was the biggest contributor to the prison boom. As the drug war dragged on through the 1990s, the federal government poured billions of dollars into efforts to stop illegal drugs from crossing the Mexican border or from landing by boat or airplane. The United States intervened in South American nations that produced cocaine, particularly Peru and Colombia, aiding local military efforts to uproot crops and battle drug lords. Meanwhile, aggressive enforcement of domestic laws against drug possession or sales filled U.S. prison cells. The antidrug campaign fell most heavily on minorities.

In fact, crime fell steadily for a decade after reaching a peak in the early 1990s. The rate of violent crime as reported by the FBI (murder, rape, robbery, aggravated assault) fell by 37 percent from 1993 to 2007, including a 40 percent drop in the number of murders. The rate of major property crimes (burglary, larceny-theft, and motor vehicle theft) fell by 31 percent over the same period. Easing fears combined with escalating costs to cause some states to rethink the reliance on prison terms.

QUICK REVIEW

Crime and Punishment

- High-profile acts of violence sparked interest in gun control.
- Some conservatives argued that the best defense against violence was gun ownership.
- The war on drugs led to a prison population boom.

Debating the death penalty. Governor George Ryan of Illinois was elected in 1998 as a conservative Republican. In January 2003, this small-town businessman emptied death row in the Illinois prison system by commuting the death sentences of 167 convicted murderers to prison terms of life or less. He asserted that his review of individual cases had led him to doubt the justice of the death-penalty system as a whole, which he said is "haunted by the demons of error—error in determining guilt and error in determining who among the guilty deserves to die."

Discussion of flaws in the application of the death penalty reveals basic disagreements about the best approach to public order. Thirty-eight of the 50 states impose the death penalty, although sixteen states have not carried out an execution since 1976. The majority of Americans have accepted capital punishment as a flawed but necessary defense for society.

In contrast, a passionate minority thinks that capital punishment is a tool so bent and blunted as to be worse than useless. They point out that the deterrent effect of capital punishment is weak at best; murder rates are often higher in death-penalty states than in similar states without the penalty. They note that African Americans and Latinos receive the death penalty far more often than whites charged with the same crimes. The nation's Roman Catholic bishops in 1999 condemned the death penalty, and in *Atkins v. Virginia* (2002) the Supreme Court forbade the execution of mentally retarded persons. The debate about capital punishment exemplifies the fault lines that divide Americans as they try to balance the demands of justice and public order.

Whitewater Arkansas real estate development in which Bill and Hillary Clinton were investors; several fraud convictions resulted from investigations into Whitewater, but evidence was not found that the Clinton's were involved in wrongdoing.

Morality and Partisanship

If the economy was the fundamental news of the later 1990s, Bill Clinton's personal life was the hot news. Years of rumors, innuendos, and lawsuits culminated in 1999 in the nation's second presidential impeachment trial. President Clinton's problems began in 1994 with the appointment of a special prosecutor to investigate possible fraud in the **Whitewater** development, an Arkansas land promotion in which Bill and Hillary Clinton had invested in the 1980s. The probe by Kenneth Starr, the independent counsel, however, expanded into a wide-ranging investigation that encompassed the firing of the White House travel-office staff early in 1993, the suicide of White House aide Vincent Foster, and the sexual behavior of the president. Meanwhile, Paula Jones had brought a lawsuit claiming sexual harassment by then-governor Clinton while she was a state worker in Arkansas. The investigation of Whitewater brought convictions of several friends and former associates of the Clintons, but no evidence pointing decisively at either Bill or Hillary Clinton.

QUICK REVIEW

From Whitewater to Impeachment

- 1994: Appointment of special prosecutor to investigate possible Whitewater fraud.
- 1994–1998: Special prosecutor conducts wide-ranging investigation.
- January 1998: Accusations of affair between President Clinton and Monica Lewinsky.
- Fall 1998: Congressional Republicans pursue impeachment.

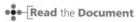

Read the **Document** at **www.myhistorylab.com** *Bill Clinton, Answers to the Articles of Impeachment (1998)*

Read the **Document** at **www.myhistorylab.com** *Articles of Impeachment against William Jefferson Clinton (1998)*

The legal landscape changed in January 1998, with allegations about an affair between the president and Monica Lewinsky, a former White House intern. Lewinsky admitted to the relationship privately and then to Starr's staff after the president had denied it in a sworn deposition for the Paula Jones case. This opened Clinton to charges of perjury and obstruction of justice.

In the fall of 1998, the Republican leaders who controlled Congress decided that Clinton's statements and misstatements justified initiating the process of impeachment. In December, the majority on the House Judiciary Committee recommended four articles of impeachment, or specific charges against the president, to the House of Representatives. By a partisan vote, the full House approved two of the charges and forwarded them to the Senate. The formal trial of the charges by the Senate began in January 1999 and ended on February 12. Moderate Republicans joined Democrats to ensure that the Senate would fall far short of the two-thirds majority required for conviction and removal from office (see Overview, Presidential Impeachment).

A NEW ECONOMY?

WHAT ROLE did new information technology play in the economic boom of the 1990s?

Within months of the impeachment trial, Americans had a new worry. In the closing months of 1999, many people stocked up on canned food and kerosene, powdered milk, ammunition, and cash. They were preparing to survive, not foreign invasion or natural disaster, but rather the possible collapse of the global computer network. Early programs had used only two digits for years in dates because memory space was precious, leading to fears that old programs would treat

2000 as 1900 or choke in electronic confusion. Europeans called the problem the "millennium bug," Americans the "Y2K" problem (for Year 2000). In fact, almost nothing happened.

In larger perspective, the Y2K worries illustrate how much the American economy had changed in the preceding decade, and how mysterious the changes seemed. More than ever, it was a global economy. And, unlike any time in the past, it was an economy that depended on electronic computing to manage and transmit vast quantities of data. The impact of the electronic revolution was still being absorbed into the structures and routines of everyday life as Americans put Y2K behind them and looked to a new century.

THE PROSPEROUS 1990S

From 1992 through 2000, Americans enjoyed nine years of continuous economic expansion. Unemployment dropped from 7.2 percent in 1992 to 4.0 percent at the start of 2000 as American businesses created more than 12 million new jobs. Key states like California rebounded from economic recession with new growth driven by high-tech industries, entertainment, and foreign trade. The stock market soared during the nineties; rising demand for shares in established blue-chip companies and new **Internet** firms swelled the value of individual portfolios, retirement accounts, and pension funds. The rate of home ownership rose after declining for 15 years. Prosperity also trickled down to Americans at the bottom of the economic ladder. The proportion of Americans in poverty dropped to 12 percent in 1999, and the gap between rich and poor began to narrow (slightly) for the first time in two decades.

Internet The system of interconnected computers and servers that allows the exchange of e-mail, posting of Web sites, and other means of instant communication.

The economic boom was great news for the federal budget. Tight spending and rising personal income turned perennial deficits into surpluses for 1998, 1999, and 2000. Reduced borrowing by the U.S. Treasury resulted in low interest rates, which further fueled corporate expansion and consumer spending. In 1997, Clinton signed a deficit-reduction bill that seemed to promise fiscal stability.

Behind the statistics were substantial gains in the efficiency of the U.S. economy. International rivals, especially Japan, experienced severe economic slumps in the mid-1990s. In the United States, in contrast, by the end of the decade the productivity of manufacturing workers was increasing more than 4 percent per year, the highest rate in a generation. Part of the gain was the payoff from the painful business restructuring and downsizing of the 1970s and 1980s. Another cause was improvements in efficiency from the full incorporation of personal computers and electronic communication into everyday life and business practice. In the later 1990s, fast-growing information-based industries seemed to be jump-starting another era of prosperity. However, many individual technology companies failed in 2001 and 2002 in a "dotcom bust" that dragged down the stock market for several years, and the real estate bubble that followed diverted investment from productive uses, leaving the United States weaker rather than stronger in relation to rising nations like China.

QUICK REVIEW

Boom Times

- United States enjoyed nine years of economic expansion between 1992 and 2000.
- Unemployment fell to 4 percent in 2000.
- The economic boom resulted in increased government revenues.

THE SERVICE ECONOMY

At the beginning of the twenty-first century, the United States was an economy of services. As fewer Americans drove tractors and toiled on assembly lines, more became service workers. The service sector includes everyone not directly involved in producing and processing physical products. Service workers range from lawyers to hair stylists, from police officers who write traffic tickets to theater employees who sell movie tickets. In 1965, services already accounted for more than half of American jobs. By the end of the 1990s, their share rose to more than 75 percent.

Service work varies greatly. At the bottom of the scale are minimum-wage jobs held mostly by women, immigrants, and the young, such as cleaning people, childcare workers, hospital orderlies, and fast-food workers. These positions offer little in terms of advancement, job security, or benefits. In contrast, many of the best new jobs are in information industries.

OVERVIEW Presidential Impeachment

Andrew Johnson, 1868	Charges:	Failure to comply with Tenure of Office Act requiring congressional approval to fire cabinet members.
	Political Lineup:	Radical Republicans against Johnson; Democrats and moderate Republicans for him.
	Actions:	Tried and acquitted by Senate.
	Underlying Issues:	Johnson's opposition to Republican plans for reconstruction of southern states after the Civil War.
Richard Nixon, 1974	Charges:	Obstruction of justice in Watergate investigation, abuse of power of federal agencies for political purposes, refusal to recognize congressional subpoena.
	Political Lineup:	Democrats and many Republicans against Nixon.
	Actions:	Charges approved by House committee; Nixon resigned before action by the full House of Representatives.
	Underlying Issues:	Nixon's construction of a secret government and his efforts to undermine integrity of national elections.
Bill Clinton, 1999	Charges:	Perjury and obstruction of justice in the investigation of sexual-misconduct allegations by Paula Jones.
	Political Lineup:	Conservative Republicans against Clinton; Democrats and some moderate Republicans for him.
	Actions:	Tried and acquitted by Senate.
	Underlying Issues:	Republican frustration with Clinton's ability to block their agenda; deep concern about Clinton's character and moral fitness for presidency.

Teaching, research, advertising, mass communications, and professional consulting depend on producing and manipulating information. All of these fields have grown. They add to national wealth by creating and applying new ideas rather than by supplying standardized products and services.

The information economy flourishes in large cities with libraries, universities, research hospitals, advertising agencies, and corporate headquarters. New York's bankers and stockbrokers made Manhattan an island of prosperity in the 1980s. Pittsburgh, with major universities and corporate headquarters, made the transition to the information economy even while its steel industry failed.

The rise of the service economy had political consequences. Rapid expansion of jobs in state and local government triggered popular revolts against state taxes that started in 1978 with passage of California's Proposition 13, which limited property taxes, and continued into the 1990s. Another growth industry was healthcare. Spending on medical and health services amounted to 15 percent of the gross domestic product in 2000, up from 5 percent in 1960. The need to share this huge expense fairly was the motivation for Medicare and Medicaid in the 1960s and the search for a national health insurance program in the 1990s and beyond.

The High-Tech Sector

The epitome of the "sunrise" economy was electronics, which grew hand-in-glove with the defense budget. The first computers in the 1940s were derived in part from wartime code-breaking efforts. Employment in computer manufacturing rose in the mid-1960s with the expansion of mainframe computing. Large machines from IBM, Honeywell, NCR, and other established corporations required substantial support facilities and staff and were used largely by universities, government agencies, and corporations. In the 1970s, new companies began to build smaller, specialized machines for such purposes as word processing. One cluster of firms sprang up outside Boston around Route 128, benefiting from proximity to MIT and other Boston-area universities. California's **Silicon Valley,** north of San Jose, took off with corporate spinoffs and civilian applications of military technologies and benefited from proximity to Stanford University.

Silicon Valley The region of California between San Jose and San Francisco that holds the nation's greatest concentration of electronics firms.

Extraordinary improvements in computing capacity drove the electronics boom. At the start of the microcomputer era, Intel co-founder Gordon Moore predicted that the number of transistors on a microchip would double every 18 months, with consequent increases in performance and drops in price. "Moore's Law" worked at least through the opening of the new century as producers moved from chips with 5,000 transistors to ones with 50,000,000. The practical result was a vast increase in the capacities and portability of computers, with personal computers and consumer electronics becoming part of everyday life in the 1990s.

An Instant Society

The spread of consumer electronics helped to create an "instant society." Americans in the 1990s learned to communicate by e-mail and to look up information on the **World Wide Web.** The United States was increasingly a society that depended on instant information and expected instant results.

World Wide Web A part of the Internet designed to allow easier navigation of the network through the use of graphical user interfaces and hypertext links between different addresses.

The Internet grew out of concerns about defense and national security. Its prototype was ARPAnet (for Advanced Research Projects Administration of the Defense Department), intended to be a communication system that could survive nuclear attack. As the Internet evolved into a system that connected universities and national weapons laboratories, the Pentagon gave up control in 1984 (when there were only 1,000 Internet-connected devices rather than the billion of 2008). Through the 1980s, it was used mainly by scientists and academics to share data and communicate by e-mail. The World Wide Web, created in 1991, expanded the Internet's uses by allowing organizations and companies to create websites that placed political and commercial information only a few clicks away from wired consumers.

Instant satisfaction was one of the principles behind the boom of dotcom businesses in 1998, 1999, and 2000. Many were services that repackaged information for quick access. Others were essentially on-line versions of mail order catalogs, but capable of listing hundreds of thousands of items. Still others were instant-delivery services designed to save consumers a trip to the video store or minimart.

Mobile telephones, or cell phones, were part of the same instant society. They exploited underutilized radio bands and communication satellites to allow wireless conversations among cells—geographic areas linked by special microwave broadcasting towers. Technological changes again drove demand. The chunky car phone built into a vehicle gave way to sleek handheld devices the size of *Star Trek* communicators and then to personal digital assistants like the iPhone and BlackBerry. Wireless phone companies originally sold their phones as emergency backups and business necessities, just as wired telephones had been sold in the first years of the twentieth century. The 5 million American cell phone subscribers of 1990 had exploded to 255 million in 2007.

QUICK REVIEW

Connections

- Spread of consumer electronics helped to create an "instant society."
- The World Wide Web expanded dramatically in the 1990s.
- Cell phone subscribers reached 255 million by 2007.

Meanwhile the twenty-first century Internet had become another inescapable method of communication. Direct travel reservation sites pushed travel agencies out of business. Young people found and kept friends with MySpace and Facebook. Columns of classified ads in newspapers shrank as craigslist expanded. Listings on eBay competed with face-to-face garage sales, and businesses invested in websites rather than Yellow Pages display ads.

Honolulu, the westernmost and southernmost of major U.S. cities, has long been a connection point between the mainland United States and the economies and cultures of the Pacific Rim and Asia.

In the World Market

Instant access to business and financial information accelerated the globalizing of the American economy. Expanding foreign commerce had become a deliberate goal of national policy with the General Agreement on Tariffs and Trade (GATT) in 1947. GATT regularized international commerce after World War II and helped to secure one of the goals of World War II by ensuring that world markets remained open to American industry. The Trade Expansion Act in 1962 authorized President Kennedy to make reciprocal trade agreements to cut tariffs by up to 50 percent so as to keep American companies competitive in the new European Common Market.

With the help of national policy and booming economies overseas, the value of U.S. imports and exports more than doubled, from 7 percent of the gross domestic product in 1965 to 16 percent in 1990—the largest percentage since World War I. Americans in the 1970s began to worry about a "colonial" status, in which the United States exported food, lumber, and minerals and imported automobiles and television sets. By the 1980s, foreign economic competitiveness and trade deficits, especially with Japan, became issues of national concern that continued into the new century, when China and India were emerging as the newest competitors.

The effects of international competition were more complex than "Japan-bashers" acknowledged. Mass-production industries, such as textiles and aluminum, suffered from cheaper and sometimes higher-quality imports, but many specialized industries and services, such as Houston's oil equipment and exploration firms, thrived. Globalization also created new regional winners and losers. In 1982, the United States began to do more business with Pacific nations than with Europe.

North American Free Trade Agreement (NAFTA) Agreement reached in 1993 by Canada, Mexico, and the United States to substantially reduce barriers to trade.

The politics of trade. More recent steps to expand the global reach of the U.S. economy were the **North American Free Trade Agreement (NAFTA)** in 1993 and a new worldwide General Agreement on Tariffs and Trade (GATT) approved in 1994. Negotiated by Republican George Bush and pushed through Congress in 1993 by Democrat Bill Clinton, NAFTA combined 25 million Canadians, 90 million Mexicans, and 250 million U.S. consumers in a single "common market" similar to that of western Europe. This enlarged free-trade zone was intended to open new markets and position the United States to compete more effectively against the European Community and Japan. The agreement may have been a holdover from the Bush years, but it matched Clinton's ideas about reforming the American economy.

NAFTA was a hard pill for many Democrats, and it revived the old debate between free traders and protectionists. Support was strongest from businesses and industries that sought foreign customers, including agriculture and electronics. Opponents included organized labor, communities already hit by industrial shutdowns, and environmentalists worried about lax controls on industrial pollution in Mexico. In contrast to the nineteenth-century arguments for protecting infant industries, new industries now looked to foreign markets, whereas uncompetitive, older firms hoped for protected domestic markets. The readjustments from NAFTA have produced obvious pain in the form of closed factories or farms made unprofitable by cheaper imports, while its gains are less visible—a new job here, larger sales there.

World Trade Organization (WTO) International organization that sets standards and practices for global trade, and the focus of international protests over world economic policy in the late 1990s.

The **World Trade Organization (WTO),** which replaced GATT in 1996, became the unexpected target of a global protest movement. Seattle officials, committed to promoting

AMERICAN VIEWS

Relief Work in Africa

In the early twenty-first century, thousands of Americans work in other countries for relief and reconstruction organizations such as the Peace Corps, CARE, and Mercy Corps, and thousands more do similar work under the sponsorship of religious groups. In 2003, Peggy Senger Parsons, an evangelical Quaker minister and trauma counselor from "far off Planet America" spent several months in the small African nation of Burundi, trying to help residents develop strategies for dealing with the impacts of civil war and endemic criminal violence. Here are some excerpts from her blog.

- **What** does Peggy Parsons's experience suggest about the spread of American culture around the world?
- **How** does the level of personal safety in a nation such as Burundi compare to that in the United States?
- **What** questions does Parsons's experience raise about the challenges of building peace and democracy in troubled and divided nations?
- **How** might religiously based work in other countries differ from efforts sponsored by the U.S. government, such as with the Peace Corps? How might it be the same?

We function in Swahili and French, mine bad and hers good. . . . I have been in the company of four children who have been giving me language and cultural tutorials, which I exchanged for introducing them to the Beatles.

Pavement is a subjective concept in Burundi. Traffic is extremely real. We fly in a zig zag pattern through cars, trucks, bicycles, and lots of little children. If you notice a lack of angels in America, it is because they are all in Burundi keeping the babies from being killed on the road. . . . And in four days I am totally immune to the sight of guys with automatic weapons. My host says that he cannot tell a rebel from a Burundi soldier and sometimes neither can they.

We have a night watchman . . . we live in a walled compound and he is there to keep us safe. His only weapon is a whistle. The children tell me that if there is trouble he whistles, and all the nearby watchmen whistle and then come running to help. Then I met Gadi the moneychanger. He walks around with rolls of money as big as softballs in every pocket and he does not carry a gun. He has a quiet gentle confidence that reminds me of every wiseguy I ever met in Chicago. I do not know what happens if you jump a moneychanger—but it must be bad enough that nobody tries. Some things are very familiar.

My traumatology students are amazing. They have come from great distances and at great sacrifice to study with me. . . . Many of the terms I need to use have no equivalent. I have learned the face that my translator makes when I give her a hard one. She signals for me to stop, and the students confer and when a consensus is reached about a newly coined phrase someone shouts *Voila!* And we have a new psychological term. My students were interviewed on Burundi National Radio. The reporter came on the second day to do a quick filler piece and stayed all afternoon and then asked to join the class. He carries a huge reel-to-reel recorder. The voices of these students went out to 22 million listeners this morning in Burundi, Congo, Rwanda, and Tanzania. They were fabulous explaining the effects of trauma and how they themselves had been helped in the class. On Friday my class thanked me for telling them the truth and for bringing them the best of myself. They compared me to a Jonah "who did not run away but ran towards her call," can't get better pay than that.

I was not prepared for the fact that my trauma class students would be such recent victims [many bearing fresh wounds from beatings or torture]. Thursday there was a bit of shooting outside of the teaching compound. I had to be told what it was—a "thump" and then a "tat, tat, tat." But it was quiet after that and we resume. After a long morning of brain physiology and learning about the left brain functions, my translator said, "Peggy have mercy on them—they say they need to sing." And so they did, all Christian music. I taught them "We Shall Overcome" and told them about Dr. King and we marched around the room singing that "I do believe, deep in my heart, that Burundi will have peace one day."

Protests against the WTO have united environmentalists and labor unions, interests that are often in opposition over domestic issues.

Seattle as a world-class city, lobbied hard to get the 1999 WTO meeting. With finance and foreign affairs ministers and heads of government expected to attend, it would give Seattle world attention. Instead, it gave the city a headache. Fifty thousand protesters converged on the meeting, held from November 30 to December 4, 1999.

Protesters were convinced that the WTO is a tool of transnational corporations that flout local labor and environmental protections in the name of "free trade" that benefits only the wealthy nations and their businesses. WTO defenders pointed to the long-term effects of open trade in raising net production in the world economy and thereby making more wealth available for developing nations. Opponents asserted, in turn, that such wealth never reaches the workers and farmers in those nations. American opponents demanded that U.S. firms, such as sportswear companies, that make their products overseas make sure that their overseas workers have decent living conditions and wages.

BROADENING DEMOCRACY

WHAT GAINS did women and minorities make in national politics in the 1990s?

Closely related to the changes in the American economy were the changing composition of the American people and the continued emergence of new participants in U.S. government. Bill Clinton's first cabinet, in which three women and four minority men balanced seven white men, recognized the makeup of the American population and marked the maturing of minorities and women as distinct political constituencies. The first cabinet appointed by George W. Bush in 2001 included four minority men and four women, one of whom was Asian American. In both administrations, the new prominence of women and minorities in the national government followed years of growing success in cities and states.

AMERICANS IN 2000

The federal census for the year 2000 found 281,400,000 Americans in the 50 states, District of Columbia, and Puerto Rico (and probably 2–3 million more residents were not counted). The increase from 1990 was 13.2 percent, or 32,700,000. It was the largest ten-year population increase in U.S. history, evidence of the nation's prosperity and its attractiveness for immigrants. More than 12 percent of Americans had been born in other countries, the highest share since 1920 (Table 31–1). One third of all Americans lived in four states: California, Texas, New York, and Florida. These were the key prizes in presidential elections.

The West grew the fastest. Fast growth implies young populations, and the states with the lowest average ages were all western: Utah, Alaska, Idaho, and Texas. The Southwest and South also had the fastest growing metropolitan areas. Among large metro areas with over 500,000 people in 2000, all 20 of the fastest growing were in the West and Southeast.

In contrast, parts of the American midlands grew slowly. Rural counties continued to empty out in Appalachia and across the Great Plains as fewer and fewer Americans were needed for mining and farming or for the small towns associated with those industries.

TABLE 31–1

Immigrants 1991–2007, by Continent and by Twenty Most Important Countries of Origin

Total	16,301,000
North America	6,410,000
Mexico	3,450,000
Dominican Republic	535,000
El Salvador	412,000
Cuba	375,000
Haiti	323,000
Jamaica	323,000
Canada	261,000
Guatemala	225,000
Asia	5,363,000
Philippines	920,000
China	872,000
India	856,000
Vietnam	636,000
Korea	318,000
Pakistan	222,000
Europe	2,352,000
Poland	261,000
Ukraine	260,000
Russia	241,000
United Kingdom	246,000
South America	1,157,000
Colombia	302,000
Africa	909,000
Oceania	90,000

Source: Statistical Abstract of the United States.

Another important trend was increasing ethnic and racial diversity (Table 31–2). Hispanics were the fastest growing group in the U.S. population. Although immigrants concentrated in the coastal and border states, Hispanics and Asian Americans were also spreading into interior states. Asians and Hispanics who had been in the United States for some time showed substantial economic success. Non-Hispanic whites are now a minority in California at 47 percent, in the District of Columbia, in Hawaii, and in New Mexico.

The changing ethnicity of the American people promises to be increasingly apparent in coming decades. Immigrants tend to be young adults who are likely to form families, and birth rates have been high among Hispanics and Asian Americans. The result is a sort of multiethnic baby boom. Over the coming decades, the effects of ethnic change will be apparent not only in schools but also in the workplace, popular culture, and politics.

Women from the Grassroots to Congress

The increasing prominence of women and family issues in national politics was a steady, quiet revolution that bore fruit in the 1990s, when the number of women in Congress more than doubled. In 1981, President Reagan appointed Arizona judge Sandra Day O'Connor to be the

TABLE 31–2

States with Highest Proportions of Minority Residents in 2000 (percentage of total population)

Hispanic	
New Mexico	42%
California	32%
Texas	32%
Arizona	25%
Nevada	20%
Asian and Pacific Islander	
Hawaii	51%
California	11%
Washington	6%
New Jersey	6%
New York	6%
African American	
Mississippi	36%
Louisiana	33%
South Carolina	30%
Georgia	29%
Maryland	28%
American Indian	
Alaska	16%
New Mexico	10%
South Dakota	8%
Oklahoma	8%
Montana	6%

first woman on the United States Supreme Court. In 1984, Walter Mondale chose New York Congresswoman Geraldine Ferraro as his vice presidential candidate. In 1993 Clinton appointed the second woman to the Supreme Court, U.S. Appeals Court judge Ruth Bader Ginsburg. Clinton appointee Janet Reno was the first woman to serve as attorney general, and Madeleine K. Albright the first to serve as secretary of state. George W. Bush continued to break new ground by naming Condoleezza Rice as his national security advisor in 2001 and as secretary of state in 2005.

at **www.myhistorylab.com**
Nancy Pelosi, Inaugural Address (2007)

Political gains for women at the national level reflected their growing importance in grassroots politics. The spreading suburbs of postwar America were "frontiers" that required concerted action to solve immediate needs like adequate schools and decent parks. Because pursuit of such community services was often viewed as "woman's work" (in contrast to the "man's work" of economic development), postwar metropolitan areas offered numerous opportunities for women to engage in volunteer civic work, learn political skills, and run for local office. Moreover, new cities and suburbs had fewer established political institutions, such as political machines and strong parties; their politics were open to energetic women. Most women in contemporary politics have been more liberal than men—a difference that political scientists attribute to women's interest in the practical problems of schools, neighborhoods, and two-earner families. But women's grassroots mobilization, especially through evangelical churches, has also strengthened groups committed to conservative social values.

Regional differences have affected women's political gains. The West has long been the part of the country most open to women in state and local government and in business.

GLOBAL CONNECTIONS

WORKING 24/7 IN BANGALORE

Bangalore is a beautiful city in the highlands of southern India. Its cool climate attracted retired British officials in the days of the British Empire, leaving a legacy of Victorian parks and wide boulevards. After India achieved independence in 1947, the new government made Bangalore a center for scientific research, leaving a legacy of four universities, dozens of technical schools, and a home-grown high-tech industry. In the 1990s, U.S. electronics companies began to establish branches and subsidiaries to take advantage of the concentration of talent, creating a new suburban landscape of technology parks and gated residential neighborhoods with a strong resemblance to Silicon Valley.

The logical extension came in the twenty-first century. Computers and telephone lines have brought Bangalore, Delhi, and other Indian cities into instant contact with American businesses and consumers. Enough U.S. companies have outsourced their customer-service operations to India to become a comic-strip joke.

The development is a logical extension of the global economy. India represents the world's second-largest concentration of English speakers after the United States. Its high-quality educational system produces a million college graduates a year. Many of them are glad to work for U.S. companies at pay that is cheap by U.S. standards but good by comparison with other opportunities in India.

Any kind of routine customer service can be outsourced—telephone catalog sales, billing and debt collection, credit card marketing, help lines for Internet providers, technical support for computer manufacturers. Tens of thousands of simple income tax returns are now processed in India each year. An American accountant scans in a customer's tax information, an Indian accountant logs on and fills out the return, the American accountant prints it out for signature.

The magic of electronics and the 12-hour time differential allow Indians to do specialized work while Americans sleep. Hospitals can transit MRIs to be read in India and get the results the next morning. Publishers can send files to be formatted and proofread while authors and editors sleep. Software companies can transmit code to be debugged overnight.

There is both a light side and a serious side to this 24/7 economy. It is amusing to learn that Indian workers practice American accents and take "phone names" that sound American; CBS reported that one young woman named Sangita becomes "Julia" because Julia Roberts is her favorite actress. But it is also important to understand that distance scarcely matters when an economy's important products take the form of information, and that information flows back and forth across the oceans linking the United States to the world in ways not seen in earlier centuries.

- In twenty-first century, is the English language the most important asset of the American economy?

Westerners have been more willing than voters in the East or South to choose women as mayors of major cities and as members of state legislatures. Many of the skills learned from politics were also useful as women played a growing role in professional and managerial occupations.

In 1991, the nomination of Judge Clarence Thomas, an African American, to the U.S. Supreme Court had ensured that everyone knew that the terms of U.S. politics were changing. Because of his conservative positions on social and civil rights issues, Thomas was a controversial nominee. Controversy deepened when law professor Anita Hill accused Thomas of harassing her sexually while she served on his staff at the Equal Employment Opportunity Commission. The accusations led to riveting hearings before a U.S. Senate committee. Critics tried to discredit Hill with vicious attacks on her character, and the committee failed to call witnesses who could have supported her claims. The public was left with Hill's plausible but unproved allegations and Thomas's equally vigorous but unproved denials. The Senate confirmed Thomas to the Supreme Court. Partisans on each side continued to believe the version that best suited their preconceptions and agendas.

Whatever the merits of her charges, Hill's badgering by skeptical senators angered millions of women. In the shadow of the hearings, women made impressive gains in the 1992 election, which pushed women's share of seats in the 50 state legislatures above 20 percent. The number of women in the U.S. Senate jumped from two to seven (and grew further to seventeen Democrats

QUICK REVIEW

Women in Government

- First woman on the U.S. Supreme Court: Sandra Day O'Connor.
- First woman U.S. attorney general: Janet Reno.
- First woman secretary of state: Madeleine Albright.

and four Republicans in 2007). The number of women serving as federal judges grew from 48 in 1981 to more than 200—roughly a quarter of the total.

Women have influenced national politics as voters as well as candidates and cabinet members. Since the 1980s, voting patterns have shown a gender gap. Women in the 1990s identified with the Democratic Party and voted for its candidates at a higher rate than men. The reasons include concerns about the effect of government spending cuts and interest in measures to support families rather than in conservative rhetoric. This gender gap has helped keep Democrats competitive and dampened the nation's conservative swing on social issues.

Minorities at the Ballot Box

The changing makeup of the American populace also helped black and Latino candidates for public office to increased success. After the racial violence of the 1960s, many black people turned to local politics to gain control of their own communities. The first black mayor of a major twentieth-century city was Carl Stokes in Cleveland in 1967. The 1973 election brought victories for Tom Bradley in Los Angeles, Maynard Jackson in Atlanta, and Coleman Young in Detroit. By 1983, three of the nation's four largest cities had black mayors. In 1989, Virginia made Douglas Wilder the first black governor in any state since Reconstruction.

The election of a minority mayor was sometimes more important for its symbolism than for the transfer of real power. Efforts to restructure the basis of city council elections, however, struck directly at the balance of power.

Most mid-sized cities stopped electing city councils by wards or districts during the first half of the twentieth century. Voting at large shifted power away from geographically concentrated ethnic groups. It favored business interests that claimed to speak for the city as a whole but could assign most of the costs of economic growth to older and poorer neighborhoods.

In the 1970s, minority leaders and community activists realized that a return to district voting could convert neighborhood segregation from a liability to a political resource. As amended in 1975, the federal Voting Rights Act allowed minorities to use the federal courts to challenge at-large voting systems that diluted the impact of their votes. Blacks and Mexican Americans used the act to reestablish city council districts in the late 1970s and early 1980s in city after city across the South and Southwest.

At the national level, minorities gradually increased their representation in Congress. Ben Nighthorse Campbell of Colorado, a Cheyenne, brought a Native American voice to the U.S. Senate in 1992. The number of African Americans in the House of Representatives topped 40 after 1992, with the help of districts drawn to concentrate black voters. Even after a series of Supreme Court cases invalidated districts drawn with race as the "predominant factor," however, African Americans held most of their gains, while the number of Latino members of Congress rose to 30 by 2009 (see Figure 31–1).

In struggling for political influence, recent immigrants have added new panethnic identities to their national identities. Hispanic activists revived the term "Chicano" to bridge the gap between recent Mexican immigrants and Latinos whose families had settled in the Southwest before the American conquest in 1848. Great gaps of experience and culture separated Chinese, Koreans, Filipinos, and Vietnamese, but they gained political recognition and influence if they dealt with other Americans as "Asians." Native Americans have similarly downplayed tribal differences in efforts to secure better opportunities for Indians as a group.

Rights and Opportunities

The increasing presence of Latinos and African Americans in public life highlighted a set of troublesome questions about the proper balance between equal rights and equal opportunities. The debates at the end of the twentieth century replayed many of the questions that European immigration raised at the century's beginning.

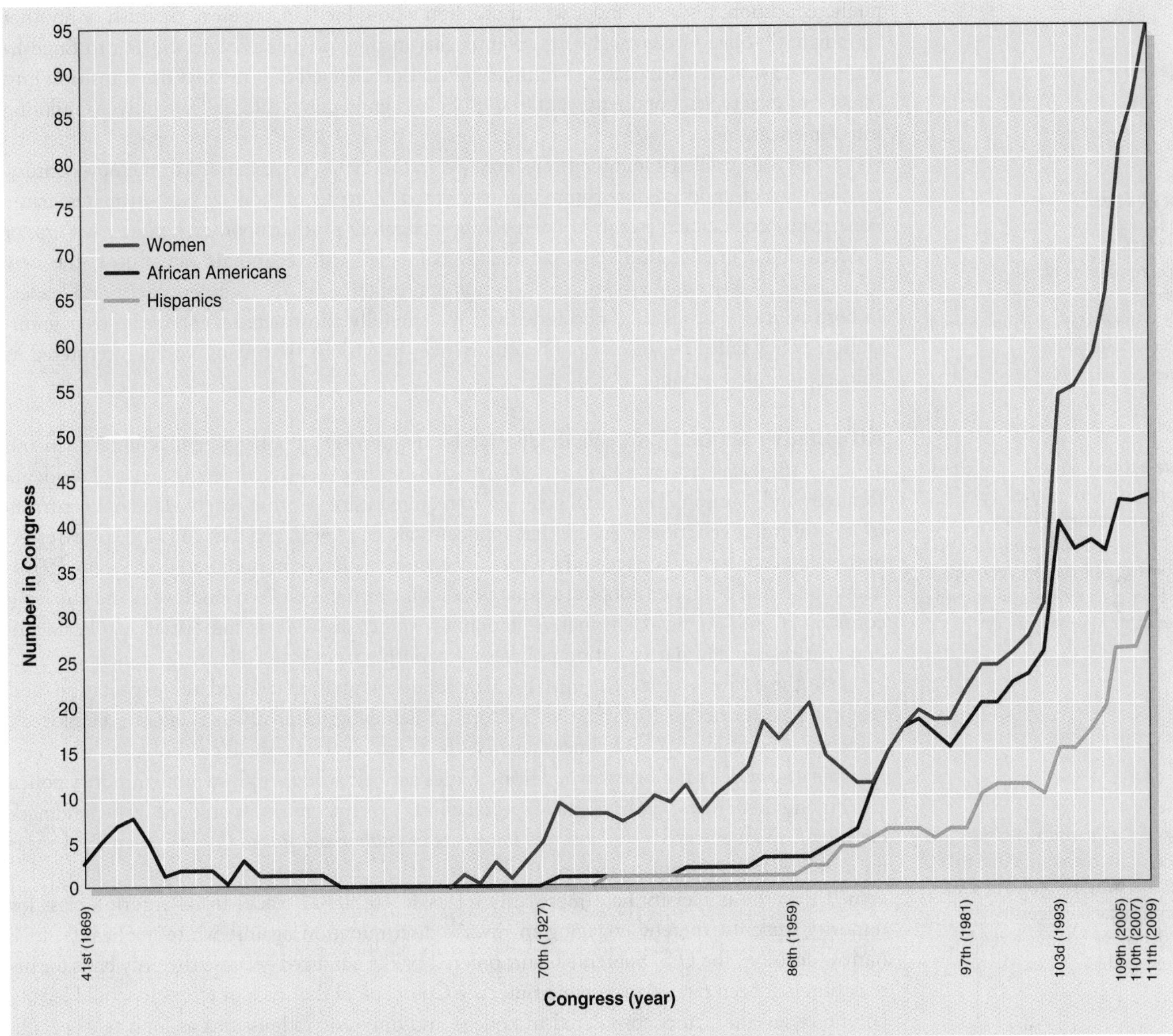

FIGURE 31–1 **Minorities and Women in Congress, 1869–2009** The number of African Americans, Hispanics, and women serving in the House of Representatives and Senate increased rapidly in the 1980s and early 1990s and more slowly in the middle 1990s. The increases reflected changing attitudes, the impact of the Voting Rights Act, and decades of political activism at the grassroots.

Illegal immigration and bilingual education. One issue is the economic impact of illegal immigration. Advocates of tight borders assert that illegal immigrants take jobs away from legal residents and eat up public assistance. Many studies, however, find that illegal immigrants fill jobs that nobody else wants. Over the long run, high employment levels among immigrants mean that their tax contributions through sales taxes and Social Security taxes and payroll deductions more than pay for their use of welfare, food stamps, and unemployment benefits, which illegal immigrants are often afraid to claim for fear of calling attention to themselves. Nevertheless, high immigration can strain local government budgets even if it benefits the nation as a whole. Partly for this reason, 60 percent of California voters approved **Proposition 187** in 1994, cutting off access to state-funded public education and healthcare for illegal immigrants.

Read the **Document** at **www.myhistorylab.com** *Illegal Immigration Reform and Immigrant Responsibility Act (1996)*

A symbolic issue was the degree to which American institutions should accommodate non–English speakers. Referendums in Alaska (1996) and Utah (2000) raised to 26 the number of states that declared English their official language. California voters in 1998 banned bilingual

Proposition 187 California legislation adopted by popular vote in California in 1994, which cuts off state-funded health and education benefits to undocumented or illegal immigrants.

public education, a system under which children whose first language was Spanish or another "immigrant" tongue were taught for several years in that language before shifting to English-language classrooms. Advocates of bilingual education claimed that it eased the transition into American society, but opponents said that it blocked immigrant children from fully assimilating into American life.

The issue of illegal immigration simmered in the 1990s, but exploded in the new century. As the total of undocumented immigrants reached 11 to 12 million by best estimates, many Americans became increasingly concerned about a porous southern border. Unlike early eras of concern about immigration that had usually coincided with economic downturns, the new immigration worries came in an era of economic prosperity. In 2007, the president and leaders in both political parties were blindsided when a carefully constructed compromise over immigration policy failed because of public outcry over provisions that many voters interpreted as amnesty for rule-breaking.

QUICK REVIEW

Divisive Issues

- The proper response to illegal immigration.
- Degree of accommodation of non–English speakers in U.S. schools.
- Affirmative action.

affirmative action A set of policies to open opportunities in business and education for members of minority groups and women by allowing race and sex to be factors included in decisions to hire, award contracts, or admit students to higher education programs.

Affirmative action. An equally divisive issue was a set of policies that originated in the 1960s as **affirmative action,** a phrase that first appeared in executive orders issued by Presidents Kennedy and Johnson. The initial goal was to require businesses that received federal contracts to "take affirmative action to ensure that applicants are employed, and that employees are treated during employment without regard for their race, creed, color, or national origin." By the 1970s, many states and cities had adopted similar policies for hiring their own employees and choosing contractors and extended affirmative action to women as well as minorities. Colleges and universities used affirmative-action policies in recruiting faculty and admitting students.

As these efforts spread, the initial goal of nondiscrimination evolved into expectations and requirements for active ("affirmative") efforts to achieve greater diversity among employees, students, or contractors. Government agencies began to set aside a small percentage of contracts for woman-owned or minority-owned firms. Cities actively worked to hire more minority police officers and firefighters. Colleges made special efforts to attract minority students. The landmark court case about affirmative action was ***University of California v. Bakke*** (1978). Alan Bakke was an unsuccessful applicant to the medical school at the University of California at Davis. He argued that the university had improperly set aside 16 of 100 places in its entering class for minority students, thereby engaging in reverse discrimination against white applicants. In a narrow decision, the U.S. Supreme Court ordered Bakke admitted because the only basis for his rejection had been race. At the same time, the Court stated that race or ethnicity could legally be one of several factors considered in college and university admissions as long as a specific number of places were not reserved for minorities.

University of California v. Bakke U.S. Supreme Court case in 1978 that allowed race to be used as one of several factors in college and university admission decisions but made rigid quotas unacceptable.

In 1996, California voters took grassroots action, approving a ballot measure to eliminate state-sponsored affirmative action. One effect was to prohibit state-funded colleges and universities from using race or ethnicity as a factor in deciding which applicants to admit. In the same year, the Supreme Court let stand a lower-court ruling in *Hopwood v. Texas,* which had forbidden the University of Texas to consider race in admission decisions. The number of black freshmen in the University of Texas dropped by half in 1997 and the number of blacks and Hispanics among first-year law students by two-thirds. The results were similar at the University of California at Berkeley, where the number of blacks among entering law students dropped from twenty to one.

In 2003, the Supreme Court affirmed the basic principle of affirmative action in two cases involving admission to the University of Michigan. Aided by supporting statements filed by major corporations and by members of the U.S. military, the Court found that promoting ethnic and racial diversity among students constitutes a compelling state interest, and it approved narrowly tailored affirmative-action programs that weigh race and ethnicity along with other admissions criteria on an individual basis. But four years later, a different majority on the Court rejected public school plans in Lexington, Kentucky, and Seattle that took race into account in deciding how to match students and schools, leaving the larger issue for further court cases.

EDGING INTO A NEW CENTURY

WHAT WERE the key elements of George W. Bush's domestic agenda?

On the evening of November 7, 2000, CBS-TV made the kind of mistake that journalists dread. Relying on questions put to a sample of voters after they cast their ballots in the presidential contest between Albert Gore Jr. and George W. Bush, the CBS newsroom first projected that Gore would win Florida and likely the election, then reversed itself and called the election for Bush, only to find that it would be days or even weeks before the votes in several pivotal states, including Florida, could be certified.

The inability to predict the outcome in 2000 was an indication of the degree to which Americans were split down the middle in their political preferences and their visions for the future. The United States entered the twenty-first century both divided and balanced, with extremes of opinion revolving around a center of basic goals and values.

THE 2000 ELECTION

On November 8, 2000, the day after their national election, Americans woke up to the news that neither Republican George W. Bush nor Democrat Albert Gore Jr. had a majority of votes in the electoral college. Although Gore held a lead in the popular vote (about 340,000 votes out of more than 100 million cast), both candidates needed a majority in Florida to win its electoral votes and the White House. After protracted protests about voting irregularities and malfunctioning voting equipment, politically divided Floridians engaged in an on-again off-again recount in key counties. The U.S. Supreme Court finally preempted the state process and ordered a halt to recounting on December 12 by the politically charged margin of 5 to 4. The result was to make Bush the winner in Florida by a few hundred votes and the winner nationwide by 271 electoral votes to 267 (see Map 31–2).

QUICK REVIEW

Election Controversy

- Al Gore secured a majority of the popular vote.
- Both sides needed Florida's contested electoral votes to secure election.
- The U.S. Supreme Court voted 5–4 to end the recount in Florida, making George W. Bush the new president.

Both Bush, governor of Texas and son of President George H. W. Bush (1989–1993), and Gore, vice president for the previous eight years, targeted their campaigns at middle Americans. Each offered to cut taxes, downsize the federal government, and protect Social Security, differing in the details rather than the broad goals. In trying to claim the political middle, they reflected the successful political message of the Clinton administration. Voters also shaved the Republican control of Congress to razor-thin margins, further undermining any chance of radical change in either a conservative or a liberal direction. To those on the political left and right who had hoped for new directions for the nation, it looked like a formula for paralysis; for the majority of Americans, it looked like stability.

In November 2002, Linda Sanchez (left) and Loretta Sanchez celebrate Linda's election to Congress from Los Angeles County. Loretta had won a congressional seat from Orange County in 1996, and Linda's victory made them the first sisters to serve simultaneously in the House of Representatives.

REAGANOMICS REVISITED

Despite the message of stability, the Bush administration took the Republican return to executive power as an opportunity to tilt domestic policy abruptly to the right. Following the example of Ronald Reagan, Bush made massive tax cuts the centerpiece of his first months in office. By starting with proposals for ten-year cuts so large that two generations of federal programs were threatened, Bush and congressional Republicans forced the Democrats to "compromise" on reductions far higher than the economy could probably support. The resulting cuts to income taxes and estate taxes were projected to total $1,350 billion over the decade, with one-third of the benefits going to families earning more than $200,000. The federal budget quickly plunged into the red, undoing the careful political balancing and fiscal discipline of the Clinton administration. Deficits were

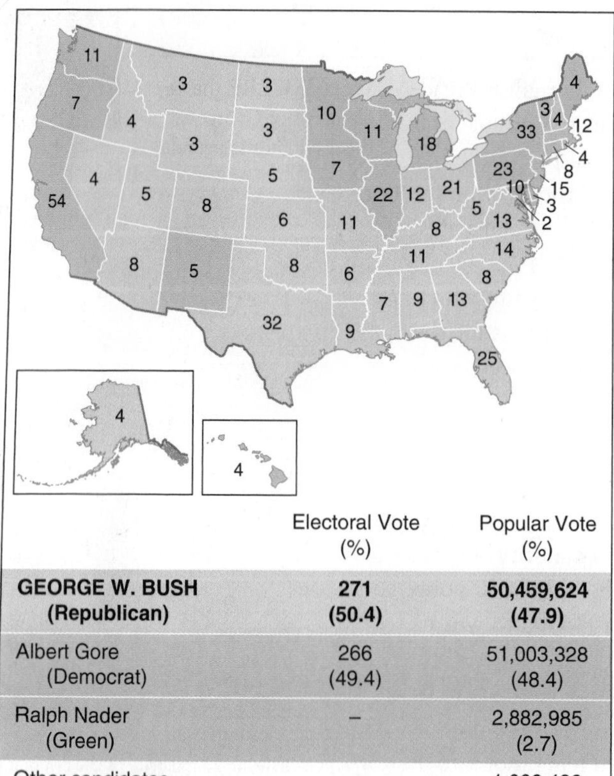

	Electoral Vote (%)	Popular Vote (%)
GEORGE W. BUSH (Republican)	**271 (50.4)**	**50,459,624 (47.9)**
Albert Gore (Democrat)	266 (49.4)	51,003,328 (48.4)
Ralph Nader (Green)	–	2,882,985 (2.7)
Other candidates	–	1,066,482 (1.0)

MAP 31–2 **The Election of 2000** In the nation's closest presidential election, Democrat Al Gore was most successful in the Northeast and Far West, while George W. Bush swept the South and won most of the Great Plains states. Green Party candidate Ralph Nader took most of his votes from Gore, in an ironic twist, helping to swing the election to Bush.

Compare this map of the 2000 election results with Map 31–1: The Election of 1992. What states did George W. Bush win that Bill Clinton won in 1992? Why was Bush able to capture these states for the Republicans?

$375 billion in 2003, $413 billion in 2004, $319 billion in 2005, and $248 billion in 2006, with more of the same forecast for the rest of the decade.

The Bush team also moved quickly to deregulate the economy. It opened many of the environmental and business regulations of the last two decades to reconsideration—from arsenic standards in drinking water to protection for wetlands to the pollution controls required of electric utilities. In many cases, the administration proposed to rely on the market through voluntary compliance and incentives to replace regulations. Vice President Dick Cheney developed a new production-oriented energy policy in consultation with energy companies but not with environmental or consumer groups. The collapse of the energy-trading company Enron in a hailstorm of criticism over deceptive accounting and shady market manipulations to create an energy crisis in California in early 2000 slowed the push to deregulate. In turn, Enron proved to be the first of many companies that had to restate earnings in 2002, depressing the stock market and raising questions about the ethics of big business and business accounting practices. Stock market declines and the evaporation of retirement savings for many workers raised doubts about the solidity of the 1990s boom and helped to hold down economic growth for a third year (see Table 31–3).

Education policy, a centerpiece of Bush's image as an innovator from his service as governor of Texas, was another legislative front. Tough battles with Congress resulted in compromise legislation, reminiscent of the 1990s, that included national testing standards, as Bush wanted, balanced by more federal funding. More important for both education and religion was the narrow decision by the Supreme Court in *Zelman v. Simmons-Harris* (2002) to uphold the use of taxpayer-funded assistance, or vouchers, to help students attend religious schools. By declaring that both religious and secular institutions can compete for government money as long as it is channeled through individuals who made "true private choices" about how to spend it, the court continued a two-decade trend to narrow the constitutional prohibition on the "establishment of religion."

QUICK REVIEW

Reagonomics Revisited: Bush's First Term

- Massive tax cuts.
- Deregulation of economy.
- Close alliance with business interests.

TABLE 31–3

Economic Inequality: 2008

	Percent of Families in Poverty	Median Household Money Income
White	11.7	$52,312
African American	24.7	$34,218
Asian	11.8	$65,637
Hispanic origin	23.2	$37,913
Native born	12.6	$51,056
Foreign born	17.8	$43,493

Source: U.S. Census.

Downsized Diplomacy

George W. Bush used his Texas ranch to escape the pressures of Washington and to cultivate his down-to-earth image.

Strong conservatives had long criticized subordinating U.S. authority and freedom of action to international agreements. The new Bush administration heeded this criticism and brought a revolutionary approach to foreign affairs. The administration repeatedly adopted unilateral or bilateral policies in preference to the complexities of negotiations with an entire range of nations.

In his first 18 months, Bush opted out of a series of treaties and negotiations on global issues, sometimes despite years of careful bargaining. In each case he pointed to specific flaws or problems, but the goal was to reduce restrictions on U.S. business and its military. The administration undercut efforts to implement the Convention on Biological Warfare because of possible adverse effects on drug companies. It refused to sign on to efforts to reduce the international trade in armaments, declined to acknowledge a new International Criminal Court that is designed to try war criminals, and ignored an international compact on the rights of women in deference to cultural conservatives. Most prominently, it refused to accept the Kyoto Agreement, aimed at combating the threat of massive environmental change through global warming resulting from the carbon dioxide released by fossil fuels, dismissing a growing scientific consensus on the problem.

Read the **Document** at **www.myhistorylab.com**
Al Gore, *Global Warming (2006)*

In the field of arms control, Bush entered office with the intention of ending the 1972 treaty that had limited the deployment of antimissile defenses by the United States and Russia in order to stabilize the arms race. The treaty had been a cornerstone of national security policy. Despite the objection of Russia, Bush formally withdrew from the treaty in December 2001. In its place he revived Ronald Reagan's idea of a Strategic Defense Initiative with proposals for new but unproven technologies to protect the United States against nuclear attacks by "rogue states." This argument was supported in 2002 by North Korea's revelation that it was pursuing a nuclear weapons program, even though it had agreed not to do so in 1994. Bush also decided not to implement the START II treaty, which had been one of the major accomplishments of his father's term as president. In its place, he worked directly to improve relations with Russia and negotiated a bilateral agreement to reduce substantially the number of nuclear warheads that Russia and the United States actively deploy (while pressing for the development of new tactical nuclear weapons). A new U.S. policy that explicitly claimed the right to act militarily to preempt potential threats confirmed the go-it-alone approach.

QUICK REVIEW

The Bush Administration Goes It Alone

- Blocked implementation of the Convention on Biological Warfare.
- Refused to acknowledge International Criminal Court.
- Refused to accept Kyoto Treaty on Global Warming.
- Decided not to implement START II arms control agreement.

PARADOXES OF POWER

HOW DID the government and the American people respond to the enormous challenges of the first decade of the twenty-first century?

The United States in the twenty-first century faced the paradox of power: the enormous economic, military, and technological capacity that allowed it to impose its will on other nations did not extend to an ability to prevent anti-American actions by deeply enraged individuals.

In the 1990s, the U.S. economy had surged while Japan stagnated, Europe marked time, and Russia verged on economic collapse. The U.S. economy in the early twenty-first century was twice the size of Japan's; California alone had economic capacity equal to France or Britain. America's lead was nurtured by research and development spending equal to that of the next six countries combined. The U.S. military budget exceeded the total military spending of the next dozen nations. The United States had the world's only global navy and a huge edge in military technology.

But the United States remained vulnerable. Huge trade deficits, massive oil imports, and a falling dollar in the early years of the new century underlined its economic vulnerability. Overseas, terrorist attacks by Islamic radicals killed 19 American soldiers at military housing in Saudi Arabia in 1996 and 17 sailors on the destroyer *Cole* while in port in the Arab nation of Yemen in 2000. Bombs at the U.S. embassies in Kenya and Tanzania in 1998 killed more than 200 people. These bombings followed the detonation of explosives in the basement garage of the World Trade Center in New York in February 1993, killing six people. New acts of terror remained a constant threat—realized in an appalling manner on September 11, 2001.

SEPTEMBER 11, 2001

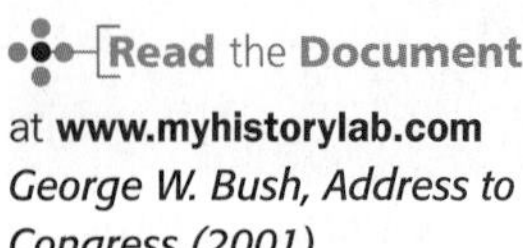

Read the **Document** at **www.myhistorylab.com** *George W. Bush, Address to Congress (2001)*

On September 11, 2001, terrorists hijacked four commercial jetliners. They crashed one plane into the Pentagon and one into each of the twin towers of the World Trade Center. Passengers on the fourth plane fought the hijackers and made sure that it crashed in the Pennsylvania mountains rather than hit a fourth target. Altogether, 479 police officers, firefighters, and other emergency workers died in the collapse of the towers. Thousands of volunteers rushed to assist rescue efforts or contribute to relief efforts. The total confirmed death toll was 2,752 in New York, 184 at the Pentagon, and 40 in Pennsylvania. A Saudi Arabian businessman who had turned against the United States because of its military presence in the Middle East and its support for Israel Osama bin Laden was probably the brains behind the attacks on the U.S. military and on diplomats overseas and the earlier blast at the World Trade Center. Operating from exile in Afghanistan, he now masterminded the new and spectacular assault.

Flames shoot from the South Tower of the World Trade Center in New York as it is struck by hijacked United Airlines Flight 15 on the morning of September 11, 2001. Smoke pours from the North Tower which had been hit sixteen minutes earlier by another hijacked aircraft.

The events of September 11 were an enormous shock to the American people, but worries about escalating terrorism were not new. Security specialists such as Defense Secretary William Cohen had been sounding the alarm through the 1990s. The U.S. Commission on National Security/21st Century, appointed by President Clinton, had included detailed warnings in its February 2001 report, although the new administration had ignored its recommendations to reorganize federal homeland security. The problem, however, had been to connect broad concerns to specific threats. It is always enormously difficult to separate and correlate key points in the vast flood of information that flows through law-enforcement and intelligence agencies. It is much easier to read the warnings after an event has occurred than to pick out the essential data before the unexpected happens—something as true about the attack on Pearl Harbor, for example, as about the attack of 9-11.

SECURITY AND CONFLICT

On September 12, President George W. Bush called the Pentagon and World Trade Center attacks "acts of war." Three days later, Congress passed a Joint Resolution that gave the president sweeping powers "to use all necessary and appropriate force against those nations, organizations, or persons he determines planned, authorized, committed, or aided the terrorist attacks that occurred on September 11, 2001." Only one member voted against the resolution—the same level of agreement that the nation showed after December 7, 1941.

The government response in the United States was a hodgepodge of security measures and arrests. Federal agents detained more than 1,000 terrorist suspects, mostly men from the Middle East, releasing some but holding hundreds without charges, evidence, or legal counsel. President Bush also declared that "enemy combatants" could be tried by special military tribunals, although domestic and international protest caused the administration to agree to more legal safeguards than originally planned. Congress passed the **PATRIOT Act** (Providing Appropriate Tools Required to Intercept and Obstruct Terrorists) in late October, which gave federal authorities substantial new capacity to conduct criminal investigations, in most provisions for the next three to five years. These included the power to request "roving" wiretaps of individuals rather than single telephones, obtain nationwide search warrants, tap information in computerized records, and detain foreigners without filing charges for up to a week. These measures raised a number of concerns about the protection of civil liberties, as noted by the several dozen members of Congress who voted against the act. The law would be renewed in 2006 with a few added provisions to protect basic constitutional and political rights.

PATRIOT Act Federal legislation adopted in 2001, in response to the terrorist attacks of September 11, intended to facilitate antiterror actions by federal law enforcement and intelligence agencies.

In November 2002, Congress approved a massive reorganization of the federal government to improve security at home. The new Department of Homeland Security includes the Immigration and Naturalization Service, Customs Service, Coast Guard, Secret Service, and Transportation Security Administration. It is the second-largest federal agency, after the Defense Department. In 2004 Congress adopted a package of reforms to improve intelligence gathering and analysis, creating the position of director of national intelligence to oversee the CIA and report directly to the president.

In contrast to the suppression of dissent during World War I or the internment of Japanese Americans during World War II, Americans in 2001 and 2002 were careful on the home front. The leaders and supporters of the War on Terror reacted to dissenting voices, particularly those from a pacifist tradition, with caustic remarks rather than repression. Censorship consisted of careful management of the news and stonewalling of requests under the Freedom of Information Act rather than direct censorship of speech and the press. Violations of civil liberties have affected individuals rather than entire groups. President Bush made an important gesture soon after September 11 by appearing at a mosque and arguing against blanket condemnation of Muslims. Ethnic profiling has resulted in heightened suspicion and surveillance of Muslims, selective enforcement of immigration laws on visitors from 20 Muslim nations, and detention of several hundred U.S. residents of Middle Eastern origin, rather than incarceration of entire ethnic groups.

In the months after 9-11, the military response overseas focused on Afghanistan, where the ruling Taliban regime was harboring bin Laden. Afghanistan had been wracked by civil war since the invasion by the Soviet Union in 1979. The Taliban, who came to power after the Soviet withdrawal and civil war, were politically and socially repressive rulers with few international friends. U.S. bombing attacks on Taliban forces began in early October 2001, and internal opposition groups in Afghanistan threw the Taliban out of power by December. Bin Laden, however, escaped with the aid of mountainous terrain and the confusion of war. The United States and NATO allies were left with an uncertain commitment to rebuild a stable Afghanistan, which remained an active war zone where resurgent Taliban activity in 2007 and 2008 threatened previous gains. On May 2, 2011, Osama bin Laden was found inside a private residence in Abbottabad, Pakistan and shot and killed by U.S. forces.

Iraq and Conflicts in the Middle East

Even while the United States was intervening in Afghanistan, the administration was extending its attention to other nations that supported or condoned anti-American terrorists or had the potential to produce chemical, biological, or nuclear weapons of mass destruction. George Bush named North Korea, Iran, and Iraq as an "axis of evil" for these reasons, and then focused on Iraq. After the Gulf War, Iraq had grudgingly accepted a United Nations requirement that it eliminate

Read the **Document** at **www.myhistorylab.com** *From Then to Now Online: America's Mission to the World*

See the **Map**
at **www.myhistorylab.com**
Present-day Africa and the Middle East

weapons of mass destruction, but gradually made UN inspections impossible. This resistance caused Bush to make the overthrow of Iraq's ruthless dictator, Saddam Hussein, the center of foreign policy. In effect, he declared one small, possibly dangerous nation to be the greatest menace the United States faced.

In addition to the direct fallout from the Persian Gulf War, the background to the deep-seated tensions in the Middle East included U.S. support of Israel amidst the deterioration of relations between Israel and the Arab Palestinians in territories occupied by Israel since 1967. The United States has consistently backed Israel since the 1960s. The cornerstones of U.S. policy have been the full endorsement of Israel's right to exist with secure borders and agreement on the right of Palestinians to a national state—in effect, a policy of coexistence. The United States helped to broker an Israel-Egypt peace agreement in 1977 and agreements pointing toward an independent Palestinian state in the 1990s. But hardline Israeli governments have repeatedly taken advantage of U.S. support from the 1980s in Lebanon (see Chapter 30) to the present.

In 2001–2002, the United States watched from the sidelines as the Israeli-Palestinian agreements for transition to a Palestinian state fell apart. Palestinian extremists and suicide bombers and an Israeli government that favored military responses locked each other into a downward spiral that turned into civil war. As a result, many Arabs identify the United States as an enemy of Arab nations and peoples. Israel's decision in 2005 to withdraw from the Gaza Strip and transfer authority there to the Palestinian government was a step toward resolution that unfortunately led to radical takeover there in 2007–2008. The deep and long-unsolvable Israeli-Palestinian conflict helps to explain anti-American terrorism among Arabs, and sometimes other Muslims.

In the spring and summer of 2002, the administration escalated threats of unilateral intervention to change the Iraqi regime and began preparations for a second war in the Persian Gulf region. On October 10, Congress authorized preemptive military action against Iraq. However, international pressure from unenthusiastic allies and from other Arab nations persuaded Bush to put diplomacy ahead of war and devote two months to making his case at the United Nations. On November 8, the UN Security Council unanimously adopted a compromise resolution that gave Iraq three and a half months to allow full and open inspections before military action might be considered. In the following months, UN inspectors searched Iraqi military sites while the United States built up forces in the Middle East in preparation for war. On March 17, 2003, Bush suspended further diplomatic efforts, and on March 19 a full scale U.S.-British invasion of Iraq began.

Read the **Document**
at **www.myhistorylab.com**
George W. Bush, Address to the Nation on the Iraq Invasion (2003)

The war to overthrow Saddam Hussein was a success as a large-scale military operation. On May 1, 2003, President Bush declared "mission accomplished"—that U.S. and British forces now controlled Iraq and major combat operations in Iraq were over.

Peace proved far more difficult than war. Reconstruction of damaged bridges, roads, water systems, and electrical systems took far longer than expected and many basic services were still fragile or nonexistent four years after the U.S. invasion. Meanwhile, American troops and relief workers were the continuing targets of car bombs, booby-trapped highways, mortar attacks, and similar guerrilla resistance. At the end of 2009, more than 4,300 U.S. soldiers had died in Iraq, over 90 percent of them after the president declared victory.

By 2007, a consensus had emerged among both critics of the war and realistic supporters that the United States had overthrown Saddam without any clear plan for next steps. Because of decisions by Secretary of Defense Donald Rumsfeld, the occupation force was inadequate in size from the start—a deficiency that a "surge" of additional U.S. forces in 2007 could not fully remedy. Early on, U.S. officials dismantled the Iraqi army and police, putting 650,000 unemployed but armed men onto the streets. The decision to shut down state industries and purge members of Saddam's political party from low-level government jobs like schoolteachers created massive unemployment. The result was the decimation of Iraq's middle class, a collapse of living standards, and the creation of roughly two million refugees who fled Iraq's new chaos for neighboring nations. However, the surge in 2007 did help to stabilize Iraq and reduce the level of violence by 2008, paving the way for gradual transfer of authority to the reconstructed Iraqi government over the next years.

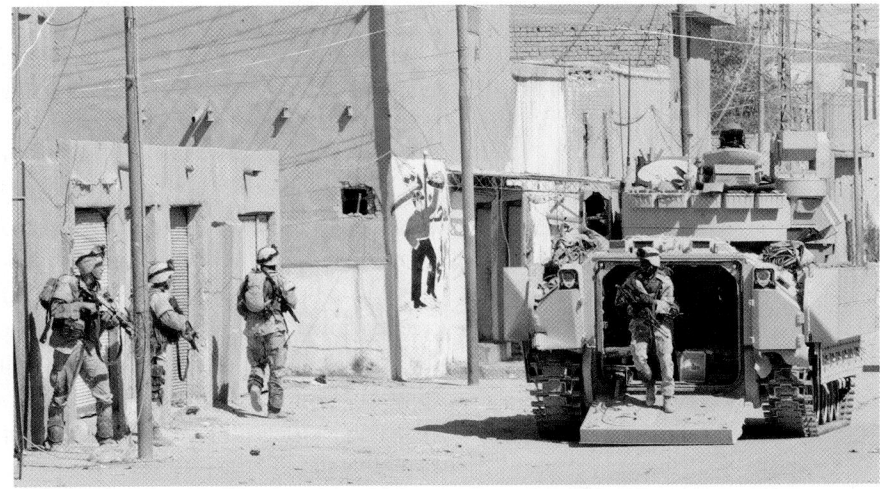

After the defeat of the Iraqi army in 2003, U.S. forces faced continuing challenges and casualties from a stubborn resistance from anti-American insurgents.

The aftermath of the war also created political problems for George Bush. A systematic search found no active production facilities or stockpiles for chemical, nuclear, or biological weapons of mass destruction. In October 2004, the final report of the U.S. bomb hunters concluded that Saddam had disbanded his chemical and nuclear weapons efforts after 1991, refuting one of the basic justifications for the war. The continuing necessity to mobilize National Guard and reserve units met heavy criticism. The need to keep an occupying army in Iraq stretched the military close to the breaking point at exactly the same time that the Taliban showed renewed strength in Afghanistan.

Hurricane and Financial Storm

Wars past and present were the pivotal issue in the 2004 election. George W. Bush argued for staying the course with the same administration. Democratic candidate John Kerry had a liberal voting record as a Massachusetts senator and decorations for meritorious service in Vietnam, but central to the Republican campaign were attacks on the veracity of his war record. A wild card was the issue of same sex marriage. Courts in Massachusetts and politicians in Oregon and San Francisco decided that legal marriage could not be denied to same sex couples. Their actions mobilized religious and cultural conservatives and led to successful ballot measures banning same sex marriage in 11 states. Bush won a solid although not overwhelming victory that helped Republicans extend their lead in Congress.

After the election, Bush reaffirmed his commitment to a U.S. presence in Iraq, where a deeply divided nation held elections for a new government early in 2005. Kurds from northern Iraq and Shiite Muslims from southern Iraq voted in large numbers and formed a coalition government. Participation was much lower among Sunni Muslims in central Iraq, who had benefited most from Saddam Hussein's regime and who were the heart of continued guerrilla resistance to the United States occupation forces. The same divisions were evident in October when Iraqis approved a new constitution that met Shiite and Kurdish desires for greater autonomy but left many Sunnis dissatisfied. Those

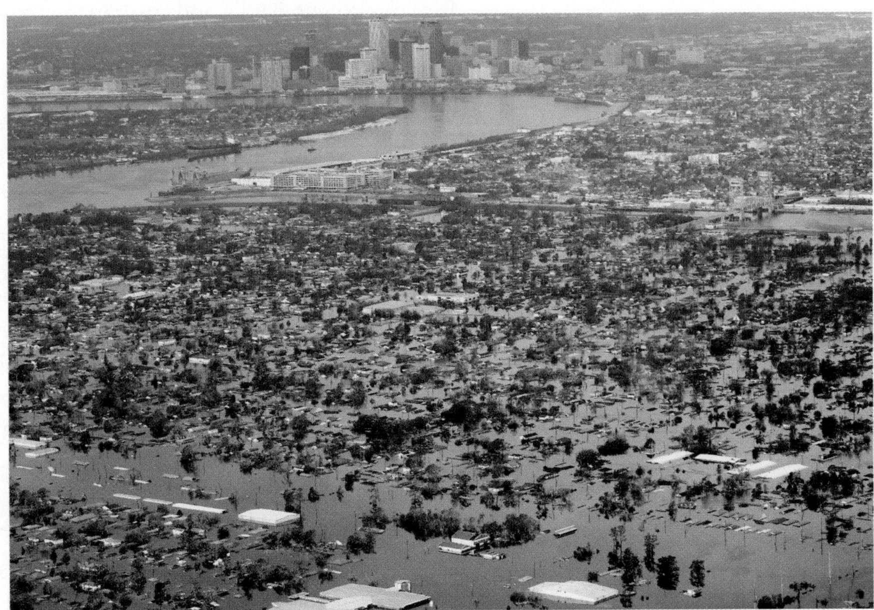

The flooding from Hurricane Katrina devastated huge expanses of low-income neighborhoods in New Orleans.

tensions played into the hands of militants who kept the level of violence among Iraqis high. Meanwhile, U.S. coalition allies such as Britain were quietly packing and leaving Iraq to its American conquerors. Nevertheless, Iraq did have a functioning government by the end of the Bush administration, opening the possibility of scaling down the U.S. military presence.

As the nation worried about the open-ended commitment in Iraq, it received a devastating reminder of vulnerability when Hurricane Katrina devastated the Gulf Coast at the end of August 2005. The storm first seemed to spare New Orleans, much of which lies below sea level, but its backlash breached levees that protected the city.

Much of the city and its surroundings flooded. Tens of thousands of residents who had not evacuated found themselves trapped in homes or huddled in overcrowded shelters. The slowness and inadequacy of the emergency response raised serious doubts about the effectiveness of the Department of Homeland Security and its Federal Emergency Management Agency and revealed the deep fault lines that still separate the poor from the larger society—exacerbated in New Orleans by the fact that most of the poor residents were African American.

Iraq and Katrina combined to deal Republicans a blow in the 2006 congressional elections, in which Democrats regained effective control of Congress for the first time in 12 years. Through 2007, as candidates of both parties jockeyed for presidential nominations, important domestic issues like immigration policy, health insurance, and the future of Social Security remained unresolved. Federal courts began to cautiously consider the basic issues of civil liberties raised by the PATRIOT Act and, even more, by the unilateral actions of the Bush administration in claiming free rein to deal with persons suspected as terrorists.

Read the **Document**
at **www.myhistorylab.com**
Dirty Politics in the 2008 Election (2007)

The Crash of 2008 upended the political jockeying with a series of stunning financial blows. The national economy began to weaken in 2007 because of pressure on housing prices. Especially in the Southwest and Southeast, housing values had inflated beyond the actual level of demand as buyers counted on the ability to resell at a high price. So-called subprime mortgage lending added to the bubble as lenders abandoned conservative practices to make incautious loans to buyers without adequate incomes and resources. Bundling these loans together and reselling them as "black box" investments added further instability. Through 2007 and into 2008, mortgage defaults increased and housing prices plummeted, knocking out one of the main props of extraordinarily high stock market indexes.

By mid-2008, declining real estate values and rising unemployment threatened the banking system, because many banks held now worthless mortgages as part of their required assets. Big investment banks and insurance companies tottered or failed and stock market indexes dropped by close to 50 percent from their highs (including a plunge of 22 percent during the second week of October), wiping out individual nest eggs and retirement accounts. Only a huge influx of government cash and guarantees saved banking from the effects of "toxic" assets, largely through the **Troubled Asset Relief Program (TARP),** which Congress approved in October 2008. TARP authorized up to $700 billion for government purchase or guarantee of illiquid and difficult-to-value mortgages and other bank assets. The federal government also used TARP funds to buy preferred stock in major banks as an additional way to shore them up.

Troubled Asset Relief Program (TARP) Federal program in 2008 to purchase or guarantee shaky bank assets to protect the economy from widespread bank failures.

The banking system stabilized in 2009 and the stock market regained about half of its losses. However, the succession of financial crises and the virtual shutdown of private construction plunged the United States into a deep recession. Small businesses found it hard to secure credit, major automobile makers declared bankruptcy, and unemployment peaked above 10 percent in October 2009 before a slow economic recovery began in 2010.

The Obama Phenomenon

Hear the **Audio**
at **www.myhistorylab.com**
The Audacity of Hope by Barack Obama, excerpt

In this context that favored Democrats, Americans in 2008 faced a presidential election campaign with two improbable candidates. The Republicans nominated John McCain, an Arizona senator who had been a prisoner of war during the Vietnam War and who cultivated a reputation as a maverick. Democrats had a hard-fought contest between Hillary Rodham Clinton, who hoped to be the first woman nominated for president by a major party, and Barack Obama, an Illinois senator who became the first African American nominee. Although Obama won the nomination with surprising ease, Democrats would have made history with either candidate.

Democrats capitalized on Republican problems with the more effective campaign. McCain divided his potential supporters by choosing Alaskan governor Sarah Palin as his vice-presidential running mate. A conservative suburban politician, Palin's short political resume and home state gave her populist appeal but left her unprepared for the national spotlight. Obama meanwhile generated enthusiasm among younger, often first-time voters as well as middle-class independents. (See Overview, Core Support for Republicans and Democrats in 2008.) The result was a solid victory in which Democrats added swing states like Virginia, North Carolina, Iowa, and Colorado to their northern and West Coast strongholds (see Map 31–3).

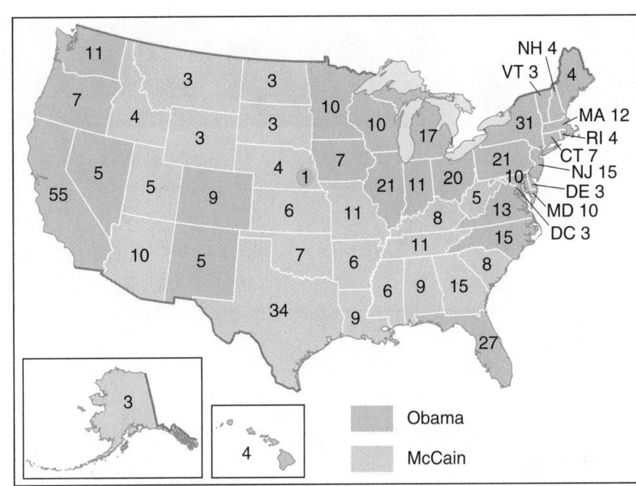

MAP 31–3 The Election of 2008 In 2008, Barack Obama won the presidency by holding the reliably Democratic Northeast and Pacific Coast and winning swing states in the Rocky Mountains (Colorado, New Mexico), the Midwest (Ohio, Indiana, Iowa), and the Southeast (Virginia, North Carolina, Florida).

Which southern states voted for Barack Obama in 2008? Does the election of 2008 indicate that Republican dominance in the South may be coming to an end?

The United States passed a tremendously important step in its national maturity by electing an African American as president, but the enthusiasm of Obama's inauguration was not enough to overcome the realities of political deadlock. Obama secured a substantial economic stimulus package to fight the deep recession, his administration began to reinvigorate protections for workers and the environment, and he tapped Sonia Sotomayor to be the first Latina on the Supreme Court. He showed his pragmatic approach by carefully assessing the situation in Afghanistan and authorizing a cautious expansion of the U.S. commitment there. The most bruising battle for the new administration came over healthcare reform, where Republicans dug in their heels against a larger federal role while Democrats tried to reconcile their liberal and conservative wings. After a year of bitter debate inside and outside Congress, President Obama in March 2010 signed a bill that promised to extend health insurance to 32 million previously uninsured Americans. It represents the greatest expansion of the federal government's social safety net since the creation of Medicare and Medicaid in 1965.

Watch the Video at **www.myhistorylab.com**
The Historical Significance of the 2008 Presidential Election

In 2010, the American people were tired of foreign wars, battered by lost retirement accounts, homes, and jobs, and impatient with a recovery that seemed to benefit bankers more than working people. They wanted someone to shake up the system, but they also feared losing what security they had. They desperately wanted change, but they showed no willingness to trust anyone to deliver it—neither Democrats nor Republicans, federal government nor corporate America. It was an enormous challenge for anyone who hoped to lead the nation into the second decade of the new century.

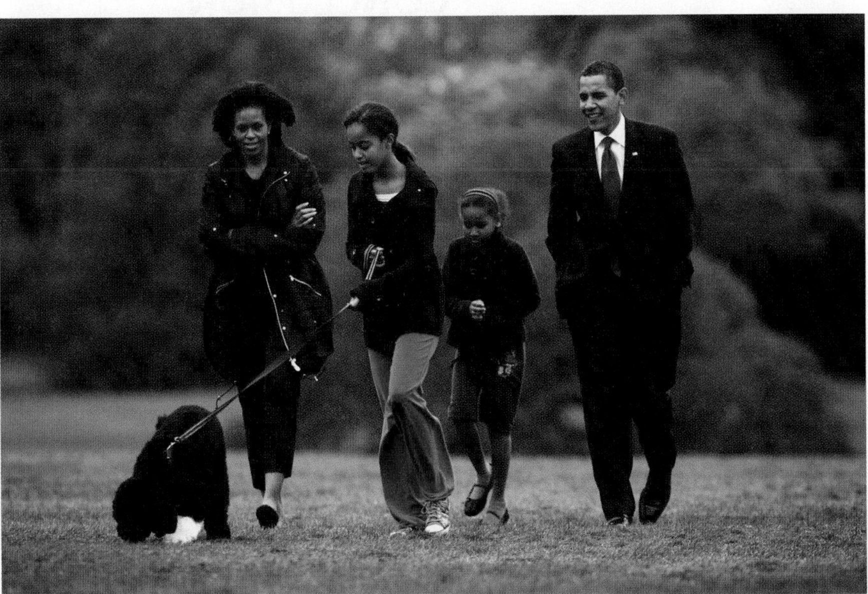

The Obama family brought youthful energy to the White House reminiscent of the Kennedy family in the 1960s and Theodore Roosevelt's family in the first years of the twentieth century.

OVERVIEW Core Support for Republicans and Democrats in 2008

	Republicans	Democrats
Age	60 and older	18–29 years old
Religion	White Protestants Evangelicals Regular church-goers	Jews
Education		Less than high school Postgraduate education
Family income		Under $50,000
Sex		Women
Race and Ethnicity	Whites	African Americans Latinos Asian Americans
Geography	South Central states Appalachian states	Pacific Coast Northeast Great Lakes states
Size of Community	Rural areas and small towns	Large cities

CONCLUSION

If there was a dominant theme that ran through the changes and challenges of the 1990s and the new century, it was interconnection. The Internet, e-mail, and cell phones brought instant communication. Corporate mismanagement affected far more people than before because of pensions and savings invested in the stock market. Whether by television or Twitter, information—and sometimes real news—traveled faster than ever before.

Despite what some might have wished, Americans also found that they could not always isolate the nation from the problems and conflicts that wracked much of the rest of the world. The Clinton administration joined international peacekeeping efforts in Bosnia and Kosovo. The Bush administration chose to ignore several international agreements, but still sought the cover of United Nations approval for action against Iraq (although it largely disregarded international opinion in its pursuit of the war).

Beyond its growing military commitments, the United States in the first years of the twenty-first century was deeply connected to the world. Travel, work and study abroad—and foreign tourists, workers, and students in the United States—improved American understanding of other nations. However, the ease and volume of travel and trade also brought problems and fears. The nation's growing diversity—closely connected to its internationalized economy—was reflected in the political gains of African Americans and Hispanics, as well as women, but the same diversity fueled battles over affirmative action and language politics. Many Americans had long worried that the United States was being flooded by illegal immigrants, and the revelation that some of the 9-11 terrorists had learned to fly in U.S. training schools compounded fears of a porous border.

International connection had other economic and environmental implications. Americans enjoyed the benefits of open trade and cheap imports, but a ballooning national debt and fast-growing trade deficits reduced the purchasing power of the dollar and made the economy dependent on investment from abroad. Hovering in the background were global environmental concerns such as global warming caused or accelerated by the massive use of fossil fuels whose combustion adds carbon dioxide to the atmosphere.

Americans have seldom made their personal journeys in isolation. We have depended on our communities and seen the consequences when the failure of community support throws us on our own, as happened to some in New Orleans in 2005. We welcome refugees from tyranny and journey across oceans to help others. In the coming decades, our community will increasingly span the entire globe as we face the challenges of economic, environmental, and political change. We—the authors of this book—look forward to learning and writing about these new journeys in the years to come.

Where to Learn More

Oklahoma City National Memorial Center Museum, Oklahoma City, Oklahoma. Exhibits about the federal building bombing and its impact on the community. http://www.oklahomacitynationalmemorial.org.

Review Questions

1. Was the U.S. political system more polarized and divided in 1992 than in 1980? How did religiously conservative Americans understand issues of foreign relations and economic policy? How did religiously liberal Americans understand the same issues? What was the gender gap in national politics in the 1990s? Why were Republicans unable to appeal to most black and Hispanic voters in 1992?
2. What were Bill Clinton's major policy accomplishments? Do these represent liberal, moderate, or conservative positions?
3. What was the Contract with America? What are other examples of a conservative political trend in the 1990s?
4. What issues were involved in Clinton's impeachment? How does the impeachment compare with the challenges to presidents Andrew Johnson and Richard Nixon?
5. Did the U.S. economy undergo fundamental changes in the 1990s? What has been the impact of the computer revolution? Of the growing importance of world markets?
6. What new directions did George W. Bush establish for U.S. domestic and foreign policy?
7. How did the terrorist attacks of September 11, 2001, change life in the United States? How did ordinary Americans respond at the time and since the attacks?
8. What are some of the reasons the experience of the United States in reconstructing Iraq after 2003 has differed from its experience in Japan and Germany after World War II?
9. What factors contributed to Democratic Party victories in the 2008 election?

Key Terms

Affirmative action (p. 894)
Contract with America (p. 880)
Internet (p. 883)
Neoliberal (p. 879)
North American Free Trade Agreement (NAFTA) (p. 886)
PATRIOT Act (p. 899)
Proposition 187 (p. 893)
Silicon Valley (p. 885)
Temporary Assistance for Needy Families (TANF) (p. 880)
Troubled Asset Relief Program (TARP) (p. 902)
University of California v. Bakke (p. 894)
Whitewater (p. 882)
World Trade Organization (WTO) (p. 886)
World Wide Web (p. 885)

myhistorylab Connections

Reinforce what you learned in this chapter by studying the many documents, images, maps, review tools, and videos available at **www.myhistorylab.com**.

Read and Review

Study and Review **Study Plan: Chapter 31**

Read the Document

Republican Contract with America (1994)

U.S. v. Timothy James McVeigh *(1997)*

Articles of Impeachment against William Jefferson Clinton (1998)

Bill Clinton, Answers to the Articles of Impeachment (1998)

Clinton Health Care Reform Proposals (1993)

Illegal Immigration Reform and Immigrant Responsibility Act (1996)

George W. Bush, Address to Congress (2001)

George W. Bush, Address to the Nation on the Iraq Invasion (2003)

Nancy Pelosi, Inaugural Address (2007)

Al Gore, Global Warming (2006)

Dirty Politics in the 2008 Election (2007)

See the Map

Settlement of the United States, c. 1998

Present-day Africa and the Middle East

Present-day Europe

Present-day World

Research and Explore

Read the Document

Personal Journeys Online

From Then to Now Online: America's Mission to the World

Exploring America: Globalization

Hear the Audio *The Audacity of Hope by Barack Obama, excerpt*

Watch the Video

Bill Clinton First Inauguration

Bill Clinton Sells Himself to America: Presidential Campaign Ad, 1992

The Historical Significance of the 2008 Presidential Election

Hear the Audio

Hear the audio files for Chapter 31 at **www.myhistorylab.com**.

The Threat of War to Democratic Institutions

HOW has the use of the PATRIOT Act and its later revisions been in line with actions of earlier American governments during wartime or times of perceived threat to the United States?

As early as 1798 and the Alien and Sedition Act of the Adams administration, American governments have been willing to suppress civil liberties in the name of national defense. Adams was fearful of French immigrants who added to the voting power of Democratic Republicans and the poisoned pens of Democratic Republicans whose newspapers torn at his public reputation. In the Civil War Lincoln suspended the right of habeas corpus in Maryland and arrested members of Congress who were known secessionists.

In the past century, the events of the eighteenth and nineteenth centuries during war were paralleled during World War I, World War II, the Cold War, and the War on Terror which began on September 11, 2001. In World War II hysteria over the Japanese attack on Pearl Harbor combined with a long-standing racism against Asians in West Coast states resulted in the imprisonment of approximately 120,000 Japanese Americans, many native-born citizens, under Roosevelt's Executive Order 9066. During the Cold War and the era of Joseph McCarthy, Americans lost their jobs, faced government investigation of the most intrusive nature, and met with public disgrace. Civil libertarians have criticized the PATRIOT Act of 2001 (Public Law 107-56) as an inappropriate curtailment of constitutional rights and a dangerous expansion of executive police powers.

. . . to prescribe military areas . . .

George W. Bush, President's Statement on H.R. 199, the "USA PATRIOT Improvement and Reauthorization Act of 2005," March 9, 2006

Today, I have signed into law H.R. 3199, the "USA PATRIOT Improvement and Reauthorization Act of 2005," and then S. 2271, the "USA PATRIOT Act Additional Reauthorizing Amendments Act of 2006." The bills will help us continue to fight terrorism effectively and to combat the use of the illegal drug methamphetamine that is ruining too many lives.

The executive branch shall construe the provisions of H.R. 3199 that call for furnishing information to entities outside the executive branch, such as sections 106A and 119, in a manner consistent with the President's constitutional authority to supervise the unitary executive branch and to withhold information the disclosure of which could impair foreign relations, national security, the deliberative processes of the Executive, or the performance of the Executive's constitutional duties.

The executive branch shall construe section 756(e)(2) of H.R. 3199, which calls for an executive branch official to submit to the Congress recommendations for legislative action, in a manner consistent with the President's constitutional authority to supervise the unitary executive branch and to recommend for the consideration of the Congress such measures as he judges necessary and expedient.

Sedition Act of 1918, May 16, 1918 (repealed 1921)

SECTION 3. Whoever, when the United States is at war, shall willfully make or convey false reports or false statements with intent to interfere with the operation or success of the military or naval forces of the United States, or to promote the success of its enemies, or shall willfully make or convey false reports, or false statements, . . . or incite insubordination, disloyalty, mutiny, or refusal of duty, in the military or naval forces of the United States, or shall willfully obstruct . . . the recruiting or enlistment service of the United States, or . . . shall willfully utter, print, write, or publish any disloyal, profane, scurrilous, or abusive language about the form of government of the United States, or the Constitution of the United States, or the military or naval forces of the United States . . . or shall willfully display the flag of any foreign enemy, or shall willfully . . . urge, incite, or advocate any curtailment of production . . . or advocate, teach, defend, or suggest the doing of any of the acts or things in this section enumerated and whoever shall by word or act support or favor the cause of any country with which the United States is at war or by word or act oppose the cause of the United States therein, shall be punished by a fine of not more than $10,000 or imprisonment for not more than twenty years, or both. . . .

Esther C. Brunauer, an employee of the State Department, testified before the Senate Subcommittee on Foreign Relations to defend herself against allegations made against her by Senator Joseph McCarthy.

Franklin D. Roosevelt, Executive Order 9066, February 19, 1942

I hereby authorize and direct the Secretary of War, and the Military Commanders whom he may from time to time designate, whenever he or any designated Commander deems such action necessary or desirable, to prescribe military areas in such places and of such extent as he or the appropriate Military Commander may determine, from which any or all persons may be excluded, and with respect to which, the right of any person to enter, remain in, or leave shall be subject to whatever restrictions the Secretary of War or the appropriate Military Commander may impose in his discretion.

The hysteria and fear following the Pearl Harbor attack resulted in the internment of 110,000 Japanese Americans in "War Relocation Centers" located in isolated areas of the West for the duration of the war. In 1944 the U.S. Supreme Court upheld this action by the government with the comment that it was a "pressing public necessity."

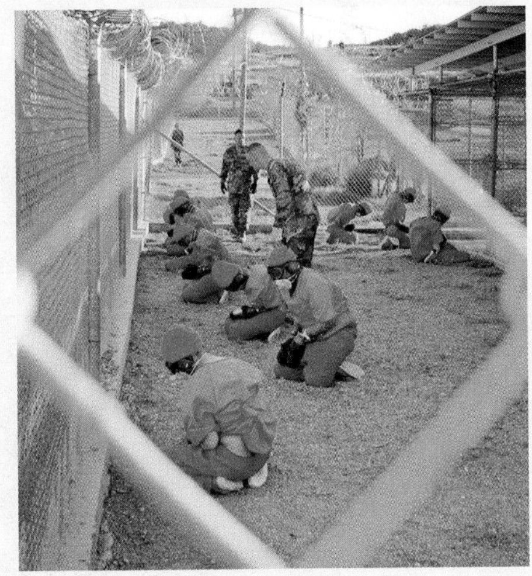

Camp X-ray detainees – Guantanamo Bay Detention Camp. In his War on Terror President Bush deemed it necessary to intern approximately 775 enemy prisoners captured in Afghanistan and elsewhere in a military facility. Bush claimed these prisoners did not possess rights under the terms of the Geneva Conventions. The U.S. Supreme Court ruled against his position in 2006 and ordered the U.S. military to extend international rights granted under the Geneva Conventions to enemy combatants to these individuals.

. . . help us continue to fight terrorism . . .

The Declaration of Independence

When in the course of human events it becomes necessary for one people to dissolve the political bands which have connected them with another and to assume, among the powers of the earth, the separate and equal station to which the laws of nature and of nature's God entitle them, a decent respect to the opinions of mankind requires that they should declare the causes which impel them to the separation.

We hold these truths to be self-evident, that all men are created equal; that they are endowed by their Creator with certain unalienable rights; that among these are life, liberty, and the pursuit of happiness. That, to secure these rights, governments are instituted among men, deriving their just powers from the consent of the governed; that, whenever any form of government becomes destructive of these ends, it is the right of the people to alter or to abolish it, and to institute a new government, laying its foundation on such principles, and organizing its powers in such form, as to them shall seem most likely to effect their safety and happiness. Prudence, indeed, will dictate that governments long established should not be changed for light and transient causes; and, accordingly, all experience hath shown that mankind are more disposed to suffer, while evils are sufferable, than to right themselves by abolishing the forms to which they are accustomed. But when a long train of abuses and usurpations, pursuing invariably the same object, evinces a design to reduce them under absolute despotism, it is their right, it is their duty, to throw off such government and to provide new guards for their future security. Such has been the patient sufferance of these colonies, and such is now the necessity which constrains them to alter their former systems of government. The history of the present King of Great Britain is a history of repeated injuries and usurpations, all having, in direct object, the establishment of an absolute tyranny over these States. To prove this, let facts be submitted to a candid world:

He has refused his assent to laws the most wholesome and necessary for the public good.

He has forbidden his governors to pass laws of immediate and pressing importance, unless suspended in their operation till his assent should be obtained; and, when so suspended, he has utterly neglected to attend to them.

He has refused to pass other laws for the accommodation of large districts of people, unless those people would relinquish the right of representation in the legislature, a right inestimable to them and formidable to tyrants only.

He has called together legislative bodies at places unusual, uncomfortable, and distant from the depository of their public records, for the sole purpose of fatiguing them into compliance with his measures.

He has dissolved representative houses, repeatedly for opposing, with manly firmness, his invasions on the rights of the people.

He has refused, for a long time after such dissolutions, to cause others to be elected; whereby the legislative powers, incapable of annihilation, have returned to the people at large for their exercise; the state remaining, in the meantime, exposed to all the danger of invasion from without and convulsions within.

He has endeavored to prevent the population of these States; for that purpose, obstructing the laws for naturalization of foreigners, refusing to pass others to encourage their migration hither, and raising the conditions of new appropriations of lands.

He has obstructed the administration of justice by refusing his assent to laws for establishing judiciary powers.

He has made judges dependent on his will alone for the tenure of their offices and the amount and payment of their salaries.

He has erected a multitude of new offices and sent hither swarms of officers to harass our people and eat out their substance.

He has kept among us, in time of peace, standing armies, without the consent of our legislatures.

He has affected to render the military independent of, and superior to, the civil power.

He has combined with others to subject us to a jurisdiction foreign to our Constitution and unacknowledged by our laws, giving his assent to their acts of pretended legislation—

For quartering large bodies of armed troops among us;

For protecting them by mock trial, from punishment for any murders which they should commit on the inhabitants of these States;

For cutting off our trade with all parts of the world;

For imposing taxes on us without our consent;

For depriving us, in many cases, of the benefit of trial by jury;

For transporting us beyond seas to be tried for pretended offences;

For abolishing the free system of English laws in a neighboring province, establishing therein an arbitrary government, and enlarging its boundaries, so as to render it at once an example and fit instrument for introducing the same absolute rule into these colonies;

For taking away our charters, abolishing our most valuable laws, and altering, fundamentally, the powers of our governments.

For suspending our own legislatures and declaring themselves invested with power to legislate for us in all cases whatsoever.

He has abdicated government here by declaring us out of his protection and waging war against us.

He has plundered our seas, ravaged our coasts, burnt our towns, and destroyed the lives of our people.

He is, at this time, transporting large armies of foreign mercenaries to complete the works of death, desolation, and tyranny already begun with circumstances of cruelty and perfidy scarcely paralleled in the most barbarous ages, and totally unworthy the head of a civilized nation.

He has constrained our fellow citizens, taken captive on the high seas, to bear arms against their country, to become the executioners of their friends and brethren, or to fall themselves by their hands.

He has excited domestic insurrections amongst us and has endeavored to bring on the inhabitants of our frontiers, the merciless Indian savages, whose known rule of warfare is an undistinguished destruction of all ages, sexes, and conditions.

In every stage of these oppressions, we have petitioned for redress in the most humble terms; our repeated petitions have been answered only by repeated injury. A prince whose character is thus marked by every act which may define a tyrant is unfit to be the ruler of a free people.

Nor have we been wanting in attention to our British brethren. We have warned them, from time to time, of attempts made by their legislature to extend an unwarrantable jurisdiction over us. We have reminded them of the circumstances of our emigration and settlement here. We have appealed to their native justice and magnanimity, and we have conjured them, by the ties of our common kindred, to disavow these usurpations, which would inevitably interrupt our connections and correspondence. They, too, have been deaf to the voice of justice and consanguinity. We must, therefore, acquiesce in the necessity which denounces our separation, and hold them, as we hold the rest of mankind, enemies in war, in peace, friends.

We, therefore, the representatives of the United States of America, in general Congress assembled, appealing to the Supreme Judge of the world for the rectitude of our intentions, do, in the name and by the authority of the good people of these colonies, solemnly publish and declare, that these united colonies are, and of right ought to be, free and independent states: that they are absolved from all allegiance to the British Crown, and that all political connection between them and the state of Great Britain is, and ought to be, totally dissolved; and that, as free and independent states, they have full power to levy war, conclude peace, contract alliances, establish commerce, and to do all other acts and things which independent states may of right do. And, for the support of this declaration, with a firm reliance on the protection of Divine Providence, we mutually pledge to each other our lives, our fortunes, and our sacred honor.

The Articles of Confederation and Perpetual Union*

Between the states of New Hampshire, Massachusetts-bay Rhode Island and Providence Plantations, Connecticut, New York, New Jersey, Pennsylvania, Delaware, Maryland, Virginia, North Carolina, South Carolina, and Georgia.

Article I

The Stile of this Confederacy shall be "The United States of America."

Article II

Each state retains its sovereignty, freedom, and independence, and every power, jurisdiction, and right, which is not by this Confederation expressly delegated to the United States, in Congress assembled.

Article III

The said States hereby severally enter into a firm league of friendship with each other, for their common defense, the security of their liberties, and their mutual and general welfare, binding themselves to assist each other, against all force offered to, or attacks made upon them, or any of them, on account of religion, sovereignty, trade, or any other pretense whatever.

Article IV

The better to secure and perpetuate mutual friendship and intercourse among the people of the different States in this Union, the free inhabitants of each of these States, paupers, vagabonds, and fugitives from justice excepted, shall be entitled to all privileges and immunities of free citizens in the several States; and the people of each State shall have free ingress and regress to and from any other State, and shall enjoy therein all the privileges of trade and commerce, subject to the same duties, impositions, and restrictions as the inhabitants thereof respectively, provided that such restrictions shall not extend so far as to prevent the removal of property imported into any State, to any other State of which the owner is an inhabitant; provided also that no imposition, duties or restriction shall be laid by any State, on the property of the United States, or either of them.

If any person guilty of, or charged with, treason, felony, or other high misdemeanor in any State, shall flee from justice, and be found in any of the United States, he shall, upon demand of the Governor or executive power of the State from which he fled, be delivered up and removed to the State having jurisdiction of his offense.

Full faith and credit shall be given in each of these States to the records, acts, and judicial proceedings of the courts and magistrates of every other State.

Article V

For the most convenient management of the general interests of the United States, delegates shall be annually appointed in such manner as the legislatures of each State shall direct, to meet in Congress on the first Monday in November, in every year, with a power reserved to each State to recall its delegates, or any of them, at any time within the year, and to send others in their stead for the remainder of the year.

No State shall be represented in Congress by less than two, nor by more than seven members; and no person shall be capable of being a delegate for more than three years in any term of six years; nor shall any person, being a delegate, be capable of holding any office under the United States, for which he, or another for his benefit, receives any salary, fees or emolument of any kind.

Each State shall maintain its own delegates in a meeting of the States, and while they act as members of the committee of the States.

In determining questions in the United States in Congress assembled, each State shall have one vote.

Freedom of speech and debate in Congress shall not be impeached or questioned in any court or place out of Congress, and the members of Congress shall be protected in their persons from arrests or imprisonments, during the time of their going to and from, and attendence on Congress, except for treason, felony, or breach of the peace.

Article VI

No State, without the consent of the United States in Congress assembled, shall send any embassy to, or receive any embassy from, or enter into any conference, agreement, alliance or treaty with any King, Prince or State; nor shall any person holding any office of profit or trust under the United States, or any of them, accept any present, emolument, office or title of any kind whatever from any King, Prince or foreign State; nor shall the United States in Congress assembled, or any of them, grant any title of nobility.

*Agreed to in Congress November 15, 1777; ratified March 1781.

No two or more States shall enter into any treaty, confederation or alliance whatever between them, without the consent of the United States in Congress assembled, specifying accurately the purposes for which the same is to be entered into, and how long it shall continue.

No State shall lay any imposts or duties, which may interfere with any stipulations in treaties, entered into by the United States in Congress assembled, with any King, Prince or State, in pursuance of any treaties already proposed by Congress, to the courts of France and Spain.

No vessel of war shall be kept up in time of peace by any State, except such number only, as shall be deemed necessary by the United States in Congress assembled, for the defense of such State, or its trade; nor shall any body of forces be kept up by any State in time of peace, except such number only, as in the judgement of the United States in Congress assembled, shall be deemed requisite to garrison the forts necessary for the defense of such State; but every State shall always keep up a well-regulated and disciplined militia, sufficiently armed and accoutered, and shall provide and constantly have ready for use, in public stores, a due number of filed pieces and tents, and a proper quantity of arms, ammunition and camp equipage.

No State shall engage in any war without the consent of the United States in Congress assembled, unless such State be actually invaded by enemies, or shall have received certain advice of a resolution being formed by some nation of Indians to invade such State, and the danger is so imminent as not to admit of a delay, till the United States in Congress assembled can be consulted; nor shall any State grant commissions to any ships or vessels of war, nor letters of marque or reprisal, except it be after a declaration of war by the United States in Congress assembled, and then only against the Kingdom or State and the subjects thereof, against which war has been so declared, and under such regulations as shall be established by the United States in Congress assembled, unless such State be infested by pirates, in which case vessels of war may be fitted out for that occasion, and kept so long as the danger shall continue, or until the United States in Congress assembled shall determine otherwise.

Article VII

When land forces are raised by any State for the common defense, all officers of or under the rank of colonel, shall be appointed by the legislature of each State respectively, by whom such forces shall be raised, or in such manner as such State shall direct, and all vacancies shall be filled up by the State which first made the appointment.

Article VIII

All charges of war, and all other expenses that shall be incurred for the common defense or general welfare, and allowed by the United States in Congress assembled, shall be defrayed out of a common treasury, which shall be supplied by the several States in proportion to the value of all land within each State, granted to or surveyed for any person, as such land and the buildings and improvements thereon shall be estimated according to such mode as the United States in Congress assembled, shall from time to time direct and appoint.

The taxes for paying that proportion shall be laid and levied by the authority and direction of the legislatures of the several States within the time agreed upon by the United States in Congress assembled.

Article IX

The United States in Congress assembled, shall have the sole and exclusive right and power of determining on peace and war, except in the cases mentioned in the sixth article; of sending and receiving ambassadors; entering into treaties and alliances, provided that no treaty of commerce shall be made whereby the legislative power of the respective States shall be restrained from imposing such imposts and duties on foreigners, as their own people are subjected to, or from prohibiting the exportation or importation of any species of goods or commodities whatsoever; of establishing rules for deciding in all cases, what captures on land or water shall be legal, and in what manner prizes taken by land or naval forces in the service of the United States shall be divided or appropriated; of granting letters of marque and reprisal in times of peace; appointing courts for the trial of piracies and felonies committed on the high seas and establishing courts for receiving and determining finally appeals in all cases of captures, provided that no member of Congress shall be appointed a judge of any of the said courts.

The United States in Congress assembled shall also be the last resort on appeal in all disputes and differences now subsisting or that hereafter may arise between two or more States concerning boundary, jurisdiction or any other causes whatever; which authority shall always be exercised in the manner following. Whenever the legislative or executive authority or lawful agent of any State in controversy with another shall present a petition to Congress stating the matter in question and praying for a hearing, notice thereof shall be given by order of Congress to the legislative or executive authority of the other State in controversy, and a day assigned for the appearance of the parties by their lawful agents, who shall then be directed to appoint by joint consent, commissioners or judges to constitute a court for hearing and determining the matter in question: but if they cannot agree, Congress shall name three persons out of each of the United States, and from the list of such persons each party shall alternately strike out one, the petitioners beginning, until the number shall be reduced to thirteen; and from that number not less than seven, nor more than nine names as Congress shall direct, shall in the presence of Congress be drawn out by lot, and the persons whose names shall be so drawn or any five of them, shall be commissioners or judges, to hear and finally determine the controversy, so always as a major part of the judges who shall hear the cause shall agree in the determination: and if either party shall neglect to attend at the day appointed, without showing reasons, which Congress shall judge sufficient, or being present shall refuse to strike, the Congress shall proceed to nominate three persons out of each State, and the secretary of Congress shall strike in behalf of such party absent or refusing; and the judgement and sentence of the court to be appointed, in the manner before prescribed, shall be final and conclusive; and if any of the parties shall refuse to submit to the authority of such court, or to appear or defend their claim or cause, the court shall nevertheless proceed to pronounce sentence, or judgement, which shall in like manner be final and decisive, the judgement or sentence and other proceedings being in either case transmitted to Congress, and lodged among the acts of Congress for the security of the parties concerned: provided that every commissioner, before he sits in judgement, shall take an oath to be administered by one of the judges of the supreme or superior court of the State, where the cause shall be tried, "well and truly to hear and determine the matter in question, according to the best of his judgement, without favor, affection or hope of reward:" provided also, that no State shall be deprived of territory for the benefit of the United States.

All controversies concerning the private right of soil claimed under different grants of two or more States, whose jurisdictions as they may respect such lands, and the States which passed such grants are adjusted, the said grants or either of them being at the same time claimed to have originated antecedent to such settlement of jurisdiction, shall on the petition of either party to the Congress of the United States, be finally determined as near as may be in the same manner as is before prescribed for deciding disputes respecting territorial jurisdiction between different States.

The United States in Congress assembled shall also have the sole and exclusive right and power of regulating the alloy and value of coin struck by their own authority, or by that of the respective States; fixing the standards of weights and measures throughout the United States; regulating the trade and managing all affairs with the Indians not members of any of the States; provided that the legislative right of any State within its own limits be not infringed or violated; establishing or regulating post offices from one State to another, throughout all the United States, and exacting such postage on the papers passing through the same as may be requisite to defray the expenses of the said office; appointing all officers of the land forces in the service of the United States, excepting regimental officers; appointing all the officers of the naval forces, and commissioning all officers whatever in the service of the United States; making rules for the government and regulation of the said land and naval forces, and directing their operations.

The United States in Congress assembled shall have authority to appoint a committee, to sit in the recess of Congress, to be denominated "A Committee of the States," and to consist of one delegate from each State; and to appoint such other committees and civil officers as may be necessary for managing the general affairs of the United States under their direction; to appoint one of their members to preside, provided that no person be allowed to serve in the office of president more than one year in any term of three years; to ascertain the necessary sums of money to be raised for the service of the United States, and to appropriate and apply the same for defraying the public expenses; to borrow money, or emit bills on the credit of the United States, transmitting every half year to the respective States an account of the sums of money so borrowed or emitted; to build and equip a navy; to agree upon the number of land forces, and to make requisitions from each State for its quota, in proportion to the number of white inhabitants in such State; which requisition shall be binding, and thereupon the legislature of each State shall appoint the regimental officers, raise the men and cloath, arm and equip them in a soldierlike manner, at the expense of the United States; and the officers and men so cloathed, armed and equipped shall march to the place appointed, and within the time agreed on by the United States in Congress assembled; but if the United States in Congress assembled shall, on consideration of circumstances judge proper that any State should not raise men, or should raise a smaller number of men than the quota thereof, such extra number shall be raised, officered, cloathed, armed and equipped in the same manner as the quota of each State, unless the legislature of such State shall judge that such extra number cannot be safely spared out in the same, in which case they shall raise, officer, cloath, arm and equip as many of such extra number as they judge can be safely spared. And the officers and men so cloathed, armed, and equipped, shall march to the place appointed, and within the time agreed on by the United States in Congress assembled.

The United States in Congress assembled shall never engage in a war, nor grant letters of marque or reprisal in time of peace, nor enter into any treaties or alliances, nor coin money, nor regulate the value thereof, nor ascertain the sums and expenses necessary for the defense and welfare of the United States, or any of them, nor emit bills, nor borrow money on the credit of the United States, nor appropriate money, nor agree upon the number of vessels of war, to be built or purchased, or the number of land or sea forces to be raised, nor appoint a commander in chief of the army or navy, unless nine States assent to the same: nor shall a question on any other point, except for adjourning from day to day be determined, unless by the votes of the majority of the United States in Congress assembled.

The Congress of the United States shall have power to adjourn to any time within the year, and to any place within the United States, so that no period of adjournment be for a longer duration than the space of six months, and shall publish the journal of their proceedings monthly, except such parts thereof relating to treaties, alliances or military operations, as in their judgement require secrecy; and the yeas and nays of the delegates of each State on any question shall be entered on the journal, when it is desired by any delegates of a State, or any of them, at his or their request shall be furnished with a transcript of the said journal, except such parts as are above excepted, to lay before the legislatures of the several States.

Article X

The Committee of the States, or any nine of them, shall be authorized to execute, in the recess of Congress, such of the powers of Congress as the United States in Congress assembled, by the consent of the nine States, shall from time to time think expedient to vest them with; provided that no power be delegated to the said Committee, for the exercise of which, by the Articles of Confederation, the voice of nine States in the Congress of the United States assembled is requisite.

Article XI

Canada acceding to this confederation, and adjoining in the measures of the United States, shall be admitted into, and entitled to all the advantages of this Union; but no other colony shall be admitted into the same, unless such admission be agreed to by nine States.

Article XII

All bills of credit emitted, monies borrowed, and debts contracted by, or under the authority of Congress, before the assembling of the United States, in pursuance of the present confederation, shall be deemed and considered as a charge against the United States, for payment and satisfaction whereof the said United States, and the public faith are hereby solemnly pledged.

Article XIII

Every State shall abide by the determination of the United States in Congress assembled, on all questions which by this confederation are submitted to them. And the Articles of this

Confederation shall be inviolably observed by every State, and the Union shall be perpetual; nor shall any alteration at any time hereafter be made in any of them; unless such alteration be agreed to in a Congress of the United States, and be afterwards confirmed by the legislatures of every State.

These articles shall be proposed to the legislatures of all the United States, to be considered, and if approved of by them, they are advised to authorize their delegates to ratify the same in the Congress of the United States; which being done, the same shall become conclusive.

The Constitution of the United States of America

We the people of the United States, in order to form a more perfect union, establish justice, insure domestic tranquillity, provide for the common defense, promote the general welfare, and secure the blessings of liberty to ourselves and our posterity, do ordain and establish this Constitution for the United States of America.

Article I

Section 1. All legislative powers herein granted shall be vested in a Congress of the United States, which shall consist of a Senate and House of Representatives.

Section 2. 1. The House of Representatives shall be composed of members chosen every second year by the people of the several States, and the electors in each State shall have the qualifications requisite for electors of the most numerous branch of the State legislature.

2. No person shall be a representative who shall not have attained to the age of twenty-five years, and been seven years a citizen of the United States, and who shall not, when elected, be an inhabitant of that State in which he shall be chosen.

3. Representatives and direct taxes[1] shall be apportioned among the several States which may be included within this Union, according to their respective numbers, which shall be determined by adding to the whole number of free persons, including those bound to service for a term of years, and excluding Indians not taxed, three fifths of all other persons.[2] The actual enumeration shall be made within three years after the first meeting of the Congress of the United States, and within every subsequent term of ten years, in such manner as they shall by law direct. The number of representatives shall not exceed one for every thirty thousand, but each State shall have at least one representative; and until such enumeration shall be made, the State of New Hampshire shall be entitled to choose three, Massachusetts eight, Rhode Island and Providence Plantations one, Connecticut five, New York six, New Jersey four, Pennsylvania eight, Delaware one, Maryland six, Virginia ten, North Carolina five, South Carolina five, and Georgia three.

4. When vacancies happen in the representation from any State, the executive authority thereof shall issue writs of election to fill such vacancies.

5. The House of Representatives shall choose their speaker and other officers; and shall have the sole power of impeachment.

Section 3. 1. The Senate of the United States shall be composed of two senators from each State, chosen by the legislature thereof,[3] for six years; and each senator shall have one vote.

2. Immediately after they shall be assembled in consequence of the first election, they shall be divided as equally as may be into three classes. The seats of the senators of the first class shall be vacated at the expiration of the second year, of the second class at the expiration of the fourth year, and of the third class at the expiration of the sixth year, so that one third may be chosen every second year; and if vacancies happen by resignation, or otherwise, during the recess of the legislature of any State, the executive thereof may make temporary appointments until the next meeting of the legislature, which shall then fill such vacancies.[4]

3. No person shall be a senator who shall not have attained to the age of thirty years, and been nine years a citizen of the United States, and who shall not, when elected, be an inhabitant of that State for which he shall be chosen.

4. The Vice President of the United States shall be President of the Senate, but shall have no vote, unless they be equally divided.

5. The Senate shall choose their other officers, and also a president pro tempore, in the absence of the Vice President, or when he shall exercise the office of the President of the United States.

6. The Senate shall have the sole power to try all impeachments. When sitting for that purpose, they shall be on oath or affirmation. When the President of the United States is tried, the chief justice shall preside: and no person shall be convicted without the concurrence of two thirds of the members present.

7. Judgment in cases of impeachment shall not extend further than to removal from office, and disqualification to hold and enjoy any office of honor, trust or profit under the United States: but the party convicted shall nevertheless be liable and subject to indictment, trial, judgment and punishment, according to law.

Section 4. 1. The times, places, and manner of holding elections for senators and representatives, shall be prescribed in each State by the legislature thereof; but the Congress may at any time by law make or alter such regulations, except as to the places of choosing senators.

2. The Congress shall assemble at least once in every year, and such meeting shall be on the first Monday in December, unless they shall by law appoint a different day.

Section 5. 1. Each House shall be the judge of the elections, returns and qualifications of its own members, and a majority of each shall constitute a quorum to do business; but a smaller number may adjourn from day to day, and may be authorized to compel the attendance of absent members, in such manner, and under such penalties as each House may provide.

[1]See the Sixteenth Amendment.
[2]See the Fourteenth Amendment.
[3]See the Seventeenth Amendment.
[4]See the Seventeenth Amendment.

2. Each House may determine the rules of its proceedings, punish its members for disorderly behavior, and, with the concurrence of two thirds, expel a member.

3. Each House shall keep a journal of its proceedings, and from time to time publish the same, excepting such parts as may in their judgment require secrecy; and the yeas and nays of the members of either House on any question shall, at the desire of one fifth of those present, be entered on the journal.

4. Neither House, during the session of Congress, shall, without the consent of the other, adjourn for more than three days, nor to any other place than that in which the two Houses shall be sitting.

SECTION 6. 1. The senators and representatives shall receive a compensation for their services, to be ascertained by law, and paid out of the Treasury of the United States. They shall in all cases, except treason, felony, and breach of the peace, be privileged from arrest during their attendance at the session of their respective Houses, and in going to and returning from the same; and for any speech or debate in either House, they shall not be questioned in any other place.

2. No senator or representative shall, during the time for which he was elected, be appointed to any civil office under the authority of the United States, which shall have been created, or the emoluments whereof shall have been increased, during such time; and no person holding any office under the United States shall be a member of either House during his continuance in office.

SECTION 7. 1. All bills for raising revenue shall originate in the House of Representatives; but the Senate may propose or concur with amendments as on other bills.

2. Every bill which shall have passed the House of Representatives and the Senate, shall, before it become a law, be presented to the President of the United States; If he approves he shall sign it, but if not he shall return it, with his objections, to that House in which it shall have originated, who shall enter the objections at large on their journal, and proceed to reconsider it. If after such reconsideration two thirds of that House shall agree to pass the bill, it shall be sent, together with the objections, to the other House, by which it shall likewise be reconsidered, and if approved by two thirds of that House, it shall become a law. But in all such cases the votes of both Houses shall be determined by yeas and nays, and the names of the persons voting for and against the bill shall be entered on the journal of each House respectively. If any bill shall not be returned by the President within ten days (Sundays excepted) after it shall have been presented to him, the same shall be a law, in like manner as if he had signed it, unless the Congress by their adjournment prevent its return, in which case it shall not be a law.

3. Every order, resolution, or vote to which the concurrence of the Senate and the House of Representatives may be necessary (except on a question of adjournment) shall be presented to the President of the United States; and before the same shall take effect, shall be approved by him, or being disapproved by him, shall be repassed by two thirds of the Senate and House of Representatives, according to the rules and limitations prescribed in the case of a bill.

SECTION 8. 1. The Congress shall have the power.

1. To lay and collect taxes, duties, imposts, and excises, to pay the debts and provide for the common defense and general welfare of the United States; but all duties, imposts, and excises shall be uniform throughout the United States.

2. To borrow money on the credit of the United States;

3. To regulate commerce with foreign nations, and among the several States, and with the Indian tribes;

4. To establish a uniform rule of naturalization, and uniform laws on the subject of bankruptcies throughout the United States;

5. To coin money, regulate the value thereof, and of foreign coin, and fix the standard of weights and measures;

6. To provide for the punishment of counterfeiting the securities and current coin of the United States;

7. To establish post offices and post roads;

8. To promote the progress of science and useful arts, by securing for limited times to authors and inventors the exclusive right to their respective writings and discoveries;

9. To constitute tribunals inferior to the Supreme Court;

10. To define and punish piracies and felonies committed on the high seas, and offenses against the law of nations;

11. To declare war, grant letters of marque and reprisal, and make rules concerning captures on land and water;

12. To raise and support armies, but no appropriation of money to that use shall be for a longer term than two years;

13. To provide and maintain a navy;

14. To make rules for the government and regulation of the land and naval forces;

15. To provide for calling forth the militia to execute the laws of the Union, suppress insurrections and repel invasions;

16. To provide for organizing, arming, and disciplining the militia, and for governing such part of them as may be employed in the service of the United States, reserving to the States respectively, the appointment of the officers, and the authority of training the militia according to the discipline prescribed by Congress;

17. To exercise exclusive legislation in all cases whatsoever, over such district (not exceeding ten miles square) as may, by cession of particular States, and the acceptance of Congress, become the seat of the government of the United States, and to exercise like authority over all places purchased by the consent of the legislature of the State in which the same shall be, for the erection of forts, magazines, arsenals, dockyards, and other needful buildings; and

18. To make all laws which shall be necessary and proper for carrying into execution the foregoing powers, and all other powers vested by this Constitution in the government of the United States, or any department or officer thereof.

SECTION 9. 1. The migration or importation of such persons as any of the States now existing shall think proper to admit, shall not be prohibited by the Congress prior to the year one thousand eight hundred and eight, but a tax or duty may be imposed on such importation, not exceeding ten dollars for each person.

2. The privilege of the writ of habeas corpus shall not be suspended, unless when in cases of rebellion or invasion the public safety may require it.

3. No bill of attainder or ex post facto law shall be passed.

4. No capitation, or other direct, tax shall be laid, unless in proportion to the census or enumeration herein-before directed to be taken.[5]

5. No tax or duty shall be laid on articles exported from any State.

6. No preference shall be given by any regulation of commerce or revenue to the ports of one State over those of another: nor shall vessels bound to, or from, one State be obliged to enter, clear, or pay duties in another.

7. No money shall be drawn from the treasury, but in consequence of appropriations made by law; and a regular statement and account of the receipts and expenditures of all public money shall be published from time to time.

8. No title of nobility shall be granted by the United States: and no person holding any office of profit or trust under them, shall, without the consent of the Congress, accept of any present, emolument, office, or title, of any kind whatever, from any king, prince, or foreign State.

SECTION 10. 1. No State shall enter into any treaty, alliance, or confederation; grant letters of marque and reprisal; coin money; emit bills of credit; make any thing but gold and silver coin a tender in payment of debts; pass any bill of attainder, ex post facto law, or law impairing the obligation of contracts, or grant, any title of nobility.

2. No State shall, without the consent of the Congress, lay any imposts or duties on imports or exports, except what may be absolutely necessary for executing its inspection laws: and the net produce of all duties and imposts laid by any State on imports or exports, shall be for the use of the treasury of the United States; and all such laws shall be subject to the revision and control of the Congress.

3. No State shall, without the consent of the Congress, lay any duty of tonnage, keep troops, or ships of war in time of peace, enter into any agreement or compact with another State, or with a foreign power, or engage in war, unless actually invaded, or in such imminent danger as will not admit of delay.

ARTICLE II

SECTION 1. 1. The executive power shall be vested in a President of the United States of America. He shall hold his office during the term of four years, and, together with the Vice President, chosen for the same term, be elected, as follows:

2. Each State shall appoint, in such manner as the legislature thereof may direct, a number of electors, equal to the whole number of senators and representatives to which the State may be entitled in the Congress: but no senator or representative, or person holding any office of trust or profit under the United States, shall be appointed an elector.

The electors shall meet in their respective States, and vote by ballot for two persons, of whom one at least shall not be an inhabitant of the same State with themselves. And they shall make a list of all the persons voted for, and of the number of votes for each; which list they shall sign and certify, and transmit sealed to the seat of the government of the United States, directed to the president of the Senate. The president of the Senate shall, in the presence of the Senate and House of Representatives, open all the certificates, and the votes shall then be counted. The person having the greatest number of votes shall be the President, if such number be a majority of the whole number of electors appointed; and if there be more than one who have such majority, and have an equal number of votes, then the House of Representatives shall immediately choose by ballot one of them for President; and if no person have a majority, then from the five highest on the list the said House shall in like manner choose the President. But in choosing the President, the votes shall be taken by States, the representation from each State having one vote; a quorum for this purpose shall consist of a member or members from two thirds of the States, and a majority of all the States shall be necessary to a choice. In every case after the choice of the President, the person having the greatest number of votes of the electors shall be the Vice President. But if there should remain two or more who have equal votes, the Senate shall choose from them by ballot the Vice President.[6]

3. The Congress may determine the time of choosing the electors, and the day on which they shall give their votes; which day shall be the same throughout the United States.

4. No person except a natural born citizen, or a citizen of the United States, at the time of the adoption of this Constitution, shall be eligible to the office of President; neither shall any person be eligible to the office who shall not have attained to the age of thirty-five years, and been fourteen years a resident within the United States.

5. In case of the removal of the President from office, or of his death, resignation, or inability to discharge the powers and duties of the said office, the same shall devolve on the Vice President, and the congress may by law provide for the case of removal, death, resignation or inability, both of the President and Vice President, declaring what officer shall then act as President, and such officer shall act accordingly until the disability be removed, or a President shall be elected.

6. The President shall, at stated times, receive for his services a compensation which shall neither be increased nor diminished during the period for which he shall have been elected, and he shall not receive within that period any other emolument from the United States, or any of them.

7. Before he enter on the execution of his office, he shall take the following oath or affirmation:—"I do solemnly swear (or affirm) that I will faithfully execute the office of President of the United States, and will to the best of my ability, preserve, protect and defend the Constitution of the United States."

SECTION 2. 1. The President shall be commander in chief of the army and navy of the United States, and of the militia of the several States, when called into the actual service of the United States; he may require the opinion in writing, of the principal officer in each of the executive departments, upon any subject relating to the duties of their respective offices, and he shall have power to grant reprieves and pardons for offenses against the United States, except in cases of impeachment.

2. He shall have power, by and with the advice and consent of the Senate, to make treaties, provided two thirds of the senators present concur; and he shall nominate, and by and with the advice and consent of the Senate, shall appoint ambassadors, other public

[5]See the Sixteenth Amendment.

[6]Superseded by the Twelfth Amendment.

ministers and consuls, judges of the Supreme Court, and all other officers of the United States, whose appointments are not herein otherwise provided for, and which shall be established by law; but the Congress may by law vest the appointment of such inferior officers, as they think proper, in the President alone, in the courts of laws, or in the heads of departments.

3. The President shall have power to fill up all vacancies that may happen during the recess of the Senate, by granting commissions which shall expire at the end of their next session.

SECTION 3. He shall from time to time give to the Congress information of the state of the Union, and recommend to their consideration such measures as he shall judge necessary and expedient; he may, on extraordinary occasions, convene both Houses, or either of them, and in case of disagreement between them with respect to the time of adjournment, he may adjourn them to such time as he shall think proper; he shall receive ambassadors and other public ministers; he shall take care that the laws be faithfully executed, and shall commission all the officers of the United States.

SECTION 4. The President, Vice President, and all civil officers of the United States, shall be removed from office on impeachment for, and conviction of, treason, bribery, or other high crimes and misdemeanors.

ARTICLE III

SECTION 1. The judicial power of the United States shall be vested in one Supreme Court, and in such inferior courts as the Congress may from time to time ordain and establish. The judges, both of the Supreme and inferior courts, shall hold their offices during good behavior, and shall, at stated times, receive for their services, a compensation, which shall not be diminished during their continuance in office.

SECTION 2. 1. The judicial power shall extend to all cases, in law and equity, arising under this Constitution, the laws of the United States, and treaties made, or which shall be made, under their authority;—to all cases of admiralty and maritime jurisdiction;—to controversies to which the United States shall be a party;[7]—to controversies between two or more States;—between a State and citizens of another State;—between citizens of different States;—between citizens of the same State claiming lands under grants of different States, and between a State, or the citizens thereof, and foreign States, citizens or subjects.

2. In all cases affecting ambassadors, other public ministers and consuls, and those in which a State shall be party, the Supreme Court shall have original jurisdiction. In all the other cases before mentioned, the Supreme Court shall have appellate jurisdiction, both as to law and fact, with such exceptions, and under such regulations as the Congress shall make.

3. The trial of all crimes, except in cases of impeachment, shall be by jury; and such trial shall be held in the State where the said crimes shall have been committed; but when not committed within any State, the trial shall be such place or places as the congress may by law have directed.

[7]See the Eleventh Amendment.

SECTION 3. 1. Treason against the United States shall consist only in levying war against them, or in adhering to their enemies, giving them aid and comfort. No person shall be convicted of treason unless on the testimony of two witnesses to the same overt act, or on confession in open court.

2. The Congress shall have power to declare the punishment of treason, but no attainder of treason shall work corruption of blood, or forfeiture except during the life of the person attained.

ARTICLE IV

SECTION 1. Full faith and credit shall be given in each State to the public acts, records, and judicial proceedings of every other State. And the Congress may by general laws prescribe the manner in which such acts, records and proceedings shall be proved, and the effect thereof.

SECTION 2. 1. The citizens of each State shall be entitled to all privileges and immunities of citizens in the several States.[8]

2. A person charged in any State with treason, felony, or other crime, who shall flee from justice, and be found in another State, shall on demand of the executive authority of the State from which he fled, be delivered up to be removed to the State having jurisdiction of the crime.

3. No person held to service or labor in one State under the laws thereof, escaping into another, shall, in consequence of any law or regulation therein, be discharged from such service or labor, but shall be delivered up on claim of the party to whom such service or labor may be due.[9]

SECTION 3. 1. New States may be admitted by the Congress into this Union; but no new State shall be formed or erected within the jurisdiction of any other State, nor any State be formed by the junction of two or more States, or parts of States, without the consent of the legislatures of the States concerned as well as of the Congress.

2. The Congress shall have power to dispose of and make all needful rules and regulations respecting the territory or other property belonging to the United States; and nothing in this Constitution shall be so construed as to prejudice any claims of the United States, or of any particular State.

SECTION 4. The United States shall guarantee to every State in this Union a republican form of government, and shall protect each of them against invasion; and on application of the legislature, or of the executive (when the legislature cannot be convened) against domestic violence.

ARTICLE V

The Congress, whenever two thirds of both Houses shall deem it necessary, shall propose amendments to this Constitution, or, on the application of the legislatures of two thirds of the several States, shall call a convention for proposing amendments, which in either case shall be valid to all intents and purposes, as part of this Constitution, when ratified by the legislatures of three fourths of the several States, or by conventions in three fourths thereof, as the one or the other

[8]See the Fourteenth Amendment, Sec. 1.
[9]See the Thirteenth Amendment.

mode of ratification may be proposed by the Congress; Provided that no amendment which may be made prior to the year one thousand eight hundred and eight shall in any manner affect the first and fourth clauses in the ninth section of the first article; and that no State, without its consent, shall be deprived of its equal suffrage in the Senate.

Article VI

1. All debts contracted and engagements entered into, before the adoption of this Constitution, shall be as valid against the United States under this Constitution, as under the Confederation.[10]

2. This Constitution, and the laws of the United States which shall be made in pursuance thereof; and all treaties made, or which shall be made, under the authority of the United States, shall be the supreme law of the land; and the judges in every State shall be bound thereby, any thing in the Constitution or laws of any State to the contrary notwithstanding.

3. The senators and representatives before mentioned, and the members of the several State legislatures, and all executive and judicial officers, both of the United States and of the several States, shall be bound by oath or affirmation to support this Constitution; but no religious test shall ever be required as a qualification to any office or public trust under the United States.

Article VII

The ratification of the conventions of nine States shall be sufficient for the establishment of this Constitution between the States so ratifying the same.

Done in Convention by the unanimous consent of the States present the seventeenth day of September in the year of our Lord one thousand seven hundred and eighty-seven, and of the independence of the United States of America the twelfth. In witness whereof we have hereunto subscribed our names.

[Signatories' names omitted]

Articles in addition to, and amendment of, the Constitution of the United States of America, proposed by Congress, and ratified by the legislatures of the several States, pursuant to the fifth article of the original Constitution.

Amendment I

[First ten amendments ratified December 15, 1791]

Congress shall make no law respecting an establishment of religion, or prohibiting the free exercise thereof; or abridging the freedom of speech, or of the press; or the right of the people peaceably to assemble, and to petition the government for a redress of grievances.

Amendment II

A well regulated militia, being necessary to the security of a free State, the right of the people to keep and bear arms, shall not be infringed.

Amendment III

No soldier shall, in time of peace be quartered in any house, without the consent of the owner, nor in time of war, but in a manner to be prescribed by law.

[10]See the Fourteenth Amendment, Sec. 4.

Amendment IV

The right of the people to be secure in their persons, houses, papers, and effects, against unreasonable searches and seizures, shall not be violated, and no warrants shall issue, but upon probable cause, supported by oath or affirmation, and particularly describing the place to be searched, and the persons or things to be seized.

Amendment V

No person shall be held to answer for a capital or otherwise infamous crime, unless on a presentment or indictment of a grand jury, except in cases arising in the land or naval forces, or in the militia, when in actual service in time of war or public danger; nor shall any person be subject for the same offense to be twice put in jeopardy of life or limb; nor shall be compelled in any criminal case to be a witness against himself, nor be deprived of life, liberty, or property, without due process of law; nor shall private property be taken for public use, without just compensation.

Amendment VI

In all criminal prosecutions, the accused shall enjoy the right to a speedy and public trial, by an impartial jury of the State and district wherein the crime shall have been committed, which district shall have been previously ascertained by law, and to be informed of the nature and cause of the accusation; to be confronted with the witnesses against him; to have compulsory process for obtaining witnesses in his favor, and to have the assistance of counsel for his defense.

Amendment VII

In suits at common law, where the value in controversy shall exceed twenty dollars, the right of trial by jury shall be preserved, and no fact tried by a jury shall be otherwise reexamined in any court of the United States, than according to the rules of the common law.

Amendment VIII

Excessive bail shall not be required, nor excessive fines imposed, nor cruel and unusual punishments inflicted.

Amendment IX

The enumeration in the Constitution of certain rights shall not be construed to deny or disparage others retained by the people.

Amendment X

The powers not delegated to the United States by the Constitution, nor prohibited by it to the States, are reserved to the States respectively, or to the people.

Amendment XI [January 8, 1798]

The judicial power of the United States shall not be construed to extend to any suit in law or equity, commended or prosecuted against one of the United States by citizens of another State, or by citizens or subjects of any foreign State.

Amendment XII [September 25, 1804]

The electors shall meet in their respective States, and vote by ballot for President and Vice President, one of whom, at least, shall not be an inhabitant of the same State with themselves; they shall name in their ballots the person voted for as President, and in distinct ballots, the person voted for as Vice President, and they shall make distinct lists of all persons voted for as President and of all persons voted for as Vice President, and of the number of votes for each, which lists they shall sign and certify, and transmit sealed to the seat of the government of the United States, directed to the President of the Senate;—The President of the Senate shall, in the presence of the Senate and House of Representatives, open all the certificates and the votes shall then be counted;—The person having the greatest number of votes for President, shall be the President, if such number be a majority of the whole number of electors appointed; and if no person have such majority, then from the persons having the highest numbers not exceeding three on the list of those voted for as President, the House of Representatives shall choose immediately, by ballot, the President. But in choosing the President, the votes shall be taken by States, the representation from each State having one vote; a quorum for this purpose shall consist of a member or members from two thirds of the States, and a majority of all the States shall be necessary to a choice. And if the House of Representatives shall not choose a President whenever the right of choice shall devolve upon them, before the fourth day of March next following, then the Vice President shall act as President, as in the case of the death or other constitutional disability of the President. The person having the greatest number of votes as Vice President shall be the Vice President, if such number be a majority of the whole number of electors appointed, and if no person have a majority, then from the two highest numbers on the list, the Senate shall choose the Vice President; a quorum for the purpose shall consist of two thirds of the whole number of Senators, and a majority of the whole number shall be necessary to a choice. But no person constitutionally ineligible to the office of President shall be eligible to that of Vice President of the United States.

Amendment XIII [December 18, 1865]

SECTION 1. Neither slavery nor involuntary servitude, except as a punishment for crime whereof the party shall have been duly convicted, shall exist within the United States, or any place subject to their jurisdiction.

SECTION 2. Congress shall have power to enforce this article by appropriate legislation.

Amendment XIV [July 28, 1868]

SECTION 1. All persons born or naturalized in the United States, and subject to the jurisdiction thereof, are citizens of the United States and of the State wherein they reside. No State shall make or enforce any law which shall abridge the privileges or immunities of citizens of the United States; nor shall any State deprive any person of life, liberty, or property, without due process of law; nor deny to any person within its jurisdiction the equal protection of the laws.

SECTION 2. Representatives shall be apportioned among the several States according to their respective numbers, counting the whole number of persons in each State, excluding Indians not taxed. But when the right to vote at any election for the choice of electors for President and Vice President of the United States, representatives in Congress, the executive and judicial officers of a State, or the members of the legislature thereof, is denied to any of the male inhabitants of such State, being twenty-one years of age, and citizens of the United States, or in any way abridged, except for participating in rebellion, or other crime, the basis of representation there shall be reduced in the proportion which the number of such male citizens shall bear to the whole number of male citizens twenty-one years of age in such State.

SECTION 3. No person shall be a senator or representative in Congress, or elector of President and Vice President, or hold any office, civil or military, under the United States, or under any State, who having previously taken an oath, as a member of Congress, or as an officer of the United States, or as a member of any State legislature, or as an executive or judicial officer of any State, to support the Constitution of the United States, shall have engaged in insurrection or rebellion against the same, or given aid or comfort to the enemies thereof. But Congress may by a vote of two thirds of each House, remove such disability.

SECTION 4. The validity of the public debt of the United States, authorized by law, including debts incurred for payment of pensions and bounties for services in suppressing insurrection or rebellion; shall not be questioned. But neither the United States nor any State shall assume or pay any debt or obligation incurred in aid of insurrection or rebellion against the United States, or any claim for the loss or emancipation of any slave; but all such debts, obligations, and claims shall be held illegal and void.

SECTION 5. The Congress shall have the power to enforce, by appropriate legislation, the provisions of this article.

Amendment XV [March 30, 1870]

SECTION 1. The right of citizens of the United States to vote shall not be denied or abridged by the United States or by any State on account of race, color, or previous condition of servitude.

SECTION 2. The Congress shall have power to enforce this article by appropriate legislation.

Amendment XVI [February 25, 1913]

The Congress shall have power to lay and collect taxes on incomes, from whatever source derived, without apportionment among the several States, and without regard to any census or enumeration.

Amendment XVII [May 31, 1913]

The Senate of the United States shall be composed of two senators from each State, elected by the people thereof, for six years; and each senator shall have one vote. The electors in each State shall have the qualifications requisite for electors of the most numerous branch of the State legislature.

When vacancies happen in the representation of any State in the Senate, the executive authority of such State shall issue writs of election to fill such vacancies: Provided, That the legislature of any State may empower the executive thereof to make temporary appointments until the people fill the vacancies by election as the legislature may direct.

This amendment shall not be so construed as to affect the election or term of any senator chosen before it becomes valid as part of the Constitution.

Amendment XVIII[11] *[January 29, 1919]*

After one year from the ratification of this article, the manufacture, sale, or transportation of intoxicating liquors within, the importation thereof into, or the exportation thereof from the United States and all territory subject to the jurisdiction thereof for beverage purposes is thereby prohibited.

The Congress and the several States shall have concurrent power to enforce this article by appropriate legislation.

This article shall be inoperative unless it shall have been ratified as an amendment to the Constitution by the legislatures of the several States, as provided in the constitution, within seven years from the date of the submission hereof to the States by Congress.

Amendment XIX [August 26, 1920]

The right of citizens of the United States to vote shall not be denied or abridged by the United States or by any State on account of sex.

Congress shall have the power to enforce this article by appropriate legislation.

Amendment XX [January 23, 1933]

SECTION 1. The terms of the President and Vice President shall end at noon on the 20th day of January and the terms of Senators and Representatives at noon on the 3rd day of January, of the years in which such terms would have ended if this article had not been ratified; and the terms of their successors shall then begin.

SECTION 2. The Congress shall assemble at least once in every year, and such meeting shall begin at noon on the 3rd day of January, unless they shall by law appoint a different day.

SECTION 3. If, at the time fixed for the beginning of the term of President, the President-elect shall have died, the Vice President-elect shall become President. If a President shall not have been chosen before the time fixed for the beginning of his term, or if the President-elect shall have failed to qualify, then the Vice President-elect shall act as President until a President shall have qualified; and the Congress may by law provide for the case wherein neither a President-elect nor a Vice President-elect shall have qualified, declaring who shall then act as President, or the manner in which one who is to act shall be selected, and such person shall act accordingly until a President or Vice President shall have qualified.

SECTION 4. The Congress may by law provide for the case of the death of any of the persons from whom, the House of Representatives may choose a President whenever the right of choice shall have devolved upon them, and for the case of the death of any of the persons from whom the Senate may choose a Vice President whenever the right of choice shall have devolved upon them.

SECTION 5. Sections 1 and 2 shall take effect on the 15th day of October following the ratification of this article.

SECTION 6. This article shall be inoperative unless it shall have been ratified as an amendment to the Constitution by the legislatures of three-fourths of the several States within seven years from the date of its submission.

[11]Repealed by the Twenty-first Amendment.

Amendment XXI [December 5, 1933]

SECTION 1. The Eighteenth Article of amendment to the Constitution of the United States is hereby repealed.

SECTION 2. The transportation or importation into any State, Territory, or possession of the United States for delivery or use therein of intoxicating liquors in violation of the laws thereof, is hereby prohibited.

SECTION 3. This article shall be inoperative unless it shall have been ratified as an amendment to the Constitution by conventions in the several States, as provided in the Constitution, within seven years from the date of the submission thereof to the States by the Congress.

Amendment XXII [March 1, 1951]

No person shall be elected to the office of the President more than twice, and no person who has held the office of President, or acted as President, for more than two years of a term to which some other person was elected President shall be elected to the office of the President more than once.

But this article shall not apply to any person holding the office of President when this article was proposed by the Congress, and shall not prevent any person who may be holding the office of President, or acting as President, during the term within which this article becomes operative from holding the office of President or acting as President during the remainder of such term.

This article shall be inoperative unless it shall have been ratified as an amendment to the Constitution by the legislatures of three-fourths of the several States within seven years from the date of its submission to the States by the Congress.

Amendment XXIII [March 29, 1961]

SECTION 1. The District constituting the seat of Government of the United States shall appoint in such manner as the Congress may direct.

A number of electors of President and Vice President equal to the whole number of Senators and Representatives in Congress to which the District would be entitled if it were a State, but in no event more than the least populous State; they shall be in addition to those appointed by the States, but they shall be considered, for the purposes of the election of President and Vice President, to be electors appointed by a State; and they shall meet in the District and perform such duties as provided by the twelfth article of amendment.

SECTION 2. The Congress shall have power to enforce this article by appropriate legislation.

Amendment XXIV [January 23, 1964]

SECTION 1. The right of citizens of the United States to vote in any primary or other election for President or Vice President, for electors for President or Vice President, or for Senator or Representative in Congress, shall not be denied or abridged by the United States or any State by reason of failure to pay any poll tax or other tax.

SECTION 2. The Congress shall have power to enforce this article by appropriate legislation.

Amendment XXV [February 10, 1967]

SECTION 1. In case of the removal of the President from office or of his death or resignation, the Vice President shall become President.

SECTION 2. Whenever there is a vacancy in the office of the Vice President, the President shall nominate a Vice President who shall take office upon confirmation by a majority of both Houses of Congress.

SECTION 3. Whenever the President transmits to the President pro tempore of the Senate and the Speaker of the House of Representatives his written declaration that he is unable to discharge the powers and duties of his office, and until he transmits to them a written declaration to the contrary, such powers and duties shall be discharged by the Vice President as Acting President.

SECTION 4. Whenever the Vice President and a majority of either the principal officers of the executive departments or of such other body as Congress may by law provide, transmit to the President pro tempore of the Senate and the Speaker of the House of Representatives their written declaration that the President is unable to discharge the powers and duties of his office, the Vice President shall immediately assume the powers and duties of the office as Acting President.

Thereafter, when the President transmits to the President pro tempore of the Senate and the Speaker of the House of Representatives his written declaration that no inability exists, he shall resume the powers and duties of his office unless the Vice President and a majority of either the principal officers of the executive departments or of such other body as Congress may by law provide, transmit within four days to the President pro tempore of the Senate and the Speaker of the House of Representatives their written declaration that the President is unable to discharge the powers and duties of his office. Thereupon Congress shall decide the issue, assembling within forty-eight hours for that purpose if not in session. If the Congress, within twenty-one days after receipt of the latter written declaration, or, if Congress is not in session, within twenty-one days after Congress is required to assemble, determines by two-thirds vote of both Houses that the President is unable to discharge the powers and duties of his office, the Vice President shall continue to discharge the same as Acting President; otherwise, the President shall resume the powers and duties of his office.

Amendment XXVI [June 30, 1971]

SECTION 1. The right of citizens of the United States who are eighteen years of age or older to vote shall not be denied or abridged by the United States or by any State on account of age.

SECTION 2. The Congress shall have power to enforce this article by appropriate legislation.

Amendment XXVII[12] *[May 7, 1992]*

No law, varying the compensation for services of the Senators and Representatives, shall take effect until an election of Representatives shall have intervened.

---

[12]James Madison proposed this amendment in 1789 together with the ten amendments that were adopted as the Bill of Rights, but it failed to win ratification at the time. Congress, however, had set no deadline for its ratification, and over the years—particularly in the 1980s and 1990s—many states voted to add it to the Constitution. With the ratification of Michigan in 1992 it passed the threshold of three-fourths of the states required for adoption, but because the process took more than 200 years, its validity remains in doubt.

Presidential Elections

Year	Number of States	Candidates	Party	Popular Vote*	Electoral Vote†	Percentage of Popular Vote
1789	11	GEORGE WASHINGTON	No party designations		69	
		John Adams			34	
		Other Candidates			35	
1792	15	GEORGE WASHINGTON	No party designations		132	
		John Adams			77	
		George Clinton			50	
		Other Candidates			5	
1796	16	JOHN ADAMS	Federalist		71	
		Thomas Jefferson	Democratic-Republican		68	
		Thomas Pinckney	Federalist		59	
		Aaron Burr	Democratic-Republican		30	
		Other Candidates			48	
1800	16	THOMAS JEFFERSON	Democratic-Republican		73	
		Aaron Burr	Democratic-Republican		73	
		John Adams	Federalist		65	
		Charles C. Pinckney	Federalist		64	
		John Jay	Federalist		1	
1804	17	THOMAS JEFFERSON	Democratic-Republican		162	
		Charles C. Pinckney	Federalist		14	
1808	17	JAMES MADISON	Democratic-Republican		122	
		Charles C. Pinckney	Federalist		47	
		George Clinton	Democratic-Republican		6	
1812	18	JAMES MADISON	Democratic-Republican		128	
		DeWitt Clinton	Federalist		89	
1816	19	JAMES MONROE	Democratic-Republican		183	
		Rufus King	Federalist		34	
1820	24	JAMES MONROE	Democratic-Republican		231	
		John Quincy Adams	Independent-Republican		1	
1824	24	JOHN QUINCY ADAMS	Democratic-Republican	108,740	84	30.5
		Andrew Jackson	Democratic-Republican	153,544	99	43.1
		William H. Crawford	Democratic-Republican	46,618	41	13.1
		Henry Clay	Democratic-Republican	47,136	37	13.2
1828	24	ANDREW JACKSON	Democrat	647,286	178	56.0
		John Quincy Adams	National Republican	508,064	83	44.0
1832	24	ANDREW JACKSON	Democrat	687,502	219	55.0
		Henry Clay	National Republican	530,189	49	42.4
		William Wirt	Anti-Masonic	33,108	7	2.6
		John Floyd			11	
1836	26	MARTIN VAN BUREN	Democrat	765,483	170	50.9
		William H. Harrison	Whig		73	
		Hugh L. White	Whig		26	
		Daniel Webster	Whig	739,795	14	49.1
		W. P. Mangum	Whig		11	

* Percentage of popular vote given for any election year may not total 100 percent because candidates receiving less than 1 percent of the popular vote have been omitted.

† Prior to the passage of the Twelfth Amendment in 1904, the electoral college voted for two presidential candidates; the runner-up became Vice-President. Data from Historical Statistics of the United States, Colonial Times to 1957 (1961), pp. 682–683, and The World Almanac.

Presidential Elections (*Continued*)

Year	Number of States	Candidates	Party	Popular Vote*	Electoral Vote†	Percentage of Popular Vote
1840	26	WILLIAM H. HARRISON	Whig	1,274,624	234	53.1
		Martin Van Buren	Democrat	1,127,781	60	46.9
1844	26	JAMES K. POLK	Democrat	1,338,464	170	49.6
		Henry Clay	Whig	1,300,097	105	48.1
		James G. Birney	Liberty	62,300		2.3
1848	30	ZACHARY TAYLOR	Whig	1,360,967	163	47.4
		Lewis Cass	Democrat	1,222,342	127	42.5
		Martin Van Buren	Free Soil	291,263		10.1
1852	31	FRANKLIN PIERCE	Democrat	1,601,117	254	50.9
		Winfield Scott	Whig	1,385,453	42	44.1
		John P. Hale	Free Soil	155,825		5.0
1856	31	JAMES BUCHANAN	Democrat	1,832,955	174	45.3
		John C. Frémont	Republican	1,339,932	114	33.1
		Millard Fillmore	American ("Know Nothing")	871,731	8	21.6
1860	33	ABRAHAM LINCOLN	Republican	1,865,593	180	39.8
		Stephen A. Douglas	Democrat	1,382,713	12	29.5
		John C. Breckinridge	Democrat	848,356	72	18.1
		John Bell	Constitutional Union	592,906	39	12.6
1864	36	ABRAHAM LINCOLN	Republican	2,206,938	212	55.0
		George B. McClellan	Democrat	1,803,787	21	45.0
1868	37	ULYSSES S. GRANT	Republican	3,013,421	214	52.7
		Horatio Seymour	Democrat	2,706,829	80	47.3
1872	37	ULYSSES S. GRANT	Republican	3,596,745	286	55.6
		Horace Greeley	Democrat	2,843,446	*	43.9
1876	38	RUTHERFORD B. HAYES	Republican	4,036,572	185	48.0
		Samuel J. Tilden	Democrat	4,284,020	184	51.0
1880	38	JAMES A. GARFIELD	Republican	4,453,295	214	48.5
		Winfield S. Hancock	Democrat	4,414,082	155	48.1
		James B. Weaver	Greenback-Labor	308,578		3.4
1884	38	GROVER CLEVELAND	Democrat	4,879,507	219	48.5
		James G. Blaine	Republican	4,850,293	182	48.2
		Benjamin F. Butler	Greenback-Labor	175,370		1.8
		John P. St. John	Prohibition	150,369		1.5
1888	38	BENJAMIN HARRISON	Republican	5,447,129	233	47.9
		Grover Cleveland	Democrat	5,537,857	168	48.6
		Clinton B. Fisk	Prohibition	249,506		2.2
		Anson J. Streeter	Union Labor	146,935		1.3
1892	44	GROVER CLEVELAND	Democrat	5,555,426	277	46.1
		Benjamin Harrison	Republican	5,182,690	145	43.0
		James B. Weaver	People's	1,029,846	22	8.5
		John Bidwell	Prohibition	264,133		2.2
1896	45	WILLIAM MCKINLEY	Republican	7,102,246	271	51.1
		William J. Bryan	Democrat	6,492,559	176	47.7

*Because of the death of Greeley, Democratic electors scattered their votes.

Presidential Elections (*Continued*)

Year	Number of States	Candidates	Party	Popular Vote*	Electoral Vote†	Percentage of Popular Vote
1900	45	WILLIAM McKINLEY	Republican	7,218,491	292	51.7
		William J. Bryan	Democrat; Populist	6,356,734	155	45.5
		John C. Woolley	Prohibition	208,914		1.5
1904	45	THEODORE ROOSEVELT	Republican	7,628,461	336	57.4
		Alton B. Parker	Democrat	5,084,223	140	37.6
		Eugene V. Debs	Socialist	402,283		3.0
		Silas C. Swallow	Prohibition	258,536		1.9
1908	46	WILLIAM H. TAFT	Republican	7,675,320	321	51.6
		William J. Bryan	Democrat	6,412,294	162	43.1
		Eugene V. Debs	Socialist	420,793		2.8
		Eugene W. Chafin	Prohibition	253,840		1.7
1912	48	WOODROW WILSON	Democrat	6,296,547	435	41.9
		Theodore Roosevelt	Progressive	4,118,571	88	27.4
		William H. Taft	Republican	3,486,720	8	23.2
		Eugene V. Debs	Socialist	900,672		6.0
		Eugene W. Chafin	Prohibition	206,275		1.4
1916	48	WOODROW WILSON	Democrat	9,127,695	277	49.4
		Charles E. Hughes	Republican	8,533,507	254	46.2
		A. L. Benson	Socialist	585,113		3.2
		J. Frank Hanly	Prohibition	220,506		1.2
1920	48	WARREN G. HARDING	Republican	16,143,407	404	60.4
		James M. Cox	Democrat	9,130,328	127	34.2
		Eugene V. Debs	Socialist	919,799		3.4
		P. P. Christensen	Farmer-Labor	265,411		1.0
1924	48	CALVIN COOLIDGE	Republican	15,718,211	382	54.0
		John W. Davis	Democrat	8,385,283	136	28.8
		Robert M. La Follette	Progressive	4,831,289	13	16.6
1928	48	HERBERT C. HOOVER	Republican	21,391,993	444	58.2
		Alfred E. Smith	Democrat	15,016,169	87	40.9
1932	48	FRANKLIN D. ROOSEVELT	Democrat	22,809,638	472	57.4
		Herbert C. Hoover	Republican	15,758,901	59	39.7
		Norman Thomas	Socialist	881,951		2.2
1936	48	FRANKLIN D. ROOSEVELT	Democrat	27,752,869	523	60.8
		Alfred M. Landon	Republican	16,674,665	8	36.5
		William Lemke	Union	882,479		1.9
1940	48	FRANKLIN D. ROOSEVELT	Democrat	27,307,819	449	54.8
		Wendell L. Willkie	Republican	22,321,018	82	44.8
1944	48	FRANKLIN D. ROOSEVELT	Democrat	25,606,585	432	53.5
		Thomas E. Dewey	Republican	22,014,745	99	46.0
1948	48	HARRY S. TRUMAN	Democrat	24,105,812	303	49.5
		Thomas E. Dewey	Republican	21,970,065	189	45.1
		J. Strom Thurmond	States' Rights	1,169,063	39	2.4
		Henry A. Wallace	Progressive	1,157,172		2.4

Presidential Elections (*Continued*)

Year	Number of States	Candidates	Party	Popular Vote*	Electoral Vote†	Percentage of Popular Vote
1952	48	DWIGHT D. EISENHOWER	Republican	33,936,234	442	55.1
		Adlai E. Stevenson	Democrat	27,314,992	89	44.4
1956	48	DWIGHT D. EISENHOWER	Republican	35,590,472	457*	57.6
		Adlai E. Stevenson	Democrat	26,022,752	73	42.1
1960	50	JOHN F. KENNEDY	Democrat	34,227,096	303†	49.9
		Richard M. Nixon	Republican	34,108,546	219	49.6
1964	50	LYNDON B. JOHNSON	Democrat	42,676,220	486	61.3
		Barry M. Goldwater	Republican	26,860,314	52	38.5
1968	50	RICHARD M. NIXON	Republican	31,785,480	301	43.4
		Hubert H. Humphrey	Democrat	31,275,165	191	42.7
		George C. Wallace	American Independent	9,906,473	46	13.5
1972	50	RICHARD M. NIXON‡	Republican	47,165,234	520**	60.6
		George S. McGovern	Democrat	29,168,110	17	37.5
1976	50	JIMMY CARTER	Democrat	40,828,929	297***	50.1
		Gerald R. Ford	Republican	39,148,940	240	47.9
		Eugene McCarthy	Independent	739,256		
1980	50	RONALD REAGAN	Republican	43,201,220	489	50.9
		Jimmy Carter	Democrat	34,913,332	49	41.2
		John B. Anderson	Independent	5,581,379		
1984	50	RONALD REAGAN	Republican	53,428,357	525	59.0
		Walter F. Mondale	Democrat	36,930,923	13	41.0
1988	50	GEORGE H. W. BUSH	Republican	48,901,046	426****	53.4
		Michael Dukakis	Democrat	41,809,030	111	45.6
1992	50	BILL CLINTON	Democrat	43,728,275	370	43.2
		George Bush	Republican	38,167,416	168	37.7
		H. Ross Perot	United We Stand, America	19,237,247		19.0
1996	50	BILL CLINTON	Democrat	45,590,703	379	49.0
		Robert Dole	Republican	37,816,307	159	41.0
		H. Ross Perot	Reform	7,866,284		8.0
2000	50	GEORGE W. BUSH	Republican	50,459,624	271	47.9
		Albert Gore, Jr.	Democrat	51,003,328	266	49.4
		Ralph Nader	Green	2,882,985		2.7
2004	50	GEORGE W. BUSH	Republican	62,040,610	286*****	50.7
		John F. Kerry	Democrat	59,028,444	251	48.3
2008	50	BARACK OBAMA	Democrat	69,456,897	365	52.9
		John McCain	Republican	59,934,814	173	45.7

*Walter B. Jones received 1 electoral vote.
† Harry F. Byrd received 15 electoral votes.
‡ Resigned August 9, 1974: Vice President Gerald R. Ford became President.
** John Hospers received 1 electoral vote.
*** Ronald Reagan received 1 electoral vote.
**** Lloyd Bentsen received 1 electoral vote.
*****John Edwards received 1 electoral vote.

GLOSSARY

Abolitionist movement A radical antislavery crusade committed to the immediate end of slavery that emerged in the three decades before the Civil War.

Acquired immune deficiency syndrome (AIDS) A complex of deadly pathologies resulting from infection with the human immunodeficiency virus (HIV).

Act for Religious Toleration The first law in America to call for freedom of worship for all Christians. It was enacted in Maryland in 1649 to quell disputes between Catholics and Protestants, but it failed to bring peace.

Actual representation The practice whereby elected representatives normally reside in their districts and are directly responsive to local interests.

Affirmative action A set of policies to open opportunities in business and education for members of minority groups and women by allowing race and sex to be factors included in decisions to hire, award contracts, or admit students to higher education programs.

Age of Enlightenment Major intellectual movement occurring in Western Europe in the late seventeenth and early eighteenth centuries. Inspired by recent scientific advances, thinkers emphasized the role of human reason in understanding the world and directing its events. Their ideas placed less emphasis on God's role in ordering worldly affairs.

Alamo Franciscan mission at San Antonio, Texas, that was the site in 1836 of a siege and massacre of Texans by Mexican troops.

Albany Plan of Union Plan put forward in 1754 by Massachusetts governor William Shirley, Benjamin Franklin, and other colonial leaders, calling for an intercolonial union to manage defense and Indian affairs. The plan was rejected by participants at the Albany Congress.

Albany Regency Popular name after 1820 for the state political machine in New York headed by Martin Van Buren.

Alien Friends Act Law passed by Congress in 1798 authorizing the president during peacetime to expel aliens suspected of subversive activities; one of the **Alien and Sedition Acts.**

Alliance for Progress Program of economic aid to Latin America during the Kennedy administration.

Allies In World War I, Britain, France, Russia, and other belligerent nations fighting against the **Central Powers** but not including the United States, which insisted upon being merely an associated nation. In World War II, the Allies fighting the **Axis Powers** included the United States as well as the Soviet Union, Great Britain, France, China, and other nations.

American Anti-Slavery Society The first national organization of abolitionists, founded in 1833.

American Colonization Society Organization, founded in 1817 by antislavery reformers, that called for gradual emancipation and the removal of freed blacks to Africa.

American Federation of Labor (AFL) Union formed in 1886 that organized skilled workers along craft lines and emphasized a few workplace issues rather than a broad social program.

American Female Moral Reform Society Organization founded in 1839 by female reformers that established homes of refuge for prostitutes and petitioned for state laws that would criminalize adultery and the seduction of women.

American Indian Movement (AIM) Group of Native American political activists who used confrontations with the federal government to publicize their case for Indian rights.

Americans with Disabilities Act Legislation in 1992 that banned discrimination against physically handicapped persons in employment, transportation, and public accommodations.

American System The program of government subsidies favored by Henry Clay and his followers to promote American economic growth and protect domestic manufacturers from foreign competition.

American system of manufacturing A technique of production pioneered in the United States in the first half of the nineteenth century that relied on precision manufacturing with the use of interchangeable parts.

American Temperance Society National organization established in 1826 by evangelical Protestants that campaigned for total abstinence from alcohol and was successful in sharply lowering per capita consumption of alcohol.

Anarchist A person who believes that all government interferes with individual liberty and should be abolished by whatever means.

Anglican Of or belonging to the Church of England, a Protestant denomination.

Anglo-American Accords Series of agreements reached in the British-American Convention of 1818 that fixed the western boundary between the United States and Canada at the 49th parallel, allowed for the joint occupation of the Oregon Country, and restored to Americans fishing rights off Newfoundland.

Annapolis Convention Conference of state delegates at Annapolis, Maryland, that issued a call in September 1786 for a convention to meet at Philadelphia in May 1787 to consider fundamental changes to the **Articles of Confederation.**

Antifederalist An opponent of the **Constitution** in the debate over its ratification.

Anti-Masons Third party formed in 1827 in opposition to the presumed power and influence of the Masonic order.

Appeal to the Colored Citizens of the World Pamphlet published in 1829 by David, a Boston free black, calling for slaves to rise up in rebellion.

Articles of Confederation Written document setting up the loose confederation of states that comprised the first national government of the United States from 1781 to 1788.

Atlanta Compromise Booker T. Washington's policy accepting segregation and **disfranchisement** for African Americans in exchange for white assistance in education and job training.

Atlantic Charter Statement of common principles and war aims developed by President Franklin Roosevelt and British Prime Minister Winston Churchill at a meeting in August 1941.

Australian ballot Secret voting and the use of official ballots rather than party tickets.

Axis Powers The opponents of the United States and its allies in World War II. The Rome–Berlin Axis was formed between Germany and Italy in 1936 and included Japan after 1940.

Aztecs A warrior people who dominated the Valley of Mexico from about 1100 until their conquest in 1519–21 by Spanish soldiers led by Hernán Cortés.

Bacon's Rebellion Violent conflict in Virginia (1675–1676), beginning with settler attacks on Indians but culminating in a rebellion led by Nathaniel Bacon against Virginia's government.

Baker v. Carr U.S. Supreme Court decision in 1962 that allowed federal courts to review the apportionment of state legislative districts and established the principle that such districts should have roughly equal populations ("one person, one vote").

Bank War The political struggle between President Andrew Jackson and the supporters of the **Second Bank of the United States.**

Battle of New Orleans Decisive American **War of 1812** victory over British troops in January 1815 that ended any British hopes of gaining control of the lower Mississippi River Valley.

Battle of Plattsburg American naval victory on Lake Champlain in September 1814 in the **War of 1812** that thwarted a British invasion from Canada.

Battle of Put-in-Bay American naval victory on Lake Erie in September 1813 in the **War of 1812** that denied the British strategic control over the Great Lakes.

Battle of the Atlantic The long struggle between German submarines and the British and U.S. navies in the North Atlantic from 1940 to 1943.

Battle of the Little Bighorn Battle in which Colonel George A. Custer and the Seventh Cavalry were defeated by the Sioux and Cheyennes under Sitting Bull and Crazy Horse in Montana in 1876.

Battles of Lexington and Concord The first two battles of the American Revolution which resulted in a total of 273 British soldiers dead, wounded, and missing and nearly 100 Americans dead, wounded, and missing.

Bay of Pigs Site in Cuba of an unsuccessful landing by 1,400 anti-Castro Cuban refugees in April 1961.

Beaver Wars Series of bloody conflicts, occurring between 1640s and 1680s, during which the Iroquois fought the French and their Indian allies for control of the fur trade in eastern North America and the Great Lakes region.

Benevolent empire Network of reform associations affiliated with Protestant churches in the early nineteenth century dedicated to the restoration of moral order.

Berlin blockade A three-hundred-day Soviet blockade of land access to United States, British, and French occupation zones in Berlin, 1948–1949.

Berlin Wall Wall erected by East Germany in 1961 and torn down in 1989 that isolated West Berlin from the surrounding areas in Communist-controlled East Berlin and East Germany.

Bill of Rights A written summary of inalienable rights and liberties.

Black codes Laws passed by states and municipalities denying many rights of citizenship to free blacks before the Civil War. Also, during the **Reconstruction era,** laws passed by newly elected southern state legislatures to control black labor, mobility, and employment.

Black Hawk's War Short 1832 war in which federal troops and Illinois militia units defeated the Sauk and Fox Indians led by Black Hawk.

Black Panthers Political and social movement among black Americans, founded in Oakland, California, in 1966 and emphasizing black economic and political power.

Black Power Philosophy emerging after 1965 that real economic and political gains for African-Americans could come only through self-help, **self-determination,** and organizing for direct political influence. Latinos and Native Americans developed their own versions as Brown Power and Red Power, respectively.

"Bleeding Kansas" Violence between pro- and antislavery forces in Kansas Territory after the passage of the **Kansas-Nebraska Act** in 1854.

Blitzkrieg German war tactic in World War II ("lightning war") involving the concentration of air and armored firepower to punch and exploit holes in opposing defensive lines.

Bolshevik Member of the communist movement in Russia that established the Soviet government after the 1917 Russian Revolution; hence, by extension, any radical or disruptive person or movement seeking to transform economic and political relationships.

Bonus Army A group of unemployed veterans who demonstrated in Washington for the payment of service bonuses, only to be dispersed violently by the U.S. Army in 1932.

Boston Massacre After months of increasing friction between townspeople and the British troops stationed in the city, on March 5,1770, British troops fired on American civilians in Boston.

Boston Tea Party Incident that occurred on December 16, 1773, in which Bostonians, disguised as Indians, destroyed £9,000 worth of tea belonging to the British East India Company in order to prevent payment of the duty on it.

British Constitution The principles, procedures, and precedents that governed the operation of the British government. These could be found in no single written document

Brook Farm A utopian community and experimental farm established in 1841 near Boston.

Brown v. Board of Education of Topeka Supreme Court decision in 1954 that declared that "separate but equal" schools for children of different races violated the **Constitution.**

Bureau of Reclamation Federal agency established in 1902 providing public funds for irrigation projects in arid regions; played a major role in the development of the West by constructing dams, reservoirs, and irrigation systems, especially beginning in the 1930s.

Cahokia Located near modern St. Louis, this was one of the largest urban centers created by Mississippian peoples, containing perhaps 30,000 residents in 1250.

Californios Persons of Spanish descent living in California.

Camp David Agreement Agreement to reduce points of conflict between Israel and Egypt, hammered out in 1977 with the help of U.S. President Jimmy Carter.

Carpetbaggers Pejorative term to describe northern transplants to the South, many of whom were Union soldiers who stayed in the South after the war.

Central Intelligence Agency (CIA) Agency that coordinates the gathering and evaluation of military and economic information on other nations, established in 1947.

Central Powers Germany and its World War I allies Austria, Turkey, and Bulgaria.

Chain migration Process common to many immigrant groups whereby one family member brings over other family members, who in turn bring other relatives and friends and occasionally entire villages.

Charles River Bridge v. Warren Bridge Supreme Court decision of 1837 that promoted economic competition by ruling that the broader rights of the community took precedence over any presumed right of monopoly granted in a corporate charter.

Cherokee War Conflict (1759–1761) on the southern frontier between the Cherokee Indians and colonists from Virginia southward. It caused South Carolina to request the aid of British troops and resulted in the surrender of more Indian land to white colonists.

Chesapeake* Incident** Attack in 1807 by the British ship ***Leopard on the American ship ***Chesapeake*** in American territorial waters that nearly provoked an Anglo-American war.

Chisholm Trail The route followed by Texas cattle raisers driving their herds north to markets at Kansas railheads.

Church of Jesus Christ of Latter-day Saints **See Mormon Church.**

Civil Rights Act of 1866 Law that defined national citizenship and specified the civil rights to which all national citizens were entitled.

Civil Rights Act of 1875 Law that prohibited racial discrimination in jury selection, public transportation, and public accommodations; declared unconstitutional by the U.S. Supreme Court in 1883.

Civil Rights Act of 1964 Federal legislation that outlawed discrimination in public accommodations and employment on the basis of race, skin color, sex, religion, or national origin.

Claims club A group of local settlers on the nineteenth-century frontier who banded together to prevent the price of their land claims from being bid up by outsiders at public land auctions.

Coercive Acts Legislation passed by Parliament in 1774; included the Boston Port Act, the Massachusetts Government Act, the Administration of Justice Act, and the **Quartering Act** of 1774.

Cold War The political and economic confrontation between the Soviet Union and the United States that dominated world affairs from 1946 to 1989.

Collective bargaining Representatives of a union negotiating with management on behalf of all members.

Colored Farmers' Alliance An organization of southern black farmers formed in Texas in 1886 in response to the **Southern Farmers' Alliance,** which did not accept black people as members.

Columbian exchange The transatlantic exchange of plants, animals, and diseases that occurred after the first European contact with the Americas.

Committees of correspondence Committees formed in Massachusetts and other colonies in the pre-Revolutionary period to keep Americans informed about British measures that would affect the colonies.

Committee of Safety Any of the extralegal committees that directed the Revolutionary movement and carried on the functions of government at the local level in the period between the breakdown of royal authority and the establishment of regular governments under the new state constitutions. Some Committees of Safety continued to function throughout the Revolutionary War.

Committee on Public Information (CPI) Government agency during World War I that sought to shape public opinion in support of the war effort through newspapers, pamphlets, speeches, films, and other media.

Communism A social structure based on the common ownership of property.

Compromise of 1850 The four-step compromise which admitted California as a free state, allowed the residents of the New Mexico and Utah territories to decide the slavery issue for themselves, ended the slave trade in the District of Columbia, and passed a new fugitive slave law to enforce the constitutional provision stating that a slave escaping into a free state shall be delivered back to the owner.

Compromise of 1877 The congressional settling of the 1876 election which installed Republican Rutherford B. Hayes in the White House and gave Democrats control of all state governments in the South.

Conciliatory Proposition Plan proposed by Lord North and adopted by the House of Commons in February 1775 whereby Parliament would "forbear" taxation of Americans in colonies whose assemblies imposed taxes considered satisfactory by the British government. The Continental Congress rejected this plan on July 31, 1775.

Confederate States of America Nation proclaimed in Montgomery, Alabama, in February 1861 after the seven states of the Lower South seceded from the United States.

Confiscation Act of 1862 Second confiscation law passed by Congress, ordering the seizure of land from disloyal Southerners and the emancipation of their slaves.

Congressional Reconstruction Name given to the period 1867–1870 when the Republican-dominated Congress controlled **Reconstruction era** policy. It is sometimes known as Radical Reconstruction, after the radical faction in the **Republican Party.**

Congress of Industrial Organizations (CIO) An alliance of industrial unions that spurred the 1930s organizational drive among the mass-production industries.

Congress of Racial Equality (CORE) Civil rights group formed in 1942 and committed to nonviolent civil disobedience, such as the 1961 "freedom rides."

Conservation The efficient management and use of natural resources, such as forests, grasslands, and rivers, as opposed to **preservation** or uncontrolled exploitation.

Constitutional Convention Convention that met in Philadelphia in 1787 and drafted the **Constitution of the United States.**

Constitutional Union Party National party formed in 1860, mainly by former **Whigs,** that emphasized allegiance to the Union and strict enforcement of all national legislation.

Constitution of the United States The written document providing for a new central government of the United States, drawn up at the **Constitutional Convention** in 1787 and ratified by the states in 1788.

Containment The policy of resisting further expansion of the Soviet bloc through diplomacy and, if necessary, military action, developed in 1947–1948.

Continental Army The regular or professional army authorized by the Second Continental Congress and commanded by General George Washington during the Revolutionary War. Better training and longer service distinguished its soldiers from the state militiamen.

Continental Association Agreement, adopted by the **First Continental Congress** in 1774 in response to the **Coercive Acts,** to cut off trade with Britain until the objectionable measures were repealed. Local committees were established to enforce the provisions of the association.

Contract theory of government The belief that government is established by human beings to protect certain rights—such as life, liberty, and property—that are theirs by natural, divinely sanctioned law and that when government protects these rights, people are obligated to obey it. But when government violates its part of the bargain (or contract) between the rulers and the ruled, the people are no longer required to obey it and may establish a new government that will do a better job of protecting them. Elements of this theory date back to the ancient Greeks; John Locke used it in his *Second Treatise on Government* (1682), and Thomas Jefferson gave it memorable expression in the Declaration of Independence, where it provides the rationale for renouncing allegiance to King George III.

Contract with America Platform on which many Republican candidates ran for Congress in 1994. Associated with House Speaker Newt Gingrich, it proposed a sweeping reduction in the role and activities of the federal government.

Copperheads A term Republicans applied to northern war dissenters and those suspected of aiding the Confederate cause during the Civil War.

Council of Economic Advisers Board of three professional economists established in 1946 to advise the president on economic policy.

Counterculture Various alternatives to mainstream values and behaviors that became popular in the 1960s, including experimentation with psychedelic drugs, communal living, a return to the land, Asian religions, and experimental art.

Country (Real Whig) ideology Strain of thought first appearing in England in the late seventeenth century in response to the growth of governmental power and a national debt. Main ideas stressed the threat to personal liberty posed by a standing army and high taxes and emphasized the need for property holders to retain the right to consent to taxation.

Coureurs de bois French for "woods runners," independent fur traders in New France.

Covenant A formal agreement or contract.

Coxey's Army A protest march of unemployed workers, led by Populist businessman Jacob Coxey, demanding inflation and a public works program during the depression of the 1890s.

Cult of domesticity The belief that women, by virtue of their sex, should stay home as the moral guardians of family life.

Culture areas Geographical regions inhabited by peoples who share similar basic patterns of subsistence and social organization.

Dartmouth College v. Woodward Supreme Court decision of 1819 that prohibited states from interfering with the privileges granted to a private corporation.

Dawes Act An 1887 law terminating tribal ownership of land and allotting some parcels of land to individual Indians with the remainder opened for white settlement.

D-Day June 6, 1944, the day of the first paratroop drops and amphibious landings on the coast of Normandy, France, in the first stage of **Operation OVERLORD** during World War II.

Declaration of Independence The document by which the Second Continental Congress announced and justified its decision (reached July 2, 1776) to renounce the colonies' allegiance to the British government. Drafted mainly by Thomas Jefferson and adopted by Congress on July 4, the declaration's indictment of the king provides a remarkably full catalog of the colonists' grievances, and Jefferson's eloquent and inspiring statement of the **contract theory of government** makes the document one of the world's great state papers.

Declaration of London Statement drafted by an international conference in 1909 to clarify international law and specify the rights of neutral nations.

Declaration of Rights and Grievances Resolves, adopted by the **Stamp Act Congress** at New York in 1765, asserting that the **Stamp Act** and other taxes imposed on the colonists without their consent, given through their colonial legislatures, were unconstitutional.

Declaration of Sentiments The resolutions passed at the **Seneca Falls. Convention** in 1848 calling for full female equality, including the right to vote.

Declaration of the Causes and Necessity of Taking Up Arms Document, written mainly by John Dickinson of Pennsylvania and adopted on July 6, 1775, by which the Second Continental Congress justified its armed resistance against British measures.

Declaratory Act Law passed in 1766 to accompany repeal of the **Stamp Act** that stated that Parliament had the authority to legislate for the colonies "in all cases whatsoever." Whether "legislate" meant tax was not clear to Americans.

Deindustrialization The process of economic change involving the disappearance of outmoded industries and the transfer of factories to new low-wage locations, with devastating effects in the Northeast and Midwest, especially in the 1970s and 1980s.

Deism Religious orientation that rejects divine revelation and holds that the workings of nature alone reveal God's design for the universe.

Democratic Party Political party formed in the 1820s under the leadership of Andrew Jackson; favored states' rights and a limited role for the federal government, especially in economic affairs.

Denmark Vesey's Conspiracy The most carefully devised slave revolt, named after its leader, a free black in Charleston. The rebels planned to seize control of Charleston in 1822 and escape to freedom in Haiti, a free black republic, but they were betrayed by other slaves, and seventy-five conspirators were executed.

Deregulation Reduction or removal of government regulations and encouragement of direct competition in many important industries and economic sectors.

Détente A lessening of tension, applied to improved American relations with the Soviet Union and China in the mid-1970s.

Disfranchisement The use of legal means to bar individuals or groups from voting.

Dixiecrats Southern Democrats who broke from the party in 1948 over the issue of civil rights and ran a presidential tickets as the States' Rights Democrats.

Dollar diplomacy The U.S. policy of using private investment in other nations to promote American diplomatic goals and business interests.

Dominion of New England James II's failed plan of 1686 to combine eight northern colonies into a single large province, to be governed by a royal appointee (Sir Edmund Andros) with an appointed council but no elective assembly. The plan ended with James's ouster from the English throne and rebellion in Massachusetts against Andros's rule.

***Dred Scott* decision** Supreme Court ruling, in a lawsuit brought by Dred Scott, a slave demanding his freedom based on his residence in a free state and a free territory with his master, that slaves could not be U.S. citizens and that Congress had no jurisdiction over slavery in the territories.

Eastern Front The area of military operations in World War II located east of Germany in eastern Europe and the Soviet Union.

Economic Recovery and Tax Act of 1981 (ERTA) A major revision of the federal income tax system.

Eighteenth Amendment Constitutional revision, ratified in 1919 and repealed in 1933, that prohibited the manufacture or sale of alcohol in the United States.

Emancipation Proclamation Decree announced by President Abraham Lincoln in September 1862 and formally issued on January 1, 1863, freeing slaves in all Confederate states still in rebellion.

Embargo Act of 1807 Act passed by Congress in 1807 prohibiting American ships from leaving for any foreign port.

Empresario An agent who received a land grant from the Spanish or Mexican government in return for organizing settlements.

Encomienda In the Spanish colonies, the grant to a Spanish settler of a certain number of Indian subjects, who would pay him tribute in goods and labor.

Enumerated products Items produced in the colonies and enumerated in acts of Parliament that could be legally shipped from the colony of origin only to specified locations, usually England and other destinations within the British Empire.

Environmental Protection Agency (EPA) Federal agency created in 1970 to oversee environmental monitoring and cleanup programs.

Era of Good Feelings The period from 1817 to 1823 in which the disappearance of the **Federalists** enabled the **Republicans** to govern in a spirit of seemingly nonpartisan harmony.

Espionage Act Law whose vague prohibition against obstructing the nation's war effort was used to crush dissent and criticism during World War I.

Fair Employment Practices Committee (FEPC) Federal agency established in 1941 to curb racial discrimination in war production jobs and government employment.

Farmers' Alliance A broad mass movement in the rural South and West during the late nineteenth century, encompassing several organizations and demanding economic and political reforms; helped create the **Populist Party.**

Fascist government Subscribing to a philosophy of governmental dictatorship that merges the interests of the state, armed forces, and big business; associated with the dictatorship of Italian leader Benito Mussolini between 1922 and 1943 and also often applied to Nazi Germany.

Federal Deposit Insurance Corporation (FDIC) Government agency that guarantees bank deposits, thereby protecting both depositors and banks.

Federal Highway Act of 1956 Measure that provided federal funding to build a nationwide system of interstate and defense highways.

Federalism The sharing of powers between the national government and the states.

Federalist A supporter of the **Constitution** who favored its ratification.

Federal Reserve Act The 1913 law that revised banking and currency by extending limited government regulation through the creation of the Federal Reserve System.

Federal Trade Commission (FTC) Government agency established in 1914 to provide regulatory oversight of business activity.

Field Order No. 15 Order by General William T. Sherman in January 1865 to set aside abandoned land along the southern Atlantic coast for forty-acre grants to freedmen; rescinded by President Andrew Johnson later that year.

Fifteenth Amendment Passed by Congress in 1869, guaranteed the right of American men to vote, regardless of race.

Fireside chats Speeches broadcast nationally over the radio in which President Franklin Roosevelt explained complex issues and programs in plain language, as though his listeners were gathered around the fireside with him.

First Continental Congress Meeting of delegates from most of the colonies held in 1774 in response to the **Coercive Acts.** The Congress endorsed the **Suffolk Resolves,** adopted the **Declaration of Rights and Grievances,** and agreed to establish the **Continental Association** to put economic pressure on Britain to repeal its objectionable measures. The Congress also wrote addresses to the king, the people of Britain, and the American people.

Fletcher v. Peck Supreme Court decision of 1810 that overturned a state law by ruling that it violated a legal contract.

Fort Sumter Begun in the late 1820s to protect Charleston, South Carolina, it became the center of national attention in April 1861 when President Lincoln attempted to provision federal troops at the fort, triggering a hostile response from on-shore Confederate forces, opening the Civil War.

Fourierist communities Short-lived utopian communities in the 1840s based on the ideas of economic cooperation and self-sufficiency popularized by the Frenchman Charles Fourier.

Fourteenth Amendment Constitutional amendment passed by Congress in April 1866 incorporating some of the features of the **Civil Rights Act of 1866.** It prohibited states from violating the civil rights of its citizens and offered states the choice of allowing black people to vote or losing representation in Congress.

Frame of Government William Penn's 1682 plan for the government of Pennsylvania, which created a relatively weak legislature and strong executive. It also contained a provision for religious freedom.

Franco-American Accord of 1800 Settlement reached with France that brought an end to the **Quasi-War** and released the United States from its 1778 alliance with France.

Freedmen's Bureau Agency established by Congress in March 1865 to provide social, educational, and economic services, advice, and protection to former slaves and destitute whites; lasted seven years.

Freedom Summer Voter registration effort in rural Mississippi organized by black and white civil rights workers in 1964.

Free silver Philosophy that the government should expand the money supply by purchasing and coining all the silver offered to it.

Free Speech Movement (FSM) Student movement at the University of California, Berkeley, formed in 1964 to protest limitations on political activities on campus.

French and Indian War The last of the Anglo-French colonial wars (1754–1763) and the first in which fighting began in North America. The war (which merged with the European conflict known as the Seven Years' War) ended with France's defeat and loss of its North American empire.

Fugitive Slave Act Law, part of the Compromise of 1850 that required authorities in the North to assist southern slave catchers and return runaway slaves to their owners.

Fundamental Constitutions of Carolina A complex plan for organizing the colony of Carolina, drafted in 1669 by Anthony Ashley Cooper and John Locke. Its provisions included a scheme for creating a hierarchy of nobles who would own vast amounts of land and wield political power; below them would be a class of freedmen and slaves. The provisions were never implemented by the Carolina colonists.

Fundamentalists Religious conservatives who believe in the literal accuracy and divine inspiration of the Bible; the name derives from an influential series of pamphlets, **The Fundamentals** (1909–1914).

Gabriel Prosser's Rebellion Slave revolt that failed when Gabriel Prosser, a slave preacher and blacksmith, organized a thousand slaves for an attack on Richmond, Virginia, in 1800. A thunderstorm upset the timing of the attack, and a slave informer alerted the whites. Prosser and twenty-five of his followers were executed.

Gag rule Procedural rule passed in the House of Representatives that prevented discussion of antislavery petitions from 1836 to 1844.

Gang system The organization and supervision of slave field hands into working teams on southern plantations.

Gentlemen's Agreement A diplomatic agreement in 1907 between Japan and the United States curtailing but not abolishing Japanese immigration.

GI Bill of Rights Legislation in June 1944 that eased the return of veterans into American society by providing educational and employment benefits.

Gibbons v. Ogden Supreme Court decision of 1824 involving coastal commerce that overturned a steamboat monopoly granted by the state of New York on the grounds that only Congress had the authority to regulate interstate commerce.

Gilded Age Term applied to late-nineteenth-century America that refers to the shallow display and worship of wealth characteristic of the period.

Glasnost Russian for "openness," applied to Mikhail Gorbachev's encouragement of new ideas and easing of political repression in the Soviet Union.

Glorious Revolution Bloodless revolt that occurred in England in 1688 when parliamentary leaders invited William of Orange, a Protestant, to assume the English throne and James II fled to France. James's ouster was prompted by fears that the birth of his son would establish a Catholic dynasty in England.

Gospel of Wealth Thesis that hard work and perseverance lead to wealth, implying that poverty is a character flaw.

Grandfather clause Rule that required potential voters to demonstrate that their grandfathers had been eligible to vote; used in some southern states after 1890 to limit the black electorate, as most black men's grandfathers had been slaves.

Grand Settlement of 1701 Separate peace treaties negotiated by Iroquois diplomats at Montreal and Albany that marked the beginning of Iroquois neutrality in conflicts between the French and the British in North America.

Grange The National Grange of the Patrons of Husbandry, a national organization of farm owners formed after the Civil War.

Granger laws State laws enacted in the Midwest in the 1870s that regulated rates charged by railroads, grain elevator operators, and other middlemen.

Great Awakening Tremendous religious revival in colonial America. Sparked by the tour of the English evangelical minister George Whitefield, the Awakening struck first in the Middle Colonies and New England in the 1740s and eventually spread to the southern colonies by the 1760s.

Great Compromise Plan proposed by Roger Sherman of Connecticut at the 1787 **Constitutional Convention** for creating a national bicameral legislature in which all states would be equally represented in the Senate and proportionally represented in the House.

Great Depression The nation's worst economic crisis, extending throughout the 1930s, producing unprecedented bank failures, unemployment, and industrial and agricultural collapse and prompting an expanded role for the federal government.

Great League of Peace and Power Confederation of five Iroquois nations—the Mohawks, Oneidas, Onondagas, Cayugas, and Senecas—formed in the fifteenth century to diminish internal conflict and increase collective strength against their enemies.

Great Migration The mass movement of African Americans from the rural South to the urban North, spurred especially by new job opportunities during World War I and the 1920s.

Great Society Theme of Lyndon Johnson's administration, focusing on poverty, education, and civil rights.

Great Uprising Unsuccessful railroad strike of 1877 to protest wage cuts and the use of federal troops against strikers; the first nationwide work stoppage in American history.

Greater East Asia Co-Prosperity Sphere Japanese goal of an East Asian economy controlled by Japan and serving the needs of Japanese industry.

Greenback Party A third party of the 1870s and 1880s that garnered temporary support by advocating currency inflation to expand the economy and assist debtors.

Gulf of Tonkin Resolution Congressional resolution in August 1964 that authorized the president to take all necessary measures to protect South Vietnam, adopted after reports of North Vietnamese attacks on U.S. navy ships in the Gulf of Tonkin off North Vietnam.

Halfway Covenant Plan adopted in 1662 by New England clergy to deal with the problem of declining church membership. It allowed adults who had been baptized because their parents were church members but who had not yet experienced conversion to have their own children baptized. Without the Halfway Covenant, these third-generation children would remain unbaptized until their parents experienced conversion.

Harlem Renaissance A new African-American cultural awareness that flourished in literature, art, and music in the 1920s.

Headright system A system of land distribution during early colonial era that granted settlers fifty acres for themselves and another fifty for each "head" (or person) they brought to the colony.

Helsinki Accords Agreement in 1975 among NATO and Warsaw Pact members that recognized European national boundaries as set after World War II and included guarantees of human rights.

Holocaust The systematic murder of millions of European Jews and others deemed undesirable by Nazi Germany.

Homestead Act Law passed by Congress in 1862 providing 160 acres of land free to anyone who would live on the plot and farm it for five years.

Hooverville Shantytown, sarcastically named after President Hoover, in which unemployed and homeless people lived in makeshift shacks, tents, and boxes. Hoovervilles cropped up in many cities in 1930 and 1931.

Horatio Alger Stories A series of best-selling tales about young rags-to-riches heroes first published in 1867 stressing the importance of neat clothes, cleanliness, thrift, and hard work. The books also highlighted the importance of chance in getting ahead and the responsibility of those better off to serve as positive role models.

Horizontal integration The merger of competitors in the same industry.

House Un-American Activities Committee Congressional committee (1938–1975) that investigated suspected Nazi and Communist sympathizers.

House of Burgesses The legislature of colonial Virginia. First organized in 1619, it was the first institution of representative government in the English colonies.

Hull House Chicago **settlement house** that became part of a broader neighborhood revitalization and immigrant assistance project led by Jane Addams.

Immigration and Nationality Act of 1965 Federal legislation that replaced the national quota system for immigration with overall limits of 170,000 immigrants per year from the Eastern Hemisphere and 120,000 per year from the Western Hemisphere.

Imperialism The policy and practice of exploiting nations and peoples for the benefit of an imperial power either directly through military occupation and colonial rule or indirectly through economic domination of resources and markets.

Impressment The British policy of forcibly enlisting American sailors into the British navy.

Indentured servant An individual—usually male but occasionally female—who contracted to serve a master for a period of four to seven years in return for payment of the servant's passage to America. Indentured servitude was the primary labor system in the Chesapeake colonies for most of the seventeenth century.

Independent Treasury System Fiscal arrangement first instituted by President Martin Van Buren in which the federal government kept its money in regional vaults ("pet banks") and transacted its business entirely in hard money.

Indian Removal Act Legislation passed by Congress in 1830 that provided funds for removing and resettling eastern Indians in the West. It granted the president the authority to use force if necessary.

Initiative Procedure by which citizens can introduce a subject for legislation, usually through a petition signed by a specific number of voters.

Intermediate-Range Nuclear Forces Treaty (INF) Disarmament agreement between the United States and the Soviet Union under which an entire class of missiles would be removed and destroyed and on-site inspections would be permitted for verification.

International Monetary Fund (IMF) International organization established in 1945 to assist nations in maintaining stable currencies.

Internet The system of interconnected computers and servers that allows the exchange of e-mail, posting of websites, and other means of instant communication.

Interstate and Defense Highways Federal legislation in 1956 committed the federal government to finance more than 40,000 miles of new limited access freeways to criss-cross the United States.

Interstate Commerce Act The 1887 law that expanded federal power over business by prohibiting pooling and discriminatory rates by railroads and establishing the first federal regulatory agency, the **Interstate Commerce Commission.**

Interstate Commerce Commission (ICC) The first federal regulatory agency, established in 1887 to oversee railroad practices.

Intolerable Acts American term for the **Coercive Acts** and the **Quebec Act.**

Irreconcilables Group of U.S. senators adamantly opposed to ratification of the **Treaty of Versailles** after World War I.

Island hopping In the Pacific Theater during World War II, the strategy in which U.S. forces seized selected Japanese-held islands while bypassing and isolating other islands held by Japan.

Jacksonian Democrats **See Democratic Party.**

Jay's Treaty Treaty with Britain negotiated in 1794 in which the United States made major concessions to avert a war over the British seizure of American ships.

Jazz Age The 1920s, so called for the popular music of the day as a symbol of the many changes taking place in the mass culture.

Jim Crow laws Segregation laws that became widespread in the South during the 1890s, named for a minstrel show character portrayed satirically by white actors in blackface.

John Brown's Raid New England abolitionist John Brown's ill-fated attempt to free Virginia's slaves with a raid on the federal arsenal at Harpers Ferry, Virginia, in 1859.

Joint-stock company Business enterprise in which a group of stockholders pooled their money to engage in trade or to fund colonizing expeditions. Joint-stock companies participated in the founding of the Virginia, Plymouth, and Massachusetts Bay colonies.

Judicial review A power implied in the **Constitution** that gives federal courts the right to review and determine the constitutionality of acts passed by Congress and state legislatures.

Judiciary Act of 1789 Act of Congress that implemented the judiciary clause of the **Constitution** by establishing the Supreme Court and a system of lower federal courts.

Kansas-Nebraska Act Law passed in 1854 creating the Kansas and Nebraska Territories but leaving the question of slavery open to residents, thereby repealing the **Missouri Compromise.**

Kellogg-Briand Pact A 1928 international treaty that denounced aggression and war but lacked provisions for enforcement.

King George's War The third Anglo-French war in North America (1744–1748), part of the European conflict known as the War of the Austrian Succession. During the North American fighting, New Englanders captured the French fortress of Louisbourg, only to have it returned to France after the peace negotiations.

King Philip's War Conflict in New England (1675–1676) between Wampanoags, Narragansetts, and other Indian peoples against English settlers; sparked by English encroachments on native lands.

King William's War The first Anglo-French conflict in North America (1689–1697), the American phase of Europe's War of the League of Augsburg. Ended in negotiated peace that reestablished the balance of power.

Knights of Labor Labor union that included skilled and unskilled workers irrespective of race or gender; founded in 1869, peaked in the 1880s, and declined when its advocacy of the eight-hour workday led to violent strikes in 1886.

Know-Nothing Party Anti-immigrant party formed from the wreckage of the **Whig Party** and some disaffected northern Democrats in 1854.

Korean War War between North Korea and South Korea (1950–1953) in which the People's Republic of China fought on the side of North Korea and the United States and other nations fought on the side of South Korea under teh auspices of the United Nations.

Ku Klux Klan Perhaps the most prominent of the vigilante groups that terrorized black people in the South during **Reconstruction Era,** founded by Confederate veterans in 1866.

Laissez-faire The doctrine that government should not intervene in the economy, especially through regulation.

Land Grant College Act Law passed by Congress in July 1862 awarding proceeds from the sale of public lands to the states for the establishment of agricultural and mechanical (later engineering) colleges. Also known as the Morrill Act, after its sponsor, Congressman Justin Morrill of Vermont.

Land Ordinance of 1785 Act passed by Congress under the **Articles of Confederation** that created the grid system of surveys by which all subsequent public land was made available for sale.

League of Nations International organization created by the **Versailles Treaty** after World War I to ensure world stability.

League of Women Voters Group formed in 1920 from the National American Woman Suffrage Association to encourage informed voting and social reforms.

Lecompton Constitution Proslavery draft written in 1857 by Kansas territorial delegates elected under questionable circumstances; it was rejected by two governors, supported by President Buchanan, and decisively defeated by Congress.

Lend-Lease Act Program begun in 1941 through which the United States transferred military equipment to Britain and other World War II allies.

Liberal Republicans Members of a reform movement within the **Republican Party** in 1872 that promoted measures to reduce government influence in the economy and restore control of southern governments to local white elites.

Liberty Bonds Interest-bearing certificates sold by the U.S. government to finance the American World War I effort.

Liberty Party The first antislavery political party, formed in 1840.

Limited Test Ban Treaty Agreement in 1963 between the United States, Britain, and the Soviet Union to halt atmospheric and underwater tests of nuclear weapons.

Lincoln-Douglas debates Series of debates in the 1858 Illinois senatorial campaign during which Democrat Stephen A. Douglas and Republican Abraham Lincoln staked out their differing opinions on the issue of slavery in the territories.

Lost Cause The phrase many white southerners applied to their Civil War defeat. They viewed the war as a noble cause but only a temporary setback in the South's ultimate vindication.

Lynching Execution, usually by a mob, without trial.

Mahanism The ideas advanced by Alfred Thayer Mahan, stressing U.S. naval, economic, and territorial expansion.

Manhattan Project The effort, using the code name Manhattan Engineer District, to develop an atomic bomb under the management of the U.S. Army Corps of Engineers during World War II.

Manifest Destiny Doctrine, first expressed in 1845, that the expansion of white Americans across the continent was inevitable and ordained by God.

Marbury v. Madison Supreme Court decision of 1803 that created the precedent of judicial review by ruling as unconstitutional part of the **Judiciary Act of 1789.**

Marshall Plan The European Recovery Program (1949), which provided U.S. economic assistance to European nations; named for Secretary of State George Marshall.

Massive retaliation Popular name for the military doctrine adopted in the 1950s, whereby the United States promised to respond to any attack on itself or its allies with massive force, including nuclear weapons.

McCarthyism Anticommunist attitudes and actions associated with Senator Joe McCarthy in the early 1950s, including smear tactics and innuendo.

McCulloch v. Maryland Supreme Court decision of 1819 upholding the constitutionality of the Second Bank of the United States and the exercise of federal powers within a state.

Medicaid Supplementary medical insurance for the poor, financed through the federal government; program created in 1965.

Medicare Basic medical insurance for the elderly, financed through the federal government; program created in 1965.

Mercantilism Economic system whereby the government intervenes in the economy for the purpose of increasing national wealth. Mercantilists advocated possession of colonies as places where the mother country could acquire raw materials not available at home.

Mexican Cession of 1848 The land ceded to the U.S. by Mexico in the Treaty of Guadalupe Hidalgo.

Middle Passage The voyage between West Africa and the New World slave colonies.

Minute Men Special companies of militia formed in Massachusetts and elsewhere beginning in late 1744. These units were composed of men who were to be ready to assemble with their arms at a minute's notice.

Missouri Compromise Sectional compromise in Congress in 1820 that admitted Missouri to the Union as a slave state and Maine as a free state and prohibited slavery in the **Louisiana Purchase** territory above 36°30′ north latitude.

Model Cities Program Effort to target federal funds to upgrade public services and economic opportunity in specifically defined urban neighborhoods between 1966 and 1974.

Molly Maguires Secret labor organization of mostly Irish miners in the Pennsylvania anthracite coal region in the decade after the Civil War. Named after a woman who led a massive protest against landlords in Ireland in the 1840s, the Maguires carried out selective murders of coal company officials until an infiltrator exposed the group in 1877 and its leaders were arrested, tried, and executed.

Monroe Doctrine Declaration by President James Monroe in 1823 that the Western Hemisphere was to be closed off to further European colonization and that the United States would not interfere in the internal affairs of European nations.

Mormon Church (Church of Jesus Christ of Latter-day Saints) Church founded in 1830 by Joseph Smith and based on the revelations in a sacred book he called the Book of Mormon.

Muckraking Journalism exposing economic, social, and political evils, so named by Theodore Roosevelt for its "raking the muck" of American society.

Mugwumps Elitist and conservative reformers who favored **sound money** and limited government and opposed tariffs and the **spoils system.**

Multinational corporation Firm with direct investments, branches, factories, and offices in a number of countries.

National Aeronautics and Space Administration (NASA) Federal agency created in 1958 to manage American space flights and exploration.

National American Woman Suffrage Association The organization, formed in 1890, that coordinated the ultimately successful campaign to achieve women's right to vote.

National Association for the Advancement of Colored People (NAACP) An interracial organization founded in 1910 dedicated to restoring African American political and social rights.

Nationalists Group of leaders in the 1780s who spearheaded the drive to replace the **Articles of Confederation** with a stronger central government.

National Origins Act of 1924 Law sharply restricting immigration on the basis of immigrants' national origins and discriminating against southern and eastern Europeans and Asians.

National Security Council (NSC) The formal policymaking body for national defense and foreign relations, created in 1947 and consisting of the president, the secretary of defense, the secretary of state, and others appointed by the president.

National Security Council Paper 68 (NSC-68) Policy statement that committed the United States to a military approach to the **Cold War.**

Nation of Islam Religious movement among black Americans that emphasizes self-sufficiency, self-help, and separation from white society.

Nativist/Nativism Favoring the interests and culture of native-born inhabitants over those of immigrants.

Nat Turner's Rebellion Uprising of slaves in Southampton County, Virginia, in the summer of 1831 led by Nat Turner that resulted in the death of fifty-five whites.

Natural rights Political philosophy that maintains that individuals have an inherent right, found in nature and preceding any government or written law, to life and liberty.

Neoliberal Advocate of or participant in the effort to reshape the **Democratic Party** for the 1990s around a policy emphasizing economic growth and competitiveness in the world economy.

New Deal The economic and political policies of the Roosevelt administration in the 1930s.

New Federalism President Richard Nixon's policy to shift responsibilities for government programs from the federal level to the states.

New Freedom Woodrow Wilson's 1912 program for limited government intervention in the economy to restore competition by curtailing the restrictive influences of trusts and protective tariffs, thereby providing opportunities for individual achievement.

New Frontier John F. Kennedy's domestic and foreign policy initiatives, designed to reinvigorate a sense of national purpose and energy.

New Harmony Short-lived utopian community established in Indiana in 1825, based on the socialist ideas of Robert Owen, a wealthy Scottish manufacturer.

New Jersey Plan Proposal of the New Jersey delegation at the 1787 **Constitutional Convention** for a strengthened national government in which all states would have equal representation in a **unicameral legislature.**

New Lights People who experienced conversion during the revivals of the **Great Awakening.**

New Nationalism Theodore Roosevelt's 1912 program calling for a strong national government to foster, regulate, and protect business, industry, workers, and consumers.

New York Draft Riot A mostly Irish-immigrant protest against conscription in New York City in July 1863 that escalated into class and racial warfare that had to be quelled by federal troops.

Niagara Movement African-American group organized in 1905 to promote racial integration, civil and political rights, and equal access to economic opportunity.

Nineteenth Amendment Constitutional revision that in 1920 established women citizens' right to vote.

Nisei U.S. citizens born of immigrant Japanese parents.

Nixon Doctrine In July, 1969, President Nixon described a new American policy toward Asia, in which the United States would honor treaty commitments but would gradually disengage and expect Asian nations to handle military defense on their own.

Nonimportation movement A tactical means of putting economic pressure on Britain by refusing to buy its exports to the colonies. Initiated in response to the taxes imposed by the **Sugar** and **Stamp acts,** it was used again against the **Townshend duties** and the **Coercive Acts.** The nonimportation movement popularized resistance to British measures and deepened the commitment of many ordinary people to a larger American community.

North American Free Trade Agreement (NAFTA) Agreement reached in 1993 by Canada, Mexico, and the United States to substantially reduce barriers to trade.

North Atlantic Treaty Organization (NATO) Military alliance of the United States, Canada, and European nations created in 1949 to protect Europe against possible Soviet aggression.

Northwest Ordinance of 1787 Legislation passed by Congress under the **Articles of Confederation** that prohibited slavery in the Northwest Territories and provided the model for the incorporation of future territories into the Union as coequal states.

Nullification A constitutional doctrine holding that a state has a legal right to declare a national law null and void within its borders.

Nullification crisis Sectional crisis in the early 1830s in which a **states' rights** party in South Carolina attempted to nullify federal law.

Office of Economic Opportunity (OEO) Federal agency that coordinated many programs of the **War on Poverty** between 1964 and 1975.

Oligopoly An industry, such as steel making or automobile manufacturing, that is controlled by a few large companies.

Olive Branch Petition Petition, written largely by John Dickinson and adopted by the Second Continental Congress on July 5, 1775, as a last effort of peace that avowed America's loyalty to George III and requested that he protect it from further aggressions. Congress continued military preparations, and the king never responded to the petition.

Omaha Platform The 1892 platform of the **Populist Party** repudiating laissez- faire and demanding economic and political reforms to aid distressed farmers and workers.

Oneida Community Utopian community established in upstate New York in 1848 by John Humphrey Noyes and his followers.

Open Door American policy of seeking equal trade and investment opportunities in foreign nations or regions.

Open shop Factory or business employing workers whether or not they are union members; in practice, such a business usually refuses to hire union members and follows antiunion policies.

Operation Desert Storm Code name for the successful offensive against Iraq by the United States and its allies in the Persian Gulf War (1991).

Operation OVERLORD U.S. and British invasion of France in June 1944 during World War II.

Oregon Trail Overland trail of more than 2,000 miles that carried American settlers from the Midwest to new settlements in Oregon, California, and Utah.

Organization of Petroleum Exporting Countries (OPEC) Cartel of oil-producing nations in Asia, Africa, and Latin America that gained substantial power over the world economy in the mid- to late 1970s by controlling the production and price of oil.

Ostend Manifesto Message sent by U.S. envoys to President Pierce from Ostend, Belgium, in 1854, stating that the United States had a "divine right" to wrest Cuba from Spain.

Pan American Union International organization originally established as the Commercial Bureau of American Republics by Secretary of State James Blaine's first Pan-American Conference in 1889 to promote cooperation among nations of the Western Hemisphere through commercial and diplomatic negotiations.

Panic of 1857 Banking crisis that caused a credit crunch in the North; it was less severe in the South, where high cotton prices spurred a quick recovery.

Pan-Indian resistance movement Movement calling for the political and cultural unification of Indian tribes in the late eighteenth and early nineteenth centuries.

PATRIOT Act Federal legislation adopted in 2001, in response to the terrorist attacks of September 11, intended to facilitate antiterror actions by federal law enforcement and intelligence agencies.

Peace of Paris Treaties signed in 1783 by Great Britain, the United States, France, Spain, and the Netherlands that ended the Revolutionary War. First in a preliminary agreement and then in the final treaty with the United States, Britain recognized the independence of the United States, agreed that the Mississippi River would be its western boundary, and permitted it to fish in some Canadian waters. Prewar debts owed by the inhabitants of one country to those of the other were to remain collectible, and Congress was to urge the states to return property confiscated from Loyalists. British troops were to evacuate United States territory without removing slaves or other property. In a separate agreement, Britain relinquished its claim to East and West Florida to Spain.

Pendleton Civil Service Act A law of 1883 that reformed the **spoils system** by prohibiting government workers from making political contributions and creating the Civil Service Commission to oversee their appointment on the basis of merit rather than politics.

Pentagon Papers Classified Defense Department documents on the history of the U.S. involvement in Vietnam, prepared in 1968 and leaked to the press in 1971.

People's Party **See Populist Party.**

Pequot War Conflict between English settlers (who had Narragansett and Mohegan allies) and Pequot Indians over control of land and trade in eastern Connecticut. The Pequots were nearly destroyed in a set of bloody confrontations, including a deadly English attack on a Mystic River village in May 1637.

Perestroika Russian for "restructuring," applied to Mikhail Gorbachev's efforts to make the Soviet economic and political systems more modern, flexible, and innovative.

Persian Gulf War War (1991) between Iraq and a U.S.-led coalition that followed Iraq's invasion of Kuwait and resulted in the expulsion of Iraqi forces from that country.

Pietists Protestants who stress a religion of the heart and the spirit of Christian living.

Pilgrims Settlers of Plymouth Colony, who viewed themselves as spiritual wanderers.

Platt Amendment A stipulation the United States had inserted into the Cuban constitution in 1901 restricting Cuban autonomy and authorizing U.S. intervention and naval bases.

Plessy v. Ferguson U.S. Supreme Court decision in 1896 affirming the constitutionality of racial segregation by law.

Pogroms Government-directed attacks against Jewish citizens, property, and villages in tsarist Russia beginning in the 1880s; a primary reason for Russian Jewish migration to the United States.

Poll tax A tax imposed on voters as a requirement for voting. Most southern states imposed poll taxes after 1900 as a way to disfranchise black people; the measures also restricted the white vote.

Pontiac's War Indian uprising (1763–1766) led by Pontiac of the Ottawas and Neolin of the Delawares. Fearful of their fate at the hands of the British after the French had been driven out of North America, the Indian nations of the Ohio River Valley and the Great Lakes area united to oust the British from the Ohio-Mississippi Valley. They failed and were forced to make peace in 1766.

Popular sovereignty A solution to the slavery crisis suggested by Michigan senator Lewis Cass by which territorial residents, not Congress, would decide slavery's fate.

Populist Party A major third party of the 1890s, also known as the **People's Party.** Formed on the basis of the **Southern Farmers' Alliance** and other reform organizations, it mounted electoral challenges against the Democrats in the South and the Republicans in the West.

Potsdam Declaration Statement issued by the United States during a meeting of U.S. president Harry Truman, British Prime Minister Winston Churchill, and Soviet premier Joseph Stalin held at Potsdam, near Berlin, in July 1945 to plan the defeat of Japan and the future of Eastern Europe and Germany. In it, the United States declared its intention to democratize the Japanese political system and reintroduce Japan into the international community and gave Japan an opening for surrender.

Predestination The belief that God decided at the moment of Creation which humans would achieve salvation.

Preparedness Military buildup in preparation for possible U.S. participation in World War I.

Preservation Protecting forests, land, and other features of the natural environment from development or destruction, often for aesthetic appreciation.

Proclamation of 1763 Royal proclamation setting the boundary known as the Proclamation Line.

Progressive Era The period of the twentieth century before World War I when many groups sought to reshape the nation's government and society in response to the pressures of industrialization and urbanization.

Prohibition A ban on the production, transportation and sale of liquor, achieved temporarily through state laws and the Eighteenth Amendment.

Prohibition Party A venerable third party still in existence that has persistently campaigned for the abolition of alcohol but has also introduced many important reform ideas into American politics.

Proposition 187 California legislation adopted by popular vote in California in 1994, which cuts off state-funded health and education benefits to undocumented or illegal immigrants.

Proprietary colony A colony created when the English monarch granted a huge tract of land to an individual or group of individuals, who became "lords proprietor." Many lords proprietor had distinct social visions for their colonies, but these plans were hardly ever implemented. Examples of proprietary colonies are Maryland, Carolina, New York (after it was seized from the Dutch), and Pennsylvania.

Protestants Europeans who supported reform of the Catholic Church in the wake of Martin Luther's critique of church practices and doctrines.

Pueblo Revolt Rebellion in 1680 of Pueblo Indians in New Mexico against their Spanish overlords, sparked by religious conflict and excessive Spanish demands for tribute.

Puritans Individuals who believed that Queen Elizabeth's reforms of the Church of England had not gone far enough in improving the church, particularly in ensuring that church members were among the saved. Puritans led the settlement of Massachusetts Bay Colony.

Putting-out system System of manufacturing in which merchants furnished households with raw materials for processing by family members.

Quakers Members of the Society of Friends, a radical religious group that arose in the mid-seventeenth century. Quakers rejected formal theology and an educated ministry, focusing instead on the importance of the "Inner Light," or Holy Spirit that dwelt within them. Quakers were important in the founding of Pennsylvania.

Quartering Acts Acts of Parliament requiring colonial legislatures to provide supplies and quarters for the troops stationed in America. Americans considered this taxation in disguise and objected. None of these acts passed during the pre-Revolutionary controversy required that soldiers be quartered in an occupied house without the owner's consent.

Quasi-War Undeclared naval war of 1797 to 1800 between the United States and France.

Quebec Act Law passed by Parliament in 1774 that provided an appointed government for Canada, enlarged the boundaries of Quebec southward to the Ohio River, and confirmed the privileges of the Catholic Church. Alarmed Americans termed this act and the **Coercive Acts** the **Intolerable Acts.**

Queen Anne's War American phase (1702–1713) of Europe's War of the Spanish Succession. At its conclusion, England gained Nova Scotia.

Radical Republicans A shifting group of Republican congressmen, usually a substantial minority, who favored the abolition of slavery from the beginning of the Civil War and later advocated harsh treatment of the defeated South.

Reagan Doctrine The policy assumption that Soviet-influenced governments in Asia, Africa, and Latin America needed to be eliminated if the United States was to win the Cold War.

Recall The process of removing an official from office by popular vote, usually after using petitions to call for such a vote.

Reconquista The long struggle (ending in 1492) during which Spanish Christians reconquered the Iberian Peninsula from Muslim occupiers, who first invaded in the eighth century.

Reconstruction Era The era (1865–1877) when the resolution of two major issues—the status of the former slaves and the terms of the Confederate states' readmission into the Union—dominated political debate.

Redeemers Southern Democrats who wrested control of governments in the former Confederacy, often through electoral fraud and violence, from Republicans beginning in 1870.

Redemptioners Similar to **indentured servants,** except that redemptioners signed labor contracts in America rather than in Europe, as indentured servants did. Shipmasters sold redemptioners into servitude to recoup the cost of their passage if they could not pay the fare upon their arrival.

Redlining Restricting mortgage credit and insurance to properties in neighborhoods defined as being high risk.

Red Scare Post–World War I public hysteria over **Bolshevik** influence in the United States directed against labor activists, radical dissenters, and some ethnic groups.

Referendum Submission of a law, proposed or already in effect, to a direct popular vote for approval or rejection.

Reformation Sixteenth-century movement to reform the Catholic Church that ultimately led to the founding of new Protestant Christian religious groups.

Regulators Vigilante groups active in the 1760s and 1770s in the western parts of North and South Carolina. The South Carolina Regulators attempted to rid the area of outlaws; the North Carolina Regulators sought to protect themselves against excessively high taxes and court costs. In both cases, westerners lacked sufficient representation in the legislature to obtain immediate redress of their grievances. The South Carolina government eventually made concessions; the North Carolina government suppressed its Regulator movement by force.

Repartimiento In the Spanish colonies, the assignment of Indian workers to labor on public works projects.

Republicanism A complex, changing body of ideas, values, and assumptions, closely related to **country ideology**, that influenced American political behavior during the eighteenth and nineteenth centuries. Derived from the political ideas of classical antiquity, Renaissance Europe, and early modern England, republicanism held that self-government by the citizens of a country, or their representatives, provided a more reliable foundation for the good society and individual freedom than rule by kings. The benefits of monarchy depended on the variable abilities of monarchs; the character of republican government depended on the virtue of the people. Republicanism therefore helped give the American Revolution a moral dimension. But the nature of republican virtue and the conditions favorable to it became sources of debate that influenced the writing of the state and federal constitutions as well as the development of political parties.

Republican Party Party that emerged in the 1850s in the aftermath of the bitter controversy over the **Kansas-Nebraska Act,** consisting of former **Whigs,** some northern Democrats, and many **Know-Nothings.**

Republican Party (Jeffersonian) Party headed by Thomas Jefferson that formed in opposition to the financial and diplomatic policies of the **Federalist Party;** favored limiting the powers of the national government and placing the interests of farmers and planters over those of financial and commercial groups; supported the cause of the French Revolution.

Rescate Procedure by which Spanish colonists would pay ransom to free Indians captured by rival natives. The rescued Indians then became workers in Spanish households.

Reservationists Group of U.S. senators favoring approval of the **Treaty of Versailles,** the peace agreement after World War I, after amending it to incorporate their reservations.

Rhode Island system During the industrialization of the early nineteenth century, the recruitment of entire families for employment in a factory.

Roe v. Wade U.S. Supreme Court decision in 1973 that disallowed state laws prohibiting abortion during the first three months (trimester) of pregnancy and established guidelines for abortion in the second and third trimesters.

Roosevelt Corollary President Theodore Roosevelt's policy asserting U.S. authority to intervene in the affairs of Latin American nations; an expansion of the **Monroe Doctrine.**

Rush-Bagot Agreement Treaty of 1817 between the United States and Britain that effectively demilitarized the Great Lakes by sharply limiting the number of ships each power could station on them.

Sabbatarian movement Reform organization founded in 1828 by Congregationalist and Presbyterian ministers that lobbied for an end to the delivery of mail on Sundays and other Sabbath violations.

"Sack of Lawrence" Vandalism and arson committed by a group of proslavery men in Lawrence, the free-state capital of Kansas Territory.

Sagebrush Rebellion Political movement in the western states in the early 1980s that called for easing of regulations on the economic use of federal lands and the transfer of some or all of those lands to state ownership.

Sand Creek Massacre The near annihilation in 1864 of Black Kettle's Cheyenne band by Colorado troops under Colonel John Chivington's orders to "kill and scalp all, big and little."

Santa Fe Trial Overland trial across the southern plains from St. Louis to New Mexico that funneled American traders and goods to Spanish-speaking settlements in the Southwest.

Scalawags Southern whites, mainly small landowning farmers and well-off merchants and planters, who supported the southern **Republican Party** during **Reconstruction** for diverse reasons; a disparaging term.

Search and destroy U.S. military tactic in South Vietnam, using small detachments to locate enemy units and then massive air, artillery, and ground forces to destroy them.

Second Bank of the United States A national bank chartered by Congress in 1816 with extensive regulatory powers over currency and credit.

Second Continental Congress An assemblage of delegates from all the colonies that convened in May 1775 after the outbreak of fighting in Massachusetts between British and American forces. It became the national government that eventually declared independence and conducted the Revolutionary War.

Second Great Awakening Series of religious revivals in the first half of the nineteenth century characterized by great G-9emotionalism in large public meetings.

Second Party System The national two-party competition between Democrats and Whigs from the 1830s through the early 1850s.

Securities and Exchange Commission (SEC) Federal agency with authority to regulate trading practices in stocks and bonds.

Sedition Act of 1918 Broad law restricting criticism of America's involvement in World War I or its government, flag, military, taxes, or officials.

Segregation A system of racial control that separated the races, initially by custom but increasingly by law during and after **Reconstruction.**

Selective Service Act of 1917 The law establishing the military draft for World War I.

Selective Service System Federal agency that coordinated military conscription before and during the Vietnam War.

Self-determination The right of a people or nation to decide on its own political allegiance or form of government without external influence.

Seneca Falls Convention The first convention for women's equality in legal rights, held in upstate New York in 1848. **See also Declaration of Sentiments.**

Separatists Members of an offshoot branch of Puritanism. Separatists believed that the Church of England was too corrupt to be reformed and hence were convinced that they must "separate" from it to save their souls. Separatists helped found Plymouth Colony.

Settlement house A multipurpose structure in a poor neighborhood that offered social welfare, educational, and homemaking services to the poor or immigrants; usually under private auspices and directed by middle-class women.

Seventeenth Amendment Constitutional change that in 1913 established the direct popular election of U.S. senators.

Shakers The followers of Mother Ann Lee, who preached a religion of strict celibacy and communal living.

Sharecropping Labor system that evolved during and after **Reconstruction** whereby landowners furnished laborers with a house, farm animals, and tools and advanced credit in exchange for a share of the laborers' crop.

Shays's Rebellion An armed movement of debt-ridden farmers in western Massachusetts in the winter of 1786–1787. The rebellion shut down courts and created a crisis atmosphere, strengthening the case of **nationalists** that a stronger central government was needed to maintain civil order in the states.

Sheppard-Towner Maternity and Infancy Act of 1921 The first federal social welfare law; funded infant and maternity health care programs in local hospitals.

Sherman Antitrust Act The first federal antitrust measure, passed in 1890; sought to promote economic competition by prohibiting business combinations in restraint of trade or commerce.

Silicon Valley The region of California between San Jose and San Francisco that holds the nation's greatest concentration of electronics firms.

Sixteenth Amendment Constitutional revision that in 1913 authorized a federal income tax.

***Slaughterhouse* cases** Group of cases resulting in one sweeping decision by the U.S. Supreme Court in 1873 that contradicted the intent of the **Fourteenth Amendment** by decreeing that most citizenship rights remained under state, not federal, control.

Slave codes Sometimes known as "black codes." A series of laws passed mainly in the southern colonies in the late seventeenth and early eighteenth centuries to define the status of slaves and codify the denial of basic civil rights to them. Also, after American independence and before the Civil War, state laws in the South defining slaves as property and specifying the legal powers of masters over slaves.

Slave Power A key concept in abolitionist and northern antislavery propaganda that depicted southern slaveholders as the driving force in a political conspiracy to promote slavery at the expense of white liberties.

Social Darwinism The application of Charles Darwin's theory of biological evolution to society, holding that the fittest and the wealthiest survive, the weak and the poor perish, and government action is unable to alter this "natural" and beneficial process.

Social Gospel movement An effort by leading Protestants to apply religious ethics to industrial conditions and thereby alleviate poverty, slums, and labor exploitation.

Socialism A social order based on government ownership of industry and worker control over corporations as a way to prevent worker exploitation.

Solid South The one-party (Democratic) political system that dominated the South from the 1890s to the 1950s.

Songhai Empire A powerful West African state that flourished between 1450 and 1591, when it fell to a Moroccan invasion.

Sons of Liberty Secret organizations in the colonies formed to oppose the **Stamp Act.** From 1765 until independence, they spoke, wrote, and demonstrated against British measures. Their actions often intimidated stamp distributors and British supporters in the colonies.

Sound money Misleading slogan that referred to a conservative policy of restricting the money supply and adhering to the gold standard.

Southeast Asia Treaty Organization (SEATO) Mutual defense alliance signed in 1954 by the United States, Britain, France, Thailand, Pakistan, the Philippines, Australia, and New Zealand.

Southern Christian Leadership Conference (SCLC) Black civil rights organization founded in 1957 by Martin Luther King Jr., and other clergy.

Southern Farmers' Alliance The largest of several organizations that formed in the post-Reconstruction South to advance the interests of beleaguered small farmers.

Southern Homestead Act Largely unsuccessful law passed in 1866 that gave black people preferential access to public lands in five southern states.

Southern Manifesto A document signed by 101 members of Congress from southern states in 1956 that argued that the Supreme Court's decision in ***Brown v. Board of Education of Topeka*** itself contradicted the **Constitution.**

Southwest Ordinance of 1790 Legislation passed by Congress that set up a government with no prohibition on slavery in U.S. territory south of the Ohio River.

Sovereignty The supreme authority of the state, including both the right to take life and to tax.

Specie Circular Proclamation issued by President Andrew Jackson in 1836 stipulating that only gold or silver could be used as payment for public land.

Spheres of influence Regions dominated and controlled by an outside power.

Spoils system The awarding of government jobs to party loyalists.

Stamp Act Law passed by Parliament in 1765 to raise revenue in America by requiring taxed, stamped paper for legal documents, publications, and playing cards. Americans opposed it as "taxation without representation" and prevented its enforcement. Parliament repealed it a year after its enactment.

Stamp Act Congress October 1765 meeting of delegates sent by nine colonies, held in New York City, that adopted the **Declaration of Rights and Grievances** and petitioned against the **Stamp Act.**

States' rights Favoring the rights of individual states over rights claimed by the national government.

Stonewall Rebellion On June 27, 1969, patrons fought back when police raided the gay Stonewall Inn in New York; the name refers to that event and to the increase in militancy by gay Americans that it symbolizes.

Stono Rebellion Uprising in 1739 of South Carolina slaves against whites; inspired in part by Spanish officials' promise of freedom for American slaves who escaped to Florida.

Strategic Arms Limitation Treaty (SALT) Signed in 1972 by the United States and the Soviet Union to slow the nuclear arms race.

Strategic Defense Initiative (SDI) President Reagan's program, announced in 1983, to defend the United States against nuclear missile attack with untested weapons systems and sophisticated technologies; also known as "Star Wars."

Student Nonviolent Coordinating Committee (SNCC) Black civil rights organization founded in 1960 and drawing heavily on younger activists and college students.

Students for a Democratic Society (SDS) The leading student organization of the New Left of the early and mid-1960s.

Subtreasury plan A program promoted by the **Southern Farmers' Alliance** in response to low cotton prices and tight credit. Farmers would store their crop in a warehouse (or "subtreasury") until prices rose, in the meantime borrowing up to 80 percent of the value of the stored crops from the government at a low interest rate.

Suffolk Resolves Militant resolves adopted in September 1774 in response to the **Coercive Acts** by representatives from the towns in Suffolk County, Massachusetts, including Boston. They termed the **Coercive Acts** unconstitutional, advised the people to arm, and called for economic sanctions against Britain. The **First Continental Congress** endorsed these resolves.

Suffrage The right to vote in a political election.

Sugar Act Law passed in 1764 to raise revenue in the American colonies. It lowered the duty from 6 pence to 3 pence per gallon on foreign molasses imported into the colonies and increased the restrictions on colonial commerce.

Sunbelt The states of the American South and Southwest.

***Sussex* Pledge** Germany's pledge during World War I not to sink merchant ships without warning, on the condition that Britain also observe recognized rules of international law.

Swann v. Charlotte-Mecklenburg Board of Education U.S. Supreme Court decision in 1971 that upheld cross-city busing to achieve the racial integration of public schools.

Sweatshops Small, poorly ventilated shops or apartments crammed with workers, often family members, who pieced together garments.

Taft-Hartley Act Federal legislation of 1947 that substantially limited the tools available to labor unions in labor-management disputes.

Tammany Hall New York City's **Democratic Party** organization, dating from well before the Civil War, that evolved into a powerful political machine after 1860, using patronage and bribes to maintain control of the city administration.

Taos Revolt Uprising of Pueblo Indians in New Mexico that broke out in January 1847 over the imposition of American rule during the Mexican War; the revolt was crushed within a few weeks.

Tariff Act of 1789 Apart from a few selected industries, this first tariff passed by Congress was intended primarily to raise revenue and not protect American manufacturers from foreign competition.

Tariff Act of 1798 Law placing a duty of 5 percent on most imported goods, designed primarily to generate revenue and not to protect American goods from foreign competition.

Tea Act of 1773 Act of Parliament that permitted the East India Company to sell tea through agents in America without paying the duty customarily collected in Britain, thus reducing the retail price. Americans, who saw the act as an attempt to induce them to pay the Townshend duty still imposed in the colonies, resisted this act through the **Boston Tea Party** and other measures.

Tejano A person of Spanish or Mexican descent born in Texas.

Teller Amendment A congressional resolution adopted in 1898 renouncing any American intention to annex Cuba.

Temperance Reform movement originating in the 1820s that sought to eliminate the consumption of alcohol.

Temporary Assistance for Needy Families (TANF) Federal program created in 1996 to replace earlier welfare programs to aid families and children; it involves explicit work requirements for receiving aid and places a time limit on benefits.

Tenement Four- to six-story residential dwelling, once common in New York and certain other cities, built on a tiny lot without regard to providing ventilation or light.

Tennessee Valley Authority (TVA) Federal regional planning agency established to promote **conservation,** produce electric power, and encourage economic development in seven southern states.

Tenure of Office Act Passed by the Republican controlled Congress in 1867 to limit presidential interference with its policies, the act prohibited the president from removing certain officeholders without the Senate's consent. President Andrew Johnson, angered at which he believed as an unconstitutional attack on presidential authority, deliberately violated the act by firing Secretary of War Edwin M. Stanton. The House responded by approving articles of impeachment against a president for the first time in American history.

Thirteenth Amendment Constitutional amendment ratified in 1865 that freed all slaves throughout the United States.

Tories A derisive term applied to loyalists in America who supported the king and Parliament just before and during the American Revolution. The term derived from late-seventeenth-century English politics when the Tory party supported the duke of York's succession to the throne as James II. Later the Tory party favored the Church of England and the crown over dissenting denominations and Parliament.

Townshend Duty Act of 1967 Act of Parliament, passed in 1767, imposing duties on colonial tea, lead, paint, paper, and glass. Designed to take advantage of the supposed American distinction between internal and external taxes, the Townshend duties were to help support government in America. The act prompted a successful colonial nonimportation movement.

Trail of Tears The forced march in 1838 of the Cherokee Indians from their homelands in Georgia to the Indian Territory in the West; thousands of Cherokees died along the way.

Transcendentalism A philosophical and literary movement centered on an idealistic belief in the divinity of individuals and nature.

Trans-Continental Treaty of 1819 Treaty between the United States and Spain in which Spain ceded Florida to the United States, surrendered all claims to the Pacific Northwest, and agreed to a boundary between the Louisiana Purchase territory and the Spanish Southwest.

Transportation revolution Dramatic improvements in transportation that stimulated economic growth after 1815 by expanding the range of travel and reducing the time and cost of moving goods and people.

Treaty of Fort Laramie The treaty acknowledging U.S. defeat in the Great Sioux War in 1868 and supposedly guaranteeing the Sioux perpetual land and hunting rights in South Dakota, Wyoming, and Montana.

Treaty of Ghent Treaty signed in December 1814 between the United States and Britain that ended the **War of 1812.**

Treaty of Greenville Treaty of 1795 in which Native Americans in the Old Northwest were forced to cede most of the present state of Ohio to the United States.

Treaty of Lancaster Negotiation in 1744 whereby Iroquois chiefs sold Virginia land speculators the right to trade at the Forks of the Ohio. Although the Iroquois had not intended this to include the right to settle in the Ohio Country, the Virginians assumed that it did. Ohio Valley Indians considered this treaty a great grievance against both the English and the Iroquois.

Treaty of Paris The formal end to British hostilities against France and Spain in February 1763.

Treaty of San Lorenzo **See Pinckney's Treaty.**

Treaty of Tordesillas Treaty negotiated by the pope in 1494 to resolve the territorial claims of Spain and Portugal. It drew a north–south line approximately 1,100 miles west of the Cape Verde Islands, granting all lands west of the line to Spain and all lands east of the line to Portugal. This limited Portugal's New World empire to Brazil but confirmed its claims in Africa and Asia.

Treaty of Versailles The treaty ending World War I and creating the **League of Nations.**

Troubled Asset Relief Program (TARP) Federal program in 2008 to purchase or guarantee shaky bank assets to protect the economy from widespread bank failures.

Truman Doctrine President Harry Truman's statement in 1947 that the United States should assist other nations that were facing external pressure or internal revolution; an important step in the escalation of the **Cold War.**

Trusts In late 19th- and early-20th-century usage, refers to monopolies that eliminated competition and fixed prices and wages in a given industry. Increasing numbers of Americans viewed these entities as threats to the free enterprise system.

Underground Railroad Support system set up by antislavery groups in the Upper South and the North to assist fugitive slaves in escaping the South.

Underwood-Simmons Tariff Act The 1913 reform law that lowered tariff rates and levied the first regular federal income tax.

Unicameral legislature A legislative body composed of a single house.

Union League A **Republican Party** organization in northern cities that became an important organizing device among freedmen in southern cities after 1865.

United States v. Cruikshank Supreme Court ruling of 1876 that overturned the convictions of some of those responsible for the Colfax Massacre, ruling that the Enforcement Act applied only to violations of black rights by states, not individuals.

University of California v. Bakke U.S. Supreme Court case in 1978 that allowed race to be used as one of several factors in college and university admission decisions but made rigid quotas unacceptable.

Valley Forge Area of Pennsylvania approximately twenty miles northwest of Philadelphia where General George Washington's continental troops were quartered from December 1777 to June 1778 while British forces occupied Philadelphia during the Revolutionary War. Approximately 2,500 men, about a quarter of those encamped there, died of hardship and disease.

Vertical integration The consolidation of numerous production functions, from the extraction of the raw materials to the distribution and marketing of the finished products, under the direction of one firm.

Viet Cong Communist rebels in South Vietnam who fought the pro-American government established in South Vietnam in 1954.

Virginia Plan Proposal of the Virginia delegation at the 1787 **Constitution Convention** calling for a national legislature in which the states would be represented according to population. The national legislature would have the explicit power to veto or overrule laws passed by state legislatures.

Virtual representation The notion, current in eighteenth-century England, that parliamentary members represented the interests of the nation as a whole, not those of the particular district that elected them.

Volstead Act The 1920 law defining the liquor forbidden under the Eighteenth Amendment and giving enforcement responsibilities to the Prohibition Bureau of the Department of the Treasury.

Voting Rights Act Legislation in 1965 that overturned a variety of practices by which states systematically denied voter registration to minorities.

Waltham system During the industrialization of the early nineteenth century, the recruitment of unmarried young women for employment in factories.

War Hawks Members of Congress, predominantly from the South and West, who aggressively pushed for a war against Britain after their election in 1810.

War Industries Board (WIB) The federal agency that reorganized industry for maximum efficiency and productivity during World War I.

War of 1812 War fought between the United States and Britain from June 1812 to January 1815 largely over British restrictions on American shipping.

War on Poverty Set of programs introduced by Lyndon Johnson between 1963 and 1966 designed to break the cycle of poverty by providing funds for job training, community development, nutrition, and supplementary education.

Warsaw Pact Military alliance of the Soviet Union and Communist nations of Eastern Europe from 1955 to 1989.

Watergate A complex scandal involving attempts to cover up illegal actions taken by administration officials and leading to the resignation of President Richard Nixon in 1974.

Webster–Ashburton Treaty Treaty signed by the United States and Britain in 1842 that settled a boundary dispute between Maine and Canada and provided for closer cooperation in suppressing the African slave trade.

Welfare capitalism A paternalistic system of labor relations emphasizing management responsibility for employee well-being. While providing some limited benefits, its function was primarily to forestall the formation of unions or public intervention.

Whig Party Political party, formed in the mid-1830s in opposition to the **Jacksonian Democrats,** that favored a strong role for the national government in promoting economic growth.

Whigs The name used by advocates of colonial resistance to British measures during the 1760s and 1770s. The Whig party in England unsuccessfully attempted to exclude the Catholic duke of York from succession to the throne as James II; victorious in the **Glorious Revolution,** the Whigs later stood for religious toleration and the supremacy of Parliament over the crown.

Whiskey Rebellion Armed uprising in 1794 by farmers in western Pennsylvania who attempted to prevent the collection of the excise tax on whiskey.

Whitewater Arkansas real estate development in which Bill and Hillary Clinton were investors; several fraud convictions resulted from investigations into Whitewater, but evidence was not found that the Clintons were involved in wrongdoing.

Wide Awakes Group of red-shirted, black-caped young men who paraded through city streets in the North extolling the virtues of the **Republican Party** during the 1860 presidential election campaign.

Wilmot Proviso The amendment offered by Pennsylvania Democrat David Wilmot in 1846 which stipulated that "as an express and fundamental condition to the acquisition of any territory from the Republic of Mexico . . . neither slavery nor involuntary servitude shall ever exist in any part of said territory."

Wobblies Popular name for the members of the Industrial Workers of the World (IWW).

Woman's Christian Temperance Union (WCTU) National organization formed after the Civil War dedicated to prohibiting the sale and distribution of alcohol.

Workingmen's Movement Associations of urban workers who began campaigning in the 1820s for free public education and a ten-hour workday.

World Bank Officially the International Bank for Reconstruction and Development, an international organization established in 1845 that assists governments around the world in economic development efforts.

World Trade Organization International organization that sets standards and practices for global trade, and the focus of international protests over world economic policy in the late 1990s.

World Wide Web Since 1991, the Web has expanded the use of the Internet by allowing organizations and companies to create websites that place political and commercial information only a few clicks away from wired consumers.

Wounded Knee Massacre The U.S. Army's brutal winter massacre in 1890 of at least two hundred Sioux men, women, and children as part of the government's assault on the tribe's Ghost Dance religion.

XYZ Affair Diplomatic incident in 1798 in which Americans were outraged by the demand of the French for a bribe as a condition for negotiating with American diplomats.

Yalta Conference Meeting of U.S. president Franklin Roosevelt, British Prime Minister Winston Churchill, and Soviet premier Joseph Stalin held in February 1945 to plan the final stages of World War II and postwar arrangements.

Yellow-dog contracts Employment agreements binding workers not to join a union.

Yellow press A deliberately sensational journalism of scandal and exposure designed to attract an urban mass audience and increase advertising revenues.

Chapter 1 CO photos: The Granger Collection, New York; © Hulton-Deutsch Collection/CORBIS; © Stapleton Collection/CORBIS; EMG Education Management Group; Service Historique de la Marine, Vincennes, France/ Lauros/Giraudon/Bridgeman Art Library; James Stanfield/National Geographic Image Collection; Getty Images Inc. - Hulton Archive; The Granger Collection, New York; The Granger Collection. Photos: p. 7: The Granger Collection, New York; p. 10: Cahokia Mounds State Historic Site; p. 12: Benin bronze plaque. National Museum of African Art, Smithsonian Institution, Washington, DC, U.S.A. Aldo Tutino/Art Resource, NY; p. 13: The Granger Collection; p. 17: Courtesy of the Library of Congress; p. 18: The Granger Collection; p. 22: Galleria Borghese, Rome, Italy/The Bridgeman Art Library; p. 26: Algonquian Indian village of Pomeiooc (North Carolina): watercolor, c1585, by John White.

Chapter 2 CO photos: Library of Congress; Photodisc/Getty Images; © Dorling Kindersley; © Bettmann/CORBIS; Courtesy of Pilgrim Hall Museum, Plymouth, Massachusetts; Courtesy of the Library of Congress; © Bettmann/CORBIS; Jonathan Carver, A TREATISE ON THE CULTURE OF THE TOBACCO PLANT (London, 1779), Manuscripts and Rare Book Division, Swem Library, College of William and Mary; The New York Public Library/Art resource, NY; Library of Congress; Courtesy of the Library of Congress. Photos: p. 35: Picture Collection, The Branch Libraries, The New York Public Library; p. 39: Ira Block/National Geographic Image Collection; p. 40: Library of Congress; p. 44: Library of Congress; p. 48: The Granger Collection, New York; p. 53: By permission of The British Library.

Chapter 3 CO photos: Library of Congress; King Philip's War Club. Published courtesy of Fruitlands Museums, Harvard, Massachusetts; Copyright ©North Wind Picture Archives/North Wind Picture Archives—All rights reserved; Library of Congress; © Dorling Kindersley, Courtesy of the Wilberforce House Museum, Hull; Courtesy of the Library of Congress; The Granger Collection; Courtesy of the Library of Congress. Photos: p. 60: Courtesy of the Library of Congress; p. 71: Royal Albert Memorial Museum, Exeter, Devon, UK/Bridgeman Art Library; p. 73: The Granger Collection, New York; p. 74: The Granger Collection, New York; p. 75: Abby Aldrich Rockefeller Folk Art Museum, The Colonial Williamsburg Foundation, Williamsburg, VA; p. 82: Courtesy of the Library of Congress; p. 83: National Museum of American History/ Smithsonian Institution; p. 83: Art Resource/Schomburg Center for Research in Black Culture.

Chapter 4 CO photos: The Granger Collection, New York; Liz McAulay © Dorling Kindersley, Courtesy of the Worthing Museum and Art Gallery; Alex Wilson © Dorling Kindersley, Courtesy of the Charlestown Shipwreck and Heritage Centre, Cornwall; © Judith Miller/Dorling Kindersley/Sara Covelli; Library of Congress; © Dorling Kindersley; Library of Congress; Library of Congress; North Wind Picture Archives; Getty Images Inc. - Hulton Archive Photos. Photos: p. 91: Samuel Scott (c. 1702–1772) "Old East India Wharf at London Bridge" (CT2825). ©Victoria & Albert Museum, London/Art Resource, NY; p. 93: Peter Cooper "The Southeast Prospect of the City of Philadelphia" ca. 1720. The Library Company of Philadelphia; p. 94: © Robert Harding World Imagery/CORBIS All Rights Reserved; p. 96: Private Collection/The Bridgeman Art Library; p. 98: The Granger Collection, New York; p. 104: Copyright © North Wind/North Wind Picture Archives— All rights reserved; p. 108: Getty Images Inc. - Hulton Archive Photos; p. 113: Benjamin West (1738–1820), "The Death of General Wolfe," 1770, Oil on canvas, 152.6_214.5 cm. Transfer from the Canadian War Memorials, 1921 (Gift of the 2nd Duke of Westminster, Eaton Hall, Cheshire, 1918). National Gallery of Canada, Ottawa, Ontario.

Chapter 5 CO photos: Courtesy of the Library of Congress; © Judith Miller/Dorling Kindersley/Sloan's; © North Wind/North Wind Picture Archives; Steve Gorton © Dorling Kindersley; © North Wind/North Wind Picture Archives; © North Wind Picture Archives—All rights reserved; Library of Congress; Courtesy of the Library of Congress; Courtesy of the Library of Congress; Getty Images Inc. - Hulton Archive Photos; Courtesy of the Library of Congress. Photos: p. 120: The Granger Collection, New York; p. 126: John Singleton Copley (1738–1815), "Samuel Adams," ca. 1772. Oil on canvas, 49 1/2 × 39 1/2 in. (125.7 cm × 100.3 cm). Deposited by the City of Boston, 30.76c. Courtesy, Museum of Fine Arts, Boston. Reproduced with permission. ©2000 Museum of Fine Arts, Boston. All Rights Reserved; p. 127: The Granger Collection; p. 130: North Wind Picture Archives; p. 133: John Singleton Copley, Portrait of Mr. and Mrs. Thomas Mifflin. Philadelphia Museum of Art: Bequest of Mrs. Esther B. Wistar to the Historical Society of Pennsylvania in 1900 and acquired by the Philadelphia Museum of Art. Accession # EW 1999-45-1, Photograph © Museum of Fine Arts, Boston; p. 136: The Granger Collection, New York.

Chapter 6 CO photos: National Museum of American History (Smithsonian); Courtesy of the Library of Congress; Independence National Historical Park; © Joseph Sohm; Visions of America/CORBIS; Photograph courtesy of the Concord Museum, Concord, MA and the archives of the Lexington Historical Society, Lexington, MA Photograph by David Bohl; Peale, Charles Willson (1741–1827). (after): George Washington after the battle of Princeton, January 3, 1777. 1779. Oil on canvas, 234.5 × 155 cm. Inv.:MV 4560. Photo: Gerard Blot. Chateaux de Versailles et de Trianon, Versailles, France. Reunion des Musées Nationaux/Art Resource, NY; Demetrio Carrasco © Dorling Kindersley; © Francis G. Mayer/CORBIS; Library of Congress; Independence National Historical Park; Library of Congress; "Paul Jones Shooting a sailor", color engraving from the Olds Collection #366, no negative number. © Collection of The New-York Historical Society. Photos: p. 147: Peale, Charles Willson (1741–1827). (after): George Washington after the battle of Princeton, January 3, 1777. 1779. Oil on canvas, 234.5 × 155 cm. Inv.:MV 4560. Photo: Gerard Blot. Chateaux de Versailles et de Trianon, Versailles, France. Reunion des Musées Nationaux/Art Resource, NY; p. 148: Library of Congress; p. 149: North Wind Picture Archives; p. 154: Courtesy of the Library of Congress; p. 157: John Trumbull (American 1756–1843), "The Surrender of Lord Cornwallis at Yorktown, 19 October 1781", 1787-c. 1828. Oil on canvas, 53.3 × 77.8 × 1.9 cm (21 × 30 5/8 × 3/4 in.)), 1832.4. Yale University Art Gallery/Art Resource., NY; p. 159: The Granger Collection, New York; p. 160: The Granger Collection; p. 166: Courtesy of the Library of Congress; p. 167: Eliot Elisofon/Getty Images/Time Life Pictures.

Chapter 7 CO photos: Courtesy of the Library of Congress; Charles Allen Munn Collection, Fordham University Library, Bronx, NY; Library of Congress; Courtesy of the Library of Congress; Courtesy of The Historical Society of Pennsylvania Collection, Atwater Kent Museum of Philadelphia; Gallery of the Republic; Courtesy National Archives, photo no. 624.0191; 4.227; The Granger Collection, New York; The Granger Collection, New York; © Bettmann/ CORBIS. Photos: p. 172: © Bettmann/CORBIS; p. 173: Getty Images Inc. - Hulton Archive Photos; p. 180: The Granger Collection; p. 186: Charles Allen Munn Collection, Fordham University Library, Bronx, NY; p. 189: Abby Aldrich Rockefeller Folk Art Museum, The Colonial Williamsburg Foundation, Williamsburg, VA.

Chapter 8 CO photos: The Granger Collection, New York; Library of Congress; Library of Congress; Getty Images Inc. - Hulton Archive Photos; Courtesy Museum of American Political Life, University of Hartford, West Hartford, CT; Courtesy of the Library of Congress; Library of Congress; The Granger Collection; "White House Historical Association (White House Collection)" (25). Photos: p. 200: Courtesy of the Library of Congress; p. 201: Collection of The New-York Historical Society, Negative number 28824c; p. 203: The Metropolitan Museum of Art, The Edward W. C. Arnold Collection of New York Prints. Bequest of Edward W. C. Arnold, 1954. (54.90.491) Photograph © 1986 The Metropolitan Museum of Art. Art Resource, NY; p. 204: The Granger Collection; p. 214: Collection of The New-York Historical Society, negative # 35609; p. 218: Courtesy of the Library of Congress; p. 219: Courtesy of the Library of Congress. Text: p. 196: United States, First Congress, 1789–1791. Kenneth R. Bowling and Helen E. Veit, eds. *Documentary History of the First Federal Congress of the United States of America, March 4, 1789-March 3, 1791*, Volume 9: *The Diary of William Maclay and Other Notes on Senate Debates*, vol. 9. pp. 11–13. © 1988 The Johns Hopkins University Press. Reprinted with permission of The Johns Hopkins University Press.

Chapter 9 CO photos: Print Collection. Miriam and Ira D. Wallach Division of Art, Prints and Photographs. The New York Public Library/Art Resource, NY. Astor, Lenox and Tilden Foundation; © CORBIS; The Granger Collection; Library of Congress; National Park Service photo; Library of Congress; Library of Congress; Courtesy of the Library of Congress; Library of Congress; Courtesy of the Library of Congress. Photos: p. 225: Jane Braddick Petticolas (1791–1852) "View of the West Front of Monticello and Garden" 1825, watercolor on paper, 13 5/8 × 18 1/18 inches. Edward Owen/Monticello/Thomas Jefferson Foundation, Inc.; p. 226: © Walters Art Museum, Baltimore/Bridgeman Art Library; p. 228: Courtesy of the Library of Congress; p. 231: Courtesy of the Library of Congress; p. 235: Courtesy of the Library of Congress; p. 237: Dagli Orti/Picture Desk, Inc./Kobal Collection; p. 239: Bettmann/Corbis.

Chapter 10 CO photos: © Bettmann/CORBIS; Courtesy, American Antiquarian Society; C Squared Studios/Getty Images, Inc.- Photodisc./Royalty Free; Library of Congress; National Numismatic Collection/Smithsonian Institution; Courtesy of the Library of Congress; Library of Congress; Courtesy of the Library of Congress; Courtesy of the Library of Congress; Library of Congress. Photos: p. 252: Collection of The New-York Historical Society, Negative # 26275; p. 253: First State Election in Detroit, Michigan, 1837, c. 1837. Thomas Mickell Burnham. Gift of Mrs. Samuel T. Carson. Photograph © 1991 The Detroit Institute of Arts/The Bridgeman Art Library, NY; p. 254: Courtesy of the Library of Congress; p. 255: CORBIS- NY; p. 256: The Granger Collection, New York; p. 258: The Granger Collection, New York; p. 262: Courtesy of the Library of Congress; p. 266: The Cincinnati Historical Society; p. 270: CORBIS- NY; p. 274: Courtesy of the Library of Congress; p. 275: The Granger Collection, New York.

Chapter 11 CO photos: The Granger Collection, New York; CORBIS- NY; Library of Congress; Library of Congress; © Dorling Kindersley; Courtesy of the Library of Congress; Library of Congress; Library of Congress; Library of Congress; Library of Congress; Courtesy of the Library of Congress. Photos: p. 282: Library of Congress; p. 284: Collection of The New-York Historical Society; p. 285: Courtesy of The New-York Historical Society, New York City; p. 287: Louisiana

State Museum; p. 290: Library of Congress; p. 290: © Bettmann/CORBIS All Rights Reserved; p. 296: The Granger Collection, New York; p. 297: Courtesy of the Library of Congress.

Chapter 12 CO photos: The Granger Collection, New York; Map of Proposed route of Erie Canal, 1811 Negative Number 420757, © Collection of the New-York Historical Society, New York City; Library of Congress; The Granger Collection; © Bettmann/CORBIS; Courtesy of the Library of Congress; Getty Images Inc. - Hulton Archive Photos; Courtesy of the Library of Congress; Library of Congress. Photos: p. 308: Collection of The New-York Historical Society, Negative #34684; p. 310: I.N. Phelps Stokes Collection, Miriam and Ira D. Wallach Division of Art, Prints and Photographs, The New York Library, Astor, Lenox and Tilden Foundations; p. 311: American Textile History Museum, Lowell, Mass.; p. 313: Courtesy of the Library of Congress; p. 314: Courtesy of the Library of Congress; p. 316: Family Group, Joesph H. Davis, American, 1811–1865, Graphite pencil and watercolor on paper, Sheet: 24.8 × 41 cm (9 3/4 × 16 1/8 in.), Museum of Fine Arts, Boston, Gift of Maxim Karolik for the proposed M. and M. Karolik Collection of American Watercolors, © 2003 Museum of Fine Arts, Boston; p. 319: CORBIS- NY; p. 323: Library of Congress; p. 323: Library of Congress; p. 331: Courtesy of the Library of Congress; p. 334: Library of Congress; p. 335: Getty Images, Inc Bridgeman.

Chapter 13 CO photos: Butler Institute of American Art, Youngstown, OH, USA/Gift of Joseph G. Butler III 1946/Bridgeman Art Library; ©Connie Ricca/CORBIS; Getty Images Inc. - Hulton Archive Photos; Peter Anderson © Dorling Kindersley; National Anthropological Archives; Library of Congress; Smithsonian American Art Museum, Washington, D.C./Art Resource, N.Y.; Courtesy of the Library of Congress; Courtesy of the Library of Congress. Photos: p. 342: The Old Print Shop Inc. Kenneth M. Newman; p. 345: Shirt, about 1860s, unknown Sioux artist Deer skin, hair, quills, feathers, paint Denver Art Museum Collection: Native Arts acquisition funds, 1947.235 © Photo by the Denver Art Museum. All Rights Reserved; p. 346: The Denver Public Library, Western History Department; p. 349: Alfred Jacob Miller, "The Interior of Fort Laramie," 1858–60. The Walters Art Museum, Baltimore; p. 350: Smithsonian American Art Museum, Washington, DC/Art Resource, NY; p. 356: Library of Congress; p. 357: Courtesy of the Library of Congress.

Chapter 14 CO photos: Courtesy of the Library of Congress; Jules Frazier/Getty Images, Inc.- Photodisc./Royalty Free; © CORBIS; Charleston Area Convention and Visitors Bureau; Library of Congress; Library of Congress; Library of Congress. Photos: p. 368: Courtesy of Elliot Koeppel, www.malakoff.com; p. 371: Courtesy of the Library of Congress; p. 372: © Bettmann/CORBIS; p. 374: The Newberry Library; p. 375: The Granger Collection, New York; p. 378: Library of Congress; p. 380: Abraham Lincoln Presidental Library & Museum (ALPLM); p. 383: The Granger Collection, New York; p. 390: Courtesy of the Library of Congress.

Chapter 15 CO photos: United States Department of the Interior; Dave King/Dorling Kindersley © Confederate Memorial Hall, New Orleans; Library of Congress; Courtesy of the Library of Congress; Courtesy of the Library of Congress; Library of Congress; Dave King/Dorling Kindersley © Confederate Memorial Hall, New Orleans; Library of Congress; Center of Military History, U.S. Army; © Bettmann/CORBIS; Courtesy of the Library of Congress. Photos: p. 400: Courtesy of the Library of Congress; p. 401: Getty Images Inc. - Hulton Archive Photos; p. 406: AP Wide World Photos; p. 406: Library of Congress; p. 409: Theodor Kaufmann (1814–1896), "On to Liberty," 1867, Oil on canvas, 36 × 56 in (91.4 × 142.2 cm). The Metropolitan Museum of Art. Gift of Erving and Joyce Wolf, 1982 (1982.443.3) Photograph © The Metropolitan Museum of Art./Art Resource, NY; p. 410: Manuscripts, Archives and Rare Books Division, Schomberg Center for Research in Black Culture, The New York Public Library. Astor, Lenox and Tilden Foundations; p. 416: Courtesy of the Library of Congress; p. 418: Culver Pictures, Inc.; p. 421: © Bettmann/CORBIS; p. 422: National Archives and Records Administration; p. 426: Courtesy of the Library of Congress; p. 428: Courtesy of the Library of Congress. Text: p. 396: From *The Civil War* by Ken Burns and Rick Burns, Geoffrey Ward, copyright © 1990, American Documentaries Inc. Used by permission of Alfred A. Knopf, a division of Random House, Inc

Chapter 16 CO photos: Courtesy of the Library of Congress; Library of Congress; Courtesy of the Library of Congress; Dorothea Lange/Library of Congress; Courtesy of the Library of Congress; The Granger Collection, New York; Library of Congress; Library of Congress; Courtesy of the Library of Congress; The Granger Collection, New York; Library of Congress. Photos: p. 438: The Granger Collection, New York; p. 440: The Granger Collection, New York; p. 442: The Granger Collection; p. 446: The Granger Collection, New York; p. 449: Courtesy of the Library of Congress; p. 451: Courtesy of the Library of Congress; p. 453: The Granger Collection, New York; p. 454: Courtesy of the Library of Congress; p. 457: Wisconsin Historical Society "WHS Image ID WHI-51721"; p. 464: North Wind Picture Archives; p. 465: North Wind Picture Archives.

Chapter 17 CO photos: Courtesy of the Library of Congress; The Granger Collection, New York; Collection of The New-York Historical Society. negative number 51391; Courtesy of the Library of Congress; Prentice Hall School Division; Courtesy of the Library of Congress; Courtesy of The North Carolina Division of Archives and History; Courtesy of the Library of Congress; Collection of The New-York Historical Society. negative number 51391. Photos: p. 471: Courtesy of the Library of Congress; p. 476: Cook Collection, Valentine Museum/Richmond History Center; p. 478: Courtesy of the Library of Congress; p. 481: Courtesy of the Library of Congress; p. 483: The Granger Collection, New York; p. 484: The Ohio Historical Society; p. 485: North Carolina Mutual Life Insurance Company; p. 488: Courtesy of the Library of Congress.

Chapter 18 CO photos: Lewis Hine/Library of Congress; Getty Images Inc. - Hulton Archive Photos; © Rykoff Collection/CORBIS; Courtesy of the Library of Congress; National Archives and Records Administration; Courtesy of the Library of Congress; Getty Images Inc. - Hulton Archive Photos; Ford Motor Company. Photos: p. 498: W. Louis Sonntag, Jr., "The Bowery at Night", watercolor, 1895. Copyright Museum of the City of New York. 32.275.2; p. 499: CORBIS- NY; p. 500: Courtesy of the Library of Congress; p. 502: Getty Images Inc. - Hulton Archive Photos; p. 502: 22 Baxter Street Court. The Jacob A. Riis Collection, Museum of the City of New York; p. 504: The Granger Collection, New York; p. 507: Courtesy of the Library of Congress; p. 509: Courtesy of The Bancroft Library. University of California, Berkeley; p. 513: Brown Brothers; p. 517: © Bettmann/CORBIS All Rights Reserved.

Chapter 19 CO photos: The Granger Collection, New York; Dave King/Dorling Kindersley © Confederate Memorial Hall, New Orleans; Courtesy of the Library of Congress; Lynton Gardiner © Dorling Kindersley, Courtesy of The American Museum of Natural History; © Dorling Kindersley; © Judith Miller/Dorling Kindersley/Cowan's Historic Americana Auctions; Courtesy of the Library of Congress; Courtesy of the Library of Congress; Underwood & Underwood/Library of Congress. Photos: p. 526: A.J. Russell/Union Pacific Historical Collection; p. 529: hide painting, George Bull Child, 1930s The L.D. and Ruth Bax Collection, 1985.106 Photograph © Denver Art Museum 2010. All Rights Reserved; p. 531: Western History Collections, University of Oklahoma Libraries. Phillips Collection 357; p. 534: Western History Collections, University of Oklahoma Libraries; p. 535: Chinese mining laborers, Idaho, 76-119.2/A, Idaho State Historical Society; p. 537: Courtesy of the Library of Congress; p. 540: Courtesy Photographic Archives, Palace of the Governors, Museum of New Mexico, Santa Fe, New Mexico/DCA Negative No.:22468; p. 542: Courtesy of the Nebraska State Historical Society; p. 544: Library of Congress.

Chapter 20 CO photos: Reproduced from the collections of the Ohio Historical Society Archives/Library; Courtesy of the Library of Congress; Courtesy of the Library of Congress; Courtesy of the Library of Congress; © Bettmann/CORBIS; Courtesy of the Library of Congress; Courtesy of the Library of Congress; Courtesy of the Library of Congress; Library of Congress. Photos: p. 555: The Granger Collection, New York; p. 555: Courtesy of the Library of Congress; p. 559: provided courtesy HarpWeek., LLC; p. 560: Courtesy of the Library of Congress; p. 564: Kansas State Historical Society; p. 567: Courtesy of the Library of Congress; p. 568: Courtesy of the Library of Congress; p. 575: The Granger Collection, New York; p. 575: Courtesy of the Library of Congress.

Chapter 21 CO photos: Denver Public Library; Courtesy of the Library of Congress; CORBIS- NY; Courtesy of the Library of Congress; © Bettmann/CORBIS; Courtesy of the Library of Congress; Courtesy National Archives, photo no. 102-LH-1986; Courtesy of the Library of Congress; The Granger Collection, New York; Courtesy of the Library of Congress. Photos: p. 580: Kheel Center, Cornell University, Ithaca, NY 14853-3901; p. 582: Courtesy of the Library of Congress; p. 583: Kheel Center, Cornell University, Ithaca, NY 14853-3901; p. 586: Courtesy of the Library of Congress; p. 588: Courtesy of the Library of Congress; p. 591: Indiana Historical Society, A70; p. 592: Courtesy of the Library of Congress; p. 596: provided courtesy HarpWeek., LLC; p. 597: Portrait #65, Courtesy of the Bancroft Library, University of California, Berkeley; p. 599: Courtesy of the Library of Congress.

Chapter 22 CO photos: The Granger Collection, New York; National Archives and Records Administration; Courtesy of the Library of Congress; Courtesy of the Library of Congress; Jonothan Potter © Dorling Kindersley; © Bettmann/CORBIS; National Archives and Records Administration; Library of Congress; Courtesy of the Library of Congress; Library of Congress; Courtesy of the Library of Congress. Photos: p. 611: Courtesy of the Library of Congress; p. 615: © Bettmann/CORBIS; p. 619: Courtesy of the Library of Congress; p. 619: Courtesy of the Library of Congress; p. 623: provided courtesy HarpWeek., LLC; p. 627: © Stock Montage, 2004; p. 628: The Granger Collection, New York; p. 629: Courtesy of the Library of Congress.

Chapter 23 CO photos: Getty Images Inc. - Hulton Archive Photos; Courtesy of the Library of Congress; Library of Congress; National Archives and Records Administration; Richard Ward © Dorling Kindersley; Library of Congress; Courtesy of the Library of Congress; Courtesy of the Library of Congress; National Archives and Records Administration. Photos: p. 640: Courtesy of the Library of Congress; p. 643: Photograph courtesy of the Hagley Museum and Library, Wilmington, Delaware; p. 644: National Archives and Records Administration; p. 647: The Granger Collection, New York; p. 650: Getty Images Inc. - Hulton Archive

Photos; p. 652: National Archives and Records Administration; 654: University of Washington Libraries, Special Collections, A. Curtis 37055; p. 655: The Granger Collection, New York; p. 656: Courtesy of the Library of Congress.
Chapter 24 CO photos: Wisconsin Historical Society/WHi-5020; EyeWire Collection/Getty Images - Photodisc-Royalty Free; © Swim Ink/CORBIS; Getty Images Inc. - Hulton Archive Photos; C Squared Studios/Getty Images Inc. RF; Wisconsin Historical Society; By permission of Campbell Soup Company; Library of Congress; Library of Congress; Courtesy of the Library of Congress; National Photo Company Collection; Courtesy of the Library of Congress; Courtesy of the Library of Congress. Photos: p. 665: Wisconsin Historical Society/WHi-5020; p. 668: Courtesy of the Library of Congress; p. 670: Courtesy of the Library of Congress; p. 671: Security Pacific Collection/Los Angeles Public Library; p. 672: By permission of Campbell Soup Company; p. 673: Frank Driggs Collection; p. 677: The Denver Public Library, Western History Collection, The Harry M. Rhoads Photograph Collection, Call Number Rh-460; p. 678: AP Wide World Photos; p. 686: CORBIS- NY; p. 687: CORBIS- NY.
Chapter 25 CO photos: Library of Congress; Courtesy of the Library of Congress; Courtesy of the Library of Congress; © CORBIS; Courtesy of the Library of Congress; Courtesy of the Library of Congress; Library of Congress; Courtesy of the Library of Congress; Library of Congress; Courtesy of the Library of Congress; Library of Congress; Library of Congress. Photos: p. 694: University of Washington Libraries, Special Collections, Lee 20102; p. 694: Courtesy of the Library of Congress; p. 697: By an unknown Associated Press photographer, July 1932/National Archives and Records Administration; p. 700: UPI/CORBIS- NY; p. 701: UPI/CORBIS- NY; p. 702: Courtesy of the Library of Congress; p. 704: UPI/CORBIS- NY; p. 706: Courtesy of the Library of Congress; p. 714: UPI/CORBIS-BETTMANN.
Chapter 26 CO photos: The Granger Collection, New York; U.S. Air Force; © CORBIS; National Archives and Records Administration; Bildarchiv PreuBischer Kulturbesitz, Berlin; National Archives and Records Administration; Poster Collection/Hoover Institution Archives; Courtesy of the Library of Congress. Photos: p. 723: Bildarchiv PreuBischer Kulturbesitz, Berlin; p. 728: National Archives and Records Administration; p. 731: AP Wide World Photos; p. 733: National Archives and Records Administration; p. 734: CORBIS- NY; p. 735: National Archives and Records Administration; p. 736: REPRINTED WITH PERMISSION OF THE DALLAS MORNING NEWS; p. 737: AP Wide World Photos; p. 744: National Archives and Records Administration; p. 746: ZUMA Press – Gamma.
Chapter 27 CO photos: Walter Sanders/LIFE/Getty Images/Time Life Pictures; CORBIS- NY; Reproduced from the Collections of the Library of Congress; MPI/Getty Images Inc. - Hulton Archive Photos; CORBIS- NY; AP Wide World Photos; Courtesy of the Library of Congress; National Archives and Records Administration, Records of the Office of the Chief Signal Officer. Photo by Sfc. Al Chang; Courtesy of the Library of Congress. Photos: p. 754: AP Wide World Photos; p. 756: UPI/CORBIS- NY; p. 756: The Granger Collection, New York; p. 758: AP Wide World Photos; p. 764: Charles Fenno Jacobs/Getty Images, Inc.; p. 766: National Archives and Records Administration; p. 772: CORBIS- NY; p. 773: UPI/CORBIS- NY; p. 774: © Bettmann/CORBIS.
Chapter 28 CO photos: UPI/CORBIS- NY; U.S. Air Force; AP Wide World Photos; Courtesy of the Library of Congress; © CORBIS; Library of Congress; Courtesy of the Library of Congress; Library of Congress; © Bettmann/CORBIS All Rights Reserved; AP Wide World Photos. Photos: p. 783: James Hanley/Photo Researchers, Inc.; p. 785: "Day dreaming" by Constantin Alajalov. © 1959 SEPS: Liscened by Curtis Publishing Co., Indianapolis, IN. All rights reserved. www.curtispublishing.com; p. 786: Getty Images Inc. - Hulton Archive Photos; p. 787: Picture Desk, Inc./Kobal Collection; p. 788: Elliott Erwitt/Magnum Photos, Inc.; p. 790: Ruth Sondak; p. 795: Cecil Stoughton, White House/John Fitzgerald Kennedy Library, Boston; p. 799: Photograph by John G. Moebes, ©News & Record, All Rights Reserved; p. 801: ©1976, Matt Herron/Take Stock-Images of Change; p. 803: Courtesy National Archives, photo no. (NLK-WHP-ST-ST1A163); p. 804: Getty Images Inc. - Hulton Archive Photos; p. 808: William Lovelace/Getty Images Inc. - Hulton Archive Photos; p. 809: Library of Congress; p. 809: Library of Congress; p. 809: Courtesy of the Library of Congress.
Chapter 29 CO photos: CORBIS- NY; Peter Anderson © Dorling Kindersley; © Royalty-Free/CORBIS; Wayne State University Archives of Labor and Urban Affairs; Trevor Melton © Dorling Kindersley; © Henry Diltz/CORBIS; © Leif Skoogfors/CORBIS All Rights Reserved; Agence France Presse/Hulton Archive/Getty Images; Getty Images Inc. - Hulton Archive Photos; AP Wide World Photos; © Wally McNamee/CORBIS. Photos: p. 816: Getty Images Inc. - Hulton Archive Photos; p. 816: CORBIS- NY; p. 817: Gene Anthony/Black Star; p. 822: © Bettmann/CORBIS All Rights Reserved; p. 823: Walter P. Reuther Library, Wayne State University; p. 823: Agence France Presse/Hulton Archive/Getty Images; p. 825: Kyo Icki Sawada/UPI/CORBIS- NY; p. 829: CORBIS- NY; p. 831: Getty Images, Inc.; p. 836: © Wally McNamee/CORBIS; p. 838: Farnood/SIPA Press.
Chapter 30 CO photos: © Bettmann/CORBIS; © Neil Beer/CORBIS; Telepress Syndicate Agency/CORBIS- NY; Joe Marquette/AP Wide World Photos; © Dorling Kindersley; Reuters/Steve Jaffe/Archive Photos; © Bettmann/CORBIS; AP Wide World Photos; Lisa Quinones/Black Star. Photos: p. 847: Corbis/CORBIS- NY; p. 849: Lynn Goldsmith/Corbis/CORBIS- NY; p. 850: ©The New Yorker Collection 2008 Koren from cartoonbank.com. All Rights Reserved; p. 853: Reuters/Steve Jaffe/Archive Photos; p. 856: AP Wide World Photos; p. 857: Regis Bossu/CORBIS- NY; p. 866: Lisa Quinones/Black Star; p. 869: Joe Marquette/AP Wide World Photos.
Chapter 31 CO photos: © Michael Ainsworth/Dallas Morning News/CORBIS All Rights Reserved; Stephen Crowley/The New York Times; © Dorling Kindersley; Photodisc/Getty Images; Geoff Dann © Dorling Kindersley, Courtesy of the Imperial War Museum, London; Courtesy of the Library of Congress; Stephen Jaffe Photography; AP Wide World Photos; © Reuters/CORBIS. Photos: p. 878: © IRA WYMAN/CORBIS SYGMA; p. 880: Mark Humphrey/AP Wide World Photos; p. 886: Mira.com/Artist Name; p. 888: Agence France Presse/Getty Images; p. 895: © Reuters/CORBIS; p. 897: © DAEMMRICH BOB/CORBIS SYGMA; p. 898: © Sean Adair/Reuters/Corbis; p. 901: Getty Images, Inc.; p. 901: David J. Phillip/AP Wide World Photos; p. 903: Getty Images; p. 909: AP Wide World Photos; p. 909: Harris and Ewing Photos Courtesy Harry S. Truman Library; p. 909: National Archives and Records Administration. Text: p. 887: Peggy Senger Parsons' blog.

A

B

C

D

E

F

H

K

L

N

O

P

S

T

X

Y

Z

GREENLAND (DENMARK)
U.S.
CANADA
ALEUTIAN ISLANDS
UNITED STATES
PACIFIC OCEAN
ATLANTIC OCEAN
MEXICO
CUBA
BAHAMAS
HAITI
PUERTO RICO (U.S.)
JAMAICA
BELIZE
HONDURAS
DOMINICAN REPUBLIC
ST. KITTS AND NEVIS
ANTIGUA AND BARBUDA
DOMINICA
ST. VINCENT AND THE GRENADINES
BARBADOS
GRENADA
TRINIDAD AND TOBAGO
GUATEMALA
EL SALVADOR
NICARAGUA
COSTA RICA
PANAMA
VENEZUELA
GUYANA
SURINAME
FRENCH GUIANA (FR)
COLOMBIA
GALAPAGOS ISLANDS (ECUADOR)
ECUADOR
PERU
BRAZIL
BOLIVIA
PARAGUAY
CHILE
ARGENTINA
URUGUAY
WESTERN SAMOA
TONGA
Tropic of Cancer
Equator
Tropic of Capricorn
Antarctic Circle
CAPE VERDE
SENEGAL
GAMBIA
GUINEA-BISSAU
GUINEA
SIERRA LEONE
LIBERIA
MAURITANIA
WESTERN SAHARA (MOROCCO)

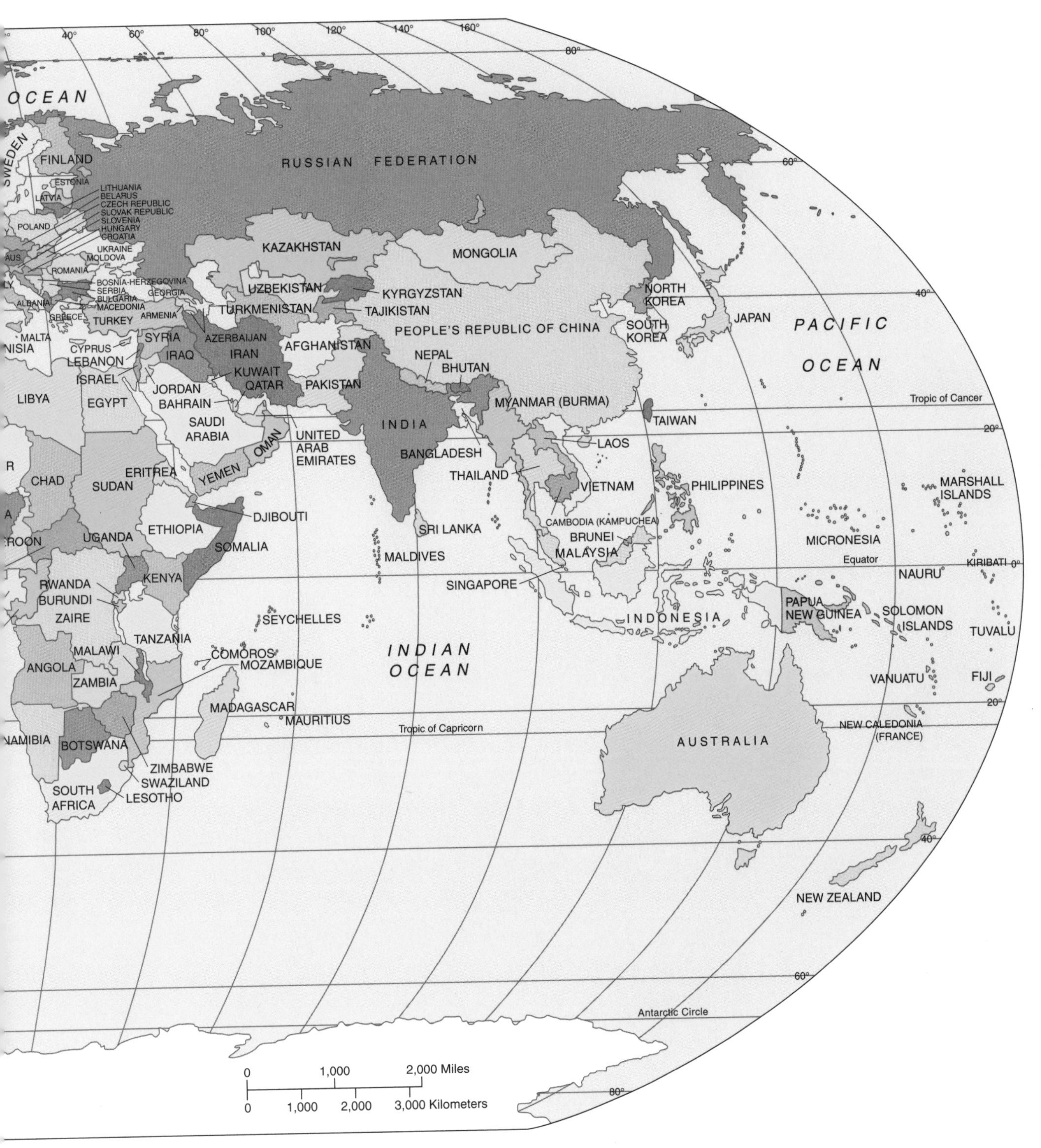

OCEAN
RUSSIAN FEDERATION
FINLAND
ESTONIA
LATVIA
LITHUANIA
BELARUS
CZECH REPUBLIC
SLOVAK REPUBLIC
SLOVENIA
HUNGARY
CROATIA
POLAND
UKRAINE
MOLDOVA
ROMANIA
BOSNIA-HERZEGOVINA
SERBIA
BULGARIA
MACEDONIA
GEORGIA
ALBANIA
GREECE
TURKEY
ARMENIA
MALTA
CYPRUS
LEBANON
ISRAEL
SYRIA
IRAQ
AZERBAIJAN
IRAN
KUWAIT
QATAR
JORDAN
BAHRAIN
SAUDI ARABIA
UNITED ARAB EMIRATES
OMAN
YEMEN
KAZAKHSTAN
UZBEKISTAN
TURKMENISTAN
KYRGYZSTAN
TAJIKISTAN
AFGHANISTAN
PAKISTAN
MONGOLIA
NORTH KOREA
SOUTH KOREA
JAPAN
PACIFIC OCEAN
PEOPLE'S REPUBLIC OF CHINA
NEPAL
BHUTAN
INDIA
BANGLADESH
MYANMAR (BURMA)
TAIWAN
LAOS
THAILAND
VIETNAM
PHILIPPINES
CAMBODIA (KAMPUCHEA)
BRUNEI
MALAYSIA
SINGAPORE
SRI LANKA
MALDIVES
LIBYA
EGYPT
CHAD
SUDAN
ERITREA
DJIBOUTI
ETHIOPIA
SOMALIA
UGANDA
KENYA
RWANDA
BURUNDI
ZAIRE
TANZANIA
SEYCHELLES
COMOROS
MOZAMBIQUE
MALAWI
ANGOLA
ZAMBIA
MADAGASCAR
MAURITIUS
NAMIBIA
BOTSWANA
ZIMBABWE
SWAZILAND
SOUTH AFRICA
LESOTHO
INDIAN OCEAN
INDONESIA
PAPUA NEW GUINEA
SOLOMON ISLANDS
MARSHALL ISLANDS
MICRONESIA
NAURU
KIRIBATI
TUVALU
VANUATU
FIJI
NEW CALEDONIA (FRANCE)
AUSTRALIA
NEW ZEALAND
Tropic of Cancer
Equator
Tropic of Capricorn
Antarctic Circle
40°
60°
80°
100°
120°
140°
160°
20°
0°
0 1,000 2,000 Miles
0 1,000 2,000 3,000 Kilometers